Concordia Bible with Notes

THE NEW TESTAMENT

Concordia Bible with Notes

THE NEW COVENANT
COMMONLY CALLED

THE NEW TESTAMENT
OF OUR LORD AND SAVIOR JESUS CHRIST

Revised Standard Version

TRANSLATED FROM THE GREEK
BEING THE VERSION SET FORTH A. D. 1611
REVISED A. D. 1881 AND A. D. 1901
COMPARED WITH THE MOST ANCIENT
AUTHORITIES AND REVISED A. D. 1946
SECOND EDITION A. D. 1971

PUBLISHED BY
William Collins Sons & Co., Ltd.
for
Concordia Publishing House
Saint Louis / London

New Testament Copyright © 1946, 1971
by
Division of Christian Education
of the National Council of the Churches of Christ
in the United States of America

Introductions, notes, and references
prepared by
Martin H. Franzmann, D. D.

Concordia Publishing House, St. Louis, Missouri
Concordia Publishing House Ltd., London, E. C. 1
Copyright © 1971 Concordia Publishing House

Library of Congress Catalog Card No. 71-152384
ISBN 0-570-00500-0

FOREWORD

The Concordia Bible with Notes published by Concordia Publishing House in 1947 was a revised edition of the original *Self-Explaining Bible* published by the American Tract Society of New York. This edition proved to be very popular with many Bible students and was therefore sold out within a few years. Unfortunately it was not possible to reprint that edition because the plates were worn out. For this reason and because of repeated requests for a Bible of this type we decided to produce an entirely new edition based on the Revised Standard Version. The Second Edition of the New Testament translation is used in this volume.

We asked Dr. Walter R. Roehrs and Dr. Martin H. Franzmann, eminent scholars of the Old and the New Testament, to prepare entirely new notes. At this time the New Testament is being made available. The entire Bible will be available in a few years.

The introductions to the various books have been prepared to present in brief form the background and important features of each book. They will help the reader gain a clear impression of the theme and purpose of the book.

The notes provide in clear, concise language explanations of passages where comment was deemed advisable.

The user of this Bible will have at his disposal a fine commentary. It will provide ideal help for the beginner, the advanced student, the teacher, and the Christian family.

OTTO A. DORN
Concordia Publishing House

PREFACE TO THE FIRST EDITION

The Revised Standard Version of the New Testament is an authorized revision of the American Standard Version, published in 1901, which was a revision of the King James Version, published in 1611.

The King James Version was itself a revision rather than a new translation. The first English version of the New Testament made by translation from the Greek was that of William Tyndale, 1525; and this became the foundation for successive versions, notably those of Coverdale, 1535; the Great Bible, 1539; Geneva, 1560; and the Bishops' Bible, 1568. In 1582 a translation of the New Testament, made from the Latin Vulgate by Roman Catholic scholars, was published at Rheims. The translators of the King James Version took into account all of these preceding versions; and comparison shows that it owes something to each of them. It kept felicitous turns of phrase and apt expressions, from whatever source, which had stood the test of public usage.

As a result of the discovery of manuscripts of the New Testament more ancient than those used by the translators in 1611, together with a marked development in Biblical studies, a demand for revision of the King James Version arose in the middle of the nineteenth century. The task was undertaken, by authority of the Church of England, in 1870. The English Revised Version was published in 1881–1885 and the American Standard Version, its variant embodying the preferences of the American scholars associated in the work, was published in 1901.

Because of unhappy experience with unauthorized publications in the two decades between 1881 and 1901, which tampered with the text of the English Revised Version in the supposed interest of the American public, the American Standard Version was copyrighted, to protect the text from unauthorized changes. In 1928 this copyright was acquired by the International Council of Religious Education, and thus passed into the ownership of the churches of the United States and Canada which were associated in this Council through their boards of education and publication.

The Council appointed a Committee of scholars to have charge of the text of the American Standard Version; and in 1937 it authorized this Committee to undertake a further revision, on the ground that there is need for a version which will "embody the best results of modern scholarship as to the meaning of the Scriptures, and express this meaning in English diction which is designed for use in public and private worship and preserves those qualities which have given to the King James Version a supreme place in English literature."

Thirty-two scholars have served as members of the Committee charged with making the revision; and they have secured the review and counsel of an Advisory Board of fifty representatives of the cooperating denominations. The Committee has worked in two Sections, one dealing with the Old Testament and one with the New Testament. Each Section has submitted its work to the scrutiny of the members of the other Section, however; and the charter of the Committee requires that all changes be agreed upon by a two-thirds vote of the total membership of the Committee. The publication of the Revised Standard Version of the Bible, containing the Old and New Testaments, was authorized by vote of the National Council of the Churches of Christ in the U. S. A. in 1951.

The King James Version of the New Testament was based upon a Greek text that was marred by mistakes, containing the accumulated errors of fourteen centuries of manuscript copying. It was essentially the Greek text of the New Testament as edited by Beza, 1589, who closely followed that published by Erasmus, 1516–1535, which was based upon a few medieval manuscripts.

The earliest and best of the eight manuscripts which Erasmus consulted was from the tenth century, and he made the least use of it because it differed most from the commonly received text; Beza had access to two manuscripts of great value, dating from the fifth and sixth centuries, but he made very little use of them because they differed from the text published by Erasmus.

We now possess many more ancient manuscripts of the New Testament, and are far better equipped to seek to recover the original wording of the Greek text. The evidence for the text of the books of the New Testament is better than for any other ancient book, both in the number of extant manuscripts and in the nearness of the date of some of these manuscripts to the date when the book was originally written.

The revisers in the 1870's had most of the evidence that we now have for the Greek text, though the most ancient of all extant manuscripts of the Greek New Testament were not discovered until 1931. But they lacked the resources which discoveries within the past eighty years have afforded for understanding the vocabulary, grammar and idioms of the Greek New Testament. An amazing body of Greek papyri has been unearthed in Egypt since the 1870's — private letters, official reports, wills, business accounts, petitions, and other such trivial, everyday recordings of the ongoing activities of human beings. In 1895 appeared the first of Adolf Deissmann's studies of these ordinary materials. He proved that many words which had hitherto been assumed to belong to what was called "Biblical Greek" were current in the spoken vernacular of the first century A. D. The New Testament was written in the Koiné, the common Greek which was spoken and understood practically everywhere throughout the Roman Empire in the early centuries of the Christian era. This development in the study of New Testament Greek has come since the work on the English Revised Version and the American Standard Version was done, and at many points sheds new light upon the meaning of the Greek text.

Another reason for revision of the King James Version is afforded by changes in English usage. The problem is presented, not so much by its archaic forms or obsolete words, as by the English words which are still in constant use but now convey different meanings from those which they had in 1611 and in the King James Version. These words were once accurate translations of the Hebrew and Greek Scriptures; but now, having changed in meaning, they have become misleading. They no longer say what the King James translators meant them to say.

The King James Version uses the word "let" in the sense of "hinder," "prevent" to mean "precede," "allow" in the sense of "approve," "communicate" for "share," "conversation" for "conduct," "comprehend" for "overcome," "ghost" for "spirit," "wealth" for "well-being," "allege" for "prove," "demand" for "ask," "take no thought" for "be not anxious," "purchase a good degree" for "gain a good standing," etc. The Greek word for "immediately" is translated in the King James Version not only by "immediately" and "straightway" but also by the terms "anon," "by and by" and "presently." There are more than three hundred such English words which are used in the King James Version in a sense substantially different from that which they now convey. It not only does the King James translators no honor, but is quite unfair to them and to the truth which they understood and expressed, to retain these words which now convey meanings they did not intend.

This preface does not undertake to set forth the lines along which the revision has proceeded. That is done in a small book entitled AN INTRODUCTION TO THE REVISED STANDARD VERSION OF THE NEW TESTAMENT, written by the members of the New Testament Section, and designed to help the general public to understand the main principles which have guided this comprehensive revision of the King James and American Standard Versions.

These principles were reaffirmed by the Committee in 1959, in connection with a study of criticisms and suggestions from various readers. As a result, a few changes have been authorized for the present and subsequent editions. Most of these are corrections of punctuation, capitalization, or footnotes. Some changes of words or phrases are made in the interest of consistency, clarity or accuracy of translation. Examples

of such changes are "bread," Matthew 7:9, 1 Corinthians 10:17; "is he," Matthew 21:9 and parallels; "the Son," Matthew 27:54, Mark 15:39; "ask nothing of me," John 16:23; "for this life only," 1 Corinthians 15:19; "the husband of one wife," 1 Timothy 3:2, 12; 5:9; Titus 1:6.

The Bible is more than an historical document to be preserved. And it is more than a classic of English literature to be cherished and admired. It is a record of God's dealing with men, of God's revelation of Himself and His will. It records the life and work of Him in whom the Word of God became flesh and dwelt among men. The Bible carries its full message, not to those who regard it simply as a heritage of the past or who praise its literary style, but to those who read it that they may discern and understand God's Word to men. That Word must not be disguised in phrases that are no longer clear or hidden under words that have changed or lost their meaning. It must stand forth in language that is direct and plain and meaningful to people today. It is our hope and our earnest prayer that this Revised Standard Version of the Bible may be used by God to speak to men in these momentous times, and to help them to understand and believe and obey His Word.

PREFACE TO THE SECOND EDITION

The Revised Standard Version Bible Committee is a continuing body, holding its meetings at regular intervals. It has become both ecumenical and international, with Protestant and Catholic members, who come from Great Britain, Canada, and the United States.

The Second Edition of the translation of the New Testament profits from textual and linguistic studies published since the Revised Standard Version New Testament was first issued in 1946. Many proposals for modification were submitted to the Committee by individuals and by two denominational committees. All of these were given careful attention by the Committee.

Two passages, the longer ending of Mark (16.9-20) and the account of the woman caught in adultery (Jn. 7.53-8.11), are restored to the text, separated from it by a blank space and accompanied by informative notes describing the various arrangements of the text in the ancient authorities. With new manuscript support two passages, Lk. 22.19b-20 and 24.51b, are restored to the text, and one passage, Lk. 22.43-44, is placed in the note, as is a phrase in Lk. 12.39. Notes are added which indicate significant variations, additions, or omissions in the ancient authorities (Mt. 9.34; Mk. 3.16; 7.4; Lk. 24. 32, 51, etc.). Among the new notes are those giving the equivalence of ancient coinage with the contemporary day's or year's wages of a laborer (Mt. 18.24, 28; 20.2, etc.). Some of the revisions clarify the meaning through rephrasing or reordering the text (see Mk. 5.42; Lk. 22.29-30; Jn. 10.33; 1 Cor. 3.9; 2 Cor. 5.19; Heb. 13.13). Even when the changes appear to be largely matters of English style, they have the purpose of presenting to the reader more adequately the meaning of the text (see Mt. 10.8; 12.1; 15.29; 17.20; Lk. 7.36; 11.17; 12.40; Jn. 16.9; Rom. 10.16; 1 Cor. 12.24; 2 Cor. 2.3; 3.5-6; etc.).

CONTENTS

ABBREVIATIONS IN NOTES

OLD TESTAMENT

Gn: Genesis
Ex: Exodus
Lv: Leviticus
Nm: Numbers
Dt: Deuteronomy
Jos: Joshua
Ju: Judges
Ru: Ruth
1 Sm: First Samuel
2 Sm: Second Samuel
1 K: First Kings
2 K: Second Kings
1 Ch: First Chronicles
2 Ch: Second Chronicles
Ez: Ezra
Neh: Nehemiah
Est: Esther
Jb: Job
Ps: Psalms
Pr: Proverbs
Ec: Ecclesiastes
SS: Song of Solomon
Is: Isaiah
Jer: Jeremiah
Lm: Lamentations
Eze: Ezekiel
Dn: Daniel
Hos: Hosea
Jl: Joel
Am: Amos
Ob: Obadiah
Jon: Jonah
Mi: Micah
Nah: Nahum
Hab: Habakkuk
Zph: Zephaniah
Hg: Haggai
Zch: Zechariah
Ml: Malachi

APOCRYPHA

1 Esd: First Esdras
2 Esd: Second Esdras
Tob: Tobit
Jdth: Judith
Ap Est: additions to
   Esther
Wis: Wisdom of Solomon
Sir: Ecclesiasticus, or the
   Wisdom of Jesus the
   Son of Sirach
Bar: Baruch
L Jer: Letter of Jeremiah
Ap Dn: additions to
   Daniel (the Prayer of
   Azariah and the Song
   of the Three Young
   Men)
Sus: Susanna
Bel: Bel and the Dragon
Man: The Prayer of
   Manasseh
1 Mac: First Maccabees
2 Mac: Second Maccabees

OT: Old Testament
NT: New Testament
RSV: Revised Standard
   Version

NEW TESTAMENT

Mt: Matthew
Mk: Mark
Lk: Luke
Jn: John
Acts
Ro: Romans
1 Co: First Corinthians
2 Co: Second Corinthians
Gl: Galatians
Eph: Ephesians
Ph: Philippians
Cl: Colossians
1 Th: First Thessalonians
2 Th: Second Thessa-
   lonians
1 Ti: First Timothy
2 Ti: Second Timothy
Tts: Titus
Phmn: Philemon
Heb: Hebrews
Ja: James
1 Ptr: First Peter
2 Ptr: Second Peter
1 Jn: First John
2 Jn: Second John
3 Jn: Third John
Jude
Rv: Revelation

THE NEW TESTAMENT

INTRODUCTION

The New Covenant, Commonly Called the New Testament, of Our Lord and Savior Jesus Christ is not, strictly speaking, one book at all: it is a collection of documents of different literary types, of varied provenance, and of different dates. And yet we rightly give these documents a common title and treat this collection as one book, for all the varied and diverse witnessing voices heard in it unite to say that which man can say only by the inspiration of the Holy Spirit: *Jesus is Lord* (1 Co 12:3). From The Gospel According to Matthew to The Revelation to John the New Testament is one great adoring acclamation of Jesus of Nazareth as Lord, an anticipation of that day when every knee shall bow to Him and "every tongue confess that Jesus Christ is Lord, to the glory of God the Father." (Ph 2:10-11)

"Lord" has become for us a rather pale and colorless term; to hear it today as the men of the New Testament want it to be heard, we need to recall what made just this title one that could inspire the ultimate loyalty of men, so that for them life became a life to be lived to the Lord and death for His sake became a crowning glory. For the men of the New Testament there was no other title which so comprehensively and compellingly expressed all that Jesus signifies for faith as "Lord." "Lord" clothed Him in His proper glory. The angel who announced the Savior's birth to shepherds proclaimed Him as "Christ the Lord" (Lk 2:11); at Pentecost Peter asserted that the God who had vindicated the Crucified and had exalted Him to glory at His own right hand, to pour out thence the Spirit upon the new people of God, had "made him both Lord and Christ" (Acts 2:36). Paul can sum up the church's confession to Jesus as Son of David and Son of God in the words, "Christ Jesus our Lord" (Ro 1:4); and "the word of faith" which the apostles proclaim says: "If you confess with your lips that Jesus is Lord . . . you will be saved" (Ro 10:9). The church awaiting His return prays, "Come, Lord Jesus!" (Rv 22:20); and "Lord" shall be the word which hails the Son and Servant of God at the end of days. (Ph 2:11)

A word that in its ordinary usage ran the gamut from respectful address ("Sir") to acknowledgment of deity thus became the New Testament church's first creed. By it men acknowledged and committed themselves to Jesus as One who by virtue of His redeeming life and death had won the right and power to rule over all times, all history, and all life, the One in whom alone they could find life and salvation, the only name given under heaven whereby men must be saved. (Acts 4:12)

When the men of the New Testament looked (with eyes of the heart enlightened by the Spirit) to the past, they beheld His Lordship there. They saw Him, at the beginning, present and active in creation, being in person the Word of God that spoke life and light for all (Jn 1:3-4; Cl 1:15-17). They knew that all history had moved toward His coming and His Lordship as toward its judgment and conclusion (Acts 17:30-31), that all God's dealing with man, every manifestation of His righteousness, climaxed in His cross (Ro 3:25-26). The Lordship of Jesus gave them the key to the understanding of the history particularly lit up by the light of God's revelation, the history of Israel prophetically recorded and interpreted in the Old Testament; they recognized their Lord as the as-yet-hidden center and heart of the history that began with the calling and blessing of Abraham. Wherever God dealt graciously with His people, their Lord was there; if God's mercy gave His people water to drink in the wilderness, the Rock from which that water sprang was Christ (1 Co 10:4). His Spirit moved Israel's prophets to utterances that intended Him (1 Ptr 1:10), so that the witness of all the prophets is witness to Him (Acts 10:42 to 43), and He is the Yes to all God's promises from of old (2 Co 1:20). Whatever tokens of God's favor had made bright Israel's way through her history, they all foretokened

3

Him, the ultimate Son of David, God's Anointed, the Christ; *the* Prophet (Acts 3:22; 7:37); *the* Passover Sacrifice that sets God's people free for the final exodus and the last deliverance (1 Co 5:7); *the* Priest-King who offers Himself as the final perfect Sacrifice and inaugurates the new and eternal covenant. (Heb 7 — 10)

However far back they might look, wherever they looked in the past, they saw the approaching glory of their Lord. The Spirit of whom Jesus had promised, "He will glorify me" (Jn 16:14), opened their eyes to see His glory also in the immediate past, in the servant's form of His ministry in the days of His flesh. They saw in John the Baptist the one sent by God to "make straight the way of the Lord" (Jn 1:23). The little sentence with which Luke introduces the raising of the widow's only son at Nain might serve as a caption over all the synoptic gospels: "The Lord . . . had compassion" (Lk 7:13); and the crowning utterance of the fourth gospel is Thomas' confession to the crucified and risen Jesus: "My Lord and my God!" (Jn 20:28)

The Spirit taught them to see the glory of His Lordship even in His Passion, just there. They saw Him as Lord "on the night when he was betrayed," when He gave Himself in self-sacrificing majesty to His own (1 Co 11:23). The "rulers of this age" who crucified Him crucified "the Lord of glory" (1 Co 2:8). Once the promised Spirit had come, they could see His whole life only in the light of His resurrection, as the glory of the Lord who went into the depths of guilt and death for mankind, the glory of Him who was "designated Son of God in power according to the Spirit of holiness by his resurrection from the dead." (Ro 1:4)

The Son of God in power is Lord of the present, "the head over all things for the church" (Eph 1:22). Men who by God's grace have become "his body, the fulness of him who fills all in all" (Eph 1:23) can and must say, "*Our* Lord reigns." He, the Lamb that was slain, is the Lord who controls all history; He and only He can take the sealed book of God's counsels from God's hand, break the seals, open the book, and speed on their way the horses that make havoc and history and so, whether they know and will it or not, carry out God's bright designs and work His sovereign will (Rv 5 — 6): for the Lamb that was slain is "Lord of lords and King of kings." (Rv 17:14)

In the world all must obey Him, and all things must serve His ends; in the church men are privileged and permitted to serve Him. Here His rule and Lordship are acknowledged, proclaimed, and praised. Here Jesus is Lord to the exclusion of all other lords, whatever other lords may lay claim to lordship over men (1 Co 8:5-6); here He is all and in all (Cl 3:11). Here His Word dwells richly, and His peace rules in men's grateful hearts (Cl 3:15-16). Whatever men may do in word or deed is done "in the name of the Lord Jesus" (Cl 3:17), so done that He is known and acknowledged as the Author of every good will and work.

Nothing can call in question this His comprehensive Lordship. Suffering cannot dim its glory for those who call Him Lord. "We rejoice in our sufferings . . . we also rejoice in God through our Lord Jesus Christ" (Ro 5:3, 11). Not even the last and mightiest enemy, before whose onset all other loyalties to lordship cease, not even death can end His reign: "If we live, we live to the Lord, and if we die, we die to the Lord; so then, whether we live or die, we are the Lord's. For to this end Christ died and lived again, that he might be Lord both of the dead and of the living." (Ro 14:8-9)

To Him men live; all living is thankfulness to Him and accountability to Him. Whatever the problems and agonies of a church may be, Paul brings them all under the judicature of the crucified Lord (1 Co). Not even the most casual action is a matter of indifference under this Lordship. James reminds his churches that where a man is seated in church, how poor and rich are treated in the house where men call Jesus Lord is a matter of paramount and eternal concern for men who "hold the faith of our Lord Jesus Christ, the Lord of glory." (Ja 2:1-13)

"Jesus is Lord," His Lordship shines forth from the past, and it illumines the present. But above all, He is Lord of the future. Under His Lordship, by the power of the Spirit bestowed by Him, the Word of the Lord grows on the thorn-infested soil of this world and brings forth fruit destined to fill the garners of God eternally (Acts). Frail earthen vessels, maligned, persecuted, dying men carry abroad the eternal treasure (2 Co 4:7-17) that outlasts all opposing powers and all the wisdom of men. The Book of Acts closes with the picture of imprisoned Paul "teaching about the Lord Jesus, quite openly and unhindered" (Acts 28:31) at Rome, the portal of the Gentile world and

the gateway to the future. To this Lord the future belongs; the Caesars of Rome who are acclaimed as "lord" by fervid subjects have no future comparable to His. Therefore the church, the people of God gathered under His Lordship, is animated by one hope (Eph 4:4), by the living, confident, and trusting expectation that her Lord will return to manifest and exercise His Lordship in open glory. When the men of the church gather to eat the bread and to drink of the cup given them by the Lord as the sign and means of His unbreakable communion with them, they do so with their eyes fixed on the future; they "proclaim the Lord's death *until he comes*" (1 Co 11:26). They pray, "Come, Lord Jesus!" (1 Co 16:22; Rv 22:20); they pray rejoicing, for they know that "the Lord is at hand" (Ph 4:5); they know that waiting for His day is a waiting "for the mercy of the Lord Jesus Christ unto eternal life." (Jude 21)

They can pray confidently and with rejoicing for their Lord's coming, for the future. For the future is no longer a dim and distant prospect; the opaque and ominous wall that separates the present from the future has grown, for them, thin and translucent. For they have received the Spirit; and the Spirit is the guarantee, the firstfruits, and the foretaste of the world to come (Eph 1:4; 2 Co 1:22; Ro 8:23). They have become "partakers of the Holy Spirit"; they "have tasted the heavenly gift . . . and have tasted . . . the powers of the age to come" (Heb 6:4-5). "Through the Spirit, by faith," they scent the fresh and eternal air of God's new world and can in that air live the life of faith working through love.

Martin Luther has caught this primal note of the New Testament witness and has expressed it with characteristic geniality and vigor in his Large Catechism:

If you are asked, "What do you believe . . . concerning Jesus Christ?" answer briefly, "I believe that Jesus Christ, true Son of God, has become my Lord." What does it mean to "become a Lord"? It means that He has redeemed me from sin, from the devil, from death, and all evil. Before this I had no

Lord and King but was captive under the power of the devil. . . . Jesus Christ, the Lord of life and righteousness and every good and blessing . . . has snatched us . . . from the jaws of hell, won us, made us free, and restored us to the Father's favor and grace. He has taken us as His own, under His protection, in order that He may rule us by His righteousness, wisdom, power, life, and blessedness.

"He has made us free . . . He has taken us as His own." Life under Jesus' Lordship is not slavery. When this Lord takes us as His own, He sets us free. He gives us the only genuine freedom that a creature of God can find. For God has created us for Himself, and our heart is restless until it finds rest in Him. We men of the 1970s are men of restless heart, and we dwell amid a nation and in a world of men of restless heart. We shall find no rest (and therefore no freedom) until we find rest in God, under the Lordship of His Son Jesus Christ. If we call Him Lord, we shall have Him for our Lord and shall be able to cease from the futile effort to go it on our own, able to lay our lives in His almighty and compassionate hands. We shall live under Him and work for Him with a purpose and meaning that reaches beyond our little today. For our Lord will hear our prayers, and He will come; history will not end with a meaningless bang nor with a despairing whimper but with the revelation of our Lord Jesus Christ.

It is the purpose of these *Notes* to help men hear the witness of the Holy Spirit in the New Testament more clearly, that they may be moved to heed the invitation to call Him Lord and serve Him in the obedience of faith and the steady buoyancy of hope. This has dictated the manner of interpretation (interpretive paraphrases of larger units rather than verse-by-verse exposition) and the selection of matter. Much that is in its own way interesting and instructive has been omitted or scantily noticed, not merely to save space but primarily to leave room for the New Testament's own major concern: that men may hear the words of Spirit-filled men who bid them call Jesus Lord.

MARTIN H. FRANZMANN

THE GOSPEL ACCORDING TO

MATTHEW

INTRODUCTION

The written gospels belong under the heading of apostolic "teaching." They are the written result of that "apostles' teaching" which Luke speaks of (Acts 2:42) as the first and basic formative element in the life of the first church. The gospels are not primarily the apostolic kerygma (proclamation of the Gospel) as we see it reflected in the sermons of Peter in the Book of Acts or summarized in Pauline passages like 1 Co 15:1-8, proclamations of the basic facts that summon men to the obedience of faith; they are the expansions of that kerygma, the apostolic teaching that builds up the church already called into being by the kerygma.

They are rightly called gospels, good news (and not "teaching") nevertheless. For they of course include all that the kerygma includes: the sending of the Messiah by God in fulfillment of His promises, the Messiah's ministry to men, culminating in His death for the sins of men, His resurrection and His exaltation and the promise of His return. They have the same basic historical outline, as a comparison between Peter's sermon in the house of Cornelius (Acts 10:34-43) and the Gospel According to Mark shows at a glance. Their content is not a biography of Jesus but the Way of the Messiah from the time that John the Baptist prepared the way before Him to the time when God raised Him from the dead; and they have the same basic intention, namely, to lay bare the redemptive meaning of the Way of the Messiah.

The goal of the apostolic kerygma is, then, that men may in faith call Jesus "Lord" in all the fullness of meaning that the word had for the apostles and for the first apostolic church. The goal of the apostolic "teaching" is that this faith may be in every sense the *obedience* of faith, that men may (as Jesus Himself put it) both call Him Lord and do what He tells them (Lk 6:46). The apostolic teaching was from the first, therefore, the natural and necessary extension of the missionary Gospel, an organic growth of the growing Word of the Lord. As our gospels show, this teaching took the form of an ever

fuller recital of the words and deeds of Jesus, a filling in of the outlines of the kerygma with the concrete details of what Jesus taught and did. This teaching thus satisfied the natural desire of the believing and hoping church to have a distinct and rounded-out picture of Him who was the object of her faith and hope; but the satisfaction of the historical interest was not the primary concern of this teaching. If it had been, one would expect the accounts to be much fuller, more nearly complete. As it is, the accounts are anything but complete; John in his old age was able to supplement the first three gospels from his own recollections, and even he makes plain that there is much that remains unwritten (Jn 20:30; 21:25). Likewise, if the historical interest were primary, we should expect the accounts to be more detailed; as it is, they are sparse and terse even in Mark, the most dramatic narrator of them all, while Matthew cuts away everything that is not *religiously* essential. And in all the evangelists much that is invaluable from a historical point of view (the exact sequence of events, for example) is disregarded. The basic interest of the teaching is religious; its aim is to confront men with the Christ (Mt 1:1; Mk 1:1), to preserve and strengthen men's faith in Him (Jn 20:31), and to bring men into a disciple's total obedience to Him. (Mt 28:20)

The gospels are genuinely historical; they record facts, and their account of Jesus' words and deeds follows a historical sequence common to the first three gospels (ministry in Galilee, a period of wanderings, last days and death and resurrection at Jerusalem). But their interest and intent are not merely historical; they do not aim merely at reconstructing a piece of the past. For them history is the dress in which the Messiah of God is clothed in order that He may be revealed and may enter men's lives as the present and powerful Christ. The gospels reflect both halves of Jesus' last words to His disciples, both the command which looks backward, "Teaching them to observe all

that I *have commanded* you," and the promise which marks Him as perpetually present, "Lo, I am with you always." (Mt 28:20)

The Gospel According to Matthew

The religiously didactic character of the gospels is very apparent in the Gospel According to Matthew. Within a generally chronological framework that is common to the first three gospels, the arrangement of the deeds and words of the Christ is topical rather than chronological. The facts are massed and marshaled in impressive and easily remembered units of three, five, and seven. Thus we have in Matthew three major divisions in the genealogy of Jesus with which the gospel opens (Mt 1:1-17), three illustrations of hypocrisy and pure piety (Mt 6:1-18), three parables of planting and growth (Mt 13:1-32). Jesus' words are presented in five great discourses (chs. 5 – 7, 10, 13, 18, 23 – 25), and in the Sermon on the Mount Matthew records five examples that illustrate the full intention of God's law (Mt 5:21-48). Jesus in this gospel pronounces seven woes on the scribes and Pharisees (Mt 23:13-36), and the great parable chapter (Mt 13) contains just seven parables. This topical arrangement is not absolutely peculiar to Matthew; Mark, for instance, twice gives a grouping of five disputes between Jesus and His Judaic adversaries, once in Galilee (Mk 2:1 – 3:6) and again in Jerusalem (Mk 11:27 – 12:44). But it is found in Matthew in a fuller and more highly developed form than in any of the other evangelists.

Another feature that illustrates the didactic character of the first gospel (again not wholly peculiar to Matthew) is Matthew's use of what one may call the "extreme case" method; that is, Matthew illustrates the bent of Jesus' will by means of words and deeds that indicate the extreme limit to which Jesus went – as we illustrate a man's generosity, for instance, by saying, "He'd give you the shirt off his back." The first discourse of Jesus in Matthew begins with the beatitude on the "poor"; Jesus promises the Kingdom and all its blessings to the beggar, to the poor in spirit (Mt 5:3); this removes every limitation from the grace of God and makes it as wide and deep as the need of man. In Matthew's account of Jesus' miracles the first three are extreme-case miracles, which illustrate the lengths to which the compassion of Jesus will go (Mt 8:1-15). Jesus heals the leper whom the Law cannot help, but must exclude from the people of God; He helps the Gentile who is outside the pale of God's people; and He restores to health the woman whom Judaism degraded to the rank of a second-rate creature of God. Now men can take the measure of the potent grace of God present and at work in the Christ. And men can measure the greatness of the divine forgiveness which Jesus brings by another extreme case, by the fact that Jesus calls a tax collector (whom the synagog branded as sinner and excluded) to be His disciple, apostle, and table companion. (Mt 9:9-13)

How rigorous and all-inclusive Jesus' call to repentance is can again be seen by the extreme case: Jesus calls the righteous to repentance; more, He imposes the call to repentance also on the men who have become His disciples (Mt 18:1-4). When Jesus bids His disciples love their *enemies*, He has removed every limitation from their loving (Mt 5:44). When He threatens Peter, the disciple who was ready to forgive seven times, with the wrath of the divine King if he will not forgive without limit, the fullness of the fraternal charity which Jesus inspires in His disciples and demands of them is spelled out in unmistakable clarity. How completely Jesus binds the disciple to Himself can be seen in the fact that Jesus makes His own cross (the climax of His life of ministry) the impulse and the standard of the disciple's ministry. (Mt 10:38; 16:24; 20:25-28)

Still another feature prominent in Matthew's evangelical teaching is the use of contrast. In the genealogy of Jesus, Matthew marks Jesus as son of Abraham and son of David, the crowning issue of Israel's history (Mt 1:1-17). The immediately following section is in sharp contrast to this: Here it is made plain that God gives to Israel what her history cannot give Israel; the Messiah is not the product of Israel's history, but God's creative intervention in that history of guilt and doom; Jesus is conceived by the Holy Spirit (Mt 1:18-23). Jesus in the Beatitudes promises to His disciples all the blessings of the kingdom of the heavens, all the glory of the world to come (5:3-9) – and puts them under the yoke of persecution "for righteousness' sake" (5:10-12). The Christ miraculously multiplies the loaves and fishes and sets a table for thousands in the wilderness (15:32-39) – and yet refuses to show a sign from heaven when the leaders of Judaism demand one (16:1-4). The woman

who spent her money lavishly to anoint the dying Christ is put in close and sharp contrast with the disciple who betrayed Him for money (26:6-13; 26:14-16). The Messiah who in sovereign grace gives Himself, His body and His blood, to His disciples and goes freely into death to inaugurate the new covenant is set side by side with the Messiah whose "soul is very sorrowful, even to death" in Gethsemane (26:26-29; 26:36-46). The Son of Man who claims a seat on the very throne of God and proclaims that He will return on the clouds of heaven (26:64), on the cross cries out, "My God, my God, why hast thou forsaken me?" (27:46). These contrasts are a sort of chiaroscuro in narrative, similar to that process in the pictorial arts which creates its impression not by the clearly drawn line but by the skillful blocking out of figures and features by means of contrasting areas of light and shade. Thus the Christ is portrayed by portraying the absoluteness of His grace for men and the absoluteness of His claim on men, by recording both His claim to an absolute communion with God, which strikes His contemporaries as blasphemous, and His full and suffering humanity, which makes Him a stumbling block to His contemporaries. It is the historical Jesus of Nazareth who is being portrayed, but He is in His every word and work portrayed and proclaimed as the Christ, the Son of God: He is *the* Son who alone of men gives God the glory that is due Him, who alone does battle with Satan and overcomes him, who alone gives His life a ransom for many. He is not a sage, so that His significance for men can be told in His words alone; He is not a hero whose deeds alone can signify what He means in history. He is the Christ, and His whole person, His words and works as a unity, must be recounted if men are to know Him, believe in Him, and have eternal life in His name.

The deep interest in the disciples of Jesus displayed by all the gospels and the amount of attention devoted to them are further testimony to their "teaching" character. In all the gospels Jesus' first Messianic act (after His baptism and temptation) is the calling of disciples; in all of them the story of Jesus' ministry is told in terms of the widening cleavage between Jesus and Israel on the one hand and the deepening communion between Jesus and His disciples on the other. And in all the gospels the supreme revelation of the Messiah, the appearance of the risen Lord, is vouchsafed to the disciples alone. But Matthew gives us the fullest account of the creation of the disciples — how Jesus called them, how He trained them, how they failed in the face of the cross, and how the risen Lord forgave and restored them. The five discourses of Jesus, which determine the structure of Matthew's Gospel, are all addressed to disciples; and the last word of Jesus in Matthew's record of Him is, "Make disciples" (28:19). The thought which is in all the gospels, that Jesus sought nothing and found nothing in the world except the men whom the Father gave Him, His disciples, comes out with especial force and clarity in Matthew. As God is known by His works, so the Christ becomes known to men by His disciples, by the men whom He called and molded in His own image.

Author of the First Gospel

Who is the author of this massive and carefully organized work? The book itself does not name its author. The ancient church, which from the first read and used the first gospel more assiduously than any other, is unanimous in attributing it to Matthew. No other claimant to authorship is ever put forward by anyone. Little is known of Matthew. Matthew, Mark, and Luke all tell us that he was a tax collector at Capernaum and therefore a member of the outcast class publicly branded by the Jewish community as "sinners." Mark and Luke call him Levi (Mk 2:14; Lk 5:27), the son of Alphaeus; only the first gospel calls him Matthew. It may be that he was originally called Levi and that Jesus gave him the name Matthew (which signifies "Gift of God"), just as He named the sons of Zebedee Boanerges and gave Simon his significant name Peter. Or he may have had two names to begin with. At any rate, we may assume that Matthew was the name by which he was best known in the Jewish Christian community and thus became the name attached to the gospel attributed to him.

Matthew is not prominent in the New Testament record of the 12 apostles. All three of the early evangelists tell the story of his call and of the feast he gave to celebrate this turning point in his life, and all three record that he was among the Twelve; but they tell the story of his calling (the only one recorded after the calling of the first four disciples) not as a part of the record of a prominent apostle but as a testimony to the supreme grace of the Christ,

who called into His fellowship and made His messenger one whom Judaism expelled and degraded (Mt 9:9-13; Mk 2:13-17; Lk 5:27-32). As a tax collector, either under the Roman government or under Herod Antipas at Capernaum, he would be a man of some education, skilled in numbers, speaking both Aramaic and Greek, and a man of substance. Early tradition has it that he first preached the Gospel to his countrymen in Palestine, originally wrote his gospel in their tongue, and later went abroad as missionary to other nations. The tradition concerning his later career is relatively late, tends to be fantastic and legendary in character, and often confuses Matthew with Matthias, so that it offers little or no basis for constructing a reliable history of Matthew the evangelist.

Theological Character of the First Gospel

The surest thing we know about Matthew is that Jesus called him as a tax collector. Like Paul, he therefore experienced the call of Jesus under circumstances which marked it most vividly as the absolute divine grace that it was. Matthew no doubt deserved the title the synagog gave him—he was a "sinner." He had, in becoming a tax collector, turned his back on the promise and the blessing given to Israel and had expressed his indifference toward the Law; he had turned to a life whose basic note was a self-seeking materialism. Jesus' call therefore meant for him a radical break with a sinful past; repentance was for him a complete 180-degree turn from sin and self to the grace of God that confronted him in Jesus. Matthew's own experience had given him an unusually keen awareness of how completely and hopelessly man's sin can separate him from God and had impressed on him with unforgettable sharpness the fact that only the grace of the Christ can recall man from that separation into fellowship with God. This gave Matthew a keen perception of two significant features in the words and works of Jesus, features prominent in his gospel.

First, Matthew clearly saw and recorded with emphasis the fact that Jesus' call to repentance is an absolute call demanding the whole man wholly. His gospel is marked by a stern and unsparing opposition to any compromise with evil, whether that compromise be a Jewish or a Christian one. He makes it clear that the call to communion with the Christ is a call to a never-ending struggle against the evil in man that is perpetually threatening this communion. It

is no accident that the words of Jesus which impose on the disciple the duty of correcting and winning the sinning brother are peculiar to Matthew and that the necessity of perpetual forgiveness toward the errant brother is reinforced by one of the most powerful of Jesus' parables, again peculiar to Matthew. (Mt 18:15-35)

Second, Matthew saw that the way to obedience can only be the way of faith, faith that is purely the attitude and action of the beggar who receives the grace of God. Jesus' call had taught him: "One there is who is good" (Mt 19:17). Only One is good, namely God; and no man dare make his own goodness count before Him. But God the Good is surely and wholly good; no man may therefore doubt His goodness and come to God with a divided heart or serve Him with half a devotion. That was the sin of scribe and Pharisee; and Matthew's Gospel is therefore the severest indictment of them in the New Testament. But Matthew indicts the scribe and Pharisee not out of personal animus but on religious grounds. He knew the hollowness and falsity of a religion that could and did degrade the sinner and thus hold him fast in his sin but could not help him by forgiving him. Scribe and Pharisee had shut up the Kingdom before him; Jesus had called him into the Kingdom.

If the call of Jesus set Matthew free from all the authorities that were leading Israel to her doom (ch. 23), it did not separate him from the Old Testament or from the God of Abraham, Isaac, and Jacob. Jesus made a true Israelite of him: His gospel is marked by a rich and constant use of the Old Testament, the fullest of any of the gospels. He sees in the Christ the consummation of Israel's history and the fulfilling of Old Testament prophecy. Of the 29 Old Testament prophecies recorded in the first gospel, 10 are peculiar to Matthew. And the influence of the Old Testament is not confined to the direct citation of the Old Testament. The Old Testament constitutes the ever-present background and the all-pervasive atmosphere of the gospel. For example, the grouping of the words of the Christ in five great discourses is no doubt intended to recall the five books of the Law and the five divisions of the Psalter. The Gospel According to Matthew is fittingly placed at the beginning of our New Testament, for it constitutes the New Testament's most powerful link with the Old.

Matthew is the most austere of the gospels,

stern in its nay to evil, uncompromising in spelling out the inexorable claim of God's grace on the disciple, almost fearfully conscious of how precarious man's hold on that grace is, summoning men to a sober and responsible adoration of the Christ. The austerity of the message is reflected in the sober, restrained, almost colorless style. A monumental quiet seems to brood over the work. The artistry of the gospel is almost entirely confined to the symmetry of its structure. It is as if Matthew had said: "We cannot embellish the Christ with words; we cannot make His grace speak more eloquently by making it speak more beautifully. Let the facts be marshaled and built up into a clear and cleanly articulated whole; let the Christ Himself appear and call men as He once called me. Let the church see how this Jesus of Nazareth once confiscated men by His gracious call. Let the church hear the call of the Christ as I once heard it, and let our human words be but the colorless and transparent vehicle of that call, and the church will remain the church of the Christ." Luke's Gospel has been called the most beautiful book in the world; the Gospel According to Matthew has been termed the most powerful book ever written. A comparison of the parable of the prodigal son, peculiar to Luke (Lk 15:11-32), and the parable of the merciless servant, peculiar to Matthew (Mt 18:23-35), serves to confirm both judgments. The parable peculiar to Luke portrays God's saving act in a warm and moving way, as the act of a father who welcomes home the errant son, and concludes with an appeal to the righteous elder brother to give his glad assent to this free forgiveness of the father. The chief emphasis is on the gratuity of the grace which has appeared in Jesus Christ, a grace offensive to the Pharisee. The parable peculiar to Matthew records God's saving act as the sovereign grace of the king who restores his indebted servant to life and freedom, and the parable is told in order to impress on the disciple what this freedom means for him: God has set him free for his fellowman, in order to forgive as freely and fully as he has been forgiven. The holy obligation which the grace of God imposes, the holy fear in which forgiven man must live by the divine Word of forgiveness in his relation to his fellowman, that is the chief emphasis here. Without the peculiar emphasis of Matthew in the gospel, the church is always in peril of becoming careless and callous, of ceasing to be church. It is no wonder that the gospel which was first written for Jewish Christians and is the most Judaic of them all became also the prime gospel of the Greeks.

Content of the Gospel According to Matthew

The gospel is symmetrically constructed, built up around the five great discourses of Jesus, each marked at its conclusion by the recurrent formula, "When Jesus had finished these sayings" (7:28; 11:1; 13:53; 19:1; 26:1). The five discourses are preceded by an introductory section and followed by the culminating conclusion of the death and resurrection of Jesus. Each of the five discourses is introduced by a recital of deeds of Jesus which prepare for the following discourse and are in turn interpreted by the discourse. Thus there are seven major divisions.

OUTLINE

Behold, Your King Is Coming to You

I. 1:1 – 4:22 Introduction: Jesus the Messianic Fulfiller
   The genealogy and seven fulfillments of prophecy.

II. 4:23 – 7:29 First Group of Messianic Deeds and Words
   The present kingdom and the call to repentance.

III. 8:1 – 10:42 Second Group of Messianic Deeds and Words
   The compassionate Shepherd-King commissions His apostles
   to seek the lost sheep of the house of Israel.

IV. 11:1 – 13:52 Third Group of Messianic Deeds and Words
   The contradicted Messiah conceals the Kingdom from those
   who have rejected it (those who "have not," 13:12) and further

reveals it to those who have accepted it (those who "have," 13:12).

V. 13:53 — 18:35 Fourth Group of Messianic Deeds and Words

Toward the new Messianic people of God, the church: The Messiah separates His disciples from the mass of old Israel, deepens His communion with His own, and shapes their relationship to one another.

VI. 19:1 — 25:46 Fifth Group of Messianic Deeds and Words

The Messiah gives His disciples a sure and responsible hope.

VII. 26:1 — 28:20 Conclusion and Climax

The Passion, death, and resurrection of the Messiah complete and crown His ministry. The risen Lord in the perfection of His grace and power gives His disciples their universal and enduring commission as His apostles.

MATTHEW

Introduction: Jesus the Messianic Fulfiller

1:1 — 4:22

THE GENEALOGY OF JESUS CHRIST (1:1-17)

1 The book of the genealogy of Jesus Christ, the son of David, the son of Abraham.

2 Abraham was the father of Isaac, and Isaac the father of Jacob, and Jacob the father of Judah and his brothers, 3 and Judah the father of Perez and Zerah by Tamar, and Perez the father of Hezron, and Hezron the father of Ram,[a] 4 and Ram[a] the father of Am·min′a·dab, and Am·min′a·dab the father of Nahshon, and Nahshon the father of Salmon, 5 and Salmon the father of Boaz by Rahab, and Boaz the father of Obed by Ruth, and Obed the father of Jesse, 6 and Jesse the father of David the king.

[a] Greek *Aram*

1:1-17 The genealogy of Jesus is hardly meant to be merely proof that Jesus is a son of David. If that were the case, Matthew had no need to go back as far as Abraham. Neither would such proof amount to much; there were thousands of sons of David in Israel, and to prove that a man is a son of David does not demonstrate that he is THE promised Son of David, the Messiah.

Rather, Matthew is linking his story of the Christ with the history of God's dealings with God's people; he is tracing the story of God's blessing, which begins with free grace of His blessing on Abraham (Gn 12:1-3) — in the face of the accumulated curses on man (Gn 3 — 11) — and is to end when the Son of Man shall say: "Come, O blessed of my Father" (Mt 25:34). The genealogy is a terse summary of the OT portion of that history.

Matthew is proclaiming the Christ as the climax of the history of God's mercy to His people (cf. 1:21). God has been in control of that history; Matthew points that up by the symmetrical form of the genealogy (3×14 generations, 1:17). God, the Lord of history, is as much in charge of Israel's generations as God, the Creator, is in charge of the 14 days of the waxing and waning of the moon. Israel's history is the history of His mercy; it rises from Abraham to the splendor of David's reign (v. 6) but then goes downward to the *deportation to Babylon* (v. 11), God's signal punishment upon His people's unfaithfulness, and ends in obscurity — Joseph is a nobody and his wife Mary an unknown.

The presence of four women in the genealogy emphasizes that this is the history of God's mercy, His free blessing. Women do not usually appear in Judaic genealogies, and these four are strange claimants of a place in this history. They are not the famous mothers of the race (Sarah, Rebecca, Rachel, Leah), but women who came by strange ways into God's people. Tamar, Rahab, and Ruth were not born Israelites; perhaps even Bathsheba, "the wife of Uriah" the Hittite, did not have a clear title to a place in Israel. Nor were they all unblemished characters. Matthew's reference to "the wife of Uriah" recalls Bathsheba's adultery; Rahab was a harlot; and Judah's words concerning Tamar ("She is more righteous than I," Gn 38:26) say more about Judah's guilt than about the innocence of hapless Tamar. These women appear, moreover, at key points in the history of Israel: Tamar beside Judah, head of the tribe of the Messianic promise (Gn 49:10); Rahab at the entry into the Promised Land; Ruth in the history of the house of Jesse, father of King David; and Bathsheba beside David as mother of King Solomon. The ancestry of the Christ tells the story of Israel's failure and of God's mercy for both Jew and Gentile. When THE Son of David appears, men can only cry, "Have mercy on us, Son of David." (9:27; 20:31)

1:1 *Book of the genealogy.* Literally "book of the generations" or "history of the origin," as in Gn 5:1, and may be the title for the whole gospel; Matthew is writing the new Genesis, the history of the new creation. (Cf. 4:15-16 and the note there)

1:3-6 For the genealogical material available to Matthew cf. Ru 4:18-22; 1 Ch 2:1-15.

1:3 *Tamar.* Cf. Gn 38.

1:5 *Rahab.* Cf. Jos 2 and 6.

Ruth. Cf. the Book of Ruth.

1:6 *David the king.* To David's house the promise of the anointed King (the Christ) was made. (Cf. 2 Sm 7:4-29; 23:1-7)

Wife of Uriah. Cf. 2 Sm 11:2 — 12:25.

And David was the father of Solomon by the wife of U·ri'ah, 7 and Solomon the father of Re·ho·bo'am, and Re·ho·bo'am the father of A·bi'jah, and A·bi'jah the father of Asa,*b* 8 and Asa*b* the father of Je·hosh'a·phat, and Je·hosh'a·phat the father of Joram, and Joram the father of Uz·zi'ah, 9 and Uz·zi'ah the father of Jotham, and Jotham the father of Ahaz, and Ahaz the father of Hez·e·ki'ah, 10 and Hez·e·ki'ah the father of Ma·nas'seh, and Ma·nas'seh the father of Amos,*c* and Amos*c* the father of Josiah, 11 and Josiah the father of Jech·o·ni'ah and his brothers, at the time of the deportation to Babylon.

12 And after the deportation to Babylon: Jech·o·ni'ah was the father of She·al'ti·el,*d* and She·al'ti·el*d* the father of Ze·rub'ba·bel, 13 and Ze·rub'ba·bel the father of A·bi'ud, and A·bi'ud the father of E·li'a·kim, and E·li'a·kim the father of Azor, 14 and Azor the father of Zadok, and Zadok the father of A'chim, and A'chim the father of E·li'ud, 15 and E·li'ud the father of El·e·a'zar, and El·e·a'zar the father of Matthan, and Matthan the father of Jacob, 16 and Jacob the father of Joseph the husband of Mary, of whom Jesus was born, who is called Christ.

17 So all the generations from Abraham to David were fourteen generations, and from David to the deportation to Babylon fourteen generations, and from the deportation to Babylon to the Christ fourteen generations.

THE SEVEN FULFILLMENTS OF PROPHECY (1:18 — 4:22)

18 Now the birth of Jesus Christ*f* took place in this way. When his mother Mary had been betrothed to Joseph, before they came together she was found to be with child of the Holy Spirit; 19 and her husband Joseph, being a just man and unwilling to put her to shame, resolved to divorce her quietly. 20 But as he considered this,

b Greek *Asaph*   *c* Other authorities read *Amon*   *d* Greek *Salathiel*   *f* Other ancient authorities read *of the Christ*

1:11 *Deportation to Babylon.* Cf. 2 K 24–25.

1:17 *Fourteen generations.* The last unit (vv. 12-16) contains only 13 generations. Perhaps one generation was lost in the copying of the text; or perhaps Matthew is hinting that there is still one generation to come—the generation of those who become free sons of God (17:25-26) through THE Son (cf. Jn 1:12-13 and Ro 8:29), the church.

1:18–4:22 Both the beginning and the end of Jesus' way on earth proved a stumbling block to the faith of His people. They looked on His obscure beginnings and said, "Is not this the carpenter's son? . . . Where then did this man get all this?" (Mt 13:55-56). They looked on His crucifixion, remembered the curse of Deuteronomy (21:23) upon the executed man, and said, "Jesus be cursed" (1 Co 12:3). Matthew proclaims that Jesus is the Christ according to the will and Word of God and cites the OT most richly just at the beginning and the end; he is saying that just here and in just this way the redeeming will of Israel's God is at work, that just here His Word is reaching the full measure of its utterance and effect. His Word is being fulfilled.

Matthew's quotations from the OT are usually very brief; but they seem to be designed to recall (for readers immersed in the OT) a larger context. One is well advised, therefore, to turn to the OT and read Matthew's quotations in their original context.

1:18-25 FIRST FULFILLMENT: IMMANUEL

1:18-25 The promise made to David (cf. 1:6) is fulfilled; by the mysterious and creative operation of His *Spirit,* God implants in the house of David

what the ruined and guilty house of David could not of itself produce, the anointed King who dawns on men like the morning light (cf. 2 Sm 23:4). The fulfillment of the promise is so great and wonderful that *Joseph, son of David,* is overwhelmed and dazed by it. He must be compelled to accept the gift of the Deliverer from sin.

The Deliverer is *Emmanuel,* "God with us" (Is 7:14). In 734 B.C. God had sent His prophet Isaiah to Ahaz, king of Judah, when he was beset by enemies from the north and was willing to barter away his freedom and the future of the people of God by subjecting himself to the Assyrian world power in return for Tiglath-pilezer's assistance in the threatening war. Isaiah sought to turn him from this suicidal course in vain. Ahaz would not believe, and so he was not "established," not held and sustained in the purposes of God (Is 7:9). Isaiah then spoke of a sign given by the Lord Himself, a sign which spelled judgment on unbelief and a blessing to faith. Ahaz might fail, but God would not; He would raise up a Deliverer for His people to fill the place left vacant by unbelieving Ahaz, a Deliverer named *Emmanuel.* Where Ahaz and all Ahaz's successors had failed, there Jesus appears; in Him God's redeeming Word reaches full measure. He is *God with us* for the defeated, hopeless people of God. (Cf. Is 7:1-25; 2 K 16:5-8)

1:18-19 *Betrothed . . . divorce.* With the betrothal the marriage bond was legally established; therefore divorce proceedings were necessary to annul the bond. Cf. Dt 22:22-24, where the violation of a betrothed virgin is punished as adultery.

1:19 *Quietly.* Without the usual public exposure of guilt.

behold, an angel of the Lord appeared to him in a dream, saying, "Joseph, son of David, do not fear to take Mary your wife, for that which is conceived in her is of the Holy Spirit; 21 she will bear a son, and you shall call his name Jesus, for he will save his people from their sins." 22All this took place to fulfil what the Lord had spoken by the prophet:
23   "Behold, a virgin shall conceive and bear a son,
          and his name shall be called Em·man'u·el"
(which means, God with us). 24 When Joseph woke from sleep, he did as the angel of the Lord commanded him; he took his wife, 25 but knew her not until she had borne a son; and he called his name Jesus.

2 Now when Jesus was born in Bethlehem of Judea in the days of Herod the king, behold, wise men from the East came to Jerusalem, saying, 2 "Where is he who has been born king of the Jews? For we have seen his star in the East, and have come to worship him." 3 When Herod the king heard this, he was troubled, and all Jerusalem with him; 4 and assembling all the chief priests and scribes of the people, he inquired of them where the Christ was to be born. 5 They told him, "In Bethlehem of Judea; for so it is written by the prophet:
6   'And you, O Bethlehem, in the land of Judah,
          are by no means least among the rulers of Judah;

1:21 *Jesus* is the Greek form of the Hebrew name Joshua (full form Jehoshua), which means: "Yahweh (the Lord, God of the covenant) is salvation." (Cf. Ps 130:7-8)

1:23 *Virgin.* Thus the Jewish translators of the Old Testament rendered the "young woman" of Is 7:14. The Hebrew word in Isaiah means "the sexually mature girl." However, the OT authors never use the term for a married woman, and in Isaiah the fatherhood of the Child is wrapped in mysterious silence — and that too in a chapter where practically every male person is identified by his descent on the father's side (Is 7:1, 2, 3, 4, 5, 6, 13, 17). Isaiah's contemporary, Micah, similarly speaks of a Deliverer of mysterious parentage (Mi 5:3). The OT is open-ended toward the virgin birth of Jesus; the NT proclaims it here and in Lk 1:26-38. In both gospels the emphasis is on "conceived by the Holy Ghost," God's creative action. Matthew calls Mary "virgin" only in the quotation from Isaiah.

1:25 *Knew her not.* Did not have intercourse with her. (Cf. Gn 4:1)

2:1-12 SECOND FULFILLMENT: RULER FROM BETHLEHEM

2:1-12 In the eighth century B. C., when Jerusalem was threatened by the Assyrian power, God through His prophet Micah promised His people that He would raise up a Ruler and Deliverer for them to give them assured freedom and lasting peace (Mi 5:1-14). He turned His people's eyes away from Jerusalem, the royal residence, center of political power; deliverance was not to come by a development of potentialities present in the people. God would make a fresh beginning in little Bethlehem, the place of small beginnings (cf. 1 Sm 16:1-13). He would bring forth from there a new David, the Messiah, and create a new order for His chastened and restored people. He opened up the future and gave His people a word of hope which could carry them through

not only the Assyrian threat but also the time of all threatening world powers, Babylonian, Persian, Greek, or Roman. *Bethlehem* is not merely a place name; it marks the divine, supernatural character of the Deliverer and the deliverance; the Deliverer would save His people from their sins (Mt 1:21; Mi 5:11-12), and not only His people — He was to "be great to the ends of the earth." (Mi 5:4)

Micah's word finds its fulfillment in Jesus; and the fulfillment is attested in a strangely wondrous way. Israel's scribes (2:4-6) are compelled to point it out to the non-Jewish King Herod and to Gentile wise men from the ends of the earth. Israel remains indifferent to the promised Ruler from Bethlehem; Israel's Idumean King Herod seeks Him out in order to destroy Him; only Gentiles, alerted by His star in the East, guided by the prophetic word and led by His star, seek Him out to worship Him. The story of the wise men is both fulfillment of prophecy (Is 60:3) and a prophecy of things to come: "Many will come from east and west . . . while the sons of the kingdom will be thrown into the outer darkness." (8:11-12)

2:1 *Herod the king,* the powerful, politically adroit, passionate, and ruthless king of the Jews called "the Great" by the Jewish historian Josephus, ruled 37 — 4 B. C. The events recorded by Matthew fall in his last troubled years, when his suspicion and brutality were at fever pitch.

Wise men. The term used, magi, originally designated a priestly class of the Medes and had come to be used generally of Eastern sages versed in knowledge of the stars.

2:2 *King of the Jews,* the Messiah, the Christ, 2:4. (Cf. Jer 23:5; Zch 9:9; Mt 27:11; Jn 1:49)

His star. Cf. Nm 24:17. The wise men were miraculously led (cf. v. 9); whether or not God employed a regular though rare conjunction of Jupiter and Saturn for this purpose is a minor question.

2:6 The quotation of Mi 5:2 is free (*in the land of Judah* replaces the original "Ephrathah," name of

for from you shall come a ruler
who will govern my people Israel.' "

7 Then Herod summoned the wise men secretly and ascertained from them what time the star appeared; [8] and he sent them to Bethlehem, saying, "Go and search diligently for the child, and when you have found him bring me word, that I too may come and worship him." [9] When they had heard the king they went their way; and lo, the star which they had seen in the East went before them, till it came to rest over the place where the child was. [10] When they saw the star, they rejoiced exceedingly with great joy; [11] and going into the house they saw the child with Mary his mother, and they fell down and worshiped him. Then, opening their treasures, they offered him gifts, gold and frankincense and myrrh. [12]And being warned in a dream not to return to Herod, they departed to their own country by another way.

13 Now when they had departed, behold, an angel of the Lord appeared to Joseph in a dream and said, "Rise, take the child and his mother, and flee to Egypt, and remain there till I tell you; for Herod is about to search for the child, to destroy him." [14]And he rose and took the child and his mother by night, and departed to Egypt, [15] and remained there until the death of Herod. This was to fulfil what the Lord had spoken by the prophet, "Out of Egypt have I called my son."

16 Then Herod, when he saw that he had been tricked by the wise men, was in a furious rage, and he sent and killed all the male children in Bethlehem and in all

David's clan), and the scribes interpret as they quote, as was customary; *by no means least* replaces Micah's "little" but gives the sense of the prophecy exactly. Bethlehem was "little" in men's eyes but not in God's. The last line *(who will govern,* etc.) is either a free reproduction of Mi 5:4 or taken from 1 Ch 11:2, where the Lord says to David: "You shall be shepherd of my people Israel, and you shall be prince over my people Israel." (The word translated *govern* is literally the verb for playing the shepherd.) Micah also has "clans of Judah": the reading *rulers of Judah* may be due to a difference in the Hebrew text employed by Matthew or the translation from which he quotes.

2:11 *Treasures . . . gold and frankincense and myrrh.* The richness of the gifts and the recollection of passages like Ps 72:10, Is 49:7, 60:10 probably gave rise to the tradition that the wise men were kings (Kaspar, Melchior, Balthasar). In Matthew the story is not that splendid. The gifts are the traditional treasures of the East. (Cf. Is 60:6; Jer 6:20; Eze 27:22)

2:13-15 THIRD FULFILLMENT: SON CALLED OUT OF EGYPT

2:13-15 Two things are worth noting concerning this "fulfillment." First, what is here being "fulfilled" is a past event and is spoken of by the prophet referred to (Hosea) in the past tense. While we confine the idea of "fulfilling" to the fulfillment of a command or a word of promise, Matthew's use of the word goes beyond these possibilities. He sees the will of God which was expressed in the act of the Exodus *(out of Egypt)* and articulated in the 8th-century prophetic word as reaching its full measure in the coming of the incarnate Son of God to effect the final exodus, the final full deliverance of His people; that is the meaning of *fulfil* here. Second, Matthew reproduces these few words of Hosea with a full consciousness of

their original context and evidently expects his readers to recall it. The context (Hos 11:1-11) speaks of the Lord's love for His people with a fervor and a boldness unparalleled in the Bible:
"When Israel was a child, I loved him,
And out of Egypt I called my son." (Hos 11:1)
In the words of Hosea, Israel's unfaithfulness rouses the anger of the Lord, who has loved so tenderly and lavishly, and He resolves to visit His wrath upon them; but His heart recoils within Him, and His compassion grows warm and tender (Hos 11:8); He will not execute His fierce anger, "for I am God and not man, the Holy One in your midst" (Hos 11:9). Because God's love is God's, it is invincible and it is creative; therefore there remains for Israel a future in which the Lord sees His repentant children come trembling home to Him (Hos 11:10). It is this lavish and holy love which must punish but will save that is reaching its full measure in the sending of the unique Son, a love that will triumph though Israel's alien King Herod may oppose it and Israel's priests and scribes remain at best indifferent to it. (Cf. 2:5-6)

2:16-18 FOURTH FULFILLMENT: RACHEL WEEPING

2:16-18 The thought of the Bible is much less individualistic than ours; a man and his ancestors, a man and his people, feel and know themselves to be one, united in their weal and woe. Thus it was no mere flight of fancy when Jeremiah heard the mother of the race, *Rachel,* weeping from her grave when Israel went into captivity (Jer 31:15). Rachel wept then; and Matthew hears her weep again, now at the climax of Israel's history of guilt and tears. Rachel weeps now when once again the redeeming purposes of God collide with man's selfish will and the mothers of Bethlehem weep for their children. Again Matthew quotes with a consciousness of the original context. Jer 30 and 31 constitute a Book of Comfort of

that region who were two years old or under, according to the time which he had ascertained from the wise men. 17 Then was fulfilled what was spoken by the prophet Jer·e·mi′ah:
18   "A voice was heard in Ramah,
      wailing and loud lamentation,
      Rachel weeping for her children;
      she refused to be consoled,
      because they were no more."

19 But when Herod died, behold, an angel of the Lord appeared in a dream to Joseph in Egypt, saying, 20 "Rise, take the child and his mother, and go to the land of Israel, for those who sought the child's life are dead." 21And he rose and took the child and his mother, and went to the land of Israel. 22 But when he heard that Ar·che·la′us reigned over Judea in place of his father Herod, he was afraid to go there, and being warned in a dream he withdrew to the district of Galilee. 23And he went and dwelt in a city called Nazareth, that what was spoken by the prophets might be fulfilled, "He shall be called a Nazarene."

3 In those days came John the Baptist, preaching in the wilderness of Judea, 2 "Repent, for the kingdom of heaven is at hand." 3 For this is he who was spoken of by the prophet I·sa′iah when he said,
      "The voice of one crying in the wilderness:
      Prepare the way of the Lord,
      make his paths straight."

God's people in the depths of their sorrow; it overflows with promises for a better day, hope for God's great future. Rachel is cheered with the words:
    "Keep your voice from weeping,
    and your eyes from tears . . . .
    There is hope for your future." (Jer 31:16-17)
For all His wrath, the Lord yearns for His "darling child," His people; and He holds out the promise of the new covenant with a people whom He has renewed by forgiving their iniquity and remembering their sin no more (Jer 31:20, 31-34), the hope for a time when the history of God's people would no longer be a history for tears.

2:16 *Tricked by the wise men.* This is of course Herod's point of view. The wise men had actually obeyed God rather than man. (Acts 5:29)

2:18 The town *Ramah* (1 Sm 10:2) lay to the north of Jerusalem; tradition, however, located Rachel's tomb south of Jerusalem near Bethlehem, where a monument to her memory existed at least as early as the fourth century after Christ.

2:19-23 FIFTH FULFILLMENT: CALLED
        A NAZARENE

2:19-23 The Christ, the King of the Jews, lives in small and obscure Nazareth, a town mentioned neither in the OT nor in Judaic writings. This, too, is part of God's design; His Word is being fulfilled. The prophets who had foretold the coming of the Messiah had spoken of His obscure beginnings. Amos had promised that the Lord would "raise up the booth of David that is fallen" (Am 9:11). In Is 9 the Child with the wondrous names ("Wonderful Counselor, Mighty God, etc.," Is 9:6) arises out of deep darkness (Is 9:2) to rule on the throne of David. It is a "shoot from the stump of Jesse," a scion from the judged and ruined royal house who ushers in the time of

righteousness and paradisal peace in Is 11. Zechariah had promised his people a humble king, "humble and riding on an ass" (Zch 9:9). The Servant Messiah of Is 53:2 comes "like a root out of dry ground." All this is fulfilled in Jesus' obscure youth in insignificant Nazareth.

2:20-21 *Land of Israel.* This designation for Palestine occurs only here in the entire NT; it has an archaic ring—the ancient promises of God concerning Israel (cf. Eze 11:17; 20:42; 36:6 ff.; 37:12) are to be fulfilled in this Child in whom "all the promises of God find their Yes" (2 Co 1:20). The Child coming from Egypt enters His own, the promised land of Israel. (Cf. Jn 1:11)

2:22 *Archelaus,* son and principal successor of Herod the Great when Herod died in 4 B. C. Joseph's fear of him was shared by his countrymen and justified by the history of Archelaus' short and violent reign. He was banished by his Roman overlord A. D. 6.

Galilee was governed by Archelaus' brother, Antipas.

2:23 *Called a Nazarene.* Some scholars see a reference here to Is 11:1, where the Hebrew word for shoot *(nezer)* bears some resemblance to the word Nazarene. But how were Greek-speaking readers to catch this? And why is a plurality of *prophets* referred to?

3:1—4:11 SIXTH FULFILLMENT: VOICE
          IN THE WILDERNESS

3:1—4:11 In Is 40 the prophet hears God pronouncing pardon to His people, still captive in Babylon, to all seeming doomed to be forever in captivity to the power of the kingdoms of this world (40:1-2). Then he hears a voice, mysteriously undefined, giving the command that a way be prepared in the wilderness for the triumphant

⁴ Now John wore a garment of camel's hair, and a leather girdle around his waist; and his food was locusts and wild honey. ⁵ Then went out to him Jerusalem and all Judea and all the region about the Jordan, ⁶ and they were baptized by him in the river Jordan, confessing their sins.

7 But when he saw many of the Pharisees and Sad′du·cees coming for baptism, he said to them, "You brood of vipers! Who warned you to flee from the wrath to come? ⁸ Bear fruit that befits repentance, ⁹ and do not presume to say to yourselves, 'We have Abraham as our father'; for I tell you, God is able from these stones to raise up

return of Israel's God, with His people, to Israel's land, that all flesh might behold the revealed glory of Him whose word will stand when all flesh fades and withers, whose coming spells good news for His people – He comes as triumphant Victor, as the Workman who has finished His task and brings His reward with Him, as the Shepherd who will tend His flock with a strong and gentle hand (40:3-11). This ancient voice achieves its full utterance – *Prepare!* – now, when in the face of Israel's utter failure and man's despair a voice is heard in the wilderness announcing the advent of the *kingdom of heaven,* proclaiming the coming of the *mightier* One in whom the Kingdom is to become a reality on earth; bidding men *repent,* to turn toward the God who is turning to them with His renewing Spirit and the dread alternative of fiery judgment on those who refuse His supreme gift. John the Baptist is that voice (cf. Jn 1:23); he *baptizes* men *for repentance,* with a baptism that confers the repentance God demands. He prepares for and ushers in the Son and Servant of God (3:17) who identified Himself with the fallen manhood of Israel by submitting to John's baptism in order to *fulfil all righteousness* (3:15) and meets and conquers the Tempter in the *wilderness,* making good the failure of His people by loving His neighbor as Himself and loving the Lord His God with all His heart. (4:11)

3:1 *Wilderness of Judea.* The southern reaches of the Jordan valley, where John baptized, were wilderness.

3:2 *Repent.* John, last and greatest of the prophets (11:9-11), renews the cry of OT prophecy. The OT prophets conceived of sin as a personal, total turning away from God; they therefore conceived of repentance as a personal and total turning to God (the usual word for repentance in Hebrew is simply "to turn"). They deprecated any merely ritual ceremony of repentance ("Rend your hearts and not your garments," Jl 2:13) and demanded that man turn personally to God in obedience, trust, and radical aversion from self and sin. This turning is God's work in man; He creates the clean heart (Ps 51:10). This last note is particularly clear in John: *Repent, for* – turn to your God, not in order to make Him turn to you but because He has in His grace turned to you. (Cf. Ro 2:4)

3:2 *Kingdom of heaven. Heaven* signifies God; it is one of a number of expressions current in Judaism as a reverential substitute for the divine name. *Kingdom of heaven* summed up for Judaic ears the God of Israel as the OT prophets pro-

claimed Him, King of creation, Lord of all history, whose kingship over His chosen people found a partial and preliminary "incarnation" in the reign of the Davidic kings. The prophets had foretold that this real but hidden reign of God would one day become manifest and universal; God would lay bare His arms finally and definitively to lead all history to its goal, to triumph over all who refused His royal mercy and to bring home to Himself His people gathered from among all nations. "The Lord will become king over all the earth." (Zch 14:9)

3:4 *Garment of camel's hair,* the traditional garb of the prophet (Zch 13:4), particularly of Elijah (2 K 1:8), whose return Malachi had foretold for the last days. (Ml 4:5)

Locusts and wild honey. Locusts were commonly eaten (cf. Lv 11:21-22), as they are by Bedouins to this day. Both the rough garb and the readily obtainable wild food of the Baptist indicate that he, like the apostles after him, did not seek his own but imparted the Word of God "without pay" (10:8). For John's austere mode of life cf. 9:14; 11:18.

3:7 *Pharisees and Sadducees* represent the religiously elite in Judaism. The Pharisees, under the tutelage of the scribes, were the scrupulous pietists of the Law; the Sadducees represented the priestly aristocracy interested in the temple and the priestly interpretation of the Law. These two parties were in opposition to each other on many points. (Cf. Acts 23:6-8)

Brood of vipers. Brood in the sense of "offspring." Their venomous, vicious character is hereditary, in the blood; they boast of being Abraham's children (3:9) but are in reality no true sons of his. For the expression cf. Mt 12:34; 23:33. For the thought cf. Jn 8:39-44, where Jesus tells the sons of Abraham that they are in reality children of the devil, the liar and killer.

The wrath to come. Like the prophets before him (e.g., Zph 1:2-18) and like Paul after him (Ro 1:18 – 3:20), John proclaims the impending wrath of God, His annihilating reaction against all ungodliness and wickedness of man. Not even the religious elite of Israel are exempt; man as man is threatened.

3:9 *Abraham as our father.* See note on 3:7, and cf. Gl 3:6-9; Ro 4:16-17.

Raise up children to Abraham. God's promise to Abraham (Gn 12:1-3) will not fail, even if Abraham's descendants fail; He will raise up children for Abraham from among the Gentiles to inherit His blessing.

children to Abraham. [10] Even now the axe is laid to the root of the trees; every tree therefore that does not bear good fruit is cut down and thrown into the fire.

[11] "I baptize you with water for repentance, but he who is coming after me is mightier than I, whose sandals I am not worthy to carry; he will baptize you with the Holy Spirit and with fire. [12] His winnowing fork is in his hand, and he will clear his threshing floor and gather his wheat into the granary, but the chaff he will burn with unquenchable fire."

[13] Then Jesus came from Galilee to the Jordan to John, to be baptized by him. [14] John would have prevented him, saying, "I need to be baptized by you, and do you come to me?" [15] But Jesus answered him, "Let it be so now; for thus it is fitting for us to fulfil all righteousness." Then he consented. [16]And when Jesus was baptized, he went up immediately from the water and behold, the heavens were opened [g] and he saw the Spirit of God descending like a dove, and alighting on him; [17] and lo, a voice from heaven, saying, "This is my beloved Son,[h] with whom I am well pleased."

4 Then Jesus was led up by the Spirit into the wilderness to be tempted by the devil. [2]And he fasted forty days and forty nights, and afterward he was hungry. [3]And the tempter came and said to him, "If you are the Son of God, command these stones to become loaves of bread." [4] But he answered, "It is written,

'Man shall not live by bread alone,

---

[g] Other ancient authorities add *to him* [h] Or *my Son, my* (or *the*) *Beloved*

3:10 For the *axe* as a symbol of divine judgment cf. Is 10:15; Mt 7:19.

3:11 *Baptize you with the Holy Spirit and with fire. Baptize* means to bestow in fullness (cf. Acts 1:5; 2-33). The *you* is plural; those who repent and believe will receive the promised blessing of the last days from the Coming One; those who disbelieve will forfeit salvation, and the wrath of God (symbolized by fire) remains on them. (Cf. Jn 3:36)

3:11-12 The Mightier One who follows John is nothing less than divine. John is not worthy to perform even the lowliest service for Him (*carry* His *sandals*); the *Holy Spirit* is His to bestow; He executes divine judgment, eternal judgment (*unquenchable fire);* the gathered *wheat* (the redeemed and renewed people of God) is His possession.

3:13-15 These verses make it clear that Jesus, in accepting the baptism of John, is freely identifying Himself with men under the wrath of God. His baptism is the first step toward the cross. Cf. Mk 10:38 and Lk 12:50, where "baptism" clearly refers to the Passion and death of Jesus.

3:15 *Fulfil all righteousness,* the purposes of God. Since this word is spoken against the background of John's proclamation of the wrath of God on all men, *righteousness* probably has the sense of "the redeeming activity of God" familiar to the Jew from the OT (e. g., Ps 103:17; Is 45:8) and familiar from Paul's proclamation (Ro 1:16-18; 3:21). For this sense in Matthew cf. 5:6; 6:33; 21:32.

3:17 *My beloved Son, with whom I am well pleased.* The wording brings to mind two OT passages, one addressed to the anointed King whom the Lord will set on His holy hill to rule over nations to the ends of the earth (Ps 2:6-8), the other addressed to the Servant whom God the Lord gives as a covenant to His people and a light to the nations (Is 42:1, 6), the Servant whose ministry carries Him into a vicarious death for the sins of many and beyond death into life and triumph (Is 52:13 – 53:12). God's approval rests on the Son and King as He makes Himself one with sinners, the Servant who is to die for all.

4:1-11 In the temptation Jesus is revealed as the obedient Son that Israel was to be (Ex 4:22-23) and never was. The devil appeals to Him as the unique *Son* whom the voice from heaven had attested at His baptism (3:17) and bids Him exploit a Son's privilege (4:3). Jesus takes His stand as man simply, as the obedient son (Israel) addressed in Dt, and wills to *live by every word that proceeds from the mouth of God* (4:4; Dt 8:3), whatever the words may impose on Him, even suffering and death (cf. 26:54). This same will, which is the theme of Dt, refuses to invert the relationship between God and man by tempting God, putting Him to the test, experimenting with Him, manipulating Him, trying to make God live by the word that proceeds from the mouth of man (4:7; Dt 6:16), but gives God a whole worship and an unquestioning service (4:10; Dt 6:13). Thus the upward-reaching satanic will is thwarted (cf. Ph 2:6), the Law is written on the heart of man (Jer 31:33) in this representative Man, and the fulfillment of all righteousness (3:15) is carried another step forward.

4:1 *Led up by the Spirit.* The confrontation with the devil comes by God's will, not by any free initiative of the devil.

4:2 *Forty days and forty nights.* The inclusion of *nights* marks the extraordinary character of this fast; the Jew ordinarily fasted only from sunrise to sunset. *Forty* is commonly used in the Bible as a round number, e.g., to indicate the usual length of a critical period. (Gn 7:4; 8:6; Ex 24:18; Nm 13:25; 1 Sm 17:16; 1 K 19:8; Eze 4:6)

4:4 *It is written.* Ps 91:11-12.

but by every word that proceeds from the mouth of God.' "
5 Then the devil took him to the holy city, and set him on the pinnacle of the temple,
6 and said to him, "If you are the Son of God, throw yourself down; for it is written,
'He will give his angels charge of you,'
and
'On their hands they will bear you up,
lest you strike your foot against a stone.' "
7 Jesus said to him, "Again it is written, 'You shall not tempt the Lord your God.' "
8Again, the devil took him to a very high mountain, and showed him all the kingdoms of the world and the glory of them; 9 and he said to him, "All these I will give you, if you will fall down and worship me." 10 Then Jesus said to him, "Begone, Satan! for it is written,
'You shall worship the Lord your God
and him only shall you serve.' "
11 Then the devil left him, and behold, angels came and ministered to him.
12 Now when he heard that John had been arrested, he withdrew into Galilee; 13 and leaving Nazareth he went and dwelt in Ca·per′na·um by the sea, in the territory of Zeb′u·lun and Naph′ta·li, 14 that what was spoken by the prophet I·sa′iah might be fulfilled:
15 "The land of Zeb′u·lun and the land of Naph′ta·li,
toward the sea, across the Jordan,
Galilee of the Gentiles—
16 the people who sat in darkness
have seen a great light,
and for those who sat in the region and shadow of death
light has dawned."
17 From that time Jesus began to preach, saying, "Repent, for the kingdom of heaven is at hand."

4:7 *Again it is written.* Only Scripture can speak against Scripture, to prevent its misuse and to interpret it rightly. The light shed by Dt 6:16 on man's basic relationship to his God lets him understand Ps 91 rightly and keeps him from confusing the confidence of faith with self-willed and self-seeking presumption.

4:9 *Fall down and worship me.* The devil asks a little compromise, one act of obeisance to himself, and in return promises that He shall reign as anointed King without struggle and pain.

4:11 *Angels came and ministered.* The Greek word for *ministered* suggests service at table; the Father gave His obedient Son the bread which He would not seek for Himself. (Cf. 6:33)

4:12-22 SEVENTH FULFILLMENT:
THE GREAT LIGHT

4:12-22 In 734 and 732 B. C. the Assyrian king Tiglath-pileser waged two campaigns against Israel and incorporated into his empire large northern tracts of the Promised Land (2 K 15:29). To Israel it seemed that the promises of God were failing; if the God of Israel "brought into contempt the land of Zebulun and the land of Naphtali" (Is 9:1), what would the end be? Where was the hope and the future of God's people? To this Isaiah replied that the promises of God hold, however great the guilt of His people and the severity of His judgment might be; the God who brought the land into contempt, even He, would "in the latter time . . . make glorious the way of the sea, the

land beyond Jordan, Galilee of the nations" (Is 9:1). And the great reversal of grace would begin just there where His judgment had first struck; in *Galilee,* contemptuously called *Galilee of the Gentiles* because of its mixed population, the *great light* of His new creation would shine. A new "Let light shine" would usher in a new epoch of salvation; for a Son, a Child, would be given to the people, a Child with names that speak the blessing of His reign on the throne of David ("Wonderful Counselor, Mighty God, Everlasting Father, Prince of Peace"), a reign of peace and justice without end, a reign established and eternally guaranteed by "the zeal of the Lord of hosts" (Is 9:2-7). This word of Isaiah is now fulfilled, now when Jesus appears, just in *Galilee of the Gentiles,* after the voice of John has been silenced by his imprisonment, to renew John's cry of the Kingdom at hand, to gather the new people of God, the first of the disciples and apostles. This is the dawn of the new creation; these called apostles could say with Paul: "The God who said, 'Let light shine out of darkness' . . . has shone in our hearts to give the light of the knowledge of the glory of God in the face of Christ." (2 Co 4:6)

4:12 *John . . . arrested.* Cf. 11:2; 14:3-5.

4:14 *Spoken by . . . Isaiah.* Is 9:1-2. Matthew is conscious of the whole Messianic context in Isaiah. (9:1-7)

4:16 *Great light,* not a mere glimmering on the horizon but the full light of the new creation.

4:17 Jesus' announcement of the coming of the

18 As he walked by the Sea of Galilee, he saw two brothers, Simon who is called Peter and Andrew his brother, casting a net into the sea; for they were fishermen. [19]And he said to them, "Follow me, and I will make you fishers of men." 20 Immediately they left their nets and followed him. [21]And going on from there he saw two other brothers, James the son of Zeb′e·dee and John his brother, in the boat with Zeb′e·dee their father, mending their nets, and he called them. 22 Immediately they left the boat and their father, and followed him.

First Group of Messianic Deeds and Words
4:23 — 7:29

23 And he went about all Galilee, teaching in their synagogues and preaching the gospel of the kingdom and healing every disease and every infirmity among the people. [24] So his fame spread throughout all Syria, and they brought him all the sick, those afflicted with various diseases and pains, demoniacs, epileptics, and paralytics, and he healed them. [25]And great crowds followed him from Galilee and the De·cap′o·lis and Jerusalem and Judea and from beyond the Jordan.

THE SERMON ON THE MOUNT (5:1 — 7:29)

5 Seeing the crowds, he went up on the mountain, and when he sat down his disciples came to him. [2]And he opened his mouth and taught them, saying:
3 "Blessed are the poor in spirit, for theirs is the kingdom of heaven.

---

kingdom, directly and logically *(for)* connected with the call to *repentance,* is identical with John's (3:2); but Matthew makes clear the distinction between the two by means of the Scripture cited to illumine each. John's call is preparatory (3:3); Jesus' announcement is word and act in one.

4:18-22 The calling of the first four disciples-apostles is the first item under the rubric "the kingdom of heaven is at hand." This is divinely royal grace in action, creating the nucleus of the new Israel. The disciples do not choose their teacher as was usual in Judaism; Jesus chooses them (cf. Jn 15:16). And there is no stress on the disciples' qualification for the call. The emphasis is on Jesus Himself, who calls with the sovereign freedom of God to Himself alone. He lays on men His gentle yoke of obedience and renunciation and promises them a life of ministry as *fishers of men* (19). The great light has fallen on men; the new people of God is coming into being, and the last great age of God has begun.

4:18 *Called Peter.* For the significance of the name cf. 16:18 note.

4:21 *Called.* As God once called Abraham (Is 51:2) and His people Israel. (Hos 11:1)

4:23 — 7:29 The account of the Messianic deeds that precedes the discourse is very brief in this unit (4:23-25). There is a sketch of Jesus' characteristic activity, just enough to identify Him as the Christ, the kingdom of heaven in person (cf. 12:28). The authority with which He teaches (7:29) is that of the One who proclaims the Kingdom, heals every disease, overcomes the powers of the devil (*demoniacs,* 4:24). His Word is a Messianic word that bestows the blessings it pronounces and moulds men in the image of the Christ. (Chs. 5 — 7)

4:23-25 JESUS' MINISTRY IN GALILEE

4:23 *Teaching in their synagogues and preaching the gospel of the kingdom.* For a vivid account of such teaching and preaching see Lk 4:14-21.

4:25 *Decapolis.* A loose federation of 10 (or more) cities, centers of Greek culture, most of them lying to the east of the Jordan. Decapolis serves to point out how far east (and north) the influence of Jesus had reached.

5:1 — 7:29 The Sermon on the Mount is the record of how Jesus moulds the will of His disciple, leading the disciple to live a life wholly drawn from God the King as He is revealed in these last days in His Son, a life which is therefore wholly lived for God the King. The gift of the Kingdom and the claim of the Kingdom (the call to repentance) are to shape the disciple's whole existence.

5:1-12 THE BEATITUDES

5:1-12 Jesus' first words mark Him as the Giver. The word *blessed* indicates that God has acted or is acting or will act for man's good (cf. e.g., Ps 32:1-2; 65:4; 84:12; Dt 33:29; Rv 14:13; 19:9). In Matthew *blessed* is always associated with God's action in Jesus Himself (11:6; 13:16-17; 16:17; 24:46). Jesus' Beatitudes therefore declare what He is and gives; they are a Messianic self-attestation.

5:3 *Poor in spirit.* To the beggarly, those whose state is such that they must look to God for everything and whose disposition is such that they do look to God for everything (the repentant), Jesus' potent Word gives the *kingdom of heaven.* God in His grace is their King; and they are permitted to enjoy and share in His reign. That reign is present *(theirs is)* for them in Jesus. The promise of the

4 "Blessed are those who mourn, for they shall be comforted.

5 "Blessed are the meek, for they shall inherit the earth.

6 "Blessed are those who hunger and thirst for righteousness, for they shall be satisfied.

7 "Blessed are the merciful, for they shall obtain mercy.

8 "Blessed are the pure in heart, for they shall see God.

9 "Blessed are the peacemakers, for they shall be called sons of God.

10 "Blessed are those who are persecuted for righteousness' sake, for theirs is the kingdom of heaven.

11 "Blessed are you when men revile you and persecute you and utter all kinds of evil against you falsely on my account. 12 Rejoice and be glad, for your reward is great in heaven, for so men persecuted the prophets who were before you.

first (5:3) and the eighth Beatitude (5:10) is the promise of the Kingdom and is in the present tense; the promises of the other Beatitudes are in the future and portray the ultimate, future blessings of the Kingdom, the final fruit of Jesus' royal ministry. (Cf. 25:34)

5:4 *Those who mourn* are "those who mourn in Zion" (Is 61:3); their mourning is the expression of their intense longing for Him who is the Comfort (Is 61:2) of the afflicted and the brokenhearted. God will comfort them (the passive verb *be comforted* indicates God's action, as often) and God's comforting is Jesus, "the Lord's Christ." (Cf. Lk 2:25-26)

5:5 Jesus' promise to the meek is practically a quotation from Ps 37:11. That psalm pictures the meek as those who trust in the Lord, commit their way to Him, are still before Him, wait patiently for Him confident that He will bring forth their vindication as the Light, will help them, deliver them, and save them because they take refuge in Him. Jesus Himself will go that way of meekness (11:29; 21:5) into death and victory. As the triumphant Messiah He will fulfill the promise of Isaiah "and decide with equity for the *meek* of the earth" (Is 11:4). Those who are His will *inherit the earth* with Him who shall have authority in heaven and on earth. (28:18)

5:6 Those who long for *righteousness,* knowing that they must die without it *(hunger and thirst), shall be satisfied—*God will give them righteousness and life. Jesus is that righteousness in person, the fulfillment of Jeremiah's promise of a Messiah whose name was to be "the Lord is our righteousness" (Jer 23:5-6). Cf. Mt 3:15 and the note there. In 5:10-11 Jesus Himself indicates that suffering for righteousness' sake and suffering for His sake are one and the same.

5:7-10 The first four Beatitudes are a unit; the persons are the same and the promise and gift of Jesus is one. Jesus is giving to those who have nothing and need everything that which answers their every need—comfort, the earth, righteousness, the Kingdom. The last four Beatitudes also are a unit. The promises bring into view the Last Judgment and the new world God the King will create. And the promises are made to men who have tasted the powers of the world to come in God's present reign, in Christ, and are manifesting

that new world in their actions even now.

5:7 *The merciful* have learned mercy from Him whom Jesus revealed as their Father (5:44-48), who desires mercy and not sacrifice (9:13; 12:7). The life they drew from God made them merciful. To them Jesus promises *mercy* in the Judgment. Cf. 25:34-40, where Jesus bestows the blessing of the Father and the inheritance of the Kingdom on the merciful.

5:8 The *pure in heart* are the men of singlehearted, pure devotion, men who have learned from the Son to live by every word that proceeds from the mouth of God to give God that obedience of faith and pure adoration which Jesus made possible by His overcoming of the Tempter (4:1-10) and His obedience unto death. They *shall see God* at the end of days. The vision of God is for Biblical thought not a mystical experience but an eschatological one. In this age men hear God's Word; they shall see His face in the world to come. (1 Co 13: 12; Rv 22:4)

5:9 The *peacemakers* are those who follow in the train of the Messianic Prince of Peace (Is 9:6), who have learned peacemaking from the meek King who speaks peace to the nations (Zch 9:10) and have by word and deed brought His peace to men (10:13). God said "This is my beloved Son" of Him who became Prince of Peace by a ministry that bound Him to men in their guilt (3:17); He will *call* those men His *sons* who witness to and serve the Son.

5:10 *Persecuted for righteousness' sake.* Jesus, God's Son and Servant, goes the way through contempt, rejection, and dying to glory and royal reign (Is 53); all sons and servants are called on to follow Him on that way: "We suffer with him in order that we may also be glorified with him" (Ro 8:17; cf. 2 Ti 2:12). To be on the path of suffering is to be on the road to the Kingdom; and the assurance of this is blessedness even now. (Ro 5:2-5)

5:11-12 To find blessedness in suffering does not come naturally to men; Jesus therefore reinforces the last Beatitude. His disciples are not merely to accept persecution and endure it stoically. They are to speak a glad and resolute yea to it and find in it the assurance that thus, in communion with the Servant Christ, they stand in the succession of the *prophets* and can look forward to a great reward.

13 "You are the salt of the earth; but if salt has lost its taste, how shall its saltness be restored? It is no longer good for anything except to be thrown out and trodden under foot by men.

14 "You are the light of the world. A city set on a hill cannot be hid. 15 Nor do men light a lamp and put it under a bushel, but on a stand, and it gives light to all in the house. 16 Let your light so shine before men, that they may see your good works and give glory to your Father who is in heaven.

17 "Think not that I have come to abolish the law and the prophets; I have come not to abolish them but to fulfil them. 18 For truly, I say to you, till heaven and earth pass away, not an iota, not a dot, will pass from the law until all is accomplished. 19 Whoever then relaxes one of the least of these commandments and teaches men so, shall be called least in the kingdom of heaven; but he who does them and teaches them shall be called great in the kingdom of heaven. 20 For I tell you, unless your righteousness exceeds that of the scribes and Pharisees, you will never enter the kingdom of heaven.

21 "You have heard that it was said to the men of old, 'You shall not kill; and whoever kills shall be liable to judgment.' 22 But I say to you that every one who is angry with his brother[i] shall be liable to judgment; whoever insults[j] his brother shall be liable to the council, and whoever says, 'You fool!' shall be liable to the hell[k] of fire. 23 So if you are offering your gift at the altar, and there remember that your brother has something against you, 24 leave your gift there before the altar and go; first be reconciled to your brother, and then come and offer your gift. 25 Make friends quickly with your accuser, while you are going with him to court, lest your accuser hand you over to the judge, and the judge to the guard, and you be put in prison; 26 truly, I say to you, you will never get out till you have paid the last penny.

[i] Other ancient authorities insert *without cause* [j] Greek *says Raca to* (an obscure term of abuse) [k] Greek *Gehenna*

5:13-16 SALT, LIGHT, CITY ON A HILL: GOOD WORKS

5:13-16 The last four Beatitudes have already indicated that the coming of the Kingdom changes and ennobles the lives of men. The poor in spirit can only receive from God; but they do receive, and God's giving makes them merciful. The present section makes clear that this must happen. *Salt* must by its very nature be salt, *light* must shine, a *city on a hill* is inevitably seen. If a disciple refuses to function as a disciple, he has ceased to be a disciple and involves judgment on himself; he has become saltless salt which can only *be thrown out* (13; cf. Jn 15:2, 6). As sons of God the disciples naturally so live and work that their Father is *glorified* — is known, acknowledged, and adored by men. (16; cf. 1 Ptr 2:12)

5:17-20 JESUS THE FULFILLER: THE NEW RIGHTEOUSNESS OF THE DISCIPLE

5:17-20 In the solitary hour of His temptation (4:1-10) Jesus had overcome Satan with three words from Deuteronomy; He had thus implicitly spoken His assent to God's ancient Word, the OT Scriptures. He now speaks this assent to the *law and the prophets* explicitly and publicly. Moreover, He marks His whole Messianic mission as determined by the entire OT Scriptures; every claim of the Law will be satisfied by Him, every condemnation of the Law will be executed upon Him (cf. Gl 3:13), every prophetic promise of

God will be fulfilled in Him (cf. 2 Co 1:20). God's new last-days act, the coming of His kingdom, is witnessed by the Law and upholds the Law (cf. Ro 3:21, 31). For the disciple the way to the new righteousness (which takes the "just requirements" of the Law more seriously than the scribe and Pharisee ever did) is through Jesus, the Fulfiller of Law and prophets. (Cf. Ro 8:3-4)

5:18 Cf. 24:35, where Jesus claims for His own Word more than He here asserts of the Law.

5:19 *The least.* Since Jesus has the written page before His mind's eye (iota . . . dot, 18), He is probably referring to basic commandments, which are least on the page, such as the Fifth Commandment, three syllables in Hebrew.

5:20 *Scribes,* the professional interpreters of the Law, and *Pharisees,* men devoted to the scrupulous fulfillment of the Law and the "tradition of the elders" (15:2), represent the apex of Judaic piety.

5:21-48 THE NEW RIGHTEOUSNESS: FIVE EXAMPLES

5:21-48 With five examples Jesus illustrates the nature of the new "exceeding" (20) righteousness. His mighty *But I say to you* reveals that He is the end of the Law (Ro 10:4); His treatment of the intention and will of the Law shows that He is the end because He is the Fulfiller and ushers in the new age.

5:21-26 The new righteousness (which "exceeds" purely legal corrections of conduct) exemplified by

27 "You have heard that it was said, 'You shall not commit adultery.' 28 But I say to you that every one who looks at a woman lustfully has already committed adultery with her in his heart. 29 If your right eye causes you to sin, pluck it out and throw it away; it is better that you lose one of your members than that your whole body be thrown into hell.*k* 30And if your right hand causes you to sin, cut it off and throw it away; it is better that you lose one of your members than that your whole body go into hell.*k*

31 "It was also said, 'Whoever divorces his wife, let him give her a certificate of divorce.' 32 But I say to you that every one who divorces his wife, except on the ground of unchastity, makes her an adulteress; and whoever marries a divorced woman commits adultery.

33 "Again you have heard that it was said to the men of old, 'You shall not swear falsely, but shall perform to the Lord what you have sworn.' 34 But I say to you, Do not swear at all, either by heaven, for it is the throne of God, 35 or by the earth, for it is his footstool, or by Jerusalem, for it is the city of the great King. 36And do not swear by your head, for you cannot make one hair white or black. 37 Let what you say be simply 'Yes' or 'No'; anything more than this comes from evil.*l*

38 "You have heard that it was said, 'An eye for an eye and a tooth for a tooth.' 39 But I say to you, Do not resist one who is evil. But if any one strikes you on the

k Greek *Gehenna*   *l* Or *the evil one*

the Fifth Commandment. The disciple sees the protecting hand of God extended not only over his brother's physical life but over his whole life, which is threatened by his fellowman's angry thought and slighting word as well as by his murderous hand.

5:22 *The council,* the supreme Jewish court, presided over by the high priest, composed of high priests, elders, and scribes.

5:24-25 *First be reconciled . . . make friends quickly.* All days since the coming of the Christ are last days (Heb 1:1) and are filled with last-days urgency. No act of worship dare delay reconciliation with the injured brother, for all roads lead to the judgment throne of God, who will punish, inevitably and severely, all loveless action (cf. 18:32-35). If God's royal favor has not made the disciple merciful (5:7), he may not look for mercy in the Last Judgment. (Ja 2:13)

5:27-32 The new righteousness exemplified by the Sixth Commandment. God is witness to the marriage covenant and "hates divorce" as much as bloody violence (Ml 2:14-16). He keeps a jealous and all-seeing watch over marriage, which is violated by the lustful look and by divorce as well as by overt adultery. From this God the disciple draws his life, and he lives his life before Him as his Father; he therefore keeps his *eye* and *hand* under iron discipline (29, 30), lest he look and lust and reach for forbidden fruit and be separated forever from his God and Father (*hell,* 30).

5:29-30 *Eye . . . hand.* In Biblical thought the various parts of the body are the expressive instruments of man's will and may stand for the whole man in action ("Turn your foot away from evil," Pr 4:27). To *pluck out* the *eye* or to *cut off the hand* therefore signifies resolute repression of sinful desire, however painful the effort may be.

5:31 The Law conceded divorce and prescribed the *certificate of divorce* (Dt 24:1-4) because the

Law could not overcome man's "hardness of heart" (19:8). But God's intention at creation was life-long indissoluble union between man and woman (19:3-6). This divine intention Jesus is now re-asserting and inscribing on the heart of his disciple.

5:32 *Except on the ground of unchastity.* Judaism in general interpreted the Mosaic prescription concerning divorce very liberally, and a man could divorce his wife for almost "any cause" (19:3). Jesus championed the cause of woman, left help-less and without honor by this procedure, but she can no more violate marriage with impunity than the husband can.

5:33-37 The new righteousness exemplified by the Law concerning oaths (Lv 19:12; Nm 30:2; Dt 23:21). Jesus applied the Fifth and Sixth Com-mandments to His disciples with radical rigor; in this case (as in the following, 38-42) He with Messianic authority sets aside the prescription of the Law entirely. He does so, however, in order that the intention of the Law may be fully realized. The Law prescribed the oath with the intention that man be reminded, on occasion at least, that he is speaking in the presence of his God. Jesus re-moves the oath in order that His disciple may speak his every *Yes* and *No* as in the presence of God.

5:34-36 The Jew tended to evade the serious-ness of the oath by artificial distinctions between binding and nonbinding oaths (23:16-22). Jesus sweeps away all such sophistry.

5:37 *From evil.* The reading of RSV note *l (the evil one)* seems preferable. It is the influence of the devil, the "father of lies" (Jn 8:44), which makes the oath a necessity in law.

5:38-42 The new righteousness exemplified by the law of retaliation (Ex 21:24; Lv 24:20; Dt 19:21). The Law cannot remove the desire for vengeance from man's heart; it can only, as it

right cheek, turn to him the other also; 40 and if any one would sue you and take your coat, let him have your cloak as well; 41 and if any one forces you to go one mile, go with him two miles. 42 Give to him who begs from you, and do not refuse him who would borrow from you.

43 "You have heard that it was said, 'You shall love your neighbor and hate your enemy.' 44 But I say to you, Love your enemies and pray for those who persecute you, 45 so that you may be sons of your Father who is in heaven; for he makes his sun rise on the evil and on the good, and sends rain on the just and on the unjust. 46 For if you love those who love you, what reward have you? Do not even the tax collectors do the same? 47And if you salute only your brethren, what more are you doing than others? Do not even the Gentiles do the same? 48 You, therefore, must be perfect, as your heavenly Father is perfect.

6 "Beware of practicing your piety before men in order to be seen by them; for then you will have no reward from your Father who is in heaven.

2 "Thus, when you give alms, sound no trumpet before you, as the hypocrites do in the synagogues and in the streets, that they may be praised by men. Truly, I say to you, they have received their reward. 3 But when you give alms, do not let your left hand know what your right hand is doing, 4 so that your alms may be in secret; and your Father who sees in secret will reward you.

were, regulate revenge, setting a limit to it *(eye for an eye)*. Jesus removes the impulse of revenge from His disciples' hearts and bids them live, as He Himself lived, in a love that recklessly exposes itself to the lovelessness of the world and the need of men.

5:43-48 The new righteousness exemplified by the law of love. The Law enjoined love for the neighbor; legalism (the attempt to find favor with God and to stand in His judgment by way of works of the Law) raised the question, "Who is my neighbor?" (Lk 10:29), and sought to limit the imperative of love by finding scope for lovelessness and hate. Jesus removes every limitation from the law of love by enjoining love for the enemy. The highest "righteousness" is love. Jesus went this way of love for the enemy before His disciples and for them; He joined Himself, in love, to men under the wrath of God when He was baptized; He loved the enemy in order to "fulfil all righteousness" (3:15). That way of love took Him to the cross, "so that in Him we might become the righteousness of God." (2 Co 5:21)

5:45 *Be sons,* literally "become sons," that is, "show yourself to be, evince yourselves as" sons of the God who loves spontaneously and freely without regard for the worthiness of the objects of His love. Sonship involves both: getting one's life from the Father and living a life of love in communion with Him.

5:46 *Even the tax collectors,* hated and despised by good Jews because of their connection with the Roman rule and their greed and dishonesty. (Cf. Lk 3:13; 19:8)

5:48 *Perfect,* in love without reservation or limit, the kind of "perfection" which Jesus held before the rich young man when He bade him sell all his possessions and give them to the poor. (19:21)

As your heavenly Father. For this use of *as* to indicate not only the pattern but also the power for right action see 20:28: "Even as the Son of man

came . . . to serve." It is the Gospel of the Father who loves His enemies and the Son who serves that makes men capable of obeying the Law and glorifying their Father in heaven.

6:1-18 THE PIETY OF THE DISCIPLE

6:1-18 The new righteousness brings with it a new piety, which Jesus illustrates by the familiar Judaic triad of *almsgiving* (2-4), *prayer* (5-15), and *fasting* (16-18). As the new righteousness of the disciple is the expression of a life derived from the Father and lived for the Father, so the new piety is distinguished by the same purity of heart, by selfless and unalloyed devotion to the Father. The Father-child relationship gives this piety its characteristic color; the phrase *your Father* occurs nine times in these 18 verses. Since the Father *sees in secret* (4, 6, 18), self-consciousness and display and applause seeking disappear from this piety. Since it is the Father who *rewards* (4, 6, 18) His child with a Father's generous and forgiving love, the disciple does not strain for merit and reward, nor does he seek his reward from men. Thus Jesus takes over the Judaic idea of reward and transforms it; the truth that lives in the idea — that man is set before God in his actions and is responsible to Him — is retained; but man no longer works in order to obtain the favor of God — he works because he is in the sunshine of God's favor.

6:2 *Hypocrites* attempt to divide their heart between God and man. Unable to trust God as their Father for His reward, they seek the reward of men's approval and admiration.

Sound no trumpet. Figurative for "Do not publicize."

6:3 *Left hand know.* Do not let your left hand point to the right hand to call attention to the act of giving.

6:4 *Sees in secret.* The Father knows the hidden deed and its hidden motive.

5 "And when you pray, you must not be like the hypocrites; for they love to stand and pray in the synagogues and at the street corners, that they may be seen by men. Truly, I say to you, they have received their reward. 6 But when you pray, go into your room and shut the door and pray to your Father who is in secret; and your Father who sees in secret will reward you.

7 "And in praying do not heap up empty phrases as the Gentiles do; for they think that they will be heard for their many words. 8 Do not be like them, for your Father knows what you need before you ask him. 9 Pray then like this:

>Our Father who art in heaven,
>Hallowed be thy name.
10 >Thy kingdom come,
>Thy will be done,
>On earth as it is in heaven.
11 >Give us this day our daily bread; *m*
12 >And forgive us our debts,
>As we also have forgiven our debtors;
13 >And lead us not into temptation,
>But deliver us from evil. *n*

14 For if you forgive men their trespasses, your heavenly Father also will forgive you; 15 but if you do not forgive men their trespasses, neither will your Father forgive your trespasses.

m Or *our bread for the morrow*

n Or *the evil one.* Other authorities, some ancient, add, in some form, *For thine is the kingdom and the power and the glory, for ever. Amen.*

6:7 *Heard for their many words.* Their prayer is a "magical" prayer; the petitioner attempts to manipulate the Godhead and make Him subservient to his own desires. The Father-child relationship (8) makes such prayer impossible.

6:9 *Hallowed be thy name.* God will hallow His name when He acts in judgment and mercy to reveal Himself finally and forever as the one good (19:17) God that He is (cf. Eze 36:22 ff., esp. 23: "vindicate the holiness of my great name").

6:10 *Thy kingdom come.* The royal reign of God "is at hand" in Jesus' Word and work (4:17; 5:3; 12:28); His coming is the beginning of the end. But the kingdom is still to "come with power" (Mk 9:1) at the end of the End, when Christ returns and bids His own inherit the kingdom prepared for them. For that day the disciple longs and prays and lives.

Thy will be done on earth. The first three petitions are really one prayer that God may fulfill His gracious purposes and come. The third petition adds the all-important idea that man is not a mere spectator of God's great act; God draws man into it and graciously employs men to achieve His purposes. Paul calls his fellow missionaries his "fellow workers for the kingdom of God." (Cl 4:11)

6:11 *Daily.* Cf. RSV note *m*. The exact translation of the rare word used in the Greek is uncertain, but it is certain that the prayer for sustenance is a modest one: "Keep us alive one day at a time."

6:12 *Debts . . . debtors.* For sin pictured as a debt cf. 5:26; 18:23-35.

As we also have forgiven. The disciple as son of God lives by every word that proceeds from His mouth; that word is the word of forgiveness, and the disciple must needs live by it in relationship to his fellowman. (Cf. 14-15 and note)

6:13 *Lead us not into temptation.* This is the prayer the disciples forgot when they failed their Lord in Gethsemane (26:36 ff.). The glad confidence of the disciple that God's name will be hallowed and His kingdom will come is mingled with a holy fear that he may fail to hallow God's name, and he trusts only in God's kindly control of his history to bring him through his encounters with the Evil One.

Deliver us from evil. The disciple knows that he is dependent on his heavenly Father for ultimate deliverance; only He can rescue him from every evil and bring him safely into the heavenly kingdom (2 Ti 4:18). And so his prayer ends as it began with the petition that God break forth in majesty and put an end to all that opposes God and endangers God's sons.

The doxology with which we close the Lord's Prayer is not part of the original text but is thoroughly in keeping with the spirit of the prayer, which seeks first God's kingdom and His righteousness, makes the petitioner dependent on God's grace, and so gives God the glory. (Cf. Ro 4:20)

6:14-15 Jesus commented on the last Beatitude (5:11-12), since man finds it difficult to find blessedness in persecution. So here he reinforces the Fifth Petition, particularly the "as we also have forgiven"; for at this point our discipleship is put to the test again and again, and endless forgiving does not come easy. For a dramatic commentary on the Fifth Petition see the parable, Mt 18:21-35. The alternate translation of RSV note *n (the evil one)* is very probable; the sense of the petition is not essentially changed thereby.

16 "And when you fast, do not look dismal, like the hypocrites, for they disfigure their faces that their fasting may be seen by men. Truly, I say to you, they have received their reward. 17 But when you fast, anoint your head and wash your face, 18 that your fasting may not be seen by men but by your Father who is in secret; and your Father who sees in secret will reward you.

19 "Do not lay up for yourselves treasures on earth, where moth and rust° consume and where thieves break in and steal, 20 but lay up for yourselves treasures in heaven, where neither moth nor rust° consumes and where thieves do not break in and steal. 21 For where your treasure is, there will your heart be also.

22 "The eye is the lamp of the body. So, if your eye is sound, your whole body will be full of light; 23 but if your eye is not sound, your whole body will be full of darkness. If then the light in you is darkness, how great is the darkness!

24 "No one can serve two masters; for either he will hate the one and love the other, or he will be devoted to the one and despise the other. You cannot serve God and mammon.ˣ

25 "Therefore I tell you, do not be anxious about your life, what you shall eat or what you shall drink, nor about your body, what you shall put on. Is not life more than food, and the body more than clothing? 26 Look at the birds of the air: they neither sow nor reap nor gather into barns, and yet your heavenly Father feeds them. Are you not of more value than they? 27And which of you by being anxious can add one cubit to his span of life?ᵖ 28And why are you anxious about clothing? Consider the lilies of the field, how they grow; they neither toil nor spin; 29 yet I tell you, even Solomon in all his glory was not arrayed like one of these. 30 But if God so clothes the grass of the field, which today is alive and tomorrow is thrown into the oven, will he not much more clothe you, O men of little faith? 31 Therefore do not be anxious, saying, 'What shall we eat?' or 'What shall we drink?' or 'What shall we wear?' 32 For the Gentiles seek all these things; and your heavenly Father knows that you need them all. 33 But seek first his kingdom and his righteousness, and all these things shall be yours as well.

34 "Therefore do not be anxious about tomorrow, for tomorrow will be anxious for itself. Let the day's own trouble be sufficient for the day.

° Or *worm* ᵖ Or *to his stature* ˣ *Mammon* is a Semitic word for money or riches

6:16 *Fasting* undertaken voluntarily by individuals was considered a meritorious religious exercise (Lk 18:12). Since fasting is an expression of sorrow for sin and urgency of prayer and therefore speaks to God of a penitent heart, making a display of it is only a piece of religious showmanship.

6:19-34 THE DISCIPLE AND HIS PROPERTY

6:19-34 Property poses a double threat to purity of heart; it tempts to avarice (19-23) and gives rise to anxiety (25-34). Whether a man seeks wealth (19) or anxiously strives for mere security (25), he is dividing his loyalty and is no longer whole-souled in his devotion to God. The avaricious man is giving his *heart,* which belongs to his God, to his *treasures;* the anxious man forgets the God who created him, the Father who will clothe and feed him—his faith shrinks (*little faith*, 30) and atrophies. To this Jesus opposes His warning: You cannot be a slave (*serve*, 24) in full-time, single service to God and property; you dare not cleave your *heart* (21). But He does more than warn; He lets God the Creator and Father grow great before His disciples' eyes (26-30) and bids them *seek first* (33) the given gift of His kingdom (5:3) and His saving righteousness (5:6) and to

trust Him who feeds the birds and clothes the lilies for all the rest. He bids His disciples go the way of the obedient Son who would not seek bread (4:3-4) but sought to let God reign in His life— God's angels set a table for Him in the wilderness. (4:11)

6:23 *The light in you,* the eye of the *heart* (21), center of man's desiring, willing, and thinking. If man's inner eye is darkened, he is blinded with a blindness more fatal than any defect of the physical eye, the *lamp of the body.* (21)

6:24 *Mammon,* a word taken over from Jesus' mother tongue (Aramaic); it means "property," "money," "wealth."

6:27 *Cubit,* about 18 inches.

6:30 *Oven.* The Palestinian oven, made of burnt clay, was heated by building a fire INSIDE it. *Grass* was commonly used as fuel.

6:34 The Fourth Petition with its request for "daily bread this day" provides the best commentary on this verse. We live one day at a time under God's care.

Trouble. Jesus does not idealize or gloss over the hard economic realities of life; they are there, and they are no fun. But our King and Father can help us deal with them.

THE DISCIPLE IN AN ALIEN WORLD (7:1-29)

7 "Judge not, that you be not judged. 2 For with the judgment you pronounce you will be judged, and the measure you give will be the measure you get. 3 Why do you see the speck that is in your brother's eye, but do not notice the log that is in your own eye? 4 Or how can you say to your brother, 'Let me take the speck out of your eye,' when there is the log in your own eye? 5 You hypocrite, first take the log out of your own eye, and then you will see clearly to take the speck out of your brother's eye.

6 "Do not give dogs what is holy; and do not throw your pearls before swine, lest they trample them under foot and turn to attack you.

7 "Ask, and it will be given you; seek, and you will find; knock, and it will be opened to you. 8 For every one who asks receives, and he who seeks finds, and to him who knocks it will be opened. 9 Or what man of you, if his son asks him for bread, will give him a stone? 10 Or if he asks for a fish, will give him a serpent? 11 If you then, who are evil, know how to give good gifts to your children, how much more will your Father who is in heaven give good things to those who ask him! 12 So whatever you wish that men would do to you, do so to them; for this is the law and the prophets.

13 "Enter by the narrow gate; for the gate is wide and the way is easy,*q* that leads to destruction, and those who enter by it are many. 14 For the gate is narrow and the way is hard, that leads to life, and those who find it are few.

15 "Beware of false prophets, who come to you in sheep's clothing but inwardly are ravenous wolves. 16 You will know them by their fruits. Are grapes gathered from thorns, or figs from thistles? 17 So, every sound tree bears good fruit, but the bad tree

q Other ancient authorities read *for the way is wide and easy*

7:1-29 The disciple as moulded by Jesus is a new sort of man. Endowed with a new righteousness whose crowning characteristic is unlimited love — love for His enemy (5:17-48), living in a childlike piety that looks only for the Father's reward (6:1-18), freed from the compulsion of both avarice and anxiety and seeking first the reign and saving righteousness of God (6:19-34) — the disciple emerges as one set off from both Gentile (5:47; 6:7, 32) and Jew (5:20), a new third race in a world of alien men. How is he to confront them? What shall his attitudes and actions toward them be?

7:1-14 THE DISCIPLE AND THE SINNER

7:1-14 In a world where the law condemns the wrongdoer and the synagog metes out the discipline of the 39 lashes (cf. 10:17; 2 Co 11:24), where the natural bent of man is to judge the other man (Ro 2:1), the disciple will be tempted to ascend God's judgment throne and condemn the sinner (7:1). This he dare not do, for he lives purely of God's forgiveness (6:12; 18:21-35), and he can only be the voice of God's forgiveness to his fellowman. If he judges, he loses God the Forgiver and will have God against him as his Judge. He wishes to win the sinner (18:15), but he can do so only by calling him to repentance, offering the forgiveness which he, the disciple, has himself received. He must, by repenting, clear his own eye of the *log* of his own sin before he can see clearly to remove the *speck* from the eye of his *brother.* (4-5)

The disciple is not authorized to execute God's judgment (Ro 12:19); neither can he play God in forcing salvation on men, exposing *what is holy* to the malice of men who refuse and resent it (6).

Jesus will not permit him to desecrate the precious thing *(pearls)* entrusted him nor to endanger himself needlessly. This does not, however, leave him helpless; he can pray in the rich assurance that his Father will hear and heed his prayer (7-11) and in the strength of the Father's good gifts employ the whole power of love. (12)

7:1 *Be not judged.* By God in the last judgment.

7:6 *What is holy.* Sacrificial meat. (Lv 22:14-16)

7:11 *You . . . who are evil.* In Jesus' eyes man at his best, man who can give his children *good gifts,* is still at bottom evil.

7:12 *This is the law and the prophets.* When men love their fellowmen as naturally, as constantly, and as instinctively as they act to protect and preserve themselves, then they are perfect, as their heavenly Father is perfect (5:48, cf. 45); then His will as proclaimed by the Law and the prophets (the OT) is being done and His kingdom comes.

7:13-14 In this world grown alien to him the disciple will be confronted with an alien majority, a mass of men indifferent to him and pursuing a course which is easier than and the exact opposite of his own. He can find the strength to resist the pressure of this majority only in the Word of his Lord; His word of threat and promise determines the value and the outcome of the two opposing ways. In the power of His Lord's Word the disciple can go through the *narrow gate* down the *hard way that leads to life.*

7:15-23 THE DISCIPLE AND FALSE PROPHECY

7:15-23 The disciples stand in this alien world as successors to the prophets of old (5:12), bearers of the Word of God. They will be confronted by

bears evil fruit. [18]A sound tree cannot bear evil fruit, nor can a bad tree bear good fruit. [19] Every tree that does not bear good fruit is cut down and thrown into the fire. [20] Thus you will know them by their fruits.

21 "Not every one who says to me, 'Lord, Lord,' shall enter the kingdom of heaven, but he who does the will of my Father who is in heaven. [22] On that day many will say to me, 'Lord, Lord, did we not prophesy in your name, and cast out demons in your name, and do many mighty works in your name?' [23]And then will I declare to them, 'I never knew you; depart from me, you evildoers.'

24 "Every one then who hears these words of mine and does them will be like a wise man who built his house upon the rock; [25] and the rain fell, and the floods came, and the winds blew and beat upon that house, but it did not fall, because it had been founded on the rock. [26]And every one who hears these words of mine and does not do them will be like a foolish man who built his house upon the sand; [27] and the rain fell, and the floods came, and the winds blew and beat against that house, and it fell; and great was the fall of it."

28 And when Jesus finished these sayings, the crowds were astonished at his teaching, [29] for he taught them as one who had authority, and not as their scribes.

Second Group of Messianic Deeds and Words

8:1 — 10:42

TEN DEEDS OF THE MESSIAH (8:1 — 9:34)

8 When he came down from the mountain, great crowds followed him; [2] and behold, a leper came to him and knelt before him, saying, "Lord, if you will, you can make me clean." [3]And he stretched out his hand and touched him, saying,

competitors, by *false prophets,* similar to the true prophets, distinguishable from the true only by their *fruits,* their output. The disciples will recognize them as men destined for judgment by the fact that their words do not lead men to Christ and the Father but bind men to themselves. The voice of false prophecy will be raised by men who call Jesus *Lord* and can validate their message with *mighty works.* The disciples will recognize them for what they are, men who will be disowned by Christ *on that day* of judgment, by the fact that they do not do what the Lord Himself did, fulfill *the will of my Father,* the will of love. (Cf. 1 Co 13:2)

7:15 *Sheep's clothing . . . ravenous wolves.* The destroying enemies (Jn 10:12) of the flock (Lk 12:32), the people of God, will appear in disguise as members of the flock. (Cf. 2 Co 11:12-15)

7:24-29 THE DISCIPLE UNDER THE WORD OF CHRIST

7:24-29 How shall the disciple attain to this higher righteousness (5:20), this pure piety (6:1), this single devotion to God and freedom from mammon (6:19), this clear-eyed wisdom that can resist the persuasion of the majority (7:13), and the lure of false prophecy (7:15)? Only by remaining under the Word of Jesus. Only by *hearing* and *doing* that Word can he build a house of life which will come through the storm of divine judgment upright and unshaken. Only he who takes Christ at His word and lives of His Word (all of it, the words that confer the gift of Christ and words that make

His claim on man) will fully know what the *crowds* sensed, how great is the *authority* of this Teacher; year by difficult year he will be more and more *astonished at his teaching.*

7:25 *Rain, floods, winds.* For the storm as a description of God's judgment cf. Eze 13:10-15.

8:1 — 9:34 Ten, number of completeness (cf. ten commandments, Ex 20; ten plagues in Egypt, Ex 7 — 11). With an account of TEN deeds Matthew records a comprehensive revelation of the authority and compassion of the Messiah and also of the twofold reaction (faith and praise, opposition and blasphemy) which that revelation provokes. With this Messianic *authority,* authority in the service of compassion (10:1, 7, 8), Jesus will send out the Twelve to the "lost sheep" (10:6); and His Word prepares them for the same twofold reaction (10:12-15, 25, etc.). Matthew punctuates the series of miracles with two accounts of nonmiraculous words and deeds which likewise illustrate Jesus' compassionate authority as it confronts men.

8:1-17 THREE DEEDS: THE COMPASSIONATE SERVANT

8:1-17 The first three deeds illustrate the Beatitude on the poor (5:3); Jesus brings the power and the grace of the Kingdom to persons in their extreme need: to the *leper* whom the Law could only shut out from the people of God, to the Gentile *centurion* excluded by Law from Israel, to the woman whom Judaic opinion considered a second-rate creature of God. He triumphs over the power of *demons* (16) who oppose and attack the work of

"I will; be clean." And immediately his leprosy was cleansed. [4]And Jesus said to him, "See that you say nothing to any one; but go, show yourself to the priest, and offer the gift that Moses commanded, for a proof to the people."[r]

5 As he entered Ca·per′na·um, a centurion came forward to him, beseeching him [6] and saying, "Lord, my servant is lying paralyzed at home, in terrible distress." [7]And he said to him, "I will come and heal him." [8] But the centurion answered him, "Lord, I am not worthy to have you come under my roof; but only say the word, and my servant will be healed. [9] For I am a man under authority, with soldiers under me; and I say to one, 'Go,' and he goes, and to another, 'Come,' and he comes, and to my slave, 'Do this,' and he does it." [10] When Jesus heard him, he marveled, and said to those who followed him, "Truly, I say to you, not even[s] in Israel have I found such faith. [11] I tell you, many will come from east and west and sit at table with Abraham, Isaac, and Jacob in the kingdom of heaven, [12] while the sons of the kingdom will be thrown into the outer darkness; there men will weep and gnash their teeth." [13]And to the centurion Jesus said, "Go; be it done for you as you have believed." And the servant was healed at that very moment.

14 And when Jesus entered Peter's house, he saw his mother-in-law lying sick with a fever; [15] he touched her hand, and the fever left her, and she rose and served him. [16] That evening they brought to him many who were possessed with demons; and he cast out the spirits with a word, and healed all who were sick. [17] This was to fulfil what was spoken by the prophet I·sa′iah, "He took our infirmities and bore our diseases."

18 Now when Jesus saw great crowds around him, he gave orders to go over to the

[r] Greek *to them* [s] Other ancient authorities read *with no one*

God, but He triumphs as the Servant whose ministry takes Him into the depths of human misery. (17)

8:2 *Leper.* For the lot of the leper under the Law cf. Lv 13–14.

8:4 *Say nothing.* Cf. 12:15-21, where Jesus is pictured as the Messiah who is the meek Servant of God, who will not call attention to Himself or assert Himself but does His merciful work for the crushed and hopeless in order that God's cause ("justice") may prevail. Jesus did not want to instigate a "popular movement" that hung on Him; He wanted men to see God at work in His deeds, to repent, and accept the royal reign of God (4:17). The Son of God takes on servant form and does His servant work "to the glory of God the Father." (Ph 2:11)

For a proof, that He came not to abolish but to fulfill (5:17), that in restoring the leper to the people He was fulfilling the law which willed that God's people be clean and whole.

8:5 *Centurion,* an officer in charge of 100 soldiers. Whether a Roman or a mercenary in the service of Herod, he would be a Gentile.

8:9 *A man under authority.* The centurion is saying: "If even I, a subordinate, can bring about effective action by my word, how much the more can You whose authority is so much greater than mine."

8:11 Again Jesus fulfills Law and prophets; the believing Gentile is brought into the people of God which began with *Abraham;* God is raising up children to Abraham. (3:9)

8:12 *Sons of the kingdom,* Israelites called into being by God their King to be "a kingdom of priests." (Ex 19:6)

8:17 Cf. Is 53:4. Matthew is recalling the Servant of the Lord promised in Isaiah, the Servant who goes the downward way of a ministry for the broken and despairing into an atoning death for the sins of "the many." Is 53:4 speaks of that vicarious death; Matthew sees this ministry-unto-death as already beginning in Jesus' deeds of healing. And one can see why, for Jesus uses His power only in service to others, never to assert Himself (8:4; 9:30). He will not let Himself be proclaimed as Messiah until He has by His self-sacrifice revealed Himself as the Messiah of the God of all grace. The miracle forces a decision upon men; it both fosters faith and makes unbelief congeal into deadly opposition (9:3, 34; Jn 11:47-48). This opposition Jesus refused to overwhelm or destroy miraculously. His deeds of mercy are therefore steps toward the cross. His life of serving and His ransoming death are an organic whole. (20:28)

8:18-22 FIRST INTERLUDE: THE CLAIM AND GIFT OF THE SON OF MAN

Jesus' response to the volunteers for discipleship (*I will follow you,* 19) reveals the *Son of man* (destined to have universal, eternal, indestructible "dominion and glory and. kingdom," Dn 7:14) going the way of Servant ministry with such restless devotion that He *has nowhere to lay his head.* He claims men for that kind of ministry, and His claim overrides every other claim, even that of filial piety toward a *father* (21-22). His claim is so high because His gift is so great; with Him is life, the only life in a world of the *dead* (22). His miracles all proclaim what this word says: "With Me is life."

other side. ¹⁹And a scribe came up and said to him, "Teacher, I will follow you wherever you go." ²⁰And Jesus said to him, "Foxes have holes, and birds of the air have nests; but the Son of man has nowhere to lay his head." ²¹Another of the disciples said to him, "Lord, let me first go and bury my father." ²² But Jesus said to him, "Follow me, and leave the dead to bury their own dead."

23 And when he got into the boat, his disciples followed him. ²⁴And behold, there arose a great storm on the sea, so that the boat was being swamped by the waves; but he was asleep. ²⁵And they went and woke him, saying, "Save, Lord; we are perishing." ²⁶And he said to them, "Why are you afraid, O men of little faith?" Then he rose and rebuked the winds and the sea; and there was a great calm. ²⁷And the men marveled, saying, "What sort of man is this, that even winds and sea obey him?"

28 And when he came to the other side, to the country of the Gad·a·renes′,ᵗ two demoniacs met him, coming out of the tombs, so fierce that no one could pass that way. ²⁹And behold, they cried out, "What have you to do with us, O Son of God? Have you come here to torment us before the time?" ³⁰ Now a herd of many swine was feeding at some distance from them. ³¹And the demons begged him, "If you cast us out, send us away into the herd of swine." ³²And he said to them, "Go." So they came out and went into the swine; and behold, the whole herd rushed down the steep bank into the sea, and perished in the waters. ³³ The herdsmen fled, and going into the city they told everything, and what had happened to the demoniacs. ³⁴And behold, all the city came out to meet Jesus; and when they saw him, they begged him to leave their neighborhood.

9 And getting into a boat he crossed over and came to his own city. ²And behold, they brought to him a paralytic, lying on his bed; and when Jesus saw their faith he said to the paralytic, "Take heart, my son; your sins are forgiven." ³And behold, some of the scribes said to themselves, "This man is blaspheming." ⁴ But Jesus, knowingᵘ their thoughts, said, "Why do you think evil in your hearts? ⁵ For which is easier, to say, 'Your sins are forgiven,' or to say, 'Rise and walk'? ⁶ But that you may

---

ᵗ Other ancient authorities read *Gergesenes;* some, *Gerasenes*   ᵘ Other ancient authorities read *seeing*

8:19 *Scribe,* interpreter of the Law; the scribes were the theological leaders of the Pharisaic party.

8:22 *The dead.* Cf. Eph 2:1.

8:23 — 9:8 THREE DEEDS: AUTHORITY OVER THE SEA, THE ENEMY, AND SIN

8:23 — 9:8 The majesty and mercy of the Lord, the God of Israel, are manifested in the deeds of Jesus; in Jesus men can behold the Lord who is Master of the dreaded chaotic sea and rescues men from its terrors (23-27; Ps 107:23-32); the Lord who stills the enemy (Ps 8:2), before whom His enemies are scattered (Ps 68:1, 21), even *the* enemy whose demonic underlings distort and torment His creature, man (28-34); the Lord who forgives iniquity and heals diseases (9:1-8; Ps 103:3; 107:17-22), whose power over sin reveals Him as the God to be feared (9:8; Ps 130:4). Just here, where the arm of the Lord is revealed in His compassionate Servant (Is 53:1), the opposition of men is provoked. The disciples may bow before the *man* whom *winds and sea obey* (8:27), and the crowds may *glorify* the *God* who has given the *Son of man authority on earth to forgive sins* (9:6, 8), but the Gadarenes will have nothing to do with a *Son of God* who costs them pigs (8:34), and the *scribes* accuse the *Son of man* of blaspheming. (9:3)

8:26 *Little faith.* Faith is little when the object of faith grows little, when the stormy sea seems greater than Jesus (cf. 14:30-31); the great faith of the Canaanite woman saw a God great enough for the needs of all. (15:28)

8:28 *Gadarenes,* citizens of Gadara, a city of the Decapolis, about 5 miles southeast of the Sea of Galilee; the *country of the Gadarenes* extended to the shore of the Sea of Galilee.

8:29 *Before the time.* The demons recognize the *Son of God* and know that He is destined to overthrow them at the appointed *time,* at the end of days (Rv 20:10, cf. 19:20). They are startled and terrified to find that the future time of God's victory projects into the present in the person of Jesus. Both the devil and the demons always recognize Jesus for what He is (4:3; Mk 1:24), the divine Victor of the last days. (Jn 12:31; 14:30; 16:11)

8:32 *Perished.* Jesus thus unmasks the power of Satan and his demons as the absolute negation of created life; Satan is THE killer. (Jn 8:44)

9:1 *His own city,* Capernaum. (Mk 2:1)

9:3 *Blaspheming.* Unless Jesus is what His deeds reveal Him to be, the scribes are in the right; because they refused to accept that revelation, they finally condemned Him to death. (26:63-66)

9:5 *Easier to say.* Both healing and forgiveness by the effective word alone are divine actions, impossible for men; but a man can speak forgiveness without authority and escape being exposed;

know that the Son of man has authority on earth to forgive sins"—he then said to the paralytic—"Rise, take up your bed and go home." ⁷And he rose and went home. ⁸ When the crowds saw it, they were afraid, and they glorified God, who had given such authority to men.

9 As Jesus passed on from there, he saw a man called Matthew sitting at the tax office; and he said to him, "Follow me." And he rose and followed him.

10 And as he sat at table ᵛ in the house, behold, many tax collectors and sinners came and sat down with Jesus and his disciples. ¹¹And when the Pharisees saw this, they said to his disciples, "Why does your teacher eat with tax collectors and sinners?" ¹² But when he heard it, he said, "Those who are well have no need of a physician, but those who are sick. ¹³ Go and learn what this means, 'I desire mercy, and not sacrifice.' For I came not to call the righteous, but sinners."

14 Then the disciples of John came to him, saying, "Why do we and the Pharisees fast, ʷ but your disciples do not fast?" ¹⁵And Jesus said to them, "Can the wedding guests mourn as long as the bridegroom is with them? The days will come, when the bridegroom is taken away from them, and then they will fast. ¹⁶And no one puts a piece of unshrunk cloth on an old garment, for the patch tears away from the garment, and a worse tear is made. ¹⁷ Neither is new wine put into old wineskins; if it is, the skins burst, and the wine is spilled, and the skins are destroyed; but new wine is put into fresh wineskins, and so both are preserved."

18 While he was thus speaking to them, behold, a ruler came in and knelt before him, saying, "My daughter has just died; but come and lay your hand on her, and she will live." ¹⁹And Jesus rose and followed him, with his disciples. ²⁰And behold, a

---

ᵛ Greek *reclined*   ʷ Other ancient authorities add *much* or *often*

---

but the word of healing will either expose him or vindicate him because the result will be verifiable now, *on earth*.

9:8 *Men.* Matthew's comment looks forward to the apostolic church, where the word of forgiveness will be spoken with divine validity (Mt 18:15, 18-20). Forgiveness will no longer be an uncertain, far-off event of the Last Judgment but an on-earth present reality.

9:9-17 SECOND INTERLUDE: JESUS IS CALLER, PHYSICIAN, BRIDEGROOM

9:9-17 The mighty deeds of Jesus are all refractions of the one "great light" (4:16) which Jesus is. The sheer unmerited grace of His call is brilliantly evident here, where He *calls* the tax collector Matthew to be His disciple and apostle (9; 10:3; cf. 4:18-22; 1 Co 15:9-10). He is the Caller of *sinners* (13). The wholeness and the efficacy of His forgiveness appear in His table fellowship with sinners; He is the Lord their Healer (cf. Ex 15:26; Hos 11:3) who does not ignore their sin but deals with it effectually. His presence is the presence of the God who *desires mercy* even as He bestows mercy (13; Hos 6:6). He is the *bridegroom* (Jer 31:32) whose presence puts an end to the night of weeping and ushers in the morn of festal song (15). His coming is the dawn of the new age and brings "new things" (Is 48:6). He is not a *patch* that can be sewn on the old garments of Judaic piety; He is *new wine* that will break the old *wineskins,* the old forms that cannot contain Him—e. g., the temple will pass away because "something greater than the temple is here." (12:6)

9:10 *Tax collectors and sinners.* Notorious sinners are meant, men separated from the *righteous*

(13) by the rigorous discipline of the synagog. Tax collectors were classed with them; the tax-farming contracts under which they worked gave ample opportunity for fraud, which they generally exploited. (Lk 3:13; 19:8)

9:14 *Fasting* expressed sorrow over sin and intensity of prayer. The presence of the forgiving Healer and Bridegroom puts an end to such sorrow and is God's answer to longing prayer.

9:15 *Taken away,* a first hint of Jesus' Passion (Is 53:8) and death and His return to His Father. In the days when the church awaits and longs for the return of her Lord, the sobriety and vigilance of her waiting may express itself in fasting.

9:18-34 FOUR DEEDS: DAVID'S SON AND LORD

9:18-34 Here, for the first time in Matthew, Jesus is addressed as *Son of David,* the Messiah (27; cf. 1:1-17). His deeds reveal Him as both David's Son and David's Lord (22:45), for He does what only divine authority can do: He "gives life to the dead" (18-26; Ro 4:17). He responds with healing to the unuttered petition of the woman who *suffered from a hemorrhage* (20-22). He opens *blind* eyes (27-31) and unseals the lips which Satan has sealed (32-34). He is the object of *faith* (22, 28, 29; cf. 8:10; 9:2). Opposition to Him necessarily takes the form of blasphemy; the *Pharisees* can seek to discredit Him only by calling diabolical what must otherwise be confessed as divine. His deeds cannot be explained away in human terms. (34; cf. 12:24)

9:20 The *fringe* (or tassel) on a garment was prescribed by the Law; it was to serve as a reminder of obedience to the Law (Nm 15:38-40). Jesus is "under the law." (Gl 4:4)

woman who had suffered from a hemorrhage for twelve years came up behind him and touched the fringe of his garment; 21 for she said to herself, "If I only touch his garment, I shall be made well." 22 Jesus turned, and seeing her he said, "Take heart, daughter; your faith has made you well." And instantly the woman was made well. 23And when Jesus came to the ruler's house, and saw the flute players, and the crowd making a tumult, 24 he said, "Depart; for the girl is not dead but sleeping." And they laughed at him. 25 But when the crowd had been put outside, he went in and took her by the hand, and the girl arose. 26And the report of this went through all that district.

27 And as Jesus passed on from there, two blind men followed him, crying aloud, "Have mercy on us, Son of David." 28 When he entered the house, the blind men came to him; and Jesus said to them, "Do you believe that I am able to do this?" They said to him, "Yes, Lord." 29 Then he touched their eyes, saying, "According to your faith be it done to you." 30And their eyes were opened. And Jesus sternly charged them, "See that no one knows it." 31 But they went away and spread his fame through all that district.

32 As they were going away, behold, a dumb demoniac was brought to him. 33And when the demon had been cast out, the dumb man spoke; and the crowds marveled, saying, "Never was anything like this seen in Israel." 34 But the Pharisees said, "He casts out demons by the prince of demons." [a]

THE COMMISSIONING AND SENDING OF THE TWELVE (9:35 – 10:42)

35 And Jesus went about all the cities and villages, teaching in their synagogues and preaching the gospel of the kingdom, and healing every disease and every infirmity. 36 When he saw the crowds, he had compassion for them, because they were harassed and helpless, like sheep without a shepherd. 37 Then he said to his disciples, "The harvest is plentiful, but the laborers are few; 38 pray therefore the Lord of the harvest to send out laborers into his harvest."

10 And he called to him his twelve disciples and gave them authority over unclean spirits, to cast them out, and to heal every disease and every infirmity. 2 The names of the twelve apostles are these: first, Simon, who is called Peter, and Andrew his brother; James the son of Zeb'e·dee, and John his brother; 3 Philip and Bartholomew; Thomas and Matthew the tax collector; James the son of Al·phae'us, and Thaddaeus; [x] 4 Simon the Ca·na·nae'an, and Judas Is·car'i·ot, who betrayed him.

[a] Other ancient authorities omit this verse
[x] Other ancient authorities read *Lebbaeus* or *Lebbaeus called Thaddaeus*

9:22 *Your faith,* not the touch or the fringe of the garment. Jesus purges her faith of traces of superstition as He responds to it.

9:23 *Flute players.* Lamentation for the dead was highly formal, involving the service of professionals; the flute was the preferred instrument of lamentation. (Jer 48:36)

9:35 – 10:42 The Messiah of compassionate authority commissions and sends His 12 apostles to Israel to speak His message, to do His deeds, to share His sufferings, and to find their life by losing it for His sake.

9:35-38 THE MOTIVE
FOR THE APOSTOLIC MISSION

9:35-38 Jesus' motive is His *compassion* (36). His people are like *sheep without a shepherd* (36), a people without a king to lead them and care for them. Man's need is God's opportunity; the *harassed and helpless* crowds are standing fields of grain to be reaped by God's mercy (37). It is God's harvest; the apostle is apostle "by the will of God" (1 Co 1:1); God, the *Lord of the harvest, sends* him, and he undertakes and carries on his work with prayer to God. (38)

9:35 Cf. 4:23, where the same general description of Jesus' activity precedes Jesus' teaching; there it precedes His sending. The apostles are men whose will the Messiah has moulded (Mt 5 – 7), who must speak of what they have seen and heard. (Mt 8 – 9)

9:36 For the picture of the people of God as a flock and the Messiah ("David") as their Shepherd-King cf. Eze 34:22-24; 37:24.

10:1-4 COMMISSIONING OF THE 12 APOSTLES

10:1-4 Jesus equips the *apostles,* His authorized emissaries, with His own compassionate *authority.* The number *twelve* is emphasized (1, 2, 5). Twelve is the number of Israel, the twelve tribes; in sending out just twelve apostles Jesus is making it clear that He is offering the gift of the Kingdom and uttering the call to repentance to all Israel (4:17), to the whole people of God and through them to the whole new people of God that is to be. (Cf. Rv 7:4-8)

10:4 *Judas . . . who betrayed him.* The twofold reaction of Israel to the Messiah is reflected in the circle of the Twelve; one proves unfaithful and turns traitor.

5 These twelve Jesus sent out, charging them, "Go nowhere among the Gentiles, and enter no town of the Samaritans, 6 but go rather to the lost sheep of the house of Israel. 7And preach as you go, saying, 'The kingdom of heaven is at hand.' 8 Heal the sick, raise the dead, cleanse lepers, cast out demons. You received without paying, give without pay. 9 Take no gold, nor silver, nor copper in your belts, 10 no bag for your journey, nor two tunics, nor sandals, nor a staff; for the laborer deserves his food. 11And whatever town or village you enter, find out who is worthy in it, and stay with him until you depart. 12As you enter the house, salute it. 13And if the house is worthy, let your peace come upon it; but if it is not worthy, let your peace return to you. 14And if any one will not receive you or listen to your words, shake off the dust from your feet as you leave that house or town. 15 Truly, I say to you, it shall be more tolerable on the day of judgment for the land of Sodom and Go·mor′rah than for that town.

16 "Behold, I send you out as sheep in the midst of wolves; so be wise as serpents and innocent as doves. 17 Beware of men; for they will deliver you up to councils, and flog you in their synagogues, 18 and you will be dragged before governors and kings for my sake, to bear testimony before them and the Gentiles. 19 When they deliver you up, do not be anxious how you are to speak or what you are to say; for what you are to say will be given to you in that hour; 20 for it is not you who speak, but the Spirit of your Father speaking through you. 21 Brother will deliver up brother to death, and the father his child, and children will rise against parents and have them put to death; 22 and you will be hated by all for my name's sake. But he who endures to

10:5-15 THE APOSTOLIC MISSION: ITS SCOPE, CONTENT, SPIRIT, AND OUTCOME

10:5-15 The SCOPE (5-6) of the apostolic mission is determined by the scope of Jesus' own mission (cf. 15:24); Jesus goes the way that God has gone, through *Israel* to the Gentiles. The Gospel comes "to the Jew first" (Ro 1:16). When Jesus has fulfilled (to the death) His ministry to Israel (Ro 15:8), the apostolic mission becomes universal (28:19); when the Seed has fallen into the ground and died, the hour of the Gentiles has struck; lifted upon the cross the Son draws all men to Himself (Jn 12:20-24, 32). The CONTENT (7-8a) of the mission is likewise that of Jesus' own: the proclamation of the *kingdom* at hand in word and deed. The SPIRIT of the mission is the spirit in which Jesus worked—no small-souled care for self (*gold, silver, bag,* etc., 9-10) but His confident dependence on God, the Lord of the harvest, who will provide *food* (10) for His workmen, who give freely what they have freely received (*without paying,* literally "as a gift." The OUTCOME (11-15) of their mission is again like that of Jesus' own (chs. 8—9): faith and unbelief, acceptance and rejection, houses that are *worthy* (because they accept) and *houses* and *towns* that are *not worthy* (because they refuse), the *peace* of God and at the end the judgment of God. Such is the scope, content, spirit, and outcome of the mission.

10:12 *Salute it.* The common Jewish greeting was "Peace!" (Cf. Lk 10:5.) That term is filled when Jesus or His apostles pronounce it, with its full and true OT sense of the soundness, wholeness, health, all's-well-between-God-and-man. (Cf. Nm 6:26)

10:14 *Shake off the dust,* as a sign that all communion with them is broken off. (Cf. Acts 13:51; 18:6)

10:15 *Sodom and Gomorrah.* The fate of these cities lived in men's memories as a signal instance of God's judgment on the wickedness of man because of his unbelief. (Cf. 11:24; Jude 7; Gn 18:16—19:28)

10:16-42 THE APOSTLE AND HIS LORD

10:16-42 The rest of the discourse makes plain and emphasizes what was implicit in the preceding words: the apostle is the living extension of his Lord. Through the apostle Christ works "by word and deed, by the power of signs and wonders, by the power of the Holy Spirit" (Ro 15:18-19; cf. 2 Co 13:3). The apostles' sufferings fill up the measure of "Christ's afflictions" (Cl 1:24); and they shall share in the vindication and triumph of the afflicted Christ. Whoever receives them, receives Him and the Father who sent Him.

10:16-23 *I send you out* (the *I* is emphatic); the defenseless Servant Christ, 12:19 ("he cannot save himself," 27:42) sends them and they can expect to repeat His history: persecution (18), betrayal (21), hatred (22) await them. But suffering will no more frustrate their mission than it frustrated His. Persecution will enable them *to bear testimony* before kings (18) and the *Spirit* given them by their *Father* will inspire their words (20). They must *endure to the end,* but in the end they *will be saved* (22); the *Son of man* will *come* and put an end forever to their life of persecution and flight in the fulfillment of their mission to Israel. (23)

10:17 *Flog you in their synagogues.* Cf. 2 Co 11:24, where Paul speaks of the 39 lashes which he received five times "at the hands of the Jews."

10:20 *Spirit . . . speaking.* Cf. the promise of the Spirit as Counselor, Jn 15:26; 16:7-11.

10:22 *Saved,* in the Last Judgment. (Cf. Ro 5:9)

the end will be saved. 23 When they persecute you in one town, flee to the next; for truly, I say to you, you will not have gone through all the towns of Israel, before the Son of man comes.

24 "A disciple is not above his teacher, nor a servant^y above his master; 25 it is enough for the disciple to be like his teacher, and the servant^y like his master. If they have called the master of the house Beelzebul, how much more will they malign those of his household.

26 "So have no fear of them; for nothing is covered that will not be revealed, or hidden that will not be known. 27 What I tell you in the dark, utter in the light; and what you hear whispered, proclaim upon the housetops. 28And do not fear those who kill the body but cannot kill the soul; rather fear him who can destroy both soul and body in hell. ^{z} 29Are not two sparrows sold for a penny? And not one of them will fall to the ground without your Father's will. 30 But even the hairs of your head are all numbered. 31 Fear not, therefore; you are of more value than many sparrows. 32 So every one who acknowledges me before men, I also will acknowledge before my Father who is in heaven; 33 but whoever denies me before men, I also will deny before my Father who is in heaven.

34 "Do not think that I have come to bring peace on earth; I have not come to bring peace, but a sword. 35 For I have come to set a man against his father, and a daughter against her mother, and a daughter-in-law against her mother-in-law; 36 and a man's foes will be those of his own household. 37 He who loves father or mother more than me is not worthy of me; and he who loves son or daughter more than me is not worthy of me; 38 and he who does not take his cross and follow me is not worthy of me. 39 He who finds his life will lose it, and he who loses his life for my sake will find it.

40 "He who receives you receives me, and he who receives me receives him who sent me. 41 He who receives a prophet because he is a prophet shall receive a prophet's reward, and he who receives a righteous man because he is a righteous man shall receive a righteous man's reward. 42And whoever gives to one of these little ones even a cup of cold water because he is a disciple, truly, I say to you, he shall not lose his reward."

^{y} Or *slave* ^{z} Greek *Gehenna*

10:23 As an indication of the time of Jesus' return this verse is enigmatic, for Jesus Himself declared that time to be a total mystery, known only to the Father (24:36). But three things are clear: (a) Jesus makes the mission to Israel a perpetual obligation of the apostles and the apostolic church; (b) the apostles need not expose their lives needlessly but are to be *wise as serpents* (16; cf. 7:6) in this too (cf. Paul's flights as recorded in Acts); (c) the coming of the Son of Man is the hope that sustains the apostle in his difficult and dangerous mission.

10:24-33 *Disciple* and *teacher*. The enmity that met Jesus did not shrink even from blasphemy; men called His divine work the work of "the prince of demons" (9:34); they identified Jesus with *Beelzebul* (25). Jesus therefore prepares His disciples for the worst; and He arms them with the best, the triple armor of His *have no fear* (26, 28, 31). As they are members of the *household* of Christ and bear the reproaches of Christ, so they shall share in His vindication and victory. When their proclamation shall have made the *hidden* Christ *known* (26) and the time of judgment comes, Christ will *acknowledge* them before the *Father* (32) and lead them to glory. They will triumph over death; their enemies, who *kill the body but cannot kill the soul* (28), shall find that Christ and

the Father are mightier than death. Christ will *deny* those who denied Him, and He who *can destroy both soul and body in hell* (28) will be their Judge.

10:25 *Beelzebul,* the prince of demons (9:34), Satan. (12:24, 26)

10:34-39 *Not peace, but a sword.* Christ is the Prince of Peace (Is 9:6). He brings peace indeed; but it is God's peace, which separates men from evil. And since men cling to their evil and refuse God's peace (cf. 12-15), the coming of the Kingdom in Christ means for them judgment, the *sword* (34) which divides and separates. The Kingdom cuts across the closest ties (35-36) and claims the sacrifice of kin (37), of honor and life (*cross,* the criminal's death, 38). For only in Christ is *life* to be found, real life, everlasting life (39; cf. 8:22); to cling to the life of this world, the doomed and forfeited life of man dead in his sins (Eph 2:1), means losing the only real life there is.

10:37 *Not worthy,* because he has refused the gift of Christ. (Cf. 13)

10:40-42 *He who receives you receives me.* Christ identifies the disciple with Himself, and Himself with God (*him who sent me,* 40). Christ, *prophet, righteous man, disciple*—these are all servants of God; God watches over His servants zealously (cf. 30) and will reward even the slightest and most

Third Group of Messianic Deeds and Words

11:1 — 13:52

THE CONTRADICTED MESSIAH (11:1 — 12:50)

11 And when Jesus had finished instructing his twelve disciples, he went on from there to teach and preach in their cities.

2 Now when John heard in prison about the deeds of the Christ, he sent word by his disciples 3 and said to him, "Are you he who is to come, or shall we look for another?" 4And Jesus answered them, "Go and tell John what you hear and see: 5 the blind receive their sight and the lame walk, lepers are cleansed and the deaf hear, and the dead are raised up, and the poor have good news preached to them. 6And blessed is he who takes no offense at me."

7 As they went away, Jesus began to speak to the crowds concerning John: "What did you go out into the wilderness to behold? A reed shaken by the wind? 8 Why then did you go out? To see a man*a* clothed in soft raiment? Behold, those who wear soft raiment are in kings' houses. 9 Why then did you go out? To see a prophet?*b* Yes, I tell you, and more than a prophet. 10 This is he of whom it is written,

'Behold, I send my messenger before thy face,
who shall prepare thy way before thee.'

11 Truly, I say to you, among those born of women there has risen no one greater

a Or *What then did you go out to see? A man . . .*
b Other ancient authorities read *What then did you go out to see? A prophet?*

effortless kindness shown to them (*cup of cold water,* 42). The apostles go forth in the consciousness that they shall scatter blessings as they go.

11:1—13:52 The contradicted Messiah conceals the Kingdom from those who have rejected it (those who *have not,* 13:12) and further reveals it to those who have accepted it (those who *have,* 13:12). The disciples are taught to recognize the Messiah in the contradicted Servant and to understand the *secrets* of the Kingdom. (12:18-21; 13:11)

11:1—12:50 When Jesus sent out the Twelve as His representatives, He taught them to expect the contradiction and enmity of man (ch. 10). In this section the root of man's contradiction is laid bare: man wants to master God. In one way or another all Jesus' contemporaries try to impose their will on Him: *John* the Baptist (11:2-3), this *generation* generally (11:16-19), *the wise and understanding* (11:25-30), the *Pharisees* (12:1-14; 12:22-32), *scribes and Pharisees* (12:38-42). Against this background of questioning, offense, and opposition the Christ looms up in fearful majesty — to oppose Him is to invoke the judgment of God both now and hereafter (11:6, 19, 20-24, 25; 12:27, 30-32, 33-37, 42, 43-45). And the greatness of the divine work which He has come to do becomes all the more apparent in the face of man's doubts and opposition. (Cf. 11:5 note; 11:11 note; 11:21, 23, 25-27; 12:6, 8, 18-21, 28, 41-42)

11:1-15 JOHN'S QUESTION FROM PRISON

11:1-15 John's question is the mildest example of man's attempt to impose his will on God. Even he, imprisoned now and helpless, wavers concerning *the deeds of the Christ* (2) and his question (3) suggests that Jesus ought to fulfill John's prophecy of the Mightier One who comes with Spirit and fire and executes judgment NOW when

John expects it and as John expects it (3:11-12). On the other hand, John's question is addressed in faith to Jesus Himself; and if Jesus is not the Coming One, John is willing to wait (*shall we look for another?*). He is still willing to submit to a Christ who does not fulfill his expectations at once. And so Jesus warns him gently (6) and answers his question. Jesus' answer (4-5) is couched in the language of the OT (Is 29:18-19; 35:5-6; 61:1), which indicates that the *deeds of the Christ* are in reality the acts of God and God's Servant which God has promised for the last days. God is present in Jesus, and Jesus is indeed *he who is to come.* (2)

John is therefore still one who has, and to him more is given (13:12). Jesus vindicates the Baptist (7-15) by reproaching the crowds for treating him as a mere spectacle to *behold* (7), a great man to *see* (8) instead of hearing and obeying his prophetic word. John is *more than a prophet,* Jesus tells them (9); he is truly the fulfillment of OT prophecy, the *messenger* and the returning *Elijah* whom the Lord had promised to send before "the great and terrible day of the Lord," the Day of Judgment (Ml 3:1; 4:5; cf. Mt 17:11; Lk 1:17). John is the greatest among those *born of women;* he heralds the advent of the Kingdom. (11-12)

11:2 *In prison.* Cf. 14:3-4.

11:3 *Who is to come.* Cf. 3:11.

11:5 The diseases listed are those which excluded a Jew from the official temple services. Jesus in restoring men to health restores them to the fellowship of the worshiping community.

11:6 *Takes no offense,* by refusing to believe or by falling away.

11:9 *To see a prophet.* God's prophets are to be heard.

11:11 *Least.* Literally "less," "smaller." This is usually interpreted to mean that even the least of

than John the Baptist; yet he who is least in the kingdom of heaven is greater than he.
[12] From the days of John the Baptist until now the kingdom of heaven has suffered violence,[c] and men of violence take it by force. [13] For all the prophets and the law prophesied until John; [14] and if you are willing to accept it, he is E·li'jah who is to come. [15] He who has ears to hear,[d] let him hear.

16 "But to what shall I compare this generation? It is like children sitting in the market places and calling to their playmates,

[17]   'We piped to you, and you did not dance;
          we wailed, and you did not mourn.'

[18] For John came neither eating nor drinking, and they say, 'He has a demon'; [19] the Son of man came eating and drinking, and they say, 'Behold, a glutton and a drunkard, a friend of tax collectors and sinners!' Yet wisdom is justified by her deeds."[e]

20 Then he began to upbraid the cities where most of his mighty works had been done, because they did not repent. [21] "Woe to you, Cho·ra'zin! woe to you, Beth-sa'i·da! for if the mighty works done in you had been done in Tyre and Sidon, they would have repented long ago in sackcloth and ashes. [22] But I tell you, it shall be more tolerable on the day of judgment for Tyre and Sidon than for you. [23]And you, Ca·per'na·um, will you be exalted to heaven? You shall be brought down to Hades. For if the mighty works done in you had been done in Sodom, it would have remained until this day. [24] But I tell you that it shall be more tolerable on the day of judgment for the land of Sodom than for you."

25 At that time Jesus declared, "I thank thee, Father, Lord of heaven and earth, that thou hast hidden these things from the wise and understanding and revealed them to babes; [26] yea, Father, for such was thy gracious will.[f] [27]All things have been

[c] Or *has been coming violently*   [d] Other ancient authorities omit *to hear*
[e] Other ancient authorities read *children* (Luke 7.35)   [f] Or *so it was well-pleasing before thee*

those who live to see the Kingdom come are more highly privileged than John. But it seems preferable to see in the word a reference to Jesus Himself: He who is an *offense* (6) in His littleness (as the Servant who uses His power in the service of mercy to others) is greater than John, for in Him the Kingdom itself is present. (Cf. 12:28)

11:12 *Kingdom . . . has suffered violence*. John is in prison, doomed to die (14:10); the apostles go out "as sheep in the midst of wolves" (10:16); the Pharisees blaspheme Jesus' work (9:34) and plot to destroy Him (12:14). But the fact that the Kingdom suffers violence is evidence that it is no longer a hope but a present reality.

11:14 *Elijah*. Cf. 17:10; Lk 1:17.

11:15 *He who has ears*. Cf. 13:9, 43. This solemn injunction, thrice repeated in this section, marks the seriousness of the hour, when he who will not *hear* (in the full sense of hearing, heeding, and obeying) will become as one who has not. Then God's judgment will take from him *even what he has*. (13:12)

11:16-19 THE PETULANT CHILDREN

11:16-19 Jesus pictures His contemporaries as children who want to call the tunes and feel snubbed when their partners do not dance to them. So they are towards God, dissatisfied with the prophet John because he is too stern, and censorious toward Jesus because He is too forgiving. They want to impose their will on God. The divine *wisdom* which sent both the austere prophet of repentance and the freely forgiving *Son of man* will be vindicated (*justified*) by the outcome of

her deeds, the results, when those who have heeded both John and Jesus shall enter into the Kingdom. (Cf. 21:31-32)

11:20-24 WOE UPON THE CITIES OF THE LAKE

11:20-24 *Capernaum*, Jesus' "own city" (9:1), and the neighboring towns of *Chorazin* and *Bethsaida* were highly favored; in Jesus' *mighty works* God was wooing them, seeking to lead them to repentance (cf. Ro 2:4). They have not accepted God's proffered gift; they shall lose even what they have and be visited by a judgment more severe than that of those notoriously wicked ancient cities, *Tyre, Sidon,* and *Sodom.*

11:23 *Hades,* realm of the dead. Jesus uses the language with which Isaiah had denounced the godless and insolent king of Babylon. (Is 14:13, 15)

11:25-30 THE SON WHO KNOWS THE FATHER

11:25-30 Jesus *knows* and is known by the Father (27); since "knowing" in Biblical usage involves personal communion between the knower and the known, Jesus here claims for Himself a unique, mutual, total communion with the *Father,* the *Lord of heaven and earth* who has *delivered all things* to Him (27)—the healing of all disease, victory over death, the Good News, the gracious inbreaking of God's kingdom. In the strength of this communion He thanks His Father for so disposing His revelation that His *gracious will* (26) is made manifest in it; the simple and unskilled *(babes)* can and do receive it, though the wisdom of the wise makes them stumble over it (they too would master God, 25). The *wise and under-*

delivered to me by my Father; and no one knows the Son except the Father, and no one knows the Father except the Son and any one to whom the Son chooses to reveal him. 28 Come to me, all who labor and are heavy laden, and I will give you rest. 29 Take my yoke upon you, and learn from me; for I am gentle and lowly in heart, and you will find rest for your souls. 30 For my yoke is easy, and my burden is light.''

12 At that time Jesus went through the grainfields on the sabbath; his disciples were hungry, and they began to pluck heads of grain and to eat. 2 But when the Pharisees saw it, they said to him, "Look, your disciples are doing what is not lawful to do on the sabbath." 3 He said to them, "Have you not read what David did, when he was hungry, and those who were with him: 4 how he entered the house of God and ate the bread of the Presence, which it was not lawful for him to eat nor for those who were with him, but only for the priests? 5 Or have you not read in the law how on the sabbath the priests in the temple profane the sabbath, and are guiltless? 6 I tell you, something greater than the temple is here. 7And if you had known what this means, 'I desire mercy, and not sacrifice,' you would not have condemned the guiltless. 8 For the Son of man is lord of the sabbath."

9 And he went on from there, and entered their synagogue. 10And behold, there was a man with a withered hand. And they asked him, "Is it lawful to heal on the sabbath?" so that they might accuse him. 11 He said to them, "What man of you, if he has one sheep and it falls into a pit on the sabbath, will not lay hold of it and lift it out? 12 Of how much more value is a man than a sheep! So it is lawful to do good on the sabbath." 13 Then he said to the man, "Stretch out your hand." And the man stretched it out, and it was restored, whole like the other. 14 But the Pharisees went out and took counsel against him, how to destroy him.

15 Jesus, aware of this, withdrew from there. And many followed him, and he healed them all, 16 and ordered them not to make him known. 17 This was to fulfil

---

standing are opposed to the Son; if scribe and Pharisee are turned against the Son, that means that He will "fail" and perish. Jesus, the obedient Son and Servant, *thanks* God for that "failure" and continues steadfast on the course which will bring Him death. He chooses still to reveal the Father; He invites men struggling under the burden of the Law and their sin to come to Him for *rest* (28), to find rest and peace for their muddled lives under the beneficent discipline of His *easy yoke,* to take up the *burden* which is *light* because He has borne it before them and for them (29-30). In the midst of contradiction Jesus reveals Himself as "God of God . . . for us men and our salvation came down from heaven . . . incarnate by the Holy Ghost . . . made man."

11:29 *Yoke.* The rabbis spoke of the "yoke of the Law"; Jesus with His Yoke is the "end of the law." (Ro 10:4)

12:1-21 LORD OF THE SABBATH AND SERVANT OF GOD

12:1-21 In the face of contradiction the Christ looms large in His merciful majesty. Reproached by the *Pharisees* for letting His disciples "thresh" (1) on the sacred *sabbath,* He recalls the example of *David's* freedom over against the temple-cultus—if David, the man after God's heart (1 Sm 13:14), had this freedom, how much more THE Son of David (1:1), the Messiah (1-4)? Jesus claims even more for Himself: He is *greater than the temple* (6), a higher and fuller presence of God among His people than God's house has been; and

if His disciples do work on the Sabbath as they attend upon Him, they no more *profane* the Sabbath than the *priests* who offer the burnt offering on the Sabbath at God's command (Nm 28:9-10). If the Pharisees had an ear for the God who desires *mercy* more than *sacrifice* (Hos 6:6), they would not condemn the *guiltless* disciples, who attend Jesus on His mission of mercy (7), and they would not be offended at the *Son of man* who is *lord of the sabbath* (8) and uses His divine authority *to do good* on the Sabbath (12), while those who carp at Him plot *to destroy him* on the Sabbath which they guard so jealously. (14)

Jesus uses His authority solely in the service of mercy; He will not destroy His destroyers but withdraws before their enmity (15). He will not even capitalize on His deeds of mercy to achieve fame (16), for He is the selfless Servant of the Lord who goes His way of quiet ministration to the hopelessly distressed (*bruised reed . . . smoldering wick,* 20) and waits for God to give Him *victory* (20). That victory means that by the power of the *Spirit* (18) the cause and revelation of God (*justice,* 18, 20) shall prevail and shall avail for all men (*Gentiles,* 18, 21).

12:3 *What David did.* 1 Sm 21:1-6.

12:4 *Bread of the Presence.* The 12 loaves of unleavened bread placed fresh every Sabbath on a table in the Holy Place of the temple as an offering. The old loaves were eaten by the priests. (Ex 25:30; Lv 24:5-9)

12:5 *In the law.* Nm 28:9-10.

12:7 *I desire mercy.* Hos 6:6; Mt 9:13.

what was spoken by the prophet I·sa′iah:

18	"Behold, my servant whom I have chosen,
	my beloved with whom my soul is well pleased.
	I will put my Spirit upon him,
	and he shall proclaim justice to the Gentiles.
19	He will not wrangle or cry aloud,
	nor will any one hear his voice in the streets;
20	he will not break a bruised reed
	or quench a smoldering wick,
	till he brings justice to victory;
21	and in his name will the Gentiles hope."

22 Then a blind and dumb demoniac was brought to him, and he healed him, so that the dumb man spoke and saw. 23And all the people were amazed, and said, "Can this be the Son of David?" 24 But when the Pharisees heard it they said, "It is only by Beelzebul, the prince of demons, that this man casts out demons." 25 Knowing their thoughts, he said to them, "Every kingdom divided against itself is laid waste, and no city or house divided against itself will stand; 26 and if Satan casts out Satan, he is divided against himself; how then will his kingdom stand? 27And if I cast out demons by Beelzebul, by whom do your sons cast them out? Therefore they shall be your judges. 28 But if it is by the Spirit of God that I cast out demons, then the kingdom of God has come upon you. 29 Or how can one enter a strong man's house and plunder his goods, unless he first binds the strong man? Then indeed he may plunder his house. 30 He who is not with me is against me, and he who does not gather with me scatters. 31 Therefore I tell you, every sin and blasphemy will be forgiven men, but the blasphemy against the Spirit will not be forgiven. 32And whoever says a word

---

12:18-21 Is 42:1-4. This is the first of the so-called Servant Songs in Isaiah, which portray a Deliverer sent by the Lord whose quiet, obedient ministry takes Him through contradiction, suffering, and rejection down into an atoning death for the salvation of both Israel and the Gentiles. Is 42:1-9; 49:1-7; 50:4-9; 52:13 — 53:12; some would include 61:1-4 also.

12:22-37 ULTIMATE CONTRADICTION OF THE CHRIST

12:22-37 Jesus' power over the *demons* moves the *people* to recognize in Him the Messiah (*Son of David,* 23). The Pharisees meet this dawning recognition with blasphemy; they assert that Jesus is in league with *Beelzebul;* they call the divine satanic (24). Jesus in His mercy seeks to win them still. "Your charge," He says, "is folly; Satan will not willingly destroy his own *kingdom* (25-26). Your charge is a self-contradiction; for your *sons,* pious men of your own group, cast out demons too, and you do not call their deeds satanic but works of piety. These *sons . . . shall be your judges* (27); they will testify that only the power of God can overcome the kingdom of Satan. You must recognize that in My deeds the *Spirit of God* is at work, not the unclean spirits of Satan; in My deeds *the kingdom of God has come upon you* (28). God is establishing His reign, promised for the last days, among you now. My power over demons is the fruit of My victory over Satan in the Temptation; I have broken the power of Satan and am plundering Satan's house." (29)

Jesus meets their contradiction with an urgent call to repentance; there is no room for contradiction; there is not even room for neutrality (30); a man must either gather the flock, the new people of God, with the Shepherd Messiah (cf. 9:36 note), or else he *scatters* the sheep of God (30). If a man contradicts the Messiah working in the power of the Spirit, he is in danger of committing the ultimate sin of *blasphemy against the Spirit,* the sin which *will not be forgiven* because it makes repentance impossible (31-32). There is still room for repentance, and so Jesus renews the Baptist's call to repentance (33-37; cf. 3:7-10). They can still become *good trees* bearing *good fruit* through God's gift of repentance if they will accept the gift; they can cease being a *brood of vipers* and become *good men* bringing *good* words out of the *good treasure* of their repentant *hearts.* But the hour is the critical hour, for every *careless* word spoken by men against the Messiah will come under God's scrutiny in the impending *judgment.* (33-37)

12:24 *By Beelzebul.* Cf. 9:34; 10:25. The form given here is to be preferred to the more familiar Beelzebub as a designation for Satan.

12:31-32 The *blasphemy against the Spirit* is conscious, stubborn, malicious opposition to divine revelation which becomes unpardonable because it cuts off the possibility of repentance. Notice that just here, when Jesus issues this most terrifying of warnings, He stresses the fullness of God's forgiveness. Paul spoke many a *word against the Son of man* when he persecuted the church; had he persisted in this after the risen Lord appeared to him, he would have been guilty of the unpardonable sin. (Cf. 1 Ti 1:13, 16)

against the Son of man will be forgiven; but whoever speaks against the Holy Spirit will not be forgiven, either in this age or in the age to come.

33 "Either make the tree good, and its fruit good; or make the tree bad, and its fruit bad; for the tree is known by its fruit. 34 You brood of vipers! how can you speak good, when you are evil? For out of the abundance of the heart the mouth speaks. 35 The good man out of his good treasure brings forth good, and the evil man out of his evil treasure brings forth evil. 36 I tell you, on the day of judgment men will render account for every careless word they utter; 37 for by your words you will be justified, and by your words you will be condemned."

38 Then some of the scribes and Pharisees said to him, "Teacher, we wish to see a sign from you." 39 But he answered them, "An evil and adulterous generation seeks for a sign; but no sign shall be given to it except the sign of the prophet Jonah. 40 For as Jonah was three days and three nights in the belly of the whale, so will the Son of man be three days and three nights in the heart of the earth. 41 The men of Nin′e·veh will arise at the judgment with this generation and condemn it; for they repented at the preaching of Jonah, and behold, something greater than Jonah is here. 42 The queen of the South will arise at the judgment with this generation and condemn it; for she came from the ends of the earth to hear the wisdom of Solomon, and behold, something greater than Solomon is here.

43 "When the unclean spirit has gone out of a man, he passes through waterless places seeking rest, but he finds none. 44 Then he says, 'I will return to my house from which I came.' And when he comes he finds it empty, swept, and put in order. 45 Then he goes and brings with him seven other spirits more evil than himself, and they enter and dwell there; and the last state of that man becomes worse than the first. So shall it be also with this evil generation."

46 While he was still speaking to the people, behold, his mother and his brothers stood outside, asking to speak to him.ᵍ 48 But he replied to the man who told him,

___

ᵍ Other ancient authorities insert verse 47, *Some one told him, "Your mother and your brothers are standing outside, asking to speak to you"*

___

12:33 *Tree . . . fruit.* Cf. 3:10.
12:34 *Brood of vipers.* Cf. 3:7.

12:38-42 DEMAND FOR A SIGN; THE SIGN OF JONAH

12:38-42 At least some of the *Pharisees* and their theological leaders, the *scribes,* remained unmoved by Jesus' warning. Their demand for a sign is a mark of their unwillingness to repent; they are an *adulterous generation* (39), men who will not commit themselves unreservedly to God's love and so come to repentance and faith in God's Messiah on God's terms. They will not accept the given revelation of Jesus' triumph over Satan and demand a special revelation, an overwhelming *sign* (cf. 16:1, "sign from heaven") which will make repentance and faith unnecessary. They are like their fathers in the wilderness who put God to the proof even though they had seen His work (Ps 95:9). They seek to master God, to dictate to Him. And Jesus, who rejects no petition, rejects their demand; no sign shall be given them except the *sign of Jonah,* no sign except the Servant Messiah who goes into death for His people's sins (*in the heart of the earth,* 40), no sign that will relieve them of the need to repent (41). The *men of Nineveh* and the *queen of the South* who acted on the revelation given them in their day will appear in the Last Judgment to bear witness against the men who refused the revelation given them in One who is a *greater* Spokesman for God than

Jonah and a *greater* King than Solomon with a *wisdom* far surpassing Solomon's.

12:40-41 Jon 1:17; 3:5.
12:40 *Three days and three nights.* Not intended as a prediction of the exact length of time that Jesus would be in the grave. After three days visible corruption set in (cf. Jn 11:39); God will not let His "Holy One see corruption." (Acts 2:27)
12:42 *Queen of the South.* 1 K 10:1-10.

12:43-50 RETURNING DEMON AND FAMILY OF JESUS

12:43-50 No neutrality is possible (cf. 12:30) over against Jesus. These two brief sections present the alternatives which confront men in Him. Those who would remain uncommitted (*this evil generation,* 45), accepting the benefits of His works but refusing to repent and believe, are like a healed demoniac; their heart is an empty house that invites the return of the augmented powers of evil, and their *last state . . . becomes worse than the first* (45). Man is never so open to the power of Satan as when he has been touched by the Christ but has not been filled by Him. Those *who do the will of my Father in heaven* (50), who accept the Christ and become good trees bearing good fruit (33) by God's planting (15:13) — for them the door of the Father's house is opened wide; they become the true *brothers* and *sisters* of Jesus, no less. (Cf. Ro 8:29)

12:43 The *unclean spirit* exists only to destroy

"Who is my mother, and who are my brothers?" 49And stretching out his hand toward his disciples, he said, "Here are my mother and my brothers! 50 For whoever does the will of my Father in heaven is my brother, and sister, and mother."

THE SECRETS OF THE KINGDOM (13:1-52)

13 That same day Jesus went out of the house and sat beside the sea. 2And great crowds gathered about him, so that he got into a boat and sat there; and the whole crowd stood on the beach. 3And he told them many things in parables, saying: "A sower went out to sow. 4And as he sowed, some seeds fell along the path, and the birds came and devoured them. 5 Other seeds fell on rocky ground, where they had not much soil, and immediately they sprang up, since they had no depth of soil, 6 but when the sun rose they were scorched; and since they had no root they withered away. 7 Other seeds fell upon thorns, and the thorns grew up and choked them. 8 Other seeds fell on good soil and brought forth grain, some a hundredfold, some sixty, some thirty. 9 He who has ears,ʰ let him hear."

10 Then the disciples came and said to him, "Why do you speak to them in parables?" 11And he answered them, "To you it has been given to know the secrets of the kingdom of heaven, but to them it has not been given. 12 For to him who has will more be given, and he will have abundance; but from him who has not, even what he has will be taken away. 13 This is why I speak to them in parables, because seeing they do not see, and hearing they do not hear, nor do they understand. 14 With them indeed is fulfilled the prophecy of I·sa′iah which says:

'You shall indeed hear but never understand,
    and you shall indeed see but never perceive.

15   For this people's heart has grown dull,
      and their ears are heavy of hearing,
      and their eyes they have closed,
    lest they should perceive with their eyes,
      and hear with their ears,
      and understand with their heart,
    and turn for me to heal them.'

ʰ Other ancient authorities add here and in verse 43 *to hear*

God's handiwork; when driven out from man, the spirit is desolate and restless.

12:50 *Sister.* Woman has her place of undiminished honor in the family of God. (Gl 3:28)

13:1-52 The parables of Jesus are plain, utilizing materials familiar to every Galilean. The people were familiar with the parable form of teaching; their rabbis used this form. And yet Jesus' parables serve to conceal as well as reveal (11-15). They conceal the *secrets of the kingdom* (11) from those who have rejected the Kingdom as revealed in the words and works of Jesus the Servant, from those who do not hold and treasure (*has not*, 12) what God has given them already in the OT, in John the Bapist, in Jesus' plain words and eloquent acts. The parables are unintelligible to them because they have thrown away the key to them, Jesus. Because they refuse to see in Jesus the coming of the Kingdom (12:28), they cannot (and by God's judgment on their unbelief shall not) see that He is sowing the Word of the Kingdom (18:3-9), that He is the Sower of God's *good seed* (37), the *treasure* of all treasures (44). Isaiah's word that hardened Israel in her unbelief finds a fresh fulfillment in them (14). On the other hand, those who *have* (hold and treasure) what God's previous revelation has given them are enriched by the parables; *more* is *given* them, and they have in *abundance*. (12, 51-52)

13:1-9 THE PARABLE OF THE SOWER

13:1-9 As Jesus' own interpretation (18-23) makes plain, the Kingdom comes in the unspectacular and vulnerable form of the *word* (19), which can be *devoured* (4), *scorched* (6), and *choked* (7). But this "failure" of the Word indicts the soil, not the sower or the seed. Man is responsible when confronted by God's Word and guilty when he fails to use it. Therefore the stern warning at the close. (9)

13:10-17 TO HIM WHO HAS . . . FROM HIM WHO HAS NOT

13:10-17 See note on 1-52 at beginning of chapter.

13:11 *Secrets.* The same word is also sometimes translated as "mysteries." See note on Cl 1:26-27.

13:14-15 Is 6:9-10. Both in Isaiah and here these words are not an eternal decree which predestines some men for salvation and dooms others to unbelief; they describe God's reaction to man's unbelief. What man has refused to hear for his salvation, he is doomed to hear for his hardening and condemnation.

16 But blessed are your eyes, for they see, and your ears, for they hear. 17 Truly, I say to you, many prophets and righteous men longed to see what you see, and did not see it, and to hear what you hear, and did not hear it.

18 "Hear then the parable of the sower. 19 When any one hears the word of the kingdom and does not understand it, the evil one comes and snatches away what is sown in his heart; this is what was sown along the path. 20As for what was sown on rocky ground, this is he who hears the word and immediately receives it with joy; 21 yet he has no root in himself, but endures for a while, and when tribulation or persecution arises on account of the word, immediately he falls away.[i] 22As for what was sown among thorns, this is he who hears the word, but the cares of the world and the delight in riches choke the word, and it proves unfruitful. 23As for what was sown on good soil, this is he who hears the word and understands it; he indeed bears fruit, and yields, in one case a hundredfold, in another sixty, and in another thirty."

24 Another parable he put before them, saying, "The kingdom of heaven may be compared to a man who sowed good seed in his field; 25 but while men were sleeping, his enemy came and sowed weeds among the wheat, and went away. 26 So when the plants came up and bore grain, then the weeds appeared also. 27And the servants[j] of the householder came and said to him, 'Sir, did you not sow good seed in your field? How then has it weeds?' 28 He said to them, 'An enemy has done this.' The servants[j] said to him, 'Then do you want us to go and gather them?' 29 But he said, 'No; lest in gathering the weeds you root up the wheat along with them. 30 Let both grow together until the harvest; and at harvest time I will tell the reapers, Gather the weeds first and bind them in bundles to be burned, but gather the wheat into my barn.' "

31 Another parable he put before them, saying, "The kingdom of heaven is like a grain of mustard seed which a man took and sowed in his field; 32 it is the smallest of all seeds, but when it has grown it is the greatest of shrubs and becomes a tree, so that the birds of the air come and make nests in its branches."

33 He told them another parable. "The kingdom of heaven is like leaven which a woman took and hid in three measures of flour, till it was all leavened."

34 All this Jesus said to the crowds in parables; indeed he said nothing to them

[i] Or stumbles   [j] Or slaves

13:16 Blessed . . . your eyes . . . your ears. Not hearing and unbelief are man's guilt; hearing and believing, however, are not merit on man's part but God's grace to him.

13:18-23 EXPLANATION OF PARABLE OF THE SOWER

13:23 Understands, comprehends, makes his own, so that his will and action are controlled by it. (Cf. Cl 1:9)

Hundredfold . . . sixty . . . thirty. God's seed thrives on good soil but not with a chemical uniformity; the response is personal and individual, for God "apportions to each one individually as He wills" (1 Co 12:11), and each man is individually responsible.

13:24-30 PARABLE OF THE WEEDS AND THE WHEAT

13:24-30 See Jesus' explanation, 36-43. God's action in establishing His kingdom provokes the counterthrust of the Evil One, who sows weeds where God sows His wheat, weeds that look like wheat. The disciples' task is not to institute an inquisition to destroy the weeds but to remember Jesus' words, "Judge not!" (7:1), and to await the hour of God's judgment and to look forward in patience to the time of their own glory. (43)

13:25 Weeds, probably bearded darnel, which looks like wheat until grown.

13:26 For the idea that the satanic appears in the guise of the divine cf. 16:22-23; 2 Co 11:3-5, 13-15. In the temptation of Jesus the Tempter quotes Scripture. (4:6)

13:31-33 PARABLES OF MUSTARD SEED AND LEAVEN

13:31-33 The homely language of garden and kitchen is used to warn men against being offended at the slight beginnings of the Kingdom as present in Jesus (cf. 11:6). The seed and the leaven have in them God's creative power and will achieve God's purposes of full growth and total penetration; the end is potentially present in the beginning. On this kingdom men may confidently fix their faith and hope.

13:32 Becomes a tree, etc. Jesus' language here is an echo of certain OT passages in which the tree is a symbol of worldwide dominion. (Eze 17:23; 31:5-6; Dn 4:9-12, 20-22)

13:33 Three measures. A large mass of dough, each measure being about 3 gallons.

13:34-35 "I WILL OPEN MY MOUTH IN PARABLES"

13:34-35 Ps 78:2 is quoted as being fulfilled. In

without a parable. 35 This was to fulfil what was spoken by the prophet: [k]
"I will open my mouth in parables,
I will utter what has been hidden since the foundation of the world."
36 Then he left the crowds and went into the house. And his disciples came to him, saying, "Explain to us the parable of the weeds of the field." 37 He answered, "He who sows the good seed is the Son of man; 38 the field is the world, and the good seed means the sons of the kingdom; the weeds are the sons of the evil one, 39 and the enemy who sowed them is the devil; the harvest is the close of the age, and the reapers are angels. 40 Just as the weeds are gathered and burned with fire, so will it be at the close of the age. 41 The Son of man will send his angels, and they will gather out of his kingdom all causes of sin and all evildoers, 42 and throw them into the furnace of fire; there men will weep and gnash their teeth. 43 Then the righteous will shine like the sun in the kingdom of their Father. He who has ears, let him hear.

44 "The kingdom of heaven is like treasure hidden in a field, which a man found and covered up; then in his joy he goes and sells all that he has and buys that field.

45 "Again, the kingdom of heaven is like a merchant in search of fine pearls, 46 who, on finding one pearl of great value, went and sold all that he had and bought it.

47 "Again, the kingdom of heaven is like a net which was thrown into the sea and gathered fish of every kind; 48 when it was full, men drew it ashore and sat down and sorted the good into vessels but threw away the bad. 49 So it will be at the close of the age. The angels will come out and separate the evil from the righteous, 50 and throw them into the furnace of fire; there men will weep and gnash their teeth.

51 "Have you understood all this?" They said to him, "Yes." 52And he said to

[k] Other ancient authorities read *the prophet Isaiah*

Matthew the word *fulfil* covers a much wider range of meaning than what we connect with it (a prediction, promise, or command is "fulfilled"). Here the connection seems to be this: Ps 78 recounts the history of Israel as the history of Israel's persistent rebellion against the ever-renewed manifestation of God's grace, a rebellion which makes that history an enigma and is marked as such by the psalmist (*parable* can also mean puzzle, enigma). That history of ungrateful revolt is climaxed in Israel's rejection of Jesus, in the people's unbelief which provokes the judgment of Jesus' speaking to them in parables (13). And so the word spoken by the psalmist reaches its full utterance, is "fulfilled," now when Jesus speaks in parables which doom the impenitent and unbelieving.

13:36-43 EXPLANATION OF PARABLE OF THE WEEDS

13:36 *Went into the house.* The rest of the discourse is spoken to the *disciples* alone.

13:37 *Son of man.* Jesus portrays Himself in terms of divine majesty; the *Son of man* owns the world (38), is Lord of the angels (41), and executes the Last Judgment (41-42); yet He remains the Servant and obedient Son who does all "to the glory of God the Father." (43; Ph 2:11; cf. 1 Co 15:28)

13:44-45 PARABLES OF THE HIDDEN TREASURE AND THE ONE PEARL

13:44-45 This pair of parables has particular

significance for Jesus' disciples. They have left all to follow Him (4:22), and they can see ever more plainly that following the contradicted Christ will involve painful renunciation. Is this renunciation worth while? Jesus' answer is: The gain of the Kingdom is so great that repentance and renunciation become a *joy.* (44)

13:47-50 PARABLE OF THE NET

13:47-50 The coming of the Kingdom is to bring both grace and judgment; the Christ is to work with both Spirit and fire (3:11). Lest His disciples grow doubtful about the reality of the Kingdom and impatient for the judgment which will *separate* (49) the evil from the righteous (as John the Baptist was tempted to do, 11:2-3), Jesus reminds them that God's judgment will come *at the close of the age* (49), after the nets of His grace have swept all waters and have *gathered fish of every kind.* (47)

13:51-52 THE SCRIBE TRAINED FOR THE KINGDOM

13:51-52 The disciple will be the *scribe* for the new people of God who call Jesus Lord; he will expound God's Word and will for men. And for this his sufficiency is from God. What the parables have given him will be part of his treasure, from which he can draw at need. And since he "has" that, more will be given him; when his ministry grows broader and more complex, he will ever and again find riches of revelation for his need. The

them, "Therefore every scribe who has been trained for the kingdom of heaven is like a householder who brings out of his treasure what is new and what is old."

Fourth Group of Messianic Deeds and Words

13:53 — 18:35

53 And when Jesus had finished these parables, he went away from there, 54 and coming to his own country he taught them in their synagogue, so that they were astonished, and said, "Where did this man get this wisdom and these mighty works? 55 Is not this the carpenter's son? Is not his mother called Mary? And are not his brothers James and Joseph and Simon and Judas? 56And are not all his sisters with us? Where then did this man get all this?" 57And they took offense at him. But Jesus said to them, "A prophet is not without honor except in his own country and in his own house." 58And he did not do many mighty works there, because of their unbelief.

14 At that time Herod the tetrarch heard about the fame of Jesus; 2 and he said to his servants, "This is John the Baptist, he has been raised from the dead; that is why these powers are at work in him." 3 For Herod had seized John and bound him and put him in prison, for the sake of He·ro′di·as, his brother Philip's wife;*l* 4 because John said to him, "It is not lawful for you to have her." 5And though he wanted to put him to death, he feared the people, because they held him to be a prophet. 6 But when Herod's birthday came, the daughter of He·ro′di·as danced before the company, and pleased Herod, 7 so that he promised with an oath to give her whatever she might ask. 8 Prompted by her mother, she said, "Give me the head of John the Baptist here on a platter." 9And the king was sorry; but because of his oaths and his guests he commanded it to be given; 10 he sent and had John beheaded in the prison, 11 and his head was brought on a platter and given to the girl, and she brought it to her mother. 12And his disciples came and took the body and buried it; and they went and told Jesus.

13 Now when Jesus heard this, he withdrew from there in a boat to a lonely place apart. But when the crowds heard it, they followed him on foot from the towns. 14As he went ashore he saw a great throng; and he had compassion on them, and healed their sick. 15 When it was evening, the disciples came to him and said, "This is a lonely

l Other ancient authorities read *his brother's wife*

theological riches of the NT writings are evidence that Jesus kept this promise to His own, as He did with all His promises.

13:53 — 18:35 Toward the new Messianic people of God, the church: The Messiah separates His disciples from the old Israel, which is rejecting Him, deepens His communion with His own, and shapes their relationship to one another in the fellowship of the church.

13:53 — 14:21 THE REJECTED, COMPASSIONATE MESSIAH

13:53 — 14:21 Jesus is rejected in *his own country* and becomes an object of superstitious fear at the court of Herod, who senses that the *powers* which he had attempted to destroy in executing John the Baptist threaten him anew in Jesus. What is happening in the village and the palace is symptomatic of what is happening in all Israel: the men of Israel are rejecting their Messiah. Jesus the unresisting Servant (12:19) *withdraws.* But even now He demonstrates His unbroken will of *compassion* for His people; He *heals the sick* and invites men to the fellowship of His table.

14:1 *Tetrarch* originally meant the ruler of the fourth part of a region, then came to be used more generally as title of a petty dependent prince such as *Herod* Antipas, who succeeded his father Herod the Great as ruler over a part of that monarch's kingdom, namely Galilee. (Lk 3:1)

14:3 *Philip,* not the tetrarch of Lk 3:1 but Philip's half brother Herod, who is not called Philip in other ancient records. Perhaps the reading given in RSV note *l* (*his brother's wife*) is to be preferred.

14:13 *Heard this,* namely Herod's reaction to His fame. For the threat posed by this reaction on the part of the man who had executed John cf. Lk 13:31.

14:15-21 Matthew records the miracle of the feeding of the 5,000 as well as that of the 4,000 (15:32-38) in a section which culminates in Jesus' discourse on fellowship (ch. 18). The common meal was more significant for the man of the ancient East generally, and for the Jew particularly, than it is for us; it established fellowship, and to violate this bond was the grossest kind of infidelity (cf. Jn 13:18; Ps 41:9). The Pharisees' objection to

place, and the day is now over; send the crowds away to go into the villages and buy food for themselves." 16 Jesus said, "They need not go away; you give them something to eat." 17 They said to him, "We have only five loaves here and two fish." 18And he said, "Bring them here to me." 19 Then he ordered the crowds to sit down on the grass; and taking the five loaves and the two fish he looked up to heaven, and blessed, and broke and gave the loaves to the disciples, and the disciples gave them to the crowds. 20And they all ate and were satisfied. And they took up twelve baskets full of the broken pieces left over. 21And those who ate were about five thousand men, besides women and children.

22 Then he made the disciples get into the boat and go before him to the other side, while he dismissed the crowds. 23And after he had dismissed the crowds, he went up on the mountain by himself to pray. When evening came, he was there alone, 24 but the boat by this time was many furlongs distant from the land,*m* beaten by the waves; for the wind was against them. 25And in the fourth watch of the night he came to them, walking on the sea. 26 But when the disciples saw him walking on the sea, they were terrified, saying, "It is a ghost!" And they cried out for fear. 27 But immediately he spoke to them, saying, "Take heart, it is I; have no fear."

28 And Peter answered him, "Lord, if it is you, bid me come to you on the water." 29 He said, "Come." So Peter got out of the boat and walked on the water and came to Jesus; 30 but when he saw the wind,*n* he was afraid, and beginning to sink he cried out, "Lord, save me." 31 Jesus immediately reached out his hand and caught him, saying to him, "O man of little faith, why did you doubt?" 32And when they got into the boat, the wind ceased. 33And those in the boat worshiped him, saying, "Truly you are the Son of God."

34 And when they had crossed over, they came to land at Gen·nes´a·ret. 35And when the men of that place recognized him, they sent round to all that region and brought to him all that were sick, 36 and besought him that they might only touch the fringe of his garment; and as many as touched it were made well.

15 Then Pharisees and scribes came to Jesus from Jerusalem and said, 2 "Why do your disciples transgress the tradition of the elders? For they do not wash their hands when they eat." 3 He answered them, "And why do you transgress the commandment of God for the sake of your tradition? 4 For God commanded, 'Honor your father and your mother,' and, 'He who speaks evil of father or mother, let him

m Other ancient authorities read *was out on the sea*   *n* Other ancient authorities read *strong wind*

Jesus' association with sinners made a point of the fact that He ate with them. (9:11; Lk 15:2)

14:16 *You give them.* Here and in the feeding of the 4,000 the disciples for the first time assist in the creative deed of Jesus; they are being taught the ministry of fellowship.

14:22-36 JESUS COMES ACROSS THE WATERS

14:22-36 Though the fellowship of the meal comes to an end, Jesus' fellowship with His own does not end. He comes to them across stormy waters and responds to the prayer of the faith that seeks Him with His enabling command, *Come.* Only *little faith* (which loses sight of the greatness of the commanding Christ) interrupts fellowship with Him. Even little faith can cry to Him and be *saved;* He is the *Lord, the Son of God,* ready to hear and mighty to save. He will be with them "always to the close of the age" (28:20). And as He is to His own, He is ready to be to all; all may *touch* His healing, seamless dress and be *made well.* (34-36)

14:25 The *fourth watch* was the last of the four periods into which the *night* was divided.

15:1-20 THE TRADITION OF THE ELDERS: WHAT DEFILES A MAN?

15:1-20 Jesus separates His disciples from the *tradition of the elders,* which interpreted and expanded the Law, often in such a way that it enabled a man to *transgress the commandment of God* with a show of legality. Jesus leads His own beyond the hypocrisy of Judaic worship, even beyond the whole legal conception of cultic purity, to a worship in purity of *heart:* Not what a man eats (cultically unclean food) but what a man thinks, desires, and speaks *defiles a man* and makes him unfit for worship and fellowship with God and his fellowman. Jesus is here transcending the dietary laws of the OT (Lv 11; Nm 19; Dt 14) but is at the same time affirming the will of the Law: that there be a pure, undefiled people of God to worship Him.

15:2 *Tradition of the elders,* the body of interpretation of (and additions to) the Law which had grown up around the Law in the Jewish schools. It enjoyed a prestige and authority practically equal to that of the Law itself. (Cf. Gl 1:14)

15:4 Ex 20:12; 21:17.

surely die.' 5 But you say, 'If any one tells his father or his mother, What you would have gained from me is given to God,^{o} he need not honor his father.' 6 So, for the sake of your tradition, you have made void the word^p of God. 7 You hypocrites! Well did I·sa'iah prophesy of you, when he said:

8   'This people honors me with their lips,
       but their heart is far from me;
9   in vain do they worship me,
       teaching as doctrines the precepts of men.' "

10 And he called the people to him and said to them, "Hear and understand: 11 not what goes into the mouth defiles a man, but what comes out of the mouth, this defiles a man." 12 Then the disciples came and said to him, "Do you know that the Pharisees were offended when they heard this saying?" 13 He answered, "Every plant which my heavenly Father has not planted will be rooted up. 14 Let them alone; they are blind guides. And if a blind man leads a blind man, both will fall into a pit." 15 But Peter said to him, "Explain the parable to us." 16And he said, "Are you also still without understanding? 17 Do you not see that whatever goes into the mouth passes into the stomach, and so passes on?^{q} 18 But what comes out of the mouth proceeds from the heart, and this defiles a man. 19 For out of the heart come evil thoughts, murder, adultery, fornication, theft, false witness, slander. 20 These are what defile a man; but to eat with unwashed hands does not defile a man."

21 And Jesus went away from there and withdrew to the district of Tyre and Sidon. 22And behold, a Canaanite woman from that region came out and cried, "Have mercy on me, O Lord, Son of David; my daughter is severely possessed by a demon." 23 But he did not answer her a word. And his disciples came and begged him, saying, "Send her away, for she is crying after us." 24 He answered, "I was sent only to the lost sheep of the house of Israel." 25 But she came and knelt before him, saying, "Lord, help me." 26And he answered, "It is not fair to take the children's bread and throw it to the dogs." 27 She said, "Yes, Lord, yet even the dogs eat the crumbs that fall from their masters' table." 28 Then Jesus answered her, "O woman, great is your faith! Be it done for you as you desire." And her daughter was healed instantly.

29 And Jesus went on from there and passed along the Sea of Galilee. And he went up on the mountain, and sat down there. 30And great crowds came to him, bringing with them the lame, the maimed, the blind, the dumb, and many others, and they put them at his feet, and he healed them, 31so that the throng wondered, when they saw the dumb speaking, the maimed whole, the lame walking, and the blind seeing; and they glorified the God of Israel.

^{o} Or *an offering* ^{p} Other ancient authorities read *law* ^{q} Or *is evacuated*

15:5-6 *Given to God.* A son might declare that the property which he was in duty bound to use for the support of his parents had been dedicated by him to God and was not therefore available for secular uses. The sacredness of such a vow was utilized to withhold support from parents, even if the property was not actually given to God. Thus a pretext of religion served to *make void the word of God.*

15:8-9. Cf. Is 29:13-14, which threatens divine judgment on the teachers of the people. For Jesus' full indictment of Pharisees and scribes see Mt 23.

15:13 For the picture of the true man of God as a *plant planted* by the *Father* cf. Is 60:21; Jn 15:2; Cl 2:7, "rooted . . . in Him" (Christ).

15:15 *Parable,* the pointed saying of v. 11.

15:21-28 THE CANAANITE WOMAN: GREAT IS YOUR FAITH

15:21-28 Jesus remains faithful to Israel even when Israel proves unfaithful to God by rejecting the Christ (cf. Ro 15:8). He upholds Israel's prerogative over against the Gentiles (24, 26). He oversteps the limitations of His mission only in response to *faith.* His help and healing is available "to everyone who has faith," whether Jew or Gentile (Ro 1:16). Such incidents as these point forward to the command to make disciples of all nations (28:19) and to the universal church.

15:28 *Great . . . faith.* Her faith is great, for she submits wholly to God and assents wholly to His way (through Israel to the world, 27), sees that the table which God set for Israel is rich enough to supply all nations (27), and is willing to accept God's grace on the lowest terms of beggary—she can pray from under the table.

15:29-39 UNFAILING MERCY OF THE MESSIAH

15:29-39 Again (cf. 14:14, 34-36) Jesus heals the sick and suffering members of His people to the glory of the *God of Israel.* Again (cf. 14:15-21) He invites thousands to the fellowship of the com-

32 Then Jesus called his disciples to him and said, "I have compassion on the crowd, because they have been with me now three days, and have nothing to eat; and I am unwilling to send them away hungry, lest they faint on the way." 33And the disciples said to him, "Where are we to get bread enough in the desert to feed so great a crowd?" 34And Jesus said to them, "How many loaves have you?" They said, "Seven, and a few small fish." 35And commanding the crowd to sit down on the ground, 36 he took the seven loaves and the fish, and having given thanks he broke them and gave them to the disciples, and the disciples gave them to the crowds. 37And they all ate and were satisfied; and they took up seven baskets full of the broken pieces left over. 38 Those who ate were four thousand men, besides women and children. 39And sending away the crowds, he got into the boat and went to the region of Mag′a·dan.

16 And the Pharisees and Sad′du·cees came, and to test him they asked him to show them a sign from heaven. 2 He answered them,[r] "When it is evening, you say, 'It will be fair weather; for the sky is red.' 3And in the morning, 'It will be stormy today, for the sky is red and threatening.' You know how to interpret the appearance of the sky, but you cannot interpret the signs of the times. 4An evil and adulterous generation seeks for a sign, but no sign shall be given to it except the sign of Jonah." So he left them and departed.

5 When the disciples reached the other side, they had forgotten to bring any bread. 6 Jesus said to them, "Take heed and beware of the leaven of the Pharisees and Sad′du·cees." 7And they discussed it among themselves, saying, "We brought no bread." 8 But Jesus, aware of this, said, "O men of little faith, why do you discuss among yourselves the fact that you have no bread? 9 Do you not yet perceive? Do you not remember the five loaves of the five thousand, and how many baskets you gathered? 10 Or the seven loaves of the four thousand, and how many baskets you gathered? 11 How is it that you fail to perceive that I did not speak about bread? Beware of the leaven of the Pharisees and Sad′du·cees." 12 Then they understood that he did not tell them to beware of the leaven of bread, but of the teaching of the Pharisees and Sad′du·cees.

13 Now when Jesus came into the district of Caes·a·re′a Phi·lip′pi, he asked his

[r] Other ancient authorities omit the following words to the end of verse 3

mon meal — *in the desert,* where the Lord once fed His people with manna. In Jesus God, the Healer of Israel, the Lord who cared for Israel in the wilderness, is present for the salvation of His people.

15:39 *Magadan,* place of uncertain location on the Sea of Galilee.

16:1-28 YOU ARE THE CHRIST:
I WILL BUILD MY CHURCH

16:1-28 Jesus separates His disciples from all Judaism. He separates them from the Pharisees and Sadducees who, for all their differences, unite in demanding from Jesus a *sign from heaven;* they ignore God's given revelation and demand a special revelation for themselves, thus disclosing themselves as an *evil and adulterous generation.* The Christ cannot give Himself to their evil and divided hearts (1-4). Jesus warns His disciples against the *leaven . . . of the teaching of the Pharisees and Sadducees;* that teaching might otherwise insinuate itself into their hearts and corrupt their faith. (5-12)

To those who do not demand a sign but live by the given revelation of God, the supreme revelation is given; the Father *reveals* to them *the Christ, the Son of the living God.* And they hear from the lips of the Christ His promise concerning the new people of God *(my church)* which shall triumph

over death. In the building of this church the disciples are given a fundamental place as believers in and confessors of the Christ. (13-20)

The confession binds the disciples to the Servant Christ who goes in hiddenness (cf. 20) and shame to His *cross* and resurrection in obedience to God's will; to oppose His way to the cross is satanic opposition to God. Jesus makes His cross the pattern of life for all who are united in His fellowship: The disciple is to *find his life* by *losing* it for the sake of the Christ, who will return in glory to *repay every man for what he has done.* (21-28)

16:3 *The signs of the times,* the words and works of Jesus which reveal that God's kingdom has drawn near.

16:4 *Adulterous,* unfaithful to God. Cf. Hos 1 – 3; Ja 4:4.

Sign of Jonah. Cf. 12:38-40.

16:5-12 The story of the forgotten bread remains obscure for us in detail, but the main point is clear. The disciples are preoccupied with the food for their bodies, even after seeing how Jesus' mighty grace can supply loaves in abundance. Jesus is concerned about the food for their faith, which the *leaven . . . of the teaching of the Pharisees and Sadducees* would corrupt.

16:13 *Caesarea Philippi* marks the northern-

disciples, "Who do men say that the Son of man is?" [14]And they said, "Some say John the Baptist, others say E·li′jah, and others Jer·e·mi′ah or one of the prophets." [15] He said to them, "But who do you say that I am?" [16] Simon Peter replied, "You are the Christ, the Son of the living God." [17]And Jesus answered him, "Blessed are you, Simon Bar-Jona! For flesh and blood has not revealed this to you, but my Father who is in heaven. [18]And I tell you, you are Peter,[s] and on this rock[t] I will build my church, and the powers of death[u] shall not prevail against it. [19] I will give you the keys of the kingdom of heaven, and whatever you bind on earth shall be bound in heaven, and whatever you loose on earth shall be loosed in heaven." [20] Then he strictly charged the disciples to tell no one that he was the Christ.

21 From that time Jesus began to show his disciples that he must go to Jerusalem and suffer many things from the elders and chief priests and scribes, and be killed, and on the third day be raised. [22]And Peter took him and began to rebuke him, saying, "God forbid, Lord! This shall never happen to you." [23] But he turned and said to Peter, "Get behind me, Satan! You are a hindrance[v] to me; for you are not on the side of God, but of men."

24 Then Jesus told his disciples, "If any man would come after me, let him deny himself and take up his cross and follow me. [25] For whoever would save his life will lose it, and whoever loses his life for my sake will find it. [26] For what will it profit a man, if he gains the whole world and forfeits his life? Or what shall a man give in return for his life? [27] For the Son of man is to come with his angels in the glory of his Father, and then he will repay every man for what he has done. [28] Truly, I say to you, there are some standing here who will not taste death before they see the Son of man coming in his kingdom."

[s] Greek *Petros*   [t] Greek *petra*   [u] Greek *the gates of Hades*   [v] Greek *stumbling block*

most limits of Jesus' ministry in Galilee; from here His course will be southward toward Jerusalem and the cross. Now Jesus binds His disciples to Himself as the Christ who must die. (Cf. 16:21; 17:22; 20:17-19)

16:14 Jesus separates His disciples not only from those who oppose Him but also from those whose "appreciation" of Him falls short of confessing Him as the Christ. They can see in Him One whose coming prepares for the Kingdom, but not the Christ in whose person the Kingdom comes.

John the Baptist. Cf. 14:2.

Elijah. Cf. Ml 4:5; Mt 11:14; 17:10-13.

16:17 *Bar-Jona,* son of Jonah. Simon's flesh-and-blood father could not reveal the Christ to him.

16:18 *Peter . . . rock.* As the RSV notes indicate, Jesus is playing on the sense of the name *(rock)* which He gave Simon (Mk 3:16; Lk 6:14; Jn 1:42). In the building which the Christ rears, Peter (and the disciples for whom he speaks in his confession) will have a fundamental position; the apostles constitute the foundation of the structure (cf. Eph 2:20; Rv 21:14). This position signifies not lordship but ministry; the apostles serve (2 Co 1:24; Mt 20:26; 1 Co 3:5; Cl 1:25). The Father reveals; the Christ builds the church, gives the promise of life, and bestows authority. The apostles remain strictly subordinate to the divine action which takes place through them (Ro 15:18); Peter is a rock because the Christ employs him as foundation stone.

Powers of death (gates of Hades). The gates of the world of the dead which do not open to release

the inhabitants of Hades will not be strong enough to hold back those whom the Christ calls; the followers of Jesus will lose their life for His sake (25), but they shall find their life in the resurrection of the dead.

16:19 *Keys,* symbols of authority. (Cf. Is 22: 21-22; Rv 1:18; 3:7)

Bind . . . loose. The apostolic witness to Christ, the Gospel, will be a divinely valid word *(in heaven).* Those who reject it will be *bound* by it, held fast under the judgment of God; those who accept and believe it will be set free *(loosed)* by it for the eternal liberty of sons of God (17:26; cf. 2 Co 2:14-17; Jn 20:23). The apostles receive this authority not as something to be held exclusively by them but in order to bestow it on the church. (Cf. 18:17-18)

16:20 *Tell no one.* The action of God will at His time and in His way proclaim and glorify the Christ. (28:18; Ph 2:9-11)

16:23 *Satan.* In his attempt to dissuade Jesus from going the Servant's way to the cross, Peter has become the voice of the Tempter (4:1-10), a *hindrance* to Jesus on His way of obedience to the Father.

On the side of God. God wills man's redemption; *men* seek their own ease and advantage. In Jesus' judgment this self-seeking will of man is satanic. (Cf. Ja 3:15)

16:24 *Cross* is to be taken literally: loss of honor and life for the sake of Christ and the Gospel.

16:28 *See the Son of man coming in his kingdom.* Peter, James, and John had a foretaste of this when they beheld Jesus' transfiguration. (17:1-8)

17 And after six days Jesus took with him Peter and James and John his brother, and led them up a high mountain apart. ²And he was transfigured before them, and his face shone like the sun, and his garments became white as light. ³And behold, there appeared to them Moses and E·li′jah, talking with him. ⁴And Peter said to Jesus, "Lord, it is well that we are here; if you wish, I will make three booths here, one for you and one for Moses and one for E·li′jah." ⁵ He was still speaking, when lo, a bright cloud overshadowed them, and a voice from the cloud said, "This is my beloved Son,ʷ with whom I am well pleased; listen to him." ⁶ When the disciples heard this, they fell on their faces, and were filled with awe. ⁷ But Jesus came and touched them, saying, "Rise, and have no fear." ⁸And when they lifted up their eyes, they saw no one but Jesus only.

9 And as they were coming down the mountain, Jesus commanded them, "Tell no one the vision, until the Son of man is raised from the dead." ¹⁰And the disciples asked him, "Then why do the scribes say that first E·li′jah must come?" ¹¹ He replied, "E·li′jah does come, and he is to restore all things; ¹² but I tell you that E·li′jah has already come, and they did not know him, but did to him whatever they pleased. So also the Son of man will suffer at their hands." ¹³ Then the disciples understood that he was speaking to them of John the Baptist.

14 And when they came to the crowd, a man came up to him and kneeling before him said, ¹⁵ "Lord, have mercy on my son, for he is an epileptic and he suffers terribly; for often he falls into the fire, and often into the water. ¹⁶And I brought him to your disciples, and they could not heal him." ¹⁷And Jesus answered, "O faithless and perverse generation, how long am I to be with you? How long am I to bear with you? Bring him here to me." ¹⁸And Jesus rebuked him, and the demon came out of him, and the boy was cured instantly. ¹⁹ Then the disciples came to Jesus privately and said, "Why could we not cast it out?" ²⁰ He said to them, "Because of your little faith. For truly, I say to you, if you have faith as a grain of mustard seed, you will say to this mountain, 'Move from here to there,' and it will move; and nothing will be impossible to you." ˣ

ʷ Or *my Son, my* (or *the*) *Beloved*
ˣ Other ancient authorities insert verse 21, "*But this kind never comes out except by prayer and fasting*"

17:1-27 TRANSFIGURED BEFORE THEM

17:1-27 The disciples did not demand a sign from heaven; they believed in the Christ, the Son of the living God, on the basis of the revelation which the Father GAVE them. To them the sign from heaven is freely given. They are privileged to behold the Son of the living God in His heavenly splendor (2), to see the Christ whom His people reject receiving the witness of the Law and the prophets (*Moses, Elijah*, 3), to hear the voice from the *bright cloud* attest the *beloved Son* and Servant (5, cf. 3:17). They learn, too, that the Christ "must suffer" (16:21); they cannot hold Him on the mountain of His glory (4). Jesus descends to resume His hidden way to the cross (9), to the world in which the contradiction of the scribes awaits Him (10), where the fate of *Elijah (John the Baptist)* is a prediction of His own end (11-13). He must face and deal with the agony of demonridden man and His disciples' littleness of faith (14-21). *The Son of man is* destined *to be delivered into the hands of men* (22). His disciples are *distressed* at that (23); but He goes in free obedience to His death, as the free Son who sets all *sons free* (26). He frees His disciples from the old doomed Israel by freeing them from the temple tax imposed on all adult members of the people. (24-27)

17:3 *Moses and Elijah* appear together in the last chapter of the last prophet of the OT, Ml 4:4-6. The disciples see confirmed Jesus' claim that He is Fulfiller of the Law and the prophets. (5:17)

17:5 *Bright cloud,* symbol of the gracious presence of God. (Cf. Ex 40:34)

17:4 *Make three booths.* Peter deemed it natural that the glory of this vision (9) should continue, that the Christ remain *transfigured,* not that He descend and resume His way to the cross. (Cf. 16:22)

17:5 Cf. 3:17 and note there. *Listen to him* marks Jesus as THE Prophet foretold in Dt 18:15-19. (Cf. Acts 3:22-23)

17:9 Cf. 16:20 and the note there.

17:10 *First Elijah must come.* According to Ml 4:5-6, Elijah was to come before "the great and terrible day of the Lord comes" and prepare the people for His coming by leading them to repentance. The *scribes* argued that Jesus could not be the Messiah, since Elijah had not yet appeared. In response to this, Jesus repeats His assertion of 11:14 that the prophecy concerning Elijah has been fulfilled in John the Baptist. (Cf. Lk 1:17)

17:20 *Little faith . . . faith as a grain of mustard seed.* Faith is little when its object is small – as here, where the disciples could not envision an absent Christ strong enough to overcome a present demon. Even the most limited (*grain*) faith can

22 As they were gathering[y] in Galilee, Jesus said to them, "The Son of man is to be delivered into the hands of men, 23 and they will kill him, and he will be raised on the third day." And they were greatly distressed.

24 When they came to Ca·per′na·um, the collectors of the half-shekel tax went up to Peter and said, "Does not your teacher pay the tax?" 25 He said, "Yes." And when he came home, Jesus spoke to him first, saying, "What do you think, Simon? From whom do kings of the earth take toll or tribute? From their sons or from others?" 26And when he said, "From others," Jesus said to him, "Then the sons are free. 27 However, not to give offense to them, go to the sea and cast a hook, and take the first fish that comes up, and when you open its mouth you will find a shekel; take that and give it to them for me and for yourself."

18 At that time the disciples came to Jesus, saying, "Who is the greatest in the kingdom of heaven?" 2And calling to him a child, he put him in the midst of them, 3 and said, "Truly, I say to you, unless you turn and become like children, you will never enter the kingdom of heaven. 4 Whoever humbles himself like this child, he is the greatest in the kingdom of heaven.

5 "Whoever receives one such child in my name receives me; 6 but whoever causes one of these little ones who believe in me to sin,[z] it would be better for him to have a great millstone fastened round his neck and to be drowned in the depth of the sea.

7 "Woe to the world for temptations to sin![a] For it is necessary that temptations come, but woe to the man by whom the temptation comes! 8And if your hand or your foot causes you to sin,[z] cut it off and throw it away; it is better for you to enter life maimed or lame than with two hands or two feet to be thrown into the eternal fire. 9And if your eye causes you to sin,[z] pluck it out and throw it away; it is better for you to enter life with one eye than with two eyes to be thrown into the hell[b] of fire.

10 "See that you do not despise one of these little ones; for I tell you that in heaven their angels always behold the face of my Father who is in heaven.[c] 12 What do you think? If a man has a hundred sheep, and one of them has gone astray, does he not leave the ninety-nine on the mountains and go in search of the one that went astray? 13And if he finds it, truly, I say to you, he rejoices over it more than over the ninety-

[y] Other ancient authorities read *abode*   [z] Greek *causes . . . to stumble*   [a] Greek *stumbling blocks*   [b] Greek *Gehenna*
[c] Other ancient authorities add verse 11, *For the Son of man came to save the lost*

lay hold of the whole power of God and *move mountains.*

17:24 *The tax.* The term used in the Greek makes it plain that the temple tax is meant. This tax was exacted from every male Jew, whether living in Palestine or abroad, from his 20th year onward. If the disciples are free of this, their freedom from Judaism is complete.

17:27 *Not to give offense.* A Jew who refused to pay the temple tax would appear to his countrymen as an outright atheist and could never hope to gain a hearing for the Gospel; therefore the disciples, though "free from all men," are to pay the tax, becoming "to the Jews . . . as a Jew, in order to win Jews" (1 Co 9:19-20). The Book of Acts shows that the first Christians of Jerusalem were obedient to their Lord in this. (Acts 2:46-47; 3:1)

First fish. Their Father will provide the money they need for the payment of the tax, for also the sea is His.

18:1-35 THE FELLOWSHIP OF THE FORGIVEN

18:1-35 The voice at the Transfiguration bade the disciples listen to Him (17:5) who went the way of ministry to the little, the lost, and the

guilty. His Word shapes the fellowship of the disciples. He breaks the will to greatness in them and bids them *turn* (repent) *and become like children* in order to enter the *kingdom of heaven* (1-4). He identifies Himself with the childlike *(one such child)* and gives His disciples eyes to behold the Christ Himself in the *little ones* who need their help (5). No punishment is too great for those who *cause one of these little ones to sin* (6); no sacrifice is too costly to avoid harming these little ones (7-9). No one in the church dares to *despise one of these little ones,* whose angels are jealous guardians over them and have constant access to the *Father* (10-11). If *one* of them is *lost,* the *Father,* the Seeking Shepherd, *goes in search* of that *one* (12-14); the church can do no less than use her word, her witness, and her prayer to that same end – to *gain* the brother (15-20). The church is made up of men who have received the extravagant forgiveness of their King. They LIVE by the Word that proceeds from His mouth, and that Word is forgiveness. If they will not live by it, they shall die by it; the wrath of the King and Father will deal with them unless they will to give the forgiveness as extravagantly (70×7) as it has been given to them. (21-35)

nine that never went astray. ¹⁴ So it is not the will of my*d* Father who is in heaven that one of these little ones should perish.

15 "If your brother sins against you, go and tell him his fault, between you and him alone. If he listens to you, you have gained your brother. ¹⁶ But if he does not listen, take one or two others along with you, that every word may be confirmed by the evidence of two or three witnesses. ¹⁷ If he refuses to listen to them, tell it to the church; and if he refuses to listen even to the church, let him be to you as a Gentile and a tax collector. ¹⁸ Truly, I say to you, whatever you bind on earth shall be bound in heaven, and whatever you loose on earth shall be loosed in heaven. ¹⁹Again I say to you, if two of you agree on earth about anything they ask, it will be done for them by my Father in heaven. ²⁰ For where two or three are gathered in my name, there am I in the midst of them."

21 Then Peter came up and said to him, "Lord, how often shall my brother sin against me, and I forgive him? As many as seven times?" ²² Jesus said to him, "I do not say to you seven times, but seventy times seven.*e*

23 "Therefore the kingdom of heaven may be compared to a king who wished to settle accounts with his servants. ²⁴ When he began the reckoning, one was brought to him who owed him ten thousand talents;*f* ²⁵ and as he could not pay, his lord ordered him to be sold, with his wife and children and all that he had, and payment to be made. ²⁶ So the servant fell on his knees, imploring him, 'Lord, have patience with me, and I will pay you everything.' ²⁷And out of pity for him the lord of that servant released him and forgave him the debt. ²⁸ But that same servant, as he went out, came upon one of his fellow servants who owed him a hundred denarii;*g* and seizing him by the throat he said, 'Pay what you owe.' ²⁹ So his fellow servant fell down and besought him, 'Have patience with me, and I will pay you.' ³⁰ He refused and went and put him in prison till he should pay the debt. ³¹ When his fellow servants saw what had taken place, they were greatly distressed, and they went and reported to their lord all that had taken place. ³² Then his lord summoned him and said to him, 'You wicked servant! I forgave you all that debt because you besought me; ³³ and should not you have had mercy on your fellow servant, as I had mercy on you?' ³⁴And in anger his lord delivered him to the jailers,*h* till he should pay all his debt. ³⁵ So also my heavenly Father will do to every one of you, if you do not forgive your brother from your heart."

---

d Other ancient authorities read *your*   *e* Or *seventy-seven times*
f This talent was more than fifteen years' wages of a laborer
g The denarius was a day's wage for a laborer   *h* Greek *torturers*

18:15 *Tell him his fault.* The Greek word used here is employed by the NT authors to convey the idea of confronting a man with his sin IN ORDER TO TURN HIM TO REPENTANCE. The *telling* attempts to *gain* the *brother.* (Cf. 1 Co 14:24-25, "convicted"; Rv 3:19, "reprove")

18:20 *Gathered in my name,* that is, Christ is the reason for their coming together.

18:23 *Servants.* In an Oriental court even the highest officials entrusted with large sums would be accounted *servants,* or slaves, of the king.

18:24 *Ten thousand talents.* A fantastically large sum; the annual income of Herod the Great is estimated at 900 talents. The talent was the equivalent of $1,000, but had a much higher purchasing power.

18:25 *Ordered . . . sold.* For enslavement for debt cf. Lv 25:39-46; 2 K 4:1.

18:28 *Denarii.* The denarius had a monetary value of about 20 cents.

19:1 – 25:46 The Christ is the future of mankind; He is the breaking-in of the new creation (4:17), the only Life in a dying world (8:22; 16:25); and before Him all men must come to receive from His judgment the final blessing or the final curse of God (16:27; 25:34, 41). (a) His Word therefore determines the hoping disciple's relationship to the orders of this passing world (marriage, children, property, 19:1–20:16). (b) His way to the cross and into life (the way of ministry, mercy, and meekness) determines the way of those who are His and would follow Him into life eternal (20:17–21:11). (c) His call to repentance, addressed to Jerusalem in its most appealing and poignant form, remains as the salutary warning to all who would escape the doom of Jerusalem and the temple (21:12–23:39). (d) His interpretation of all history as a history moving toward His return and serving as the sign that points the hope of men to His return will preserve His disciples in a hope which keeps them steady, faithful, and unafraid while they perform their mission in the world. (24:1–25:46)

Fifth Group of Messianic Deeds and Words

19:1 — 25:46

HOPE WITHIN THE ORDERS OF THIS WORLD (19:1 — 20:16)

19 Now when Jesus had finished these sayings, he went away from Galilee and entered the region of Judea beyond the Jordan; 2 and large crowds followed him, and he healed them there.

3 And Pharisees came up to him and tested him by asking, "Is it lawful to divorce one's wife for any cause?" 4 He answered, "Have you not read that he who made them from the beginning made them male and female, 5 and said, 'For this reason a man shall leave his father and mother and be joined to his wife, and the two shall become one flesh'? 6 So they are no longer two but one flesh. What therefore God has joined together, let not man put asunder." 7 They said to him, "Why then did Moses command one to give a certificate of divorce, and to put her away?" 8 He said to them, "For your hardness of heart Moses allowed you to divorce your wives, but from the beginning it was not so. 9 And I say to you: whoever divorces his wife, except for unchastity,^{j} and marries another, commits adultery." ^{k}

10 The disciples said to him, "If such is the case of a man with his wife, it is not expedient to marry." 11 But he said to them, "Not all men can receive this saying, but only those to whom it is given. 12 For there are eunuchs who have been so from birth, and there are eunuchs who have been made eunuchs by men, and there are eunuchs who have made themselves eunuchs for the sake of the kingdom of heaven. He who is able to receive this, let him receive it."

13 Then children were brought to him that he might lay his hands on them and pray. The disciples rebuked the people; 14 but Jesus said, "Let the children come to me, and do not hinder them; for to such belongs the kingdom of heaven." 15 And he laid his hands on them and went away.

16 And behold, one came up to him, saying, "Teacher, what good deed must I do, to have eternal life?" 17 And he said to him, "Why do you ask me about what is good? One there is who is good. If you would enter life, keep the commandments." 18 He said to him, "Which?" And Jesus said, "You shall not kill, You shall not commit

^{j} Other ancient authorities, after *unchastity*, read *makes her commit adultery*
^{k} Other ancient authorities insert *and he who marries a divorced woman commits adultery*

(19:1 — 25:46, see previous page)
19:1 — 20:16 HOPE WITHIN THE ORDERS OF THIS WORLD: MARRIAGE, CHILDREN, PROPERTY

1) 19:1-12 Marriage
Marriage is the Creator's primal ordinance for His world (*beginning,* 4, 8). Man may not violate its sanctity by *divorce;* even what *Moses allowed* because of men's *hardness of heart* has become a thing of the past, now that Jesus is ushering in the new age in which God's primal will holds. Neither may man arbitrarily renounce marriage because he deems it *expedient* to avoid the high claim that marriage imposes on him; celibacy is a gift at God's disposal (cf. 1 Co 7:7, 17), granted to some *for the sake of* His eternal *kingdom.*

19:3 *Divorce . . . for any cause?* There were differences among the rabbis on the interpretation of Dt 24:1-4, which permitted divorce (cf. 7); a considerable number held that the husband could divorce his wife *for any cause* however slight.

19:5 Cf. Gn 1:27; 2:24.

19:12 *Eunuchs.* Jesus in this statement uses the word eunuch in three senses, all of them referring to men capable of forgoing marriage: (a) men born

with feeble sexuality; (b) the normal sense, castrated males; (c) men of resolute will who can renounce marriage *for the sake of the kingdom,* i. e., to be able to devote all their time and energies to the service of God their King.

2) 19:13-15 Children
What Jesus had said about the child in illustration of the nature of fellowship of the church (18:3 ff.) is repeated here in the context of the hoping church. He who is Lord of the future has a heart and blessing for the child.

3) 19:16 — 20:16 Property
a. The peril of possessions
Where man is husband and father, the question of property is serious and unavoidable. Possessions can impede a man in his hope and keep him from the way to *eternal life* (16). Since only God is good, a man must do the impossible: turn from all other goods and *follow* Him who is the present God. Only the grace of the good God, with whom *all things are possible,* can *save* men from the clutch of possessions.

19:17 *Why . . . ask me about what is good?* Jesus will not permit any one to seek the good anywhere but in God and in His Word. (Cf. Mi 6:8)

adultery, You shall not steal, You shall not bear false witness, [19] Honor your father and mother, and, You shall love your neighbor as yourself." [20] The young man said to him, "All these I have observed; what do I still lack?" [21] Jesus said to him, "If you would be perfect, go, sell what you possess and give to the poor, and you will have treasure in heaven; and come, follow me." [22] When the young man heard this he went away sorrowful; for he had great possessions.

23 And Jesus said to his disciples, "Truly, I say to you, it will be hard for a rich man to enter the kingdom of heaven. [24]Again I tell you, it is easier for a camel to go through the eye of a needle than for a rich man to enter the kingdom of God." [25] When the disciples heard this they were greatly astonished, saying, "Who then can be saved?" [26] But Jesus looked at them and said to them, "With men this is impossible, but with God all things are possible." [27] Then Peter said in reply, "Lo, we have left everything and followed you. What then shall we have?" [28] Jesus said to them, "Truly, I say to you, in the new world, when the Son of man shall sit on his glorious throne, you who have followed me will also sit on twelve thrones, judging the twelve tribes of Israel. [29]And every one who has left houses or brothers or sisters or father or mother or children or lands, for my name's sake, will receive a hundredfold,[l] and inherit eternal life. [30] But many that are first will be last, and the last first.

20 "For the kingdom of heaven is like a householder who went out early in the morning to hire laborers for his vineyard. [2]After agreeing with the laborers for a denarius[m] a day, he sent them into his vineyard. [3]And going out about the third hour he saw others standing idle in the market place; [4] and to them he said, 'You go into the vineyard too, and whatever is right I will give you.' So they went. [5] Going out again about the sixth hour and the ninth hour, he did the same. [6]And about the eleventh hour he went out and found others standing; and he said to them, 'Why do you stand here idle all day?' [7] They said to him, 'Because no one has hired us.' He said to them, 'You go into the vineyard too.' [8]And when evening came, the owner of the vineyard said to his steward, 'Call the laborers and pay them their wages, beginning with the last, up to the first.' [9]And when those hired about the eleventh hour came, each of them received a denarius. [10] Now when the first came, they thought they would receive more; but each of them also received a denarius. [11]And on receiving it they grumbled at the householder, [12] saying, 'These last worked only one hour, and you have made them equal to us who have borne the burden of the day and the scorching heat.' [13] But he replied to one of them, 'Friend, I am doing you no wrong; did you not agree with me for a denarius? [14] Take what belongs to you, and go; I choose to give to this last as I give to you. [15]Am I not allowed to do what I choose with what belongs to me? Or do you begrudge my generosity?'[n] [16] So the last will be first, and the first last."

THE WAY OF THE CHRIST (20:17 — 21:11)

17 And as Jesus was going up to Jerusalem, he took the twelve disciples aside,

---

[l] Other ancient authorities read *manifold*　　[m] The denarius was a day's wage for a laborer
[n] Or *is your eye evil because I am good?*

19:21 *Perfect,* as the Father in heaven is perfect in a whole and perfect love. (Cf. 5:48)

19:25 *Astonished* is a weak translation; the Greek word connotes a mixture of amazement and fear. The disciples feel struck by this word; if property has such a hold on man, no man can consider himself "safe."

b. The peril of renunciation

There is peril also for those who do renounce property for the sake of the hope of eternal life. Jesus' promise to them is one of lavish generosity; they shall reign with Him *(throne) in the new world* and shall find recompense for all they have abandoned in the generous fellowship of the church (29). But these *first* recipients of His grace can lose their favored place if they question His

generosity toward others who receive that same generous grace. It is as dangerous to try to keep God's grace to oneself as it is to keep possessions to oneself.

19:28 *Judging* here probably has the broader sense of "ruling." Cf. Ju 2:16, 18, where the "judges" are leaders rather than judges.

19:30 *First will be last.* The parable of 20:1-16 is designed to explain this enigmatic statement. To work in the vineyard is privilege and the pay is pure grace; to question that grace for others is to lose it for oneself.

20:17 — 21:11 THE WAY OF THE CHRIST: MINISTRY, MERCY, MEEKNESS

20:17 — 21:11 Jesus' third prediction of His

and on the way he said to them, [18] "Behold, we are going up to Jerusalem; and the Son of man will be delivered to the chief priests and scribes, and they will condemn him to death, [19] and deliver him to the Gentiles to be mocked and scourged and crucified, and he will be raised on the third day."

20 Then the mother of the sons of Zeb′e·dee came up to him, with her sons, and kneeling before him she asked him for something. [21]And he said to her, "What do you want?" She said to him, "Command that these two sons of mine may sit, one at your right hand and one at your left, in your kingdom." [22] But Jesus answered, "You do not know what you are asking. Are you able to drink the cup that I am to drink?" They said to him, "We are able." [23] He said to them, "You will drink my cup, but to sit at my right hand and at my left is not mine to grant, but it is for those for whom it has been prepared by my Father." [24]And when the ten heard it, they were indignant at the two brothers. [25] But Jesus called them to him and said, "You know that the rulers of the Gentiles lord it over them, and their great men exercise authority over them. [26] It shall not be so among you; but whoever would be great among you must be your servant, [27] and whoever would be first among you must be your slave; [28] even as the Son of man came not to be served but to serve, and to give his life as a ransom for many."

29 And as they went out of Jericho, a great crowd followed him. [30]And behold, two blind men sitting by the roadside, when they heard that Jesus was passing by, cried out,[o] "Have mercy on us, Son of David!" [31] The crowd rebuked them, telling them to be silent; but they cried out the more, "Lord, have mercy on us, Son of David!" [32]And Jesus stopped and called them, saying, "What do you want me to do for you?" [33] They said to him, "Lord, let our eyes be opened." [34]And Jesus in pity touched their eyes, and immediately they received their sight and followed him.

21 And when they drew near to Jerusalem and came to Beth′pha·ge, to the Mount of Olives, then Jesus sent two disciples, [2] saying to them, "Go into the village opposite you, and immediately you will find an ass tied, and a colt with her; untie them and bring them to me. [3] If any one says anything to you, you shall say, 'The Lord has need of them,' and he will send them immediately." [4] This took place to fulfil what was spoken by the prophet, saying,
[5]   "Tell the daughter of Zion,
        Behold, your king is coming to you,
        humble, and mounted on an ass,
        and on a colt, the foal of an ass."

[o] Other ancient authorities insert *Lord*

Passion and death concludes, as do the previous ones, with the assurance that *he will be raised on the third day* (19); the way of the Christ leads to life.

1) 20:17-28 The Way of the Christ: Ministry

Jesus quells the will to greatness in His disciples by inverting all human standards of greatness; the greatness of man is the greatness demonstrated by the Son of Man, ministry to the full, self-expending love as seen in Jesus' vicarious suffering and death.

20:17-19 The third and most detailed of the predictions of the Passion and resurrection (cf. 16:21; 17:22-23). New are: the delivering of the Son of Man to the Gentiles, the mockery and scourging, and death by crucifixion.

20:22 *Drink the cup.* The cup is a frequent OT symbol for suffering, especially suffering under the judgment of God. (Ps 11:6; 75:8; Is 51:17, 22)

20:28 *Ransom for many,* the price paid for the release of all men — *many* is here used in the inclusive Semitic sense of "all." (Cf. 1 Ti 2:5-6; 1 Ptr 1:18)

2) 20:29-34 The Way of the Christ: Mercy

The way of the *Son of David,* the Messiah, is the way of *mercy,* which opens the blind eyes of men and enables them to *follow Him* into eternal life.

3) 21:1-11 The Way of the Christ: Meekness

Jesus comes to Jerusalem to die as the meek King foretold by Zechariah (see note on 21:5). The way of meekness has the promise of eternal victory.

21:1 *Bethphage,* a village not far from the descent of the Mount of Olives. When Jesus reached this point, His approach could be seen from Jerusalem.

21:5 *Your king is coming to you,* Zch 9:9, with the introductory phrase *(Tell the daughter of Zion)* supplied from Is 62:11. Jesus fulfills the promise which the Lord gave through Zechariah: The people of God will be saved by a God-given King who comes without the trappings of power, depending on God for victory, with no weapon but the word which speaks "peace to the nations" (Zch 9:10). His coming signifies peace for all na-

6 The disciples went and did as Jesus had directed them; 7 they brought the ass and the colt, and put their garments on them, and he sat thereon. 8 Most of the crowd spread their garments on the road, and others cut branches from the trees and spread them on the road. 9And the crowds that went before him and that followed him shouted, "Hosanna to the Son of David! Blessed is he who comes in the name of the Lord! Hosanna in the highest!" 10And when he entered Jerusalem, all the city was stirred, saying, "Who is this?" 11And the crowds said, "This is the prophet Jesus from Nazareth of Galilee."

JESUS CALLS JERUSALEM TO REPENTANCE (21:12 — 23:39)

12 And Jesus entered the temple of God[p] and drove out all who sold and bought in the temple, and he overturned the tables of the money-changers and the seats of those who sold pigeons. 13 He said to them, "It is written, 'My house shall be called a house of prayer'; but you make it a den of robbers."

14 And the blind and the lame came to him in the temple, and he healed them. 15 But when the chief priests and the scribes saw the wonderful things that he did, and the children crying out in the temple, "Hosanna to the Son of David!" they were indignant; 16 and they said to him, "Do you hear what these are saying?" And Jesus said to them, "Yes; have you never read,

    'Out of the mouth of babes and sucklings
    thou hast brought perfect praise'?"

17And leaving them, he went out of the city to Beth′a·ny and lodged there.

18 In the morning, as he was returning to the city, he was hungry. 19And seeing a fig tree by the wayside he went to it, and found nothing on it but leaves only. And he said to it, "May no fruit ever come from you again!" And the fig tree withered at once. 20 When the disciples saw it they marveled, saying, "How did the fig tree wither at once?" 21And Jesus answered them, "Truly, I say to you, if you have faith and never doubt, you will not only do what has been done to the fig tree, but even if you say to this mountain, 'Be taken up and cast into the sea,' it will be done. 22And whatever you ask in prayer, you will receive, if you have faith."

[p] Other ancient authorities omit *of God*

---

tions, not only for Israel. The fact that He comes mounted on an ass points up His humility; He rides not the horses and chariots of the warrior but the ordinary man's peaceful beast of burden.

Humble, literally "meek," which emphasizes that total dependence on God which gives a man the strength to endure in the confidence that God will vindicate him. See Ps 37 for a portrait of the meek man.

21:9 *Hosanna,* literally "save now." From its use in the liturgy of the Feast of Tabernacles, the words of Ps 118:25-26 seem to have become a word of acclamation and associated with the Messianic hope. But it is possible that *Hosanna* retains its original sense of "save" and that the words are a prayer to God to vindicate (save, give victory to) His Messiah from heaven above *(in the highest).*

In the name of the Lord. His coming is under the authority of the Lord, to accomplish His will. He is the Lord's Anointed.

21:12 — 23:39 Three temple incidents (21:12-22), three parables (21:23 — 22:14), three disputes (22:15-40), Jesus' Messianic manifesto (22:41-46), and Jesus' sad and vehement indictment of the hollow piety of scribe and Pharisee (23:1-39) spell out for the last time the message of Jesus to His people: "Repent, for the kingdom of heaven is at hand." (4:17)

21:12-22 THREE TEMPLE INCIDENTS: REPENT

21:12-22 Jesus' cleansing of the temple is an indictment of His people's externalized and commercialized worship which has made of the *house of prayer* a *den of robbers* (12-13). The temple authorities are *indignant* at the *wonderful things* Jesus did for the *blind and the lame* in the temple precincts and would have Jesus silence the praises of the *children;* Jesus' words point them to the God of the OT who brings forth *perfect praise out of the mouth of babes* (14-17). The blasting of the *fig tree* symbolizes Jesus' judgment on a piety that supports a costly temple and a great ritual but produces no fruit for the Messiah of mercy, ministry, and meekness (18-19). To this hollow piety the *faith* which can move mountains and has Jesus' promise stands in sharp contrast. (20-22)

21:13 *House of prayer.* Cf. Is 56:7. In its context the word of Isaiah, like that of Zechariah, has in it a promise for all nations. (Is 56:6-8)

Den of robbers. Jer 7:11. As robbers use their den to escape arrest and plan new misdeeds, so the men of Israel use the temple and its cultus to escape the consequences of their sins and to plan new sins.

21:16 *Out of the mouth of babes.* Cf. Ps 8:2. The opening verses of the psalm express the psalmist's

23 And when he entered the temple, the chief priests and the elders of the people came up to him as he was teaching, and said, "By what authority are you doing these things, and who gave you this authority?" 24 Jesus answered them, "I also will ask you a question; and if you tell me the answer, then I also will tell you by what authority I do these things. 25 The baptism of John, whence was it? From heaven or from men?" And they argued with one another, "If we say, 'From heaven,' he will say to us, 'Why then did you not believe him?' 26 But if we say, 'From men,' we are afraid of the multitude; for all hold that John was a prophet." 27 So they answered Jesus, "We do not know." And he said to them, "Neither will I tell you by what authority I do these things.

28 "What do you think? A man had two sons; and he went to the first and said, 'Son, go and work in the vineyard today.' 29And he answered, 'I will not'; but afterward he repented and went. 30And he went to the second and said the same; and he answered, 'I go, sir,' but did not go. 31 Which of the two did the will of his father?" They said, "The first." Jesus said to them, "Truly, I say to you, the tax collectors and the harlots go into the kingdom of God before you. 32 For John came to you in the way of righteousness, and you did not believe him, but the tax collectors and the harlots believed him; and even when you saw it, you did not afterward repent and believe him.

33 "Hear another parable. There was a householder who planted a vineyard, and set a hedge around it, and dug a wine press in it, and built a tower, and let it out to tenants, and went into another country. 34 When the season of fruit drew near, he sent his servants to the tenants, to get his fruit; 35 and the tenants took his servants and beat one, killed another, and stoned another. 36Again he sent other servants, more than the first; and they did the same to them. 37Afterward he sent his son to them, saying, 'They will respect my son.' 38 But when the tenants saw the son, they said to themselves, 'This is the heir; come, let us kill him and have his inheritance.' 39And they took him and cast him out of the vineyard, and killed him. 40 When therefore the owner of the vineyard comes, what will he do to those tenants?" 41 They said to him, "He will put those wretches to a miserable death, and let out the vineyard to other tenants who will give him the fruits in their seasons."

42 Jesus said to them, "Have you never read in the scriptures:
'The very stone which the builders rejected
has become the head of the corner;
this was the Lord's doing,
and it is marvelous in our eyes'?

adoration of the mighty Creator who can assert His will, execute His purposes, and silence His enemies with the slightest of means, the words of children (cf. 1 Co 1:27-29). Jesus sees His Father's almighty hand at work in the cries of these children; God, Jesus is certain, is leading the Son of David to victory.

21:23 — 22:14 THREE PARABLES OF REPENTANCE: TWO SONS, VINEYARD, MARRIAGE FEAST

21:23 — 22:14 In the parables Jesus spreads out before the men of Israel all the riches God has given them and still offers them. They are by God's grace God's *sons,* God's trusted tenant workmen, and God's *invited* guests. He therefore bids them give God a son's obedience and the fruits of the vineyard which the *tenants* owe the Owner, to come to the *marriage feast* of their King without delay, without excuses, and dressed in the festal *garment* of obedience to His Word. God's kindness is wooing them; but if they will not learn the seriousness of the hour from His kindness, they will learn it from His wrath (21:41, 43; 22:5, 6, 13), that wrath which cuts off all hope forever.

21:25 *From heaven,* i. e., from God. *Heaven* was a Judaic designation for God; cf. kingdom of heaven = kingdom of God.

21:27 *Neither will I tell you.* If they will not acknowledge John as the voice sent by God to call them to repentance and to offer them forgiveness, Jesus cannot tell them of His *authority;* that authority is revealed in ministry and mercy to men who know and feel their need of mercy.

21:32 *In the way of righteousness,* i. e., the way that offered salvation. For *righteousness* in this sense cf. 5:6; 6:33.

21:33 *Planted a vineyard.* For the vineyard as a picture of God's people, the object of His love and care, cf. Is 5:1-7.

21:36-37 *Servants . . . son.* The prophets (cf. Am 3:7) have made their plea; now the Son is making His. It is the final hour.

21:42 *Stone which the builders rejected.* Ps 118: 22-23. The psalm gives thanks to the Lord who has given victory to one (probably the king) who

⁴³ Therefore I tell you, the kingdom of God will be taken away from you and given to a nation producing the fruits of it."ᵠ

45 When the chief priests and the Pharisees heard his parables, they perceived that he was speaking about them. ⁴⁶ But when they tried to arrest him, they feared the multitudes, because they held him to be a prophet.

22 And again Jesus spoke to them in parables, saying, ² "The kingdom of heaven may be compared to a king who gave a marriage feast for his son, ³ and sent his servants to call those who were invited to the marriage feast; but they would not come. ⁴Again he sent other servants, saying, 'Tell those who are invited, Behold, I have made ready my dinner, my oxen and my fat calves are killed, and everything is ready; come to the marriage feast.' ⁵ But they made light of it and went off, one to his farm, another to his business, ⁶ while the rest seized his servants, treated them shamefully, and killed them. ⁷ The king was angry, and he sent his troops and destroyed those murderers and burned their city. ⁸ Then he said to his servants, 'The wedding is ready, but those invited were not worthy. ⁹ Go therefore to the thoroughfares, and invite to the marriage feast as many as you find.' ¹⁰And those servants went out into the streets and gathered all whom they found, both bad and good; so the wedding hall was filled with guests.

11 "But when the king came in to look at the guests, he saw there a man who had no wedding garment; ¹² and he said to him, 'Friend, how did you get in here without a wedding garment?' And he was speechless. ¹³ Then the king said to the attendants, 'Bind him hand and foot, and cast him into the outer darkness; there men will weep and gnash their teeth.' ¹⁴ For many are called, but few are chosen."

15 Then the Pharisees went and took counsel how to entangle him in his talk. ¹⁶And they sent their disciples to him, along with the He·ro′di·ans, saying, "Teacher, we know that you are true, and teach the way of God truthfully, and care for no man;

ᵠ Other ancient authorities add verse 44, "*And he who falls on this stone will be broken to pieces; but when it falls on any one, it will crush him*"

---

fought against overwhelming odds and triumphed solely by the help of the Lord. Perhaps Jesus recalled also the words which preceded the ones He quoted:

"I shall not die, but I shall live,
and recount the deeds of the Lord." (17)

21:46 *Tried to arrest him.* Cf. 22:15. Jesus' pleading call to repentance falls on deaf ears; the impenitent are cutting off their future and their hope.

22:11 *Wedding garment.* The guest is invited by the free grace of the King; he need not earn his invitation, which goes out to *bad and good.* But to come without the *wedding garment* is to despise the grace of the King and desecrate it; this invites judgment. The man without the festal garment is like salt that does not salt and is therefore cast out (5:13). Where grace is received and yet not allowed to shape man's conduct, it is received in vain. (2 Co 6:1)

22:14 *Many . . . called . . . few . . . chosen.* God's call, His invitation, goes out to all Israel (3), to all men, bad and good (10); but God's love working through His Word achieves its goal only in the *few,* whose response to God's call marks them as God's *chosen,* His elect.

22:15-40 THE CALL TO REPENTANCE
IN THE THREE DISPUTES

22:15-40 Jesus utilizes even the attempts *to entangle him in his talk* (15) to press home His call to repentance. He bids the Pharisees (who

put Him to the test with the question concerning *taxes paid to Caesar*) do what the parable of the vineyard enjoined on them: give *God the things that are God's* (15-22), as He was doing when He went to the cross.

When the *Sadducees* attempt to cast doubt on the *resurrection* with their calculated question, He seeks to turn them to the *scriptures* which He obeyed to the death (cf. 26:54) and to give them eyes for the *power of God* which He trusted to raise Him on the third day. (23-33)

He directed the *lawyer* who tested Him with his question concerning *the great commandment in the law* to the overriding and unifying will of God in the Law: *love* for God and man in unbroken unity; obedience to that will took Jesus to the cross in obedience to His Father and as a ransom for all men. (34-40)

22:16 The presence of the *Herodians* is explained by the nature of the question put to Jesus. The question is designed to test His Messianic claim and to confront Him with a dilemma. If He permits payment of *taxes to Caesar,* He will discredit Himself as Messiah—for would not the Messiah put an end to the hated Roman domination? If, however, He forbids payment of the taxes, He will put forward a Messianic claim that makes Him politically suspect. The Herodians, partisans of the Herods who depended on Roman rule, would be quick to inform the Roman authorities. In either case Jesus would be disposed of by men who considered Him dangerous.

for you do not regard the position of men. 17 Tell us, then, what you think. Is it lawful to pay taxes to Caesar, or not?" 18 But Jesus, aware of their malice, said, "Why put me to the test, you hypocrites? 19 Show me the money for the tax." And they brought him a coin.*r* 20And Jesus said to them, "Whose likeness and inscription is this?" 21 They said, "Caesar's." Then he said to them, "Render therefore to Caesar the things that are Caesar's, and to God the things that are God's." 22 When they heard it, they marveled; and they left him and went away.

23 The same day Sad'du·cees came to him, who say that there is no resurrection; and they asked him a question, 24 saying, "Teacher, Moses said, 'If a man dies, having no children, his brother must marry the widow, and raise up children for his brother.' 25 Now there were seven brothers among us; the first married, and died, and having no children left his wife to his brother. 26 So too the second and third, down to the seventh. 27After them all, the woman died. 28 In the resurrection, therefore, to which of the seven will she be wife? For they all had her."

29 But Jesus answered them, "You are wrong, because you know neither the scriptures nor the power of God. 30 For in the resurrection they neither marry nor are given in marriage, but are like angels*s* in heaven. 31And as for the resurrection of the dead, have you not read what was said to you by God, 32 'I am the God of Abraham, and the God of Isaac, and the God of Jacob'? He is not God of the dead, but of the living." 33And when the crowd heard it, they were astonished at his teaching.

34 But when the Pharisees heard that he had silenced the Sad'du·cees, they came together. 35And one of them, a lawyer, asked him a question, to test him. 36 "Teacher, which is the great commandment in the law?" 37And he said to him, "You shall love the Lord your God with all your heart, and with all your soul, and with all your mind. 38 This is the great and first commandment. 39And a second is like it, You shall love your neighbor as yourself. 40 On these two commandments depend all the law and the prophets."

41 Now while the Pharisees were gathered together, Jesus asked them a question, 42 saying, "What do you think of the Christ? Whose son is he?" They said to him, "The son of David." 43 He said to them, "How is it then that David, inspired by the Spirit,*t* calls him Lord, saying,

44   'The Lord said to my Lord,
           Sit at my right hand,
           till I put thy enemies under thy feet'?

45 If David thus calls him Lord, how is he his son?" 46And no one was able to answer him a word, nor from that day did any one dare to ask him any more questions.

r Greek *a denarius*   *s* Other ancient authorities add *of God*   *t* Or *David in the Spirit*

22:17 *Lawful.* The question is religious: Could the people of God help maintain an alien pagan power without proving disloyal to their God? Some in Israel answered that question with a violent no and fomented rebellion against Rome (the Zealots).

22:21 Jesus' answer implies that there need be no clash of loyalties; they can pay the coin minted in Rome to the Roman emperor and still give *God the things that are God's:* a son's obedience, a workman's service, an invited guest's response. (21:28 – 22:14)

22:23-28 The Sadducees' question implies that the *resurrection,* by assigning one woman to seven husbands, contradicts the Law and cannot therefore be a true belief.

22:24 *Moses said.* Dt 25:5.

22:30 *Marriage.* The Sadducees attributed to Jesus the Pharisees' conception of the life of the world to come as merely a more splendid continuation of this present life. Jesus rejects this conception.

22:32 *I am the God of Abraham,* etc. Ex 3:6.

22:40 *Depend,* literally "hang"; take away the basic command of love and the whole OT *(the law and the prophets)* collapses.

22:41-46 JESUS' MESSIANIC MANIFESTO

22:41-46 Jesus calls *the Pharisees* to repentance by showing them how their conception of the *Christ* falls altogether short of the OT promise of the Christ. They hope for a *son of David,* great and powerful, who will deliver them from Roman rule and make them great. Jesus uses Ps 110 to give them a really religious conception of the Christ. Jesus looks not to Jerusalem, Mount Zion, and the throne of David but to heaven and the throne of God; the greatness of the Christ is not that He is *son of David* (that is His humiliation) but that He is David's *Lord,* before whom all *enemies* will be brought low. It was for this Messianic claim that Jesus was called blasphemer and condemned to die. (26:63-66)

23 Then said Jesus to the crowds and to his disciples, 2 "The scribes and the Pharisees sit on Moses' seat; 3 so practice and observe whatever they tell you, but not what they do; for they preach, but do not practice. 4 They bind heavy burdens, hard to bear,ᵘ and lay them on men's shoulders; but they themselves will not move them with their finger. 5 They do all their deeds to be seen by men; for they make their phylacteries broad and their fringes long, 6 and they love the place of honor at feasts and the best seats in the synagogues, 7 and salutations in the market places, and being called rabbi by men. 8 But you are not to be called rabbi, for you have one teacher, and you are all brethren. 9 And call no man your father on earth, for you have one Father, who is in heaven. 10 Neither be called masters, for you have one master, the Christ. 11 He who is greatest among you shall be your servant; 12 whoever exalts himself will be humbled, and whoever humbles himself will be exalted.

13 "But woe to you, scribes and Pharisees, hypocrites! because you shut the kingdom of heaven against men; for you neither enter yourselves, nor allow those who

ᵘ Other ancient authorities omit *hard to bear*

23:1-39 WOE TO YOU, SCRIBES AND PHARISEES

23:1-39 Jerusalem and the temple are like a fig tree rich in leaves and devoid of fruit (21:18-19), hopelessly doomed. The false and empty piety that doomed them was the piety of the *scribes and the Pharisees;* they shaped and influenced the religion of Judaism more than any one else. Jesus' last call to repentance is therefore a last indictment of their piety. Their will is at every point a contradiction of the will of Christ. Christ comes to fulfill the Law and the prophets, and His whole life is determined by the Word of God (cf., e. g., 26: 54, 56); they *sit on Moses' seat* as the guardians and interpreters of the Word of God and *preach, but do not practice* (3). Christ comes in merciful ministry and gives the heavy-burdened rest (11: 28-29); they *lay heavy burdens on men's shoulders* but *themselves* will not lift a *finger* to *move them* (4). Christ comes in meekness and goes the way of the Servant (11:29; 12:18-21); they *do all their deeds to be seen by men,* cultivate their own greatness, and forfeit the reward of God by seeking their reward of men (5-7; cf. 6:2-3) – they are the very opposite of what Jesus is and what His followers are to be (8-12). Christ opens the Kingdom to the poor and the child (5:3; 18:3; 19:14); they *shut the kingdom of heaven against men* (13). Christ the Son makes His followers children of the Father, free sons (5:45; 17:26); they make their convert *(proselyte) a child of hell* (15). Christ is the Light (4:16) and the Shepherd who guides and tends the harassed and helpless flock (9:36); they are *blind guides* who lead their followers into destruction (cf. 15:14) with their frivolous teaching concerning the oath (16-22), whereas Christ made His disciples' simple yes and no an oath, words spoken in the presence of God, the remembering Witness (5:37). For Christ the *weightier matters of the law* (23) loomed large – He held firm in His God even unto death *(faith,* 23) and served Him who desires *mercy* (9:13), in order that He might bring God's *justice* to victory; they are punctilious in *tithing,* as they ought to be, but withdraw from the pressure of the Law when it lays claim to their hearts,

their love (23). The Christ is a clear cup filled with the goodness of God, the Giver who gives freely to all, unposed in His transparent goodness; they have hearts that belie their fair appearance, hearts filled with *rapacity* and *iniquity* (25-28). For Christ the word of the prophets was a word to live and die by (5:17; 26:56); they disclaimed connection with the *fathers who shed the blood of the prophets,* but they no more obey the prophetic word than their fathers did (29-31). Thus they unite themselves in guilt with their fathers (32-33), will continue in the ways of their fathers (34), and will suffer the judgment that concludes the guilty history of their people. (35-36)

Harsh as these words of Jesus are, they are still a part of His call to repentance. His is the voice of the *hen* that *gathers her brood under her wings,* concerned and compassionate (37). The temple will be abandoned by God; the house of God which they have made *their house* and a den of robbers (21:13) will be *forsaken and desolate.* But when the Christ returns, there will be men of Israel among those who hail His coming. (39)

23:2 *Sit on Moses' seat.* They are the recognized expositors of the Law.

23:3 *Whatever they tell you.* After what Jesus has said of the tradition of the elders in 15:3-6, this can hardly include all the additions to and corruptions of the Law which were embodied in that tradition; but the word of Moses remains sacred.

23:5 *Phylacteries,* amulets, bands worn on the arm or forehead; they contained verses of Scripture. The purpose in wearing them was to remind man of the law of the Lord (Ex 13:9; Dt 6:8); by making them *broad* the scribes and Pharisees used them to advertise their piety.

Fringes, or tassels, enjoined by the Law as a reminder of "the commandments of the Lord" (Nm 15:38-41), were made long to call attention to the wearer's piety. Jesus Himself wore the fringe on His garment, in the sense intended by the Law. (9:20)

23:7 *Rabbi,* title of respect, means literally "My great one."

would enter to go in.[v] [15] Woe to you, scribes and Pharisees, hypocrites! for you traverse sea and land to make a single proselyte, and when he becomes a proselyte, you make him twice as much a child of hell[w] as yourselves.

16 "Woe to you, blind guides, who say, 'If any one swears by the temple, it is nothing; but if any one swears by the gold of the temple, he is bound by his oath.' [17] You blind fools! For which is greater, the gold or the temple that has made the gold sacred? [18]And you say, 'If any one swears by the altar, it is nothing; but if any one swears by the gift that is on the altar, he is bound by his oath.' [19] You blind men! For which is greater, the gift or the altar that makes the gift sacred? [20] So he who swears by the altar, swears by it and by everything on it; [21] and he who swears by the temple, swears by it and by him who dwells in it; [22] and he who swears by heaven, swears by the throne of God and by him who sits upon it.

23 "Woe to you, scribes and Pharisees, hypocrites! for you tithe mint and dill and cummin, and have neglected the weightier matters of the law, justice and mercy and faith; these you ought to have done, without neglecting the others. [24] You blind guides, straining out a gnat and swallowing a camel!

25 "Woe to you, scribes and Pharisees, hypocrites! for you cleanse the outside of the cup and of the plate, but inside they are full of extortion and rapacity. [26] You blind Pharisee! first cleanse the inside of the cup and of the plate, that the outside also may be clean.

27 "Woe to you, scribes and Pharisees, hypocrites! for you are like whitewashed tombs, which outwardly appear beautiful, but within they are full of dead men's bones and all uncleanness. [28] So you also outwardly appear righteous to men, but within you are full of hypocrisy and iniquity.

29 "Woe to you, scribes and Pharisees, hypocrites! for you build the tombs of the prophets and adorn the monuments of the righteous, [30] saying, 'If we had lived in the days of our fathers, we would not have taken part with them in shedding the blood of the prophets.' [31] Thus you witness against yourselves, that you are sons of those who murdered the prophets. [32] Fill up, then, the measure of your fathers. [33] You serpents, you brood of vipers, how are you to escape being sentenced to hell?[w] [34] Therefore I send you prophets and wise men and scribes, some of whom you will kill and crucify, and some you will scourge in your synagogues and persecute from town to town, [35] that upon you may come all the righteous blood shed on earth, from the blood of innocent Abel to the blood of Zech·a·ri′ah the son of Bar·a·chi′ah, whom you murdered between the sanctuary and the altar. [36] Truly, I say to you, all this will come upon this generation.

37 "O Jerusalem, Jerusalem, killing the prophets and stoning those who are sent to you! How often would I have gathered your children together as a hen gathers her brood under her wings, and you would not! [38] Behold, your house is forsaken and desolate.[x] [39] For I tell you, you will not see me again, until you say, 'Blessed is he who comes in the name of the Lord.' "

THE SIGN OF CHRIST'S COMING (24:1 — 25:46)

24 Jesus left the temple and was going away, when his disciples came to point out to him the buildings of the temple. [2] But he answered them, "You see all

[v] Other authorities add here (or after verse 12) verse 14, *Woe to you, scribes and Pharisees, hypocrites! for you devour widows' houses and for a pretense you make long prayers; therefore you will receive the greater condemnation*
[w] Greek *Gehenna*   [x] Other ancient authorities omit *and desolate*

23:23 *Justice, mercy, faith.* For a similar summary of God's claim upon His people see Mi 6:8.

23:33 *Serpents . . . brood of vipers.* Cf. 3:7; 12:34.

23:35 *Abel . . . Zechariah.* The first (Gn 4:8) and the last (2 Ch 24:21) murder of an innocent man recorded in the OT. 2 Chronicles was the last book in the Jewish arrangement of the OT.

Son of Barachiah. The Zechariah *murdered between the sanctuary and the altar* was the son of Jehoiada (2 Ch 24:20-22). The prophet Zechariah was son of Barachiah (Zch 1:1). The con-

fusion here may be the result of a well-intentioned but mistaken note made by some copyist of the text.

23:38 *Your house,* the temple. Cf. Jer 12:7; possibly, however, "your land and people" is meant.

24:1-31 ALL HISTORY THE SIGN OF HIS COMING

24:1-31 Jesus does not answer the question, *When will this be?* (3). He will not permit His disciples to speculate concerning His return; instead He shapes their hope as a vigilant and

these, do you not? Truly, I say to you, there will not be left here one stone upon another, that will not be thrown down."

3 As he sat on the Mount of Olives, the disciples came to him privately, saying, "Tell us, when will this be, and what will be the sign of your coming and of the close of the age?" 4And Jesus answered them, "Take heed that no one leads you astray. 5 For many will come in my name, saying, 'I am the Christ,' and they will lead many astray. 6And you will hear of wars and rumors of wars; see that you are not alarmed; for this must take place, but the end is not yet. 7 For nation will rise against nation, and kingdom against kingdom, and there will be famines and earthquakes in various places: 8 all this is but the beginning of the birth-pangs.

9 "Then they will deliver you up to tribulation, and put you to death; and you will be hated by all nations for my name's sake. 10And then many will fall away,ʸ and betray one another, and hate one another. 11And many false prophets will arise and lead many astray. 12And because wickedness is multiplied, most men's love will grow cold. 13 But he who endures to the end will be saved. 14And this gospel of the kingdom will be preached throughout the whole world, as a testimony to all nations; and then the end will come.

15 "So when you see the desolating sacrilege spoken of by the prophet Daniel,

ʸ Or *stumble*

responsible expectation by teaching them to read in all history the *sign* of His *coming* and *the close of the age*. All history is the sign; they are to see in all history, with its false hopes (5), its wars and disasters, and its apparently meaningless *sufferings* (8), the work of God carrying out His will (*must*, 6) as He moves toward final judgment. (1-8)

The history of the church is the sign. God will be at work in His persecuted, stumbling church manifesting His strength in her weakness. The task of the church will be accomplished; the *gospel* will be universally proclaimed, and then the *end will come*. (9-14)

All history alerts the disciple for the end of history. In that history the fall of Jerusalem has a unique place; in Jerusalem the drama of God's offer of His grace in the Son and man's rejection of that grace, with the resultant judgment, are a miniature of the close of the age. Jesus has separated His own inwardly from the doomed city, and they need not share its fate; they are to flee. (15-20)

Jesus' words on the close of the age are anything but a precise forecast of events; the line between the fall of Jerusalem and the end is left indistinct; the *great tribulation* (21) which the kindly providence of God will shorten *for the sake of the elect* (22), the false and fevered Messianic hopes which mark that time of tribulation (23-26) — these might refer to either event or both. But there will be no room for doubt about the *coming of the Son of man* when He comes; it will be manifest and universal, like *lightning* that emblazons the whole heaven (27), sudden as the appearance of *vultures* where a carcass is (28), accompanied by cosmic convulsions (29) at which *all the tribes of the earth will mourn* (30) and His *elect* will rejoice as at the fruition of their long and strenuous hope. (31)

24:5 *In my name*, claiming the authority of the Christ.

24:6 *This must take place*. Cf. Rv 1:1: The whole Book of Revelation is the inspired commentary to these words of Jesus, tracing even in the most fearful and diabolical disasters the working of God toward His end.

24:8 *Birth-pangs*. The pains of a travailing mother have an end and a purpose. The sufferings are no whim of fate; rather in them God is working out His purposes toward a happy end.

24:12 *Men's love will grow cold*. The bitter disillusionment which comes when men *betray* their brothers in the faith (10), the harsh necessity of exposing *false prophets* and separating the church from them (11) — these things, together with the constant pressure of being *hated by all nations* (9), put a strain on Christian love that threatens to destroy it. (Cf. Rv 2:2-7)

24:15 *The desolating sacrilege*. Cf. Dn 9:27; 11:31; 12:11. The first reference of Daniel's prophecy was probably to the action of Antiochus Epiphanes (168 B.C.), who erected a pagan idol and altar in the temple, thereby desecrating it so that no Israelite could worship the Lord there; this made the holy place desolate (cf. 1 Mac 1:54). Jesus warns His disciples that a similar desecration would foretoken the fall of Jerusalem. Some see the fulfillment of this word in the Roman emperor Caligula's attempt (Λ. D. 38) to set up a statue of himself (as deified) in the Jerusalem temple, an attempt that horrified all Jewry. Luke 21:20 speaks of the presence of (pagan) armies surrounding Jerusalem as foretokening "that its DESOLATION has come near," and this is probably the nearer reference. Roman emperors, with their claim to divine honors, will be God's instrument in turning the splendor of the temple into the forsaken and desolate house of which Jesus had spoken. (23:38)

Let the reader understand. Let him read the word of Daniel and take it to heart as a word that speaks to him in his situation.

standing in the holy place (let the reader understand), [16] then let those who are in Judea flee to the mountains; [17] let him who is on the housetop not go down to take what is in his house; [18] and let him who is in the field not turn back to take his mantle. [19]And alas for those who are with child and for those who give suck in those days! [20] Pray that your flight may not be in winter or on a sabbath. [21] For then there will be great tribulation, such as has not been from the beginning of the world until now, no, and never will be. [22]And if those days had not been shortened, no human being would be saved; but for the sake of the elect those days will be shortened. [23] Then if any one says to you, 'Lo, here is the Christ!' or 'There he is!' do not believe it. [24] For false Christs and false prophets will arise and show great signs and wonders, so as to lead astray, if possible, even the elect. [25] Lo, I have told you beforehand. [26] So, if they say to you, 'Lo, he is in the wilderness,' do not go out; if they say, 'Lo, he is in the inner rooms,' do not believe it. [27] For as the lightning comes from the east and shines as far as the west, so will be the coming of the Son of man. [28] Wherever the body is, there the eagles [z] will be gathered together.

29 "Immediately after the tribulation of those days the sun will be darkened, and the moon will not give its light, and the stars will fall from heaven, and the powers of the heavens will be shaken; [30] then will appear the sign of the Son of man in heaven, and then all the tribes of the earth will mourn, and they will see the Son of man coming on the clouds of heaven with power and great glory; [31] and he will send out his angels with a loud trumpet call, and they will gather his elect from the four winds, from one end of heaven to the other.

32 "From the fig tree learn its lesson: as soon as its branch becomes tender and puts forth its leaves, you know that summer is near. [33] So also, when you see all these things, you know that he is near, at the very gates. [34] Truly, I say to you, this generation will not pass away till all these things take place. [35] Heaven and earth will pass away, but my words will not pass away.

[z] Or vultures

24:19 Flight would be especially difficult and dangerous for women *with child* and for nursing mothers burdened and delayed by the necessity of caring for a baby.

24:20 *In winter . . . on a sabbath.* When inclement weather or religious scruples might tempt them to put off flight.

24:26 *In the wilderness.* Cf. Acts 21:38.

24:28 *Body . . . eagles (vultures).* A carcass attracts vultures with uncanny certainty. With the same certainty the Son of Man will appear to deliver and judge.

24:29 The language used to depict the convulsion of the universe is from the OT: Is 24:21; 34:4; Jl 2:30, 31. Jesus introduces no "novelties" in speaking of the last things; His emphasis is religious and personal, on the return of the *Son of man* (30) and the *gathering* of *His elect.*

24:30 *The sign of the Son of man* is the appearing of the Son of Man in His *power* and *glory.*

24:32 – 25:46 THE SIGN OF HIS COMING:
        YOU MUST BE READY

24:32 – 25:46 Jesus is not the great forecaster of the future; His words are designed to give His disciples a sure and responsible hope, to make them ready for His coming. Only a third of His words in Matthew's record of His teaching on last things are predictive (24:1-31); the rest are directly and explicitly admonitory. Six parables and a magnificent depiction of the Last Judgment are all directed to the paramount question in all NT teaching on the last things: "What sort of persons ought you to be in your lives of holiness and godliness waiting for and hastening [or "earnestly desiring"] the coming of the day of God?" (2 Ptr 3:11-12)

24:32-35 The parable of the fig tree frees the disciples from excited impatience in their hoping; they can await the coming of their Lord as they await the coming of *summer* with patience, knowing that it is in the Creator's hands. His work has begun; the tree is budding, their Lord is near. This they know from His sure, eternal *words.*

24:34 *This generation* can refer to the Jews (Mt 11:16; 12:39, 41, 42, 45; 16:4). For all the severity of God's judgment on Israel, its history shall not end with the destruction of the temple and the fall of Jerusalem; there is a place for Israel in the new and eternal people of God. Or the reference can be one of time; Jesus' contemporaries dare not think of *all these things* as an event in the distant future; the end of Jerusalem ushers in the end, and all men live henceforth under the tension and responsibility of "these last days." (Heb 1:2)

24:35 *My words.* Jesus' words surpass even the words of the Law in their enduring validity (cf. 5:18). Only One who is very God of very God can speak thus of His Word.

36 "But of that day and hour no one knows, not even the angels of heaven, nor the Son,[a] but the Father only. [37]As were the days of Noah, so will be the coming of the Son of man. [38] For as in those days before the flood they were eating and drinking, marrying and giving in marriage, until the day when Noah entered the ark, [39] and they did not know until the flood came and swept them all away, so will be the coming of the Son of man. [40] Then two men will be in the field; one is taken and one is left. [41] Two women will be grinding at the mill; one is taken and one is left. [42] Watch therefore, for you do not know on what day your Lord is coming. [43] But know this, that if the householder had known in what part of the night the thief was coming, he would have watched and would not have let his house be broken into. [44] Therefore you also must be ready; for the Son of man is coming at an hour you do not expect.

45 "Who then is the faithful and wise servant, whom his master has set over his household, to give them their food at the proper time? [46] Blessed is that servant whom his master when he comes will find so doing. [47] Truly, I say to you, he will set him over all his possessions. [48] But if that wicked servant says to himself, 'My master is delayed,' [49] and begins to beat his fellow servants, and eats and drinks with the drunken, [50] the master of that servant will come on a day when he does not expect him and at an hour he does not know, [51] and will punish[b] him, and put him with the hypocrites; there men will weep and gnash their teeth.

25 "Then the kingdom of heaven shall be compared to ten maidens who took their lamps and went to meet the bridegroom.[c] [2] Five of them were foolish, and five were wise. [3] For when the foolish took their lamps, they took no oil with them; [4] but the wise took flasks of oil with their lamps. [5]As the bridegroom was delayed, they all slumbered and slept. [6] But at midnight there was a cry, 'Behold, the bridegroom! Come out to meet him.' [7] Then all those maidens rose and trimmed their lamps. [8]And the foolish said to the wise, 'Give us some of your oil, for our lamps are going out.' [9] But the wise replied, 'Perhaps there will not be enough for us and for you; go rather to the dealers and buy for yourselves.' [10]And while they went to buy, the bridegroom came, and those who were ready went in with him to the marriage feast; and the door was shut. [11]Afterward the other maidens came also, saying, 'Lord, lord, open to us.' [12] But he replied, 'Truly, I say to you, I do not know you.' [13] Watch therefore, for you know neither the day nor the hour.

14 "For it will be as when a man going on a journey called his servants and en-

---

[a] Other ancient authorities omit *nor the Son*   [b] Or *cut him in pieces*   [c] Other ancient authorities add *and the bride*

24:36-44 The parables of the *days of Noah* and of the *thief* in the night both stress the complete incalculability of the coming of the Son of Man. The *days of Noah* were deceptively normal days, and the householder does not know the hour of the thief's coming—he knows only the cost of unreadiness. *Therefore you . . . must* be *ready*.

24:36 Cf. Acts 1:6-7.

24:37 *Days of Noah*. Gn 6:5 — 7:24.

24:40 *One man is taken* by the Son of Man when He gathers in His elect (31); *and one is left*, to be eternally separated from God. Cf. John the Baptist's image of the wheat and chaff, 3:12.

24:43 *Thief*. Cf. 1 Th 5:2; 2 Ptr 3:10; Rv 3:3; 16:15. The suddenness of the coming of the Son of Man, which cuts off all possibility of forecast and calculation, makes the disciples' hope one of perpetual vigilance *(watch)*.

24:45-51 The disciple is to be composed and ready; this means that he must be *faithful and wise* in the service of His coming Lord. The reward for faithful service is generous, out of all proportion to the service rendered (47). The penalty for unfaithful folly is a fearful one.

24:45 *Servant . . . over his household* (cf. 49, *beat his fellow servants*). The promise and warning are addressed particularly to leaders in the church.

24:51 *Hypocrites*. The "Christian" hypocrite, whose profession of faith is not reflected in his practise, will be dealt with as severely as the Judaic hypocrite (23:33), "For God shows no partiality." (Ro 2:11)

25:1-13 The parable of the wise and foolish maidens makes clear that the disciple, whose life has been made the evening before the festival, dare not merely luxuriate in his hope; he lives by it in responsible readiness. He lives and hopes as a member of the church; but the church cannot hope for him or *be ready* for him. Each man moves toward the end in personal responsibility and individual vigilance. Otherwise he forfeits forever the joy of communion with his Lord.

25:12 *I do not know you*. "You are not Mine." (Cf. 7:23)

25:13 *Watch*. Be on the alert.

25:14-30 The parable of the *talents* portrays the Christ entrusting His property and business to His *servants*. Every gift of the Christ imposes its

trusted to them his property; 15 to one he gave five talents,*d* to another two, to another one, to each according to his ability. Then he went away. 16 He who had received the five talents went at once and traded with them; and he made five talents more. 17 So also, he who had the two talents made two talents more. 18 But he who had received the one talent went and dug in the ground and hid his master's money. 19 Now after a long time the master of those servants came and settled accounts with them. 20And he who had received the five talents came forward, bringing five talents more, saying, 'Master, you delivered to me five talents; here I have made five talents more.' 21 His master said to him, 'Well done, good and faithful servant; you have been faithful over a little, I will set you over much; enter into the joy of your master.' 22And he also who had the two talents came forward, saying, 'Master, you delivered to me two talents; here I have made two talents more.' 23 His master said to him, 'Well done, good and faithful servant; you have been faithful over a little, I will set you over much; enter into the joy of your master.' 24 He also who had received the one talent came forward, saying, 'Master, I knew you to be a hard man, reaping where you did not sow, and gathering where you did not winnow; 25 so I was afraid, and I went and hid your talent in the ground. Here you have what is yours.' 26 But his master answered him, 'You wicked and slothful servant! You knew that I reap where I have not sowed, and gather where I have not winnowed? 27 Then you ought to have invested my money with the bankers, and at my coming I should have received what was my own with interest. 28 So take the talent from him, and give it to him who has the ten talents. 29 For to every one who has will more be given, and he will have abundance; but from him who has not, even what he has will be taken away. 30And cast the worthless servant into the outer darkness; there men will weep and gnash their teeth.'

31 "When the Son of man comes in his glory, and all the angels with him, then he will sit on his glorious throne. 32 Before him will be gathered all the nations, and he will separate them one from another as a shepherd separates the sheep from the goats, 33 and he will place the sheep at his right hand, but the goats at the left. 34 Then the King will say to those at his right hand, 'Come, O blessed of my Father, inherit the kingdom prepared for you from the foundation of the world; 35 for I was hungry and

d This talent was more than fifteen years' wages of a laborer

claim on the recipient and asks of him fidelity, whether the gift be large or small. The Christ rewards with the lavishness of grace; the faithful two-talent man receives the same great reward as the faithful five-talent man; both feast with their Lord (see note on 21). The Christ measures a man not by what he has received but by his fidelity in what he has received. Therefore the Law which governs revelation (*to every one who has,* 29, cf. 13:12) also governs ministry, service; and therefore the *one talent,* the free gift of divine grace, dare not be neglected. To neglect it is to desecrate the grace of God.

25:15 *According to his ability.* The gift is seen to be the opportunity of serving the Christ.

25:21 *Joy of your master.* Cf. 23. *Joy* is probably used in the sense (found in Judaic writings) of festive dinner, banquet; the faithful servants enter into the joyous fellowship of the meal with their master. (Cf. 26:29)

25:27 *Invested my money with the bankers.* Even a course which involved minimal effort and imagination would have met with the master's approval. As he gives to "each according to his ability" (15), he is ready to reward accordingly.

25:31-46 THE LAST JUDGMENT

25:31-46 The great Shepherd who *separates*

the sheep from the goats (32) once said: "He who is not with me is against me, and he who does not gather with me scatters" (12:30). That is what determines now, in the judgment; the separation takes place before any deed of man is mentioned. Whether a man has been against Him or for Him has been documented in his deeds; deeds of mercy done or left undone have been man's yea or nay to Christ. The merciful will find mercy in the judgment, as Jesus had promised (5:7)—and mercy it is, for the Judge buries all their failures in forgiving silence and remembers only their deeds of mercy. The unmerciful have committed themselves to the unmerciful enemy of God and share his doom, that *eternal fire* which God did not design for man.

25:32 *All the nations,* to whom the Servant ministered (12:18) and gave hope; who had the Gospel proclaimed to them (24:14); who hated the disciples for the sake of Christ's name. (24:9)

25:32 *Sheep . . . goats.* Cf. Eze 34:17-24.

25:34 *Blessed of my Father.* God's work of *blessing,* begun in His creation (Gn 1:22), continued in history (Gn 12:2), active in the worship and life of His people (Nm 6:24; Eph 1:3), comes to its eternal climax here.

26:1—28:20 The Passion, death, and resurrection of the Messiah complete and crown His min-

you gave me food, I was thirsty and you gave me drink, I was a stranger and you welcomed me, 36 I was naked and you clothed me, I was sick and you visited me, I was in prison and you came to me.' 37 Then the righteous will answer him, 'Lord, when did we see thee hungry and feed thee, or thirsty and give thee drink? 38And when did we see thee a stranger and welcome thee, or naked and clothe thee? 39And when did we see thee sick or in prison and visit thee?' 40And the King will answer them, 'Truly, I say to you, as you did it to one of the least of these my brethren, you did it to me.' 41 Then he will say to those at his left hand, 'Depart from me, you cursed, into the eternal fire prepared for the devil and his angels; 42 for I was hungry and you gave me no food, I was thirsty and you gave me no drink, 43 I was a stranger and you did not welcome me, naked and you did not clothe me, sick and in prison and you did not visit me.' 44 Then they also will answer, 'Lord, when did we see thee hungry or thirsty or a stranger or naked or sick or in prison, and did not minister to thee?' 45 Then he will answer them, 'Truly, I say to you, as you did it not to one of the least of these, you did it not to me.' 46And they will go away into eternal punishment, but the righteous into eternal life.''

Conclusion and Climax

26:1 — 28:20

PASSION AND DEATH (26:1 — 27:66)

26 When Jesus had finished all these sayings, he said to his disciples, 2 "You know that after two days the Passover is coming, and the Son of man will be delivered up to be crucified."

3 Then the chief priests and the elders of the people gathered in the palace of the high priest, who was called Ca′ia·phas, 4 and took counsel together in order to arrest Jesus by stealth and kill him. 5 But they said, "Not during the feast, lest there be a tumult among the people."

6 Now when Jesus was at Beth′a·ny in the house of Simon the leper, 7 a woman came up to him with an alabaster flask of very expensive ointment, and she poured it on his head, as he sat at table. 8 But when the disciples saw it, they were indignant, saying, "Why this waste? 9 For this ointment might have been sold for a large sum, and given to the poor." 10 But Jesus, aware of this, said to them, "Why do you trouble the woman? For she has done a beautiful thing to me. 11 For you always have the poor with you, but you will not always have me. 12 In pouring this ointment on my body she has done it to prepare me for burial. 13 Truly, I say to you, wherever this gospel is preached in the whole world, what she has done will be told in memory of her."

14 Then one of the twelve, who was called Judas Is·car′i·ot, went to the chief priests 15 and said, "What will you give me if I deliver him to you?" And they paid him thirty pieces of silver. 16And from that moment he sought an opportunity to betray him.

---

istry. The risen Lord in the perfection of His grace and power gives His disciples their universal and enduring commission as His apostles.

26:1-16 PRELUDE TO THE PASSION

26:1-16 The opening of the Passion story sounds most of the notes heard in that account; the majestic certitude of the Christ who goes of set purpose to His death (2) and shapes the future of the universal Gospel (13); the determined enmity of the leaders of the people (3-5); the devotion of a woman to the dying Christ (6-13); the failure of Jesus' disciples—they all object to the generous gesture of the woman (8), and Judas agrees to betray Him. (14-15)

26:2 *Passover.* See note on 26:26.

You know. Jesus had predicted His death thrice: 16:21; 17:22-23; 20:17-19. Jesus knows that His "hour" is at hand.

Will be delivered up. The passive voice indicates God's action. (Cf. Ro 8:32)

26:6 *Simon the leper,* mentioned only here and Mk 14:3. Apparently he had been healed of his leprosy by Jesus.

26:12 *Ointment . . . burial.* For the anointing of the dead cf. Mk 14:8; Lk 23:56.

26:15 *They paid him.* Judas has become the opposite of a disciple and apostle. He had received from Jesus "without pay" (10:8); he betrays Jesus for pay.

17 Now on the first day of Unleavened Bread the disciples came to Jesus, saying, "Where will you have us prepare for you to eat the passover?" 18 He said, "Go into the city to a certain one, and say to him, 'The Teacher says, My time is at hand; I will keep the passover at your house with my disciples.'" 19And the disciples did as Jesus had directed them, and they prepared the passover.

20 When it was evening, he sat at table with the twelve disciples;*e* 21 and as they were eating, he said, "Truly, I say to you, one of you will betray me." 22And they were very sorrowful, and began to say to him one after another, "Is it I, Lord?" 23 He answered, "He who has dipped his hand in the dish with me, will betray me. 24 The Son of man goes as it is written of him, but woe to that man by whom the Son of man is betrayed! It would have been better for that man if he had not been born." 25 Judas, who betrayed him, said, "Is it I, Master?"*f* He said to him, "You have said so."

26 Now as they were eating, Jesus took bread, and blessed, and broke it, and gave it to the disciples and said, "Take, eat; this is my body." 27And he took a cup, and when he had given thanks he gave it to them, saying, "Drink of it, all of you; 28 for this is my blood of the*g* covenant, which is poured out for many for the forgiveness of sins. 29 I tell you I shall not drink again of this fruit of the vine until that day when I drink it new with you in my Father's kingdom."

30 And when they had sung a hymn, they went out to the Mount of Olives. 31 Then Jesus said to them, "You will all fall away because of me this night; for it is written, 'I

e Other authorities omit *disciples*   *f* Or *Rabbi*   *g* Other ancient authorities insert *new*

26:17-29 THE LAST PASSOVER, THE NEW PASSOVER

26:17-29 The obedient suffering Servant is in charge of His own history; Jesus determines the place of the *passover* meal (17-19), unmasks His betrayer, and pronounces God's judgment on him (20-25). He makes *bread* and *wine* the vehicles of His self-giving, atoning death and establishes the new *covenant* of the *forgiveness of sins* (26-28). He looks forward confidently to the *new,* eternal fellowship of the meal in His *Father's kingdom* in the world to come. (29)

26:17 *Unleavened Bread,* the term used to designate the Passover (cf. 2) AND the 7-day festival which followed.

26:19 *Prepared the passover.* For the ritual of the Passover meal see Ex 12.

26:23 *Dipped his hand in the dish.* The outrageousness of the betrayal by Judas is underscored; he is violating the sacred bond of table fellowship. (Cf. Ps 41:9; Jn 13:18)

26:24 *As it is written . . . woe to that man.* God can use the wrong of man to carry out His settled purpose *(written);* but that does not excuse man's wrong. (Cf. Ro 3:5-8)

26:25 *You have said so.* Cf. 26:64; 27:11. There is a mysterious reticence in the way Jesus speaks His Yes to the questions of the disciple who betrayed Him, the Jewish council which condemned Him, and the Roman governor who executed Him.

26:26 *As they were eating.* In the course of the meal of the Passover, which commemorated the "passing over" or sparing of Israel when the first-born of Egypt were slain (Ex 12; 13:3-9), Christ institutes the new Passover based on His self-sacrifice (cf. 1 Co 5:7); on the memorial day of the first covenant He establishes the new *covenant* promised for the new age.

Covenant evokes many OT memories: the Lord's covenant with Israel (Ex 24:6-8); His promise to David (2 Sm 23:5; Ps 89:3, 4, 28), the Servant who is the "covenant to the people" (Is 42:6), the ancient promise of a new covenant to supersede the one which unfaithful Israel had broken (Jer 31:31-34; Eze 16:60; 34:25; 37:26; Is 54:10; 55:3; 61:8). In establishing the covenant, a gracious God takes the initiative to establish fellowship between Himself and estranged man, to create a new order of things where His grace and will prevail. In using the term *covenant* of His death, Jesus marks His dying as God's grace toward man, His deed for man, His gift toward man. God is saying: "I will be your God."

26:30-56 THE STRICKEN SHEPHERD AND THE SCATTERED FLOCK

26:30-56 Jesus knows that He must drink the cup of God's judgment on man's sin alone and unsustained, and He accepts the burden laid on Him. He predicts the defection of His disciples and Peter's denial (30-35). He prays, in a genuinely human agony, for the strength to align His will with the Father's, while His disciples *sleep* (36-46). Strengthened and unwavering (46), He faces the *crowd* come to arrest Him and the disciple who betrays Him, stays the hand of the disciple who would defend Him with the *sword,* and goes the way marked out for Him by the *scriptures,* while His disciples *forsook him and fled.* (47-56)

26:30 *Hymn.* The singing of the Hallel (Pss 113 to 118) was a regular part of the Passover ritual. Jesus' last hours are worship, filled with hymns, Scripture, and prayer.

26:31 *Strike the shepherd.* Zechariah the prophet had spoken of the death of a Good Shepherd of God's people who was to perish by the judicial

will strike the shepherd, and the sheep of the flock will be scattered.' ³² But after I am raised up, I will go before you to Galilee." ³³ Peter declared to him, "Though they all fall away because of you, I will never fall away." ³⁴ Jesus said to him, "Truly, I say to you, this very night, before the cock crows, you will deny me three times." ³⁵ Peter said to him, "Even if I must die with you, I will not deny you." And so said all the disciples.

36 Then Jesus went with them to a place called Geth·sem′a·ne, and he said to his disciples, "Sit here, while I go yonder and pray." ³⁷And taking with him Peter and the two sons of Zeb′e·dee, he began to be sorrowful and troubled. ³⁸ Then he said to them, "My soul is very sorrowful, even to death; remain here, and watch*ʰ* with me." ³⁹And going a little farther he fell on his face and prayed, "My Father, if it be possible, let this cup pass from me; nevertheless, not as I will, but as thou wilt." ⁴⁰And he came to the disciples and found them sleeping; and he said to Peter, "So, could you not watch*ʰ* with me one hour? ⁴¹ Watch*ʰ* and pray that you may not enter into temptation; the spirit indeed is willing, but the flesh is weak." ⁴²Again, for the second time, he went away and prayed, "My Father, if this cannot pass unless I drink it, thy will be done." ⁴³And again he came and found them sleeping, for their eyes were heavy. ⁴⁴ So, leaving them again, he went away and prayed for the third time, saying the same words. ⁴⁵ Then he came to the disciples and said to them, "Are you still sleeping and taking your rest? Behold, the hour is at hand, and the Son of man is betrayed into the hands of sinners. ⁴⁶ Rise, let us be going; see, my betrayer is at hand."

47 While he was still speaking, Judas came, one of the twelve, and with him a great crowd with swords and clubs, from the chief priests and the elders of the people. ⁴⁸ Now the betrayer had given them a sign, saying, "The one I shall kiss is the man; seize him." ⁴⁹And he came up to Jesus at once and said, "Hail, Master!"*ⁱ* And he kissed him. ⁵⁰ Jesus said to him, "Friend, why are you here?"*ʲ* Then they came up and laid hands on Jesus and seized him. ⁵¹And behold, one of those who were with Jesus stretched out his hand and drew his sword, and struck the slave of the high priest, and cut off his ear. ⁵² Then Jesus said to him, "Put your sword back into its place; for all who take the sword will perish by the sword. ⁵³ Do you think that I cannot appeal to my Father, and he will at once send me more than twelve legions of angels? ⁵⁴ But how then should the scriptures be fulfilled, that it must be so?" ⁵⁵At that hour Jesus said to the crowds, "Have you come out as against a robber, with swords and clubs to capture me? Day after day I sat in the temple teaching, and you did not seize me. ⁵⁶ But all this has taken place, that the scriptures of the prophets might be fulfilled." Then all the disciples forsook him and fled.

57 Then those who had seized Jesus led him to Ca′ia·phas the high priest, where the scribes and the elders had gathered. ⁵⁸ But Peter followed him at a distance, as far as the courtyard of the high priest, and going inside he sat with the guards to see

---

ʰ Or *keep awake*   *ⁱ* Or *Rabbi*   *ʲ* Or *do that for which you have come*

---

action of God (by His "sword," Zch 13:7). The immediate effect of the Shepherd's death was to be a dispersal of the flock, a time of trial and sifting for the people of God; the ultimate effect would be the restoration of a trusting and confessing people of God. (Zch 13:7-9)

26:36 *Gethsemane,* an olive yard east of Jerusalem.

26:37 *Sons of Zebedee.* James and John.

26:38 *My soul is sorrowful.* Ps 42:5, 11; 43:5.

26:39 *This cup.* Cf. 20:22 note.

26:41 *The spirit is willing.* Cf. Ps 51:12. The *willing spirit* is God's gift to man; it arises from "joy in His salvation." The *flesh* is man in his frailty and unwillingness to accept God's salvation.

26:49 *Kiss.* For the kiss as an expression of honor for a teacher (*Master,* rabbi) cf. Lk 7:45.

26:52 *Perish by the sword.* Jesus' word refers

particularly to those who, like the Zealots, attempt to achieve religious ends by military-political means.

26:55 *Robber.* The term was also used to designate a political revolutionary, a Zealot, such as Barabbas was (called "robber" in Jn 18:40 and "rebel" in Mk 15:7, cf. Lk 23:19).

26:57-75 THE TRIAL BEFORE CAIAPHAS AND PETER'S DENIAL

26:57-75 Jesus endures in silence the waves of malice that sweep over Him: the *false testimony,* the charge of *blasphemy,* the decision that He must die, and the mockery designed to discredit His Messianic claim. He is the Servant who "opened not his mouth" when the Lord laid on Him "the iniquity of us all" (Is 53:6-7). He endures in silence, and He endures alone; Peter the "first" of

the end. [59] Now the chief priests and the whole council sought false testimony against Jesus that they might put him to death, [60] but they found none, though many false witnesses came forward. At last two came forward [61] and said, "This fellow said, 'I am able to destroy the temple of God, and to build it in three days.' " [62]And the high priest stood up and said, "Have you no answer to make? What is it that these men testify against you?" [63] But Jesus was silent. And the high priest said to him, "I adjure you by the living God, tell us if you are the Christ, the Son of God." [64] Jesus said to him, "You have said so. But I tell you, hereafter you will see the Son of man seated at the right hand of Power, and coming on the clouds of heaven." [65] Then the high priest tore his robes, and said, "He has uttered blasphemy. Why do we still need witnesses? You have now heard his blasphemy. [66] What is your judgment?" They answered, "He deserves death." [67] Then they spat in his face, and struck him; and some slapped him, [68] saying, "Prophesy to us, you Christ! Who is it that struck you?"

[69] Now Peter was sitting outside in the courtyard. And a maid came up to him, and said, "You also were with Jesus the Galilean." [70] But he denied it before them all, saying, "I do not know what you mean." [71]And when he went out to the porch, another maid saw him, and she said to the bystanders, "This man was with Jesus of Nazareth." [72]And again he denied it with an oath, "I do not know the man." [73]After a little while the bystanders came up and said to Peter, "Certainly you are also one of them, for your accent betrays you." [74] Then he began to invoke a curse on himself and to swear, "I do not know the man." And immediately the cock crowed. [75]And Peter remembered the saying of Jesus, "Before the cock crows, you will deny me three times." And he went out and wept bitterly.

27 When morning came, all the chief priests and the elders of the people took counsel against Jesus to put him to death; [2] and they bound him and led him away and delivered him to Pilate the governor.

[3] When Judas, his betrayer, saw that he was condemned, he repented and brought back the thirty pieces of silver to the chief priests and the elders, [4] saying, "I have

His disciples and apostles (10:2) denies Him – his iniquity, too, becomes part of the burden laid on the one obedient Servant.

26:61 *Destroy the temple.* The charge is a distortion of a word of Jesus recorded in Jn 2:19, where Jesus marked His opponents as the destroyers of the temple and Himself as the Restorer of what they had destroyed. (Cf. Jn 2:21-22)

26:64 *You have said.* Cf. 26:25 note.

Power. Judaic expression for God.

Son of man . . . coming on clouds. Jesus in His "good confession" combines two of the mightiest Messianic utterances of the OT, Ps 110:1 (cf. Mt 22:43-45) and Dn 7:13-14, where the *Son of man* is pictured in the light of the heavenly world, as Judge over the kingdoms of this world and as recipient of a universal and imperishable kingdom.

26:65 *Blasphemy.* Cf. 9:3. Galilee and Jerusalem bring the same charge against the Son of Man who looks to His rightful place at God's right hand. Jesus is to be executed because of His claim to deity.

26:67-68 *Spat . . . struck . . . slapped . . . you Christ.* Cf. Is 50:6, a word concerning the Servant. The mistreatment of Jesus by His judges is to justify their verdict; if He is so defenseless, He cannot be the Messiah, the Son of the Blessed.

27:1-31 THE TRIAL BEFORE PILATE

27:1-31 Jesus' prediction that His people would "deliver him to the Gentiles to be mocked and scourged and crucified" (20:19) is fulfilled. And Jesus' prediction that "the Son of man is to be delivered into the hands of MEN" (17:22) is fulfilled too. Men – Jew, disciple, Gentile – are guilty of His death; and none can evade that guilt. The remorse of Judas and the return of the silver (3-10) cannot clear Judas; his fate is a terrifying prediction of the fate of all who "profaned the blood" of the Son of God (Heb 10:29). The men of Israel cannot evade responsibility by delivering Jesus to Pilate (2, 11-14); the choice between Jesus and Barabbas is their choice and makes Pilate's verdict their verdict (15-23). And no *washing* can sweeten Pilate's *hands;* he *releases Barabbas, scourges Jesus* and *delivers him to be crucified* (24-26); and it is soldiery under his command that completes the parallel between Jew and Gentile by *mocking* the *King of the Jews* (27-31) just as His own people had mocked Him (26:67-68). The trial of Jesus is a miniature of the guilt of mankind.

27:1-2 Legal tradition demanded that in the case of capital offenses the trial had to extend over two days and the verdict had to be reached in the daytime. This second meeting seems to have been held to meet that requirement. *Took counsel.* Better: "decided."

27:3 *Repented.* The Greek word here is not the usual one for *repent.* Better: "felt remorse"; not the same as the "repentance that leads to salvation." (2 Co 7:10)

sinned in betraying innocent blood." They said, "What is that to us? See to it yourself." 5And throwing down the pieces of silver in the temple, he departed; and he went and hanged himself. 6 But the chief priests, taking the pieces of silver, said, "It is not lawful to put them into the treasury, since they are blood money." 7 So they took counsel, and bought with them the potter's field, to bury strangers in. 8 Therefore that field has been called the Field of Blood to this day. 9 Then was fulfilled what had been spoken by the prophet Jer·e·mi'ah, saying, "And they took the thirty pieces of silver, the price of him on whom a price had been set by some of the sons of Israel, 10 and they gave them for the potter's field, as the Lord directed me."

11 Now Jesus stood before the governor; and the governor asked him, "Are you the King of the Jews?" Jesus said, "You have said so." 12 But when he was accused by the chief priests and elders, he made no answer. 13 Then Pilate said to him, "Do you not hear how many things they testify against you?" 14 But he gave him no answer, not even to a single charge; so that the governor wondered greatly.

15 Now at the feast the governor was accustomed to release for the crowd any one prisoner whom they wanted. 16And they had then a notorious prisoner, called Bar-ab'bas.k 17 So when they had gathered, Pilate said to them, "Whom do you want me to release for you, Bar-ab'bask or Jesus who is called Christ?" 18 For he knew that it was out of envy that they had delivered him up. 19 Besides, while he was sitting on the judgment seat, his wife sent word to him, "Have nothing to do with that righteous man, for I have suffered much over him today in a dream." 20 Now the chief priests and the elders persuaded the people to ask for Bar-ab'bas and destroy Jesus. 21 The governor again said to them, "Which of the two do you want me to release for you?" And they said, "Bar-ab'bas." 22 Pilate said to them, "Then what shall I do with Jesus who is called Christ?" They all said, "Let him be crucified." 23And he said, "Why, what evil has he done?" But they shouted all the more, "Let him be crucified."

24 So when Pilate saw that he was gaining nothing, but rather that a riot was beginning, he took water and washed his hands before the crowd, saying, "I am innocent of this man's blood;l see to it yourselves." 25And all the people answered, "His blood be on us and on our children!" 26 Then he released for them Bar-ab'bas, and having scourged Jesus, delivered him to be crucified.

27 Then the soldiers of the governor took Jesus into the praetorium, and they gathered the whole battalion before him. 28And they stripped him and put a scarlet robe upon him, 29 and plaiting a crown of thorns they put it on his head, and put a reed in his right hand. And kneeling before him they mocked him, saying, "Hail, King of the Jews!" 30And they spat upon him, and took the reed and struck him on

k Other ancient authorities read Jesus Barabbas
l Other authorities read this righteous blood or this righteous man's blood

27:6 It is not lawful. Tainted money could not be brought into the house of the Lord. (Cf. Dt 23:18)

27:9 Jeremiah. The passage quoted is basically Zch 11:12-13; reminiscences of Jer 32:6-15; 18:2-3 probably led to the citing of Jeremiah's name. The language of the Zechariah passage is mysterious and the text uncertain; therefore the fulfillment connection is hard to trace. Common to Zechariah and Matthew is the thought that One whom the Lord appointed to be Shepherd over His people is rejected by them and held cheap—thirty pieces of silver are the indemnity money to be paid for the killing of a slave. (Ex 21:32)

27:11 King of the Jews, a political messianic pretender, a revolutionary and therefore dangerous to Rome.

You have said so. Cf. 26:25, 64.

27:14 No answer. Again (cf. 26:63) the Servant suffers silently. (Is 53:7)

27:17 Barabbas means "son of Abbas" (cf. 16:17); there is considerable probability in the read-

ing given in RSV note k, Jesus Barabbas. There would then be a tragic contrast between the Jesus whom Israel produced (Barabbas) and the Jesus the Christ whom God gave to Israel as Savior (1:21); the one was liberated by his people, the other was sent to the cross although said to be innocent. (Cf. 27:19)

27:18 Out of envy. Jn 11:47-48 is an eloquent commentary on this statement.

27:19 Three Gentiles attest Jesus' innocence in Matthew: Pilate's wife, Pilate (23-24), and the centurion. (54)

27:25 On us and on our children. Those who spin fables about a hereditary curse upon the Jews ignore the fact that it was not God who uttered this imprecation, that the apostles went to the Jews first and offered them forgiveness, and that "the gifts and call of God are irrevocable." (Ro 11:29)

27:27 Praetorium, the palace of the Roman governor.

the head. [31]And when they had mocked him, they stripped him of the robe, and put his own clothes on him, and led him away to crucify him.

32 As they went out, they came upon a man of Cy·re'ne, Simon by name; this man they compelled to carry his cross. [33]And when they came to a place called Gol'go·tha (which means the place of a skull), [34] they offered him wine to drink, mingled with gall; but when he tasted it, he would not drink it. [35]And when they had crucified him, they divided his garments among them by casting lots; [36] then they sat down and kept watch over him there. [37]And over his head they put the charge against him, which read, "This is Jesus the King of the Jews." [38] Then two robbers were crucified with him, one on the right and one on the left. [39]And those who passed by derided him, wagging their heads [40] and saying, "You who would destroy the temple and build it in three days, save yourself! If you are the Son of God, come down from the cross." [41] So also the chief priests, with the scribes and elders, mocked him, saying, [42] "He saved others; he cannot save himself. He is the King of Israel; let him come down now from the cross, and we will believe in him. [43] He trusts in God; let God deliver him now, if he desires him; for he said, 'I am the Son of God.' " [44]And the robbers who were crucified with him also reviled him in the same way.

45 Now from the sixth hour there was darkness over all the land[m] until the ninth hour. [46]And about the ninth hour Jesus cried with a loud voice, "Eli, Eli, la'ma sabach-tha'ni?" that is, "My God, my God, why hast thou forsaken me?" [47]And some of the bystanders hearing it said, "This man is calling E·li'jah." [48]And one of them at once ran and took a sponge, filled it with vinegar, and put it on a reed, and gave it to him to drink. [49] But the others said, "Wait, let us see whether E·li'jah will come to save him."[n] [50]And Jesus cried again with a loud voice and yielded up his spirit.

[m] Or *earth*

[n] Other ancient authorities insert *And another took a spear and pierced his side, and out came water and blood*

27:27-31 The mockery of Gentile soldiery is parallel to that of Judaic scribes and elders (26: 67). Jesus once told His brothers: "The WORLD . . . hates me because I testify of it that its works are evil." (Jn 7:7)

Only here does the Messiah appear with the title and insignia of royalty; thus, by suffering He comes to kingship. (Cf. Ph 2:9)

27:32-66 THE CRUCIFIXION, DEATH, AND BURIAL OF JESUS

27:32-66 Old Israel rejects the King sent to her; the beginning of the history of the new Israel, the Twelve, is a sad chapter of failure. A stranger carries the cross for the Christ (32); a hitherto unknown disciple provides for His burial (57-60); only the devotion of women remains constant (55-56, 61). Jesus dies alone, and He tastes death to the full, "numbered with the transgressors" (38, 44; Is 53:12), forsaken by God (46), fully conscious to the last (34, 50). But the Father attests the Son even now when He gives Him the cup to drink, in catastrophic *darkness* (45), in the rent curtain of the temple, in earthquake, and in the *rising of the saints fallen asleep* (51-53); the mockery under the cross is made to publish once more all that Jesus is and claims to be (39-43); a Gentile centurion is *filled with awe* at this crucified criminal and calls Him *Son of God* (54). The language of the account is rich in reminiscences of the OT; Matthew saw that these things were no mere accident—the drink offered to

Jesus (34, 48), the casting of lots for His garments (36), Jesus' crucifixion in the company of transgressors (44)—in all this Scripture is being fulfilled; God's will is being done. Jesus had gone this way in the assurance that it was God's will ("must," 16:21; "is to be," 17:22), that will also was that "He be raised on the third day." No posted guard, no *seal* of Roman security, no *secure sepulchre* can frustrate that will. (62-66)

27:32 *Compelled.* Literally "to requisition, press into service."

27:34 *Wine . . . mingled with gall.* A narcotic to help deaden the pain. Jesus' refusal expresses His will to drink the cup of suffering to the full.

27:39 *Wagging their heads.* Ps 22:7. A gesture of mockery.

27:45 *Sixth . . . until the ninth hour.* Noon till three.

Darkness. Amos had prophesied that the Lord God would "make the sun go down at noon and darken the earth in broad daylight" (Am 8:9) on the day of threatened judgment against His people. Cf. Am 8:2: "The end has come upon my people Israel."

27:46 *Eli.* Ps 22:1. In the hour when He is forsaken, He still calls God *my God.* He is the Servant "who walks in darkness and has no light, yet . . . relies upon his God." (Is 50:10)

27:47 *Calling Elijah.* Elijah was celebrated in Judaic legend as helper in time of need.

27:48 *Vinegar.* Sour wine.

27:50 *Cried with a loud voice.* It was probably

51 And behold, the curtain of the temple was torn in two, from top to bottom; and the earth shook, and the rocks were split; [52] the tombs also were opened, and many bodies of the saints who had fallen asleep were raised, [53] and coming out of the tombs after his resurrection they went into the holy city and appeared to many. [54] When the centurion and those who were with him, keeping watch over Jesus, saw the earthquake and what took place, they were filled with awe, and said, "Truly this was the Son[x] of God!"

55 There were also many women there, looking on from afar, who had followed Jesus from Galilee, ministering to him; [56] among whom were Mary Magdalene, and Mary the mother of James and Joseph, and the mother of the sons of Zeb'e·dee.

57 When it was evening, there came a rich man from Ar·i·ma·the'a, named Joseph, who also was a disciple of Jesus. [58] He went to Pilate and asked for the body of Jesus. Then Pilate ordered it to be given to him. [59]And Joseph took the body, and wrapped it in a clean linen shroud, [60] and laid it in his own new tomb, which he had hewn in the rock; and he rolled a great stone to the door of the tomb, and departed. [61] Mary Magdalene and the other Mary were there, sitting opposite the sepulchre.

62 Next day, that is, after the day of Preparation, the chief priests and the Pharisees gathered before Pilate [63] and said, "Sir, we remember how that impostor said, while he was still alive, 'After three days I will rise again.' [64] Therefore order the sepulchre to be made secure until the third day, lest his disciples go and steal him away, and tell the people, 'He has risen from the dead,' and the last fraud will be worse than the first." [65] Pilate said to them, "You have a guard[o] of soldiers; go, make it as secure as you can."[p] [66] So they went and made the sepulchre secure by sealing the stone and setting a guard.

THE RESURRECTION (28:1-20)

28 Now after the sabbath, toward the dawn of the first day of the week, Mary Magdalene and the other Mary went to see the sepulchre. [2]And behold, there was a great earthquake; for an angel of the Lord descended from heaven and came and rolled back the stone, and sat upon it. [3] His appearance was like lightning, and his raiment white as snow. [4]And for fear of him the guards trembled and became like dead men. [5] But the angel said to the women, "Do not be afraid; for I know that you seek Jesus who was crucified. [6] He is not here; for he has risen, as he said. Come, see the place where he[q] lay. [7] Then go quickly and tell his disciples that he has risen from the dead, and behold, he is going before you to Galilee; there you will see him. Lo, I have told you." [8] So they departed quickly from the tomb with fear and great joy, and ran to tell his disciples. [9]And behold, Jesus met them and said, "Hail!" And they came up and took hold of his feet and worshiped him. [10] Then Jesus said to them,

---

[x] Or a son [o] Or Take a guard [p] Greek know [q] Other ancient authorities read the Lord

---

for this that Jesus had accepted the sour wine (48). He departed from life consciously; His death was not His fate but His act.

27:51-53 The torn curtain of the temple, the shaken earth, the opened tombs, and the exclamation of the centurion mark the significance of the hour. The rending of the curtain which divided the Holy of Holies from the Holy Place (Ex 26:33) signifies that God no longer dwells in His house; it is "forsaken and desolate" (23:38). Others take it to signify that the Holy of Holies is now open to all believers (cf. Heb 6:19; 10:19-22). The shaking of the earth is a frequent feature in many of the OT theophanies (appearances of God); here God is manifesting Himself, in the death of the Servant the arm of the Lord is being revealed (Is 53:1); the saints proceeding from their tombs and appearing in the holy city indicate that Christ's death is the victory over death, that He is the firstborn from the dead. The exclamation of the centurion and those who were with him, Gentiles all, indicates that in His dying the Christ has fulfilled His ministry to the Jew and now goes to all nations to assert His Lordship over all.

27:57 Joseph . . . a disciple. John adds that he was a disciple "secretly, for fear of the Jews" (Jn 19:38). This may account for Matthew's previous silence concerning him.

27:62 Day of Preparation. The day before the Sabbath, when preparation for the Sabbath was made.

27:66 Sealing the stone. The presence of the seal made any violation of the grave an offense against Roman authority. (Cf. Dn 6:17)

28:1-20 The supreme event of the gospel is economically told. The actual event of the resurrection is, as in all the gospels, veiled in the silence of awe; only the annunciation of the resurrection is dramatically narrated (2-3). Wondrous as the crowning event is, it retains continuity with the

"Do not be afraid; go and tell my brethren to go to Galilee, and there they will see me."

11 While they were going, behold, some of the guard went into the city and told the chief priests all that had taken place. 12And when they had assembled with the elders and taken counsel, they gave a sum of money to the soldiers 13 and said, "Tell people, 'His disciples came by night and stole him away while we were asleep.' 14And if this comes to the governor's ears, we will satisfy him and keep you out of trouble." 15 So they took the money and did as they were directed; and this story has been spread among the Jews to this day.

16 Now the eleven disciples went to Galilee, to the mountain to which Jesus had directed them. 17And when they saw him they worshiped him; but some doubted. 18And Jesus came and said to them, "All authority in heaven and on earth has been given to me. 19 Go therefore and make disciples of all nations, baptizing them in the name of the Father and of the Son and of the Holy Spirit, 20 teaching them to observe all that I have commanded you; and lo, I am with you always, to the close of the age."

previous history of Jesus. There is the same determined opposition by the leadership of His people (11-15), the same devotion inspired in womankind (1), the same genuine humanity of Jesus (*took hold of his feet,* 9), the same instability in His disciples (*some doubted,* 17), the same *Galilee* that witnessed the calling of the first disciples (10, 16). Jesus remains the Forgiver and Restorer; the angel calls men who had forfeited their right to discipleship *his disciples* still (7), and Jesus calls men who had forsaken and denied Him His *brethren* (10). The *authority* of Jesus (18) emerges into the full light of Easter, but it is of a piece with His "authority on earth to forgive sins" (9:6); His compassionate authority makes the disciples' apostolate an apostolate to *all nations* (19), no longer confined to the lost sheep of the house of Israel. His authority gives the grace of Baptism and the gift of His teaching to all mankind and promises the abiding power of His presence *always, to the close of the age* (20). One *name* (19) unites the *Son* with *the Father* and *the Spirit;* Jesus' Godhead is apparent now, and in that God-head He is Servant—His will is to *make disciples* still. (19)

28:19 *Baptizing . . . in the name. In the name of* was a term used in Judaism to indicate that a man was being effectually COMMITTED TO something or someone. E. g., a man circumcised "in the name of the covenant" was committed to the covenant, brought under its blessing and placed under its obligations. A man baptized *in the name of the Father* has God as his Father; baptized *in the name of the Son,* he receives all the benefits of the Son's redeeming act; baptized *in the name of the Spirit,* he receives the life-giving, life-sustaining power and presence of the Spirit. Baptism is the enacted Gospel of the Trinity.

28:20 *Commanded.* Jesus is not a new lawgiver, as Matthew's account of His teaching has shown. His command is given to men baptized in His name, men with whom He is present as their crucified and risen Lord. *Command* calls for what Paul calls "the obedience of faith" (Ro 1:5). For the command contained in the gift of Baptism cf. Ro 6:3-14.

THE GOSPEL ACCORDING TO

MARK

INTRODUCTION

1 The second gospel begins with the words, "The beginning of the gospel of Jesus Christ, the Son of God." This is too comprehensive and solemn a phrase to be the title of the opening section only, as some have thought, the part which deals with John the Baptist and Jesus' baptism and His temptation, the preparation for Jesus' Messianic ministry. It is designed to be the title to the whole work, and it is a significant one. Mark's book aims to set before the readers the record of the beginning and origin of that Good News which they knew and believed, that powerful and saving Word of God which the Son of God first proclaimed in word and deed (1:14-15), a word which was still the voice of Christ when proclaimed to men by human apostles and evangelists. Mark is answering the question of converts who, once they had heard the basic kerygma (Gospel), naturally and rightly asked, "How did this great Good News that has revolutionized our lives begin? What is its history? Tell us more of the strong Son of God who loved us and gave Himself for us. Recount for us His words and works, which will make clear His will for us who have become His own." Mark is doing what Luke did when he wrote "an orderly account" for Theophilus, in order that he might know the truth concerning *the things of which he had been informed* (Lk 1:3-4). Mark's book is "teaching"; it is the filling in of the outline of the kerygma for Christian readers. This is confirmed by many details in the book itself; for instance, the noun "gospel" occurs seven times in this gospel, while it occurs only four times in Matthew's much longer work and not at all in Luke and John. And it is in Mark's Gospel that Jesus identifies "gospel" so closely with His own person that the two are practically one entity, as when He says, "Whoever loses his life for my sake *and the gospel's* will save it." (Mk 8:35; cf. 10:29)

2 The earliest tradition of the church confirms this view of the gospel as "teaching." Papias, bishop of Hierapolis, writing about A. D. 130 and citing as his authority the "Elder John" (perhaps John the apostle, certainly a man close to the apostolic age), writes concerning the second gospel: "Mark, having become Peter's interpreter, wrote down accurately, though not in order, as many as he remembered of the things said or done by the Lord. For he neither had heard the Lord nor followed Him, but at a later time, as I said, [he followed] Peter, *who delivered his instructions* according to the needs [of the occasion] . . . ." Other early notices locate this preaching of Peter's and Mark's recording of it in Italy, more specifically in Rome. An early prolog to the gospel (one of the so-called Anti-Marcionite prologs) says that Mark wrote his record of Peter's preaching "in the regions of Italy," and Clement of Alexandria reports an early tradition that Mark wrote his gospel in Rome at the request of those who had heard Peter preach there. Since Christianity had been established in Italy and Rome long before Peter ever worked there, both these notices are taken most naturally as referring to a *teaching* activity of Peter in Rome rather than to a strictly missionary activity.

Author of the Gospel

3 Mark (referred to in the New Testament also as John and as John Mark, Acts 13:5, 13; 12:12) was the son of a certain Mary who owned a house in Jerusalem. At the time of Peter's imprisonment, A. D. 44, Jerusalem Christians assembled there for prayer, and it was thither that Peter turned when he was miraculously released from prison. Peter evidently knew the family, and since he calls Mark his "son" in 1 Ptr 5:13, we may assume that Mark was converted by him. In A. D. 46 Mark accompanied Paul and Barnabas on the first missionary journey as far as Perga in Pamphylia, whence he returned to Jerusalem (Acts 13:13). Barnabas wished to take his cousin Mark along on the second missionary journey also, but Paul objected so violently that the two missionaries parted ways (Acts 15:37 ff.). Barnabas took Mark with him to Cyprus. Mark was with Paul

again during the first Roman imprisonment according to Phmn 24 (A. D. 59 — 61), and Paul bespeaks a warm welcome for him on the part of the Christians of Colossae (Cl 4:10-11 f). In 1 Ptr 5:13 Peter includes greetings from his "son" Mark to the Christians of Asia Minor; apparently he had worked there and was known there. Mark was with Peter in Rome at the time when he wrote first Peter in the early sixties. A few years later, at the time of Paul's last imprisonment, he was again in Asia Minor. Paul urges Timothy to bring Mark with him when he comes to Rome (2 Ti 4:11). This is the last New Testament notice of Mark. According to the church historian Eusebius, Mark was the founder of the church at Alexandria in Egypt and its first bishop. He is said to have died a martyr's death there.

4 Early tradition is unanimous in ascribing the second gospel to Mark, the interpreter of Peter. There is one bit of evidence in the gospel itself which also points, although only indirectly, to Mark. Only this gospel records the incident of the young man who ran away naked at the arrest of Jesus (Mk 14:51-52). Since no other convincing reason can be found for the inclusion of this detail, many scholars assume that the young man was Mark himself; the evangelist is thus appending his signature, as it were, to the gospel. It may even be that the house of Mark's mother, Mary, was the house in whose upper room our Lord celebrated the Passover with His disciples on the night in which He was betrayed.

Place and Date of Writing

5 The style and character of the gospel itself, which make it probable that the book was written for Gentile readers, confirm the tradition that Mark wrote his gospel in Rome. The gospel is therefore to be dated in the sixties of the first century, since Peter did not reach Rome until his later years. Some of the early witnesses declare that Mark wrote after the death of Peter. This would necessitate a date after A. D. 64. But since the tradition is not unanimous on this point, there can be no absolute certainty on it.

Characteristics of Mark's Gospel

6 The Gospel According to Mark is a gospel of action. As compared with Matthew, Mark emphasizes the deeds of Jesus. The deeds of Jesus are by no means isolated from His words; the word is Jesus' instrument in His deeds too; He speaks, and it is done. And Mark, besides giving two longer discourses of Jesus (4:1-34; 13:1-37), repeatedly emphasizes the centrality of the word in the ministry of Jesus and the effect of its authority on men, 1:14, 22, 38-39 f.; 2:2, 13; 4:1; 6:1-7; 9:7; 10:1; 11:18; cf. also 8:38. But it is chiefly by His works that Jesus is marked as the Proclaimer and the Bringer of the almighty grace of the kingdom of God, as the anointed King in whom man can trust, the Son of God in whom man can believe.

7 The Gospel According to Mark is Peter's Gospel. Papias' statement that Mark "became Peter's interpreter" can be variously interpreted; but his assertion that Mark's Gospel incorporates the preaching of Peter is certainly confirmed by the character of the gospel itself; it begins with Peter's call (1:16); it reaches its critical point when Peter in the name of the Twelve confesses the Christ (8:29); it closes with a message from the risen Lord to His disciples *and Peter* (16:7). Peter's house is the center of operations at Capernaum (1:29), the followers of Jesus are called "Simon and those who were with him" (1:36), and Mark's use of an indefinite "they" for the disciples is most naturally understood as reproducing Peter's use of "we" (e.g., 1:21; 6:53). The resemblance of the structure of the gospel to that of Peter's sermon in the house of Cornelius (Acts 10:34-43) points in the same direction.

8 The many vivid and dramatic touches in the gospel which mark the account as that of an eyewitness also reflect the preaching of Peter and are quite in keeping with what we know of his warm, vivacious, and volatile nature. The expressions, bearing, gestures, and feelings of Jesus are often noted, as is the effect of His words and deeds on the disciples and the multitudes. The narrative frequently drops into the vivid historical present, and Jesus' words are usually given in direct speech. The occasional reproduction of Jesus' words in His own tongue is probably also an echo of Peter's concrete and vivid narrative. (E.g., 5:41; 7:34)

9 The ancient tradition that Mark wrote his gospel for Gentiles, specifically at the request of Roman Christians, is confirmed by the gospel itself. Hebrew and Aramaic expressions are elucidated (3:17; 5:41; 7:11; 15:22), and Jewish customs are explained (7:2-4; 15:42). The evangelist himself quotes the Old Testament explicitly but once (1:2),

although his narrative shows by allusion and echo that the narrator is conscious of the Old Testament background of the gospel story (e.g., 9:2-8; cf. Ex 24:12 ff.; 12:1-12, cf. Is 5:1 ff.). Mark reduces Greek money to terms of Roman currency (12:42) and ex- plains an unfamiliar Greek term by means of a Latin one (15:16, *praetorium*); and Latin- isms, that is, the direct taking over of Latin terms into the Greek, are more frequent in Mark's language than in that of the other evangelists.

OUTLINE
The Good News of Jesus Christ, the Son of God

I. 1:1-45 Christ's Coming Ushers in Promised Reign of God

II. 2:1–3:6 Christ's Coming Provokes Contradiction: Five Galilean Disputes

III. 3:7–8:30 Christ's Response to Contradiction

IV. 8:31–10:31 Christ Imprints Cross on Life of His Disciples

V. 10:32–13:37 Christ Goes to Jerusalem

VI. 14:1–16:20 Christ's Suffering, Death, and Resurrection

MARK

Christ's Coming Ushers in Promised Reign of God

1:1-45

1 The beginning of the gospel of Jesus Christ, the Son of God.[a]
2 As it is written in I·sa′iah the prophet,[b]
"Behold, I send my messenger before thy face,
who shall prepare thy way;
3 the voice of one crying in the wilderness:
Prepare the way of the Lord,
make his paths straight—"
4 John the baptizer appeared[c] in the wilderness, preaching a baptism of repentance for the forgiveness of sins. 5And there went out to him all the country of Judea, and all the people of Jerusalem; and they were baptized by him in the river Jordan, confessing their sins. 6 Now John was clothed with camel's hair, and had a leather girdle around his waist, and ate locusts and wild honey. 7And he preached, saying, "After me comes he who is mightier than I, the thong of whose sandals I am not worthy to stoop down and untie. 8 I have baptized you with water; but he will baptize you with the Holy Spirit."

9 In those days Jesus came from Nazareth of Galilee and was baptized by John in the Jordan. 10And when he came up out of the water, immediately he saw the heavens opened and the Spirit descending upon him like a dove; 11 and a voice came from heaven, "Thou art my beloved Son;[d] with thee I am well pleased."

12 The Spirit immediately drove him out into the wilderness. 13And he was in the wilderness forty days, tempted by Satan; and he was with the wild beasts; and the angels ministered to him.

[a] Other ancient authorities omit *the Son of God*   [b] Other ancient authorities read *in the prophets*
[c] Other ancient authorities read *John was baptizing*   [d] Or *my Son, my* (or *the*) *Beloved*

1:1 *Beginning of the gospel.* This is best taken as the title of the whole gospel. See the Introduction, par. 1.

1:1-13 THE PREPARATION FOR HIS COMING

1:1-13 *John the baptizer* prepares men for Christ's coming by his *baptism of repentance for the forgiveness of sins* and by his announcement of the coming of the *mightier* One with His gift of the *Holy Spirit.* (2-8)

Jesus is prepared for His coming ministry by submitting to John's baptism, an act by which He marks His solidarity with sinful man; by being endowed with the fullness of the Spirit; by being hailed *from heaven* as the *Son* and Servant of God; by overcoming the temptation of Satan *in the wilderness.* He appears as the embodiment of the new, true Israel, who obeys and triumphs where the old Israel disobeyed and failed.

1:2 *Isaiah the prophet.* Mark introduces the quotation from Isaiah concerning the *voice* (3; Is 40:3) with Malachi's word concerning the messenger (Ml 3:1). For the significance of the prophetic voice cf. Mt 3:1–4:11 note.

Messenger. Malachi had promised God's people that the hoped-for coming of the Lord would not come unheralded; there would be a warning messenger to prepare them before He came to judge and purify. (Ml 3:1-4)

1:4 *John the baptizer.* Cf. Mt 3:1-12 and the notes there for the ministry of John.

1:9-11 *Jesus . . . baptized by John.* Cf. Mt 3:13-17 note.

1:12-13 The temptation. Cf. Mt 4:1-13 note.

1:13 *Tempted by Satan.* This phrase does not imply that the temptation lasted 40 days; the temptation was the significant climax of His 40-day sojourn in the wilderness.

Was with the wild beasts. Only Mark has this feature. It may be merely an indication of the rigors of Jesus' wilderness sojourn; but more probably it signifies that Jesus is the new Man to whom all beasts are subject as they were to Adam (Gn 1:26; 2:19-20), that with the coming of Jesus there has dawned the Messianic age of paradisal peace of which Isaiah spoke (Is 11:6-9), that the covenant of peace promised by Ezekiel is being inaugurated. (Eze 34:25-31)

14 Now after John was arrested, Jesus came into Galilee, preaching the gospel of God, [15] and saying, "The time is fulfilled, and the kingdom of God is at hand; repent, and believe in the gospel."

16 And passing along by the Sea of Galilee, he saw Simon and Andrew the brother of Simon casting a net in the sea; for they were fishermen. [17]And Jesus said to them, "Follow me and I will make you become fishers of men." [18]And immediately they left their nets and followed him. [19]And going on a little farther, he saw James the son of Zeb'e·dee and John his brother, who were in their boat mending the nets. [20]And immediately he called them; and they left their father Zeb'e·dee in the boat with the hired servants, and followed him.

21 And they went into Ca·per'na·um; and immediately on the sabbath he entered the synagogue and taught. [22]And they were astonished at his teaching, for he taught them as one who had authority, and not as the scribes. [23]And immediately there was in their synagogue a man with an unclean spirit; [24] and he cried out, "What have you to do with us, Jesus of Nazareth? Have you come to destroy us? I know who you are, the Holy One of God." [25] But Jesus rebuked him, saying, "Be silent, and come out of him!" [26]And the unclean spirit, convulsing him and crying with a loud voice, came out of him. [27]And they were all amazed, so that they questioned among themselves, saying, "What is this? A new teaching! With authority he commands even the unclean spirits, and they obey him." [28]And at once his fame spread everywhere throughout all the surrounding region of Galilee.

29 And immediately he[e] left the synagogue, and entered the house of Simon and Andrew, with James and John. [30] Now Simon's mother-in-law lay sick with a fever, and immediately they told him of her. [31]And he came and took her by the hand and lifted her up, and the fever left her; and she served them.

32 That evening, at sundown, they brought to him all who were sick or possessed with demons. [33]And the whole city was gathered together about the door. [34]And he healed many who were sick with various diseases, and cast out many demons; and he would not permit the demons to speak, because they knew him.

35 And in the morning, a great while before day, he rose and went out to a lonely place, and there he prayed. [36]And Simon and those who were with him pursued him, [37] and they found him and said to him, "Every one is searching for you." [38]And he said to them, "Let us go on to the next towns, that I may preach there also; for that is why I came out." [39]And he went throughout all Galilee, preaching in their synagogues and casting out demons.

[e] Other ancient authorities read *they*

1:14-45 CHRIST'S COMING IN MIGHT
           AND MERCY

1:14-45 Jesus ANNOUNCES that the promised and long-awaited (*fulfilled*, 15) *kingdom of God is at hand* and calls men to repentance and faith, bidding them turn to the God who is at this decisive hour turning in might and mercy to them. (14-15)

Jesus ENACTS the good news of God's reign by His sovereign call to discipleship (16-20), His word of authority which *even the unclean spirits must obey* (21-28), His healing of the *sick* and the *possessed* (29-34), His cleansing of the *leper* (40-42). Yet, though His *fame spreads* (28, 37, 45), He remains the selfless Son and Servant who works for the glory of God, to whom He *prays* (35), whose law He obeys (44). God shall at His time glorify His Servant-Son, not the demons (24-25, 34), not men who do not as yet understand the significance of His mighty acts. (43-44)

1:14 *Gospel of God.* Both the saving action and His saving proclamation are God's, two aspects

or phases of His one royal reign. (Cf. 2 Co 5:18-19, "God RECONCILED . . . entrusting to us the MESSAGE of reconciliation")

1:15 *The time is fulfilled.* The word for *time* implies "decisive time," the great moment foretold by the OT prophets in which God's final offer of His grace and His final summons to accept it and live by it appear in history. For this sense of time cf. Mt 26:18; Lk 19:44; Ro 5:6 ("right time").

Kingdom of God. Cf. Mt 3:2 note.

1:16-20 Calling of disciples. Cf. Mt 4:18-22 note.

1:24 *Holy One of God.* The unclean spirits are confronted by the Bearer of the Holy Spirit (8, 10) and recognize in Him the One destined to destroy them, since no compromise is possible between the Holy and the unclean.

1:27 *New teaching! . . . unclean spirits . . . obey him.* The authority of Jesus' Word establishes itself (teaching, 22); the power to *command* the *unclean spirits* only confirms it. With Jesus word and deed do not fall apart, as is so often the case with men; speech and act are one. (Cf. 2:8-11)

1:32 *At sundown.* The Sabbath ended at sun-

40 And a leper came to him beseeching him, and kneeling said to him, "If you will, you can make me clean." 41 Moved with pity, he stretched out his hand and touched him, and said to him, "I will; be clean." 42And immediately the leprosy left him, and he was made clean. 43And he sternly charged him, and sent him away at once, 44 and said to him, "See that you say nothing to any one; but go, show yourself to the priest, and offer for your cleansing what Moses commanded, for a proof to the people."*f* 45 But he went out and began to talk freely about it, and to spread the news, so that Jesus*g* could no longer openly enter a town, but was out in the country; and people came to him from every quarter.

Christ's Coming Provokes Contradiction

2:1 — 3:6

2 And when he returned to Ca·per'na·um after some days, it was reported that he was at home. 2And many were gathered together, so that there was no longer room for them, not even about the door; and he was preaching the word to them. 3And they came, bringing to him a paralytic carried by four men. 4And when they could not get near him because of the crowd, they removed the roof above him; and when they had made an opening, they let down the pallet on which the paralytic lay. 5And when Jesus saw their faith, he said to the paralytic, "My son, your sins are forgiven." 6 Now some of the scribes were sitting there, questioning in their hearts, 7 "Why does this man speak thus? It is blasphemy! Who can forgive sins but God alone?" 8And immediately Jesus, perceiving in his spirit that they thus questioned within themselves, said to them, "Why do you question thus in your hearts? 9 Which is easier, to say to the paralytic, 'Your sins are forgiven,' or to say, 'Rise, take up your pallet and walk'? 10 But that you may know that the Son of man has authority on earth to forgive sins"—he said to the paralytic— 11 "I say to you, rise, take up your pallet and go home." 12And he rose, and immediately took up the pallet and went out before them all; so that they were all amazed and glorified God, saying, "We never saw anything like this!"

13 He went out again beside the sea; and all the crowd gathered about him, and he taught them. 14And as he passed on, he saw Levi the son of Al·phae'us sitting at the tax office, and he said to him, "Follow me." And he rose and followed him.

15 And as he sat at table in his house, many tax collectors and sinners were sitting with Jesus and his disciples; for there were many who followed him. 16And the scribes of*h* the Pharisees, when they saw that he was eating with sinners and tax collectors, said to his disciples, "Why does he eat*i* with tax collectors and sinners?" 17And when

f Greek *to them*   *g* Greek *he*   *h* Other ancient authorities read *and*
i Other ancient authorities add *and drink*

down, and men could carry their *sick* and *possessed* without fear of violating the Law.

1:40-45 The healing of the leper. Cf. Mt 8:1-4 note.

1:45 *Openly enter a town.* Jesus did not want a fevered "Messianic movement"; He wanted repentant and believing men (15). The mob excitement generated by His presence in a crowded town would have frustrated His purpose.

2:1 — 3:6 In the account of five disputes in Galilee Mark shows how "religious" man (that is, man who wants to make his own legal righteousness count before God and therefore resists the grace of God) contradicts Christ and the Kingdom. Scribe and Pharisee oppose: the divine forgiveness pronounced by Jesus (2:1-12); Jesus' free fellowship at table with repentant sinners (2:13-17); Jesus the Bridegroom who brings the festal joy of the new age (2:18-22); the Son of Man who is Lord

even of the Sabbath (2:23-28); the Healer who saves life on the Sabbath, while they (the jealous guardians of its sanctity) plan to kill on the Sabbath. (3:1-6)

2:1-12 Healing of the paralytic. Cf. Mt 8:23 — 9:8 note and notes on Mt 9:1, 3, 5, 8.

2:12 *Amazed . . . glorified God . . ."we never saw anything like this!"* Here the uniqueness of Jesus' authority breaks upon men; they see in Him the glory of the God of Israel, the Lord "who forgives . . . iniquity, who heals . . . diseases." (Ps 103:3)

2:13-17 Calling of Levi and eating with sinners. Cf. Mt 9:9-13. See notes on Mt 9:9-17 and 9:10, 14, 15.

2:14 *Levi.* The first gospel calls him Matthew and includes "Matthew the tax collector" in the list of the Twelve (Mt 9:9; 10:3); perhaps Levi came to be known as Matthew ("gift of the Lord") in the Christian community.

Jesus heard it, he said to them, "Those who are well have no need of a physician, but those who are sick; I came not to call the righteous, but sinners."

18 Now John's disciples and the Pharisees were fasting; and people came and said to him, "Why do John's disciples and the disciples of the Pharisees fast, but your disciples do not fast?" 19And Jesus said to them, "Can the wedding guests fast while the bridegroom is with them? As long as they have the bridegroom with them, they cannot fast. 20 The days will come, when the bridegroom is taken away from them, and then they will fast in that day. 21 No one sews a piece of unshrunk cloth on an old garment; if he does, the patch tears away from it, the new from the old, and a worse tear is made. 22And no one puts new wine into old wineskins; if he does, the wine will burst the skins, and the wine is lost, and so are the skins; but new wine is for fresh skins."*j*

23 One sabbath he was going through the grainfields; and as they made their way his disciples began to pluck heads of grain. 24And the Pharisees said to him, "Look, why are they doing what is not lawful on the sabbath?" 25And he said to them, "Have you never read what David did, when he was in need and was hungry, he and those who were with him: 26 how he entered the house of God, when A·bi'a·thar was high priest, and ate the bread of the Presence, which it is not lawful for any but the priests to eat, and also gave it to those who were with him?" 27And he said to them, "The sabbath was made for man, not man for the sabbath; 28 so the Son of man is lord even of the sabbath."

3 Again he entered the synagogue, and a man was there who had a withered hand. 2And they watched him, to see whether he would heal him on the sabbath, so that they might accuse him. 3And he said to the man who had the withered hand, "Come here." 4And he said to them, "Is it lawful on the sabbath to do good or to do harm, to save life or to kill?" But they were silent. 5And he looked around at them with anger, grieved at their hardness of heart, and said to the man, "Stretch out your hand." He stretched it out, and his hand was restored. 6 The Pharisees went out, and immediately held counsel with the He·ro'di·ans against him, how to destroy him.

Christ's Response to Contradiction

3:7—8:30

7 Jesus withdrew with his disciples to the sea, and a great multitude from Galilee followed; also from Judea 8 and Jerusalem and Id·u·me'a and from beyond the Jordan and from about Tyre and Sidon a great multitude, hearing all that he did,

j Other ancient authorities omit *but new wine is for fresh skins*

2:18-22 Jesus the Bridegroom. Cf. Mt 9:14-17. See notes on Mt 9:9-17 and 9:14, 15.

2:23-28 Plucking grain on the Sabbath. Cf. Mt 12:1-8. See notes on Mt 12:1-21 and 12:3, 4.

2:26 *Abiathar*. The *high priest* in the OT story of *David* and the (sacred) *bread of the Presence* is called Ahimelech (1 Sm 21:1); his son was Abiathar (1 Sm 22:20), closely associated with David. Some important manuscripts omit the reference to Abiathar, as do Matthew and Luke.

2:27-28 *Sabbath was made for man, not man for the sabbath; so the Son of man is lord even of the sabbath.* Jesus saw in the law of God one unified will, that of love (12:28-34). The God who asks love of man is the God who shows love to man — even the rabbis asserted that *the sabbath was made for man* (in order to relax the sabbath-law in cases of dire necessity) but the idea that a man can be *lord . . . of the sabbath* was unheard of in Judaism, and rightly so; Jesus can override the Sabbath only because He is *the Son of man* who

brings the love of a forgiving God to man (2:10), who comes to serve and to give His life as a ransom for many (10:45). The love of God makes Jesus the end of the Law.

3:1-6 *To save life or to kill on the sabbath*. Cf. Mt 12:9-14. See note on Mt 12:1-21. If the Sabbath was made for man and is, as the Lord's Day, the day on which His love is to be manifested, it is the Pharisees, not Jesus, who are violating the Sabbath. (6)

3:5 *Anger* mingled with grief is Jesus' reaction to those who in *their hardness of heart* have no eyes for the divine goodness and mercy revealed to them in the works of Jesus.

3:6 *Herodians*, partisans of the Herods and Roman rule, whose cooperation would be needed *to destroy* Jesus since the Jewish authorities did not have the right to inflict capital punishment. (Jn 18:31)

3:7—8:30 Three motifs dominate this section of the gospel. First, the contradicted Christ main-

came to him. 9And he told his disciples to have a boat ready for him because of the crowd, lest they should crush him; 10 for he had healed many, so that all who had diseases pressed upon him to touch him. 11And whenever the unclean spirits beheld him, they fell down before him and cried out, "You are the Son of God." 12And he strictly ordered them not to make him known.

13 And he went up on the mountain, and called to him those whom he desired; and they came to him. 14And he appointed twelve,*k* to be with him, and to be sent out to preach 15 and have authority to cast out demons: 16 Simon*x* whom he surnamed Peter; 17 James the son of Zeb'e·dee and John the brother of James, whom he surnamed Bo·a·ner'ges, that is, sons of thunder; 18Andrew, and Philip, and Bartholomew, and Matthew, and Thomas, and James the son of Al·phae'us, and Thaddaeus, and Simon the Ca·na·nae'an, 19 and Judas Is·car'i·ot, who betrayed him.

Then he went home; 20 and the crowd came together again, so that they could not even eat. 21And when his family heard it, they went out to seize him, for people were saying, "He is beside himself." 22And the scribes who came down from Jerusalem said, "He is possessed by Beelzebul, and by the prince of demons he casts out the demons." 23And he called them to him, and said to them in parables, "How can Satan

k Other ancient authorities add *whom also he named apostles*
x Other authorities read *demons.* 16 *So he appointed the twelve: Simon*

tains His will of mercy toward all who will accept the gracious reign of God present in His words and works. He heals, frees men from the power of demons, raises the dead, invites men in great numbers to the fellowship of the common meal, and gives a Gentile woman part in the abundant mercies of the God of Israel. The appointment and sending of the Twelve is the declaration of His mercy to the whole of Israel (12 tribes).

Second, the cleavage between Christ and those who oppose Him becomes ever sharper and deeper. The line of demarcation is drawn between Jesus and His "friends," the scribes and Pharisees, His fellow townsmen, those who are willing to call Him prophet but not to confess Him as the Christ. The death of John the Baptist is prophetic of Jesus' own fate. But even the bitterest opposition cannot make Him swerve from His course as the obedient Son and the Servant Christ. He withdraws before opposition, silences the demons who proclaim Him Son of God, "cannot" do mighty works in the face of His townsmen's unbelief, and refuses to give the sign from heaven that would satisfy arrogant unbelief. He executes judgment only by speaking in parables, which take from the man who has not even what he has.

Third, Christ deepens the communion between Himself and His disciples until they, and they alone, are capable of confessing Him as Christ. He appoints the Twelve to be with Him and gives them a share in His Messianic task and declares His disciples to be His true family. His teaching in parables is for His disciples a deepened revelation of the kingdom of God which equips them for their future task as His apostles. He permits them to witness His victory of death and comes to them across the waters. He evokes from them the confession which He had refused from the demons, the confession of faith which sets them apart from both His enemies and His admirers and binds them wholly to Himself forever, the confession: "You are the Christ."

3:7-12 JESUS WITHDRAWS, HEALS MANY, SILENCES DEMONS

3:7 *Jesus withdrew;* He meets the will to destroy Him (6) with the will to serve as the quiet Servant of God who "will not wrangle or cry aloud." (Mt 12:19-20 f.; 12:15-21)

3:12 *Ordered them not to make him known.* Not the defeated demons in their terror but the men given Him by God shall confess Him before men, in faith. (13-19)

3:13-19 THE APPOINTMENT OF THE TWELVE

3:13 *Called.* Cf. Mt 4:21 note.

3:14 *Appointed,* literally "made"; the apostles are His creation. (Cf. 2 Co 4:5-6)

3:16 *Surnamed Peter.* For the significance of the name cf. Mt 16:18 note.

3:17 *Surnamed Boanerges . . . sons of thunder,* probably because of their impetuous, "stormy" temperament. (9:38; Lk 9:54)

3:18 *Cananaean.* The name which distinguishes this Simon from Simon Peter indicates that he had been a member of the fiercely nationalistic Jewish party, the Zealots. (Cf. Lk 6:15; Acts 1:13)

3:20-30 BY THE PRINCE OF DEMONS HE CASTS OUT DEMONS: BLASPHEMY AGAINST HOLY SPIRIT

3:20-30 For the *Beelzebul* controversy (the deepest cleavage between Jesus and His contemporaries) and the warning concerning the *blasphemy against the Holy Spirit* see Mt 12:22-37 note.

3:20 *They could not even eat. They* are Jesus and His disciples, a particularly clear case of how the "we" of Peter's preaching shines through in Mark's account. See the Introduction, par. 7.

3:21 *His family.* Cf. 31, "his mother . . . brothers." This verse illustrates how Jesus' consuming passion for ministry was misunderstood and misinterpreted even by family and friends.

cast out Satan? 24If a kingdom is divided against itself, that kingdom cannot stand. 25And if a house is divided against itself, that house will not be able to stand. 26And if Satan has risen up against himself and is divided, he cannot stand, but is coming to an end. 27But no one can enter a strong man's house and plunder his goods, unless he first binds the strong man; then indeed he may plunder his house.

28 "Truly, I say to you, all sins will be forgiven the sons of men, and whatever blasphemies they utter; 29but whoever blasphemes against the Holy Spirit never has forgiveness, but is guilty of an eternal sin"— 30for they had said, "He has an unclean spirit."

31 And his mother and his brothers came; and standing outside they sent to him and called him. 32And a crowd was sitting about him; and they said to him, "Your mother and your brothers*l* are outside, asking for you." 33And he replied, "Who are my mother and my brothers?" 34And looking around on those who sat about him, he said, "Here are my mother and my brothers! 35Whoever does the will of God is my brother, and sister, and mother."

4 Again he began to teach beside the sea. And a very large crowd gathered about him, so that he got into a boat and sat in it on the sea; and the whole crowd was beside the sea on the land. 2And he taught them many things in parables, and in his teaching he said to them: 3 "Listen! A sower went out to sow. 4And as he sowed, some seed fell along the path, and the birds came and devoured it. 5 Other seed fell on rocky ground, where it had not much soil, and immediately it sprang up, since it had no depth of soil; 6 and when the sun rose it was scorched, and since it had no root it withered away. 7 Other seed fell among thorns and the thorns grew up and choked it, and it yielded no grain. 8And other seeds fell into good soil and brought forth grain, growing up and increasing and yielding thirtyfold and sixtyfold and a hundredfold." 9And he said, "He who has ears to hear, let him hear."

10 And when he was alone, those who were about him with the twelve asked him concerning the parables. 11And he said to them, "To you has been given the secret of the kingdom of God, but for those outside everything is in parables; 12 so that they may indeed see but not perceive, and may indeed hear but not understand; lest they should turn again, and be forgiven." 13And he said to them, "Do you not understand this parable? How then will you understand all the parables? 14 The sower sows the word. 15And these are the ones along the path, where the word is sown; when they hear, Satan immediately comes and takes away the word which is sown in them. 16And these in like manner are the ones sown upon rocky ground, who, when they hear the word, immediately receive it with joy; 17 and they have no root in themselves, but endure for a while; then, when tribulation or persecution arises on account of the word, immediately they fall away.*m* 18And others are the ones sown among thorns; they are those who hear the word, 19 but the cares of the world, and the delight

l Other early authorities add *and your sisters*   *m* Or *stumble*

3:31-35 THE FAMILY OF JESUS

3:31-35 Cf. Mt 12:43-50 note.

3:35 *Sister.* Woman has her place of undiminished honor in the family of God. (Gl 3:28)

4:1-9 THE PARABLE OF THE SOWER

4:1-9 Cf. Mt 13:1-9 note; 13:18-23 note.

4:10-25 THE PURPOSE OF TEACHING IN PARABLES

4:10-12, 21-25 Cf. Mt 13:1-52 note; 13:10-17.

4:13-20 Cf. Mt 13:18-23 note.

4:11 *The secret of the kingdom.* The phrase recalls the vision of Dn 2. The "secret" is the fact that the Kingdom "is at hand" in the person of Jesus (1:15); in His Word and work God is revealing what He had promised through Daniel for "the latter days," the establishment of a kingdom by "the God of heaven," which shall put an end to the kingdoms of this world but shall itself never be destroyed (Dn 2:28, 44-45). See the whole of Dn 2 for a portrayal of the kingdom of God as opposed to earthly kingdoms, coming in unspectacular form ("a stone . . . cut out by no human hand," 34) as a kingdom not of this world but finally and eternally triumphant. To have this secret is God's gift; to have it not is the guilt of refusing God's revelation (cf. 25) and calls forth God's judgment, as Isaiah had pronounced it. (12; cf. Is 6:9-10)

4:13 *Understand this parable . . . understand all the parables?* The key to the parable of the sower is Jesus as the presence of God's kingdom among men. And He is the key to all the parables; the parable of the self-growing seed (26-29) and of the mustard seed (30-32) also tell His story.

in riches, and the desire for other things, enter in and choke the word, and it proves unfruitful. 20 But those that were sown upon the good soil are the ones who hear the word and accept it and bear fruit, thirtyfold and sixtyfold and a hundred-fold."

21 And he said to them, "Is a lamp brought in to be put under a bushel, or under a bed, and not on a stand? 22 For there is nothing hid, except to be made manifest; nor is anything secret, except to come to light. 23 If any man has ears to hear, let him hear." 24And he said to them, "Take heed what you hear; the measure you give will be the measure you get, and still more will be given you. 25 For to him who has will more be given; and from him who has not, even what he has will be taken away."

26 And he said, "The kingdom of God is as if a man should scatter seed upon the ground, 27 and should sleep and rise night and day, and the seed should sprout and grow, he knows not how. 28 The earth produces of itself, first the blade, then the ear, then the full grain in the ear. 29 But when the grain is ripe, at once he puts in the sickle, because the harvest has come."

30 And he said, "With what can we compare the kingdom of God, or what parable shall we use for it? 31 It is like a grain of mustard seed, which, when sown upon the ground, is the smallest of all the seeds on earth; 32 yet when it is sown it grows up and becomes the greatest of all shrubs, and puts forth large branches, so that the birds of the air can make nests in its shade."

33 With many such parables he spoke the word to them, as they were able to hear it; 34 he did not speak to them without a parable, but privately to his own disciples he explained everything.

35 On that day, when evening had come, he said to them, "Let us go across to the other side." 36And leaving the crowd, they took him with them in the boat, just as he was. And other boats were with him. 37And a great storm of wind arose, and the waves beat into the boat, so that the boat was already filling. 38 But he was in the stern, asleep on the cushion; and they woke him and said to him, "Teacher, do you not care if we perish?" 39And he awoke and rebuked the wind, and said to the sea, "Peace! Be still!" And the wind ceased, and there was a great calm. 40 He said to them, "Why are you afraid? Have you no faith?" 41And they were filled with awe, and said to one another, "Who then is this, that even wind and sea obey him?"

4:21-25 If the message of the parable is the story of Jesus Christ, the Son of God (1:1), if it is the Gospel of God (1:14), it must and will emerge from the hiddenness of the parable's veiled utterance and *come to light*. In that coming to light the apostles have a decisive role to play (3:14, "be sent out to preach"); it is therefore of crucial importance that they should have *ears to hear* and *take heed what* they *hear*. The *measure* of obedience to the word which they give will be the measure of the blessing which they will *get* in their ministry; fidelity is all. (Cf. 1 Co 4:1-2)

4:25 *To him who has*. In the Gospel of Matthew Jesus applies this standard to both revelation (Mt 13:12) and ministry (Mt 25:29). Here too both ideas are present.

4:26-29 PARABLE OF SEED GROWING SECRETLY

4:26-29 This parable, only in Mark, conveys both a warning and a word of encouragement to Jesus' disciples. However important their role may be (21-25), they are not to imagine that the Kingdom is their kingdom or its triumph their triumph; the Kingdom remains God's mysteriously creative work. He is "Lord of the harvest" (Mt 9:38). This serves for encouragement also; however slow and unspectacular the "progress" of the Kingdom may be, the outcome is in the sure hands of the Creator. Men may pray, "Thy kingdom come," with patience and confidence.

4:29 *Harvest*. Cf. Mt 9:37; Jn 4:35.

4:30-34 PARABLE OF THE MUSTARD SEED

4:30-34 Cf. Mt 13:31-33 note.

4:33 *As they were able to hear it,* that is, in terms familiar to their experience (sower, seed, mustard seed). The parables speak plainly to those who have not rejected Jesus, the key to the parables.

4:35-41 THE STILLING OF THE STORM

4:35-41 Cf. Mt 8:23 – 9:8 note and 8:26 note.

The story is told in simple language, and the details of the account *(other boats, boat was already filling, cushion, said to one another)* leave the impression that the details come from one who experienced the event. The account indicates strongly that Mark "became Peter's interpreter." (Cf. Introduction, par. 7)

4:39 The disciples are made conscious of their frail humanity in the presence of this Lord of the waves. Jesus deepens His communion with the disciples by using His power in the service of compassion for them and by using the event to build up their faith. (40)

5 They came to the other side of the sea, to the country of the Ger´a·senes.[n] 2And when he had come out of the boat, there met him out of the tombs a man with an unclean spirit, 3 who lived among the tombs; and no one could bind him any more, even with a chain; 4 for he had often been bound with fetters and chains, but the chains he wrenched apart, and the fetters he broke in pieces; and no one had the strength to subdue him. 5 Night and day among the tombs and on the mountains he was always crying out, and bruising himself with stones. 6And when he saw Jesus from afar, he ran and worshiped him; 7 and crying out with a loud voice, he said, "What have you to do with me, Jesus, Son of the Most High God? I adjure you by God, do not torment me." 8 For he had said to him, "Come out of the man, you unclean spirit!" 9And Jesus[o] asked him, "What is your name?" He replied, "My name is Legion; for we are many." 10And he begged him eagerly not to send them out of the country. 11 Now a great herd of swine was feeding there on the hillside; 12 and they begged him, "Send us to the swine, let us enter them." 13 So he gave them leave. And the unclean spirits came out, and entered the swine; and the herd, numbering about two thousand, rushed down the steep bank into the sea, and were drowned in the sea.

14 The herdsmen fled, and told it in the city and in the country. And people came to see what it was that had happened. 15And they came to Jesus, and saw the demoniac sitting there, clothed and in his right mind, the man who had had the legion; and they were afraid. 16And those who had seen it told what had happened to the demoniac and to the swine. 17And they began to beg Jesus[p] to depart from their neighborhood. 18And as he was getting into the boat, the man who had been possessed with demons begged him that he might be with him. 19 But he refused, and said to him, "Go home to your friends, and tell them how much the Lord has done for you, and how he has had mercy on you." 20And he went away and began to proclaim in the De·cap´o·lis how much Jesus had done for him; and all men marveled.

21 And when Jesus had crossed again in the boat to the other side, a great crowd gathered about him; and he was beside the sea. 22 Then came one of the rulers of the synagogue, Ja´i·rus by name; and seeing him, he fell at his feet, 23 and besought him, saying, "My little daughter is at the point of death. Come and lay your hands on her, so that she may be made well, and live." 24And he went with him.

And a great crowd followed him and thronged about him. 25And there was a woman who had had a flow of blood for twelve years, 26 and who had suffered much under many physicians, and had spent all that she had, and was no better but rather grew worse. 27 She had heard the reports about Jesus, and came up behind him in the crowd and touched his garment. 28 For she said, "If I touch even his garments, I shall

[n] Other ancient authorities read *Gergesenes*, some *Gadarenes* [o] Greek *he* [p] Greek *him*

5:1-20 THE DEMONIAC OF GERASA

5:1-20 Cf. Mt 8:28-34 note; cf. Mt 8:23 — 9:8 note. The line of demarcation between Jesus and men is very apparent here, where some want to rid themselves of Him (because He costs them swine) and one man becomes the messenger of His mercy. All marvel; not all respond. (20)

5:1 *Gerasenes.* Both here and in Matthew and Luke the manuscripts fluctuate between Gerasenes, Gergesenes, and Gadarenes.

5:9 *Legion,* the largest unit of the Roman army; then used to indicate any large number. (Cf. Mt 26:53)

5:13 *Drowned in the sea.* Many are offended at the death of the swine here. We had best honor the decision of Him who made both swine and man and gave His life for man.

5:18 *Begged him that he might be with him.* Jesus alone determines who shall be with Him; He calls and appoints. (1:20; 3:14)

5:19 *Go home . . . and tell them.* This contrasts strangely with Jesus' usual command that healed persons tell no one (1:44; 7:36; 8:26). The exception may be due to the fact that the miracle took place in Gentile territory (swine, 11; Decapolis, 20), so that the proclamation of "how much the Lord has done for you" would not impede Jesus' real mission but might serve as preparation for a later mission to the Gentiles in that region.

5:20 *Decapolis.* (Cf. Mt 4:25 note.)

5:21-43 JAIRUS' DAUGHTER AND THE WOMAN WITH THE FLOW OF BLOOD

5:21-43 Cf. Mt 9:18-34 note; 9:20, 22, 23 notes. In these two mighty acts the majesty of Him whom men dare to contradict is apparent. He is Lord not only over the sea and the demons but over death itself; and His vigilant compassion can hear and answer the unuttered petition of the woman who dared only to touch His garment. He who has eyes to see and ears to hear cannot rank Him with John or Elijah or one of the prophets (8:28); He must be confessed as the Christ. (8:29)

be made well." [29]And immediately the hemorrhage ceased; and she felt in her body that she was healed of her disease. [30]And Jesus, perceiving in himself that power had gone forth from him, immediately turned about in the crowd, and said, "Who touched my garments?" [31]And his disciples said to him, "You see the crowd pressing around you, and yet you say, 'Who touched me?' " [32]And he looked around to see who had done it. [33] But the woman, knowing what had been done to her, came in fear and trembling and fell down before him, and told him the whole truth. [34]And he said to her, "Daughter, your faith has made you well; go in peace, and be healed of your disease."

35 While he was still speaking, there came from the ruler's house some who said, "Your daughter is dead. Why trouble the Teacher any further?" [36] But ignoring[q] what they said, Jesus said to the ruler of the synagogue, "Do not fear, only believe." [37]And he allowed no one to follow him except Peter and James and John the brother of James. [38] When they came to the house of the ruler of the synagogue, he saw a tumult, and people weeping and wailing loudly. [39]And when he had entered, he said to them, "Why do you make a tumult and weep? The child is not dead but sleeping." [40]And they laughed at him. But he put them all outside, and took the child's father and mother and those who were with him, and went in where the child was. [41] Taking her by the hand he said to her, "Talitha cumi"; which means, "Little girl, I say to you, arise." [42]And immediately the girl got up and walked (she was twelve years of age), and they were immediately overcome with amazement. [43]And he strictly charged them that no one should know this, and told them to give her something to eat.

6 He went away from there and came to his own country; and his disciples followed him. [2]And on the sabbath he began to teach in the synagogue; and many who heard him were astonished, saying, "Where did this man get all this? What is the wisdom given to him? What mighty works are wrought by his hands! [3] Is not this the carpenter, the son of Mary and brother of James and Joses and Judas and Simon, and are not his sisters here with us?" And they took offense[r] at him. [4]And Jesus said to them, "A prophet is not without honor, except in his own country, and among his own kin, and in his own house." [5]And he could do no mighty work there, except that he laid his hands upon a few sick people and healed them. [6]And he marveled because of their unbelief.

And he went about among the villages teaching.

7 And he called to him the twelve, and began to send them out two by two, and gave them authority over the unclean spirits. [8] He charged them to take nothing for their journey except a staff; no bread, no bag, no money in their belts; [9] but to wear sandals and not put on two tunics. [10]And he said to them, "Where you enter a house, stay there until you leave the place. [11]And if any place will not receive you and they refuse to hear you, when you leave, shake off the dust that is on your feet for a testimony against them." [12] So they went out and preached that men should repent.

[q] Or overhearing. Other ancient authorities read hearing   [r] Or stumbled

---

5:33 *Fear and trembling.* Since a woman with a flow of blood was unclean according to the Law, she feared rebuke from the Man whom her touch had defiled. But Jesus, who had touched and healed the unclean leper (1:41), cannot be defiled.

5:40 *They laughed.* This is the only place in the NT where Jesus' presence evokes laughter, just where He manifests Himself as Overcomer of death, which silences laughter.

6:1-6a JESUS REJECTED AT NAZARETH

6:1-6a The men of Nazareth are *astonished* at the *wisdom* and the *mighty works* of Jesus of Nazareth but take *offense* at the *carpenter* whose *mother, brothers,* and *sisters* they know so well. Their *unbelief* makes revelation impossible; He who met every need of man with God's creative power but gave no sign to questioning and de-

manding unbelief (cf. 8:11-13) *could do no mighty work there.*

6:3 *Son of Mary and brother of James.* The much-debated question whether the brothers of Jesus were children of Joseph and Mary born after Jesus or children of Joseph by a previous marriage or Jesus' cousins will probably never be settled to everyone's satisfaction. The first suggestion (that they were children of Joseph and Mary) seems the most natural.

6:6b-13 THE SENDING OF THE TWELVE

6:6b-13 Cf. Mt 10:1-4; 10:5-15 notes. Jesus draws His disciples closer to Himself by employing them in the extension of His Messianic mission.

6:7 *The twelve.* Cf. 3:13-19.

6:12 *Men should repent. Repent* is shorthand for the message summed up in 1:15.

13And they cast out many demons, and anointed with oil many that were sick and healed them.

14 King Herod heard of it; for Jesus's name had become known. Some[t] said, "John the baptizer has been raised from the dead; that is why these powers are at work in him." 15 But others said, "It is E·li'jah." And others said, "It is a prophet, like one of the prophets of old." 16 But when Herod heard of it he said, "John, whom I beheaded, has been raised." 17 For Herod had sent and seized John, and bound him in prison for the sake of He·ro'di·as, his brother Philip's wife; because he had married her. 18 For John said to Herod, "It is not lawful for you to have your brother's wife." 19And He·ro'di·as had a grudge against him, and wanted to kill him. But she could not, 20 for Herod feared John, knowing that he was a righteous and holy man, and kept him safe. When he heard him, he was much perplexed; and yet he heard him gladly. 21 But an opportunity came when Herod on his birthday gave a banquet for his courtiers and officers and the leading men of Galilee. 22 For when He·ro'di·as' daughter came in and danced, she pleased Herod and his guests; and the king said to the girl, "Ask me for whatever you wish, and I will grant it." 23And he vowed to her, "Whatever you ask me, I will give you, even half of my kingdom." 24And she went out, and said to her mother, "What shall I ask?" And she said, "The head of John the baptizer." 25And she came in immediately with haste to the king, and asked, saying, "I want you to give me at once the head of John the Baptist on a platter." 26And the king was exceedingly sorry; but because of his oaths and his guests he did not want to break his word to her. 27And immediately the king sent a soldier of the guard and gave orders to bring his head. He went and beheaded him in the prison, 28 and brought his head on a platter, and gave it to the girl; and the girl gave it to her mother. 29 When his disciples heard of it, they came and took his body, and laid it in a tomb.

30 The apostles returned to Jesus, and told him all that they had done and taught. 31And he said to them, "Come away by yourselves to a lonely place, and rest a while." For many were coming and going, and they had no leisure even to eat. 32And they went away in the boat to a lonely place by themselves. 33 Now many saw them going, and knew them, and they ran there on foot from all the towns, and got there ahead of them. **34As he went ashore he saw a great throng, and he had compassion on them, because they were like sheep without a shepherd; and he began to teach them many** things. 35And when it grew late, his disciples came to him and said, "This is a lonely place, and the hour is now late; 36 send them away, to go into the country and villages round about and buy themselves something to eat." 37 But he answered them, "You give them something to eat." And they said to him, "Shall we go and buy two hundred denarii[u] worth of bread, and give it to them to eat?" 38And he said to them, "How many loaves have you? Go and see." And when they had found out, they said, "Five, and two fish." 39 Then he commanded them all to sit down by companies upon the green grass. 40 So they sat down in groups, by hundreds and by fifties. 41And taking the five loaves and the two fish he looked up to heaven, and blessed, and broke the loaves, and gave them to the disciples to set before the people; and he divided the two fish among them all. 42And they all ate and were satisfied. 43And they took up twelve

---

[s] Greek *his*   [t] Other ancient authorities read *he*   [u] The denarius was a day's wage for a laborer

---

6:13 *Anointed with oil.* Healing by anointing with oil is mentioned only here and in Ja 5:14 as an act involving the power of God (Lk 10:34 records common medicinal practice). Neither passage explains the significance of the oil; James stresses the power of the accompanying prayer.

6:14-29 THE DEATH OF JOHN THE BAPTIST

6:14-29 Cf. Mt 14:1-12 note. Herod senses that in Jesus the *powers* which he thought he had banished when he executed John are *at work;* the disquieting voice of God calling him to account has not been silenced. The death of John the Baptist, told here and not in its natural place in the

sequence of events (cf. 1:14), is prophetic of Jesus' fate (cf. Mk 9:12-13; Mt 17:12-13). Both in the village (1-6) and in the royal court men are turning against Him; the cleavage deepens because of His teaching.

6:30-44 THE RETURN OF THE TWELVE AND THE FEEDING OF THE 5,000

6:30-44 Cf. Mt 14:15-21 note. The contradicted Christ still invites men to Himself by offering them the fellowship of the meal which His *compassion* (34) provides.

6:41 *Blessed.* Jesus speaks the blessing as a Jewish housefather would at his table.

baskets full of broken pieces and of the fish. 44And those who ate the loaves were five thousand men.

45 Immediately he made his disciples get into the boat and go before him to the other side, to Beth·sa'i·da, while he dismissed the crowd. 46And after he had taken leave of them, he went up on the mountain to pray. 47And when evening came, the boat was out on the sea, and he was alone on the land. 48And he saw that they were making headway painfully, for the wind was against them. And about the fourth watch of the night he came to them, walking on the sea. He meant to pass by them, 49 but when they saw him walking on the sea they thought it was a ghost, and cried out; 50 for they all saw him, and were terrified. But immediately he spoke to them and said, "Take heart, it is I; have no fear." 51And he got into the boat with them and the wind ceased. And they were utterly astounded, 52 for they did not understand about the loaves, but their hearts were hardened.

53 And when they had crossed over, they came to land at Gen·nes'a·ret, and moored to the shore. 54And when they got out of the boat, immediately the people recognized him, 55 and ran about the whole neighborhood and began to bring sick people on their pallets to any place where they heard he was. 56And wherever he came, in villages, cities, or country, they laid the sick in the market places, and besought him that they might touch even the fringe of his garment; and as many as touched it were made well.

7 Now when the Pharisees gathered together to him, with some of the scribes, who had come from Jerusalem, 2 they saw that some of his disciples ate with hands defiled, that is, unwashed. 3 (For the Pharisees, and all the Jews, do not eat unless they wash their hands, [v] observing the tradition of the elders; 4 and when they come from the market place, they do not eat unless they purify [w] themselves; [o]and there are many other traditions which they observe, the washing of cups and pots and vessels of bronze. [x]) 5And the Pharisees and the scribes asked him, "Why do your disciples not live [y] according to the tradition of the elders, but eat with hands defiled?" 6And he said to them, "Well did I·sa'iah prophesy of you hypocrites, as it is written,

'This people honors me with their lips,
    but their heart is far from me;
7   in vain do they worship me,
    teaching as doctrines the precepts of men.'
8   You leave the commandment of God, and hold fast the tradition of men."

9 And he said to them, "You have a fine way of rejecting the commandment of God, in order to keep your tradition! 10 For Moses said, 'Honor your father and your mother'; and, 'He who speaks evil of father or mother, let him surely die'; 11 but you say, 'If a man tells his father or his mother, What you would have gained from me is Corban' (that is, given to God) [z]— 12 then you no longer permit him to do anything for his father or mother, 13 thus making void the word of God through your tradition which you hand on. And many such things you do."

14 And he called the people to him again, and said to them, "Hear me, all of you, and understand: 15 there is nothing outside a man which by going into him can defile him; but the things which come out of a man are what defile him." [a] 17And when he had entered the house, and left the people, his disciples asked him about the parable. 18And he said to them, "Then are you also without understanding? Do you not see

[v] One Greek word is of uncertain meaning and is not translated   [w] Other ancient authorities read *baptize*
[o] Other ancient authorities read *and they do not eat anything from the market unless they purify it*
[x] Other ancient authorities add *and beds*   [y] Greek *walk*   [z]Or *an offering*
[a] Other ancient authorities add verse 16, "*If any man has ears to hear, let him hear*"

6:45-56 JESUS WALKS ON THE SEA

   6:45-56 Cf. Mt 14:22-36

   6:48 *Fourth watch of the night.* Cf. Mt 14:25 note.

   6:52 *They did not understand about the loaves.* If their *hearts* had not been dulled by unbelief (*hardened*), they could have known that He who multiplied the *loaves* could come to them, not as a ghost (49) but as a person, and bring peace to them.

   6:56 *Fringe of his garment.* Cf. 5:28. The compassion that reached out to the woman is there for all who will follow her example.

7:1-23 THE TRADITION OF THE ELDERS:
          WHAT DEFILES A MAN

   7:1-23 Cf. Mt 15:1-20 note.

   7:11 *Corban,* literally "offering." Matthew translates the word ("*given to God*"). Cf. Mt 15:5-6 note.

that whatever goes into a man from outside cannot defile him, [19] since it enters, not his heart but his stomach, and so passes on?"[b] (Thus he declared all foods clean.) [20]And he said, "What comes out of a man is what defiles a man. [21] For from within, out of the heart of man, come evil thoughts, fornication, theft, murder, adultery, [22] coveting, wickedness, deceit, licentiousness, envy, slander, pride, foolishness. [23]All these evil things come from within, and they defile a man."

[24] And from there he arose and went away to the region of Tyre and Sidon.[c] And he entered a house, and would not have any one know it; yet he could not be hid. [25] But immediately a woman, whose little daughter was possessed by an unclean spirit, heard of him, and came and fell down at his feet. [26] Now the woman was a Greek, a Sy·ro·phoe·ni′cian by birth. And she begged him to cast the demon out of her daughter. [27]And he said to her, "Let the children first be fed, for it is not right to take the children's bread and throw it to the dogs." [28] But she answered him, "Yes, Lord; yet even the dogs under the table eat the children's crumbs." [29]And he said to her, "For this saying you may go your way; the demon has left your daughter." [30]And she went home, and found the child lying in bed, and the demon gone.

[31] Then he returned from the region of Tyre, and went through Sidon to the Sea of Galilee, through the region of the De·cap′o·lis. [32]And they brought to him a man who was deaf and had an impediment in his speech; and they besought him to lay his hand upon him. [33]And taking him aside from the multitude privately, he put his fingers into his ears, and he spat and touched his tongue; [34] and looking up to heaven, he sighed, and said to him, "Eph·pha′tha," that is, "Be opened." [35]And his ears were opened, his tongue was released, and he spoke plainly. [36]And he charged them to tell no one; but the more he charged them, the more zealously they proclaimed it. [37]And they were astonished beyond measure, saying, "He has done all things well; he even makes the deaf hear and the dumb speak."

8 In those days, when again a great crowd had gathered, and they had nothing to eat, he called his disciples to him, and said to them, [2] "I have compassion on the crowd, because they have been with me now three days, and have nothing to eat; [3] and if I send them away hungry to their homes, they will faint on the way; and some of them have come a long way." [4]And his disciples answered him, "How can one feed these men with bread here in the desert?" [5]And he asked them, "How many loaves have you?" They said, "Seven." [6]And he commanded the crowd to sit down on the ground; and he took the seven loaves, and having given thanks he broke them and gave

[b] Or is evacuated   [c] Other ancient authorities omit and Sidon

---

7:19 *Thus he declared all foods clean.* Later on the Lord had to remind Peter of this. (Acts 10:9-15)

7:22 *Foolishness* is not only intellectual but moral and religious. Cf. the use of "fool" in Lk 12:20-21 of the man who "lays up treasure for himself, and is not rich toward God."

7:24-30 THE SYROPHOENICIAN WOMAN

7:24-30 Cf. Mt 15:21-28 note.

7:26 *A Greek, a Syrophoenician by birth,* a Greek-speaking inhabitant of Syrophoenicia, a district so called because ancient Phoenicia belonged to the Roman province of Syria and to distinguish it from Libophoenicia around Carthage.

7:31-37 HE HAS DONE ALL THINGS WELL

7:31-37 The mercy of Christ restores the deaf man to health and to the society from which his impediment had shut him out. The response of those who witnessed the act of restoration (37, *done all things well*) recalls the "very good" of creation (Gn 1:31). The coming of the Kingdom is the new creation. (Cf. Is 35:5-6; Mt 11:5)

7:33 *Spat.* Cf. 8:23; Jn 9:33. This feature is found only in cases where communication with the person to be healed is difficult; since spittle was held to have curative powers in Judaism (both by itself and in connection with magical spells), the action indicates to the deaf man the presence of the Healer. The cure is brought about simply by the mighty word of Jesus (34), which eliminates any idea of magic.

8:1-10 THE FEEDING OF THE 4,000

8:1-10 The great gesture of offered fellowship is repeated (cf. 6:30-44). It is difficult to say whether the account of the feeding of 4,000 is intended merely to emphasize by repetition Jesus' will of mercy to the multitudes (cf. the repeated accounts of Sabbath controversies, expulsion of demons, etc.) or has independent significance. Some see such independent significance indicated by the time and locale of this feeding: as the feeding of the 5,000 followed the sending and return of the Twelve (6:30; cf. 6:7) and concludes and crowns the ministry of Jesus in Galilee, the feeding of the 4,000 follows Jesus' wanderings in non-Israelite territory (7:24, 31) and is Jesus' gesture of fellow-

them to his disciples to set before the people; and they set them before the crowd. [7]And they had a few small fish; and having blessed them, he commanded that these also should be set before them. [8]And they ate, and were satisfied; and they took up the broken pieces left over, seven baskets full. [9]And there were about four thousand people. [10]And he sent them away; and immediately he got into the boat with his disciples, and went to the district of Dal·ma·nu′tha.[d]

11 The Pharisees came and began to argue with him, seeking from him a sign from heaven, to test him. [12]And he sighed deeply in his spirit, and said, "Why does this generation seek a sign? Truly, I say to you, no sign shall be given to this generation." [13]And he left them, and getting into the boat again he departed to the other side.

14 Now they had forgotten to bring bread; and they had only one loaf with them in the boat. [15]And he cautioned them, saying, "Take heed, beware of the leaven of the Pharisees and the leaven of Herod."[e] [16]And they discussed it with one another, saying, "We have no bread." [17]And being aware of it, Jesus said to them, "Why do you discuss the fact that you have no bread? Do you not yet perceive or understand? Are your hearts hardened? [18] Having eyes do you not see, and having ears do you not hear? And do you not remember? [19] When I broke the five loaves for the five thousand, how many baskets full of broken pieces did you take up?" They said to him, "Twelve." [20] "And the seven for the four thousand, how many baskets full of broken pieces did you take up?" And they said to him, "Seven." [21]And he said to them, "Do you not yet understand?"

22 And they came to Beth-sa′i·da. And some people brought to him a blind man, and begged him to touch him. [23]And he took the blind man by the hand, and led him out of the village; and when he had spit on his eyes and laid his hands upon him, he asked him, "Do you see anything?" [24]And he looked up and said, "I see men; but they look like trees, walking." [25] Then again he laid his hands upon his eyes; and he looked intently and was restored, and saw everything clearly. [26]And he sent him away to his home, saying, "Do not even enter the village."

27 And Jesus went on with his disciples, to the villages of Caes·a·re′a Phi·lip′pi; and on the way he asked his disciples, "Who do men say that I am?" [28]And they told

---

[d] Other ancient authorities read *Magadan* or *Magdala*   [e] Other ancient authorities read *the Herodians*

---

ship toward those Gentile regions. The children of God's household (Israel) are fed first; then the Gentiles partake of His bounty. (7:27-28)

8:10 *Dalmanutha.* Location unknown.

8:11-13 DEMAND FOR A SIGN FROM HEAVEN

8:11-13 For the impiety that lies in the demand for a sign, cf. Mt 12:38-42 note. The "sign of Jonah" of which Jesus speaks in Matthew is not the kind of *sign from heaven* the Pharisees expect. In both gospels Jesus refuses the sign, and the cleavage between Him and Judaic leadership widens. Men who come to Jesus to *argue* and *test* Him cannot find the way to the Christ; Jesus must in sorrow *(sighed deeply)* leave them to the judgment their unbelief invites; they continue their demand for a sign at the cross. (15:32)

8:14-21 THE LEAVEN OF THE PHARISEES AND THE LEAVEN OF HEROD

8:14-21 Cf. Mt 16:5-12 note.

8:15 *Leaven of Herod* (or *Herodians*). Leaven (fermented dough used to make new dough rise) penetrates imperceptibly but irresistibly (cf. Mt 13:33). The rabbis used the term to designate the evil impulse in man, and that is probably the meaning here. For all their differences, the *Pharisees* in their arrogant self-centered religi-

osity and Herod, or the Herodians, in their self-seeking political machinations are at one in their impulse of opposition to Jesus Christ (3:6; 12:13). Their example and influence can ruin the disciples, whose hold on Jesus is still a shaky one. (17-21)

8:18 *Eyes . . . ears.* The grace and power of Christ, who gives sight to the blind, hearing to the deaf, and speech to the dumb (7:37; cf. 7:32-36; 8:22-26), has made but slow headway in their unperceptive hearts.

8:22-26 HEALING THE BLIND AT BETHSAIDA

8:23 *Spit.* Cf. 7:33 note; Jn 9:6.

8:27-30 YOU ARE THE CHRIST

8:27-30 Here as always in His relationship to His disciples (cf. call, apostolate) Jesus takes the initiative. He has separated His disciples from those who oppose Him; now He draws the line between disciples who believe in Him and *men* who admire Him and "appreciate" Him and binds them to Himself for better or worse, life or death, (cf. 35) and forever.

8:28 *John the Baptist.* Cf. 6:14.

Elijah. Cf. 6:15; Mt 11:14; 17:10; Lk 1:17. "Men" see in Jesus only one who plays a preliminary and preparatory role in the coming of the Kingdom. (Ml 4:5-6)

him, "John the Baptist; and others say, E·li′jah; and others one of the prophets." ²⁹And he asked them, "But who do you say that I am?" Peter answered him, "You are the Christ." ³⁰And he charged them to tell no one about him.

Christ Imprints Cross on Life of His Disciples
8:31 – 10:31

31 And he began to teach them that the Son of man must suffer many things, and be rejected by the elders and the chief priests and the scribes, and be killed, and after three days rise again. ³²And he said this plainly. And Peter took him, and began to rebuke him. ³³ But turning and seeing his disciples, he rebuked Peter, and said, "Get behind me, Satan! For you are not on the side of God, but of men."

34 And he called to him the multitude with his disciples, and said to them, "If any man would come after me, let him deny himself and take up his cross and follow me. ³⁵ For whoever would save his life will lose it; and whoever loses his life for my sake and the gospel's will save it. ³⁶ For what does it profit a man, to gain the whole world and forfeit his life? ³⁷ For what can a man give in return for his life? ³⁸ For whoever is ashamed of me and of my words in this adulterous and sinful generation, of him will the Son of man also be ashamed, when he comes in the glory of his Father with the holy angels." ¹And he said to them, "Truly, I say to you, there are some standing here who will not taste death before they see that the kingdom of God has come with power."

2 And after six days Jesus took with him Peter and James and John, and led them up a high mountain apart by themselves; and he was transfigured before them, ³ and his garments became glistening, intensely white, as no fuller on earth could bleach them. ⁴And there appeared to them E·li′jah with Moses; and they were talking to Jesus. ⁵And Peter said to Jesus, "Master,ᶠ it is well that we are here; let us make three booths, one for you and one for Moses and one for E·li′jah." ⁶ For he did not know what to say, for they were exceedingly afraid. ⁷And a cloud overshadowed them, and a voice came out of the cloud, "This is my beloved Son;ᵍ listen to him." ⁸And suddenly looking around they no longer saw any one with them but Jesus only.

ᶠ Or *Rabbi*   ᵍ Or *my Son, my* (or *the*) *Beloved*

8:30 *Tell no one.* Cf. Mt 16:20 note.

8:31 – 10:31 By His prediction of His Passion (8:31-33), by making the way of the cross the pattern of His disciples' way (8:34 – 9:1), by going down from the mountain of transfiguration to the contradiction and agony of men (9:2-29), by teaching that the greatness of the disciple lies in unspectacular ministry to the child (9:30-37), a greatness which is free of narrowhearted exclusiveness (9:38-41) and marked by self-denial (9:42-50) – by these means Christ puts the imprint of His cross on the life of His disciples. They are to go the way of the cross to glory; but they are to go this way within the orders which God has established for this world. Therefore Christ shapes their relationship to marriage, children, and property. (10:1-31)

8:31 – 9:1 THE WAY OF THE CROSS

8:31 – 9:1 Jesus predicts His Passion, saying this plainly (8:32). He brands as satanic any will, even Peter's, which would oppose that way. He makes His way to the cross the pattern of the disciple's way; the disciple is to be ready to *lose his life* in the service of Christ in order to *save his life.*

8:32 *Rebuke him.* In Peter's mind the idea of the cross and of the Christ are contradictory; he feels that Jesus is contradicting the confession of 8:29 when He predicts His cross.

8:33 *Seeing his disciples.* Peter has by his rash words endangered the faith of all the disciples; therefore the public and emphatic rebuke of Jesus.

Behind me. The disciple is to follow after Jesus, not to dictate the way of Jesus.

Satan . . . on the side . . . of men. Cf. Mt 16:23 note.

Side of God. God wills the cross; He gives the Son the cup which He drinks. (Cf. 10:38; 14:36)

8:38 *Adulterous.* Unfaithful to the covenant God who was a husband to Israel. (Jer 31:32; Hos 1 – 3)

9:1 Cf. 9:9; Mt 16:28 note.

9:2-29 THE TRANSFIGURATION

9:2-29 Cf. Mt 17:1-27 note (to 23).

9:2 *After six days.* Since indications of time-sequence are rare in Mark, this note is probably intended to link the Transfiguration closely with the confession of Peter in 8:29 and the prediction of 8:31. It provides a commentary on the words "and after three days rise again" – Peter, James, and John have a glimpse of the glory which awaits the Christ beyond the cross.

9 And as they were coming down the mountain, he charged them to tell no one what they had seen, until the Son of man should have risen from the dead. [10] So they kept the matter to themselves, questioning what the rising from the dead meant. [11]And they asked him, "Why do the scribes say that first E·li′jah must come?" [12]And he said to them, "E·li′jah does come first to restore all things; and how is it written of the Son of man, that he should suffer many things and be treated with contempt? [13] But I tell you that E·li′jah has come, and they did to him whatever they pleased, as it is written of him."

14 And when they came to the disciples, they saw a great crowd about them, and scribes arguing with them. [15]And immediately all the crowd, when they saw him, were greatly amazed, and ran up to him and greeted him. [16]And he asked them, "What are you discussing with them?" [17]And one of the crowd answered him, "Teacher, I brought my son to you, for he has a dumb spirit; [18] and wherever it seizes him, it dashes him down; and he foams and grinds his teeth and becomes rigid; and I asked your disciples to cast it out, and they were not able." [19]And he answered them, "O faithless generation, how long am I to be with you? How long am I to bear with you? Bring him to me." [20]And they brought the boy to him; and when the spirit saw him, immediately it convulsed the boy, and he fell on the ground and rolled about, foaming at the mouth. [21]And Jesus[h] asked his father, "How long has he had this?" And he said, "From childhood. [22]And it has often cast him into the fire and into the water, to destroy him; but if you can do anything, have pity on us and help us." [23]And Jesus said to him, "If you can! All things are possible to him who believes." [24] Immediately the father of the child cried out[i] and said, "I believe; help my unbelief!" [25]And when Jesus saw that a crowd came running together, he rebuked the unclean spirit, saying to it, "You dumb and deaf spirit, I command you, come out of him, and never enter him again." [26]And after crying out and convulsing him terribly, it came out, and the boy was like a corpse; so that most of them said, "He is dead." [27] But Jesus took him by the hand and lifted him up, and he arose. [28]And when he had entered the house, his disciples asked him privately, "Why could we not cast it out?" [29]And he said to them, "This kind cannot be driven out by anything but prayer."[j]

30 They went on from there and passed through Galilee. And he would not have any one know it; [31] for he was teaching his disciples, saying to them, "The Son of man will be delivered into the hands of men, and they will kill him; and when he is killed, after three days he will rise." [32] But they did not understand the saying, and they were afraid to ask him.

33 And they came to Ca·per′na·um; and when he was in the house he asked them, "What were you discussing on the way?" [34] But they were silent; for on the way they had discussed with one another who was the greatest. [35]And he sat down and called the twelve; and he said to them, "If any one would be first, he must be last of all and

[h] Greek *he* [i] Other ancient authorities add *with tears* [j] Other ancient authorities add *and fasting*

9:14 *Scribes arguing with them* (the disciples), probably on the basis of their failure to heal the demoniac boy (18, 28), which the scribes would use to discredit their Master.

9:15 *Were greatly amazed.* The reason for their amazement is not stated; perhaps something of the glory of the Transfiguration still lingered about Jesus. Others compare 10:32, where Jesus' resolute devotion to death creates amazement in the disciples.

9:29 *Prayer* and faith are here closely linked. "All things are possible to him who believes" (23), and faith works through prayer.

9:30-50 HE WAS TEACHING HIS DISCIPLES

9:30-50 Jesus teaches His disciples, and His teaching is the cross, His own cross (30-32) and His disciples'; the cross puts an end to the question of who is *the greatest* (34) and makes him great

who is *servant of all* (35). The disciple finds his greatness in service to the *child,* the little one who needs his help; in serving the child he serves Christ and God Himself (37). The disciple goes the way of the servant, with no self-seeking motives; this makes him generous and open-hearted toward every recognition of Christ and every slight service rendered to them because of Christ (38-41). This greatness found in service makes the disciple scrupulous toward the *little ones who believe in* Christ, capable of heroic self-sacrifice in their behalf, lest he cause them to sin. They are to become men *salted with fire* (cleansed of self by God's discipline), *salt* that seasons and preserves, and men working together, *at peace with one another.* (42-50)

9:30-32 The second of the three major predictions of the Passion. (Cf. 8:31; 10:32-33)

9:32 *Afraid to ask him.* Cf. 10:32 note; Lk 9:45.

servant of all." [36]And he took a child, and put him in the midst of them; and taking him in his arms, he said to them, [37] "Whoever receives one such child in my name receives me; and whoever receives me, receives not me but him who sent me."

38 John said to him, "Teacher, we saw a man casting out demons in your name,[k] and we forbade him, because he was not following us." [39] But Jesus said, "Do not forbid him; for no one who does a mighty work in my name will be able soon after to speak evil of me. [40] For he that is not against us is for us. [41] For truly, I say to you, whoever gives you a cup of water to drink because you bear the name of Christ, will by no means lose his reward.

42 "Whoever causes one of these little ones who believe in me to sin,[l] it would be better for him if a great millstone were hung round his neck and he were thrown into the sea. [43]And if your hand causes you to sin,[l] cut it off; it is better for you to enter life maimed than with two hands to go to hell,[m] to the unquenchable fire.[n] [45]And if your foot causes you to sin,[l] cut it off; it is better for you to enter life lame than with two feet to be thrown into hell.[m] [n] [47]And if your eye causes you to sin,[l] pluck it out; it is better for you to enter the kingdom of God with one eye than with two eyes to be thrown into hell,[m] [48] where their worm does not die, and the fire is not quenched. [49] For every one will be salted with fire.[o] [50] Salt is good; but if the salt has lost its saltness, how will you season it? Have salt in yourselves, and be at peace with one another."

10 And he left there and went to the region of Judea and beyond the Jordan, and crowds gathered to him again; and again, as his custom was, he taught them.

2 And Pharisees came up and in order to test him asked, "Is it lawful for a man to divorce his wife?" [3] He answered them, "What did Moses command you?" [4] They said, "Moses allowed a man to write a certificate of divorce, and to put her away." [5] But Jesus said to them, "For your hardness of heart he wrote you this commandment. [6] But from the beginning of creation, 'God made them male and female.' [7] 'For this reason a man shall leave his father and mother and be joined to his wife,[p] [8] and the two shall become one flesh.' So they are no longer two but one flesh. [9] What therefore God has joined together, let not man put asunder."

10 And in the house the disciples asked him again about this matter. [11]And he said to them, "Whoever divorces his wife and marries another, commits adultery against her; [12] and if she divorces her husband and marries another, she commits adultery."

13 And they were bringing children to him, that he might touch them; and the disciples rebuked them. [14] But when Jesus saw it he was indignant, and said to them, "Let the children come to me, do not hinder them; for to such belongs the kingdom of

---

[k] Other ancient authorities add *who does not follow us*　　[l] Greek *stumble*　　[m] Greek *Gehenna*
[n] Verses 44 and 46 (which are identical with verse 48) are omitted by the best ancient authorities
[o] Other ancient authorities add *and every sacrifice will be salted with salt*
[p] Other ancient authorities omit *and be joined to his wife*

9:37 *One such child . . . receives me.* Cf. Mt 18:1-35 note.

9:38 *In your name,* on Your authority. Cf. Acts 16:18 for the formula.

9:48 *Worm . . . fire.* The language is that of Is 66:24, which describes the place of punishment of those who have rebelled against the Lord in terms of the place where the refuse of Jerusalem was destroyed, the valley of Hinnom (Gehenna).

9:49 *Salted with fire.* To be acceptable to God, every sacrifice had to be salted with salt (Lv 2:13). So to be an acceptable servant of God and Christ, the disciple must be purified by the fire of self-denial (43-47), which God uses to make him a fit servant. For fire as God's means of purifying His servants cf. Ml 3:2-3. For the apostolic ministry pictured as sacrifice cf. Ph 2:17.

9:50 *Have salt in yourselves.* If they are thus (49)

purified for service, they can fulfill their function of being "the salt of the earth." (Mt 5:13)

Peace with one another, instead of vying for greatness. (34)

10:1-31 MARRIAGE, CHILDREN, AND PROPERTY

10:1-31 Cf. Mt 19:1 – 20:16 notes. The way of the cross does not evade the obligations and temptations of family and money but meets them and deals with them in faith. Marriage is to be the pure communion which God the Creator ordained (1-12). Children are to be received, honored, and imitated as the objects of the love of God the King (13-16). God the only Good can free them from the fatal hold of property, and He will provide for all who renounce the created blessings for His sake and give them *eternal life in the age to come.* (17-31)

God. ¹⁵ Truly, I say to you, whoever does not receive the kingdom of God like a child shall not enter it." ¹⁶And he took them in his arms and blessed them, laying his hands upon them.

17 And as he was setting out on his journey, a man ran up and knelt before him, and asked him, "Good Teacher, what must I do to inherit eternal life?" ¹⁸And Jesus said to him, "Why do you call me good? No one is good but God alone. ¹⁹ You know the commandments: 'Do not kill, Do not commit adultery, Do not steal, Do not bear false witness, Do not defraud, Honor your father and mother.' " ²⁰And he said to him, "Teacher, all these I have observed from my youth." ²¹And Jesus looking upon him loved him, and said to him, "You lack one thing; go, sell what you have, and give to the poor, and you will have treasure in heaven; and come, follow me." ²²At that saying his countenance fell, and he went away sorrowful; for he had great possessions.

23 And Jesus' looked around and said to his disciples, "How hard it will be for those who have riches to enter the kingdom of God!" ²⁴And the disciples were amazed at his words. But Jesus said to them again, "Children, how hard it isʳ to enter the kingdom of God! ²⁵ It is easier for a camel to go through the eye of a needle than for a rich man to enter the kingdom of God." ²⁶And they were exceedingly astonished, and said to him,ˢ "Then who can be saved?" ²⁷ Jesus looked at them and said, "With men it is impossible, but not with God; for all things are possible with God." ²⁸ Peter began to say to him, "Lo, we have left everything and followed you." ²⁹ Jesus said, "Truly, I say to you, there is no one who has left house or brothers or sisters or mother or father or children or lands, for my sake and for the gospel, ³⁰ who will not receive a hundredfold now in this time, houses and brothers and sisters and mothers and children and lands, with persecutions, and in the age to come eternal life. ³¹ But many that are first will be last, and the last first."

Christ Goes to Jerusalem

10:32 – 13:37

32 And they were on the road, going up to Jerusalem, and Jesus was walking ahead of them; and they were amazed, and those who followed were afraid. And taking the twelve again, he began to tell them what was to happen to him, ³³ saying, "Behold, we are going up to Jerusalem; and the Son of man will be delivered to the chief priests and the scribes, and they will condemn him to death, and deliver him to the Gentiles; ³⁴ and they will mock him, and spit upon him, and scourge him, and kill him; and after three days he will rise."

ʳ Other ancient authorities add *for those who trust in riches*   ˢ Other ancient authorities read *to one another*

(10:1-31, see previous page)

10:31 *First will be last.* The parable of the workers in the vineyard is Jesus' own commentary on this saying. Cf. Mt 20:1-16. Cf. notes at Mt 19:27 – 20:16 and 19:30.

10:32 – 13:37 The cross pronounces doom on the empty, self-centered piety of Jerusalem (the old Israel) and gives the disciples, the new Israel, their hope of glory. Three phases may be distinguished: (a) Christ binds His disciples to Himself as the Servant Messiah (10:32-52). (b) Christ confronts Jerusalem with His Messianic claim and His call to repentance (11:1 – 12:37). (c) Christ separates His disciples from the scribes, the teachers of Israel. All three find their conclusion in the discourse of ch. 13, in which Jesus predicts doom for Jerusalem and deliverance for His own.

10:32-52 CHRIST BINDS HIS DISCIPLES
            TO HIMSELF

10:32-52 Jesus claims His disciples for Himself

as the dying Servant Christ. He predicts His death for the third time; Israel's leaders will reject Him, condemn Him to death, and deliver Him to the Gentiles for execution (10:32-34). He is forced to remind His disciples again that participation in His future glory comes only by participation in His suffering, that the measure of all greatness is the self-giving greatness of the Son of Man who serves to the utmost, to the giving of His life for the ransoming of the "many" (10:35-45); and He once more sums up His whole serving and saving ministry in one mighty deed: He opens the eyes of blind Bartimaeus in order that the new, seeing man may follow Him "on the way." (10:46-52)

10:32-45 Cf. Mt 20:17-28 notes.

10:32 *They were amazed ... afraid.* Cf. 9:32. They were filled with awe at the sight of Him who took His way to the cross in full consciousness of His destiny and its significance for the destiny of mankind.

35 And James and John, the sons of Zeb'e·dee, came forward to him, and said to him, "Teacher, we want you to do for us whatever we ask of you." ³⁶And he said to them, "What do you want me to do for you?" ³⁷And they said to him, "Grant us to sit, one at your right hand and one at your left, in your glory." ³⁸ But Jesus said to them, "You do not know what you are asking. Are you able to drink the cup that I drink, or to be baptized with the baptism with which I am baptized?" ³⁹And they said to him, "We are able." And Jesus said to them, "The cup that I drink you will drink; and with the baptism with which I am baptized, you will be baptized; ⁴⁰ but to sit at my right hand or at my left is not mine to grant, but it is for those for whom it has been prepared." ⁴¹And when the ten heard it, they began to be indignant at James and John. ⁴²And Jesus called them to him and said to them, "You know that those who are supposed to rule over the Gentiles lord it over them, and their great men exercise authority over them. ⁴³ But it shall not be so among you; but whoever would be great among you must be your servant, ⁴⁴ and whoever would be first among you must be slave of all. ⁴⁵ For the Son of man also came not to be served but to serve, and to give his life as a ransom for many."

46 And they came to Jericho; and as he was leaving Jericho with his disciples and a great multitude, Bar·ti·mae'us, a blind beggar, the son of Ti·mae'us, was sitting by the roadside. ⁴⁷And when he heard that it was Jesus of Nazareth, he began to cry out and say, "Jesus, Son of David, have mercy on me!" ⁴⁸And many rebuked him, telling him to be silent; but he cried out all the more, "Son of David, have mercy on me!" ⁴⁹And Jesus stopped and said, "Call him." And they called the blind man, saying to him, "Take heart; rise, he is calling you." ⁵⁰And throwing off his mantle he sprang up and came to Jesus. ⁵¹And Jesus said to him, "What do you want me to do for you?" And the blind man said to him, "Master,ᵗ let me receive my sight." ⁵²And Jesus said to him, "Go your way; your faith has made you well." And immediately he received his sight and followed him on the way.

11 And when they drew near to Jerusalem, to Beth'pha·ge and Beth'a·ny, at the Mount of Olives, he sent two of his disciples, 2 and said to them, "Go into the village opposite you, and immediately as you enter it you will find a colt tied, on which no one has ever sat; untie it and bring it. 3 If any one says to you, 'Why are you doing this?' say, 'The Lord has need of it and will send it back here immediately.' " ⁴And they went away, and found a colt tied at the door out in the open street; and they untied it. ⁵And those who stood there said to them, "What are you doing, untying the colt?" ⁶And they told them what Jesus had said; and they let them go. ⁷And they brought the colt to Jesus, and threw their garments on it; and he sat upon it. ⁸And many spread their garments on the road, and others spread leafy branches which they had cut from the fields. ⁹And those who went before and those who followed cried out, "Hosanna! Blessed is he who comes in the name of the Lord! ¹⁰ Blessed is the kingdom of our father David that is coming! Hosanna in the highest!"

11 And he entered Jerusalem, and went into the temple; and when he had looked round at everything, as it was already late, he went out to Beth'a·ny with the twelve.

ᵗ Or *Rabbi*

10:38 *Baptism with which I am baptized.* Cf. Mt 3:13-15 note. The baptism to which Jesus refers is His being plunged into suffering and death. (Cf. Lk 12:50)

10:42 *Supposed to rule,* that is, are recognized as rulers.

10:46-52 Cf. Mt 20:29-34 note. On Jesus as the Servant prophesied in Isaiah cf. Mt 8:17 and 12:18-21 notes.

10:46 *Bartimaeus* means son of *Timaeus.* Cf. Bar-Jona, Mt 16:17.

11:1—12:37 CHRIST CONFRONTS JERUSALEM

11:1—12:37 In deed and word Jesus confronts

Jerusalem, the capital and heart of Israel, with His Messianic claim and call to repentance.

11:1-11 THE MESSIANIC ENTRY

11:1-11 Cf. Mt 21:1-11 notes.

11:3 *The Lord has need.* This is the first time in Mark that Jesus calls Himself Lord; this act is a royal requisitioning.

11:10 *Blessed is the kingdom of our father David.* The promise given to David (2 Sm 7:16; Ps 89:3, 4, 20, 21, 27, 28, 29, 35, 36), the long-cherished hope of the Messiah is being fulfilled. The blessing of His reign *(kingdom)* is about to descend on His people.

12 On the following day, when they came from Beth'a·ny, he was hungry. [13]And seeing in the distance a fig tree in leaf, he went to see if he could find anything on it. When he came to it, he found nothing but leaves, for it was not the season for figs. [14]And he said to it, "May no one ever eat fruit from you again." And his disciples heard it.

15 And they came to Jerusalem. And he entered the temple and began to drive out those who sold and those who bought in the temple, and he overturned the tables of the money-changers and the seats of those who sold pigeons; [16] and he would not allow any one to carry anything through the temple. [17]And he taught, and said to them, "Is it not written, 'My house shall be called a house of prayer for all the nations'? But you have made it a den of robbers." [18]And the chief priests and the scribes heard it and sought a way to destroy him; for they feared him, because all the multitude was astonished at his teaching. [19]And when evening came they[u] went out of the city.

20 As they passed by in the morning, they saw the fig tree withered away to its roots. [21]And Peter remembered and said to him, "Master,[v] look! The fig tree which you cursed has withered." [22]And Jesus answered them, "Have faith in God. [23] Truly, I say to you, whoever says to this mountain, 'Be taken up and cast into the sea,' and does not doubt in his heart, but believes that what he says will come to pass, it will be done for him. [24] Therefore I tell you, whatever you ask in prayer, believe that you have received[a] it, and it will be yours. [25]And whenever you stand praying, forgive, if you have anything against any one; so that your Father also who is in heaven may forgive you your trespasses." [w]

27 And they came again to Jerusalem. And as he was walking in the temple, the chief priests and the scribes and the elders came to him, [28] and they said to him, "By what authority are you doing these things, or who gave you this authority to do them?" [29] Jesus said to them, "I will ask you a question; answer me, and I will tell you by what authority I do these things. [30] Was the baptism of John from heaven or from men? Answer me." [31]And they argued with one another, "If we say, 'From heaven,' he will say, 'Why then did you not believe him?' [32] But shall we say, 'From men'?"—they were afraid of the people, for all held that John was a real prophet. [33] So they answered Jesus, "We do not know." And Jesus said to them, "Neither will I tell you by what authority I do these things."

12 And he began to speak to them in parables. "A man planted a vineyard, and set a hedge around it, and dug a pit for the wine press, and built a tower, and let it out to tenants, and went into another country. [2] When the time came, he sent a

[u] Other ancient authorities read *he*   [v] Or *Rabbi*   [a] Other ancient authorities read *are receiving*
[w] Other ancient authorities add verse 26, "*But if you do not forgive, neither will your Father who is in heaven forgive your trespasses*"

11:12-26 THE CALL TO REPENTANCE IN DEED

11:12-26 Cf. Mt 21:12-22. By His cleansing of the temple (15-18) and His blasting of the fig tree (12-14, 20-26) Jesus pronounces judgment on the self-centered and fruitless piety of Israel and therewith calls His people to repentance.

11:13 *For it was not the season for figs.* These words and the note in 14, "And his disciples heard it" (the curse on the fig tree), indicate that Jesus' action is a symbolic one intended for the instruction of His disciples. Jesus' curse upon the fig tree is not the petulant reaction of one disappointed in hope of refreshment; it is His word of judgment on the fruitless piety of His people. For the image and the idea cf. Mi 7:1-4.

11:16 *Carry anything through the temple*, that is, use the temple courts as a commercial street like any other. "There shall no longer be a trader in the house of the Lord of hosts on that day." (Zch 14:21)

11:25 Cf. Mt 6:12, 14-15 notes.

11:27-33 THE CALL TO REPENTANCE IN WORD: BY WHAT AUTHORITY?

11:27-33 Cf. Mt 21:25, 27. By refusing to validate His *authority* for the Jewish authorities who have not heeded John the Baptist's call to repentance (his baptism) Jesus once more imposes that call to repentance upon them; if they will not heed that call, they can never know the authority of the Christ and be blessed by it.

11:33 *Neither will I tell you.* They have refused to be told when God spoke to them in John's baptism and in Jesus' word and deed. Now they shall not be told—except by the cross and resurrection of Jesus.

12:1-12 THE CALL TO REPENTANCE IN WORD: THE PARABLE OF THE VINEYARD

12:1-12 Cf. Mt 21:33, 36, 42, 46 notes. The parable of the rebellious tenants presses home Jesus' call to repentance; it calls upon Israel's leaders to give God what is God's, to beware of the fearful

servant to the tenants, to get from them some of the fruit of the vineyard. ³And they took him and beat him, and sent him away empty-handed. ⁴Again he sent to them another servant, and they wounded him in the head, and treated him shamefully. ⁵And he sent another, and him they killed; and so with many others, some they beat and some they killed. ⁶ He had still one other, a beloved son; finally he sent him to them, saying, 'They will respect my son.' ⁷ But those tenants said to one another, 'This is the heir; come, let us kill him, and the inheritance will be ours.' ⁸And they took him and killed him, and cast him out of the vineyard. ⁹ What will the owner of the vineyard do? He will come and destroy the tenants, and give the vineyard to others. ¹⁰ Have you not read this scripture:

> 'The very stone which the builders rejected
> has become the head of the corner;
> ¹¹   this was the Lord's doing,
> and it is marvelous in our eyes'?"

12 And they tried to arrest him, but feared the multitude, for they perceived that he had told the parable against them; so they left him and went away.

13 And they sent to him some of the Pharisees and some of the He·ro'di·ans, to entrap him in his talk. ¹⁴And they came and said to him, "Teacher, we know that you are true, and care for no man; for you do not regard the position of men, but truly teach the way of God. Is it lawful to pay taxes to Caesar, or not? ¹⁵ Should we pay them, or should we not?" But knowing their hypocrisy, he said to them, "Why put me to the test? Bring me a coin,ˣ and let me look at it." ¹⁶And they brought one. And he said to them, "Whose likeness and inscription is this?" They said to him, "Caesar's." ¹⁷ Jesus said to them, "Render to Caesar the things that are Caesar's, and to God the things that are God's." And they were amazed at him.

18 And Sad'du·cees came to him, who say that there is no resurrection; and they asked him a question, saying, ¹⁹ "Teacher, Moses wrote for us that if a man's brother dies and leaves a wife, but leaves no child, the manʸ must take the wife, and raise up children for his brother. ²⁰ There were seven brothers; the first took a wife, and when he died left no children; ²¹ and the second took her, and died, leaving no children; and the third likewise; ²² and the seven left no children. Last of all the woman also died. ²³ In the resurrection whose wife will she be? For the seven had her as wife."

24 Jesus said to them, "Is not this why you are wrong, that you know neither the scriptures nor the power of God? ²⁵ For when they rise from the dead, they neither marry nor are given in marriage, but are like angels in heaven. ²⁶And as for the dead being raised, have you not read in the book of Moses, in the passage about the bush, how God said to him, 'I am the God of Abraham, and the God of Isaac, and the God of Jacob'? ²⁷ He is not God of the dead, but of the living; you are quite wrong."

28 And one of the scribes came up and heard them disputing with one another, and seeing that he answered them well, asked him, "Which commandment is the first of all?" ²⁹ Jesus answered, "The first is, 'Hear, O Israel: The Lord our God, the

---

ˣ Greek *a denarius* ʸ Greek *his brother*

---

fate that awaits them if they disobey, and to realize that they cannot prevent the triumph of the Christ and the rise of a new people of God. Jesus calls in vain. (12)

12:13-34 THE CALL TO REPENTANCE IN WORD: THREE DISPUTES

12:13-34 Cf. Mt 22:15-40. In His disputes with the *Pharisees and Herodians,* with the *Sadducees,* and the *scribes,* Jesus again shows what separates Israel's leading men from the Son whom God has sent to them. The Pharisees (13-17) scruple about *paying taxes to Caesar* but will not give God what is God's—Jesus goes to the cross because He is "on the side of God" (8:33), in order that God's grace and righteousness may prevail. The Sad-

ducees with their rational denial of the *resurrection* (18-27) know neither the *scriptures* nor the *power of God*—Jesus can go to the cross because He knows that the Scriptures direct Him to the cross (9:12) and that the power of the living God will raise Him on the third day and seat Him at God's right hand (12:36). The scribe (28:34) searches amid the manifold commandments of God and cannot for all His searching be sure of the primal will of God—Jesus goes to the cross sure of the will of God; He goes with a whole *love* for God which binds Him in love to man.

12:13 *Herodians.* Cf. Mt 22:16 note.

12:28 *Which commandment is the first?* First in the sense of foremost, most important, most prominent.

Lord is one; [30] and you shall love the Lord your God with all your heart, and with all your soul, and with all your mind, and with all your strength.' [31] The second is this, 'You shall love your neighbor as yourself.' There is no other commandment greater than these." [32] And the scribe said to him, "You are right, Teacher; you have truly said that he is one, and there is no other but he; [33] and to love him with all the heart, and with all the understanding, and with all the strength, and to love one's neighbor as oneself, is much more than all whole burnt offerings and sacrifices." [34] And when Jesus saw that he answered wisely, he said to him, "You are not far from the kingdom of God." And after that no one dared to ask him any question.

35 And as Jesus taught in the temple, he said, "How can the scribes say that the Christ is the son of David? [36] David himself, inspired by [z] the Holy Spirit, declared,

> 'The Lord said to my Lord,
> Sit at my right hand,
> till I put thy enemies under thy feet.'

[37] David himself calls him Lord; so how is he his son?" And the great throng heard him gladly.

38 And in his teaching he said, "Beware of the scribes, who like to go about in long robes, and to have salutations in the market places [39] and the best seats in the synagogues and the places of honor at feasts, [40] who devour widows' houses and for a pretense make long prayers. They will receive the greater condemnation."

41 And he sat down opposite the treasury, and watched the multitude putting money into the treasury. Many rich people put in large sums. [42] And a poor widow came, and put in two copper coins, which make a penny. [43] And he called his disciples to him, and said to them, "Truly, I say to you, this poor widow has put in more than all those who are contributing to the treasury. [44] For they all contributed out of their abundance; but she out of her poverty has put in everything she had, her whole living."

13 And as he came out of the temple, one of his disciples said to him, "Look, Teacher, what wonderful stones and what wonderful buildings!" [2] And Jesus said to him, "Do you see these great buildings? There will not be left here one stone upon another, that will not be thrown down."

---

[z] Or *himself, in*

12:29-31 Cf. Dt 6:4-5; Lv 19:18.

12:32 *You are right, Teacher.* The scribe's approval of Jesus' answer is natural enough. The question of the unifying principle of the Law, the commandment which expressed the will underlying all the 613 commandments of the Law was much discussed in the schools, and answers like that of Jesus were given. But only Jesus wrote the answer with His whole life and death.

12:33 *More than . . . sacrifices.* Cf. 1 Sm 15:22; Hos 6:6.

12:34 *You are not far from the kingdom of God.* One who so grasps the will of God the King is but one step removed from the recognition that in Jesus, the anointed King (the Christ), this will is being fulfilled.

12:35-37 JESUS' MESSIANIC CLAIM: DAVID'S SON AND LORD

12:35-37 Cf. Mt 22:41-46 note; Mk 14:63-64, where Jesus is condemned to die as a blasphemer for making this Messianic claim in the words of Ps 110:1. Here it becomes crystal clear that Jesus is, according to the old saying, "either God or not a good man."

12:38-44 THE SCRIBES AND THE POOR WIDOW

12:38-44 Cf. Mt 23:1-39 note. Jesus warns His disciples against the *scribes,* who in their pride and self-seeking introduce a fatal cleavage into their piety and become blind guides to the people for whom they are responsible. They fail both in their lives and in their responsibility and will therefore receive the greater condemnation. The selfless piety of the *poor widow,* who gives *her whole living* to the one good God, loving Him with her whole heart and trusting Him for her future, stands in sharp contrast to that of the scribes — she is, in Jesus' judgment, "not far from the kingdom of God," like the scribe who recognized that the will of God is love. (34)

12:38 *Long robes,* garments which mark them as men of piety and learning.

12:40 *Devour widows' houses,* an extreme case of the "extortion and rapacity" with which Jesus reproaches them in Mt 23:25.

12:41 *The treasury,* trumpet-shaped containers set up in the court of the women in the temple for receiving the contributions of the faithful.

13:1-37 JESUS PREDICTS FALL OF JERUSALEM AND DELIVERANCE OF HIS ELECT

13:1-37 Cf. Mt 24:1-31 note. The fall of the temple is the beginning of the end (1-2). Henceforth all history is to be for Jesus' disciples the *sign* (4) which alerts them to the coming of the

3 And as he sat on the Mount of Olives opposite the temple, Peter and James and John and Andrew asked him privately, 4 "Tell us, when will this be, and what will be the sign when these things are all to be accomplished?" 5And Jesus began to say to them, "Take heed that no one leads you astray. 6 Many will come in my name, saying, 'I am he!' and they will lead many astray. 7And when you hear of wars and rumors of wars, do not be alarmed; this must take place, but the end is not yet. 8 For nation will rise against nation, and kingdom against kingdom; there will be earthquakes in various places, there will be famines; this is but the beginning of the birth-pangs.

9 "But take heed to yourselves; for they will deliver you up to councils; and you will be beaten in synagogues; and you will stand before governors and kings for my sake, to bear testimony before them. 10And the gospel must first be preached to all nations. 11And when they bring you to trial and deliver you up, do not be anxious beforehand what you are to say; but say whatever is given you in that hour, for it is not you who speak, but the Holy Spirit. 12And brother will deliver up brother to death, and the father his child, and children will rise against parents and have them put to death; 13 and you will be hated by all for my name's sake. But he who endures to the end will be saved.

14 "But when you see the desolating sacrilege set up where it ought not to be (let the reader understand), then let those who are in Judea flee to the mountains; 15 let him who is on the housetop not go down, nor enter his house, to take anything away; 16 and let him who is in the field not turn back to take his mantle. 17And alas for those who are with child and for those who give suck in those days! 18 Pray that it may not happen in winter. 19 For in those days there will be such tribulation as has not been from the beginning of the creation which God created until now, and never will be. 20And if the Lord had not shortened the days, no human being would be saved; but for the sake of the elect, whom he chose, he shortened the days. 21And then if any one says to you, 'Look, here is the Christ!' or 'Look, there he is!' do not believe it. 22 False Christs and false prophets will arise and show signs and wonders, to lead astray, if possible, the elect. 23 But take heed; I have told you all things beforehand.

24 "But in those days, after that tribulation, the sun will be darkened, and the moon will not give its light, 25 and the stars will be falling from heaven, and the powers in the heavens will be shaken. 26And then they will see the Son of man coming in clouds with great power and glory. 27And then he will send out the angels, and gather his elect from the four winds, from the ends of the earth to the ends of heaven.

28 "From the fig tree learn its lesson: as soon as its branch becomes tender and puts forth its leaves, you know that summer is near. 29 So also, when you see these things taking place, you know that he is near, at the very gates. 30 Truly, I say to you, this generation will not pass away before all these things take place. 31 Heaven and earth will pass away, but my words will not pass away.

32 "But of that day or that hour no one knows, not even the angels in heaven, nor the Son, but only the Father. 33 Take heed, watch;a for you do not know when the

a Other ancient authorities add and pray

end: the war-torn history of the world (3-8), the history of the persecuted church and the universal preaching of the *gospel* in the power of the Spirit and in spite of man's failures (9-13), the appearance of the *desolating sacrilege* and the coming of the great tribulation at the fall of Jerusalem, together with the appearance of *false Christs* in those fevered times (14-23)—all constitute the sign which points to the coming of the *Son of man* in *power and glory* to *gather* in *his elect* from all the earth (24-27). The parable of the *fig tree* prepares the disciples to live through that history in calm and patient hope; Jesus' enduring *words* assure them that all this history is in the hands of the Creator whose faithful working they see in the approach of summer year by year (28-31); the parable of the returning master of the house

makes their hope a vigilant and responsible expectation of their returning Lord. (32-37)

13:9 *Beaten in synagogues.* Cf. Acts 5:40; 2 Co 11:24.

13:10 *Must . . . be preached.* The same overruling divine will that controls wars and rumors of wars (7) will cause the Gospel to speed and triumph amid disasters.

13:14 *Desolating sacrilege.* Cf. Mt 24:15 note.

Where it ought not to be, in the holy land and place.

Let the reader understand both the reference to the prophecy of Daniel (Dn 12:11; 9:27) and the warning of Jesus recorded here, which is based on Daniel's word.

13:27 *From the ends of the earth to the ends of heaven.* This seems to be a fusion of two expres-

time will come. 34 It is like a man going on a journey, when he leaves home and puts his servants in charge, each with his work, and commands the doorkeeper to be on the watch. 35 Watch therefore—for you do not know when the master of the house will come, in the evening, or at midnight, or at cockcrow, or in the morning—36 lest he come suddenly and find you asleep. 37And what I say to you I say to all: Watch."

Christ's Suffering, Death, and Resurrection

14:1 – 16:20

14 It was now two days before the Passover and the feast of Unleavened Bread. And the chief priests and the scribes were seeking how to arrest him by stealth, and kill him; 2 for they said, "Not during the feast, lest there be a tumult of the people."

3 And while he was at Beth′a·ny in the house of Simon the leper, as he sat at table, a woman came with an alabaster flask of ointment of pure nard, very costly, and she broke the flask and poured it over his head. 4 But there were some who said to themselves indignantly, "Why was the ointment thus wasted? 5 For this ointment might have been sold for more than three hundred denarii,*b* and given to the poor." And they reproached her. 6 But Jesus said, "Let her alone; why do you trouble her? She has done a beautiful thing to me. 7 For you always have the poor with you, and whenever you will, you can do good to them; but you will not always have me. 8 She has done what she could; she has anointed my body beforehand for burying. 9And truly, I say to you, wherever the gospel is preached in the whole world, what she has done will be told in memory of her."

10 Then Judas Is·car′i·ot, who was one of the twelve, went to the chief priests in order to betray him to them. 11And when they heard it they were glad, and promised to give him money. And he sought an opportunity to betray him.

12 And on the first day of Unleavened Bread, when they sacrificed the passover lamb, his disciples said to him, "Where will you have us go and prepare for you to eat the passover?" 13And he sent two of his disciples, and said to them, "Go into the

b The denarius was a day's wage for a laborer

sions: "from one end of the earth to the other" and "from horizon to horizon."

13:37 *What I say to you I say to all.* The disciples are to transmit this admonition to the church.

14:1 – 16:20 Cf. Mt 26 – 28 notes. Jesus goes alone into His death. His disciples all fail Him; Judas betrays Him (14:10-11, 43-50), the three cannot watch with Him one hour (14:32-42), all flee at His arrest (14:26-31, 43-52), and Peter denies Him (14:66-72). His people reject Him (14:1-2, 43-46, 53-65; 15:1-15); all join in mocking the condemned and dying King of Israel (15:29-32). Gentile (Roman) justice abandons Him to the fury of His people (15:1-15), and Gentile soldiers mock Him (15:16-20). He is forsaken by His God (15:34). He suffers in full and simple humanity; witness the agony in Gethsemane (14:32-42) and His cry from the cross (15:34). And yet He endures with the quiet majesty of the Son of God; He is the Sufferer, and yet He is in charge. He unmasks the betrayer (14:17-21); He gives His dying self to His disciples (14:22-25); He sings the Passover psalms in praise of God the Deliverer at the very hour of His arrest (14:26); He foretells the failure of His disciples (14:27-31); He rebukes His captors (14:48-49), is silent and composed before the Sanhedrin (14:61) and before Pilate (15:4-5), makes no answer to those who mock Him (15:

16-20, 29-32), and departs in full consciousness with a loud cry (15:37). His death is His voluntary act; by His shed blood He inaugurates the new covenant (14:23-24), and in His dying He drinks the cup of God's judgment upon the sin of man (15:33-39; cf. 10:38 note; 14:36). The ransom for many is paid. (Cf. 10:45)

His resurrection is enacted forgiveness; the risen Christ restores to His fellowship the disciples, who had failed Him, and Peter, who had denied Him (16:7). He sends His disciples out to *all the world* to preach the Gospel to all creation for the salvation of all men – *all the world* includes the Israel that had rejected Him and killed Him. (16:15, 20)

14:1-11 PRELUDE TO THE PASSION

14:1-11 Cf. Mt 26:1-16 note.

14:1 *Passover.* Cf. Mt 26:26 note.

14:3 *Nard,* an aromatic plant from which a fragrant oil was extracted.

14:12-25 THE LAST PASSOVER, THE NEW PASSOVER

14:12-25 Cf. Mt 26:17-29 note.

14:13 *A man carrying a jar of water.* Since women ordinarily fetched water (cf. Jn 4:28), a man carrying a water jar would be conspicuous.

city, and a man carrying a jar of water will meet you; follow him, [14] and wherever he enters, say to the householder, 'The Teacher says, Where is my guest room, where I am to eat the passover with my disciples?' [15]And he will show you a large upper room furnished and ready; there prepare for us." [16]And the disciples set out and went to the city, and found it as he had told them; and they prepared the passover.

17 And when it was evening he came with the twelve. [18]And as they were at table eating, Jesus said, "Truly, I say to you, one of you will betray me, one who is eating with me." [19] They began to be sorrowful, and to say to him one after another, "Is it I?" [20] He said to them, "It is one of the twelve, one who is dipping bread into the dish with me. [21] For the Son of man goes as it is written of him, but woe to that man by whom the Son of man is betrayed! It would have been better for that man if he had not been born."

22 And as they were eating, he took bread, and blessed, and broke it, and gave it to them, and said, "Take; this is my body." [23]And he took a cup, and when he had given thanks he gave it to them, and they all drank of it. [24]And he said to them, "This is my blood of the[c] covenant, which is poured out for many. [25] Truly, I say to you, I shall not drink again of the fruit of the vine until that day when I drink it new in the kingdom of God."

26 And when they had sung a hymn, they went out to the Mount of Olives. [27]And Jesus said to them, "You will all fall away; for it is written, 'I will strike the shepherd, and the sheep will be scattered.' [28] But after I am raised up, I will go before you to Galilee." [29] Peter said to him, "Even though they all fall away, I will not." [30]And Jesus said to him, "Truly, I say to you, this very night, before the cock crows twice, you will deny me three times." [31] But he said vehemently, "If I must die with you, I will not deny you." And they all said the same.

32 And they went to a place which was called Geth·sem′a·ne; and he said to his disciples, "Sit here, while I pray." [33]And he took with him Peter and James and John, and began to be greatly distressed and troubled. [34]And he said to them, "My soul is very sorrowful, even to death; remain here, and watch."[d] [35]And going a little farther, he fell on the ground and prayed that, if it were possible, the hour might pass from him. [36]And he said, "Abba, Father, all things are possible to thee; remove this cup from me; yet not what I will, but what thou wilt." [37]And he came and found them sleeping, and he said to Peter, "Simon, are you asleep? Could you not watch[d] one hour? [38] Watch[d] and pray that you may not enter into temptation; the spirit indeed is willing, but the flesh is weak." [39]And again he went away and prayed, saying the same words. [40]And again he came and found them sleeping, for their eyes were very heavy; and they did not know what to answer him. [41]And he came the third time, and said to them, "Are you still sleeping and taking your rest? It is enough; the hour has come; the Son of man is betrayed into the hands of sinners. [42] Rise, let us be going; see, my betrayer is at hand."

43 And immediately, while he was still speaking, Judas came, one of the twelve, and with him a crowd with swords and clubs, from the chief priests and the scribes and the elders. [44] Now the betrayer had given them a sign, saying, "The one I shall kiss is the man; seize him and lead him away under guard." [45]And when he came, he went up to him at once, and said, "Master!"[e] And he kissed him. [46]And they laid hands on him and seized him. [47] But one of those who stood by drew his sword, and struck the slave of the high priest and cut off his ear. [48]And Jesus said to them, "Have you come out as against a robber, with swords and clubs to capture me? [49] Day after day I was with you in the temple teaching, and you did not seize me. But let the scriptures be fulfilled." [50]And they all forsook him, and fled.

51 And a young man followed him, with nothing but a linen cloth about his body; and they seized him, [52] but he left the linen cloth and ran away naked.

[c] Other ancient authorities insert *new*　　[d] Or *keep awake*　　[e] Or *Rabbi*

14:26-52 THE STRICKEN SHEPHERD AND
　　　THE SCATTERED FLOCK

14:26-52 Cf. Mt 26:30-56 note.
14:51-52 The story of the young man who ran away is peculiar to Mark; the young man may be Mark himself. See the Introduction, par. 4.

Naked. Cf. Am 2:16, where it is said that "in that day," when God's judgment strikes the sin of His people, "he who is stout of heart among

53 And they led Jesus to the high priest; and all the chief priests and the elders and the scribes were assembled. 54And Peter had followed him at a distance, right into the courtyard of the high priest; and he was sitting with the guards, and warming himself at the fire. 55 Now the chief priests and the whole council sought testimony against Jesus to put him to death; but they found none. 56 For many bore false witness against him, and their witness did not agree. 57And some stood up and bore false witness against him, saying, 58 "We heard him say, 'I will destroy this temple that is made with hands, and in three days I will build another, not made with hands.'" 59 Yet not even so did their testimony agree. 60And the high priest stood up in the midst, and asked Jesus, "Have you no answer to make? What is it that these men testify against you?" 61 But he was silent and made no answer. Again the high priest asked him, "Are you the Christ, the Son of the Blessed?" 62And Jesus said, "I am; and you will see the Son of man seated at the right hand of Power, and coming with the clouds of heaven." 63And the high priest tore his garments, and said, "Why do we still need witnesses? 64 You have heard his blasphemy. What is your decision?" And they all condemned him as deserving death. 65And some began to spit on him, and to cover his face, and to strike him, saying to him, "Prophesy!" And the guards received him with blows.

66 And as Peter was below in the courtyard, one of the maids of the high priest came; 67 and seeing Peter warming himself, she looked at him, and said, "You also were with the Nazarene, Jesus." 68 But he denied it, saying, "I neither know nor understand what you mean." And he went out into the gateway.*f* 69And the maid saw him, and began again to say to the bystanders, "This man is one of them." 70 But again he denied it. And after a little while again the bystanders said to Peter, "Certainly you are one of them; for you are a Galilean." 71 But he began to invoke a curse on himself and to swear, "I do not know this man of whom you speak." 72And immediately the cock crowed a second time. And Peter remembered how Jesus had said to him, "Before the cock crows twice, you will deny me three times." And he broke down and wept.

15 And as soon as it was morning the chief priests, with the elders and scribes, and the whole council held a consultation; and they bound Jesus and led him away and delivered him to Pilate. 2And Pilate asked him, "Are you the King of the Jews?" And he answered him, "You have said so." 3And the chief priests accused him of many things. 4And Pilate again asked him, "Have you no answer to make? See how many charges they bring against you." 5 But Jesus made no further answer, so that Pilate wondered.

6 Now at the feast he used to release for them one prisoner for whom they asked. 7And among the rebels in prison, who had committed murder in the insurrection, there was a man called Bar·ab′bas. 8And the crowd came up and began to ask Pilate to do as he was wont to do for them. 9And he answered them, "Do you want me to release for you the King of the Jews?" 10 For he perceived that it was out of envy that the chief priests had delivered him up. 11 But the chief priests stirred up the crowd to have him release for them Bar·ab′bas instead. 12And Pilate again said to them, "Then what shall I do with the man whom you call the King of the Jews?" 13And they cried out again, "Crucify him." 14And Pilate said to them, "Why, what evil has he done?" But they shouted all the more, "Crucify him." 15 So Pilate, wishing to satisfy the crowd, released for them Bar·ab′bas; and having scourged Jesus, he delivered him to be crucified.

16 And the soldiers led him away inside the palace (that is, the praetorium); and they called together the whole battalion. 17And they clothed him in a purple cloak, and plaiting a crown of thorns they put it on him. 18And they began to salute him, "Hail, King of the Jews!" 19And they struck his head with a reed, and spat upon him, and they knelt down in homage to him. 20And when they had mocked him, they

f Or *fore-court.* Other ancient authorities add *and the cock crowed*

the mighty shall flee away naked." "That day" of judgment has come, and no man can stand before it save One.

14:53-72 THE TRIAL BEFORE CAIAPHAS
AND PETER'S DENIAL

14:53-72 Cf. Mt 26:57-75 note.

14:62 *I am.* Cf. 6:50; 13:6. The words are spoken in the usual style of the OT declarations of the Lord (cf. Ex 3:14; Dt 32:39) and may include a claim to deity.

15:1-20 THE TRIAL BEFORE PILATE

15:1-20 Cf. Mt 27:1-31 note.

stripped him of the purple cloak, and put his own clothes on him. And they led him out to crucify him.

21 And they compelled a passer-by, Simon of Cy·re′ne, who was coming in from the country, the father of Alexander and Rufus, to carry his cross. 22And they brought him to the place called Gol′go·tha (which means the place of a skull). 23And they offered him wine mingled with myrrh; but he did not take it. 24And they crucified him, and divided his garments among them, casting lots for them, to decide what each should take. 25And it was the third hour, when they crucified him. 26And the inscription of the charge against him read, "The King of the Jews." 27And with him they crucified two robbers, one on his right and one on his left.*g* 29And those who passed by derided him, wagging their heads, and saying, "Aha! You who would destroy the temple and build it in three days, 30 save yourself, and come down from the cross!" 31 So also the chief priests mocked him to one another with the scribes, saying, "He saved others; he cannot save himself. 32 Let the Christ, the King of Israel, come down now from the cross, that we may see and believe." Those who were crucified with him also reviled him.

33 And when the sixth hour had come, there was darkness over the whole land*h* until the ninth hour. 34And at the ninth hour Jesus cried with a loud voice, "E·lo′i, E·lo′i, la′ma sabach-tha′ni?" which means, "My God, my God, why hast thou forsaken me?" 35And some of the bystanders hearing it said, "Behold, he is calling E·li′jah." 36And one ran and, filling a sponge full of vinegar, put it on a reed and gave it to him to drink, saying, "Wait, let us see whether E·li′jah will come to take him down." 37And Jesus uttered a loud cry, and breathed his last. 38And the curtain of the temple was torn in two, from top to bottom. 39And when the centurion, who stood facing him, saw that he thus*i* breathed his last, he said, "Truly this man was the Son*x* of God!"

40 There were also women looking on from afar, among whom were Mary Magdalene, and Mary the mother of James the younger and of Joses, and Sa·lo′me, 41 who, when he was in Galilee, followed him, and ministered to him; and also many other women who came up with him to Jerusalem.

42 And when evening had come, since it was the day of Preparation, that is, the day before the sabbath, 43 Joseph of Ar·i·ma·the′a, a respected member of the council, who was also himself looking for the kingdom of God, took courage and went to Pilate, and asked for the body of Jesus. 44And Pilate wondered if he were already dead; and summoning the centurion, he asked him whether he was already dead.*j* 45And when he learned from the centurion that he was dead, he granted the body to Joseph. 46And he bought a linen shroud, and taking him down, wrapped him in the linen shroud, and laid him in a tomb which had been hewn out of the rock; and he rolled a stone against the door of the tomb. 47 Mary Magdalene and Mary the mother of Joses saw where he was laid.

16 And when the sabbath was past, Mary Magdalene, and Mary the mother of James, and Sa·lo′me, bought spices, so that they might go and anoint him. 2And very early on the first day of the week they went to the tomb when the sun had risen. 3And they were saying to one another, "Who will roll away the stone for us from

g Other ancient authorities insert verse 28, *And the scripture was fulfilled which says, "He was reckoned with the transgressors"* *h* Or *earth* *i* Other ancient authorities insert *cried out and* *x* Or *a son*
j Other ancient authorities read *whether he had been some time dead*

15:21-47 THE CRUCIFIXION, DEATH, AND BURIAL OF JESUS

15:21-47 Cf. Mt 27:32-66 note.

15:21 *The father of Alexander and Rufus.* Simon and his sons were evidently well known to the church (or churches) for whom Mark wrote. If the Rufus of Ro 16:13 is identical with Simon's son, he was a member of one of the churches in Rome.

15:23 *Mingled with myrrh,* as a narcotic to dull the pain.

15:29 *Aha!* An expression of scornful wonder.

15:43 *Joseph . . . member of the council . . . took courage.* For a member of the council which had condemned Jesus to identify Himself thus with Jesus, publicly and at considerable expense, was an act of great courage. It would seem that Joseph in *looking for the kingdom of God* saw and welcomed its coming in Jesus.

15:44 *Wondered if,* or better, "was surprised that he" was "already dead." The suffering of the crucified was usually prolonged.

16:1-20 THE RESURRECTION

16:1-20 Cf. Mt 28:1-20 note.

the door of the tomb?" [4]And looking up, they saw that the stone was rolled back — it was very large. [5]And entering the tomb, they saw a young man sitting on the right side, dressed in a white robe; and they were amazed. [6]And he said to them, "Do not be amazed; you seek Jesus of Nazareth, who was crucified. He has risen, he is not here; see the place where they laid him. [7] But go, tell his disciples and Peter that he is going before you to Galilee; there you will see him, as he told you." [8]And they went out and fled from the tomb; for trembling and astonishment had come upon them; and they said nothing to any one, for they were afraid.

[9] Now when he rose early on the first day of the week, he appeared first to Mary Magdalene, from whom he had cast out seven demons. [10] She went out and told those who had been with him, as they mourned and wept. [11]But when they heard that he was alive and had been seen by her, they would not believe it.

[12] After this he appeared in another form to two of them, as they were walking into the country. [13]And they went back and told the rest, but they did not believe them.

[14] Afterward he appeared to the eleven themselves as they sat at table; and he upbraided them for their unbelief and hardness of heart, because they had not believed those who saw him after he had risen. [15]And he said to them, "Go into all the world and preach the gospel to the whole creation. [16]He who believes and is baptized will be saved; but he who does not believe will be condemned. [17]And these signs will accompany those who believe: in my name they will cast out demons; they will speak in new tongues; [18]they will pick up serpents, and if they drink any deadly thing, it will not hurt them; they will lay their hands on the sick, and they will recover."

[19] So then the Lord Jesus, after he had spoken to them, was taken up into heaven, and sat down at the right hand of God. [20]And they went forth and preached everywhere, while the Lord worked with them and confirmed the message by the signs that attended it. Amen.[k]

[k]Some of the most ancient authorities bring the book to a close at the end of verse 8. One authority concludes the book by adding after verse 8 the following: *But they reported briefly to Peter and those with him all that they had been told. And after this, Jesus himself sent out by means of them, from east to west, the sacred and imperishable proclamation of eternal salvation.* Other authorities include the preceding passage and continue with verses 9-20. In most authorities verses 9-20 follow immediately after verse 8; a few authorities insert additional material after verse 14.

16:7 *And Peter.* The special mention of Peter was occasioned by the fact that he had not only fled with the rest but had also denied Jesus in spite of his assurances.

16:8 *Trembling . . . astonishment . . . afraid.* It may be that the book which tells of the "beginning of the gospel of Jesus Christ, the Son of God" (1:1), ended here on this note of astonished fear and awe. This note is a recurrent one in Mark; men are awed and overwhelmed at Jesus' word of authority which even demons must obey (2:12); at the Son of God who stills the storm and walks across the waters (4:41; 6:51); at the Son of Man who has power to heal and to forgive sins on earth (2:12); at Him who conquers death with a word (5:42); at the glory of the transfigured beloved Son (9:6); at the Christ who goes in unshaken majesty toward Jerusalem and the cross (10:32). All this recurs in higher potency at the resurrection; these trembling women know, what every disciple of the Risen One comes to know, that in

this Son of God all the compassion and power of God is present, that there is only one thing to do — to fall down before Him and own Him as Lord and God, serve Him, and work out your salvation with fear and trembling, for here in Him God is at work giving men the will and the power to work according to His good pleasure (Ph 2:12-13). It is a solemn close to the gospel; the moment when all choices in life narrow down to one choice is a solemn one. It is the occurrence of that moment, then, that set the Good News going through the world; and it is the recurrence of that moment, ever and again, that keeps it going until the Christ, the Son of God, shall return.

16:9-10 Cf. Jn 20:11-18; Lk 24:10-11.

16:12-13 Cf. Lk 24:13-27.

16:14-18 Cf. Lk 24:36-49; Jn 20:19-23, 26-31; Mt 28:16.

16:15-16 Cf. Mt 28:18-20.

16:19 Cf. Lk 24:50-53; Acts 1:4-14.

THE GOSPEL ACCORDING TO

LUKE

INTRODUCTION

The third gospel is the most outspokenly "teaching" gospel of them all. This is already obvious from the dedicatory preface (Lk 1:1-4) in which the author promises Theophilus a full and orderly account of things Theophilus to some extent already knows, in order that he may have reliable information concerning the things he has been taught. Luke is not proclaiming the Gospel for the first time to Theophilus and his Gentile readers generally; rather, he intends to expand and fill in the already familiar basic outline of the Gospel message with a full account of what Jesus did and taught (cf. Acts 1:1). This is borne out by the fullness and completeness of his narrative; it is likewise confirmed by the fact that Luke extends his narrative in the Acts of the Apostles to include not only what Jesus "began to do and teach," but also the continued activity of the exalted Lord through His messengers by the power of the Spirit. The words of the preface, "accomplished *among us,*" indicate that Luke had this extension of the account in mind from the very beginning; he is, like Mark, going to tell the beginning of the Gospel of Jesus Christ; but he is going to carry on the account of it to include the triumphant progress of the Gospel from Jerusalem to Rome, the center of the world. He is recording that mighty growth of the Word of the Lord which he and his readers have come to know as the power of God in their own experience. The Spirit of God guided the mind of Luke to see that a man has not come to know the Christ fully until he has come to know also the church which the exalted Christ by His Word and through His messengers creates.

The Gospel According to Luke, with its companion volume, the Acts of the Apostles, is teaching designed for Gentiles. The name Theophilus is best taken as a real name, not merely as a symbolical designation of the Christian reader; the adjective "most excellent" (1:3) would mark him as a man of some standing in society—Paul and Tertullus use the same term in addressing the

Roman procurators Felix and Festus (Acts 24:2; 26:25). Luke was following a literary custom of antiquity in dedicating his work to Theophilus. The man to whom the book was dedicated often bore the cost of the publication and the distribution of the book; and this may well have been the case with Theophilus. Since the work follows the contemporary conventions of Greek literature, it would follow that it was designed for Greek readers. And the content of the work confirms this inference.

Author

The ancient church from the second half of the second century onward uniformly ascribes the third gospel and the Acts of the Apostles to Luke, "the beloved physician," Paul's companion on his journeys and his faithful friend in his imprisonment. He was probably a Gentile, for Paul distinguishes him from his Jewish co-workers (Cl 4:10-11, 14). He joined Paul at Troas during the second missionary journey, as the use of the first person plural in Acts 16:11 indicates, accompanied Paul as far as Philippi on that journey and apparently remained there for the next seven years. He rejoined Paul A. D. 56 when Paul passed through Philippi on his last journey to Jerusalem and was with him continually thereafter. According to 2 Ti 4:11 he was with Paul in his last imprisonment also.

The evidence of the two books themselves confirms the ancient tradition. The gospel and Acts have one author: Both are addressed to Theophilus, and they are markedly alike in language and style; they also show structural similarities. Now, the author of Acts in a number of places speaks in the first person plural (the so-called "we" passages, e.g., Acts 16:11-17; 20:5 – 21:18; 27:1 – 28:16), thus indicating that he was an eyewitness of the events recorded. Since these "we" passages are in the same style as the rest of the work and fit naturally into the whole narrative, they can hardly be assigned to another author. This marks the

author as a companion of Paul. Of all the known companions of Paul, only Titus and Luke come seriously into consideration; the rest are excluded by the content of the narrative itself or made unlikely by their obscurity. If the ancient church were guessing at the author, it might well have picked Titus, who is more prominent than Luke in the letters of Paul. The tradition which assigns the third gospel and Acts to Luke is therefore in all probability a genuine tradition and is to be trusted.

Scholars have naturally examined the language of Luke to see whether it betrays the physician. The first findings of research in this area greatly exaggerated the medical character of Luke's language. Later investigation has shown that much which had been labeled "medical" was not specifically medical at all but part of the common language of cultured men of the day. But if the language of Luke is not sufficiently medical in character to *prove* that he was a physician, it does confirm the ancient tradition insofar as there is nothing in it which makes it unlikely or impossible that the writer was a physician.

Characteristics of Luke's Gospel

Formally, the work of Luke is obviously the most literary and the most thoroughly Greek of the first three gospels. The preface with its formal structure, its conformity to Greek literary custom, its reference to the work of other writers, and its claim to painstaking and systematic research as the basis of an ordered and articulated account plainly bespeaks an acceptance of the work as a piece of Greek literature. The extensive proportions of the two-book work, its long perspective and broad scope, are in keeping with its announced literary intentions. The language and style have a purity and an elegance which set the work apart from the other gospels. Hebrew and Aramaic words are in general avoided; Latinisms are relatively rare. But the work is in no sense a compromise with Greek thought and spirit, even in style. Especially when the narrative moves on Palestinian soil, as in the gospel and the first 12 chapters of Acts, the style reflects the Semitically colored language of the Septuagint (the Greek translation of the Old Testament). And the gospel, for all its fullness, remains a gospel; it does not become a Greek biography. Likewise, the Acts of the Apostles is sacred history of a unique sort, the history not of heroic men but of the embattled and triumphant Word of the Lord.

The material peculiar to Luke emphasizes the absoluteness and the fullness of the forgiving grace which came into the world in the person of Jesus. Jesus' first Messianic words are "gracious words" (Lk 4:22); they reveal Him as the compassionate Servant of the Lord who brings good news to the poor, sight to the blind, liberty to the oppressed; His coming is the beginning of the great Year of Jubilee, the divinely appointed amnesty for all mankind (Lk 4:16-21). The story of Peter's call makes clear that the summons to discipleship is an act of divine forgiveness (Lk 5:1-11). The story of the sinful woman who anointed Jesus' feet, with its parable of the two debtors, shows how Jesus looked on forgiveness as the source and wellspring of ministering love (Lk 7:36-50). In the parable of the barren fig tree (Lk 13:6-9) Jesus pictures Himself as the Intercessor for a people under the judgment of God. In the moving parables of the prodigal son and the Pharisee and the publican the free and gracious forgiveness of God is put in sharp antithesis to the legalistic harshness and pride of Pharisaic piety (Lk 15:11-32; 18:9-14). The motif is continued in the story of Zacchaeus (Lk 19:1-10); one could inscribe over the whole gospel the Messianic words in which that story culminates: "The Son of man came to seek and to save the lost" (Lk 19:10). It is found in the shadow of the cross—Jesus intercedes for the disciple who will deny Him (Lk 22:31 to 34)—and on the cross itself; Jesus opens the gates of Paradise to the criminal beside Him (Lk 23:42-43). And the risen Christ sends out His disciples to preach repentance and forgiveness of sins in His name. (Lk 24:47)

The Christ of the third gospel is the Seeker of the lost, the Savior of the lowly. His birth is announced to the shepherds, whom good Jews suspected and despised (Lk 2:8-20), and He is branded by the righteous in Israel as one who "receives sinners and eats with them" (Lk 15:2). Of a piece with this picture of Jesus as the compassionate and condescending Savior is the special attention paid to women in this gospel, for woman was not highly regarded in Judaism or in the ancient world generally. The infancy story is Mary's story, not Joseph's as in Matthew; and Luke dwells more than the other evangelists on Jesus' relationship to women: Mary and Martha (Lk 10:38-42), the widow of Nain (Lk 7:11 to 17), the sinful woman (Lk 7:36-50), the

women on the *via dolorosa* (Lk 23:27-31)—
these are peculiar to Luke's account. And
two parables dealing with women are peculiar to Luke also: the parable of the lost coin
(Lk 15:8-10) and that of the importunate
widow. (Lk 18:1-8)

The third gospel emphasizes the universality of Jesus' grace and Saviorhood. It is
richly imbued with Old Testament language
and thought, and the portions peculiar to
Luke are pronouncedly Palestinian in
coloring—no other gospel gives us such
sympathetic portraits of the pure Judaic
piety which waited for the fulfillment of
God's promises as the first chapters of Luke.
Yet all that characterizes Jesus' earthly
ministry as limited to Israel recedes into the
background. Jesus' interpretation of the
Law, which occupies so broad a space in
Matthew (Mt 5:17-48), has no counterpart in
Luke. Luke does not tell of Jesus' dispute
with the scribes and Pharisees concerning
the tradition of the elders (Mt 15:1-20), nor
does he tell the story of the Syrophoenician
woman with its emphasis on Israel's prior
claim to the Gospel (Mt 15:21-28). His is the
universal, missionary outlook; he fits the
life of Jesus into world history; the names of
Augustus and Tiberius appear only in Luke
(Lk 2:1 ff.; 3:1 ff.). His genealogy of Jesus
does not stop with Abraham, but goes back
to Adam, the father of all mankind (Lk 3:23
to 38), and thus points up the universal significance of the Christ. Little touches here
and there keep this motif of universality
before the reader; for example, Luke alone
records the fact that soldiers, who would be
Gentiles, came to be baptized by John (3:14);
no other evangelist shows such an interest in
Samaritans as Luke (Lk 9:52 ff.; 17:11 ff.;
10:29 ff.); his gospel looks forward to the day
when Samaria would receive with joy the
Word of God (Acts 8:8, 14), when Peter would
be divinely led to preach the Gospel to a
Roman centurion (Acts 10), to the time when
the Word of the Lord would grow and prevail mightily until it reached "the end of the
earth." (Acts 1:8)

Perhaps it is because of Luke's emphasis
on the completely gratuitous character of
the grace of God in Christ, that Fatherly
grace which makes man merciful and sets
him free for a love that sees in never-ending
ministry its obvious task (Lk 17:7-10), that
there is in Luke's Gospel a corresponding
emphasis on the radical antithesis between
mammon and the kingdom of God. The
evangelist who so completely took the mea-

sure of God's transfiguring grace had a keen
eye also for those elements of Jesus' teaching
which warned against the disfiguring power
of wealth. The Magnificat of Mary sings of
the God who has filled the hungry with good
things and has sent the rich away empty
(Lk 1:53). Only Luke records the Baptist's
admonition, "He who has two coats, let him
share with him who has none" (Lk 3:11).
Only Luke records the woe upon the rich as
the counterpart to the beatitude upon the
poor (Lk 6:24). Only Luke tells of Jesus'
rebuke to the man who wanted His help in
getting his legal rights as heir: "Man, who
made me a judge or divider over you?" (Lk
12:14-15). Only Luke has the parables which
speak of the false security of the rich (Lk 12:
16-21) and of the wrong and right use of
riches. (Lk 16:19-31; 16:1-9)

The evangelist who was to write the
Gospel of the Holy Spirit (as Acts has aptly
been called) naturally emphasizes the
activity of the Holy Spirit in the life of the
Baptist (Lk 1:15, 17) and in the life and ministry of Jesus (Lk 1:35; 3:22; 4:1, 14, 18;
10:21). The "acceptable year of the Lord" is
in Luke's Gospel greeted by a burst of inspired song. Elizabeth, "filled with the
Spirit," hails the mother of the Lord (Lk
1:41-42); Zechariah "was filled with the Holy
Spirit and prophesied" over the child of his
old age, the forerunner of the Lord (Lk 1:67
to 79). The Holy Spirit was upon Simeon (Lk
2:25) and, "inspired by the Spirit" (Lk 2:27),
he hailed the Child in his arms as God's
salvation in person (Lk 2:29-32). The Messiah's gift will be the baptism with the
Spirit (Lk 3:16); His disciples have the
promise of the Spirit for their witness to the
world (Lk 12:11, 12; 24:49). The Holy Spirit
is the heavenly Father's best gift to His own.
(Lk 11:13)

Scholars are inclined to see the influence
of Paul in these religious emphases of Luke's
Gospel; the emphasis on the absoluteness of
God's grace in Christ, on the universality of
Christ's redeeming work, and on the Spirit
as the mark and the power of the new age is
certainly central to Paul's proclamation too.
The Lucan antithesis between mammon and
the kingdom of God has its counterpart in
Paul's antithesis of flesh and Spirit. And
since Paul performed his apostolic ministry
to the music of prayer and thanksgiving and
perpetually admonished his churches to
prayer, it may be that Luke's emphasis on
prayer owes something to Paul too. He does
go beyond the other evangelists in depicting

Jesus at prayer (Lk 3:21; 5:16; 6:12; 9:18; 9:28-29; 22:41 ff.; 23:34, 46) and in recording Jesus' teaching on prayer. Jesus, in Luke's Gospel, illustrates the difference between a false, self-righteous piety and the genuine piety of repentance by recounting the *prayers* of the Pharisee and the tax collector (Lk 18:9-14); and two parables of encouragement to prayer are peculiar to Luke. (Lk 11:5-8; 18:1-8)

If Matthew's Gospel is at once the most austere and the most compelling of the gospels, if Mark's is the most vivid and dramatic recital of the deeds of the Christ, Luke's is the warmest and most winning story of them all. It is Luke who has filled the church with the moving music of the New Testament canticles; it is Luke's Nativity story that has most decisively shaped the church's Christmas celebration. And the church's teaching has been immeasurably enriched by the warmth and pathos of such Lucan narratives as those of the widow of Nain, Jesus weeping over Jerusalem, the look of Jesus that called Peter to repentance, Jesus' words to the weeping daughters of Jerusalem, and the story of the walk to Emmaus.

Content of Luke's Gospel

The basic outline of Luke is that of Mark's Gospel. Luke prefaces this Marcan outline with an extensive account of the infancy and youth of both John the Baptist and Jesus, expands the Marcan account by means of two major insertions (Lk 6:20 – 8:3 between Mk 3:19 and 3:20; and Lk 9:51 – 18:14 between Mk 9:50 and 10:1) and by considerable additional material in the narrative of the Passion and Resurrection. He rather inexplicably omits the material covered by Mark 6:45 to 8:26. The peculiar quality of Luke's highly original work cannot therefore be very well indicated by an outline, which is consequently kept brief here. An appreciation of the individual accent of the third gospel is best gained (a) by studying the material peculiar to it, and (b) by a study of Luke-Acts as a unified whole.

OUTLINE

THE GOSPEL ACCORDING TO

LUKE

1 Inasmuch as many have undertaken to compile a narrative of the things which
have been accomplished among us, 2 just as they were delivered to us by those
who from the beginning were eyewitnesses and ministers of the word, 3 it seemed
good to me also, having followed all things closely[a] for some time past, to write an
orderly account for you, most excellent The·oph'i·lus, 4 that you may know the truth
concerning the things of which you have been informed.

John and Jesus: Forerunner and Messiah
1:5 − 2:52

5 In the days of Herod, king of Judea, there was a priest named Zech·a·ri'ah,[b]
of the division of A·bi'jah; and he had a wife of the daughters of Aaron, and her name
was Elizabeth. 6And they were both righteous before God, walking in all the commandments and ordinances of the Lord blameless. 7 But they had no child, because
Elizabeth was barren, and both were advanced in years.

8 Now while he was serving as priest before God when his division was on duty,
9 according to the custom of the priesthood, it fell to him by lot to enter the temple of
the Lord and burn incense. 10And the whole multitude of the people were praying
outside at the hour of incense. 11And there appeared to him an angel of the Lord
standing on the right side of the altar of incense. 12And Zech·a·ri'ah was troubled when

[a] Or accurately   [b] Greek Zacharias

1:1-4 PREFACE

1:1-4 Cf. the Introduction. The preface is done in
the manner of a Greek historian and gives an
account of the purpose and manner of Luke's work
as historian. But the historian is an evangelist
concerned with *the things ... accomplished among
us* (1), accomplished BY GOD in fulfillment of His
promises.

1:3 *Followed.* The word denotes careful investigation.

1:5 − 2:52 Paul says of the "gospel of God" that
it is the Gospel "which he promised beforehand
through his prophets in the holy scriptures" (Ro
1:2). All the evangelists bear him out in this.
Matthew links his story with that of Abraham and
David and sees the way of the Messiah illumined
step for step by the Word of the prophets (Mt 1 − 4).
For Mark the Gospel begins "as it is written in
Isaiah the prophet" (Mk 1:2). John harks back to
the creation (Jn 1:1) and to Moses (Jn 1:17). The
first two chapters of Luke, all material peculiar to
Luke, also hark back to God's ancient Word. The
style, in marked contrast to the finished Greek
period of the preface, is the stately and archaic
simplicity of OT narrative and the balanced
architecture of OT poetry. The material is charged
with OT ideas, language, institutions, historical
figures. But all serves to point up the fact that the
Gospel is the Gospel of God, the fulfillment of
His purpose and promise; all points to the great

new thing, to the good news (1:19; 2:10) of what
God is doing now, in the last days.

1:5-25 ANNUNCIATION OF BIRTH OF JOHN

1:5-25 The *good news* (19) is first spoken amid
the sanctities of the Old Covenant (the priesthood
and the temple) at the burning of the incense. To
an aged priest and his barren wife the angel announces the birth of a son who is to be the vessel of
God's grace, the dedicated prophet and Spirit-
filled forerunner who shall prepare the hearts of
his people for the coming of the Lord. The God
with whom no thing is impossible has spoken;
before Him the questioning of man must fall
silent. Man can only receive, in the total subject of
faith, the *words which will be fulfilled in their
time.*

1:5 *Herod, king of Judea.* Cf. Mt 2:1 note. Luke
uses *Judea* in the wider sense of the whole region
occupied by the Jews, all Palestine, not only of the
southern division. (Cf. 23:5)

Division of Abijah. The 8th of the 24 divisions
into which the priests were divided, each class
serving one week at a time. (1 Ch 24:10, 19)

1:7 *Barren ... advanced in years.* Like Abraham
and Sarah, to whom the son of the promise was
given against all human probabilities. (Gn 18:
10-14)

1:10 *Hour of incense.* Incense was offered twice
daily, morning and evening (Ex 30:7-8). For

he saw him, and fear fell upon him. [13] But the angel said to him, "Do not be afraid, Zech·a·ri′ah, for your prayer is heard, and your wife Elizabeth will bear you a son, and you shall call his name John.

[14]   And you will have joy and gladness,
              and many will rejoice at his birth;
[15]   for he will be great before the Lord,
              and he shall drink no wine nor strong drink,
              and he will be filled with the Holy Spirit,
              even from his mother's womb.
[16]   And he will turn many of the sons of Israel to the Lord their God,
[17]   and he will go before him in the spirit and power of E·li′jah,
              to turn the hearts of the fathers to the children,
              and the disobedient to the wisdom of the just,
              to make ready for the Lord a people prepared."

[18]And Zech·a·ri′ah said to the angel, "How shall I know this? For I am an old man, and my wife is advanced in years." [19]And the angel answered him, "I am Gabriel, who stand in the presence of God; and I was sent to speak to you, and to bring you this good news. [20]And behold, you will be silent and unable to speak until the day that these things come to pass, because you did not believe my words, which will be fulfilled in their time." [21]And the people were waiting for Zech·a·ri′ah, and they wondered at his delay in the temple. [22]And when he came out, he could not speak to them, and they perceived that he had seen a vision in the temple; and he made signs to them and remained dumb. [23]And when his time of service was ended, he went to his home.

24 After these days his wife Elizabeth conceived, and for five months she hid herself, saying, 25 "Thus the Lord has done to me in the days when he looked on me, to take away my reproach among men."

26 In the sixth month the angel Gabriel was sent from God to a city of Galilee named Nazareth, 27 to a virgin betrothed to a man whose name was Joseph, of the house of David; and the virgin's name was Mary. [28]And he came to her and said,

---

incense as symbolizing prayer cf. Ps 141:2; Rv 5:8; 8:3-4.

1:13 *Call his name John.* John signifies, "the Lord, the God of the covenant, has been gracious." God Himself, through the angel, gives the significant name. (Cf. Mt 1:21)

1:15 *Great.* John is the only man in the NT (besides our Lord, 1:32) to be called great in a good sense.

Drink no wine. John is to be wholly consecrated to God, like the Nazirite (Nm 6:1-21; Ju 13) of the OT. His sufficiency for the task assigned to him is from God; *he will be filled with the Holy Spirit.* (Cf. Mi 3:8)

1:16 *Turn* is the regular OT term for repentance. (Cf. 1 K 18:37)

1:17 *Spirit and power of Elijah.* Cf. Mt 11:14; 17:13. Through Malachi God had promised to send "Elijah the prophet" before the coming of "the great and terrible day of the Lord," to "turn the hearts" of His people (i.e., lead them to repentance), lest the coming of God find them unprepared and so prove disastrous to them (Ml 4:5-6). Now the great day of the Lord is dawning, and the promised forerunner will appear. His coming is a manifestation of the grace of the Lord. (Cf. 13 note)

Turn the hearts of the fathers to the children. Ml 4:5. The *fathers,* the pious men of old who awaited the fulfillment of God's promises (1:55,

72), will no longer be ashamed of the children who have abandoned the old hope and the old ways.

1:19 *Gabriel.* Cf. Dn 8:16; 9:21.

Stand in the presence of God, as His servant, to carry out His commands. Cf. Gn 41:46, where the phrase "stand in the presence of" is translated "entered the service of."

1:22 *Could not speak,* i.e., to pronounce the blessing which concluded the service.

1:24 *Hid herself.* Zechariah was forbidden to speak (20); Elizabeth voluntarily refrained from speaking of the wondrous promise of God *for five months* until it had become obvious that the words spoken by God's messenger would "be fulfilled in their time." (20)

1:25 *Reproach.* For the reproach, disgrace, of childlessness cf. Gn 30:23; 1 Sm 1:11.

1:26-38 ANNUNCIATION OF BIRTH OF JESUS

1:26-38 The annunciation to Mary is narrated in strict parallel to the story of the annunciation to Zechariah (angelic messenger; "troubled" recipient; calming of fear; promise of one who "will be great"; sign given, introduced by "and behold"; assurance of fulfillment); both stories are part of the one Gospel. But there is progression and heightening as well as parallelism. There is in the story of the annunciation to Mary a heightened emphasis on the initiative and the working of God; this is God's Gospel indeed, dominated by

"Hail, O favored one, the Lord is with you!"[c] 29 But she was greatly troubled at the saying, and considered in her mind what sort of greeting this might be. 30And the angel said to her, "Do not be afraid, Mary, for you have found favor with God. 31And behold, you will conceive in your womb and bear a son, and you shall call his name Jesus.

32　　　He will be great, and will be called the Son of the Most High;
　　　　　and the Lord God will give to him the throne of his father David,
33　　　and he will reign over the house of Jacob for ever;
　　　　　and of his kingdom there will be no end."

34And Mary said to the angel, "How shall this be, since I have no husband?" 35And the angel said to her,

　　　　　"The Holy Spirit will come upon you,
　　　　　and the power of the Most High will overshadow you;
　　　　　therefore the child to be born[d] will be called holy,
　　　　　the Son of God.

36And behold, your kinswoman Elizabeth in her old age has also conceived a son; and this is the sixth month with her who was called barren. 37 For with God nothing will be impossible." 38And Mary said, "Behold, I am the handmaid of the Lord; let it be to me according to your word." And the angel departed from her.

39 In those days Mary arose and went with haste into the hill country, to a city of Judah, 40 and she entered the house of Zech·a·ri′ah and greeted Elizabeth. 41And when Elizabeth heard the greeting of Mary, the babe leaped in her womb; and Elizabeth was filled with the Holy Spirit 42 and she exclaimed with a loud cry, "Blessed are you among women, and blessed is the fruit of your womb! 43And why is this granted me, that the mother of my Lord should come to me? 44 For behold, when the voice of your greeting came to my ears, the babe in my womb leaped for joy. 45And blessed is she who believed that there would be[e] a fulfilment of what was spoken to her from the Lord." 46And Mary said,

　　　　　"My soul magnifies the Lord,
47　　　and my spirit rejoices in God my Savior,

c Other ancient authorities add "Blessed are you among women!"
d Other ancient authorities add of you　e Or believed, for there will be

---

Him: here are God's messengers, God's *favor,* God's Word, God's *Spirit,* the *power* of the God with whom nothing is impossible, and above all the grace of God which gives to Israel and mankind the *Son of God to reign for ever* on the *throne of . . . David.* God's Gospel is good news "concerning his Son" (Ro 1:3), and it is genuine news of an event on earth, in history. The *Son of the Most High* enters David's line (*his father David,* 32); He comes into the flesh and the world, a world as concrete as Galilee, Nazareth, Joseph, Mary, a mother's womb. The combined supernatural wonder and the earthiness of the whole Gospel are here; and it is this Gospel of peace *on earth* that creates faith: *Let it be to me according to your word.* (38)

1:31 The wording recalls the promise of Immanuel (Is 7:14; cf. Mt 1:18-25 note). The name *Jesus* ("the Lord is salvation") is an unfolding of the meaning of Immanuel ("God with us").

1:32 *His father David.* God implants His Son in David's line.

1:32-33 *Throne . . . reign for ever.* For the eternal reign of the Son of David, the Messiah, cf. 2 Sm 7:8-17.

1:35 *Holy Spirit.* Cf. Mt 1:18-25 note.

1:39-56 THE MEETING OF THE TWO MOTHERS: THE MAGNIFICAT

1:39-56 The meeting of the two favored mothers (commonly called the Visitation) pulls together the two stories which have hither run parallel but separate. Mary beholds the promised sign (1:36), and experiences more than was promised: she hears from the lips of her inspired kinswoman the Spirit's confirmation of the message of Gabriel concerning herself and her Son, her own blessedness, and her Son's Lordship (39-45). The obedient and submissive faith of her who called herself "the handmaid of the Lord" (1:38) becomes the exultant faith which finds expression in Mary's song, the Magnificat. (46-55)

1:44 *Babe . . . leaped for joy.* There is nothing extraordinary in the fact itself that a babe leaps in the womb. But it is significant and a thing of wonder that this babe, the forerunner of the Messiah, leaped at just this moment, when Mary's greeting reached Elizabeth's ears.

1:42, 45 *Blessed . . . believed.* Mary is blessed because God has favored her and she has accepted and welcomed His favor in faith. She has heard and kept the Word of God. (11:27-28)

1:46-55 The Magnificat, so called from the first

48 for he has regarded the low estate of his handmaiden.
For behold, henceforth all generations will call me blessed;
49 for he who is mighty has done great things for me,
and holy is his name.
50 And his mercy is on those who fear him
from generation to generation.
51 He has shown strength with his arm,
he has scattered the proud in the imagination of their hearts,
52 he has put down the mighty from their thrones,
and exalted those of low degree;
53 he has filled the hungry with good things,
and the rich he has sent empty away.
54 He has helped his servant Israel,
in remembrance of his mercy,
55 as he spoke to our fathers,
to Abraham and to his posterity for ever."

56And Mary remained with her about three months, and returned to her home.

57 Now the time came for Elizabeth to be delivered, and she gave birth to a son. 58And her neighbors and kinsfolk heard that the Lord had shown great mercy to her, and they rejoiced with her. 59And on the eighth day they came to circumcise the child; and they would have named him Zech·a·ri′ah after his father, 60 but his mother said, "Not so; he shall be called John." 61And they said to her, "None of your kindred is called by this name." 62And they made signs to his father, inquiring what he would have him called. 63And he asked for a writing tablet, and wrote, "His name is John." And they all marveled. 64And immediately his mouth was opened and his tongue loosed, and he spoke, blessing God. 65And fear came on all their neighbors. And all these things were talked about through all the hill country of Judea; 66 and all who heard them laid them up in their hearts, saying, "What then will this child be?" For the hand of the Lord was with him.

67 And his father Zech·a·ri′ah was filled with the Holy Spirit, and prophesied, saying,

word of the song in the Latin Bible ("magnifies"), is the song of the "handmaid of the Lord," a song of faith (cf. 45). She sings of the God who, *holy* and *mighty,* has in mercy condescended to make her the object and instrument of His redeeming work (46-49). The vocabulary of her faith is the vocabulary of the OT, the song of Hannah (1 Sm 2:1-10) and the doxological language of the Psalms and prophets. In the light of God's new revelation the old "prophetic word" is "made more sure" for her (2 Ptr 1:19). She sees in her own history the continuation of the story of the divine *mercy* which *is on those who fear* their *God* and *Savior* (50); more than that, she sees that story drawing to its triumphant close, she sees the dawn of the final fulfillment of all God's promises to His people (55). That final triumph is, for her faith, so certain that she speaks of it (as also many OT prophets did) as already accomplished; God HAS triumphed in His sovereign mercy to *those of low degree,* to the *hungry;* while the *proud,* the *mighty,* and the *rich,* the self-sufficient and self-assertive men who feel no need of His mercy and refuse it, are overridden and destroyed. The blessing promised to *Abraham* (Gn 12:1-3) for all the families of the earth is breaking forth to do its work in all the earth; in the face of God's gracious action all human standards of greatness are inverted, all human greatness melts away.

1:48 *Regarded,* looked upon with favor and acted in love toward. Cf. 9:38, where the father of the afflicted boy asks Jesus "to look upon" his son, i.e., to have mercy on him and heal him.

1:49 *Holy is his name.* He reveals Himself *(name)* in such a way that He makes known the uniqueness of His mighty and merciful Godhead.

1:57-80 BIRTH OF JOHN: THE BENEDICTUS

1:57-80 The story moves on the earth; the sympathetic joy of neighbors and kinsfolk at the arrival of Elizabeth's boy and their kindly aunt-and-uncle officiousness at the naming of the child are homely touches. But this commonplace neighbor-and-relatives atmosphere is only the background and foil to the action of God, which makes men *marvel* and *fear* as they sense the presence of the *hand of the Lord* (63, 65, 66). God has given the child when all hope for children was past; God gives the child its significant name (cf. 1:13); God opens the mouth of Zechariah and gives him the *Holy Spirit* in order that he may *prophesy.* This is God's good news, and glory is given to Him: *Blessed be the Lord God of Israel.* (68)

1:64 *Blessing God.* The content of this blessing, praise, and thanksgiving is given in the Benedictus. (68-79)

1:67 *Prophesied.* Declared and interpreted the will and work of God, present and future.

68   "Blessed be the Lord God of Israel,
       for he has visited and redeemed his people,
69   and has raised up a horn of salvation for us
       in the house of his servant David,
70   as he spoke by the mouth of his holy prophets from of old,
71   that we should be saved from our enemies,
       and from the hand of all who hate us;
72   to perform the mercy promised to our fathers,
       and to remember his holy covenant,
73   the oath which he swore to our father Abraham, 74 to grant us
       that we, being delivered from the hand of our enemies,
       might serve him without fear,
75   in holiness and righteousness before him all the days of our life.
76   And you, child, will be called the prophet of the Most High;
       for you will go before the Lord to prepare his ways,
77   to give knowledge of salvation to his people
       in the forgiveness of their sins,
78   through the tender mercy of our God,
       when the day shall dawn upon*f* us from on high
79   to give light to those who sit in darkness and in the shadow of death,
       to guide our feet into the way of peace."

80And the child grew and became strong in spirit, and he was in the wilderness till the day of his manifestation to Israel.

2 In those days a decree went out from Caesar Augustus that all the world should be enrolled. 2 This was the first enrollment, when Qui·ri′ni·us was governor of Syria. 3And all went to be enrolled, each to his own city. 4And Joseph also went up

f Or *whereby the dayspring will visit.* Other ancient authorities read *since the dayspring has visited*

1:68-79 The Benedictus. "Benedictus" is the first word of Zechariah's song in the Latin Bible and means *blessed*. Like the Magnificat, the Benedictus is couched in the language of the OT, the characteristic speech of the pious who were "looking for the consolation of Israel" (2:25). The first strophe hails the dawn of Messianic salvation (68-75); the second proclaims the role which John is to play, as the *prophet of the Most High*, in this drama of redemption (76-79). Zechariah's prophecy celebrates the fidelity of the *Lord God of Israel* who has not forgotten *his people* nor *his servant David;* He has made a *promise* and fulfilled it, established a *covenant* and maintained it, sworn an *oath* and kept it. His people can rest secure in the hope that His *tender mercy* will complete what is now begun; they shall be delivered from their enemies and be enabled to *serve* their God *without fear* in *holiness and righteousness.* For God is dealing not only with their enemies but with all that thwarted and corrupted His people's service to Him in the past; He is dealing with their *sins.* He brings *salvation* and *forgiveness;* His people shall see *light* and life and shall worship their God in *peace.* (79)

1:68 *Visited.* He has come to help His people. Cf. Ja 1:27 — to "visit orphans and widows in their affliction" means to relieve their affliction, to help them.

1:69 *Horn of salvation.* The horn is a symbol of victorious strength. Cf. 1 Sm 2:10, where "horn" is translated with "power."

1:73 *Oath . . . to . . . Abraham.* Cf. Gn 22:16-18,

where the promise is repeated in the form of an oath.

Serve. The Greek word implies religious service, a life lived as worship to God. It was for such service that God had called Israel out of Egypt. (Ex 4:23)

1:78 The *day* (or *dayspring*) . . . *from on high* is the coming of the Messiah. Cf. Is 9:1-7 and Mt 4:12-22 note.

1:79 *Peace* has a more comprehensive meaning in Biblical speech than in ordinary English usage, denoting total soundness, health, wholeness (cf. 2:14). The coming of the Messiah will create a world in which all is as God wills it, divinely normal.

1:80 *In the wilderness . . . manifestation.* Since the discovery of the remains of the Essene community at Qumran in the Judean wilderness, there has been much speculation as to whether John may not have been a member of that "order." All that the gospel account tells us is that he grew up in solitude, apart from the corrupting influences of his people, and did not enter the priesthood. He was being preserved and kept for the *day of his manifestation,* the time when God would commission him and install him in his office. (Cf. 3:2)

2:1-20 THE BIRTH OF JESUS

2:1-20 How silently, how silently
     The wondrous gift is given.

This story has been so transfigured by Christian legend, song, and art that it is difficult to read it afresh in the simplicity of Luke's narrative. The

from Galilee, from the city of Nazareth, to Judea, to the city of David, which is called Bethlehem, because he was of the house and lineage of David, 5 to be enrolled with Mary, his betrothed, who was with child. 6And while they were there, the time came for her to be delivered. 7And she gave birth to her first-born son and wrapped him in swaddling cloths, and laid him in a manger, because there was no place for them in the inn.

8 And in that region there were shepherds out in the field, keeping watch over their flock by night. 9And an angel of the Lord appeared to them, and the glory of the Lord shone around them, and they were filled with fear. 10And the angel said to them, "Be not afraid; for behold, I bring you good news of a great joy which will come to all the people; 11 for to you is born this day in the city of David a Savior, who is Christ the Lord. 12And this will be a sign for you: you will find a babe wrapped in swaddling cloths and lying in a manger." 13And suddenly there was with the angel a multitude of the heavenly host praising God and saying,

14   "Glory to God in the highest,
         and on earth peace among men with whom he is pleased!"*g*

15 When the angels went away from them into heaven, the shepherds said to one another, "Let us go over to Bethlehem and see this thing that has happened, which the Lord has made known to us." 16And they went with haste, and found Mary and Joseph, and the babe lying in a manger. 17And when they saw it they made known the saying which had been told them concerning this child; 18 and all who heard it wondered at what the shepherds told them. 19 But Mary kept all these things, pondering them in her heart. 20And the shepherds returned, glorifying and praising God for all they had heard and seen, as it had been told them.

21 And at the end of eight days, when he was circumcised, he was called Jesus, the name given by the angel before he was conceived in the womb.

g Other ancient authorities read *peace, good will among men*

gift of God IS given "silently." Jesus comes into the world sharing with His people the degradation of foreign, pagan domination. The Roman emperor *Augustus* and the Roman *governor Quirinius* "dictate" the place of His birth. From the beginning "the Son of man has nowhere to lay his head" (9:58). He is bedded in a *manger;* and He is *wrapped* in *swaddling cloths* like any Jewish baby. The news of His birth is proclaimed only to unhonored *shepherds,* for whom His lowliness is to be the *sign* (12, 16) that identifies Him.

The "wondrousness" of the gift is marked by the Word of God, by which the angelic messengers of God interpret the event as God's act for us men and for our salvation. Not the child but the interpretive word has the radiant *glory* and the song of the *heavenly host.* That word is *good news of a great joy,* the fulfillment of God's promise to *David* for *all the people* of God, news of a *Savior,* a Deliverer who brings radical deliverance from man's desperation, the anointed King who has the right and the might *(Lord)* to carry out God's gracious purpose for man, to bring God's *peace* to men who have no claim to it but receive it gratis from His sovereign and spontaneous grace (*is pleased,* 14). Thus God is glorified, in the glory of His grace, and is praised by the tongues of angels (13) and of men. (20)

From this interpretive word fresh light falls on the lowliness of the Christ's beginnings. Not the Romans but God, the Lord of history, dictated the place of Jesus' birth; He is fulfilling His promise of a Deliverer from little *Bethlehem,* the *city of David*

(Mi 5:2-4; Mt 2:1-6 notes). God brought the Deliverer down into the depth of man's misery, that He might deliver man by taking up the burden of man's misery Himself. God picked shepherds to be the first recipients of the good news for the poor, that all men may be given ears to hear the good news to the poor.

2:1-2 *Enrolled.* The *enrollment* instituted by Augustus (31 B. C. — A. D. 14) was a census of the whole population designed to enable a complete and equitable taxation. It was made according to families in their native cities. According to documents discovered in Egypt, it was customary to take such a census every 14 years. The exact date of the census mentioned here and the part of *Quirinius* in it remain uncertain.

2:8 *Shepherds,* according to Jewish sources, were among the poor and despised in Palestine. They were suspected of dishonesty. A third-century rabbi expresses surprise at the fact that David can compare God with a shepherd. (Ps 23)

2:14 *God* has His *glory,* is manifested and acknowledged and adored as God, *in the highest,* now when in sending the Savior He creates *peace* (wholeness, health, well-being in every sense) on *earth* purely out of grace (the word translated *pleased* emphasizes the sovereign freedom and spontaneity of His favor).

2:21-40 THE CIRCUMCISION OF JESUS AND
         THE PRESENTATION IN THE TEMPLE

2:21-40 Jesus is "born under the law" (Gl 4:4); He is incorporated in the people of God by the rite

22 And when the time came for their purification according to the law of Moses, they brought him up to Jerusalem to present him to the Lord 23 (as it is written in the law of the Lord, "Every male that opens the womb shall be called holy to the Lord") 24 and to offer a sacrifice according to what is said in the law of the Lord, "a pair of turtledoves, or two young pigeons." 25 Now there was a man in Jerusalem, whose name was Simeon, and this man was righteous and devout, looking for the consolation of Israel, and the Holy Spirit was upon him. 26 And it had been revealed to him by the Holy Spirit that he should not see death before he had seen the Lord's Christ. 27 And inspired by the Spirit[h] he came into the temple; and when the parents brought in the child Jesus, to do for him according to the custom of the law, 28 he took him up in his arms and blessed God and said,

29   "Lord, now lettest thou thy servant depart in peace,
      according to thy word;
30   for mine eyes have seen thy salvation
31   which thou hast prepared in the presence of all peoples,
32   a light for revelation to the Gentiles,
      and for glory to thy people Israel."

33 And his father and his mother marveled at what was said about him; 34 and Simeon blessed them and said to Mary his mother,

    "Behold, this child is set for the fall and rising of many in Israel,
      and for a sign that is spoken against
35   (and a sword will pierce through your own soul also),
      that thoughts out of many hearts may be revealed."

36 And there was a prophetess, Anna, the daughter of Pha·nu'el, of the tribe of Asher; she was of a great age, having lived with her husband seven years from her virginity, 37 and as a widow till she was eighty-four. She did not depart from the temple, worshiping with fasting and prayer night and day. 38 And coming up at that very hour she gave thanks to God, and spoke of him to all who were looking for the redemption of Jerusalem.

39 And when they had performed everything according to the law of the Lord,

[h] Or in the Spirit

---

of circumcision (21), which is prescribed by the Law and commits Him to the keeping of the Law (Gn 17:12-14; Lv 12:3; Ro 2:25). The purification of the mother and the presentation of the firstborn Son are carried out according to the law of Moses. (22-24)

Here, as He goes the way of obedience to the Law, in His Father's house two prophetic voices bear witness to the Messianic Child. Simeon, moved by the Spirit, recognizes that his time of waiting witness is over; the consolation of Israel, the Lord's Christ, has come, and the Lord whose faithful prophet-servant he had been will now let him depart in peace, his work done. In the language of OT prophecy (Is 40:5; 52:10; 42:6; 49:6, 9; 25:7; 46:13) he hails the Child in his arms as thy [Lord's] salvation in person, a salvation wrought by the ministry of a Servant Messiah who is to serve and suffer for the salvation of all peoples, for the Gentiles as well as His people. Even Jesus' parents marveled at this revelation, which for the first time speaks of the universal mission of Mary's Son (33). Jesus is to be the Servant Messiah who goes through contradiction and suffering (Is 50:5-6) to His ultimate and universal redeeming triumph. He will be a sign of God's present gracious working, but a sign spoken against (34); men will fail or refuse to see in Him the Lord's

salvation, and the ways of men will divide before Him. Some will stumble at Him in unbelief and so fall in their unbelief, others will see the saving arm of the Lord revealed in Him as He suffers and dies for the sins of all (Is 53), will repent and believe and find in Him a rising to new life (34). None can remain neutral over against Him; the thoughts of men's hearts will become manifest before Him (35). They will either call the Crucified Lord or will call Him accursed (1 Co 12:3). His mother, blessed among women, cannot be spared the pain of being mother of the Servant (sword, 35).

A second prophetic voice confirms the prophecy of Simeon; the venerable prophetess Anna speaks of the Christ to all those quiet hopers in Israel who were looking for the redemption of Jerusalem. (36-38; Is 52:9)

2:21 Name given by the angel. Cf. 1:31 note.

2:22 Purification . . . present. Cf. Lv 12:2-8; Ex 13:2, 12, 15.

2:29-30 Simeon's song is called the Nunc Dimittis after the opening words in the Latin Bible. It is usually sung in the post-Communion liturgy.

2:29 Servant. For the prophets as servants cf., e.g., Jer 26:5; 29:19; 35:15; Am 3:7; Zch 1:6.

2:34 Sign. Cf. 11:30.

Fall and rising. Cf. Is 8:14-15.

they returned into Galilee, to their own city, Nazareth. 40And the child grew and became strong, filled with wisdom; and the favor of God was upon him.

41 Now his parents went to Jerusalem every year at the feast of the Passover. 42And when he was twelve years old, they went up according to custom; 43 and when the feast was ended, as they were returning, the boy Jesus stayed behind in Jerusalem. His parents did not know it, 44 but supposing him to be in the company they went a day's journey, and they sought him among their kinsfolk and acquaintances; 45 and when they did not find him, they returned to Jerusalem, seeking him. 46After three days they found him in the temple, sitting among the teachers, listening to them and asking them questions; 47 and all who heard him were amazed at his understanding and his answers. 48And when they saw him they were astonished; and his mother said to him, "Son, why have you treated us so? Behold, your father and I have been looking for you anxiously." 49And he said to them, "How is it that you sought me? Did you not know that I must be in my Father's house?" 50And they did not understand the saying which he spoke to them. 51And he went down with them and came to Nazareth, and was obedient to them; and his mother kept all these things in her heart.

52 And Jesus increased in wisdom and in stature,*i* and in favor with God and man.

The Ministry of John the Baptist

3:1-22

3 In the fifteenth year of the reign of Ti·be′ri·us Caesar, Pontius Pilate being governor of Judea, and Herod being tetrarch of Galilee, and his brother Philip tetrarch of the region of It·u·rae′a and Trach·o·ni′tis, and Ly·sa′ni·as tetrarch of Ab′i·le′ne, 2 in the high-priesthood of Annas and Ca′ia·phas, the word of God came to John the

i Or *years*

2:40 *Filled with wisdom.* Wisdom, comprehensive insight into the will and work of God, is a characteristic of the Messiah. (Is 11:2)

2:41-52 THE BOY JESUS IN HIS
    FATHER'S HOUSE

2:41-52 The one recorded incident from Jesus' boyhood shows Him walking the path of obedience. The story begins with His obedience to the Law which established the *Passover* and prescribed its celebration (Ex 12:1-6; 23:15; Dt 16:1-8); it ends with Jesus' obedience to His parents, obedience to the Fourth Commandment, which He later defended so fiercely against the encroachments of Judaic tradition (Mt 15:4). In this setting we hear His first words. In these words God is, for the first time in Luke, expressly called Jesus' *Father.* In these words Jesus expresses His high consciousness of His mission and office; His life is to be uniquely a human life wholly lived to God, a life which is in all its parts and in every aspect an act of worship, as man's life ought to be and never had been. He *must be in* His *Father's house,* obedient in the place and for the salvation of all. Here begins the career of obedience "unto death, even death on a cross" (Ph 2:8). Here for the first time Mary has a premonition of the sword that is to pierce her soul. (Cf. 35)

2:41 Cf. Dt 16:1-8; Ex 23:15.

2:44 *Company.* A village or group of villages would make up a caravan for the pilgrimage to Jerusalem. The custom then was probably the same as in modern times, with the women and little children in the lead, followed by the men, while older children stayed with either parent. A 12-year-old would therefore not necessarily be missed until nightfall.

2:48 *Anxiously.* The Greek word thus translated is somewhat stronger, expressing pain. Cf. Acts 20:38, where it is rendered "sorrowing."

2:51 *His mother kept all these things in her heart.* Some scholars see here a hint that Mary herself was Luke's source of information for the events of Jesus' childhood.

2:52 *Wisdom.* Cf. 2:40. The wording is traditional, used in the OT of the growing up of Samson and Samuel, (Ju 13:24; 1 Sm 2:26)

3:1-20 Cf. Mt 3:1-17 notes.

3:1-9 THE VOICE IN THE WILDERNESS

3:1-9 Cf. Mt 3:1-10 notes.

3:1-2 In keeping with this markedly universal outlook, Luke connects the history of John with general history, dating the beginning of his ministry by listing the secular and religious authorities of the time.

3:1 *Fifteenth year of . . . Tiberius.* Either A. D. 28/29 or 26/27, depending on whether one dates from the year in which Tiberius succeeded Augustus or from the year when he was associated with Augustus as coruler.

3:1 *Tetrarch,* originally "ruler of the fourth part of a country," then used more loosely to designate any dependent prince with less than royal power and dignity.

3:2 *High-priesthood of Annas and Caiaphas.* Annas was deposed from the high-priesthood in A. D. 15 but continued to have great influence in

son of Zech·a·ri′ah in the wilderness; ³ and he went into all the region about the Jordan, preaching a baptism of repentance for the forgiveness of sins. ⁴As it is written in the book of the words of I·sa′iah the prophet,

> "The voice of one crying in the wilderness:
> Prepare the way of the Lord,
> make his paths straight.

5
> Every valley shall be filled,
> and every mountain and hill shall be brought low,
> and the crooked shall be made straight,
> and the rough ways shall be made smooth;

6
> and all flesh shall see the salvation of God."

7 He said therefore to the multitudes that came out to be baptized by him, "You brood of vipers! Who warned you to flee from the wrath to come? ⁸ Bear fruits that befit repentance, and do not begin to say to yourselves, 'We have Abraham as our father'; for I tell you, God is able from these stones to raise up children to Abraham. ⁹ Even now the axe is laid to the root of the trees; every tree therefore that does not bear good fruit is cut down and thrown into the fire."

10 And the multitudes asked him, "What then shall we do?" ¹¹And he answered them, "He who has two coats, let him share with him who has none; and he who has food, let him do likewise." ¹² Tax collectors also came to be baptized, and said to him, "Teacher, what shall we do?" ¹³And he said to them, "Collect no more than is appointed you." ¹⁴ Soldiers also asked him, "And we, what shall we do?" And he said to them, "Rob no one by violence or by false accusation, and be content with your wages."

15 As the people were in expectation, and all men questioned in their hearts concerning John, whether perhaps he were the Christ, ¹⁶ John answered them all, "I baptize you with water; but he who is mightier than I is coming, the thong of whose sandals I am not worthy to untie; he will baptize you with the Holy Spirit and with fire. ¹⁷ His winnowing fork is in his hand, to clear his threshing floor, and to gather the wheat into his granary, but the chaff he will burn with unquenchable fire."

18 So, with many other exhortations, he preached good news to the people. ¹⁹ But Herod the tetrarch, who had been reproved by him for He·ro′di·as, his brother's wife, and for all the evil things that Herod had done, ²⁰ added this to them all, that he shut up John in prison.

21 Now when all the people were baptized, and when Jesus also had been baptized

---

the Sanhedrin, the Jewish high council. Four of his sons and his son-in-law Caiaphas became high priests. Caiaphas held office from A. D. 18 to 36. Jn 18:13, 24 indicate that Annas and Caiaphas collaborated closely, although Caiaphas alone "was high priest that year." (Jn 11:49)

The word of God came. This is a phrase frequently used in the OT for the calling of a prophet (e.g., Jer 1:4; Hos 1:1; Jon 1:1). The word of the prophet is God's Word, entrusted to the prophet.

3:4-6 Is 40:3-5. Luke quotes Isaiah more fully than the other evangelists to state explicitly the universal significance of the action of God which begins with the ministry of the Baptist (*all flesh,* 6).

3:10-14 JOHN INSTRUCTS THE PENITENT

3:10-14 Luke alone records the words with which Jesus spells out the meaning of "fruits that befit repentance" (8). Those "fruits" are simple acts of social kindliness, beginning at once there in the desolate regions where John baptized, where nights are cold (*coats*) and *food* is not readily obtainable for those who come without adequate

provisions (11). Men are not summoned to leave their professions (even the profession of a *tax collector,* which Pharisaic piety looked upon as a dubious one at best, cf. 15:1-2) but to act honestly in their professions. The *soldiers,* probably mercenaries in the service of Herod Antipas, included non-Jews; here is a first fulfillment of the promise that "all flesh" shall see the salvation of God. (6)

3:15-20 PROMISE OF THE MIGHTIER ONE:
JOHN SHUT UP IN PRISON

3:15-20 Cf. Mt 3:1 ff.

3:15 *The people were in expectation.* Luke alone records the reaction of the people which occasioned John's witness to the coming Mightier One and his own subservient role.

3:18-20 Luke does not record the execution of John (Mt 14:1-12; Mk 6:17-18); it is presupposed in 9:7-9.

3:21-22 THE BAPTISM OF JESUS

3:21-22 Cf. Mt 3:13-17 notes. Luke's account links Jesus' baptism with that of *all the people,* thus marking the fact that Jesus is making Him-

and was praying, the heaven was opened, 22 and the Holy Spirit descended upon him in bodily form, as a dove, and a voice came from heaven, "Thou art my beloved Son;*j* with thee I am well pleased."*k*

Jesus' Galilean Ministry
3:23 — 9:50

23 Jesus, when he began his ministry, was about thirty years of age, being the son (as was supposed) of Joseph, the son of Heli, 24 the son of Matthat, the son of Levi, the son of Melchi, the son of Jan'na·i, the son of Joseph, 25 the son of Mat·ta·thi'as, the son of Amos, the son of Nahum, the son of Esli, the son of Naggai, 26 the son of Maath, the son of Mat·ta·thi'as, the son of Sem'e·in, the son of Josech, the son of Joda, 27 the son of Jo·a'nan, the son of Rhesa, the son of Ze·rub'ba·bel, the son of She·al'ti·el,*l* the son of Neri, 28 the son of Melchi, the son of Addi, the son of Cosam, the son of El·ma'dam, the son of Er, 29 the son of Joshua, the son of El·i·e'zer, the son of Jorim, the son of Matthat, the son of Levi, 30 the son of Simeon, the son of Judah, the son of Joseph, the son of Jonam, the son of E·li'a·kim, 31 the son of Melea, the son of Menna, the son of Mat'ta·tha, the son of Nathan, the son of David, 32 the son of Jesse, the son of Obed, the son of Boaz, the son of Sala, the son of Nahshon, 33 the son of Am·min'a·dab, the son of Admin, the son of Arni, the son of Hezron, the son of Perez, the son of Judah, 34 the son of Jacob, the son of Isaac, the son of Abraham, the son of Terah, the son of Nahor, 35 the son of Serug, the son of Reu, the son of Peleg, the son of Eber, the son of Shelah, 36 the son of Ca·i'nan, the son of Ar·phax'ad, the son of Shem, the son of Noah, the son of Lamech, 37 the son of Methuselah, the son of Enoch, the son of Jared, the son of Ma·ha'la·le·el, the son of Ca·i'nan, 38 the son of Enos, the son of Seth, the son of Adam, the son of God.

4 And Jesus, full of the Holy Spirit, returned from the Jordan, and was led by the Spirit 2 for forty days in the wilderness, tempted by the devil. And he ate nothing in those days; and when they were ended, he was hungry. 3 The devil said to him, "If you are the Son of God, command this stone to become bread." 4And Jesus answered him, "It is written, 'Man shall not live by bread alone.' " 5And the devil took him up, and showed him all the kingdoms of the world in a moment of time, 6 and said to him, "To you I will give all this authority and their glory; for it has been delivered to me, and I give it to whom I will. 7 If you, then, will worship me, it shall all be yours." 8And Jesus answered him, "It is written,

> 'You shall worship the Lord your God,
>   and him only shall you serve.' "

j Or *my Son, my* (or *the*) *Beloved*   *k* Other ancient authorities read *today I have begotten thee*
l Greek *Salathiel*

---

self one with His people in their need. The reference to Jesus' *praying* is peculiar to Luke also; Jesus is aligning His will with the will of the Father (cf. 22:42) and submitting to baptism "to fulfil all righteousness." (Cf. Mt 3:13-15 note)

3:23-38 THE GENEALOGY OF JESUS

3:23-38 Cf. Mt 1:1-17 note. As in Matthew, the symmetry of numbers indicates God's control of the history that culminates in the incarnation of the Son of God. There are 77 names in the genealogy, in groupings that are multiples of 7 (21 names from *Jesus* to *Zerubbabel*, 21 names from *Shealtiel* to *Nathan*, 14 names from *David* to *Isaac*, 21 names from *Abraham* to *Adam*). While Matthew's genealogy (from Abraham through David to Jesus) leads up to Him "who will save HIS PEOPLE from their sins" (Mt 1:21), that of Luke leads up to Him who is the Savior of all sons of Adam, all mankind, the One in whom "ALL FLESH

shall see the salvation of God" (Lk 3:6; cf 2:32). Efforts to harmonize the two genealogies have not been altogether successful. A useful suggestion is that Matthew traces the royal line, while Luke traces physical descent.

3:38 *Son of Adam, the son of God.* In Jesus the new creation begins (2 Co 5:17); through faith in Christ Jesus men can all become sons of God again. (Gl 3:26)

4:1-13 THE TEMPTATION OF JESUS

4:1-13 Cf. Mt 4:1-11 note. Two features distinguish Luke's account from that of Mt: (a) Luke inverts the order of the last two temptations, so that the final temptation takes place in *Jerusalem* (9), and Jerusalem is in his gospel the place of Jesus' suffering and death (9:31, 51, 53; cf. 13:22; 13:33, 34; 17:11; 18:31; 19:11, 28). Thus the temptation is marked at the beginning of the "trials" of Jesus (22:28, the same word in Greek as "tempta-

⁹And he took him to Jerusalem, and set him on the pinnacle of the temple, and said to him, "If you are the Son of God, throw yourself down from here; ¹⁰ for it is written,
    'He will give his angels charge of you, to guard you,'
¹¹ and
    'On their hands they will bear you up,
    lest you strike your foot against a stone.' "
¹²And Jesus answered him, "It is said, 'You shall not tempt the Lord your God.' "
¹³And when the devil had ended every temptation, he departed from him until an opportune time.

14 And Jesus returned in the power of the Spirit into Galilee, and a report concerning him went out through all the surrounding country. ¹⁵And he taught in their synagogues, being glorified by all.

16 And he came to Nazareth, where he had been brought up; and he went to the synagogue, as his custom was, on the sabbath day. And he stood up to read; ¹⁷ and there was given to him the book of the prophet I·sa′iah. He opened the book and found the place where it was written,
18   "The Spirit of the Lord is upon me,
    because he has anointed me to preach good news to the poor.
    He has sent me to proclaim release to the captives
    and recovering of sight to the blind,
    to set at liberty those who are oppressed,
19   to proclaim the acceptable year of the Lord."
²⁰And he closed the book, and gave it back to the attendant, and sat down; and the eyes of all in the synagogue were fixed on him. ²¹And he began to say to them, "Today this scripture has been fulfilled in your hearing." ²²And all spoke well of him, and wondered at the gracious words which proceeded out of his mouth; and they said, "Is not this Joseph's son?" ²³And he said to them, "Doubtless you will quote to me this proverb, 'Physician, heal yourself; what we have heard you did at Ca·per′na·um,

tion"), which culminate in His Passion and death. (b) The second distinctive feature is related to the first; *the devil . . . departed* from Jesus *until an opportune time;* that final opportune time is the Passion, when "Satan entered into Judas" to betray his Lord (22:3), when Satan sought to sift Jesus' disciples like wheat (22:31), when Jesus greeted His captors with the words: "This is your hour, and the power of darkness" (22:53). Thus Luke marks Jesus' whole career as an unshrinking and victorious confrontation with the power of the Evil One. Cf. also 10:18; 11:18-22; 13:16; Acts 10:38; 26:18. The Son of God goes forth to war.

4:14-30 NAZARETH REJECTS JESUS

4:14-30 Luke sums up Jesus' activity in *Galilee* with *he taught in their synagogues* (15); and it is as Teacher that He confronts His home city *Nazareth.* He teaches as any Jewish teacher might, in the synagog, *on the sabbath,* on the basis of an OT text, standing to read and sitting to teach as custom prescribed. But then He appears as One who teaches *in the power of the Spirit* (14) who had descended upon Him at His baptism (3:22). The beloved Son is not merely another expounder of the prophetic Word; He is the fulfillment of that Word (21). He stands before the men of Nazareth as the Spirit-filled Anointed One of God, with the gift of *good news to the poor, release* for the *captives, sight* for the *blind, liberty* for the *oppressed* — with His appearing the new exodus begins (18). As He proclaims *the acceptable year of the Lord* (19),

the great Year of Jubilee when God sets all right again, that is no longer a promise but a reality; the year of the Lord is beginning as men hear it proclaimed by Him. (21)

Men were astonished at His *gracious words;* but they were also offended that Joseph's son, the hometown boy, should assume the authority to speak to them. And when He refused to validate His authority with a sign (23), but pointed to the Scriptures instead, to make plain to them that God's sovereign grace can (and will) be bestowed on Gentile Sidonians and Syrians if Israel will not accept it — when He added His stringent call to repentance to His proffer of the good news (24-27), they were *filled with wrath* (28) and prepared to execute judgment on this blasphemer (29). Already Jesus is the Sign that is spoken against (2:34) who proves to be the fall of many just because God has set Him for the rising of many. Jesus goes toward the cross, and the Gospel will go to the Gentiles.

4:18-19 Is 61:1-2. Significantly, Jesus omits the second half of 61:2, "and the day of vengeance of our God." He offers the free grace of God; God's vengeance will come on all who refuse His grace.

4:19 *The acceptable year.* The background idea is probably that of the Year of Jubilee, every 50th year, a holy year, the "year of liberty" (Ez 46:17), when property reverted to its original owners, debts were remitted, and Israelite slaves were set free (Lv 25:8-24; 27:17-24; Nm 36:4). In this last great Year of Jubilee all captives everywhere shall be set free and all will be made well.

do here also in your own country.' " [24]And he said, "Truly, I say to you, no prophet is acceptable in his own country. [25] But in truth, I tell you, there were many widows in Israel in the days of E·li′jah, when the heaven was shut up three years and six months, when there came a great famine over all the land; [26] and E·li′jah was sent to none of them but only to Zar′e·phath, in the land of Sidon, to a woman who was a widow. [27]And there were many lepers in Israel in the time of the prophet E·li′sha; and none of them was cleansed, but only Na′a·man the Syrian." [28] When they heard this, all in the synagogue were filled with wrath. [29]And they rose up and put him out of the city, and led him to the brow of the hill on which their city was built, that they might throw him down headlong. [30] But passing through the midst of them he went away.

31 And he went down to Ca·per′na·um, a city of Galilee. And he was teaching them on the sabbath; [32] and they were astonished at his teaching, for his word was with authority. [33]And in the synagogue there was a man who had the spirit of an unclean demon; and he cried out with a loud voice, [34] "Ah![m] What have you to do with us, Jesus of Nazareth? Have you come to destroy us? I know who you are, the Holy One of God." [35] But Jesus rebuked him, saying, "Be silent, and come out of him!" And when the demon had thrown him down in the midst, he came out of him, having done him no harm. [36]And they were all amazed and said to one another, "What is this word? For with authority and power he commands the unclean spirits, and they come out." [37]And reports of him went out into every place in the surrounding region.

38 And he arose and left the synagogue, and entered Simon's house. Now Simon's mother-in-law was ill with a high fever, and they besought him for her. [39]And he stood over her and rebuked the fever, and it left her; and immediately she rose and served them.

40 Now when the sun was setting, all those who had any that were sick with various diseases brought them to him; and he laid his hands on every one of them and healed them. [41]And demons also came out of many, crying, "You are the Son of God!" But he rebuked them, and would not allow them to speak, because they knew that he was the Christ.

42 And when it was day he departed and went into a lonely place. And the people sought him and came to him, and would have kept him from leaving them; [43] but he said to them, "I must preach the good news of the kingdom of God to the other cities also; for I was sent for this purpose." [44]And he was preaching in the synagogues of Judea.[n]

5   While the people pressed upon him to hear the word of God, he was standing by the lake of Gen·nes′a·ret. [2]And he saw two boats by the lake; but the fishermen had gone out of them and were washing their nets. [3] Getting into one of the boats, which was Simon's, he asked him to put out a little from the land. And he sat down

---

[m] Or *Let us alone*   [n] Other ancient authorites read *Galilee*

4:25 *Elijah*. Cf. 1 K 17:1, 8-16; 18:1.

4:27 *Elisha*. Cf. 2 K 5:1-14.

4:29 *Throw him down headlong*. This points to stoning, the punishment which the Law prescribed for blasphemy (Lv 24:10-16). The guilty person was thrown down backward from a wall or cliff; and if he survived, heavy stones were cast on him.

4:31-44 THE WORD WITH AUTHORITY

4:31-44 In 4:15 Lk has described Jesus' activity in Galilee as teaching, even though He evidently performed mighty deeds in Capernaum, as 4:23 indicates. The mighty deeds (such as the expulsion of a demon here) are but manifestations of *the word . . . with authority* (32) of the person of Christ. The Word is emphasized throughout this section. Jesus *rebuked* the fever of *Simon's mother-in-law* (39) and *rebuked* the *demons* (41). He owes

the *good news of the kingdom of God* to all Israel (43) and goes *preaching in the synagogues of Judea*. (44)

4:31-37 Cf. Mk 1:21-28, esp. 1:27 note.

4:38-41 Cf. Mt 8:17 note; Mk 1:32.

4:42-44 Cf. Mk 1:35-38.

5:1-11 THE CALLING OF SIMON PETER AND HIS PARTNERS

5:1-11 Cf. Mt 4:18-22 note. The "word with authority" (4:32) dominates the story. That Word of Jesus, here expressly designated as *word of God,* drew the people to Jesus (1), commandeered Peter's boat (3), creatively produced the great catch of fish contrary to all human likelihood and all fishermen's experience (4-7), removed the fear of Simon Peter when he fell down at Jesus' knees desperately aware of his sinfulness in the presence of this almighty goodness and giving (8), and

and taught the people from the boat. [4]And when he had ceased speaking, he said to Simon, "Put out into the deep and let down your nets for a catch." [5]And Simon answered, "Master, we toiled all night and took nothing! But at your word I will let down the nets." [6]And when they had done this, they enclosed a great shoal of fish; and as their nets were breaking, [7] they beckoned to their partners in the other boat to come and help them. And they came and filled both the boats, so that they began to sink. [8] But when Simon Peter saw it, he fell down at Jesus' knees, saying, "Depart from me, for I am a sinful man, O Lord." [9] For he was astonished, and all that were with him, at the catch of fish which they had taken; [10] and so also were James and John, sons of Zeb′e·dee, who were partners with Simon. And Jesus said to Simon, "Do not be afraid; henceforth you will be catching men." [11]And when they had brought their boats to land, they left everything and followed him.

12 While he was in one of the cities, there came a man full of leprosy; and when he saw Jesus, he fell on his face and besought him, "Lord, if you will, you can make me clean." [13]And he stretched out his hand, and touched him, saying, "I will; be clean." And immediately the leprosy left him. [14]And he charged him to tell no one; but "go and show yourself to the priest, and make an offering for your cleansing, as Moses commanded, for a proof to the people."[o] [15] But so much the more the report went abroad concerning him; and great multitudes gathered to hear and to be healed of their infirmities. [16] But he withdrew to the wilderness and prayed.

17 On one of those days, as he was teaching, there were Pharisees and teachers of the law sitting by, who had come from every village of Galilee and Judea and from Jerusalem; and the power of the Lord was with him to heal.[p] [18]And behold, men were bringing on a bed a man who was paralyzed, and they sought to bring him in and lay him before Jesus;[q] [19] but finding no way to bring him in, because of the crowd, they went up on the roof and let him down with his bed through the tiles into the midst before Jesus. [20]And when he saw their faith he said, "Man, your sins are forgiven you." [21]And the scribes and the Pharisees began to question, saying, "Who is this that speaks blasphemies? Who can forgive sins but God only?" [22] When Jesus perceived their questionings, he answered them, "Why do you question in your hearts? [23] Which is easier, to say, 'Your sins are forgiven you,' or to say, 'Rise and walk'? [24] But that you may know that the Son of man has authority on earth to forgive sins"—he said to the man who was paralyzed—"I say to you, rise, take up your bed and go home." [25]And immediately he rose before them, and took up that on which he lay, and went home, glorifying God. [26]And amazement seized them all, and they glorified God and were filled with awe, saying, "We have seen strange things today."

27 After this he went out, and saw a tax collector, named Levi, sitting at the tax office; and he said to him, "Follow me." [28]And he left everything, and rose and followed him.

29 And Levi made him a great feast in his house; and there was a large company of tax collectors and others sitting at table[r] with them. [30]And the Pharisees and their scribes murmured against his disciples, saying, "Why do you eat and drink with tax collectors and sinners?" [31]And Jesus answered them, "Those who are well have no

---

[o] Greek *to them*   [p] Other ancient authorities read *was present to heal them*   [q] Greek *him*   [r] Greek *reclining*

summoned him to his apostolic ministry (10). That Word produced in Peter and his partners the ready will to leave everything and follow Jesus (11). They were called to renunciation and ministry; but above all, they were called (as Peter later expressed it) to "obtain a blessing." (1 Ptr 3:9)

5:1 *Lake of Gennesaret.* The Sea of Galilee.

5:8 *Lord* represents a higher degree of respect and awe than the *Master* of Peter's first response. (5)

5:9 The word translated *astonished* indicates an awe-filled recognition of how great the distance is between the Holy One of God and sinful man, how undeserved His favor, how intolerable His pres-

ence for man on any terms but that of the forgiveness of sins. (Cf. 1:77)

5:12-16 THE LEPER MADE CLEAN

    5:12-16 Cf. Mt 8:1-4 notes.

5:17-26 "YOUR SINS ARE FORGIVEN. RISE AND WALK"

    5:17-26 Cf. Mt 9:1-8 notes; cf. Mt 8:23 – 9:8 note.

5:27-39 THE CALLING OF LEVI: THE PHYSICIAN AND THE BRIDEGROOM

    5:27-39 Cf. Mt 9:9-17 note.

need of a physician, but those who are sick; 32 I have not come to call the righteous, but sinners to repentance."

33 And they said to him, "The disciples of John fast often and offer prayers, and so do the disciples of the Pharisees, but yours eat and drink." 34And Jesus said to them, "Can you make wedding guests fast while the bridegroom is with them? 35 The days will come, when the bridegroom is taken away from them, and then they will fast in those days." 36 He told them a parable also: "No one tears a piece from a new garment and puts it upon an old garment; if he does, he will tear the new, and the piece from the new will not match the old. 37And no one puts new wine into old wineskins; if he does, the new wine will burst the skins and it will be spilled, and the skins will be destroyed. 38 But new wine must be put into fresh wineskins. 39And no one after drinking old wine desires new; for he says, 'The old is good.' "[s]

6 On a sabbath,[t] while he was going through the grainfields, his disciples plucked and ate some heads of grain, rubbing them in their hands. 2 But some of the Pharisees said, "Why are you doing what is not lawful to do on the sabbath?" 3And Jesus answered, "Have you not read what David did when he was hungry, he and those who were with him: 4 how he entered the house of God, and took and ate the bread of the Presence, which it is not lawful for any but the priests to eat, and also gave it to those with him?" 5And he said to them, "The Son of man is lord of the sabbath."

6 On another sabbath, when he entered the synagogue and taught, a man was there whose right hand was withered. 7And the scribes and the Pharisees watched him, to see whether he would heal on the sabbath, so that they might find an accusation against him. 8 But he knew their thoughts, and he said to the man who had the withered hand, "Come and stand here." And he rose and stood there. 9And Jesus said to them, "I ask you, is it lawful on the sabbath to do good or to do harm, to save life or to destroy it?" 10And he looked around on them all, and said to him, "Stretch out your hand." And he did so, and his hand was restored. 11 But they were filled with fury and discussed with one another what they might do to Jesus.

12 In these days he went out to the mountain to pray; and all night he continued in prayer to God. 13And when it was day, he called his disciples, and chose from them twelve, whom he named apostles; 14 Simon, whom he named Peter, and Andrew his brother, and James and John, and Philip, and Bartholomew, 15 and Matthew, and Thomas, and James the son of Al-phae'us, and Simon who was called the Zealot, 16 and Judas the son of James, and Judas Is-car'i-ot, who became a traitor.

17 And he came down with them and stood on a level place, with a great crowd of his disciples and a great multitude of people from all Judea and Jerusalem and the

[s] Other ancient authorities read better
[t] Other ancient authorities read On the second first sabbath (on the second sabbath after the first)

5:39 The meaning of this verse, only in Lk, remains obscure. Perhaps Jesus is warning those who will not join His disciples in the festive freedom which His forgiving presence brings against clinging to the old ways out of mere attachment to old tradition and pious habit.

6:1-11 TWO SABBATH CONTROVERSIES

6:1-11 Cf. Mt 12:1-14 note. Besides these two Sabbath controversies which he has in common with Mt and Mk, Lk records two others (13:10-17; 14:1-6) peculiar to his gospel.

6:12-16 JESUS APPOINTS 12 APOSTLES

6:12-16 Cf. Mt 10:1-4 note; Mk 3:13-19. The notice that Jesus spent the night before the appointment in prayer (12) occurs only in Lk and marks the solemnity of the act. Jesus is at one with the will of His Father as He begins that extension of His activity through authorized and empowered messengers (9:1) which shall reach "to the end of the earth." (Acts 1:8)

6:17-49 THE SERMON ON THE PLAIN

6:17-49 Cf. Mt 5:1 — 7:29 notes. A brief introduction (17-19) indicates that Jesus' ministry has attracted not only a great crowd of his disciples but a great multitude of people, interested but not yet committed, from among all Jewry (all Judea and Jerusalem) and from regions as far away as Tyre and Sidon to the west, where many Jews lived. The time has come to extend His ministry through His disciples, and it is they who are addressed in the sermon. (20)

To His disciples, first, the Gospel of God's free royal favor to the poor (20-26); second, the imperative of freely giving and forgiving love (27-38); and third, the injunction of a ministry (lead, 39) which is an expression of their faithful and obedient discipleship. (39-49)

seacoast of Tyre and Sidon, who came to hear him and to be healed of their diseases; [18] and those who were troubled with unclean spirits were cured. [19]And all the crowd sought to touch him, for power came forth from him and healed them all.

20 And he lifted up his eyes on his disciples, and said:

"Blessed are you poor, for yours is the kingdom of God.

21 "Blessed are you that hunger now, for you shall be satisfied.

"Blessed are you that weep now, for you shall laugh.

22 "Blessed are you when men hate you, and when they exclude you and revile you, and cast out your name as evil, on account of the Son of man! [23] Rejoice in that day, and leap for joy, for behold, your reward is great in heaven; for so their fathers did to the prophets.

24 "But woe to you that are rich, for you have received your consolation.

25 "Woe to you that are full now, for you shall hunger.

"Woe to you that laugh now, for you shall mourn and weep.

26 "Woe to you, when all men speak well of you, for so their fathers did to the false prophets.

27 "But I say to you that hear, Love your enemies, do good to those who hate you, [28] bless those who curse you, pray for those who abuse you. [29] To him who strikes you on the cheek, offer the other also; and from him who takes away your coat do not withhold even your shirt. [30] Give to every one who begs from you; and of him who takes away your goods do not ask them again. [31]And as you wish that men would do to you, do so to them.

32 "If you love those who love you, what credit is that to you? For even sinners love those who love them. [33]And if you do good to those who do good to you, what credit is that to you? For even sinners do the same. [34]And if you lend to those from whom you

6:20-26 GOOD NEWS TO THE POOR

6:20-26 The good news is proclaimed (as anticipated in the Magnificat, 1:51-53) as the great reversal of the standards and orders of this age in the dawning new age. The *poor,* whose only riches is the *Son of man* (22), whose lot *now* is *hunger,* tears, and dishonor *on account of the Son of man,* they have cause for joy; God is their King and will lead them through the darkness of sorrow and persecution into His perfect *day.* The *rich* and the *full,* who have chosen to live by bread alone (4:4), who live and *laugh* now and enjoy honor in the age for which they live, the age whose short view and selfish standards determine the pattern of their lives—they shall share the fate of the *false prophets* of old, who turned their people from repentance and hope to present enjoyment and perished with their people under the judgment of God.

6:20-21 *Poor . . . hunger . . . weep.* Cf. Mt 5:3, 4, 6 notes.

6:22-23. Cf. Mt 5:11 note.

6:22 *Exclude,* i. e., from the community, especially the worshiping community. (Cf. Jn 9:22; 12:42; 16:2)

Cast out your name as evil. Cast out is probably the equivalent of a Hebrew term meaning "to publish abroad" (cf. Dt 22:14, 19). The disciples will be reviled and slandered. (Mt 5:11)

6:23 *In that day,* the day of the Lord (cf. Zph 1:7) when God's judgment will deal with the malice of His enemies and His grace will vindicate and *reward* all who have suffered for His sake.

6:24 *Rich* is not merely an economic designation;

the word designates men like the rich man of 16:19-31 whose riches blinded him to the misery of Lazarus and left him no time for Moses and the prophets, or the rich fool of 12:16-21 whose riches shut him up completely with his own concerns, so that he laid up "treasures for himself" and was "not rich toward God." (Cf. Ja 5:1-6)

6:26 *False prophets.* Cf. Mi 2:1-6, 11.

6:27-38 BE SONS OF THE MOST HIGH

6:27-38 The response of the disciples to the love of God shown to them as to the poor, the hungry, the mourners; their response to Him who has given them a hope so sure and strong that they are able to endure dishonor with joy (20-23)—their response is to *love.* "We love because he first loved us" (1 Jn 4:19). This love is to have on it the mark of its divine origin (*sons of the Most High,* 35; *your Father is merciful,* 36). It is love for the *enemies* with no thought for the worthiness of its object (27-28), love that is willing to expose itself to abuse, love simply according to the Golden Rule (29-31), love as different from normal human mutual amiability as God's love is from man's; He is their *Father,* and they derive their capacity for love from Him who *is kind to the ungrateful and the selfish* (32-36). They have found in God the Judge as He is revealed in Jesus the *merciful* God who forgives and gives (cf. 5:1-11); as sons of the Forgiver and Giver they can *forgive* (not *judge* and *condemn*) and can hope for His overwhelmingly generous reward. (37-38)

6:27-30 Cf. Mt 5:38-42 note.

6:31 Cf. Mt 7:12 note.

6:32-36. Cf. Mt 5:43-48 note.

hope to receive, what credit is that to you? Even sinners lend to sinners, to receive as much again. 35 But love your enemies, and do good, and lend, expecting nothing in return;[v] and your reward will be great, and you will be sons of the Most High; for he is kind to the ungrateful and the selfish. 36 Be merciful, even as your Father is merciful.

37 "Judge not, and you will not be judged; condemn not, and you will not be condemned; forgive, and you will be forgiven; 38 give, and it will be given to you; good measure, pressed down, shaken together, running over, will be put into your lap. For the measure you give will be the measure you get back."

39 He also told them a parable: "Can a blind man lead a blind man? Will they not both fall into a pit? 40A disciple is not above his teacher, but every one when he is fully taught will be like his teacher. 41 Why do you see the speck that is in your brother's eye, but do not notice the log that is in your own eye? 42 Or how can you say to your brother, 'Brother, let me take out the speck that is in your eye,' when you yourself do not see the log that is in your own eye? You hypocrite, first take the log out of your own eye, and then you will see clearly to take out the speck that is in your brother's eye.

43 "For no good tree bears bad fruit, nor again does a bad tree bear good fruit; 44 for each tree is known by its own fruit. For figs are not gathered from thorns, nor are grapes picked from a bramble bush. 45 The good man out of the good treasure of his heart produces good, and the evil man out of his evil treasure produces evil; for out of the abundance of the heart his mouth speaks.

46 "Why do you call me 'Lord, Lord,' and not do what I tell you? 47 Every one who comes to me and hears my words and does them, I will show you what he is like: 48 he is like a man building a house, who dug deep, and laid the foundation upon rock; and when a flood arose, the stream broke against that house, and could not shake it, because it had been well built.[w] 49 But he who hears and does not do them is like a man who built a house on the ground without a foundation; against which the stream broke, and immediately it fell, and the ruin of that house was great."

7 After he had ended all his sayings in the hearing of the people he entered Ca·per'-na·um. 2 Now a centurion had a slave who was dear[x] to him, who was sick and at the point of death. 3 When he heard of Jesus, he sent to him elders of the Jews, asking

[v] Other ancient authorities read *despairing of no man*
[w] Other ancient authorities read *founded upon the rock*   [x] Or *valuable*

6:35 *Selfish.* This seems rather a mild translation of the Greek word used here, which can mean "evil, bad, base, worthless, vicious," and is used of Satan as the Evil One, e. g., Mt 13:19.

6:37-38 Cf. Mt 7:1-2 note.

6:38 *Good measure ... put into your lap.* The lap is literally the fold of the loose garment as it falls from the chest over the girdle; this pouchlike place was used as a pocket, here for carrying grain (cf. 2 K 4:39). In Is 40:11 the Lord is pictured as carrying a lamb in this fold of the garment.

6:39-49 ONE FULLY TAUGHT WILL BE LIKE HIS TEACHER

6:39-49 The disciples are to become apostles (6:14), representatives of their Lord, called to *lead* the new people of God (39), as He leads; they will have His task of opening the eyes of the *blind* (4:18). If they are not to be blind leaders of the blind (like the scribes and Pharisees who led men to their ruin, Mt 15:14), they must be *fully taught,* in order to be *like* their *teacher* (40). To lead the blind, they need clarity of vision; they can lead men to repentance only as forgiven leaders, as men who have taken the *log* out of their *own eye* by repentance (39-42). They can, moreover, lead

men only by being what they proclaim, *good trees* bearing *good fruit, good men* producing good from the treasury of their *hearts* (43-45). In a word, they can fulfill their function by hearing and doing the *words* of their Lord, by taking up His teaching into their mind, heart, and will. Thus their life will be a *house built upon rock,* stable and unshaken when the house *without a foundation* (the house of those who pay only lip service to their Lord, 46) falls in *ruin* under the judgment of their Lord. (46-49)

6:40 *Fully taught,* i. e., completely fitted out, put into perfect working order, as the Greek word suggests.

6:49 *It fell,* an illustration of how the Child in Simeon's arms is "set for the fall . . . of many." (2:34; cf. Is 30:12-13)

7:1-10 HEALING THE CENTURION'S SLAVE

7:1-10 Cf. Mt 8:1-17 note. Peculiar to Lk is the intercession of the Jewish *elders* on behalf of the Gentile *centurion* (3-5). Since the centurion *loves* their *nation* and built them their *synagogue* (5), he is probably one of those Gentiles who were drawn to the monotheism of the synagog and attended the worship services there without,

him to come and heal his slave. ⁴And when they came to Jesus, they besought him earnestly, saying, "He is worthy to have you do this for him, ⁵ for he loves our nation, and he built us our synagogue." ⁶And Jesus went with them. When he was not far from the house, the centurion sent friends to him, saying to him, "Lord, do not trouble yourself, for I am not worthy to have you come under my roof; ⁷ therefore I did not presume to come to you. But say the word, and let my servant be healed. ⁸ For I am a man set under authority, with soldiers under me: and I say to one, 'Go,' and he goes; and to another, 'Come,' and he comes; and to my slave, 'Do this,' and he does it." ⁹ When Jesus heard this he marveled at him, and turned and said to the multitude that followed him, "I tell you, not even in Israel have I found such faith." ¹⁰And when those who had been sent returned to the house, they found the slave well.

11 Soon afterward*ʸ* he went to a city called Nain, and his disciples and a great crowd went with him. ¹²As he drew near to the gate of the city, behold, a man who had died was being carried out, the only son of his mother, and she was a widow; and a large crowd from the city was with her. ¹³And when the Lord saw her, he had compassion on her and said to her, "Do not weep." ¹⁴And he came and touched the bier, and the bearers stood still. And he said, "Young man, I say to you, arise." ¹⁵And the dead man sat up, and began to speak. And he gave him to his mother. ¹⁶ Fear seized them all; and they glorified God, saying, "A great prophet has arisen among us!" and "God has visited his people!" ¹⁷And this report concerning him spread through the whole of Judea and all the surrounding country.

18 The disciples of John told him of all these things. ¹⁹And John, calling to him two of his disciples, sent them to the Lord, saying, "Are you he who is to come, or shall we look for another?" ²⁰And when the men had come to him, they said, "John the Baptist has sent us to you, saying, 'Are you he who is to come, or shall we look for another?' " ²¹ In that hour he cured many of diseases and plagues and evil spirits, and on many that were blind he bestowed sight. ²²And he answered them, "Go and tell John what you have seen and heard: the blind receive their sight, the lame walk, lepers are cleansed, and the deaf hear, the dead are raised up, the poor have good news preached to them. ²³And blessed is he who takes no offense at me."

24 When the messengers of John had gone, he began to speak to the crowds concerning John: "What did you go out into the wilderness to behold? A reed shaken by the wind? ²⁵ What then did you go out to see? A man clothed in soft clothing? Behold, those who are gorgeously appareled and live in luxury are in kings' courts. ²⁶ What then did you go out to see? A prophet? Yes, I tell you, and more than a prophet. ²⁷ This is he of whom it is written,
>'Behold, I send my messenger before thy face,
>who shall prepare thy way before thee.'

ʸ Other ancient authorities read Next day

---

however, submitting to circumcision or obligating themselves to keep the whole Law. Such Gentiles appear frequently in Acts as among the first to accept the Gospel message of Paul, and it is probably for this reason that Lk stresses this feature. Even here Christ appears as the Light of the Gentiles (2:32; for this type of Gentile in Acts, called "devout," "you that fear God," "devout converts to Judaism," "worshiper of God," cf. Acts 10:2; 13:16, 26, 43, 50; 16:14; 17:4, 17; 18:7).

7:11-17 RAISING OF WIDOW'S SON AT NAIN

7:11-17 Recorded by Lk alone. This is the first narrative in which the evangelist calls Jesus *Lord* (13). That divine authority for which distance was no obstacle (6-8) and the grace which reached beyond Israel to help a believing Gentile centurion (9) are here conjoined in Jesus' *compassion* for the *widow* and His word of power to the *only*

son lying dead—here is the Lord, "the day" which has dawned "from on high to give light to those . . . in the shadow of death" (1:78-79). Here is cause for holy *fear;* here is reason for *glorifying God;* the long-awaited *prophet* "mighty in deed and word" (24:19) has appeared (16). The prophecy of Zechariah is being fulfilled: "Blessed be the Lord God of Israel, for he has visited and redeemed his people." (1:68) The Gospel preached to the poor is a power; the dead are raised up. (22)

7:13 *Had compassion.* The Greek word used here is used only to designate the compassion of God or of Christ (Mt 9:36; 14:14; 15:32; 18:27; 20:34; Mk 1:41; 9:22; Lk 15:20). The one exception is the compassion of the Good Samaritan. (Lk 10:33)

7:16 *Great prophet.* Cf. Dt 18:15, 18; Acts 3:22-23. *Visited.* Cf. 1:68 note.

7:18-30 JOHN'S QUESTION FROM PRISON

7:18-30 Cf. Mt 11:1-15 note.

28 I tell you, among those born of women none is greater than John; yet he who is least in the kingdom of God is greater than he." 29 (When they heard this all the people and the tax collectors justified God, having been baptized with the baptism of John; 30 but the Pharisees and the lawyers rejected the purpose of God for themselves, not having been baptized by him.)

31 "To what then shall I compare the men of this generation, and what are they like? 32 They are like children sitting in the market place and calling to one another,

'We piped to you, and you did not dance;

we wailed, and you did not weep.'

33 For John the Baptist has come eating no bread and drinking no wine; and you say, 'He has a demon.' 34 The Son of man has come eating and drinking; and you say, 'Behold, a glutton and a drunkard, a friend of tax collectors and sinners!' 35 Yet wisdom is justified by all her children."

36 One of the Pharisees asked him to eat with him, and he went into the Pharisee's house, and took his place at table. 37And behold, a woman of the city, who was a sinner, when she learned that he was at table in the Pharisee's house, brought an alabaster flask of ointment, 38 and standing behind him at his feet, weeping, she began to wet his feet with her tears, and wiped them with the hair of her head, and kissed his feet, and anointed them with the ointment. 39 Now when the Pharisee who had invited him saw it, he said to himself, "If this man were a prophet, he would have known who and what sort of woman this is who is touching him, for she is a sinner." 40And Jesus answering said to him, "Simon, I have something to say to you." And he answered, "What is it, Teacher?" 41 "A certain creditor had two debtors; one owed five hundred denarii, and the other fifty. 42 When they could not pay, he forgave them both. Now which of them will love him more?" 43 Simon answered, "The one, I suppose, to whom he forgave more." And he said to him, "You have judged rightly." 44 Then turning toward the woman he said to Simon, "Do you see this woman? I entered your house, you gave me no water for my feet, but she has wet my feet with her tears and wiped them with her hair. 45 You gave me no kiss, but from the time I came in she has not ceased to kiss my feet. 46 You did not anoint my head with oil, but she has anointed my feet with ointment. 47 Therefore I tell you, her sins, which are many, are forgiven, for she loved much; but he who is forgiven little, loves little." 48And he said to her, "Your sins are forgiven." 49 Then those who were at table with him began to say among themselves, "Who is this, who even forgives sins?" 50And he said to the woman, "Your faith has saved you; go in peace."

7:29-30 Peculiar to Lk. Cf. Mt 21:31-32. This is Lk's comment on the people's reaction to John's baptism of repentance.

7:29 *Having been baptized*—perhaps better, "by accepting John's baptism of repentance."

Justified God. They declared that God had dealt righteously with them in dealing with them as sinners and offering them entry into His kingdom by way of repentance and forgiveness. (3:3)

7:30 *The Pharisees and the lawyers,* who sought salvation by way of the Law, *rejected the purpose of God,* "who desires all men to be saved" (1 Ti 2:4), by refusing John's baptism. They sought to establish their own righteousness and "did not submit to God's." (Ro 10:3)

Lawyers, experts in the Mosaic law.

7:31-35 WE PIPED . . . YOU DID NOT DANCE

7:31-35 Cf. Mt 11:16-19 note.

7:34 *Friend of tax collectors and sinners.* This was a stone of stumbling for Pharisee and scribe (cf. 15:1-2 note); they were offended at free forgiveness, whether proclaimed by John (30) or enacted by Jesus. (Cf. 9:21)

7:35 The *wisdom* of God *is justified by all her children.* The new people of God made up of forgiven sinners and accepted outcasts will at the end inherit the Kingdom (cf. Mt 21:31-32), while those who in their self-sufficiency have refused God's grace will perish; thus the *children* of God, created by His wise redemptive counsels, will demonstrate that "the foolishness of God is wiser than men." (1 Co. 1:25)

7:36-50 A MAN HAD TWO DEBTORS: THE SINFUL WOMAN

7:36-50 Recorded only by Lk. Jesus' contemporaries complained that He was "a friend of sinners" (34). Jesus' host, *Simon the Pharisee,* was making the same complaint when he saw Jesus' accepting the lavish devotion of a sinful woman (37-38) and concluded that Jesus was no *prophet*—would not a prophet know what *sort of woman* was *touching him* and shrink from such contact with a *sinner,* as every good *Pharisee* did (39)? Jesus' answer to Simon's unspoken objection (which constitutes the heart of the story) proves Him to be a prophet indeed; He sees the sin in Simon's heart and with

8 Soon afterward he went on through cities and villages, preaching and bringing the good news of the kingdom of God. And the twelve were with him, 2 and also some women who had been healed of evil spirits and infirmities: Mary, called Magdalene, from whom seven demons had gone out, 3 and Joanna, the wife of Chuza, Herod's steward, and Susanna, and many others, who provided for them *z* out of their means.

4 And when a great crowd came together and people from town after town came to him, he said in a parable: 5 "A sower went out to sow his seed; and as he sowed, some fell along the path, and was trodden under foot, and the birds of the air devoured it. 6And some fell on the rock; and as it grew up, it withered away, because it had no moisture. 7And some fell among thorns; and the thorns grew with it and choked it. 8And some fell into good soil and grew, and yielded a hundredfold." As he said this, he called out, "He who has ears to hear, let him hear."

9 And when his disciples asked him what this parable meant, 10 he said, "To you it has been given to know the secrets of the kingdom of God; but for others they are in parables, so that seeing they may not see, and hearing they may not understand. 11 Now the parable is this: The seed is the word of God. 12 The ones along the path are those who have heard; then the devil comes and takes away the word from their hearts, that they may not believe and be saved. 13And the ones on the rock are those who, when they hear the word, receive it with joy; but these have no root, they believe for a while and in time of temptation fall away. 14And as for what fell among the thorns, they are those who hear, but as they go on their way they are choked by the cares and riches and pleasures of life, and their fruit does not mature. 15And as for that in the good soil, they are those who, hearing the word, hold it fast in an honest and good heart, and bring forth fruit with patience.

16 "No one after lighting a lamp covers it with a vessel, or puts it under a bed, but puts it on a stand, that those who enter may see the light. 17 For nothing is hid that

z Other ancient authorities read *him*

prophetic authority calls him to repentance. The parable of the *two debtors* (40-43) makes it plain that all men are sinners and all need a "friend of sinners" if they are to have a friend at all. All men are in God's debt, and only divine release from that debt, great or small, can release a man for a life of *love* (42, 47). And then Simon learns that the Prophet who sat at table with him (36) is not only a friend of sinners; He *forgives sins* with divine authority (to the shocked astonishment of Simon's guests, 49) and sends the forgiven sinner, who believed in the Friend of sinners, whose *faith* was active in abundant *love*, with the assurance of salvation (*saved*) and in *peace* (50). Again we hear the "gracious words" of the Anointed of the Lord, and again we sense the contradiction they evoke. (Cf. 4:18-30)

7:39 *A prophet . . . would have known.* Cf. Jn 4:16, 29.

7:41 A *denarius* was a day's wage for a laborer. (Mt 20:2)

7:47 *For she loved much.* The greatness of her love is evidence of the reality of the forgiveness; she could not have loved much if her *many sins* had not been *forgiven.*

8:1-3 JESUS' COMPANIONS ON HIS TRAVELS

8:1-3 The presence of the *twelve* is noted; they are being trained for their apostolic mission by being witnesses of the *good news of the kingdom of God* proclaimed by Jesus in word and deed. Cf. Mk 3:14: "He appointed twelve, TO BE WITH HIM, and

to be sent out to preach." (Cf. also Lk 9:1-2, 6.) The *women* who accompanied Jesus and *provided* for Him and His disciples *out of their means* are examples of those who "loved much" (7:47) because of the forgiving grace which they had experienced (2). Jesus' kindly and respectful attitude toward women is in striking contrast to that of Judaism generally and of the rabbis in particular; He accepts their services, calls woman His "sister" in the household of God (Mt 12:50), and is entirely free of the painful scrupulosity which marked the rabbis' association with womankind—the pure and free association here described would have been unthinkable for them.

8:2 *Mary Magdalene.* Cf. Mt 27:56; 28:1; Jn 20:1.

8:3 *Joanna.* Cf. Lk 24:10.

Chuza, Herod's steward, either a manager of some of Herod's properties or a political official in his service. Jesus' influence had extended even to court circles.

Susanna, otherwise unknown.

8:4-15 THE PARABLE OF THE SOWER

8:4-15 Cf. Mt 13:1-9 note; Mt 13:1-52 note.

8:16-21 TAKE HEED HOW YOU HEAR

8:16-21 These words are addressed primarily to the disciples (9) and reinforce the encouragement and warning of the parable of the sower (4-15). The Word of God is an imperiled Word, exposed to the attack of the devil, the power of temptations, and the pressure of both care and pleasure (11-14).

shall not be made manifest, nor anything secret that shall not be known and come to light. 18 Take heed then how you hear; for to him who has will more be given, and from him who has not, even what he thinks that he has will be taken away."

19 Then his mother and his brothers came to him, but they could not reach him for the crowd. 20And he was told, "Your mother and your brothers are standing outside, desiring to see you." 21 But he said to them, "My mother and my brothers are those who hear the word of God and do it."

22 One day he got into a boat with his disciples, and he said to them, "Let us go across to the other side of the lake." So they set out, 23 and as they sailed he fell asleep. And a storm of wind came down on the lake, and they were filling with water, and were in danger. 24And they went and woke him, saying, "Master, Master, we are perishing!" And he awoke and rebuked the wind and the raging waves; and they ceased, and there was a calm. 25 He said to them, "Where is your faith?" And they were afraid, and they marveled, saying to one another, "Who then is this, that he commands even wind and water, and they obey him?"

26 Then they arrived at the country of the Ger'a·senes,[a] which is opposite Galilee. 27And as he stepped out on land, there met him a man from the city who had demons; for a long time he had worn no clothes, and he lived not in a house but among the tombs. 28 When he saw Jesus, he cried out and fell down before him, and said with a loud voice, "What have you to do with me, Jesus, Son of the Most High God? I beseech you, do not torment me." 29 For he had commanded the unclean spirit to come out of the man. (For many a time it had seized him; he was kept under guard, and bound with chains and fetters, but he broke the bonds and was driven by the demon into the desert.) 30 Jesus then asked him, "What is your name?" And he said, "Legion"; for many demons had entered him. 31And they begged him not to command them to depart into the abyss. 32 Now a large herd of swine was feeding there on the hillside; and they begged him to let them enter these. So he gave them leave. 33 Then the demons came out of the man and entered the swine, and the herd rushed down the steep bank into the lake and were drowned.

34 When the herdsmen saw what had happened, they fled, and told it in the city and in the country. 35 Then people went out to see what had happened, and they came to Jesus, and found the man from whom the demons had gone, sitting at the feet of Jesus, clothed and in his right mind; and they were afraid. 36And those who had seen it told them how he who had been possessed with demons was healed. 37 Then all the people of the surrounding country of the Ger'a·senes[a] asked him to depart from them; for they were seized with great fear; so he got into the boat and returned. 38 The man from whom the demons had gone begged that he might be with him; but he sent him away, saying, 39 "Return to your home, and declare how much God has done for you." And he went away, proclaiming throughout the whole city how much Jesus had done for him.

[a] Other ancient authorities read *Gadarenes*, others *Gergesenes*

But where it is heard and held fast in "an honest and good heart," there it yields bountifully (15). The disciple is to *take heed* that his heart be a good and honest heart ("heart" includes understanding and will). In the good and honest heart the Word is a functioning Word, a *lamp . . . on a stand* that gives *light* (16). The Word has a future and opens up the future; on the lips of the disciple it will make *manifest* the now-hidden presence of the Kingdom, the Messianic glory now veiled by the form of the Servant (17). To *hear* that Word is of crucial importance. Not to "have" it (really have it, hold it fast in a good and honest heart) invokes the judgment of God who will *take away* the neglected gift. To have it is to enter into the ever-increasing riches of God's future (*will more be given,* 18). For those who *hear and do* the Word the future holds no less a blessing than membership in the family of God (*my mother and my brothers,* 21).

8:22-25 JESUS STILLS THE STORM

8:22-25 Cf. Mt 8:23-27 note. The *disciples* (22) witness the power of Jesus' word (*rebuked the wind and the raging waves,* 24); their *faith,* still weak and wavering, grows stronger as they *marveled* in holy *fear* at Him who *commands even wind and water* (25), evincing the power of God as proclaimed in the OT (Ps 65:7; 89:9; 107:23-29), power employed for their protection. They could learn to say of Jesus what the psalmist said of God: "By dread deeds thou dost answer us with deliverance." (Ps 65:5)

8:26-39 THE GERASENE DEMONIAC

8:26-39 Cf. Mt 8:28-34 notes; Mk 5:1-20 note.

40 Now when Jesus returned, the crowd welcomed him, for they were all waiting for him. [41]And there came a man named Ja′i·rus, who was a ruler of the synagogue; and falling at Jesus' feet he besought him to come to his house, [42] for he had an only daughter, about twelve years of age, and she was dying.

As he went, the people pressed round him. [43]And a woman who had had a flow of blood for twelve years[b] and could not be healed by any one, [44] came up behind him, and touched the fringe of his garment; and immediately her flow of blood ceased. [45]And Jesus said, "Who was it that touched me?" When all denied it, Peter[c] said, "Master, the multitudes surround you and press upon you!" [46] But Jesus said, "Some one touched me; for I perceive that power has gone forth from me." [47]And when the woman saw that she was not hidden, she came trembling, and falling down before him declared in the presence of all the people why she had touched him, and how she had been immediately healed. [48]And he said to her, "Daughter, your faith has made you well; go in peace."

49 While he was still speaking, a man from the ruler's house came and said, "Your daughter is dead; do not trouble the Teacher any more." [50] But Jesus on hearing this answered him, "Do not fear; only believe, and she shall be well." [51]And when he came to the house, he permitted no one to enter with him, except Peter and John and James, and the father and mother of the child. [52]And all were weeping and bewailing her; but he said, "Do not weep; for she is not dead but sleeping." [53]And they laughed at him, knowing that she was dead. [54] But taking her by the hand he called, saying, "Child, arise." [55]And her spirit returned, and she got up at once; and he directed that something should be given her to eat. [56]And her parents were amazed; but he charged them to tell no one what had happened.

9 And he called the twelve together and gave them power and authority over all demons and to cure diseases, 2 and he sent them out to preach the kingdom of God and to heal. [3]And he said to them, "Take nothing for your journey, no staff, nor bag, nor bread, nor money; and do not have two tunics. [4]And whatever house you enter, stay there, and from there depart. [5]And wherever they do not receive you, when you leave that town shake off the dust from your feet as a testimony against them." [6]And they departed and went through the villages, preaching the gospel and healing everywhere.

7 Now Herod the tetrarch heard of all that was done, and he was perplexed, because it was said by some that John had been raised from the dead, 8 by some that E·li′jah had appeared, and by others that one of the old prophets had risen. 9 Herod said, "John I beheaded; but who is this about whom I hear such things?" And he sought to see him.

[b] Other ancient authorities add *and had spent all her living upon physicians*
[c] Other ancient authorities add *and those who were with him*

8:40-49 JESUS RAISES JAIRUS' DAUGHTER

8:40-49 Cf. Mt 9:18-26 notes.

9:1-6 THE SENDING OF THE TWELVE

9:1-6 Cf. Mt 9:35 – 10:42 note. Cf. also Lk 10:1-12, the instruction given to the Seventy. The *twelve,* whose appointment is recorded in 6:13, have been "fully taught" by the words and works of Jesus to be "like their teacher" (6:40). They are *sent out* to be the living extensions of their Lord, with His *authority over all demons* (1; cf. 8:26-33), His authority to *cure diseases* (1) and *to heal* (2; cf. 7:1-10), and *to preach the kingdom of God* (2, 6; cf. 6:20-23; 7:22). Jesus implants in them also His own freedom from care, His certainty that the Father will provide (3-4). His sobering Word (6:22; 7:31-35) has prepared them for the shock of the rejection of the Gospel (5), and His meekness in the face of doubt and opposition has taught them that though they may and

must announce the judgment of God on unbelief (5, *a testimony against them*), they are not called on to execute judgment. (Cf. 6:37)

9:5 *Shake off the dust from your feet,* as a sign that they are annulling all connection with them and leaving them to their self-willed fate. Cf. Acts 18:6, where Paul tells those who oppose and revile him as witness to Jesus Christ, "Your blood be upon your heads!"

9:7-9 THE PERPLEXITY OF HEROD

9:7-9 Cf. Mk 6:14-29 note. The mission of the Twelve brought news of Jesus to the court of Herod. The suspicious perplexity of *Herod* Antipas is part of the gathering cloud of opposition which increasingly darkens the way of Jesus from here on (9:22, 23, 31, 44). We hear of his plan to kill Jesus in 13:31; and the words *he sought to see him* (9) point forward to Herod's role in the Passion story. (23:6-12, esp. 8)

10 On their return the apostles told him what they had done. And he took them and withdrew apart to a city called Beth-sa′i-da. ¹¹ When the crowds learned it, they followed him; and he welcomed them and spoke to them of the kingdom of God, and cured those who had need of healing. ¹² Now the day began to wear away; and the twelve came and said to him, "Send the crowd away, to go into the villages and country round about, to lodge and get provisions; for we are here in a lonely place." ¹³ But he said to them, "You give them something to eat." They said, "We have no more than five loaves and two fish—unless we are to go and buy food for all these people." ¹⁴ For there were about five thousand men. And he said to his disciples, "Make them sit down in companies, about fifty each." ¹⁵And they did so, and made them all sit down. ¹⁶And taking the five loaves and the two fish he looked up to heaven, and blessed and broke them, and gave them to the disciples to set before the crowd. ¹⁷And all ate and were satisfied. And they took up what was left over, twelve baskets of broken pieces.

18 Now it happened that as he was praying alone the disciples were with him; and he asked them, "Who do the people say that I am?" ¹⁹And they answered, "John the Baptist; but others say, E·li′jah; and others, that one of the old prophets has risen." ²⁰And he said to them, "But who do you say that I am?" And Peter answered, "The Christ of God." ²¹ But he charged and commanded them to tell this to no one, ²² saying, "The Son of man must suffer many things, and be rejected by the elders and chief priests and scribes, and be killed, and on the third day be raised."

23 And he said to all, "If any man would come after me, let him deny himself and take up his cross daily and follow me. ²⁴ For whoever would save his life will lose it; and whoever loses his life for my sake, he will save it. ²⁵ For what does it profit a man if he gains the whole world and loses or forfeits himself? ²⁶ For whoever is ashamed of me and of my words, of him will the Son of man be ashamed when he comes in his glory and the glory of the Father and of the holy angels. ²⁷ But I tell you truly, there are some standing here who will not taste death before they see the kingdom of God."

28 Now about eight days after these sayings he took with him Peter and John and James, and went up on the mountain to pray. ²⁹And as he was praying, the appearance of his countenance was altered, and his raiment became dazzling white. ³⁰And behold, two men talked with him, Moses and E·li′jah, ³¹ who appeared in glory and spoke of his departure, which he was to accomplish at Jerusalem. ³² Now Peter and those who were with him were heavy with sleep, and when they wakened they saw his glory and the two men who stood with him. ³³And as the men were parting from him, Peter said to

---

9:10-17 THE RETURN OF THE TWELVE
AND THE FEEDING OF THE 5,000

9:10 The *apostles,* by the nature of their commission, are required to render an account of their activity. *Bethsaida* lay outside Herod's domain; perhaps that is why Jesus withdrew thither.

9:11-17 For the feeding of the 5,000 cf. Mt 14:15-21 note.

9:11 *Spoke to them of the kingdom of God.* These words, only in Lk, point up the significance of the feeding of the multitudes. Where God reigns, the hungry are fed (6:2) and runaway sons are permitted to eat at the Father's table. (15:23)

9:13 *You give them something to eat.* The *you* is emphatic; Jesus is training the Twelve and challenging their faith.

9:18-27 THE CHRIST OF GOD AND THE CROSS

9:18-27 Cf. Mt 16:1-28 note. The confession to Jesus, to the Christ as the Christ who must suffer and die, Jesus' command that the disciples refrain from proclaiming Him as the Christ, and the imprinting of the cross on the whole life of the disciple—these are common to Mt, Mk, and Lk.

Peculiar to Lk and characteristic of him is his reference to Jesus as *praying* (18) at this decisive moment. And Lk alone speaks of taking up one's cross *daily* (23)—the way of the cross is accepted with the daily prayer, "Thy will be done." Lk has no reference to Peter's objection to the cross and Jesus' rebuke. (Mt 16:22-23)

9:28-36 THE TRANSFIGURATION

9:28-36 Cf. Mt 17:1-27 notes. The chief peculiarities of Lk's account are his reference to Jesus' *praying* (28, 29), his indication of the content of the conversation between Jesus and *Moses* and *Elijah* (31), and the designation of Jesus as *my Chosen* by the heavenly voice. (35)

9:31 *Spoke of his departure . . . at Jerusalem.* The departure which Jesus *was to accomplish* at Jerusalem is His dying, which is not a fate that He endures but a deed which He accomplishes, dying freely, of His own will. The Greek word for *departure* is "exodus"; this indicates that Jesus' death will not be defeat but triumph, since it sets His people free. The Servant Messiah will "set at liberty those who are oppressed" (4:18) in the last great Exodus.

Jesus, "Master, it is well that we are here; let us make three booths, one for you and one for Moses and one for E·li'jah"—not knowing what he said. ³⁴As he said this, a cloud came and overshadowed them; and they were afraid as they entered the cloud. ³⁵And a voice came out of the cloud, saying, "This is my Son, my Chosen;ᵈ listen to him!" ³⁶And when the voice had spoken, Jesus was found alone. And they kept silence and told no one in those days anything of what they had seen.

37 On the next day, when they had come down from the mountain, a great crowd met him. ³⁸And behold, a man from the crowd cried, "Teacher, I beg you to look upon my son, for he is my only child; ³⁹ and behold, a spirit seizes him, and he suddenly cries out; it convulses him till he foams, and shatters him, and will hardly leave him. ⁴⁰And I begged your disciples to cast it out, but they could not." ⁴¹ Jesus answered, "O faithless and perverse generation, how long am I to be with you and bear with you? Bring your son here." ⁴² While he was coming, the demon tore him and convulsed him. But Jesus rebuked the unclean spirit, and healed the boy, and gave him back to his father. ⁴³And all were astonished at the majesty of God.

But while they were all marveling at everything he did, he said to his disciples, ⁴⁴ "Let these words sink into your ears; for the Son of man is to be delivered into the hands of men." ⁴⁵ But they did not understand this saying, and it was concealed from them, that they should not perceive it; and they were afraid to ask him about this saying.

46 And an argument arose among them as to which of them was the greatest. ⁴⁷ But when Jesus perceived the thought of their hearts, he took a child and put him by his side, ⁴⁸ and said to them, "Whoever receives this child in my name receives me, and whoever receives me receives him who sent me; for he who is least among you all is the one who is great."

49 John answered, "Master, we saw a man casting out demons in your name, and we forbade him, because he does not follow with us." ⁵⁰ But Jesus said to him, "Do not forbid him; for he that is not against you is for you."

Jesus' Travel Ministry

9:51 – 18:30

51 When the days drew near for him to be received up, he set his face to go to Jerusalem. ⁵²And he sent messengers ahead of him, who went and entered a village of the Samaritans, to make ready for him; ⁵³ but the people would not receive him, because his face was set toward Jerusalem. ⁵⁴And when his disciples James and John

---

ᵈ Other ancient authorities read *my Beloved*

9:35 *My Chosen.* This title recalls the Lord's word concerning His Servant who will save His people: "Behold my servant . . . my chosen, in whom my soul delights" (Is 42:1). On the Servant cf. Mt 8:17 note; 12:18-21 note.

9:37-50 IMPERFECT FAITH OF DISCIPLES

9:37-50 Jesus' Galilean ministry is drawing to its close. His disciples have witnessed much, heard much, gone forth to proclaim, confessed the Christ of God – and yet their faith (which the impending Passion will put to so rigorous a test) remains imperfect. They cannot heal the epileptic boy in Jesus' absence (37-43a) and must hear Jesus' disappointed cry of *O faithless and perverse generation* (41); not in them but in Jesus alone is the *majesty of God* made manifest (43). Jesus' second prediction of His Passion (44) leaves them baffled and *afraid;* they cannot yet take in and endure the thought that the *Son of man is to be delivered into the hands of men* (44-45). They cannot yet wholly

grasp the thought that the only greatness that matters is Jesus' kind of greatness, the greatness of self-forgetting ministry to the *child,* ministry performed for one who needs it because he needs it (46-48). They have not yet attained to the large-heartedness which can rejoice in any service performed by anyone in Jesus' name and for His glory (49-50; cf. Ph 1:15-18). Accompanied by men still beset by such weaknesses, Jesus "set his face to go to Jerusalem" (51) to suffer and die alone.

9:51 – 18:30 This section contains much material that is peculiar to Luke and characteristic of his gospel, especially the so-called Travel Account. (9:51 – 18:14)

9:51-56 HOSTILITY IN SAMARIA

9:51-56 The hostility between Jews and *Samaritans* was intense and notorious (cf. Jn 4:9). When a Samaritan *village* expressed this hostility by refusing to *receive* Jesus and His company, *James*

saw it, they said, "Lord, do you want us to bid fire come down from heaven and consume them?" *e* 55 But he turned and rebuked them.*f* 56And they went on to another village.

57 As they were going along the road, a man said to him, "I will follow you wherever you go." 58And Jesus said to him, "Foxes have holes, and birds of the air have nests; but the Son of man has nowhere to lay his head." 59 To another he said, "Follow me." But he said, "Lord, let me first go and bury my father." 60 But he said to him, "Leave the dead to bury their own dead; but as for you, go and proclaim the kingdom of God." 61Another said, "I will follow you, Lord; but let me first say farewell to those at my home." 62 Jesus said to him, "No one who puts his hand to the plow and looks back is fit for the kingdom of God."

10 After this the Lord appointed seventy*g* others, and sent them on ahead of him, two by two, into every town and place where he himself was about to come. 2And he said to them, "The harvest is plentiful, but the laborers are few; pray therefore the Lord of the harvest to send out laborers into his harvest. 3 Go your way; behold, I send you out as lambs in the midst of wolves. 4 Carry no purse, no bag, no sandals; and salute no one on the road. 5 Whatever house you enter, first say, 'Peace be to this house!' 6And if a son of peace is there, your peace shall rest upon him; but if not, it shall return to you. 7And remain in the same house, eating and drinking what they provide, for the laborer deserves his wages; do not go from house to house. 8 Whenever you enter a town and they receive you, eat what is set before you; 9 heal the sick in it and say to them, 'The kingdom of God has come near to you.' 10 But whenever you enter a town and they do not receive you, go into its streets and say, 11 'Even the dust of your town that clings to our feet, we wipe off against you; nevertheless know this, that the kingdom of God has come near.' 12 I tell you, it shall be more tolerable on that day for Sodom than for that town.

13 "Woe to you, Cho·ra′zin! woe to you, Beth-sa′i·da! for if the mighty works done in you had been done in Tyre and Sidon, they would have repented long ago, sitting in sackcloth and ashes. 14 But it shall be more tolerable in the judgment for

---

e Other ancient authorities add *as Elijah did*
f Other ancient authorities add *and he said, "You do not know what manner of spirit you are of; for the Son of man came not to destroy men's lives but to save them"*
g Other ancient authorities read *seventy-two*

---

and John, those impetuous and fiery "sons of thunder" (Mk 3:17), wished to use their apostolic authority to avenge this insult to their Master by calling down fire on the village, as Elijah had once done (2 K 1:9-16). Jesus lived the love He had taught (6:27-36) and *rebuked* His vengeful disciples as He was wont to rebuke the demons (55; cf., e. g., 4:35, 41). Lk includes more instances of Jesus' concern for Samaritans than the other evangelists (10:29-37; 17:11-19); this incident makes it clear that such concern sprang from pure love, love for the enemy, not from any experience of Samaritan kindness.

9:51 *Set his face.* Cf. Is 50:7.

9:52 *Samaritans,* a people of mixed blood and illegitimate worship, were regarded as unclean and despised by the Jews, and they responded in kind. The concern for these outcasts continues in Acts. (1:8; 8:1-25; 9:31; 15:3)

9:57-62 WHAT IT MEANS TO FOLLOW JESUS

9:57-62 For 9:57-60 cf. Mt 8:18-22 note.

9:62 Only in Lk. He who would follow Jesus must "set his face" steadfastly forward, as Jesus did (9:51); nothing has priority over the *kingdom of God.*

10:1-20 THE SENDING AND THE RETURN
OF THE 70 MESSENGERS

10:1-20 The mission of the Seventy (or Seventy-two) is peculiar to Lk. The number 70 (or 72) is the traditional number of the non-Jewish peoples in the world (Gn 10) just as 12 is the number of the tribes of Israel (Mt 10:1-4 note). The choice of this number indicates the ultimate universality of Jesus' saving mission (cf. 2:32) and prepares for the march of the Gospel to the end of the earth in Acts.

10:1-12 Cf. Mt 9:37-38; 10:5-15 note.

10:1 *Two by two,* according to the rule of Dt 19:15, which required two witnesses (cf. 2 Co 13:1). The apostolic church followed the same practice. (Acts 8:14; 13:2; 15:39-40)

10:6 *Son of peace,* one who accepts and welcomes the "peace on earth" which God is giving through His Son to "men with whom he is pleased." (2:14)

10:7-8 *Not go from house to house . . . eat what is set before you.* Cf. 9:4. One believer's house is to be their base of operation (cf. Acts 9:43; 16:15; 17:7; 18:3); and they need not worry about whether the food set before them is "clean" or "unclean" according to Pharisaic standards.

10:13-15 Cf. Mt 11:20-24 note.

Tyre and Sidon than for you. ¹⁵And you, Ca·per′na·um, will you be exalted to heaven? You shall be brought down to Hades.

16 "He who hears you hears me, and he who rejects you rejects me, and he who rejects me rejects him who sent me."

17 The seventy*ᵍ* returned with joy, saying, "Lord, even the demons are subject to us in your name!" ¹⁸And he said to them, "I saw Satan fall like lightning from heaven. ¹⁹ Behold, I have given you authority to tread upon serpents and scorpions, and over all the power of the enemy; and nothing shall hurt you. ²⁰ Nevertheless do not rejoice in this, that the spirits are subject to you; but rejoice that your names are written in heaven."

21 In that same hour he rejoiced in the Holy Spirit and said, "I thank thee, Father, Lord of heaven and earth, that thou hast hidden these things from the wise and understanding and revealed them to babes; yea, Father, for such was thy gracious will.*ʰ* ²²All things have been delivered to me by my Father; and no one knows who the Son is except the Father, or who the Father is except the Son and any one to whom the Son chooses to reveal him."

23 Then turning to the disciples he said privately, "Blessed are the eyes which see what you see! ²⁴ For I tell you that many prophets and kings desired to see what you see, and did not see it, and to hear what you hear, and did not hear it."

25 And behold, a lawyer stood up to put him to the test, saying, "Teacher, what shall I do to inherit eternal life?" ²⁶ He said to him, "What is written in the law? How do you read?" ²⁷And he answered, "You shall love the Lord your God with all your heart, and with all your soul, and with all your strength, and with all your mind; and your neighbor as yourself." ²⁸And he said to him, "You have answered right; do this, and you will live."

29 But he, desiring to justify himself, said to Jesus, "And who is my neighbor?" ³⁰ Jesus replied, "A man was going down from Jerusalem to Jericho, and he fell among robbers, who stripped him and beat him, and departed, leaving him half dead. ³¹ Now by chance a priest was going down that road; and when he saw him he passed by on the other side. ³² So likewise a Levite, when he came to the place and saw him, passed by on the other side. ³³ But a Samaritan, as he journeyed, came to where he was; and when he saw him, he had compassion, ³⁴ and went to him and bound up his wounds, pouring on oil and wine; then he set him on his own beast and brought him to an inn, and took care of him. ³⁵And the next day he took out two denarii*ⁱ* and gave them to the innkeeper, saying, 'Take care of him; and whatever

---

ᵍ Other ancient authorities read *seventy-two*   *ʰ* Or *so it was well-pleasing before thee*
ⁱ The denarius was a day's wage for a laborer

10:16 Cf. Mt 10:40-42 note.

10:17-20 The 70 *return with joy*. They had discovered that, poor and "powerless" as they were, they had in the *name* of Jesus (all that Jesus is and signifies for man) a power which even the *demons* could not resist. Jesus confirms them in the joy of their success; their triumph over the hosts of Satan, He tells them, was the carrying out of His own triumph over Satan. Jesus *saw Satan fall . . . from heaven;* since Jesus triumphantly faced him in His temptation, He has freed all men from Satan's power. Satan has lost his place as the accuser of man (cf. Rv 12:7-10). But joy in "success," even success in Jesus' name, can be a treacherous thing for man; it can turn his faith from the power of God toward his own religious prowess. And so Jesus turns the eye of His messengers away from the sight of the scattering hosts of Satan to the cause and grounds of their victory: *Your names are written in heaven.* They have triumphed because God, in bringing them to Jesus, has made them His own, citizens of the city of God, sons and servants of God who find their deepest joy where Jesus found His, in fulfilling the will of their Father in heaven. (Cf. Jn 15:10-11)

10:21-24 JESUS THANKS HIS FATHER

10:21-22 Cf. Mt 11:25-30 note. Peculiar to Lk and characteristic of him is the notice that Jesus rejoiced *in the Holy Spirit.*

10:23-24 Cf. Mt 13:16 note. Jesus thanks His Father for making the revelation of His power and grace accessible to all by revealing them even "to babes" (21). If the "wise and understanding" let their wisdom blind them to God's revelation, that is their guilt; if the "babes" receive the revelation of God promised by *prophets* and behold the promised King, the Messiah, *desired* by *kings* of old, that is pure grace. They are *blessed*, favored by God.

10:25-37 THE GOOD SAMARITAN

10:25-37 Jesus was not the only Jew who recog-

more you spend, I will repay you when I come back.' [36] Which of these three, do you think, proved neighbor to the man who fell among the robbers?" [37] He said, "The one who showed mercy on him." And Jesus said to him, "Go and do likewise."

38 Now as they went on their way, he entered a village; and a woman named Martha received him into her house. [39]And she had a sister called Mary, who sat at the Lord's feet and listened to his teaching. [40] But Martha was distracted with much serving; and she went to him and said, "Lord, do you not care that my sister has left me to serve alone? Tell her then to help me." [41] But the Lord answered her, "Martha, Martha, you are anxious and troubled about many things; [42] one thing is needful.[j] Mary has chosen the good portion, which shall not be taken away from her."

11 He was praying in a certain place, and when he ceased, one of his disciples said to him, "Lord, teach us to pray, as John taught his disciples." [2]And he said to them, "When you pray, say:

"Father, hallowed be thy name. Thy kingdom come. [3] Give us each day our daily bread;[k] [4] and forgive us our sins, for we ourselves forgive every one who is indebted to us; and lead us not into temptation."

5 And he said to them, "Which of you who has a friend will go to him at midnight and say to him, 'Friend, lend me three loaves; [6] for a friend of mine has arrived on a journey, and I have nothing to set before him'; [7] and he will answer from within, 'Do not bother me; the door is now shut, and my children are with me in bed; I cannot get up and give you anything'? [8] I tell you, though he will not get up and give him anything because he is his friend, yet because of his importunity he will rise and give

[j] Other ancient authorities read *few things are needful, or only one*   [k] Or *our bread for the morrow*

nized that the beating heart of the *law* is *love,* that love for *God* and love for the *neighbor* constitute the way to *eternal life.* The *lawyer,* skilled in the Law and confident that he was qualified to test Jesus on points of Law, recognized it too. His answer to Jesus' counterquestion wins Jesus' full approval (25-28; cf. Mt 22:34-39). But then the gulf which separates the piety of Judaism from that of Jesus becomes apparent. The lawyer recognizes that he, the tester, is being tested when Jesus tells him, *Do this, and you will live* (28). And so he seeks to *justify himself* in his lovelessness. The Law is, after all, not all that clear, he maintains; *neighbor* needs definition. Jesus' reply, the story of the Good Samaritan, makes it plain that the problem is not one of definition. Neighbor is not a generality to be defined but an individual to be met. God, who governs all happenings down to and including the fall of the sparrow (12:6), will "define" neighbor for you by laying him across your road half dead, in need of you. You need not take steps to define and find him; you will have to take steps to avoid him, as the *priest* and the *Levite* did. The Law is clear, and the imperative of love is inescapable; even a *Samaritan* could hear and heed it. In the last analysis the question is not one of mind (who is?) but of will—how can I *prove neighbor* to the man across my path? Five men are confronted by the Law. The lawyer, priest, and Levite evaded it. The Samaritan in the simplicity of his heart obeyed it. Jesus went on to the cross in an unbroken unity of love for God and all His half-dead neighbors and fulfilled it.

10:31-32 *Priest . . . Levite,* both serving in the temple, both in the service of the God whose love offered man communion with Himself and forgive-

ness in the house where He made His name dwell. They avoided the simple duty of love, perhaps out of fear that the man left half dead might die and so pollute them. (Cf. Lv 21:1)

10:38-42 MARY AND MARTHA

10:38-42 Only in Lk. The story is an illustration in terms of common life of the priority of the Word over bread, which Jesus had asserted in His temptation. (4:4)

10:39 *Sat at the Lord's feet.* Cf. Acts 22:3, where Paul uses the expression to describe his relationship to his teacher Gamaliel. The rabbis refused to teach women the Law; here as always Jesus' attitude toward woman is in striking contrast to the general attitude of Judaism. (Cf. 8:1-3 note)

10:42 For the hearing of the Word as the *good portion* cf. 8:15, 21; 11:28.

11:1-13 LORD, TEACH US TO PRAY

11:1 *As John taught his disciples.* Cf. 5:33. The example of John and Jesus' own example of constant prayer, emphasized by Lk, give rise to the disciples' request.

11:2b-4 Cf. Mt 6:9-15 notes. Lk's form of the Lord's Prayer has 5 petitions, as over against the 7 in Mt ("Thy will be done" and "Deliver us from evil" being absent from Lk). This free variation in the form of the prayer as preserved by the inspired evangelists indicates that the Spirit led them to see in Jesus' words a pattern of prayer to be followed rather than a rigid formula to be memorized and repeated; the substance of Jesus' instruction in prayer remains the same.

11:5-8 The parable of the man "bothering" his friend for the loan of *three loaves at midnight* is Jesus' comment on the word "Father" (2), the

him whatever he needs. 9And I tell you, Ask, and it will be given you; seek, and you will find; knock, and it will be opened to you. 10 For every one who asks receives, and he who seeks finds, and to him who knocks it will be opened. 11 What father among you, if his son asks for¹ a fish, will instead of a fish give him a serpent; 12 or if he asks for an egg, will give him a scorpion? 13 If you then, who are evil, know how to give good gifts to your children, how much more will the heavenly Father give the Holy Spirit to those who ask him!"

14 Now he was casting out a demon that was dumb; when the demon had gone out, the dumb man spoke, and the people marveled. 15 But some of them said, "He casts out demons by Beelzebul, the prince of demons"; 16 while others, to test him, sought from him a sign from heaven. 17 But he, knowing their thoughts, said to them, "**Every kingdom divided against itself is laid waste, and a divided household falls.**18And if Satan also is divided against himself, how will his kingdom stand? For you say that I cast out demons by Beelzebul. 19And if I cast out demons by Beelzebul, by whom do your sons cast them out? Therefore they shall be your judges. 20 But if it is by the finger of God that I cast out demons, then the kingdom of God has come upon you. 21 When a strong man, fully armed, guards his own palace, his goods are in peace; 22 but when one stronger than he assails him and overcomes him, he takes away his armor in which he trusted, and divides his spoil. 23 He who is not with me is against me, and he who does not gather with me scatters.

24 "When the unclean spirit has gone out of a man, he passes through waterless places seeking rest; and finding none he says, 'I will return to my house from which I came.' 25And when he comes he finds it swept and put in order. 26 Then he goes and brings seven other spirits more evil than himself, and they enter and dwell there; and the last state of that man becomes worse than the first."

27 As he said this, a woman in the crowd raised her voice and said to him, "Blessed is the womb that bore you, and the breasts that you sucked!" 28 But he said, "Blessed rather are those who hear the word of God and keep it!"

29 When the crowds were increasing, he began to say, "This generation is an evil

---

¹ Other ancient authorities insert *bread, will give him a stone; or if he asks for*

---

address of the prayer. "Father" probably reproduces the "Abba" of Jesus' mother tongue; "Abba" was the child's familiar address to his father, with all of a child's confidence and *importunity* (8) in it. Jesus reveals to us a God whom we can bother, who welcomes His children's importunity.

11:9-13 Cf. Mt 7:7-11. The argument is from the less to the greater; if even human fathers, evil though they be at best, can and do give good gifts to their children, how much the more will *the heavenly Father* give the best of all gifts, *the Holy Spirit,* to His own? If men dare hope for that gift, they may confidently expect all good gifts. (Cf. Mt 6:33)

11:14-32 REACTIONS TO JESUS: ADMIRATION, BLASPHEMY, SEEKING A SIGN

11:14-32 Cf. Mt 12:22-45 notes. Jesus casts out a *demon,* and His mighty deed provokes a threefold response. There is, first, astonished admiration: *The people marveled* (14). There is, second, blasphemous contradiction: *He casts out demons by Beelzebul, the prince of demons* (15). There is, third, the reserved skepticism which demands conclusive proof: *Others, to test him, sought from him a sign from heaven.*

Jesus answers the blasphemers by pointing out (17-22) the folly and danger of interpreting His power over the demons as anything but as His overcoming of Satan (the *strong man,* 21) and

the coming of the *kingdom of God* (20). Now neutrality is impossible (23); and no one can remain empty who refuses the presence of the Christ — the powers of Satan will fill that vacuum. (24-26)

Jesus answers the sign-seeking skeptics (29-32) with the promise of the *sign of Jonah* (29), a call to repentance, and the threat of *judgment* on those who have refused *something greater* than the revelation given through prophet and king of old *(Jonah, Solomon).*

Jesus' answer to those who respond with nothing stronger than admiration is contained in His reply to the admiring woman (27-28, peculiar to Lk) who called *blessed* the mother of so brilliant a Son. This is no time for admiration; this is the critical hour in which only one thing matters: to *hear and keep the word* which God is in these last days speaking by His Son. (Cf. Heb 1:1-2; 2:3-4)

11:20 *The finger of God* is a symbol of God's irresistible power and unquestionable authority. Pharaoh's magicians recognized the finger of God in the plagues by which the Lord smote Egypt and set His people free (Ex 8:19); and the "tables of stone" which recorded God's will for His covenant people were "written with the finger of God" (Ex 31:18). The psalmist is filled with awe and humble adoration when he beholds the heavens, the work of the "fingers" of God (Ps 8:3-4). God the Deliverer, the Lawgiver, the Creator is at work in this mighty and delivering deed of Jesus.

generation; it seeks a sign, but no sign shall be given to it except the sign of Jonah. [30] For as Jonah became a sign to the men of Nin′e·veh, so will the Son of man be to this generation. [31] The queen of the South will arise at the judgment with the men of this generation and condemn them; for she came from the ends of the earth to hear the wisdom of Solomon, and behold, something greater than Solomon is here. [32] The men of Nin′e·veh will arise at the judgment with this generation and condemn it; for they repented at the preaching of Jonah, and behold, something greater than Jonah is here.

[33] "No one after lighting a lamp puts it in a cellar or under a bushel, but on a stand, that those who enter may see the light. [34] Your eye is the lamp of your body; when your eye is sound, your whole body is full of light; but when it is not sound, your body is full of darkness. [35] Therefore be careful lest the light in you be darkness. [36] If then your whole body is full of light, having no part dark, it will be wholly bright, as when a lamp with its rays gives you light."

[37] While he was speaking, a Pharisee asked him to dine with him; so he went in and sat at table. [38] The Pharisee was astonished to see that he did not first wash before dinner. [39] And the Lord said to him, "Now you Pharisees cleanse the outside of the cup and of the dish, but inside you are full of extortion and wickedness. [40] You fools! Did not he who made the outside make the inside also? [41] But give for alms those things which are within; and behold, everything is clean for you.

[42] "But woe to you Pharisees! for you tithe mint and rue and every herb, and neglect justice and the love of God; these you ought to have done, without neglecting the others. [43] Woe to you Pharisees! for you love the best seat in the synagogues and salutations in the market places. [44] Woe to you! for you are like graves which are not seen, and men walk over them without knowing it."

[45] One of the lawyers answered him, "Teacher, in saying this you reproach us also." [46] And he said, "Woe to you lawyers also! for you load men with burdens hard to bear, and you yourselves do not touch the burdens with one of your fingers. [47] Woe to you! for you build the tombs of the prophets whom your fathers killed. [48] So you are witnesses and consent to the deeds of your fathers; for they killed them, and you build their tombs. [49] Therefore also the Wisdom of God said, 'I will send them prophets and apostles, some of whom they will kill and persecute,' [50] that the blood of all the prophets, shed from the foundation of the world, may be required of this generation, [51] from the blood of Abel to the blood of Zech·a·ri′ah, who perished between the altar and the sanctuary. Yes, I tell you, it shall be required of this generation. [52] Woe to you lawyers! for you have taken away the key of knowledge; you did not enter yourselves, and you hindered those who were entering."

[53] As he went away from there, the scribes and the Pharisees began to press him

11:33-36 BE CAREFUL LEST THE LIGHT IN YOU BE DARKNESS

11:33-36 God has not obscured the light of His revelation; Jesus is not *a lamp* set *under a bushel* basket; He is a lamp set on a *stand* for all to *see*. His words and works are clear (33). But as the unsound *eye* deprives the body of the light, though the light is present in all fullness (34), so the unsound eye of unbelief can deprive the whole man of the light which is designed to make man's life *wholly bright*, fully illuminated by the gracious revelation of God. These words are a warning attached to 11:14-32, where the various reactions of men to Jesus' revelatory deed are all examples of the unsound eye that leaves men in darkness.

11:37-54 JESUS' WOE TO THE PHARISEES AND THE LAWYERS

11:37-54 In three woes on the *Pharisees* and three on their theological guides and leaders, the *lawyers* (scribes), Jesus exposes the falsity of the piety that resists Him and plots to entrap Him (53-54). For the substance of Jesus' indictment cf. Mt 23:1-39 note.

11:38 *Not . . . wash before dinner,* as the tradition of the elders prescribed. Cf. Mt 15:2 note on the authority of the tradition.

11:40-41 *He who made.* The God who made man made the whole man, *outside* and *inside,* and so man owes his whole self to God; giving oneself to Him with undivided devotion is the basis of all genuine piety *(alms)* and is a purity which transcends the Pharisaic anxiety about "clean" and "unclean." (Cf. Mt 15:10-20)

11:44 *Walk over them,* and are made unclean by contact with the dead. The Pharisaic piety, displayed and admired, corrupts men's piety.

11:49 *The Wisdom of God said. Wisdom* is the personified wisdom of God (cf. 7:35). They will continue to resist God's counsels (7:30) to their own destruction.

hard, and to provoke him to speak of many things, [54] lying in wait for him, to catch at something he might say.

THE DISCIPLES IN THIS WORLD (12:1-59)

12 In the meantime, when so many thousands of the multitude had gathered together that they trod upon one another, he began to say to his disciples first, "Beware of the leaven of the Pharisees, which is hypocrisy. [2] Nothing is covered up that will not be revealed, or hidden that will not be known. [3] Therefore whatever you have said in the dark shall be heard in the light, and what you have whispered in private rooms shall be proclaimed upon the housetops.

[4] "I tell you, my friends, do not fear those who kill the body, and after that have no more that they can do. [5] But I will warn you whom to fear: fear him who, after he has killed, has power to cast into hell; [m] yes, I tell you, fear him! [6] Are not five sparrows sold for two pennies? And not one of them is forgotten before God. [7] Why, even the hairs of your head are all numbered. Fear not; you are of more value than many sparrows.

[8] "And I tell you, every one who acknowledges me before men, the Son of man also will acknowledge before the angels of God; [9] but he who denies me before men will be denied before the angels of God. [10] And every one who speaks a word against the Son of man will be forgiven; but he who blasphemes against the Holy Spirit will not be forgiven. [11] And when they bring you before the synagogues and the rulers and the authorities, do not be anxious how or what you are to answer or what you are to say; [12] for the Holy Spirit will teach you in that very hour what you ought to say."

[13] One of the multitude said to him, "Teacher, bid my brother divide the inheritance with me." [14] But he said to him, "Man, who made me a judge or divider over you?" [15] And he said to them, "Take heed, and beware of all covetousness; for

[m] Greek *Gehenna*

12:1-59 In the presence of a great *multitude* Jesus instructs *his disciples* on the quality of their life in this world as they wait and work in the hope of the world to come. Their life in this world is to be in sharp contrast to the *hypocrisy* of the *Pharisees;* it is the life of the pure in heart (1-34). It is a life animated by a lively hope which keeps them vigilant and faithful, alert and open-eyed to the realities of the world's last days. (35-59)

12:1-34 THE DISCIPLES IN THE WORLD: PURITY OF HEART

12:1-34 To be pure in heart is to will one thing only, to have your heart fixed, whole and undivided, on the supreme *treasure* of your life (34), to *seek* the *kingdom* of God and trust Him wholly (31). To this purity of heart the hypocritical piety of the Pharisees (which dominated the Judaic world about them) posed an insidious threat; it could work imperceptibly but pervasively, like *leaven,* to corrupt their heart and make them incapable of life in the light (1-3). Purity of heart has in it a holy fear of God, the inescapable Judge, a fear which drives out every other fear of men. In the heart of Jesus' *friends* this holy fear co-exists with a pure trust in Him who has numbered the *hairs of your head,* so that fear is ever and again swallowed up in fearless faith (4-7). Fearless faith leads to fearless confession in the power of the *Holy Spirit,* that supreme gift of God (cf. 11:13), the Spirit so strong and terrible that men

who *blaspheme* Him can no longer hope to be *forgiven.* (4-12)

Purity of heart cannot coexist with *covetousness* (15) and care (*anxious about your life,* 22); both blind a man to God's governance and goodness in his life and give priority to *barns* (18), *food,* and *clothing* (23) in his heart, priority over the *kingdom* and the *Father.* Both make man incapable of that largehearted, reckless generosity which provides him with *treasure in the heavens.* (13-34)

12:1 *Pharisees . . . hypocrisy.* Cf. 11:37-54 note; Mt 23:1-39 note. Hypocrisy is the characteristic of the man who attempts to divide his heart between God and self.

12:2-3 *Revealed . . . known,* etc. Hypocrisy cannot succeed; it will be exposed and convicted.

12:4-9 Cf. Mt 10:24-33 note.

12:4 *My friends.* Since they are not only servants (cf. 37) of Christ but His friends, who "know what their Master is doing" (Jn 15:14-15), they are doubly responsible and have full grounds for confident trust in God.

12:10 Cf. Mt 12:31-32 note and Mt 12:22-37 note.

12:12 *Spirit.* Cf. Mt 10:20; Jn 15:26; 16:7-11 (the Spirit as Counselor).

12:13 *Divide the inheritance.* The scribes, or "lawyers," were often called on to adjudicate cases of this sort. Jesus, who came to free men from the clutches of covetousness (15), will not let Himself be used in the service of men's covetings.

12:15 *Life* is God's gift, and no acquisitions of man can either safeguard (20) or prolong it (25).

a man's life does not consist in the abundance of his possessions." [16]And he told them a parable, saying, "The land of a rich man brought forth plentifully; [17] and he thought to himself, 'What shall I do, for I have nowhere to store my crops?' [18]And he said, 'I will do this: I will pull down my barns, and build larger ones; and there I will store all my grain and my goods. [19]And I will say to my soul, Soul, you have ample goods laid up for many years; take your ease, eat, drink, be merry.' [20] But God said to him, 'Fool! This night your soul is required of you; and the things you have prepared, whose will they be?' [21] So is he who lays up treasure for himself, and is not rich toward God.' "

22 And he said to his disciples, "Therefore I tell you, do not be anxious about your life, what you shall eat, nor about your body, what you shall put on. [23] For life is more than food, and the body more than clothing. [24] Consider the ravens: they neither sow nor reap, they have neither storehouse nor barn, and yet God feeds them. Of how much more value are you than the birds! [25]And which of you by being anxious can add a cubit to his span of life?[n] [26] If then you are not able to do as small a thing as that, why are you anxious about the rest? [27] Consider the lilies, how they grow; they neither toil nor spin;[o] yet I tell you, even Solomon in all his glory was not arrayed like one of these. [28] But if God so clothes the grass which is alive in the field today and tomorrow is thrown into the oven, how much more will he clothe you, O men of little faith! [29]And do not seek what you are to eat and what you are to drink, nor be of anxious mind. [30] For all the nations of the world seek these things; and your Father knows that you need them. [31] Instead, seek his[p] kingdom, and these things shall be yours as well.

32 "Fear not, little flock, for it is your Father's good pleasure to give you the kingdom. [33] Sell your possessions, and give alms; provide yourselves with purses that do not grow old, with a treasure in the heavens that does not fail, where no thief approaches and no moth destroys. [34] For where your treasure is, there will your heart be also.

---

[n] Or *to his stature*   [o] Other ancient authorities read *Consider the lilies; they neither spin nor weave*
[p] Other ancient authorities read *God's*

12:16-21 The rich fool who *lays up treasure for himself* (21) is completely self-centered; he speaks only to himself (*soul,* 19), with no thought for his fellowman or his God. He is the classic case of the man in whom the thorns of the "riches and pleasures of life" have "choked out" the Word of God which bids him love God and his neighbor. (8:7, 14)

12:21 *Rich toward God,* in his relationship to God, the one relationship that counts supremely and endures forever. (Cf. 33)

12:21-31 Cf. Mt 6:19-34 note.

12:32 The *Father* who out of free and sovereign grace (*good pleasure*) gives no less a gift than His *kingdom* can be trusted to provide; the only logical thing to do is to follow in the footsteps of His lavish love.

12:35-59 THE DISCIPLE IN THE WORLD:
A LIVELY HOPE

12:35-59 Their lively hope is to make the disciples vigilant and ready, *like men . . . waiting for their master to come home.* The reward for vigilance is astonishingly great—the returning *master* will *serve* His *servants!* But their vigilance must be constant, for the *Son of man* will come as a *thief* in the night; no one knows the *hour* of His coming. His disciples know only how costly an error it will be to miss that hour. (35-40)

Their lively hope is to make them responsible, *faithful and wise stewards* of their *master's household.* The reward is, according to human standards of merit, ridiculously high; the returning master will *set them over all his possessions.* The punishment of the *unfaithful* will be correspondingly severe; *to whom much is given, of him will much be required.* (41-48)

Their lively hope is at the same time to be a sober, open-eyed recognition of the seriousness of the present hour. Before that blessed time when they shall sit at their Master's table enjoying the ministry of His love, before the time when they shall be coheirs with Christ (cf. Ro 8:17), there lies the time of fiery trial (49) when the cross (50) shall confront men with a decision and create a *division* which will cut across all ties of kinship (49-53). The vigilant, responsible disciple will, unlike the unheeding *multitudes,* be able *to interpret . . . the present time,* to read the weather signals of God's approaching storm. (54-56)

Their lively hope is therefore held and lived under the shadow of the approaching judgment (*magistrate, judge, officer, prison,* 58). As they live in hope of forgiveness, they live a life that has on it the mark of forgiveness. They forgive and seek forgiveness lest any offended brother stand as their *accuser* on that last and fateful day. (57-59)

35 "Let your loins be girded and your lamps burning, 36 and be like men who are waiting for their master to come home from the marriage feast, so that they may open to him at once when he comes and knocks. 37 Blessed are those servants whom the master finds awake when he comes; truly, I say to you, he will gird himself and have them sit at table, and he will come and serve them. 38 If he comes in the second watch, or in the third, and finds them so, blessed are those servants! 39 But know this, that if the householder had known at what hour the thief was coming, he*q* would not have left his house to be broken into. 40 You also must be ready; for the Son of man is coming at an unexpected hour."

41 Peter said, "Lord, are you telling this parable for us or for all?" 42And the Lord said, "Who then is the faithful and wise steward, whom his master will set over his household, to give them their portion of food at the proper time? 43 Blessed is that servant whom his master when he comes will find so doing. 44 Truly, I say to you, he will set him over all his possessions. 45 But if that servant says to himself, 'My master is delayed in coming,' and begins to beat the menservants and the maidservants, and to eat and drink and get drunk, 46 the master of that servant will come on a day when he does not expect him and at an hour he does not know, and will punish*r* him, and put him with the unfaithful. 47And that servant who knew his master's will, but did not make ready or act according to his will, shall receive a severe beating. 48 But he who did not know, and did what deserved a beating, shall receive a light beating. Every one to whom much is given, of him will much be required; and of him to whom men commit much they will demand the more.

49 "I came to cast fire upon the earth; and would that it were already kindled! 50 I have a baptism to be baptized with; and how I am constrained until it is accomplished! 51 Do you think that I have come to give peace on earth? No, I tell you, but rather division; 52 for henceforth in one house there will be five divided, three against two and two against three; 53 they will be divided, father against son and son against father, mother against daughter and daughter against her mother, mother-in-law against her daughter-in-law and daughter-in-law against her mother-in-law."

54 He also said to the multitudes, "When you see a cloud rising in the west, you say at once, 'A shower is coming'; and so it happens. 55And when you see the south wind blowing, you say, 'There will be scorching heat'; and it happens. 56 You hypocrites! You know how to interpret the appearance of earth and sky; but why do you not know how to interpret the present time?

57 "And why do you not judge for yourselves what is right? 58As you go with your accuser before the magistrate, make an effort to settle with him on the way, lest he drag you to the judge, and the judge hand you over to the officer, and the officer put you in prison. 59 I tell you, you will never get out till you have paid the very last copper."

REPENTANCE, HEALING, PARABLES, HEROD'S PLAN (13:1-35)

13 There were some present at that very time who told him of the Galileans whose blood Pilate had mingled with their sacrifices. 2And he answered them,

q Other ancient authorities add *would have watched and*   *r* Or *cut him in pieces*

12:35 *Loins be girded.* Be ready to serve. (Cf. 37)

12:41-42 *For us or for all?* All disciples are servants; the apostles, for whom Peter is speaking, are servants with a special responsibility as *stewards,* men *set over his household,* all the servants, *to give them their portion of food at the proper time.* What applies to the apostles applies to all who hold positions of ministering leadership. (Cf. 1 Co 4:1-2; Tts 1:7; 1 Ptr 4:7)

12:47-48 *Severe beating . . . light beating.* Responsibility is in proportion to knowledge; to the disciples "it has been given to know the secrets of the kingdom of God" (8:9), and they must face up to their greater responsibility.

12:49 *I came to cast fire upon the earth.* Peculiar to Lk. The *fire* is probably fiery trial, the suffering of those who will take up their cross and follow Jesus and the agonizing conflict and cruel divisions which the Gospel of the Crucified will create. Jesus wishes *that it were already kindled* in order that the result of His work, the new people of God tested and purified by fire, may emerge.

12:50 *A baptism to be baptized with.* For Jesus' suffering and death as a baptism, an immersion into agony, cf. Mk 10:38 note and OT passages like Ps 69:14-15; 144:7.

How I am constrained! The constraint is both His eagerness to fulfill the will of God and that horror of death expressed in Gethsemane.

13:1-9 REPENT, OR YOU WILL ALL PERISH

13:1-9 Recorded by Lk only. The Pharisees

"Do you think that these Galileans were worse sinners than all the other Galileans, because they suffered thus? 3 I tell you, No; but unless you repent you will all likewise perish. 4 Or those eighteen upon whom the tower in Si·lo′am fell and killed them, do you think that they were worse offenders than all the others who dwelt in Jerusalem? 5 I tell you, No; but unless you repent you will all likewise perish."

6 And he told this parable: "A man had a fig tree planted in his vineyard; and he came seeking fruit on it and found none. 7And he said to the vinedresser, 'Lo, these three years I have come seeking fruit on this fig tree, and I find none. Cut it down; why should it use up the ground?' 8And he answered him, 'Let it alone, sir, this year also, till I dig about it and put on manure. 9And if it bears fruit next year, well and good; but if not, you can cut it down.' "

10 Now he was teaching in one of the synagogues on the sabbath. 11And there was a woman who had had a spirit of infirmity for eighteen years; she was bent over and could not fully straighten herself. 12And when Jesus saw her, he called her and said to her, "Woman, you are freed from your infirmity." 13And he laid his hands upon her, and immediately she was made straight, and she praised God. 14 But the ruler of the synagogue, indignant because Jesus had healed on the sabbath, said to the people, "There are six days on which work ought to be done; come on those days and be healed, and not on the sabbath day." 15 Then the Lord answered him, "You hypocrites! Does not each of you on the sabbath untie his ox or his ass from the manger, and lead it away to water it? 16And ought not this woman, a daughter of Abraham whom Satan bound for eighteen years, be loosed from this bond on the sabbath day?" 17As he said this, all his adversaries were put to shame; and all the people rejoiced at all the glorious things that were done by him.

18 He said therefore, "What is the kingdom of God like? And to what shall I compare it? 19 It is like a grain of mustard seed which a man took and sowed in

interpreted a disaster which befell a man as an indication that the man involved was being punished by God for some particularly dreadful sin. Thus they could remain aloof and secure in their own sense of righteousness; they did "not know how to interpret the present time" and remained "hypocrites" (12:56). Jesus teaches them "how to interpret the present time." Two recent disasters, the slaughter of the *Galileans* and the construction accident which killed 18 men at the *tower in Siloam* in Jerusalem, are tokens and portents of the judgment of God which impends over *all unless* they *repent.* Roman armies will shed more blood than *Pilate* did, and the collapsing walls of besieged *Jerusalem* will bury not 18 but thousands. All Israel is like a fruitless *fig tree* living under the suspended sentence of *Cut it down!* And yet God's love is still at work to move His people to repentance; the Gardener still digs and nurtures the tree to save it from its doom. "Note then the kindness . . . of God." (Ro 11:22)

13:1 The incident of *Pilate* killing *Galileans* while they were engaged in *sacrifice* is otherwise unknown but is of a piece with known instances of his brutal disregard for the religious feelings of the people whom he governed.

13:4 *Tower in Siloam.* Siloam was a pool which formed part of the water-supply system of Jerusalem; the collapse of the tower probably occurred during construction on the water system.

13:10-17 JESUS FREES A DAUGHTER OF
     ABRAHAM FROM SATAN'S BONDAGE

13:10-17 Recorded by Luke only. "God's kind-

ness is meant to lead" Israel "to repentance" (Ro 2:4). The *ought* (16), the must, of God's merciful will governs the whole life of Jesus (2:49; 4:43; 9:22; 13:33; 17:25; 19:5; 22:37; 24:7, 44). That ought impels Jesus to His deed of mercy toward the *woman* whom demonic power (*spirit of infirmity,* 11) bent and bowed. She must be set free, for she is a *daughter of Abraham;* and God has made a promise "to Abraham and to his posterity for ever" (1:55), a promise of blessing (Gn 12:2). She must be set free *on the sabbath,* for God's blessing rests on the Sabbath (Gn 2:3). She must be set free, for the mercy of God will not allow Satan to usurp His creation forever. And God's kindness does lead some men to repentance; the daughter of Abraham *praised God* (13), and *all the people rejoiced at all the glorious things that were done* by Jesus (17). But His kindness collides with the *hypocrites* whose cloven piety will make a Sabbath exception for their *ox or ass* in order that "life, their life, may go on," but will not permit God to do His work of mercy on the Sabbath in order that His gift of life, life freed from Satan, may go on (15). Thus Jesus woos His people; the example of the *ruler of the synagogue* (14) shows that He woos in vain: "You would not!" (13:34)

13:18-21 MUSTARD SEED AND THE LEAVEN

13:18-21 Cf. Mt 13:31-33 note. Jesus is not discouraged and Israel need not be offended by the littleness of the beginnings of the *kingdom of God;* these little beginnings have in them the promise and pledge of future greatness.

his garden; and it grew and became a tree, and the birds of the air made nests in its branches."

20 And again he said, "To what shall I compare the kingdom of God? 21 It is like leaven which a woman took and hid in three measures of flour, till it was all leavened."

22 He went on his way through towns and villages, teaching, and journeying toward Jerusalem. 23And some one said to him, "Lord, will those who are saved be few?" And he said to them, 24 "Strive to enter by the narrow door; for many, I tell you, will seek to enter and will not be able. 25 When once the householder has risen up and shut the door, you will begin to stand outside and to knock at the door, saying, 'Lord, open to us.' He will answer you, 'I do not know where you come from.' 26 Then you will begin to say, 'We ate and drank in your presence, and you taught in our streets.' 27 But he will say, 'I tell you, I do not know where you come from; depart from me, all you workers of iniquity!' 28 There you will weep and gnash your teeth, when you see Abraham and Isaac and Jacob and all the prophets in the kingdom of God and you yourselves thrust out. 29And men will come from east and west, and from north and south, and sit at table in the kingdom of God. 30And behold, some are last who will be first, and some are first who will be last."

31 At that very hour some Pharisees came, and said to him, "Get away from here, for Herod wants to kill you." 32And he said to them, "Go and tell that fox, 'Behold, I cast out demons and perform cures today and tomorrow, and the third day I finish my course. 33 Nevertheless I must go on my way today and tomorrow and the day following; for it cannot be that a prophet should perish away from Jerusalem.' 34 O Jerusalem, Jerusalem, killing the prophets and stoning those who are sent to you! How often would I have gathered your children together as a hen gathers her brood under her wings, and you would not! 35 Behold, your house is forsaken. And I tell you, you will not see me until you say, 'Blessed is he who comes in the name of the Lord!' "

SALT IS GOOD: THE PHARISEES AND THE MULTITUDES (14:1-35)

14 One sabbath when he went to dine at the house of a ruler who belonged to the Pharisees, they were watching him. 2And behold, there was a man before him who had dropsy. 3And Jesus spoke to the lawyers and Pharisees, saying, "Is it

---

13:22-30 WILL THOSE WHO ARE SAVED BE FEW?

13:22-30 Jesus will not permit anyone to be a spectator at the drama of salvation. He will not allow men to ask theoretical questions like, *Will those who are saved be few?* (23). (Theoretical questions put off repentance and do not lead to faith.) Jesus' answer is therefore not a statement but a command: *Strive* (24). Strive to take up God's call into your heart and will, though it be against the grain and in the face of the majority. Strive now before it is too late, now before the *door* is *shut* forever on men who can claim historical knowledge of Jesus but have not been moved to repentance and faith by Him and cannot be acknowledged by Him (25-28). Strive in fear and trembling lest all the grace of God which made you *first* (the promise to *Abraham* and the living oracles of the *prophets,* 28) prove to be grace given in vain and the *last,* long distant from God (Eph 2:11-22), come from the four corners of the earth to accept the invitation which you have rejected (14:18-24) and sit down to the feast (29-30) which "the Lord of hosts will make for all people." (Is 25:6)

13:31-35 I MUST GO ON MY WAY

13:31-35 We can guess why *Herod* Antipas

wants to kill Jesus; he who had found the Baptist uncomfortable, a man to be gotten out of the way (3:19-20; 9:7-9), would not be happy with the Man who had come "to cast fire upon the earth" (12:49). We are not told why the *Pharisees* informed Jesus of Herod's plan (31). The center of interest lies in Jesus' response. Not Herod, Jesus declares, but God shall determine the time and place of His death; *today and tomorrow* and on the day following (day by day) He is listening for the striking of God's clock. At God's time He *must* and will finish His course where God wills it, in *Jerusalem.* The city that has heard and *killed* the *prophets,* God's servants, shall hear the voice of God's Son also. Then He will pour out His life and intercede for transgressors. The will of self-sacrificing love that impels Jesus toward Jerusalem finds eloquent expression in His cry of injured love over Jerusalem (34-35; cf. Mt 23:37-39 and note on Mt 23:1-39, last paragraph).

14:1-35 Jesus sought and found nothing on earth but men. Whether He is talking with *Pharisees* at dinner (1) or summoning *multitudes* (25) to *renounce all* and be His *disciples* (33), He is seeking and saving men. And it is His will to make men *salt* of the earth (34) — whole men of God, men in whom nature and function are one, men who are what they profess and DO what they

lawful to heal on the sabbath, or not?" 4 But they were silent. Then he took him and healed him, and let him go. 5And he said to them, "Which of you, having a son⁸ or an ox that has fallen into a well, will not immediately pull him out on a sabbath day?" 6And they could not reply to this.

7 Now he told a parable to those who were invited, when he marked how they chose the places of honor, saying to them, 8 "When you are invited by any one to a marriage feast, do not sit down in a place of honor, lest a more eminent man than you be invited by him; 9 and he who invited you both will come and say to you, 'Give place to this man,' and then you will begin with shame to take the lowest place. 10 But when you are invited, go and sit in the lowest place, so that when your host comes he may say to you, 'Friend, go up higher'; then you will be honored in the presence of all who sit at table with you. 11 For every one who exalts himself will be humbled, and he who humbles himself will be exalted."

12 He said also to the man who had invited him, "When you give a dinner or a banquet, do not invite your friends or your brothers or your kinsmen or rich neighbors, lest they also invite you in return, and you be repaid. 13 But when you give a feast, invite the poor, the maimed, the lame, the blind, 14 and you will be blessed, because they cannot repay you. You will be repaid at the resurrection of the just."

15 When one of those who sat at table with him heard this, he said to him, "Blessed is he who shall eat bread in the kingdom of God!" 16 But he said to him, "A man once gave a great banquet, and invited many; 17 and at the time for the banquet he sent his servant to say to those who had been invited, 'Come; for all is now ready.' 18 But they all alike began to make excuses. The first said to him, 'I have bought a field, and I must go out and see it; I pray you, have me excused.' 19And another said, 'I have bought five yoke of oxen, and I go to examine them; I pray you, have me excused.'

⁸ Other ancient authorities read an ass

are, who express their saltness by salting whatever they touch. Moreover, His words to both Pharisees and multitudes make sense only as the words of One who can claim men wholly because He is giving Himself to them wholly; as the healing mercy of God, the inviting voice of God in person.

14:1-24 JESUS AND THE PHARISEES

14:1-6 The healing of the man with dropsy (peculiar to Lk). To the Pharisees, entrenched in their legal piety and keeping a suspiciously watchful eye on the breaker of the *sabbath* (1), Jesus presents the healing mercy of God in His own person; He *heals* the dropsical *man before him* on the Sabbath, on God's Day. For the Pharisees mercy on the Sabbath is the exception (5); for Jesus mercy on all days is the rule (3). They can become good salt only by breaking their stubborn silence (4, 6) and speaking a glad assent to the healing mercy of God present in Jesus. (Cf. 15:31-32)

14:1 *Watching* maliciously, lying in wait to see whether Jesus would violate the Sabbath as He had done before. (6:6 ff.; 13:10 ff.)

14:7-14 Found only in Lk. Jesus is not lecturing on table manners or giving rules on party-giving. The scene before Him offers the material for a *parable* (7) concerning men's faith in God the Exalter (11) and Rewarder (14). Jesus did not exalt Himself; He went the way of obedient ministry into the depths, the way of the merciful Servant, trusting in God to exalt Him at His time

and in His way (cf. Ph 2:6-11). He resisted the satanic temptation to greatness (4:5-8) and lavished his power and love on the *poor, the maimed, the lame, the blind* (13). He loved and served men who could not *repay, because* they could not repay (14). He loved with the love of the Most High (6:35). In summoning the Pharisee from his self-seeking and self-interest to this selfless way, Jesus is inviting them to Himself and to a share in His great reward. Thus they can become good salt.

14:11 *Will be humbled . . . be exalted.* The passive voice, as often, indicates divine action. (Cf., e.g., 6:21)

14:14 *The resurrection of the just.* This does not exclude a resurrection of those who "shall awake . . . to shame and everlasting contempt" (Dn 12:2). Jesus is speaking to the hope of the Pharisee, whom He called "just" or "righteous" in contrast to flagrant sinners. (Cf. 15:7; 5:32)

14:15-24 Cf. Mt 22:1-10. The Pharisee shares with Jesus the hope of partaking in God's feast in the future *kingdom of God* (15; cf. 13:29; 22:16). What the Pharisee in his comfortable hope does not see, what his concern for *field, oxen,* and to be *married* (18-20) blinds him to is the fact that the future kingdom is making its claim on him now, that now in the person of Jesus "the kingdom of God is in the midst" of them (17:21). With the coming Jesus God is saying, *Come; for all is now ready* (17). Jesus is God's invitation to the feast; through Him God *compels* men and *fills* His *house* (23) with guests. To evade Him is to be excluded from the great *banquet* of God. (24)

²⁰And another said, 'I have married a wife, and therefore I cannot come.' ²¹ So the servant came and reported this to his master. Then the householder in anger said to his servant, 'Go out quickly to the streets and lanes of the city, and bring in the poor and maimed and blind and lame.' ²²And the servant said, 'Sir, what you commanded has been done, and still there is room.' ²³And the master said to the servant, 'Go out to the highways and hedges, and compel people to come in, that my house may be filled. ²⁴ For I tell you,^a none of those men who were invited shall taste my banquet.' "

25 Now great multitudes accompanied him; and he turned and said to them, ²⁶ "If any one comes to me and does not hate his own father and mother and wife and children and brothers and sisters, yes, and even his own life, he cannot be my disciple. ²⁷ Whoever does not bear his own cross and come after me, cannot be my disciple. ²⁸ For which of you, desiring to build a tower, does not first sit down and count the cost, whether he has enough to complete it? ²⁹ Otherwise, when he has laid a foundation, and is not able to finish, all who see it begin to mock him, ³⁰ saying, 'This man began to build, and was not able to finish.' ³¹ Or what king, going to encounter another king in war, will not sit down first and take counsel whether he is able with ten thousand to meet him who comes against him with twenty thousand? ³²And if not, while the other is yet a great way off, he sends an embassy and asks terms of peace. ³³ So therefore, whoever of you does not renounce all that he has cannot be my disciple.

34 "Salt is good; but if salt has lost its taste, how shall its saltness be restored? ³⁵ It is fit neither for the land nor for the dunghill; men throw it away. He who has ears to hear, let him hear."

JESUS, THE SEEKER OF THE LOST (15:1-32)

15 Now the tax collectors and sinners were all drawing near to hear him. ²And the Pharisees and the scribes murmured, saying, "This man receives sinners and eats with them."

3 So he told them this parable: ⁴ "What man of you, having a hundred sheep, if he has lost one of them, does not leave the ninety-nine in the wilderness, and go after

^a The Greek word for *you* here is plural

14:21-23 The verses point to the inclusion of the Gentile, the theme of the Book of Acts. (Cf. 24:47)

14:25-35 JESUS AND THE MULTITUDES

14:25-35 Since Jesus is God's future, the only future that matters (cf. 14:15-24), it is not enough to accompany Him (25), man must come to Him (26). Man must be ready to turn his back on the dearest things this life holds for him: family (26), *life*, and honor (both given up in the criminal's death on the *cross*, 26-27), *all that he has* (33). He must do so with open-eyed sobriety and *count the cost* (28); romantic enthusiasm, illusions about victory without war — these will not do. Only discipleship, only faith in Jesus Christ will make a man *good salt*; only living and active faith will save him from the fate of salt that *has lost its taste*. *He who has ears to hear, let him hear* (35) the words not of a stern ascetic moralist but of Jesus Christ, the Wisdom of God and the Power of God. (Cf. 1 Co 1:24)

15:1-32 Once again (cf. 5:29-30) Jesus' free and forgiving association with *sinners* provokes the dissent of the "righteous," *the Pharisees and the scribes* (1-2). In three parables Jesus seeks to open the eyes of the dissenters to the wonder and glory of the history which is taking place before their eyes; it is the beginning of the last chapter of the story of the Lord who has promised to seek and save the lost (Eze 34:16; cf. Lk 19:10). The twin parables of the lost sheep (3-7) and the lost coin (8-10) make it plain: God is in Christ seeking His own; these *sinners* are His creatures, in whom He has an owner's interest (cf. Jn 10:11-17), for whose return He is willing to take trouble, to *seek diligently* (8), at whose recovery He and all His angels rejoice exceedingly (10). There is *joy in heaven* (7) now when Jesus admits sinners to table fellowship with Himself; shall there be murmuring on earth? (1)

This searching question is implicit in the first two parables; it becomes explicit in the third parable (11-32), which tells the same story in the personal terms of father and son, waiting love, repentance and return, free forgiveness, and exuberant joy. The parable of the prodigal son ends with the conversation between the rejoicing father and the angry *elder son*, the righteous who stayed home and *served* and *never disobeyed* his father's *command* (29). In the father's remarkably gentle and winning rebuke (31-32) Jesus is wooing the righteous to speak a joyous assent to His mission — not without pointing to their deep disease; their self-seeking will. In the end the elder son and the prodigal son both suffer from the same disease, self-seeking. The younger son said, *Give me* (12); the elder son said, *You never gave me.* (29)

15:2 *Eats with them.* For the significance of

the one which is lost, until he finds it? [5]And when he has found it, he lays it on his shoulders, rejoicing. [6]And when he comes home, he calls together his friends and his neighbors, saying to them, 'Rejoice with me, for I have found my sheep which was lost.' [7] Just so, I tell you, there will be more joy in heaven over one sinner who repents than over ninety-nine righteous persons who need no repentance.

8 "Or what woman, having ten silver coins,[t] if she loses one coin, does not light a lamp and sweep the house and seek diligently until she finds it? [9]And when she has found it, she calls together her friends and neighbors, saying, 'Rejoice with me, for I have found the coin which I had lost.' [10] Just so, I tell you, there is joy before the angels of God over one sinner who repents."

11 And he said, "There was a man who had two sons; [12] and the younger of them said to his father, 'Father, give me the share of property that falls to me.' And he divided his living between them. [13] Not many days later, the younger son gathered all he had and took his journey into a far country, and there he squandered his property in loose living. [14]And when he had spent everything, a great famine arose in that country, and he began to be in want. [15] So he went and joined himself to one of the citizens of that country, who sent him into his fields to feed swine. [16]And he would gladly have fed on[u] the pods that the swine ate; and no one gave him anything. [17] But when he came to himself he said, 'How many of my father's hired servants have bread enough and to spare, but I perish here with hunger! [18] I will arise and go to my father, and I will say to him, "Father, I have sinned against heaven and before you; [19] I am no longer worthy to be called your son; treat me as one of your hired servants."' [20]And he arose and came to his father. But while he was yet at a distance, his father saw him and had compassion, and ran and embraced him and kissed him. [21]And the son said to him, 'Father, I have sinned against heaven and before you; I am no longer worthy to be called your son.'[v] [22] But the father said to his servants, 'Bring quickly the best robe, and put it on him; and put a ring on his hand, and shoes on his feet; [23] and bring the fatted calf and kill it, and let us eat and make merry; [24] for this my son was dead, and is alive again; he was lost, and is found.' And they began to make merry.

25 "Now his elder son was in the field; and as he came and drew near to the house, he heard music and dancing. [26]And he called one of the servants and asked what this meant. [27]And he said to him, 'Your brother has come, and your father has killed the fatted calf, because he has received him safe and sound.' [28] But he was angry and refused to go in. His father came out and entreated him, [29] but he answered his father, 'Lo, these many years I have served you, and I never disobeyed your command; yet you never gave me a kid, that I might make merry with my friends. [30] But when this son of yours came, who has devoured your living with harlots, you killed for him the fatted calf!' [31]And he said to him, 'Son, you are always with me, and all that is mine is yours. [32] It was fitting to make merry and be glad, for this your brother was dead, and is alive; he was lost, and is found.' "

[t] The drachma, rendered here by *silver coin,* was about a day's wage for a laborer
[u] Other ancient authorities read *filled his belly with*
[v] Other ancient authorities add *treat me as one of your hired servants*

the common meal cf. Mt 14:15-21 note.

15:8-32 Only in Lk.

15:8 *Ten silver coins.* The ten coins probably were part of her dowry and adorned her headdress, a treasured possession.

15:11-32 Only in Lk.

15:13 *Gathered all he had,* i. e., converted it into cash.

15:15-16 *Feed swine . . . no one gave him.* A Jew could hardly sink lower than this: herding the unclean animals and filching their fodder for food.

15:21 *Called your son.* The father does not allow him to finish his prepared speech of repentance (cf. 19, "treat me as one of your hired servants"); the penitent, returning son is son with full honors

(22-23). God's forgiveness is instant and total. (Cf. Mi 7:18-19)

15:22 For the *robe* as a symbol of forgiveness cf. Zch 3:4.

15:29 *Many years I have served you.* The elder son felt that he had been dealt with unfairly. He had worked for the good of the home all his life; the younger brother had squandered everything he had received.

15:31 *You are always with me.* That is what life under the covenant means: constant communion with God.

15:32 *Your brother was dead.* Cf. Eph 2:1-2, "dead through the trespasses and sins in which you once walked."

THE POSSIBILITIES AND PERILS OF MAMMON (16:1-31)

16 He also said to the disciples, "There was a rich man who had a steward, and charges were brought to him that this man was wasting his goods. ²And he called him and said to him, 'What is this that I hear about you? Turn in the account of your stewardship, for you can no longer be steward.' ³And the steward said to himself, 'What shall I do, since my master is taking the stewardship away from me? I am not strong enough to dig, and I am ashamed to beg. ⁴ I have decided what to do, so that people may receive me into their houses when I am put out of the stewardship.' ⁵ So, summoning his master's debtors one by one, he said to the first, 'How much do you owe my master?' ⁶ He said, 'A hundred measures of oil.' And he said to him, 'Take your bill, and sit down quickly and write fifty.' ⁷ Then he said to another, 'And how much do you owe?' He said, 'A hundred measures of wheat.' He said to him, 'Take your bill, and write eighty.' ⁸ The master commended the dishonest steward for his shrewdness; for the sons of this world *ʷ* are more shrewd in dealing with their own generation than the sons of light. ⁹And I tell you, make friends for yourselves by means of unrighteous mammon, *ᵃ* so that when it fails they may receive you into the eternal habitations.

10 "He who is faithful in a very little is faithful also in much; and he who is dishonest in a very little is dishonest also in much. ¹¹ If then you have not been faithful in the unrighteous mammon, *ᵃ* who will entrust to you the true riches? ¹²And if you have not been faithful in that which is another's, who will give you that which is your own? ¹³ No servant can serve two masters; for either he will hate the one and love the other, or he will be devoted to the one and despise the other. You cannot serve God and mammon." *ᵃ*

ʷ Greek *age*   *ᵃ Mammon* is a Semitic word for money or riches

16:1-31 *Mammon* is a word from Jesus' mother tongue, Aramaic, and means "possessions." Luke's Gospel is particularly rich in Jesus' teaching on mammon. (See Introduction.) This whole chapter is devoted to the subject. Jesus speaks of the possibilities of mammon to His *disciples,* and of the perils of mammon to the *Pharisees, who were lovers of money.* In both cases He speaks of man's use of mammon in view of man's long future; man's use of mammon can lead to the *eternal habitations* (9) or to the eternal *place of torment.* (28)

16:1-13 THE POSSIBILITIES OF MAMMON: THE DISHONEST STEWARD

16:1-13 *Mammon,* property, can serve eternally useful ends if it is used with *shrewdness* (8); the disciples can learn that shrewdness from the example of an unscrupulous rascal like the dishonest steward. Shrewdness is the ability to appraise a situation realistically, to find ways and means to meet the situation, and to employ the means and ways vigorously and consistently toward gaining one's desired end. In this, and in this alone, the steward is exemplary. He knows that his time is short, that he must work with what he has while there still is time; and he does work with it shrewdly and boldly. And so he ensures his future against degradation and want (3). He wins out by giving away what he has while he still has it. This the disciples are to imitate, not the dishonesty but the prudence. They are to know that they are stewards, whose property is entrusted to them for a short time by Another; that they are to work with that property while they can, giving away deliberately and recklessly

with an eye to the future and its *eternal habitations* (9). Thus they will provide themselves with "purses that do not grow old, with a treasure in the heavens that does not fail." (1-9; cf. 12:33)

Mammon, Jesus adds (10-13), is but a *very little* thing compared with the *true riches* which are theirs. But in this little thing they can and must demonstrate their faithfulness; in it they can show their singlehearted devotion to their one Master; they can *serve* only one Master, God. But in their prudence learned from Jesus they can make mammon serve God's cause and their own eternal welfare. (10-13)

16:1 *Wasting his goods.* That is what the tax collectors who drew near to Jesus (15:1) and men like the younger son of the parable had done (15:13, 30); they had wasted God's goods. Now, as disciples of Jesus, they still have a little time to use wisely the goods entrusted to them, as Zacchaeus did (19:8) when salvation came to his house. (19:9)

16:8 *The master.* The steward's master, cf. 3, 5; even the man who had suffered from the steward's dishonesty had to admire his *shrewdness* as a "smart operator." *The sons of this world,* the men who live for and by the profits of this age, have a keener eye for shrewdness on their level and in men of their own kind than the Christian has.

Sons of light, the men who derive their being and character from the light that has dawned on the world in Jesus Christ. (1:78-79; 2:32; Acts 26:23)

16:9 *They may receive you.* They are the people helped and won by the disciples' generosity. What was done to them was done to Christ and God

14 The Pharisees, who were lovers of money, heard all this, and they scoffed at him. 15 But he said to them, "You are those who justify yourselves before men, but God knows your hearts; for what is exalted among men is an abomination in the sight of God.

16 "The law and the prophets were until John; since then the good news of the kingdom of God is preached, and every one enters it violently. 17 But it is easier for heaven and earth to pass away, than for one dot of the law to become void.

18 "Every one who divorces his wife and marries another commits adultery, and he who marries a woman divorced from her husband commits adultery.

19 "There was a rich man, who was clothed in purple and fine linen and who feasted sumptuously every day. 20And at his gate lay a poor man named Lazarus, full of sores, 21 who desired to be fed with what fell from the rich man's table; moreover the dogs came and licked his sores. 22 The poor man died and was carried by the angels to Abraham's bosom. The rich man also died and was buried; 23 and in Hades, being in torment, he lifted up his eyes, and saw Abraham far off and Lazarus in his bosom. 24And he called out, 'Father Abraham, have mercy upon me, and send Lazarus to dip the end of his finger in water and cool my tongue; for I am in anguish in this flame.' 25 But Abraham said, 'Son, remember that you in your lifetime received your good things, and Lazarus in like manner evil things; but now he is comforted here, and you are in anguish. 26And besides all this, between us and you a great chasm has been fixed, in order that those who would pass from here to you may not be able, and none may cross from there to us.' 27And he said, 'Then I beg you, father, to send him to my

---

(9:48) and receives the gracious reward of life in their *eternal habitations.*

16:14-31 THE PERILS OF MAMMON: THE RICH MAN AND LAZARUS

16:14-31 The *Pharisees,* known not only from the NT but also from Judaic sources as *lovers of money, scoffed* at Jesus (14). They saw no conflict between serving God and mammon (13). When John the Baptist came with the call to repentance and the gift of forgiveness by Baptism, these men did not "justify God" as "the people and the tax collectors" did by accepting God's judgment on their sin and His forgiveness for their sin (7:29 note). They "rejected the purpose of God" by refusing Baptism (7:30) and continued to *justify* themselves *before men* (15) with their hollow and pretentious piety. Jesus tries once more to open their eyes to the reality of their present situation and of their impending future. *God,* He tells them, *knows* them for what they are, for He knows their *hearts* (15). They have heard *the law and the prophets* from childhood on; they have heard *John* the Baptist; they are hearing *the good news of the kingdom of God,* and they see man hazarding all to enter that proclaimed kingdom (*enters it violently,* 16). They know from Jesus' own teaching that the Gospel does not "overthrow the law" but "upholds the law" (17; cf. Ro 3:31). And yet they continue to flout the sanctity of marriage which the Law commands and the Gospel upholds. No word of God has turned them from their self-serving distortion of the Law, from their self-exaltation, their worship of themselves, which makes them an *abomination* (an idol) in the *sight of God.* (15)

The story of the *rich man* and *Lazarus* (19-31) makes terrifyingly clear what is the future of men who attempt to serve both God and mammon. Mammon has made the rich man blind to the need of the neighbor whom God has put at *his gate,* inescapably visible. Mammon has made the rich man deaf to the voice of God in *Moses and the prophets,* which he had. His heart was not fixed in love on God or man; his heart lay where his treasure was (*purple and fine linen . . . feasted sumptuously;* 19). At the great reversal which Mary had hailed in the Magnificat, Lazarus is filled with good things and the rich is sent empty away, into the *place of torment* (cf. 1:51-53). Too late he realizes that the Word of God is more precious than gold, than fine gold. Too late he learns that those who have not heeded the Law and the prophets have made impossible the greater gift of God, the word of one risen from the dead. He and his *brothers* have not really had the gift of the Law and the prophets; "from him who has not, even what he thinks that he has will be taken away." (8:18)

16:20 *Lazarus* is the only person in Jesus' parables who is given a name; the name is therefore significant. It means "God is my help" and indicates that the poor man is not merely destitute but one who is "poor in spirit," wholly dependent on God. (Cf. Mt 5:3 note)

16:21 *Dogs . . . licked his sores.* Since dogs, lean and hungry scavengers of the streets, are regarded as unclean (Mt 7:6), this feature serves to mark the extremity of the poor man's misery.

16:22 *Abraham's bosom,* the place of honor (Jn 13:23) at the great feast in the world to come (Lk 13:28-29; Mt 8:11). God has "exalted those of low degree." (1:52)

father's house, 28 for I have five brothers, so that he may warn them, lest they also come into this place of torment.' 29 But Abraham said, 'They have Moses and the prophets; let them hear them.' 30And he said, 'No, father Abraham; but if some one goes to them from the dead, they will repent.' 31 He said to him, 'If they do not hear Moses and the prophets, neither will they be convinced if some one should rise from the dead.' "

SERVICE AND HEALING (17:1-19)

17 And he said to his disciples, "Temptations to sin*x* are sure to come; but woe to him by whom they come! 2 It would be better for him if a millstone were hung round his neck and he were cast into the sea, than that he should cause one of these little ones to sin.*y* 3 Take heed to yourselves; if your brother sins, rebuke him, and if he repents, forgive him; 4 and if he sins against you seven times in the day, and turns to you seven times, and says, 'I repent,' you must forgive him."

5 The apostles said to the Lord, "Increase our faith!" 6And the Lord said, "If you had faith as a grain of mustard seed, you could say to this sycamine tree, 'Be rooted up, and be planted in the sea,' and it would obey you.

7 "Will any one of you, who has a servant plowing or keeping sheep, say to him when he has come in from the field, 'Come at once and sit down at table'? 8 Will he not rather say to him, 'Prepare supper for me, and gird yourself and serve me, till I eat and drink; and afterward you shall eat and drink'? 9 Does he thank the servant because he did what was commanded? 10 So you also, when you have done all that is commanded you, say, 'We are unworthy servants; we have only done what was our duty.' "

11 On the way to Jerusalem he was passing along between Sa·mar′i·a and Galilee. 12And as he entered a village, he was met by ten lepers, who stood at a distance 13 and

---

x Greek *stumbling blocks*   *y* Greek *stumble*

16:31 *If some one should rise from the dead.* Perhaps a hint of the coming resurrection of Jesus and the renewed proclamation of the Gospel to Israel, "beginning from Jerusalem" (24:47). Even then no "sign" will be given to those who demand one; Jesus will appear to His disciples — all others will be dependent on the Word.

17:1-10 THE DISCIPLES' SERVICE:
FAITH WORKING THROUGH LOVE

17:1-10 For 1-2 cf. Mt 18:6-9; for 3-4 cf. Mt 18:15, 21-22; for 5-6 cf. Mt 17:20 note. 7-10 is peculiar to Lk.

Jesus lays on *his disciples* (1), who are to be *apostles* of their *Lord*, living extensions of His ministering love, a burden that only *faith* (5) can bear: He asks of them a love which will in holy fear avoid putting *temptations to sin* (or *stumbling blocks*, 1) in the way of *little ones* (2), the weak and wavering brothers, easily shocked, readily misled. Paul's words in Ro 14:13 – 15:2 show what loving consideration, what disciplined self-sacrifice this involves. Jesus asks of His disciples a readiness to forgive the penitent brother which knows no limits (*seven times in the day*, 4). He asks of them a servant's (slave's) total devotion which works with no thought of reward, a love which considers a *duty done* the least that love can do (7-10). No wonder that the disciples make the request, *Increase our faith* (5). And Jesus does increase it when He assures them that it is not the power of their believing but the power of the

God in whom they believe that achieves the impossible — the firmly rooted *sycamine tree . . . rooted up* (6), bearing patiently with little ones, forgiving without limit.

17:7 No master of a slave is expected to serve his servants; but Jesus will do the unexpected. To those who work in faith and love, with no thought of reward, He gives the reward which none may claim and only He can give: "He will gird himself and have them sit at table, and he will come and serve them." (12:37; cf. Rv 3:20)

17:11-19 THE HEALING OF THE 10 LEPERS

17:11-19 Peculiar to Lk. *Faith* (19) links this third story involving Samaritans (cf. 9:52-55; 10:30-37) with the preceding; as faith is manifested in considerate, self-denying love (17:1-2), in forgiving (17:3-4), and in service to the Lord (17:7-10), so it is in the nature of faith *to . . . give praise to God* (18; cf. Ro 4:20). The common tragedy of leprosy united the Samaritan with nine Jews in their misery; his *faith* unites him with Jesus and makes him a member of the new people of God, while the Jews who accept the gifts of the Messiah but will not believe in Him and *give thanks* to God for Him are excluded. (Cf. Mt 8:11-12)

17:12 *Village.* Judaic interpretation of the Law (Lv 13 – 14) excluded *lepers* from Jerusalem and walled cities but permitted them to live in segregation in or near unwalled villages.

At a distance, as prescribed in Lv 13:45-46.

lifted up their voices and said, "Jesus, Master, have mercy on us." 14 When he saw them he said to them, "Go and show yourselves to the priests." And as they went they were cleansed. 15 Then one of them, when he saw that he was healed, turned back, praising God with a loud voice; 16 and he fell on his face at Jesus' feet, giving him thanks. Now he was a Samaritan. 17 Then said Jesus, "Were not ten cleansed? Where are the nine? 18 Was no one found to return and give praise to God except this foreigner?" 19And he said to him, "Rise and go your way; your faith has made you well."

THE PRESENCE AND THE COMING OF THE KINGDOM (17:20 — 18:30)

20 Being asked by the Pharisees when the kingdom of God was coming, he answered them, "The kingdom of God is not coming with signs to be observed; 21 nor will they say, 'Lo, here it is!' or 'There!' for behold, the kingdom of God is in the midst of you." *z*

22 And he said to the disciples, "The days are coming when you will desire to see one of the days of the Son of man, and you will not see it. 23And they will say to you, 'Lo, there!' or 'Lo, here!' Do not go, do not follow them. 24 For as the lightning flashes and lights up the sky from one side to the other, so will the Son of man be in his day.*a* 25 But first he must suffer many things and be rejected by this generation.

z Or *within you* *a* Other ancient authorities omit *in his day*

17:14 *Show yourselves to the priests.* Cf. Lv 14:2-32.

17:18 *Was no one found?* Jesus laments over the unbelief and ingratitude of His people, represented here by the nine lepers (cf. 19:41-44); He does not revoke the gift of healing. His is the divine love that "risks betrayal." (Luther)

17:20—18:30 Faith (17:1-19) and hope are inseparable; this section speaks of hope. The units of this section are held together by the idea of the presence and the future coming of the kingdom of God. The question of the *Pharisees* is a question concerning the *when* of the reign of God (17:20-21); Jesus speaks to His disciples of *one of the days of the Son of man*, which is another way of speaking of the Kingdom (17:22-37); the parable of the *widow* and the *judge* encourages continual, unflagging prayer for the coming of the Son of Man in glory (18:1-8); the story of the *Pharisee* and the *publican* points toward the future judgment when the self-righteous *will be humbled* and the penitently humble *will be exalted* (18:9-14); Jesus' welcoming of the *children* speaks of man's entry into the *kingdom* (18:15-17); the *ruler's* question is concerned with *eternal life,* and Jesus' answer concerns entry into the *kingdom of God* (18:18-30). The whole mystery of the Kingdom, present in the person of Jesus, won or lost by man's response to Him now, and coming incalculably and gloriously in the future, is presented here.

17:20-21 PHARISEES' QUESTION CONCERNING
THE COMING OF THE KINGDOM

17:20-21 The healing of the 10 lepers (11-19) may have prompted the Pharisees' question. Their rabbis equated the healing of a leper with the resurrection of a dead man; and the resurrection of the dead was a sure *sign* of the arrival of the long-awaited Kingdom. Jesus' answer cuts off all calculation of time and place concerning the future Kingdom and seeks to open their eyes for the beginning of "the acceptable year of the Lord" (4:19), the dawn of the Kingdom in His own words and works now, spoken and done *in the midst* of them (cf. 19:20). The Pharisee felt sure of his place in the Kingdom (14:15) and needed only to be assured of its arrival; Jesus' answer implies that the drawing near of the Kingdom is not a time for observation but for repentance. (Cf. Mt 4:17; Mk 1:15)

17:22-37 THE HOPE OF THE DISCIPLE:
THE DAY OF THE SON OF MAN

17:22-37 Jesus' words to His *disciples* are somber and sobering words, full of pastoral concern for them. The *Son of man . . . must suffer* (25) before He can "enter into his glory" (24:26); and His own must follow Him on that path of suffering (cf. Ro 8:17). Therefore their longing for the return of the Son of Man in glory will be intense (22). They must not let that intensity of hope make them credulous toward misleading voices (23); they need no word but the Word of their Lord, and it assures them that *the Son of man . . . in his day* will be as inescapably apparent in His glorious coming as *lightning flashes* to illumine the sky from horizon to horizon (24). They must never lose the intensity of their hope and become so enmeshed in the normal concerns of life that the return of the Son of Man comes upon them unawares and proves their destruction. The *days of Noah* and the *days of Lot* should warn them against that, those "normal" days which ended suddenly in judgment by *flood* and *fire* (26-30). The example of *Lot's wife* warns them of the danger of the one last look backward at the perishing world; no desire for self-preservation dare tempt them to *gain* their *life* and so, at the last moment, *lose it* (31-34). That last moment will bring terribly unexpected divisions; the ties of this world will be sundered forever (35-36). Jesus cuts off all curious ques-

26As it was in the days of Noah, so will it be in the days of the Son of man. 27 They ate, they drank, they married, they were given in marriage, until the day when Noah entered the ark, and the flood came and destroyed them all. 28 Likewise as it was in the days of Lot—they ate, they drank, they bought, they sold, they planted, they built, 29but on the day when Lot went out from Sodom fire and sulphur rained from heaven and destroyed them all— 30 so will it be on the day when the Son of man is revealed. 31 On that day, let him who is on the housetop, with his goods in the house, not come down to take them away; and likewise let him who is in the field not turn back. 32 Remember Lot's wife. 33 Whoever seeks to gain his life will lose it, but whoever loses his life will preserve it. 34 I tell you, in that night there will be two in one bed; one will be taken and the other left. 35 There will be two women grinding together; one will be taken and the other left."*b* 37And they said to him, "Where, Lord?" He said to them, "Where the body is, there the eagles*c* will be gathered together."

18 And he told them a parable, to the effect that they ought always to pray and not lose heart. 2 He said, "In a certain city there was a judge who neither feared God nor regarded man; 3 and there was a widow in that city who kept coming to him and saying, 'Vindicate me against my adversary.' 4 For a while he refused; but afterward he said to himself, 'Though I neither fear God nor regard man, 5 yet because this widow bothers me, I will vindicate her, or she will wear me out by her continual coming.' " 6And the Lord said, "Hear what the unrighteous judge says. 7And will not God vindicate his elect, who cry to him day and night? Will he delay long over them? 8 I tell you, he will vindicate them speedily. Nevertheless, when the Son of man comes, will he find faith on earth?"

9 He also told this parable to some who trusted in themselves that they were righteous and despised others: 10 "Two men went up into the temple to pray, one a Pharisee and the other a tax collector. 11 The Pharisee stood and prayed thus with himself, 'God, I thank thee that I am not like other men, extortioners, unjust, adulterers, or even like this tax collector. 12 I fast twice a week, I give tithes of all that I get.' 13 But the tax collector, standing far off, would not even lift up his eyes to heaven, but beat his breast, saying, 'God, be merciful to me a sinner!' 14 I tell you, this man went down to his house justified rather than the other; for every one who exalts himself will be humbled, but he who humbles himself will be exalted."

b Other ancient authorities add verse 36, "*Two men will be in the field; one will be taken and the other left*"
c Or *vultures*

tioning; the eagles of God *will be gathered together* for judgment at the time of this world's death (*body,* corpse) which only God knows. (37)

17:26 *Days of Noah.* Cf. Gn 6:5-8; 7:6-24; Mt 24:37-39.

17:28 *Days of Lot.* Cf. Gn 18:20-33; 19:24-25.

17:35 *One . . . taken,* that is, taken to Himself by the Son of Man when He comes to gather His elect. (Cf. Mt 24:31)

18:1-8 THE HOPE OF THE DISCIPLE: PRAY AND NOT LOSE HEART

18:1-8 Peculiar to Lk. As in the case of the dishonest steward (16:1-9), Jesus uses an extreme case to make His point. If even an irreverent and *unrighteous judge* will finally heed the plea of a *widow* who has no money to bribe him and no prestige or influence to sway him, how much the more will not a righteous *God* give ear to the prayers of those whom His love has made His *elect* and *vindicate them speedily?* God will keep faith, Jesus says, with those who long and pray for the day of the Son of Man; and He concludes with the searching question: Will you keep faith?

18:9-30 WILL THE SON OF MAN FIND FAITH ON EARTH?

18:9-30 Will the Son of Man, when He comes, find faith on earth (cf. 8)? He will find faith in men like the crushed and contrite *tax collector* who throws himself unconditionally upon the mercy of God (13); *he who humbles himself* in faith *will be exalted* on that day (14). He will find faith in the childlike who *receive* at God's hand the *kingdom of God* (17), dependent on Him and looking to Him. He will find it in him who has permitted God to do what is *impossible with men* (27)—turn him from serving mammon to serving God (18-27). He will find it in those who, trusting in Jesus' promise of *eternal life,* have *left* all and *followed* Him. (28-30)

18:9-14 Peculiar to Lk. The piety of the *Pharisee* and of the *tax collector* finds expression in their prayers. The Pharisee's righteousness has made him contemptuous and loveless and self-centered; he prays *with himself* and gives thanks that he is *not like other men* (11). The praying tax collector *beats his breast* in desperation, prays the

15 Now they were bringing even infants to him that he might touch them; and when the disciples saw it, they rebuked them. [16] But Jesus called them to him, saying, "Let the children come to me, and do not hinder them; for to such belongs the kingdom of God. [17] Truly, I say to you, whoever does not receive the kingdom of God like a child shall not enter it."

18 And a ruler asked him, "Good Teacher, what shall I do to inherit eternal life?" [19]And Jesus said to him, "Why do you call me good? No one is good but God alone. [20] You know the commandments: 'Do not commit adultery, Do not kill, Do not steal, Do not bear false witness, Honor your father and mother.' " [21]And he said, "All these I have observed from my youth." [22]And when Jesus heard it, he said to him, "One thing you still lack. Sell all that you have and distribute to the poor, and you will have treasure in heaven; and come, follow me." [23] But when he heard this he became sad, for he was very rich. [24] Jesus looking at him said, "How hard it is for those who have riches to enter the kingdom of God! [25] For it is easier for a camel to go through the eye of a needle than for a rich man to enter the kingdom of God." [26] Those who heard it said, "Then who can be saved?" [27] But he said, "What is impossible with men is possible with God." [28]And Peter said, "Lo, we have left our homes and followed you." [29]And he said to them, "Truly, I say to you, there is no man who has left house or wife or brothers or parents or children, for the sake of the kingdom of God, [30] who will not receive manifold more in this time, and in the age to come eternal life."

Jesus' Last Days in Jerusalem

18:31 — 21:38

31 And taking the twelve, he said to them, "Behold, we are going up to Jerusalem, and everything that is written of the Son of man by the prophets will be accomplished. [32] For he will be delivered to the Gentiles, and will be mocked and shamefully treated and spit upon; [33] they will scourge him and kill him, and on the third day he will rise." [34] But they understood none of these things; this saying was hid from them, and they did not grasp what was said.

35 As he drew near to Jericho, a blind man was sitting by the roadside begging; [36] and hearing a multitude going by, he inquired what this meant. [37] They told him, "Jesus of Nazareth is passing by." [38]And he cried, "Jesus, Son of David, have mercy on me!" [39]And those who were in front rebuked him, telling him to be silent; but he cried out all the more, "Son of David, have mercy on me!" [40]And Jesus stopped, and commanded him to be brought to him; and when he came near, he asked him, [41] "What do you want me to do for you?" He said, "Lord, let me receive my sight." [42]And Jesus said to him, "Receive your sight; your faith has made you well." [43]And immediately he received his sight and followed him, glorifying God; and all the people, when they saw it, gave praise to God.

19 He entered Jericho and was passing through. [2]And there was a man named Zac·chae'us; he was a chief tax collector, and rich. [3]And he sought to see who Jesus was, but could not, on account of the crowd, because he was small of stature.

---

prayer of Ps 51:1, and receives the promise of Ps 51:17: "The sacrifice acceptable to God is a broken spirit; a broken and contrite heart, O God, thou wilt not despise." He goes *down to his house justified* (14). The great promise of the future *(will be exalted)* has restored and renewed him even now.

18:15-17 Cf. Mt 19:13-15 note.

18:18-30 Cf. Mt 19:16-29 note.

18:31-34 THIRD PREDICTION OF THE PASSION

18:31-34 Cf. Mt 20:17-19 note. In this third formal prediction of the Passion (cf. 9:22; 9:44) the accent peculiar to Lk is the fact that Jesus goes to His death in order that *everything that is*

written . . . by the prophets may be *accomplished* (31) and that His disciples do not *grasp what was said* (34). Both point forward to Jesus' final instruction to His disciples after His resurrection. (Cf. 24:25-26, 44-47)

18:35-43 THE HEALING OF THE BLIND MAN AT JERICHO

18:35-43 Cf. Mt 20:29-34 note.

19:1-10 ZACCHAEUS: TODAY SALVATION HAS COME TO THIS HOUSE

19:1-10 Peculiar to Lk. In this last incident before Jesus' entry into Jerusalem all that has characterized Lk's account of Jesus' ministry

4 So he ran on ahead and climbed up into a sycamore tree to see him, for he was to pass that way. 5And when Jesus came to the place, he looked up and said to him, "Zac·chae'us, make haste and come down; for I must stay at your house today." 6 So he made haste and came down, and received him joyfully. 7And when they saw it they all murmured, "He has gone in to be the guest of a man who is a sinner." 8And Zac-chae'us stood and said to the Lord, "Behold, Lord, the half of my goods I give to the poor; and if I have defrauded any one of anything, I restore it fourfold." 9And Jesus said to him, "Today salvation has come to this house, since he also is a son of Abraham. 10 For the Son of man came to seek and to save the lost."

11 As they heard these things, he proceeded to tell a parable, because he was near to Jerusalem, and because they supposed that the kingdom of God was to appear immediately. 12 He said therefore, "A nobleman went into a far country to receive a kingdom and then return. 13 Calling ten of his servants, he gave them ten pounds,ᵉ and said to them, 'Trade with these till I come.' 14 But his citizens hated him and sent an embassy after him, saying, 'We do not want this man to reign over us.' 15 When he returned, having received the kingdom, he commanded these servants, to whom he had given the money, to be called to him, that he might know what they had gained by trading. 16 The first came before him, saying, 'Lord, your pound has made ten pounds more.' 17And he said to him, 'Well done, good servant! Because you have been faithful in a very little, you shall have authority over ten cities.' 18And the

ᵉ The mina, rendered here by *pound,* was about three months' wages for a laborer

appears in concentrated form. Jesus as *Son of man* is come to do God's own work: *to seek and to save the lost* (cf. Eze 34:16). He is the promised Savior in person (2:11). The lost is the outcast *tax collector,* lost in greed, victim of mammon, forgetful of God's promise and unmindful of His law. The God of *Abraham,* however, has not forgotten His promise (9; cf. 1:54-55, 73; 13:16) and brings His free and undeserved *salvation* (1:69, 71, 77) to the house of this disobedient *son of Abraham;* the joy of the new age is there (*joyfully,* 6; cf. 1:14; 2:10; 10:20; 13:17). This course Jesus *must* (5) follow in obedience to His Father's will (cf. 2:49; 4:43; 9:22; 17:25; 22:37; 24:7, 26, 44; 13:16, 33). His people objected to this free grace of His way at the beginning in Nazareth (4:22-29); and now, with Jerusalem in sight, *all murmured* (7) at His grace to the tax collector. And so this course leads to His rejection by His people, to the cross.

19:1-2 *Jericho . . . chief tax collector.* Jericho was the winter capital of Herod and then of Archelaus, his son; it had a rich export from its balsam groves and was an important customs station. Zacchaeus' post was no doubt a highly remunerative one.

19:8-9 *Salvation* came to Zacchaeus' *house* simply because he *also* was a *son of Abraham* and heir of the promise. This "kindness" of God led him "to repentance" (Ro 2:4), and this repentance manifested itself in his generosity to the poor and the *fourfold* restitution to men whom he had *defrauded,* which was more than the Law required (cf. Lv 6:5; Nm 5:5-7) except for stolen cattle and sheep. (Ex 22:1)

19:11-27 THE PARABLE OF THE POUNDS

19:11-27 Similar to Mt 25:14-30 but not identical. Most striking Lukan feature is the rebellion of the citizens against their king. (14, 27)

As Jesus draws *near to Jerusalem* (11) amid opposition (cf. 19:7) and expectation (*kingdom of God . . . appear immediately,* 11), He speaks a parable which makes plain His purpose as King of the Kingdom and what that purpose means for men. Jesus will not claim or even fight for His kingly power in Jerusalem; He will *receive* it in *a far country* from Another's hand (12; cf. 22:29). Then He will return in *kingly power* and glory to reward and judge. Meanwhile—the chief stress lies on this "meanwhile"—His opponents may still learn to lay aside their fatal enmity before the Final Judgment cuts them down (14, 27). He calls on His people to repent before it is too late (cf. 19:41-44; 23:28-31). Meanwhile those who have acknowledged His royal claim on them are to await His return as faithful workers with what has been entrusted to them, fortified by hope of a splendid reward (17, 19) and sobered by the prospect of being found unfaithful in the King's scrutiny. (20-26)

19:11 *Kingdom . . . appear.* Cf. 17:20-21.

19:12-14 Jesus takes His material from a piece of history that many of His hearers would remember. Upon the death of Herod the Great, Herod's son and principal successor, Archelaus, was confronted by a hostile people. His situation was further complicated by the intrigues of his brother and rival Herod Antipas. He therefore went to Rome to have his claim to the throne confirmed by the emperor Augustus. While he was in Rome, a deputation of Jews arrived petitioning the emperor to do away with Herodian rule altogether and allow the Jews to live according to their own laws.

19:16-18 *Your pound has made.* The good servant claims no credit for his successful trading. The king's *pound* has done the king's work. Cf. Paul's description of his apostolic "success," Ro 15:17-19.

second came, saying, 'Lord, your pound has made five pounds.' ¹⁹And he said to him, 'And you are to be over five cities.' ²⁰ Then another came, saying, 'Lord, here is your pound, which I kept laid away in a napkin; ²¹ for I was afraid of you, because you are a severe man; you take up what you did not lay down, and reap what you did not sow.' ²² He said to him, 'I will condemn you out of your own mouth, you wicked servant! You knew that I was a severe man, taking up what I did not lay down and reaping what I did not sow? ²³ Why then did you not put my money into the bank, and at my coming I should have collected it with interest?' ²⁴And he said to those who stood by, 'Take the pound from him, and give it to him who has the ten pounds.' ²⁵ (And they said to him, 'Lord, he has ten pounds!') ²⁶ 'I tell you, that to every one who has will more be given; but from him who has not, even what he has will be taken away. ²⁷ But as for these enemies of mine, who did not want me to reign over them, bring them here and slay them before me.' "

28 And when he had said this, he went on ahead, going up to Jerusalem. ²⁹ When he drew near to Beth′pha·ge and Beth′a·ny, at the mount that is called Olivet, he sent two of the disciples, ³⁰ saying, "Go into the village opposite, where on entering you will find a colt tied, on which no one has ever yet sat; untie it and bring it here. ³¹ If any one asks you, 'Why are you untying it?' you shall say this, 'The Lord has need of it.' " ³² So those who were sent went away and found it as he had told them. ³³And as they were untying the colt, its owners said to them, "Why are you untying the colt?" ³⁴And they said, "The Lord has need of it." ³⁵And they brought it to Jesus, and throwing their garments on the colt they set Jesus upon it. ³⁶And as he rode along, they spread their garments on the road. ³⁷As he was now drawing near, at the descent of the Mount of Olives, the whole multitude of the disciples began to rejoice and praise God with a loud voice for all the mighty works that they had seen, ³⁸ saying, "Blessed is the King who comes in the name of the Lord! Peace in heaven and glory in the highest!" ³⁹And some of the Pharisees in the multitude said to him, "Teacher, rebuke your disciples." ⁴⁰ He answered, "I tell you, if these were silent, the very stones would cry out."

19:17-19 *Ten . . . five cities.* The good servants' reward is wholly at the king's discretion since it is of his grace. Both participate in his reign. (Cf. 22:28-30; Mt 19:28)

19:20 *Napkin,* or "face cloth, handkerchief." The wicked servant kept the money safe but did nothing with it.

19:22 *Condemn you out of your own mouth.* "Judge you by your own standard." The servant's conception of his lord was a false one (as the lord's generous treatment of the faithful servants shows), but he is unfaithful even on the basis of that conception; even though obsessed by fear, he might have performed a safe and slight ministry. (23; cf. Mt 25:27 note)

19:24-26 The action does not seem "equitable" to men. And it is not, since the whole operation is not one of equity but of sheer "unreasonable" grace—being entrusted with the king's property and business is grace (as Paul calls his apostolate, Eph 3:8), the reward given for service, whether great or small, is grace. (Cf. Mt 25:14-30 note)

19:28-40 JESUS ENTERS JERUSALEM

19:28-40 Cf. Mt 21:1-11 note; Mk 11:3, 10 notes.

19:37-38 *Blessed is the King . . . peace . . . glory.* These words recall the message of the angel (2:11) and the song of the heavenly host (2:14) at the birth of the *King,* the Anointed (Christ). The *multitude of the disciples* have *seen* how the *mighty works* of Jesus have fulfilled the angelic promise of peace and joy on earth; His expulsion of demons, His merciful healings, His triumph over death, His forgiving proclamation of the Good News have spelled out that promise in act. They know that He is the promised King who speaks peace to the nations (Zch 9:9; cf. Is 9:6). There is *peace in heaven;* the God who gives His people and mankind such a King wills peace for man. The King may still be King incognito and may still have a journey to go into a far land (12), but God's will shall be done, and He shall have His *glory in the highest,* that is, He shall be known, acknowledged, and adored as the great and good God that He is. The praise of the disciples, like the song of Mary (1:46-55 note) anticipates that final triumph of His great goodness.

19:39-40 The *Pharisees* consider such a Messianic acclamation imprudent (if not foolish) and dangerous; the Roman authorities would not tolerate Messianic pretenders. Jesus' answer is that God's will must be done, that God will raise up witnesses to His anointed King from the *very stones* if men will not witness to Him. For the crying stone as witness cf. Hab 2:11. Jesus' answer could also be rendered to mean: "If my disciples are silenced, the very stones of Jerusalem will *cry out;* the judgment of God on Jerusalem which will not leave one of Jerusalem's stones upon another (44; 21:6) will be a tragic witness to the fact that those who acclaimed Jesus as King were in the right and those who tried to

41 And when he drew near and saw the city he wept over it, ⁴² saying, "Would that even today you knew the things that make for peace! But now they are hid from your eyes. ⁴³ For the days shall come upon you, when your enemies will cast up a bank about you and surround you, and hem you in on every side, ⁴⁴ and dash you to the ground, you and your children within you, and they will not leave one stone upon another in you; because you did not know the time of your visitation."

45 And he entered the temple and began to drive out those who sold, ⁴⁶ saying to them, "It is written, 'My house shall be a house of prayer'; but you have made it a den of robbers."

47 And he was teaching daily in the temple. The chief priests and the scribes and the principal men of the people sought to destroy him; ⁴⁸ but they did not find anything they could do, for all the people hung upon his words.

20 One day, as he was teaching the people in the temple and preaching the gospel, the chief priests and the scribes with the elders came up ² and said to him, "Tell us by what authority you do these things, or who it is that gave you this authority." ³ He answered them, "I also will ask you a question; now tell me, ⁴ Was the baptism of John from heaven or from men?" ⁵And they discussed it with one another, saying, "If we say, 'From heaven,' he will say, 'Why did you not believe him?' ⁶ But if we say, 'From men,' all the people will stone us; for they are convinced that John was a prophet." ⁷ So they answered that they did not know whence it was. ⁸And Jesus said to them, "Neither will I tell you by what authority I do these things."

9 And he began to tell the people this parable: "A man planted a vineyard, and let it out to tenants, and went into another country for a long while. ¹⁰ When the time came, he sent a servant to the tenants, that they should give him some of the fruit of the vineyard; but the tenants beat him, and sent him away empty-handed. ¹¹And he sent another servant; him also they beat and treated shamefully, and sent him away empty-handed. ¹²And he sent yet a third; this one they wounded and cast out. ¹³ Then the owner of the vineyard said, 'What shall I do? I will send my beloved son; it may be they will respect him.' ¹⁴ But when the tenants saw him, they said to themselves, 'This is the heir; let us kill him, that the inheritance may be ours.' ¹⁵And they cast him out of the vineyard and killed him. What then will the owner of the vineyard do to them? ¹⁶ He will come and destroy those tenants, and give the vineyard to others." When they heard this, they said, "God forbid!" ¹⁷ But he looked at them and said, "What then is this that is written:

'The very stone which the builders rejected
has become the head of the corner'?

---

silence their acclamation were in the wrong." This latter seems the more probable interpretation.

19:41-48 THE GUILT OF JERUSALEM

19:41-48 The King whose coming means peace (38 note) weeps over the city that has refused and is refusing *the things that make for peace,* the city that will not recognize the times of God's gracious *visitation;* the Prince of Peace is forced to predict war, siege, and destruction for the guilty city (41-44). The men of Jerusalem have made the *house of prayer,* God's temple, a *den of robbers* (45-46). In unwearied compassion Jesus continues His mission to Jerusalem, *teaching daily in the temple;* but Jerusalem's authorities respond by seeking *to destroy him.* (47-48)

19:44 *Visitation.* Cf. 1:68 note.

19:46 *Den of robbers.* Cf. Mt 21:13 note and 21:12-22 note.

20:1-8 WHO GAVE YOU THIS AUTHORITY?

20:1-8 Cf. Mt 21:23-27, esp. 21:27 note. To men

who have "rejected the purpose of God for themselves" by refusing the gift of repentance and forgiveness which the *baptism of John* offered, to men who have refused to repent (7:30), Jesus "cannot" speak of His *authority.* For His authority is the authority "to forgive sins" (5:24) and "to seek and to save the lost" (19:10), an authority which men who refuse to face up to their sin and their lostness cannot comprehend. Jesus is *preaching the gospel* (1) whose power only the forgiven can know.

20:9-18 THE PARABLE OF THE VINEYARD LET TO TENANTS

20:9-18 Cf. notes on Mt 21:23—22:14; 21:33; 21:36-37; 21:42; and 21:46.

20:18 The saying concerning the destructive effect of the *stone* is based on Is 8:14-15 and Dn 2:34-35, cf. 44-45. The point in both passages is that he who resists the saving purposes of God will be destroyed.

18 Every one who falls on that stone will be broken to pieces; but when it falls on any one it will crush him.''

19 The scribes and the chief priests tried to lay hands on him at that very hour, but they feared the people; for they perceived that he had told this parable against them. 20 So they watched him, and sent spies, who pretended to be sincere, that they might take hold of what he said, so as to deliver him up to the authority and jurisdiction of the governor. 21 They asked him, ''Teacher, we know that you speak and teach rightly, and show no partiality, but truly teach the way of God. 22 Is it lawful for us to give tribute to Caesar, or not?'' 23 But he perceived their craftiness, and said to them, 24 ''Show me a coin.ᶠ Whose likeness and inscription has it?'' They said, ''Caesar's.'' 25 He said to them, ''Then render to Caesar the things that are Caesar's, and to God the things that are God's.'' 26And they were not able in the presence of the people to catch him by what he said; but marveling at his answer they were silent.

27 There came to him some Sad'du·cees, those who say that there is no resurrection, 28 and they asked him a question, saying, ''Teacher, Moses wrote for us that if a man's brother dies, having a wife but no children, the manᵍ must take the wife and raise up children for his brother. 29 Now there were seven brothers; the first took a wife, and died without children; 30 and the second 31 and the third took her, and likewise all seven left no children and died. 32Afterward the woman also died. 33 In the resurrection, therefore, whose wife will the woman be? For the seven had her as wife.''

34 And Jesus said to them, ''The sons of this age marry and are given in marriage; 35 but those who are accounted worthy to attain to that age and to the resurrection from the dead neither marry nor are given in marriage, 36 for they cannot die any more, because they are equal to angels and are sons of God, being sons of the resurrection. 37 But that the dead are raised, even Moses showed, in the passage about the bush, where he calls the Lord the God of Abraham and the God of Isaac and the God of Jacob. 38 Now he is not God of the dead, but of the living; for all live to him.'' 39And some of the scribes answered, ''Teacher, you have spoken well.'' 40 For they no longer dared to ask him any question.

41 But he said to them, ''How can they say that the Christ is David's son? 42 For David himself says in the Book of Psalms,

'The Lord said to my Lord,
Sit at my right hand,
43   till I make thy enemies a stool for thy feet.'
44   David thus calls him Lord; so how is he his son?''

45 And in the hearing of all the people he said to his disciples, 46 ''Beware of the scribes, who like to go about in long robes, and love salutations in the market places and the best seats in the synagogues and the places of honor at feasts, 47 who devour widows' houses and for a pretense make long prayers. They will receive the greater condemnation.''

21 He looked up and saw the rich putting their gifts into the treasury; 2 and he saw a poor widow put in two copper coins. 3And he said, ''Truly I tell you, this

---

ᶠ Greek denarius   ᵍ Greek his brother

20:19-26 TRIBUTE TO CAESAR

20:19-26 Cf. Mt 22:15-40 note and 22:16, 17, 21 notes.

20:27-40 THE SADDUCEES' QUESTION
CONCERNING THE RESURRECTION

20:27-40 Cf. Mt 22:15-40 note and 22:23-33 notes.

20:35 That age, used in contrast to ''this age'' (34), is a Judaic expression used to indicate the world to come.

20:36 They cannot die any more, and so there is no need of procreation.

Sons of the resurrection. Their nature and life is

determined by the resurrection and the life of the world to come.

20:41-44 JESUS' MESSIANIC MANIFESTO

20:41-44 Cf. Mt 22:41-46 note.

20:45-47 BEWARE OF THE SCRIBES

20:45-47 For Jesus' indictment of the scribes cf. 11:45-52. For the particular vices of honor-seeking, avarice, and hypocrisy cf. Mt 23:5-7, 12, 25, 28; Mk 12:40; and Mt 23:1-39 note; Mk 12:38-44 note.

21:1-4 THE POOR WIDOW'S GIFT

21:1-4 Cf. Mk 12:38-44 note.

poor widow has put in more than all of them; 4 for they all contributed out of their abundance, but she out of her poverty put in all the living that she had."

5 And as some spoke of the temple, how it was adorned with noble stones and offerings, he said, 6 "As for these things which you see, the days will come when there shall not be left here one stone upon another that will not be thrown down." 7And they asked him, "Teacher, when will this be, and what will be the sign when this is about to take place?" 8And he said, "Take heed that you are not led astray; for many will come in my name, saying, 'I am he!' and, 'The time is at hand!' Do not go after them. 9And when you hear of wars and tumults, do not be terrified; for this must first take place, but the end will not be at once."

10 Then he said to them, "Nation will rise against nation, and kingdom against kingdom; 11 there will be great earthquakes, and in various places famines and pestilences; and there will be terrors and great signs from heaven. 12 But before all this they will lay their hands on you and persecute you, delivering you up to the synagogues and prisons, and you will be brought before kings and governors for my name's sake. 13 This will be a time for you to bear testimony. 14 Settle it therefore in your minds, not to meditate beforehand how to answer; 15 for I will give you a mouth and wisdom, which none of your adversaries will be able to withstand or contradict. 16 You will be delivered up even by parents and brothers and kinsmen and friends, and some of you they will put to death; 17 you will be hated by all for my name's sake. 18 But not a hair of your head will perish. 19 By your endurance you will gain your lives.

20 "But when you see Jerusalem surrounded by armies, then know that its desolation has come near. 21 Then let those who are in Judea flee to the mountains, and let those who are inside the city depart, and let not those who are out in the country enter it; 22 for these are days of vengeance, to fulfil all that is written. 23Alas for those who are with child and for those who give suck in those days! For great distress shall be upon the earth and wrath upon this people; 24 they will fall by the edge of the sword, and be led captive among all nations; and Jerusalem will be trodden down by the Gentiles, until the times of the Gentiles are fulfilled.

21:5-36 JESUS' PROPHECY OF THE FUTURE

21:5-36 For the whole topic cf. Mt 24:1 – 25:46 notes; Mk 13:1-37 note; Lk 17:22-37 note and 17:20 – 18:30 note.

Jesus' words concerning the future and the end are prophecy; "he who prophesies speaks to men for their upbuilding and encouragement and consolation" (1 Co 14:3). Jesus does predict, as the OT prophets did before Him, the nearer and the farther and the farthest future: the destruction of the temple (6), the coming of false prophets and false Christs (8), wars and disasters in the world (10-11), persecution and martyrdom for the church (12-17), the fall of Jerusalem (20-24), the fainting anxiety of the world in the last days and the coming of the Son of Man (25-28). But His predictions are the framework and scaffolding of the structure of His commands, warnings, and promises, which serve to upbuild, encourage, and console His disciples and His church in the last days, that they *may have strength to escape all these things that will take place, and to stand before the Son of man,* sure of their justification and final victory. (36)

21:5-19 BY YOUR ENDURANCE YOU WILL GAIN YOUR LIVES

21:5-19 Jesus predicts the destruction of the temple but refuses to answer the curious question of *when* or to give *the sign* (7) which would enable

men to calculate the coming of the disaster. Rather, He uses the occasion to warn His disciples against false and feverish hopes (8) and to safeguard them against panic terror; all disasters are part of God's plan *(must first take place),* and He alone will determine and declare the time of the *end* (9). Even the sufferings of the church are no accident; God will use them for the spreading of His Word *(testimony,* 13), and the Christ will give His own the *mouth and wisdom* which will make their testimony powerful and fruitful (13, 15). They are in God's hand, and no power of their enemies and no treachery of their friends can harm them (12, 15, 16); *not a hair of your head will perish* (18). They can be so confident of God's future that they will have the power to endure the present, even if the present means death, and so *gain* their *lives* forever. (19)

21:5 *Offerings,* votive gifts presented to the temple by princes and private individuals for its adornment.

21:9 *The end will not be at once.* Cf. 2 Th 2:1-2, where Paul calms a feverish excitement of hope to restore the church to confidence and obedience. (13-15; cf. 3:3-13)

21:20-24 THE DESOLATION OF JERUSALEM

21:20-24 Jesus predicts the fall of Jerusalem at the hand of *Gentile armies* (20, 24). His prophetic care for His disciples opens their eyes to see in this event the fulfillment of *all that is written* (22), so

25 "And there will be signs in sun and moon and stars, and upon the earth distress of nations in perplexity at the roaring of the sea and the waves, 26 men fainting with fear and with foreboding of what is coming on the world; for the powers of the heavens will be shaken. 27And then they will see the Son of man coming in a cloud with power and great glory. 28 Now when these things begin to take place, look up and raise your heads, because your redemption is drawing near."

29 And he told them a parable: "Look at the fig tree, and all the trees; 30 as soon as they come out in leaf, you see for yourselves and know that the summer is already near. 31 So also, when you see these things taking place, you know that the kingdom of God is near. 32 Truly, I say to you, this generation will not pass away till all has taken place. 33 Heaven and earth will pass away, but my words will not pass away.

34 "But take heed to yourselves lest your hearts be weighed down with dissipation and drunkenness and cares of this life, and that day come upon you suddenly like a snare; 35 for it will come upon all who dwell upon the face of the whole earth. 36 But watch at all times, praying that you may have strength to escape all these things that will take place, and to stand before the Son of man."

37 And every day he was teaching in the temple, but at night he went out and lodged on the mount called Olivet. 38And early in the morning all the people came to him in the temple to hear him.

Jesus' Passion, Death, Resurrection, and Ascension

22:1 — 24:53

22 Now the feast of Unleavened Bread drew near, which is called the Passover. 2And the chief priests and the scribes were seeking how to put him to death; for they feared the people.

3 Then Satan entered into Judas called Is·car'i·ot, who was of the number of the twelve; 4 he went away and conferred with the chief priests and officers how he might betray him to them. 5And they were glad, and engaged to give him money.

---

that in this respect, too, they can have the OT "prophetic word made more sure" (2 Ptr 1:19). The men who constitute the new Israel need not share in the fate of old Israel; Jesus bids them flee the doomed city and land (21) when the long-foretold *days of vengeance* and the time of God's *wrath* upon His disobedient *people* come (22, 23). The phrase *the times of the Gentiles* (24) points them to their future mission to the Gentiles, portrayed by Lk in Acts (Cf. Acts 28:25-28; Ro 11:11-12; 11:25)

21:20 *Surrounded by armies.* Cf. 19:43.

Desolation. An echo of Dn 9:27; 11:31; 12:11; cf. Mt 24:15 note.

21:22 *Days of vengeance . . . written.* Cf. Dt 32:28-35; Jer 5:29; Hos 9:7.

21:23 *Those . . . with child.* The blessing of motherhood will only intensify their *distress.*

21:24 *Trodden down by the Gentiles.* Cf. Is 63:18-19.

21:25-28 THE COMING OF THE SON OF MAN

21:25-28 Amid the agony of a collapsing world, amid the intolerable *fear* and *foreboding* of men for whom the coming of the *Son of man . . . with power and great glory* signifies destruction, the disciples can *look up and raise* their *heads* in joyous expectation; they know this Son of Man as their Savior who brings their ultimate *redemption.* (Cf. Dn 7:13-14, 17-18)

21:25 *Roaring of the sea.* At creation God set

bounds to the sea: "Thus far shall you come, and no farther, and here shall your proud waves be stayed." (Jb 38:11; cf. Ps 65:8.) Now God's ancient order disintegrates to make way for His new creation; and the failing of the ancient order is terrifying to men without hope.

21:29-38 ASSURANCE AND ADMONITION

21:29-36 For 29-33 cf. Mt 24:32-35. The *parable* of the *fig tree* and Jesus' assurance concerning His enduring *words* give the disciples' hope a firm basis. They need not fear for God and the coming of His kingdom; they need to live in holy fear lest this world's pleasures and cares *weigh* them *down* and leave them unprepared for the coming of *that day.* Vigilant, unceasing prayer is called for.

21:36 *Stand before,* as your Judge who shall pronounce your acquittal. Cf. Mt 25:34; for the expression cf. Rv 6:17.

21:37-38 A summary of Jesus' activity during His last days in Jerusalem.

22:1-6 THE PLOT TO DESTROY JESUS

22:1-6 Cf. Mt 26:1-16 note.

22:1 *Unleavened Bread . . . called the Passover.* Strictly speaking these are two separate festivals, the day of Passover and the 7-day feast of Unleavened Bread which followed directly the Passover (Lv 23:4-6). But since the Passover could be celebrated only in Jerusalem (Dt 16:2, 5-6), the

⁶ So he agreed, and sought an opportunity to betray him to them in the absence of the multitude.

7 Then came the day of Unleavened Bread, on which the passover lamb had to be sacrificed. ⁸ So Jesus*ʰ* sent Peter and John, saying, "Go and prepare the passover for us, that we may eat it." ⁹ They said to him, "Where will you have us prepare it?" ¹⁰ He said to them, "Behold, when you have entered the city, a man carrying a jar of water will meet you; follow him into the house which he enters, ¹¹ and tell the house-holder, 'The Teacher says to you, Where is the guest room, where I am to eat the passover with my disciples?' ¹²And he will show you a large upper room furnished; there make ready." ¹³And they went, and found it as he had told them; and they prepared the passover.

14 And when the hour came, he sat at table, and the apostles with him. ¹⁵And he said to them, "I have earnestly desired to eat this passover with you before I suffer; ¹⁶ for I tell you I shall not eat it*ⁱ* until it is fulfilled in the kingdom of God." ¹⁷And he took a cup, and when he had given thanks he said, "Take this, and divide it among yourselves; ¹⁸ for I tell you that from now on I shall not drink of the fruit of the vine until the kingdom of God comes." ¹⁹And he took bread, and when he had given thanks he broke it and gave it to them, saying, "This is my body which is given for you. Do this in remembrance of me." ²⁰And likewise the cup after supper, saying, "This cup which is poured out for you is the new covenant in my blood.*ʲ* ²¹ But behold the hand of him who betrays me is with me on the table. ²² For the Son of man goes as it has been determined; but woe to that man by whom he is betrayed!" ²³And they began to question one another, which of them it was that would do this.

24 A dispute also arose among them, which of them was to be regarded as the

ʰ Greek *he*   *ⁱ* Other ancient authorities read *never eat it again*
ʲ Other authorities omit, in whole or in part, verses 19b-20 *(which is given... in my blood).*

two festivals tended to merge for people outside Jerusalem and Palestine, especially for Gentiles like Lk's readers.

22:3 *Satan entered into Judas.* When Satan left Jesus after the temptation, he did so "until an opportune time" (4:13); the opportune time for his final assault on Jesus has now come, and Judas becomes the instrument of the "power of darkness" (22:53). Cf. also 22:31; Jn 6:70-71; 13:2, 27.

22:4 *Officers,* the men in charge of the temple police; the head captain ranked next to the high priest in authority. Cf. 52; Acts 4:1; 5:24, 26.

22:5 *Give him money.* Cf. Mt 26:15 note.

22:7-23 THE LAST SUPPER

22:7-23 Cf. Mt 26:17-29 note.

22:7 *Day of Unleavened Bread.* Cf. 22:1 note.

22:12 *Furnished* with couches on which the participants reclined while eating. The word translated "sat at table" in 14 means literally "reclined."

22:14 *The hour* probably signifies both the hour of the Passover and the climactic hour of Jesus' ministry. (Cf. 22:53; Jn 7:30; 8:20; 12:23, 27; 13:1; 17:1)

22:15-16 *Passover ... fulfilled in the kingdom of God.* Cf. Mt 26:26 note. All that the Passover signified and the feast of the Passover memorialized will be fully revealed and accomplished in the future, consummated kingdom of God to which Jesus looks forward; God's elective love for His people, His mighty deliverance, His covenant-will of fellowship with man. Jesus is interpreting His death as a divine act of deliverance in these words and preparing His disciples for the Lord's Supper.

22:17 *Cup . . . divide it among yourselves.* The significance of this first cup (cf. 19-20 note), recorded only by Lk, is left somewhat mysterious. The Passover ritual of Jesus' day prescribed individual cups for the participants; Jesus offers His disciples a common cup, to be shared by them all. The context speaks of Jesus' impending Passion ("suffer," 15) and the future "kingdom of God" (16, 18). The first cup, then, signifies that a man receives, as a gift, his share in the coming kingdom; and that He receives it as a gift from Him who is destined (22) to suffer (15), to give His body (19) and His blood (20) in order that God's final covenant (20) may be established.

22:20 *New covenant in my blood.* Cf. Mt 26:26 note. The word *new* recalls especially Jer 31:31-34 with its emphasis on the forgiveness of sins.

22:22 Cf. Mt 26:24 note.

22:24-38 JESUS TEACHING AT TABLE

22:24-38 Lk frequently portrays Jesus teaching at table (cf. 7:36 ff.; 10:38 ff.; 11:37 ff.; 14:1 ff.), and he here records material largely peculiar to him. Each of the three units of Jesus' discourse (24-30; 31-34; 35-38) is related to Jesus' impending Passion.

22:24-30 THE WAY TO GREATNESS

22:24-30 The old *dispute* (cf. 9:46-48) as to who *was to be regarded as greatest* breaks out once more. Jesus makes plain once more that greatness is not won by the upward reach for *lordship* and *authority* but on the downward way of self-denying service, following in the footsteps of the King who

greatest. 25And he said to them, "The kings of the Gentiles exercise lordship over them; and those in authority over them are called benefactors. 26 But not so with you; rather let the greatest among you become as the youngest, and the leader as one who serves. 27 For which is the greater, one who sits at table, or one who serves? Is it not the one who sits at table? But I am among you as one who serves.

28 "You are those who have continued with me in my trials; 29 and I assign to you, as my Father assigned to me, a kingdom, 30 that you may eat and drink at my table in my kingdom, and sit on thrones judging the twelve tribes of Israel.

31 "Simon, Simon, behold, Satan demanded to have you,^{k} that he might sift you^k like wheat, 32 but I have prayed for you that your faith may not fail; and when you have turned again, strengthen your brethren." 33And he said to him, "Lord, I am ready to go with you to prison and to death." 34 He said, "I tell you, Peter, the cock will not crow this day, until you three times deny that you know me."

35 And he said to them, "When I sent you out with no purse or bag or sandals, did you lack anything?" They said, "Nothing." 36 He said to them, "But now, let him who has a purse take it, and likewise a bag. And let him who has no sword sell his mantle and buy one. 37 For I tell you that this scripture must be fulfilled in me, 'And he was reckoned with transgressors'; for what is written about me has its fulfilment." 38And they said, "Look, Lord, here are two swords." And he said to them, "It is enough."

39 And he came out, and went, as was his custom, to the Mount of Olives; and

^{k} The Greek word for *you* here is plural; in verse 32 it is singular

is among them *as one who serves* (24-27). (Cf. Mt 20:17-28 note.) In the last analysis greatness is not "won" by man at all; it comes to the followers of Jesus as His free gift to them and is a greatness beyond all deserving; table fellowship and co-regency with Him in His *kingdom* (28-30). (Cf. Mt 20:20-28)

22:27 *As one who serves.* At the Passover feast the reclining guests were waited on by a servant; on this one night even the poorest Israelite was great and free. Some interpreters think that Jesus actually waited on His disciples at this feast, thus providing a first fulfillment of His promise in 12:37. However that may be, Jesus is referring to His whole life's work as a Servant ministry, to be crowned by His dying as "a ransom for many." (Cf. 37 note; Mt 20:28)

22:28 *My trials.* Here used generally of all the hardships of His way. (Cf. Acts 20:19)

22:29-30 *I assign.* The verb translated *assign* belongs to the same word family as "covenant" (20) and underscores the fact that participation in the festal joy and royal power *(thrones)* of the *kingdom* is Jesus' free gift.

22:31-34 SIMON, I HAVE PRAYED FOR YOU

22:31-34 Satan's last attack on Jesus (cf. 3 note) will be an attack on His disciples too. He will *demand to have* them, as he once "demanded" Job (Jb 1:6-12), and will *sift* them, shake and disturb them, in order to get some of the *wheat* of God's harvest for himself, as he has already gotten Judas (3). *Simon's* confidence in himself (33) is an indication that he is especially vulnerable to Satan's attack; self-confidence and the confidence of faith are two different things. Jesus, Servant to the last, intercedes for him (the Servant intercedes for transgressors, 23:34 note; cf. Is 53:12). Thus

Simon's failure in his denial will not prove to be his final downfall; in repentance (*turned again,* 32) he will replace self-confidence with confidence in his Lord and so find the strength to *strengthen* his *brethren.* (32)

22:32 *Strengthen your brethren.* Cf. the Introduction to 1 Ptr.

22:35-38 BUY A SWORD

22:35-38 Jesus goes to a criminal's death, *reckoned with transgressors* (37; Is 53:12). The disciples will *now* (36) be witnesses to the Crucified, the one declared accursed by Israel's leadership according to their law (cf. Gl 3:13; 1 Co 12:3; Dt 21:23). The old carefree days of the first mission of the Twelve and the Seventy are over (35; 9:3; 10:4). Their mission will become an embattled progress through hostile territory—the martyrdom of Stephen and the execution of James are landmarks on that road (Acts 7; 12:1-2). Jesus' command to provide equipment for the journey and to *buy* a *sword* (even if it means selling one's *mantle* to get it, 36) is probably a figurative way of bidding the disciples brace themselves for this new situation. Jesus' way is not the way of power and warfare (cf. 25-26); and He could hardly have called two swords *enough* (38) if He had planned a Messianic war.

22:37 *Reckoned with transgressors.* Is 53:12. For Jesus as the Servant cf. Mt 12:18-21 note.

22:39-46 JESUS' AGONY OF PRAYER

22:39-46 Cf. Mt 26:30-56 note. The scene in Gethsemane (Lk uses only the more general designation *Mount of Olives*) reveals as hardly another the genuine humanity of the Son of God; and Lk lays special stress on this humanity with his reference to the physical *agony* of Jesus at prayer

the disciples followed him. 40And when he came to the place he said to them, "Pray that you may not enter into temptation." 41And he withdrew from them about a stone's throw, and knelt down and prayed, 42 "Father, if thou art willing, remove this cup from me; nevertheless not my will, but thine, be done." *l* 45And when he rose from prayer, he came to the disciples and found them sleeping for sorrow, 46 and he said to them, "Why do you sleep? Rise and pray that you may not enter into temptation."

47 While he was still speaking, there came a crowd, and the man called Judas, one of the twelve, was leading them. He drew near to Jesus to kiss him; 48 but Jesus said to him, "Judas, would you betray the Son of man with a kiss?" 49And when those who were about him saw what would follow, they said, "Lord, shall we strike with the sword?" 50And one of them struck the slave of the high priest and cut off his right ear. 51 But Jesus said, "No more of this!" And he touched his ear and healed him. 52 Then Jesus said to the chief priests and officers of the temple and elders, who had come out against him, "Have you come out as against a robber, with swords and clubs? 53 When I was with you day after day in the temple, you did not lay hands on me. But this is your hour, and the power of darkness."

54 Then they seized him and led him away, bringing him into the high priest's house. Peter followed at a distance; 55 and when they had kindled a fire in the middle of the courtyard and sat down together, Peter sat among them. 56 Then a maid, seeing him as he sat in the light and gazing at him, said, "This man also was with him." 57 But he denied it, saying, "Woman, I do not know him." 58And a little later some one else saw him and said, "You also are one of them." But Peter said, "Man, I am not." 59And after an interval of about an hour still another insisted, saying, "Certainly this man also was with him; for he is a Galilean." 60 But Peter said, "Man, I do not know what you are saying." And immediately, while he was still speaking, the cock crowed. 61And the Lord turned and looked at Peter. And Peter remembered the word of the Lord, how he had said to him, "Before the cock crows today, you will deny me three times." 62And he went out and wept bitterly.

63 Now the men who were holding Jesus mocked him and beat him; 64 they also blindfolded him and asked him, "Prophesy! Who is it that struck you?" 65And they spoke many other words against him, reviling him.

66 When day came, the assembly of the elders of the people gathered together, both chief priests and scribes; and they led him away to their council, and they said,

---

l Other ancient authorities add verses 43 and 44: 43*And there appeared to him an angel from heaven, strengthening him.* 44*And being in an agony he prayed more earnestly; and his sweat became like great drops of blood falling down upon the ground.*

---

(44). The appearance of the *angel from heaven, strengthening him* (43) is another "human" touch; it recalls the story of the prophet Elijah at a point when that man of God was wearied and discouraged. (1 K 19:4-8)

22:39 *As was his custom.* Cf. 21:37. Jesus is taking the initiative, confronting his captors in a place where they knew He could be found.

22:40 *Temptation.* Cf. 31-34.

22:47-53 THE ARREST: THIS IS YOUR HOUR

22:47-53 Cf. Mt 26:30-56 note. If Gethsemane lays bare the humanity of Jesus, the arrest reveals the free majesty with which *the Son of man* (48) goes to His death. Touches peculiar to Lk emphasize this majestic freedom. Jesus' reproach to Judas exposes his treachery in all its ugliness (48). In healing the slave of the high priest He continues His ministry as physician (cf. 5:31) and at the same time protects His disciples against reprisals (51). And He makes clear to His captors at what a fearful cost they have made this hour their hour; they

have sold themselves to *the power of darkness.* (53; cf. 3 note)

22:54-65 PETER DENIES JESUS

22:54-65 Cf. Mt 26:57-75 note. Lk hardly notices the nocturnal hearing conducted in *the high priest's house* (54; cf. Mt 26:57-68); the mockery recorded in 63-65 presupposes such a hearing and an adverse verdict. Lk concentrates on Peter's denial; Lk alone records that *the Lord turned and looked at Peter* (61). We are not told what all was in that look — reproach, sorrow, appeal — but Peter must have read in that look the unfailing love of the Lord who had interceded for him; his faith did not fail utterly. (32)

22:59 *A Galilean,* recognizable by his dialect. (Mt 26:73)

22:63-65 Cf. Mt 26:67-68 note.

22:66-71 JESUS BEFORE THE COUNCIL

22:66-71 Lk's account of Jesus' hearing before the council is highly condensed, concentrating

67 "If you are the Christ, tell us." But he said to them, "If I tell you, you will not believe; 68 and if I ask you, you will not answer. 69 But from now on the Son of man shall be seated at the right hand of the power of God." 70And they all said, "Are you the Son of God, then?" And he said to them, "You say that I am." 71And they said, "What further testimony do we need? We have heard it ourselves from his own lips."

JESUS CONDEMNED AND CRUCIFIED (23:1-56)

23 Then the whole company of them arose, and brought him before Pilate. 2And they began to accuse him, saying, "We found this man perverting our nation, and forbidding us to give tribute to Caesar, and saying that he himself is Christ a king." 3And Pilate asked him, "Are you the King of the Jews?" And he answered him, "You have said so." 4And Pilate said to the chief priests and the multitudes, "I find no crime in this man." 5 But they were urgent, saying, "He stirs up the people, teaching throughout all Judea, from Galilee even to this place."

6 When Pilate heard this, he asked whether the man was a Galilean. 7And when he learned that he belonged to Herod's jurisdiction, he sent him over to Herod, who was himself in Jerusalem at that time. 8 When Herod saw Jesus, he was very glad, for he had long desired to see him, because he had heard about him, and he was hoping to see some sign done by him. 9 So he questioned him at some length; but he made no answer. 10 The chief priests and the scribes stood by, vehemently accusing him. 11And Herod with his soldiers treated him with contempt and mocked him; then, arraying him in gorgeous apparel, he sent him back to Pilate. 12And Herod and Pilate became friends with each other that very day, for before this they had been at enmity with each other.

13 Pilate then called together the chief priests and the rulers and the people, 14 and said to them, "You brought me this man as one who was perverting the people; and

on the crucial point of Jesus' claim to be the Christ and *Son of God* (67, 70). (Cf. Mt 26:67-68 note)

22:66 *When day came.* For the legal technicality involved cf. Mt 27:1-2 note.

22:67-68 *You will not believe . . . you will not answer.* It was not Jesus' silence but their unbelief and stubbornness which had veiled His Messiahship from their eyes. Cf. 20:1-8 note, where they refused Him an answer; and 20:41-44 note, where they received His Messianic self-attestation (given in terms of Ps 110 and Dn 7, as now, 69) with unbelieving silence.

23:1-5 JESUS BROUGHT BEFORE PILATE

23:1-5 Cf. Mt 27:1-31 note for the whole trial before Pilate.

Before the council the charge is religious (22:66-71). Before the Roman governor it is political. The attempt to make Jesus appear politically dangerous employs half-truths; Jesus did indeed claim to be *Christ a king,* but not king in the sense that Pilate was inclined to understand it—He looked to God alone for victory (20:41-45) and quelled His followers' attempt at violence (22:49-51). The accusers do not even shrink from the direct lie (*forbidding . . . tribute to Caesar,* 2; cf. 20:25). Pilate's examination of Jesus (presupposed by Lk here but not recounted, cf. 14) leads him to make the first of three declarations of Jesus' innocence. (4; cf. 14, 22)

23:5 *All Judea,* i. e., all Palestine.

23:6-12 JESUS SENT OVER TO HEROD

23:6-12 Only in Lk. Cf. Acts 4:27.

The presence of *Herod in Jerusalem* at Passover time afforded Pilate a chance to evade his responsibility of pronouncing judgment on Jesus. Herod thus becomes the second witness to Jesus' innocence (cf. 15; Dt 19:15). Herod, no longer fearful of Jesus (13:31-33) but still curious (9:7-9), *was hoping to see some sign done by* Jesus. Jesus refused to answer the questions of the man whom He had once dismissed as "that fox" with no power to control His ministry (13:32 note), and He refused, as always, to use His miraculous power to defend or advance Himself (*sign;* cf. 4:3; 11:16, 29). Herod dismissed Him with *contempt;* the *gorgeous apparel* is intended to mock the impotent and captive Messianic pretender.

23:12 *Became friends.* Pilate had acknowledged Herod's jurisdiction over Jesus (7), and Herod had remanded the case to Pilate (11) for final adjudication. This exchange of courtesies ended the *enmity* between the men who had long been jealous rivals for power. One may see beneath the political surface an indication of the "world's" unanimity of opposition to Jesus. (Cf. Jn 7:7; 15:18)

23:13-25 PILATE DELIVERS JESUS UP TO HIS ACCUSERS

23:13-25 Cf. Mt 27:1-31 note. Pilate makes two more attempts to secure Jesus' *release:* the offer of a compromise punishment of flogging (*chastise,* 16) and of the choice between *Barabbas* and Jesus (18-19). But His accusers' *voices prevailed.*

23:18 *Barabbas'* story is briefly told by Lk, as if he could presuppose knowledge of it on the part of his readers. (Cf. Mt 27:15-26; 27:17 note)

after examining him before you, behold, I did not find this man guilty of any of your charges against him; [15] neither did Herod, for he sent him back to us. Behold, nothing deserving death has been done by him; [16] I will therefore chastise him and release him." *m*

18 But they all cried out together, "Away with this man, and release to us Bar·ab´-bas"—[19] a man who had been thrown into prison for an insurrection started in the city, and for murder. [20] Pilate addressed them once more, desiring to release Jesus; [21] but they shouted out, "Crucify, crucify him!" [22]A third time he said to them, "Why, what evil has he done? I have found in him no crime deserving death; I will therefore chastise him and release him." [23] But they were urgent, demanding with loud cries that he should be crucified. And their voices prevailed. [24] So Pilate gave sentence that their demand should be granted. [25] He released the man who had been thrown into prison for insurrection and murder, whom they asked for; but Jesus he delivered up to their will.

26 And as they led him away, they seized one Simon of Cy·re´ne, who was coming in from the country, and laid on him the cross, to carry it behind Jesus. [27]And there followed him a great multitude of the people, and of women who bewailed and lamented him. [28] But Jesus turning to them said, "Daughters of Jerusalem, do not weep for me, but weep for yourselves and for your children. [29] For behold, the days are coming when they will say, 'Blessed are the barren, and the wombs that never bore, and the breasts that never gave suck!' [30] Then they will begin to say to the mountains, 'Fall on us'; and to the hills, 'Cover us.' [31] For if they do this when the wood is green, what will happen when it is dry?"

32 Two others also, who were criminals, were led away to be put to death with him. [33]And when they came to the place which is called The Skull, there they crucified him, and the criminals, one on the right and one on the left. [34]And Jesus said, "Father,

m Here, or after verse 19, other ancient authorities add verse 17, *Now he was obliged to release one man to them at the festival*

23:25 *Jesus he delivered up to their will.* Historians have puzzled over Pilate's evasive and compliant attitude during the trial of Jesus; he had previously demonstrated a brutal disregard for the feelings of his subjects (cf. 13:1). There is some evidence that Pilate's dealings with the high priest Caiaphas had been such that he was not free to resist pressure from that quarter. Others point out that the political situation in Rome had changed drastically just before this time and that Pilate's position had become so insecure that he could ill afford to besmirch an already soiled record with another arbitrary execution. The evidence is only indirect; but Pilate was removed from office in A. D., 37, and Caiaphas was deposed as high priest in the same year, and this lends some plausibility to these conjectures.

23:26-31 THE ROAD TO GOLGOTHA

23:26-31 The incident of the crossbearer *Simon of Cyrene,* which marks the utter forsakenness of Jesus, is common to Mt, Mk, and Lk. Cf. Mt 27: 32 note. The story of the wailing *daughters of Jerusalem* is peculiar to Lk. Such wailing was customary; Jesus' words to the women were unique. Jesus had often foretold the fall of Jerusalem, its temple, and its people (11:50-51; 13: 34-35; 19:11-27; 20:9-19; 21:20-24). He wept when He entered the city for the last time (19: 41-44), and His last words as He left were a last call to repentance in the form of a prediction of Jerusalem's doom.

23:31 Men will prefer annihilation to the fearful judgment of God which confronts them. (Cf. Hos 10:8; Rv 6:16)

They do this. "They" is a Judaic way of referring to God. The RSV translators elsewhere render it by means of the passive voice (cf. 6:38, where "will be put" renders a verb that says literally, "they will put").

Green wood . . . dry. If God's judgment, thought of as a consuming fire (3:9, 16, 17; 17:29), does not spare even God's Son, the green wood not ready for the fire (not ripe for judgment), but delivers Him up thus (cf. Ro 8:32), what will become of those who have refused God's mercy and have in their impenitence become dry wood ripe for judgment?

23:32-38 THE CRUCIFIXION

23:32-38 Cf. Mt 27:32-66 note. Jesus is "reckoned with transgressors" (22:37; Is 53:12). The Servant at the apex of His servanthood, when He "pours out his soul to death" (Is 53:12) as Savior of mankind, is *mocked* for His impotence to save by the *rulers* of His people and by the Roman *soldiers;* there is mockery even in the *inscription* which was hung over Him (cf. Jn 19:19-22). But just here, in the depths, the power of the Servant to save is revealed; His inconquerable love intercedes for transgressors (34; peculiar to Lk) as He "bears the sins of many." (Is 53:12)

23:33 *Skull,* translation of the Aramaic "Golgotha." Why so called remains obscure.

23:34 *Forgive them.* Cf. Stephen's prayer, Acts 7:60.

forgive them; for they know not what they do."[n] And they cast lots to divide his
garments. 35 And the people stood by, watching; but the rulers scoffed at him, saying,
"He saved others; let him save himself, if he is the Christ of God, his Chosen One!"
36 The soldiers also mocked him, coming up and offering him vinegar, 37 and saying,
"If you are the King of the Jews, save yourself!" 38 There was also an inscription over
him,[o] "This is the King of the Jews."

39 One of the criminals who were hanged railed at him, saying, "Are you not the
Christ? Save yourself and us!" 40 But the other rebuked him, saying, "Do you not
fear God, since you are under the same sentence of condemnation? 41 And we indeed
justly; for we are receiving the due reward of our deeds; but this man has done nothing
wrong." 42 **And he said, "Jesus, remember me when you come into[p] your kingdom."**
43 And he said to him, "Truly, I say to you, today you will be with me in Paradise."

44 It was now about the sixth hour, and there was darkness over the whole land[q]
until the ninth hour, 45 while the sun's light failed;[r] and the curtain of the temple was
torn in two. 46 Then Jesus, crying with a loud voice, said, "Father, into thy hands I
commit my spirit!" And having said this he breathed his last. 47 Now when the centurion saw what had taken place, he praised God, and said, "Certainly this man was
innocent!" 48 And all the multitudes who assembled to see the sight, when they saw
what had taken place, returned home beating their breasts. 49 And all his acquaintances
and the women who had followed him from Galilee stood at a distance and saw these
things.

50 Now there was a man named Joseph from the Jewish town of Ar·i·ma·the′a.
He was a member of the council, a good and righteous man, 51 who had not consented
to their purpose and deed, and he was looking for the kingdom of God. 52 This man
went to Pilate and asked for the body of Jesus. 53 Then he took it down and wrapped
it in a linen shroud, and laid him in a rock-hewn tomb, where no one had ever yet

[n] Other ancient authorities omit the sentence *And Jesus . . . what they do*
[o] Other ancient authorities add *in letters of Greek and Latin and Hebrew* [p] Other ancient authorities read *in*
[q] Or *earth* [r] Or *the sun was eclipsed.* Other ancient authorities read *the sun was darkened*

They know not what they do. Cf. Acts 3:17; 13:27; 1 Ti 1:13 note.

23:35 *Chosen One,* a designation of the Servant. (Is 42:1; cf. 9:35 note)

23:39-43 THE PENITENT CRIMINAL

23:39-43 Jesus' second word from the cross (43) is the word of Him "who justifies the ungodly" (Ro 4:5), for it assigns to the *criminal* (who ceases to justify himself and throws himself unreservedly on His royal mercy, 42) a place in *Paradise,* the abode of the righteous dead. Whosoever is in communion with Jesus *(with me)* has entered the great *today* of "great joy" (2:10-11), of "the acceptable year of the Lord" (4:19-21) of forgiveness and healing (5:26, cf. 17-25), of "salvation" in fulfillment of the promise made to Abraham (19:5, 9). This word is a promise to Israel; the way of faith to Jesus and to justification is still open "to the Jew first" (Ro 1:16; Acts 1–12). The diverse reaction of the two criminals is a prophecy of the course of the Gospel through Israel (and mankind) as a savor of life and a savor of death.

23:40 *Fear God,* basic to repentance, faith, and salvation. (Rv 14:7)

23:42 *Remember me.* To be remembered by the divine mercy is to be helped. (Cf. Ps 106:4, 6; Lk 1:54, 72)

23:44-56 THE DEATH AND BURIAL OF JESUS

23:44-56 The characteristic feature of Lk's account of Jesus' death is the third word which Jesus speaks from the cross in the third gospel (46). As at the beginning of His ministry, at the temptation and in the synagog at Nazareth (4: 1-19), so at the close the Scriptures are Jesus' life element. He dies with a prayer from the Psalter on His lips (Ps 31:5). The whole of His unwavering trust in His Father, which made Him the Man of prayer and the Teacher of prayer, lives in this last word. The whole of the psalm should be considered in this connection (perhaps Jesus prayed it through).

23:45 *Sun's light failed.* Cf. Mt 27:45 note.

Curtain of the temple. Cf. Mt 27:51-53 note.

23:47 *Centurion . . . praised God.* Jesus' whole mission was "to the glory of God the Father" (Ph 2:11). Cf. 5:8; 7:16; 9:43; 13:13; 17:15; 18:43; 19:8, 37, where Jesus' might and mercy leads men to praise, or glorify, God.

23:48 *Beating their breasts,* as a sign of grief. (Cf. 18:13)

23:49 *Stood at a distance.* Cf. Ps 38:11; 88:8, 18. The echo of the Psalms intensifies the note of Jesus' desolation. His disciples have severed the bond of discipleship; Lk does not call them "disciples" from 22:45 on. Only Jesus' forgiving grace can restore what they have destroyed.

23:53-56 The burial was hasty and provisional only (cf. 56); the Law demanded that an executed criminal be buried "the same day" (Dt 21:22-23), and the *sabbath* began at sunset.

been laid. ⁵⁴ It was the day of Preparation, and the sabbath was beginning.ˢ ⁵⁵ The women who had come with him from Galilee followed, and saw the tomb, and how his body was laid; ⁵⁶ then they returned, and prepared spices and ointments.

On the sabbath they rested according to the commandment.

THE RESURRECTION AND ASCENSION (24:1-53)

24 But on the first day of the week, at early dawn, they went to the tomb, taking the spices which they had prepared. ²And they found the stone rolled away from the tomb, ³ but when they went in they did not find the body.ᵗ ⁴ While they were perplexed about this, behold, two men stood by them in dazzling apparel; ⁵ and as they were frightened and bowed their faces to the ground, the men said to them, "Why do you seek the living among the dead?ᵘ ⁶ Remember how he told you, while he was still in Galilee, ⁷ that the Son of man must be delivered into the hands of sinful men, and be crucified, and on the third day rise." ⁸And they remembered his words, ⁹ and returning from the tomb they told all this to the eleven and to all the rest. ¹⁰ Now it was Mary Magdalene and Joanna and Mary the mother of James and the other women with them who told this to the apostles; ¹¹ but these words seemed to them an idle tale, and they did not believe them.ᵛ

13 That very day two of them were going to a village named Em·ma′us, about seven milesʷ from Jerusalem, ¹⁴ and talking with each other about all these things that had happened. ¹⁵ While they were talking and discussing together, Jesus himself drew near and went with them. ¹⁶ But their eyes were kept from recognizing him. ¹⁷And he said to them, "What is this conversation which you are holding with each

---

ˢ Greek *was dawning*   ᵗ Other ancient authorities add *of the Lord Jesus*
ᵘ Other ancient authorities add *He is not here, but has risen*
ᵛ Other ancient authorities add verse 12, *But Peter rose and ran to the tomb; stooping and looking in, he saw the linen cloths by themselves; and he went home wondering at what had happened*
ʷ Greek *sixty stadia;* some ancient authorities read *a hundred and sixty stadia*

24:1-53 Lk's resurrection story is the indispensable transition to his story of the apostolic mission and church in the Book of Acts. Of Jesus' many post-resurrection appearances (1 Co 15: 5-8), he records only appearances that took place in or near Jerusalem; for it is in Jerusalem that the apostolic story begins (48, 49; Acts 1:4). And the story of the risen Christ is the story of the creation of *witnesses* to Him (48; Acts 1:8). Men do not become witnesses on their own initiative but by a divine act; and the whole account is marked by this divine initiative. God leads men from sorrow and unbelief to faith and joy; His messengers, His Son, His Word, and the promise of His Spirit control the course of events.

God creates witnesses; and He makes them witness to facts: the *stone rolled away* (2); the empty tomb (3); a Man who walks on a Palestinian road toward a *village* with a name, interprets the familiar Bible of the Jews, and *breaks bread* (13-30); a Man (no disembodied *spirit*) with *hands* and *feet*, a body of *flesh and bones* to be *seen* and *handled;* a Man who eats *broiled fish;* a Man who has been *crucified,* who spoke *words* to be remembered (14-44) — of such hard stuff the witness of the apostolic Gospel is to be made. It is to be not myth but news.

But faith is not a conclusion drawn by man from bare facts; *repentance and forgiveness of sins* (47) is given to men by the divine revelation which illumines and interprets the facts. *Perplexed* (4), *frightened* (5), *sad* (17), *startled, frightened,* and superstitious (37) people become witnesses in the

full Biblical sense by the operation of the word of angels (5) and the *remembered words* of Jesus (8); when Jesus *interprets* and *opens* up the OT Word of God for them (27) and God *opens their eyes* (31); when *the Lord appears* (34) and *opens their minds* through the *scriptures* to the saving significance of His suffering and death (46-47). Then they become witnesses wholly claimed by the Lord to whom they witness, empowered by the Spirit whom He sends (49), with a message designed by God to claim men wholly (*repentance,* 47). The witnessing apostles are the first examples of men who are a new creation in Christ (2 Co 5:17). Through them Jesus can continue all that He "began to do and teach." (Acts 1:1) While He *blessed them, he parted from them.* (51)

24:1-11 (12) THE EMPTY TOMB

24:4 *Two men . . . in dazzling apparel.* Angels. (Cf. Acts 1:10)

24:6 *Remember how he told you.* Cf. 9:22, 44.

24:12 RSV prints this verse in a footnote in agreement with the opinion of most scholars that it was added to the text by copyists on the basis of Jn 20:3-10 and in view of Lk 24:24.

24:13-35 EMMAUS: KNOWN IN THE BREAKING OF THE BREAD

24:13 *Emmaus* ("warm springs"). Location is uncertain.

24:16 *Their eyes were kept.* Cf. 31, "Their eyes were opened." Revelation is given when and where God pleases.

other as you walk?" And they stood still, looking sad. 18 Then one of them, named Cle′o·pas, answered him, "Are you the only visitor to Jerusalem who does not know the things that have happened there in these days?" 19And he said to them, "What things?" And they said to him, "Concerning Jesus of Nazareth, who was a prophet mighty in deed and word before God and all the people, 20 and how our chief priests and rulers delivered him up to be condemned to death, and crucified him. 21 But we had hoped that he was the one to redeem Israel. Yes, and besides all this, it is now the third day since this happened. 22 Moreover, some women of our company amazed us. They were at the tomb early in the morning 23 and did not find his body; and they came back saying that they had even seen a vision of angels, who said that he was alive. 24 Some of those who were with us went to the tomb, and found it just as the women had said; but him they did not see." 25And he said to them, "O foolish men, and slow of heart to believe all that the prophets have spoken! 26 Was it not necessary that the Christ should suffer these things and enter into his glory?" 27And beginning with Moses and all the prophets, he interpreted to them in all the scriptures the things concerning himself.

28 So they drew near to the village to which they were going. He appeared to be going further, 29 but they constrained him, saying, "Stay with us, for it is toward evening and the day is now far spent." So he went in to stay with them. 30 When he was at table with them, he took the bread and blessed, and broke it, and gave it to them. 31And their eyes were opened and they recognized him; and he vanished out of their sight. 32 They said to each other, "Did not our hearts burn within us ᶜ while he talked to us on the road, while he opened to us the scriptures?" 33And they rose that same hour and returned to Jerusalem; and they found the eleven gathered together and those who were with them, 34 who said, "The Lord has risen indeed, and has appeared to Simon!" 35 Then they told what had happened on the road, and how he was known to them in the breaking of the bread.

36 As they were saying this, Jesus himself stood among them.ˣ 37 But they were startled and frightened, and supposed that they saw a spirit. 38And he said to them, "Why are you troubled, and why do questionings rise in your hearts? 39 See my hands and my feet, that it is I myself; handle me, and see; for a spirit has not flesh and bones as you see that I have."ʸ 41And while they still disbelieved for joy, and wondered, he said to them, "Have you anything here to eat?" 42 They gave him a piece of broiled fish, 43 and he took it and ate before them.

44 Then he said to them, "These are my words which I spoke to you, while I was still with you, that everything written about me in the law of Moses and the prophets and the psalms must be fulfilled." 45 Then he opened their minds to understand the scriptures, 46 and said to them, "Thus it is written, that the Christ should suffer and

---

ᶜ Other ancient authorities omit *within us*   ˣ Other ancient authorities add *and said to them, "Peace to you!"*
ʸ Other ancient authorities add verse 40, *And when he had said this, he showed them his hands and his feet*

24:18 *Cleopas* is identified by some with the Clopas of Jn 19:25, to whom early tradition assigns considerable importance in the history of the Jerusalem church. He may be one of the "eyewitnesses" referred to in Lk 1:2.

Visitor to Jerusalem, for the celebration of the Passover, which drew visitors from all Palestine and the Dispersion.

24:25 *Slow of heart. Heart* in Biblical usage includes the whole inner man, feeling and willing and understanding.

24:30 *Took the bread . . . broke it.* The Guest takes the position of the father of the house and distributes the bread. The disciples recognize Him in His characteristic role of Giver and Provider (9:16; 22:19); as such He will be with His disciples, present in His Supper, "known . . . in the breaking of the bread." (35)

24:32 *Hearts burn within us.* The phrase describes the warm glow of dawning recognition and nascent faith.

24:34 *The Lord. Lord,* not used in Lk since 22:61, expresses the joyous rigor of their reborn faith. (Cf. Ro 10:9-10)

Appeared to Simon. Cf. 1 Co 15:5 ("Cephas" is the Aramaic form of "Peter").

24:36-49 THE RISEN CHRIST AND
HIS WITNESSES

24:44 *While I was still with you.* The resurrection does not reduce Jesus' previous ministry to insignificance but rather lets it be seen in its true significance.

Moses . . . prophets . . . psalms, the three divisions of the OT canon.

24:45 *Opened their minds.* For the contrast (the OT read without insight into its character as witness to Christ) cf. 2 Co 3:14-16.

on the third day rise from the dead, [47] and that repentance and forgiveness of sins should be preached in his name to all nations, [z] beginning from Jerusalem. [48] You are witnesses of these things. [49] And behold, I send the promise of my Father upon you; but stay in the city, until you are clothed with power from on high."

[50] Then he led them out as far as Beth′a·ny, and lifting up his hands he blessed them. [51] While he blessed them, he parted from them, and was carried up into heaven.[a] [52] And they[b] returned to Jerusalem with great joy, [53] and were continually in the temple blessing God.

[z] Or *nations. Beginning from Jerusalem you are witnesses*
[a] Other ancient authorities omit *and was carried up into heaven*
[b] Other ancient authorities add *worshiped him, and*

24:47 *Beginning from Jerusalem.* Jesus' intercession for those who crucified Him has been heard. (23:34)

24:49 *The promise of my Father,* the Holy Spirit. (Cf. Acts 2:16-21, 32-33)

24:50-53 WHILE HE BLESSED THEM,
            HE PARTED FROM THEM

24:50-53 The story of God's dealings with man is the story of His blessing from creation (Gn 1:22) to the consummation (Mt 25:34). The story of the incarnate Son fitly ends with His parting (and enduring, Acts 3:26) blessing. In the strong

assurance of that blessing His disciples *returned to Jerusalem* and the beginning of the worldwide task that awaits them there *with great joy, blessing God* for the blessing which He has bestowed on them: "Blessed be the God and Father of our Lord Jesus Christ, who has blessed us in Christ." (Eph 1:3)

24:50 *Bethany,* village on the Mount of Olives about 2 miles from Jerusalem.

24:53 *In the temple,* the first part of Lk's two-volume story ends where it began (1:9), in the house of God where He gives His blessing and His people respond with blessing.

THE GOSPEL ACCORDING TO

JOHN

INTRODUCTION

Occasion and Purpose of the Gospel

1 The central and controlling purpose of the gospel is stated by John himself: "Now Jesus did many other signs in the presence of the disciples, which are not written in this book; but these are written that you may believe that Jesus is the Christ, the Son of God, and that believing you may have life in his name" (Jn 20:30-31). The book is not a missionary appeal; it addresses Christians and seeks to deepen and strengthen their faith in Jesus as the Christ. It does so by recounting and interpreting the words and deeds of Jesus, His "signs," or significant actions. It is therefore, like the first three gospels, "teaching" in the sense of Acts 2:42. Like the other gospels, it no doubt had behind it a long history of oral teaching; it is, as ancient tradition also indicates, the result of John's many years of oral apostolic witness to Christ in the churches of Asia Minor. Some scholars see indications that the book had its origin in the worship life of the church of Asia Minor in such features of the gospel as its simple but exalted style, its dramatic structure, its highly selective way of dealing with the career of Jesus, and its rich use of the solemn "I am" sayings of Jesus. They may well be right.

2 John's teaching did not take place in a vacuum. The church that he taught was in the world, a church in conflict and under temptation. And we can tell from the gospel's particular emphases what some of the conflicts and temptations were. The Gospel of the Crucified was a stumbling block to the Jew and folly to the Greek in John's day as it had been in Paul's (1 Co 1:23). The fierce hatred of the Jews of Asia had pursued Paul (Acts 20:19; 21:27); we find the same embittered Jewish offense at the cross active in Smyrna against Christians a generation after John at the time of the martyrdom of Polycarp. And in the letters to the churches at Smyrna and Philadelphia in Revelation (most probably written within a few years of the time of the Gospel of John) we find

references to Jews opposed to the church, "those who say that they are Jews and are not, but are a synagogue of Satan" (Rv 2:9; 3:9; cf. John 8:44). Conflict with the Jews had not ended with the death of Jesus nor with the death of Paul. Rather, according to the witness of the fourth gospel, it persisted in intensified form; the Gospel of John presents the conflict between Jesus and the Jews in even stronger colors than does the Gospel of Matthew. He speaks of the Jews for the most part simply as "Jews." He knows the distinctive coloring of the various Jewish parties, but the distinction between Pharisees and Sadducees is no longer of importance to him or his readers. John speaks of his people simply as of the people who rejected Jesus as their Messiah, and "Jew" is practically equivalent to "unbelieving Jew" (Jn 2:18, 20; 5:10, 16, 18; 6:41, 52; 7:13; 9:22, etc.). The "Jews" are the opponents of Jesus, blind and stubborn in their refusal to recognize Him, persecuting Him with an ever-mounting hatred. They deny that He is the Son of God (Jn 5:18; 8:40-59); they seek His life (Jn 5:18; 8:40, 59; 10:31, 39; 11:8, 50), and in all things they show themselves not as true children of Abraham but as children of the devil (Jn 8:39-44). Jesus predicts that this hatred will persist; they will deem it a service to God if they kill Jesus' disciples (Jn 16:2). The Spirit whom Jesus will send will enable His disciples to continue the struggle He had in His lifetime carried on against His opponents. (Jn 16:2-4, 7-11)

3 This feature of John's Gospel may be due in part to the fact that he devotes so much space to Jesus' ministry in Jerusalem, where opposition to Jesus was concentrated most strongly. But only in part; it is due chiefly to the fact that the lines have been drawn by Israel's national rejection of her Messiah, that judgment has been executed on Jerusalem and a gulf has been fixed between the ancient people of God and the new Israel, the church. But this does not mean that the fourth gospel has an anti-Semitic

bias. John is at one with the other evangelists and with Paul (Ro 9:1-5) in his positive
appreciation of what the Jew had by the
grace of God received and in his hope that
the Jew may still receive of that grace.
John's harsh indictment of the Jew is therefore to be construed as a call to repentance
addressed to the Jew. It is in the fourth
gospel that Jesus declares to the Samaritan
woman that "salvation is from the Jews"
(Jn 4:22); the Scripture given to the Jews
is for the Jesus of John the supreme authority as it is for the Jesus of Matthew
(e. g., Jn 10:35). The flock for which the Good
Shepherd dies is a flock gathered out of
Israel (Jn 10:16); the hour of the Gentiles,
the hour for the Greeks who would see Jesus,
is yet to come (Jn 10:16; 12:20, 32). Israel's
own high priest must declare that Jesus is
the One who dies for the whole people (Jn
11:50-51). The title of the Crucified is "King
of the Jews" (Jn 19:19). Jesus is "King of
Israel" (Jn 1:49), and the gospel still pleads
with the Jew to become an "Israelite indeed,"
an Israelite "in whom is no guile," by
acknowledging Israel's King as Nathanael
acknowledged Him (Jn 1:47). This motif is
so strong that one modern scholar has advanced and defended the theory that the
fourth gospel is primarily a missionary appeal addressed to the Jew — an overstatement, of course, but an indication of the
tendency of the gospel.

4 Another less direct form of Judaic
opposition to Jesus and His church is also
combated by the fourth gospel. Some in
Israel became disciples of John the Baptist
but did not accept his witness to Jesus as
the Christ. They continued to exist as a separate group or sect, and apparently their
reverent esteem for the Baptist was such
that they assigned to him the titles and
functions of the Messiah. The incident recorded in Acts 19:1-7 (Paul's encounter with
"disciples" who knew only the baptism of
John) would seem to indicate that this movement had spread as far as Ephesus, where
the fourth gospel was written. This would
account for the fact that the fourth gospel
emphasizes that the Baptist has his significance and honor in his subordination to
Jesus as the Christ: "He was not the light,
but came to bear witness to the light" (Jn
1:8); in John's account of him the Baptist
will accept no title of honor, but calls himself
merely the voice in the wilderness — his
whole significance lies in his function as the
herald of the Christ (Jn 1:19-23). He must de-

crease, as the Messiah must increase; and
he finds his perfect joy in the Christ's increasing (Jn 3:28-30). He points his disciples
to the Lamb of God, who takes away the sin
of the world (Jn 1:29-36). But the evangelist
is not minded to belittle the true stature of
the Baptist; he sees in him "a man sent from
God" (Jn 1:6), a valid and mighty witness to
the only Son from the Father (Jn 1:14-15).
John alone records the witness of the people
to John ("Everything that John said about
this man was true," Jn 10:41), and he alone
records the words with which Jesus Himself
places His seal on the Baptist's mission:
"You sent to John, and he has borne witness
to the truth. . . . He was a burning and
shining lamp." (Jn 5:33, 35)

5 The Gospel was a stumbling block to
the Jew and foolishness to the Greek. And
the Gospel of John is directed also against
a Greek perversion of the Gospel, which was
in effect a denial of the Gospel. According
to the second-century father Irenaeus, the
Gospel of John was written to combat the
heresy of Cerinthus. This is hardly the whole
purpose of the gospel, but John's emphatic
declaration that the eternal Son, the Word,
"became flesh" (Jn 1:14) does seem to be
aimed at one of the tenets of the sect of
Cerinthus. For Cerinthus denied that the
"heavenly Christ" had been identified with
man, the creature of flesh, in any real and
lasting way; he maintained that not the
Christ but only the man Jesus (in whom the
Christ had dwelt guest-fashion from the
time of His baptism onward up to the eve of
His Passion) had suffered and died. This
could also be the historical background to
the fact that in the fourth gospel and in it
alone Jesus is hailed at the very beginning
of His ministry as the dying Christ, as "the
Lamb of God" (Jn 1:29), and is at the end
of His ministry worshiped by Thomas as the
Crucified. Thomas says, "My Lord and my
God," to the Christ who bears on His body
the marks of the crucifixion (Jn 20:27-28).
Perhaps John's insistence in the opening
verses of his gospel that "all things were
made through him [the Word], and without
him was not anything made that was made"
(Jn 1:3) is also pointed at Cerinthus, who
maintained that the world was created not
by the highest God who sent the heavenly
Christ into the world, but by a power which
had separated itself from God. The fact that
the First Letter of John is patently directed
against a heresy like that of Cerinthus lends
great plausibility to the suggestion that the

gospel, too, has a polemical point aimed at Cerinthus.

Content of the Gospel

6 John begins his gospel with a compressed, thematic statement that contains in essence the message of the whole book (Jn 1:1-18). Everything that follows is really only a fuller and more profound development of this statement, an unfolding of all that is implicit in it. The recital of the words and deeds of Jesus that follows does not pretend to be a complete record of Jesus' activity (Jn 20:30); the words and deeds are freely selected from a much larger mass of material (some of it, no doubt, familiar to John's readers from the other gospels) freely arranged and told in stylized form, with one aim only: to proclaim what Jesus is and signifies; to present Jesus to men as John and his fellow witnesses had been led by the Spirit to behold Him, as the very Word of God, the only Son in whom God has uttered His whole will for man, the grace and truth of God in person and enacted in the history of a human life witnessed by men.

7 The movement of the gospel is therefore not so much movement in a straight line as in spiral form, a spiral that rises higher and higher and grows wider and wider but remains always over the same area, the area marked out by the first 18 verses of the gospel. For example, the theme of the cross is already stated in the first unit, 1:10-11: "The world knew him not . . . his own people received him not." It recurs in the witness of the Baptist in 1:29: "Behold, the Lamb of God, who takes away the sin of the world!" This spiral comes around to it again in 3:14: "As Moses lifted up the serpent in the wilderness, so must the Son of man be lifted up," and again and again — in 6:51: "The bread which I shall give for the life of the world is my flesh"; in 8:28: "When you have lifted up the Son of man, then you will know that I am he"; in 10:11: "I am the good shepherd. The good shepherd lays down his life for the sheep"; in 12:24: "Truly, truly, I say to you, unless a grain of wheat falls into the earth and dies, it remains alone; but if it dies, it bears much fruit"; and in 12:31-32: "Now is the judgment of this world, now shall the ruler of this world be cast out; and I, when I am lifted up from the earth, will draw all men to myself," to mention only a few passages. The spiral movement touches the cross again in ch. 13, for the cross is the luminous background of Jesus' action when He washes His disciples' feet (13:1-20). The spiral movement of the cross runs through the last discourses of Jesus (e. g., 15:13, 18-21; 16:20). This movement does not cease at the actual crucifixion; it goes on over the narrative of Jesus' appearance to Thomas — Thomas beholds the Crucified (Jn 20:25-29) — and continues over the narrative of Jesus' last conversation with Peter, for Jesus' words, "Feed my sheep" (21:15-19), unmistakably recall the Good Shepherd who lays down His life for the sheep.

OUTLINE

JOHN

Theme: The Eternal Word of God in the Flesh

1:1-18

1 In the beginning was the Word, and the Word was with God, and the Word was God. 2 He was in the beginning with God; 3 all things were made through him, and without him was not anything made that was made. 4 In him was life,*a* and the life was the light of men. 5 The light shines in the darkness, and the darkness has not overcome it.

6 There was a man sent from God, whose name was John. 7 He came for testimony, to bear witness to the light, that all might believe through him. 8 He was not the light, but came to bear witness to the light.

9 The true light that enlightens every man was coming into the world. 10 He was in the world, and the world was made through him, yet the world knew him not. 11 He came to his own home, and his own people received him not. 12 But to all who received him, who believed in his name, he gave power to become children of God; 13 who were born, not of blood nor of the will of the flesh nor of the will of man, but of God.

14 And the Word became flesh and dwelt among us, full of grace and truth; we have beheld his glory, glory as of the only Son from the Father. 15 (John bore witness to him, and cried, "This was he of whom I said, 'He who comes after me ranks before me, for he was before me.' ") 16And from his fulness have we all received, grace upon grace. 17 For the law was given through Moses; grace and truth came through Jesus Christ. 18 No one has ever seen God; the only Son,*b* who is in the bosom of the Father, he has made him known.

a Or *was not anything made. That which has been made was life in him*   *b* Other ancient authorities read *God*

1:1-5 THE ETERNAL WORD

1:1-5 He whom John and his fellow disciples had known as Jesus, the Man in history (cf. 17), was not of this world (8:23). *In the beginning,* before the world began, He *was with God* as God's *Word,* personally united with God as God's speaking, willing, and working, so closely united with God that He must be confessed as *God* (cf. 20:28). He is not creature but Creator of *all things;* in Him God called into being matter and flesh and called them "very good" (Gn 1:31). The *life* which only God has and can impart (5:26) was in Him and was designed to bless mankind (*light of men,* 4). The powers of evil (*darkness,* 5), mysteriously present and maliciously at work in God's good world, have opposed that life but have not *overcome* Him; He remains God's No to all evil.

1:6-13 THE WORD SPOKEN TO MEN: THE LIGHT OF THE WORLD

1:6-13 As in Mt, Mk, and Lk, the history of the incarnate Word begins with the ministry of John the Baptist, the first master of the fourth evangelist (1:35-40). The great glory of the Baptist – his only glory – is that he was witness to the Word spoken to men, to the Light coming into the world, in order that men might believe in the Light and have life by that Light through him. (6-8)

The coming of the Light revealed how deep and evil was the darkness (cf. 5) that opposed Him. The *world* would not listen to the Word; it would not acknowledge the Light (*knew him not,* 10). His *own people,* prepared for His coming by the voices of prophecy from Moses (cf. 17) to John, loved darkness rather than light and *received him not* (11); their answer to His coming was the cross. But the authority of the Word and the trueness of the Light are not thereby called in question; all who *received him,* all who *believed in his name,* trusted in Him and surrendered themselves to Him as to God's final Word and God's creative Light – they found in Him life from God and with God (*born . . . of God,* 13; *children of God,* 12).

1:14-18 THE WORD GIVEN TO THE DISCIPLES: GRACE AND TRUTH

1:14-18 Simple statement (1-13) gives way to warm personal confession (*us; we,* 14; *we,* 16). The excited cry, "We have found the Messiah" (2:41), with which the disciples first proclaimed Him finds an echo here. They have believed in His name and have found in Him divine *grace*

The Word Is Spoken to All Israel

1:19—4:54

THE WITNESS OF JOHN THE BAPTIST (1:19-34)

19 And this is the testimony of John, when the Jews sent priests and Levites from Jerusalem to ask him, "Who are you?" 20 He confessed, he did not deny, but confessed, "I am not the Christ." 21And they asked him, "What then? Are you E·li′jah?" He said, "I am not." "Are you the prophet?" And he answered, "No." 22 They said to him then, "Who are you? Let us have an answer for those who sent us. What do you say about yourself?" 23 He said, "I am the voice of one crying in the wilderness, 'Make straight the way of the Lord,' as the prophet I·sa′iah said."

24 Now they had been sent from the Pharisees. 25 They asked him, "Then why are you baptizing, if you are neither the Christ, nor E·li′jah, nor the prophet?" 26 John answered them, "I baptize with water; but among you stands one whom you do not know, 27 even he who comes after me, the thong of whose sandal I am not worthy to untie." 28 This took place in Beth′a·ny beyond the Jordan, where John was baptizing.

29 The next day he saw Jesus coming toward him, and said, "Behold, the Lamb of God, who takes away the sin of the world! 30 This is he of whom I said, 'After me comes a man who ranks before me, for he was before me.' 31 I myself did not know him; but for this I came baptizing with water, that he might be revealed to Israel." 32And John bore witness, "I saw the Spirit descend as a dove from heaven, and it remained on him. 33 I myself did not know him; but he who sent me to baptize with water said to me, 'He on whom you see the Spirit descend and remain, this is he who baptizes with the Holy Spirit.' 34And I have seen and have borne witness that this is the Son of God."

THE CALL AND CONFESSION OF THE FIRST DISCIPLES (1:35-51)

35 The next day again John was standing with two of his disciples; 36 and he looked at Jesus as he walked, and said, "Behold, the Lamb of God!" 37 The two disciples heard him say this, and they followed Jesus. 38 Jesus turned, and saw them following, and said to them, "What do you seek?" And they said to him, "Rabbi" (which means

which has gone the whole way to man (*became flesh and dwelt among us,* 14) in man's darkness, the grace of the eternal *Word,* grace in which God's *truth* is present (14); grace that is one with *glory,* the holiness of God manifested in Him who is the *only Son* (14), through whom alone men receive power to become sons of God (12). There is none who can be ranked with Him or compared with Him; not John the Baptist, who himself confessed the towering superiority of the One who came after him (15); not the disciples, who remain only and always the recipients of His grace (16); not Moses for all his dignity as mediator of the Law, for Moses could not give what his word demanded and promised—*grace* and *truth* became a reality only in the Word made flesh (*came through Jesus Christ,* 17). Not any man, for no man *has ever seen God* as the only Son has seen Him; He, the trusted Companion of His Father (*in the bosom,* alone *made him known.* (18)

1:19—4:54 This first section is an unfolding of the thematic words: "He came to his own home" (1:11). All three divisions of the land of Israel (Judea, Samaria, Galilee) are scenes of the revelation.

1:19-34 Cf. 1:6-8; 15. "He . . . came to bear witness to the light" (1:8). In that act of witnessing

John himself sees his whole and only function. When questioned by an official delegation from Jerusalem, he disclaims every title or honor that will detract from the Light. He, John, is not the *Christ* (20), not the looked for *Elijah* of the last days (21); not the *prophet* like Moses whom God promised to raise up for His people (21; cf. Dt 18:15). He is only the *voice . . . in the wilderness* (23; Is 40:1 ff.). Only his cry signifies. John's baptism has its whole significance as preparation for the revelation of Him who is to come, the Unknown who can no longer remain unknown (21-28). *He* will bring the last-days baptism with the Spirit, for He is the *Lamb of God,* the sacrifice for the world's sin which God provides. On Him the *Spirit* promised for the Messianic descendant of Jesse (Is 11:2) rests; He is the Eternal, the Son of God. (29-34)

1:35-51 "The Word became flesh and dwelt among us" (1:14). That was John's first statement concerning his discipleship. The story of the beginnings of discipleship is "flesh," down-to-earth history. Natural and normal associations play their part in bringing men within earshot of the Word: a master's word points two disciples to the Lamb of God (36), brother brings brother (40-42), and a man of Bethsaida tells a fellow townsman

Teacher), "where are you staying?" 39 He said to them, "Come and see." They came and saw where he was staying; and they stayed with him that day, for it was about the tenth hour. 40 One of the two who heard John speak, and followed him, was Andrew, Simon Peter's brother. 41 He first found his brother Simon, and said to him, "We have found the Messiah" (which means Christ). 42 He brought him to Jesus. Jesus looked at him, and said, "So you are Simon the son of John? You shall be called Cephas" (which means Peter*c*).

43 The next day Jesus decided to go to Galilee. And he found Philip and said to him, "Follow me." 44 Now Philip was from Beth-sa'i-da, the city of Andrew and Peter. 45 Philip found Na·than'a·el, and said to him, "We have found him of whom Moses in the law and also the prophets wrote, Jesus of Nazareth, the son of Joseph." 46 Na·than'a·el said to him, "Can anything good come out of Nazareth?" Philip said to him, "Come and see." 47 Jesus saw Na·than'a·el coming to him, and said of him, "Behold, an Israelite indeed, in whom is no guile!" 48 Na·than'a·el said to him, "How do you know me?" Jesus answered him, "Before Philip called you, when you were under the fig tree, I saw you." 49 Na·than'a·el answered him, "Rabbi, you are the Son of God! You are the King of Israel!" 50 Jesus answered him, "Because I said to you, I saw you under the fig tree, do you believe? You shall see greater things than these." 51And he said to him, "Truly, truly, I say to you, you will see heaven opened, and the angels of God ascending and descending upon the Son of man."

FIRST SIGN: JESUS MANIFESTS HIS GLORY (2:1-12)

2 On the third day there was a marriage at Cana in Galilee, and the mother of Jesus was there; 2 Jesus also was invited to the marriage, with his disciples. 3 When the wine gave out, the mother of Jesus said to him, "They have no wine." 4And Jesus said to her, "O woman, what have you to do with me? My hour has not yet come." 5 His mother said to the servants, "Do whatever he tells you." 6 Now six stone jars were

c From the word for *rock* in Aramaic and Greek, respectively

(43-45). Jesus' first words to His first disciples are simplicity itself: *What do you seek? . . . Come and see.* (38-39)

Yet through this flesh the Word's eternal glory shines: the voice proclaims Him as God's final and universal sacrifice (36). The ancient words of promise inevitably find their goal in Him (45). He knows "what is in man" (cf. 2:25), and this knowledge has a shattering effect on the skeptic Nathanael (47-49). The first five disciples cannot but confess Him as *the Messiah* (41), *the King of Israel, the Son of God.* (49)

And this was but a foretaste and token of the glory they were to behold in Him; greater things awaited them (50). The disciples' first and overwhelming experience of Him was the experience of His grace (cf. 1:16). They turned to Him as to the Lamb of God, God's sufficient answer to their desperate need as members of a sinful world (36; cf. 29). He took the initiative (*What do you seek?* 38) and invited them to His lodgings and received them at His table (see note on v. 39). He bade an undistinguished Philip follow Him (43). When He called Simon *Cephas,* that was grace; for He spoke of a ministry that Simon would be privileged and enabled to perform, a partaking in the Christ's own work of building a new temple (cf. 2:19), a new Israel (cf. Mt 16:16-19). His grace forgave Nathanael his sneer at Nazareth and reached out to fulfill the heart's desire of that guileless Israelite (45-49). His promise of *greater things* is a promise of "grace upon grace." The

disciples shall see in the Word become flesh the work of the God who opens heaven and comes down, who seeks, establishes, and maintains fellowship with man in the person of One who calls Himself *the Son of man.* (50-51)

1:39 *About the tenth hour,* 4 p. m., when the main meal of the day was eaten.

2:1-12 Jesus first manifests His glory by giving; the gift speaks anew His Father's blessing on the creation that came into being through Him (1:3), on the creaturely flesh which He has made His own (1:14). Jesus blesses marriage by His presence at the wedding feast and by His giving blesses the wine that makes glad the heart of man. He gives in obedience to the Father, awaiting the hour which He has ordained (4) in sovereign independence of all others, even of His kindly mother (3-4). He gives royally; the gift is lavish in both quantity and quality (6, 10). Jesus' first sign is like the last sign recorded by John in that both are extreme-case signs. As the last sign (ch. 11) shows — by Jesus' mastery over death — that there is no limit to His power to give, so the first sign shows that there is no limit to His will to give; even the slightest need (the embarrassment of a host and the dampening of festal pleasure) is enough to evoke His compassionate aid. The disciples are to know how freely and confidently they may ask in His name. (14:13; 15:16)

2:4 *O woman.* There is nothing disrespectful in this form of address.

2:6 *Jewish rites of purification.* Cf. Mk 7:3-4.

standing there, for the Jewish rites of purification, each holding twenty or thirty gallons. 7 Jesus said to them, "Fill the jars with water." And they filled them up to the brim. 8 He said to them, "Now draw some out, and take it to the steward of the feast." So they took it. 9 When the steward of the feast tasted the water now become wine, and did not know where it came from (though the servants who had drawn the water knew), the steward of the feast called the bridegroom 10 and said to him, "Every man serves the good wine first; and when men have drunk freely, then the poor wine; but you have kept the good wine until now." 11 This, the first of his signs, Jesus did at Cana in Galilee, and manifested his glory; and his disciples believed in him.

12 After this he went down to Ca·per′na·um, with his mother and his brothers and his disciples; and there they stayed for a few days.

THE CLEANSING OF THE TEMPLE (2:13-22)

13 The Passover of the Jews was at hand, and Jesus went up to Jerusalem. 14 In the temple he found those who were selling oxen and sheep and pigeons, and the money-changers at their business. 15And making a whip of cords, he drove them all, with the sheep and oxen, out of the temple; and he poured out the coins of the money-changers and overturned their tables. 16And he told those who sold the pigeons, "Take these things away; you shall not make my Father's house a house of trade." 17 His disciples remembered that it was written, "Zeal for thy house will consume me." 18 The Jews then said to him, "What sign have you to show us for doing this?" 19 Jesus answered them, "Destroy this temple, and in three days I will raise it up." 20 The Jews then said, "It has taken forty-six years to build this temple, and will you raise it up in three days?" 21 But he spoke of the temple of his body. 22 When therefore he was raised from the dead, his disciples remembered that he had said this; and they believed the scripture and the word which Jesus had spoken.

FAITH: THE CONVERSATION WITH NICODEMUS (2:23 — 3:21)

23 Now when he was in Jerusalem at the Passover feast, many believed in his name when they saw the signs which he did; 24 but Jesus did not trust himself to them,

2:10 The steward is worldly wise, well versed in the ways of drinkers; but he is an objective witness to the reality of the miracle.

2:11 *Signs,* the miracles in their significance as the revelation of the mind and will of God. (Cf. 6:26)

2:13-22 The disciples, John said, beheld the glory of the incarnate Word as "the glory of the only Son," a glory the Son received "from the Father" in obedient self-subordination to the Father (1:14). The obedient Son is zealous for the honor of His Father's house, the temple. He will not have men attempt to serve God and mammon in its hallowed precincts (13-16; cf. Mt 6:24). He is challenged by the temple authorities: If He is reforming Israel's worship with an assumption of prophetic (or even Messianic) authority, He must authenticate Himself by performing a *sign,* a miraculous demonstration of His authority (18). Jesus, who leaves no believing petition unanswered, refuses as always the sign which will satisfy the demand of the impenitent. He gives the authorities a riddling answer (19), one which even His disciples understood fully only after His resurrection (22). But, though it posed a riddle, it was unmistakably a call to repentance. The course which they are pursuing, Jesus is telling them, will bring the judgment of God on the desecrated temple; the future of the people of God lies, not with the custodians of the temple or even with the temple itself but with the Son whom they will resist, defeat, and kill. He will arise from the dead as the new and living temple, the center and focus for the worship of men (19). The sneer with which *the Jews* answer His call to repentance (20) makes it clear that Jesus knew what was in their hearts when He refused their demand for a sign. The lines are drawn; His people will not receive Him (1:11). But to those who do receive Him He manifests His glory as much in this refusal of a sign as in the doing of a sign. His disciples' faith grows. They see in Him the ultimate meaning of the OT words concerning the Righteous Sufferer (Ps 69:9) and come to know Him as One whose Word has the same unbreakable force as that of their Sacred Scriptures. (22; cf. 10:35)

2:13 *Passover.* It is characteristic of John that he dwells on Jesus' appearances in Jerusalem at the great festivals, concerning which the other gospels are silent, although the words of Jesus in Mt 23:37 and Lk 13:34; 19:41 presuppose a ministry in Jerusalem also.

2:19 *Three days,* the time when observable corruption of a corpse sets in; cf. 11:39, "dead four days."

2:23 — 3:21 The eternal Son gives power to become children of God to all who believe in His name (1:12). What is believing? What does faith

25 because he knew all men and needed no one to bear witness of man; for he himself knew what was in man.

3 Now there was a man of the Pharisees, named Nicodemus, a ruler of the Jews. 2 This man came to Jesus*d* by night and said to him, "Rabbi, we know that you are a teacher come from God; for no one can do these signs that you do, unless God is with him." 3 Jesus answered him, "Truly, truly, I say to you, unless one is born anew,*e* he cannot see the kingdom of God." 4 Nicodemus said to him, "How can a man be born when he is old? Can he enter a second time into his mother's womb and be born?" 5 Jesus answered, "Truly, truly, I say to you, unless one is born of water and the Spirit, he cannot enter the kingdom of God. 6 That which is born of the flesh is flesh, and that which is born of the Spirit is spirit.*f* 7 Do not marvel that I said to you, 'You must be born anew.'*e* 8 The wind*f* blows where it wills, and you hear the sound of it, but you do not know whence it comes or whither it goes; so it is with every one who is born of the Spirit." 9 Nicodemus said to him, "How can this be?" 10 Jesus answered him, "Are you a teacher of Israel, and yet you do not understand this? 11 Truly, truly, I say to you, we speak of what we know, and bear witness to what we have seen; but you do not receive our testimony. 12 If I have told you earthly things and you do not believe, how can you believe if I tell you heavenly things? 13 No one has ascended into heaven but he who descended from heaven, the Son of man.*g* 14And as Moses lifted up the serpent in the wilderness, so must the Son of man be lifted up, 15 that whoever believes in him may have eternal life."*h*

16 For God so loved the world that he gave his only Son, that whoever believes in him should not perish but have eternal life. 17 For God sent the Son into the world, not to condemn the world, but that the world might be saved through him. 18 He who believes in him is not condemned; he who does not believe is condemned already, because he has not believed in the name of the only Son of God. 19And this is the judgment, that the light has come into the world, and men loved darkness rather than light, because their deeds were evil. 20 For every one who does evil hates the light, and does not come to the light, lest his deeds should be exposed. 21 But he who does what is true comes to the light, that it may be clearly seen that his deeds have been wrought in God.

d Greek *him*　*e* Or *from above*　*f* The same Greek word means both *wind* and *spirit*
g Other ancient authorities add *who is in heaven*
h Some interpreters hold that the quotation continues through verse 21

involve? The brief notice concerning the *many* who *believed . . . when they saw the signs which he did* (2:23) — a faith which Jesus could not accept (2:24) — seems designed to raise this question, and the conversation with Nicodemus (3:1-21) seems designed to answer it. The word *believe* occurs 8 times in these 24 verses (as over against 5 times in the preceding 73 verses).

Believing is more that seeing *signs* and being somehow drawn to Him who performs them. Jesus knows *what* is *in man* and knows that the stance of the sympathetic spectator is not the stance of faith; He cannot give Himself to the spectator. (2:23-25)

Believing is more than a good man's sincere religious interest in Jesus as a *teacher come from God* (3:1-2); Jesus' brusque disregard of Nicodemus' compliment makes that plain (3:3). To believe is to let God be God (*kingdom of God,* 3:3, 5); it is living with and on the miracle, where God is the sole agent. Faith lives on the miracle of a new birth *from above* (3:3, 5), birth by the *water* of John's baptism and by the Spirit baptism given by the Son of God (3:5; cf. 1:32-33). Faith cannot ask, as Nicodemus does, *How can this be?*

(3:9; cf. 3:4), for man can raise the question of *how* only in the domain of man, the domain of *the flesh;* the *Spirit* is beyond his questioning. Man can find an analogy for the mystery of the Spirit's working in the mysterious ways of God's creation, in the *wind* whose sound he hears and whose reality he feels without being able to explain its coming and going (3:8). The *teacher of Israel* can find the record and reality of the Spirit in the Sacred Scriptures on which he bases his teaching (3:10; cf. e. g., Eze 36:27). The miracle of the prophets (with whom Jesus associates Himself as THE Prophet, *we,* 3:11) can help him toward a believing encounter with the greater miracle of the *Son of man,* the valid witness of *heavenly things . . . who has descended from heaven.* (3:12-13)

The *teacher of Israel* can find in the record of *Moses* (Nm 21:4-9) the miracle of the love of God manifested to a people who had by rebellion against Him (Nm 21:5, 7) forfeited all right to His love — he can find there a similitude for the miracle of the supreme love which will cause the *Son of man* to *be lifted up* to the cross and to the throne of God (3:14; cf. 8:28; 12:32, 34). But this does not exempt him from the total submission of

THE LAST WITNESS OF JOHN THE BAPTIST (3:22-36)

22 After this Jesus and his disciples went into the land of Judea; there he remained with them and baptized. 23 John also was baptizing at Ae′non near Salim, because there was much water there; and people came and were baptized. 24 For John had not yet been put in prison.

25 Now a discussion arose between John's disciples and a Jew over purifying. 26And they came to John, and said to him, "Rabbi, he who was with you beyond the Jordan, to whom you bore witness, here he is, baptizing, and all are going to him." 27 John answered, "No one can receive anything except what is given him from heaven. 28 You yourselves bear me witness, that I said, I am not the Christ, but I have been sent before him. 29 He who has the bride is the bridegroom; the friend of the bridegroom, who stands and hears him, rejoices greatly at the bridegroom's voice; therefore this joy of mine is now full. 30 He must increase, but I must decrease."*i*

31 He who comes from above is above all; he who is of the earth belongs to the earth, and of the earth he speaks; he who comes from heaven is above all. 32 He bears witness to what he has seen and heard, yet no one receives his testimony; 33 he who receives his testimony sets his seal to this, that God is true. 34 For he whom God has sent utters the words of God, for it is not by measure that he gives the Spirit; 35 the Father loves the Son, and has given all things into his hand. 36 He who believes in the Son has eternal life; he who does not obey the Son shall not see life, but the wrath of God rests upon him.

THE WOMAN OF SAMARIA (4:1-42)

4 Now when the Lord knew that the Pharisees had heard that Jesus was making and baptizing more disciples than John 2 (although Jesus himself did not baptize, but only his disciples), 3 he left Judea and departed again to Galilee. 4 He had to pass

i Some interpreters hold that the quotation continues through verse 36

faith; it can but help him to *believe* in the Son of Man and so find *eternal life* in Him (3:15). The miracle of God's love for His people can prepare him for faith in the uncaused, universal love of God for the *world* in rebellion against Him, the love which *gave* the *only Son* for the life of the enemy, the love which wrought salvation and *eternal life* for all (3:16). Faith cannot ask *how* in the face of this miracle; and faith dare not ask for reasons, for faith is the desperate reach for life in the midst of death, in the face of judgment and condemnation (3:18). And judgment is not a far-off event; the judgment is taking place now, in the unbelief of men who *love darkness,* which dooms them and does not want to be *exposed* by the *light* (3:19-20). For unbelief the Last Judgment has moved into the present. But for faith the final miracle takes place; the believer moves from the passivity of being born and being loved to the activity of doing *what is true,* of enacting the truth in *deeds* that have God's hallmark on them, deeds *wrought in God.* (3:21)

3:22-36 The Baptist, the witness through whom men come to faith (1:6-8), is a man of faith. He lives on the miracle and therefore knows that all men live on God's giving (27). His disciples' anxiety for their master's honor therefore leaves him unmoved; he is content to play the subordinate role which God has assigned to him (28). He is more than content; he rejoices, as the bridegroom's friend rejoices in the bridegroom's joy, in the fact that the will of God (*must,* 30) has decreed that the increasing Light should reduce to insignificance

the burning and shining lamp of the witness to the Light (30; cf. 5:33). No mists of selfish ambition becloud his vision of the Light; he can witness to Him fully because he witnesses freely; the One whom John attests comes *from above,* from God, and is *above all,* high over the witness John, who is and speaks *of the earth* (31); *He* is eye- and ear-witness to the world of God from which He comes (32); possessed of the Spirit in unprecedented fullness. He utters the very *words of God* (34); one with the Father who *loves* Him, He is the Bearer of all God's counsels, the Executor of all God's purposes for men (35). The believing witness to the Light is a credible witness to the cruciality of faith when he declares that he who *believes in the Son* attests that God is faithful to His promises (33) and *has* the promised *eternal life* in the Son; whoever will not yield to Him the obedience of faith has willed to remain under the *wrath of God.* (36)

3:22 *He . . . baptized.* Cf. 4:2, where baptizing is restricted to Jesus' disciples. Through them He (Jesus) baptized.

3:33 *Sets his seal to this,* that is, attests, certifies, acknowledges.

3:34 *Not by measure . . . he* (the Father) *gives the Spirit* (to the Son). This distinguishes Jesus from all other recipients of the Spirit (judges, Ju 6:34; kings, 1 Sm 16:13; prophets, Mi 3:8; cf. 1:33).

4:1-42 Nicodemus, high-minded Pharisee, ruler, and teacher of Israel; John the Baptist, witness, voice, friend of the Bridegroom, a shining lamp in Israel; and, third, the *woman of Samaria,* these are

through Sa·mar′i·a. 5 So he came to a city of Sa·mar′i·a, called Sychar, near the field that Jacob gave to his son Joseph. 6 Jacob's well was there, and so Jesus, wearied as he was with his journey, sat down beside the well. It was about the sixth hour.

7 There came a woman of Sa·mar′i·a to draw water. Jesus said to her, "Give me a drink." 8 For his disciples had gone away into the city to buy food. 9 The Samaritan woman said to him, "How is it that you, a Jew, ask a drink of me, a woman of Sa·mar′-i·a?" For Jews have no dealings with Samaritans. 10 Jesus answered her, "If you knew the gift of God, and who it is that is saying to you, 'Give me a drink,' you would have asked him, and he would have given you living water." 11 The woman said to him, "Sir, you have nothing to draw with, and the well is deep; where do you get that living water? 12Are you greater than our father Jacob, who gave us the well, and drank from it himself, and his sons, and his cattle?" 13 Jesus said to her, "Every one who drinks of this water will thirst again, 14 but whoever drinks of the water that I shall give him will never thirst; the water that I shall give him will become in him a spring of water welling up to eternal life." 15 The woman said to him, "Sir, give me this water, that I may not thirst, nor come here to draw."

16 Jesus said to her, "Go, call your husband, and come here." 17 The woman answered him, "I have no husband." Jesus said to her, "You are right in saying, 'I have no husband'; 18 for you have had five husbands, and he whom you now have is not your husband; this you said truly." 19 The woman said to him, "Sir, I perceive that you are a prophet. 20 Our fathers worshiped on this mountain; and you say that in Jerusalem is the place where men ought to worship." 21 Jesus said to her, "Woman, believe me, the hour is coming when neither on this mountain nor in Jerusalem will you worship the Father. 22 You worship what you do not know; we worship what we know, for salvation is from the Jews. 23 But the hour is coming, and now is, when the true worshipers will worship the Father in spirit and truth, for such the Father seeks to worship him. 24 God is spirit, and those who worship him must worship in spirit and truth." 25 The woman said to him, "I know that Messiah is coming (he who is called Christ); when he comes, he will show us all things." 26 Jesus said to her, "I who speak to you am he."

27 Just then his disciples came. They marveled that he was talking with a woman, but none said, "What do you wish?" or, "Why are you talking with her?" 28 So the woman left her water jar, and went away into the city, and said to the people, 29 "Come, see a man who told me all that I ever did. Can this be the Christ?" 30 They went out of the city and were coming to him.

31 Meanwhile the disciples besought him, saying, "Rabbi, eat." 32 But he said to them, "I have food to eat of which you do not know." 33 So the disciples said to one

---

an ill-assorted company. For she was alien to Jewry; no good Jew would set his lip to a Samaritan water jar (9). She was walled in by sectarian pride and prejudice (12); hemmed in by a low horizon of physical desires and satisfactions (15); and, living with her sixth man, she had a past and a present that she preferred to be ambiguous about (16-18). And yet she joins that company of witnesses of which John was the first (39). If the story of Nicodemus shows that nothing less than faith will avail, her story makes it plain that nothing more than faith is needed. (4:21-26)

The love of Jesus, which could be brusque with the teacher of Israel, deals gently with this sorry slut of Samaria. Gradually and patiently He leads her to see in Him more than a tired, thirsty, and impertinent Jew (9), to see in Him more than a mysteriously arresting personality who has a gift to give (10-15), a prophet who can divine her secret sins and can point her beyond the competing claims of Mount Gerizim in Samaria and Mount Zion in Jerusalem to a new and true worship in which all men may join, a worship made possible and acceptable by the gift of the Spirit and His revelation of the truth (16-24). He leads her, finally, to a dawning recognition of Him as the Christ whose coming resolves the religious riddles of the past (25-26, 29). He makes her a believer and a witness, and she enjoys a witness's reward; her fellow townsmen come to Jesus, prevail on Him to stay with them, and find in Him the Savior who, though He asserts the primacy of the Jew in God's counsels of salvation (22), excludes no one from salvation, the *Savior of the world*. (28-30, 39-42)

For Jesus this bit of evangelization done in transit on His way to Galilee (3-4) was no little thing. He was doing the will of His Father who seeks worshipers (23), and that was the *food* He lived on (32-34). He, the patient Sower, sees the fields which His disciples shall reap *already white for harvest* and *rejoices* with these *reapers* who *shall reap that for which others* (John the Baptist, Jesus) *have labored* (35-38). The Savior of the world looks

another, "Has any one brought him food?" 34 Jesus said to them, "My food is to do the will of him who sent me, and to accomplish his work. 35 Do you not say, 'There are yet four months, then comes the harvest'? I tell you, lift up your eyes, and see how the fields are already white for harvest. 36 He who reaps receives wages, and gathers fruit for eternal life, so that sower and reaper may rejoice together. 37 For here the saying holds true, 'One sows and another reaps.' 38 I sent you to reap that for which you did not labor; others have labored, and you have entered into their labor."

39 Many Samaritans from that city believed in him because of the woman's testimony, "He told me all that I ever did." 40 So when the Samaritans came to him, they asked him to stay with them; and he stayed there two days. 41And many more believed because of his word. 42 They said to the woman, "It is no longer because of your words that we believe, for we have heard for ourselves, and we know that this is indeed the Savior of the world."

SECOND SIGN: THE HEALING OF THE OFFICIAL'S SON (4:43-54)

43 After the two days he departed to Galilee. 44 For Jesus himself testified that a prophet has no honor in his own country. 45 So when he came to Galilee, the Galileans welcomed him, having seen all that he had done in Jerusalem at the feast, for they too had gone to the feast.

46 So he came again to Cana in Galilee, where he had made the water wine. And at Ca·per′na·um there was an official whose son was ill. 47 When he heard that Jesus had come from Judea to Galilee, he went and begged him to come down and heal his son, for he was at the point of death. 48 Jesus therefore said to him, "Unless you see signs and wonders you will not believe." 49 The official said to him, "Sir, come down before my child dies." 50 Jesus said to him, "Go; your son will live." The man believed the word that Jesus spoke to him and went his way. 51As he was going down, his servants met him and told him that his son was living. 52 So he asked them the hour when he began to mend, and they said to him, "Yesterday at the seventh hour the fever left him." 53 The father knew that was the hour when Jesus had said to him, "Your son will live"; and he himself believed, and all his household. 54 This was now the second sign that Jesus did when he had come from Judea to Galilee.

The Word Is Rejected by Israel

5:1—12:50

THE HEALING AT BETHESDA ON THE SABBATH (5:1-47)

5 After this there was a feast of the Jews, and Jesus went up to Jerusalem. 2 Now there is in Jerusalem by the Sheep Gate a pool, in Hebrew called Beth-za′tha,ʲ which has five porticoes. 3 In these lay a multitude of invalids, blind, lame, paralyzed.ᵏ 5 One man was there, who had been ill for thirty-eight years. 6 When

---

ʲ Other ancient authorities read *Bethesda*, others *Bethsaida*
ᵏ Other ancient authorities insert, wholly or in part, *waiting for the moving of the water; 4 for an angel of the Lord went down at certain seasons into the pool, and troubled the water: whoever stepped in first after the troubling of the water was healed of whatever disease he had*

---

down the missionary road that leads through Samaria into the far corners of the world, and His joy is full.

4:43-54 Jesus' second (cf. 2:11) *sign* in Galilee again shows Jesus as the Giver. He is curiously reserved and austere in His giving. He chides the poor father who has ridden 18 miles to get help for his dying son (48). But He holds back and chides, not because He is unwilling to give but because He is minded to give the petitioner more than he asks for. And He does give Him more; He gives him his son, and He gives him a faith in His Word (50) that is independent of signs and won-

ders, a faith that can endure beyond the crisis which evoked it, a faith that lives and communicates itself to others (*and all his household,* 53).

4:48 *Unless you see signs.* The *you* is plural, "you Galileans." (Cf. 45)

5:1—12:50 The thematic word, "His own people received him not" (1:11), is not forgotten in the first four chs. (cf. 2:23-25; 3:11; 3:32; 4:44). But it is in chs. 5—12 that this theme is fully developed and becomes a dominant motif of the narratives and discourses in which Jesus reveals Himself amid a hostile and obdurate people.

5:1-18 Jesus brought the grace and truth of

Jesus saw him and knew that he had been lying there a long time, he said to him, "Do you want to be healed?" 7 The sick man answered him, "Sir, I have no man to put me into the pool when the water is troubled, and while I am going another steps down before me." 8 Jesus said to him, "Rise, take up your pallet, and walk." 9And at once the man was healed, and he took up his pallet and walked.

Now that day was the sabbath. 10 So the Jews said to the man who was cured, "It is the sabbath, it is not lawful for you to carry your pallet." 11 But he answered them, "The man who healed me said to me, 'Take up your pallet, and walk.' " 12 They asked him, "Who is the man who said to you, 'Take up your pallet, and walk'?" 13 Now the man who had been healed did not know who it was, for Jesus had withdrawn, as there was a crowd in the place. 14Afterward, Jesus found him in the temple, and said to him, "See, you are well! Sin no more, that nothing worse befall you." 15 The man went away and told the Jews that it was Jesus who had healed him. 16And this was why the Jews persecuted Jesus, because he did this on the sabbath. 17 But Jesus answered them, "My Father is working still, and I am working." 18 This was why the Jews sought all the more to kill him, because he not only broke the sabbath but also called God his own Father, making himself equal with God.

19 Jesus said to them, "Truly, truly, I say to you, the Son can do nothing of his own accord, but only what he sees the Father doing; for whatever he does, that the Son does likewise. 20 For the Father loves the Son, and shows him all that he himself is doing; and greater works than these will he show him, that you may marvel. 21 For as the Father raises the dead and gives them life, so also the Son gives life to whom he will. 22 The Father judges no one, but has given all judgment to the Son, 23 that all may honor the Son, even as they honor the Father. He who does not honor the Son does not honor the Father who sent him. 24 Truly, truly, I say to you, he who hears my word and believes him who sent me, has eternal life; he does not come into judgment, but has passed from death to life.

25 "Truly, truly, I say to you, the hour is coming, and now is, when the dead will hear the voice of the Son of God, and those who hear will live. 26 For as the Father has life in himself, so he has granted the Son also to have life in himself, 27 and has given him authority to execute judgment, because he is the Son of man. 28 Do not marvel at this; for the hour is coming when all who are in the tombs will hear his voice 29 and come forth, those who have done good, to the resurrection of life, and those who have done evil, to the resurrection of judgment.

30 "I can do nothing on my own authority; as I hear, I judge; and my judgment is just, because I seek not my own will but the will of him who sent me. 31 If I bear witness to myself, my testimony is not true; 32 there is another who bears witness to

---

God into the life of a hopeless invalid; He did so with characteristically quiet unobtrusiveness (*had withdrawn,* 13). He made clear to the healed man that the whole restorative grace of God had touched his life and that this grace dare not be received in vain (*sin no more,* 14). His deed brought Him into conflict with His people because He had broken the jealously guarded Sabbath in doing it (18). The conflict became a deadly conflict when Jesus pleaded in His defense that He was acting thus in oneness with His Father, the Creator who has been working ceaselessly from creation onward, on weekdays and holy days alike (*is working still,* 17). In the eyes of His people He was defending sacrilege with blasphemy when He called God His Father, making Himself equal with God. (18)

5:19-29 Jesus' reply to this charge is simply the declaration of the mystery of His Sonship. He is not MAKING Himself equal with God when He calls Him Father in this unique sense; His Sonship is enacted in obedience (19) and is lived under the law enunciated by the Baptist: "No one can

receive anything except what is GIVEN HIM FROM HEAVEN" (3:27). The initiative is not His own but His Father's; the Father's love for the obedient Son puts all things into the Son's hands (19-20): the eternal issues of life and death (21) and the judgment, which is God's own prerogative (22; cf. Dt 32:35). The Father crowns the Son with His own glory and honor; therefore the Son's Word is the divine two-edged sword of *judgment* and *eternal life* (24), both now and hereafter (25, 28); now, for the underived *life* of God is present now, in the *Son of man,* and is given to man now (cf. 24); the alternative is judgment from the Son of Man now (27); hereafter, for the voice heard now (25) will be heard again at the Last Day to open tombs and to make manifest the judgment which is being enacted now. (28-29)

5:30-37a The Son has witnesses who live and can tell of the truth and selflessness of His Sonship. There is the testimony of *John,* who called Him both Lamb of God (1:29, 36) and Son of God (1:34); His testimony counts, not because it is a

me, and I know that the testimony which he bears to me is true. ³³ You sent to John, and he has borne witness to the truth. ³⁴ Not that the testimony which I receive is from man; but I say this that you may be saved. ³⁵ He was a burning and shining lamp, and you were willing to rejoice for a while in his light. ³⁶ But the testimony which I have is greater than that of John; for the works which the Father has granted me to accomplish, these very works which I am doing, bear me witness that the Father has sent me. ³⁷And the Father who sent me has himself borne witness to me. His voice you have never heard, his form you have never seen; ³⁸ and you do not have his word abiding in you, for you do not believe him whom he has sent. ³⁹ You search the scriptures, because you think that in them you have eternal life; and it is they that bear witness to me; ⁴⁰ yet you refuse to come to me that you may have life. ⁴¹ I do not receive glory from men. ⁴² But I know that you have not the love of God within you. ⁴³ I have come in my Father's name, and you do not receive me; if another comes in his own name, him you will receive. ⁴⁴ How can you believe, who receive glory from one another and do not seek the glory that comes from the only God? ⁴⁵ Do not think that I shall accuse you to the Father; it is Moses who accuses you, on whom you set your hope. ⁴⁶ If you believed Moses, you would believe me, for he wrote of me. ⁴⁷ But if you do not believe his writings, how will you believe my words?"

FEEDING THE 5,000 IN GALILEE (6:1-71)

6 After this Jesus went to the other side of the Sea of Galilee, which is the Sea of Ti·be′ri·as. ²And a multitude followed him, because they saw the signs which he did on those who were diseased. ³ Jesus went up on the mountain, and there sat

man's word but because He was a *lamp* kindled by God Himself; the Jews themselves have, for a time at least, delighted in that *light* (33-35). There is the witness of the *works* which the Father has *granted* Him to *accomplish;* the working Word that gladdens and restores is God's Word spoken for the need of man (36). And the Father's voice has testified to the Son at His baptism. (37; cf. 1:33, 34)

5:37b-47 The Accused now becomes the Accuser of His accusers: "You who are so zealous for God's Sabbath and God's honor," He asserts, "do not even know the God for whom your unenlightened zeal (cf. Ro 10:2) contends. If His *word,* the *scriptures,* had really found a home in your hearts (*abiding in you,* 38) as well as in your searching minds (39), you could recognize the authentic accent of the eternal Word, who has heard and seen God; you would believe Him and find in Him *eternal* life (39, 40). If your selfish love for the *glory* that lives from man to man (44) had not killed in you the *love of God* (42), you would *receive* the Son who unselfishly comes in His *Father's name* (43), doing His will, seeking His glory, not *glory from men* (41). As it is, you can believe only a messiah who is as self-centered as yourselves (43b). The *Moses . . . on whom you set your hope* (45) stands before the Father as your accuser: 'You have not *believed his writings* in their essential import, as witnesses to Me.'" (45-47; cf. 1:45; 3:14)

6:1-71 The story of the feeding of the 5,000 (Jesus' enacted invitation to fellowship) and its sequel, the story of Jesus' coming to His disciples across the waters (the enactment of Jesus' unconquerable will to fellowship with His own) are familiar to us, as they probably were to John's

first readers, from the accounts in the first three gospels. (Cf., e. g., Mt 14:1-33). Peculiar to the fourth gospel (aside from details, such as the reference to the *Passover,* 4) is the emphasis on Jesus' deeds as *signs,* as wondrous acts which point beyond themselves, from the gift to the Giver (cf. 26). John had previously recorded Jesus' mistrust of a "faith" that feeds on signs alone; He could not "trust himself" to such a faith (2:23-25); the sequel to the story of the feeding in John (v. 15) makes plain why He who "knew what is in man" could not give Himself to such a faith; such a faith has room in it for the self-seeking will of man, man who will not be taught and drawn to Jesus by the Father (44-45) but seeks by force to *make* Him King whom only the Father can make both King and Lord (cf. Acts 2:36). The faith which feeds on signs is an appetite that grows by what it feeds on; it cannot rest in the revelation of the given sign but demands another. (26)

Jesus' discourse on the bread of life makes clear the true significance and the real function of the sign (26-71). The sign of the multiplied loaves points beyond itself, beyond the *food which perishes* to *the food which endures to eternal life* (27), beyond any *works of God* (28) which man in his zeal can do to the one *work of God* which God in His grace does, to faith in the *Son of man* whom God has sent, not only to give (34) but to be *the true bread from heaven* that *gives life to the world* (32, 33, 35). Jesus in His person is the *bread of life* (35, 48), eternal life (40, 51); His person is the Word become flesh (cf. 1:14). The *bread which* He *shall give for the life of the world is* His *flesh* (51), the flesh of the Lamb of God (1:29), of the Crucified whose *blood* (53, 55, 56) is shed for the life of the world. Whosoever eats that flesh and drinks that

down with his disciples. 4 Now the Passover, the feast of the Jews, was at hand. 5 Lifting up his eyes, then, and seeing that a multitude was coming to him, Jesus said to Philip, "How are we to buy bread, so that these people may eat?" 6 This he said to test him, for he himself knew what he would do. 7 Philip answered him, "Two hundred denarii[l] would not buy enough bread for each of them to get a little." 8 One of his disciples, Andrew, Simon Peter's brother, said to him, 9 "There is a lad here who has five barley loaves and two fish; but what are they among so many?" 10 Jesus said, "Make the people sit down." Now there was much grass in the place; so the men sat down, in number about five thousand. 11 Jesus then took the loaves, and when he had given thanks, he distributed them to those who were seated; so also the fish, as much as they wanted. 12 And when they had eaten their fill, he told his disciples, "Gather up the fragments left over, that nothing may be lost." 13 So they gathered them up and filled twelve baskets with fragments from the five barley loaves, left by those who had eaten. 14 When the people saw the sign which he had done, they said, "This is indeed the prophet who is to come into the world!"

15 Perceiving then that they were about to come and take him by force to make him king, Jesus withdrew again to the mountain by himself.

16 When evening came, his disciples went down to the sea, 17 got into a boat, and started across the sea to Ca·per′na·um. It was now dark, and Jesus had not yet come to them. 18 The sea rose because a strong wind was blowing. 19 When they had rowed about three or four miles,[m] they saw Jesus walking on the sea and drawing near to the boat. They were frightened, 20 but he said to them, "It is I; do not be afraid." 21 Then they were glad to take him into the boat, and immediately the boat was at the land to which they were going.

22 On the next day the people who remained on the other side of the sea saw that there had been only one boat there, and that Jesus had not entered the boat with his disciples, but that his disciples had gone away alone. 23 However, boats from Ti·be′ri·as came near the place where they ate the bread after the Lord had given thanks. 24 So when the people saw that Jesus was not there, nor his disciples, they themselves got into the boats and went to Ca·per′na·um, seeking Jesus.

25 When they found him on the other side of the sea, they said to him, "Rabbi, when did you come here?" 26 Jesus answered them, "Truly, truly, I say to you, you seek me, not because you saw signs, but because you ate your fill of the loaves. 27 Do

---

l The denarius was a day's wage for a laborer　　*m* Greek *twenty-five* or *thirty stadia*

---

blood (in the sacrament which the dying Son of Man instituted as the perpetual memorial of His death and as the vehicle of its blessing) *has eternal life* and shall be raised up by the Son of Man *at the last day* (54), for he shall be in abiding communion with Him who shares the life of the Father, Source and Creator of all life. (57)

At every word which Jesus speaks the sign grows more luminous and points to greater things than God gave to His people through *Moses* (31, 32, 49, 58; cf. 1:17). Inevitably the sign becomes "a sign that is spoken against" (Lk 2:34). The *Jews murmur* when the *son of Joseph* (41) lays claim to divine Sonship and descent from heaven (38-40); they *dispute among themselves* (52) when the grace of the Son of Man and the love of the Father confront them with the incredible gift of eternal life in the flesh and blood of the Son of Man, given "for us Christians to eat and to drink." Even *many of* the *disciples* find the words of Jesus a *hard saying* and *take offense* at them, drawing back and forsaking His fellowship (66) just when they encounter the "greater things" which Jesus had promised, just when they behold the full glory of the Son of Man. (Cf. 1:50-51)

But the sign has not been given and interpreted in vain; it is given in order that men "may believe that Jesus is the Christ, the Son of God, and that believing" they "may have life in his name" (20:30). In *Simon Peter* (68) and the *twelve* (67) there is born a faith that cannot lose its hold on Him who has *the words of eternal life,* even in the face of the diabolical attack which has made *Judas . . . one of the twelve* (71) its victim.

6:4 *The Passover . . . was at hand.* The memorial feast of the Exodus (Ex 12) recalls Moses, the first deliverer of Israel, and the gift of manna (cf. 6:31, 32, 49, 58). The theme announced in 1:17 is being developed.

6:14 *The prophet.* The promised prophet of Dt 18:15, 18-19 and the Messiah were closely associated in Judaic thinking, cf. 6:15 *(king)* and 7:40-41.

6:23 *Tiberias,* a city on the west shore of the Sea of Galilee, founded by Herod Antipas and named for the Roman emperor Tiberius. The Sea of Galilee came to be called after the city. (6:1)

6:27 *God the Father set his seal.* Cf. 3:33 note.

not labor for the food which perishes, but for the food which endures to eternal life, which the Son of man will give to you; for on him has God the Father set his seal." 28 Then they said to him, "What must we do, to be doing the works of God?" 29 Jesus answered them, "This is the work of God, that you believe in him whom he has sent." 30 So they said to him, "Then what sign do you do, that we may see, and believe you? What work do you perform? 31 Our fathers ate the manna in the wilderness; as it is written, 'He gave them bread from heaven to eat.' " 32 Jesus then said to them, "Truly, truly, I say to you, it was not Moses who gave you the bread from heaven; my Father gives you the true bread from heaven. 33 For the bread of God is that which comes down from heaven, and gives life to the world." 34 They said to him, "Lord, give us this bread always."

35 Jesus said to them, "I am the bread of life; he who comes to me shall not hunger, and he who believes in me shall never thirst. 36 But I said to you that you have seen me and yet do not believe. 37All that the Father gives me will come to me; and him who comes to me I will not cast out. 38 For I have come down from heaven, not to do my own will, but the will of him who sent me; 39 and this is the will of him who sent me, that I should lose nothing of all that he has given me, but raise it up at the last day. 40 For this is the will of my Father, that every one who sees the Son and believes in him should have eternal life; and I will raise him up at the last day."

41 The Jews then murmured at him, because he said, "I am the bread which came down from heaven." 42 They said, "Is not this Jesus, the son of Joseph, whose father and mother we know? How does he now say, 'I have come down from heaven'?" 43 Jesus answered them, "Do not murmur among yourselves. 44 No one can come to me unless the Father who sent me draws him; and I will raise him up at the last day. 45 It is written in the prophets, 'And they shall all be taught by God.' Every one who has heard and learned from the Father comes to me. 46 Not that any one has seen the Father except him who is from God; he has seen the Father. 47 Truly, truly, I say to you, he who believes has eternal life. 48 I am the bread of life. 49 Your fathers ate the manna in the wilderness, and they died. 50 This is the bread which comes down from heaven, that a man may eat of it and not die. 51 I am the living bread which came down from heaven; if any one eats of this bread, he will live for ever; and the bread which I shall give for the life of the world is my flesh."

52 The Jews then disputed among themselves, saying, "How can this man give us his flesh to eat?" 53 So Jesus said to them, "Truly, truly, I say to you, unless you eat the flesh of the Son of man and drink his blood, you have no life in you; 54 he who eats my flesh and drinks my blood has eternal life, and I will raise him up at the last day. 55 For my flesh is food indeed, and my blood is drink indeed. 56 He who eats my flesh and drinks my blood abides in me, and I in him. 57As the living Father sent me, and I live because of the Father, so he who eats me will live because of me. 58 This is the bread which came down from heaven, not such as the fathers ate and died; he who eats this bread will live for ever." 59 This he said in the synagogue, as he taught at Ca·per′na·um.

60 Many of his disciples, when they heard it, said, "This is a hard saying; who can listen to it?" 61 But Jesus, knowing in himself that his disciples murmured at it, said to them, "Do you take offense at this? 62 Then what if you were to see the Son of man ascending where he was before? 63 It is the spirit that gives life, the flesh is of no avail;

6:31 *He gave them bread from heaven.* Ps 105:40; cf. 78:24; Neh 9:15.

6:34 *Give us this bread always.* Cf. 4:15.

6:45 *Written in the prophets.* Cf. Jer 31:34; Is 54:13.

6:62 *What if you were to see the Son of man ascending where he was before?* Then they would have all the more reason to take offense, for the Son of Man will ascend to where He was before by going to the cross, to a criminal's death.

6:63 *Spirit . . . flesh . . . words.* When Jesus has ascended where He was before, He will bestow the Spirit on those who believe in Him (7:39). The Spirit will lead those who believe into all truth (16:13); He will enable the believer to apprehend that the *flesh* of Jesus, which in itself is of *no more avail* than any human flesh, is the sacrifice of the Lamb of God, given for the life of the world (6:51). The Spirit will recall and confirm in the believer the *words* of Jesus which gave His flesh

the words that I have spoken to you are spirit and life. [64] But there are some of you that do not believe." For Jesus knew from the first who those were that did not believe, and who it was that would betray him. [65]And he said, "This is why I told you that no one can come to me unless it is granted him by the Father."

[66] After this many of his disciples drew back and no longer went about with him. [67]Jesus said to the twelve, "Do you also wish to go away?" [68]Simon Peter answered him, "Lord, to whom shall we go? You have the words of eternal life; [69] and we have believed, and have come to know, that you are the Holy One of God." [70] Jesus answered them, "Did I not choose you, the twelve, and one of you is a devil?" [71] He spoke of Judas the son of Simon Is·car′i·ot, for he,one of the twelve, was to betray him.

JESUS AND JERUSALEM (7:1 – 11:54)

7 After this Jesus went about in Galilee; he would not go about in Judea, because the Jews[n] sought to kill him. [2] Now the Jews' feast of Tabernacles was at hand. [3] So his brothers said to him, "Leave here and go to Judea, that your disciples may see the works you are doing. [4] For no man works in secret if he seeks to be known openly. If you do these things, show yourself to the world." [5] For even his brothers did not believe in him. [6] Jesus said to them, "My time has not yet come, but your time is always here. [7] The world cannot hate you, but it hates me because I testify of it that its works are evil. [8] Go to the feast yourselves; I am not[o] going up to this feast, for my time has not yet fully come." [9] So saying, he remained in Galilee.

[10] But after his brothers had gone up to the feast, then he also went up, not publicly but in private. [11] The Jews were looking for him at the feast, and saying, "Where is he?" [12]And there was much muttering about him among the people. While some said, "He is a good man," others said, "No, he is leading the people astray." [13] Yet for fear of the Jews no one spoke openly of him.

[n] Or Judeans
[o] Other ancient authorities add yet

this significance and power (14:26); thus the Spirit will give life.

6:64 Some...that do not believe. For such neither the witness of the Spirit nor the words of Jesus have any force.

6:69 The Holy One of God. The use of this term indicates that Peter is confessing more than the term "Christ" (or "Messiah") commonly connoted. In his confession in Mt 16:16 this "more" is expressed in the words "the Son of the living God." Peter is confessing the deity of his Lord.

6:70 One of you is a devil. As one "inspired" by the devil (13:2, 27), Judas has become so much a part of the diabolical attack on Jesus (cf. 14:30) as to be identified with him.

7:1 – 11:54 The Word has been rejected in Galilee (ch. 6). Jesus goes from Galilee to Judea in order that the Word may be spoken to the full and for the last time (7:6, 8) to Jerusalem, the heart and center of Israel. The Word of grace and truth is offered to Israel in the person of Him who makes man's body whole (7:23), who promises rivers of living waters (the Spirit) to a parched land, who is the Light of the world (8:12) and brings man freedom from sin and death (8:32, 51), who opens blind eyes (ch. 9) and goes into death as the Good Shepherd who lays down His life for the sheep (10:11, 14), who is the Resurrection and the Life (11:25). The Word is spoken in that Jesus shows His people the "many good works from the Father" (10:32) which declare God's love for the

world. It is man's obduracy, not God's intent, that makes these days of bitter and fierce contention; Jerusalem represents the mankind which loved darkness rather than light (cf. 3:19) when the men of Jerusalem impulsively take up stones (8:59; 10:31) and at last deliberately resolve (11:47, 57) to destroy Him who is the Light of mankind.

7:1-13 JESUS GOES TO JERUSALEM:
    JESUS AND HIS BROTHERS

7:1-13 Jesus' manner of removing from Galilee to Jerusalem illustrates the cleavage between Jesus and His people. His unbelieving (5) brothers cannot understand a Brother who is so wholly one with God that His time is completely in His Father's hands (6, 8) and His whole life is a walking indictment of the world's evil works (7). He goes at God's time (10) and in private (10), the quiet way of the Servant and obedient Son, to confront a people as yet wavering and uncertain about Him (12), although within the circles of official Judaism (the Jews, 13) the decision has been made against Him. (Cf. 7:25, 32, 44-52)

7:2 Feast of Tabernacles, the third of three great annual festivals of Israel, in October, celebrated by constructing booths (tabernacles) of fruit and palm trees to commemorate the years of wandering when Israel dwelt in tents. (Lv 23:40-42)

7:6, 8 My time. The time is that of His "glorification" by dying (12:23-24) for the sins of the world. (11:50-52)

14 About the middle of the feast Jesus went up into the temple and taught. 15 The Jews marveled at it, saying, "How is it that this man has learning,^{p} when he has never studied?" 16 So Jesus answered them, "My teaching is not mine, but his who sent me; 17 if any man's will is to do his will, he shall know whether the teaching is from God or whether I am speaking on my own authority. 18 He who speaks on his own authority seeks his own glory; but he who seeks the glory of him who sent him is true, and in him there is no falsehood. 19 Did not Moses give you the law? Yet none of you keeps the law. Why do you seek to kill me?" 20 The people answered, "You have a demon! Who is seeking to kill you?" 21 Jesus answered them, "I did one deed, and you all marvel at it. 22 Moses gave you circumcision (not that it is from Moses, but from the fathers), and you circumcise a man upon the sabbath. 23 If on the sabbath a man receives circumcision, so that the law of Moses may not be broken, are you angry with me because on the sabbath I made a man's whole body well? 24 Do not judge by appearances, but judge with right judgment."

25 Some of the people of Jerusalem therefore said, "Is not this the man whom they seek to kill? 26And here he is, speaking openly, and they say nothing to him! Can it be that the authorities really know that this is the Christ? 27 Yet we know where this man comes from; and when the Christ appears, no one will know where he comes from." 28 So Jesus proclaimed, as he taught in the temple, "You know me, and you know where I come from? But I have not come of my own accord; he who sent me is true, and him you do not know. 29 I know him, for I come from him, and he sent me." 30 So they sought to arrest him; but no one laid hands on him, because his hour had not yet come. 31 Yet many of the people believed in him; they said, "When the Christ appears, will he do more signs than this man has done?"

32 The Pharisees heard the crowd thus muttering about him, and the chief priests and Pharisees sent officers to arrest him. 33 Jesus then said, "I shall be with you a little longer, and then I go to him who sent me; 34 you will seek me and you will not find me; where I am you cannot come." 35 The Jews said to one another, "Where does this man intend to go that we shall not find him? Does he intend to go to the Dispersion among the Greeks and teach the Greeks? 36 What does he mean by saying, 'You will seek me and you will not find me,' and, 'Where I am you cannot come'?"

37 On the last day of the feast, the great day, Jesus stood up and proclaimed, "If any one thirst, let him come to me and drink. 38 He who believes in me, as^q the scripture has said, 'Out of his heart shall flow rivers of living water.' " 39 Now this he said about the Spirit, which those who believed in him were to receive; for as yet the Spirit had not been given, because Jesus was not yet glorified.

^{p} Or *this man knows his letters*　　^{q} Or *let him come to me, and let him who believes in me drink. As*

7:14 – 8:59 CONTROVERSY AT THE FEAST
OF TABERNACLES

7:14-52 Jesus forces a decision upon His wavering (12) people. He confronts them with His *teaching* (16): they cannot call it the teaching of a good man (cf. 12), a learned rabbi versed in inherited rabbinical lore, to be *marveled at* (15). His teaching is a divine Word, to be known and recognized as such in obedience to the *will* of God (17), marked by its selfless candor as the Word of the obedient Son *who seeks the glory of him who sent him* (18). Men who have not obeyed the voice of God heard in the *law* given them by *Moses* are ill-prepared to hear God's voice in the teaching of the Son; inevitably, they must join the ranks of those who hate the Son because He testifies that their works are evil (7) and finally *seek to kill* Him. (19)

Jesus confronts them with His *deed* (21) of heal-

ing on the Sabbath (cf. ch. 5); that, too, is not something they may merely *marvel at* (21). It is the work of God (cf. 5:17), as much a doing of His will as a circumcision performed on the Sabbath *that the law of Moses may not be broken* (23). Those who *judge with right judgment* (24), a judgment that desires the will of God, are able to look beyond the *appearances* of illegality to the real character of the deed and call it good.

Jesus confronts them with His impending (25, 32) death. That death will not be a successful countermeasure taken by *chief priests and Pharisees* (32) against one who "is leading the people astray" (12). It will be the Son's free act of returning to His Father (33) that will remove Him forever from the pursuit of men (34). The Son's free act will bring the blessing of the *Spirit* on those who have *believed in Him* (39). In that free act of love the Son will be *glorified.* (39)

The result: *there was a division among the*

40 When they heard these words, some of the people said, "This is really the prophet." 41 Others said, "This is the Christ." But some said, "Is the Christ to come from Galilee? 42 Has not the scripture said that the Christ is descended from David, and comes from Bethlehem, the village where David was?" 43 So there was a division among the people over him. 44 Some of them wanted to arrest him, but no one laid hands on him.

45 The officers then went back to the chief priests and Pharisees, who said to them, "Why did you not bring him?" 46 The officers answered, "No man ever spoke like this man!" 47 The Pharisees answered them, "Are you led astray, you also? 48 Have any of the authorities or of the Pharisees believed in him? 49 But this crowd, who do not know the law, are accursed." 50 Nicodemus, who had gone to him before, and who was one of them, said to them, 51 "Does our law judge a man without first giving him a hearing and learning what he does?" 52 They replied, "Are you from Galilee too? Search and you will see that no prophet is to rise from Galilee."

8 53 They went each to his own house, 1 but Jesus went to the Mount of Olives. 2 Early in the morning he came again to the temple; all the people came to him, and he sat down and taught them. 3 The scribes and the Pharisees brought a woman who had been caught in adultery, and placing her in the midst 4 they said to him, "Teacher, this woman has been caught in the act of adultery. 5 Now in the law Moses commanded us to stone such. What do you say about her?" 6 This they said to test him, that they might have some charge to bring against him. Jesus bent down and wrote with his finger on the ground. 7 And as they continued to ask him, he stood up and said to them, "Let him who is without sin among you be the first to throw a stone at her." 8 And once more he bent down and wrote with his finger on the ground. 9 But when they heard it, they went away, one by one, beginning with the eldest, and Jesus was left alone with the woman standing before him. 10 Jesus looked up and said to her, "Woman, where are they? Has no one condemned you?" 11 She said, "No one, Lord." And Jesus said, "Neither do I condemn you; go, and do not sin again." *r*

12 Again Jesus spoke to them, saying, "I am the light of the world; he who follows me will not walk in darkness, but will have the light of life." 13 The Pharisees then

---

r The most ancient authorities omit 7.53-8.11; other authorities add the passage here or after 7.36 or after 21.25 or after Luke 21.38, with variations of text

---

people over him (43). The division runs deep; reactions are as various as the sneer of those who call Jesus possessed (20) or deliberately misunderstand His allusion to His death to be a reference to a proposed trip into the Dispersion, to *teach the Greeks* (35) or the passing inclination of others to suspect that the *authorities* are not, after all, serious in their opposition to *the Christ* (26) and to see in Jesus the promised *prophet* and the expected *Christ* (40, 41) — or the reaction of *many of the people* (31) in whom the dawning recognition of the Christ was not suppressed by their preconceptions concerning Him (27, 41-42), the *many who believed in him* (31). Even in the camp of the authorities who sought to kill Him (25) and *sent officers to arrest Him* (32) there is uncertainty and wavering. The *officers,* who returned overawed by Jesus' words (46), and *Nicodemus,* who ventured a timid objection to the illegality of their procedure (51) were shouted down (47-49; 52). But it is clear that the last word has not yet been said.

7:53 – 8:11 THE WOMAN TAKEN IN ADULTERY

7:53 – 8:11 The section is in all likelihood a later insertion into the text of the fourth gospel. Many

of the ancient manuscripts omit this section, and it is unknown to commentators of the Greek church down to the 11th century. Further doubt is thrown on this section as a part of the fourth gospel by the fact that other manuscripts insert it at Jn 7:36 or Jn 21:24, while still others insert it after Lk 21:38. Besides, the section differs from the fourth gospel in language and style. The story is probably true, a genuine part of the story of Jesus; but it can hardly be a part of the gospel which John wrote.

8:12-59 CONTROVERSY CONTINUED:
SON OF GOD AND SONS OF THE DEVIL

8:12-59 The controversy of ch. 7 is continued (*again,* 12). The time and place (*temple,* 20, 59) are the same. But Jesus' interlocutors are no longer "the people" (7:12, 20, 31, 40, 43) but official Judaism (*Pharisees,* 8:13; *the Jews,* 8:31, 48, 52). The center of dispute is the question of fatherhood: Whose Son am I? Whose sons are you? This question becomes the expressly stated point of dispute only in the third major section of the controversy (31-59); but the question is in the air from the beginning and determines Jesus' speech concern-

said to him, "You are bearing witness to yourself; your testimony is not true." [14] Jesus answered, "Even if I do bear witness to myself, my testimony is true, for I know whence I have come and whither I am going, but you do not know whence I come or whither I am going. [15] You judge according to the flesh, I judge no one. [16] Yet even if I do judge, my judgment is true, for it is not I alone that judge, but I and he[s] who sent me. [17] In your law it is written that the testimony of two men is true; [18] I bear witness to myself, and the Father who sent me bears witness to me." [19] They said to him therefore, "Where is your Father?" Jesus answered, "You know neither me nor my Father; if you knew me, you would know my Father also." [20] These words he spoke in the treasury, as he taught in the temple; but no one arrested him, because his hour had not yet come.

21 Again he said to them, "I go away, and you will seek me and die in your sin; where I am going, you cannot come." [22] Then said the Jews, "Will he kill himself, since he says, 'Where I am going, you cannot come'?" [23] He said to them, "You are from below, I am from above; you are of this world, I am not of this world. [24] I told you that you would die in your sins, for you will die in your sins unless you believe that I am he." [25] They said to him, "Who are you?" Jesus said to them, "Even what I have told you from the beginning.[t] [26] I have much to say about you and much to judge; but he who sent me is true, and I declare to the world what I have heard from him." [27] They did not understand that he spoke to them of the Father. [28] So Jesus said, "When you have lifted up the Son of man, then you will know that I am he, and that I do nothing on my own authority but speak thus as the Father taught me. [29]And he who sent me is with me; he has not left me alone, for I always do what is pleasing to him." [30]As he spoke thus, many believed in him.

31 Jesus then said to the Jews who had believed in him, "If you continue in my

[s] Other ancient authorities read *the Father*
[t] Or *Why do I talk to you at all?*

ing the validity of His witness to Himself, the first formal point of difference between Him and His interlocutors (12-20; note 14, 16, 18, 19), as it does His words concerning His death, the second point of dispute. (21-30; note 23; 26-27; 28, 29)

8:12-20 Jesus witnesses to Himself as *the light of the world* (13). To the *Pharisees'* objection that the unsupported witness of one man *is not true,* Jesus responds that His testimony is valid even on the terms of the Law, on which they take their stand (*your law,* 17; cf. Dt 19:15); the *Father* (from whom He comes and to whom He returns, whom He knows and the Pharisees do not, 14, 19) is the great Second Witness to Him (18). Their blindness toward the Son, born of their enmity toward Him (cf. 20b), blinds them to the Father too. (19)

8:12 *Light of the world.* Jesus is making a Messianic claim (Is 42:6; 49:6; 60:1-3; cf. Mt 5:14, where Jesus calls His disciples, who shall witness to Him, "the light of the world"). There may be an allusion here to the ceremonial of the Feast of Tabernacles (7:2), which included both libations of water (cf. 7:37-38) and a great illumination of the entire temple area.

8:15 *I judge* (i.e., condemn) *no one.* Cf. 3:17.

8:21-30 Jesus speaks of His death, allusively but unmistakably (*I go away,* 21; cf. 22). The leaders of Israel, wilfully blind to the fact that His death is the death of the Lamb of God, a sacrifice *pleasing* to God (29), can only answer with a sneer (22, *will he kill himself?*). They will die *in* their *sins,* the sin of unbelief (24; cf. 16:9). They cannot believe; trapped in their own world (*from below . . . of this world,* 23), they will not accept Jesus' testimony to

Himself (25, cf. 21). Too late, when they have *lifted up the Son of man* to the cross (and to glory), they will learn the truth (28), that He is God of God and Light of Light (*I am he,* 28), one with the Father and obedient to Him (28) in life and in death.

8:26 *Much to say . . . and much to judge.* The mission of the Son is to save the world, not to condemn it (3:17); yet, when God's saving intent collides with man's unbelief, judgment results. Jesus can therefore say of Himself, "I judge no one" (8:15), and with equal truth, "For judgment I came into this world." (9:39)

8:28 *I am he.* For Judaic ears, attuned to the OT, these words contain a claim to deity (cf. Is 43:10, 25). For a similar use of this absolute *I am* in this gospel cf. 8:58, 13:19; 18:5-8.

8:31-59 "As he spoke thus, many believed in him" (30). Jesus seeks to exploit this faith (however imperfect it may be and however transitory it may prove to be). He offers to *the Jews who had believed in him* (31) all that He can give to faith: His Word, the truth, the freedom of free sons of God—the full blessing of obedient discipleship (32). As He made His offer to them, He reveals more and more fully what His Sonship is: His full communion with the Father, which makes His Word God's Word (38), His free obedience to the One who sent Him (42), His valid witness to God as the free Son unmarred and unenslaved by sin (45-46), His unalloyed devotion to the Father's *honor* (49), His serene confidence that the Father will glorify Him who does not seek His own glory (50, 54)—until He blazes upon them in the glory

word, you are truly my disciples, 32 and you will know the truth, and the truth will make you free." 33 They answered him, "We are descendants of Abraham, and have never been in bondage to any one. How is it that you say, 'You will be made free'?"

34 Jesus answered them, "Truly, truly, I say to you, every one who commits sin is a slave to sin. 35 The slave does not continue in the house for ever; the son continues for ever. 36 So if the Son makes you free, you will be free indeed. 37 I know that you are descendants of Abraham; yet you seek to kill me, because my word finds no place in you. 38 I speak of what I have seen with my Father, and you do what you have heard from your father."

39 They answered him, "Abraham is our father." Jesus said to them, "If you were Abraham's children, you would do what Abraham did, 40 but now you seek to kill me, a man who has told you the truth which I heard from God; this is not what Abraham did. 41 You do what your father did." They said to him, "We were not born of fornication; we have one Father, even God." 42 Jesus said to them, "If God were your Father, you would love me, for I proceeded and came forth from God; I came not of my own accord, but he sent me. 43 Why do you not understand what I say? It is because you cannot bear to hear my word. 44 You are of your father the devil, and your will is to do your father's desires. He was a murderer from the beginning, and has nothing to do with the truth, because there is no truth in him. When he lies, he speaks according to his own nature, for he is a liar and the father of lies. 45 But, because I tell the truth, you do not believe me. 46 Which of you convicts me of sin? If I tell the truth, why do you not believe me? 47 He who is of God hears the words of God; the reason why you do not hear them is that you are not of God."

48 The Jews answered him, "Are we not right in saying that you are a Samaritan and have a demon?" 49 Jesus answered, "I have not a demon; but I honor my Father, and you dishonor me. 50 Yet I do not seek my own glory; there is One who seeks it and he will be the judge. 51 Truly, truly, I say to you, if any one keeps my word, he will never see death." 52 The Jews said to him, "Now we know that you have a demon. Abraham died, as did the prophets; and you say, 'If any one keeps my word, he will never taste death.' 53 Are you greater than our father Abraham, who died? And the prophets died! Who do you claim to be?" 54 Jesus answered, "If I glorify myself, my glory is nothing; it is my Father who glorifies me, of whom you say that he is your God. 55 But you have not known him; I know him. If I said, I do not know him, I

---

of eternal Godhead (*I am*, 58). As His self-attestation mounts, the opposition to Him mounts also, and His opponents reveal ever more clearly whose sons *they* are. They claim to be Abraham's free sons (descended from free-born Isaac and not from the slave woman's son, Ishmael), but their enslavement to sin gives the lie to their claim that they are free; and their actions belie their claim to kinship with believing and obedient Abraham— *he* never opposed a murderous will to God's truth (41). They have lost title also to the privilege of being sons of God, which the OT conferred upon them (e. g., Ex 4:22-23; Hos 11:1; Is 1:2; Ml 1:6), for they have not acted as sons of God. They do not love Him whom the Father loves (42). Not Abraham's sons, not God's sons—they have in fact become sons of the devil, committed to his will to destroy what is God's and to his primeval (cf. Gn 3) and unceasing denial of the truth (44). They cannot bear to hear the words of Him who speaks God's Word, and so they *seek to kill* (40) Him who has *told them the truth which* He *heard from God.* Whatever faith they may have had has melted away in the fires of this conflict; they who were ready to believe are now prepared to stone. (59)

8:32 *The truth will make you free.* The truth

which Jesus reveals—and is (1:17)—will make them free of the enslavement of sin (34), free for God, free to abide forever in the Father's house. (35)

8:33 *Have never been in bondage.* The Egyptian bondage, the Babylonian captivity, and the Roman domination are bondage, to be sure, but Israel has remained Israel through all that and has not become just another pagan people without God and without hope.

Descendants of Abraham. Jesus does not deny their descent from Abraham, but their real kinship with Abraham. (Cf. 39-40)

8:41 *We were not born of fornication.* The *we* is emphatic; perhaps a slur on Jesus' birth is intended; as the virgin's son, He is slandered as illegitimate.

8:44 *A murderer from the beginning.* Cf. Gn 3, where the Tempter's lie brought death into the world.

8:48 *Samaritan.* For the bitterness between Jews and Samaritans cf. 4:9. Just why the Jew should call Jesus a Samaritan is not clear. Perhaps the reason is that the Samaritans, too, cast doubt on the Jews' claim to be the true and only descendants of Abraham.

should be a liar like you; but I do know him and I keep his word. 56 Your father Abraham rejoiced that he was to see my day; he saw it and was glad." 57 The Jews then said to him, "You are not yet fifty years old, and have you seen Abraham?"*u* 58 Jesus said to them, "Truly, truly, I say to you, before Abraham was, I am." 59 So they took up stones to throw at him; but Jesus hid himself, and went out of the temple.

9 As he passed by, he saw a man blind from his birth. 2And his disciples asked him, "Rabbi, who sinned, this man or his parents, that he was born blind?" 3 Jesus answered, "It was not that this man sinned, or his parents, but that the works of God might be made manifest in him. 4 We must work the works of him who sent me, while it is day; night comes, when no one can work. 5As long as I am in the world, I am the light of the world." 6As he said this, he spat on the ground and made clay of the spittle and anointed the man's eyes with the clay, 7 saying to him, "Go, wash in the pool of Si·lo′am" (which means Sent). So he went and washed and came back seeing. 8 The neighbors and those who had seen him before as a beggar, said, "Is not this the man who used to sit and beg?" 9 Some said, "It is he"; others said, "No, but he is like him." He said, "I am the man." 10 They said to him, "Then how were your eyes opened?" 11 He answered, "The man called Jesus made clay and anointed my eyes and said to me, 'Go to Si·lo′am and wash'; so I went and washed and received my sight." 12 They said to him, "Where is he?" He said, "I do not know."

13 They brought to the Pharisees the man who had formerly been blind. 14 Now it was a sabbath day when Jesus made the clay and opened his eyes. 15 The Pharisees again asked him how he had received his sight. And he said to them, "He put clay on my eyes, and I washed, and I see." 16 Some of the Pharisees said, "This man is not from God, for he does not keep the sabbath." But others said, "How can a man who is a sinner do such signs?" There was a division among them. 17 So they again said to the blind man, "What do you say about him, since he has opened your eyes?" He said, "He is a prophet."

18 The Jews did not believe that he had been blind and had received his sight, until they called the parents of the man who had received his sight, 19 and asked them, "Is this your son, who you say was born blind? How then does he now see?" 20 His parents answered, "We know that this is our son, and that he was born blind; 21 but how he now sees we do not know, nor do we know who opened his eyes. Ask him; he is of age, he will speak for himself." 22 His parents said this because they feared the Jews, for the Jews had already agreed that if any one should confess him to be Christ, he was to be put out of the synagogue. 23 Therefore his parents said, "He is of age, ask him."

u Other ancient authorities read *has Abraham seen you?*

8:58 *Before Abraham was, I am.* For the force of *I am* cf. 8:28 note.

9:1-41 THE GIFT OF SIGHT AND THE JUDGMENT OF BLINDNESS

9:1-41 The Light of the world (5; cf. 8:12) shines in healing beneficence on man, giving sight (6-7) and creating faith (35-38; cf. 17). But men love darkness (3:19), and the most fervid lovers of darkness are the men who deem themselves already in the light, the Pharisees (13), *the disciples of Moses* (28), jealous guardians of God's sabbath (16) and God's honor (24), quick to judge and to *cast out* (16, 34), tyrannizing over the conscience of the comman man (22-23), indignant at the suggestion that the light they walk by may be darkness (40, *Are we also blind?*). And so He who proclaims Himself the *light of the world* (5) and is sent to do the gracious *works of* the *God* who loved this dark world (3:16) is compelled by man's unbelief to proclaim: *For judgment I came into this world, that those who do not see may see, and that*

those who see may become blind (39). Those who lack the light shall have it as the free gift of the Son of Man; those who refuse the light shall have the darkness which they have loved, as God's judgment on their unbelief; *your guilt remains.* (41)

9:1-4 Jesus imposes on His disciples the rule of "Judge not!" (cf. Mt 7:1); the God whom the Son makes known (1:18) is the God of grace and truth (1:17). It is *the works of him* that Jesus and His disciples must do while it is day, before the night of God's judgment descends. (*We* [Jesus and His disciples, as light of the world, cf. Mt 5:14] must work, 4.) The disciples of Moses in their blindness judge and condemn; the disciples of Jesus serve God, who loves the world.

9:7 *Siloam . . . Sent.* The name *Siloam* is derived from the Hebrew word meaning "to send." The *Sent* One is God's Son. He, not some power inherent in the waters of the pool, gives sight to the man born blind.

9:22 *Be put out of the synagogue,* i. e., be excommunicated from the fellowship of God's people.

24 So for the second time they called the man who had been blind, and said to him, "Give God the praise; we know that this man is a sinner." 25 He answered, "Whether he is a sinner, I do not know; one thing I know, that though I was blind, now I see." 26 They said to him, "What did he do to you? How did he open your eyes?" 27 He answered them, "I have told you already, and you would not listen. Why do you want to hear it again? Do you too want to become his disciples?" 28 And they reviled him, saying, "You are his disciple, but we are disciples of Moses. 29 We know that God has spoken to Moses, but as for this man, we do not know where he comes from." 30 The man answered, "Why, this is a marvel! You do not know where he comes from, and yet he opened my eyes. 31 We know that God does not listen to sinners, but if any one is a worshiper of God and does his will, God listens to him. 32 Never since the world began has it been heard that any one opened the eyes of a man born blind. 33 If this man were not from God, he could do nothing." 34 They answered him, "You were born in utter sin, and would you teach us?" And they cast him out.

35 Jesus heard that they had cast him out, and having found him he said, "Do you believe in the Son of man?" *v* 36 He answered, "And who is he, sir, that I may believe in him?" 37 Jesus said to him, "You have seen him, and it is he who speaks to you." 38 He said, "Lord, I believe"; and he worshiped him. 39 Jesus said, "For judgment I came into this world, that those who do not see may see, and that those who see may become blind." 40 Some of the Pharisees near him heard this, and they said to him, "Are we also blind?" 41 Jesus said to them, "If you were blind, you would have no guilt; but now that you say, 'We see,' your guilt remains.

10 "Truly, truly, I say to you, he who does not enter the sheepfold by the door but climbs in by another way, that man is a thief and a robber; 2 but he who enters by the door is the shepherd of the sheep. 3 To him the gatekeeper opens; the sheep hear his voice, and he calls his own sheep by name and leads them out. 4 When he has brought out all his own, he goes before them, and the sheep follow him, for they know his voice. 5 A stranger they will not follow, but they will flee from him, for they do not know the voice of strangers." 6 This figure Jesus used with them, but they did not understand what he was saying to them.

7 So Jesus again said to them, "Truly, truly, I say to you, I am the door of the sheep. 8 All who came before me are thieves and robbers; but the sheep did not heed them. 9 I am the door; if any one enters by me, he will be saved, and will go in and out and find pasture. 10 The thief comes only to steal and kill and destroy; I came that they may have life, and have it abundantly. 11 I am the good shepherd. The good

v Other ancient authorities read *the Son of God*

9:34 *You were born in utter sin.* The Pharisees judge; they interpret the man's blindness as a judgment of God on his parents. (Cf. 2)

9:41 *You say, 'We see.'* For the Pharisees' claim to vision, knowledge, and the consequent right and capacity to judge others cf. 16, 24, 28, 29, 34.

10:1-21 JESUS THE DOOR OF THE SHEEP
AND THE GOOD SHEPHERD

10:1-21 Jesus is still conversing with the Pharisees (cf. 9:40). Using the familiar picture of Israel as the flock of God (cf. e. g., Eze 34), He accuses the leaders of Israel of being *thieves and robbers* (8), men who by stealth or violence have despoiled and destroyed God's people (10; cf. Eze 34:1-6). Only through Him will Israel get true shepherds; He is the *door* of the sheepfold through whom the true shepherds, whom the sheep can recognize and trust (3-5), have access to the flock of God; through His guarding and fostering care Israel, no longer "the lost sheep of the house of Israel" (cf. Mt 9:36; 10:5), will be God's protected (*saved,* 9) and tended (*find pasture,* 9) flock. More than that: in Him

Israel will get a *shepherd* who deserves the name (11, 14), devoted unto death to His own; no selfish *hireling* (12, 13), He freely lays down His life that *they may have life, and have it abundantly* (10). This Shepherd-King who dies that the flock may live shall be great "to the ends of the earth" (Mi 5:4); such is the compulsion of His love (*must,* 16) that He will join men of all nations to His own in Israel and thus create *one flock,* one new Israel, under one *shepherd* (16), known and obeyed by His flock (14, 16), united with Him in a love like that which unites the Father and the Son (15, 17). — Again there is *division among the Jews* (19). *Again* the charge is made by *many* that *he has a demon* (20); *others* recognize that the charge rings hollow when leveled at one whose word and deed, far from being the expression of demonic hatred for the creation of God, breathes God's own love for God's misled and suffering people. (21)

10:3 *The gatekeeper,* the man who stands guard over the sheepfold at night.

10:6 *This figure Jesus used,* i. e., He spoke to them in this picture language.

shepherd lays down his life for the sheep. 12 He who is a hireling and not a shepherd, whose own the sheep are not, sees the wolf coming and leaves the sheep and flees; and the wolf snatches them and scatters them. 13 He flees because he is a hireling and cares nothing for the sheep. 14 I am the good shepherd; I know my own and my own know me, 15 as the Father knows me and I know the Father; and I lay down my life for the sheep. 16And I have other sheep, that are not of this fold; I must bring them also, and they will heed my voice. So there shall be one flock, one shepherd. 17 For this reason the Father loves me, because I lay down my life, that I may take it again. 18 No one takes it from me, but I lay it down of my own accord. I have power to lay it down, and I have power to take it again; this charge I have received from my Father."

19 There was again a division among the Jews because of these words. 20 Many of them said, "He has a demon, and he is mad; why listen to him?" 21 Others said, "These are not the sayings of one who has a demon. Can a demon open the eyes of the blind?"

22 It was the feast of the Dedication at Jerusalem; 23 it was winter, and Jesus was walking in the temple, in the portico of Solomon. 24 So the Jews gathered round him and said to him, "How long will you keep us in suspense? If you are the Christ, tell us plainly." 25 Jesus answered them, "I told you, and you do not believe. The works that I do in my Father's name, they bear witness to me; 26 but you do not believe, because you do not belong to my sheep. 27 My sheep hear my voice, and I know them, and they follow me; 28 and I give them eternal life, and they shall never perish, and no one shall snatch them out of my hand. 29 My Father, who has given them to me, w is greater than all, and no one is able to snatch them out of the Father's hand. 30 I and the Father are one."

31 The Jews took up stones again to stone him. 32 Jesus answered them, "I have shown you many good works from the Father; for which of these do you stone me?" 33 The Jews answered him, "It is not for a good work that we stone you but for blasphemy; because you, being a man, make yourself God." 34 Jesus answered them, "Is

w Other ancient authorities read *What my Father has given to me*

10:15 *Knows . . . know.* This knowing is the personal communion of love. (Cf. 17)

10:18 *Of my own accord . . . this charge I have received.* Such is Jesus' love for the Father who loves Him (15) that desire and duty do not conflict in Him; the Father's will and His desire are one.

10:22-42 "IF YOU ARE THE CHRIST, TELL US PLAINLY"

10:22-42 *The Jews,* whether out of uncertainty, as they profess (24), or from the desire to involve Jesus in conflict with Rome if He proclaims Himself the *Christ,* the King of the Jews (cf. 19:14-15), ask Jesus the Messianic question and demand an unambiguous answer (24). Jesus replies: *I told you* (25). His words in Jerusalem (cf. chs. 5, 7, 8) have blazoned forth the Christ; the *works which* He has done in the *Father's name . . . bear witness* to Him as the Healer of men (ch. 5), the Opener of blind eyes (ch. 9), the Christ in whom all God's promises find their Yes (cf. 2 Co 1:20). They do not lack evidence; they lack faith (25-26). They have not listened to the voice of the Good Shepherd and have not followed Him (cf. 27); their unbelief has shut them out from *eternal life,* from the sure protection of the Son's almighty *hand* (28), of God's own hand (29), for the Son and the Father *are one.* (30)

At this *"blasphemy"* (33), the *Jews* take up

stones again to stone him (31). Jesus points once more to the witness of His *many good works from the Father* (32) and meets the charge of blasphemy with an appeal to His opponents' own Sacred Scriptures (*your law,* 34), that inviolable revelation of the mind and will of God (35). He has not, He asserts, *made* Himself *God* in equating His hand with the hand of God (cf. 29-30). The Father has done that by consecrating Him and sending Him into the world as a *man* (33) among men (36). If the God whose voice they hear in their *law* can address as *gods* the men to whom *the word of God came* (35; Ps 82:6), where is the blasphemy when He who speaks God's Word and is God's Word calls Himself the *Son of God* (36)? His words are pure, and His works are the *works of* His *Father* (37). He cannot but repeat His "blasphemous" claim: *The Father is in me and I am in the Father* (38). The old claim arouses once more the old opposition: *Again they tried to arrest him.* (39)

Jesus *escaped from their hands* (39); His hour has not yet come. But He can no longer await that hour in Jerusalem; He goes *across the Jordan* and remains at the scene of John's baptizing (cf. 1:28). There the witness of John bears belated fruit: *Many believed in him there.* (42)

10:22 *Feast of the Dedication.* This feast, celebrated in October-November, celebrated the cleansing of the temple after it had been desecrated by Antiochus Epiphanes. (1 Mac 4:52-59)

it not written in your law, 'I said, you are gods'? 35 If he called them gods to whom the word of God came (and scripture cannot be broken), 36 do you say of him whom the Father consecrated and sent into the world, 'You are blaspheming,' because I said, 'I am the Son of God'? 37 If I am not doing the works of my Father, then do not believe me; 38 but if I do them, even though you do not believe me, believe the works, that you may know and understand that the Father is in me and I am in the Father." 39Again they tried to arrest him, but he escaped from their hands.

40 He went away again across the Jordan to the place where John at first baptized, and there he remained. 41And many came to him; and they said, "John did no sign, but everything that John said about this man was true." 42And many believed in him there.

11 Now a certain man was ill, Lazarus of Beth'a·ny, the village of Mary and her sister Martha. 2 It was Mary who anointed the Lord with ointment and wiped his feet with her hair, whose brother Lazarus was ill. 3 So the sisters sent to him, saying, "Lord, he whom you love is ill." 4 But when Jesus heard it he said, "This illness is not unto death; it is for the glory of God, so that the Son of God may be glorified by means of it."

5 Now Jesus loved Martha and her sister and Lazarus. 6 So when he heard that he was ill, he stayed two days longer in the place where he was. 7 Then after this he said

10:35 *Called them gods to whom the word of God came.* The words of Ps 82:6 are addressed to unjust judges who have abused the power entrusted to them by *the word of God* which authorized them. For the bearer of God's Word as "god" cf. Ex 4:16.

11:1-54 THE RAISING OF LAZARUS: JESUS THE RESURRECTION AND THE LIFE

11:1-54 The seventh sign recorded by John is the supreme sign. He who creatively gives wine to make glad the heart of man (ch. 2), who by His Word gives healing to the sick (chs. 4 – 5), who sets a table in the wilderness and comes to His own across the waters (ch. 6) in token of His will to dwell with man and bless him, who gives sight to the blind (ch. 9) – He now gives life to the dead in token of His will to be the resurrection and the life for man. (11:25-26)

The raising of Lazarus is marked out emphatically as a "sign," as the enacted Word of God which reveals God to man. Jesus is portrayed as solely and sovereignly in charge of the action; the Word of life speaks in this deed. In obedience to His Father's will *he* determines the time and manner of the resurrection of Lazarus. He delays the resurrection of His friend in a way that would appear arbitrary and harsh were it not for the evangelist's express assurance that His love is active in this arbitrary harshness (5); He stays away from Bethany when He is most needed there, *two days* beyond the critical time (6, cf. 21, 32). He goes to Bethany when His going is a going into certain death (8, 16), in the calm certitude which His obedient oneness with His Father gives Him; He knows that the working day of *twelve hours* which His Father has assigned Him (9-10; cf. 9:4) is not yet over. He restores to life a man who is *four days* dead, when corruption has set in (17, 39), when all human experience cries out, "Too late!"

when faith can be only faith in the God "who gives life to the dead and calls into existence the things that do not exist." (Ro 4:17)

The sign is acted doxology; it is done *for the glory of God* (4, cf. 40). In that glory the *Son of God* is *glorified;* He prays at the door of the tomb for the given gift, in order that men may know that the Father has sent Him (42) and may believe that in Him God is giving mankind the resurrection and the life, now, in the hour of His presence among men (25). The enacted Word that glorifies God is spoken to Jerusalem, to the city and the people for whose faith Jesus has been wrestling all this time (chs. 7 – 10); men of nearby Jerusalem are present to comfort the mourning sisters and hear the cry which speaks eternal life to all who will believe: *Lazarus, come out!* (43; cf. 19, 31)

The Word is being spoken in the flesh; this is the climax of the signs done by *Jesus* (20:30), the Man who loves (3, 5), who is *deeply moved in spirit and troubled* (33, 38), who weeps (35) and prays. (41)

The final sign creates faith in *many of the Jews* (45; cf. 12:11, 17-18); it also brings the opposition of the *chief priests and Pharisees* (47) to a head. Official Judaism fears a Messianic movement that will erupt in violence and bring down on them the intervening arm of Rome to put an end to the last remnants of Israel's national-political existence (48, 50). The *Pharisees* see clearly enough the end which they must pursue; they cannot let Jesus *go on thus* (48); Caiaphas sees the means to this end: it is *expedient* that Jesus *should die* (50). And so the intention of Israel's leaders to destroy Him, manifest before this, becomes their resolve to destroy Him (53). The decision is made; the actual trial before the council will be a formality, so much a mere formality that John does not even record it in his account of the Passion. (Cf. 18:12-27 note)

11:2 *Who anointed the Lord.* Cf. 12:3. Matthew and Mark also record the anointing (Mt 26:6-13;

to the disciples, "Let us go into Judea again." 8 The disciples said to him, "Rabbi, the Jews were but now seeking to stone you, and are you going there again?" 9 Jesus answered, "Are there not twelve hours in the day? If any one walks in the day, he does not stumble, because he sees the light of this world. 10 But if any one walks in the night, he stumbles, because the light is not in him." 11 Thus he spoke, and then he said to them, "Our friend Lazarus has fallen asleep, but I go to awake him out of sleep." 12 The disciples said to him, "Lord, if he has fallen asleep, he will recover." 13 Now Jesus had spoken of his death, but they thought that he meant taking rest in sleep. 14 Then Jesus told them plainly, "Lazarus is dead; 15 and for your sake I am glad that I was not there, so that you may believe. But let us go to him." 16 Thomas, called the Twin, said to his fellow disciples, "Let us also go, that we may die with him."

17 Now when Jesus came, he found that Lazarus[x] had already been in the tomb four days. 18 Beth'a·ny was near Jerusalem, about two miles[y] off, 19 and many of the Jews had come to Martha and Mary to console them concerning their brother. 20 When Martha heard that Jesus was coming, she went and met him, while Mary sat in the house. 21 Martha said to Jesus, "Lord, if you had been here, my brother would not have died. 22And even now I know that whatever you ask from God, God will give you." 23 Jesus said to her, "Your brother will rise again." 24 Martha said to him, "I know that he will rise again in the resurrection at the last day." 25 Jesus said to her, "I am the resurrection and the life;[z] he who believes in me, though he die, yet shall he live, 26 and whoever lives and believes in me shall never die. Do you believe this?" 27 She said to him, "Yes, Lord; I believe that you are the Christ, the Son of God, he who is coming into the world."

28 When she had said this, she went and called her sister Mary, saying quietly, "The Teacher is here and is calling for you." 29And when she heard it, she rose quickly and went to him. 30 Now Jesus had not yet come to the village, but was still in the place where Martha had met him. 31 When the Jews who were with her in the house, consoling her, saw Mary rise quickly and go out, they followed her, supposing that she was going to the tomb to weep there. 32 Then Mary, when she came where Jesus was and saw him, fell at his feet, saying to him, "Lord, if you had been here, my brother would not have died." 33 When Jesus saw her weeping, and the Jews who came with her also weeping, he was deeply moved in spirit and troubled; 34 and he said, "Where have you laid him?" They said to him, "Lord, come and see." 35 Jesus wept. 36 So the Jews said, "See how he loved him!" 37 But some of them said, "Could not he who opened the eyes of the blind man have kept this man from dying?"

38 Then Jesus, deeply moved again, came to the tomb; it was a cave, and a stone lay upon it. 39 Jesus said, "Take away the stone." Martha, the sister of the dead man, said to him, "Lord, by this time there will be an odor, for he has been dead four days." 40 Jesus said to her, "Did I not tell you that if you would believe you would see the glory of God?" 41 So they took away the stone. And Jesus lifted up his eyes and said, "Father, I thank thee that thou hast heard me. 42 I knew that thou hearest me always, but I have said this on account of the people standing by, that they may believe that thou didst send me." 43 When he had said this, he cried with a loud voice, "Lazarus, come out." 44 The dead man came out, his hands and feet bound with bandages, and his face wrapped with a cloth. Jesus said to them, "Unbind him, and let him go."

45 Many of the Jews therefore, who had come with Mary and had seen what he did, believed in him; 46 but some of them went to the Pharisees and told them what Jesus had done. 47 So the chief priests and the Pharisees gathered the council, and said, "What are we to do? For this man performs many signs. 48 If we let him go on

[x] Greek he   [y] Greek fifteen stadia   [z] Other ancient authorities omit and the life

Mk 14:3-9); only John identifies the woman as Mary.
11:8 Seeking to stone you. Cf. 8:59; 10:31.
11:16 Twin is the translation of the Aramaic word Thomas.
11:17 Four days. Cf. 39.
11:22 Cf. 41.

11:25 I am the resurrection. With the coming of Him in whom is the life that is the light of men (1:3) the resurrection is no longer merely a far-off event at the last day (24); it is a presently effective reality. He who believes in Him "HAS eternal life; he . . . HAS PASSED from death to life." (5:24)
11:48 Holy place, the temple.

thus, every one will believe in him, and the Romans will come and destroy both our holy place[a] and our nation." [49] But one of them, Ca'ia·phas, who was high priest that year, said to them, "You know nothing at all; [50] you do not understand that it is expedient for you that one man should die for the people, and that the whole nation should not perish." [51] He did not say this of his own accord, but being high priest that year he prophesied that Jesus should die for the nation, [52] and not for the nation only, but to gather into one the children of God who are scattered abroad. [53] So from that day on they took counsel how to put him to death.

[54] Jesus therefore no longer went about openly among the Jews, but went from there to the country near the wilderness, to a town called E'phra·im; and there he stayed with the disciples.

THE RESULT OF JESUS' MINISTRY (11:55 — 12:50)

[55] Now the Passover of the Jews was at hand, and many went up from the country to Jerusalem before the Passover, to purify themselves. [56] They were looking for Jesus and saying to one another as they stood in the temple, "What do you think? That he will not come to the feast?" [57] Now the chief priests and the Pharisees had given orders that if any one knew where he was, he should let them know, so that they might arrest him.

12 Six days before the Passover, Jesus came to Beth'a·ny, where Lazarus was, whom Jesus had raised from the dead. [2] There they made him a supper; Martha served, and Lazarus was one of those at table with him. [3] Mary took a pound of costly ointment of pure nard and anointed the feet of Jesus and wiped his feet with her hair; and the house was filled with the fragrance of the ointment. [4] But Judas Is·car'i·ot, one of his disciples (he who was to betray him), said, [5] "Why was this ointment not sold for three hundred denarii[b] and given to the poor?" [6] This he said, not that he cared for the poor but because he was a thief, and as he had the money box he used to take what was put into it. [7] Jesus said, "Let her alone, let her keep it for the day of my burial. [8] The poor you always have with you, but you do not always have me."

[9] When the great crowd of the Jews learned that he was there, they came, not only on account of Jesus but also to see Lazarus, whom he had raised from the dead. [10] So the chief priests planned to put Lazarus also to death, [11] because on account of him many of the Jews were going away and believing in Jesus.

[a] Greek *our place*   [b] The denarius was a day's wage for a laborer

---

11:51 *But being high priest that year he prophesied.* Under Roman rule the high priesthood had ceased to be a lifelong office. Caiaphas, *high priest that year,* the year in which Jesus concluded His ministry, is compelled by God to utter more than he intends or knows. Like Balaam of old, he must speak what God puts in his mouth. (Nm 23:12)

11:54 *Ephraim,* a small town NE. of Jerusalem; its precise location is not known.

11:55 — 12:50 The sign of the resurrection of Lazarus has made Jesus a man of note, sought after by the Passover pilgrims in Jerusalem (11:55-57); Mary's anointing of Him is a token of the devotion He has inspired in His own (12:1-8); a crowd hails the *King of Israel* at His entry into Jerusalem (12:9-19); Greek proselytes present at the Passover seek Him out (12:20-22); even among the authorities there are many who believe in Him, though they cannot find the courage to confess Him (12:42-43). But to Israel as a whole the Word has been spoken in vain: Judas, one of the Twelve, will betray Him (12:4-6); the chief priests and Pharisees, the most influential group in Israel,

are hardened against Him (11:57; 12:19, 42). Jesus knows that His Passion impends. *The hour has come for the Son of man to be glorified* (23). The seed must fall into the ground and die before it can bear much fruit — life for the world is won by dying (12:23-26). The agony of Gethsemane is already in the air as the Son, to glorify His Father's name, prepares to do battle with the *ruler of this world,* to overcome him by the cross (*I am lifted up from the earth,* 32), and so to draw all men to Himself (27-34). The Light of the world has but a little while to shine (12:35-36); the Word of God, spoken by the Son to save mankind, will on the Last Day judge those who have rejected it in unbelief. (12:44-50)

11:55 *To purify themselves.* An Israelite had to be ritually clean to participate in the Passover (Nm 9:1-14). One who had become unclean had to undergo a purifying ceremony. (Nm 19:11-13; cf. 18:28)

12:11 *Were going away,* i. e., deserting the Jewish faith. For *going away* as a term for abandoning a religious allegiance cf. 6:67.

12 The next day a great crowd who had come to the feast heard that Jesus was coming to Jerusalem. [13] So they took branches of palm trees and went out to meet him, crying, "Hosanna! Blessed is he who comes in the name of the Lord, even the King of Israel!" [14]And Jesus found a young ass and sat upon it; as it is written,

[15]   "Fear not, daughter of Zion;
         behold, your king is coming,
         sitting on an ass's colt!"

[16] His disciples did not understand this at first; but when Jesus was glorified, then they remembered that this had been written of him and had been done to him. [17] The crowd that had been with him when he called Lazarus out of the tomb and raised him from the dead bore witness. [18] The reason why the crowd went to meet him was that they heard he had done this sign. [19] The Pharisees then said to one another, "You see that you can do nothing; look, the world has gone after him."

20 Now among those who went up to worship at the feast were some Greeks. [21] So these came to Philip, who was from Beth-sa′i·da in Galilee, and said to him, "Sir, we wish to see Jesus." [22] Philip went and told Andrew; Andrew went with Philip and they told Jesus. [23]And Jesus answered them, "The hour has come for the Son of man to be glorified. [24] Truly, truly, I say to you, unless a grain of wheat falls into the earth and dies, it remains alone; but if it dies, it bears much fruit. [25] He who loves his life loses it, and he who hates his life in this world will keep it for eternal life. [26] If any one serves me, he must follow me; and where I am, there shall my servant be also; if any one serves me, the Father will honor him.

27 "Now is my soul troubled. And what shall I say? 'Father, save me from this hour'? No, for this purpose I have come to this hour. [28] Father, glorify thy name." Then a voice came from heaven, "I have glorified it, and I will glorify it again." [29] The crowd standing by heard it and said that it had thundered. Others said, "An angel has spoken to him." [30] Jesus answered, "This voice has come for your sake, not for mine. [31] Now is the judgment of this world, now shall the ruler of this world be cast out; [32] and I, when I am lifted up from the earth, will draw all men to myself." [33] He said this to show by what death he was to die. [34] The crowd answered him, "We have heard from the law that the Christ remains for ever. How can you say that the Son of man must be lifted up? Who is this Son of man?" [35] Jesus said to them, "The light is with you for a little longer. Walk while you have the light, lest the darkness overtake you; he who walks in the darkness does not know where he goes. [36] While you have the light, believe in the light, that you may become sons of light."

When Jesus had said this, he departed and hid himself from them. [37] Though he had done so many signs before them, yet they did not believe in him; [38] it was that

---

12:13 *Hosanna.* Cf. Mt 21:9 note.

12:15 Cf. Mt 21:5 note.

12:20-22 *Philip . . . Andrew.* Both these disciples have Greek names and were probably more familiar than the other disciples with the Greek language and Greek-speaking people of Palestine, such as these *Greeks* probably were.

12:25-26 The way Jesus goes, through death to glory, is to be the way of His disciples too, the way of those who *follow* and serve Him.

12:27 *Now is my soul troubled.* Cf. Jesus' words in Gethsemane, Mt 26:38; Mk 14:34; Lk 22:44.

12:28 *I have glorified it, and I will glorify it again.* God has glorified His name, His revealed self, through the words and deeds of the Son whom He sent into the world (cf. 11:4, 40); He will glorify it again in the death and resurrection of the Son whom He has given to be the Lamb of God, the sacrifice for the sins of the world. (1:29; cf. 13:31-32; 17:1)

12:29 *An angel has spoken to him.* Cf. Acts 23:9.

12:31 *Now is the judgment of this world, now*

shall the ruler of this world be cast out. The ruler of this world is the devil, the evil one (14:30; 16:19; cf. 1 Jn 5:19). *Now* in the hour of Jesus' crucifixion (cf. 32-33), it is apparently Jesus who is being judged; but in reality the *world* which hates (3:20; 7:7; 15:18, 23, 24) and seeks to destroy the Son is coming under *judgment.* The world hates and seeks to destroy Him under the leadership and inspiration of the ruler of this world; when he comes to assail Jesus, he finds in Him a human love for God and obedience to God which is proof against His temptation (14:30-31). The Accuser therefore loses his place as the Accuser of mankind when the Son of Man whose love embraces all mankind overcomes him (cf. Rv 12:10); the love and obedience of the Son convict the murderous lord of lies (8:44); HE is judged (16:11), and those who have willed to be ruled by him are judged with him. (16:33; cf. Mt 25:41)

12:33 *By what death he was to die,* that is, crucifixion; for this sense of "lifted up" cf. 8:28.

12:38 *The word spoken by the prophet Isaiah*

the word spoken by the prophet I·sa'iah might be fulfilled:
> "Lord, who has believed our report,
> and to whom has the arm of the Lord been revealed?"

39 Therefore they could not believe.
For I·sa'iah again said,

40
> "He has blinded their eyes and hardened their heart,
> lest they should see with their eyes and perceive with their heart,
> and turn for me to heal them."

41 I·sa'iah said this because he saw his glory and spoke of him. 42 Nevertheless many even of the authorities believed in him, but for fear of the Pharisees they did not confess it, lest they should be put out of the synagogue: 43 for they loved the praise of men more than the praise of God.

44 And Jesus cried out and said, "He who believes in me, believes not in me but in him who sent me. 45And he who sees me sees him who sent me. 46 I have come as light into the world, that whoever believes in me may not remain in darkness. 47 If any one hears my sayings and does not keep them, I do not judge him; for I did not come to judge the world but to save the world. 48 He who rejects me and does not receive my sayings has a judge; the word that I have spoken will be his judge on the last day. 49 For I have not spoken on my own authority; the Father who sent me has himself given me commandment what to say and what to speak. 50And I know that his commandment is eternal life. What I say, therefore, I say as the Father has bidden me."

The Word Is Received by the Disciples

13:1 – 17:26

FAREWELL MEAL, FOOTWASHING, THE BETRAYER (13:1-30)

13 Now before the feast of the Passover, when Jesus knew that his hour had come to depart out of this world to the Father, having loved his own who were in the world, he loved them to the end. 2And during supper, when the devil had already put it into the heart of Judas Is·car'i·ot, Simon's son, to betray him, 3 Jesus, knowing that the Father had given all things into his hands, and that he had come from God and was going to God, 4 rose from supper, laid aside his garments, and girded himself with a towel. 5 Then he poured water into a basin, and began to wash the

concerning the Suffering Servant of God who goes through suffering, degradation, and death to exaltation and glory (Is 52:13 – 53:12), bearing the sins of many, was an incredible word for the prophet's contemporaries (Is 53:1). When the Word became flesh and appeared among men in a servant's form, Isaiah's prophecy concerning the Suffering Servant was *fulfilled;* fulfilled, too, was the prophetic word which pictured His people's unbelief and their rejection of the Servant.

12:39-40 The fearful judgment of obduration once pronounced on God's people by *Isaiah* (Is 6:10) is repeated in the history of Jesus; here too God's judgment locks men up in their unbelief. They would not believe; they are condemned to become men who *could not believe.*

12:43 *Loved the praise of men more than the praise of God.* Cf. 5:44.

13:1 – 17:26 "To all who received him, who believed in his name, he gave power to become children of God" (1:12). The record of Jesus' last meal with His disciples and of His last words to His disciples is the record of His giving, ministering love: *He loved them to the end* (13:1). He enacts His ministering love for His disciples in the

footwashing. By identifying the betrayer, He shows them the way His ministering love must go, the way of the cross. Thus He imposes on them His commandment of love (13:2-38). He prepares His disciples for the time when they shall be separated from His bodily presence, by revealing to them what they will gain by His departure: He promises that the Father will send them the Spirit. The Spirit shall be their Counselor in their conflict with the world, lead them into all the truth, and complete the presence of the Christ among them (chs. 14 – 16). Even when Jesus is praying for His own glorification (17:1-6), His disciples are remembered (17:2b-3), and the bulk of His prayer is intercession for His disciples (17:7-19), for those who shall come to faith through their Word (17:20-23), for all who are His by the Father's giving. (17:24-26)

13:1-30 The first paragraph (1-11), which portrays the act of footwashing, begins and ends with words that connect this act of Jesus with His Passion (*his hour had come,* 1; *he knew who was to betray him,* 11). This menial act is the act of Him who "came . . . to serve, and to give his life as a ransom for many" (Mt 20:28). In His inter-

disciples' feet, and to wipe them with the towel with which he was girded. 6 He came to Simon Peter; and Peter said to him, "Lord, do you wash my feet?" 7 Jesus answered him, "What I am doing you do not know now, but afterward you will understand." 8 Peter said to him, "You shall never wash my feet." Jesus answered him, "If I do not wash you, you have no part in me." 9 Simon Peter said to him, "Lord, not my feet only but also my hands and my head!" 10 Jesus said to him, "He who has bathed does not need to wash, except for his feet,*c* but he is clean all over; and you *x* are clean, but not every one of you." 11 For he knew who was to betray him; that was why he said, "You are not all clean."

12 When he had washed their feet, and taken his garments, and resumed his place, he said to them, "Do you know what I have done to you? 13 You call me Teacher and Lord; and you are right, for so I am. 14 If I then, your Lord and Teacher, have washed your feet, you also ought to wash one another's feet. 15 For I have given you an example, that you also should do as I have done to you. 16 Truly, truly, I say to you, a servant*d* is not greater than his master; nor is he who is sent greater than he who sent him. 17 If you know these things, blessed are you if you do them. 18 I am not speaking of you all; I know whom I have chosen; it is that the scripture may be fulfilled, 'He who ate my bread has lifted his heel against me.' 19 I tell you this now, before it takes place, that when it does take place you may believe that I am he. 20 Truly, truly, I say to you, he who receives any one whom I send receives me; and he who receives me receives him who sent me."

21 When Jesus had thus spoken, he was troubled in spirit, and testified, "Truly, truly, I say to you, one of you will betray me." 22 The disciples looked at one another, uncertain of whom he spoke. 23 One of his disciples, whom Jesus loved, was lying close to the breast of Jesus; 24 so Simon Peter beckoned to him and said, "Tell us who it is of whom he speaks." 25 So lying thus, close to the breast of Jesus, he said to him, "Lord, who is it?" 26 Jesus answered, "It is he to whom I shall give this morsel when I have dipped it." So when he had dipped the morsel, he gave it to Judas, the son of Simon Is·car'i·ot. 27 Then after the morsel, Satan entered into him. Jesus said to him, "What you are going to do, do quickly." 28 Now no one at the table knew why he said

c Other ancient authorities omit *except for his feet*   *d* Or *slave*   *x* The Greek word for *you* here is plural

pretation of the act (12-20) Jesus makes plain how His free gift of Himself (*part in me*, 8) commits His disciples to a life like that of their *Teacher and Lord* (13-14). They can find blessedness in Him (17), believe in Him, their ministering Lord who squanders His service on His betrayer (18-19), and can be credible and valid messengers of Him (20), only in following His example by washing one another's feet. (14-15)

Jesus is *troubled in spirit* (21) at the harsh reality of His Passion, now present in the person of His betrayer. He identifies His betrayer with a word from the Psalter (26; Ps 41:9) and an action (the giving of the morsel dipped in the common bowl, 26) which lay bare the full horror of the betrayer's sin and hint (at the least) that the Betrayed retains unshaken that trust in God of which the psalmist spoke: "By this I know that thou art pleased with me, in that my enemy has not triumphed over me. But thou hast upheld me because of my integrity, and set me in thy presence for ever." (Ps 41:11-12)

13:7 *Afterward you will understand:* "After you have failed Me and denied Me and My forgiving love has restored you, you will realize how completely you are dependent on My Servant ministry to you." (Cf. 21:15-19)

13:10 *He who has bathed does not need to wash,*

except for his feet. The forgiven man (*he who has bathed*) can be wholly and forever sure of God's forgiveness; "The Lamb of God TAKES AWAY the sin of the world" (1:29); but in their life with one another the disciples are in danger of forfeiting the divine forgiveness by failing to forgive as they have been forgiven—hence the need for repeated footwashing as a mutual ministry. (14; cf. Mt 18: 21-35)

13:16 *He who is sent.* The Greek word is the same as the word for "apostle." Jesus puts the disciples in mind of their future ministry. (Cf. 20:21)

13:19 *I am he.* For the connotation of deity in this phrase cf. 8:28 note. The fact that Jesus will be betrayed need not shake the disciples' faith in Him as divine; the fact that He foreknows and foretells the betrayal reveals that He goes into death freely; death is His sovereign act, not a fate to which He helplessly submits. (Cf. 10:17-18)

13:23 *One of his disciples, whom Jesus loved.* This is in all probability John, the son of Zebedee, to whom tradition assigns the authorship of the fourth gospel. The beloved disciple appears again in 19:26; 20:2, 3, 4, 8; 21:7, 20-23; in two other passages an unnamed disciple figures, and he is probably to be identified with the beloved disciple. (1:40; 18:15-16)

13:27 *Satan entered into him.* The expression

this to him. [29] Some thought that, because Judas had the money box, Jesus was telling him, "Buy what we need for the feast"; or, that he should give something to the poor. [30] So, after receiving the morsel, he immediately went out; and it was night.

JESUS' LAST WORDS TO HIS DISCIPLES, I (13:31 — 14:31)

31 When he had gone out, Jesus said, "Now is the Son of man glorified, and in him God is glorified; [32] if God is glorified in him, God will also glorify him in himself, and glorify him at once. [33] Little children, yet a little while I am with you. You will seek me; and as I said to the Jews so now I say to you, 'Where I am going you cannot come.' [34]A new commandment I give to you, that you love one another; even as I have loved you, that you also love one another. [35] By this all men will know that you are my disciples, if you have love for one another."

here is stronger than that of 13:2 ("the devil ... put it into the heart of Judas"); Judas has become completely the instrument of Satan, the murderer from the beginning. (Cf. 8:44)

13:29 *That he should give something to the poor.* Judas was treasurer and almoner for Jesus and the Twelve. (Cf. 12:6)

13:30 *It was night.* The literal fact has symbolic significance; Judas has shut himself out from the Light of the world, and the daylight hours in which Jesus does the works of the Father who sent Him are over. (Cf. 11:9; 12:46)

13:31 — 14:31 John records two farewell discourses of Jesus; the first (13:31 — 14:31) is delivered in the room in which the supper was eaten, the second (chs. 15 — 16) at an unspecified place. In 13:31 — 14:31 Jesus is bracing His disciples for the shock of His departure and strengthening them for their life and work as His disciples and witnesses after His departure.

This first discourse begins and ends on a note of assured victory. Judas has departed to "do quickly" (at Jesus' behest!) what Satan has impelled him to do (13:27-30). *Now,* Jesus says, ... *God is glorified* (13:31); *now,* in the Passion of the *Son of man,* God is reaching the goal of all His ways; the glory that He will not give to another shall be His, manifestly and forever. God is glorified; and the *ruler of this world* is defeated; He is *coming* to fight a battle that he has already lost; *he has no power over* the Son who loves and obeys even unto death (14:30-31). The reality and seriousness of Jesus' suffering is not forgotten or evaded; Jesus knows that He goes a way which He must go bitterly alone (13:33); not even the intensest devotion will enable Peter, or any man, to go with Him into the depths (13:36-38). Out of the strength of His own assurance of victory Jesus is able to strengthen His disciples. His death is not the end of all that He has meant for them but the beginning of all that He can mean for them. He gives them a vision of the final fullness of the grace upon grace (1:16) which they shall receive from Him; He will return and take them to Himself, to their place in the Father's house, which He has Himself prepared for them (14:2-3; cf. 14: 18-19, 28). They shall live, in the full sense of "living," as the Son lives, possessed of life from the Father (14:28; cf. 5:26), a life victorious over death.

Meanwhile, they shall not be left desolate; their life is not to be only a life of hope. They know their final home, and they know the *way* there, for they know Him by faith who is *the way, and the truth, and the life* (14:6). Knowing Him, they know the Father to whose house they are going (14:7), for Jesus *is in the Father and the Father in* Him (14:11). The love of the Father and the love of the Son will fill their lives (14:23-24): They can believe with a new certitude (14:1) and pray with new confidence (14:13). They can obey the "new commandment" of mutual love (13:34; cf. 14:15, 21) and are empowered to do the *works* that the Christ did in the days of His flesh (*works that I do,* 14:12) and the *greater works* which the Christ at God's right hand will do through them (14:12). Those who do the works of the Christ must expect the opposition which He met. To meet, endure, and overcome that opposition, Christ will give His disciples *the Spirit* whose mark and gift is *the truth* that sets men free (14:17; cf. 8:32); the Spirit will be in future what the Christ has been heretofore, the *Counselor* (*another Counselor,* 14:16), the advocate and spokesman for the disciples; He will make the departed and exalted Christ a Christ at hand for them by teaching the disciples all things, by bringing to their remembrance all that Christ has taught them; they will not mourn an absent Teacher; He will be with them in the powerful Word and witness of the Spirit. (14:26-27)

Peace will be theirs; Jesus leaves them peace, not as a gracious wish (*as the world gives,* 14:27) but as His gift, bestowed in a Word that conveys what it expresses (14:27). Their *hearts* need not *be troubled* at His departure; they need not *be afraid* for the future (14:27); they can and should rejoice that Jesus is going to the almighty and gracious Father. (14:28)

13:31 *Glorified.* Cf. 12:28 note.

13:34 *A new commandment.* The commandment enjoining brotherly love is as old as Lv 19:18; but is new because it has received a new depth and new power in Him who loved us and gave Himself for us. (Cf. 1 Jn 2:7-8)

36 Simon Peter said to him, "Lord, where are you going?" Jesus answered, "Where I am going you cannot follow me now; but you shall follow afterward." 37 Peter said to him, "Lord, why cannot I follow you now? I will lay down my life for you." 38 Jesus answered, "Will you lay down your life for me? Truly, truly, I say to you, the cock will not crow, till you have denied me three times.

14 "Let not your hearts be troubled; believe[e] in God, believe also in me. 2 In my Father's house are many rooms; if it were not so, would I have told you that I go to prepare a place for you? 3And when I go and prepare a place for you, I will come again and will take you to myself, that where I am you may be also. 4And you know the way where I am going."[f] 5 Thomas said to him, "Lord, we do not know where you are going; how can we know the way?" 6 Jesus said to him, "I am the way, and the truth, and the life; no one comes to the Father, but by me. 7 If you had known me, you would have known my Father also; henceforth you know him and have seen him."

8 Philip said to him, "Lord, show us the Father, and we shall be satisfied." 9 Jesus said to him, "Have I been with you so long, and yet you do not know me, Philip? He who has seen me has seen the Father; how can you say, 'Show us the Father'? 10 Do you not believe that I am in the Father and the Father in me? The words that I say to you I do not speak on my own authority; but the Father who dwells in me does his works. 11 Believe me that I am in the Father and the Father in me; or else believe me for the sake of the works themselves.

12 "Truly, truly, I say to you, he who believes in me will also do the works that I do; and greater works than these will he do, because I go to the Father. 13 Whatever you ask in my name, I will do it, that the Father may be glorified in the Son; 14 if you ask[g] anything in my name, I will do it.

15 "If you love me, you will keep my commandments. 16And I will pray the Father, and he will give you another Counselor, to be with you for ever, 17 even the Spirit of truth, whom the world cannot receive, because it neither sees him nor knows him; you know him, for he dwells with you, and will be in you.

18 "I will not leave you desolate; I will come to you. 19 Yet a little while, and the world will see me no more, but you will see me; because I live, you will live also. 20 In that day you will know that I am in my Father, and you in me, and I in you. 21 He who has my commandments and keeps them, he it is who loves me; and he who loves me will be loved by my Father, and I will love him and manifest myself to him." 22 Judas (not Is·car′i·ot) said to him, "Lord, how is it that you will manifest yourself to us, and not to the world?" 23 Jesus answered him, "If a man loves me, he will keep my word, and my Father will love him, and we will come to him and make our home with him. 24 He who does not love me does not keep my words; and the word which you hear is not mine but the Father's who sent me.

25 "These things I have spoken to you, while I am still with you. 26 But the Counselor, the Holy Spirit, whom the Father will send in my name, he will teach you all things, and bring to your remembrance all that I have said to you. 27 Peace I leave with

[e] Or *you believe*   [f] Other ancient authorities read *where I am going you know, and the way you know*
[g] Other ancient authorities add *me*

13:36 *You shall follow afterward.* Cf. 21:18-19, where Jesus foretells Peter's martyrdom.

14:2 *Would I have told you that I go to prepare a place for you?* John records no word of Jesus that corresponds word for word to what Jesus refers to here; but 12:26 contains the substance of the promise to which Jesus is referring.

14:12 *Greater works than these will he do.* Jesus' works were done in the shadow of the cross, and His activity was confined to Israel. The disciples' works will be done in the light of the resurrection, in the power of the Spirit sent by the exalted Christ (14:15-17, 25-26), and will embrace the world of the Gentiles too. Cf. Jesus' words concerning His mission to the Greeks after His

suffering, death, and resurrection. (12:20-24)

14:17 *For he* (the Spirit) *dwells with you,* now in the words and works of Jesus, on whom the Spirit descended and remained (1:32), to whom the Father gave the Spirit "not by measure" (3:34) but in fullness. *And will be in you,* after Jesus' death, when their worldwide ministry begins. (14:16, 25-26; 16:4-11)

14:22 Judas' question is answered indirectly in the following verses. The world, under the domination of the ruler of this world, cannot love Jesus or keep His Word (23-24), cannot receive the Spirit of truth because it is ruled by the lie and the father of lies. (26, cf. 17)

14:27 *Peace . . . my peace . . . not as the world*

you; my peace I give to you; not as the world gives do I give to you. Let not your hearts be troubled, neither let them be afraid. 28 You heard me say to you, 'I go away, and I will come to you.' If you loved me, you would have rejoiced, because I go to the Father; for the Father is greater than I. 29And now I have told you before it takes place, so that when it does take place, you may believe. 30 I will no longer talk much with you, for the ruler of this world is coming. He has no power over me; 31 but I do as the Father has commanded me, so that the world may know that I love the Father. Rise, let us go hence.

JESUS' LAST WORDS TO HIS DISCIPLES, II (15:1 – 16:33)

15 "I am the true vine, and my Father is the vinedresser. 2 Every branch of mine that bears no fruit, he takes away, and every branch that does bear fruit he prunes, that it may bear more fruit. 3 You are already made clean by the word which I have spoken to you. 4Abide in me, and I in you. As the branch cannot bear fruit by itself, unless it abides in the vine, neither can you, unless you abide in me. 5 I am the vine, you are the branches. He who abides in me, and I in him, he it is that bears much fruit, for apart from me you can do nothing. 6 If a man does not abide in me, he is cast forth as a branch and withers; and the branches are gathered, thrown into the fire and burned. 7 If you abide in me, and my words abide in you, ask whatever you will, and it shall be done for you. 8 By this my Father is glorified, that you bear much fruit, and so prove to be my disciples. 9As the Father has loved me, so have I loved you; abide in my love. 10 If you keep my commandments, you will abide in my love,

gives. Peace was a common form of greeting. On Jesus' lips the word is filled once more with the fullness of meaning which it had in the OT, where the blessing pronounced on God's people by the sons of Aaron culminates in "and give you *peace*" (Nm 6:26), where the promised Messiah bears the significant title, "Prince of *Peace*" (Is 9:6, cf. 7), where the Lord's "covenant of *peace*" with His people ensures that total wholeness, soundness, and health which only God can give (Eze 34:25-31; 37:26-28): "I will be their God, and they shall be my people." (Eze 37:27)

14:28 *The Father is greater than I.* The Son, the Word made flesh, can in His obedient self-subordination speak thus of Himself. Believing man can only echo Thomas' cry: "My Lord and my God!" (20:28)

15:1 – 16:33 The second farewell discourse (cf. 13:31 – 14:31 note) has much in common with the first (13:31 – 14:31). But there is a new emphasis on the fullness and strength of the disciples' union and communion with Jesus: this is expressed most explicitly in the figure of the vine and the branches (15:1-17); but the same motif runs through Jesus' words on their exposure to the world's hatred for His sake (15:18 – 16:4), on the Spirit whom He will bestow on them (16:5-15), and on the *little while* which must elapse before their reunion with Him shall give them *full joy.* (16:16-33)

15:1-17 UNION WITH JESUS: THE VINE AND THE BRANCHES

15:1-17 The figure of the *vine* and the *branches* emphasizes the vitally organic nature of the disciples' communion with their Teacher and Lord. He initiates that communion (16), and they remain forever dependent on Him; they can *bear fruit* only by virtue of their continuing union with Him (4-5). Jesus' comment on the figure makes clear

what the figure in itself cannot express: that their union with Him is conscious, personal union, involving responsibility and God's judgment on infidelity (2, 6), involving the conscious resolve to do His will which finds expression in prayer (7), in keeping His commandment of love, and in sharing the joy of their Lord (11). The *branch* is no mere mystically vegetable appendage to the *vine;* Jesus' disciple is not merely *servant* to His Lord (15), high and honorable as the title servant is – it dignifies Moses and the prophets (Jos 1:2; Am 3:7; Jer 7:25) and Paul bears it proudly (e. g., Ro 1:1). Jesus' disciple is not an ignorant servant (or slave) who obeys because he must; he is a *friend* who acts freely and gladly because he knows what his Master is doing, namely, the will of the Father. (14-15)

15:1 *The true vine.* The vine is an OT figure for Israel (Is 5:7; Jer 2:21; Eze 19:10-14). That vine has, as Jeremiah complained, "turned degenerate and become a wild vine" (Jer 2:21); man now becomes a member of God's people and has a place in God's house (14:2), not by membership in Israel but by being incorporated in the *true vine,* the Son who is all that God's "firstborn" (Ex 4:22), Israel, failed to be.

15:2 *Fruit.* Since the vine is a person and the branches are persons, it seems natural to think of the fruit as persons also, as those who come to faith through the disciples' Word (17:20). Jesus is laying a missionary, apostolic obligation upon His disciples. (Cf. 20:21)

15:3 *You are already made clean.* The word translated as "prunes" in the preceding verse means literally "to make clean."

15:5 *You can do nothing.* Jesus' prediction of Peter's denial (13:37-38) and of His disciples' defection (16:31-33) are concrete exemplifications of the truth of this saying. The disciples "on their own" are failures.

just as I have kept my Father's commandments and abide in his love. 11 These things I have spoken to you, that my joy may be in you, and that your joy may be full.

12 "This is my commandment, that you love one another as I have loved you. 13 Greater love has no man than this, that a man lay down his life for his friends. 14 You are my friends if you do what I command you. 15 No longer do I call you servants,[h] for the servant[i] does not know what his master is doing; but I have called you friends, for all that I have heard from my Father I have made known to you. 16 You did not choose me, but I chose you and appointed you that you should go and bear fruit and that your fruit should abide; so that whatever you ask the Father in my name, he may give it to you. 17 This I command you, to love one another.

18 "If the world hates you, know that it has hated me before it hated you. 19 If you were of the world, the world would love its own; but because you are not of the world, but I chose you out of the world, therefore the world hates you. 20 Remember the word that I said to you, 'A servant[i] is not greater than his master.' If they persecuted me, they will persecute you; if they kept my word, they will keep yours also. 21 But all this they will do to you on my account, because they do not know him who sent me. 22 If I had not come and spoken to them, they would not have sin; but now they have no excuse for their sin. 23 He who hates me hates my Father also. 24 If I had not done among them the works which no one else did, they would not have sin; but now they have seen and hated both me and my Father. 25 It is to fulfil the word that is written in their law, 'They hated me without a cause.' 26 But when the Counselor comes, whom I shall send to you from the Father, even the Spirit of truth, who proceeds from the Father, he will bear witness to me; 27 and you also are witnesses, because you have been with me from the beginning.

16 "I have said all this to you to keep you from falling away. 2 They will put you out of the synagogues; indeed, the hour is coming when whoever kills you

[h] Or *slaves* [i] Or *slave*

15:18—16:4a THE WORLD'S HATRED

15:18—16:4a The Jesus who loved His own to the end (13:1) has assured His disciples that they can continue in His love as surely as He Himself abides in the Father's love (15:9-10). It is His love for them that forewarns them of the world's hatred and forearms them against it (16:1). Because they are identified with Christ as He is identified with the Father (15:18, 21), because His choice of them has made them alien to the world (19), the world will hate them. As surely as they are servants of this Lord, so surely will they inherit the hatred of the world which persecuted Him and ignored His Word (20; cf. 1:10-11). That hatred will be the satanic hatred of men who have heard and seen and have rejected the words and deeds of Jesus which revealed the Father, the hatred of men who *have* sin (15:22, 24) as their demonic master (cf. 8:34) because they have rejected Him who is God's forgiving grace and truth. The satanic impulse will disguise itself as religious zeal; these men will excommunicate and kill to the greater glory of God (16:2; cf. 2 Co 11: 14-15). But the world's hatred shall not triumph; the light that shines in this darkness of hate shall not be quenched (cf. 1:5). The Spirit's witness and the disciples' inspired witness will continue and shall prevail.

15:18 *World . . . hated me.* Cf. 7:7.

15:20 *The word that I said to you.* Cf. 13:16.

15:24 *They have seen and hated both me and my*

Father. They have seen but have not accepted and acknowledged; therefore Jesus can say both: "They have seen," and, "They do not know" (15:21). Love opens the eyes of faith; hatred blinds them. (Cf. 16:3)

15:25 *Word . . . written in their law.* Ps 35:19; 69:4. For *law* in the comprehensive sense of "Old Testament" cf. 10:34.

15:26 *The Counselor . . . will bear witness.* This anticipates the theme of 16:4b-15.

15:27 *You also are witnesses.* For the united witness of the Spirit and the disciples cf. Acts 5:32.

16:4b-15 THE COUNSELOR WHOM JESUS SENDS

16:4b-15 *Now* that Jesus is leaving them, the disciples are keenly and sadly aware of their own helplessness; what can they do without Him against the concerted hatred of the world? If they had the wit to ask the right question, *Where are you going?* (5), Jesus would give them the answer that would remove the *sorrow* that *has filled* their *hearts* (6); for Jesus is going to the *Father,* and that is *to* their *advantage,* for He will send (7) the *Counselor* "from the Father" (15:26); and the Counselor's witness will do what no human eloquence or persuasion can do: it will *convince* (8), that is, expose the world's wrong and call the *world* to repentance. The world that hates and crucifies Jesus for the sin of blasphemy (10:33; cf. 8:59; 19:7) is still blind to *sin;* since Jesus has come to be "the Lamb of God, who takes away the

will think he is offering service to God. ³And they will do this because they have not known the Father, nor me. ⁴ But I have said these things to you, that when their hour comes you may remember that I told you of them.

"I did not say these things to you from the beginning, because I was with you. ⁵ But now I am going to him who sent me; yet none of you asks me, 'Where are you going?' ⁶ But because I have said these things to you, sorrow has filled your hearts. ⁷ Nevertheless I tell you the truth: it is to your advantage that I go away, for if I do not go away, the Counselor will not come to you; but if I go, I will send him to you. ⁸And when he comes, he will convince ˣ the world concerning sin and righteousness and judgment: ⁹concerning sin, because they do not believe in me; ¹⁰concerning righteousness, because I go to the Father, and you will see me no more; ¹¹concerning judgment, because the ruler of this world is judged.

12 "I have yet many things to say to you, but you cannot bear them now. ¹³ When the Spirit of truth comes, he will guide you into all the truth; for he will not speak on his own authority, but whatever he hears he will speak, and he will declare to you the things that are to come. ¹⁴ He will glorify me, for he will take what is mine and declare it to you. ¹⁵All that the Father has is mine; therefore I said that he will take what is mine and declare it to you.

16 "A little while, and you will see me no more; again a little while, and you will see me." ¹⁷ Some of his disciples said to one another, "What is this that he says to us, 'A little while, and you will not see me, and again a little while, and you will see me';

ˣ Or convict

sin of the world" (1:29), there is but one sin that shuts a man out from the God who loves the world, the rejection of God's proffered forgiveness: *They do not believe in me* (9). The world that asserts, "We have a law, and by that law he ought to die, because he has made himself the Son of God" (19:7), is still blind to *righteousness* (8-9); the only righteousness that avails is in Him who dies for the world's sin and goes in triumph *to the Father,* removed from sight but present to faith (10). The world that bullies Pilate into executing *judgment* by crucifying the King who bears witness to the truth (19:12-16; cf. 18:37) does not know what judgment is being executed when this King dies: *The ruler* of this world is judged (11; cf. 12:31 note). The Spirit who witnesses through the witnessing disciples will present the crucified and exalted Christ as God's atonement for man's sin, God's righteousness for unrighteous man, God's judgment on the murderous and lying ruler of this world. Men will behold Him as He really is in that inspired witness, and men will repent.

To the disciples the Counselor will present the Christ in all the fullness of His glory, a glory they are not yet equipped to comprehend (12-15). The gospels, and indeed all the apostolic writings of the NT, witness to the fact that Jesus kept His promise concerning the Counselor, that men who once understood their Lord so ill (cf. e. g., 2:22; 12:16) were guided by the Spirit *into all the truth* (13) and learned to understand Him so well that their written witness to His glory has become the inexhaustible treasure of His church.

16:4 *Because I was with you,* to keep you and guard you. (Cf. 17:12)

16:12 *You cannot bear them now.* Not until men have been broken by their own failure (13:37-38; 16:31-32) and have been restored by Jesus' for-

giving grace (cf. 20:17 "my brethren"; 20:19 "Peace be with you"; cf. 21:15-19)—not until then are they ripe for the full revelation of His glory.

16:16-33 A LITTLE WHILE: PASSING SORROW AND LASTING JOY

16:16-33 Jesus sees in one perspective His resurrection and His return in glory at the end of days; the *little while* (16) of which He speaks is both the three days of His entombment and the time until His second coming. Jesus explains to His puzzled (16:17-18) disciples: The approaching time of separation *will* be a time of sorrow, the time of the world's triumphant joy at its apparent victory over the buried and unseen (cf. 16:10) Son of God (20); but it will be only a little while and that little while will not be a time of hopeless sorrow. The disciples' sorrow at the departure of their Lord will be like the sorrow of a *woman in travail,* real and poignant but also sorrow which has a goal and a hope. The agony will be followed, and swallowed up, by *joy* over the new life *born into the world* (21). When their Lord returns (from the grave and in His second coming), the *sorrow* of the disciples will be *turned into joy* which no man can take from them (22). All the questions which have perplexed and troubled them will be answered (23; *you will ask me no questions*); all the desires of their heart will be fulfilled by the *Father* who *loves* them who *have loved* Him and *believed* in Him whom the Father has sent (27). The Son will have given them a sonship that can ask of God with a child's freedom and a child's assurance. The disciples will have the strength and courage to endure the *tribulation* which they must endure *in the world,* for they know that they are held securely by Him who has *overcome the world.* (33)

and, 'because I go to the Father'?" [18] They said, "What does he mean by 'a little while'? We do not know what he means." [19] Jesus knew that they wanted to ask him; so he said to them, "Is this what you are asking yourselves, what I meant by saying, 'A little while, and you will not see me, and again a little while, and you will see me'? [20] Truly, truly, I say to you, you will weep and lament, but the world will rejoice; you will be sorrowful, but your sorrow will turn into joy. [21] When a woman is in travail she has sorrow, because her hour has come; but when she is delivered of the child, she no longer remembers the anguish, for joy that a child[j] is born into the world. [22] So you have sorrow now, but I will see you again and your hearts will rejoice, and no one will take your joy from you. [23] In that day you will ask nothing of me. Truly, truly, I say to you, if you ask anything of the Father, he will give it to you in my name. [24] Hitherto you have asked nothing in my name; ask, and you will receive, that your joy may be full.

[25] "I have said this to you in figures; the hour is coming when I shall no longer speak to you in figures but tell you plainly of the Father. [26] In that day you will ask in my name; and I do not say to you that I shall pray the Father for you; [27] for the Father himself loves you, because you have loved me and have believed that I came from the Father. [28] I came from the Father and have come into the world; again, I am leaving the world and going to the Father."

[29] His disciples said, "Ah, now you are speaking plainly, not in any figure! [30] Now we know that you know all things, and need none to question you; by this we believe that you came from God." [31] Jesus answered them, "Do you now believe? [32] The hour is coming, indeed it has come, when you will be scattered, every man to his home, and will leave me alone; yet I am not alone, for the Father is with me. [33] I have said this to you, that in me you may have peace. In the world you have tribulation; but be of good cheer, I have overcome the world."

JESUS' FAREWELL PRAYER (17:1-26)

17 When Jesus had spoken these words, he lifted up his eyes to heaven and said, "Father, the hour has come; glorify thy Son that the Son may glorify thee, [2] since thou hast given him power over all flesh, to give eternal life to all whom thou hast given him. [3] And this is eternal life, that they know thee the only true God, and Jesus Christ whom thou hast sent. [4] I glorified thee on earth, having accomplished the work which thou gavest me to do; [5] and now, Father, glorify thou me in thy own presence with the glory which I had with thee before the world was made.

[j] Greek *a human being*

16:20 *Your sorrow will turn into joy.* Cf. 20:20.

16:23 *Ask . . . ask.* The first *ask* means "ask" in the sense of "ask questions, inquire"; the second *ask* is "ask" in the sense of "request."

16:24 *You have asked nothing in my name.* To ask, make a request, in Jesus' name is to ask on the basis of Jesus' completed mission as the Son sent by the Father. Similarly, the Father will give in Jesus' name (23) when He gives to those who have loved and believed in the Son sent by the Father.

16:32 *You will be scattered . . . and leave me alone.* Cf. Mt 26:31 note.

17:1-26 Now that *the* supreme *hour* of His life on earth has come, Jesus prays. He prays for Himself (1-5), asking the Father for the promised gift (cf. 12:28) of glorification through suffering and death, that His own may have *eternal life* in the knowledge of the *only true God* who so loved the world that He gave His only Son for the world's salvation (cf. 3:16), that thus the obedient son, *Jesus Christ,* may *glorify* the Father and then return to His primordial place of glory with the Father. (5)

He prays for His disciples (6-19), the men whom the Father has given Him (6), who have *received* and *believed the words* (8) from the Father and have kept His *word;* the men in whom the Son achieves the glory (10) that is rightly His as the Savior who consecrates Himself as a Sacrifice (19) for their sins. He prays that the Father may preserve them in an alien (16) and hostile (14) world, may *sanctify them in the truth* (17) of His *word* and so equip them to be apostles of the Son sent to save the world. (18)

He prays also for His future disciples, those who shall come to faith in Him through the Word of His witness (20-26). He asks that they *may all be one* (21), *perfectly one* (23), united with one another as Jesus is united with the Father and united with Jesus and the Father, that there may be an unbroken line of valid witnesses (the Son, the Son's disciples, and the disciples' disciples), witnesses to the Father's love which works in and

6 "I have manifested thy name to the men whom thou gavest me out of the world; thine they were, and thou gavest them to me, and they have kept thy word. 7 Now they know that everything that thou hast given me is from thee; 8 for I have given them the words which thou gavest me, and they have received them and know in truth that I came from thee; and they have believed that thou didst send me. 9 I am praying for them; I am not praying for the world but for those whom thou hast given me, for they are thine; 10 all mine are thine, and thine are mine, and I am glorified in them. 11And now I am no more in the world, but they are in the world, and I am coming to thee. Holy Father, keep them in thy name, which thou hast given me, that they may be one, even as we are one. 12 While I was with them, I kept them in thy name, which thou hast given me; I have guarded them, and none of them is lost but the son of perdition, that the scripture might be fulfilled. 13 But now I am coming to thee; and these things I speak in the world, that they may have my joy fulfilled in themselves. 14 I have given them thy word; and the world has hated them because they are not of the world, even as I am not of the world. 15 I do not pray that thou shouldst take them out of the world, but that thou shouldst keep them from the evil one.ᵏ 16 They are not of the world, even as I am not of the world. 17 Sanctify them in the truth; thy word is truth. 18As thou didst send me into the world, so I have sent them into the world. 19And for their sake I consecrate myself, that they also may be consecrated in truth.

20 "I do not pray for these only, but also for those who believe in me through their word, 21 that they may all be one; even as thou, Father, art in me, and I in thee, that they also may be in us, so that the world may believe that thou hast sent me. 22 The glory which thou hast given me I have given to them, that they may be one even as we are one, 23 I in them and thou in me, that they may become perfectly one, so that the world may know that thou hast sent me and hast loved them even as thou hast loved me. 24 Father, I desire that they also, whom thou hast given me, may be with me where I am, to behold my glory which thou hast given me in thy love for me before the foundation of the world. 25 O righteous Father, the world has not known thee, but I have known thee; and these know that thou hast sent me. 26 I made known to them thy name, and I will make it known, that the love with which thou hast loved me may be in them, and I in them."

The Word Speaks God's Grace and Truth

18:1 — 20:31

THE ARREST (18:1-11)

18 When Jesus had spoken these words, he went forth with his disciples across the Kidron valley, where there was a garden, which he and his disciples entered. 2 Now Judas, who betrayed him, also knew the place; for Jesus often met there with

---

ᵏ Or *from evil*

---

through them all (21, 23). He prays that all those whom the Father has given Him, all who know the Son and have learned from Him God's name, "Father," *may be with* Him to behold His ancient and eternal glory. (24)

17:9 *I am not praying for the world.* Jesus' prayer for the world's salvation is contained in His prayer for His witnesses (21, 23, "that the world may believe . . . may know").

17:11 *Keep them in thy name,* that is, keep them as what they have become by the revelation given in the Son who has manifested God's name to them.

17:12 *That the scripture might be fulfilled.* Cf. 13:18; Ps 41:9.

17:17 *Sanctify them.* Separate them from all evil and make them Thine own, for service to Thee. (Cf. 18)

17:19 *I consecrate myself.* Cf. 10:36, where the action of consecrating is ascribed to the Father; the Son does freely what He owes as obedience to the Father. (Cf. 10:18 note)

17:25 *O righteous Father.* God is righteous both in His judgment on the world that has rejected Him *(not known thee)* and in His glorification of the obedient Son and of those who believe in Him *(know that thou hast sent me).*

18:1 — 20:31 In the Passion, death, and resurrection of Jesus His disciples behold His glory, the glory of the Good Shepherd who dies for His flock, the glory of the King whose kingdom is not of this world, the glory of the ministering Lord who on the cross commits His mother to the disciple whom He loves, the glory of the Word made flesh in full human reality, who said, "I thirst." It is the glory of the Savior of the world who cried, "It

his disciples. ³ So Judas, procuring a band of soldiers and some officers from the chief priests and the Pharisees, went there with lanterns and torches and weapons. ⁴ Then Jesus, knowing all that was to befall him, came forward and said to them, "Whom do you seek?" ⁵ They answered him, "Jesus of Nazareth." Jesus said to them, "I am he." Judas, who betrayed him, was standing with them. ⁶ When he said to them, "I am he," they drew back and fell to the ground. ⁷Again he asked them, "Whom do you seek?" And they said, "Jesus of Nazareth." ⁸ Jesus answered, "I told you that I am he; so, if you seek me, let these men go." ⁹ This was to fulfil the word which he had spoken, "Of those whom thou gavest me I lost not one." ¹⁰ Then Simon Peter, having a sword, drew it and struck the high priest's slave and cut off his right ear. The slave's name was Malchus. ¹¹ Jesus said to Peter, "Put your sword into its sheath; shall I not drink the cup which the Father has given me?"

THE HEARING BEFORE ANNAS AND PETER'S DENIAL (18:12-27)

12 So the band of soldiers and their captain and the officers of the Jews seized Jesus and bound him. ¹³ First they led him to Annas; for he was the father-in-law of Ca′ia·phas, who was high priest that year. ¹⁴ It was Ca′ia·phas who had given counsel to the Jews that it was expedient that one man should die for the people.

15 Simon Peter followed Jesus, and so did another disciple. As this disciple was known to the high priest, he entered the court of the high priest along with Jesus, ¹⁶ while Peter stood outside at the door. So the other disciple, who was known to the high priest, went out and spoke to the maid who kept the door, and brought Peter in. ¹⁷ The maid who kept the door said to Peter, "Are not you also one of this man's disciples?" He said, "I am not." ¹⁸ Now the servants[l] and officers had made a charcoal fire, because it was cold, and they were standing and warming themselves; Peter also was with them, standing and warming himself.

19 The high priest then questioned Jesus about his disciples and his teaching. ²⁰ Jesus answered him, "I have spoken openly to the world; I have always taught in synagogues and in the temple, where all Jews come together; I have said nothing secretly. ²¹ Why do you ask me? Ask those who have heard me, what I said to them;

[l] Or *slaves*

is finished," the glory of the risen Lord of life who breathed on them with creative breath and gave them the Holy Spirit for their apostolic task, the glory of the Lord and God who overwhelmed the stubborn doubt of Thomas and called them blessed who, without seeing, believe.

18:1-11 Jesus went out to meet the onset of the ruler of this world with a resolute, "rise, let us go hence" (14:30-31). His resolution does not fail Him now when He is confronted by the betrayer in the flesh and sees in the friend who ate His bread (13:18) the incarnation of the will of Satan (cf. 13: 2, 27). The quiet majesty with which He takes the initiative, goes to meet His captors, questions them (4, 7), and gives Himself into their hands has a shattering effect on them (6). He loves His own to the end; the Good Shepherd goes freely (cf. 4) into death in order that His flock may live (8-9; cf. 10:11). And He remains to the end the obedient Son who cannot but *drink the cup* of suffering *which the Father has given* Him. (11)

18:9 *The word which He had spoken*. Cf. 17:12.

18:10 Only the fourth gospel identifies the wielder of the sword as *Peter* and gives the name of the high priest's slave, *Malchus*.

18:11 *Drink the cup*. For the cup as a symbol of suffering under the punitive judgment of God cf. Mt 20:22 note; 26:39.

18:12-27 The most remarkable feature of this part of John's narrative is that it practically omits the story of Jesus' trial before the high council of His people (cf., e. g., Mt 26:57-68). The hearing before Annas (12-13; 19-23) is not a trial, and Jesus' appearance before Caiaphas is just mentioned (24). They are hardly more than the background to the story of Peter's denial (15-18; 25-27). The reason for this omission is not far to seek; John has already portrayed the "trial" of Jesus before His own people; the record of chs. 7—12 makes clear that they have in effect tried and condemned Him. See the note on 11:1-54, especially the last paragraph.

18:13 *Annas*. See Lk 3:2 note. John continues to call *Annas the high priest* despite the fact that he had been deposed by the Roman governor in the year 15 (15, 19; cf. 22). The office of high priest was by law a lifelong office, and Annas enjoyed great respect and exerted great influence for many years after he had been deposed.

18:14 Cf. 11:49-51.

18:15 *Another disciple*. See 13:23 note.

18:19 *Questioned Jesus about his disciples*. The question was probably designed to incriminate the disciples, so that they too might be prosecuted. Jesus shields them (20-21), as He had shielded them at His arrest in the garden. (8)

they know what I said." ²² When he had said this, one of the officers standing by struck Jesus with his hand, saying, "Is that how you answer the high priest?" ²³ Jesus answered him, "If I have spoken wrongly, bear witness to the wrong; but if I have spoken rightly, why do you strike me?" ²⁴Annas then sent him bound to Ca'ia·phas the high priest.

25 Now Simon Peter was standing and warming himself. They said to him, "Are not you also one of his disciples?" He denied it and said, "I am not." ²⁶ One of the servants*¹* of the high priest, a kinsman of the man whose ear Peter had cut off, asked, "Did I not see you in the garden with him?" ²⁷ Peter again denied it; and at once the cock crowed.

THE TRIAL BEFORE PILATE (18:28 — 19:16)

28 Then they led Jesus from the house of Ca'ia·phas to the praetorium. It was early. They themselves did not enter the praetorium, so that they might not be defiled, but might eat the passover. ²⁹ So Pilate went out to them and said, "What accusation do you bring against this man?" ³⁰ They answered him, "If this man were not an evildoer, we would not have handed him over." ³¹ Pilate said to them, "Take him yourselves and judge him by your own law." The Jews said to him, "It is not lawful for us to put any man to death." ³² This was to fulfil the word which Jesus had spoken to show by what death he was to die.

33 Pilate entered the praetorium again and called Jesus, and said to him, "Are you the King of the Jews?" ³⁴ Jesus answered, "Do you say this of your own accord, or did others say it to you about me?" ³⁵ Pilate answered, "Am I a Jew? Your own nation and the chief priests have handed you over to me; what have you done?" ³⁶ Jesus answered, "My kingship is not of this world; if my kingship were of this world, my servants would fight, that I might not be handed over to the Jews; but my kingship is not from the world." ³⁷ Pilate said to him, "So you are a king?" Jesus

¹ Or *slaves*

18:27 *The cock crowed.* Cf. 13:38.

18:28 — 19:16 The disciples, taught by the Spirit who glorifies the Son (16:14), behold the glory of their Lord in His Passion (see note on 18:1 — 20:31); they behold there too, and just there, the Light of the world; but the Light shines in darkness, and the darkness struggles fiercely, though unsuccessfully, to overcome the Light (1:5). The nation for whom He dies (11:50-51) is in the forefront of that struggle. The nation whose peculiar glory it is that "to them belong . . . the giving of the law" (Ro 9:4) is punctilious in the observance of the lesser matters of the Law (18:22, 28), but uses the Law to rid itself of the Light of the world that exposes its deeds as evil (3:19; 19:7). "Of their race, according to the flesh, is the Christ" (Ro 9:5); yet they choose *Barabbas,* the *robber,* in preference to Him (18:40), and deny the anointed King God gave them (19:15), and will *have no king but Caesar.* (19:15)

But it is not only His nation that seeks to kill the King and quench the Light. Judas, who became their willing tool, may have *the greater sin* (19:11), but the Gentile world, too, takes part in the struggle and shares the guilt. Pilate, representative of the Gentile world, holder of a *power* given him *from above* (19:11), chosen to be the custodian of God's wrath upon the wrongdoer (cf. Ro 13:4), will not use that power to protect the Man whose innocence he has thrice attested (18:38; 19:4, 6). The divinely appointed guardian of truth and justice shrugs off his responsibility with a skeptical, "What is truth?" and hands over

the incarnate grace and truth of God *to be crucified.* (18:38; 19:16)

The *world* united to overcome the Light, and Pilate spoke better than he knew when he presented the scourged and thorn-crowned King of the Jews, robed in purple, with the words, *Behold the man!* (19:5). He is indeed THE Man, not the Jew merely, but the Man on whom the sin of mankind is visited, in whom the hope of the world lies hid.

18:28 *The praetorium,* the headquarters of the Roman governor. *That they might not be defiled,* by entering the dwelling of a Gentile. Defilement would exclude them from the celebration of the *passover.* (Cf. 11:55 note)

18:32 *By what death he was to die.* Jesus' prediction that He would be "lifted up" (8:28; 12:32) is fulfilled by His crucifixion, the Roman form of punishment, not by stoning, the Jewish form of punishment for blasphemers.

18:34 Jesus' question determines whether Pilate's inquiry concerning the "King of the Jews" is prompted, like that of the Magi (Mt 2:2), by a religious interest in Him or is merely formal and official. Pilate's reply both here (35) and later (38) makes clear his indifference toward any Messianic claim (except insofar as it might prove a threat to Roman rule) and to the whole world of "truth" (divine revelation) that Jesus represents. He is not "of the truth."

18:36-37 Jesus declares His kingship in terms which a Gentile can understand. He is no king whose followers fight for Him that He may gain

answered, "You say that I am a king. For this I was born, and for this I have come into the world, to bear witness to the truth. Every one who is of the truth hears my voice." 38 Pilate said to him, "What is truth?"

After he had said this, he went out to the Jews again, and told them, "I find no crime in him. 39 But you have a custom that I should release one man for you at the Passover; will you have me release for you the King of the Jews?" 40 They cried out again, "Not this man, but Bar·ab′bas!" Now Bar·ab′bas was a robber.

19 Then Pilate took Jesus and scourged him. 2And the soldiers plaited a crown of thorns, and put it on his head, and arrayed him in a purple robe; 3 they came up to him, saying, "Hail, King of the Jews!" and struck him with their hands. 4 Pilate went out again, and said to them, "See, I am bringing him out to you, that you may know that I find no crime in him." 5So Jesus came out, wearing the crown of thorns and the purple robe. Pilate said to them, "Behold the man!" 6 When the chief priests and the officers saw him, they cried out, "Crucify him, crucify him!" Pilate said to them, "Take him yourselves and crucify him, for I find no crime in him." 7 The Jews answered him, "We have a law, and by that law he ought to die, because he has made himself the Son of God." 8 When Pilate heard these words, he was the more afraid; 9 he entered the praetorium again and said to Jesus, "Where are you from?" But Jesus gave no answer. 10 Pilate therefore said to him, "You will not speak to me? Do you not know that I have power to release you, and power to crucify you?" 11 Jesus answered him, "You would have no power over me unless it had been given you from above; therefore he who delivered me to you has the greater sin."

12 Upon this Pilate sought to release him, but the Jews cried out, "If you release this man, you are not Caesar's friend; every one who makes himself a king sets himself against Caesar." 13 When Pilate heard these words, he brought Jesus out and sat down on the judgment seat at a place called The Pavement, and in Hebrew, Gab′ba·tha. 14 Now it was the day of Preparation of the Passover; it was about the sixth hour. He said to the Jews, "Behold your King!" 15 They cried out, "Away with him, away with him, crucify him!" Pilate said to them, "Shall I crucify your King?" The chief priests answered, "We have no king but Caesar." 16 Then he handed him over to them to be crucified.

THE CRUCIFIXION, DEATH, AND BURIAL OF JESUS (19:17-42)

17 So they took Jesus, and he went out, bearing his own cross, to the place called the place of a skull, which is called in Hebrew Gol′go·tha. 18 There they crucified him, and with him two others, one on either side, and Jesus between them. 19 Pilate also wrote a title and put it on the cross; it read, "Jesus of Nazareth, the King of the Jews."

and hold a throne; no Roman governor need suspect Him of seditious intent. His kingship lies on another plane altogether; He is come *to bear witness to the truth* of God that sets men free from the lust for being king or making kings.

19:6 *The officers.* The "officers of the Jews" (18: 12, 18) are meant.

19:7 *A law,* particularly the law against blasphemy, Lv 24:16.

Made himself the Son of God. Cf. 10:33.

19:11 *Power ... given you from above.* Cf. Ro 13:1.

He who delivered me, Judas, the instrument of Satan. (13:2, 27)

19:12 *You are not Caesar's friend.* The emperor Tiberius' chronic suspiciousness (there were many trials for sedition and treason during his reign) and Pilate's far-from-unblemished record as governor made this veiled threat a powerful one.

19:13 *The Pavement . . . Gabbatha.* The Pavement could be either a place paved with stones (conspicuous in a city whose streets were largely unpaved) or a place covered with mosaic. The meaning of the Hebrew term *Gabbatha* is uncertain.

19:14 *Preparation for the Passover ... sixth hour.* The sixth hour is noon; the Preparation for the Passover is, properly, the "eve of the Passover." On the afternoon of the preparation the paschal lambs were slain; Jesus, the true Lamb (1:29; cf. 1 Co 5:7), gives the OT shadow its substance by dying at the appointed time. (Cf. 19:36 note)

Behold your King! Pilate speaks more truly than he, by his mocking words, intends.

19:17-42 Jesus dies, as He has lived, fulfilling His Father's will according to the Scriptures (24, 28, 36, 37); He dies a real human death, mindful of the parental ties that bind Him to humanity (25-27), suffering human pain (28, *I thirst*); but He dies as the divine Good Shepherd who lays down His life of His own accord (28, *knowing that all was now finished*).

20 Many of the Jews read this title, for the place where Jesus was crucified was near the city; and it was written in Hebrew, in Latin, and in Greek. 21 The chief priests of the Jews then said to Pilate, "Do not write, 'The King of the Jews,' but, 'This man said, I am King of the Jews.' " 22 Pilate answered, "What I have written I have written."

23 When the soldiers had crucified Jesus they took his garments and made four parts, one for each soldier; also his tunic. But the tunic was without seam, woven from top to bottom; 24 so they said to one another, "Let us not tear it, but cast lots for it to see whose it shall be." This was to fulfil the scripture,

"They parted my garments among them,
and for my clothing they cast lots."

25 So the soldiers did this. But standing by the cross of Jesus were his mother, and his mother's sister, Mary the wife of Clopas, and Mary Magdalene. 26 When Jesus saw his mother, and the disciple whom he loved standing near, he said to his mother, "Woman, behold, your son!" 27 Then he said to the disciple, "Behold, your mother!" And from that hour the disciple took her to his own home.

28 After this Jesus, knowing that all was now finished, said (to fulfil the scripture), "I thirst." 29 A bowl full of vinegar stood there; so they put a sponge full of the vinegar on hyssop and held it to his mouth. 30 When Jesus had received the vinegar, he said, "It is finished"; and he bowed his head and gave up his spirit.

31 Since it was the day of Preparation, in order to prevent the bodies from remaining on the cross on the sabbath (for that sabbath was a high day), the Jews asked Pilate that their legs might be broken, and that they might be taken away. 32 So the soldiers came and broke the legs of the first, and of the other who had been crucified with him; 33 but when they came to Jesus and saw that he was already dead, they did not break his legs. 34 But one of the soldiers pierced his side with a spear, and at once there came out blood and water. 35 He who saw it has borne witness—his testimony is true, and he knows that he tells the truth—that you also may believe. 36 For these things took place that the scripture might be fulfilled, "Not a bone of him shall be broken." 37 And again another scripture says, "They shall look on him whom they have pierced."

38 After this Joseph of Ar·i·ma·the′a, who was a disciple of Jesus, but secretly, for fear of the Jews, asked Pilate that he might take away the body of Jesus, and Pilate gave him leave. So he came and took away his body. 39 Nicodemus also, who had at first come to him by night, came bringing a mixture of myrrh and aloes, about a hundred pounds' weight. 40 They took the body of Jesus, and bound it in linen cloths with the spices, as is the burial custom of the Jews. 41 Now in the place where he was crucified there was a garden, and in the garden a new tomb where no one had ever been laid. 42 So because of the Jewish day of Preparation, as the tomb was close at hand, they laid Jesus there.

19:22 *What I have written I have written.* Cf. 19. By God's governance of history the stubbornness of the Roman governor, weary of altercations with a people he does not respect and cannot understand, ensures the proclamation of the truth. Nathanael's confession at the beginning of Jesus' ministry finds a strange echo at its close: "You are the King of Israel!" (1:49)

19:24 *To fulfil the scripture.* Cf. Ps 22:18.

19:26 *The disciple whom he loved.* Cf. 13:23 note.

19:28 *To fulfil the scripture.* Cf. Ps 69:21.

19:29 *Hyssop,* a small bushy plant with aromatic leaves. Since the short stalk of this plant seems to be ill adapted to the purpose of bringing the *vinegar* to the lips of the crucified, some scholars have conjectured that the text has suffered in transmission: *hyssopos* has been mistakenly written for a word of similar appearance *(hyssos)* which means javelin.

19:31 *Preparation.* Cf. 19:14 note.

That sabbath was a high day, since it coincided with the Passover.

Legs . . . broken, to ensure a speedy death.

19:34 *Blood and water.* Some see here a symbolism pointing to the Lord's Supper and Baptism.

19:35 *He who saw it,* the beloved disciple of v. 26, eyewitness of the events and author of the gospel. (Cf. 21:24)

You, plural, the readers of the gospel.

19:36 *That the scripture might be fulfilled.* The reference is either to the Passover lamb (Ex 12:46; Nm 9:12) or to Ps 34:19-20, which speaks of God's care for the righteous in delivering him out of his afflictions: "He keeps all his bones; not one of them is broken."

19:37 *Another scripture.* Zch 12:10.

THE RISEN LORD (20:1-29)

20 Now on the first day of the week Mary Magdalene came to the tomb early, while it was still dark, and saw that the stone had been taken away from the tomb. 2 So she ran, and went to Simon Peter and the other disciple, the one whom Jesus loved, and said to them, "They have taken the Lord out of the tomb, and we do not know where they have laid him." 3 Peter then came out with the other disciple, and they went toward the tomb. 4 They both ran, but the other disciple outran Peter and reached the tomb first; 5 and stooping to look in, he saw the linen cloths lying there, but he did not go in. 6 Then Simon Peter came, following him, and went into the tomb; he saw the linen cloths lying, 7 and the napkin, which had been on his head, not lying with the linen cloths but rolled up in a place by itself. 8 Then the other disciple, who reached the tomb first, also went in, and he saw and believed; 9 for as yet they did not know the scripture, that he must rise from the dead. 10 Then the disciples went back to their homes.

11 But Mary stood weeping outside the tomb, and as she wept she stooped to look into the tomb; 12 and she saw two angels in white, sitting where the body of Jesus had lain, one at the head and one at the feet. 13 They said to her, "Woman, why are you weeping?" She said to them, "Because they have taken away my Lord, and I do not know where they have laid him." 14 Saying this, she turned round and saw Jesus standing, but she did not know that it was Jesus. 15 Jesus said to her, "Woman, why are you weeping? Whom do you seek?" Supposing him to be the gardener, she said to him, "Sir, if you have carried him away, tell me where you have laid him, and I will take him away." 16 Jesus said to her, "Mary." She turned and said to him in Hebrew, "Rab·bo′ni!" (which means Teacher). 17 Jesus said to her, "Do not hold me, for I have not yet ascended to the Father; but go to my brethren and say to them, I am ascending to my Father and your Father, to my God and your God." 18 Mary Magdalene went and said to the disciples, "I have seen the Lord"; and she told them that he had said these things to her.

19 On the evening of that day, the first day of the week, the doors being shut where the disciples were, for fear of the Jews, Jesus came and stood among them and said to them, "Peace be with you." 20 When he had said this, he showed them his hands and his side. Then the disciples were glad when they saw the Lord. 21 Jesus said to them again, "Peace be with you. As the Father has sent me, even so I send you." 22 And when he had said this, he breathed on them, and said to them, "Receive the Holy Spirit. 23 If you forgive the sins of any, they are forgiven; if you retain the sins of any, they are retained."

24 Now Thomas, one of the twelve, called the Twin, was not with them when Jesus came. 25 So the other disciples told him, "We have seen the Lord." But he said to them, "Unless I see in his hands the print of the nails, and place my finger in the mark of the nails, and place my hand in his side, I will not believe."

20:1-29 The disciples are fully assured of the reality of the resurrection; they are to know: "Because I live, you will live also" (14:19). The silent witness of the empty tomb is enough for one of the two disciples to whom it was granted: *He saw and believed* (8). Mary sees the Good Shepherd who "calls his own sheep by name" (10:3, 14), the familiar *Teacher* (16) but already bound for that world whither she cannot follow now (17). To the ten disciples huddled behind shut doors *for fear of the Jews* (19) He manifests Himself as the crucified Victor (20), bestows on them His *peace* (21), and the *Holy Spirit*, who is to be the power of their apostolate (21, *so I send you*). Doubting *Thomas* cannot remain *faithless* (27) when he beholds the Crucified with the marks of battle and the tokens of victory on His body; believing,

Thomas bows before Him: *My Lord and my God!*

20:4 *The other disciple.* Cf. 13:23 note.

20:6-7 The orderly disposition of the *linen cloths* and the *napkin* is evidence that this is not the work of grave robbers. (Cf. 13, 15)

20:9 *For as yet they did not know the scriptures, that he must rise from the dead.* Since their minds were not yet opened to understand the Scriptures (in the sense of Lk 24:45-46) as witnessing to Jesus' resurrection, the faith of the "other disciple" (8) is all the more remarkable.

20:17 *My brethren . . . my Father and your Father . . . my God and your God.* Every word expresses the completeness of the atonement wrought by Jesus: "It is finished" indeed. (19:30)

20:20 *The disciples were glad.* Cf. 16:20,22.

20:23 Cf. Mt 16:19; 18:18.

26 Eight days later, his disciples were again in the house, and Thomas was with them. The doors were shut, but Jesus came and stood among them, and said, "Peace be with you." 27 Then he said to Thomas, "Put your finger here, and see my hands; and put out your hand, and place it in my side; do not be faithless, but believing." 28 Thomas answered him, "My Lord and my God!" 29 Jesus said to him, "Have you believed because you have seen me? Blessed are those who have not seen and yet believe."

CONCLUSION: THE PURPOSE OF THE GOSPEL (20:30-31)

30 Now Jesus did many other signs in the presence of the disciples, which are not written in this book; 31 but these are written that you may believe that Jesus is the Christ, the Son of God, and that believing you may have life in his name.

Afterword: Jesus, Peter, and the Beloved Disciple

21:1-25

21 After this Jesus revealed himself again to the disciples by the Sea of Ti·be'-ri·as; and he revealed himself in this way. 2 Simon Peter, Thomas called the Twin, Na·than'a·el of Cana in Galilee, the sons of Zeb'e·dee, and two others of his disciples were together. 3 Simon Peter said to them, "I am going fishing." They said to him, "We will go with you." They went out and got into the boat; but that night they caught nothing.

4 Just as day was breaking, Jesus stood on the beach; yet the disciples did not know that it was Jesus. 5 Jesus said to them, "Children, have you any fish?" They answered him, "No." 6 He said to them, "Cast the net on the right side of the boat, and you will find some." So they cast it, and now they were not able to haul it in, for the quantity of fish. 7 That disciple whom Jesus loved said to Peter, "It is the Lord!" When Simon Peter heard that it was the Lord, he put on his clothes, for he was stripped for work, and sprang into the sea. 8 But the other disciples came in the boat, dragging the net full of fish, for they were not far from the land, but about a hundred yards*m* off.

9 When they got out on land, they saw a charcoal fire there, with fish lying on it, and bread. 10 Jesus said to them, "Bring some of the fish that you have just caught." 11 So Simon Peter went aboard and hauled the net ashore, full of large fish, a hundred and fifty-three of them; and although there were so many, the net was not torn. 12 Jesus said to them, "Come and have breakfast." Now none of the disciples dared ask him, "Who are you?" They knew it was the Lord. 13 Jesus came and took the bread and gave it to them, and so with the fish. 14 This was now the third time that Jesus was revealed to the disciples after he was raised from the dead.

15 When they had finished breakfast, Jesus said to Simon Peter, "Simon, son of John, do you love me more than these?" He said to him, "Yes, Lord; you know that I love you." He said to him, "Feed my lambs." 16A second time he said to him, "Simon,

m Greek *two hundred cubits*

20:30-31 Cf. Introduction, par. 1.

21:1-25 The afterword, whether written by John himself or by followers of John (cf. 24, *we know*), records the risen Christ's third manifestation of Himself to His disciples (14; cf. 20:19, 26). Once more, this time in Galilee and amid the everyday occupations of a fisherman, they behold Him in the glory of His gracious Lordship. He admits His own to the fellowship of the common meal (1-14). His forgiving love thrice restores to his apostolic shepherd's task *Simon*, who had denied Him thrice (15-17) and makes him once more Peter, the rock on whom the Christ will build His church (1:42; cf. Mt 16:18). He appoints for Peter the death by which he is to *glorify God* (18-19). He alone determines the fate of *the dis-*

ciple whom He loved (20-23). It is this disciple, the apostle determined wholly by his Lord, who witnesses to the Word in the written Word, and the men who have come to faith and have found life through that Word (cf. 20:31) *know* (what millions of readers have come to know with unshakable certainty since) *that his testimony is true.* (24)

21:11 *Large fish, a hundred and fifty-three of them.* The number 153, and indeed the whole story of the catch of fish, have often been interpreted allegorically as indicating the worldwide mission of the apostles. But the text itself contains no hint that it is to be understood allegorically, and the most natural explanation of the number 153 would seem to be that there were 153 fish in the net.

son of John, do you love me?" He said to him, "Yes, Lord; you know that I love you." He said to him, "Tend my sheep." 17 He said to him the third time, "Simon, son of John, do you love me?" Peter was grieved because he said to him the third time, "Do you love me?" And he said to him, "Lord, you know everything; you know that I love you." Jesus said to him, "Feed my sheep. 18 Truly, truly, I say to you, when you were young, you girded yourself and walked where you would; but when you are old, you will stretch out your hands, and another will gird you and carry you where you do not wish to go." 19 (This he said to show by what death he was to glorify God.) And after this he said to him, "Follow me."

20 Peter turned and saw following them the disciple whom Jesus loved, who had lain close to his breast at the supper and had said, "Lord, who is it that is going to betray you?" 21 When Peter saw him, he said to Jesus, "Lord, what about this man?" 22 Jesus said to him, "If it is my will that he remain until I come, what is that to you? Follow me!" 23 The saying spread abroad among the brethren that this disciple was not to die; yet Jesus did not say to him that he was not to die, but, "If it is my will that he remain until I come, what is that to you?"

24 This is the disciple who is bearing witness to these things, and who has written these things; and we know that his testimony is true.

25 But there are also many other things which Jesus did; were every one of them to be written, I suppose that the world itself could not contain the books that would be written.

21:19 *By what death he was to glorify God,* that is, by martyrdom. Reliable tradition has it that Peter died a martyr's death, probably by crucifixion, in Rome under Nero.

THE

ACTS OF THE APOSTLES

(The Second Half of Luke's Gospel)

INTRODUCTION

Title of the Work

1 "Acts of the Apostles" can hardly be the title given to the second part of his work by Luke himself. As an indication of the content it is inaccurate. Of the apostles only Peter and Paul are really leading figures. John appears a few times in the early chapters and then disappears; James the son of Zebedee appears only as a martyr, with one short sentence devoted to his execution. On the other hand, men who are not apostles play a considerable role in the narrative — Stephen, Philip, Barnabas, Silas, Agabus. Furthermore, if the title were to be understood in the sense suggested by similar works current in antiquity, such as the Acts of Alexander by Callisthenes or the Acts of Hannibal by Sosylus, it could actually be misleading. It would suggest a narrative of human heroism and achievement. Of course the very term "apostle," as defined by Jesus and used by the apostles themselves, should have excluded that idea, for the apostle is by definition nothing of himself and everything by virtue of the commission given him by his Lord. But would Luke have selected a title which even suggested the idea of human greatness? His

book tells the story of men only because and insofar as men are instrumental in the growth and triumph of the Word of the Lord. The Book of Acts is to be thought of as the direct continuation of Luke's Gospel, with the exalted Christ as its dominant figure. (Acts 1:1)

Content of the Acts of the Apostles

2 Luke has himself outlined the structure of his work by inserting summarizing statements at six points in it (Acts 6:7; 9:31; 12:24; 16:5; 19:20; 28:31). Each of the units marks a step in the progress of the Word of the Lord on its way from Jerusalem to Rome. It is probably not accidental that the first five of the summarizing statements alternate in stressing the Word (6:7; 12:24; 19:20) and the church (9:31; 16:5), while the last one (28:31) gives the content (kingdom of God; Lordship of Jesus) which makes the Word a creative power that has built and shall build the church. Where the Word is spoken, even though it be by "defeated" men in prison, there God the King, revealed in Jesus the Lord, is gathering the new people of God, the church, which multiplied despite opposition.

OUTLINE

I. 1:1 — 6:7 The Word of the Lord in Jerusalem

   The Spirit-filled apostolic Word creates and sustains in Jerusalem a church which overcomes internal tensions and triumphs and grows despite outside opposition.

   Summarizing statement: "And the word of God increased; and the number of the disciples multiplied greatly in Jerusalem, and a great many of the priests were obedient to the faith." (6:7)

II. 6:8 — 9:31 The Word of the Lord Triumphs over Persecution

   The Word goes to Samaria, and the persecutor Saul becomes the Lord's chosen instrument.

   Summarizing statement: "So the church throughout all Judea

and Galilee and Samaria had peace and was built up; and walking in the fear of the Lord and in the comfort of the Holy Spirit it was multiplied." (9:31)

III. 9:32–12:25 The Word of the Lord Becomes a Light to the Gentiles (cf. Acts 26:23)

Peter, mighty in deed and word, preached the Gospel to the Roman centurion. The Word goes to Antioch in Syria and creates a predominantly Gentile church there (Barnabas and Saul). Peter is rescued "from the hand of Herod and from all that the Jewish people were expecting"; he is preserved to promote the growth of the Word by championing Gentile freedom from the Law (Acts 15:7-11), while the persecuting king is destroyed.

Summarizing statement: "But the word of God grew and multiplied." (12:24)

IV. 13:1–16:5 The Word of the Lord Unites Jew and Gentile in One, Free Church

Paul's first missionary journey; the Judaistic controversy and its resolution at the Jerusalem Council.

Summarizing statement: "So the churches were strengthened in the faith, and they increased in numbers daily." (16:5)

V. 16:6–19:20 The Word of the Lord Goes in Conflict and Triumph to Macedonia, Achaia, and Asia

The second and third missionary journeys of Paul.

Summarizing statement: "So the word of the Lord grew and prevailed mightily." (19:20)

VI. 19:21–28:31 The Power of the Word of the Lord Made Perfect in Weakness

Paul the prisoner witnesses before "rulers and authorities" (Lk 12:11) and brings his Gospel to Rome.

Summarizing statement: "Preaching the kingdom of God and teaching about the Lord Jesus Christ quite openly and unhindered." (28:31)

Purpose of Acts

3 It may be, as some scholars have supposed, that the purpose of Acts is to make plain to the Roman world that Christianity is no treasonable, subversive movement but is innocent of any politically dangerous intent; its preachers may be "turning the world upside down" (Acts 17:6), but not in any sense that threatens the stability of the empire. It has often been pointed out that Luke repeatedly notes that Roman officials find Christianity politically innocuous (e. g., Acts 18:14-15; 23:29; 25:18-19; 26:32). But that purpose is at most a secondary one. The prime intent of the work is religious. It portrays the impact of the risen and exalted Christ on the wide world. The Christ confronts men in the inspired Word of the messengers whom He Himself has chosen. He confronts all sorts and conditions of men—Jews, Samaritans, Greeks, Romans, the high and the lowly, the king and the cripple, suave metropolitan philosophers and superstitious, excitable louts of the hinterland. He confronts them all with the gracious claim of His saving Lordship. Whether the response be the submission of faith or the resistance of unbelief or the mockery of skepticism, He is the Lord before whom the ways of men divide, as the Christ who is gathering the new people of God from among all the nations of the earth.

4 The book does not pretend to be a history of the first church or even a history of early missions; it would be woefully incomplete as either of the two. It is the con-

tinuation of the story of the Christ and can therefore be as selective in recording the facts of history as the Gospel itself. Of all the ways which the Gospel went, Luke selects just one, the high road to Rome. And even that segment of the total history of missions is not fully portrayed. There are, for instance, large gaps in the record of the career of Paul; both his 2-year ministry at Corinth and his 3-year ministry at Ephesus are merely illustrated by means of typical incidents rather than chronicled. The whole work illustrates rather than chronicles the course of the Word that proclaims and presents the Christ. Luke selects incidents and actions that illumine and bring out in clear outline the impact of that Word on men, the tensions and conflicts that ensue when the Word of the Lord is heard, and the triumphant progress of that Word despite tensions and conflicts.

5 If we understand the book thus on its own terms, the ending no longer appears strange or weak. Many have found the ending puzzling and inadequate: Why is the outcome of Paul's trial not told? Either his release or martyrdom would seem to constitute a more fitting conclusion to the work than the one Luke has seen fit to give it. Some scholars have suggested that Luke perhaps intended to add a third volume to his work, one that would round out and conclude the story by recounting Paul's release, his voyage to Spain, and his martyr's death. But there is no real indication that Luke intended such a continuation of his book; neither is the suggestion very plausible that Luke did not record the outcome of Paul's trial because the outcome was martyrdom, and he did not wish to conclude his account of the victorious Gospel on a sad and negative note. To judge from Luke's account of the martyrdom of Stephen (Acts 7:54-60) and from Paul's own attitude toward martyrdom as recorded by Luke (Acts 20:24; 21:13), neither Luke nor Paul looked on martyrdom as something negative and depressing.

6 The fact is that the present ending makes sense both as the conclusion of Acts and as the conclusion of the two-part work. It is not merely the end but the conclusion of Acts; the goal pointed to in Acts 1:8 has been reached: the Gospel is being proclaimed in Rome, the capital of the world; it has stepped through the door that opens into all the world. That is the fact that counts; before it any man's fate, even Paul's, pales into insignificance. And the present ending is a meaningful conclusion to the whole work. When Jesus "began to do and to teach" in His own city Nazareth, He offered His people God's free forgiveness on the basis of a word from Isaiah (Lk 4:18-21). He had met with objection and resistance from His own people even then (Lk 4:22-23, 28-30). And He had hinted that the Word they were rejecting would go to the Gentiles (Lk 4:24-27). Jesus' prediction is now being fulfilled; the Jews of Rome are following the course set by the Jews of Galilee and Jerusalem and the cities of Asia and Macedonia and Achaia. They are rejecting the proffered good news of God. The prophet Isaiah is heard once more, this time uttering words of fearful judgment on a people who will not hear (Acts 28:25-27). But God's purposes are being worked out nevertheless: "This salvation of God has been sent to the Gentiles; they will listen." (Acts 28:28)

ACTS OF THE APOSTLES

The Word of the Lord in Jerusalem

1:1–6:7

THE LINK WITH LUKE, THE 40 DAYS, THE ASCENSION (1:1-11)

1 In the first book, O The·oph′i·lus, I have dealt with all that Jesus began to do and teach, 2 until the day when he was taken up, after he had given commandment through the Holy Spirit to the apostles whom he had chosen. 3 To them he presented himself alive after his passion by many proofs, appearing to them during forty days, and speaking of the kingdom of God. 4And while staying[a] with them he charged them not to depart from Jerusalem, but to wait for the promise of the Father, which, he said, "you heard from me, 5 for John baptized with water, but before many days you shall be baptized with the Holy Spirit."

6 So when they had come together, they asked him, "Lord, will you at this time restore the kingdom to Israel?" 7 He said to them, "It is not for you to know times or seasons which the Father has fixed by his own authority. 8 But you shall receive power when the Holy Spirit has come upon you; and you shall be my witnesses in Jerusalem and in all Judea and Sa·mar′i·a and to the end of the earth." 9And when he had said this, as they were looking on, he was lifted up, and a cloud took him out of their sight. 10And while they were gazing into heaven as he went, behold, two men stood by them in white robes, 11 and said, "Men of Galilee, why do you stand looking into heaven? This Jesus, who was taken up from you into heaven, will come in the same way as you saw him go into heaven."

THE WAITING DISCIPLES (1:12-14)

12 Then they returned to Jerusalem from the mount called Olivet, which is near Jerusalem, a sabbath day's journey away; 13 and when they had entered, they went up to the upper room, where they were staying, Peter and John and James and Andrew, Philip and Thomas, Bartholomew and Matthew, James the son of Al·phae′us and Simon the Zealot and Judas the son of James. 14All these with one accord devoted

a Or *eating*

1:1–6:7 The Spirit-filled apostolic Word, spoken by men under the command and promise of the Lord Jesus (1:8), creates and sustains in Jerusalem a church which overcomes internal tensions and triumphs and grows despite outside opposition.

1:1-11 The first verse clearly marks Acts as the continuation of Luke's Gospel; the gospel is referred to as the *first book, Theophilus* is addressed again as at the beginning of the gospel (Lk 1:1-4), and the words *Jesus began to do and teach* imply that this second volume will recount what Jesus will continue to do and teach by His Spirit through His apostles. This continuity with the gospel is marked also in the account of the 40 days (1:2-5), which harks back to the *passion* (3) and portrays Jesus as continuing His teaching of the *kingdom of God,* the theme of His teaching in the gospel (e. g., 4:43; 8:1; 9:2, 11; 11:20). At the Ascension the *cloud* which receives Jesus recalls the cloud at the Transfiguration in the gospel (Lk 9:34). And the words of the *two men . . . in white robes*

(10) maintain the link with the gospel history (*Men of Galilee . . . will come in the same way,* 11).

1:4 *The promise of the Father,* the promised Holy Spirit. (Cf. Lk 24:49; Jn 14:16, 26; 15:26)

1:7-8 Jesus turns the thoughts of His disciples away from the idea of a reign in Israel toward a ministry by the power of the Spirit in the wide world.

1:8 *Jerusalem . . . Judaea . . . Samaria . . . end of the earth.* These stages of the progress of the Gospel indicate the structure of Acts. (Cf. Introduction)

1:12-14 The example and teaching of Jesus (cf. Introduction to Luke's Gospel, par. 14) had made of His disciples men of prayer; *with one accord devoted themselves to prayer.* (14)

1:12 *Mount called Olivet,* the Mount of Olives. *A sabbath day's journey,* the distance a pious Jew may travel on the Sabbath, about 800 yards.

1:14 *Mary.* The last mention of the mother of our Lord in the NT.

themselves to prayer, together with the women and Mary the mother of Jesus, and with his brothers.

THE ENROLLMENT OF MATTHIAS AMONG THE APOSTLES (1:15-26)

15 In those days Peter stood up among the brethren (the company of persons was in all about a hundred and twenty), and said, 16 "Brethren, the scripture had to be fulfilled, which the Holy Spirit spoke beforehand by the mouth of David, concerning Judas who was guide to those who arrested Jesus. 17 For he was numbered among us, and was allotted his share in this ministry. 18 (Now this man bought a field with the reward of his wickedness; and falling headlong[b] he burst open in the middle and all his bowels gushed out. 19And it became known to all the inhabitants of Jerusalem, so that the field was called in their language A·kel′da·ma, that is Field of Blood.) 20 For it is written in the book of Psalms,

'Let his habitation become desolate,
and let there be no one to live in it';

and

'His office let another take.'

21 So one of the men who have accompanied us during all the time that the Lord Jesus went in and out among us, 22 beginning from the baptism of John until the day when he was taken up from us—one of these men must become with us a witness to his resurrection." 23And they put forward two, Joseph called Bar′sab·bas, who was surnamed Justus, and Mat·thi′as. 24And they prayed and said, "Lord, who knowest the hearts of all men, show which one of these two thou hast chosen 25 to take the place in this ministry and apostleship from which Judas turned aside, to go to his own place." 26And they cast lots for them, and the lot fell on Mat·thi′as; and he was enrolled with the eleven apostles.

PENTECOST (2:1-13)

2 When the day of Pentecost had come, they were all together in one place. 2And suddenly a sound came from heaven like the rush of a mighty wind, and it filled all the house where they were sitting. 3And there appeared to them tongues as of fire, distributed and resting on each one of them. 4And they were all filled with the Holy Spirit and began to speak in other tongues, as the Spirit gave them utterance.

5 Now there were dwelling in Jerusalem Jews, devout men from every nation under

[b] Or *swelling up*

1:15-26 When Jesus appointed the 12 apostles (Lk 6:13), He was offering His Messianic grace and laying His Messianic claim to the 12 tribes, to ALL Israel. After Jesus' intercession for the people who crucified Him (Lk 23:34), that offer and claim is to be stated anew. Therefore Judas *must* be replaced (22); God wills that all Israel be confronted with the crucified and risen Christ (cf. 2:36; 3:25-26) and so be offered His forgiveness anew. (Cf. Lk 24:47)

1:16 *Mouth of David,* in the Psalter. Cf. 20 *(book of Psalms).*

1:18-19 Cf. Mt 27:3-10.

1:20 Cf. Ps 69:25; 109:8.

1:22 *The baptism of John* marks the beginning of the Gospel record in all the evangelists.

1:26 *They cast lots.* The casting of lots to determine the will of God is an OT provision; cf. e. g., Lv 16:8-10. This is the last instance of it (BEFORE Pentecost) in the Bible.

2:1-13 The church follows in the footsteps of the church's Lord. When Jesus emerged from Nazareth to undertake His public ministry in Israel (Lk 3:23), He was prepared and heralded for that

ministry by a manifest, "dramatic" bestowal of the Holy Spirit descending upon Him "in bodily form, as a dove" (Lk 3:22). So His church, emerging from the prayerful quiet of the upper room (Acts 1:13-14), was prepared by a miraculous bestowal of the Spirit, manifested in the power of wind and fire (2:2-3), for a ministry of witness in word (2:14-36, 38-40) and deed. (2:42-47)

2:1 *Pentecost.* The term means "fiftieth" (day) and designates the Feast of Weeks celebrated at the end of the grain harvest seven weeks after the Passover (Lv 23:15; Dt 16:9). This feast of grateful recognition of the goodness of the Creator drew Jewish pilgrims from all over the world to Jerusalem. (Cf. 9-11)

2:2-3 *Like the rush . . . as of fire.* The mysterious and mighty manifestation of the Spirit is recorded in language that is suggestive rather than descriptive.

2:4 *Speak in other tongues.* Cf. 2:6, 8, 11. The curse of Babel is canceled (Gn 11:7, 9); the church is enabled by the Spirit to speak to men of all nations in their own tongues and will become the new people of God gathered out of all nations,

heaven. 6And at this sound the multitude came together, and they were bewildered, because each one heard them speaking in his own language. 7And they were amazed and wondered, saying, "Are not all these who are speaking Galileans? 8And how is it that we hear, each of us in his own native language? 9 Parthians and Medes and Elamites and residents of Mes·o·po·ta′mi·a, Judea and Cap·pa·do′ci·a, Pontus and Asia, 10 Phryg′i·a and Pam·phyl′i·a, Egypt and the parts of Libya belonging to Cy-re′ne, and visitors from Rome, both Jews and proselytes. 11 Cretans and Arabians, we hear them telling in our own tongues the mighty works of God." 12And all were amazed and perplexed, saying to one another, "What does this mean?" 13 But others mocking said, "They are filled with new wine."

WITNESS IN WORD AND DEED (2:14-47)

14 But Peter, standing with the eleven, lifted up his voice and addressed them, "Men of Judea and all who dwell in Jerusalem, let this be known to you, and give ear to my words. 15 For these men are not drunk, as you suppose, since it is only the third hour of the day; 16 but this is what was spoken by the prophet Joel:

17   'And in the last days it shall be, God declares,
             that I will pour out my Spirit upon all flesh,
             and your sons and your daughters shall prophesy,
             and your young men shall see visions,
             and your old men shall dream dreams;
18   yea, and on my menservants and my maidservants in those days
             I will pour out my Spirit; and they shall prophesy.
19   And I will show wonders in the heaven above
             and signs on the earth beneath,
             blood, and fire, and vapor of smoke;
20   the sun shall be turned into darkness
             and the moon into blood,
             before the day of the Lord comes,
             the great and manifest day.
21   And it shall be that whoever calls on the name of the Lord shall be saved.'

22 "Men of Israel, hear these words: Jesus of Nazareth, a man attested to you by God with mighty works and wonders and signs which God did through him in your midst, as you yourselves know— 23 this Jesus, delivered up according to the definite plan and foreknowledge of God, you crucified and killed by the hands of lawless men. 24 But God raised him up, having loosed the pangs of death, because it was not possible for him to be held by it. 25 For David says concerning him,

God's harvest of a new mankind united in Christ.

2:12-13 The history of the church is the continuation of that of Jesus (cf. 1:1-11 note); again there is "a division among the Jews because of these words" (Jn 10:19-21). Some are led to ask and seek, others mock.

2:14-47 "Beginning with . . . scripture he told . . . the good news of Jesus" (Acts 8:35). The words with which Luke describes Philip's witness to the Ethiopian eunuch are an apt characterization of all NT proclamation. (Cf. Jesus' proclamation in Nazareth, Lk 4:16-21.) Peter interprets the Pentecost miracle as the fulfillment of the OT prophecy of Joel which promised the outpouring of the Spirit *upon all flesh* (17) for the last days (Jl 2:28-32). That outpouring would usher in the day of God's final reckoning, the *day of the Lord . . . great and manifest* (20). On that day only he who *calls on the name of the Lord shall be saved* (21). And that Lord, Peter proclaims, is none other than *Jesus of Nazareth,* whom God attested to

His people *with mighty works and wonders and signs* (22), whom *God raised up,* vindicated and glorified, though His people *crucified* Him (32, 36). He is the Giver of the Spirit; He is the Lord who will judge; He is the *Lord and Christ* on whose name men must call in order to be saved from *this crooked generation* of men who have rejected Him. (40)

2:15 *The third hour,* about 9 a. m., too early for any but the most dissolute to be *drunk.* The charge is dismissed as the absurdity it is, rather than rebutted.

2:22-36 This part of Peter's sermon is concerned to show that Jesus is the *Lord* of v. 25, that His crucifixion was not an untoward accident but a part of God's *definite plan* for His Servant (23), that God reversed the verdict of men upon Him by raising Him from the dead, as *David* had foreseen and foretold (Ps 16:8-11; Acts 2:25-34), that David's greater Son has indeed been manifested (*made,* 36) as *both Lord and Christ* by God Himself.

'I saw the Lord always before me,
    for he is at my right hand that I may not be shaken;
26   therefore my heart was glad, and my tongue rejoiced;
    moreover my flesh will dwell in hope.
27   For thou wilt not abandon my soul to Hades,
    nor let thy Holy One see corruption.
28   Thou hast made known to me the ways of life;
    thou wilt make me full of gladness with thy presence.'

29 "Brethren, I may say to you confidently of the patriarch David that he both died and was buried, and his tomb is with us to this day. 30 Being therefore a prophet, and knowing that God had sworn with an oath to him that he would set one of his descendants upon his throne, 31 he foresaw and spoke of the resurrection of the Christ, that he was not abandoned to Hades, nor did his flesh see corruption. 32 This Jesus God raised up, and of that we all are witnesses, 33 Being therefore exalted at the right hand of God, and having received from the Father the promise of the Holy Spirit, he has poured out this which you see and hear. 34 For David did not ascend into the heavens; but he himself says,

'The Lord said to my Lord, Sit at my right hand,
35   till I make thy enemies a stool for thy feet.'

36 Let all the house of Israel therefore know assuredly that God has made him both Lord and Christ, this Jesus whom you crucified."

37 Now when they heard this they were cut to the heart, and said to Peter and the rest of the apostles, "Brethren, what shall we do?" 38And Peter said to them, "Repent, and be baptized every one of you in the name of Jesus Christ for the forgiveness of your sins; and you shall receive the gift of the Holy Spirit. 39 For the promise is to you and to your children and to all that are far off, every one whom the Lord our God calls to him." 40And he testified with many other words and exhorted them, saying, "Save yourselves from this crooked generation." 41 So those who received his word were baptized, and there were added that day about three thousand souls. 42And they devoted themselves to the apostles' teaching and fellowship, to the breaking of bread and the prayers.

43 And fear came upon every soul; and many wonders and signs were done through the apostles. 44And all who believed were together and had all things in common; 45 and they sold their possessions and goods and distributed them to all, as any had need. 46And day by day, attending the temple together and breaking bread in their homes, they partook of food with glad and generous hearts, 47 praising God and having favor with all the people. And the Lord added to their number day by day those who were being saved.

HEALING THE LAME BEGGAR AND CONFLICT WITH AUTHORITIES (3:1 – 4:31)

3 Now Peter and John were going up to the temple at the hour of prayer, the ninth hour. 2And a man lame from birth was being carried, whom they laid daily at that gate of the temple which is called Beautiful to ask alms of those who entered

---

2:30 *God had sworn with an oath.* Ps 132:11.

2:34 Ps 110:1 is added to the witness of Ps 16 to indicate that Jesus' resurrection signified not only survival but Lordship and the glory of being enthroned with God; Jesus *did* (what could not be said of the speaker of the psalm) . . . *ascend into the heavens,* there to reign and triumph.

2:39 *Whom the Lord our God calls.* When men "call on the name of the Lord" (12), that is the result of God's effectual calling to them.

2:41-47 The operation of the Spirit transformed not only the disciples' crude Galilean speech (7) but their whole inner life, making it a life centered in the apostles' inspired *teaching,* a life of *fellowship* at the Table of their Lord (*breaking of bread*

and of *prayer,* a new life marked by an active communal love (44-45) and a high-hearted (*glad and generous hearts,* 46) adoration of God. Thus their works reinforced the witness of their words; men sensed the presence of the divine among them, *and fear came upon every soul* (43); the whole demeanor of the disciples among their people, whether in the public worship in the *temple* (46) or *in their homes* (46), was such that it won them *favor with all the people* (47), and the Lord used it to win men (47, *added to their number*).

3:1 – 4:31 The apostles Peter and John did what they as apostles of Christ had to do; they were poor, yet equipped by Christ to make many rich (2 Co 6:10). To the lame beggar at the Beautiful

the temple. ³ Seeing Peter and John about to go into the temple, he asked for alms. ⁴And Peter directed his gaze at him, with John, and said, "Look at us." ⁵And he fixed his attention upon them, expecting to receive something from them. ⁶ But Peter said, "I have no silver and gold, but I give you what I have; in the name of Jesus Christ of Nazareth, walk." ⁷And he took him by the right hand and raised him up; and immediately his feet and ankles were made strong. ⁸And leaping up he stood and walked and entered the temple with them, walking and leaping and praising God. ⁹And all the people saw him walking and praising God, ¹⁰ and recognized him as the one who sat for alms at the Beautiful Gate of the temple; and they were filled with wonder and amazement at what had happened to him.

11 While he clung to Peter and John, all the people ran together to them in the portico called Solomon's, astounded. ¹²And when Peter saw it he addressed the people, "Men of Israel, why do you wonder at this, or why do you stare at us, as though by our own power or piety we had made him walk? ¹³ The God of Abraham and of Isaac and of Jacob, the God of our fathers, glorified his servant*ᶜ* Jesus, whom you delivered up and denied in the presence of Pilate, when he had decided to release him. ¹⁴ But you denied the Holy and Righteous One, and asked for a murderer to be granted to you, ¹⁵ and killed the Author of life, whom God raised from the dead. To this we are witnesses. ¹⁶And his name, by faith in his name, has made this man strong whom you see and know; and the faith which is through Jesus*ᵈ* has given the man this perfect health in the presence of you all.

ᶜ Or *child*   *ᵈ* Greek *him*

Gate of the temple they gave the riches of Christ's healing compassion, so that *leaping up,* he *walked* (3:8). They spoke—as they had to speak—as witnesses of Christ in Jerusalem (1:8); they dared not let this deed of God's Servant Jesus be attributed to their *own power or piety* (3:12). The apostle of Christ must point men away from himself *to the God of Abraham and of Isaac and of Jacob* and *his servant Jesus* (3:13). It was their simple fidelity to the charge given them by their Lord that led to their first collision with the Jewish authorities, not any provocative manifesto issued in the name of the rejected Messiah nor any planned program of opposition to Judaism. In fact the apostles (like their Lord before them) went all the way to seek and find the lost sheep of the house of Israel where they lived. They went to Israel's temple at the appointed hour to pray (3:1), they spoke in the language of Israel's sacred book, in terms of the *God of Abraham and of Isaac and of Jacob* (3:13), in terms of the *servant* whose fate and significance (for Israel and all nations) Isaiah had foretold (3:13, 26) in terms of *Moses'* promise of a *prophet* like himself (Dt 18:15-16, 23), One whose word would spell weal or woe to every soul as it was accepted or rejected, in terms of God's *covenant* with *Abraham* with its promise of blessing for *all the families of the earth* (3:25; Gn 22:18). They spoke of God's amnesty for His people's *wickedness* (3:26). And when they were called to account by the high court of their people (4:5), they spoke simply as the *Holy Spirit* (4:8) prompted them, silent neither concerning the guilt of those who had *crucified Jesus Christ of Nazareth* (4:10) nor concerning the *salvation* (4:12) which God was offering His people, in spite of all, in the name of the Crucified (4:12). Moreover, in the prayer and praise with which the church responded to the

persecution at the hands of their fellow Jews there is no trace of any vengeful spirit. These men of the church bow before the Creator and Lord of history (4:23-26) who guides the actions of kings, governors, and nations to do what God's *hand* and *plan had predestined to take place* (4:27-28; cf. Ps 2:1-2). They commit their future to God's almighty hand (*look upon their threats,* 4:29), but they do not pray for revenge; they ask for boldness in their speech and for the gift of healing in their deeds (4:29-30). They go in the meek way of the *servant* Jesus and are confirmed in this course by a renewed outpouring of the Holy Spirit and a clear manifestation of the Spirit's presence among them (*the place . . . was shaken,* 4:31).

If the men of Israel were to suffer the doom of being hardened in their sin, as Isaiah had threatened (cf. Acts 28:26-27), and so leave the Gentiles to inherit the promised salvation of God, the guilt was Israel's, not the apostles' or their Lord's. *They* had spoken God's final offer of salvation to the full, inspired and moved by the Spirit.

3:1 *Hour of prayer . . . the ninth hour.* The hour of prayer coincided with the offering of the two daily sacrifices, early in the morning and at the ninth hour. (3 p. m.)

3:2 *Beautiful,* probably to be identified with an Eastern gate which a contemporary source describes as made of Corinthian bronze and "far exceeding in value those plated with silver and set in gold."

3:11 *Portico called Solomon's.* Cf. Jn 10:23. This portico soon became a regular gathering place for the Christians in the early days at Jerusalem. (Cf. 5:12)

3:14 *Righteous One.* Cf. Is 53:11; Acts 7:52; 22:14; Ja 5:6; 1 Jn 2:1.

17 "And now, brethren, I know that you acted in ignorance, as did also your rulers. 18 But what God foretold by the mouth of all the prophets, that his Christ should suffer, he thus fulfilled. 19 Repent therefore, and turn again, that your sins may be blotted out, that times of refreshing may come from the presence of the Lord, 20 and that he may send the Christ appointed for you, Jesus, 21 whom heaven must receive until the time for establishing all that God spoke by the mouth of his holy prophets from of old. 22 Moses said, 'The Lord God will raise up for you a prophet from your brethren as he raised me up. You shall listen to him in whatever he tells you. 23And it shall be that every soul that does not listen to that prophet shall be destroyed from the people.' 24And all the prophets who have spoken, from Samuel and those who came afterwards, also proclaimed these days. 25 You are the sons of the prophets and of the covenant which God gave to your fathers, saying to Abraham, 'And in your posterity shall all the families of the earth be blessed.' 26 God, having raised up his servant,[c] sent him to you first, to bless you in turning every one of you from your wickedness."

4 And as they were speaking to the people, the priests and the captain of the temple and the Sad'du·cees came upon them, 2 annoyed because they were teaching the people and proclaiming in Jesus the resurrection from the dead. 3And they arrested them and put them in custody until the morrow, for it was already evening. 4 But many of those who heard the word believed; and the number of the men came to about five thousand.

5 On the morrow their rulers and elders and scribes were gathered together in Jerusalem, 6 with Annas the high priest and Ca'ia·phas and John and Alexander, and all who were of the high-priestly family. 7And when they had set them in the midst, they inquired, "By what power or by what name did you do this?" 8 Then Peter, filled with the Holy Spirit, said to them, "Rulers of the people and elders, 9 if we are being examined today concerning a good deed done to a cripple, by what means this man has been healed, 10 be it known to you all, and to all the people of Israel, that by the name of Jesus Christ of Nazareth, whom you crucified, whom God raised from the dead, by him this man is standing before you well. 11 This is the stone which was rejected by you builders, but which has become the head of the corner. 12And there is salvation in no one else, for there is no other name under heaven given among men by which we must be saved."

13 Now when they saw the boldness of Peter and John, and perceived that they were uneducated, common men, they wondered; and they recognized that they had been with Jesus. 14 But seeing the man that had been healed standing beside them, they had nothing to say in opposition. 15 But when they had commanded them to

---

3:17 *You acted in ignorance.* Cf. Lk 23:34; 1 Ti 1: 13. For the opposite cf. Heb 10:26, "If we sin deliberately after receiving the knowledge of the truth," and Heb 6:4-6 note.

3:25 *Sons of the prophets and of the covenant,* destined to inherit the promise spoken by the prophets and the blessing promised by the covenant. (Cf. 26)

3:26 *To you first, to bless you.* Cf. Ro 1:16.

4:1-2 The *Sadducees,* members of the party in which the priestly aristocracy was most influential, would naturally be in the forefront of opposition to Christianity for two reasons: (1) They sought to remain on good terms with the Romans and therefore looked with suspicion on any Messianic movement which might bring on Roman intervention and put an end to their privileged priestly position (cf. Jn 11:48). (2) They denied the resurrection of the dead in principle (cf. Mt 22:23; Lk 20:27; Acts 23:8). When the Christians proclaimed the resurrection of the dead in Jesus (a Messianic "Pretender" whom the Romans had

executed!), they were politically unacceptable and theologically offensive to the Sadducees.

4:1 The *captain of the temple,* an officer in charge of the temple guard (composed of Levites) and responsible for preserving order in the temple. He was second in authority only to the high priest. (Cf. 5:24, 26)

4:6 *Annas* and *Caiaphas.* Although Annas had been deposed from the high priesthood about A. D. 15, he continued to be so influential during the high priesthood of his sons and his son-in-law Caiaphas (cf. Jn 18:13) that he was regarded as virtual high priest, as here. Cf. Lk 3:2, where his name is coupled with that of Caiaphas in dating the beginning of the Baptist's ministry.

John and *Alexander* cannot be identified.

4:9 *Examined . . . concerning a good deed.* Cf. the words of Jesus in Jn 10:31.

4:11 Cf. Mt 21:42, where Jesus cites Ps 118:22 to interpret His mission and its significance in the same sense.

go aside out of the council, they conferred with one another, [16] saying, "What shall we do with these men? For that a notable sign has been performed through them is manifest to all the inhabitants of Jerusalem, and we cannot deny it. [17] But in order that it may spread no further among the people, let us warn them to speak no more to any one in this name." [18] So they called them and charged them not to speak or teach at all in the name of Jesus. [19] But Peter and John answered them, "Whether it is right in the sight of God to listen to you rather than to God, you must judge; [20] for we cannot but speak of what we have seen and heard." [21] And when they had further threatened them, they let them go, finding no way to punish them, because of the people; for all men praised God for what had happened. [22] For the man on whom this sign of healing was performed was more than forty years old.

23 When they were released they went to their friends and reported what the chief priests and the elders had said to them. [24] And when they heard it, they lifted their voices together to God and said, "Sovereign Lord, who didst make the heaven and the earth and the sea and everything in them, [25] who by the mouth of our father David, thy servant,[c] didst say by the Holy Spirit,

'Why did the Gentiles rage,
    and the peoples imagine vain things?
[26]   The kings of the earth set themselves in array,
    and the rulers were gathered together,
    against the Lord and against his Anointed'—[e]

[27] for truly in this city there were gathered together against thy holy servant[c] Jesus, whom thou didst anoint, both Herod and Pontius Pilate, with the Gentiles and the peoples of Israel, [28] to do whatever thy hand and thy plan had predestined to take place. [29] And now, Lord, look upon their threats, and grant to thy servants[f] to speak thy word with all boldness, [30] while thou stretchest out thy hand to heal, and signs and wonders are performed through the name of thy holy servant[c] Jesus." [31] And when they had prayed, the place in which they were gathered together was shaken; and they were all filled with the Holy Spirit and spoke the word of God with boldness.

"ALL THE WORDS OF THIS LIFE" (4:32 – 6:7)

32 Now the company of those who believed were of one heart and soul, and no one said that any of the things which he possessed was his own, but they had every-

[c] Or *child*   [e] Or *Christ*   [f] Or *slaves*

4:25-26 Ps 2:1-2.
4:27 *Herod.* Cf. Lk 23:6-12.
4:32 – 6:7 The angel of the Lord released the imprisoned apostles in order that they might *go and stand in the temple and speak to the people all the words of this Life* (5:20), the new life made possible by the resurrection of Jesus from the dead. Those words by the power of the Spirit create the life of God's new world in the midst of the old; they are words to be lived and words that must be spoken (4:20). In the midst of the old world they can be lived and spoken only amid a constant struggle. (Paul calls on Christians to put on the "armor of light" in order to live "as in the day," Ro 13:12-13.)

The *words of this Life* created in the young church that unanimity of *heart and soul* (4:32) which the Spirit inspires, a unanimity that did not remain sentiment and theory; it expressed itself in the sacrificial giving of *lands and houses* for the needs of the community – *they had everything in common* (4:32). But the church had not only the encouragement of the example of a *Barnabas* (4:36-37), rightly named *Son of encourage-*

ment; the church had to endure the shock of seeing an *Ananias* and a *Sapphira* attempting the fearful blasphemy of lying to the Holy Spirit and of putting His omniscient majesty to the test (5:3, 9). The church had to endure the salutary but shattering experience of the *great fear* that *came upon the whole church and upon all who heard of these things* (5:11) when God's judgment laid the blasphemers dead at their feet (5:1-11). The *words of this Life* become "fragrance of death" (2 Co 2:16) to those who will not bow before them.

The Word of life had to be spoken; and the apostles spoke it so vigorously that their Sadducee opponents had reason to complain that the apostles had *filled Jerusalem with* their *teaching* (5:28). The disciples' prayer that God would stretch out His hand to heal and do signs and wonders through the name of His holy Servant Jesus (4:30) was heard. So strongly did God reinforce their words with the many signs and wonders done by the hands of the apostles that the people *held them in high honor* (5:13). But they did not escape renewed persecution; and though officialdom dealt cautiously with them (5:26), the new hearing

thing in common. ³³And with great power the apostles gave their testimony to the resurrection of the Lord Jesus, and great grace was upon them all. ³⁴ There was not a needy person among them, for as many as were possessors of lands or houses sold them, and brought the proceeds of what was sold ³⁵ and laid it at the apostles' feet; and distribution was made to each as any had need. ³⁶ Thus Joseph who was surnamed by the apostles Bar′na·bas (which means, Son of encouragement), a Levite, a native of Cyprus, ³⁷ sold a field which belonged to him, and brought the money and laid it at the apostles' feet.

5 But a man named An·a·ni′as with his wife Sap·phi′ra sold a piece of property, ² and with his wife's knowledge he kept back some of the proceeds, and brought only a part and laid it at the apostles' feet. ³ But Peter said, "An·a·ni′as, why has Satan filled your heart to lie to the Holy Spirit and to keep back part of the proceeds of the land? ⁴ While it remained unsold, did it not remain your own? And after it was sold, was it not at your disposal? How is it that you have contrived this deed in your heart? You have not lied to men but to God." ⁵ When An·a·ni′as heard these words, he fell down and died. And great fear came upon all who heard of it. ⁶ The young men rose and wrapped him up and carried him out and buried him.

7 After an interval of about three hours his wife came in, not knowing what had happened. ⁸And Peter said to her, "Tell me whether you sold the land for so much." And she said, "Yes, for so much." ⁹ But Peter said to her, "How is it that you have agreed together to tempt the Spirit of the Lord? Hark, the feet of those that have buried your husband are at the door, and they will carry you out." ¹⁰ Immediately she fell down at his feet and died. When the young men came in they found her dead, and they carried her out and buried her beside her husband. ¹¹And great fear came upon the whole church, and upon all who heard of these things.

12 Now many signs and wonders were done among the people by the hands of the apostles. And they were all together in Solomon's Portico. ¹³ None of the rest dared join them, but the people held them in high honor. ¹⁴And more than ever believers were added to the Lord, multitudes both of men and women, ¹⁵ so that they even carried out the sick into the streets, and laid them on beds and pallets, that as Peter came by at least his shadow might fall on some of them. ¹⁶ The people also

before the council (5:27) confronted the apostles with Sadducees so *enraged* that they *wanted to kill them* (5:33); only the prudent words of the Pharisaic teacher of the Law, Gamaliel (5:34-39), restrained them so far that they were content, for the time being, with a renewed enjoinder to silence and a flogging (5:40) before releasing the apostles.

Threats and flogging could not silence the inspired witnesses to *Jesus as the Christ* (5:42); but the apostles' devotion to their prime task of *prayer and . . . ministry of the word* (6:4) was impeded, or at least threatened, by an internal dissension concerning the *daily distribution* of support to the widows (6:1); but God gave the church men *full of the Spirit and of wisdom* (6:3) so that the *words of this Life* could be both lived and proclaimed with no confusion of priorities. Luke can look back on the checkered history of the Word in Jerusalem with the calm and confident words: *The word of God increased; and the number of the disciples multiplied greatly.* (6:7)

4:36 *Barnabas,* first mentioned here, is a telling example of the validity of Jesus' law: "To him who has will more be given, and he will have abundance" (Mt 13:12). He has "the words of this Life" and accepts the claim these words make on him,

sharing actively in the life of the church. And to him more is given. He takes the initiative in binding Paul (Saul) and the Jerusalem church together (9:27); he is privileged to be the emissary of the Jerusalem church to the new Gentile church in Antioch (11:22-23); he is associated with Paul in administering the charity of Gentile Antioch toward Judaic Jerusalem (11:30; 12:25) and in Paul's first missionary thrust into the Gentile world (Acts 13 – 15). Paul's mention of him in 1 Co 9:6 shows that he remained throughout his richly blessed ministry the same selfless, generous man whom we meet here, "a good man, full of the Holy Spirit and of faith," as Luke characterizes him in 11:24.

Son of encouragement. How this meaning is derived from the name Barnabas is not clear. It was probably his gift of encouraging speech that earned him the name. (The word translated "exhorted" in 11:23 can also be translated "encouraged.")

5:4 These words show how completely voluntary the sharing of property was. The term "Christian communism," sometimes applied to this aspect of the life of the Jerusalem church, is at best misleading.

5:12 *Solomon's Portico.* Cf. 3:11.

gathered from the towns around Jerusalem, bringing the sick and those afflicted with unclean spirits, and they were all healed.

17 But the high priest rose up and all who were with him, that is, the party of the Sad′du·cees, and filled with jealousy 18 they arrested the apostles and put them in the common prison. 19 But at night an angel of the Lord opened the prison doors and brought them out and said, 20 "Go and stand in the temple and speak to the people all the words of this Life." 21And when they heard this, they entered the temple at daybreak and taught.

Now the high priest came and those who were with him and called together the council and all the senate of Israel, and sent to the prison to have them brought. 22 But when the officers came, they did not find them in the prison, and they returned and reported, 23 "We found the prison securely locked and the sentries standing at the doors, but when we opened it we found no one inside." 24 Now when the captain of the temple and the chief priests heard these words, they were much perplexed about them, wondering what this would come to. 25And some one came and told them, "The men whom you put in prison are standing in the temple and teaching the people." 26 Then the captain with the officers went and brought them, but without violence, for they were afraid of being stoned by the people.

27 And when they had brought them, they set them before the council. And the high priest questioned them, 28 saying, "We strictly charged you not to teach in this name, yet here you have filled Jerusalem with your teaching and you intend to bring this man's blood upon us." 29 But Peter and the apostles answered, "We must obey God rather than men. 30 The God of our fathers raised Jesus whom you killed by hanging him on a tree. 31 God exalted him at his right hand as Leader and Savior, to give repentance to Israel and forgiveness of sins. 32And we are witnesses to these things, and so is the Holy Spirit whom God has given to those who obey him."

33 When they heard this they were enraged and wanted to kill them. 34 But a Pharisee in the council named Ga·ma′li·el, a teacher of the law, held in honor by all the people, stood up and ordered the men to be put outside for a while. 35And he said to them, "Men of Israel, take care what you do with these men. 36 For before these days Theudas arose, giving himself out to be somebody, and a number of men, about four hundred, joined him; but he was slain and all who followed him were dispersed and came to nothing. 37After him Judas the Galilean arose in the days of the census and drew away some of the people after him; he also perished, and all who followed him were scattered. 38 So in the present case I tell you, keep away from these men and let them alone; for if this plan or this undertaking is of men, it will fail; 39 but if it is of God, you will not be able to overthrow them. You might even be found opposing God!"

40 So they took his advice, and when they had called in the apostles, they beat

---

5:17 *Sadducees.* Cf. 4:1-2 note.

5:21 *Senate,* another name for the supreme council (Sanhedrin) composed of high priests, elders, and scribes. (Cf. 4:15)

5:24 *Captain of the temple.* Cf. 4:1 note.

5:26 *Stoned by the people.* Stoning was the punishment appointed for blasphemy (Lv 24:15-16). The people would construe an attack on men so signally distinguished by marks of God's favor (cf. 12) and characterized by sanctity of life as a blasphemous act.

5:30 *Hanging him on a tree.* The OT language (Dt 21:22-23) recalls the fact that one thus executed was considered to be cursed by God. (Cf. 1 Co 12:3)

5:31-32 *We are witnesses . . . and so is the Holy Spirit.* Cf. Jn 15:26-27. Any man with eyes and ears could have been a witness to Jesus' crucifixion; only men endowed with the *Spirit* could

testify that the Crucified is *Leader and Savior* in whom God offers *Israel repentance* and *forgiveness of sins.*

5:34 *Gamaliel,* renowned and long-remembered *teacher of the law,* referred to by Paul as his teacher in 22:3. For the differences in teaching and temper (and consequently in their attitude toward Christianity) between Sadducee and Pharisee cf. 23:6-10.

5:36 *Theudas,* otherwise unknown. A Theudas mentioned by the Jewish historian Josephus as a false messiah arose some years after (A. D. 44) the events here recorded by Luke.

5:37 *Judas the Galilean,* leader of a rebellion against Rome when the Roman legate stated Rome's claim to lordship over Israel in drastic terms by ordering a *census* (for purposes of taxation) taken. Judas and his followers found in this an intolerable conflict with God's own lordship

them and charged them not to speak in the name of Jesus, and let them go. 41 Then they left the presence of the council, rejoicing that they were counted worthy to suffer dishonor for the name. 42And every day in the temple and at home they did not cease teaching and preaching Jesus as the Christ.

6 Now in these days when the disciples were increasing in number, the Hel'len·ists murmured against the Hebrews because their widows were neglected in the daily distribution. 2And the twelve summoned the body of the disciples and said, "It is not right that we should give up preaching the word of God to serve tables. 3 Therefore, brethren, pick out from among you seven men of good repute, full of the Spirit and of wisdom, whom we may appoint to this duty. 4 But we will devote ourselves to prayer and to the ministry of the word." 5And what they said pleased the whole multitude, and they chose Stephen, a man full of faith and of the Holy Spirit, and Philip, and Proch'o·rus, and Ni·ca'nor, and Timon, and Par'me·nas, and Nic'o·laus, a proselyte of Antioch. 6 These they set before the apostles, and they prayed and laid their hands upon them.

7 And the word of God increased; and the number of the disciples multiplied greatly in Jerusalem, and a great many of the priests were obedient to the faith.

The Word of the Lord Triumphs over Persecution

6:8 — 9:31

8 And Stephen, full of grace and power, did great wonders and signs among the people. 9 Then some of those who belonged to the synagogue of the Freedmen (as it was called), and of the Cy·re'ni·ans, and of the Alexandrians, and of those from Cilicia and Asia, arose and disputed with Stephen. 10 But they could not withstand the wisdom and the Spirit with which he spoke. 11 Then they secretly instigated men,

---

over His people. His followers were later known as Zealots. Cf. Lk 6:15; Acts 1:13; for the census cf. Lk 2:1-2 note.

5:41 *Rejoicing . . . suffer dishonor.* Cf. Lk 6:22-23.

6:5 The names indicate that the seven chosen to supervise the charitable work were Hellenists (6:1); one of them was not a born Jew but a convert to Judaism *(proselyte).*

6:7 This is the first of six summarizing statements (cf. 9:31; 12:24; 16:5; 19:20; 28:31) with which Luke indicates the plan, or pattern, of his history. (Cf. Introduction, par. 2)

6:8 — 9:31 Persecution could not halt the progress of the Word in Jerusalem (cf. 6:7). The Word sped on and triumphed over and through persecution. Neither could persecution halt the march of the Word from Jerusalem to Samaria and the Gentile world. Three men are prominent in that movement: Stephen (6:8 — 8:2), Philip (8:4-40), and Saul (Paul, 9:1-30). Through Stephen, one of the seven (6:1-6), the line of division between Christianity and Judaism was sharply drawn, and it was through him that persecution broke out, not only on the apostles but on the whole church. The persecution that scattered the church also scattered abroad the Gospel. Philip, another of the seven (6:5), escaped from the jurisdiction of the Jerusalem authorities into Samaria and planted the Gospel there; and it was Philip who baptized an Ethiopian eunuch, excluded from the ancient people of God both because he was a Gentile and because he was a eunuch (Dt 23:1). So the promise of Is 56:3-5 and the prayer of Ps 68:31 were ful-

filled in this foreigner, and the universally inclusive character of the new people of God found an unforgettable expression. The third man involved in this stage of the progress of the Word was Saul, the faithful Pharisee and zealous devotee of Judaic tradition (cf. Gl 1:14) who spearheaded the new persecution of the church and carried it beyond Jerusalem to Damascus (9:2). The light that broke on Saul near Damascus, when the Lord laid claim to His chosen instrument (9:15), was destined to break through Saul the persecutor turned Paul the apostle (cf. 13:9 note) on the whole Gentile world. (26:23)

6:8 *Full of grace and power.* Cf. 6:3, 6, 10. The seven were never intended to be narrow specialists in welfare work.

6:9 *Synagogue of the Freedmen.* Jerusalem had literally hundreds of synagogs at this time, some of which were designed to serve special national or linguistic groups. The *Freedmen* were evidently Jewish men who had been Roman captives or sons of such captives and had been liberated. They would naturally be Greek-speaking Jews rather than "Hebrews" (6:1), and the synagog named after them would be one in which the Greek language was used (this would hold also of the synagogs of the *Cyrenians, Alexandrians, those from Cilicia and Asia* — if indeed we are to think of them as separate synagogs; perhaps one synagog served all these Greek-speaking groups). Such men would naturally carry on their dispute with a Greek-speaking Jew like Stephen.

6:11-14 Cf. Lk 23:1-2. Luke points up the paral-

who said, "We have heard him speak blasphemous words against Moses and God." [12]And they stirred up the people and the elders and the scribes, and they came upon him and seized him and brought him before the council, [13] and set up false witnesses who said, "This man never ceases to speak words against this holy place and the law; [14] for we have heard him say that this Jesus of Nazareth will destroy this place, and will change the customs which Moses delivered to us." [15]And gazing at him, all who sat in the council saw that his face was like the face of an angel.

7 And the high priest said, "Is this so?" [2]And Stephen said:

"Brethren and fathers, hear me. The God of glory appeared to our father Abraham, when he was in Mes·o·po·ta′mi·a, before he lived in Haran, [3] and said to him, 'Depart from your land and from your kindred and go into the land which I will show you.' [4] Then he departed from the land of the Chal·de′ans, and lived in Haran. And after his father died, God removed him from there into this land in which you are now living; [5] yet he gave him no inheritance in it, not even a foot's length, but promised to give it to him in possession and to his posterity after him, though he had no child. [6]And God spoke to this effect, that his posterity would be aliens in a land belonging to others, who would enslave them and ill-treat them four hundred years. [7] 'But I will judge the nation which they serve,' said God, 'and after that they shall come out and worship me in this place.' [8]And he gave him the covenant of circumcision. And so Abraham became the father of Isaac, and circumcised him on the eighth day; and Isaac became the father of Jacob, and Jacob of the twelve patriarchs.

[9] "And the patriarchs, jealous of Joseph, sold him into Egypt; but God was with him, [10] and rescued him out of all his afflictions, and gave him favor and wisdom before Pharaoh, king of Egypt, who made him governor over Egypt and over all his household. [11] Now there came a famine throughout all Egypt and Canaan, and great affliction, and our fathers could find no food. [12] But when Jacob heard that there was grain in Egypt, he sent forth our fathers the first time. [13]And at the second visit Joseph made himself known to his brothers, and Joseph's family became known to Pharaoh. [14]And Joseph sent and called to him Jacob his father and all his kindred, seventy-five souls; [15] and Jacob went down into Egypt. And he died, himself and our fathers, [16] and they were carried back to Shechem and laid in the tomb that Abraham had bought for a sum of silver from the sons of Hamor in Shechem.

[17] "But as the time of the promise drew near, which God had granted to Abraham, the people grew and multiplied in Egypt [18] till there arose over Egypt another king who had not known Joseph. [19] He dealt craftily with our race and forced our fathers to expose their infants, that they might not be kept alive. [20]At this time Moses was born, and was beautiful before God. And he was brought up for three months in his father's house; [21] and when he was exposed, Pharaoh's daughter adopted him and brought him up as her own son. [22]And Moses was instructed in all the wisdom of the Egyptians, and he was mighty in his words and deeds.

[23] "When he was forty years old, it came into his heart to visit his brethren, the sons of Israel. [24]And seeing one of them being wronged, he defended the oppressed man and avenged him by striking the Egyptian. [25] He supposed that his brethren understood that God was giving them deliverance by his hand, but they did not understand. [26]And on the following day he appeared to them as they were quarreling and would have reconciled them, saying, 'Men, you are brethren, why do you wrong

lel between the trial of Stephen and that of Jesus. (Cf. Mt 26:59-66)

7:1-53 Stephen's defense, apparently a mere survey of the history of Israel, is in fact a pointed answer to the charges brought against him (6:11-14). His narrative, based on OT Scriptures, makes plain that the *God of glory* (2; cf. Ps 29, esp. v. 3) works where He wills, independent of any "holy place," including the temple. He performed His mighty acts in distant and "unholy" lands, calling Abraham in *Mesopotamia* (2), making *holy ground* of a spot in the *wilderness of Mount Sinai*

when He appeared to Moses (30-33), performing signs and wonders through Moses *in Egypt and at the Red Sea and in the wilderness* (36). All through the decisive, foundation-laying portion of its history Israel had no temple (44); and after Solomon had built a house for Israel's God (47), Isaiah spoke the Word of the Lord which declared that no house could contain the Creator of heaven and earth (48-50; Is 66:1-2). The temple could not be the ultimate expression of God's presence among His people; Judaic zeal for the temple is branded by Scripture itself as fanatical and misplaced, and

each other?' 27 But the man who was wronging his neighbor thrust him aside, saying, 'Who made you a ruler and a judge over us? 28 Do you want to kill me as you killed the Egyptian yesterday?' 29At this retort Moses fled, and became an exile in the land of Midian, where he became the father of two sons.

30 "Now when forty years had passed, an angel appeared to him in the wilderness of Mount Sinai, in a flame of fire in a bush. 31 When Moses saw it he wondered at the sight; and as he drew near to look, the voice of the Lord came, 32 'I am the God of your fathers, the God of Abraham and of Isaac and of Jacob.' And Moses trembled and did not dare to look. 33And the Lord said to him, 'Take off the shoes from your feet, for the place where you are standing is holy ground. 34 I have surely seen the ill-treatment of my people that are in Egypt and heard their groaning, and I have come down to deliver them. And now come, I will send you to Egypt.'

35 "This Moses whom they refused, saying, 'Who made you a ruler and a judge?' God sent as both ruler and deliverer by the hand of the angel that appeared to him in the bush. 36 He led them out, having performed wonders and signs in Egypt and at the Red Sea, and in the wilderness for forty years. 37 This is the Moses who said to the Israelites, 'God will raise up for you a prophet from your brethren as he raised me up.' 38 This is he who was in the congregation in the wilderness with the angel who spoke to him at Mount Sinai, and with our fathers; and he received living oracles to give to us. 39 Our fathers refused to obey him, but thrust him aside, and in their hearts they turned to Egypt, 40 saying to Aaron, 'Make for us gods to go before us; as for this Moses who led us out from the land of Egypt, we do not know what has become of him.' 41And they made a calf in those days, and offered a sacrifice to the idol and rejoiced in the works of their hands. 42 But God turned and gave them over to worship the host of heaven, as it is written in the book of the prophets:

> 'Did you offer to me slain beasts and sacrifices,
>   forty years in the wilderness, O house of Israel?

43   And you took up the tent of Moloch,
>   and the star of the god Rephan,
>   the figures which you made to worship;
>   and I will remove you beyond Babylon.'

44 "Our fathers had the tent of witness in the wilderness, even as he who spoke to Moses directed him to make it, according to the pattern that he had seen. 45 Our fathers in turn brought it in with Joshua when they dispossessed the nations which God thrust out before our fathers. So it was until the days of David, 46 who found favor in the sight of God and asked leave to find a habitation for the God of Jacob. 47 But it was Solomon who built a house for him. 48 Yet the Most High does not dwell in houses made with hands; as the prophet says,

49   'Heaven is my throne,
>   and earth my footstool.
>   What house will you build for me, says the Lord,
>   or what is the place of my rest?

50   Did not my hand make all these things?'

51 "You stiff-necked people, uncircumcised in heart and ears, you always resist the Holy Spirit. As your fathers did, so do you. 52 Which of the prophets did not your fathers persecute? And they killed those who announced beforehand the coming of

---

Israel's fury at any doubt cast on its permanence is not an expression of holy zeal.

The record of Israel is not a record of holy zeal for what is God's; rather it is a record of rebellion and apostasy. The nation which betrayed Joseph (9), rejected and disobeyed Moses (35, 39), turned from the living God to idols (40-43), persecuted the prophets (52), killed the men of God *who announced beforehand the coming of the Righteous One,* the Christ (52), *betrayed and murdered the Righteous One when He appeared* (52), a nation that *did not keep* the Law for which they profess such zeal (53)—how dare they crown their persistent resistance to the Holy Spirit (51) by attempting to silence the Spirit who speaks in Stephen (cf. 6:10)? When they stop their ears to evade the force of Stephen's words, that is of a piece with the fact that they have stopped their ears to the voice of the Law itself, which pointed beyond itself, beyond Moses to the Prophet promised for latter days. (37; cf. 3:22-23; Dt 18:15, 18)

7:42-43 Cf. Amos 5:25-27, quoted freely.

the Righteous One, whom you have now betrayed and murdered, [53] you who received the law as delivered by angels and did not keep it."

54 Now when they heard these things they were enraged, and they ground their teeth against him. [55] But he, full of the Holy Spirit, gazed into heaven and saw the glory of God, and Jesus standing at the right hand of God; [56] and he said, "Behold, I see the heavens opened, and the Son of man standing at the right hand of God." [57] But they cried out with a loud voice and stopped their ears and rushed together upon him. [58] Then they cast him out of the city and stoned him; and the witnesses laid down their garments at the feet of a young man named Saul. [59]And as they were stoning Stephen, he prayed, "Lord Jesus, receive my spirit." [60]And he knelt down and cried with a loud voice, "Lord, do not hold this sin against them." And when he had said this, he fell asleep. [1]And Saul was consenting to his death.

And on that day a great persecution arose against the church in Jerusalem; and they were all scattered throughout the region of Judea and Sa·mar′i·a, except the apostles. [2] Devout men buried Stephen, and made great lamentation over him. [3] But Saul was ravaging the church, and entering house after house, he dragged off men and women and committed them to prison.

4 Now those who were scattered went about preaching the word. [5] Philip went down to a city of Sa·mar′i·a, and proclaimed to them the Christ. [6]And the multitudes with one accord gave heed to what was said by Philip, when they heard him and saw the signs which he did. [7] For unclean spirits came out of many who were possessed, crying with a loud voice; and many who were paralyzed or lame were healed. [8] So there was much joy in that city.

9 But there was a man named Simon who had previously practiced magic in the city and amazed the nation of Sa·mar′i·a, saying that he himself was somebody great. [10] They all gave heed to him, from the least to the greatest, saying, "This man is that power of God which is called Great." [11]And they gave heed to him, because for a long time he had amazed them with his magic. [12] But when they believed Philip as he preached good news about the kingdom of God and the name of Jesus Christ, they were baptized, both men and women. [13] Even Simon himself believed, and after being baptized he continued with Philip. And seeing signs and great miracles performed, he was amazed.

14 Now when the apostles at Jerusalem heard that Sa·mar′i·a had received the word of God, they sent to them Peter and John, [15] who came down and prayed for them that they might receive the Holy Spirit; [16] for it had not yet fallen on any of them, but they had only been baptized in the name of the Lord Jesus. [17] Then they laid their hands on them and they received the Holy Spirit. [18] Now when Simon saw that the Spirit was given through the laying on of the apostles' hands, he offered them money, [19] saying, "Give me also this power, that any one on whom I lay my hands may receive the Holy Spirit." [20] But Peter said to him, "Your silver perish with you, because you thought you could obtain the gift of God with money! [21] You have neither part nor lot in this matter, for your heart is not right before God. [22] Repent therefore of this wickedness of yours, and pray to the Lord that, if possible, the intent of your

---

7:56 *Son of man,* Jesus' most characteristic self-designation, occurs some 80 times in the gospels but only here, on the lips of the first martyr, outside the gospels.

7:59-60 Stephen prays to his Lord (Jesus), as Jesus had prayed to the Father. (Cf. Lk 23:46; 23:34)

8:1 *Saul was consenting to his death.* Cf. 22:19-20.

Except the apostles. The apostles probably felt bound to remain in Jerusalem, where their first duty lay; as "Hebrews" (6:1) they had less to fear than men like Stephen and Philip from an outbreak directed primarily at "Hellenists." The men

of the NT neither fear martyrdom nor seek it.

Samaria. Cf. 1:8. The second stage of the church's witness as foretold by Jesus is now reached.

8:9-24 *Simon.* Later generations wove many legends about the figure of Simon, but for Luke the point seems to be that this is the first of a series of confrontations between Christianity and the world of pagan *magic.* (9; cf. 13:6-12; 16:16-18; 19:11-20)

8:20 *Obtain the gift of God with money.* The difference between the world of magic with its murky self-seeking and the world of the Gospel is sharply illumined by this statement. Witnesses to the

heart may be forgiven you. 23 For I see that you are in the gall of bitterness and in the bond of iniquity." 24And Simon answered, "Pray for me to the Lord, that nothing of what you have said may come upon me."

25 Now when they had testified and spoken the word of the Lord, they returned to Jerusalem, preaching the gospel to many villages of the Samaritans.

26 But an angel of the Lord said to Philip, "Rise and go toward the south*g* to the road that goes down from Jerusalem to Gaza." This is a desert road. 27And he rose and went. And behold, an Ethiopian, a eunuch, a minister of the Can′da·ce, queen of the Ethiopians, in charge of all her treasure, had come to Jerusalem to worship 28 and was returning; seated in his chariot, he was reading the prophet I·sa′iah. 29And the Spirit said to Philip, "Go up and join this chariot." 30 So Philip ran to him, and heard him reading I·sa′iah the prophet, and asked, "Do you understand what you are read- ing?" 31And he said, "How can I, unless some one guides me?" And he invited Philip to come up and sit with him. 32 Now the passage of the scripture which he was reading was this:

> "As a sheep led to the slaughter
> or a lamb before its shearer is dumb,
> so he opens not his mouth.
> 33 In his humiliation justice was denied him.
> Who can describe his generation?
> For his life is taken up from the earth."

34And the eunuch said to Philip, "About whom, pray, does the prophet say this, about himself or about some one else?" 35 Then Philip opened his mouth, and begin- ning with this scripture he told him the good news of Jesus. 36And as they went along the road they came to some water, and the eunuch said, "See, here is water! What is to prevent my being baptized?"*h* 38And he commanded the chariot to stop, and they both went down into the water, Philip and the eunuch, and he baptized him. 39And when they came up out of the water, the Spirit of the Lord caught up Philip; and the eunuch saw him no more, and went on his way rejoicing. 40 But Philip was found at A·zo′tus, and passing on he preached the gospel to all the towns till he came to Caes- a·re′a.

9 But Saul, still breathing threats and murder against the disciples of the Lord, went to the high priest 2 and asked him for letters to the synagogues at Damascus, so that if he found any belonging to the Way, men or women, he might bring them bound to Jerusalem. 3 Now as he journeyed he approached Damascus, and suddenly a light from heaven flashed about him. 4And he fell to the ground and heard a voice saying to him, "Saul, Saul, why do you persecute me?" 5And he said, "Who are you, Lord?" And he said, "I am Jesus, whom you are persecuting; 6 but rise and enter the city, and you will be told what you are to do." 7 The men who were traveling with him stood speechless, hearing the voice but seeing no one. 8 Saul arose from the ground; and when his eyes were opened, he could see nothing; so they led him by the

---

g Or *at noon*
h Other ancient authorities add all or most of verse 37, *And Philip said, "If you believe with all your heart, you may." And he replied, "I believe that Jesus Christ is the Son of God."*

Christ not only receive but also give "without pay." (Mt 10:8)

8:23 *Gall of bitterness . . . bond of iniquity.* To Peter's enlightened vision the man whom blind superstition accepted as "somebody great" (9) and hailed as "that power of God which is called Great" (10) appears as the victim of the bitter poison and enslaving power of sin.

8:27 *Minister,* a court official *in charge of* the queen's treasury. (*Candace* is a title rather than a proper name.) His visit to Jerusalem and his interest in the OT indicate that he was in some sense a proselyte to Judaism.

8:32-33 Cf. Is 53:7-8, a prophecy of Jesus, the

Suffering Servant who suffers vicariously for the sins of many.

8:40 *Philip was found at Azotus.* The vagueness of the language reflects the mysteriousness of the Spirit's action. (39)

9:1-19 For the conversion of Saul cf. 22:3-21; 26:9-20; Gl 1:13-17.

9:2 *The Way.* This designation of Christianity is found only in Acts (19:9, 23; 22:4; 24:14, 22) as a name applied by Christians to themselves (cf. 24:14). The origin of the term remains obscure.

9:4 *Persecute me.* Whosoever persecutes the church, the body of Christ, persecutes the Head of the church, Christ.

hand and brought him into Damascus. 9And for three days he was without sight, and neither ate nor drank.

10 Now there was a disciple at Damascus named An·a·ni′as. The Lord said to him in a vision, "An·a·ni′as." And he said, "Here I am, Lord." 11And the Lord said to him, "Rise and go to the street called Straight, and inquire in the house of Judas for a man of Tarsus named Saul; for behold, he is praying, 12 and he has seen a man named An·a·ni′as come in and lay his hands on him so that he might regain his sight." 13 But An·a·ni′as answered, "Lord, I have heard from many about this man, how much evil he has done to thy saints at Jerusalem; 14 and here he has authority from the chief priests to bind all who call upon thy name." 15 But the Lord said to him, "Go, for he is a chosen instrument of mine to carry my name before the Gentiles and kings and the sons of Israel; 16 for I will show him how much he must suffer for the sake of my name." 17 So An·a·ni′as departed and entered the house. And laying his hands on him he said, "Brother Saul, the Lord Jesus who appeared to you on the road by which you came, has sent me that you may regain your sight and be filled with the Holy Spirit." 18And immediately something like scales fell from his eyes and he regained his sight. Then he rose and was baptized, 19 and took food and was strengthened.

For several days he was with the disciples at Damascus. 20And in the synagogues immediately he proclaimed Jesus, saying, "He is the Son of God." 21And all who heard him were amazed, and said, "Is not this the man who made havoc in Jerusalem of those who called on this name? And he has come here for this purpose, to bring them bound before the chief priests." 22 But Saul increased all the more in strength, and confounded the Jews who lived in Damascus by proving that Jesus was the Christ.

23 When many days had passed, the Jews plotted to kill him, 24 but their plot became known to Saul. They were watching the gates day and night, to kill him; 25 but his disciples took him by night and let him down over the wall, lowering him in a basket.

26 And when he had come to Jerusalem he attempted to join the disciples; and they were all afraid of him, for they did not believe that he was a disciple. 27 But Bar′na·bas took him, and brought him to the apostles, and declared to them how on the road he had seen the Lord, who spoke to him, and how at Damascus he had preached boldly in the name of Jesus. 28 So he went in and out among them at Jerusalem, 29 preaching boldly in the name of the Lord. And he spoke and disputed against the Hel′len·ists; but they were seeking to kill him. 30And when the brethren knew it, they brought him down to Caes·a·re′a, and sent him off to Tarsus.

31 So the church throughout all Judea and Galilee and Sa·mar′i·a had peace and was built up; and walking in the fear of the Lord and in the comfort of the Holy Spirit it was multiplied.

The Word of the Lord a Light to the Gentiles

9:32 – 12:25

32 Now as Peter went here and there among them all, he came down also to the saints that lived at Lydda. 33 There he found a man named Ae·ne′as, who had been

9:10 *Here I am.* The response implies a willingness to obey the voice heard in the vision. (Cf. Gn 22:1, 7, 11; 1 Sm 3:4; Is 6:8)

9:15 *To carry my name.* Cf. Paul's own words, Ro 15:20.

9:23-25 Cf. 2 Co 11:32-33.

9:31 *Peace . . . built up . . . multiplied.* This calm doxology for triumph through persecution is the second of Luke's six summarizing conclusions marking stages in the progress of the Gospel from Jerusalem to Rome. (Cf. Introduction, par. 2)

9:32 – 12:25 Luke's record has already made it plain that the living and active Word could not

be contained in Jerusalem; it had to break forth and begin its conquering progress through the world, in Samaria and beyond. As subsequent events were to show (e. g., ch. 15), the transition of the Word from the Judaic to the Gentile world would be fraught with the danger to the church that the admission of Gentiles would cause a cleavage between Judaic and Gentile Christianity. This section of Acts (9:32 – 12:25) reveals how the Lord of the church moved to avert that danger as He dealt with His servants Peter, Barnabas, and Saul (Paul) and with His new people in Jerusalem. Peter, mighty in word and deed (9:32-43), is di-

bedridden for eight years and was paralyzed. ³⁴And Peter said to him, "Ae·ne′as, Jesus Christ heals you; rise and make your bed." And immediately he rose. ³⁵And all the residents of Lydda and Sharon saw him, and they turned to the Lord.

36 Now there was at Joppa a disciple named Tabitha, which means Dorcas.ˣ She was full of good works and acts of charity. ³⁷In those days she fell sick and died; and when they had washed her, they laid her in an upper room. ³⁸Since Lydda was near Joppa, the disciples, hearing that Peter was there, sent two men to him entreating him, "Please come to us without delay." ³⁹So Peter rose and went with them. And when he had come, they took him to the upper room. All the widows stood beside him weeping, and showing tunics and other garments which Dorcas made while she was with them. ⁴⁰But Peter put them all outside and knelt down and prayed; then turning to the body he said, "Tabitha, rise." And she opened her eyes, and when she saw Peter she sat up. ⁴¹And he gave her his hand and lifted her up. Then calling the saints and widows he presented her alive. ⁴²And it became known throughout all Joppa, and many believed in the Lord. ⁴³And he stayed in Joppa for many days with one Simon, a tanner.

10 At Caes·a·re′a there was a man named Cornelius, a centurion of what was known as the Italian Cohort, ² a devout man who feared God with all his household, gave alms liberally to the people, and prayed constantly to God. ³About the ninth hour of the day he saw clearly in a vision an angel of God coming in and saying to him, "Cornelius." ⁴And he stared at him in terror, and said, "What is it, Lord?" And he said to him, "Your prayers and your alms have ascended as a memorial before God. ⁵And now send men to Joppa, and bring one Simon who is called Peter; ⁶ he is lodging with Simon, a tanner, whose house is by the seaside." ⁷When the angel who spoke to him had departed, he called two of his servants and a devout soldier from among those that waited on him, ⁸ and having related everything to them, he sent them to Joppa.

9 The next day, as they were on their journey and coming near the city, Peter went up on the housetop to pray, about the sixth hour. ¹⁰And he became hungry and desired something to eat; but while they were preparing it, he fell into a trance ¹¹ and saw the heaven opened, and something descending, like a great sheet, let down by four corners upon the earth. ¹² In it were all kinds of animals and reptiles and birds of the air.

ˣ The name Tabitha in Aramaic and the name Dorcas in Greek mean *gazelle*

vinely taught to overcome his Judaic exclusiveness (10:9-29); as he is moved to bring the Gospel to the Gentile Roman centurion Cornelius he sees the wideness of God's mercy with new eyes and associates freely with men whom he had previously considered unclean (10:34-35); Barnabas the Levite (4:36) is sent by the Jerusalem church to Antioch in Syria, where the Word had called into being a predominantly Gentile church (11:20-21); he rejoiced (11:23) at the grace of God which united Antioch and Jerusalem, Gentile and Jew, in one new people of God. And through Barnabas, that *good man full of the Holy Spirit and of faith* (11:24), Saul is drawn into the work among the Gentiles in Antioch. The bond established between Gentile and Judaic Christians by the sending of Barnabas to Antioch is further strengthened when the Gentile Christians of Antioch are moved to respond to the need of Judaic Christians in Jerusalem and send help by the hand of Barnabas and Saul (11:27-30; 12:25). Palestinian Christians learned that an accommodation with Judaism was not to be hoped for. Judaism spoke a hard no to the Gospel by its approval of Herod's action in executing the apostle James and imprisoning Peter (12:1-3). James is not replaced by a new apostle, as Judas was at the beginning (1:15-26 note);

the 12 tribes have heard, but in vain, the witness of the 12 messengers of Jesus. But Peter is rescued *from the hand of Herod and from all that the Jewish people were expecting* (12:11) to continue God's offer of grace to "a disobedient and contrary people" (Ro 10:21; cf. Gl 2:7, 9) and to become the champion of Gentile freedom from the Law (Acts 15:7-11), while the judgment of God strikes the king who had made himself the persecuting arm of Judaism. (12:20-23)

9:34 *Jesus Christ heals you.* These words are the perfect brief interpretation of the nature of the mighty deeds wrought by apostles. (Cf. Ro 15:18-19)

10:1 *Italian Cohort.* The cohort, the tenth part of a legion, numbered 600 men or more, with auxiliary cavalry in addition. The name *Italian* indicates that the troops had been mustered in Italy and were probably Roman citizens.

10:2 As often in Acts (10:22, 35; 16:14; 17:4, 17), the words used to describe Cornelius indicate a Gentile who has been drawn to Judaism and has in some sense been "converted" to the Jewish faith. They are frequently the most receptive hearers of the Gospel. The term "worshiper" (18:7) is also found in this sense. Cornelius gave generous help to the Jewish people.

13And there came a voice to him, "Rise, Peter; kill and eat." 14 But Peter said, "No, Lord; for I have never eaten anything that is common or unclean." 15And the voice came to him again a second time, "What God has cleansed, you must not call common." 16 This happened three times, and the thing was taken up at once to heaven.

17 Now while Peter was inwardly perplexed as to what the vision which he had seen might mean, behold, the men that were sent by Cornelius, having made inquiry for Simon's house, stood before the gate 18 and called out to ask whether Simon who was called Peter was lodging there. 19And while Peter was pondering the vision, the Spirit said to him, "Behold, three men are looking for you. 20 Rise and go down, and accompany them without hesitation; for I have sent them." 21And Peter went down to the men and said, "I am the one you are looking for; what is the reason for your coming?" 22And they said, "Cornelius, a centurion, an upright and God-fearing man, who is well spoken of by the whole Jewish nation, was directed by a holy angel to send for you to come to his house, and to hear what you have to say." 23 So he called them in to be his guests.

The next day he rose and went off with them, and some of the brethren from Joppa accompanied him. 24And on the following day they entered Caes·a·re′a. Cornelius was expecting them and had called together his kinsmen and close friends. 25 When Peter entered, Cornelius met him and fell down at his feet and worshiped him. 26 But Peter lifted him up, saying, "Stand up; I too am a man." 27And as he talked with him, he went in and found many persons gathered; 28 and he said to them, "You yourselves know how unlawful it is for a Jew to associate with or to visit any one of another nation; but God has shown me that I should not call any man common or unclean. 29 So when I was sent for, I came without objection. I ask then why you sent for me."

30 And Cornelius said, "Four days ago, about this hour, I was keeping the ninth hour of prayer in my house; and behold, a man stood before me in bright apparel, 31 saying, 'Cornelius, your prayer has been heard and your alms have been remembered before God. 32 Send therefore to Joppa and ask for Simon who is called Peter; he is lodging in the house of Simon, a tanner, by the seaside.' 33 So I sent to you at once, and you have been kind enough to come. Now therefore we are all here present in the sight of God, to hear all that you have been commanded by the Lord."

34 And Peter opened his mouth and said: "Truly I perceive that God shows no partiality, 35 but in every nation any one who fears him and does what is right is acceptible to him. 36 You know the word which he sent to Israel, preaching good news of peace by Jesus Christ (he is Lord of all), 37 the word which was proclaimed throughout all Judea, beginning from Galilee after the baptism which John preached: 38 how God anointed Jesus of Nazareth with the Holy Spirit and with power; how he went about doing good and healing all that were oppressed by the devil, for God was with him. 39And we are witnesses to all that he did both in the country of the Jews and in Jerusalem. They put him to death by hanging him on a tree; 40 but God raised him on the third day and made him manifest; 41 not to all the people but to us who were chosen by God as witnesses, who ate and drank with him after he rose from the dead. 42And he commanded us to preach to the people, and to testify that he is the one ordained by God to be judge of the living and the dead. 43 To him all the prophets bear witness that every one who believes in him receives forgiveness of sins through his name."

44 While Peter was still saying this, the Holy Spirit fell on all who heard the word. 45And the believers from among the circumcised who came with Peter were amazed, because the gift of the Holy Spirit had been poured out even on the Gentiles. 46 For they heard them speaking in tongues and extolling God. Then Peter declared, 47 "Can any one forbid water for baptizing these people who have received the Holy Spirit just as we have?" 48And he commanded them to be baptized in the name of Jesus Christ. Then they asked him to remain for some days.

10:14 *Common or unclean.* The two words are synonyms, designating foods prohibited by the Law.

10:25-26 Cf. 3:12; 14:14-15. The apostles are selfless men and consistently refuse to accept any honor due their Lord, in complete antithesis to the human tendency as seen, for instance, in Herod. (12:22)

11 Now the apostles and the brethren who were in Judea heard that the Gentiles also had received the word of God. 2 So when Peter went up to Jerusalem, the circumcision party criticized him, 3 saying, "Why did you go to uncircumcised men and eat with them?" 4 But Peter began and explained to them in order: 5 "I was in the city of Joppa praying; and in a trance I saw a vision, something descending, like a great sheet, let down from heaven by four corners; and it came down to me. 6 Looking at it closely I observed animals and beasts of prey and reptiles and birds of the air. 7And I heard a voice saying to me, 'Rise, Peter; kill and eat.' 8 But I said, 'No, Lord; for nothing common or unclean has ever entered my mouth.' 9 But the voice answered a second time from heaven, 'What God has cleansed you must not call common.' 10 This happened three times, and all was drawn up again into heaven. 11At that very moment three men arrived at the house in which we were, sent to me from Caes·a·re′a. 12And the Spirit told me to go with them, making no distinction. These six brethren also accompanied me, and we entered the man's house. 13And he told us how he had seen the angel standing in his house and saying, 'Send to Joppa and bring Simon called Peter; 14 he will declare to you a message by which you will be saved, you and all your household.' 15As I began to speak, the Holy Spirit fell on them just as on us at the beginning. 16And I remembered the word of the Lord, how he said, 'John baptized with water, but you shall be baptized with the Holy Spirit.' 17 If then God gave the same gift to them as he gave to us when we believed in the Lord Jesus Christ, who was I that I could withstand God?" 18 When they heard this they were silenced. And they glorified God, saying, "Then to the Gentiles also God has granted repentance unto life."

19 Now those who were scattered because of the persecution that arose over Stephen traveled as far as Phoe·nic′i·a and Cyprus and Antioch, speaking the word to none except Jews. 20 But there were some of them, men of Cyprus and Cy·re′ne, who on coming to Antioch spoke to the Greeks*i* also, preaching the Lord Jesus. 21And the hand of the Lord was with them, and a great number that believed turned to the Lord. 22 News of this came to the ears of the church in Jerusalem, and they sent Bar′na·bas to Antioch. 23 When he came and saw the grace of God, he was glad; and he exhorted them all to remain faithful to the Lord with steadfast purpose; 24 for he was a good man, full of the Holy Spirit and of faith. And a large company was added to the Lord. 25 So Bar′na·bas went to Tarsus to look for Saul; 26 and when he had found him, he brought him to Antioch. For a whole year they met with*j* the church, and taught a large company of people; and in Antioch the disciples were for the first time called Christians.

27 Now in these days prophets came down from Jerusalem to Antioch. 28And one of them named Ag′a·bus stood up and foretold by the Spirit that there would be a great famine over all the world; and this took place in the days of Claudius. 29And the disciples determined, every one according to his ability, to send relief to the brethren who lived in Judea; 30 and they did so, sending it to the elders by the hand of Bar′na·bas and Saul.

12 About that time Herod the king laid violent hands upon some who belonged to the church. 2 He killed James the brother of John with the sword; 3 and when

i Other ancient authorities read *Hellenists*   *j* Or *were guests of*

11:2 *The circumcision party,* those Judaic Christians who insisted that Gentiles could come into the new people of God only via Judaism, i. e., by submitting to circumcision and the law of Moses. (Cf. 15:1, 5; Gl 2:11-12)

11:8 *Common or unclean.* Cf. 10:14 note.

11:17 Cf. 15:7-8.

11:18 *They were silenced,* not necessarily convinced, a hint that the objection advanced by the circumcision party (11:2) would be heard again. (Cf. 15:1, 5)

11:22 The Jerusalem church continues the practice begun in Samaria (8:14-17) of establishing and fostering solidarity between the old and the new churches.

11:26 *For the first time called Christians.* The term "Christian" was first applied to the followers of Jesus by outsiders; in all three NT occurrences the term is either used by outsiders (here and 26:28) or reflects their attitude. (1 Ptr 4:16)

11:28 *Claudius,* Roman emperor A. D. 41 – 54.

12:1 *Herod the king.* Herod Agrippa I, grandson of Herod the Great, was reared in Rome, where he found friends among members of the Imperial family. Through the favor of various Roman emperors he greatly expanded his territory until

he saw that it pleased the Jews, he proceeded to arrest Peter also. This was during the days of Unleavened Bread. [4]And when he had seized him, he put him in prison, and delivered him to four squads of soldiers to guard him, intending after the Passover to bring him out to the people. [5] So Peter was kept in prison; but earnest prayer for him was made to God by the church.

6 The very night when Herod was about to bring him out, Peter was sleeping between two soldiers, bound with two chains, and sentries before the door were guarding the prison; [7] and behold, an angel of the Lord appeared, and a light shone in the cell; and he struck Peter on the side and woke him, saying, "Get up quickly." And the chains fell off his hands. [8]And the angel said to him, "Dress yourself and put on your sandals." And he did so. And he said to him, "Wrap your mantle around you and follow me." [9]And he went out and followed him; he did not know that what was done by the angel was real, but thought he was seeing a vision. [10] When they had passed the first and the second guard, they came to the iron gate leading into the city. It opened to them of its own accord, and they went out and passed on through one street; and immediately the angel left him. [11]And Peter came to himself, and said, "Now I am sure that the Lord has sent his angel and rescued me from the hand of Herod and from all that the Jewish people were expecting."

12 When he realized this, he went to the house of Mary, the mother of John whose other name was Mark, where many were gathered together and were praying. [13]And when he knocked at the door of the gateway, a maid named Rhoda came to answer. [14] Recognizing Peter's voice, in her joy she did not open the gate but ran in and told that Peter was standing at the gate. [15] They said to her, "You are mad." But she insisted that it was so. They said, "It is his angel!" [16] But Peter continued knocking; and when they opened, they saw him and were amazed. [17] But motioning to them with his hand to be silent, he described to them how the Lord had brought him out of the prison. And he said, "Tell this to James and to the brethren." Then he departed and went to another place.

18 Now when day came, there was no small stir among the soldiers over what had become of Peter. [19]And when Herod had sought for him and could not find him, he examined the sentries and ordered that they should be put to death. Then he went down from Judea to Caes·a·re′a, and remained there.

20 Now Herod was angry with the people of Tyre and Sidon; and they came to him in a body, and having persuaded Blastus, the king's chamberlain, they asked for peace, because their country depended on the king's country for food. [21] On an appointed day Herod put on his royal robes, took his seat upon the throne, and made an oration to them. [22]And the people shouted, "The voice of a god, and not of man!" [23] Immediately an angel of the Lord smote him, because he did not give God the glory; and he was eaten by worms and died.

24 But the word of God grew and multiplied.

25 And Bar′na·bas and Saul returned from[k] Jerusalem when they had fulfilled their mission, bringing with them John whose other name was Mark.

[k] Other ancient authorities read to

it practically equaled that of his grandfather, Herod the Great. At the same time he sought and won the favor of his subjects by presenting himself to them as devotee and champion of Judaism. His willingness to accept divine honors, after the manner of pagan rulers (12:22), indicates that his Judaism was more of the surface than of the substance.

12:3 Days of Unleavened Bread, the seven days immediately following and closely associated with the Passover. (Ex 12:8; 13:3-10)

12:12 John . . . Mark. Cf. Introduction to Mark's Gospel.

12:17 James, the brother of the Lord, appears here as the acknowledged leader of the Jerusalem church. (Cf. Gl 1:19; 2:9, 12; and Introduction to Letter of James)

12:24 The third of Luke's summarizing statements (cf. Introduction, par. 2). In spite of internal tensions and outside persecution, the word of God grew and multiplied.

12:25 Cf. 11:27-30.

13:1 – 16:5 Paul's first missionary journey (chs. 13 – 14), the Judaistic controversy and its resolution at the Jerusalem Council (ch. 15). See Introduction to Galatians, pars. 1-11.

13:2 Set apart. The verb used suggests the idea of consecration for a particular task. (Cf. Ro 1:1)

13:5 John. Cf. 12:12 note and Introduction to Mark's Gospel.

The Word of the Lord Unites Jew and Gentile

13:1 — 16:5

13 Now in the church at Antioch there were prophets and teachers, Bar´na·bas, Simeon who was called Niger, Lucius of Cy·re´ne, Man´a·en a member of the court of Herod the tetrarch, and Saul. ² While they were worshiping the Lord and fasting, the Holy Spirit said, "Set apart for me Bar´na·bas and Saul for the work to which I have called them." ³ Then after fasting and praying they laid their hands on them and sent them off.

4 So, being sent out by the Holy Spirit, they went down to Se·leu´cia; and from there they sailed to Cyprus. ⁵ When they arrived at Sal´a·mis, they proclaimed the word of God in the synagogues of the Jews. And they had John to assist them. ⁶ When they had gone through the whole island as far as Paphos, they came upon a certain magician, a Jewish false prophet, named Bar-Je´sus. ⁷ He was with the proconsul, Ser´gi·us Paulus, a man of intelligence, who summoned Bar´na·bas and Saul and sought to hear the word of God. ⁸ But El´y·mas the magician (for that is the meaning of his name) withstood them, seeking to turn away the proconsul from the faith. ⁹ But Saul, who is also called Paul, filled with the Holy Spirit, looked intently at him ¹⁰ and said, "You son of the devil, you enemy of all righteousness, full of all deceit and villainy, will you not stop making crooked the straight paths of the Lord? ¹¹And now, behold, the hand of the Lord is upon you, and you shall be blind and unable to see the sun for a time." Immediately mist and darkness fell upon him and he went about seeking people to lead him by the hand. ¹² Then the proconsul believed, when he saw what had occurred, for he was astonished at the teaching of the Lord.

13 Now Paul and his company set sail from Paphos, and came to Perga in Pamphyl´i·a. And John left them and returned to Jerusalem; ¹⁴ but they passed on from Perga and came to Antioch of Pi·sid´i·a. And on the sabbath day they went into the synagogue and sat down. ¹⁵After the reading of the law and the prophets, the rulers of the synagogue sent to them, saying, "Brethren, if you have any word of exhortation for the people, say it." ¹⁶ So Paul stood up, and motioning with his hand said:

"Men of Israel, and you that fear God, listen. ¹⁷ The God of this people Israel chose our fathers and made the people great during their stay in the land of Egypt, and with uplifted arm he led them out of it. ¹⁸And for about forty years he bore with *m* them in the wilderness. ¹⁹And when he had destroyed seven nations in the land of

---

m Other ancient authorities read *cared for* (Deut 1.31)

13:8 *Magician.* Cf. 8:9-24.

That is the meaning of his name. The explanatory note is not clear; Bar-Jesus (6) does not mean "magician," and that meaning can be given to *Elymas* only by indirect and unconvincing ways. Perhaps all that Luke intends to say is that the magician had two names, one Jewish and the other Greek, as Saul (Paul) did. (9)

13:9 *Saul, who is also called Paul.* As a Roman citizen (22:27-28) Saul/Paul no doubt had both a Jewish and a Roman name from his youth. Luke at this point, where the Gospel moves into the larger Roman world, begins to call him by his Roman name and mentions him before Barnabas, whereas hitherto Barnabas has been named first. In the Roman world the initiative lies with Paul.

13:10 *Son of the devil.* The expression is Hebraic, indicating that the magician derives his nature and character as opponent of the Gospel from the devil.

13:15 *Word of exhortation.* Cf. Heb 13:22 note.

13:16 *You that fear God,* proselytes. Cf. 10:2 note.

13:16-41 Paul's first recorded sermon in the synagog at Pisidian Antioch reads like an expansion of the summary of the Gospel which Paul himself gives in Ro 1:1-5: "The gospel of God which he promised beforehand through his prophets in the holy scriptures, the gospel concerning his Son, who was descended from David according to the flesh and designated Son of God in power according to the Spirit of holiness by his resurrection from the dead, Jesus Christ our Lord, through whom we have received grace." Paul proclaims the Gospel of God; it is His Word concerning His saving action. "God" is the first word of the sermon (17), and He is the acting subject throughout the history that runs from Abraham (*our fathers,* 17) to Jesus (17-30). He proclaims a Gospel which God "promised beforehand": the record of *this people Israel* (17) is the record of a history which runs toward the fulfillment of God's promise to Israel for all nations (32-33), and the voices of psalmist and prophet "in the holy scriptures" are the abiding interpretative witnesses to God's saving act in the cross and resurrection (33, 34,

Canaan, he gave them their land as an inheritance, for about four hundred and fifty years. 20And after that he gave them judges until Samuel the prophet. 21 Then they asked for a king; and God gave them Saul the son of Kish, a man of the tribe of Benjamin, for forty years. 22And when he had removed him, he raised up David to be their king; of whom he testified and said, 'I have found in David the son of Jesse a man after my heart, who will do all my will.' 23 Of this man's posterity God has brought to Israel a Savior, Jesus, as he promised. 24 Before his coming John had preached a baptism of repentance to all the people of Israel. 25And as John was finishing his course, he said, 'What do you suppose that I am? I am not he. No, but after me one is coming, the sandals of whose feet I am not worthy to untie.'

26 "Brethren, sons of the family of Abraham, and those among you that fear God, to us has been sent the message of this salvation. 27 For those who live in Jerusalem and their rulers, because they did not recognize him nor understand the utterances of the prophets which are read every sabbath, fulfilled these by condemning him. 28 Though they could charge him with nothing deserving death, yet they asked Pilate to have him killed. 29And when they had fulfilled all that was written of him, they took him down from the tree, and laid him in a tomb. 30 But God raised him from the dead; 31 and for many days he appeared to those who came up with him from Galilee to Jerusalem, who are now his witnesses to the people. 32And we bring you the good news that what God promised to the fathers, 33 this he has fulfilled to us their children by raising Jesus; as also it is written in the second psalm,

> 'Thou art my Son,
> today I have begotten thee.'

34And as for the fact that he raised him from the dead, no more to return to corruption, he spoke in this way,

> 'I will give you the holy and sure blessings of David.'

35 Therefore he says also in another psalm,

> 'Thou wilt not let thy Holy One see corruption.'

36 For David, after he had served the counsel of God in his own generation, fell asleep, and was laid with his fathers, and saw corruption; 37 but he whom God raised up saw no corruption. 38 Let it be known to you therefore, brethren, that through this man forgiveness of sins is proclaimed to you, 39 and by him every one that believes is freed from everything from which you could not be freed by the law of Moses. 40 Beware, therefore, lest there come upon you what is said in the prophets:

41   'Behold, you scoffers, and wonder, and perish;
> for I do a deed in your days,
> a deed you will never believe, if one declares it to you.' "

42 As they went out, the people begged that these things might be told them the next sabbath. 43And when the meeting of the synagogue broke up, many Jews and devout converts to Judaism followed Paul and Bar′na·bas, who spoke to them and urged them to continue in the grace of God.

44 The next sabbath almost the whole city gathered together to hear the word of God. 45 But when the Jews saw the multitudes, they were filled with jealousy, and contradicted what was spoken by Paul, and reviled him. 46And Paul and Bar′na·bas

---

35). Paul's Gospel is emphatically God's Gospel "concerning his Son"; Paul's recital of the history of Israel leaps over a thousand years from *David* (22), the recipient of the Messianic promise (2 Sm 7:8-16), to the *Savior, Jesus,* the fulfillment of the promise (23); and *John* the Baptist is assigned a place in that history which is characterized as strictly preliminary (24) and subordinate (25) to that of the Son. The Son, according to Paul's Gospel, is the incarnation and revelation of God's grace. Every man of Israel knew that the OT history of Israel is a record of Israel's persistent failure and God's indomitable grace; that grace overruled even Israel's ultimate failure and

crowning disobedience (the rejection of the Son and Savior, 27-28) by raising His Son *from the dead* and raising up witnesses and evangelists to attest to His guilty people the *good news* of the fulfillment of *what God promised to the fathers* (31-32). What the Law could not do, God has done: Israel is free, *freed* by the forgiveness of sins proclaimed in Jesus. Before this incredible miracle of grace Israel must bow in fear and faith. (40-41)

13:39 *Freed.* The original has Paul's word "justified" here; they are "freed" by the acquitting verdict of God. (Cf. Ro 8:3)

13:46 *It was necessary ... first to you.* The prom-

spoke out boldly, saying, "It was necessary that the word of God should be spoken first to you. Since you thrust it from you, and judge yourselves unworthy of eternal life, behold, we turn to the Gentiles. 47 For so the Lord has commanded us, saying,

'I have set you to be a light for the Gentiles,
that you may bring salvation to the uttermost parts of the earth.' "

48 And when the Gentiles heard this, they were glad and glorified the word of God; and as many as were ordained to eternal life believed. 49And the word of the Lord spread throughout all the region. 50 But the Jews incited the devout women of high standing and the leading men of the city, and stirred up persecution against Paul and Bar′na·bas, and drove them out of their district. 51 But they shook off the dust from their feet against them, and went to I·co′ni·um. 52And the disciples were filled with joy and with the Holy Spirit.

14 Now at I·co′ni·um they entered together into the Jewish synagogue, and so spoke that a great company believed, both of Jews and of Greeks. 2 But the unbelieving Jews stirred up the Gentiles and poisoned their minds against the brethren. 3 So they remained for a long time, speaking boldly for the Lord, who bore witness to the word of his grace, granting signs and wonders to be done by their hands. 4 But the people of the city were divided; some sided with the Jews, and some with the apostles. 5 When an attempt was made by both Gentiles and Jews, with their rulers, to molest them and to stone them, 6 they learned of it and fled to Lystra and Derbe, cities of Lyc·a·o′ni·a, and to the surrounding country; 7 and there they preached the gospel.

8 Now at Lystra there was a man sitting, who could not use his feet; he was a cripple from birth, who had never walked. 9 He listened to Paul speaking; and Paul, looking intently at him and seeing that he had faith to be made well, 10 said in a loud voice, "Stand upright on your feet." And he sprang up and walked. 11And when the crowds saw what Paul had done, they lifted up their voices, saying in Lyc·a·o′ni·an, "The gods have come down to us in the likeness of men!" 12 Bar′na·bas they called Zeus, and Paul, because he was the chief speaker, they called Hermes. 13And the priest of Zeus, whose temple was in front of the city, brought oxen and garlands to the gates and wanted to offer sacrifice with the people. 14 But when the apostles Bar′-na·bas and Paul heard of it, they tore their garments and rushed out among the multitude, crying, 15 "Men, why are you doing this? We also are men, of like nature with you, and bring you good news, that you should turn from these vain things to a living God who made the heaven and the earth and the sea and all that is in them. 16 In past generations he allowed all the nations to walk in their own ways; 17 yet he did not leave himself without witness, for he did good and gave you from heaven rains and fruitful seasons, satisfying your hearts with food and gladness." 18 With these words they scarcely restrained the people from offering sacrifice to them.

19 But Jews came there from Antioch and I·co′ni·um; and having persuaded the people, they stoned Paul and dragged him out of the city, supposing that he was dead.

---

ise was given to Israel (32, 34); the fulfillment in Jesus, Son of David and Son of God, was enacted in Israel (33); Jesus commanded His disciples to preach repentance and forgiveness of sins to all nations, "beginning from Jerusalem," (Lk 24:47-49). For this "necessity" of proclaiming Jesus "to the Jew first" in Paul's own writings cf. Ro 1:16.

13:47 Cf. Is 49:6; Lk 2:32. The word spoken concerning the Servant Messiah is applied by Paul to the servants of the Servant in whom He speaks and acts. (Cf. Ro 15:18; 2 Co 13:3)

13:51 Shook off the dust from their feet, as a sign that all communion between them had been ended by their unbelief and enmity. (Cf. 18:6; Mt 10:14)

14:11-12 "The gods have come down to us" . . . Zeus . . . Hermes. Zeus, chief god of the Greeks, and Hermes, messenger of the gods, were linked in a local cult, and a story retold by the Roman poet Ovid tells how an old couple, Philemon and Barrcis, entertained the two gods unawares when they came down . . . in the likeness of men. It was this familiar story that led the natives to identify Paul and Barnabas as gods and to attempt to honor them with sacrifice.

14:14 Tore their garments, as a sign of grief and horror at the idolatrous action. Cf. Mt 26:65, where the high priest reacts to Jesus "blasphemy" with the same action.

14:15 Turn from these vain things to a living God. For Paul's own summary of his preaching to pagans cf. 1 Th 1:9-10. In Acts 17:21-31 Luke gives a fuller account of Paul's preaching to pagan hearers, when Paul cannot, as in the synagog, presuppose a knowledge of the OT. (Cf. 13:16-41)

14:17 Not . . . without witness. Cf. Ro 1:19-20.

14:19 Stoned Paul. Cf. 2 Co 11:25.

20 But when the disciples gathered about him, he rose up and entered the city; and on the next day he went on with Bar′na·bas to Derbe. 21 When they had preached the gospel to that city and had made many disciples, they returned to Lystra and to I·co′ni·um and to Antioch, 22 strengthening the souls of the disciples, exhorting them to continue in the faith, and saying that through many tribulations we must enter the kingdom of God. 23 And when they had appointed elders for them in every church, with prayer and fasting, they committed them to the Lord in whom they believed.

24 Then they passed through Pi·sid′i·a, and came to Pam·phyl′i·a. 25 And when they had spoken the word in Perga, they went down to At·ta·li′a; 26 and from there they sailed to Antioch, where they had been commended to the grace of God for the work which they had fulfilled. 27 And when they arrived, they gathered the church together and declared all that God had done with them, and how he had opened a door of faith to the Gentiles. 28 And they remained no little time with the disciples.

15 But some men came down from Judea and were teaching the brethren, "Unless you are circumcised according to the custom of Moses, you cannot be saved." 2 And when Paul and Bar′na·bas had no small dissension and debate with them, Paul and Bar′na·bas and some of the others were appointed to go up to Jerusalem to the apostles and the elders about this question. 3 So, being sent on their way by the church, they passed through both Phoe·nic′i·a and Sa·mar′i·a, reporting the conversion of the Gentiles, and they gave great joy to all the brethren. 4 When they came to Jerusalem, they were welcomed by the church and the apostles and the elders, and they declared all that God had done with them. 5 But some believers who belonged to the party of the Pharisees rose up, and said, "It is necessary to circumcise them, and to charge them to keep the law of Moses."

6 The apostles and the elders were gathered together to consider this matter. 7 And after there had been much debate, Peter rose and said to them, "Brethren, you know that in the early days God made choice among you, that by my mouth the Gentiles should hear the word of the gospel and believe. 8 And God who knows the heart bore witness to them, giving them the Holy Spirit just as he did to us; 9 and he made no distinction between us and them, but cleansed their hearts by faith. 10 Now therefore why do you make trial of God by putting a yoke upon the neck of the disciples which neither our fathers nor we have been able to bear? 11 But we believe that we shall be saved through the grace of the Lord Jesus, just as they will."

12 And all the assembly kept silence; and they listened to Bar′na·bas and Paul as they related what signs and wonders God had done through them among the Gentiles. 13 After they finished speaking, James replied, "Brethren, listen to me. 14 Simeon has related how God first visited the Gentiles, to take out of them a people for his name. 15 And with this the words of the prophets agree, as it is written,

16   'After this I will return,
        and I will rebuild the dwelling of David, which has fallen;
        I will rebuild its ruins,
        and I will set it up,

14:23 *Appointed elders.* Cf. Tts 1:5. The apostolic mission aims, not at a loose, enthusiastic "movement" but at a church solidly rooted and grounded, as is evidenced not only by the appointment of elders but also by Paul's practice of revisiting already evangelized territory (cf., e.g., Acts 15:36; 16:4-5), his ministry by letter, and his frequent employment of emissaries to the churches.

15:1 – 16:5 For the origin and significance of the tension that led to the Apostolic Council and the resolution of the tension cf. Introduction to Galatians, pars. 1-11.

15:5 *Circumcise them, and to charge them,* the newly converted Gentiles concerning whose conversion Paul and Barnabas had reported. (3-4)

15:7-9 For Peter's experience cf. 10:1 – 11:18.

15:10 *Why do you make trial of God by putting*

a yoke, etc.? As Peter's experience has shown (7-9) and as the experience of Paul and Barnabas will show (12), God has gone His way of free grace (11) with the Gentiles; no man has the right to experiment with God, to see whether He will go man's way, i. e., the way of *putting a yoke* (of the Law) *upon the neck of the disciples* which God Himself has not imposed. To experiment with God is the way of magic, not of faith.

15:13 *James.* For the position and influence of James, the brother of our Lord, in Judaic Christianity cf. 12:17 and Introduction to Letter of James.

15:15-18 James quotes from the prophet Amos (9:11-12) concerning the inclusion of the Gentiles in the promised Messianic salvation; his use of the plural "prophets" indicates that the sentiment

17   that the rest of men may seek the Lord,
          and all the Gentiles who are called by my name,
18   says the Lord, who has made these things known from of old.'
19 Therefore my judgment is that we should not trouble those of the Gentiles who turn to God, 20 but should write to them to abstain from the pollutions of idols and from unchastity and from what is strangled[n] and from blood. 21 For from early generations Moses has had in every city those who preach him, for he is read every sabbath in the synagogues.''

22 Then it seemed good to the apostles and the elders, with the whole church, to choose men from among them and send them to Antioch with Paul and Bar·na·bas. They sent Judas called Bar'sab·bas, and Silas, leading men among the brethren, 23 with the following letter: "The brethren, both the apostles and the elders, to the brethren who are of the Gentiles in Antioch and Syria and Cilicia, greeting. 24 Since we have heard that some persons from us have troubled you with words, unsettling your minds, although we gave them no instructions, 25 it has seemed good to us, having come to one accord, to choose men and send them to you with our beloved Bar'-na·bas and Paul, 26 men who have risked their lives for the sake of our Lord Jesus Christ. 27 We have therefore sent Judas and Silas, who themselves will tell you the same things by word of mouth. 28 For it has seemed good to the Holy Spirit and to us to lay upon you no greater burden than these necessary things: 29 that you abstain from what has been sacrificed to idols and from blood and from what is strangled[n] and from unchastity. If you keep yourselves from these, you will do well. Farewell.''

30 So when they were sent off, they went down to Antioch; and having gathered the congregation together, they delivered the letter. 31 And when they read it, they rejoiced at the exhortation. 32 And Judas and Silas, who were themselves prophets, exhorted the brethren with many words and strengthened them. 33 And after they had spent some time, they were sent off in peace by the brethren to those who had sent them.[o] 35 But Paul and Bar·na·bas remained in Antioch, teaching and preaching the word of the Lord, with many others also.

36 And after some days Paul said to Bar'na·bas, "Come, let us return and visit the brethren in every city where we proclaimed the word of the Lord, and see how they are.'' 37 And Bar'na·bas wanted to take with them John called Mark. 38 But Paul thought best not to take with them one who had withdrawn from them in Pam·phyl'i·a, and had not gone with them to the work. 39 And there arose a sharp contention, so that they separated from each other; Bar'na·bas took Mark with him and sailed away to Cyprus, 40 but Paul chose Silas and departed, being commended by the brethren to the grace of the Lord. 41 And he went through Syria and Cilicia, strengthening the churches.

16 And he came also to Derbe and to Lystra. A disciple was there, named Timothy, the son of a Jewish woman who was a believer; but his father was a Greek. 2 He was well spoken of by the brethren at Lystra and I·co'ni·um. 3 Paul wanted

---

n Other early authorities omit *and from what is strangled*
o Other ancient authorities insert verse 34, *But it seemed good to Silas to remain there*

---

is not only that of Amos. (Cf., e. g., Is 11:9-10; 42:4, 6; 49:6; Jer 12:14-17)

15:20-21 Cf. 15:15-18 note, where the advice of James appears as the official request of Judaic to Gentile Christians.

15:22 *Judas . . . Barsabbas.* Known only from this passage and vv. 27 and 32.

Silas, known also by the Latinized form of his name, Silvanus, becomes prominent in the history of Gentile missions (Acts 15:40 and chs. 16—18; cf. 2 Co 1:19; 1 Th 1:1; 2 Th 1:1), associated both with Paul and Peter (1 Ptr 5:12; cf. Introduction to First Peter).

15:28 *These necessary things.* Cf. Introduction to Galatians, par. 10.

15:37 *John called Mark.* Cf. Introduction to Mark's Gospel.

15:38 *Withdrawn from them in Pamphylia.* Cf. 13:13.

16:1 *Timothy.* Cf. Introduction to First Timothy.

16:3 *Circumcised him because of the Jews . . . in those places.* When, as in the case of the Gentile Titus, circumcision was demanded by men intent on putting the yoke of the Law on the neck of Gentile disciples (Acts 15:10; Gl 2:3-5), Paul would not yield. Here in the case of Timothy, son of a Jewish mother, Paul of his own free will marked his future companion and co-worker as a member of Israel in order not to offend the Jews. Paul's willingness to "become all things to all men" in

Timothy to accompany him; and he took him and circumcised him because of the Jews that were in those places, for they all knew that his father was a Greek. ⁴As they went on their way through the cities, they delivered to them for observance the decisions which had been reached by the apostles and elders who were at Jerusalem. ⁵ So the churches were strengthened in the faith, and they increased in numbers daily.

The Word of the Lord Goes to Europe and Asia Minor

16:6–19:20

THE CALL TO MACEDONIA (16:6-10)

6 And they went through the region of Phryg′i·a and Galatia, having been forbidden by the Holy Spirit to speak the word in Asia. ⁷And when they had come opposite Mysia, they attempted to go into Bi·thyn′i·a, but the Spirit of Jesus did not allow them; ⁸ so, passing by Mysia, they went down to Troas. ⁹And a vision appeared to Paul in the night: a man of Macedonia was standing beseeching him and saying, "Come over to Macedonia and help us." ¹⁰And when he had seen the vision, immediately we sought to go on into Macedonia, concluding that God had called us to preach the gospel to them.

order that he "might by all means save some" (1 Co 9:22; cf. 19-23) gave him an astonishing flexibility.

16:5 *So the churches,* etc. The fourth of Luke's summarizing statements (cf. 6:7; 9:31; 12:24), coming as it does at the close of a series of events that had in them the seeds of discord and dissolution, is illuminated by words written by the apostle who played so signal a role in those events: "Speaking the truth in love, we are to grow up in every way into him who is the head, into Christ, from whom the whole body, joined and knit together by every joint with which it is supplied, when each part is working properly, makes bodily growth and upbuilds itself in love." (Eph 4:15-16)

16:6–19:20 Luke concludes this section with the words: "So the word of the Lord grew and prevailed mightily" (19:20). His language is strong, stronger than that of previous summary statements (cf. 6:7; 9:31; 12:24; 16:5), but not too strong for the facts. The half-dozen years spanned by this portion of the record witnessed the progress of the Word of the Lord through an area far greater than that covered by any previous period—toward the close of this period Paul could write to the Christians of Rome: "From Jerusalem and as far round as Illyricum [in NW. Greece] I have fully preached the gospel of Christ" (Ro 15:19), and he could look to Rome and Spain as the next necessary stage of his missionary travels (Ro 15:23-24, 28). This period saw the crossing of the Gospel from Asia to Europe (16:10-12) and saw it firmly planted in two strategic centers, Ephesus in Asia and Corinth in Europe.

The Word prevailed in the face of opposition and conflict. Whether the opposition came from the synagog (17:5-8, 13; 18:6, 12-17), from Gentile superstition and avarice (16:16-24), from itinerant Jewish exorcists (19:13), or from the indifference of philosophic Athenians (17:23), it succeeded in inflicting on the bearers of the Word beatings,

imprisonment, and enforced untimely departure from their chosen field of activity. It did not succeed in hindering the progress of the Word even when it invoked the strong arm of Roman law; Luke's exultant summary is a reading of the facts as the Spirit illumines them and is justified praise of the God who watched over His Word to make it prevail in spite of all opposition, by the guidance of His Spirit (16:6-7), by visions (16:8; 18:9), by the still, small voice that opened the heart of Lydia (16:14), and by the earthquake that shook the prisoners free in the jail at Philippi (16:26) and made the trembling jailer ask the question that is the opened door to the Gospel, "Men, what must I do to be saved?" (16:30)

16:6-10 God is in charge, even of the itinerary. His Spirit (which is the Spirit of His Son Jesus continuing the work He had begun on earth, 16:7; cf. 1:1) turns His messengers back from the next logical step, the evangelization of the rest of Asia Minor, and calls them to cross over to Europe and preach the Gospel in Macedonia.

16:6 *Phrygia and Galatia,* that is, that part of the Roman province of Galatia which was both a part of the ancient area of Phrygia and a part of Galatia, scene of Paul's labors on the first missionary journey.

16:6 *Asia,* the Roman province of that name in western Asia Minor, whose capital was Ephesus.

16:6-8 The Spirit cuts off the "logical" lines of advance to the west *(Asia)* and the north *(Bithynia)* and leads Paul and his companions to *Troas* in NW. Asia Minor and to Macedonia in northern Greece.

16:10 *We sought to go on into Macedonia.* The change from the third person plural of vv. 6, 7, 8 to *we* indicates that Luke joined Paul's party at Troas. Other "we" sections in Acts besides 16:10-17 are 20:5-16; 21:1-18; 27:1–28:16; they are probably Luke's way of indicating that he was an eyewitness of the events there recorded.

PHILIPPI (16:11-40)

11 Setting sail therefore from Troas, we made a direct voyage to Sam′o·thrace, and the following day to Neapolis, 12 and from there to Phi·lip′pi, which is the leading city of the district*x* of Macedonia, and a Roman colony. We remained in this city some days; 13 and on the sabbath day we went outside the gate to the riverside, where we supposed there was a place of prayer; and we sat down and spoke to the women who had come together. 14 One who heard us was a woman named Lydia, from the city of Thy·a·ti′ra, a seller of purple goods, who was a worshiper of God. The Lord opened her heart to give heed to what was said by Paul. 15And when she was baptized, with her household, she besought us, saying, "If you have judged me to be faithful to the Lord, come to my house and stay." And she prevailed upon us.

16 As we were going to the place of prayer, we were met by a slave girl who had a spirit of divination and brought her owners much gain by soothsaying. 17 She followed Paul and us, crying, "These men are servants of the Most High God, who proclaimed to you the way of salvation." 18And this she did for many days. But Paul was annoyed, and turned and said to the spirit, "I charge you in the name of Jesus Christ to come out of her." And it came out that very hour.

19 But when her owners saw that their hope of gain was gone, they seized Paul and Silas and dragged them into the market place before the rulers; 20 and when they had brought them to the magistrates they said, "These men are Jews and they are disturbing our city. 21 They advocate customs which it is not lawful for us Romans to accept or practice." 22 The crowd joined in attacking them; and the magistrates tore the garments off them and gave orders to beat them with rods. 23And when they had inflicted many blows upon them, they threw them into prison, charging the jailer to keep them safely. 24 Having received this charge, he put them into the inner prison and fastened their feet in the stocks.

25 But about midnight Paul and Silas were praying and singing hymns to God, and the prisoners were listening to them, 26 and suddenly there was a great earthquake, so that the foundations of the prison were shaken; and immediately all the doors were opened and every one's fetters were unfastened. 27 When the jailer woke and saw that the prison doors were open, he drew his sword and was about to kill himself, supposing that the prisoners had escaped. 28 But Paul cried with a loud voice, "Do not harm yourself, for we are all here." 29And he called for lights and rushed in, and trembling with fear he fell down before Paul and Silas, 30 and brought them out and said, "Men, what must I do to be saved?" 31And they said, "Believe in the Lord Jesus, and you will be saved, you and your household." 32And they spoke the word of the Lord to him and to all that were in his house. 33And he took them the same hour of the night, and washed their wounds, and he was baptized at once, with all his family. 34 Then he brought them up into his house, and set food before them; and he rejoiced with all his household that he had believed in God.

35 But when it was day, the magistrates sent the police, saying, "Let those men go." 36And the jailer reported the words to Paul, saying, "The magistrates have sent to let you go; now therefore come out and go in peace." 37 But Paul said to them, "They have beaten us publicly, uncondemned, men who are Roman citizens, and have thrown us into prison; and do they now cast us out secretly? No! let them come them-

---

x The Greek text is uncertain

16:11-40 Cf. Introduction to Philippians.

16:11 *Neapolis,* the port city of Philippi.

16:12 *A Roman colony.* Cf. Introduction to Philippians, par. 1.

16:13 *Riverside . . . a place of prayer,* an unofficial open-air place of worship for the Jews of Philippi. Paul as usual offers the Gospel "to the Jew first." (Ro 1:16; cf. Acts 13:46 note)

16:14 *A worshiper of God.* A convert to Judaism.

16:21 *Not lawful for us Romans.* As members of a Roman colony (cf. 16:12 note) the Philippians enjoyed and no doubt prided themselves on Roman citizenship.

16:22 *Beat them with rods.* Cf. 2 Co 11:25.

16:31 *Believe in the Lord Jesus.* For the title *Lord* as a summary of all that Jesus signifies for faith cf. Ro 10:9; 1 Co 12:3.

16:37 *Uncondemned,* without the due process of law to which a Roman citizen was entitled. (Cf. Acts 22:24-29)

selves and take us out." 38 The police reported these words to the magistrates, and they were afraid when they heard that they were Roman citizens; 39 so they came and apologized to them. And they took them out and asked them to leave the city. 40 So they went out of the prison, and visited Lydia; and when they had seen the brethren, they exhorted them and departed.

THESSALONICA (17:1-9)

17 Now when they had passed through Am·phip´o·lis and Apollonia, they came to Thes·sa·lon´i·ca, where there was a synagogue of the Jews. 2And Paul went in, as was his custom, and for three weeks*p* he argued with them from the scriptures, 3 explaining and proving that it was necessary for the Christ to suffer and to rise from the dead, and saying, "This Jesus, whom I proclaim to you, is the Christ." 4And some of them were persuaded, and joined Paul and Silas; as did a great many of the devout Greeks and not a few of the leading women. 5 But the Jews were jealous, and taking some wicked fellows of the rabble, they gathered a crowd, set the city in an uproar, and attacked the house of Jason, seeking to bring them out to the people. 6And when they could not find them, they dragged Jason and some of the brethren before the city authorities, crying, "These men who have turned the world upside down have come here also, 7 and Jason has received them; and they are all acting against the decrees of Caesar, saying that there is another king, Jesus." 8And the people and the city authorities were disturbed when they heard this. 9And when they had taken security from Jason and the rest, they let them go.

BEROEA (17:10-15)

10 The brethren immediately sent Paul and Silas away by night to Be·roe´a; and when they arrived they went into the Jewish synagogue. 11 Now these Jews were more noble than those in Thes·sa·lon´i·ca, for they received the word with all eagerness, examining the scriptures daily to see if these things were so. 12 Many of them therefore believed, with not a few Greek women of high standing as well as men. 13 But when the Jews of Thes·sa·lon´i·ca learned that the word of God was proclaimed by Paul at Be·roe´a also, they came too, stirring up and inciting the crowds. 14 Then the brethren immediately sent Paul off on his way to the sea, but Silas and Timothy remained there. 15 Those who conducted Paul brought him as far as Athens; and receiving a command for Silas and Timothy to come to him as soon as possible, they departed.

ATHENS (17:16-34)

16 Now while Paul was waiting for them at Athens, his spirit was provoked within him as he saw that the city was full of idols. 17 So he argued in the synagogue with

p Or *sabbaths*

17:1-9 Cf. Introduction to Letters to the Thessalonians.

17:4 *Devout Greeks.* Converts to Judaism.

17:7 *Acting against the decrees of Caesar . . . another king, Jesus.* The Jews attempt to make the Gospel of Jesus appear politically dangerous, subversive to the Roman state. (Cf. 18:13; 24:5)

17:9 *Taken security.* Paul's host, Jason, and the rest of his friends were bound under penalty to see to it that the disturbance would not recur.

17:10-15 The men of the synagog at Beroea proved more *noble* than those of Thessalonica, i. e., they gave the Gospel a hearing on its own terms, "in accordance with the [OT] scriptures" (cf. 1 Co 15:3-4), with the result that *many of them . . . believed* (12). But again the apostle was forced to leave before the founding of a church in Beroea was really completed.

17:16-34 "The Greeks seek wisdom" (1 Co 1:22),

Paul wrote to the Corinthians some 5 years after his visit to Athens. In this respect the Athenians were the most Greek of the Greeks, and the intellectual vigor which made 5th-century and 4th-century Athens "the eye of Greece" was not yet entirely spent; the intellectual climate of Athens favored philosophy (18), and the *foreigners who lived there* (21) were attracted thither by the cultural atmosphere of Athens (*telling or hearing something new,* 21). But if Athens was the scene of the triumph of human wisdom, it was also the scene of wisdom's signal failure: "The world did not know God through wisdom" (1 Co 1:21). *The city was full of idols* (16), and the *very religious* (22) men of Athens were haunted by the fear that haunts all polytheism, namely, that some god or goddess might have been overlooked and offended; the altar with the *inscription, To an unknown god* (23) testified to this fear and so to the failure

the Jews and the devout persons, and in the market place every day with those who chanced to be there. 18 Some also of the Ep·i·cu·re′an and Stoic philosophers met him. And some said, "What would this babbler say?" Others said, "He seems to be a preacher of foreign divinities"—because he preached Jesus and the resurrection. 19And they took hold of him and brought him to the Ar·e·op′a·gus, saying, "May we know what this new teaching is which you present? 20 For you bring some strange things to our ears; we wish to know therefore what these things mean." 21 Now all the Athenians and the foreigners who lived there spent their time in nothing except telling or hearing something new.

22 So Paul, standing in the middle of the Ar·e·op′a·gus, said: "Men of Athens, I perceive that in every way you are very religious. 23 For as I passed along, and observed the objects of your worship, I found also an altar with this inscription, 'To an unknown god.' What therefore you worship as unknown, this I proclaim to you. 24 The God who made the world and everything in it, being Lord of heaven and earth, does not live in shrines made by man, 25 nor is he served by human hands, as though he needed anything, since he himself gives to all men life and breath and everything. 26And he made from one every nation of men to live on all the face of the earth, having determined allotted periods and the boundaries of their habitation, 27 that they should seek God, in the hope that they might feel after him and find him. Yet he is not far from each one of us, 28 for

'In him we live and move and have our being';
as even some of your poets have said,
'For we are indeed his offspring.'

29 Being then God's offspring, we ought not to think that the Deity is like gold, or silver, or stone, a representation by the art and imagination of man. 30 The times of ignorance God overlooked, but now he commands all men everywhere to repent, 31 because he has fixed a day on which he will judge the world in righteousness by a man whom he has appointed, and of this he has given assurance to all men by raising him from the dead."

32 Now when they heard of the resurrection of the dead, some mocked; but others said, "We will hear you again about this." 33 So Paul went out from among them. 34 But some men joined him and believed, among them Di·o·nys′i·us the Ar·e·op′-a·gite and a woman named Dam′a·ris and others with them.

of wisdom. It is to this fear and failure that Paul attached in his address (22-31). He points men away from the sorry splendors of their idolatry to the one true God, the almighty Creator whom no *shrines made by man* (24) can contain, the Lord of all history who attests Himself to man by His works (25) and wills to be found by man (27). God has in His long patience *overlooked* (30) man's guilty failure to find Him, but the time of His forbearance is drawing to a close, the *day on which he will judge the world in righteousness* (31) is near; and the Judge is *appointed,* the Man whom He has raised from the dead. For all the difference of approach and method, Paul's proclamation to the Greek is one with his proclamation to the Jew; he is "testifying both to Jews and Greeks of repentance to God and of faith in our Lord Jesus Christ" (Acts 20:21), the Deliverer and Judge of both Jew and Greek. Human wisdom is not easily persuaded of its failure; the mind boggles at the miracle of the resurrection of the dead. *Some mocked,* while others clothe their rejection in a polite request that the matter be discussed further (32). *But some . . . believed* (34), and these "some" (cf. 1 Co 9:22) are the future of the church and of the world.

17:18 *Epicurean and Stoic philosophers* represent the two most widely held philosophic faiths (and faiths they were rather than philosophies, strictly speaking) of late antiquity.

Babbler. This contemptuous term, used literally of birds that pick up seeds, designated a person who picked up scraps of learning and culture and paraded without having made them really his own.

17:19 *Areopagus,* name of a hill near the Acropolis of Athens and of an ancient court which sat there. In Paul's day this court was primarily concerned with matters of education and religion. As a "preacher of foreign divinities" (18) Paul would come under this scrutiny.

17:22 *Religious.* The term used could be used in either a derogatory ("superstitious") or a positive sense ("religious"). Paul's use of it is probably neutral; his subsequent words indicate that he does not intend to be either insulting or laudatory.

17:24 *Does not live in shrines made by man.* Cf. Is 42:5; 66:1-2. (Acts 7:49-50)

17:27 Cf. Ro 1:19-21.

17:28 The quotations are from two Greek poets, Epimenides (cf. Tts 1:12 note) and Aratus. The wise Greeks sensed the presence and working of God, yet did not turn from their idols to respond to Him with thanks and praise. (Ro 1:21)

17:30 *Times of ignorance God overlooked.* Cf. Ro 3:25.

CORINTH (18:1-17)

18 After this he left Athens and went to Corinth. ²And he found a Jew named Aq′ui·la, a native of Pontus, lately come from Italy with his wife Priscilla, because Claudius had commanded all the Jews to leave Rome. And he went to see them; ³ and because he was of the same trade he stayed with them, and they worked, for by trade they were tentmakers. ⁴And he argued in the synagogue every sabbath, and persuaded Jews and Greeks.

5 When Silas and Timothy arrived from Macedonia, Paul was occupied with preaching, testifying to the Jews that the Christ was Jesus. ⁶And when they opposed and reviled him, he shook out his garments and said to them, "Your blood be upon your heads! I am innocent. From now on I will go to the Gentiles." ⁷And he left there and went to the house of a man named Ti′ti·us*q* Justus, a worshiper of God; his house was next door to the synagogue. ⁸ Crispus, the ruler of the synagogue, believed in the Lord, together with all his household; and many of the Corinthians hearing Paul believed and were baptized. ⁹And the Lord said to Paul one night in a vision, "Do not be afraid, but speak and do not be silent; ¹⁰ for I am with you, and no man shall attack you to harm you; for I have many people in this city." ¹¹And he stayed a year and six months, teaching the word of God among them.

12 But when Gallio was proconsul of A·cha′ia, the Jews made a united attack upon Paul and brought him before the tribunal, ¹³ saying, "This man is persuading men to worship God contrary to the law." ¹⁴ But when Paul was about to open his mouth, Gallio said to the Jews, "If it were a matter of wrongdoing or vicious crime, I should have reason to bear with you, O Jews; ¹⁵ but since it is a matter of questions about words and names and your own law, see to it yourselves; I refuse to be a judge of these things." ¹⁶And he drove them from the tribunal. ¹⁷And they all seized Sos′thenes, the ruler of the synagogue, and beat him in front of the tribunal. But Gallio paid no attention to this.

q Other early authorities read *Titus*

18:1-17 Corinth proved to be the farthest reach and the most important evangelization center of the second missionary journey (Acts 15:36 – 18:22). For the character and subsequent history of the church in Corinth see Introduction to Letters to the Corinthians. Paul was encouraged to extend the time of his ministry there (11) by the fact that he encountered *Aquila* and *Priscilla*, fellow Jews (2) and followers of the same trade (3) who became his "fellow workers in Christ Jesus," deserving of the gratitude of Paul and of "all the churches of the Gentiles" (Ro 16:4). His meeting with them was an encouragement in another respect also: it enabled him to maintain himself by working at his trade (3) and so to "make the gospel free of charge" (1 Co 9:18; cf. 2 Co 11:7-11) to his converts in Corinth. But the decisive encouragement came from the Lord Himself, who appeared to Paul in a vision in the night and promised him fruitful labors and protection against attack (10). The Lord kept both promises; the church grew (cf. 8) despite the hostility of the synagog (6); and the *united attack* of the Jews on Paul before the tribunal of the Roman proconsul Gallio (12-17) failed of its purpose.

18:2 *Claudius . . . commanded all the Jews to leave Rome.* Claudius (Roman emperor A. D. 41 – 54) virtually commanded the Jews to leave Rome because of their turbulent behavior by banning their assemblies; since this deprived devout Jews of opportunity to worship, they were forced to leave. The action of Claudius probably affected Jewish Christians also, though it is not clear whether Aquila and his wife had been converted in Rome or were won for Christ by Paul in Corinth.

18:3 *Tentmakers.* Tents made out of the felted cloth of goat's hair were produced in Cilicia, Paul's home province.

18:5 *Silas and Timothy arrived from Macedonia.* Cf. 17:15 and 1 Th 3:6.

Was occupied with, or perhaps better, "wholly absorbed in," *preaching.* Timothy's report concerning the fidelity of the Thessalonian church relieved Paul of anxiety over the young congregation, and he could throw himself into the work at Corinth with renewed vigor. (Cf. 1 Th 3:1-8)

18:12 *Gallio . . . proconsul of Achaia.* With headquarters in Corinth, Gallio was proconsul of Achaia either A. D. 51 – 52 or 52 – 53.

18:13 *Contrary to the law.* Gallio perceived that the *law* involved was not the Roman law but Jewish law and therefore refused to recognize the charge brought against Paul. (Cf. 14-15)

18:17 The mistreatment of *Sosthenes* was not an official Roman action but an outburst of popular anti-Semitic feeling on the part of bystanders. Some identify this Sosthenes, *the ruler of the synagogue,* with the Sosthenes whom Paul calls "our brother" in 1 Co 1:1; if the two are identical (possible but not certain), one must assume that Sosthenes was later converted and became,

THE RETURN TO ANTIOCH (18:18-23)

18 After this Paul stayed many days longer, and then took leave of the brethren and sailed for Syria, and with him Priscilla and Aq'ui·la. At Cen·chre'ae he cut his hair, for he had a vow. 19And they came to Eph'e·sus, and he left them there; but he himself went into the synagogue and argued with the Jews. 20 When they asked him to stay for a longer period, he declined; 21 but on taking leave of them he said, "I will return to you if God wills," and he set sail from Eph'e·sus.

22 When he had landed at Caes·a·re'a, he went up and greeted the church, and then went down to Antioch. 23After spending some time there he departed and went from place to place through the region of Galatia and Phryg'i·a, strengthening all the disciples.

EPHESUS (18:24 — 19:20)

24 Now a Jew named A·pol'los, a native of Alexandria, came to Eph'e·sus. He was an eloquent man, well versed in the scriptures., 25 He had been instructed in the way of the Lord; and being fervent in spirit, he spoke and taught accurately the things concerning Jesus, though he knew only the baptism of John. 26 He began to speak boldly in the synagogue; but when Priscilla and Aq'ui·la heard him, they took him and expounded to him the way of God more accurately. 27And when he wished to cross to A·cha'ia, the brethren encouraged him, and wrote to the disciples to receive him. When he arrived, he greatly helped those who through grace had believed, 28 for he powerfully confuted the Jews in public, showing by the scriptures that the Christ was Jesus.

19 While A·pol'los was at Corinth, Paul passed through the upper country and came to Eph'e·sus. There he found some disciples. 2And he said to them, "Did you receive the Holy Spirit when you believed?" And they said, "No, we have never even heard that there is a Holy Spirit." 3And he said, "Into what then were you baptized?" They said, "Into John's baptism." 4And Paul said, "John baptized with the baptism of repentance, telling the people to believe in the one who was to come after him, that is, Jesus." 5 On hearing this, they were baptized in the name of the Lord Jesus. 6And when Paul had laid his hands upon them, the Holy Spirit came on them; and they spoke with tongues and prophesied. 7 There were about twelve of them in all.

8 And he entered the synagogue and for three months spoke boldly, arguing and pleading about the kingdom of God; 9 but when some were stubborn and disbelieved, speaking evil of the Way before the congregation, he withdrew from them, taking the disciples with him, and argued daily in the hall of Tyrannus.ʳ 10 This continued for two years, so that all the residents of Asia heard the word of the Lord, both Jews and Greeks.

11 And God did extraordinary miracles by the hands of Paul, 12 so that handkerchiefs or aprons were carried away from his body to the sick, and diseases left them and the evil spirits came out of them. 13 Then some of the itinerant Jewish

ʳ Other ancient authorities add *from the fifth hour to the tenth*

like Paul, a member of the church he had once persecuted.

18:18 *Cenchreae,* the eastern seaport of Corinth on the isthmus.

Cut his hair, for he had a vow. For the provisions of the Nazirite vow cf. Nm 6 and Acts 21:23-26. There is nothing to indicate the purpose of the vow, nor is it altogether clear who had taken the vow, Paul or Aquila.

18:22 *The church,* i. e., the Jerusalem church. *Antioch* in Syria, Paul's missionary base. (Cf. 13:1-3; 15:35)

18:23 *Galatia and Phrygia.* Cf. 16:6 note.

18:24 — 19:20 For a survey of Paul's ministry at Ephesus cf. Introduction to First Corinthians, pars. 1-6.

18:25 *He knew only the baptism of John,* the baptism of promise, which had been superseded

by the baptism of fulfillment "in the name of the Lord Jesus" (19:4-5) and the gift of the Holy Spirit. (19:6)

18:27 *Wished to cross to Achaia.* For an account of Apollos' influence in Achaia, particularly at Corinth, cf. Introduction to First Corinthians, pars. 10-11.

19:2 *Never even heard that there is a Holy Spirit,* that is, that the Holy Spirit has been bestowed upon the new people of God, the church (cf. Jn 7:39). Disciples of John the Baptist (such as these disciples were, 19:1) would have heard of the Holy Spirit (Mt 3:11) if they did not already know of Him from the OT.

19:3 *John's baptism.* Cf. 18:25 note.

19:6 Cf. 8:17; 10:44-45; 11:15.

19:9 *The hall of Tyrannus.* The Greek word for *hall* indicates a place where a school meets,

exorcists undertook to pronounce the name of the Lord Jesus over those who had evil spirits, saying, "I adjure you by the Jesus whom Paul preaches." [14] Seven sons of a Jewish high priest named Sceva were doing this. [15] But the evil spirit answered them, "Jesus I know, and Paul I know; but who are you?" [16]And the man in whom the evil spirit was leaped on them, mastered all of them, and overpowered them, so that they fled out of that house naked and wounded. [17]And this became known to all residents of Eph'e·sus, both Jews and Greeks; and fear fell upon them all; and the name of the Lord Jesus was extolled. [18] Many also of those who were now believers came, confessing and divulging their practices. [19]And a number of those who practiced magic arts brought their books together and burned them in the sight of all; and they counted the value of them and found it came to fifty thousand pieces of silver. [20] So the word of the Lord grew and prevailed mightily.

The Power of the Word of the Lord

19:21 — 28:31

FINAL CONFLICT IN EPHESUS: "GREAT IS ARTEMIS" (19:21-41)

21 Now after these events Paul resolved in the Spirit to pass through Macedonia and A·cha'ia and go to Jerusalem, saying, "After I have been there, I must also see Rome." [22]And having sent into Macedonia two of his helpers, Timothy and E·ras'tus, he himself stayed in Asia for a while.

a lecture hall. Tyrannus is otherwise unknown.

19:14 *Sons of a Jewish high priest named Sceva.* There is no record of a Jewish high priest with this name. Sceva is a name of Latin origin; perhaps the high priest in question bore a Hebrew and a Latin name (as Saul/Paul did) and could be identified if his Hebrew name were known.

19:19 *Brought their books together and burned them,* thus publicly renouncing their magical practices. The books were books of magic, for which Ephesus was famous.

19:21 — 28:31 As Paul was about to leave Ephesus, he "resolved in the Spirit to . . . go to Jerusalem, saying, 'After I have been there, I *must* also see Rome'" (19:21). The *must* that impelled him toward Jerusalem and to Rome was the *must* of the will of his Lord, who appeared to him in Jerusalem and said, "As you have testified about me at Jerusalem, so you *must* bear witness also at Rome" (23:11). It was a Christlike way that he went; it was a way of love, for he went bringing gifts. "I came to bring to my nation alms and offerings," he said at his trial before Felix (24:17). He attached great importance to these alms and offerings, for he saw in them the concrete expression of what he had written to the Corinthians concerning the members of the body of Christ: "If one member suffers, all suffer together" (1 Co 12:26); in these gifts of Gentile to Jewish Christians he saw the miracle of the unity of the church being enacted. (Ro 15:25-29; cf. 15:7-9)

Paul knew that the way he was going was a dangerous one (Ro 15:31). He knew how much his unbelieving fellow countrymen hated him and how desperately they wanted him out of the way; he had been in "danger from his own people" more than once before (2 Co 11:26). His fears were

confirmed at Corinth, where a "plot was made against him by the Jews as he was about to set sail for Syria" (20:3) and Paul was forced to change his itinerary to avoid death. And as he journeyed toward Jerusalem, the Spirit warned him, directly and through the voice of prophecy, that "imprisonment and afflictions" awaited him. (20:22-24; cf. 21:4, 10-11)

And yet he went willingly and resolutely to Jerusalem, for he saw in this bringing of gifts to Jerusalem a piece of the ministry which he had received from the Lord Jesus, "to testify to the gospel of the grace of God" (20:24). To whom did Paul want to testify? To his Jewish Christian brethren surely; the gift from the Gentile churches would speak unmistakably to them of the universal grace of God. But surely also to his Jewish "kinsmen by race" who had not yet obeyed the Gospel. Their hatred of him had not engendered hatred in his heart; his mission to the Gentiles did not mean the end of his love for his kinsmen or the cessation of his efforts on their behalf (Ro 9:1-5; 10:1; 11:13, 14). "I came to bring *to my nation* alms and offerings," Paul said pointedly at his trial (24:17); he evidently hoped that the sight of gifts pouring into Jerusalem from Gentile lands, to which the Jew had hitherto looked in vain for kindness, might open the eyes of at least some to the grace of God and its "inexpressible gift."

Luke marks this way of Paul's as a Christlike way, one of giving, of suffering, of love for his people the Jews. Even externally the life of Paul has on it the imprint of his Lord's life: the time of travels is followed by a time of imprisonment and suffering. The parallelism between the Lord and His apostle is apparent in the story of the

23 About that time there arose no little stir concerning the Way. ²⁴ For a man named De·me′tri·us, a silversmith, who made silver shrines of Ar′te·mis, brought no little business to the craftsmen. ²⁵ These he gathered together, with the workmen of like occupation, and said, "Men, you know that from this business we have our wealth. ²⁶And you see and hear that not only at Eph′e·sus but almost throughout all Asia this Paul has persuaded and turned away a considerable company of people, saying that gods made with hands are not gods. ²⁷And there is danger not only that this trade of ours may come into disrepute but also that the temple of the great goddess Ar′te·mis may count for nothing, and that she may even be deposed from her magnificence, she whom all Asia and the world worship."

28 When they heard this they were enraged, and cried out, "Great is Ar′te·mis of the E·phe′sians!" ²⁹ So the city was filled with the confusion; and they rushed together into the theater, dragging with them Gaius and Ar·is·tar′chus, Macedonians who were Paul's companions in travel. ³⁰ Paul wished to go in among the crowd, but the disciples would not let him; ³¹ some of the A′si·archs also, who were friends of his, sent to him and begged him not to venture into the theater. ³² Now some cried one thing, some another; for the assembly was in confusion, and most of them did not know why they had come together. ³³ Some of the crowd prompted Alexander, whom the Jews had put forward. And Alexander motioned with his hand, wishing to make a defense to the people. ³⁴ But when they recognized that he was a Jew, for about two hours they all with one voice cried out, "Great is Ar′te·mis of the E·phe′sians!" ³⁵And when the town clerk had quieted the crowd, he said, "Men of Eph′e·sus, what man is there who does not know that the city of the E·phe′sians is temple keeper of the great Ar′te·mis, and of the sacred stone that fell from the sky?ˢ ³⁶ Seeing then

ˢ The meaning of the Greek is uncertain

arrest and imprisonment of Paul. Like Jesus, he is tried before the Sanhedrin (22:30 – 23:10; cf. Lk 22:66-70), before the Roman procurator (24:1-23; 25:6-12; cf. Lk 23:1-5, 13-25), and before a Jewish king, Herod Agrippa II (25:23 – 26:32; cf. Lk 23:6-12). And he resembles Jesus in this too that he tries to the last to bring the men of Jerusalem under the wings of the Christ who can save them (cf. Mt 23:37); even when the Jerusalem mob was screaming for his blood, he once more addressed them in their own tongue, and sought even then to gain a hearing by stressing all that he and they had in common by the grace of God.

Paul appealed to his people in vain. He was imprisoned at Jerusalem, removed to Caesarea when the fury of his people again threatened his life (23:12-35), and imprisoned there for two years under the procurator Felix, who hoped for a bribe from Paul or his friends (24:26), and when that was not forthcoming left Paul in prison at the end of his term, "desiring to do the Jews a favor" (24:27). When even the fair and conscientious Festus, Felix's successor as procurator, wanted to prolong his already long-drawn trial by transferring him for trial to Jerusalem, Paul made use of his privilege as a Roman citizen and appealed to Caesar. (25:11)

"You have appealed to Caesar; to Caesar you shall go," Festus said (25:12). Paul was sent to Rome. The long voyage to Rome with its dangers and disasters, through all which Paul was led safely to the goal set for him by his Lord, is, as it were, an epitome of his whole career as an apostle of Jesus Christ; again the strength of the Lord was made perfect in His apostle's weakness.

Jesus' promise that Paul would testify to Him at Rome was fulfilled (23:11); and Jesus' more sweeping promise to the Twelve (1:8), was fulfilled also; the Gospel is being proclaimed in Rome, the capital of the world; it has stepped through the door which opens into all the world, to the ends of the earth. Paul is seen at the close of Acts "preaching the kingdom of God and teaching about the Lord Jesus Christ quite openly and unhindered." (28:31)

19:21-41 Cf. Introduction to First Corinthians, par. 6.

19:24 The *silver shrines of Artemis* were probably sold to the worshipers to be used as votive gifts in the temple of Artemis, one of the seven wonders of the ancient world.

19:26 *Gods made with hands are not gods.* Cf. 17:24-25, 29.

19:31 *Asiarchs,* men of substance and influence, prominent in the cult of emperor worship, known for their loyalty to Rome. The details of the nature of their office are not known.

19:35 *Town clerk,* the principal municipal officer of Ephesus, whom the Roman government would hold responsible for civic disorders. Translators have used terms like "chancellor," "secretary of state," and "mayor" in their attempts to convey the importance of this office.

Temple keeper of the great Artemis, an honorific title of which the Ephesians were evidently proud, found in inscriptions and on coins.

Sacred stone that fell from the sky, probably a meteorite which, from its resemblance to a many-breasted female figure, was identified with the Ephesian mother-goddess Artemis.

that these things cannot be contradicted, you ought to be quiet and do nothing rash. 37 For you have brought these men here who are neither sacrilegious nor blasphemers of our goddess. 38 If therefore De·me'tri·us and the craftsmen with him have a complaint against any one, the courts are open, and there are proconsuls; let them bring charges against one another. 39 But if you seek anything further,[t] it shall be settled in the regular assembly. 40 For we are in danger of being charged with rioting today, there being no cause that we can give to justify this commotion." 41And when he had said this, he dismissed the assembly.

THROUGH GREECE TO TROAS (20:1-12)

20 After the uproar ceased, Paul sent for the disciples and having exhorted them took leave of them and departed for Macedonia. 2 When he had gone through these parts and had given them much encouragement, he came to Greece. 3 There he spent three months, and when a plot was made against him by the Jews as he was about to set sail for Syria, he determined to return through Macedonia. 4 So'pa·ter of Be·roe'a, the son of Pyrrhus, accompanied him; and of the Thessalonians, Ar·is·tar'chus and Secundus; and Gaius of Derbe, and Timothy; and the Asians, Tych'i·cus and Troph'i·mus. 5 These went on and were waiting for us at Troas, 6 but we sailed away from Phi·lip'pi after the days of Unleavened Bread, and in five days we came to them at Troas, where we stayed for seven days.

7 On the first day of the week, when we were gathered together to break bread, Paul talked with them, intending to depart on the morrow; and he prolonged his speech until midnight. 8 There were many lights in the upper chamber where we were gathered. 9And a young man named Eu'ty·chus was sitting in the window. He sank into a deep sleep as Paul talked still longer; and being overcome by sleep, he fell down from the third story and was taken up dead. 10 But Paul went down and bent over him, and embracing him said, "Do not be alarmed, for his life is in him." 11And when Paul had gone up and had broken bread and eaten, he conversed with them a long while, until daybreak, and so departed. 12And they took the lad away alive, and were not a little comforted.

TO MILETUS: PAUL'S FAREWELL TO ELDERS OF EPHESUS (20:13-38)

13 But going ahead to the ship, we set sail for Assos, intending to take Paul aboard there; for so he had arranged, intending himself to go by land. 14And when he met us at Assos, we took him on board and came to Mi·ty·le'ne. 15And sailing from there we came the following day opposite Chios; the next day we touched at Samos; and[u] the day after that we came to Mi·le'tus. 16 For Paul had decided to sail past Eph'e·sus, so that he might not have to spend time in Asia; for he was hastening to be at Jerusalem, if possible, on the day of Pentecost.

17 And from Mi·le'tus he sent to Eph'e·sus and called to him the elders of the church. 18And when they came to him, he said to them:

---

[t] Other ancient authorities read *about other matters*　[u] Other ancient authorities add *after remaining at Trogyllium*

19:38-40 *The courts are open, and there are proconsuls,* that is, the regular channels of government provided by Roman rule are sufficient for the redress of any real grievances. Tumultuous proceedings are unnecessary as well as dangerous, since the Romans would take a grave view of them.

20:3 *There he spent three months.* Paul probably spent much of this time at Corinth, where he wrote his Letter to the Romans. Cf. Introduction to Romans.

20:4 *Sopater . . . Aristarchus,* etc. The men named were probably representatives of the Gentile churches who brought the gifts of the Gentiles to the poor saints of Jerusalem. (Cf. 1 Co 16:3-4)

20:6 *Days of Unleavened Bread,* the seven days following the Passover and so closely associated with that feast that the two terms are practically interchangeable.

20:8 The presence of *many lights* is noted as accounting for the sleepiness of Eutychus (8); the burning of many oil lamps would create an oppressive atmosphere.

20:5-6 *Us . . . we.* Cf. 16:10 note. Luke rejoins Paul at Philippi.

20:16 *The day of Pentecost.* Cf. 2:1 note.

20:18-35 Luke has recorded addresses of Paul the missionary speaking to Jews in their synagog (13:16-41) and to Gentiles, both the wise (17:22-31) and the foolish (14:15-17). It is only in this farewell address to the elders of Ephesus that Luke presents Paul the pastor speaking to Christians. As

"You yourselves know how I lived among you all the time from the first day that I set foot in Asia, [19] serving the Lord with all humility and with tears and with trials which befell me through the plots of the Jews; [20] how I did not shrink from declaring to you anything that was profitable, and teaching you in public and from house to house, [21] testifying both to Jews and to Greeks of repentance to God and of faith in our Lord Jesus Christ. [22] And now, behold, I am going to Jerusalem, bound in the Spirit, not knowing what shall befall me there; [23] except that the Holy Spirit testifies to me in every city that imprisonment and afflictions await me. [24] But I do not account my life of any value nor as precious to myself, if only I may accomplish my course and the ministry which I received from the Lord Jesus, to testify to the gospel of the grace of God. [25] And now, behold, I know that all you among whom I have gone preaching the kingdom will see my face no more. [26] Therefore I testify to you this day that I am innocent of the blood of all of you, [27] for I did not shrink from declaring to you the whole counsel of God. [28] Take heed to yourselves and to all the flock, in which the Holy Spirit has made you overseers, to care for the church of God[v] which he obtained with the blood of his own Son.[w] [29] I know that after my departure fierce wolves will come in among you, not sparing the flock; [30] and from among your own selves will arise men speaking perverse things, to draw away the disciples after them. [31] Therefore be alert, remembering that for three years I did not cease night or day to admonish every one with tears. [32] And now I commend you to God and to the word of his grace, which is able to build you up and to give you the inheritance among all those who are sanctified. [33] I coveted no one's silver or gold or apparel. [34] You yourselves know that these hands ministered to my necessities, and to those who were with me. [35] In all things I have shown you that by so toiling one must help the weak, remembering the words of the Lord Jesus, how he said, 'It is more blessed to give than to receive.' "

36 And when he had spoken thus, he knelt down and prayed with them all. [37] And they all wept and embraced Paul and kissed him, [38] sorrowing most of all because of the word he had spoken, that they should see his face no more. And they brought him to the ship.

FROM MILETUS TO JERUSALEM (21:1-16)

21 And when we had parted from them and set sail, we came by a straight course to Cos, and the next day to Rhodes, and from there to Pat'a·ra.[x] [2] And having found a ship crossing to Phoe·nic'i·a, we went aboard, and set sail. [3] When we had come in sight of Cyprus, leaving it on the left we sailed to Syria, and landed at Tyre;

[v] Other ancient authorities read *of the Lord*   [w] Greek *with the blood of his Own* or *with his own blood*
[x] Other ancient authorities add *and Myra*

he faces these elders for what in all probability is the last time (25), he recalls his missionary ministry among them, a ministry marked by fidelity to his Lord and *humility* toward men amid the *trials* and *tears* of his imperiled life as missionary, how he had resisted the temptation to abridge his Gospel or to restrict his audience for the sake of "success" (18-21). He turns to the future. He himself faces *imprisonment and afflictions,* but that is not what concerns him. What does concern him is that he remains faithful unto death in the ministry his Lord has given him and run true in the course He has set for him (22-24). The future of the church in Ephesus, too, is dark. The new people of God (*flock,* 28) will be beset by both foe and traitor (29-30). The elders must therefore be alert and vigilant in the exercise of their office, as Paul has been in his; he has given them the Word of life fully and faithfully; no man has lost eternal life by any fault of his (26-27, 31). Paul's charge to the elders has been sober and uncompromising (28-31); he gives them the heart and the strength to execute

it by his promise. He commends them to the Word of divine grace, which has been his own sufficiency all his days, a Word that has power to build them up and to carry them through the dark days ahead into God's bright final future (32). They can live of that grace and hope for that future if they follow Paul's example of self-giving, which has the blessing and promise of the Lord Jesus. (34-35)

20:23 *The Holy Spirit testifies to me,* probably through Christian prophets such as Agabus. (21:10-11)

20:26 *I am innocent of the blood of all of you.* Cf. 18:6.

20:29 *Fierce wolves . . . not sparing the flock.* For the people of God as the *flock* of God, and *wolves* (false prophets and teachers) as enemies of the flock, cf. Mt 7:15.

20:34 *These hands ministered to my necessities.* Cf. 1 Co 4:12; 9:3-18; 2 Co 11:7-11; 12:13; 1 Th 2:3-10; 2 Th 3:7-9.

20:35 *The words of the Lord Jesus.* This word of our Lord is not recorded in the gospels.

for there the ship was to unload its cargo. ⁴And having sought out the disciples, we stayed there for seven days. Through the Spirit they told Paul not to go on to Jerusalem. ⁵And when our days there were ended, we departed and went on our journey; and they all, with wives and children, brought us on our way till we were outside the city; and kneeling down on the beach we prayed and bade one another farewell. ⁶ Then we went on board the ship, and they returned home.

7 When we had finished the voyage from Tyre, we arrived at Ptol·e·ma′is; and we greeted the brethren and stayed with them for one day. ⁸ On the morrow we departed and came to Caes·a·re′a; and we entered the house of Philip the evangelist, who was one of the seven, and stayed with him. ⁹And he had four unmarried daughters, who prophesied. ¹⁰ While we were staying for some days, a prophet named Ag′a·bus came down from Judea. ¹¹And coming to us he took Paul's girdle and bound his own feet and hands, and said, "Thus says the Holy Spirit, 'So shall the Jews at Jerusalem bind the man who owns this girdle and deliver him into the hands of the Gentiles.'" ¹² When we heard this, we and the people there begged him not to go up to Jerusalem. ¹³ Then Paul answered, "What are you doing, weeping and breaking my heart? For I am ready not only to be imprisoned but even to die at Jerusalem for the name of the Lord Jesus." ¹⁴And when he would not be persuaded, we ceased and said, "The will of the Lord be done."

15 After these days we made ready and went up to Jerusalem. ¹⁶And some of the disciples from Caes·a·re′a went with us, bringing us to the house of Mnason of Cyprus, an early disciple, with whom we should lodge.

THE REQUEST OF THE JERUSALEM CHURCH (21:17-26)

17 When we had come to Jerusalem, the brethren received us gladly. ¹⁸ On the following day Paul went in with us to James; and all the elders were present. ¹⁹After greeting them, he related one by one the things that God had done among the Gentiles through his ministry. ²⁰And when they heard it, they glorified God. And they said to him, "You see, brother, how many thousands there are among the Jews of those who have believed; they are all zealous for the law, ²¹ and they have been told about you that you teach all the Jews who are among the Gentiles to forsake Moses, telling them not to circumcise their children or observe the customs. ²² What then is to be done? They will certainly hear that you have come. ²³ Do therefore what we tell you. We have four men who are under a vow; ²⁴ take these men and purify yourself along with them and pay their expenses, so that they may shave their heads. Thus all will know that there is nothing in what they have been told about you but that you yourself live in observance of the law. ²⁵ But as for the Gentiles who have believed, we have sent a letter with our judgment that they should abstain from what has been sacrificed to idols and from blood and from what is strangled*ʸ* and from unchastity." ²⁶ Then Paul took the men, and the next day he purified himself with them and went into the temple, to give notice when the days of purification would be fulfilled and the offering presented for every one of them.

ʸ Other early authorities omit and from what is strangled

21:4 *Having sought out the disciples, we stayed there.* Passages like this (cf. 8, 16) show the relevance of the admonitions to Christian hospitality in the letters of Paul (Ro 12:13; 1 Ti 3:2; 5:10; Tts 1:8), Peter (1 Ptr 4:9) and Heb 13:2.

21:8 *Philip the evangelist . . . one of the seven.* Cf. 6:5; 8:5-13, 26-40.

21:10 *Agabus.* Cf. 11:28.

21:11 *Took Paul's girdle.* Like the OT prophets, Agabus reinforces his message by symbolic action. (Cf. 1 K 11:29-36; Is 20:2-4; Eze 4:1-17)

21:13 *Breaking my heart,* that is, "trying to break down my resolve." (Cf. 14)

21:18 For James as leader of the Jerusalem church cf. 12:17 note.

21:21 *Teach . . . the Jews . . . not to circumcise their children.* The report that reached Jerusalem was a distortion of Paul's teaching regarding Christian freedom from the Law. For Paul's true position concerning circumcision cf. 16:3 note and 1 Co 7:17-19.

21:22-24 Paul is to purge himself of the suspicion that he has become a traitor to the religion of his fathers and to his people by publicly associating himself with *four men . . . under a vow,* a Nazirite vow (cf. 18:18 note), and by paying the considerable *expenses* involved in the sacrificial ceremony of purification.

21:25 *We have sent a letter.* Cf. 15:20, 23-29; 16:4; and Introduction to Galatians.

21:26 Paul's consent to the request of the

PAUL'S ARREST IN THE TEMPLE (21:27-40)

27 When the seven days were almost completed, the Jews from Asia, who had seen him in the temple, stirred up all the crowd, and laid hands on him, 28 crying out, "Men of Israel, help! This is the man who is teaching men everywhere against the people and the law and this place; moreover he also brought Greeks into the temple, and he has defiled this holy place." 29 For they had previously seen Troph'i·mus the E·phe'sian with him in the city, and they supposed that Paul had brought him into the temple. 30 Then all the city was aroused, and the people ran together; they seized Paul and dragged him out of the temple, and at once the gates were shut. 31And as they were trying to kill him, word came to the tribune of the cohort that all Jerusalem was in confusion. 32 He at once took soldiers and centurions, and ran down to them; and when they saw the tribune and the soldiers, they stopped beating Paul. 33 Then the tribune came up and arrested him, and ordered him to be bound with two chains. He inquired who he was and what he had done. 34 Some in the crowd shouted one thing, some another; and as he could not learn the facts because of the uproar, he ordered him to be brought into the barracks. 35And when he came to the steps, he was actually carried by the soldiers because of the violence of the crowd; 36 for the mob of the people followed, crying, "Away with him!"

37 As Paul was about to be brought into the barracks, he said to the tribune, "May I say something to you?" And he said, "Do you know Greek? 38Are you not the Egyptian, then, who recently stirred up a revolt and led the four thousand men of the Assassins out into the wilderness?" 39 Paul replied, "I am a Jew, from Tarsus in Cilicia, a citizen of no mean city; I beg you, let me speak to the people." 40And when he had given him leave, Paul, standing on the steps, motioned with his hand to the people; and when there was a great hush, he spoke to them in the Hebrew language, saying:

PAUL SPEAKS FOR THE LAST TIME TO HIS PEOPLE (22:1-21)

22 "Brethren and fathers, hear the defense which I now make before you." 2 And when they heard that he addressed them in the Hebrew language, they were the more quiet. And he said:

3 "I am a Jew, born at Tarsus in Cilicia, but brought up in this city at the feet of Ga·ma'li·el, educated according to the strict manner of the law of our fathers, being zealous for God as you all are this day. 4 I persecuted this Way to the death, binding and delivering to prison both men and women, 5 as the high priest and the whole council of elders bear me witness. From them I received letters to the brethren, and

Jerusalem church is in keeping with what he has written. (1 Co 9:20)

21:27 *The seven days* required for the rite of purification for a Nazirite who had incurred defilement. (Cf. Nm 6:9)

Jews from Asia. Paul's break with the synagog at Ephesus (19:9) and his subsequent missionary success (19:10) apparently had made the Jews of Asia especially bitter toward him (cf. 20:19). They were present in Jerusalem for Pentecost. (20:16)

21:28 *Brought Greeks into the temple.* Gentiles were permitted in the outer court of the temple, but for a Gentile to enter the inner precincts was an offense punishable by death.

21:30 *All the city was aroused.* Religious-national feelings ran high at the time of the great festivals. The Roman garrison, quartered in the fortress Antonia adjacent to the temple precincts (cf. 31, 34), was often reinforced on these occasions in expectation of disorders like the one recorded here. (30-35)

21:31 *Tribune,* Roman officer in command of a *cohort,* a division of the legion.

21:36 *"Away with him!"* The crowd raised the same cry concerning Jesus at His trial. (Lk 23:18)

21:38 *Egyptian.* The tribune had identified Paul with an Egyptian impostor who had appeared in Jerusalem a few years before. He claimed to be a prophet and promised his followers that the walls of Jerusalem would fall before him and that the Roman power would be overcome. When Roman troops quashed the attempted revolt, the Egyptian disappeared.

The Assassins were Jews whose zeal for the cause of Jewish freedom led them to assassinate Jews suspected of collaboration with the Romans. Men of this type would join in revolts such as the Egyptian fomented.

22:1-21 Paul's last words to his people are a monument to his inextinguishable love for Israel (cf. Ro 9:1-5; 10:1-2; 11:13-14). His every word is designed to win the men who had just attempted to kill him (21:31) and would soon cry for his blood again (22:22). He speaks to them in their mother tongue (21:40), not without effect (22:2). His mode of address (*Brethren and fathers,* 22:1) and his first words to them (*I am a Jew,* 22:3) avow

I journeyed to Damascus to take those also who were there and bring them in bonds to Jerusalem to be punished.

6 "As I made my journey and drew near to Damascus, about noon a great light from heaven suddenly shone about me. [7]And I fell to the ground and heard a voice saying to me, 'Saul, Saul, why do you persecute me?' [8]And I answered, 'Who are you, Lord?' And he said to me, 'I am Jesus of Nazareth whom you are persecuting.' [9] Now those who were with me saw the light but did not hear the voice of the one who was speaking to me. [10]And I said, 'What shall I do, Lord?' And the Lord said to me, 'Rise, and go into Damascus, and there you will be told all that is appointed for you to do.' [11]And when I could not see because of the brightness of that light, I was led by the hand by those who were with me, and came into Damascus.

12 "And one An·a·ni'as, a devout man according to the law, well spoken of by all the Jews who lived there, [13] came to me, and standing by me said to me, 'Brother Saul, receive your sight.' And in that very hour I received my sight and saw him. [14]And he said, 'The God of our fathers appointed you to know his will, to see the Just One and to hear a voice from his mouth; [15] for you will be a witness for him to all men of what you have seen and heard. [16]And now why do you wait? Rise and be baptized, and wash away your sins, calling on his name.'

17 "When I had returned to Jerusalem and was praying in the temple, I fell into a trance [18] and saw him saying to me, 'Make haste and get quickly out of Jerusalem, because they will not accept your testimony about me.' [19]And I said, 'Lord, they themselves know that in every synagogue I imprisoned and beat those who believed in thee. [20]And when the blood of Stephen thy witness was shed, I also was standing by and approving, and keeping the garments of those who killed him.' [21]And he said to me, 'Depart; for I will send you far away to the Gentiles.' "

THE RESULT OF PAUL'S ADDRESS TO HIS COUNTRYMEN (22:22-30)

22 Up to this word they listened to him; then they lifted up their voices and said, "Away with such a fellow from the earth! For he ought not to live." [23]And as they cried out and waved their garments and threw dust into the air, [24] the tribune commanded him to be brought into the barracks, and ordered him to be examined by scourging, to find out why they shouted thus against him. [25] But when they had tied him up with the thongs, Paul said to the centurion who was standing by, "Is it lawful for you to scourge a man who is a Roman citizen, and uncondemned?" [26] When the centurion heard that, he went to the tribune and said to him, "What are you about to do? For this man is a Roman citizen." [27] So the tribune came and said to him, "Tell me, are you a Roman citizen?" And he said, "Yes." [28] The tribune answered, "I bought this citizenship for a large sum." Paul said, "But I was born a citizen." [29] So those who were about to examine him withdrew from him instantly; and the

his kinship with them. He has been *brought up* in their city, has studied under their revered teacher *Gamaliel, educated according to the strict manner of the law* of the Jewish fathers who are both their fathers and his, *zealous for God* as they *are this day* (3; cf. Ro 10:2). The man through whom the blinded persecutor received his sight and saw his new Lord was *a devout man according to the law, well spoken of by all the Jews who lived there,* in Damascus (12-13); this man, *Ananias,* acted in obedience to *the God of our fathers* and spoke of Christ in terms familiar to the Jews from their OT (*Just One,* 14; cf. Is 53:11). And Paul's own impulse and desire had been to witness to his Lord among the Jews (17-20); it was the overruling word of his Lord that sent him to the Gentiles (21), not some dissatisfaction with or resentment toward his people. The substance of Paul's words, too, is thoroughly Jewish; his appeal to them is the *narrative* of his conversion.

The Jew was accustomed from his OT to appeal by narrative; he rightly called the books which we call "historical books" the Former Prophets (Joshua through 2 Kings).

22:22-30 At the word "Gentiles" (21) the prejudice and fury of the mob breaks out anew (22-23; cf. 21:28). The tribune decides to interrogate Paul under torture (24) but is deterred from this course when he discovers that Paul is a Roman citizen (25-29). *Desiring to know the real reason why the Jews accused* Paul, he determines to bring him before the council. (30)

22:24 *Examined by scourging.* This third-degree manner of obtaining evidence was common enough; but to apply it to a Roman citizen was illegal. (Cf. 25-26)

22:25 *Tied him up,* preparatory to scourging. *Uncondemned,* without due process of law. (Cf. 16:37)

22:28 *For a large sum.* The tribune evidently

tribune also was afraid, for he realized that Paul was a Roman citizen and that he had bound him.

30 But on the morrow, desiring to know the real reason why the Jews accused him, he unbound him, and commanded the chief priests and all the council to meet, and he brought Paul down and set him before them.

PAUL DIVIDES THE COUNCIL (23:1-11)

23 And Paul, looking intently at the council, said, "Brethren, I have lived before God in all good conscience up to this day." 2And the high priest An·a·ni′as commanded those who stood by him to strike him on the mouth. 3 Then Paul said to him, "God shall strike you, you whitewashed wall! Are you sitting to judge me according to the law, and yet contrary to the law you order me to be struck?" 4 Those who stood by said, "Would you revile God's high priest?" 5And Paul said, "I did not know, brethren, that he was the high priest; for it is written, 'You shall not speak evil of a ruler of your people.' "

6 But when Paul perceived that one part were Sad′du·cees and the other Pharisees, he cried out in the council, "Brethren, I am a Pharisee, a son of Pharisees; with respect to the hope and the resurrection of the dead I am on trial." 7And when he had said this, a dissension arose between the Pharisees and the Sad′du·cees; and the assembly was divided. 8 For the Sad′du·cees say that there is no resurrection, nor angel, nor spirit; but the Pharisees acknowledge them all. 9 Then a great clamor arose; and some of the scribes of the Pharisees' party stood up and contended, "We find nothing wrong in this man. What if a spirit or an angel spoke to him?" 10And when the dissension became violent, the tribune, afraid that Paul would be torn in pieces by them, commanded the soldiers to go down and take him by force from among them and bring him into the barracks.

11 The following night the Lord stood by him and said, "Take courage, for as you have testified about me at Jerusalem, so you must bear witness also at Rome."

THE JEWISH PLOT AGAINST PAUL BETRAYED (23:12-22)

12 When it was day, the Jews made a plot and bound themselves by an oath neither to eat nor drink till they had killed Paul. 13 There were more than forty who made this conspiracy. 14And they went to the chief priests and elders, and said, "We have strictly bound ourselves by an oath to taste no food till we have killed Paul. 15 You therefore, along with the council, give notice now to the tribune to bring him down to you, as though you were going to determine his case more exactly. And we are ready to kill him before he comes near."

16 Now the son of Paul's sister heard of their ambush; so he went and entered the barracks and told Paul. 17And Paul called one of the centurions and said, "Take this young man to the tribune; for he has something to tell him." 18 So he took him and brought him to the tribune and said, "Paul the prisoner called me and asked me to bring this young man to you, as he has something to say to you." 19 The tribune took him by the hand, and going aside asked him privately, "What is it that you have to

doubted that a man such as he saw before him had the means to purchase Roman citizenship, as he himself had done.

23:1-11 "With me it is a very small thing that I should be judged . . . by any human court," Paul had written to the Corinthians (1 Co 4:3). The Jewish high court certainly demonstrated that this very human court was not competent to judge an apostle of Jesus Christ. The presiding high priest, Ananias, begins proceedings with a gross illegality, exposing himself as the *whitewashed wall* that he is (2-3). The members of the council are hopelessly and violently at variance, *Sadducee* against *Pharisee*. Paul, serenely independent of the judgment of men, utilizes the split between Pharisee and Sadducee to remove himself from the judicature of men incompetent to judge him (6-10). There is only One who is competent to judge the apostle, and His word is one of assurance *(take courage)* and promise. (11)

23:1 *In all good conscience.* Cf. 2 Ti 1:3.

23:3 *You whitewashed wall,* whose fair exterior conceals from the eyes of men the weakness of the structure doomed to the judgment of God. (Cf. Eze 13:10-16)

23:5 Paul's words may be ironic: "I did not recognize as *God's high priest* one who acted in so ungodly and unpriestly a way."

You shall not speak, etc. Cf. Ex 22:28.

23:8 *No resurrection.* Cf. Lk 20:27.

tell me?" 20And he said, "The Jews have agreed to ask you to bring Paul down to the council tomorrow, as though they were going to inquire somewhat more closely about him. 21 But do not yield to them; for more than forty of their men lie in ambush for him, having bound themselves by an oath neither to eat nor drink till they have killed him; and now they are ready, waiting for the promise from you." 22 So the tribune dismissed the young man, charging him, "Tell no one that you have informed me of this."

PAUL IS SENT TO THE ROMAN GOVERNOR AT CAESAREA (23:23-35)

23 Then he called two of the centurions and said, "At the third hour of the night get ready two hundred soldiers with seventy horsemen and two hundred spearmen to go as far as Caes·a·re′a. 24Also provide mounts for Paul to ride, and bring him safely to Felix the governor." 25And he wrote a letter to this effect:
26 "Claudius Lys′i·as to his Excellency the governor Felix, greeting. 27 This man was seized by the Jews, and was about to be killed by them, when I came upon them with the soldiers and rescued him, having learned that he was a Roman citizen. 28And desiring to know the charge on which they accused him, I brought him down to their council. 29 I found that he was accused about questions of their law, but charged with nothing deserving death or imprisonment. 30And when it was disclosed to me that there would be a plot against the man, I sent him to you at once, ordering his accusers also to state before you what they have against him."
31 So the soldiers, according to their instructions, took Paul and brought him by night to An·tip′a·tris. 32And on the morrow they returned to the barracks, leaving the horsemen to go on with him. 33 When they came to Caes·a·re′a and delivered the letter to the governor, they presented Paul also before him. 34 On reading the letter, he asked to what province he belonged. When he learned that he was from Cilicia 35 he said, "I will hear you when your accusers arrive." And he commanded him to be guarded in Herod's praetorium.

PAUL BEFORE FELIX THE ROMAN GOVERNOR (24:1-23)

24 And after five days the high priest An·a·ni′as came down with some elders and a spokesman, one Ter·tul′lus. They laid before the governor their case against Paul; 2 and when he was called, Ter·tul′lus began to accuse him, saying:
"Since through you we enjoy much peace, and since by your provision, most excellent Felix, reforms are introduced on behalf of this nation, 3 in every way and everywhere we accept this with all gratitude. 4 But, to detain you no further, I beg you in your kindness to hear us briefly. 5 For we have found this man a pestilent fellow, an agitator among all the Jews throughout the world, and a ringleader of the sect of the Nazarenes. 6 He even tried to profane the temple, but we seized him. z 8 By examining him yourself you will be able to learn from him about everything of which we accuse him."
9 The Jews also joined in the charge, affirming that all this was so.
10 And when the governor had motioned to him to speak, Paul replied:
"Realizing that for many years you have been judge over this nation, I cheerfully

---

z Other ancient authorities add *and we would have judged him according to our law.* 7 *But the chief captain Lysias came and with great violence took him out of our hands,* 8 *commanding his accusers to come before you.*

23:23 *Third hour of the night,* about 9 p. m.
23:34 *Cilicia,* a Roman province whose inhabitants would come under Roman jurisdiction.
23:35 *Herod's praetorium.* The governor's headquarters *(praetorium)* in Caesarea was situated in a building which had been Herod the Great's palace.
24:1-23 Paul's first trial before the governor ends inconclusively (22, *put them off*). Paul answers the second of the two charges brought against him (attempted profanation of the temple, 6) by pointing out that his stay in Jerusalem has

been brief *(twelve days,* 11) and peaceable (12). As to the first charge *(ringleader of the sect of the Nazarenes,* i. e., Christians, 5), he admits it freely (14) but insists that he occupies the same religious ground as his opponents *(law ... prophets,* 14; the hope of Israel, 15), implying that the case is one of a theological difference within Judaism, one which a Roman court is neither willing nor able to adjudicate (cf. Gallio's attitude, 18:14-15). If he has in fact been an *agitator among . . . the Jews* (5), the "agitation" he has provoked is theological, not political. (20-21; cf. 23:6-10)

make my defense. [11]As you may ascertain, it is not more than twelve days since I went up to worship at Jerusalem; [12] and they did not find me disputing with any one or stirring up a crowd, either in the temple or in the synagogues, or in the city. [13] Neither can they prove to you what they now bring up against me. [14] But this I admit to you, that according to the Way, which they call a sect, I worship the God of our fathers, believing everything laid down by the law or written in the prophets, [15] having a hope in God which these themselves accept, that there will be a resurrection of both the just and the unjust. [16] So I always take pains to have a clear conscience toward God and toward men. [17] Now after some years I came to bring to my nation alms and offerings. [18]As I was doing this, they found me purified in the temple, without any crowd or tumult. But some Jews from Asia— [19] they ought to be here before you and to make an accusation, if they have anything against me. [20] Or else let these men themselves say what wrongdoing they found when I stood before the council, [21] except this one thing which I cried out while standing among them, 'With respect to the resurrection of the dead I am on trial before you this day.' "

22 But Felix, having a rather accurate knowledge of the Way, put them off, saying, "When Lys'i·as the tribune comes down, I will decide your case." [23] Then he gave orders to the centurion that he should be kept in custody but should have some liberty, and that none of his friends should be prevented from attending to his needs.

PAUL AND FELIX AND DRUSILLA (24:24-27)

24 After some days Felix came with his wife Dru·sil'la, who was a Jewess; and he sent for Paul and heard him speak upon faith in Christ Jesus. [25]And as he argued about justice and self-control and future judgment, Felix was alarmed and said, "Go away for the present; when I have an opportunity I will summon you." [26]At the same time he hoped that money would be given him by Paul. So he sent for him often and conversed with him. [27] But when two years had elapsed, Felix was succeeded by Por'ci·us Festus; and desiring to do the Jews a favor, Felix left Paul in prison.

PAUL BEFORE FESTUS: THE APPEAL TO CAESAR (25:1-12)

25 Now when Festus had come into his province, after three days he went up to Jerusalem from Caes·a·re'a. [2]And the chief priests and the principal men of the Jews informed him against Paul; and they urged him, [3] asking as a favor to have the man sent to Jerusalem, planning an ambush to kill him on the way. [4] Festus replied that Paul was being kept at Caes·a·re'a, and that he himself intended to go there shortly. [5] "So," said he, "let the men of authority among you go down with me, and if there is anything wrong about the man, let them accuse him."

6 When he had stayed among them not more than eight or ten days, he went down to Caes·a·re'a; and the next day he took his seat on the tribunal and ordered Paul to be brought. [7]And when he had come, the Jews who had gone down from Jerusalem stood about him, bringing against him many serious charges which they could not prove. [8] Paul said in his defense, "Neither against the law of the Jews, nor against the temple, nor against Caesar have I offended at all." [9] But Festus, wishing to do the Jews a favor, said to Paul, "Do you wish to go up to Jerusalem, and there be tried on these charges before me?" [10] But Paul said, "I am standing before Caesar's tribunal,

24:1 *Tertullus*, otherwise unknown.

24:14 *The Way.* Cf. 9:2 note.

24:14-15 *Law . . . prophets . . . hope.* For Paul's attitude toward the OT Scriptures cf. Ro 3:21; 15:4.

24:18 *Jews from Asia.* Cf. 21:27 note.

24:21 *I cried out while standing among them.* Cf. 23:6.

24:24-27 Roman and Jewish historians agree in giving *Felix* a bad character; his Jewish wife, *Drusilla*, had left her first husband to marry him. Whatever prompted him to ask Paul to *speak upon faith in Christ Jesus* (24), he could not have ex-

pected and certainly did not relish talk of *justice and self-control and future judgment* (25). With a past like his, and with such a wife beside him, it is no wonder he was *alarmed* (25) and cut the interview short.

24:27 *Desiring to do the Jews a favor,* probably to offset the bitterness engendered by his administration, a bitterness so great that the Jews sent a deputation to Rome to bring charges against Felix.

25:1-12 The new trial before Festus produces nothing really new; prosecution and defense are the same as in the trial before Felix (6-8; cf.

where I ought to be tried; to the Jews I have done no wrong, as you know very well. [11] If then I am a wrongdoer, and have committed anything for which I deserve to die, I do not seek to escape death; but if there is nothing in their charges against me, no one can give me up to them. I appeal to Caesar." [12] Then Festus, when he had conferred with his council, answered, "You have appealed to Caesar; to Caesar you shall go."

THE ARRIVAL OF AGRIPPA (25:13-22)

13 Now when some days had passed, A·grip'pa the king and Ber·ni'ce arrived at Caes·a·re'a to welcome Festus. [14]And as they stayed there many days, Festus laid Paul's case before the king, saying, "There is a man left prisoner by Felix; [15] and when I was at Jerusalem, the chief priests and the elders of the Jews gave information about him, asking for sentence against him. [16] I answered them that it was not the custom of the Romans to give up any one before the accused met the accusers face to face, and had opportunity to make his defense concerning the charge laid against him. [17] When therefore they came together here, I made no delay, but on the next day took my seat on the tribunal and ordered the man to be brought in. [18] When the accusers stood up, they brought no charge in his case of such evils as I supposed; [19] but they had certain points of dispute with him about their own superstition and about one Jesus, who was dead, but whom Paul asserted to be alive. [20] Being at a loss how to investigate these questions, I asked whether he wished to go to Jerusalem and be tried there regarding them. [21] But when Paul had appealed to be kept in custody for the decision of the emperor, I commanded him to be held until I could send him to Caesar." [22]And A·grip'pa said to Festus, "I should like to hear the man myself." "Tomorrow," said he, "you shall hear him."

THE HEARING BEFORE KING AGRIPPA (25:23 – 26:23)

23 So on the morrow A·grip'pa and Ber·ni'ce came with great pomp, and they entered the audience hall with the military tribunes and the prominent men of the city. Then by command of Festus Paul was brought in. [24]And Festus said, "King A·grip'pa and all who are present with us, you see this man about whom the whole Jewish people petitioned me, both at Jerusalem and here, shouting that he ought not to live any longer. [25] But I found that he had done nothing deserving death; and as he himself appealed to the emperor, I decided to send him. [26] But I have nothing definite to write to my lord about him. Therefore I have brought him before you, and, especially before you, King A·grip'pa, that, after we have examined him, I may have something to write. [27] For it seems to me unreasonable, in sending a prisoner, not to indicate the charges against him."

26 A·grip'pa said to Paul, "You have permission to speak for yourself." Then Paul stretched out his hand and made his defense:

2 "I think myself fortunate that it is before you, King A·grip'pa, I am to make my defense today against all the accusations of the Jews, [3] because you are especially familiar with all customs and controversies of the Jews; therefore I beg you to listen to me patiently.

24:2-21). When Festus is inclined to make a conciliatory gesture to the Jews by shifting the trial to Jerusalem (9), Paul makes use of his privilege as a Roman citizen to lodge an appeal to have his case tried in Rome where neither Jewish prejudice nor plotting (cf. 7) would preclude a fair hearing.

25:13 *Agrippa the king.* Herod Agrippa II, son of Herod Agrippa I (Acts 12:1-4, 20-23), the last of the Herodians, had attained and held his power by his devotion and subservience to Rome; hence his prompt courtesy call on the newly arrived Roman governor. Drusilla, wife of Felix, was his sister, as was *Bernice.* There was scandalous gossip, apparently not unfounded, that his relationship with Bernice was incestuous. Embarrassed by the fact that he had on his hands an

appeal case which he did not understand (cf. 26-27), Festus welcomed the opportunity to consult with one "especially familiar with all customs and controversies of the Jews." (26:2)

25:23 – 26:23 Paul speaks in defense of his Gospel for the last time on Jewish soil, before the last Jewish king. As in his words to the mob in the temple court (ch. 22), he stresses the continuity between his Judaic past and his present position as an apostle of Jesus Christ; the Gospel he proclaims is the fulfillment of the promise made to his Jewish fathers, the fulfilled content of the hope of the 12 tribes of Israel. That Paul should be accused *for this* Jewish *hope by Jews* (7) is supreme and tragic irony. (4-8)

Paul admits that he had once been as blind to

4 "My manner of life from my youth, spent from the beginning among my own nation and at Jerusalem, is known by all the Jews. 5 They have known for a long time, if they are willing to testify, that according to the strictest party of our religion I have lived as a Pharisee. 6And now I stand here on trial for hope in the promise made by God to our fathers, 7 to which our twelve tribes hope to attain, as they earnestly worship night and day. And for this hope I am accused by Jews, O king! 8 Why is it thought incredible by any of you that God raises the dead?

9 "I myself was convinced that I ought to do many things in opposing the name of Jesus of Nazareth. 10And I did so in Jerusalem; I not only shut up many of the saints in prison, by authority from the chief priests, but when they were put to death I cast my vote against them. 11And I punished them often in all the synagogues and tried to make them blaspheme; and in raging fury against them, I persecuted them even to foreign cities.

12 "Thus I journeyed to Damascus with the authority and commission of the chief priests. 13At midday, O king, I saw on the way a light from heaven, brighter than the sun, shining round me and those who journeyed with me. 14And when we had all fallen to the ground, I heard a voice saying to me in the Hebrew language, 'Saul, Saul, why do you persecute me? It hurts you to kick against the goads.' 15And I said, 'Who are you, Lord?' And the Lord said, 'I am Jesus whom you are persecuting. 16 But rise and stand upon your feet; for I have appeared to you for this purpose, to appoint you to serve and bear witness to the things in which you have seen me and to those in which I will appear to you, 17 delivering you from the people and from the Gentiles—to whom I send you 18 to open their eyes, that they may turn from darkness to light and from the power of Satan to God, that they may receive forgiveness of sins and a place among those who are sanctified by faith in me.'

19 "Wherefore, O King A·grip′pa, I was not disobedient to the heavenly vision, 20 but declared first to those at Damascus, then at Jerusalem and throughout all the country of Judea, and also to the Gentiles, that they should repent and turn to God and perform deeds worthy of their repentance. 21 For this reason the Jews seized me in the temple and tried to kill me. 22 To this day I have had the help that comes from God, and so I stand here testifying both to small and great, saying nothing but what the prophets and Moses said would come to pass: 23 that the Christ must suffer, and that, by being the first to rise from the dead, he would proclaim light both to the people and to the Gentiles."

THE EFFECT OF PAUL'S WORDS (26:24-32)

24 And as he thus made his defense, Festus said with a loud voice, "Paul, you are mad; your great learning is turning you mad." 25 But Paul said, "I am not mad, most excellent Festus, but I am speaking the sober truth. 26 For the king knows about these things, and to him I speak freely; for I am persuaded that none of these things has escaped his notice, for this was not done in a corner. 27 King A·grip′pa, do you believe the prophets? I know that you believe." 28And A·grip′pa said to Paul, "In a short time

the purpose and working of God in Jesus as his accusers now are (9-11). It was not until "the God who said, 'Let light shine out of darkness,'" had shone in his heart "to give the light of the knowledge of the glory of God in the face of Christ" (2 Co 4:6) that he had ceased to persecute Jesus and begun to proclaim Him to Jew and Gentile. (12-18)

He could not be *disobedient to the heavenly vision* (19) that burst on him near Damascus, no more than he could disobey the voice of God that spoke to him from the OT (22). The threat of death cannot deter him, for he is sure of God's help as he continues Christ's own work in proclaiming *light both to the people* (Israel) *and to the Gentiles.* (19-23)

26:4 *My manner of life from my youth.* Cf. 22:3.

26:6 *On trial for hope in the promise.* Cf. 23:6.

26:9-18 Cf. 9:1-8; 22:4-16.

26:9 *Opposing the name of Jesus,* that is, opposing all that *Jesus* stands for, all that He signifies for those who believe in Him.

26:14 *To kick against the goads,* to resist the divine Driver who is leading you in His way.

26:18 Cf. Cl 1:13.

Sanctified, made God's own, His "saints."

26:22 *What the prophets and Moses said.* Cf. Lk 24:44-47.

26:23 *Light both to the people and to the Gentiles.* Cf. Is 42:7, 16.

26:24-32 Both Festus and the king are, it seems, more deeply affected by Paul's words than they care to be. Both fight their way back into the cooler realm of common sense, Festus by his

you think to make me a Christian!" 29And Paul said, "Whether short or long, I would to God that not only you but also all who hear me this day might become such as I am—except for these chains."

30 Then the king rose, and the governor and Ber·ni′ce and those who were sitting with them; 31 and when they had withdrawn, they said to one another, "This man is doing nothing to deserve death or imprisonment." 32And A·grip′pa said to Festus, "This man could have been set free if he had not appealed to Caesar."

THE STORMY VOYAGE TO ROME (27:1-44)

27 And when it was decided that we should sail for Italy, they delivered Paul and some other prisoners to a centurion of the Augustan Cohort, named Julius. 2And embarking in a ship of Ad·ra·myt′ti·um, which was about to sail to the ports along the coast of Asia, we put to sea, accompanied by Ar·is·tar′chus, a Macedonian from Thes·sa·lon′i·ca. 3 The next day we put in at Sidon; and Julius treated Paul kindly, and gave him leave to go to his friends and be cared for. 4And putting to sea from there we sailed under the lee of Cyprus, because the winds were against us. 5And when we had sailed across the sea which is off Cilicia and Pam·phyl′i·a, we came to Myra in Lyc′i·a. 6 There the centurion found a ship of Alexandria sailing for Italy, and put us on board. 7 We sailed slowly for a number of days, and arrived with difficulty off Cnidus, and as the wind did not allow us to go on, we sailed under the lee of Crete off Salmone. 8 Coasting along it with difficulty, we came to a place called Fair Havens, near which was the city of La·se′a.

9 As much time had been lost, and the voyage was already dangerous because the fast had already gone by, Paul advised them, 10 saying, "Sirs, I perceive that the voyage will be with injury and much loss, not only of the cargo and the ship, but also of our lives." 11 But the centurion paid more attention to the captain and to the owner of the ship than to what Paul said. 12And because the harbor was not suitable to winter in, the majority advised to put to sea from there, on the chance that somehow they could reach Phoenix, a harbor of Crete, looking northeast and southeast,a and winter there.

13 And when the south wind blew gently, supposing that they had obtained their purpose, they weighed anchor and sailed along Crete, close inshore. 14 But soon a tempestuous wind, called the northeaster, struck down from the land; 15 and when the ship was caught and could not face the wind, we gave way to it and were driven. 16And running under the lee of a small island called Cauda,b we managed with difficulty to secure the boat; 17 after hoisting it up, they took measuresc to undergird the ship; then, fearing that they should run on the Syrtis, they lowered the gear, and so were driven. 18As we were violently storm-tossed, they began next day to throw the cargo overboard; 19 and the third day they cast out with their own hands the tackle of the ship. 20And when neither sun nor stars appeared for many a day, and no small tempest lay on us, all hope of our being saved was at last abandoned.

21 As they had been long without food, Paul then came forward among them and said, "Men, you should have listened to me, and should not have set sail from Crete and incurred this injury and loss. 22 I now bid you take heart; for there will be no loss of life among you, but only of the ship. 23 For this very night there stood by me an angel of the God to whom I belong and whom I worship, 24 and he said, 'Do not

a Or *southwest and northwest*   b Other ancient authorities read *Clauda*   c Greek *helps*

bluff *you are mad* (24), Agrippa with a feeble joke when confronted by Paul's personal appeal (27-28). Both agree that Paul is innocent. (31-32)

27:1 *Augustan Cohort*. The cohort was one tenth of a legion; cohorts stationed in Palestine numbered 760 infantry and 240 cavalry. An Augustan cohort is known to have been stationed in Syria at this time, but the origin and significance of the term *Augustan* is not clear.

27:9 *The fast*. The Day of Atonement, the great annual fast day in Israel (Lv 16), is meant, the

modern Yom Kippur. The time is autumn, when travel by sea became dangerous and shipping was normally suspended until spring. (Cf. 12)

27:17 *Undergird the ship*. To prevent the wooden hull from breaking up in rough weather, it was reinforced by ropes passed under the ship and wrapped around it.

Syrtis, sandbanks off the coast of north Africa south of Crete, feared by sailors.

27:24 Cf. 23:11.

be afraid, Paul; you must stand before Caesar; and lo, God has granted you all those who sail with you.' 25 So take heart, men, for I have faith in God that it will be exactly as I have been told. 26 But we shall have to run on some island."

27 When the fourteenth night had come, as we were drifting across the sea of A′dri·a, about midnight the sailors suspected that they were nearing land. 28 So they sounded and found twenty fathoms; a little farther on they sounded again and found fifteen fathoms. 29And fearing that we might run on the rocks, they let out four anchors from the stern, and prayed for day to come. 30And as the sailors were seeking to escape from the ship, and had lowered the boat into the sea, under pretense of laying out anchors from the bow, 31 Paul said to the centurion and the soldiers, "Unless these men stay in the ship, you cannot be saved." 32 Then the soldiers cut away the ropes of the boat, and let it go.

33 As day was about to dawn, Paul urged them all to take some food, saying, "Today is the fourteenth day that you have continued in suspense and without food, having taken nothing. 34 Therefore I urge you to take some food; it will give you strength, since not a hair is to perish from the head of any of you." 35And when he had said this, he took bread, and giving thanks to God in the presence of all he broke it and began to eat. 36 Then they all were encouraged and ate some food themselves. 37 (We were in all two hundred and seventy-six*d* persons in the ship.) 38And when they had eaten enough, they lightened the ship, throwing out the wheat into the sea.

39 Now when it was day, they did not recognize the land, but they noticed a bay with a beach, on which they planned if possible to bring the ship ashore. 40 So they cast off the anchors and left them in the sea, at the same time loosening the ropes that tied the rudders; then hoisting the foresail to the wind they made for the beach. 41 But striking a shoal*e* they ran the vessel aground; the bow stuck and remained immovable, and the stern was broken up by the surf. 42 The soldiers' plan was to kill the prisoners, lest any should swim away and escape; 43 but the centurion, wishing to save Paul, kept them from carrying out their purpose. He ordered those who could swim to throw themselves overboard first and make for the land, 44 and the rest on planks or on pieces of the ship. And so it was that all escaped to land.

WINTER IN MALTA (28:1-10)

28 After we had escaped, we then learned that the island was called Malta. 2And the natives showed us unusual kindness, for they kindled a fire and welcomed us all, because it had begun to rain and was cold. 3 Paul had gathered a bundle of sticks and put them on the fire, when a viper came out because of the heat and fastened on his hand. 4 When the natives saw the creature hanging from his hand, they said to one another, "No doubt this man is a murderer. Though he has escaped from the sea, justice has not allowed him to live." 5 He, however, shook off the creature into the fire and suffered no harm. 6 They waited, expecting him to swell up or suddenly fall down dead; but when they had waited a long time and saw no misfortune come to him, they changed their minds and said that he was a god.

7 Now in the neighborhood of that place were lands belonging to the chief man of the island, named Publius, who received us and entertained us hospitably for three days. 8 It happened that the father of Publius lay sick with fever and dysentery; and Paul visited him and prayed, and putting his hands on him healed him. 9And when this had taken place, the rest of the people on the island who had diseases also came and were cured. 10 They presented many gifts to us;*f* and when we sailed, they put on board whatever we needed.

FROM MALTA TO ROME (28:11-16)

11 After three months we set sail in a ship which had wintered in the island, a ship of Alexandria, with the Twin Brothers as figurehead. 12 Putting in at Syracuse,

---

d Other ancient authorities read *seventy-six* or *about seventy-six*   *e* Greek *place of two seas*
f Or *honored us with many honors*

27:27 *Adria*, the Adriatic Sea, although its limits are not the same as in modern usage.

28:4 *Justice* is probably thought of as a person-

ified power, and the word might therefore well be capitalized.

28:6 *Said that he was a god.* Cf. 14:8-13.

we stayed there for three days. 13And from there we made a circuit and arrived at Rhe′gi·um; and after one day a south wind sprang up, and on the second day we came to Pu·te′o·li. 14 There we found brethren, and were invited to stay with them for seven days. And so we came to Rome. 15And the brethren there, when they heard of us, came as far as the Forum of Ap′pi·us and Three Taverns to meet us. On seeing them Paul thanked God and took courage. 16And when we came into Rome, Paul was allowed to stay by himself, with the soldier that guarded him.

PAUL AND THE JEWS OF ROME (28:17-29)

17 After three days he called together the local leaders of the Jews; and when they had gathered, he said to them, "Brethren, though I had done nothing against the people or the customs of our fathers, yet I was delivered prisoner from Jerusalem into the hands of the Romans. 18 When they had examined me, they wished to set me at liberty, because there was no reason for the death penalty in my case. 19 But when the Jews objected, I was compelled to appeal to Caesar—though I had no charge to bring against my nation. 20 For this reason therefore I have asked to see you and speak with you, since it is because of the hope of Israel that I am bound with this chain." 21And they said to him, "We have received no letters from Judea about you, and none of the brethren coming here has reported or spoken any evil about you. 22 But we desire to hear from you what your views are; for with regard to this sect we know that everywhere it is spoken against."

23 When they had appointed a day for him, they came to him at his lodging in great numbers. And he expounded the matter to them from morning till evening, testifying to the kingdom of God and trying to convince them about Jesus both from the law of Moses and from the prophets. 24And some were convinced by what he said, while others disbelieved. 25 So, as they disagreed among themselves, they departed, after Paul had made one statement: "The Holy Spirit was right in saying to your fathers through I·sa′iah the prophet:

26　　'Go to this people, and say,
　　　You shall indeed hear but never understand,
　　　and you shall indeed see but never perceive.
27　　For this people's heart has grown dull,
　　　and their ears are heavy of hearing,
　　　and their eyes they have closed;
　　　lest they should perceive with their eyes,
　　　and hear with their ears,
　　　and understand with their heart,
　　　and turn for me to heal them.'

28:15 *Paul thanked God and took courage.* His Lord had fulfilled His promise (23:11); the long-cherished wish that he might see Rome also (19:21; Ro 1:13; 15:22, 29, 32) has been granted; and the fact that Roman Christians have come some 40 miles to meet him is heartwarming assurance that his letter to them has borne fruit; the Roman Christians will not disappoint Paul's hope that he may be "sped on his journey" to Spain by their assistance. (Ro 15:24)

28:17-29 In Rome Paul brings the Gospel to the Jew first, as has been his consistent practice. He invites the local leaders of the Jews to his quarters and explains to them why he has come to Rome as a prisoner (17-20): He has done nothing against his people (17)—nor has he any charge to bring against the people he still calls *my nation* (19). He is innocent of any offense against Roman law (18). *Because of the hope of Israel,* he is *bound with this chain* (20). This hope is fulfilled in Jesus, proclaimed by Paul—and rejected by the Jews.

There is implicit in Paul's account a call to repentance and a plea for a fair hearing.

The Jewish leaders are willing to give him a hearing (21-22), and on the appointed day Paul confronts them on the basis of their Scriptures with the hope of Israel fulfilled: *the kingdom of God,* God's reign, as actualized and established by *Jesus* (23). And once more Paul learns by experience that "not all who are descended from Israel belong to Israel" (Ro 9:6); *some were convinced . . . while others disbelieved* (24). When Jesus began His ministry in Nazareth, He invited His fellow townsmen to inherit the hope of Israel with words of glad promise from Isaiah (Lk 4:18-19; Is 61:1-2). Even then the response of His people was such that He hinted that the Good News would pass from them to the Gentiles (Lk 4:23-27). Now it is Paul's bitter duty to dismiss his departing fellow Jews with a word of Isaiah's of quite another kind: the people who *will* not hear the voice of their God fall under His fearful

28 Let it be known to you then that this salvation of God has been sent to the Gentiles; they will listen."*g*

THE WORD IS NOT BOUND (28:30-31)

30 And he lived there two whole years at his own expense,*h* and welcomed all who came to him, 31 preaching the kingdom of God and teaching about the Lord Jesus Christ quite openly and unhindered.

g Other ancient authorities add verse 29, *And when he had said these words, the Jews departed, holding much dispute among themselves* *h* Or *in his own hired dwelling*

judgment; they shall not hear it (25-27), and the salvation they have refused will go to the Gentiles. (28)

28:28 *To the Gentiles.* Cf. 13:46.

28:30-31 Paul remains a prisoner, but Jesus' own message of the *kingdom of God* (cf. 1:3) and Paul's witness to Him as *the Lord,* the royal reign of God in person, sound forth nevertheless *quite openly and unhindered,* and the end of that sounding forth is not yet.

THE LETTER OF PAUL TO THE

ROMANS

INTRODUCTION

1 It is historically natural and fitting that the Letter to the Romans has always been of special interest and import to Western Christendom. For with this letter Paul is looking westward. The hope of coming to Rome was one he had been cherishing "for many years" at the time of writing (15:23). He had met Aquila and Priscilla as early as the year 50. An edict of Emperor Claudius banishing all Jews from Rome had brought that couple, destined to be so dear and so valuable to him, to Corinth, where Paul was then beginning his work. They could tell him of the church (or, more accurately, churches) in that key city of the empire, its life, its problems, and its possibilities, especially its possibilities as a missionary center for the western part of the Roman Empire. It was this last point that was no doubt of greatest interest to Paul, whose missionary strategy had as its chief object the founding of churches in the key cities of the empire. That strategy had carried him from Antioch to Corinth and Ephesus.

The Occasion of the Letter

2 It was probably in late summer A.D. 55, when Paul was about to conclude his work at Ephesus and was about to return to Jerusalem with the offering gathered among the Gentiles for the poverty-stricken saints of Jerusalem, that he gave expression to his long-cherished hope of going to Rome: "After I have been there, I must also see Rome" (Acts 19:21). He spoke of that hope again when he wrote to the Corinthians from Macedonia a few weeks later: "Our hope is that as your faith increases, our field among you may be greatly enlarged, so that we may preach the gospel in lands beyond you" (2 Co 10:15-16). "Lands beyond you"—this expression coming from a man who had been working his way westward "from Jerusalem and as far round as Illyricum" in northwestern Greece (Ro 15:19) surely points to the West.

3 The letter itself enables us to fix the time of writing fairly closely. Paul is about to conclude his work in the East, so that he no longer has "any room for work in these regions" between Jerusalem and Illyricum (Ro 15:23; cf. 15:19). He is about to go to Jerusalem with the collection gathered in Macedonia and Achaia (Ro 15:25-27; cf. 2 Co 8 and 9). All this points to the close of the so-called third missionary journey and the winter A.D. 55–56.

4 The place of writing is fairly certain also. Paul spent three months in southern Greece at the close of his third missionary journey. He had promised the Corinthians that he would stay with them or "even spend the winter" with them (1 Co 16:6). Corinth would therefore seem to be the most likely place of writing. This is confirmed by three notices in the letter itself. In 16:23 Paul sends greetings from "Erastus, the city treasurer"; Erastus is associated with Corinth in 2 Ti 4:20, and an inscription found at Corinth mentions an Erastus as a city official there. In Ro 16:1 Paul commends to the brethren at Rome a woman named Phoebe, a deaconess of the church at Cenchreae, the eastern harbor town of Corinth (she is probably the bearer of the Letter to the Romans). In Ro 16:23 Paul mentions Gaius as his host and transmits his greetings to the Romans. One Gaius was a member of the church at Corinth (1 Co 1:14); but since Gaius was a very common Roman name, this is not a particularly weighty piece of evidence.

5 The above paragraph assumes that ch. 16 is an original and integral part of the letter. Many scholars doubt this and are inclined to see in this chapter a letter, undoubtedly by Paul (with the possible exception of vv. 25-27), addressed to the church at Ephesus, which somehow got attached to the Letter to the Romans when the letters of Paul were collected. The arguments for this hypothesis are chiefly the following: (1) The letter seems to come to a close at 15:33 with a benediction such as is common at the close of a Pauline letter. (2) The closing doxology (16:25-27) is placed at

various points in the ancient manuscripts; some place it after 14:23, some after 15:33, and some after 16:23. This is thought to indicate that ch. 16 was not a fixed part of the letter in the manuscript tradition. (3) Paul greets 26 people in this chapter; it seems unlikely that Paul had so many friends in Rome, whereas it would be very natural for him to have so many friends in Ephesus, the scene of more than two years' missionary activity. (4) It seems unlikely that Aquila and Priscilla would change their place of residence so often as this chapter, as a part of the Letter to the Romans, would indicate. They have moved from Rome to Corinth, from Corinth to Ephesus, and thence again to Rome (Acts 18:2, 19; Ro 16:3); and a few years later they are once more in Ephesus (2 Ti 4:19). (5) The stern warning of 16:17-20 is not prepared for by anything in the first 15 chapters; the tone of the warning seems to be more brusque and authoritative than Paul's usually tactful way of addressing a church he has not himself founded and does not know personally.

6 These arguments are not conclusive. (1) 15:33 *is* a closing benediction, but a lengthy postscript to the letter is not inherently improbable. (2) The varying position of the doxology points to varying liturgical usage in the churches; they probably did not all read the last chapter or chapters in their public worship. This says nothing about the original length of the letter, for even the manuscripts that place the doxology early contain all 16 chapters of the letter. (3) We have no way of telling how many friends Paul might have had at Rome. It seems unlikely, however, that he would single out some two dozen persons for personal greetings in writing to Ephesus, where he knew and was known by all members of the church; that would be tactless, and Paul was not a tactless man. In a letter to an unknown church it would be natural for him to single out those whom he knew personally for special greetings and thus draw nearer to the church as a whole. (4) The movements of Aquila and Priscilla really present no problem. Travel was relatively easy and safe within the Roman Empire, so that people with business interests could move freely in the pursuit of commercial advantages; and besides, Aquila and Priscilla would probably move with the Gospel. (5) We do not know the historical situation well enough to judge whether the stern

warning of 16:17-20 would be probable or improbable in a letter to the Romans. Chapters 12–15 bristle with strong imperatives; Paul tempers the brusqueness of his imperatives there with a tactful reference to the Romans' Christian maturity and capacity for mutual correction (15:14). He likewise tempers the brusqueness of Ro 16: 17-20 by acknowledging the Romans' exemplary obedience to the Gospel (16:19). To conclude: it is difficult to explain how a letter to Ephesus got so firmly attached to the Letter to the Romans, and there is not a single outright witness for the omission of the chapter in all the manuscripts that have come down to us. Any hypothesis that separates the last chapter from the rest of the letter must be supported by weightier arguments than those hitherto advanced.

The Purpose of the Letter

7 Paul wrote his Letter to the Romans from Corinth during the winter A.D. 55–56. His purpose in writing it is delicately but clearly stated in the letter itself. The letter is to prepare for his visit to Rome. But Rome is not his ultimate goal. It cannot be, for Paul has made it his ambition as apostle to the Gentiles "to preach the gospel, not where Christ has already been named," lest he "build on another man's foundation" (Ro 15:20). The apostle's task is to lay foundations, not to build on foundations already laid by others (1 Co 3:10). The foundation has long since been laid in Rome. Paul's language in the Letter to the Romans indicates that the church there had been in existence for some time; the faith of the Roman Christians is already being proclaimed "in all the world" (1:8); their obedience is known to all (16:19); Paul has longed for many years to come to them (15:23). Non-Christian sources indicate that there was a church in Rome at least as early as A.D. 49 and probably earlier. Neither Paul nor any other early source points to any single outstanding personality as founder of the Roman church; Christianity probably came to Rome through the agency of a number of nameless men such as the "visitors from Rome" who were present in Jerusalem at Pentecost (Acts 2:10) and later returned to Rome, bringing with them the Word of God "sent to Israel, preaching good news of peace by Jesus Christ." (Acts 10:36)

8 The "visitors from Rome" present at Pentecost were in all probability Jews, and the church at Rome was no doubt strongly

Jewish in its beginnings. At the time when Paul wrote to the Romans the church was no longer predominantly Jewish; indeed, Paul speaks of it and to it as a basically Gentile church (1:13-15; cf. 1:5-6; 11:13, 28-31). But there remained in it, no doubt, a strong Jewish-Christian element. The presence of this element helps explain why Paul in this letter expounds his Gospel by setting it in contrast to Judaism (the works of the Law, circumcision, descent from Abraham) and why he speaks at such length (chs. 9—11) of the relationship between the old Israel and the new Israel, the church.

9 Paul plans to spend some time in Rome to enrich and be enriched by his association with the Roman Christians and to proclaim the Gospel there (1:11-13; 15:24). But he is looking beyond Rome to Spain (15:24-28). Paul hopes to be "sped on his way" there by the Romans (15:24). The expression "to be sped on one's way" seems to have become almost technical for the support, both moral and material, given to missionaries by established churches or individual Christians (Acts 20:38; 21:5; 1 Co 16:6, 11; 2 Co 1:16; Tts 3:13; 3 Jn 6). Paul evidently hopes that Rome may become his missionary base in the West, what Syrian Antioch had been for him in the East.

10 This explains why the Letter to the Romans, a letter written merely to *prepare* for his visit to Rome, is so deep and massive a treatment of the Gospel, which Paul proclaims and now intends to proclaim in the West. Everything that we know of Paul's missionary preaching and missionary methods (for example, his practice of revisiting already established churches and his continued contact with them by letter or by means of personal emissaries) makes it clear that he did not aim at creating a vague, emotional, and enthusiastic movement but rather the firmly rooted, grounded, and established church of God in which the Word of Christ dwelt richly. What he looked for and strove for in a church that was to be his base in the West was a full and thoroughgoing common understanding of the Gospel. At his former base in the East this common understanding was something he could presuppose. Antioch had been deeply influenced by Barnabas, and Paul himself had preached and taught at Antioch for a full year before the Holy Spirit sent him forth on his wider mission to the Gentiles (Acts 11:26; 13:1-3). What a year's ministry had accomplished in the East, a brief visit and a single letter had to accomplish in the West. That letter had to be a full and rich one.

The Content of the Letter

11 The theme of the letter is announced in 1:16-17; it is the Gospel as the power of God for salvation. This theme is developed in four great movements of thought that unfold the creative power of the Gospel (1:18—15:13). This body of the letter is preceded and followed by sections that make clear Paul's relationship as apostle to that Gospel and the relationship of the Romans to the Gospel's westward movement. The following outline may serve as a guide:

OUTLINE

I. 1:1-15 Introduction

II. 1:16—15:13 The Gospel That Goes Westward
   A. The Gospel Creates a New Status for Man. 1:16—5:21
      1. The Old Status: Man Under the Revelation of the Wrath of God. 1:16—3:20
      2. The New Status: Man Under the Revelation of the Righteousness of God. 3:21—5:21
   B. The Gospel Creates a New Life in Man. 6:1—8:39
      1. Man Is Freed from Sin. Ch. 6
      2. Man Is Freed from the Law. Ch. 7
      3. Man Is Freed from Death. Ch. 8
   C. The Gospel Creates a New Israel out of Jew and Gentile. 9:1—11:36
      1. God's Freedom to Create His Israel as He Wills. 9:1-29

THE LETTER OF PAUL TO THE

ROMANS

INTRODUCTION: GREETINGS, THANKSGIVING, AND PRAYER (1:1-15)

1 Paul, a servant[a] of Jesus Christ, called to be an apostle, set apart for the gospel of God ² which he promised beforehand through his prophets in the holy scriptures, ³ the gospel concerning his Son, who was descended from David according to the flesh ⁴ and designated Son of God in power according to the Spirit of holiness by his resurrection from the dead, Jesus Christ our Lord, ⁵ through whom we have received grace and apostleship to bring about the obedience of faith for the sake of his name among all the nations, ⁶ including yourselves who are called to belong to Jesus Christ;

7 To all God's beloved in Rome, who are called to be saints:
Grace to you and peace from God our Father and the Lord Jesus Christ.

8 First, I thank my God through Jesus Christ for all of you, because your faith is proclaimed in all the world. ⁹ For God is my witness, whom I serve with my spirit in the gospel of his Son, that without ceasing I mention you always in my prayers, ¹⁰ asking that somehow by God's will I may now at last succeed in coming to you. ¹¹ For I long to see you, that I may impart to you some spiritual gift to strengthen you, ¹² that is, that we may be mutually encouraged by each other's faith, both yours and mine. ¹³ I want you to know, brethren, that I have often intended to come to you (but thus far have been prevented), in order that I may reap some harvest among you as well as among the rest of the Gentiles. ¹⁴ I am under obligation both to Greeks and to barbarians, both to the wise and to the foolish: ¹⁵ so I am eager to preach the gospel to you also who are in Rome.

[a] Or *slave*

1:1-7 GREETINGS: PAUL, THE BEARER OF THE GOSPEL

1:1-7 Paul's greeting follows a common ancient letter form: The sender (1) to the recipients (7a), greetings (7b). But it differs from the ancient form in two points; for one thing the first element (naming of the sender) is greatly expanded, a feature found only in ancient OFFICIAL letters; for another, the whole is given a distinctly Christian character and content. It is Paul's confession to the *grace* (cf. 5) which *called* and consecrated (*set apart,* 1) him to be an accredited and authorized messenger of Christ (*apostle,* 1), bearer of the Gospel which proclaims Him universally (*among all nations,* 5) as *Son of David* and *Son of God in power,* the risen *Lord* (3-4) to whom every knee must bow for His glory (*obedience of faith for the sake of his name,* 5). By virtue of this God-given authority he invokes on the Roman people of God (*called to be saints,* 7) the undeserved re-creating favor of God (*grace,* 7) and His *peace* (7), the well-being of divine health which God's fatherly grace revealed in the *Lord Jesus Christ* creates for men. (7)

1:1 *Servant* (or *slave*) expresses Paul's total subjection and devotion to his Lord and at the same time states a high claim; he stands in the succession of men of God of the OT who were permitted to speak His Word and execute His

purposes: Moses (Jos 1:2), Joshua (Jos 24:29), David (Ps 78:70), and the prophets (Am 3:7; Jer 7:25; Dn 9:6). Jesus Himself applied the title to His apostles. (Mt 10:24-25; Jn 13:16)

1:2 *Promised . . . prophets . . . holy scriptures.* God's Gospel is the culmination of His revelation, the fulfillment of His promises; therefore Paul cherishes, together with Jesus and all the men of the NT, the ancient OT writings as Holy Scriptures, God's own Word.

1:5 *Grace and apostleship.* Cf. 1 Co 15:10; Eph 3:8; 1 Ti 1:12-14.

Among all the nations. The universal Lordship of Christ makes Paul's apostleship universal. Hence his great interest in Rome, that crossroads of the nations, and in lands beyond Rome, like Spain. (Cf. 15:24, 28)

1:7 *God's beloved . . . called . . . saints.* The combination constitutes a good description of what the Bible means by saints; men whom God in His love has called to be His own and serve Him.

Lord is the most comprehensive confession of Jesus in His significance for faith. (Cf. 10:9-13; Ph 2:11)

1:8-15 THE APOSTLE'S THANKSGIVING AND PRAYER

1:8-15 Paul gives thanks for the *faith* (8) of the Roman church. Faith is so essential to the Christian life that he uses the term to designate the

The Gospel Creates a New Status for Man

1:16 – 5:21

THE OLD STATUS: MAN UNDER THE WRATH OF GOD (1:16 – 3:20)

16 For I am not ashamed of the gospel: it is the power of God for salvation to every one who has faith, to the Jew first and also to the Greek. 17 For in it the righteousness of God is revealed through faith for faith; as it is written, "He who through faith is righteous shall live."[b]

18 For the wrath of God is revealed from heaven against all ungodliness and wickedness of men who by their wickedness suppress the truth. 19 For what can be known about God is plain to them, because God has shown it to them. 20 Ever since the

[b] Or *The righteous shall live by faith*

whole existence and activity of the Roman Christians. The life of faith in Rome has been so active and effective that it has made worldwide news; and the apostle, dedicated to bringing about "the obedience of faith . . . among all nations" (5) must needs follow and foster the course of that life with his prayers. He prays to God that he may fulfill his long-cherished desire (cf. Acts 19:21) to visit Rome in order to *reap some harvest* (13) of men won for Christ among them and to *strengthen* (and be strengthened by, 12) them for the task of carrying the Gospel to the western regions beyond Rome. (Cf. 15:24)

1:13 *Harvest*. For the metaphor cf. Mt 9:37-38; 1 Co 3:6-9; 9:10-12.

1:14-15 *I am under obligation . . . I am eager.* Under the grace of God, duty and desire become one in the bearer of the Gospel.

1:16-17 THEME OF THE LETTER

1:16-17 Paul is eager to preach the Gospel to the men of Rome, his gateway to the West. With that he has reached the point where he must deal at length with that which impels him Romeward and westward. He now states the theme which is to occupy him for the rest of the letter: the Gospel as the *power of God for salvation,* the revelation of the *righteousness of God,* to all believers. He is *not ashamed* of the Gospel, though his missionary experience has taught him that the *Jew* finds the good news of a crucified Messiah offensive and the intellectual *Greek* finds it foolishness (1 Co 1:23) and knows that he will meet both Jew and Greek again in Rome; for he knows that the Gospel is not a product of Judaic dreams and not a plausible system of thought competing with plausible systems devised by the Greek. He knows that the Gospel is no less than the power of God which can effect the salvation of man, a radical deliverance out of man's desperate situation (cf. Ex 14:13; 15:2). The Gospel is power because in it a revelation takes place; by it God makes Himself known and makes Himself count among men. The Gospel is news of God's action through His Son (cf. 1:3-4), a saving action which gives men the gift of the righteousness of God. Gift it is, for it asks of the hearer only the receptive yes of faith, and it creates that faith in the

hearer; it is revealed for faith. And the Gospel has for it the witness of God's prophets, through whom God promised His Gospel beforehand (1:2). In the day when the whole hope of God's people seemed cut off, Habakkuk had uttered the great word which pronounced the unbreakable connection between faith, righteousness, and life: *He who through faith is righteous shall live.* (Hab 2:4)

1:16 *To the Jew first.* To the Jew the promises had been made, and so the good news of their fulfillment comes to him first. Paul was mindful of this as missionary; wherever he came, he preached first in the synagog (Acts 13:14-16, 46), and in his work among the Gentiles he never lost sight of his fellow Jews. (Ro 11:13-14)

1:18-32 THE WRATH OF GOD ON IDOLATRY

1:18-32 The Gospel is the power of God to deliver man out of a desperate situation. It is a desperate situation; for man is under the revelation, the making known and making felt, of the *wrath of God,* God's fearfully destructive reaction to man's *ungodliness and wickedness.* Men *suppress the truth,* the truth of truths, the encountered reality of God and His will for man (*decree,* 32). They know God but will *not honor him as God or give thanks to him* (21). In their folly (22) they seek independence of God but cannot free themselves from Him wholly, and so they exchange *the glory of the immortal God* for gods of their own devising, worshiping and serving *the creature rather than the Creator* (24-25). God is not mocked; He uses the very wickedness of man, that dubious liberty which they sought when they fled from the Creator by suppressing the truth, to punish their ungodliness. God gives men up, judicially, to the wickedness they wanted by giving them more of it than they wanted; He delivers them up to the degradation of their unleashed sensuality (24), to the debasement of sexual perversion (26-27), to the *base mind* which sets man against man and makes men hell to each other in the social order that was designed by God to be their protection and blessing. (28-32)

1:18 *From heaven.* It is as inescapable as the revelation of God's wrath at the end of days (2:5). All days since the coming of God's Son are "last

creation of the world his invisible nature, namely, his eternal power and deity, has been clearly perceived in the things that have been made. So they are without excuse; 21 for although they knew God they did not honor him as God or give thanks to him, but they became futile in their thinking and their senseless minds were darkened. 22 Claiming to be wise, they became fools, 23 and exchanged the glory of the immortal God for images resembling mortal man or birds or animals or reptiles.

24 Therefore God gave them up in the lusts of their hearts to impurity, to the dishonoring of their bodies among themselves, 25 because they exchanged the truth about God for a lie and worshiped and served the creature rather than the Creator, who is blessed for ever! Amen.

26 For this reason God gave them up to dishonorable passions. Their women exchanged natural relations for unnatural, 27 and the men likewise gave up natural relations with women and were consumed with passion for one another, men committing shameless acts with men and receiving in their own persons the due penalty for their error.

28 And since they did not see fit to acknowledge God, God gave them up to a base mind and to improper conduct. 29 They were filled with all manner of wickedness, evil, covetousness, malice. Full of envy, murder, strife, deceit, malignity, they are gossips, 30 slanderers, haters of God, insolent, haughty, boastful, inventors of evil, disobedient to parents, 31 foolish, faithless, heartless, ruthless. 32 Though they know God's decree that those who do such things deserve to die, they not only do them but approve those who practice them.

2 Therefore you have no excuse, O man, whoever you are, when you judge another; for in passing judgment upon him you condemn yourself, because you, the judge, are doing the very same things. 2 We know that the judgment of God rightly falls upon those who do such things. 3 Do you suppose, O man, that when you judge those who do such things and yet do them yourself, you will escape the judgment of God? 4 Or do you presume upon the riches of his kindness and forbearance and patience? Do you not know that God's kindness is meant to lead you to repentance? 5 But by your hard and impenitent heart you are storing up wrath for yourself on the day of wrath when God's righteous judgment will be revealed. 6 For he will render to every man according to his works: 7 to those who by patience in well-doing seek for glory and honor and immortality, he will give eternal life; 8 but for those who are factious and do not obey the truth, but obey wickedness, there will be wrath and fury. 9 There will be tribulation and distress for every human being who does evil, the Jew first and also the Greek, 10 but glory and honor and peace for every one who does good, the Jew first and also the Greek. 11 For God shows no partiality.

days" (Heb 1:2), and the revelation of wrath in these days is the upbeat of that last dreadful music of damnation.

1:29-31 All the vices listed here have this in common: they rend the fabric of society and make an agony of communal life.

2:1-11 THE WRATH OF GOD THE JUDGE UPON THE MAN WHO JUDGES HIS FELLOWMAN

2:1-11 Many of Paul's contemporaries, both Jews and Greeks, would concur with his condemnation of the idolatry and immorality of the pagan world and assent to his proclamation of the wrath of God on them. They would thereby exempt themselves from the judgment proclaimed and feel secure in their ethical superiority to the libertine, the pervert, and the antisocial criminal. Paul's aim is to stop every mouth and to make all the world, including the ethical world, accountable to God (3:19); otherwise he cannot bring men to the obedience of faith. As long as a man still has the strength and confidence to judge his fellow-

man, he is not ready to receive, in the beggary of faith, the radical rescue of the righteousness of God. Paul therefore proceeds to proclaim the judgment of God on these judges of mankind. In assenting to God's judgment on others they are (he tells them) passing judgment on themselves, for they are equally guilty of suppressing the truth when they commit, in refined form perhaps, the wickedness they condemn. No man dare think that he is the one exception to God's judgment; no man dare see in the forbearing kindness of God toward himself a license to continue in his sin; when God's *kindness is meant to lead* him, not to a sense of security but to *repentance* (3-4). The Judge whom the ethical men have been applauding is a righteous and impartial Judge, who will judge men not by the quality of their ethical judgments but by their deeds.

2:10 *The Jew first.* Cf. 1:16. If the Jew misused his priority in the grace of God, he has a priority in punishment, as his own prophets have warned him. (Am 3:2)

12 All who have sinned without the law will also perish without the law, and all who have sinned under the law will be judged by the law. 13 For it is not the hearers of the law who are righteous before God, but the doers of the law who will be justified. 14 When Gentiles who have not the law do by nature what the law requires, they are a law to themselves, even though they do not have the law. 15 They show that what the law requires is written on their hearts, while their conscience also bears witness and their conflicting thoughts accuse or perhaps excuse them 16 on that day when, according to my gospel, God judges the secrets of men by Christ Jesus.

17 But if you call yourself a Jew and rely upon the law and boast of your relation to God 18 and know his will and approve what is excellent, because you are instructed in the law, 19 and if you are sure that you are a guide to the blind, a light to those who are in darkness, 20 a corrector of the foolish, a teacher of children, having in the law the embodiment of knowledge and truth— 21 you then who teach others, will you not teach yourself? While you preach against stealing, do you steal? 22 You who say that one must not commit adultery, do you commit adultery? You who abhor idols, do you rob temples? 23 You who boast in the law, do you dishonor God by breaking the law? 24 For, as it is written, "The name of God is blasphemed among the Gentiles because of you."

25 Circumcision indeed is of value if you obey the law; but if you break the law, your circumcision becomes uncircumcision. 26 So, if a man who is uncircumcised

The proclamation of the impartial judgment of God on every man according to his works is really one great question addressed to man: "You knew Me; did you honor and thank Me by doing My will?" But God Himself has made a great distinction between the Jew and the rest of mankind. He made His covenant with Israel and gave His law to Israel alone. The one great question therefore breaks down into two questions. Concerning the Gentiles: Did the nations without the Law know God? Can God hold them accountable? Concerning the Jew: He knew God, no doubt; the only question concerning him is, Did he do God's will? Paul deals with these two questions in 2:12-24.

2:12-16 THE QUESTION CONCERNING THE GENTILE

2:12-16 All who sin will perish, each man being judged on the basis of the revelation God has given him. The deed is what counts, whether it is done by a Jew who possesses the Law or by a Gentile who has it not. The deed will decide in the judgment; the deed is the great leveler between Gentile and Jew. And yet the Jew is guided in his action by the written Law, the direct, express Word of God. But, Paul says, God has attested His will to the Gentile too; the finger of God has written on his heart what the Law requires. The deeds of the Gentiles testify to that. So does their conscience. The voice of conscience may be howled down by the voice of mad desire or reasoned out of court by the perverse logic of the base mind. But it is still there; the thoughts which Gentile men think upon their deeds are still *conflicting thoughts,* some for the prosecution, some for the defense. Each Gentile carries about in his heart a secret miniature of the Last Judgment as it were. It will no longer be secret when the Last Judgment comes. On that day God will judge the *secrets of men.* Judgment according to works is

clearly not a judgment on the bare, external deed; a man is judged by the deeds with which he has expressed the hidden motions of his heart.

2:16 *According to my gospel.* Over against the idea that the Gospel of free grace is an invitation to continue in sin (6:1; cf. 3:8; Ph 3:18-19) Paul solemnly asserts that "his" Gospel is the Gospel of God, the Gospel of that divine grace which can forgive and overcome sin but cannot compromise with sin. The Christ of "his" Gospel is the Judge of man as surely as He is his Savior (2 Co 5:10). Paul is servant and apostle of the Christ who spoke judgment on salt that loses its saltness (Mt 5:13) and kept His disciples mindful of the fact that a man's life moves on a path that takes him to his Judge. (Mt 5:25-26; 7:1; 16:27)

2:17-24 THE QUESTION CONCERNING THE JEW

2:17-24 The Jew knows God's will and proudly fancies himself the destined teacher and enlightener of mankind. Only he does not keep the Law, which is his pride; he brings disgrace on his God by flouting it.

To sum up: The Gentile is a law to himself; the Jew has and knows the Law. Both, when they sin, suppress the truth; both are without excuse.

2:21-22 Paul's indictment of the Jew is the same as Jesus': "They preach, but do not practice." (Mt 23:3)

2:22 *Abhor idols . . . rob temples.* The Jew expresses his contempt for idols by robbing their temples, but in that act he gives his heart to the idol Mammon.

2:23-24 What Isaiah (52:5) and Ezekiel (36:20) once said of the captive people of God must be said now of the Jew who boasts of the Law but does not obey it. Both provoke the blasphemous taunt: "Where is your God?"

2:25-29 CIRCUMCISION AND THE LAW

2:25-29 Not the mere possession of the Law

keeps the precepts of the law, will not his uncircumcision be regarded as circumcision? [27] Then those who are physically uncircumcised but keep the law will condemn you who have the written code and circumcision but break the law. [28] For he is not a real Jew who is one outwardly, nor is true circumcision something external and physical. [29] He is a Jew who is one inwardly, and real circumcision is a matter of the heart, spiritual and not literal. His praise is not from men but from God.

3 Then what advantage has the Jew? Or what is the value of circumcision? [2] Much in every way. To begin with, the Jews are entrusted with the oracles of God. [3] What if some were unfaithful? Does their faithlessness nullify the faithfulness of God? [4] By no means! Let God be true though every man be false, as it is written,

"That thou mayest be justified in thy words,
and prevail when thou art judged."

[5] But if our wickedness serves to show the justice of God, what shall we say? That God is unjust to inflict wrath on us? (I speak in a human way.) [6] By no means! For then how could God judge the world? [7] But if through my falsehood God's truthfulness abounds to his glory, why am I still being condemned as a sinner? [8] And why not do evil that good may come?—as some people slanderously charge us with saying. Their condemnation is just.

makes the Jew a Jew. Long before the giving of the Law, God made His covenant with father Abraham and his descendants and set on it the sign and seal of circumcision. In circumcision God incised on the flesh of the Jew His pledge "I will be your God" (cf. Gn 17). Could the Jew, then, thus marked and honored by God, be made to stand on a level with the Gentiles in the judgment? Would not the enduring covenantal sacrament shield him from the wrath of God? Paul replies: Circumcision is the sign both of God's gift and of His claim to the Jews; the covenant puts the Jew under both the promise and the command of God, and he is called on to speak his Amen to the promise by obeying the command (cf. Dt 10:16; Jer 4:4; 6:10). Circumcision is no magic spell, but God's personal dealing with responsible man. If a man breaks the Law, the covenant of God, circumcision cannot save him; it indicts him. The obedient Gentile, uncircumcised though he be, succeeds to the position of the disobedient Jew. More than that, since he has been obedient where the Jew has failed, he is in person the living condemnation of the Jew who with God's law before him and God's mark upon him yet breaks the Law. The true Jew is in fact not an ethnic quantity at all. A line must be drawn between the physical Jew and the Jew in heart whose *praise is . . . from God,* (29), on whom God's good pleasure rests.

2:29 *Praise.* Paul is alluding to the root meaning of the name Judah, from which "Jew" is derived. When Judah was born, his mother cried out, "I will praise the Lord" (Gn 29:35), and Jacob's blessing on his son Judah, the bearer of the Messianic promise, was, "Your brothers shall praise you." (Gn 49:8)

3:1-20 THE JEW'S OBJECTIONS AND PAUL'S REPLIES

3:1-20 Three times the objection to Paul's indictment is heard (1, 5, 9a); Paul's reply follows in each case, in vv. 2-4, 6-8, and 9b-20. This last section with its cluster of quotations from the OT and two summarizing sentences (19-20) rounds off not only the dialog with the Jew but the whole major section which begins at 1:18.

The first Judaic objection is: "If possession of the Law and circumcision does not avail in the Judgment, at the one point where it matters supremely, what advantage DOES the Jew have?" The Jew is asking the question in order to evade the call to repentance that is contained in the proclamation of the wrath and the impartial judgment of God. Paul, seeking by all means to save some (1 Co 9:22), honors the question and deals seriously with it. He concentrates in his reply on the one great advantage of the Jew: he has been *entrusted with the oracles of God* (2). To him God gave Law and Promise; to him he spoke by His servants the prophets and in the last days by His Son (cf. Mt 21:37; Heb 1:1). With these utterances the Jew was entrusted; what God spoke to the children of Abraham was intended for a blessing on all the families of the earth (Gn 12:3; 18:18; 22:17-18; 26:4). Paul's reply meets the uttered objection and anticipates another related objection ("If the blessing is contingent upon our obedience to these oracles, where is our advantage?"). He remembers the faithful remnant in Israel who remained faithful (11:5). The failure of others does not call into question the validity and power of the Word given to Israel. God is still faithful to His given Word. To deny that this Word, present and still speaking, is an advantage is to utter blasphemy, a denial of the bedrock affirmation of OT and NT, the affirmation that God is true, that His Word holds whatever else may break. Where God's will and man's collide, it is axiomatic for faith that the will of man is false. This faith speaks in the words of the psalmist (4) who will not attempt to conceal or excuse his sin but confesses it freely (Paul's brief quotation is intended to recall the context of Ps 51:3-4) in order that God may be seen to be the righteous God that He is and all men may be still

9 What then? Are we Jews any better off?[c] No, not at all; for I[d] have already charged that all men, both Jews and Greeks, are under the power of sin, 10 as it is written:

    "None is righteous, no, not one;

11   no one understands, no one seeks for God.

12   All have turned aside, together they have gone wrong;

    no one does good, not even one."

13   "Their throat is an open grave,

    they use their tongues to deceive."

    "The venom of asps is under their lips."

14   "Their mouth is full of curses and bitterness."

15   "Their feet are swift to shed blood,

16   in their paths are ruin and misery,

17   and the way of peace they do not know."

18   "There is no fear of God before their eyes."

19 Now we know that whatever the law says it speaks to those who are under the law, so that every mouth may be stopped, and the whole world may be held accountable to God. 20 For no human being will be justified in his sight by works of the law, since through the law comes knowledge of sin.

THE NEW STATUS: MAN UNDER THE RIGHTEOUSNESS OF GOD (3:21 — 5:21)

21 But now the righteousness of God has been manifested apart from law, although the law and the prophets bear witness to it, 22 the righteousness of God through faith in Jesus Christ for all who believe. For there is no distinction; 23 since all have sinned and fall short of the glory of God, 24 they are justified by his grace as a gift, through the redemption which is in Christ Jesus, 25 whom God put forward as an expiation by his blood, to be received by faith. This was to show God's righteousness, because in his divine forbearance he had passed over former sins; 26 it was to prove at the present time that he himself is righteous and that he justifies him who has faith in Jesus.

[c] Or *at any disadvantage?*   [d] Greek *we*

and know that He is God of all men. (Cf. Ps 46:10)

The second objection (5) attaches itself to Paul's previous reply: "If God always *prevails when* He is *judged,* does not the history of our nation, blackened as it is by our unfaithfulness, show forth God's justice, His fidelity to the covenant which we broke—can He still in justice *inflict wrath* on us for what in the last analysis glorifies Him?" Paul replies (6-8) that the Jew's objection proves too much: since God's sovereign control of history overrules the sin of all men, to His glory, every sinner could make this plea and God would have to abdicate as (what both Jew and Christian confess Him to be) Judge of the world. Even Paul, whom the Jew hated and despised as a renegade to the faith of his fathers, whose Gospel seemed to them an open invitation to sin for the greater glory of God, even he would no longer be condemned. Paul pauses to pronounce judgment on those who caricature his Gospel as they do: *Their condemnation is just.* (8)

The third objection is no longer a reasoned one, but irony: "Are we Jews actually worse off?" (This rendering or the one given in RSV note *c* is to be preferred to the one given in the text, as fitting better in this context). Paul's answer (9b-20) is what he has been maintaining all along: All men stand equally guilty before the tribunal of God. But Paul repeats with a difference. (a) Here sin appears as a *power* ruling over men (cf. 5:12, 21;

6:6, 7, 12, 14, etc.). (b) Paul enforces his indictment of man with the witness of the OT, its verdict on man. This is the Jew's Bible speaking to his people; this the Jew cannot evade. His Psalter (Ps 14:1-3; 5:9; 140:3; 10:7; 36:1) and his prophets (Is 59:7-8) combine to *stop* his *mouth* (19). The last sentence of Paul's reply (20) introduces two new thoughts that he will treat more fully later: man's inability to find acceptance before God by way of *works of the law* (man's own effort to win the acquitting verdict of God) and the Law's uncanny effect on man under the domination of sin, that of *the knowledge of sin* (20); through man's confrontation with the Law, sin becomes a powerful reality in man's life. (Cf. ch. 7)

Thus every mouth pleading in man's defense is stopped. The old status of man under sin and wrath is, for man, irrevocable and fixed. If he is to have a new status, he can obtain it only if God, his Judge, creates it, and he can receive it only as His gift, by faith.

3:21-31 *But now* God has spoken, and all mankind must fall silent. His Word is acquittal, full and free (*as a gift,* 24). This is judicial action, but it is *apart from law* (21), indeed it violates all legal justice. Legal justice can recognize the fact that a man is righteous: only God's righteousness can make a man righteous. God makes man a gift of His acquittal and gives him, effectually, the status of righteousness, lets him stand and

27 Then what becomes of our boasting? It is excluded. On what principle? On the principle of works? No, but on the principle of faith. 28 For we hold that a man is justified by faith apart from works of law. 29 Or is God the God of Jews only? Is he not the God of Gentiles also? Yes, of Gentiles also, 30 since God is one; and he will justify the circumcised on the ground of their faith and the uncircumcised through their faith. 31 Do we then overthrow the law by this faith? By no means! On the contrary, we uphold the law.

4 What then shall we say about*e* Abraham, our forefather according to the flesh? 2 For if Abraham was justified by works, he has something to boast about, but not before God. 3 For what does the scripture say? "Abraham believed God, and it was reckoned to him as righteousness." 4 Now to one who works, his wages are not reckoned as a gift but as his due. 5And to one who does not work but trusts him who justifies the ungodly, his faith is reckoned as righteousness. 6 So also David pronounces a blessing upon the man to whom God reckons righteousness apart from works:

7   "Blessed are those whose iniquities are forgiven, and whose sins are covered;
8   blessed is the man against whom the Lord will not reckon his sin."

9 Is this blessing pronounced only upon the circumcised, or also upon the uncir-

e Other ancient authorities read *was gained by*

count as righteous in His sight. He bestows righteousness on man (cf. Ph 3:9). That is pure grace, gratuitous favor, against all man's deserving. This acquitting and restoring grace is lavish, generous, without reserve. But it is neither sentimental nor arbitrary. It does not simply ignore sin. God deals with sin; in His grace He remains the God of justice. His freely given acquittal has a solid basis in the *redemption* which He Himself has provided *in Christ Jesus*. God's grace was a holy, costly grace. He ransomed men from their ruined past "with the precious blood of Christ" (1 Ptr 1:19). He did not spare His son but "gave him up for us all" (8:32). He restored man to communion with Himself by providing the perfect and availing sacrifice (*expiation*, 25) in His Son. In going the way of grace to the utmost by way of redemption and sacrifice God has asserted His righteousness to the utmost. In passing over sins in the past, He did so with this hour and this act of love and justice in view. When He now justifies the man *who has faith in Jesus* (26), there is no "as if" in that acquitting verdict; it is a serious, executed verdict. All merit of man disappears; all *boasting* of man is silenced. There is now room only for the faith which receives everything from God and gives all glory to God: the believing Greek sheds his sorry wisdom, leaves his idols (1:22-23), and bows down before his God. The believing Jew strips off the filthy rags of his own righteousness (Is 64:6), drops his high pretensions, and finds the God of Abraham who justifies the ungodly (4:5), a God greater than the God he knew when he worshiped Him as the God of the Law; for if the Law given to the Jew is God's first and last word, God is *God of the Jews only* (29), not the God of all. But He is manifested now in His acquitting Word to all who have faith as the Lord of all, Jew and Gentile alike. The First Commandment, and every other commandment that reveals His will, is made to stand and count in this new revelation made to faith. Men who believe do what the Law requires,

what men suppressing the truth have failed to do: they glorify God. (1:21; 4:20)

4:1-25 JUSTIFICATION THROUGH FAITH: THE DECISIVE CASE OF ABRAHAM

4:1-25 *What then shall we say about Abraham?* (1) Paul dare not ignore Abraham if he would win the Jew, for Judaic legend had made of Abraham a "works" hero, one who had kept the Law (revealed to him by special dispensation four centuries before Sinai) perfectly—for the Jew, Abraham was clearly justified by works. Moreover, Paul's loyalty to the OT Scripture (1:2, 17; 3:21) made it imperative that he speak of Abraham; for according to Scripture, God's dealing with Abraham represents the first and basic step in the creation of the people of God; if Paul represents God as acting now, in Christ, in a way that contradicts that first and primal act, he is flouting the authority of God's Word. And the question then is not merely one of formal authority; it is theological. If the Gospel of Paul is God's Gospel, it must remain in harmony with God's earlier revelation of Himself. The case of Abraham will decide whether Paul is proclaiming the mighty acts of the Creator and Redeemer revealed in the OT (as Paul himself avers), or is indeed, as the Athenians once suspected (Acts 17:18), introducing an alien God.

Paul therefore uses the OT itself to demonstrate that Abraham was justified through faith, *apart from works* (1-8); through faith, without circumcision (9-12), through faith, without the Law. (13-15)

WITHOUT WORKS (1-8): In the one place where Genesis speaks of Abraham's righteousness (15:6), it speaks not of Abraham's doing but of his believing. Here God was acting, and Abraham remained passive; God reckoned his faith to him as righteousness. God opened up the future for him and all mankind by forgiving him with that free and total forgiveness of which David sang (Ps

cumcised? We say that faith was reckoned to Abraham as righteousness. [10] How then was it reckoned to him? Was it before or after he had been circumcised? It was not after, but before he was circumcised. [11] He received circumcision as a sign or seal of the righteousness which he had by faith while he was still uncircumcised. The purpose was to make him the father of all who believe without being circumcised and who thus have righteousness reckoned to them, [12] and likewise the father of the circumcised who are not merely circumcised but also follow the example of the faith which our father Abraham had before he was circumcised.

13 The promise to Abraham and his descendants, that they should inherit the world, did not come through the law but through the righteousness of faith. [14] If it is the adherents of the law who are to be the heirs, faith is null and the promise is void. [15] For the law brings wrath, but where there is no law there is no transgression.

16 That is why it depends on faith, in order that the promise may rest on grace and be guaranteed to all his descendants—not only to the adherents of the law but also to those who share the faith of Abraham, for he is the father of us all, [17] as it is written, "I have made you the father of many nations"—in the presence of the God in whom he believed, who gives life to the dead and calls into existence the things that do not exist. [18] In hope he believed against hope, that he should become the father of many nations; as he had been told, "So shall your descendants be." [19] He did not weaken in faith when he considered his own body, which was as good as dead because he was about a hundred years old, or when he considered the barrenness of Sarah's womb. [20] No distrust made him waver concerning the promise of God, but he grew strong in his faith as he gave glory to God, [21] fully convinced that God was able to do what he had promised. [22] That is why his faith was "reckoned to him as righteousness." [23] But the words, "it was reckoned to him," were written not for his sake alone, [24] but for ours also. It will be reckoned to us who believe in him that raised from the dead Jesus our Lord, [25] who was put to death for our trespasses and raised for our justification.

5 Therefore, since we are justified by faith, we[f] have peace with God through our Lord Jesus Christ. [2] Through him we have obtained access[g] to this grace in which we stand, and we[h] rejoice in our hope of sharing the glory of God. [3] More than that,

[f] Other ancient authorities read *let us*   [g] Other ancient authorities add *by faith*   [h] Or *let us*

Abraham's faith depended wholly on the promise (20), for he saw the possibility of life and blessing in God alone, in God who gives life to the 32:1-2) and so of His free grace made him a blessing.

WITHOUT CIRCUMCISION (9-12): The Judaic teachers contended that the blessing pronounced by Ps 32 applied only to the circumcised, specifically to the Israelites on the Day of Atonement (Lv 16). Paul shows from the OT record that Abraham came under the blessing of Ps 32 before he received circumcision, the sign and seal of his justification. The reckoned righteousness received by faith (Gn 15) and the gift of circumcision are two chapters and (according to the rabbis) 29 years apart. Thus in the case of Abraham faith counted supremely, and all men of faith, not only the circumcised, can claim Abraham as father.

WITHOUT THE LAW (13-15): Where God promises, God is at work, not demanding but giving. Where the law of God demands works of man, there is wrath of God over against the failure of man, and there can be no justification. But where the promise is, God's creative giving deals and does away with man's transgression and unites man with his God. If God's word to Abraham is promise, it must be pure promise, unmixed with and unadulterated by the demands of the Law.

dead and calls into existence the things that do not exist (17); he saw in himself only death (18-19), and so he gave glory to God alone, the sole Author and Giver of life as He is the sole Author of righteousness.

Abraham's faith is the prototype and exemplar of the Christian's faith (23-25). The Christian sees in Christ's death the hopelessness and inevitable dying of man, sees in His resurrection the divinely given sole possibility of life for man, because it is God's righteousness for man. And the Christian lives by his hold on the redeeming Word of God, the Gospel, which proclaims and gives him Christ as his righteousness and life.

4:2 *Something to boast about.* Thus Abraham would be a refutation of what Paul said in 3:27.

4:5 *Justifies the ungodly.* Perhaps the most pointed formulation of justification in the NT. Forgiveness as pure gift (cf. 3:24) to man under the wrath of God. (Cf. 1:18)

4:13 *Promise . . . that they should inherit the world.* Paul uses the language with which Judaic teachers used to paraphrase God's promises to Abraham.

5:1-11 THE NEW STATUS: PEACE WITHOUT END

5:1-11 Our new status before God is no neutral state. Being justified does not mean merely that

we[h] rejoice in our sufferings, knowing that suffering produces endurance, 4 and endurance produces character, and character produces hope, 5 and hope does not disappoint us, because God's love has been poured into our hearts through the Holy Spirit which has been given to us.

6 While we were still weak, at the right time Christ died for the ungodly. 7 Why, one will hardly die for a righteous man—though perhaps for a good man one will dare even to die. 8 But God shows his love for us in that while we were yet sinners Christ died for us. 9 Since, therefore, we are now justified by his blood, much more shall we be saved by him from the wrath of God. 10 For if while we were enemies we were reconciled to God by the death of his Son, much more, now that we are reconciled, shall we be saved by his life. 11 Not only so, but we also rejoice in God through our Lord Jesus Christ, through whom we have now received our reconciliation.

12 Therefore as sin came into the world through one man and death through sin, and so death spread to all men because all men sinned—13 sin indeed was in the world before the law was given, but sin is not counted where there is no law. 14 Yet death reigned from Adam to Moses, even over those whose sins were not like the transgression of Adam, who was a type of the one who was to come.

15 But the free gift is not like the trespass. For if many died through one man's trespass, much more have the grace of God and the free gift in the grace of that one man Jesus Christ abounded for many. 16And the free gift is not like the effect of that one man's sin. For the judgment following one trespass brought condemnation, but the free gift following many trespasses brings justification. 17 If, because of one man's trespass, death reigned through that one man, much more will those who receive the abundance of grace and the free gift of righteousness reign in life through the one man Jesus Christ.

18 Then as one man's trespass led to condemnation for all men, so one man's act of righteousness leads to acquittal and life for all men. 19 For as by one man's disobedience many were made sinners, so by one man's obedience many will be made righteous. 20 Law came in, to increase the trespass; but where sin increased, grace abounded all the more, 21 so that, as sin reigned in death, grace also might reign through righteousness to eternal life through Jesus Christ our Lord.

[h] Or let us

we have "gotten off" unpunished. It means *peace* in the full sense given to that word by the OT, that divinely normal state in which we have access to God and His grace, grace as the power that enables us to stand and play our part according to the will of God. Peace fills the present, and it opens up a future that is cause for exultation: *sharing* in the very *glory of God.* That bright prospect makes present *suffering,* too, a cause for rejoicing, for faith can recognize in suffering that same unparalleled love of God that has justified us contrary to all our deserving; and suffering, by tempering us and strengthening us, gives us that sure *hope* which only the Spirit-given knowledge of the love of God can inspire: the reconciling love that sought and found us when we were *still weak* (6), incapable of response; *ungodly* (6) and *sinners* (8), *enemies* (10) of the Christ who died for us—that love assures us that the *wrath of God* (9) which looms up at the end of all men's ways to destroy them does not loom up at the end of our new way; the living Christ, once dead for our salvation, looms up, and He will save us from the wrath to come. *We . . . rejoice in God.* (11)

5:12-21 THE OLD AND THE NEW:
ADAM AND CHRIST

5:12-21 From his vantage point of exultant certainty Paul looks back and surveys the ground he has traveled. All that he has said of sin and grace, of Law and Gospel, of man's old status under the judgment of God and his new status under the acquittal of God, he sums up once more in the monumental comparison-and-contrast between Adam and Christ. After stating the first half of the comparison-contrast (12), he inserts two parenthetical thoughts; one (13-14) is designed to support his statement that *all men sinned* in the death-dealing primal sin of Adam, head of the human race, that the sway of death over mankind is due to mankind's solidarity in sin with Adam—what else could explain the unbroken universal sway of death during the period without Law between Adam and Moses?

The other parenthesis (15-17) safeguards the unique glory of Christ against the misunderstanding that Christ and Adam are equal forces in the life of mankind. Three times Paul asserts the positive, vital, creative plus on the side of Christ. Then (19-20) two pithy statements enunciate the comparison-contrast between Adam's trespass and disobedience and Christ's act of righteousness and obedience, both universally effective in their result for all mankind. A brief (20-21) conclusion points up the subordinate and negative role of the Law in the desperate situation

The Gospel Creates a New Life in Man

6:1 — 8:39

MAN IS FREED FROM SIN (6:1-23)

6 What shall we say then? Are we to continue in sin that grace may abound? 2 By no means! How can we who died to sin still live in it? 3 Do you not know that all of us who have been baptized into Christ Jesus were baptized into his death? 4 We were buried therefore with him by baptism into death, so that as Christ was raised from the dead by the glory of the Father, we too might walk in newness of life.

5 For if we have been united with him in a death like his, we shall certainly be united with him in a resurrection like his. 6 We know that our old self was crucified with him so that the sinful body might be destroyed, and we might no longer be enslaved to sin. 7 For he who has died is freed from sin. 8 But if we have died with Christ, we believe that we shall also live with him. 9 For we know that Christ being raised from the dead will never die again; death no longer has dominion over him. 10 The death he died he died to sin, once for all, but the life he lives he lives to God. 11 So you also must consider yourselves dead to sin and alive to God in Christ Jesus.

12 Let not sin therefore reign in your mortal bodies, to make you obey their passions. 13 Do not yield your members to sin as instruments of wickedness, but yield yourselves to God as men who have been brought from death to life, and your members to God as instruments of righteousness. 14 For sin will have no dominion over you, since you are not under law but under grace.

created by the sin of Adam and resolved triumphantly by the grace of God. Grace has established a reign whose gift to man is righteousness. That reign means life, unbroken, full, eternal life. That grace, reign, righteousness, life — all are through Jesus Christ, our Lord.

5:12 *Therefore.* Since Christ is the key Figure in the history of God's dealing with man (cf. the frequent use of "through" Christ or "by" Christ in the preceding, 1:5; 1:8; 2:16; 5:1-2), He may be compared to another key figure in that history, Adam.

5:14 *Type.* In Adam was prefigured in black the bright figure of Him who would, like Adam, by His action determine the history of all mankind and be the Beginning, Head, and Representative of a new mankind.

6:1 — 8:39 The creative force of the Gospel as God's power for man's salvation is not exhausted in creating a new status for man; it creates a new life in man, and it is to this aspect of salvation that Paul devotes the next three chapters. His Gospel proclaims the same act which gives man his new status through faith, namely, the death and resurrection of God's Son, as giving man a new life lived in the obedience of faith: for that act of God frees man for obedience. It liberates him from the power of sin (ch. 6, esp., 6:3-4, 11), from the Law (ch. 7, esp. 7:4-6), and from death. (Ch. 8, esp. 8:3-4, 10-11)

6:1-14 FREED FROM SIN BY SHARING IN
       CHRIST'S DEATH AND RESURRECTION
       THROUGH BAPTISM

6:1-14 If increasing sin means abounding grace (5:20), a satanic kind of logic might conclude that man might well *continue in sin* (1). But such logic is impossible for the man of faith. For faith knows that man cannot fly in the face of an action of God's. By an action of God's, by the death and resurrection of His Son, made ours in our baptism, continuing in sin has become not only reprehensible but impossible, as impossible as reversing the irreversible act of Christ's death and resurrection. That death and resurrection embraced us all and ushers us into a wholly new kind of life, the resurrection-life of Christ, in which there is no room for sinning. Paul's proclamation in vv. 5-10 is but an underscoring of this double statement: (a) the reality of our union with Christ through Baptism; (b) the wholly new quality of our resurrection-life.

Three times he asserts the reality of our union with the dying and resurrected Christ (5, 6, 8). A real death has taken place, a death-and-burial death, as Jesus' was (4); a criminal's death (*crucified,* 6) which destroyed our old, active criminal self (*sinful body,* 6) and set us free for righteousness; a death that opens up a future in which we may live as Christ now lives, His back forever turned to sin, *to God* (10). Our present life gets its character, direction, and purpose from the fact that we shall live with Him who now lives a life beyond death; a life lived wholly to God, now that He has died an atoning death, once for all, to sin. Now, and not until now, Paul utters his first imperatives (11-13). Now that his word has revealed the way trodden by Christ before us and for us, he can bid us enter on that way. And he gives us courage and strength to enter by pronouncing the promise: *Sin will have no dominion over you . . . you are . . . under grace* (14). We enter, not under the compulsion of Law but under the power of enabling grace.

15 What then? Are we to sin because we are not under law but under grace? By no means! 16 Do you not know that if you yield yourselves to any one as obedient slaves, you are slaves of the one whom you obey, either of sin, which leads to death, or of obedience, which leads to righteousness? 17 But thanks be to God, that you who were once slaves of sin have become obedient from the heart to the standard of teaching to which you were committed, 18 and, having been set free from sin, have become slaves of righteousness. 19 I am speaking in human terms, because of your natural limitations. For just as you once yielded your members to impurity and to greater and greater iniquity, so now yield your members to righteousness for sanctification.

20 When you were slaves of sin, you were free in regard to righteousness. 21 But then what return did you get from the things of which you are now ashamed? The end of those things is death. 22 But now that you have been set free from sin and have become slaves of God, the return you get is sanctification and its end, eternal life. 23 For the wages of sin is death, but the free gift of God is eternal life in Christ Jesus our Lord.

MAN IS FREED FROM THE LAW (7:1-25)

7 Do you not know, brethren—for I am speaking to those who know the law—that the law is binding on a person only during his life? 2 Thus a married woman is bound by law to her husband as long as he lives; but if her husband dies she is discharged from the law concerning the husband. 3Accordingly, she will be called an adulteress if she lives with another man while her husband is alive. But if her husband dies she is free from that law, and if she marries another man she is not an adulteress.

4 Likewise, my brethren, you have died to the law through the body of Christ, so that you may belong to another, to him who has been raised from the dead in order that we may bear fruit for God. 5 While we were living in the flesh, our sinful passions, aroused by the law, were at work in our members to bear fruit for death. 6 But now we are discharged from the law, dead to that which held us captive, so that we serve not under the old written code but in the new life of the Spirit.

7 What then shall we say? That the law is sin? By no means! Yet, if it had not been for the law, I should not have known sin. I should not have known what it is to covet

6:15-23 FREED FROM SIN AND ENSLAVED TO RIGHTEOUSNESS THROUGH THE WORD

6:15-23 Being *under grace* does not revive the old wild dream of "continuing in sin." Rather, it forces us to face facts and gives us the power to face them and joy in facing them. One set of facts is grim: the fact that we cannot "take or leave sin"—sin takes us, enslaves us (16), and rewards us with the due reward *(wages) of death* (23). Being *free in regard to righteousness* (20) is the most dubious of dubious liberties. The other set of facts is glorious: God Himself has freed us from that dubious liberty by Himself committing us to His Word *(standard of teaching,* 17) and making us obedient to it. He has made us slaves to Him "whom to serve is perfect liberty." He has caught us up into His work of making God's men of us *(sanctification,* 19-22) and holds out to us His *free gift of . . . eternal life in Christ Jesus our Lord* (23). God's facts are infinitely better than our tawdry dreams.

7:1-25 Paul has drawn a sharp division between the Gospel and the Law (3:28; cf. 3:20). The working and effect of the Law is the opposite of that of the Gospel, negative and destructive. It indicts the Jew (2:17-24) and renders all men accountable to God (3:19). It makes sin a known and experienced reality in man's life (3:20) and therefore

"brings wrath" (4:15); it increases the trespass initiated by Adam (5:20). Men can live to God only when grace replaces Law as the impelling power in their lives (6:14). Why does the Law, the Word of God, have this uncanny effect on man, and why must man be liberated from it if he is to be God's saint? Paul answers this question in 7:7-25. Before that he answers another, related question: How is it possible that man be liberated from the Law, that holy, just, and good (7:12) Word of God?

7:1-6 HOW CAN MAN BE FREED FROM THE LAW?

7:1-6 Liberation from the Law is not an arbitrary act of man. It is a liberation on the Law's own terms, by death, which severs legal ties, as the analogy of marriage shows. By God's action we died to the Law *through the body of Christ* (4) and were set free by Him that we might *serve* Him in the *new life* bestowed by His *Spirit.*

7:6 *New life of the Spirit.* This, the first reference to the Spirit, points forward to the theme of ch. 8, "the law of the Spirit of life in Christ Jesus." (8:2)

7:7-25 WHY MUST MAN BE LIBERATED FROM THE LAW?

7:7-25 The Law is *holy* and its commandment is *holy and just and good* (12). But sin, that diabolic power, manifests itself in its true colors (13) by

if the law had not said, "You shall not covet." 8 But sin, finding opportunity in the commandment, wrought in me all kinds of covetousness. Apart from the law sin lies dead. 9 I was once alive apart from the law, but when the commandment came, sin revived and I died; 10 the very commandment which promised life proved to be death to me. 11 For sin, finding opportunity in the commandment, deceived me and by it killed me. 12 So the law is holy, and the commandment is holy and just and good.

13 Did that which is good, then, bring death to me? By no means! It was sin, working death in me through what is good, in order that sin might be shown to be sin, and through the commandment might become sinful beyond measure. 14 We know that the law is spiritual; but I am carnal, sold under sin. 15 I do not understand my own actions. For I do not do what I want, but I do the very thing I hate. 16 Now if I do what I do not want, I agree that the law is good. 17 So then it is no longer I that do it, but sin which dwells within me. 18 For I know that nothing good dwells within me, that is, in my flesh. I can will what is right, but I cannot do it. 19 For I do not do the good I want, but the evil I do not want is what I do. 20 Now if I do what I do not want, it is no longer I that do it, but sin which dwells within me.

21 So I find it to be a law that when I want to do right, evil lies close at hand. 22 For I delight in the law of God, in my inmost self, 23 but I see in my members another law at war with the law of my mind and making me captive to the law of sin which dwells in my members. 24 Wretched man that I am! Who will deliver me from this body of death? 25 Thanks be to God through Jesus Christ our Lord! So then, I of myself serve the law of God with my mind, but with my flesh I serve the law of sin.

MAN IS FREED FROM DEATH (8:1-39)

8 There is therefore now no condemnation for those who are in Christ Jesus. 2 For the law of the Spirit of life in Christ Jesus has set me free from the law of sin and death. 3 For God has done what the law, weakened by the flesh, could not do: sending his own Son in the likeness of sinful flesh and for sin,[i] he condemned sin in the flesh, 4 in order that the just requirement of the law might be fulfilled in us, who walk not according to the flesh but according to the Spirit. 5 For those who live according to the flesh set their minds on the things of the flesh, but those who live according to the Spirit set their minds on the things of the Spirit. 6 To set the mind on the flesh is death, but to set the mind on the Spirit is life and peace. 7 For the mind that is set on the flesh is hostile to God; it does not submit to God's law, indeed it cannot; 8 and those who are in the flesh cannot please God.

---

[i] Or *and as a sin offering*

---

using just that good Word of God to rouse in man the dormant will of opposition to God which destroys him. Paul illustrates this working of the Law (as misused by the power of sin) from both his early life (7-13) and from his experience with the Law as a Christian (14-25). It was contact with the Law, confronting him as the *commandment*, that first gave sin its deadly power in his life (9-11). Paul the Christian, when confronted by the Law, becomes a man rent by an agonizing inner struggle (14-24) from which only Christ can and does release him. (25)

7:7 *Covet* has a wider scope than the English word "covet" commonly indicates, namely, all the self-centered desiring of man which ignores or opposes the will of God.

7:8 *Lies dead.* Is dormant and therefore inactive.

7:11 *Sin . . . deceived me.* The tragic history of the Fall (Gn 3) was reenacted in Paul's life; sin is personified in the role of the Tempter.

7:14 *Sold under sin.* Not the old slavery of pre-conversion days, where total slave-devotion (6:20) made any other tie impossible; here the claim of

sin is offset and opposed by an anterior and superior claim. (15-17)

7:24 *Body of death.* The unceasing encroachment of sin (21-23) threatens ever and again to make the body a "sinful body" (6:6), the expressive instrument of the sinner's revolt against God, and thus to doom it to death.

8:1-8 THE ESTABLISHMENT OF THE LAW OF THE SPIRIT OF LIFE

8:1-8 Where sin reigns, there is death (6:16, 21, 23). Where Jesus Christ is Lord, sin is overcome and the Law no longer controls and condemns; there is a new "law," a new and compelling order of things which sets men free from the old dark orders of sin and death. Christ's order is the order of righteousness and life, presented and enforced by the Spirit of life. This new order of the Spirit of life was inaugurated by the sending of Christ. The Law could not break the old order, for it could not overcome the *flesh*, man's innate will of opposition to God. God did overcome it by sending His Son into the flesh, wholly identified

9 But you are not in the flesh, you are in the Spirit, if in fact the Spirit of God dwells in you. Any one who does not have the Spirit of Christ does not belong to him. [10] But if Christ is in you, although your bodies are dead because of sin, your spirits are alive because of righteousness. [11] If the Spirit of him who raised Jesus from the dead dwells in you, he who raised Christ Jesus from the dead will give life to your mortal bodies also through his Spirit which dwells in you.

12 So then, brethren, we are debtors, not to the flesh, to live according to the flesh—[13] for if you live according to the flesh you will die, but if by the Spirit you put to death the deeds of the body you will live. [14] For all who are led by the Spirit of God are sons of God. [15] For you did not receive the spirit of slavery to fall back into fear, but you have received the spirit of sonship. When we cry, "Abba! Father!" [16] it is the Spirit himself bearing witness with our spirit that we are children of God, [17] and if children, then heirs, heirs of God and fellow heirs with Christ, provided we suffer with him in order that we may also be glorified with him.

18 I consider that the sufferings of this present time are not worth comparing with the glory that is to be revealed to us. [19] For the creation waits with eager longing for the revealing of the sons of God; [20] for the creation was subjected to futility, not of its own will but by the will of him who subjected it in hope; [21] because the creation itself will be set free from its bondage to decay and obtain the glorious liberty of the children of God. [22] We know that the whole creation has been groaning in travail together until now; [23] and not only the creation, but we ourselves, who have the first fruits of the Spirit, groan inwardly as we wait for adoption as sons, the redemption of our bodies. [24] For in this hope we were saved. Now hope that is seen is not hope. For who hopes for what he sees? [25] But if we hope for what we do not see, we wait for it with patience.

with man, to endure a penal and sacrificial (*as a sin offering*, 3; RSV note *i*) death for man's sin. By His death the Spirit, God's own creative and renewing presence, was released for man and creates new possibilities of obedience in man; now the *just requirement of the law* (4) can be fulfilled—there can be a people of God living in love with God and one another where the Spirit is at work. Nothing less than this action of God and this Spirit of God will overcome man's fleshly, deathward bent and give him life and peace under God. The indwelling Spirit (ch. 8) triumphs over indwelling sin. (Ch. 7)

8:1 *Therefore . . . no condemnation . . . in Christ Jesus. Therefore* is the logic of faith, which reasons thus: Whatever I lack and need I find in Christ. If the Law condemns (ch. 7), it follows that there is acquittal *(no condemnation)* in Christ.

8:9-17 THE PRESENT LIFE OF THE CHRISTIAN UNDER THE NEW LAW

8:9-17 Life in the Spirit—and that is what the Christian life is, if it be Christian (9)—is life with a future. The grave is not its goal; the indwelling of the Spirit is the sure pledge that our *mortal bodies* (11) will be raised from death as Jesus' body was.

Life in the Spirit is life with a purpose.—We are bound (*debtors,* 12) to live the new life of freedom under the law of the Spirit of life, on pain of death; we are led by the Spirit to lead the Son's life of obedience to the Father whom we can address with the familiarity of a child's love (*Abba!* 15) by the prompting of the Spirit. As *heirs of God and fellow heirs with Christ* (17) we can go steadfastly down the road of Christ through suffering to glory.

8:15 *Abba.* In Jesus' mother tongue this word was the child's address to its father, the word Jesus Himself (who did not lose a child's dependence and trust in manhood) used to address His Father at the supreme crisis of His life (Mk 14:36; cf. Gl 4:6). The Spirit who brought to remembrance all that Jesus had told His disciples (Jn 14:26) implanted the word in the prayers of the church in its original form.

8:18-39 THE FUTURE OF THE CHRISTIAN UNDER THE NEW LAW

8:18-39 The glory that awaits the suffering fellow heirs of Christ is so great that present sufferings cannot outweigh it (18) nor can Paul describe it. He pictures it by describing the greatness of the longing it evokes. All *creation . . . subjected to futility* by the fall of man (20; cf. Gn 3) and destined to participate in the final *glorious liberty of the children of God* (21) longs for the day when it shall be set free from *its bondage to decay* (21). Men, who possess in the Spirit a foretaste and a pledge of that glory, *groan inwardly* (23) in the intensity of their longing for the day when their sonship shall be freely manifested and fully enjoyed, when their bodies shall be transformed into glorious bodies (Ph 3:21), fit instruments to serve Him whom they can call Abba even now. Even the *Spirit* (26), who prompts the Christian's prayers, joins in the universal longing and *intercedes* for saints in their stammering weakness when they pray, "Thy kingdom come!" That glory is as certain as it is great (28-30). For those who know the unparalleled love of God for them and love Him because He first loved them, for such men a golden chain of unbreakable certitude links

26 Likewise the Spirit helps us in our weakness; for we do not know how to pray as we ought, but the Spirit himself intercedes for us with sighs too deep for words. [27]And he who searches the hearts of men knows what is the mind of the Spirit, because[j] the Spirit intercedes for the saints according to the will of God.

28 We know that in everything God works for good[k] with those who love him,[l] who are called according to his purpose. [29] For those whom he foreknew he also predestined to be conformed to the image of his Son, in order that he might be the first-born among many brethren. [30]And those whom he predestined he also called; and those whom he called he also justified; and those whom he justified he also glorified.

31 What then shall we say to this? If God is for us, who is against us? [32] He who did not spare his own Son but gave him up for us all, will he not also give us all things with him? [33] Who shall bring any charge against God's elect? It is God who justifies; [34] who is to condemn? Is it Christ Jesus, who died, yes, who was raised from the dead, who is at the right hand of God, who indeed intercedes for us?[m] [35] Who shall separate us from the love of Christ? Shall tribulation, or distress, or persecution, or famine, or nakedness, or peril, or sword? [36]As it is written,

"For thy sake we are being killed all the day long;
we are regarded as sheep to be slaughtered."

[37] No, in all these things we are more than conquerors through him who loved us. [38] For I am sure that neither death, nor life, nor angels, nor principalities, nor things present, nor things to come, nor powers, [39] nor height, nor depth, nor anything else in all creation, will be able to separate us from the love of God in Christ Jesus our Lord.

The Gospel Creates a New Israel out of Jew and Gentile

9:1 — 11:36

GOD'S FREEDOM TO CREATE HIS ISRAEL AS HE WILLS (9:1-29)

9 I am speaking the truth in Christ, I am not lying; my conscience bears me witness in the Holy Spirit, [2] that I have great sorrow and unceasing anguish in my heart. [3] For I could wish that I myself were accursed and cut off from Christ for the

[j] Or *that*   [k] Other ancient authorities read *in everything he works for good*, or *everything works for good*
[l] Greek *God*   [m] Or *It is Christ Jesus . . . for us*

all actions of God together, from His first motion of eternal predestining love to the crowning act which will give to His firstborn glorified Son a host of glorified brethren.

Standing on this height, Paul leads all Christendom in a song of triumphant certitude (31-39): He who in the unsparing sanctity of His love gave up His Son for us all will give us no less than all. The Judge of mankind has spoken; no one can reverse His verdict. Christ sits enthroned beside His Father; who dares to raise a voice against His intercession for us? No sufferings, no powers seen or unseen, no aspect or dimension of all creation can henceforth *separate us from the love of God in Christ Jesus our Lord.* (39)

9:1 — 11:36 As surely as the Gospel creates a new status for man before God (chs. 1 — 5) and creates a new life in man that sets him free to serve God by the power of His Spirit (chs. 6 — 8), so surely it creates a new Israel, a new people of God in the last days. The new Israel has a continuity with the old; its members can call Abraham "father" (4:12) and walk in the footsteps of his faith (4:12). But

there is also a tragic and disturbing discontinuity; there are many Gentile sons of believing Abraham, but few from among the Jews who "follow the example of the faith" of Abraham (4:12). It is quite natural, then, that when Paul comes to speak of the new Israel, he should do so with constant reference to the old Israel, as he does in chapters 9 — 11, and should begin with the nature of Israel's election (what makes Israel the people of God, ch. 9) and with the reason for the rejection of old Israel (ch. 10), before turning to the prospect of the new, inclusive Israel (*all Israel*, 11:26), the church of God chosen from among both Jews and Gentiles. (Ch. 11)

9:1-5 PAUL MOURNS FOR ISRAEL

9:1-5 Paul writes no cool and thoughtful essay on "The Problem of the Jew"; he mourns, as all sons of Abraham must, for his *kinsmen by race* (3), as Jesus mourned (Mt 23:37-39; Lk 19:41-42), and he is ready (as once Moses was, Ex 32:32) to lose all for their gain (3), if that were possible. He cannot but mourn as he recalls the greatness

sake of my brethren, my kinsmen by race. 4 They are Israelites, and to them belong the sonship, the glory, the covenants, the giving of the law, the worship, and the promises; 5 to them belong the patriarchs, and of their race, according to the flesh, is the Christ. God who is over all be blessed for ever.[n] Amen.

6 But it is not as though the word of God had failed. For not all who are descended from Israel belong to Israel, 7 and not all are children of Abraham because they are his descendants; but "Through Isaac shall your descendants be named." 8 This means that it is not the children of the flesh who are the children of God, but the children of the promise are reckoned as descendants. 9 For this is what the promise said, "About this time I will return and Sarah shall have a son." 10And not only so, but also when Rebecca had conceived children by one man, our forefather Isaac, 11 though they were not yet born and had done nothing either good or bad, in order that God's purpose of election might continue, not because of works but because of his call, 12 she was told, "The elder will serve the younger." 13As it is written, "Jacob I loved, but Esau I hated."

14 What shall we say then? Is there injustice on God's part? By no means! 15 For he says to Moses, "I will have mercy on whom I have mercy, and I will have compassion on whom I have compassion." 16 So it depends not upon man's will or exertion, but upon God's mercy. 17 For the scripture says to Pharaoh, "I have raised you up for the very purpose of showing my power in you, so that my name may be proclaimed

[n] Or Christ, who is God over all, blessed for ever

of God's gifts to them (4-5), gifts squandered now by Israel's disobedience and unbelief.

9:4 Israelites, the sacred name which marks the Jews as elect and favored recipients of the revelation, the grace, and the promises of God. (Cf. Eph 2:12)

Sonship. Cf. Ex 4:22-23; Hos 11:1.

The glory. Cf. Ex 16:7, 10; 24:16; 40:34-35; 1 K 8:10-11.

The giving of the law spelled out for Israel the claim of the covenant.

The covenants, in which God said, "I will be your God," to Abraham (Gn 15:18), to the whole people (Ex 24), to David (2 Sm 23:5). Cf. also the promise of the "new and final covenant" with His people in Jer 31:31-34; Eze 34:25-31.

9:5 God who is over all. The reading given in RSV note n is to be preferred. (a) The statement of Christ's Godhead is needed to balance the statement according to the flesh. (b) It was Jesus' claim to Godhead that led to His people's rejection of Him (cf. Mk 2:7; Jn 5:18; 8:18; 10:33) and led them to execute Him for blasphemy (Mt 26:65-66). (c) The doxology to God, which comes in naturally at 1:25, does not seem to fit so well here.

9:6-13 THE WORD OF GOD HAS NOT FAILED

9:6-13 If Israel is cause for mourning, does that mean that the Word of God, which called Israel into being and shaped Israel's history, has failed? If the Word of God can fail, the church has no grounds for faith and hope; for the church lives and dies in the power of God's Word. Paul looks into the history that the Word of God has made and sees there the revelation of God's will which will solve the mystery of unbelieving Israel: Not all who are descended from Israel belong to Israel (6). If the physical descendants of Israel have

failed, that does not mean that God's Word has failed; God's Word has always made a distinction between the essential Israel and the physical descendants of Israel, as the cases of Isaac and Ishmael (7-9) and Jacob and Esau show (10-13). Paul is saying: "If you would know where Israel, God's people, is, look where God's promise is at work creating Israel." See there how the Word of God in sovereign freedom works: not the children of the flesh . . . are the children of God, but the children of the promise are reckoned as descendants (8); God creates His Israel as He wills.

9:14-29 GOD HAS NOT BEEN UNJUST

9:14-29 In emphasizing the fact that the unbelief of physical Israel does not call in question the power of God's Word to Israel, Paul has asserted the free sovereignty of God boldly, to the point of ambiguity. The question can arise: Is not this freedom mere arbitrariness, a tyrannic assertion of His will because it is His will? Is God, after all, unjust? Paul anticipates the question and answers it (a) by pointing to God's revelation of Himself in the OT (for that, and not some abstract notion of "justice," is the only standard to be applied to God's action) and showing there, in God's dealing with faithful Moses and rebellious Pharaoh (15 to 18), the unquestionably sovereign mercy and judgment of God; (b) by asserting the absolute authority over man which is God's as man's Creator—an authority which He has, moreover, used in the service of His mercy (19-24); (c) by citing the words of Hosea and Isaiah which prefigured and foretold the history of God's undeserved compassion on the Gentiles and His rejection of the mass of Israel. (25-29)

9:15 To Moses. The name is emphatic by its position in the Greek. Even Moses, whose inno-

in all the earth." ¹⁸ So then he has mercy upon whomever he wills, and he hardens the heart of whomever he wills.

19 You will say to me then, "Why does he still find fault? For who can resist his will?" ²⁰ But who are you, a man, to answer back to God? Will what is molded say to its molder, "Why have you made me thus?" ²¹ Has the potter no right over the clay, to make out of the same lump one vessel for beauty and another for menial use? ²² What if God, desiring to show his wrath and to make known his power, has endured with much patience the vessels of wrath made for destruction, ²³ in order to make known the riches of his glory for the vessels of mercy, which he has prepared beforehand for glory, ²⁴ even us whom he has called, not from the Jews only but also from the Gentiles?

25   As indeed he says in Ho·se′a,
        "Those who were not my people
        I will call 'my people,'
        and her who was not beloved
        I will call 'my beloved.' "

26   "And in the very place where it was said to them, 'You are not my people,'
        they will be called 'sons of the living God.' "

27 And I·sa′iah cries out concerning Israel: "Though the number of the sons of Israel be as the sand of the sea, only a remnant of them will be saved; ²⁸ for the Lord will execute his sentence upon the earth with rigor and dispatch." ²⁹And as I·sa′iah predicted,
        "If the Lord of hosts had not left us children,
        we would have fared like Sodom and been made like Go·mor′rah."

GOD'S JUSTICE IN REJECTING ANCIENT ISRAEL (9:30 — 10:21)

30 What shall we say, then? That Gentiles who did not pursue righteousness have attained it, that is, righteousness through faith; ³¹ but that Israel who pursued the righteousness which is based on law did not succeed in fulfilling that law. ³² Why?

cence amid Israel's apostasy the Lord Himself attested (Ex 32:33), could stand before God and live only on terms of His free mercy.

9:18. This is one side of the argument; that more can and must be said about man's responsibility (and consequent guilt) when confronted by God, is clear from what follows in 9:30 – 10:21. Paul's argument here is convincing only for those who share with him two convictions (which he can presuppose on the part of Christian readers – and on the part of the Jew, for that matter: (a) the conviction that the OT is the Word of God, an adequate disclosure of His being and will; (b) that God Himself, as disclosed in His Word, is the standard of righteousness. – Paul is illustrating the righteousness of God in His present actions by pointing to God's words and deeds of old and making plain that His actions are all of a piece.

9:19 For the same kind of question, based on similar reasoning, cf. 3:5-8 note.

9:20-21 For the image of the *potter* and the *clay* cf. Is 29:16; 45:9; 64:8; and esp. Jer 18:6.

9:22-24 When a man has bowed before the revelation of Scripture (14-18) and has submitted in obedience to his Creator (19-21), he is enabled to look into God's ways and see in them the logic of God's mercy. How can there be any talk of God's injustice, in the light of His great forbearance and His all-inclusive (*called . . . Jews . . . also . . . Gentiles,* 24) mercy?

9:25 *Hosea.* If the free majesty and boundless

reach of God's love is such that He can restore to Himself an Israel which had forfeited every right to be His *beloved people,* it is but a small step in the inclusion of the Gentiles in His people.

9:27-29 *Isaiah.* If the number of Jews included in the ultimate people of God seems pitifully small, still that is what Israel's prophets had foretold. (Is 1:9; cf. 10:22)

9:30 – 10:21 The tenor of Paul's proclamation thus far (9:1-29) has been: "Be still, and know that I am God" (Ps 46:10). God is free to call His people into being and to form it as He wills. If Israel has now become a vessel of His wrath, while Gentiles now praise Him for His mercy (cf. 15:9), no one can say that His Word has failed or that His ways have been arbitrary. But there is another equally important aspect to the fall of Israel: Israel's guilty unbelief. And so Paul must point to Israel's guilt and say: "If you will not believe, surely you shall not be established" (Is 7:9). The section 9:30-33 forms a transition from the first theme to the second. It looks backward, emphasizing God's sovereignty: He lays the stone in Zion (33), that is, establishes and reveals the way of salvation; man may stumble over it or be saved by it, but man can neither lay the stone nor question Him who lays it. The section also looks forward to ch. 10 in its emphasis on the necessity of faith (9:32-33) and the guilt of unbelief.

Paul speaks in ch. 10 as the compassionate intercessor for His people, not as their judge (1).

Because they did not pursue it through faith, but as if it were based on works. They have stumbled over the stumbling stone, 33 as it is written,

"Behold, I am laying in Zion a stone that will make men stumble,
a rock that will make them fall;
and he who believes in him will not be put to shame."

10 Brethren, my heart's desire and prayer to God for them is that they may be saved. 2 I bear them witness that they have a zeal for God, but it is not enlightened. 3 For, being ignorant of the righteousness that comes from God, and seeking to establish their own, they did not submit to God's righteousness. 4 For Christ is the end of the law, that every one who has faith may be justified.

5 Moses writes that the man who practices the righteousness which is based on the law shall live by it. 6 But the righteousness based on faith says, Do not say in your heart, "Who will ascend into heaven?" (that is, to bring Christ down) 7 or "Who will descend into the abyss?" (that is, to bring Christ up from the dead). 8 But what does it say? The word is near you, on your lips and in your heart (that is, the word of faith which we preach); 9 because, if you confess with your lips that Jesus is Lord and believe in your heart that God raised him from the dead, you will be saved. 10 For man believes with his heart and so is justified, and he confesses with his lips and so is saved. 11 The scripture says, "No one who believes in him will be put to shame." 12 For there is no distinction between Jew and Greek; the same Lord is Lord of all and bestows his riches upon all who call upon him. 13 For, "every one who calls upon the name of the Lord will be saved."

14 But how are men to call upon him in whom they have not believed? And how are they to believe in him of whom they have never heard? And how are they to hear without a preacher? 15And how can men preach unless they are sent? As it is written, "How beautiful are the feet of those who preach good news!" 16 But they have not all obeyed the gospel; for I·sa′iah says, "Lord, who has believed what he has heard from us?" 17 So faith comes from what is heard, and what is heard comes by the preaching of Christ.

18 But I ask, have they not heard? Indeed they have; for

"Their voice has gone out to all the earth,
and their words to the ends of the world."

19Again I ask, did Israel not understand? First Moses says,

"I will make you jealous of those who are not a nation;
with a foolish nation I will make you angry."

20 Then I·sa′iah is so bold as to say,

"I have been found by those who did not seek me;
I have shown myself to those who did not ask for me."

21 But of Israel he says, "All day long I have held out my hands to a disobedient and contrary people."

He must in love lay bare the guilt of their unenlightened *zeal* (2): When Israel was confronted by the revelation of God's saving righteousness in Christ, it was being summoned to believe, find righteousness, and live. But Israel ignored the proffered righteousness and chose to go its own way and to establish its own righteousness on the basis of the Law, which God superseded by the sending of Christ (*end of the law,* 4). That wrong choice was disobedience (*did not submit,* 3) and unbelief and therefore guilt (cf. 21). The right choice had inevitably to be made; man, whether Jew or Greek, had to choose between Moses' "Do!" and the "It is done" proclaimed in the Gospel (5-13). The right choice could be made; God saw to that: every link in the golden chain which binds men in faith to the Lord has been forged by Him. He has sent His heralds; they have proclaimed Christ, and men have come to faith and called upon His name for their salvation (14-17). The

foolish nation of the Gentiles has heard and understood; *those who did not seek* (20) the Lord have found Him. If Israel did not *confess* and *believe* (9-10), but disobeyed and contradicted instead (21), the fault is clearly Israel's; they have ignored the outstretched, pleading hands of God.

9:33 *Laying in Zion a stone.* Cf. Is 8:14 and 28:16. Since Zion is the citadel of the anointed king of Israel, the salvation promised is that given in the anointed King, the Messiah. (Cf. 1 Ptr 2:4-6)

10:15 *How beautiful are the feet.* Cf. Is 52:7. As in the days when God took up His kingly power and freed His people from Babylon, so now when His kingdom comes in Christ, His heralds go forth to bring the good news to captive men.

10:18 *Their voice has gone out.* Cf. Ps 19:1-4, which speaks of the heavens that tell the glory of God, of the firmament which proclaims His handiwork, of the ordered times and seasons which proclaim the God who ordered them. Paul is imply-

GOD'S WISDOM IN THE CREATION OF HIS NEW ISRAEL (11:1-36)

11 I ask, then, has God rejected his people? By no means! I myself am an Israelite, a descendant of Abraham, a member of the tribe of Benjamin. 2 God has not rejected his people whom he foreknew. Do you not know what the scripture says of E·li′jah, how he pleads with God against Israel? 3 "Lord, they have killed thy prophets, they have demolished thy altars, and I alone am left, and they seek my life." 4 But what is God's reply to him? "I have kept for myself seven thousand men who have not bowed the knee to Baal." 5 So too at the present time there is a remnant, chosen by grace. 6 But if it is by grace, it is no longer on the basis of works; otherwise grace would no longer be grace.

7 What then? Israel failed to obtain what it sought. The elect obtained it, but the rest were hardened, 8 as it is written,

"God gave them a spirit of stupor,
eyes that should not see and ears that should not hear,
down to this very day."

9And David says,

"Let their table become a snare and a trap,
a pitfall and a retribution for them;
10   let their eyes be darkened so that they cannot see,
and bend their backs for ever."

11 So I ask, have they stumbled so as to fall? By no means! But through their trespass salvation has come to the Gentiles, so as to make Israel jealous. 12 Now if their trespass means riches for the world, and if their failure means riches for the Gentiles, how much more will their full inclusion mean!

---

ing: When God, the almighty Creator, wants to be heard, He will be heard. He who has all powers in heaven and on earth at His command can (and does) raise up men to preach His Gospel. That Gospel has been "fully preached" (15:19). The men of Israel have heard it, no doubt of that.

11:1-36 God is free, and Israel is guilty; chs. 9 and 10 would suffice "to justify the ways of God to man." But it is not Paul's mission to provide a theodicy, to vindicate God; he is an apostle of Jesus Christ (1:1), who knew that there are no limits to the creative possibilities of God (Mt 19:26) and could see in the hopeless spectacle of the lost sheep of Israel the harvest field of God. Paul, His servant, has the mind of Christ. Paul has, moreover, been set apart for the Gospel of God (1:1) and serves the Creator, whose Word has never failed (9:6), whose Word says, "Let light shine out of darkness" (2 Co 4:6; Gn 1:3; cf. Is 9:2). His Word can make light shine even out of Israel's present darkness; His Word has uses for the dead branches cut from the tree of Israel (11:17), for Israel hardened in resistance to God (11:25). For God's almighty love is in that Word. A proclamation of God's Gospel which stops at theodicy would be an incomplete proclamation; beyond God's freedom (ch. 9) and justice (ch. 10) the illimitable wisdom of God opens up prospects for His new people of which an apostle must speak. (Ch. 11)

11:1-10 THE PRESENT STATE OF ISRAEL

11:1-10 The present case of Israel is cause for mourning. The majority of the Israelites are a spectacle for tears: men whom God has petrified in their stony resistance to the truth (*hardened*, 7),

whose verdict Paul pronounces in terms of Isaiah (8; cf. Is 29:10) and Ps 69:22-23 (9-10). But in that darkness of doom a light shines nevertheless, the light of God's sheer grace, which has preserved a believing *remnant* (5) in Israel. Paul himself is living proof that *God has not rejected his people* (2), His chosen ones. God's Word has reached him and is working through him; while one Israelite fulfills Israel's function of bearing witness to Israel's God, Israel exists; Israel is not rejected (1). And Paul knows that he is not a lone true Israelite (His fellow apostles were all Jews!). No more than *Elijah* was of old, when he felt alone amid an unbelieving nation (2-4; cf. 1 K 19:10, 14). God's assurance to Elijah (1 K 19:18) is an assurance to Paul; he knows that he belongs to a *remnant, chosen by grace* (5), that the history of Israel has not ended in the extinction of Israel.

11:9 *Let their table become a snare and a trap* Ps 69:22 depicts the enemies of the righteous sufferer as feasting in their triumph over him. The righteous sufferer calls on his God to vindicate him: their table, symbol of their triumphant security, is to be their doom.

11:11-16 GOD'S USES FOR ISRAEL

11:11-16 The wisdom of God can make even Israel's *trespass* (11) and Israel's *rejection* (15) serve His saving purposes. Paul has seen with his own eyes how Jewish rejection of the Word of God has served to send that Word of life out among the Gentiles to enrich (*riches for the world,* 12) men of Pisidian Antioch (Acts 13:45-47) and Corinth (Acts 18:5-6). In bringing *reconciliation* to the *world* of the nations (15), God has not forgotten His ancient people, the *first fruits* of His harvest

13 Now I am speaking to you Gentiles. Inasmuch then as I am an apostle to the Gentiles, I magnify my ministry 14 in order to make my fellow Jews jealous, and thus save some of them. 15 For if their rejection means the reconciliation of the world, what will their acceptance mean but life from the dead? 16 If the dough offered as first fruits is holy, so is the whole lump; and if the root is holy, so are the branches.

17 But if some of the branches were broken off, and you, a wild olive shoot, were grafted in their place to share the richness*o* of the olive tree, 18 do not boast over the branches. If you do boast, remember it is not you that support the root, but the root that supports you. 19 You will say, "Branches were broken off so that I might be grafted in." 20 That is true. They were broken off because of their unbelief, but you stand fast only through faith. So do not become proud, but stand in awe. 21 For if God did not spare the natural branches, neither will he spare you. 22 Note then the kindness and the severity of God: severity toward those who have fallen, but God's kindness to you, provided you continue in his kindness; otherwise you too will be cut off. 23And even the others if they do not persist in their unbelief, will be grafted in, for God has the power to graft them in again. 24 For if you have been cut from what is by nature a wild olive tree, and grafted, contrary to nature, into a cultivated olive tree, how much more will these natural branches be grafted back into their own olive tree.

25 Lest you be wise in your own conceits, I want you to understand this mystery, brethren: a hardening has come upon part of Israel, until the full number of the Gentiles come in, 26 and so all Israel will be saved; as it is written,

> "The Deliverer will come from Zion,
>
> he will banish ungodliness from Jacob";

27   "and this will be my covenant with them

when I take away their sins."

o Other ancient authorities read *rich root*

and the *root* (16) of the tree that is the people of God (cf. 17-24); what happens to Gentiles has its effect on Israel also. God is wooing Israel when He makes *Israel jealous* (11, 14). When God receives into His new people those Israelites won by Paul's work among the Gentiles, will that not be His proper work (cf. 4:17) of bringing *life from the dead* (15), a triumph of His creative grace in Christ Jesus?

11:14 *Save some of them.* Paul does not envision a mass conversion of the nation Israel. This is important for the interpretation of "all Israel" in 11:26.

11:17-24 THE TREE AND THE BRANCHES

11:17-24 The new people of God is a fair *olive tree* (17). Cultivating that tree bears witness to the *kindness and the severity of God* (22). His kindness has given the Gentile (*a wild olive tree,* 24) his place and life in that tree; it was an extravagant kindness, one that sovereignly ignored the rules of horticulture (normally and naturally, cultivated branches are engrafted on the wild plant; the reverse is *contrary to nature,* 24). His severity was provoked by *unbelief* (20); God's judgment struck the natural branches because they had, un- naturally, by unbelief, refused life from Him. The Gentile has no cause for smug complacency; rather let him *stand in awe* (20). That same severity can deal unsparingly with him (21), and that same kindness can restore the natural branches, now removed and withered by His judgment (24), to

their native tree. The Gentile dare not boast; and the Jew (and all who mourn for him) need not despair.

11:25-27 THE MYSTERY

11:25-27 Paul states in another form what he has already said in the figure of the tree and the branches. This form he calls *mystery,* a prophetic utterance concerning God's hidden counsels, which only God can reveal. There are three elements in this mystery: (1) The hardening of Israel is only partial, and there is still a time of grace for Israel; (2) this time of grace will endure *until the full number of the Gentiles come in,* that is, to the end of this age, when judgment comes; until the end of this age, the coming in of the Gentiles will continue to provoke Israel to jealousy, and God will thus continue to call Israel to repentance; (3) *and so* — by God's wise governance of the history of Gentile and Jew — *all Israel* (the whole of God's people from among Gentiles and Jews) *will be saved.* What the image of the tree and the branches opened up as something possible (23-24), the mystery asserts as an action of God. What God can do, He will do. Under the blessing of His Messianic (*Zion,* 26) deliverance, under the new covenant of forgiveness (27), all God's people, cleansed and restored, will come home to Him.

11:26-27 Paul combines the basic thought of Is 59:20-21 with touches from Ps 14:7 and Ps 53:6; the picture of the new *covenant* contains reminis- cences of Jer 31:33-34.

28As regards the gospel they are enemies of God, for your sake; but as regards election they are beloved for the sake of their forefathers. 29 For the gifts and the call of God are irrevocable. 30 Just as you were once disobedient to God but now have received mercy because of their disobedience, 31 so they have now been disobedient in order that by the mercy shown to you they also may*p* receive mercy. 32 For God has consigned all men to disobedience, that he may have mercy upon all.

33 O the depth of the riches and wisdom and knowledge of God! How unsearchable are his judgments and how inscrutable his ways!

34   "For who has known the mind of the Lord,
           or who has been his counselor?"

35   "Or who has given a gift to him
           that he might be repaid?"

36 For from him and through him and to him are all things. To him be glory for ever. Amen.

The Gospel Creates a New Worship for the New People of God
12:1 – 15:13

ALL LIFE IN THE CHURCH AND IN THE WORLD A SPIRITUAL WORSHIP (12:1 – 13:14)

12 I appeal to you therefore, brethren, by the mercies of God, to present your bodies as a living sacrifice, holy and acceptable to God, which is your spiritual worship. 2 Do not be conformed to this world*q* but be transformed by the renewal of your mind, that you may prove what is the will of God, what is good and acceptable and perfect.*r*

3 For by the grace given to me I bid every one among you not to think of himself more highly than he ought to think, but to think with sober judgment, each according

p Other ancient authorities add *now*   *q* Greek *age*   *r* Or *what is the good and acceptable and perfect will of God*

11:28-32 ENEMIES AND BELOVED

11:28-32 Israel as a nation has refused the *gospel*, which offered them righteousness and life; that has made them *enemies* of God (28). As surely as God lifts up His countenance upon the Gentiles who call Jesus Lord, so surely His face is set against the men who persecute His church and say that Jesus is accursed. And yet, no simple scheme of guilt and punishment can enclose the mysterious workings of the Word of God. God is God and not man; His *election*, His *gifts and the call* have their cause and origin in Him alone; they are not generated by the goodness of man and do not evaporate before the badness of man. They remain *irrevocable* so far as His will to give is concerned. The history of man, Gentile and Jew alike, is a history of his disobedience. The disobedience of the Jew was the occasion of mercy shown to the Gentile, but they did not merit that mercy by any previous obedience of their own. *God has consigned all men to disobedience* (32). By strange ways His wisdom has brought all men to that dead end where man must turn and face the wrath of God, must cease to boast, must cease to offer excuses, must throw himself in total surrender on the mercy of Him whose wrath He fears, in order that the passionate Pursuer of His enemies may at last have mercy on them all.

11:33-36 DOXOLOGY

11:33-36 All men end up in beggary (11:32);

only God is rich, and only He is wise; no one can give Him counsel (34), and no one can earn His favor (35) in the work that is solely His: the salvation of man. He stands at the beginning as the Creator of all, the Giver of all gifts. He holds the reins of man's sorry history in His wise, almighty hands. He shall bring His creation home, that all may witness to His glory everlastingly.

12:1-2 THE GOSPEL BASIS

12:1-2 The new people of God are universal, and their worship is total. The whole living man presents his acting self *(bodies)* as a living *sacrifice* to God in a true *(spiritual)* dedication of all his powers, including his intelligence *(prove what is the will of God)*. The call to worship is therefore not based on the compulsion of Law but on the inspiration of the Gospel. The Gospel, which sheds abroad in man's heart *the mercies of God*, turns man from conformity to *this* self-seeking and dying *world* and *transforms* him into the true worshiper living his renewed life to God in faith (3-8), love (9-11), and hope. (12-21)

12:3-8 THE RENEWED LIFE A LIFE OF FAITH

12:3-8 Faith that is born of the mercies of God and lives of them spells the end of pride (3) and makes of a man a soberly functioning member of the *one body in Christ*, the new people of God (5). Whether his new worship is by way of the vocal ministries of *prophecy* (6, declaring the will of

to the measure of faith which God has assigned him. 4 For as in one body we have many members, and all the members do not have the same function, 5 so we, though many, are one body in Christ, and individually members one of another. 6 Having gifts that differ according to the grace given to us, let us use them: if prophecy, in proportion to our faith; 7 if service, in our serving; he who teaches, in his teaching; 8 he who exhorts, in his exhortation; he who contributes, in liberality; he who gives aid, with zeal; he who does acts of mercy, with cheerfulness.

9 Let love be genuine; hate what is evil, hold fast to what is good; 10 love one another with brotherly affection; outdo one another in showing honor. 11 Never flag in zeal, be aglow with the Spirit, serve the Lord. 12 Rejoice in your hope, be patient in tribulation, be constant in prayer. 13 Contribute to the needs of the saints, practice hospitality.

14 Bless those who persecute you; bless and do not curse them. 15 Rejoice with those who rejoice, weep with those who weep. 16 Live in harmony with one another; do not be haughty, but associate with the lowly;⁸ never be conceited. 17 Repay no one evil for evil, but take thought for what is noble in the sight of all. 18 If possible, so far as it depends upon you, live peaceably with all. 19 Beloved, never avenge your-selves, but leave it† to the wrath of God; for it is written, "Vengeance is mine, I will repay, says the Lord." 20 No, "if your enemy is hungry, feed him; if he is thirsty, give him drink; for by so doing you will heap burning coals upon his head." 21 Do not be overcome by evil, but overcome evil with good.

13 Let every person be subject to the governing authorities. For there is no authority except from God, and those that exist have been instituted by God. 2 Therefore he who resists the authorities resists what God has appointed, and those who resist will incur judgment. 3 For rulers are not a terror to good conduct, but to bad. Would you have no fear of him who is in authority? Then do what is good, and you will receive his approval, 4 for he is God's servant for your good. But if you do wrong, be afraid, for he does not bear the sword in vain; he is the servant of God to

---

⁸ Or *give yourselves to humble tasks*   † Greek *give place*

God to God's people in each new situation) or *teaching* (7, probably instruction in the church's first Bible, the OT) or *exhortation* (8, the warm and winning word that moves men to action according to the will of God) or in the silently winning witness of *service* (7) or generous contribution (8) or giving *aid* (8) or *acts of mercy* (8)—all is done in the knowledge and conviction that they are recipients and stewards of the mercies of God, empowered and circumscribed by Him (*according to the measure of faith . . . assigned*, 3).

12:9-11 THE RENEWED LIFE A LIFE OF LOVE

12:9-11 Faith and love are inseparable; faith is always faith working through love (Gl 5:6). Love animated and informed by faith is holy love; it speaks God's No to *evil*, while holding *fast to what is good* as it dispenses the mercies of God in *brotherly affection* and self-effacing humility (10). Faith, inspired by *the Spirit* (11), knows that all love is a service rendered to *the Lord* (11); no one dare offer Him the unclean ministry of a senti-mental love that makes human pride or blurs the line between good and evil with a tear.

12:12-21 THE RENEWED LIFE A LIFE OF HOPE

12:12-21 *Hope* is faith looking forward, rejoicing in the future provided by the mercies of God (cf. 8:19-39). The assurance of that great future gives the believer patience in present tribulation and constancy in prayer (cf. 8:26-27); it gives him

the generous largeness of heart which can *con-tribute to the needs of the saints* (13), can love and bless even the enemy and the persecutors (14), can enter with ready sympathy into other men's laughter and tears (15), can preserve harmony and quell pride (18), can forego vengeance in the as-surance the Lord who reserves vengeance to Him-self (19; Dt 32:35) "will vindicate his people and have compassion on his servants" (Dt 32:36). The only "vengeance" open to the man of hope is the vengeance of undeserved love, which heaps *burn-ing coals* of agonizing contrition upon the head of the enemy (20; Pr 25:21-22). Thus Christian hope triumphs by overcoming *evil with good.* To do evil in return for evil is defeat, is to *be overcome by evil* and so to lose all that glorious victory and future which Christ, who overcomes evil with good, has won for us.

13:1-7 THE RENEWED LIFE WITHIN THE ORDERS OF THIS WORLD

13:1-7 Ch. 13 repeats the emphasis of ch. 12 on faith (1-7), love (8-10), and hope (11-14). To faith it is given to recognize in *the governing authorities* (1) an order that *God has appointed* for His good ends and man's benefit (2), to see in Caesar *God's servant* (4) and in Caesar's *sword* (symbol of Caesar's power over life and death) the consecrated instrument of *God's wrath* (5) and to obey *for the sake of conscience* (5), to pay not only *taxes* and *revenue* but also the heart's tribute of *respect* and

execute his wrath on the wrongdoer. 5 Therefore one must be subject, not only to avoid God's wrath but also for the sake of conscience. 6 For the same reason you also pay taxes, for the authorities are ministers of God, attending to this very thing. 7 Pay all of them their dues, taxes to whom taxes are due, revenue to whom revenue is due, respect to whom respect is due, honor to whom honor is due.

8 Owe no one anything, except to love one another; for he who loves his neighbor has fulfilled the law. 9 The commandments, "You shall not commit adultery, You shall not kill, You shall not steal, You shall not covet," and any other commandment, are summed up in this sentence, "You shall love your neighbor as yourself." 10 Love does no wrong to a neighbor; therefore love is the fulfilling of the law.

11 Besides this you know what hour it is, how it is full time now for you to wake from sleep. For salvation is nearer to us now than when we first believed; 12 the night is far gone, the day is at hand. Let us then cast off the works of darkness and put on the armor of light; 13 let us conduct ourselves becomingly as in the day, not in reveling and drunkenness, not in debauchery and licentiousness, not in quarreling and jealousy. 14 But put on the Lord Jesus Christ, and make no provision for the flesh, to gratify its desires.

THE WEAK AND THE STRONG IN FAITH UNITED IN ONE WORSHIP (14:1 — 15:13)

14 As for the man who is weak in faith, welcome him, but not for disputes over opinions. 2 One believes he may eat anything, while the weak man eats only vegetables. 3 Let not him who eats despise him who abstains, and let not him who abstains pass judgment on him who eats; for God has welcomed him. 4 Who are you to pass judgment on the servant of another? It is before his own master that he stands or falls. And he will be upheld, for the Master is able to make him stand.

honor to this ambiguous representative of God (7). No area of life, however "secular," is exempted from the claim of total worship.

13:8-10 THE DEBT OF LOVE

13:8-10 Paul's preaching of faith does not overthrow the Law but upholds it (3:31). Believing men are expected to pay what is due, wherever it is due (7). *Love* does not stop at what is due but works unceasingly to pay the debt of love perpetually owed, never marked "paid in full." Where love born of faith, born of the mercies of God, lives and works, the just requirement of the Law has been fulfilled; there is no wrong that the Law must condemn. The will of God, "what is good and acceptable and perfect" is "proved" (12:2), known, and done. (9-10)

13:11-14 LIFE AS IN THE DAY

13:11-14 The summons to pay the debt of love (8-10) is reinforced by a (*Besides this,* 11) hymn of hope (11-14). To know God's *hour* (11; cf. 3:26), His appointed time of final salvation, as the imminent hour that it is, involves acting on that knowledge; means being aroused from *sleep,* from ignorance of and indifference to one's opportunities and duties. The hour when the night of this age of sin and death is far gone and the great day of God's new world of righteousness and life is at hand — that hour is one that challenges the renewed man to resist the still potent forces of darkness and bear militant witness to the reality of the inbreaking day, to live a whole life as in the coming *day* (13) in a bodily witness to the day and its righteousness; renewed man professes his hope in things as concrete and ordinary as his atti-

tude toward sex and alcohol and the peaceable preservation of society (13). Only the renewed man can do this, the man who makes his baptism his daily dress and clothes Himself in the Christ in whom he has been clothed at baptism (cf. Gl 3:27). With *Jesus Christ* for his *Lord* he can turn his back on the old concerns of his *flesh* and live a life launched forward into the eternal day. (14)

14:1 — 15:13 Unanimity is essential to the life of the new worshiping people of God. That this unanimity does not involve a monotonous uniformity of faith, Paul has already shown in 12:3-8, where he stressed the individuality of faith in the varied ministries in the church, where "gifts that differ according to the grace given" (12:6) to each believer serve not to disrupt but to maintain and further the unanimity and health of the church. Differences in faith make themselves felt and create tensions in other areas also. Not all are equally strong in faith. To some it is given to see the new life and worship steadily and to see it whole in all its implications for action. They walk through life untroubled by scruples, with a glad and free self-confidence. These are the strong in faith. Others have not the power of faith to appropriate for themselves at once and altogether the liberty for which their Lord has set them free (Gl 5:1); they walk more timidly and circumspectly than the strong, troubled by doubts and inhibitions. These are the weak in faith.

Paul uses differences of conviction concerning food and drink and the observance of holy days to exemplify his teaching here; it may be that in Rome the weak were Judaic Christians, coming from a part in which dietary prescriptions ("clean" and "unclean" foods) and strict Sabbath obser-

5 One man esteems one day as better than another, while another man esteems all days alike. Let every one be fully convinced in his own mind. 6 He who observes the day, observes it in honor of the Lord. He also who eats, eats in honor of the Lord, since he gives thanks to God; while he who abstains, abstains in honor of the Lord and gives thanks to God. 7 None of us lives to himself, and none of us dies to himself. 8 If we live, we live to the Lord, and if we die, we die to the Lord; so then, whether we live or whether we die, we are the Lord's. 9 For to this end Christ died and lived again, that he might be Lord both of the dead and of the living.

10 Why do you pass judgment on your brother? Or you, why do you despise your brother? For we shall all stand before the judgment seat of God; 11 for it is written,

"As I live, says the Lord, every knee shall bow to me,
   and every tongue shall give praise[u] to God."

12 So each of us shall give account of himself to God.

13 Then let us no more pass judgment on one another, but rather decide never to put a stumbling block or hindrance in the way of a brother. 14 I know and am persuaded in the Lord Jesus that nothing is unclean in itself; but it is unclean for any one who thinks it unclean. 15 If your brother is being injured by what you eat, you are no longer walking in love. Do not let what you eat cause the ruin of one for whom Christ died. 16 So do not let your good be spoken of as evil. 17 For the kingdom of God is not food and drink but righteousness and peace and joy in the Holy Spirit; 18 he who thus serves Christ is acceptable to God and approved by men. 19 Let us then pursue what makes for peace and for mutual upbuilding. 20 Do not, for the sake of food, destroy the work of God. Everything is indeed clean, but it is wrong for any one to make others fall by what he eats; 21 it is right not to eat meat or drink wine or do anything that makes your brother stumble.[v] 22 The faith that you have, keep between yourself and God; happy is he who has no reason to judge himself for what he approves. 23 But he who has doubts is condemned, if he eats, because he does not act from faith; for whatever does not proceed from faith is sin.[w]

[u] Or confess   [v] Other ancient authorities add or be upset or be weakened
[w] Other authorities, some ancient, insert here Ch 16.25-27

vance were important for piety; while the Gentiles, not so conditioned by their past, breathed more easily in the free atmosphere of the church—they were the "strong." At any rate these differences were not, for all their external character, a trifling matter; they were a matter of faith, and so a matter of central concern in a community of believers; and the difference in attitude toward foods would affect the common meal, so important in the life of the early church as the symbol and expression of fellowship (cf. 1 Co 11). Paul first addresses both groups together (14:1-12), then the strong alone (14:13—15:6), and then again appeals to both. (15:7-13)

14:1-12 TO THE WEAK AND THE STRONG

14:1-12 Paul, characteristically, first espouses the cause of the weak; the weak man is to find a real welcome in the new people of God; he is not merely to be accepted in order that the strong may argue him out of his misguided opinions (1). That would be contempt (3), which has no place in a community of love whose law is: "Outdo one another in showing honor" (12:10). The weak is tempted to pass judgment (3) on the brother whose strong freedom looks to the weak dangerously like religious indifference and a disregard of the danger lurking in such freedom. Paul reminds the censorious, worrying weak brother that he has no reason to worry and no right to judge. The strong man in his freedom has been received by

God (3) and has a Master who can sustain him in his freedom (4). In fact we all, weak and strong alike, have one Lord, whom we serve in all that we do, to whom we live and die, and each of us is accountable to God Himself for his service to that Master.

14:13—15:6 TO THE STRONG

14:13—15:6 Paul identifies himself with the strong (14:14; 15:1, we who are strong) and states their obligation of love both negatively (14:13-23) and positively (15:1-6). Negatively: Whatever does not proceed from faith is sin (23)—even the practicing of a freedom of faith without regard for its injurious effect on the weaker brother is sin; for to leave the path of love and to injure the brother (15), to misuse one's freedom so as to cause the ruin of one for whom Christ died (15), to bring disrepute upon his Christian liberty (your good, 16) by employing it ruthlessly (16), to destroy the work of God in a man, his faith and salvation (20), to make men stumble (21) and fall (20) by one's own swaggering walk of freedom, to indulge in freedom in such a way that one's conscience becomes uncertain (doubts, 23) about it— these are not fruits of faith. Positively: Faith looks to Christ, and the life of faith gets its content and shape from the life of Christ; He did not please himself (15:3) but gave Himself so wholly to a life lived for others (the weak who needed Him most) that His righteous countrymen reproached Him

15 We who are strong ought to bear with the failings of the weak, and not to please ourselves; 2 let each of us please his neighbor for his good, to edify him. 3 For Christ did not please himself; but, as it is written, "The reproaches of those who reproached thee fell on me." 4 For whatever was written in former days was written for our instruction, that by steadfastness and by the encouragement of the scriptures we might have hope. 5 May the God of steadfastness and encouragement grant you to live in such harmony with one another, in accord with Christ Jesus, 6 that together you may with one voice glorify the God and Father of our Lord Jesus Christ.

7 Welcome one another, therefore, as Christ has welcomed you, for the glory of God. 8 For I tell you that Christ became a servant to the circumcised to show God's truthfulness, in order to confirm the promises given to the patriarchs, 9 and in order that the Gentiles might glorify God for his mercy. As it is written,

> "Therefore I will praise thee among the Gentiles,
> and sing to thy name";

10 and again it is said,

> "Rejoice, O Gentiles, with his people";

11 and again,

> "Praise the Lord, all Gentiles,
> and let all the peoples praise him";

12 and further I·sa′iah says,

> "The root of Jesse shall come,
> he who rises to rule the Gentiles;
> in him shall the Gentiles hope."

13 May the God of hope fill you with all joy and peace in believing, so that by the power of the Holy Spirit you may abound in hope.

Conclusion

15:14 — 16:27

14 I myself am satisfied about you, my brethren, that you yourselves are full of goodness, filled with all knowledge, and able to instruct one another. 15 But on some points I have written to you very boldly by way of reminder, because of the grace given me by God 16 to be a minister of Christ Jesus to the Gentiles in the priestly service of the gospel of God, so that the offering of the Gentiles may be acceptable, sanctified by the Holy Spirit. 17 In Christ Jesus, then, I have reason to be proud of my work for God. 18 For I will not venture to speak of anything except what Christ has wrought through me to win obedience from the Gentiles, by word and deed, 19 by

for the prodigal liberality of His grace and thereby reproached God for sending His Son to seek the lost. The cry of the psalmist became the cry of the Christ: *The reproaches of those who reproached thee fell on me* (Ps 69:9; 15:3). Christ found the pattern of His life in the OT Scriptures, and the church of the last days that would serve and love in *accord with Christ Jesus* (15:5) can find the pattern and power for its life there too, and so find strength to rise above tensions and difficulties to a life of hope-filled unanimous doxology. (15:4-6)

15:7-13 TO ALL: WELCOME ONE ANOTHER

15:7-13 The *welcome* which binds brother to brother, despite the difficulties and tensions caused by the difference between the weak and strong, is the church's echo of Christ's welcome; that costly welcome (it cost Him His life) revealed God's love to the full, and so glorified Him (7). God's love in Christ spanned greater and graver differences than those which separate vegetarians from those who eat meat; it embraced both Jew

and Gentile (to whom God faithfully kept His promises, 8) and (in whom God's undeserved and unexpected mercy awakened songs of praise, 9). The fulfillment of the promises made to Israel (*patriarchs,* 8) brought the fulfillment of the promises made for the Gentiles in the OT (9-12). The God who gave these promises and fulfilled them in Jesus Christ is *the God of hope* (13); all men may confidently lay their future in His hands. He can give to both the strong and the weak the *joy and peace* they need for living and worshiping together. Joy and peace can be theirs by *believing,* by receiving from God. Thus, by God's working, by the power of God's Spirit, they can *abound* in hope. They can meet the severest demands made on their love with kindly evenness of mind. (13)

15:14-33 THE APOSTLE'S PLANS:
JERUSALEM, ROME, SPAIN

15:14-33 By his letter Paul has already imparted a generous installment of the "spiritual gift" he had promised to impart to the saints of Rome when

the power of signs and wonders, by the power of the Holy Spirit, so that from Jerusalem and as far round as Il·lyr′i·cum I have fully preached the gospel of Christ, [20] thus making it my ambition to preach the gospel, not where Christ has already been named, lest I build on another man's foundation, [21] but as it is written,

"They shall see who have never been told of him,
and they shall understand who have never heard of him."

22 This is the reason why I have so often been hindered from coming to you. [23] But now, since I no longer have any room for work in these regions, and since I have longed for many years to come to you, [24] I hope to see you in passing as I go to Spain, and to be sped on my journey there by you, once I have enjoyed your company for a little. [25]At present, however, I am going to Jerusalem with aid for the saints. [26] For Macedonia and A·cha′ia have been pleased to make some contribution for the poor among the saints at Jerusalem; [27] they were pleased to do it, and indeed they are in debt to them, for if the Gentiles have come to share in their spiritual blessings, they ought also to be of service to them in material blessings. [28] When therefore I have completed this, and have delivered to them what has been raised,[x] I shall go on by way of you to Spain; [29] and I know that when I come to you I shall come in the fulness of the blessing[y] of Christ.

30 I appeal to you, brethren, by our Lord Jesus Christ and by the love of the Spirit, to strive together with me in your prayers to God on my behalf, [31] that I may be delivered from the unbelievers in Judea, and that my service for Jerusalem may be acceptable to the saints, [32] so that by God's will I may come to you with joy and be refreshed in your company. [33] The God of peace be with you all. Amen.

16 I commend to you our sister Phoebe, a deaconess of the church at Cen·chre′ae, [2] that you may receive her in the Lord as befits the saints, and help her in whatever she may require from you, for she has been a helper of many and of myself as well.

[x] Greek *sealed to them this fruit*
[y] Other ancient authorities insert *of the gospel*

he should come to them (1:11). He, "called to be an apostle" (1:1), has set before them once more *by way of reminder* (15:15) what it means to be "called to be saints" (1:7). Now he can disclose to them more fully his plans (cf. 1:10-13) and invite the church, newly strengthened by his spiritual gift, to an active "partnership in the Gospel." (Cf. Ph 1:5)

An apostle's plans are not his own, to make or alter as he pleases; for the apostle is an instrument in the hands of the Trinity: God has given him grace to be a minister of Christ Jesus, and the offering which his priestly ministry presents to God (Gentiles won to the obedience of faith) is *sanctified by the Holy Spirit* (16). Therefore the apostle cannot move westward, to Rome and Spain, until God's business has been finished in the East, until he has *fully preached* the Gospel of God where God wants it preached (19-21), until he has strengthened the tie that binds the new Israel into one by presenting to the *saints at Jerusalem* the Gentiles' *contribution* of love. Only then can he come to Rome in the high-hearted assurance that he comes *in the fulness of the blessing of Christ.* (29)

Paul draws the called saints into the orbit of the called apostle by requesting two services of them. He asks that their prayers accompany him to Jerusalem, where he has cause to fear both the rancor of his inveterate enemies, *the unbelievers in Judea,* and the suspicions of Judaic Christians (31; cf. Acts 21:20-26). He wishes, moreover, *to*

be sped on his *journey* (24) by the churches of Rome—this "speeding on," as passages like Ti 3:13-14; 3 Jn 6; 1 Co 16:6, 11; 2 Co 1:16 show, could include a variety of services rendered to a missionary on his travels: e. g., letters of recommendation, guides, information, money. Thus the Gospel creates the apostolic, missionary church.

16:1-16, 21-24 COMMENDATION AND GREETINGS

16:1-16, 21-24 Paul's commendation of Phoebe, deaconess of Cenchreae (1-2), his greetings to members of the Roman church personally known to him (3-16), and the greetings from his co-workers and companions (21-23) give us a revealing glimpse of the energetic and many-sided life of the early church. Some of those named had worked and suffered with Paul in the East (3, 4, 7, 9); all knew him and could tell the Roman Christians what manner of man was soliciting their sympathy and aid for work in the West. The number of women in the list is remarkable, and Paul's characterization of them is no less remarkable; the apostle who enjoined silence on woman in the public worship of the church (1 Co 14:34) obviously was no smug male belittler of womankind. The mobility of the first Christians is documented here too; men and women from all over the Mediterranean world are met in Rome; that mobility is coupled with a sense of churchmanship which is anything but parochial or provincial. Paul can write: *All the churches of Christ greet*

3 Greet Prisca and Aq′ui·la, my fellow workers in Christ Jesus, [4] who risked their necks for my life, to whom not only I but also all the churches of the Gentiles give thanks; [5] greet also the church in their house. Greet my beloved E·pae′ne·tus, who was the first convert in Asia for Christ. [6] Greet Mary, who has worked hard among you. [7] Greet An·dro·ni′cus and Junias, my kinsmen and my fellow prisoners; they are men of note among the apostles, and they were in Christ before me. [8] Greet Am·pli·a′tus, my beloved in the Lord. [9] Greet Urbanus, our fellow worker in Christ, and my beloved Stachys. [10] Greet A·pel′les, who is approved in Christ. Greet those who belong to the family of A·ris·to·bu′lus. [11] Greet my kinsman He·ro′di·on. Greet those in the Lord who belong to the family of Narcissus. [12] Greet those workers in the Lord, Try·phae′na and Try·pho′sa. Greet the beloved Persis, who has worked hard in the Lord. [13] Greet Rufus, eminent in the Lord, also his mother and mine. [14] Greet A·syn′cri·tus, Phlegon, Hermes, Patrobas, Hermas, and the brethren who are with them. [15] Greet Phi·lol′o·gus, Julia, Nereus and his sister, and Olympas, and all the saints who are with them. [16] Greet one another with a holy kiss. All the churches of Christ greet you.

17 I appeal to you, brethren, to take note of those who create dissensions and difficulties, in opposition to the doctrine which you have been taught; avoid them. [18] For such persons do not serve our Lord Christ, but their own appetites,[z] and by fair and flattering words they deceive the hearts of the simple-minded. [19] For while your obedience is known to all, so that I rejoice over you, I would have you wise as to what is good and guileless as to what is evil; [20] then the God of peace will soon crush Satan under your feet. The grace of our Lord Jesus Christ be with you.[a]

21 Timothy, my fellow worker, greets you; so do Lucius and Jason and So·sip′a·ter, my kinsmen.

22 I Ter′ti·us, the writer of this letter, greet you in the Lord.

23 Gaius, who is host to me and to the whole church, greets you. E·ras′tus, the city treasurer, and our brother Quartus, greet you.[b]

25 Now to him who is able to strengthen you according to my gospel and the preaching of Jesus Christ, according to the revelation of the mystery which was kept

[z] Greek *their own belly* (Phil 3.19)
[a] Other ancient authorities omit this sentence
[b] Other ancient authorities insert verse 24, *The grace of our Lord Jesus Christ be with you all. Amen.*

you (16) — all the churches know of Paul's plans, all accompany him with their prayers, all bespeak a welcome for him in Rome.

16:5 *The church in their house.* The house-church seems to have been normal for Rome, as it was for most of the early church. Cf. 14 and 15, "the brethren who are with them . . . the saints who are with them."

16:17-20 THE APOSTLE'S WARNING

16:17-20 This note of warning comes unexpectedly and abruptly; if we recall the nature of the early church's service of worship (at which Paul's letters were read, cf. Cl 4:16), the occasion of the warning is clear. The picture of such a service shimmers through here (16-20). The assembled church has heard the apostolic Word; the solemn celebration of the Lord's Supper is about to begin. The assembly expresses its solidarity in the Lord by the exchange of the holy kiss (16; cf. 1 Th 5:26; 2 Co 13:12; esp. 1 Co 16:20-22). Having thus spoken a corporate yea to their Lord, the worshipers speak their inevitable nay to all who deny His Lordship and exclude them from their communion (cf. the anathema of 1 Co 16:22, "accursed"). Here the anathema takes the form of a stern warning against men who, for all their de-

ceptively winning eloquence (*fair and flattering words,* 18), are serving themselves and not the Lord, disrupting the church (*dissensions,* 17) and endangering her faith (*difficulties,* 17; literally "stumbling blocks"), *in opposition to the doctrine . . . taught* in all Christendom (17). No church may tolerate or compromise with them, least of all the Roman church, conspicuous among all Christians by her position and by her record of fidelity (19). *Avoid them* (17), that is the only possible course, the only wise (19) course when confronted by such satanic intrusions into the church; then God will give the victory and resolve all dissensions with His peace. (20)

16:25-27 CONCLUDING DOXOLOGY

16:25-27 Paul began the body of his letter with an affirmation of the power of God at work in the Gospel (1:16); the whole letter has set forth the past and present workings of that power for salvation. Paul closes with a hymn in praise of the God of power. He is a God at hand, able to sustain the Romans in their conspicuous and responsible position, able to strengthen them for the greater tasks which Paul's coming will open up for them. His Word is near them. Paul's Gospel itself is that Word; it can strengthen them because Jesus

secret for long ages 26 but is now disclosed and through the prophetic writings is made known to all nations, according to the command of the eternal God, to bring about the obedience of faith— 27 to the only wise God be glory for evermore through Jesus Christ! Amen.

Christ is preaching in Paul's Gospel. And Jesus Christ is the disclosure of God's *mystery* (25), the revelation of His long counsels of salvation which worked in strange and secret ways for long ages, hidden in the sad and inconspicuous history of His little people Israel. In Christ that plan is now disclosed and is working on the stage of universal history to the ends of the earth. All nations shall know the Christ; the *prophetic writings* (26) of the OT are the interpretive witnesses to what the eternal God has revealed in Christ. Thus men will be brought to the obedience of faith. The Romans need not fear; whatever apostolic task they undertake will not be undertaken in vain. They need but bow with Paul in adoration before the God whose wisdom (27) guides all history to His goal, to the glory of His grace. Whatever serves that glory cannot fail.

THE FIRST LETTER OF PAUL TO THE
CORINTHIANS

INTRODUCTION

1 Paul wrote his letters to Corinth during the period of his life commonly known as his third missionary journey (A. D. 52—56). The heart of that journey was the nearly 3-year ministry in the great metropolis of Asia Minor, Ephesus; it was preceded by a revisitation of the churches founded on the first missionary journey and followed by a revisitation of the European churches of Macedonia and Achaia founded on the second journey.

2 Paul himself had prepared the way for his ministry in Ephesus by his visit to Ephesus on his return from Corinth to Palestine at the close of the second journey (Acts 18:19-21). The men of the synagog were so much moved by his words that they asked him to stay on. He promised to return to Ephesus and left Aquila and Priscilla there. As their contact with Apollos shows (Acts 18:24-26), they did not remain silent concerning the faith that was in them. Through them the learned and eloquent Apollos became a full-fledged witness to the Christ (Acts 18:26) and thus further prepared the way for Paul. Perhaps the 12 "disciples" who knew only the baptism of John and had not heard of the outpouring of the Holy Spirit in the last days (Acts 19:1-7) had been won by Apollos. Paul baptized them and laid hands on them that they might receive the Holy Spirit. Thus his work at Ephesus began. The beginning was slight, only 12 men, but the foundation was, as always, essentially his own (Ro 15:20), and he built on it with a will.

3 That will generated conflict. Luke's account of Paul's Ephesian ministry is anything but complete. He gives no chronicle of it, but presents it as a series of three conflicts, each of which results in a triumph for the cause of the apostle of Christ. The first conflict was with the synagog (Acts 19:8-10). Paul was here permitted to witness in the synagog for an unusually long period, for 3 months, and with considerable success. The Jews of the province of Asia were therefore particularly bitter against him, and it

was they who later instigated the riot in Jerusalem which led to Paul's arrest and imprisonment (Acts 21:27-28). As was inevitable, the break with the synagog came: "Some were stubborn and disbelieved, speaking evil of the Way before the congregation" (Acts 19:9), and Paul withdrew from the synagog to continue his teaching in the school of Tyrannus. He continued there for 2 years, and the conflict with Judaism proved to be a triumph for the Word of the Lord: "All the residents of Asia heard the word of the Lord, both Jews and Greeks." (Acts 19:10)

4 The second conflict generated by the Christ-centered will of Paul was the conflict with magic, for which Ephesus was notorious (Acts 19:11-20). The fact that "God did extraordinary miracles by the hands of Paul" (Acts 19:11) made the superstitious look upon Christianity as a new and more potent kind of magic; but the experience of the Jewish exorcists who sought to use the names of Jesus and Paul in their trade made it plain that Jesus is Lord in personal and august power, a Lord who can defend His name against misuse by those who deem Him a power which they can manipulate and employ. "The name of the Lord Jesus was extolled," and the conscience of believers was quickened—the line between magic and religion was sharply and critically drawn for them by this incident. They confessed their wrong and burned their infamous Ephesian books of charms and incantations, and "the word of the Lord grew and prevailed mightily" (Acts 19:20). The magical word by which men sought power grew impotent before the divine word.

5 The third and most dangerous conflict was the conflict with the commercialized state religion of Ephesus (Acts 19:23-41). The zeal of the silversmith Demetrius and his guild was something less than a purely religious fervor; but the fury of the guild members and of the huge, shouting city mob they aroused is nevertheless an illustration of the demonic power which Paul in his

First Letter to the Corinthians describes as at work in the worship of gods that are no gods (1 Co 10:19-20). The fury of that demonic power fell on Paul and the Christians of Ephesus; but the conflict led to a vindication of Paul and his followers, so that Paul could leave Ephesus with an unsullied reputation and with the respect of men like the Asiarchs and the town clerk (the most important city official of Ephesus). This was something Paul valued; soon after he left Ephesus he wrote the words: "We aim at what is honorable not only in the Lord's sight but also in the sight of men." (2 Co 8:21; cf. Cl 4:5-6)

6 Luke himself gives a hint that the Ephesian years were filled with difficulties and dangers beyond those noted by him in his account of those years. He records the words of Paul to the elders of Ephesus which speak of the trials that befell him through the plottings of the Jews (Acts 20:19), tells of the Jewish plot against Paul's life at Corinth a little later (Acts 20:3), and notes that the Jews of Asia were especially rancorous in their hatred of Paul (Acts 21:27). Paul's letters of this period further fill in the picture of this time as a period of perils. Paul speaks in First Corinthians of the fact that his great opportunity at Ephesus has as its cast shadow the presence of many adversaries (1 Co 16:9), and that he has "fought with beasts at Ephesus" (1 Co 15:32) — whether the expression is to be taken literally or, as is more probable, figuratively, it is a vivid expression of extreme peril. In the opening verses of Second Corinthians Paul gives thanks for an unlooked-for divine deliverance from desperate danger in the province of Asia (2 Co 1:8-10). And when he speaks in his Letter to the Romans of the fact that Aquila and Priscilla have risked their necks for him, he is probably referring to the Ephesian period also. (Ro 16:4)

7 Paul is no bloodless saint on a gold background. He held life dear just because he had committed it wholly to the Christ, and he hoped to live to see his Lord when He returned in glory (1 Co 15:51; 2 Co 5:1-5). While he was ready to sacrifice his life (Acts 20:24), he was not ready to waste it. And so he suffered in a genuinely human way. He feared in the face of perils and was racked by his fears. But in his human frailty, which he never denied but rather asserted (1 Co 2:3-4), he held in faith to the fact that all things that are and that happen

are from God the Father and are mediated by the Lord Jesus Christ, so that he saw in everything that befell him God's fatherly dealings with him and the Lordship of Christ exercised over him and through him (1 Co 8:6). He experienced again and again the truth of what his Lord had told him: "My grace is sufficient for you, for my power is made perfect in weakness" (2 Co 12:9). Thus a period marked by perils was for Paul also an exhilarating one; we see him in the letters of this period welcoming suffering as essential to the Christian life and a salutary part of it (Ro 5:3-5; 8:35-39) and boasting of his perils and afflictions as being the glory of his life as an apostle. He is employing high irony when he contrasts the assured complacency of the Corinthians with his own sorry and embattled existence (1 Co 4:8-13), and the only boast he really permits himself over against the boasting of his detractors in Corinth is a glorying in his sufferings (2 Co 11:23-33). He sees in the paradox of "dying, and behold we live" (2 Co 6:9) the apex of his apostolate.

8 It was a perilous period; it was also a strenuous one. The evangelization of Ephesus was also the evangelization of the province of Asia. Whether men like Epaphras, who brought the Gospel to Colossae in the interior, worked under the direct supervision of Paul or not cannot be made out; certainly he and others like him must have consulted Paul frequently in the course of their work, as Epaphras did later on when heresy threatened the inland cities (Cl 1:7-8; 4:12). The sending of Timothy and Erastus to Macedonia (Acts 19:22) indicates that the churches there, too, needed help. But Paul's dealings with his beloved, brilliant, and wayward child, the church of Corinth, give us the most vivid picture of what Paul meant when he spoke of the daily pressure of "anxiety for all the churches" (2 Co 11:28). If the growth of the Word of the Lord in this period meant conflict, if it meant "fighting without," it also meant for Paul an intense personal and pastoral anxiety; it meant "fear within." (2 Co 7:5)

9 The church of Corinth was a brilliantly endowed church, "enriched . . . with all speech and all knowledge . . . not lacking in any spiritual gift" (1 Co 1:5, 7). Corinth had had the benefit of a much longer ministry by Paul than any of the other Greek cities. Paul was the "father" of the Corinthian Christians: their life in Christ had

his unmistakable and ineradicable imprint on it. We can gauge from Acts and from Paul's letters what it meant to have Paul for a father, how rich a heritage this father gave his children. (Cf. 2 Co 12:14)

10   They had also had the benefit of the ministry of Apollos, the eloquent and fervent Alexandrian, powerful in the Scriptures (Acts 18:24). His coming to Corinth with letters of recommendation from Ephesus (Acts 18:27-28) apparently led to a renewed contact with the synagog in Corinth, which had previously broken with Paul (Acts 18:6-8): "He powerfully confuted the Jews *in public,* showing by the scriptures that the Christ was Jesus" (Acts 18:28). Perhaps it was Apollos who won for Christ the ruler of the synagog, Sosthenes, whom the crowd had beaten before the tribunal of Gallio (Acts 18:17). Paul includes Sosthenes with himself in the sending of his First Letter to the Corinthians (1 Co 1:1). If this Sosthenes is a Corinthian converted by Apollos, the fact that Paul thus singles him out is significant; Paul is telling the clique-ridden church of Corinth: Here is one who received the Gospel from Apollos and is one with me in all that I am telling you, just as Apollos himself is. (1 Co 3:5-9; 16:12)

11   At the time when Paul wrote his first letter there were in the Corinthian church those who said, "I belong to Cephas" (1 Co 1:12). They professed a special allegiance to Simon Peter, and they used the original Aramaic form of his official name (Cephas). This would indicate that they were Jews who had come to Corinth from one of the eastern Judaic churches which Peter had evangelized. The presence of these Christians from the fields where Peter had worked no doubt meant an enrichment of the church at Corinth; but it also created tensions. The various components of the young church — the original converts of Paul, the converts of Apollos, and the new arrivals from the east — could not as yet, or would not, unite in that free and richly various oneness which Paul described as essential to the life of the church (1 Co 12). Apollos himself had worked in complete harmony with Paul; no shadow of blame attached to him, as every mention of him in the first letter shows. But there were those, converts or admirers of Apollos, who compared this personable, energetic, and brilliant preacher with Paul and found him more to their liking than Paul, the bondman of God who had come to Corinth "in weakness and in much

fear and trembling" (1 Co 2:3), who candidly described himself as "unskilled in speaking" (2 Co 11:6), and preached the *crucified* Christ with single-minded insistence (1 Co 2:2). The new arrivals from the east, the Cephas people, quite naturally felt themselves to be the representatives of a maturer, more original kind of Christianity than that of the churches founded by Paul. They had received the Word from Peter, the "first" of the apostles, who had seen the Lord Jesus and had lived with Him; Paul was in their eyes an apostle of not quite equal rank with the Twelve, the child "untimely born" (1 Co 15:8), not really a full member of the apostolic brotherhood. They felt as charter members of an old, honorable club might feel toward newer members, who besides being new would not be members at all if *they* had not generously relaxed the rules a bit.

12   The church was full of tensions and ferment, and the church's outward situation did nothing to improve its inward state. This church lived in Corinth, where all the brilliance of the Greek mind and all the vagaries of the Greek will mingled with an influx of Oriental religiosity to produce a moral climate which even the Greeks found singularly vicious.

13   The Corinthian church had, moreover, never been tried, refined, and unified by persecution. The policy of noninterference which the Roman proconsul Gallio had enunciated to the Jews (Acts 18:14-16) apparently remained in force with his successors, and while the church no doubt had to endure the social pressures and animosities which any consistent opposition to the prevailing culture and religiosity evoked, it was safe from Jewish vindictiveness and governmental coercion. The Christians of Corinth waited for the "revealing of our Lord Jesus Christ" (1 Co 1:7), but they were tempted more than other churches to make themselves comfortable and at home in the world while they waited. They enjoyed security, and they had leisure to speculate about the implications of the Gospel, since they were not called on to affirm the Gospel in action in the face of persecution.

14   Such was the climate of the church life in Corinth. All that was potentially harmful and disruptive in it was crystallized and intensified by the emergence of a fourth group in the congregation. Since Paul never fully describes this group, it is difficult to get a clear picture of these people, and some-

times it is impossible to see where the line between them and the Cephas people, for instance, is being drawn. But the following would seem to be a fair characterization of them: They came from outside the Corinthian church. Paul distinguishes them from those who professed allegiance to himself or to Apollos, the men who had worked at Corinth (1 Co 1:12). His words in 2 Co 11:4 explicitly mark this group as new arrivals in Corinth: "If some one *comes* and preaches another Jesus than the one we preached . . . ." Paul's contemptuous reference in 2 Co 3:1 to "some" who need letters of recommendation makes it probable that they came with such letters from one of the eastern churches (which need not imply that any of the eastern churches was necessarily responsible for the teaching which they developed at Corinth). They were Judaic and proud of it, Hebrews, Israelites, descendants of Abraham (2 Co 11:22). But they were not Judaizers of the sort that had disturbed the churches of Galatia; we hear nothing of circumcision and the reimposition of the Mosaic law in connection with these men. One can imagine that they claimed to be the inheritors of the true Judaic-Christian tradition and for that reason felt themselves uniquely qualified to lead the church beyond the first stages of that tradition into the full riches of knowledge and freedom in Christ.

15 What they brought into Corinth was a brilliant and persuasive kind of liberalism which operated (as liberalism characteristically does) with genuinely Christian slogans and catchwords. If, according to Paul, they preached "another Jesus," *they* no doubt claimed that they were preaching the genuine Jesus; if they proclaimed a "different gospel" and had and imparted a "different spirit," it was Paul who said so, not they; they claimed that their gospel was the true Gospel and their spirit the true Spirit of God (2 Co 11:4). The slogan which they brought with them (or developed in the course of their activities at Corinth) was as Christian as a slogan can be: "I belong to Christ" (1 Co 1:12; 2 Co 10:7). Paul himself uses the phrase to designate the Christian. (1 Co 3:23; cf. Ro 8:9)

16 They exalted the Christ and awaited His return; they treasured His gift of the Spirit and set great store by the gifts given by the Spirit (2 Co 11:4; cf. 1 Co 7:40). But they exalted the Christ as the Giver of knowledge and treasured the gifts of the Spirit

primarily as a means to knowledge of God, as the way to wisdom (1 Co 3:18-20; 8:1-3, 10, 11; 13:9). And this knowledge, they claimed, made them free; the knowledge and wisdom they possessed carried them beyond any previous revelation of God, beyond the Old Testament Scriptures, beyond anything contained in the apostolic Word. Before this ultimate knowledge of God, which they claimed to possess, all previous standards became meaningless, all former ties were dissolved, all the old taboos were gone: "All things are lawful for me"—that was their boast (1 Co 6:12; 10:23). It was an intellectually appealing and an intoxicating message they brought; it is not surprising that they attracted followers and deeply influenced the whole church.

17 Their deep influence on the life of the church was also harmful in the extreme. We can trace its beginnings in Paul's reference to a letter (now lost) which he had written to the Corinthians before our present first letter (1 Co 5:9). In that earlier letter Paul had demanded of the Corinthians that they refuse to have fellowship with "immoral men." This demand was questioned by the church, perhaps even rejected as being unclear and impracticable. (1 Co 5:9-11)

18 Perhaps it was "Chloe's people" (1 Co 1:11) who delivered Paul's earlier letter to Corinth; they would then have seen and could report to Paul how it was received, how the church broke up into factions over the issues involved (1 Co 1—4). It was probably they who reported to Paul the conditions which resulted from this new proclamation of absolute liberty at Corinth; they could tell Paul why his letter was questioned and contradicted: the new teachers were saying that the new knowledge set men free, and at least one Corinthian Christian had drastically used that liberty (1 Co 5:1): Why should not a man be free to "live with" his father's wife (probably his stepmother) after his father's death? What the Old Testament said no longer bound him (Dt 22:30; 27:20), and the authority of Jesus and His apostles had been superseded by the new revelation of the Spirit. The Corinthian church as a whole not only tolerated this immorality but was even "arrogant" about it (1 Co 5:2); these men felt that they were demonstrating their spiritual maturity in tolerating it. The people of Chloe could tell Paul, too, of the breakdown of discipline in the church, how differences between Christian brethren

were no longer being settled in the church but were being taken to pagan courts; the preachers of the new freedom had no interest in or taste for the serious and painful business of keeping the church pure by calling erring brethren to repentance (1 Co 6:1-11). Paul has to hammer home the most elementary moral facts in his attempt to pierce the complacency of the people intoxicated by the new freedom. (1 Co 6:9-11)

19 The new liberty preached in Corinth conceded to the Christian man the freedom to associate with prostitutes. The law which demanded sexual purity of them was being put on the same level with the law concerning clean and unclean foods (1 Co 6:12-20) — or at least the satisfaction of sexual desire was being put on the same level with the satisfaction of hunger (1 Co 6:13). The fact that the Apostolic Council had expressly laid the abstaining from immorality on the consciences of the Gentile Christians made no impression in Corinth. (Acts 15:29)

20 Not everyone at Corinth was so completely swept away by the eloquent rationalism of the new teachers or so deeply intoxicated by the liberty they offered that he asked no questions or raised no objections. Men like Stephanas (1 Co 16:15) and Fortunatus and Achaicus (1 Co 16:17) saw that it was high time that Paul be consulted explicitly and at length on the questions raised by the new theology of knowledge and freedom, and they saw to it that he was consulted. The congregation wrote Paul a letter (1 Co 7:1) and laid before him a series of questions on points where it was becoming evident that the teaching of the new teachers was not only different from Paul's but was contradicting it.

21 The first question concerned marriage (1 Co 7). The form that Paul's answer to their question takes makes it tolerably clear what direction the new teachers were taking here. Pursuing their ideal of religious self-fulfillment, they saw in marriage merely an impediment to the religious life and were intent on making the church an association of celibates without regard for the moral dangers involved in this mass imposition of celibacy, without regard for the authority of the Lord Jesus, who had blessed little children and had declared the bond which united man and woman to be inviolable (Mt 19:3-9, 13-15) and made celibacy a gift reserved for those "to whom it is given" (Mt 19:11). They were running counter to the thinking and practice of the apostles also, for the apostles saw in the family and all natural orders primarily vehicles which the grace of God might employ — "You will be saved, *you and your household*," Paul told the jailer at Philippi (Acts 16:31). But the new teachers not only sought to keep men and women from marriage (the passage on the "unmarried" and the "betrothed" takes cognizance of this, 1 Co 7:25-38); they also apparently permitted men and women to free themselves of their spouses, especially pagan spouses, in order to be "free for the Lord," again in contradiction to the express command of Jesus (1 Co 7:10-11). Perhaps the license which they conceded with regard to association with harlots (1 Co 6:12-20) is connected with this attitude toward marriage: If a man could not be continent and yet wished to be free of the impediment of marriage, the association with the harlot would be a solution, since "all things are lawful for me." (1 Co 6:12)

22 To the question, "May a Christian eat food that has been offered as a sacrifice to idols?" (1 Co 8 — 10), the new teachers had a ready and simple answer: "All of us possess knowledge" (1 Co 8:1), which meant, since knowledge gives liberty, that "all things are lawful," including the sacrificial meats consecrated to idols. In their self-centered piety, puffed up as they were by knowledge, they did not consider what harm their freedom might do to the brother whose knowledge was not yet deep and firm enough to make him capable of exercising such freedom. In their complacent self-assurance they did not pause to consider that demonic powers are at work behind all false worship of false gods, though the gods themselves are nothing. They disregarded the warning example of Israel recorded for them in the Old Testament. They flouted the example of the apostles, whose knowledge was as great as theirs, whose wisdom was more profound and certainly more sober and realistic than theirs. Paul has to remind the Corinthians: "Be imitators of me, as I am of Christ." (1 Co 11:1)

23 But it was not only in the family and in private life that the intoxication of the new liberty was working mischief; it infected the worship life of the church too (1 Co 11 — 14). Women were asserting their newfound liberty by appearing at worship without the veil, which was the badge of their womanliness and their recognition of the place God the Creator and Redeemer

(1 Co 11:3, 8) had assigned to them (1 Co 11:2-16). They were also adding to the confusion of an already chaotic public worship by an unwomanly assumption of a teaching authority which neither Jesus nor the apostles had given them (1 Co 14:33-36). But the voice of Jesus, the voice of His apostles, the practice of the churches of God (1 Co 11:16) did not deter the proponents and adherents of the new liberty; they were "disposed to be contentious" nevertheless.

24   This spirit of rampant individualism made the common fellowship meals of the church a scene of feasting and carousing in which the rich disregarded the poor and made of the Lord's Supper, celebrated in connection with the common meal, anything but the *Lord's* Supper. The Supper which commemorated and made effectively present the utter self-giving and self-sacrifice of the Lord Jesus Christ and was designed to unite the Lord's people in the eating of the one loaf and the partaking of the one cup became the scene and the means of man's self-assertion and of division (1 Co 11:17-34). When knowledge is the capstone of the religious structure and love no longer rules (1 Co 13), decency and order are sacrificed, edification is no longer possible, the salutary commands of the apostle are disregarded (1 Co 14:37-38), and the example of the churches of God everywhere means nothing. (1 Co 14:36)

25   All that characterizes the "Christ-men" appears in a concentrated and a peculiarly clear form in their denial of the bodily resurrection of the dead (1 Co 15)—their false spirituality, which disregarded and degraded the body and all things natural; their false conception of knowledge, which made them manipulators of ideas; who could disregard the central fact of all history, the bodily resurrection of Jesus Christ from the dead; their false conception of freedom, which moved them to oppose themselves and their ideas not only to Paul but to all the apostles and to the Old Testament witness to Christ as well. In their intoxication of liberty (Paul has to tell them to come to their right mind, to sober up, 1 Co 15:34) they felt free to sacrifice the central fact of the apostolic proclamation to Greek prejudice—to the Greek the idea of a bodily resurrection was particularly offensive, as the reaction of the Stoics and Epicureans at Athens to Paul's preaching of the resurrection shows. (Acts 17:32)

26   It has become abundantly clear by now that when these men said, "We belong to Christ," they were saying it in an exclusive sense, as a fighting slogan. The liberty which their "knowledge" gave them, their "freedom" in the Spirit, necessarily involved a break with the authority of Paul, who had planted the Word in Corinth; there is some evidence to indicate that they considered Paul superseded and unnecessary to the church at Corinth and claimed that he would not come to Corinth again; Paul's words in 1 Co 4:18-19 hint as much: "Some are arrogant, as though I were not coming to you. But I will come to you soon, if the Lord wills, and I will find out not the talk of these arrogant people but their power." A break with Paul necessarily meant a break with Apollos, who had watered where Paul had planted; and it meant a break with all apostolic authority. Paul's words concerning their arrogance (1 Co 4:18-19) and their contentiousness (1 Co 11:16; 14:38) seem to indicate that they were highly autocratic and contemptuous of any power but their own, a fact confirmed by the bitter irony of Paul's reproach to the Corinthians in 2 Co 11:20-21: "You bear it if a man makes slaves of you, or preys upon you, or takes advantage of you, or puts on airs, or strikes you in the face." They and those who were most completely taken in by them thus constituted a clique in the church; and as a clique produces more cliques by way of reaction, there ensued that sorry and divided state of the church which Paul deals with so powerfully in the first four chapters of his first letter. At Corinth the line between the church (where Christ alone is Lord) and the world (where *men* head movements and command loyalties) was being perilously blurred.

27   Our present first letter is Paul's response to this situation, as he had learned it from Chloe's people, from Stephanas, Fortunatus, and Achaicus, and from the letter of the Corinthian church. If all the problems at Corinth have a common root, all Paul's responses to the various derangements and sins in the church also have a common denominator. The first letter, for all its variety, is one unified answer, one brilliant demonstration of how a genuinely apostolic authority makes itself felt. And the common denominator, the unifying power, is the cross of Jesus Christ seen in its full significance by the light of the resurrection.

28   Paul operates with the slogans of the new leaders, but by relating them all to the cross he gives them a radically different content. If they extolled the Christ as the Giver of knowledge and freedom, Paul exalts Him as the Lord of glory who was crucified by the rulers of this world. If they empty the cross of its power (1 Co 1:17), he is resolved to know nothing but the cross (1 Co 2:2); and he sets the cross squarely in the center of the church again, the cross which with its pure and all-inclusive grace lays a total claim on man, body and soul, for a life lived wholly to God (1 Co 6:19-20). The cross, which pronounces an annihilating judgment on all human greatness and on all human pretenses to wisdom, cuts off all boasting of man and marks as monstrous and unnatural any clustering about great men in schools and factions that give their loyalty to men rather than to Christ.

29   If they boast of possessing the Spirit and foster a spirituality which disregards the body and feeds the religious ego, Paul interprets the Spirit by the cross, by that event in history in which the Son of God suffered in the flesh for men in the flesh, that event in which God spoke His unmistakable yea to the body which He had created. Paul proclaims a Spirit who dwells in the human body and lays a consecrating claim on it (1 Co 6:19). He proclaims a Spirit who enables men to say that *Jesus* is Lord (that is, Jesus the Crucified whom the Jews call the Accursed because He hung on the tree, 1 Co 12:3, cf. Gl 3:13), a Spirit who gives gifts to the church "for the common good" (1 Co 12:7), whose highest gift is the love which does not seek its own. (1 Co 13)

30   If they boast a knowledge which makes them "wise in this age" (1 Co 3:18), a knowledge which puffs men up (1 Co 8:1) and makes them boast of men and creates cliques clustered about men, Paul proclaims the offensive wisdom of the cross (1 Co 2:6-13), which brings man low, both Jew and Greek, and makes him glory in the Lord alone. Paul proclaims a whole and unabridged grace of God, the grace of the cross, and that grace gives a knowledge which is not primarily *man's* knowing at all, but man's being known by God; it means that a man has a knowledge that matters when God knows him (that is, loves, chooses, and calls him), and man is thus enabled to love God. (1 Co 8:1-3)

31   If they have and exercise a freedom which overrides all authority, exalts the self of man, and disregards the brother, Paul proclaims the freedom of the Christian man, who is lord of all things because he is the Christ's (1 Co 3:21-22) and in this his freedom comes under the law of Christ and enslaves himself to all men in order that he may by all means save some (1 Co 9:21-22). Paul knows freedom as freedom from sin and self, a being set free for ministry to one's fellowman.

32   These are the basic convictions underlying Paul's full and many-sided treatment of all the questions posed by the situation in Corinth. No outline of the letter can do justice to it. The following may suffice to indicate the scope of the letter.

OUTLINE

CORINTHIANS

Factions in the Church

1:1 — 4:21

INTRODUCTION: GREETINGS AND THANKSGIVING (1:1-9)

1 Paul, called by the will of God to be an apostle of Christ Jesus, and our brother Sos'the·nes,

2 To the church of God which is at Corinth, to those sanctified in Christ Jesus, called to be saints together with all those who in every place call on the name of our Lord Jesus Christ, both their Lord and ours:

3 Grace to you and peace from God our Father and the Lord Jesus Christ.

4 I give thanks to God[a] always for you because of the grace of God which was given you in Christ Jesus, 5 that in every way you were enriched in him with all speech and all knowledge—6 even as the testimony to Christ was confirmed among you— 7 so that you are not lacking in any spiritual gift, as you wait for the revealing of our Lord Jesus Christ; 8 who will sustain you to the end, guiltless in the day of our Lord Jesus Christ. 9 God is faithful, by whom you were called into the fellowship of his Son, Jesus Christ our Lord.

THE FOLLY OF DISSENSIONS (1:10-17)

10 I appeal to you, brethren, by the name of our Lord Jesus Christ, that all of you agree and that there be no dissensions among you, but that you be united in the same mind and the same judgment. 11 For it has been reported to me by Chloe's people that there is quarreling among you, my brethren. 12 What I mean is that each one of

[a] Other ancient authorities read *my God*

1:1 — 4:21 The Gospel of the Crucified is the opposite of that wisdom of this world which fosters human greatness and creates factions centering in men. The cross of Christ destroys all human greatness. If men in the Corinthian church seek "wisdom" and create factions, Paul seeks the unity of the church by subjecting all men to the Crucified and decries all parties, including the one called after himself.

1:1-9 The salutation (1-3) follows ancient epistolary practice but has been made thoroughly Christian in all three of its members (sender— recipients—greeting). The sender Paul identifies himself as *called* and authorized messenger of Christ Jesus; the recipients are characterized as *called to be saints*, separated and sanctified members of God's one holy people; and the greeting invokes on the readers the characteristically NT blessings of God's undeserved, effective favor *(grace)* and that well-being and wholeness which God's favor creates *(peace)*.

1:1 *Sosthenes.* Former ruler of the synagog at Corinth (Acts 18:17), probably converted by Apollos. Cf. Introduction, par. 10.

1:1-2 *Called . . . to be an apostle . . . called to be saints.* The parallelism is significant; Paul is already calling on the Corinthians to be "imitators" of himself. (4:16; 11:1)

1:2 *Saints together with all,* etc. Paul even here is warning his readers against that opinionated individualism he so stingingly rebukes in 14:36.

1:4-9 The customary thanksgiving dwells on the richness of the church's endowment. To some this has seemed like a hollow compliment in view of the sorry state of the church as revealed in the following chapters. But Paul is not complimenting the church; he is thanking God, the reality of whose gracious gifts is not made doubtful by the fact that some of the recipients have misused them. *God is faithful,* Paul is saying—"have you been faithful?" (9)

1:7 *Revealing of . . . Jesus Christ,* on the Last Day. (Cf. Cl 3:4)

1:10-17 God who is faithful has called men "into the fellowship of his Son Jesus Christ OUR Lord" (9). To Him all are subject (as all have been baptized in His name); even the greatest and most brilliant are servants (cf. 3:5). To make little gods of human leaders is to call in question the unique Lordship of the Crucified, to forget what baptism in His name signifies (commitment to Him, incorporation in Him, cf. 12:12-13), to lose sight of the true nature of the *gospel* as *power.*

1:11 *Chloe's people.* Cf. Introduction, par. 18.

1:12 For the factions in Corinth cf. Introduction, pars. 9-19.

you says, "I belong to Paul," or "I belong to A·pol′los," or "I belong to Cephas," or "I belong to Christ." 13 Is Christ divided? Was Paul crucified for you? Or were you baptized in the name of Paul? 14 I am thankful[b] that I baptized none of you except Crispus and Gaius; 15 lest any one should say that you were baptized in my name. 16 (I did baptize also the household of Steph′a·nas. Beyond that, I do not know whether I baptized any one else.) 17 For Christ did not send me to baptize but to preach the gospel, and not with eloquent wisdom, lest the cross of Christ be emptied of its power.

THE WORD OF THE CROSS AS THE POWER OF GOD (1:18 — 2:5)

18 For the word of the cross is folly to those who are perishing, but to us who are being saved it is the power of God. 19 For it is written,
    "I will destroy the wisdom of the wise,
      and the cleverness of the clever I will thwart."
20 Where is the wise man? Where is the scribe? Where is the debater of this age? Has not God made foolish the wisdom of the world? 21 For since, in the wisdom of God, the world did not know God through wisdom, it pleased God through the folly of what we preach to save those who believe. 22 For Jews demand signs and Greeks seek wisdom, 23 but we preach Christ crucified, a stumbling block to Jews and folly to Gentiles, 24 but to those who are called, both Jews and Greeks, Christ the power of God and the wisdom of God. 25 For the foolishness of God is wiser than men, and the weakness of God is stronger than men.

26 For consider your call, brethren; not many of you were wise according to worldly standards, not many were powerful, not many were of noble birth; 27 but God chose what is foolish in the world to shame the wise, God chose what is weak in the world to shame the strong, 28 God chose what is low and despised in the world, even things that are not, to bring to nothing things that are, 29 so that no human being might boast in the presence of God. 30 He is the source of your life in Christ Jesus, whom God made our wisdom, our righteousness and sanctification and redemption; 31 therefore, as it is written, "Let him who boasts, boast of the Lord."

2 When I came to you, brethren, I did not come proclaiming to you the testimony[c] of God in lofty words or wisdom. 2 For I decided to know nothing among you except Jesus Christ and him crucified. 3And I was with you in weakness and in much fear and trembling; 4 and my speech and my message were not in plausible words of wisdom, but in demonstration of the Spirit and of power, 5 that your faith might not rest in the wisdom of men but in the power of God.

[b] Other ancient authorities read *I thank God*   [c] Other ancient authorities read *myster* (or *secret*)

1:13 *Crucified . . . baptized.* For the connection between Christ's death and baptism in His name cf. Ro 6:3-4.

1:14 Paul's irony is not intended to depreciate Baptism, on which he sets the highest value (cf., e.g., 6:11, "washed"; 12:12-13; Ro 6:1-11). Rather, it (like the reference to the Crucified in 13) draws attention away from Paul to his Lord. For the practice of leaving the act of baptism to subordinates of the apostle cf. Acts 10:48.

Crispus. Leader of the synagog in Corinth, converted by Paul. (Acts 18:8)

Gaius. Cf. Ro 16:23. Whether he is to be identified with the Gaius of Acts 19:29 and 20:4 is doubtful.

1:17 *Eloquent* [human] *wisdom* empties the cross of its power because it substitutes an attainment of man (his system persuasively reasoned and rationally accepted) for God's mighty act of deliverance.

1:18 — 2:5 The cross of Christ (17) and the *word of the cross* are God's action for us men and for our salvation (cf. 2 Co 5:18-19); therefore both are

the power of God (cf. Ro 1:16-17). This power is not recognized and known by a critical examination of it but by being *saved* and being *called* by it (18, 24). Its divine character is made manifest by the very fact that it does not meet the expectations and demands of men, neither of the *Jews,* who expect to be overwhelmed into salvation by *signs* which make repentance and faith unnecessary, nor by the *Greeks,* who expect to be reasoned and argued into a salvation that they find rationally acceptable (22-23). The Gospel is not "according to man" (Gl 1:11). A man would have made a beginning in Corinth with converts of another kind (1:26-31); God worked in sovereign freedom when He called Corinthians. He worked as only God can work, creatively (*chose . . . things that are not,* 28; *he is the source of your life,* 30). A man would have chosen a messenger of another kind (2:1-5), not a Paul with his *weakness . . . fear and trembling* (2:3) and his lack of *plausible words of wisdom* (2:4). God's work of rescue has excluded all self-assertion of man (*boast* 29, 31; cf. Ro 3:27) and has

THE WORD OF THE CROSS AS THE WISDOM OF GOD (2:6-16)

6 Yet among the mature we do impart wisdom, although it is not a wisdom of this age or of the rulers of this age, who are doomed to pass away. 7 But we impart a secret and hidden wisdom of God, which God decreed before the ages for our glorification. 8 None of the rulers of this age understood this; for if they had, they would not have crucified the Lord of glory. 9 But, as it is written,

"What no eye has seen, nor ear heard,
nor the heart of man conceived,
what God has prepared for those who love him,"

10 God has revealed to us through the Spirit. For the Spirit searches everything, even the depths of God. 11 For what person knows a man's thoughts except the spirit of the man which is in him? So also no one comprehends the thoughts of God except the Spirit of God. 12 Now we have received not the spirit of the world, but the Spirit which is from God, that we might understand the gifts bestowed on us by God. 13And we impart this in words not taught by human wisdom but taught by the Spirit, interpreting spiritual truths to those who possess the Spirit.*d*

14 The unspiritual*e* man does not receive the gifts of the Spirit of God, for they are folly to him, and he is not able to understand them because they are spiritually discerned. 15 The spiritual man judges all things, but is himself to be judged by no one. 16 "For who has known the mind of the Lord so as to instruct him?" But we have the mind of Christ.

GOD'S WORD AND GOD'S SERVANTS (3:1 — 4:7)

3 But I, brethren, could not address you as spiritual men, but as men of the flesh, as babes in Christ. 2 I fed you with milk, not solid food; for you were not ready

d Or *interpreting spiritual truths in spiritual language;* or *comparing spiritual things with spiritual*
e Or *natural*

made men's *faith . . . rest* in Him who alone can be its resting place. (2:5)

1:19 Cf. Is 29:14; Ps 33:10.

1:21 *World did not know God through wisdom,* the wisdom, namely, of God manifested in His creation, which men beheld and "knew" and yet refused to thank and glorify the wise Creator (Ro 1:19-23). For the connection between wisdom and creation in Biblical thought cf. Jb 28:20-28; Pr 8:1, 22-31.

1:22 *Jews* and *Greeks* represent mankind, especially mankind at its "best," the religiously favored and the intellectual elite.

Jews demand signs. Cf. Mt 12:38; 16:1; Jn 4:48; 6:30.

Greeks seek wisdom. Cf. Acts 17:20-21, 31-32; when Paul speaks of God's judgment and the resurrection of Jesus, the Greeks are no longer interested.

1:24 *Called.* For the effectual call of God cf. 1:1-2 and Ro 8:28-30. *Wisdom* (cf. 30) points forward to the theme developed in 2:6 ff. (the Gospel as the wisdom of God).

1:28 *Things that are not.* Cf. Ro 4:17.

1:31 *Let him who boasts.* Cf. Jer 9:23-24.

2:2 *And him crucified.* Cf. Introduction, pars. 27 and 28.

2:4 *Spirit.* Cf. 3:12-13.

2:6-16 The Word of the cross is also a word of *wisdom* (cf. 1:24, 30); indeed it is the only wisdom which gives God's answer to man's predicament and makes final, perfect sense. But only the *mature* (6) can recognize it as such, that is, only those who have experienced its saving power as God's call

(1:18, 24). They are those who have accepted the *gifts bestowed* by God (12), who *love him* for His inexpressible favors (9). They have parted ways forever with the *wisdom of this age* and *of the rulers of this age* (6, 8); they in their self-seeking drive have no understanding for God's gracious purposes and collide with them — the rulers of this age *crucified the Lord of glory* (8). For them God's loving wisdom remains a *secret and hidden* thing (7). To those who have experienced the love of God and have responded to His love, He reveals His wisdom *through the Spirit* (10). The Spirit is God's valid (10-11) and only (14) Interpreter. By the power of the Spirit man can leave this age and enter into the new world of God (cf. Heb 6:4-5) where he is free and independent of all the judgments of this age (15); the *mind of Christ,* no less, is his. (16)

2:6 *Rulers of this age . . . doomed to pass away.* The new world of God, prepared by His self-giving love, will pass judgment on and destroy all self-seeking (Mt 20:25) powers. (Cf. 13:8, 13)

2:7 *Decreed . . . glorification.* Cf. Ro 8:28-30.

2:9 *It is written.* No such passage is found in our OT. For the thought in the OT cf. Is 52:13; 64:4; 65:17.

2:13 *Interpreting,* etc. The first alternative reading given in RSV note *d* ("interpreting spiritual truths in spiritual language") seems to fit the context better.

2:16 Cf. Is 40:13. The passage 40:1-31 is a mighty hymn on God's sovereign power in the service of His saving love.

3:1 — 4:7 Now that Paul has made clear the

for it; and even yet you are not ready, 3 for you are still of the flesh. For while there is jealousy and strife among you, are you not of the flesh, and behaving like ordinary men? 4 For when one says, "I belong to Paul," and another, "I belong to A·pol′los," are you not merely men?

5 What then is A·pol′los? What is Paul? Servants through whom you believed, as the Lord assigned to each. 6 I planted, A·pol′los watered, but God gave the growth. 7 So neither he who plants nor he who waters is anything, but only God who gives the growth. 8 He who plants and he who waters are equal, and each shall receive his wages according to his labor. 9 For we are God's fellow workers; you are God's field, God's building.

10 According to the grace of God given to me, like a skilled master builder I laid a foundation, and another man is building upon it. Let each man take care how he builds upon it. 11 For no other foundation can any one lay than that which is laid, which is Jesus Christ. 12 Now if any one builds on the foundation with gold, silver, precious stones, wood, hay, straw— 13 each man's work will become manifest; for the Day will disclose it, because it will be revealed with fire, and the fire will test what sort of work each one has done. 14 If the work which any man has built on the foundation survives, he will receive a reward. 15 If any man's work is burned up, he will suffer loss, though he himself will be saved, but only as through fire.

16 Do you not know that you are God's temple and that God's Spirit dwells in you? 17 If any one destroys God's temple, God will destroy him. For God's temple is holy, and that temple you are.

18 Let no one deceive himself. If any one among you thinks that he is wise in this age, let him become a fool that he may become wise. 19 For the wisdom of this world is folly with God. For it is written, "He catches the wise in their craftiness," 20 and again, "The Lord knows that the thoughts of the wise are futile." 21 So let no one boast of men. For all things are yours, 22 whether Paul or A·pol′los or Cephas or the world or life or death or the present or the future, all are yours; 23 and you are Christ's; and Christ is God's.

---

nature of the Gospel as the power and wisdom of God, he can hope to be understood when he speaks of the place and function of men as proclaimers of that wise and potent Word. Men such as *Paul* and *Apollos* cannot be heads of rival cliques (3:3-4), as the Corinthians would have them be; they are merely *servants* (3:5; 4:1) *God's fellow workers* (3:9), planters and waterers for Him who creatively *gives the growth* (3:6, 9); they are merely *stewards of the mysteries of God,* accountable to God for their stewardship (4:1-5; cf. 3:12-15). The church which they found and foster is not theirs but God's —*God's field, God's building* (3:9), *God's temple* indwelt by *God's Spirit* (3:16-17). If the Corinthians really want to be what they claim to be, *spiritual men,* and no longer *babes in Christ* (3:1), no longer *men of the flesh, ordinary men, merely men* trapped in the wisdom of this age (3:1-4), they must learn so to regard these proclaimers and themselves. They dare not make Paul or Apollos the ultimate focus of their loyalties (3:4), the ground of their boasting, and the occasion of their conceited rivalries (3:21; 4:6). They do not *belong* to Paul or Apollos (3:4); these men are part of God's great gift to them and they are bap-tized in His name (2:7-8; 1:13), they *are Christ's* and so belong to God (3:23). Thus they may learn . . . *not to go beyond what is written,* that Word of God which exalts God and silences the pre-

tensions of men. (Cf. the quotations from the OT at 1:19, 31; 2:9, 16; 3:19-20)

3:1 *Men of the flesh. Flesh* designates man in his natural state of alienation from and enmity against God (Ro 8:5-8; note the antithesis to "Spirit"), incapable of communion with God as "unspiritual man" (2:14). Cf. "ordinary men" (3), "merely men" (4). Paul is raising the question whether the Corinthians may not have received the grace of God in vain.

3:13 *Day . . . fire.* The Day is the Day of Judg-ment; fire is a common symbol of God's judgment, which *will test* the *work done* by the proclaimers of the Word. For God's judgment as a consuming fire cf., e.g., Ml 3:2; 4:1; Mt 3:11-12.

3:15 *Saved . . . only as through fire.* Even the careless workman is not excluded from the for-giving compassion of God. But Paul repeats his warning ("Let each man take care how he builds," 10) in the sternest terms; the careless workman is playing with an eternal fire. For the expression cf. Zch 3:2; Jude 23.

3:16-17 *God's temple.* Cf. 6:19; 2 Co 6:16. God's temple, the church, is being destroyed when men substitute the wisdom of this age for the folly of the cross. (18-20)

3:19-20 *It is written.* Jb 5:13; Ps 94:11.

3:21 *All things are yours.* Cf. Ro 8:32, 37-39.

3:23 *You are Christ's,* who has bought you "with a price" (6:20; 7:23; cf. Acts 20:28). Paul is giving

4 This is how one should regard us, as servants of Christ and stewards of the mysteries of God. 2 Moreover it is required of stewards that they be found trustworthy. 3 But with me it is a very small thing that I should be judged by you or by any human court. I do not even judge myself. 4 I am not aware of anything against myself, but I am not thereby acquitted. It is the Lord who judges me. 5 Therefore do not pronounce judgment before the time, before the Lord comes, who will bring to light the things now hidden in darkness and will disclose the purposes of the heart. Then every man will receive his commendation from God.

6 I have applied all this to myself and A·pol'los for your benefit, brethren, that you may learn by us not to go beyond what is written, that none of you may be puffed up in favor of one against another. 7 For who sees anything different in you? What have you that you did not receive? If then you received it, why do you boast as if it were not a gift?

BE IMITATORS OF ME (4:8-21)

8 Already you are filled! Already you have become rich! Without us you have become kings! And would that you did reign, so that we might share the rule with you! 9 For I think that God has exhibited us apostles as last of all, like men sentenced to death; because we have become a spectacle to the world, to angels and to men. 10 We are fools for Christ's sake, but you are wise in Christ. We are weak, but you are strong. You are held in honor, but we in disrepute. 11 To the present hour we hunger and thirst, we are ill-clad and buffeted and homeless, 12 and we labor, working with our own hands. When reviled, we bless; when persecuted, we endure; 13 when slandered, we try to conciliate; we have become, and are now, as the refuse of the world, the offscouring of all things.

14 I do not write this to make you ashamed, but to admonish you as my beloved children. 15 For though you have countless guides in Christ, you do not have many fathers. For I became your father in Christ Jesus through the gospel. 16 I urge you, then, be imitators of me. 17 Therefore I sent*g* to you Timothy, my beloved and faithful child in the Lord, to remind you of my ways in Christ, as I teach them everywhere

g Or *am sending*

the party slogan "I belong to Christ" (1:12; cf. Introduction, pars. 14-15) its true meaning by referring it to Christ crucified.

Christ is God's. God has given "all authority in heaven and on earth" (Mt 28:18; cf. 11:27) to His anointed King, His obedient Son. (Cf. 15:27-28)

4:3 *Judged by you or by any human court.* Cf. 2:15. As a spiritual man (7:40) Paul cannot submit to any judgment based on the standards of the wisdom of this age, such as the Corinthians have passed on him and Apollos. (3:4; 4:6)

4:7 *Who sees anything different in you?* Better, "Who distinguishes you," that is, marks *you* (singular, "any one of you") out as something special? You all have *received* apostles and teachers as gifts from the ascended Christ (Eph 4:7-12); you cannot therefore boast of any one of them as your private claim to distinction.

4:8-21 Paul, "called . . . to be an apostle of Christ Jesus" (1:1), goes the way of Jesus the Crucified, the way which the wise in this age reject as folly (10; cf. Mt 11:25), the way of weakness, deprivation, dishonor, and death, losing his life for Christ's sake in order to find it in Him (cf. Mt 16:25). With biting irony he indicts the Corinthians, men "called to be saints" (1:2), for leaving the way of their sainthood—Jesus' beatitudes upon the poor, hungry, and persecuted no longer apply to them (cf. Mt 5:3, 6, 10). In their arrogance they are no longer the meek to whom Jesus promised the earth

as their inheritance (Mt 5:5), no longer imitators of their meek apostle (12-13) and *father in Christ Jesus* (15). Paul points to their underlying disease, of which their factions are a symptom; they have left the cross behind them in pursuing the mirage of wisdom and power. In calling on them to be *imitators* of himself (16), he is, for all his bitter language, summoning them back as his *beloved children* (14) to the one and enduring source of wisdom and power and life, to the *gospel* (15). *Timothy's* mission to them is to reinforce the apostle's plea that they become once more the "apostolic" church.

4:9 *Last of all . . . men sentenced . . . spectacle to the world.* Paul seems to envision a sort of procession of doomed men, of which the apostles are the last and saddest lot. The whole world, both *angels and men,* looks uncomprehendingly on their sufferings.

4:13 *Refuse . . . offscouring* are words of abuse expressing profound contempt.

4:15 *Father . . . through the gospel.* Cf. 1:30; Phmn 10.

4:16 *Imitators.* Imitation involves acceptance of the apostolic Word and submission to apostolic authority as well as emulation. (Cf. 11:1; Ph 3:17; 1 Th 1:6; 2 Th 3:7, 9)

4:17 *Timothy.* Cf. 16:10.

Ways, Paul's proclamation and instruction. For *way* in this sense cf. Ps 25:4-5.

in every church. 18 Some are arrogant, as though I were not coming to you. 19 But I will come to you soon, if the Lord wills, and I will find out not the talk of these arrogant people but their power. 20 For the kingdom of God does not consist in talk but in power. 21 What do you wish? Shall I come to you with a rod, or with love in a spirit of gentleness?

Moral Problems

5:1 — 6:20

INCEST (5:1-13)

5 It is actually reported that there is immorality among you, and of a kind that is not found even among pagans; for a man is living with his father's wife. 2And you are arrogant! Ought you not rather to mourn? Let him who has done this be removed from among you.

3 For though absent in body I am present in spirit, and as if present, I have already pronounced judgment 4 in the name of the Lord Jesus on the man who has done such a thing. When you are assembled, and my spirit is present, with the power of our Lord Jesus, 5 you are to deliver this man to Satan for the destruction of the flesh, that his spirit may be saved in the day of the Lord Jesus.ʰ

6 Your boasting is not good. Do you not know that a little leaven leavens the whole lump? 7 Cleanse out the old leaven that you may be a new lump, as you really are unleavened. For Christ, our paschal lamb, has been sacrificed. 8 Let us, therefore, celebrate the festival, not with the old leaven, the leaven of malice and evil, but with the unleavened bread of sincerity and truth.

ʰ Other ancient authorities omit *Jesus*

4:18-19 *Arrogant . . . arrogant people.* For the arrogance of the men who were opposing and belittling Paul at Corinth cf. 2 Co 10—13, esp. 11:20.

5:1—6:20 Cf. Introduction, pars. 16-19. Paul deals with three cases of a gross misuse of Christian liberty.

5:1-13 Paul jars the Corinthians out of complacent (*arrogant,* 2; *boasting,* 6) misuse of their Christian liberty by calling for immediate and rigorous discipline on the *man . . . living with his father's wife* (1). As the ancient people of God were liberated from bondage in order to serve God (Ex 4:23), so it is with the new people: the Passover sacrifice of Christ (*our paschal lamb,* 7) has liberated the church for a life of *sincerity and truth* (8). The Christian life is to be a perpetual celebration of liberation from sin, not an indulgence in liberty to sin.

5:1 *Not . . . even among pagans.* Not only the OT law (Dt 22:30; 27:20) but also Greek and Roman law forbade such incestuous unions. The example of Oedipus, who blinded himself when he discovered that he had (unwittingly) married his father's wife, is an expression of the revulsion which even pagans felt.

5:2 *Mourn,* undertake the sad duty of discipline rather than be *arrogant* about their supposed achievement of liberty.

5:3-5 Though the apostle has *already pronounced judgment,* he cannot act alone, for he does not "lord it over" their faith (2 Co 1:24). Apostle and apostolic church act together with the power of Him who is Lord over them both.

5:5 *Deliver this man to Satan.* Cf. 1 Ti 1:20. Excommunication is meant (cf. 13), for the "whole world" outside the church "is in the power of the evil one" (1 Jn 5:19). The intention of the act of excommunication is that the man be ultimately *saved* in the *day* of judgment. The flesh, his opposition to the will of God (cf. 3:1 note), will be destroyed when he realizes whither his sin has brought him; and when he turns in repentance to the *Lord Jesus,* his Judge and his Forgiver, his *spirit* will *be saved.*

5:6 *Little leaven . . . whole lump.* Cf. Mt 13:33; Gl 5:9. This cuts off the plea that the man's offense is "only one" case, or an "exceptional case." The solidarity of the church is such that all members are affected by each member, for better or worse. (Cf. 12:26)

5:7-8 *Unleavened bread* was eaten at the Passover, the feast which commemorated Israel's deliverance from Egyptian bondage. It symbolizes the complete break with the past (Ex 12:8, 14-20; 13:3-10; Dt 16:1-4). So the Christian Passover, in which Christ is the *paschal lamb* that *has been sacrificed,* ushers in a new era in which the *malice and evil* of the past are done away with.

As you really are unleavened, i.e., pure, clean. The Christian is called on to enact in his living what God's redeeming act has made him to be. *Truth* is not only to be known but to be obeyed (Ro 2:8), to be done (Jn 3:21; 1 Jn 1:6); the opposite of truth is "wickedness," "wrong," "walking in darkness."

9 I wrote to you in my letter not to associate with immoral men; 10 not at all meaning the immoral of this world, or the greedy and robbers, or idolaters, since then you would need to go out of the world. 11 But rather I wrote^i to you not to associate with any one who bears the name of brother if he is guilty of immorality or greed, or is an idolater, reviler, drunkard, or robber—not even to eat with such a one. 12 For what have I to do with judging outsiders? Is it not those inside the church whom you are to judge? 13 God judges those outside. "Drive out the wicked person from among you."

LITIGATION (6:1-11)

6 When one of you has a grievance against a brother, does he dare go to law before the unrighteous instead of the saints? 2 Do you not know that the saints will judge the world? And if the world is to be judged by you, are you incompetent to try trivial cases? 3 Do you not know that we are to judge angels? How much more, matters pertaining to this life! 4 If then you have such cases, why do you lay them before those who are least esteemed by the church? 5 I say this to your shame. Can it be that there is no man among you wise enough to decide between members of the brotherhood, 6 but brother goes to law against brother, and that before unbelievers?

7 To have lawsuits at all with one another is defeat for you. Why not rather suffer wrong? Why not rather be defrauded? 8 But you yourselves wrong and defraud, and that even your own brethren.

9 Do you not know that the unrighteous will not inherit the kingdom of God? Do not be deceived; neither the immoral, nor idolaters, nor adulterers, nor sexual perverts, 10 nor thieves, nor the greedy, nor drunkards, nor revilers, nor robbers will inherit the kingdom of God. 11And such were some of you. But you were washed, you were sanctified, you were justified in the name of the Lord Jesus Christ and in the Spirit of our God.

SEXUAL IMMORALITY (6:12-20)

12 "All things are lawful for me," but not all things are helpful. "All things are lawful for me," but I will not be enslaved by anything. 13 "Food is meant for the stomach and the stomach for food"—and God will destroy both one and the other. The body is not meant for immorality, but for the Lord, and the Lord for the body.

^{i} Or *now I write*

5:9 *In my letter.* Cf. Introduction, par. 17.

5:11 *Not even to eat.* The bond created by participation in the common meal was strongly felt (cf. Mt 14:15-21 note). Not to eat with a man was to exclude him from fellowship.

5:12 *Judging outsiders . . . those inside the church . . . you are to judge.* God reserves judgment on the world to Himself (Mt 7:1; Ro 12:19); the Christians are to judge those inside the church, in the sense that they confront them with their sin and call them to repentance. (Mt 18:15-18; 1 Co 5:3-5)

5:13 Cf. Dt 17:7; 19:19; 22:21, 24; 24:7.

6:1-11 The new people of God have by virtue of their baptism (*washed,* 11) been *sanctified* and *justified in the name of the Lord Jesus Christ and in the Spirit of our God* (11); they belong to Christ (3:22) and are therefore destined to *judge the world* and *angels* with Him (2-3). They belong, as men endowed with God's Spirit, to the new world of God and cannot therefore commit their task of dealing with brothers at variance with one another to the powers of this judged and dying world.

6:7 *Defeat for you,* because it is a decline from the level at which the saints (2) really live as heirs of the future (1-3) in obedience to the Word of Jesus (Mt 5:39-42). Here too they have become

"men of the flesh," "ordinary men," "merely men." (3:1, 3, 4)

6:12-20 Cf. Introduction, pars. 16 and 19. Paul quotes a catchword of the proponents of "freedom" at Corinth (*All things are lawful for me,* 12) and a bit of the reasoning with which they defended their position that the spiritual man of knowledge is free to associate with prostitutes: sexual indulgence, they claimed, is on a par with the satisfaction of hunger, a morally indifferent part of life in this passing age (13). Then he exposes their specious catchword and murky reasoning to the light of the cross. The Christ who died for man's sins declared that to indulge in sin is to be *enslaved* to sin (12; Jn 8:34), and from that enslavement His cross has ransomed man (*bought with a price,* 20), with a whole redemption of the whole corporeal person. His grace has laid claim to man's body (*for the Lord,* 13), marked it for resurrection and eternal life (14), made it a member of Himself (15), a temple of the *Holy Spirit* (19), a place of inviolable sanctity—no longer man's to do with as he pleases (*not your own,* 19) but the instrument of his worship (20; cf. Ro 12:1). If the Corinthians *join* this body *to a prostitute* (16), they are desecrating what the cross has made holy; if they indulge in this enslaving freedom, they are denying their

¹⁴And God raised the Lord and will also raise us up by his power. ¹⁵ Do you not know that your bodies are members of Christ? Shall I therefore take the members of Christ and make them members of a prostitute? Never! ¹⁶ Do you not know that he who joins himself to a prostitute becomes one body with her? For, as it is written, "The two shall become one flesh." ¹⁷ But he who is united to the Lord becomes one spirit with him. ¹⁸ Shun immorality. Every other sin which a man commits is outside the body; but the immoral man sins against his own body. ¹⁹ Do you not know that your body is a temple of the Holy Spirit within you, which you have from God? You are not your own; ²⁰you were bought with a price. So glorify God in your body.

Celibacy and Marriage

7:1-40

7 Now concerning the matters about which you wrote. It is well for a man not to touch a woman. ² But because of the temptation to immorality, each man should have his own wife and each woman her own husband. ³ The husband should give to his wife her conjugal rights, and likewise the wife to her husband. ⁴ For the wife does not rule over her own body, but the husband does; likewise the husband does not rule over his own body, but the wife does. ⁵ Do not refuse one another except perhaps by agreement for a season, that you may devote yourselves to prayer; but then come together again, lest Satan tempt you through lack of self-control. ⁶ I say this by way of concession, not of command. ⁷ I wish that all were as I myself am. But each has his own special gift from God, one of one kind and one of another.

8 To the unmarried and the widows I say that it is well for them to remain single as I do. ⁹ But if they cannot exercise self-control, they should marry. For it is better to marry than to be aflame with passion.

10 To the married I give charge, not I but the Lord, that the wife should not separate from her husband ¹¹(but if she does, let her remain single or else be

---

"only Master and Lord, Jesus Christ" (Jude 4). The bodily character of this act, far from making the act indifferent, makes it particularly heinous.

7:1-40 The same depreciation of the body and man's bodily life which found expression in an easy conscience on fornication (6:12-20) gave rise at Corinth to an uneasy conscience concerning marriage and fostered an impulse toward universal celibacy. The church's letter to Paul (*matters about which you wrote*, 1) probably quoted a catchword of the new teaching: *It is well for a man not to touch a woman* (1) and indicated the problems to which the application of this principle had given rise. Married people were conducting ascetic experiments to which they were not always equal (2-5). Some were considering divorce from their spouses, especially pagan spouses, as a way toward a fuller religious life (10-16). The *unmarried and the widows* were being made uncertain regarding their right to marry or remarry (8-9, 25-28, 39-40). Whatever the exact meaning of 36-38 (see note on the passage), it indicates the same uneasiness of conscience regarding marriage as the rest. Paul answers the questions fully, and his answers are as sober and evangelically fair as the assertions of the new teaching were one-sided and legalistic.

Christ, he tells his church, has *bought* men *with a price* (7:23) and has destined them for glory. Their life within the orders of this world (marriage, slavery, commerce) has a provisional, next-to-the-last character, for *the form of this world is*

passing away to give place to the new world of God. As redeemed men they are to have a loose hold on the things of this world (29-31) and are to aim always at an *undivided devotion to the Lord* who has bought them (35). That gives celibacy its value and place in the life of the church, one that Paul is the first to appreciate, being himself celibate (7, 8, 26, 38, 40). But celibacy is a gift which only the free grace of God can give (7); man cannot simply claim or take it for himself, much less impose it as a rule on others without regard for their limitations. Moreover, if life in this world has a provisional, preliminary character, it also has a preparatory character; men are to live their present lives in the faith that God's *call* has summoned them to be His own in the place where they are and to serve Him there (17-24). They may not in blind enthusiasm set out blithely to free themselves of the marriage bond which the Word of their redeeming Lord has hallowed (10); and they dare not attempt a self-chosen course of celibate devotion which will plunge them into sin. (2-5; 9, 36)

7:1 *You wrote.* Cf. Introduction, par. 20, and 8:1; 11:2; 12:1; 16:1.

7:4 Even in these down-to-earth words on the physical aspect of marriage it is clear that erotic love is transfigured by that specifically Christian love which does not seek its own (13:4-7); spouses simply exist for each other.

7:10 *The Lord.* Jesus has no specific word on the wife's seeking a divorce, since under Jewish law

reconciled to her husband)—and that the husband should not divorce his wife.

12 To the rest I say, not the Lord, that if any brother has a wife who is an unbeliever, and she consents to live with him, he should not divorce her. 13 If any woman has a husband who is an unbeliever, and he consents to live with her, she should not divorce him. 14 For the unbelieving husband is consecrated through his wife, and the unbelieving wife is consecrated through her husband. Otherwise, your children would be unclean, but as it is they are holy. 15 But if the unbelieving partner desires to separate, let it be so; in such a case the brother or sister is not bound. For God has called us^l to peace. 16 Wife, how do you know whether you will save your husband? Husband, how do you know whether you will save your wife?

17 Only, let every one lead the life which the Lord has assigned to him, and in which God has called him. This is my rule in all the churches. 18 Was any one at the time of his call already circumcised? Let him not seek to remove the marks of circumcision. Was any one at the time of his call uncircumcised? Let him not seek circumcision. 19 For neither circumcision counts for anything nor uncircumcision, but keeping the commandments of God. 20 Every one should remain in the state in which he was called. 21 Were you a slave when called? Never mind. But if you can gain your freedom, avail yourself of the opportunity.^x 22 For he who was called in the Lord as a slave is a freedman of the Lord. Likewise he who was free when called is a slave of Christ. 23 You were bought with a price; do not become slaves of men. 24 So, brethren, in whatever state each was called, there let him remain with God.

25 Now concerning the unmarried,^y I have no command of the Lord, but I give my opinion as one who by the Lord's mercy is trustworthy. 26 I think that in view of the present^m distress it is well for a person to remain as he is. 27Are you bound to a wife? Do not seek to be free. Are you free from a wife? Do not seek marriage. 28 But if you marry, you do not sin, and if a girl^z marries she does not sin. Yet those who marry will have worldly troubles, and I would spare you that. 29 I mean, brethren, the appointed time has grown very short; from now on, let those who have wives live as though they had none, 30 and those who mourn as though they were not mourning, and those who rejoice as though they were not rejoicing, and those who buy as though they had no goods, 31 and those who deal with the world as though they had no dealings with it. For the form of this world is passing away.

^l Other ancient authorities read *you*   ^x Or *make use of your present condition instead*   ^y Greek *virgins*
^m Or *impending*   ^z Greek *virgin*

she could not sue for divorce. But His word on the inviolability of marriage, Mt 19:6, covers the case.

7:11 *If she does.* Better, "If she is already divorced."

Remain single. She is free to remarry only after the death of her husband. (39-40)

7:12 *To the rest,* to those married to pagan spouses.

I . . . not the Lord. Although Paul is emphatic about his apostolic authority (1:1; 7:25; 7:40) and goes so far as to assert that "Christ is speaking in" him (2 Co 13:3; cf. Ro 15:18), he distinguishes carefully between his word and a word uttered by Jesus in the days of His flesh.

7:14 *Unbelieving husband is consecrated through his wife.* Consecration is, as 16 shows, not the same as salvation; the wife's faith does not automatically "save" the unbelieving husband. The thought seems, rather, to be this: When God in His grace called the woman, He called her as she was, in the closest of human associations with an unbeliever; His grace reached her even so and is sufficient for her even so. The pagan husband is, whether he wills and knows it or not, partner in a Christian marriage and is in that respect consecrated by the divine grace which is over that

marriage. The Christian wife can and may "remain with God" in that state in which she was called (24). She is not living in an unhallowed union, and the *children* of her marriage are not *unclean* but destined to be part of the holy temple of God (3:16-17) by the grace of Baptism, as she well knew when she brought her children to be baptized.

7:16 Both apostle and the church know that they can only "by all means save SOME." (9:22)

7:17 Paul generalizes from his statement concerning mixed marriage (12-16) and illustrates his *rule* with the examples of circumcision (18-19) and slavery. (21-22)

7:23 Christians, redeemed *with a price,* are "to be judged by no one" (2:15); they would *become slaves of men* if they accepted and acted on the judgment of men concerning the importance and significance of such things as circumcision (18-19) or slavery. (21-22)

7:26 *Present distress,* the time of the "great tribulation" which precedes the return of Christ. (Cf. 7:29; Mt 24:21, 29; Lk 23:29)

7:31 *The form of this world is passing away,* and the new age, when marriage will be no more, is at hand. (Mt 22:30)

32 I want you to be free from anxieties. The unmarried man is anxious about the affairs of the Lord, how to please the Lord; 33 but the married man is anxious about worldly affairs, how to please his wife, 34 and his interests are divided. And the unmarried woman or girl*z* is anxious about the affairs of the Lord, how to be holy in body and spirit; but the married woman is anxious about worldly affairs, how to please her husband. 35 I say this for your own benefit, not to lay any restraint upon you, but to promote good order and to secure your undivided devotion to the Lord.

36 If any one thinks that he is not behaving properly toward his betrothed,*z* if his passions are strong, and it has to be, let him do as he wishes: let them marry—it is no sin. 37 But whoever is firmly established in his heart, being under no necessity but having his desire under control, and has determined this in his heart, to keep her as his betrothed,*z* he will do well. 38 So that he who marries his betrothed*z* does well; and he who refrains from marriage will do better.

39 A wife is bound to her husband as long as he lives. If the husband dies, she is free to be married to whom she wishes, only in the Lord. 40 But in my judgment she is happier if she remains as she is. And I think that I have the Spirit of God.

The Eating of Meat Offered to Idols

8:1 – 11:1

8   Now concerning food offered to idols: we know that "all of us possess knowledge." "Knowledge" puffs up, but love builds up. 2 If any one imagines that he knows something, he does not yet know as he ought to know. 3 But if one loves God, one is known by him.

z Greek *virgin*

7:36-38 As translated in the RSV, the *any one* of 36 is an engaged man who has determined to keep his relationship to his *betrothed* a purely spiritual one, *to keep her as his betrothed* (37). Paul's advice to such is the same as that given to the unmarried and the widows, 8-9; marriage is no sin — *he who marries his betrothed does well,* but for him to whom it is given, to *refrain from marriage* is *better.*

But it is more likely that the *any one* of 36 is the father of the girl. The word translated *betrothed* in 36, 37, 38 is in the Greek simply "virgin"; and the word translated *marries* is regularly used for "giving in marriage" by the father. The passage ought then probably be rendered thus: "If any one thinks that he is not behaving properly toward his virgin (daughter, by not allowing her to marry), if she is fully mature and it ought so to be, let him do as he wishes; let them (the daughter and the young man involved) marry — it is no sin. But whoever is firmly established in his heart, being under no necessity but in control of his will and has determined this in his heart, to keep her as his virgin (daughter), he will do well. So that he who gives his virgin in marriage does well, and he who refrains from giving her in marriage will do better."

7:39-40 Apparently an appendage to 10-11, 15. (Cf. 7:11 note.)

7:39 *In the Lord,* that is, to a fellow Christian, with a full sense of what Christian marriage involves.

8:1 – 11:1 Cf. Introduction, pars. 16 and 22. *Food offered to idols* (8:1) became a problem for Christians because in sacrifices to pagan deities only a part of the sacrificial animal was actually offered to the deity; the rest was either *sold in the meat*

market (10:25) or eaten at festal meals *in an idol's temple* (8:10; cf. 10:27). It was understandable that some Christians were troubled in conscience about partaking of food thus "contaminated" by close contact with abhorrent idolatry. The men of *knowledge* (8:1), blithely confident in the *liberty* (8:9) which their knowledge gave them, overrode the scruples of these weaker brothers by partaking freely and publicly (8:10) of food offered to idols. Paul, fair as always, first assents fully to what is true in the claim that knowledge gives liberty (8:1-6; 10:19-20, 27, 29); the Christian knows the exclusive sovereignty of his God and Lord and is forever free from all other gods and lords (8:5-6). Then Paul proceeds to purge knowledge of self-will and pride by pointing out the obligation of love to those who do *not . . . possess this knowledge* as they do (8:7-13) — the weak brother ruined by the strong man's knowledge. He then points to his own apostolic ministry as the example of self-denying, self-giving love which made him, free as he was, the *slave to all* (9:1-23), leading a life that knows harsh self-discipline (9:24-27). This discipline of the Christ whom Paul "imitates" and summons the strong and knowledgeable to imitate (10:31 – 11:1), is the yoke of the Christ to whose self-giving love they owe their existence (8:6), who died for the brother whom they despise and ruin (8:11), the incarnate Lord *Jesus* (9:1), whose redemptive blessings they know and experience in the Supper of the Lord. (10: 16-17; cf. 10:1-4)

This Lord had tempered the boldness of His disciples' faith with holy fear when he taught them to pray (Mt 6:13) and when He bade them watch and pray that they might not enter into tempta-

4 Hence, as to the eating of food offered to idols, we know that "an idol has no real existence," and that "there is no God but one." 5 For although there may be so-called gods in heaven or on earth—as indeed there are many "gods" and many "lords" —6 yet for us there is one God, the Father, from whom are all things and for whom we exist, and one Lord, Jesus Christ, through whom are all things and through whom we exist.

7 However, not all possess this knowledge. But some, through being hitherto accustomed to idols, eat food as really offered to an idol; and their conscience, being weak, is defiled. 8 Food will not commend us to God. We are no worse off if we do not eat, and no better off if we do. 9 Only take care lest this liberty of yours somehow become a stumbling block to the weak. 10 For if any one sees you, a man of knowledge, at table in an idol's temple, might he not be encouraged, if his conscience is weak, to eat food offered to idols? 11And so by your knowledge this weak man is destroyed, the brother for whom Christ died. 12 Thus, sinning against your brethren and wounding their conscience when it is weak, you sin against Christ. 13 Therefore, if food is a cause of my brother's falling, I will never eat meat, lest I cause my brother to fall.

9 Am I not free? Am I not an apostle? Have I not seen Jesus our Lord? Are not you my workmanship in the Lord? 2 If to others I am not an apostle, at least I am to you; for you are the seal of my apostleship in the Lord.

3 This is my defense to those who would examine me. 4 Do we not have the right to our food and drink? 5 Do we not have the right to be accompanied by a wife,[n] as the other apostles and the brothers of the Lord and Cephas? 6 Or is it only Bar'na·bas

[n] Greek *a sister as wife*

---

tion on the night in which He was betrayed (Mt 26:41). Paul imitates his Lord in this too. He deepens the knowledge of the knowing (*I want you to know*, 10:1) with the knowledge that he who *thinks that he stands* may, but for the grace of God, yet *fall* (10:12-13), as Israel once fell in spite of all that God had given her (10:1-11). He sobers the knowing in their careless contempt of idols by pointing to the fact that the idol-nonentity becomes a demonic reality when worshiped, a reality with which no worshiper of God can come to terms. (10:14-22)

Then, having laid a foundation of selfless love and reverent fear, Paul can give brief and down-to-earth directions concerning contact with food offered to idols.

These chapters, together with Ro 14—15, are the classic apostolic treatment of the use and misuse of the liberty with which Christ has set us free. (Gl 5:13)

8:1 and 4 Cf. Introduction, par. 16. The words set off by quotation marks in the text are probably slogans used by the new leaders. For the knowledge-love relationship cf. 13:2.

8:2 For the radical reconstruction effected in man's thinking by the Gospel cf. Paul's words of wisdom, 3:18.

8:3 *Is known by him* (God). Real "knowledge" is not an attainment of man but God's gift to man, not so much a knowing as a being-known, that is, being loved, chosen, and called by God. Cf. Mt 11:27, where Jesus describes knowledge of the Father as His free gift to weary and heavy laden, and Ro 8:29 ("foreknew") note.

8:5 *Lord* was a common title of deity in oriental religions, many of which had become popular in the Roman world, and was used of the deified Roman emperor.

8:6 For the *Father* as Source and Goal of creation and history cf. Ro 11:36. For *Jesus Christ* as Mediator of both creation and salvation cf. Jn 1:3; Cl 1:16-20; Heb 1:13.

8:7 *Accustomed to idols,* as real and influential powers in their life. (Cf. 12:2)

As really offered to an idol. Cf. 10:19-20.

8:8 *Food will not commend,* that is, as the second half of the verse shows, the eating of or abstaining from certain foods. Our eating and drinking is done "to the glory of God" (10:31) when it is motivated by love for the brother. (8:13)

8:10 *Encouraged,* literally "built up," the same Greek word as in 8:1. Those who made such reckless use of their liberty as is here described evidently argued that their example "built up" the weaker brother, encouraged him to become equally free; Paul's pastoral insight rejects such rough measures as injurious and destructive—the weak conscience is "defiled" (7), "wounded" (12), and the weak man "falls" and is "destroyed" (13, 11) since he is led to act in violation of his conscience. (Cf. Ro 14:14)

9:1-2 Paul develops further the thought of 8:13. He is as *free* as anybody (cf. 8:9; 9:19) and has "rights" (3, 5, 6, 12, 18) of a special kind as *apostle,* authenticated by his own history (*seen Jesus,* cf. 15:8) and by the existence of the apostolic church which his ministry has produced *(seal).*

9:5 *Accompanied by a wife.* This would increase the burden laid on the churches who supported the apostles.

Cephas, the Aramaic form of Peter's name.

9:6-14. Paul demonstrates his *right* to maintenance by the church from the principle of equity in the occupations of ordinary life (7; cf. 10-12), by the principle laid down by the Law in the OT (8-10, 13) and by an appeal to the command of

and I who have no right to refrain from working for a living? 7 Who serves as a soldier at his own expense? Who plants a vineyard without eating any of its fruit? Who tends a flock without getting some of the milk?

8 Do I say this on human authority? Does not the law say the same? 9 For it is written in the law of Moses, "You shall not muzzle an ox when it is treading out the grain." Is it for oxen that God is concerned? 10 Does he not speak entirely for our sake? It was written for our sake, because the plowman should plow in hope and the thresher thresh in hope of a share in the crop. 11 If we have sown spiritual good among you, is it too much if we reap your material benefits? 12 If others share this rightful claim upon you, do not we still more?

Nevertheless, we have not made use of this right, but we endure anything rather than put an obstacle in the way of the gospel of Christ. 13 Do you not know that those who are employed in the temple service get their food from the temple, and those who serve at the altar share in the sacrificial offerings? 14 In the same way, the Lord commanded that those who proclaim the gospel should get their living by the gospel.

15 But I have made no use of any of these rights, nor am I writing this to secure any such provision. For I would rather die than have any one deprive me of my ground for boasting. 16 For if I preach the gospel, that gives me no ground for boasting. For necessity is laid upon me. Woe to me if I do not preach the gospel! 17 For if I do this of my own will, I have a reward; but if not of my own will, I am entrusted with a commission. 18 What then is my reward? Just this: that in my preaching I may make the gospel free of charge, not making full use of my right in the gospel.

19 For though I am free from all men, I have made myself a slave to all, that I might win the more. 20 To the Jews I became as a Jew, in order to win Jews; to those under the law I became as one under the law—though not being myself under the law—that I might win those under the law. 21 To those outside the law I became as one outside the law—not being without law toward God but under the law of Christ—that I might win those outside the law. 22 To the weak I became weak, that I might win the weak. I have become all things to all men, that I might by all means save some. 23 I do it all for the sake of the gospel, that I may share in its blessings.

24 Do you not know that in a race all the runners compete, but only one receives the prize? So run that you may obtain it. 25 Every athlete exercises self-control in all things. They do it to receive a perishable wreath, but we an imperishable. 26 Well, I do not run aimlessly, I do not box as one beating the air; 27 but I pommel my body and subdue it, lest after preaching to others I myself should be disqualified.

---

i Jesus. When he waived his right (15), he was waiving indisputable rights.

9:9 *Law*. Dt 25:4. The apostle, who had an ear for the groaning of subhuman creation and knew of a promise and a hope that embraced all creation (Ro 8:18-22), can hardly be thought of as denying God's care for all His creatures, or that oxen are beneath His dignity. But he is saying very dramatically that God's provision for threshing *oxen* embodies a principle of His rule over all creation.

9:12 *Obstacle in the way of the gospel*. The suspicion that the apostle was preaching for gain would be such an obstacle (cf. 1 Th 2:5; Acts 20:33; 3 Jn 7). Even at Corinth Paul had to ward off that suspicion. (2 Co 12:14-18)

9:13 *Temple service*. Nm 18:8-32; Dt 18:1-3. Paul occasionally speaks of his own ministry as "the PRIESTLY service of the gospel." (Ro 15:16)

9:14 *The Lord commanded*. Mt 10:10; Lk 10:7-8.

9:15-18 Paul's talk of *boasting* (15, 16) and *reward* (17, 18) has a strange ring coming from a man who so rigorously excludes all boasting of

man from man's relationship to God (1:29; Ro 3:27). It can be understood only in the context of grace; we hear Paul speaking of his *ground for boasting* again in 15:10, when he says: "I worked harder [or more abundantly] than any of them." There his boast is preceded and followed by a thankful acknowledgment of the sole working of God's grace in and through him. So here, boasting and reward are an exultant recognition of the divine grace which has made him not merely an obedient slave with a *necessity . . . laid upon* him (16-17) who can claim no reward for doing what he ought (cf. Lk 17:7-10)—this grace has made him an "imitator" of Christ (11:1), a free son giving freely (*of my own will*, 17; *free of charge*, 18), as the Son gave (Gl 1:4; 2:20; cf. Mt 10:8). Thus he can look to sharing in His master's joy (Mt 25:21). All is of grace, and so Paul's "boasting" is in the last analysis a boasting "of the Lord." (1:31)

9:19-27 "Love builds up" (8:1). Paul's single desire to build the living church not only led him to renounce the financial support that was his due (9:3-18); it also made him a *slave to all* (19), in

10 I want you to know, brethren, that our fathers were all under the cloud, and all passed through the sea, 2 and all were baptized into Moses in the cloud and in the sea, 3 and all ate the same supernatural*o* food 4 and all drank the same supernatural*o* drink. For they drank from the supernatural*o* Rock which followed them, and the Rock was Christ. 5 Nevertheless with most of them God was not pleased; for they were overthrown in the wilderness.

6 Now these things are warnings for us, not to desire evil as they did. 7 Do not be idolaters as some of them were; as it is written, "The people sat down to eat and drink and rose up to dance." 8 We must not indulge in immorality as some of them did, and twenty-three thousand fell in a single day. 9 We must not put the Lord*p* to the test, as some of them did and were destroyed by serpents; 10 nor grumble, as some of them did and were destroyed by the Destroyer. 11 Now these things happened to them as a warning, but they were written down for our instruction, upon

o Greek *spiritual*   *p* Other ancient authorities read *Christ*

---

obedience to the *law of Christ* (cf. Gl 6:2). He became *all things to all men* (22), to the *Jews . . . under the law* (20), to Gentiles *outside the law* (21), to the *weak* Christian brothers (22). He sought and found the Jew where he lived, under the Law, never flouting Judaic sanctities, never belittling the high majesty of the Law or casting doubt on the promises given to Israel or concealing the fact that the Gospel is given "to the Jew first" (Ro 1:16). He sought and found the Gentile where he was, outside the Law, without imposing the Law on him, fighting for the Gentile's freedom from the Law (cf. Gl). Chapters 8 – 10 of 1 Co are abiding evidence of how he entered sympathetically into the fears and scruples of the weak, dealing gently with them like a nurse or a father (1 Th 2:7, 11), shielding them from the offense of the inconsiderate strong. He pursues this course with the intense devotion of an *athlete* in training (24-25), in the knowledge that only he who lives and shares the *gospel . . . may share in its blessings* (23) and in the somber realization that he must yet face the judgment of his Lord (cf. 4:4) and may yet be *disqualified* in the race and lose the prize. (27; cf. Ph 3:14)

10:1-22 Paul remembers what the "wise" and "strong" ignore: that God's grace and gifts put man into a personal and responsible relationship to Him; they do not "insure" man against sin and judgment magically and automatically. Ancient Israel is a warning example; Israel experienced the same wondrously working grace that Christians have experienced in their baptism, Israel had a *supernatural* supper given by the Lord to nurture His presence in the church. And yet Israel fell and provoked the judgment of God (1-10). From Israel's history the new Israel of the last days, the church, may learn: *Let any one who thinks that he stands take heed lest he fall* (12). —Not that the Christians live in sheer terror; they know that the *faithful God* who called them into the fellowship of His Son (cf. 1:9) remains protectively in charge of their embattled lives (13). —But the warning stands; the *worship of idols* stands in complete opposition to the worship of God. The communion with the Crucified ever renewed and nurtured in the *table of the Lord* is total and exclusive and makes any other com-

munion a communion with *demons*. The *Lord* who gives His *body* and *blood* in His *cup* and at His *table* is a jealous Lord (22) – what "strong" man dare fancy that he can challenge His Lordship with impunity? (14-22). (The implication seems to be that any eating of meat offered to idols which concedes reality to the idols does challenge His Lordship.)

10:2 *Baptized into Moses.* To mark the parallel between Israel and the church, Paul calls the Exodus (*cloud . . . sea, Ex* 13:21; 14:22, 29) a baptism. There in the Exodus (as now in Baptism) God was acting graciously for man's salvation (Ex 14: 13; 15:2). In both cases the person of the mediator (Moses, Christ) is of decisive importance, so that baptism is *into* him. That Christ's mediation of salvation lies on a higher level than that of Moses goes without saying. (Cf. Jn 1:17)

10:3-4 The comparison between Israel's manna and water from the Rock (*supernatural food . . . drink*) and the Christian's Supper of the Lord again marks the parallel between Israel and the church and brings the warning of Israel's history close to home.

Rock . . . followed . . . was Christ. In speaking of the *Rock which followed* Paul is employing a bit of Judaic tradition, which deduced from the two accounts of water from the rock (Ex 17:6; Nm 20: 11) that the *Rock followed* Israel through the wilderness. In saying that the *Rock was Christ* he is looking back on Israel's history from the vantage point of its culmination in Jesus Christ and is saying: Wherever we find God graciously at work for man, there the Christ is present; all the past history of salvation has Christ as its hidden center – in Him all the spoken and acted "promises of God find their Yes." (2 Co 1:20)

10:5-11 For the record of Israel's sins in the *wilderness* and God's judgment upon them cf. for 10:5 (*overthrown in the wilderness*) Nm 14:29-30; for 10:6 (*desire evil*) Nm 11:4, 34; for 10:7 (*idolaters*) Ex 32:4-6; for 10:8 (*indulge in immorality . . . fell in a single day*) Nm 25:1-18; for 10:9 (*put the Lord to the test . . . serpents*) Nm 21:5-6; for 10:10 (*grumble . . . destroyed*) Nm 16:30-49.

10:10 *Destroyer.* God's destroying angel. (Cf. 1 Ch 21:12, 15)

whom the end of the ages has come. 12 Therefore let any one who thinks that he stands take heed lest he fall. 13 No temptation has overtaken you that is not common to man. God is faithful, and he will not let you be tempted beyond your strength, but with the temptation will also provide the way of escape, that you may be able to endure it.

14 Therefore, my beloved, shun the worship of idols. 15 I speak as to sensible men; judge for yourselves what I say. 16 The cup of blessing which we bless, is it not a participation*q* in the blood of Christ? The bread which we break, is it not a participation*q* in the body of Christ? 17 Because there is one bread, we who are many are one body, for we all partake of the one bread. 18 Consider the people of Israel;*a* are not those who eat the sacrifices partners in the altar? 19 What do I imply then? That food offered to idols is anything, or that an idol is anything? 20 No, I imply that what pagans sacrifice they offer to demons and not to God. I do not want you to be partners with demons. 21 You cannot drink the cup of the Lord and the cup of demons. You cannot partake of the table of the Lord and the table of demons. 22 Shall we provoke the Lord to jealousy? Are we stronger than he?

23 "All things are lawful," but not all things are helpful. "All things are lawful," but not all things build up. 24 Let no one seek his own good, but the good of his neighbor. 25 Eat whatever is sold in the meat market without raising any question on the ground of conscience. 26 For "the earth is the Lord's, and everything in it." 27 If one of the unbelievers invites you to dinner and you are disposed to go, eat whatever is set before you without raising any question on the ground of conscience. 28 (But if some one says to you, "This has been offered in sacrifice," then out of consideration for the man who informed you, and for conscience' sake— 29 I mean his conscience, not yours—do not eat it.) For why should my liberty be determined by another man's scruples? 30 If I partake with thankfulness, why am I denounced because of that for which I give thanks?

31 So, whether you eat or drink, or whatever you do, do all to the glory of God. 32 Give no offense to Jews or to Greeks or to the church of God, 33 just as I try to please all men in everything I do, not seeking my own

q Or *communion*   *a* Greek *Israel according to the flesh*

10:14-22 The Corinthian Christians know how deep and vital a thing *participation* (16) in the divine is, how it dominates and shapes the life of the participants. They know this from the Lord's Supper, in which they encounter and are blessed by the very presence of their incarnate, redeeming Lord (*blood, body,* 16); their common nurture in their common partaking of the one *bread* (in which their one Lord is really and effectively present) creates a common life (*one body,* 17). They know this also from the Scriptures written for their instruction (cf. 11); the priests who according to the Law (Lv 7:6; cf. 1 Co 9:13) *eat the sacrifices* are by that act *partners in the altar* and of the Godhead whose presence the altar signifies; "the Lord is their inheritance" (Dt 18:1-5). From the depth and reality of this participation in the divine they can *judge for* themselves (15) how dangerous and entrapping a participation in the pseudo-divine, the demonic, must be. In partaking of the *cup* and *table of demons,* they are giving the demons power over them (for what a man gives his heart to becomes his god, cf. Mt 6:21; Eph 5:5; Cl 3:5); they *provoke the Lord* who alone is entitled to power over them *to jealousy,* challenging His authority over them. (22)

10:16 *Is it not . . . ?* Paul's use of the rhetorical question shows that he is appealing to a belief commonly held in the church; he is arguing from

the real presence of Christ, not about it. (Cf. 11: 27-29)

10:20 *To demons.* Cf. Dt 32:17.

10:22 *Provoke . . . to jealousy.* Cf. Dt 32:21.

10:23–11:1 Paul's pastoral wisdom has instilled faith (8:4-6), love (8:7–9:27), and fear (10:1-22)— on that basis he can give succinct advice: Even the weakest of consciences can grow strong enough to eat meat that has come from the idol's temple to the common *market;* the sovereign claim of the Creator (26) is not questioned here. The strong in his strength can forgo his freedom in a situation where another's conscience is involved, with his inner freedom unimpaired. What matters finally is that all life be lived *to the glory of God;* and God is glorified when men become *imitators* of the apostle of Christ and thus of *Christ* Himself, who went the servant's way, *not seeking* His *own advantage, but that of many, that they may be saved,* to the glory of His Father. (Cf. Ph 2:11)

10:23 *All things are lawful.* Cf. 6:12.

10:26 *The earth is the Lord's.* Cf. Ps 24:1; 50:12.

10:28 *Offered in sacrifice.* The expression, different from that used in 8:1, etc., indicates that the informer is convinced to some degree of the reality of the god to whom meat has been offered.

10:30 *I give thanks.* The act of thanksgiving acknowledges the fact that it is God's creation (26) and His gift. (Cf. Ro 14:6; 1 Ti 4:4-5)

11 advantage, but that of many, that they may be saved. ¹ Be imitators of me, as I am of Christ.

Disorders in the Worship Life of the Church
11:2 — 14:40
WOMAN IN THE CHURCH (11:2-16)

2 I commend you because you remember me in everything and maintain the traditions even as I have delivered them to you. ³ But I want you to understand that the head of every man is Christ, the head of a woman is her husband, and the head of Christ is God. ⁴Any man who prays or prophesies with his head covered dishonors his head, ⁵ but any woman who prays or prophesies with her head unveiled dishonors her head—it is the same as if her head were shaven. ⁶ For if a woman will not veil herself, then she should cut off her hair; but if it is disgraceful for a woman to be shorn or shaven, let her wear a veil. ⁷ For a man ought not to cover his head, since he is the image and glory of God; but woman is the glory of man. ⁸ (For man was not made from woman, but woman from man. ⁹ Neither was man created for woman, but woman for man.) ¹⁰ That is why a woman ought to have a veil[r] on her head, because of the angels. ¹¹ (Nevertheless, in the Lord woman is not independent of man nor man of woman; ¹² for as woman was made from man, so man is now born of woman. And all things are from God.) ¹³ Judge for yourselves; is it proper for a woman to pray to God with her head uncovered? ¹⁴ Does not nature itself teach you that for a man to wear long hair is degrading to him, ¹⁵ but if a woman has long hair, it is her pride? For her hair is given to her for a covering. ¹⁶ If any one is disposed to be contentious, we recognize no other practice, nor do the churches of God.

THE LORD'S SUPPER (11:17-34)

17 But in the following instructions I do not commend you, because when you come together it is not for the better but for the worse. ¹⁸ For, in the first place, when

[r] Greek *authority* (the veil being a symbol of this)

11:2 — 14:40 Cf. Introduction, pars. 23 and 24.

11:2-16. Cf. Introduction, par. 23. Paul reverts to the question of woman's place in the church in 14:34-36, where he treats the question of her role in the public assemblies of instruction and worship. Here he establishes the basic fact that woman's place in the church dare not involve a denial of her place as God's creature, as woman. Within the pattern of the customs and values of the first church a woman did deny her womanliness if she prayed or prophesied *with her head unveiled* (5, cf. 6). Dropping the *veil* signified that she was flouting the will of Him who has placed an *authority* over her (10 and RSV note *r*); she has her true place in an order of subordination: *God — Christ — man — woman* (3). The fact that Christ, the Son of God, is included in this order makes clear that this "subordination" has nothing servile or degrading about it; Christ is "subordinated" as the freely obeying, loving Son who seeks the glory of His Father and finds the goal and climax of His ministry in laying all that His ministry has won at His Father's feet (15:28; cf. Ph 2:11). Within this order set by God at creation (8-9; cf. Gn 2:21-23) man and woman have their place as Christians (*in the Lord*, 11) and live their lives together, complementing each other — Paul leaves no room for male pride when he assigns headship to the man. (11-12)

That is Paul's main argument based on the Genesis account of creation and the fact of the incarnate Christ; he closes with an appeal to his readers' "natural" sense of fitness (*nature . . . teach*, 13-15) and to the example of the apostles and the apostolic churches. (16)

11:2 Paul is evidently acknowledging the church's profession of loyalty to him and his teaching (*traditions . . . delivered*), probably quoting from their letter. (Cf. 7:1)

11:3 *Head of,* authority over.

Head of Christ is God. Cf. 3:23 note.

11:6 *Cut off her hair.* Ironic: let her go the whole way in denying her womanliness — if she would "dishonor her head" (5) by removing the badge of her womanliness, let her dishonor it utterly.

11:7 *Glory,* here, in connection with *image,* in the sense of "reflection of the glory." (Gn 1:26)

11:8 Cf. Gn 2:21-23.

11:12 *All things are from God.* The same God who made woman "a helper fit for him" (Gn 2:18) made her also "the mother of all living." (Gn 3:20)

11:17-34 Cf. Introduction, par. 24. The Lord's Supper is the Supper of the Lord of glory crucified for man (2:8); it is the gift of His cross effectually present in the church to enrich and unify the church. To make of it man's supper, a meal wherein the Lord's real and redeeming bodily presence is not recognized, to make of it the scene

you assemble as a church, I hear that there are divisions among you; and I partly believe it, [19] for there must be factions among you in order that those who are genuine among you may be recognized. [20] When you meet together, it is not the Lord's supper that you eat. [21] For in eating, each one goes ahead with his own meal, and one is hungry and another is drunk. [22] What! Do you not have houses to eat and drink in? Or do you despise the church of God and humiliate those who have nothing? What shall I say to you? Shall I commend you in this? No, I will not.

23 For I received from the Lord what I also delivered to you, that the Lord Jesus on the night when he was betrayed took bread, [24] and when he had given thanks, he broke it, and said, "This is my body which is for[s] you. Do this in remembrance of me." [25] In the same way also the cup, after supper, saying, "This cup is the new covenant in my blood. Do this, as often as you drink it, in remembrance of me." [26] For as often as you eat this bread and drink the cup, you proclaim the Lord's death until he comes.

27 Whoever, therefore, eats the bread or drinks the cup of the Lord in an unworthy manner will be guilty of profaning the body and blood of the Lord. [28] Let a man examine himself, and so eat of the bread and drink of the cup. [29] For any one who eats and drinks without discerning the body eats and drinks judgment upon himself. [30] That is why many of you are weak and ill, and some have died.[t] [31] But if we judged ourselves truly, we should not be judged. [32] But when we are judged by the Lord, we are chastened[u] so that we may not be condemned along with the world.

33 So then, my brethren, when you come together to eat, wait for one another— [34] if any one is hungry, let him eat at home—lest you come together to be condemned. About the other things I will give directions when I come.

THE USE OF SPIRITUAL GIFTS (12:1 — 14:40)

12 Now concerning spiritual gifts,[x]brethren, I do not want you to be uninformed. [2] You know that when you were heathen, you were led astray to dumb idols, however you may have been moved. [3] Therefore I want you to understand that no

[s] Other ancient authorities read *broken for*   [t] Greek *have fallen asleep* (as in 15.6, 20)
[u] Or *when we are judged we are being chastened by the Lord*   [x] Or *spiritual persons*

of man's carousing and the expression of his factious and contemptous self-will is to invite the judgment of God on His church.

11:18-19 In the chemistry of God's rule over the church *divisions must* harden into *factions* in order that the false and the *genuine* be *recognized* as they openly confront each other and the truth win out.

11:21-22 The common meal, an expression of fellowship (cf. Acts 2:42, 46) and love, lost that character when each one went *ahead with the meal* which he had brought, thus *humiliating those who had nothing.*

Houses to eat in, if physical nurture and enjoyment were the whole purpose of the meal. A common meal during which the Lord's Supper is celebrated has quite another character.

11:23-26 Cf. Mt 26:26-28; Mk 14:22-24; Lk 22: 19-20, and the notes there.

11:23 *Received from the Lord.* The significance and sanctity of the Supper do not rest on any intermediate human authority but derive from the Lord Himself.

11:24-25 *In remembrance of me.* Cf. Lk 22:19. *Remembrance* includes a believing recall and a grateful recognition and confession of the divine redemptive action. (Cf. Ps 6:5)

11:26 *You proclaim the Lord's death.* The body and the blood as interpreted by the words of the Lord Himself ("for you") point to the crucified Lord of glory. *Until he comes* points to the risen and returning Lord of glory, an echo of Jesus' word concerning His future fellowship with His disciples in Mt 26:29 and Mk 14:25, when He instituted His Supper.

11:27 *In an unworthy manner.* As 29 makes plain, the "unworthiness" lies in not *discerning the body* in its sanctity and significance for man, eating and acting as if the present Lord were not present but had failed to keep His promise, as if His redemptive death did not signify, as if His "Drink of it, all of you," did not bind all His disciples together. The "unworthiness" is impenitence and unbelief. Cf. the "worthy" of Mt 10: 11, 13.

11:32 *Chastened.* The Lord's judgments are disciplinary and corrective, designed to create repentance and to lead men to righteousness and life. (Cf. Heb 12:5-11)

12:1 — 14:40 Cf. Introduction, par. 24. The Holy Spirit puts men under the Lordship of Jesus, the Crucified; the gifts which the Spirit bestows are therefore to be the expression of the Lord's self-giving will and are to be used in mutual ministration for the church, the body of Christ, where (as in the human body) no member can be solitary and self-sufficient and all members are necessary (ch. 12). The highest gift of the Spirit is the gift of

one speaking by the Spirit of God ever says "Jesus be cursed!" and no one can say "Jesus is Lord" except by the Holy Spirit.

4 Now there are varieties of gifts, but the same Spirit; 5 and there are varieties of service, but the same Lord; 6 and there are varieties of working, but it is the same God who inspires them all in every one. 7 To each is given the manifestation of the Spirit for the common good. 8 To one is given through the Spirit the utterance of wisdom, and to another the utterance of knowledge according to the same Spirit, 9 to another faith by the same Spirit, to another gifts of healing by the one Spirit, 10 to another the working of miracles, to another prophecy, to another the ability to distinguish between spirits, to another various kinds of tongues, to another the interpretation of tongues. 11All these are inspired by one and the same Spirit, who apportions to each one individually as he wills.

12 For just as the body is one and has many members, and all the members of the body, though many, are one body, so it is with Christ. 13 For by one Spirit we were all baptized into one body—Jews or Greeks, slaves or free—and all were made to drink of one Spirit.

14 For the body does not consist of one member but of many. 15 If the foot should say, "Because I am not a hand, I do not belong to the body," that would not make it any less a part of the body. 16And if the ear should say, "Because I am not an eye, I do not belong to the body," that would not make it any less a part of the body. 17 If the whole body were an eye, where would be the hearing? If the whole body were an ear, where would be the sense of smell? 18 But as it is, God arranged the organs in the body, each one of them, as he chose. 19 If all were a single organ, where would the body be? 20As it is, there are many parts, yet one body. 21 The eye cannot say to the hand, "I have no need of you," nor again the head to the feet, "I have no need of you." 22 On the contrary, the parts of the body which seem to be weaker are indispensable, 23 and those parts of the body which we think less honorable we invest with the greater honor, and our unpresentable parts are treated with greater modesty, 24 which our

that indispensable love which sets man free for ministry (ch. 13). No gift of the Spirit is being used rightly when it is used to foster individualism in worship and creates a confusion which does not edify. The God who gave His Son to be the Peace of the world is a God of peace and not of confusion; He would have *all things . . . done decently and in order.* (Ch. 14)

12:1 *Spiritual gifts,* gifts "inspired" by the Holy Spirit (11), apportioned to various individuals in the church "for the common good" (7). For a list of such gifts (not intended to be exhaustive), see 8-10, 28, and cf. Ro 12:6-8.

12:2 *Led astray,* by demonic "spirits" (cf. 10:20). Man is never autonomous; as he is subject either to sin or righteousness (Ro 6:18, 22), so he is inspired either by a spirit that leads him to reject Jesus as the Accursed (cf. Gl 3:13) or by the Spirit, who leads him to confess Jesus as Lord. (3)

12:3 *Jesus is Lord.* This has been appropriately called the church's first creed. To confess Jesus as Lord is to anticipate the universal acclamation that will hail Him Lord at the end of days (Ph 2: 9-11) and to enter into the salvation of the last days even now. (Ro 10:9)

12:9 *Faith.* In distinction from the faith which is the common and indispensable possession of all Christians, this is that peculiar "measure of faith" (Ro 12:3) given to some, which enables them "to move mountains" (13:2; Mt 17:20; 21:21). Men with this gift draw their life so wholly from God and can live their life so wholly for God that they dare things deemed impossible.

12:10 *Distinguish between spirits,* whether they are demonic (cf. 2 note) or of God, of Christ or of antichrist. (1 Jn 4:1-3)

Kinds of tongues, glossolalia, a kind of devotional utterance inspired by the Spirit which does not engage the mind of the speaker as prophetic speech does (14:13-19) and remains unintelligible to the hearers unless interpreted to them by one endowed with the gift of *interpretation* (14:6-9). Paul prizes the gift of tongues both for himself and the church (14:5, 18, 39) but is constrained to protest against an exaggerated estimate and an irresponsible, self-centered use of it (ch. 14). It is significant that he mentions this gift last both here and in 2:28.

12:12 *So it is with Christ.* One would expect "with the church"; the fact that Paul says *Christ* shows how close the tie between Christ and His church is.

12:13 *Made to drink,* i. e., "given to drink" (there is no thought of compulsion). The reference is to the Lord's Supper.

12:22-24 *Parts of the body . . . weaker . . . less honorable . . . unpresentable.* Jesus' concern for the "little ones" in His church (Mt 18:5, 10, 14) is reflected in Paul's words here. He is protecting the less brilliantly endowed members of the church against the disregard and contempt of the Corinthian admiration society. The analogy of the body's less honorable members enables Paul to make two points: God, Creator and Redeemer, has put them where they are, and He has made them an indispensable part of the whole organism.

more presentable parts do not require. But God has so composed the body, giving the greater honor to the inferior part, 25 that there may be no discord in the body, but that the members may have the same care for one another. 26 If one member suffers, all suffer together; if one member is honored, all rejoice together.

27 Now you are the body of Christ and individually members of it. 28And God has appointed in the church first apostles, second prophets, third teachers, then workers of miracles, then healers, helpers, administrators, speakers in various kinds of tongues. 29Are all apostles? Are all prophets? Are all teachers? Do all work miracles? 30 Do all possess gifts of healing? Do all speak with tongues? Do all interpret? 31 But earnestly desire the higher gifts.

And I will show you a still more excellent way.

13 If I speak in the tongues of men and of angels, but have not love, I am a noisy gong or a clanging cymbal. 2And if I have prophetic powers, and understand all mysteries and all knowledge, and if I have all faith, so as to remove mountains, but have not love, I am nothing. 3 If I give away all I have, and if I deliver my body to be burned,[v] but have not love, I gain nothing.

4 Love is patient and kind; love is not jealous or boastful; 5 it is not arrogant or rude. Love does not insist on its own way; it is not irritable or resentful; 6 it does not rejoice at wrong, but rejoices in the right. 7 Love bears all things, believes all things, hopes all things, endures all things.

8 Love never ends; as for prophecies, they will pass away; as for tongues, they will cease; as for knowledge, it will pass away. 9 For our knowledge is imperfect and our prophecy is imperfect; 10 but when the perfect comes, the imperfect will pass away. 11 When I was a child, I spoke like a child, I thought like a child, I reasoned like a child; when I became a man, I gave up childish ways. 12 For now we see in a mirror dimly, but then face to face. Now I know in part; then I shall understand fully, even as I have been fully understood. 13 So faith, hope, love abide, these three; but the greatest of these is love.

14 Make love your aim, and earnestly desire the spiritual gifts, especially that you may prophesy. 2 For one who speaks in a tongue speaks not to men but to God; for no one understands him, but he utters mysteries in the Spirit. 3 On the other hand, he who prophesies speaks to men for their upbuilding and encouragement and consolation. 4 He who speaks in a tongue edifies himself, but he who prophesies

[v] Other ancient authorities read *body that I may glory*

12:28 *Apostles . . . prophets . . . teachers.* Cf. Eph 4:11 note.

12:31 *The higher gifts,* those that especially serve the common good (7), which are a manifestation of love (ch. 13), for the upbuilding of the church. (Ch. 14)

13:1 *Tongues of men and of angels,* the overprized gift at Corinth. (Cf. 12:10 note, 28; ch. 14)

Gong . . . cymbal, sound that signifies nothing.

Love. The question whether Paul is speaking of love for God or for man is beside the point. Both are meant; words like "patient" and "kind" (4) indicate that love for man is included, and the close connection between love and faith and hope (13, cf. 7) shows that love for God is included also. Paul sees the two as a unity, as Jesus did. (Mt 22: 34-40; cf. Mt 22:15-40 note)

13:2 *Faith.* Cf. 12:9 note.

13:3 *Body . . . burned.* Even the heroic grace of martyrdom is valueless if it is not an expression of love as Christ's death was, a death "for many."

13:4 *Not jealous.* The word *not* occurs six times (eight times in the Greek) in the enumeration of the qualities of love, an indication that this love runs against the grain of man's normal willing and doing. It is not of this age or this world but a gift

from God, an anticipation of the world to come. (Cf. 8-13)

13:7 *Love* is able to bear up under all pressures that threaten to suppress it *(bears, endures)* because it is completely open to God *(believes all things)* and to God's great future for men *(hopes all things).* For the intrinsic connection between love and hope cf. Cl 1:4; Ro 13:8-11; between love and faith, Gl 5:6; 1 Ti 1:5.

13:12 *Dimly,* because the divine reality is apprehended at second hand, by reflection, mediately rather than with the immediacy of *face to face* encounter.

13:13 *Faith, hope, love.* Cf. 7 note. As these three coexist in necessary connection now, so they will *abide,* continue in eternity, together; love is *greatest* because without it even a faith which removes mountains (2) and a hope that expends its life in hope of the world to come (3) is void and valueless.

14:3 *Speaks to men for their upbuilding.* Cf. 12:7, "for the common good." This is the major emphasis of the chapter: 4, 5, 6 ("benefit"), 12, 17, 19 ("instruct"), 25 ("he will worship God"), 26, 31 ("learn . . . be encouraged"). Gifts receive their place and value in accordance with their power to edify all;

edifies the church. [5] Now I want you all to speak in tongues, but even more to prophesy. He who prophesies is greater than he who speaks in tongues, unless some one interprets, so that the church may be edified.

6 Now, brethren, if I come to you speaking in tongues, how shall I benefit you unless I bring you some revelation or knowledge or prophecy or teaching? [7] If even lifeless instruments, such as the flute or the harp, do not give distinct notes, how will any one know what is played? [8]And if the bugle gives an indistinct sound, who will get ready for battle? [9] So with yourselves; if you in a tongue utter speech that is not intelligible, how will any one know what is said? For you will be speaking into the air. [10] There are doubtless many different languages in the world, and none is without meaning; [11] but if I do not know the meaning of the language, I shall be a foreigner to the speaker and the speaker a foreigner to me. [12] So with yourselves; since you are eager for manifestations of the Spirit, strive to excel in building up the church.

13 Therefore, he who speaks in a tongue should pray for the power to interpret. [14] For if I pray in a tongue, my spirit prays but my mind is unfruitful. [15] What am I to do? I will pray with the spirit and I will pray with the mind also; I will sing with the spirit and I will sing with the mind also. [16] Otherwise, if you bless [w] with the spirit, how can any one in the position of an outsider [x] say the "Amen" to your thanksgiving when he does not know what you are saying? [17] For you may give thanks well enough, but the other man is not edified. [18] I thank God that I speak in tongues more than you all; [19] nevertheless, in church I would rather speak five words with my mind, in order to instruct others, than ten thousand words in a tongue.

20 Brethren, do not be children in your thinking; be babes in evil, but in thinking be mature. [21] In the law it is written, "By men of strange tongues and by the lips of foreigners will I speak to this people, and even then they will not listen to me, says the Lord." [22] Thus, tongues are a sign not for believers but for unbelievers, while prophecy is not for unbelievers but for believers. [23] If, therefore, the whole church assembles and all speak in tongues, and outsiders or unbelievers enter, will they not say that you are mad? [24] But if all prophesy, and an unbeliever or outsider enters, he is convicted by all, he is called to account by all, [25] the secrets of his heart are disclosed; and so, falling on his face, he will worship God and declare that God is really among you.

26 What then, brethren? When you come together, each one has a hymn, a lesson, a revelation, a tongue, or an interpretation. Let all things be done for edification. [27] If any speak in a tongue, let there be only two or at most three, and each in turn; and let one interpret. [28] But if there is no one to interpret, let each of them keep silence in church and speak to himself and to God. [29] Let two or three prophets speak, and let the others weigh what is said. [30] If a revelation is made to another sitting by, let the first be silent. [31] For you can all prophesy one by one, so that all may learn and all be encouraged; [32] and the spirits of prophets are subject to prophets. [33] For God is not a God of confusion but of peace.

[w] That is, *give thanks to God*   [x] Or *him that is without gifts*

therefore prophecy (inspired preaching) is superior to the self-edifying (4) gift of tongues. (5)

14:13-19 The word *mind* occurs four times in seven verses. The letters of Paul witness to the intense intellectual activity which the Spirit produces. Anti-intellectualism will find small comfort in the apostolic Word, which recognizes man's mind as a gift from God.

14:21-25 *In the law. Law* is used for the OT generally. (Cf. Ro 3:19, where Psalms are called "law.") The quotation is from Is 28:11-12; there the prophet threatens the people who have sneered (Is 28:9-10) at the clear prophetic Word: God will speak to them in an unclear fashion *by men of strange tongues* as a punishment on their impenitence and unbelief, "that they may go, and fall backward, and be broken, and snared, and taken"

(Is 28:13). Thus the unintelligible language of strange *tongues* becomes a *sign,* a token of God's presence and activity, *for unbelievers,* to harden them judgmentally in their unbelief; while the clear speech of *prophecy* becomes a token of God's present activity *for believers* to establish and confirm them in their faith. They will not call men *mad* who speak openly for God; they will repent and *worship God.*

14:29 *Weigh what is said.* Cf. 1 Th 5:19-21.

14:32-33 *The spirits of prophets are subject to prophets.* The prophets may not evade responsibility for the unedifying confusion by pleading that inspiration compels them to speak; prophets are not mad dervishes but clear-minded and responsible spokesmen of the God of wholesome order *(peace).*

As in all the churches of the saints, 34 the women should keep silence in the churches. For they are not permitted to speak, but should be subordinate, as even the law says. 35 If there is anything they desire to know, let them ask their husbands at home. For it is shameful for a woman to speak in church. 36 What! Did the word of God originate with you, or are you the only ones it has reached?

37 If any one thinks that he is a prophet, or spiritual, he should acknowledge that what I am writing to you is a command of the Lord. 38 If any one does not recognize this, he is not recognized. 39 So, my brethren, earnestly desire to prophesy, and do not forbid speaking in tongues; 40 but all things should be done decently and in order.

The Resurrection of the Dead

15:1-58

SIGNIFICANCE OF RESURRECTION OF CHRIST (15:1-34)

15 Now I would remind you, brethren, in what terms I preached to you the gospel, which you received, in which you stand, 2 by which you are saved, if you hold it fast—unless you believed in vain.

3 For I delivered to you as of first importance what I also received, that Christ died for our sins in accordance with the scriptures, 4 that he was buried, that he was raised on the third day in accordance with the scriptures, 5 and that he appeared to Cephas, then to the twelve. 6 Then he appeared to more than five hundred brethren at one time, most of whom are still alive, though some have fallen asleep. 7 Then he appeared

14:34-35 *Women . . . keep silence.* In 11:3-16 Paul had established the basic rule for the behavior of woman: Even in prayer and prophecy, where she is her most religious and spiritual self, woman is not to forget or deny her created womanliness. This is now applied to woman's behavior *in the churches,* the assemblies or meetings. What the *law says* (Gn 3:16) is upheld by the Gospel: Woman is to be *subordinate* and not assume a function in the church beyond that which her Lord has assigned to her. (Cf. 1 Ti 2:11-12; 1 Ptr 3:1; Eph 5:22-33)

14:36 The church at Corinth is neither the first nor the only church and cannot therefore claim a privileged position on this point; the *word of God* rules all churches equally.

14:37 *Command of the Lord,* since Christ speaks in Paul (2 Co 13:3; Ro 15:18) and his word is God's Word to men. (1 Th 2:13)

14:38 *He is not recognized,* that is, not recognized by Christ as His own. If he continues in disobedience to the apostolic Word, he must expect to hear his Lord say to him on the Last Day: "I never knew you." (Mt 7:23)

15:1-58 Cf. Introduction, par. 25. To the vaporings of *some* who deny the resurrection of Christ by denying the resurrection of the dead in Christ, Paul opposes his trenchant and detailed proclamation of the central significance of the resurrection of Christ and clears the question of the manner of the bodily resurrection of the dead.

15:1-34 The resurrection of the dead stands or falls with the firmly attested fact of the resurrection of the Christ who *died for our sins;* Paul marshals the witnesses to that fact (1-11). So firmly established is the link between the two, between the resurrection of the Christ and the

resurrection of those who are His, that the reverse is also true: The resurrection of Christ stands or falls with the resurrection of the Christian dead. And if the resurrection of Christ falls, all is lost; the cross is indeed "emptied of its power" (1:17), for no mere martyr's death can assure the forgiveness of sins; what the apostles are proclaiming is nothing and worse than nothing, a lie; what the church believes is nothing; and the church's hope is nothing. Christian suffering and martyrdom have lost all point and purpose (12-19; 29-32). *But in fact Christ has been raised from the dead* (20)—and that fact is the all-controlling fact of all history. As surely as *all men* are, under the judgment of God, in a solidarity of dying *in Adam,* so surely all men are, by God's acquitting judgment, destined to *be made alive,* destined to share in His reign, in His triumph over death, and in His final obeisance to the Father, *that God may be everything to every one* (20-28). And yet the Corinthians have listened to *some* who *have no knowledge of God,* for all their vaunted knowledge and wisdom. In their intoxicated delusion they have admitted into their midst *bad company* that will ruin them morally by tampering with the fact on which the whole Christian life depends. (32-34)

15:3-4 Scholars are generally agreed that these sentences are a quotation from an early Christian catechism.

15:4 *Was raised.* The tense of *raised* in Greek is different from that of the preceding two verbs, being a present perfect, which indicates completed action with enduring results; Paul is emphasizing the fact that the resurrection of Christ is of enduring force and significance.

15:5 *Cephas,* Peter. Cf. 1:12.

15:7 *James,* most likely James the brother of

to James, then to all the apostles. ⁸ Last of all, as to one untimely born, he appeared also to me. ⁹ For I am the least of the apostles, unfit to be called an apostle, because I persecuted the church of God. ¹⁰ But by the grace of God I am what I am, and his grace toward me was not in vain. On the contrary, I worked harder than any of them, though it was not I, but the grace of God which is with me. ¹¹ Whether then it was I or they, so we preach and so you believed.

12 Now if Christ is preached as raised from the dead, how can some of you say that there is no resurrection of the dead? ¹³ But if there is no resurrection of the dead, then Christ has not been raised; ¹⁴ if Christ has not been raised, then our preaching is in vain and your faith is in vain. ¹⁵ We are even found to be misrepresenting God, because we testified of God that he raised Christ, whom he did not raise if it is true that the dead are not raised. ¹⁶ For if the dead are not raised, then Christ has not been raised. ¹⁷ If Christ has not been raised, your faith is futile and you are still in your sins. ¹⁸ Then those also who have fallen asleep in Christ have perished. ¹⁹ If for this life only we have hoped in Christ, we are of all men most to be pitied.

20 But in fact Christ has been raised from the dead, the first fruits of those who have fallen asleep. ²¹ For as by a man came death, by a man has come also the resurrection of the dead. ²² For as in Adam all die, so also in Christ shall all be made alive. ²³ But each in his own order: Christ the first fruits, then at his coming those who belong to Christ. ²⁴ Then comes the end, when he delivers the kingdom to God the Father after destroying every rule and every authority and power. ²⁵ For he must reign until he has put all his enemies under his feet. ²⁶ The last enemy to be destroyed is death. ²⁷ "For God ^z has put all things in subjection under his feet." But when it says, "All things are put in subjection under him," it is plain that he is excepted who put all things under him. ²⁸ When all things are subjected to him, then the Son himself will also be subjected to him who put all things under him, that God may be everything to every one.

29 Otherwise, what do people mean by being baptized on behalf of the dead? If the dead are not raised at all, why are people baptized on their behalf? ³⁰ Why am I in peril every hour? ³¹ I protest, brethren, by my pride in you which I have in Christ Jesus our Lord, I die every day! ³² What do I gain if, humanly speaking, I fought with

^z Greek *he*

Jesus, prominent in the first church. Cf Introduction to the Letter of James.

All the apostles, apparently a larger group than the original 12 (5), men commissioned by the risen Christ. (Cf. Ro 16:1-16 note)

15:8 *One untimely born.* Paul did not come to apostleship in the normal way, as a disciple of the Lord on earth (cf. Acts 1:21-22); thus he appears as an abnormal and violent birth.

15:11 *Believed,* came to believe, were brought to faith.

15:17 *Still in your sins.* For the same thought stated positively (salvation is by faith in the risen Christ) cf. Ro 10:9.

15:21-22 *Adam . . . Christ.* Cf. Ro 5:12-21 note.

15:23 *First fruits.* Christ is the beginning and the guarantee of the full harvest of the resurrection of the dead.

15:25 *Enemies under his feet.* Cf. Ps 110:1; Mt 22:41-44.

15:27 *All things . . . in subjection.* Cf. Ps 8:6. In the "man" (21) Jesus Christ the psalmist's word concerning man becomes full truth. (Cf. Heb 2:5-9)

15:28 *The Son himself will also be subjected.* Christ's whole Servant ministry and His subsequent exaltation are both "to the glory of God the Father." (Cf. Ph 2:11 note)

15:29 *Baptized on behalf of the dead.* Since baptism on behalf of the dead is not explained or even mentioned elsewhere in the NT, one can only conjecture what Paul is referring to here. Many conjectures have been made, none really satisfactory. One that meets the conditions of Paul's argument is this: A man is moved to accept the faith and be baptized by the pleadings of a dying relative or friend; he receives baptism *on behalf of* (for) *the dead,* i. e., in the hope of meeting the beloved person in the life of the world to come. If there is no resurrection and no life in the world to come, such an action is obviously foolish.

15:31 *By my pride in you.* For Paul's proud delight in his churches as the "crown" of his sufferings and labors, the "seal" of his apostleship in the Lord, cf. 9:2; 2 Co 1:14; 1 Th 2:19-20. Paul can exult in his work and in his converts only as one who has led them into eternal life by implanting in them "Christ . . . the hope of glory." (Cl 1:27, cf. 24)

15:32 *Fought with beasts,* probably a figurative expression for facing extreme danger; Paul had "many adversaries" at Ephesus (16:9), and he is probably referring to an incident in Ephesus when he speaks of a great "affliction" and a "deadly peril" in the province of Asia. (2 Co 1:8-10)

15:32 *Let us eat,* etc. Cf. Is 22:13, where the saying is found in the mouth of desperate and reckless men who have refused God's call to repentance.

beasts at Eph′e·sus? If the dead are not raised, "Let us eat and drink, for tomorrow we die." [33] Do not be deceived: "Bad company ruins good morals." [34] Come to your right mind, and sin no more. For some have no knowledge of God. I say this to your shame.

MANNER OF RESURRECTION OF THE DEAD (15:35-58)

35 But some one will ask, "How are the dead raised? With what kind of body do they come?" [36] You foolish man! What you sow does not come to life unless it dies. [37]And what you sow is not the body which is to be, but a bare kernel, perhaps of wheat or of some other grain. [38] But God gives it a body as he has chosen, and to each kind of seed its own body. [39] For not all flesh is alike, but there is one kind for men, another for animals, another for birds, and another for fish. [40] There are celestial bodies and there are terrestrial bodies; but the glory of the celestial is one, and the glory of the terrestrial is another. [41] There is one glory of the sun, and another glory of the moon, and another glory of the stars; for star differs from star in glory.

42 So is it with the resurrection of the dead. What is sown is perishable, what is raised is imperishable. [43] It is sown in dishonor, it is raised in glory. It is sown in weakness, it is raised in power. [44] It is sown a physical body, it is raised a spiritual body. If there is a physical body, there is also a spiritual body. [45] Thus it is written, "The first man Adam became a living being"; the last Adam became a life-giving spirit. [46] But it is not the spiritual which is first but the physical, and then the spiritual. [47] The first man was from the earth, a man of dust; the second man is from heaven. [48]As was the man of dust, so are those who are of the dust; and as is the man of heaven, so are those who are of heaven. [49] Just as we have borne the image of the man of dust, we shall[a] also bear the image of the man of heaven. [50] I tell you this, brethren: flesh and blood cannot inherit the kingdom of God, nor does the perishable inherit the imperishable.

51 Lo! I tell you a mystery. We shall not all sleep, but we shall all be changed, [52] in a moment, in the twinkling of an eye, at the last trumpet. For the trumpet will sound, and the dead will be raised imperishable, and we shall be changed. [53] For this

[a] Other ancient authorities read *let us*

15:33 *Bad company*, etc. Paul is quoting from a play by Menander, a popular dramatist.

Good morals. For the moral power of the resurrection cf. Ro 6:4, 12-14.

15:34 *Come to your right mind.* Literally "Sober up!" Only one who is intoxicated on the heady wine of the "new theology" could dream of abandoning the bright sobriety of the resurrection hope.

Knowledge of God. To know God in faith is to know Him as the God "who gives life to the dead." (Ro 4:17)

15:35-58 Those who deny the resurrection of the dead are foolish enough to ask: *How are the dead raised? With what kind of body do they come?* (35). They thereby reveal their ignorance of God (cf. 34), who with His lavish creative power gives each of His creatures its own fit kind of body and beauty; for Him the death of the seed is the occasion for a new *life* (36-41). He can as certainly create a new, *spiritual* body for His new creature, the man in Christ, as He created a physical body for the man in Adam. He can bridge the gulf that separates *flesh and blood* from His future *kingdom*, by clothing *mortal* men with *immortality* (42-53). How can the Corinthians listen to *foolish men* who in their ignorance of God cast to the winds the *victory* over sin and death given them *through* the *Lord Jesus Christ*, that triumphant certainty of life which makes men not theological theorists or debaters

but *steadfast, immovable, always abounding in the work of the Lord?* (54-58)

15:38 *God gives it a body.* Paul is arguing not from "nature" but from God the Creator, who can provide body (38), flesh (39), and glory (40) as He wills.

15:44 *Spiritual body. Spiritual* may mean simply "supernatural" (the word is so translated in 10:3-4), or may designate a body which is the perfect dwelling and instrument of the Spirit (cf. 6:19), the kind of body for which those who have "the first fruits of the Spirit" so intensely long. (Ro 8:23)

15:45 *The first . . . Adam.* Cf. Gn 2:7.

The last Adam, Christ.

15:46 *Not the spiritual which is first but the physical.* Paul is arguing against an idea current in Judaism that the first man is an ideal man, the redeemer; Jesus, "the last Adam" (45), the "man from heaven" (47), the *spiritual* man (conceived by the Spirit, endued with the Spirit, working in the power of the Spirit) is the Redeemer, He alone.

15:50 *Flesh and blood cannot inherit the kingdom.* Cf. 53: "This perishable nature must put on the imperishable." Paul stresses both the continuity and the discontinuity between man's present existence and his existence in the world to come. The words "put on" provide the link between the two.

perishable nature must put on the imperishable, and this mortal nature must put on immortality. 54 When the perishable puts on the imperishable, and the mortal puts on immortality, then shall come to pass the saying that is written:

"Death is swallowed up in victory."

55   "O death, where is thy victory?
O death, where is thy sting?"

56 The sting of death is sin, and the power of sin is the law. 57 But thanks be to God, who gives us the victory through our Lord Jesus Christ.

58 Therefore, my beloved brethren, be steadfast, immovable, always abounding in the work of the Lord, knowing that in the Lord your labor is not in vain.

Practical and Personal Matters

16:1-24

16 Now concerning the contribution for the saints: as I directed the churches of Galatia, so you also are to do. 2 On the first day of every week, each of you is to put something aside and store it up, as he may prosper, so that contributions need not be made when I come. 3And when I arrive, I will send those whom you accredit by letter to carry your gift to Jerusalem. 4 If it seems advisable that I should go also, they will accompany me.

5 I will visit you after passing through Macedonia, for I intend to pass through Macedonia, 6 and perhaps I will stay with you or even spend the winter, so that you may speed me on my journey, wherever I go. 7 For I do not want to see you now just in passing; I hope to spend some time with you, if the Lord permits. 8 But I will stay in Eph'e·sus until Pentecost, 9 for a wide door for effective work has opened to me, and there are many adversaries.

10 When Timothy comes, see that you put him at ease among you, for he is doing the work of the Lord, as I am. 11 So let no one despise him. Speed him on his way in peace, that he may return to me; for I am expecting him with the brethren.

12 As for our brother A·pol'los, I strongly urged him to visit you with the other brethren, but it was not at all his will[b] to come now. He will come when he has opportunity.

[b] Or *God's will for him*

15:54 *Death is swallowed up,* etc. Cf. Is 25:8.

15:55 Cf. Hos 13:14.

15:56 Here Paul establishes the connection between Adam as the author of death for all men and Adam as the source of guilt and sin in all men (cf. Ro 5:12-21 note). It is *sin* that gives *death* power over men, sin is the *sting,* or goad, with which death impels men into his realm; "because of one man's trespass, death reigns over men" (Ro 5:17). The *law* is the *power of sin;* sin (personified) grows powerful when man is confronted by the Law and rebels against the will of God (Ro 7:7-11). Thus the Law comes in "to increase the trespass." (Ro 5:20)

15:58 *Work of the Lord.* Faith in the risen Lord made a worker of Paul (10), and it will make workers of the men of the church.

**16:1-4 THE COLLECTION FOR THE
SAINTS AT JERUSALEM**

16:1-4 For the *contribution for the saints* and what it meant for the apostle cf. Ro 15:25-28; 2 Co 8 and 9; and Introduction to 2 Co, par. 6.

16:4 *Advisable that I should go.* The journey to Jerusalem would be dangerous for Paul. Cf. Ro 15:25, 30-31; Acts 20:22-24; 21:10-12; and the

story of Paul's arrest in Jerusalem, which led to his imprisonment in Caesarea and Rome (Acts 20: 27 — 28:31). See also the Introduction to the Captivity Letters (Eph, Ph, Cl, Phmn).

16:5-9 PAUL'S TRAVEL PLANS

16:5 *Visit you.* Cf. 4:18-21; 11:34

16:8 *Pentecost,* the Hebrew Feast of Weeks. (Ex 34:22; Dt 16:10)

16:9 *Door.* For the figurative sense of *door* as "opportunity" cf. 2 Co 2:12; Cl 4:3.

16:10-12 TIMOTHY AND APOLLOS

16:10 *Timothy . . . put him at ease.* Cf. 4:17 and Introduction to 2 Co, par. 1. The request to put him at ease is accounted for by Timothy's inclination to timidity (2 Ti 1:7) and the tensions that had arisen (and were to increase) between Paul and the Corinthian church.

16:12 *Apollos.* Cf. Introduction, pars. 10 and 11. Both Paul's affectionate tone in speaking of him and Apollos' refusal to come to Corinth at a time when his presence would tend to intensify the factionalism in the church testify to the cordial and harmonious relationship between the two men.

13 Be watchful, stand firm in your faith, be courageous, be strong. [14] Let all that you do be done in love.

15 Now, brethren, you know that the household of Steph′a·nas were the first converts in A·cha′ia, and they have devoted themselves to the service of the saints; [16] I urge you to be subject to such men and to every fellow worker and laborer. [17] I rejoice at the coming of Steph′a·nas and Fortunatus and A·cha′i·cus, because they have made up for your absence; [18] for they refreshed my spirit as well as yours. Give recognition to such men.

19 The churches of Asia send greetings. Aq′ui·la and Prisca, together with the church in their house, send you hearty greetings in the Lord. [20]All the brethren send greetings. Greet one another with a holy kiss.

21 I, Paul, write this greeting with my own hand. [22] If any one has no love for the Lord, let him be accursed. Our Lord, come![c] [23] The grace of the Lord Jesus be with you. [24] My love be with you all in Christ Jesus. Amen.

[c] Greek *Maranatha*

16:13-20 ADMONITION, COMMENDATIONS, AND GREETINGS

16:15-17 *Stephanas . . . Fortunatus . . . Achaicus.* Cf. Introduction, par. 20.

16:18 *Refreshed my spirit as well as yours.* The presence of these three stalwarts refreshed Paul's spirit by bringing him assurance of the church's desire to continue in obedience to their apostle (11:2) and by providing him with accurate, first-hand information. Their presence with Paul in Ephesus refreshes the spirit of the Corinthian church because it assures the faithful that their concerns are known to their father in Christ and will be dealt with.

16:19 *Aquila* and *Prisca.* Cf. Ro 16:3 note.

16:20 *Holy kiss.* Cf. Ro 16:16; 1 Ptr 5:14. The exchange of the kiss marked the congregation as one family in Christ.

16:21-24 AUTOGRAPH CONCLUSION

16:21 *With my own hand.* For Paul's habit of adding a greeting in his own handwriting to his dictated letters cf. Gl 6:11; Cl 4:18; 2 Th 3:17.

16:22 *Our Lord come!* Paul gives this prayer for the return of the Lord in Aramaic: *Maranatha.* The original language was probably retained in the liturgy of Greek-speaking churches, as were terms like "amen," "hosanna," and "hallelujah."

CORINTHIANS

INTRODUCTION

For the history of Paul's previous association with the Corinthian church see the Introduction to First Corinthians.

The Coming of Timothy

1 Paul had in his first letter prepared the church of Corinth for a coming visit by Timothy. That visit was designed by Paul to reinforce and carry further the work which his letter was designed to do, namely, to bring the Corinthians back from their flight out of Christian reality into an intoxicated and enthusiastic individualism, back to the cross, back to where Paul stood: "I urge you . . . be imitators of me. Therefore I sent to you Timothy . . . to remind you of my ways in Christ, as I teach them . . . in every church" (1 Co 4:16-17). What those "ways in Christ" were the immediately preceding context makes plain: Paul ironically contrasts the blissful state of the Corinthians, who have become kings, who are rich and reign, are wise and strong and held in honor, with the apostles' wretched and unfinished state under the cross, men sentenced to death, a spectacle for angels and men to gaze on, fools, weak, in disrepute, hungry, thirsty, ill-clad, homeless, the meekly enduring, toilworn refuse of the world (1 Co 4:8-13). Paul anticipates that Timothy's task will not be a pleasant one and that the reception he will get may be less than amiable (1 Co 16:10-11). Timothy's stay was brief, and since Second Corinthians says nothing of it, we know nothing of its results except what we can infer from the events that followed.

Paul's Intermediate Visit to Corinth

2 Timothy soon returned to Paul, who thus quickly learned how his letter had been received and how things stood at Corinth. What he heard moved him to interrupt his work at Ephesus and to proceed to Corinth at once. This is the second visit, which is implied by 2 Co 13:1-2; 12:21, the "painful visit" to which Paul alludes in 2 Co 2:1. Timothy's report had made clear to Paul that the influence of the new teachers had spread farther and gone deeper than he had realized. There were not only "some" who were arrogant (1 Co 4:18), "some" who denied the central content of the apostolic proclamation (1 Co 15:12); the whole church was infected and endangered – the very existence of the "temple of God" (1 Co 3:17) was being threatened. Immediate action was necessary, drastic action which had to be taken personally. The visit therefore proved to be a painful one for the Corinthians, who were rudely shaken out of their dreaming self-assurance by the home truths which their apostle had to tell them (2 Co 2:2; 13:2); but it was a painful visit for Paul too, for the opposition to him, under the leadership of the men who claimed to be Christ's, proved strong. They must have been bold, intellectually vigorous, and capable men – they were able to face Paul and keep a sizable part of the congregation with them. Just what form Paul's dealings with the church took cannot be clearly made out, but this much is plain: Paul was convinced that fellowship with the new leaders was no longer possible, that a break had to be made (2 Co 13:2); he left Corinth, however, without immediately forcing the issue. He still trusted that the church would come to see the necessity for the break as clearly as he himself saw it and left with the promise that he would return to Corinth when his work in Ephesus was done and would pay the church a double visit, both before and after the proposed revisitation of the Macedonian churches (2 Co 1:15-16). This was of course a change from the travel plans Paul had announced in 1 Co 16:5-6.

The Severe Letter

3 What follows now is the obscurest part of an obscure history. Paul's trust that the church would see the light and would walk in that light was apparently disappointed. There occurred an incident which strained still further the already strained relations between Paul and the church. Paul speaks of

one who did an injury which caused him pain (2 Co 2:5), an injury not directly to Paul himself but affecting him. Since Paul does not indicate the nature of the wrong done him, we can only conjecture what it may have been. Perhaps one of the men loyal to Paul suffered violence at the hands of an opponent in the heat of party strife. At any rate, the offense was so flagrant and involved the authority of Paul so immediately that the church could not ignore it and still be in any sense "his" church, still esteem him as apostle and father in Christ. Paul therefore changed his plans once more; instead of going directly to Corinth from Ephesus, he first proceeded northward toward Macedonia by way of Troas. Before leaving Asia he wrote a letter (now lost) to which he refers as a "severe" letter, a letter written "with many tears" (2 Co 2:4). This letter summoned the church to repentance in no uncertain terms: The wrongdoer must be dealt with and disciplined, and the church must return in obedience to its apostle. Paul dispatched the letter by the hand of Titus and instructed Titus to rejoin him at Troas and report on its effect.

The Report of Titus

4   Titus had not yet returned to Troas when Paul arrived there (2 Co 2:12); and so Paul, in an agony of doubt concerning the outcome of Titus' mission, left Troas and proceeded to Macedonia (2 Co 2:13). And God, who comforts the downcast, comforted him by the coming of Titus (2 Co 7:5-6). For Titus brought good news. The church at Corinth had heeded Paul's summons to repentance, had bowed to his authority, had disciplined the offender, who had also repented and asked for forgiveness. The church was ready to forgive him and only awaited Paul's assent to such a course before granting forgiveness. The church thus cleansed and restored by repentance longed to see Paul again, in order that the ties so long strained and endangered might be confirmed and strengthened once more. (2 Co 2:6; 7:7-16)

5   That was the positive side of Titus' report, and Paul welcomed it with that exuberant gratitude with which he received every good gift of God; he did not let the fact that there was another side to the report, a negative one, dampen his joy. Titus' news was not all good. The offender at Corinth had been punished by the "majority" of the congregation only, not by all (2 Co 2:6).

There were still those at Corinth who held to the new teachers. Neither Paul's visit nor his severe letter had silenced the men who maliciously misinterpreted his every word and action, for example, his change in his travel plans (2 Co 1:17) or his letters (2 Co 1:13), and sought always to undermine his apostolic authority. It was probably their influence that had brought to a standstill a project which Paul had promoted with such energy and with such good initial success: the collection for the poor saints at Jerusalem.

Occasion of Paul's Second Letter to the Corinthians

6   The unfinished task of the collection for the saints of Jerusalem was the occasion of Paul's fourth letter to the church at Corinth, our present Second Corinthians, but only the occasion. Dear as the success of that undertaking was to Paul's heart and much as he valued the collection as an expression of the unity between the Gentile and the Judaic church, it is not the central concern of his letter. That is rather the reestablishment of a full and pure understanding of his authority as "apostle of Jesus Christ by the will of God." His desire to make clear forever to the Corinthians wherein the glory and power of his ministry lay is the dominant impulse in his writing. This concern dominates the first section (chs. 1–7), which looks to the past, wherein Paul welcomes the penitent advances of the majority of the church, forgives the disciplined wrongdoer and bespeaks the love of the church for him, and appeals for a renewal of the full communion of love which had been characteristic of his association with the church of Corinth from of old. It dominates the last section of the letter also, where Paul looks forward to his coming visit to Corinth and deals rigorously and definitively with his detractors and their hangers-on (chs. 10–13). And that concern has left its marks also on the chapters (8–9) which deal with the collection; here we see in action that peculiarly divine apostolic authority which seeks nothing for itself, but all for Christ, which will not autocratically lord it over men's faith, but works with men for their joy in Christ (2 Co 1:24). This authority is essentially the vehicle of the potent claim of the grace of the Lord Jesus Christ; therefore it will not command, but need only advise (8:8,10). It is an expression of the Lordship of Christ (8:5),

which can expect and claim obedience only because it is centered wholly in God, the Father of the Lord Jesus Christ, in His power (8:5), His gifts and goodness (8:16; 9:7, 8, 11, 12,15), and has His glory for its goal. (9:13)

Effect of the Letter

7 Paul spent the three winter months A. D. 55—56 in Greece, shortly after the second letter was dispatched to Corinth (Acts 20:2-3), and he there wrote his Letter to the Romans, most likely at Corinth itself. In Romans he looks back over his work in the eastern Mediterranean area as finished and looks westward with serenity and confidence (Ro 15:14-33). No doubt the second letter had done the work it was intended to do, and the reconciliation with Corinth was complete.

Value of the Letter

8 Second Corinthians is certainly one of the most difficult of Paul's letters—which is not to say that it was difficult or obscure for its first readers; they lived in the situation which we must laboriously reconstruct. Since the hints given by the letter itself are not always full enough to permit a complete and accurate reconstruction of the situation, the letter is for us difficult, an angel to be wrestled with if we would receive a blessing. But the blessing is a rich one and worth the wrestling.

9 The letter resembles the Letter to the Galatians in being richly autobiographical; we here see Paul the man in all the human frailty and the human agony which he never attempts to conceal. But Paul the man cannot be separated from Paul the apostle of Jesus Christ by the will of God. And the letter reveals the apostle with a fullness that even Galatians cannot rival. As in Galatians, we see the apostle engaged in battle, here a battle for his very existence as apostle to the Corinthians; and in battle a man shows what he truly is. The battle which Paul wages in this letter reveals him down to the very roots and bases of his apostolic existence. We learn from this revelation that battle must be, and why it must be, in the church of the God and the Prince of peace, that lines must be drawn and where they must be drawn; we learn that Satan is at work even in that which passes for an advanced and superior form of Christianity, that his weapon is always the plausible lie which imitates the truth—one must never forget how very "nice" and very

"Christian" the men of the Christ party must have appeared to be. We learn that battle is necessary in the life of the church and can be salutary for its life.

10 We learn also that the necessity of battle need not harden the battler; the church that fights for truth need not lose the love it had at first, as the church at Ephesus did (Rv 2:4); the first seven chapters of this letter are a witness to the fact that the love which "does not rejoice at wrong, but rejoices in the right" (1 Co 13:6) is the only genuine love. Luther had these chapters especially in mind when he wrote of Second Corinthians: "In his first epistle St. Paul dealt severely with the Corinthians on many points and poured sharp wine into their wounds and terrified them; therefore he now . . . also pours oil into their wounds and is wondrously gracious to them."

11 As an apostle, Paul is a "man in Christ," a man whose whole existence and activity is shaped and formed by the single fact of Him in whom God reconciled the world to Himself. There is hardly a more vivid documentation of this lived Christianity than Second Corinthians. No aspect of Paul's life is exempt from Christ; if he says, "Yes, I will come " or "No, I shall not come," he can say it only in the light of the great Yes which God has spoken to all His promises in Christ (1:20). He can speak of Christian giving only in terms of the grace of our Lord Jesus (8:9). His suffering is the mark of the Christ imprinted on his life.

12 As an apostle Paul is a man in whom Christ speaks; he is the earthen vessel that conveys the treasure of the Christ. Paul is here fighting for his apostolate; that means, he is fighting for the Christ, for the apostolate is nothing less than the power and the presence of Christ among men. Men will find the treasure in this earthen vessel, or they will not find it at all; they will behold the light of the knowledge of the glory of God in the face of Christ in the apostolate, or they will not behold it at all. There is nothing like this letter to bind the church to the apostolic Word of the New Testament. The Reformation's embattled emphasis on *Sola Scriptura* finds powerful justification in this embattled epistle.

13 Through conflict to triumph—Second Corinthians was born of conflict; and the triumph which Christ worked through it is not limited to the restoration of the Corinthian church of the first century. By it the church can triumph still.

OUTLINE

I. 1:1–7:16 Retrospect: Paul's Authority and Ministry in Corinth

    A. 1:1-11 Ministry Under the God of All Comfort

    B. 1:12–2:17 The Ministry of Divine Triumph

    C. 3:1-3 The Ministry Commended by Christ

    D. 3:4–4:6 The Ministry of the New Covenant

    E. 4:7–5:10 The Ministry of Imparting Life of Jesus to Men

    F. 5:11–6:10 The Ministry of Reconciliation

    G. 6:11–7:4 The Ministry of God's Exclusive Appeal

    H. 7:5-16 Titus' Report: The Joyful Prospect of Reconciliation

II. 8:1–9:15 The Present: Collection for Saints of Jerusalem

    A. 8:1-7 The Example of the Churches of Macedonia

    B. 8:8-15 You Know the Grace of the Lord Jesus Christ

    C. 8:16–9:5 Commendation of Titus and Two Brothers

    D. 9:6-15 God Loves a Cheerful Giver

III. 10:1–13:14 Prospect: Paul's Impending Visit to Corinth

    A. 10:1-18 Paul's Defense Against the Charges of His Opponents

    B. 11:1–12:21 Paul's "Foolish" Boasting

    C. 13:1-14 Paul's Impending Visit and Conclusion

THE SECOND LETTER OF PAUL TO THE

CORINTHIANS

Retrospect: Paul's Authority and Ministry in Corinth
1:1—7:16

MINISTRY UNDER THE GOD OF ALL COMFORT (1:1-11)

1 Paul, an apostle of Christ Jesus by the will of God, and Timothy our brother. To the church of God which is at Corinth, with all the saints who are in the whole of A·cha′ia:
2 Grace to you and peace from God our Father and the Lord Jesus Christ.

3 Blessed be the God and Father of our Lord Jesus Christ, the Father of mercies and God of all comfort, 4 who comforts us in all our affliction, so that we may be able to comfort those who are in any affliction, with the comfort with which we ourselves are comforted by God. 5 For as we share abundantly in Christ's sufferings, so through Christ we share abundantly in comfort too.*a* 6 If we are afflicted, it is for your comfort and salvation; and if we are comforted, it is for your comfort, which you experience when you patiently endure the same sufferings that we suffer. 7 Our hope for you is unshaken; for we know that as you share in our sufferings, you will also share in our comfort.

8 For we do not want you to be ignorant, brethren, of the affliction we experienced in Asia; for we were so utterly, unbearably crushed that we despaired of life itself. 9 Why, we felt that we had received the sentence of death; but that was to make us rely not on ourselves but on God who raises the dead; 10 he delivered us from so deadly a peril, and he will deliver us; on him we have set our hope that he will deliver us again. 11 You also must help us by prayer, so that many will give thanks on our behalf for the blessing granted us in answer to many prayers.

THE MINISTRY OF DIVINE TRIUMPH (1:12—2:17)

12 For our boast is this, the testimony of our conscience that we have behaved in the world, and still more toward you, with holiness and godly sincerity, not by earthly

a Or *For as the sufferings of Christ abound for us, so also our comfort abounds through Christ*

1:1—7:16 These 7 chapters are actually the thanksgiving with which Paul regularly opens his letters (cf., e.g., 1 Co 1:4-9); it is here, as in 1 Th, executed on a monumental scale, as an awed and grateful retrospective survey of the ministry which God in His grace has assigned to him, a ministry that binds him to the church of Corinth with a bond nothing human dare undo.

1:1-11 The ministry with which God has entrusted him is pure grace, and the grace of God sustains him in it. He designates himself as *apostle . . . by the will of God* (1), that divine will which has made him the vehicle of *grace . . . and peace* to men, and opens with a thanksgiving to the *Father of our Lord Jesus Christ* who had delivered him from *deadly peril* in the province of Asia, giving him *comfort* in order that he might be able to comfort others in the strength thus given him, the strength, namely, to *rely* solely *on God who raises the dead.* (9)

1:1 *Timothy.* Cf. Introduction, par. 1.

Achaia, the Roman province comprising the southern half of Greece, of which Corinth was the capital. The inclusion of the *saints . . . in the whole of Achaia* in the greeting may indicate that the unsettling tendencies and events in Corinth had affected other churches in the province also.

1:5 *Share . . . in Christ's sufferings.* Cf. Cl 1:24 note.

1:8 *Asia.* The Roman province of Asia is meant. Ephesus was capital of that province, and the events referred to may have occurred there. Cf. 1 Co 16:8-9 ("many adversaries").

1:9 For *God who raises the dead* as object of the faith which despairs of itself and expects everything from His unlimited power cf. Ro 4:17-18.

1:11 Paul involves the church in his ministry; their *prayer* will set off a chain reaction of *blessing granted,* and "thanksgiving, to the glory of God" (4:15). The apostle is sent, faith is created, the church exists and functions to the end that He be glorified.

1:12—2:17 The grace of Paul's apostolic ministry makes his life a life full of agonizing stress;

wisdom but by the grace of God. ¹³ For we write you nothing but what you can read and understand; I hope you will understand fully, ¹⁴ as you have understood in part, that you can be proud of us as we can be of you, on the day of the Lord Jesus.

15 Because I was sure of this, I wanted to come to you first, so that you might have a double pleasure;ᵇ ¹⁶ I wanted to visit you on my way to Macedonia, and to come back to you from Macedonia and have you send me on my way to Judea. ¹⁷ Was I vacillating when I wanted to do this? Do I make my plans like a worldly man, ready to say Yes and No at once? ¹⁸As surely as God is faithful, our word to you has not been Yes and No. ¹⁹ For the Son of God, Jesus Christ, whom we preached among you, Silvanus and Timothy and I, was not Yes and No; but in him it is always Yes. ²⁰ For all the promises of God find their Yes in him. That is why we utter the Amen through him, to the glory of God. ²¹ But it is God who establishes us with you in Christ, and has commissioned us; ²² he has put his seal upon us and given us his Spirit in our hearts as a guarantee.

23 But I call God to witness against me—it was to spare you that I refrained from coming to Corinth. ²⁴ Not that we lord it over your faith; we work with you for your

2 joy, for you stand firm in your faith. ¹ For I made up my mind not to make you another painful visit. ² For if I cause you pain, who is there to make me glad but the one whom I have pained? ³And I wrote as I did, so that when I came I might not suffer pain from those who should have made me rejoice, for I felt sure of all of you, that my joy would be the joy of you all. ⁴ For I wrote you out of much affliction and anguish of heart and with many tears, not to cause you pain but to let you know the abundant love that I have for you.

5 But if any one has caused pain, he has caused it not to me, but in some measure— not to put it too severely—to you all. ⁶ For such a one this punishment by the majority is enough; ⁷ so you should rather turn to forgive and comfort him, or he may be overwhelmed by excessive sorrow. ⁸ So I beg you to reaffirm your love for him. ⁹ For this is why I wrote, that I might test you and know whether you are obedient in everything. ¹⁰Any one whom you forgive, I also forgive. What I have forgiven, if I have forgiven anything, has been for your sake in the presence of Christ, ¹¹ to keep Satan from gaining the advantage over us; for we are not ignorant of his designs.

ᵇ Other ancient authorities read *favor*

---

he has had to endure the malice of men who mis-interpreted his letters and read all manner of subtleties into his transparent *holiness and . . . sincerity* (1:12-14), men who used his change of plans regarding his forthcoming visit to Corinth to charge him with vacillation and unreliability, whereas he had in fact delayed his coming to Corinth in order to *spare* (1:23) the church. He has relied, not on *earthly wisdom* but on the *grace of God* which leads him to act in love always (1:15 – 2:4). And that grace has triumphed; Paul stands vindicated as the proclaimer of the Christ who is God's Yes of fulfillment to all His promises. The church over whose disobedience he has travailed has repented; the offending brother has been disciplined, and Paul pleads that they *reaffirm* their *love for him* (2:8; cf. Introduction, par. 3). *Thanks be to God,* Paul breaks out (2:14) even before he has told of his meeting with Titus, who brought him the comforting news (cf. 7:5-16; Introduction, par. 4), *who in Christ always leads us in triumph.* (2:5-17)

1:12 *For.* "I feel confident of your prayers, *for* I have done nothing to forfeit your confidence and concern," Paul says.

1:14 *Understood in part,* a hint that there are some tensions remaining in the relationship of the church to the apostle; with these Paul intends

to deal in chs. 10 – 13. The *day of the Lord Jesus,* when the purposes of every heart will be disclosed (1 Co 4:5), will put an end to all misunderstandings and tensions.

1:15-16 Paul's plans as projected in 1 Co 16:5 did not provide for two visits to Corinth; perhaps Paul had mentioned this double visit in a letter or by messenger. Now circumstances have moved him to change back to his original plan.

1:20 *We utter the Amen through him.* As God has affirmed and fulfilled all His promises IN Christ, so the church speaks its *Amen* in thanksgiving, praise, and prayer THROUGH Him who is the fulfillment of all promises and the ruling Lord of the church.

1:22 *Seal . . . Spirit.* Cf. Eph 1:13.

Guarantee. Literally "down payment," which in ancient times was a sizable portion of the whole.

2:4 *I wrote you . . . with many tears.* Cf. Introduction, par. 3.

2:10 *You forgive . . . I also forgive.* For Paul's apostolic desire that the church be a mature church capable of independent Christian action cf. 1 Co 5:1-5; 2 Co 13:1-10 note.

2:11 *Satan . . . gaining the advantage over us.* Where the church fails in forgiving and restoring love, Satan (the accuser of men before God, cf. Rv 12:10) has gained a victory.

12 When I came to Troas to preach the gospel of Christ, a door was opened for me in the Lord; [13] but my mind could not rest because I did not find my brother Titus there. So I took leave of them and went on to Macedonia.

14 But thanks be to God, who in Christ always leads us in triumph, and through us spreads the fragrance of the knowledge of him everywhere. [15] For we are the aroma of Christ to God among those who are being saved and among those who are perishing, [16] to one a fragrance from death to death, to the other a fragrance from life to life. Who is sufficient for these things? [17] For we are not, like so many, peddlers of God's word; but as men of sincerity, as commissioned by God, in the sight of God we speak in Christ.

THE MINISTRY COMMENDED BY CHRIST (3:1-3)

3 Are we beginning to commend ourselves again? Or do we need, as some do, letters of recommendation to you, or from you? [2] You yourselves are our letter of recommendation, written on your[c] hearts, to be known and read by all men; [3] and you show that you are a letter from Christ delivered by us, written not with ink but with the Spirit of the living God, not on tablets of stone but on tablets of human hearts.

THE MINISTRY OF THE NEW COVENANT (3:4 — 4:6)

4 Such is the confidence that we have through Christ toward God. [5] Not that we are competent of ourselves to claim anything as coming from us; our competence is from God, [6] who has made us competent to be ministers of a new covenant, not in a written code but in the Spirit; for the written code kills, but the Spirit gives life.

7 Now if the dispensation of death, carved in letters on stone, came with such splendor that the Israelites could not look at Moses' face because of its brightness,

c Other ancient authorities read our

2:14 *Triumph.* Paul is probably thinking of the splendid triumphal processions with which the Caesars and their generals celebrated their victories of human power. Paul's triumph is the triumph of God's grace in Christ.

2:15-16 *Aroma . . . fragrance . . . death . . . life.* What Paul describes in terms of light in 4:6 ("light of the knowledge of the glory of God in the face of Christ"), he here describes as an aroma. That aroma is a reviving and life-giving fragrance to those who accept the Gospel in faith, but a death-dealing fragrance to those who refuse it. The action of the Gospel is not a chemical action but a personal one and is therefore an action "through faith for faith" (Ro 1:17), calling for faith and creating faith. Where it is resisted, the aroma of life becomes the fragrance of *death.*

2:17 *For we are not . . . peddlers of God's word.* Paul dares to answer his question, "Who is sufficient for these things?" (2:16) with a bold, "We are!" because his "sufficiency is from God" (3:5) and his power is the power of His Word, which he does not dilute or adulterate as peddlers do their wares. (Cf. 4:2)

Commissioned by God, in the sight of God. As he is aware of the divine SOURCE of his "sufficiency," so he is aware of his responsibility to Him who has given it to him.

3:1-3 Since his sufficiency is from God (cf. 4), Paul needs no *letters* of men to recommend him in his ministry; the church which his apostolic ministry has by God's grace created stands, open to inspection by all men (2), as his letter of recommendation, *a letter from Christ . . . written . . . with the Spirit of the living God* (3). One thus commended by the Trinity does not need to buttress

his authority (as the "Christ-men" apparently did) with letters from men.

3:2 *Your hearts,* where the Word of God has been received and faith created. (Cf. Ro 10:10)

3:4 — 4:6 God has given Paul his sufficiency as a minister of God's new covenant to exercise a ministry, not of the *written code* of the Law which condemns and kills but a ministry of the *Spirit* which justifies and *gives life,* a ministry not of transient and fading *splendor* (7) (such as Moses' legal ministry was) but of surpassing and enduring glory, which gives him a boldness (12) which Moses could not have and which Israel cannot know until she *turns to the Lord, Christ,* a boldness in the Lord whose *Spirit* gives man freedom to look upon the face of God and carries the apostle (and all who receive his liberating Word) *from one degree of glory to another* (3:18). This boldness brings with it a pure and candid honesty (4:2), for the apostle is no self-seeking, devious proclaimer of himself but of *Jesus Christ as Lord* (5) with himself as *servant* of man, servant to the Servant Jesus (*for Jesus' sake,* 5). He proclaims what can be known only as God's work, His miracle of the new creation, the dawn of the new first day, *the light of the knowledge of the glory of God in the face of Christ.* (4:6)

3:6 *New covenant.* Cf. Jer 31:31-33; Lk 22:20; 1 Co 11:25; Heb 8:8-10; 10:16. In sharp contrast to the demand and compulsion of the old legal covenant, the new covenant is God's free proffer of forgiveness, which inwardly renews man and inspires in him a will that is in harmony with God's will.

3:7 *Splendor . . . could not look at Moses' face.* Cf. Ex 34·29-34.

fading as this was, [8] will not the dispensation of the Spirit be attended with greater splendor? [9] For if there was splendor in the dispensation of condemnation, the dispensation of righteousness must far exceed it in splendor. [10] Indeed, in this case, what once had splendor has come to have no splendor at all, because of the splendor that surpasses it. [11] For if what faded away came with splendor, what is permanent must have much more splendor.

12 Since we have such a hope, we are very bold, [13] not like Moses, who put a veil over his face so that the Israelites might not see the end of the fading splendor. [14] But their minds were hardened; for to this day, when they read the old covenant, that same veil remains unlifted, because only through Christ is it taken away. [15] Yes, to this day whenever Moses is read a veil lies over their minds; [16] but when a man turns to the Lord the veil is removed. [17] Now the Lord is the Spirit, and where the Spirit of the Lord is, there is freedom. [18]And we all, with unveiled face, beholding[d] the glory of the Lord, are being changed into his likeness from one degree of glory to another; for this comes from the Lord who is the Spirit.

4   Therefore, having this ministry by the mercy of God,[e] we do not lose heart. [2] We have renounced disgraceful, underhanded ways; we refuse to practice cunning or to tamper with God's word, but by the open statement of the truth we would commend ourselves to every man's conscience in the sight of God. [3]And even if our gospel is veiled, it is veiled only to those who are perishing. [4] In their case the god of this world has blinded the minds of the unbelievers, to keep them from seeing the light of the gospel of the glory of Christ, who is the likeness of God. [5] For what we preach is not ourselves, but Jesus Christ as Lord, with ourselves as your servants[f] for Jesus' sake. [6] For it is the God who said, "Let light shine out of darkness," who has shone in our hearts to give the light of the knowledge of the glory of God in the face of Christ.

THE MINISTRY OF IMPARTING LIFE OF JESUS TO MEN (4:7 — 5:10)

7 But we have this treasure in earthen vessels, to show that the transcendent power belongs to God and not to us. [8] We are afflicted in every way, but not crushed; per-

[d] Or reflecting   [e] Greek as we have received mercy   [f] Or slaves

3:13 *Put a veil over his face.* Cf. Ex 34:33-35.

3:15 *Whenever Moses is read a veil lies over their minds.* As the veil which Moses put over his face concealed from the Israelites the transient character of the old covenant and its orders (12), so now when the Law (Moses) is read they cannot see the real significance of the Law as WITNESS, together with the prophets, to the newly revealed righteousness of God in the Gospel. (Cf. Ro 3:21)

3:16 *When a man turns to the Lord,* that is, comes to Christ, then he recognizes that "Christ is the END OF THE LAW, that every one who has FAITH may be justified." (Ro 10:4)

3:17 *The Lord is the Spirit.* Cf. 6. Since the Lord (Christ) is present among His people, known, and operative by the power of the Spirit, the two are so closely associated in God's working and in the church's experience that Paul can simply identify them in order to emphasize the fact that God's new order of things ("new covenant . . . life," 6; "righteousness . . . splendor," 9; "glory," 18) is experienced by man IN CHRIST. (Cf. 5:17)

3:18 *From one degree of glory,* in this present life with the rich endowment of gifts and blessings bestowed on us by the Spirit, *to another,* in the world to come, where "the Lord Jesus Christ . . . will change our lowly body to be like his glorious body." (Ph 3:20-21)

4:4 *The god of this world.* Since the world is mankind in its opposition to God (cf. Ja 4:4), Satan as the inspirer and leader of that opposition is god of this world. Cf. "the ruler of this world" in Jn 12:31; 14:30; 16:11.

4:6 *Let light shine.* Cf. Gn 1:3; 2 Co 5:17.

4:7 — 5:10 The glory of the apostolic ministry is solely God's, not man's; therefore the frailty and the sufferings of the men who exercise this ministry, as men who are *afflicted, perplexed, persecuted,* and *struck down* (8-9), take nothing from its glory, for it is just in their weakness that *the transcendent power* of God is manifested (7); in their defeat and dying the new life of Jesus is being released for men (10-12). And so suffering and the prospect of dying do not discourage these ministers of God; they work in the faith that the God who raised Jesus from the dead will raise them also with Jesus (12), in the courageous certitude that the as-yet-unseen glory of the new creation will enfold them in an eternal splendor which far outweighs their present light weight of momentary affliction (17-18), in the knowledge that the Spirit given them by God is His pledge of a new and eternal bodily life (cf. 5:5). They long to be at home with their Lord, clothed with the new body which God will give them; but this longing does not make them weak and inert dreamers — it makes them strong and courageous

plexed, but not driven to despair; 9 persecuted, but not forsaken; struck down, but not destroyed; 10 always carrying in the body the death of Jesus, so that the life of Jesus may also be manifested in our bodies. 11 For while we live we are always being given up to death for Jesus' sake, so that the life of Jesus may be manifested in our mortal flesh. 12 So death is at work in us, but life in you.

13 Since we have the same spirit of faith as he had who wrote, "I believed, and so I spoke," we too believe, and so we speak, 14 knowing that he who raised the Lord Jesus will raise us also with Jesus and bring us with you into his presence. 15 For it is all for your sake, so that as grace extends to more and more people it may increase thanksgiving, to the glory of God.

16 So we do not lose heart. Though our outer nature is wasting away, our inner nature is being renewed every day. 17 For this slight momentary affliction is preparing for us an eternal weight of glory beyond all comparison, 18 because we look not to the things that are seen but to the things that are unseen; for the things that are seen are transient, but the things that are unseen are eternal.

5 For we know that if the earthly tent we live in is destroyed, we have a building from God, a house not made with hands, eternal in the heavens. 2 Here indeed we groan, and long to put on our heavenly dwelling, 3 so that by putting it on we may not be found naked. 4 For while we are still in this tent, we sigh with anxiety; not that we would be unclothed, but that we would be further clothed, so that what is mortal may be swallowed up by life. 5 He who has prepared us for this very thing is God, who has given us the Spirit as a guarantee.

6 So we are always of good courage; we know that while we are at home in the body we are away from the Lord, 7 for we walk by faith, not by sight. 8 We are of good courage, and we would rather be away from the body and at home with the Lord. 9 So whether we are at home or away, we make it our aim to please him. 10 For we must all appear before the judgment seat of Christ, so that each one may receive good or evil, according to what he has done in the body.

THE MINISTRY OF RECONCILIATION (5:11 — 6:10)

11 Therefore, knowing the fear of the Lord, we persuade men; but what we are is known to God, and I hope it is known also to your conscience. 12 We are not commending ourselves to you again but giving you cause to be proud of us, so that you may be

workers, men who make it their *aim* to please the Christ before whose judgment seat they must all appear to give an account of their working. (5:6-10)

4:7 *Earthen vessels.* Vessels of earthenware, fragile and to be valued only for their content, the life-giving Gospel.

4:12 *Death is at work in us,* the persecuted and endangered proclaimers of the Gospel, *but life in you,* the recipients of the Gospel with its life-giving fragrance. (Cf. 2:14-16)

4:13 *I believed, and so I spoke.* Cf. Ps 116:10.

4:15 *It may increase thanksgiving.* The apostle lives and dies in the pattern set by His Lord, "to the glory of God the Father." (Ph 2:11, cf. 5-11)

4:17 Cf. Ro 8:18.

5:1 *Earthly tent,* the "mortal body" (Ro 6:12), "dead because of sin" (Ro 8:10), which the on-slaughts of man can destroy; the *building from God, a house not made with hands* is the body as it is destined to be when God has raised and glorified it (1 Co 15:42-53). This new, glorious body is thought of as prepared and ready for redeemed man *in the heavens,* a new garment ready to be worn in glory.

5:2 Cf. Ro 8:23.

5:3 *Found naked,* in a disembodied state.

5:4 *Unclothed* in death; *further clothed* at the return of the Lord. (Cf. 1 Co 15:51-55)

5:5 *Spirit as a guarantee.* Cf. Eph 1:13-14.

5:8 *Rather be away from the body.* Though Paul shrinks from the thought of the "nakedness" which physical death brings (cf. 5:3), the thought of being *at home with the Lord* (which is "far better," Ph 1:23) overcomes that fear.

5:11 — 6:10 The apostle works to win (*persuade,* 11) men, but with a high independence over against the praise or blame of men. Whether men esteem him mad (*beside ourselves,* 13) because of the fervor of his commitment to Christ or sane (*in our right mind,* 13) because of his shrewd planning as the wise master builder of the church (cf. 1 Co 3:10) — that is of small moment to him; his "madness" and his "sanity" are both in the service of his apostolic ministry, manifestations of his love for God and for men. His ministry moves between the two poles of *the fear of the Lord* (11) who will judge all men (10), on the one hand, and the compelling impulse of the love of Christ who died for all men in order that all might live for Him (14-15), on the other hand. Human standards do not apply to this ministry, for it is

able to answer those who pride themselves on a man's position and not on his heart. [13] For if we are beside ourselves, it is for God; if we are in our right mind, it is for you. [14] For the love of Christ controls us, because we are convinced that one has died for all; therefore all have died. [15]And he died for all, that those who live might live no longer for themselves but for him who for their sake died and was raised.

16 From now on, therefore, we regard no one from a human point of view; even though we once regarded Christ from a human point of view, we regard him thus no longer. [17] Therefore, if any one is in Christ, he is a new creation;[g] the old has passed away, behold, the new has come. [18]All this is from God, who through Christ reconciled us to himself and gave us the ministry of reconciliation; [19] that is, in Christ God was reconciling[h] the world to himself, not counting their trespasses against them, and entrusting to us the message of reconciliation. [20] So we are ambassadors for Christ, God making his appeal through us. We beseech you on behalf of Christ, be reconciled to God. [21] For our sake he made him to be sin who knew no sin, so that in him we might become the righteousness of God.

6 Working together with him, then, we entreat you not to accept the grace of God in vain. [2] For he says,
"At the acceptable time I have listened to you,
and helped you on the day of salvation."
Behold, now is the acceptable time; behold, now is the day of salvation. [3] We put no obstacle in any one's way, so that no fault may be found with our ministry, [4] but as servants of God we commend ourselves in every way: through great endurance, in afflictions, hardships, calamities, [5] beatings, imprisonments, tumults, labors, watching, hunger; [6] by purity, knowledge, forbearance, kindness, the Holy Spirit, genuine love, [7] truthful speech, and the power of God; with the weapons of righteousness for the right hand and for the left; [8] in honor and dishonor, in ill repute and good repute. We are treated as impostors, and yet are true; [9] as unknown, and yet well known; as dying, and behold we live; as punished, and yet not killed; [10] as sorrowful, yet always rejoicing; as poor, yet making many rich; as having nothing, and yet possessing everything.

[g] Or *creature*   [h] Or *God was in Christ reconciling*

nothing less than the divinely given ministry of reconciliation; it gets its content and authority from that reconciling act in Christ by which God's new creation has broken victoriously into the present evil world, to make new all things and to make the old world and its standards irrelevant and obsolete. The apostle is nothing less than the ambassador for the Christ who knew no sin but was made by God to be sin (or a sin offering) for sinful man, in order that sinful man might find the righteousness of God in Him (5:16-21). God Himself makes His appeal for reconciliation through the apostle; now, in God's *acceptable time*, in His *day of salvation*, God's appeal is being heard in the ministry which has on it the marks of DIVINE greatness and power. Paul lists nine examples of human hardships and sufferings in which the divine strength is manifested (6:4-5); he gives nine examples of the divine gracious power which appears and works in God's afflicted messengers (6:6-7), and in nine pairs of contrasts he rounds out the picture of the apostolate, humanly insignificant and defeated, divinely significant and triumphant (6:8-9): *dying, and behold we live.* (6:9)

5:11 *Persuade,* that is, seek to persuade, appeal to.

5:12 *Those who pride themselves,* etc., the supporters of the "Christ-men."

5:16 *Regarded Christ from a human point of view.* To Paul the Jew, Jesus the Servant Messiah failed to measure up to his expectation of the King who would glorify His people; and Jesus the Crucified appeared as One accursed by God, cf. 1 Co 12:3; Gl 3:13. Now (*no longer,* 16), with eyes enlightened by the Spirit, he can see Him as the power and the wisdom of God in person, the One in whom God reconciled the world to Himself. (19)

6:1 *Accept the grace of God in vain.* The grace is received in vain, squandered and wasted, when (as in the case of the "Christ-men" and their following) it is made to serve the interests of human pride and self-seeking. (Cf. 2 Co 11:20)

6:2 *At the acceptable time,* etc. Is 49:8.

6:4 *Commend ourselves in every way,* not by obtaining letters of commendation from men (3:1) but by going the way of self-expending *servants of God,* who follow in the footsteps of the Servant Jesus Christ, suffering as He suffered, serving as He served, and "making many rich" (10), as He enriched mankind by His very poverty. (8:9)

6:7 *Weapons . . . for the right hand and for the left,* for both offense and defense.

6:10 *Possessing everything.* In Christ they are heirs of the world (Ro 4:13), of "all things." (Ro 8:32)

THE MINISTRY OF GOD'S EXCLUSIVE APPEAL (6:11 — 7:4)

11 Our mouth is open to you, Corinthians; our heart is wide. 12 You are not restricted by us, but you are restricted in your own affections. 13 In return—I speak as to children—widen your hearts also.

14 Do not be mismated with unbelievers. For what partnership have righteousness and iniquity? Or what fellowship has light with darkness? 15 What accord has Christ with Be′li·al?*i* Or what has a believer in common with an unbeliever? 16 What agreement has the temple of God with idols? For we are the temple of the living God; as God said,

> "I will live in them and move among them,
> and I will be their God,
> and they shall be my people.

17   Therefore come out from them,
> and be separate from them, says the Lord,
> and touch nothing unclean;
> then I will welcome you,

18   and I will be a father to you,
> and you shall be my sons and daughters,
> says the Lord Almighty."

7 Since we have these promises, beloved, let us cleanse ourselves from every defilement of body and spirit, and make holiness perfect in the fear of God.

2 Open your hearts to us; we have wronged no one, we have corrupted no one, we have taken advantage of no one. 3 I do not say this to condemn you, for I said before that you are in our hearts, to die together and to live together. 4 I have great confidence in you; I have great pride in you; I am filled with comfort. With all our affliction, I am overjoyed.

TITUS' REPORT: THE JOYFUL PROSPECT OF RECONCILIATION (7:5-16)

5 For even when we came into Macedonia, our bodies had no rest but we were afflicted at every turn—fighting without and fear within. 6 But God, who comforts the downcast, comforted us by the coming of Titus, 7 and not only by his coming but

i Greek *Beliar*

6:11—7:4 The church lives by perpetual repentance (cf. the first of Luther's 95 Theses). The church at Corinth can be a real church, an apostolic church, the "church of God at Corinth" (1:1) only by heeding the appeal of God spoken through the apostle. Reconciliation with Paul (so freely and generously offered by him, 7:11-13) can take place only as a piece of the church's renewed reconciliation with God. And so Paul reminds the Corinthian church that the appeal of God the Reconciler is an exclusive appeal; reconciliation with God calls for a radical break with all that opposes God. He reminds them that if God is their Father and they are His sons and daughters, it behooves them to *come out* from the world around them, to *touch nothing unclean* (6:17) and to *cleanse* themselves *from every defilement of body and spirit, and make holiness* (their consecration to God) *perfect in the fear of God* (7:1). Paul is once more combating the secularized Christianity with which he had dealt in 1 Co. When they have opened their hearts to God, then they can open their hearts to their apostle, who loves them as his *children* (6:13) with the forgiving, reconciling love of God: *You are in our hearts, to die together and to live together.* (7:3)

6:12 *Not restricted by us.* Nothing in Paul, in whom the Holy Spirit works "forbearance, kind-

ness . . . genuine love" (6:6), hinders reconciliation; the Corinthians are restricted, hindered, and impeded by their *own affections,* which are divided between God and what opposes God. (Cf. 14-16)

6:15 *Belial,* literally "Worthlessness," here used of the embodiment of all "worthlessness," the devil.

6:16 *Temple.* For the church as the temple of God cf. 1 Co 3:16-17.

As God said. The following cento of OT passages (16-18) consists of quotations from Lv 26:11-12; Eze 37:27; Is 52:11; Jer 51:45; Hos 1:10; Is 43:6.

7:2 *We have wronged no one,* etc. Cf. 12:16-17 and chs. 10—13 generally. These statements reflect charges brought against Paul by his opponents at Corinth.

7:5-16 Now at last Paul tells what he had been on the verge of telling at 2:13 but could not before he had given thanks to God for His gift; now he tells of his meeting with Titus and of Titus' report of the Corinthians' repentance. And now the note of thanksgiving with which Paul began and which has been the constant undertone in all his portrayal of his apostolate is heard once more full and clear. Paul is comforted (6, 13) and rejoices (9, 13, 16); he cannot say it often enough, all the more so since the Corinthians' repentant

also by the comfort with which he was comforted in you, as he told us of your longing, your mourning, your zeal for me, so that I rejoiced still more. 8 For even if I made you sorry with my letter, I do not regret it (though I did regret it), for I see that that letter grieved you, though only for a while. 9As it is, I rejoice, not because you were grieved, but because you were grieved into repenting; for you felt a godly grief, so that you suffered no loss through us. 10 For godly grief produces a repentance that leads to salvation and brings no regret, but worldly grief produces death. 11 For see what earnestness this godly grief has produced in you, what eagerness to clear yourselves, what indignation, what alarm, what longing, what zeal, what punishment! At every point you have proved yourselves guiltless in the matter. 12 So although I wrote to you, it was not on account of the one who did the wrong, nor on account of the one who suffffered the wrong, but in order that your zeal for us might be revealed to you in the sight of God. 13 Therefore we are comforted.

And besides our own comfort we rejoiced still more at the joy of Titus, because his mind has been set at rest by you all. 14 For if I have expressed to him some pride in you, I was not put to shame; but just as everything we said to you was true, so our boasting before Titus has proved true. 15And his heart goes out all the more to you, as he remembers the obedience of you all, and the fear and trembling with which you received him. 16 I rejoice, because I have perfect confidence in you.

The Present: Collection for Saints of Jerusalem

8:1—9:15

THE EXAMPLE OF THE CHURCHES OF MACEDONIA (8:1-7)

8 We want you to know, brethren, about the grace of God which has been shown in the churches of Macedonia, 2 for in a severe test of affliction, their abundance of joy and their extreme poverty have overflowed in a wealth of liberality on their part. 3 For they gave according to their means, as I can testify, and beyond their means, of their own free will, 4 begging us earnestly for the favor of taking part in the relief of the saints— 5 and this, not as we expected, but first they gave themselves to the Lord and to us by the will of God. 6Accordingly we have urged Titus that as he had already made a beginning, he should also complete among you this gracious work. 7 Now as you excel in everything—in faith, in utterance, in knowledge, in all earnestness, and in your love for us—see that you excel in this gracious work also.

YOU KNOW THE GRACE OF THE LORD JESUS CHRIST (8:8-15)

8 I say this not as a command, but to prove by the earnestness of others that your love also is genuine. 9 For you know the grace of our Lord Jesus Christ, that though

behavior has been a source of comfort and joy to Titus also. (7, 13, 15)

7:10 *Godly grief . . . repentance . . . salvation . . . worldly grief produces death.* One is reminded of the contrast between the penitent tears of Peter (Mt 26:75) and the suicidal remorse of Judas. (Mt 17:3-10)

7:11 *What punishment!* Cf. 2:5-11, esp. 2:6.

7:12 Paul is seeking, not punishment for the offender (note how he appeals for a loving treatment of him in 2:7-8) but the building up of the whole church (cf. 13:10). For the probable reconstruction of the event referred to, see Introduction, par. 3.

8:1—9:15 Paul turns from the retrospective thanksgiving for all that God has given him and the Corinthians in his ministry of reconciliation (chs. 1—7) to the present and the common task which will be the expression and confirmation

of the reconciliation between him and his church (chs. 8—9). He closed his account concerning Titus' report with the words: "I rejoice, because I have perfect confidence in you" (7:16). The two chapters in which he gives directions for the completion of the collection are an expression of that confidence, tactful and gentle though his directions are.

8:1-7 Paul holds up the example of the Macedonian churches, who in their poverty and affliction (see Introduction to Philippians) gave *beyond their means* (8:3) — because the grace of God moved them to *give themselves* (8:5) to the Lord and to His apostle. When men give themselves, their money is given too.

8:7 *You excel in everything,* etc. Cf. 1 Co 1:4-7.

8:8-15 Paul will not command them; he reminds them instead of what they already know—of the grace of the Lord Jesus Christ, who became poor

he was rich, yet for your sake he became poor, so that by his poverty you might become rich. ¹⁰And in this matter I give my advice: it is best for you now to complete what a year ago you began not only to do but to desire, ¹¹ so that your readiness in desiring it may be matched by your completing it out of what you have. ¹² For if the readiness is there, it is acceptable according to what a man has, not according to what he has not. ¹³ I do not mean that others should be eased and you burdened, ¹⁴ but that as a matter of equality your abundance at the present time should supply their want, so that their abundance may supply your want, that there may be equality. ¹⁵As it is written, "He who gathered much had nothing over, and he who gathered little had no lack."

COMMENDATION OF TITUS AND TWO BROTHERS (8:16 – 9:5)

16 But thanks be to God who puts the same earnest care for you into the heart of Titus. ¹⁷ For he not only accepted our appeal, but being himself very earnest he is going to you of his own accord. ¹⁸ With him we are sending the brother who is famous among all the churches for his preaching of the gospel; ¹⁹ and not only that, but he has been appointed by the churches to travel with us in this gracious work which we are carrying on, for the glory of the Lord and to show our good will. ²⁰ We intend that no one should blame us about this liberal gift which we are administering, ²¹ for we aim at what is honorable not only in the Lord's sight but also in the sight of men. ²²And with them we are sending our brother whom we have often tested and found earnest in many matters, but who is now more earnest than ever because of his great confidence in you. ²³As for Titus, he is my partner and fellow worker in your service; and as for our brethren, they are messengersʲ of the churches, the glory of Christ. ²⁴ So give proof, before the churches, of your love and of our boasting about you to these men.

9 Now it is superfluous for me to write to you about the offering for the saints, ² for I know your readiness, of which I boast about you to the people of Macedonia, saying that A·cha′ia has been ready since last year; and your zeal has stirred up most of them. ³ But I am sending the brethren so that our boasting about you may not prove vain in this case, so that you may be ready, as I said you would be; ⁴ lest if some Macedonians come with me and find that you are not ready, we be humiliated—to say nothing of you—for being so confident. ⁵ So I thought it necessary to urge the brethren to go on to you before me, and arrange in advance for this gift you have promised, so that it may be ready not as an exaction but as a willing gift.

GOD LOVES A CHEERFUL GIVER (9:6-15)

6 The point is this: he who sows sparingly will also reap sparingly, and he who sows

ʲ Greek apostles

for the enrichment of men and so provides them with the pattern and the power for their giving. And Paul reminds them of what they have already accomplished; they had set about the gathering of the collection as early as the previous year.

8:13-14 *Equality.* The church is the body of Christ in which all members work together equally for the common good. Cf. 1 Co 12:12-26 with 12:7.

8:15 *As it is written.* Cf. Ex 16:18. As God disposed His gift of bread from heaven for His people, so that no one had superfluity and no one lacked, so His church is to administer its charity.

8:16 – 9:5 Paul is sending Titus, an eager volunteer (16-17), and two other brothers in charge of the collection to aid the Corinthians in the task which will prove their love and make good Paul's boast concerning them, lest Paul (and the Corinthians themselves) be put to shame when he comes to Corinth with the representatives of the Macedonian churches and finds the Corinthians not ready.

8:18 *The brother.* Neither this brother nor the one mentioned in 22 can be identified.

8:19 *Appointed by the churches.* Cf. 1 Co 16:3-4.

8:23 *The glory of Christ.* In their willing charity the Christ who gave Himself into poverty that men might be rich (8:9) is manifested to men in the glory of His grace.

9:2 *Achaia.* Cf. 1:1 note.

9:5 *An exaction.* That is what a gift given only under pressure would be, not a *willing gift.*

9:6-15 Paul reminds the Corinthians that generous giving reaps a great harvest; not only will the God who loves a cheerful giver reward such giving; also, God will be glorified in the thanksgiving of the recipients of the gift. As in the description of his apostolic ministry (chs. 1–7), so here also in the exercise of his ministry (chs. 8–9) Paul's first and last word is in praise of the grace

bountifully will also reap bountifully. 7 Each one must do as he has made up his mind, not reluctantly or under compulsion, for God loves a cheerful giver. 8And God is able to provide you with every blessing in abundance, so that you may always have enough of everything and may provide in abundance for every good work. 9As it is written,

> "He scatters abroad, he gives to the poor;
> his righteousness^k endures for ever."

10 He who supplies seed to the sower and bread for food will supply and multiply your resources^l and increase the harvest of your righteousness.^{k} 11 You will be enriched in every way for great generosity, which through us will produce thanksgiving to God; 12 for the rendering of this service not only supplies the wants of the saints but also overflows in many thanksgivings to God. 13 Under the test of this service, you^m will glorify God by your obedience in acknowledging the gospel of Christ,‛ and by the generosity of your contribution for them and for all others; 14 while they long for you and pray for you, because of the surpassing grace of God in you. 15 Thanks be to God for his inexpressible gift!

Prospect: Paul's Impending Visit to Corinth

10:1—13:14

PAUL'S DEFENSE AGAINST THE CHARGES OF HIS OPPONENTS (10:1-18)

10 I, Paul, myself entreat you, by the meekness and gentleness of Christ—I who am humble when face to face with you, but bold to you when I am away!— 2 I beg of you that when I am present I may not have to show boldness with such con-

^{k} Or benevolence ^{l} Greek sowing ^{m} Or they

of God: That Gentiles are bound to Jews in such fellowship that Jewish need provokes a Gentile gift, that this gift is the fire which sends up clouds of grateful incense in Jerusalem to the glory of the God who is Lord of Jew and Gentile both, that is grace, grace greater than man's words can tell. *Thanks be to God for his inexpressible gift!* (9:15)

9:7 *God loves a cheerful giver.* Pr 22:8, according to the ancient Greek version (as an addition to the Hebrew text translated in English versions).

9:8 Cf. Ph 4:19.

9:9 Is 55:10. *Righteousness,* God's fidelity to His covenant, is often used of His acts of love and deliverance for His people. Cf. 1 Sm 12:7, where the RSV rightly renders the word as "saving deed."

10:1—13:14 Paul has spoken the word of conciliation to the full; he has set before the eyes of the Corinthians all the wondrous grace of God which has united him with them in the past (chs. 1—7). He has enlarged on the task which now unites them in a common effort of love (chs. 8—9). But between Paul and the Corinthians there still falls the shadow of the men who say, "We belong to Christ," in their peculiar and exclusive sense. They stand in the way of full conciliation. And there is no possibility of conciliation with them; they have given no indication of a change of heart. Being what they are, they MUST oppose Paul, for Paul is the opponent of all human greatness, including his own. He is opposed to all factions and all parties in the church, the "Pauline" party included (cf. 1 Co 1:12-13). Paul upholds and affirms all that they have sought to override and supersede—the OT Scriptures, the

commands of Jesus, the apostolate as the vehicle of the presence and power of Christ, an earthen vessel perhaps, but the vessel which God Himself has chosen and therefore the only vessel. Paul interprets all the terms which they used as slogans ("freedom," "knowledge," "Spirit," "the Lordship of Christ") in a sense radically different from theirs. There is no possibility of compromise here, no prospect of conciliation; and so the message of conciliation must show the hard and cutting edge of its exclusiveness—Paul must unmask them for what they are, satanic messengers who destroy the work of God, and must bid the Corinthians come out from them and be separate from them.

Paul had touched on the attitudes, methods, and accusations of his opponents as early as his first letter (1 Co 4:18-21; 7:40; 14:37), and the anathema on those who have no love for the Lord (1 Co 16:22) is no doubt intended primarily for them. There are indications in the first section of the second letter too that Paul is seeking conciliation in an atmosphere charged with calumny and controversy (cf., e.g., 2 Co 1:12-14; 2:6; 3:1-3; 4:2, 5; 5:11 ff.; 6:3). But it is not until now, when the word for conciliation has been fully spoken, that he meets his adversaries and their charges head on.

10:1-12 THE CHARGES OF PAUL'S OPPONENTS, WITH PAUL'S REPLY

Their charges, as Paul enumerates them, are: Paul is humble when face to face with the Corinthians and bold only when absent; he terrifies

fidence as I count on showing against some who suspect us of acting in worldly fashion. ³ For though we live in the world we are not carrying on a worldly war, ⁴ for the weapons of our warfare are not worldly but have divine power to destroy strongholds. ⁵ We destroy arguments and every proud obstacle to the knowledge of God, and take every thought captive to obey Christ, ⁶ being ready to punish every disobedience, when your obedience is complete.

7 Look at what is before your eyes. If any one is confident that he is Christ's, let him remind himself that as he is Christ's, so are we. ⁸ For even if I boast a little too much of our authority, which the Lord gave for building you up and not for destroying you, I shall not be put to shame. ⁹ I would not seem to be frightening you with letters. ¹⁰ For they say, "His letters are weighty and strong, but his bodily presence is weak, and his speech of no account." ¹¹ Let such people understand that what we say by letter when absent, we do when present. ¹² Not that we venture to class or compare ourselves with some of those who commend themselves. But when they measure themselves by one another, and compare themselves with one another, they are without understanding.

13 But we will not boast beyond limit, but will keep to the limits God has apportioned us, to reach even to you. ¹⁴ For we are not overextending ourselves, as though we did not reach you; we were the first to come all the way to you with the gospel of Christ. ¹⁵ We do not boast beyond limit, in other men's labors; but our hope is that as your faith increases, our field among you may be greatly enlarged, ¹⁶ so that we may preach the gospel in lands beyond you, without boasting of work already done in another's field. ¹⁷ "Let him who boasts, boast of the Lord." ¹⁸ For it is not the man who commends himself that is accepted, but the man whom the Lord commends.

PAUL'S "FOOLISH" BOASTING (11:1 — 12:21)

11 I wish you would bear with me in a little foolishness. Do bear with me! ² I feel a divine jealousy for you, for I betrothed you to Christ to present you as a pure bride to her one husband. ³ But I am afraid that as the serpent deceived Eve by his cunning, your thoughts will be led astray from a sincere and pure devotion to Christ. ⁴ For if some one comes and preaches another Jesus than the one we preached, or if you receive a different spirit from the one you received, or if you accept a different

---

them with his letters, but his bodily presence is weak, and his speech is of no account (10:9-10); he acts *in worldly fashion,* blustering when he can and stepping softly when he must. This proves that he is not one who "belongs to Christ" in the sense and to the degree that they, his bold and persuasive opponents, can claim to belong to Him. (10:7)

Paul's answer is simply this: Do not force me to demonstrate the authority divinely given me, an authority given for building up the church, not for destruction, an authority which therefore has the patience to wait for repentance and its fruits before it performs the necessary but painful task of destruction by judgment (10:4-6), an authority which my opponents, since they know nothing but themselves and must judge others by their own self-centered standards (10:12), cannot even understand.

10:1 *I, Paul, myself, entreat you.* As the *myself* indicates, the last four chapters of the letter are probably a greatly extended autograph conclusion, such as we find, e.g., in Gl 6:11-18.

By the meekness and gentleness of Christ. The terms of this adjuration already put the humility and unworldly "inconsistency" of Paul in their true light. When he exposes himself thus to the

criticism of opponents, "Christ," the gentle and meek, "is speaking in" him. (13:3)

10:13-18 PAUL'S AUTHORITY AS APOSTLE

10:13-18 Over against the self-commendation of his detractors (12, 18) Paul sets the fact that the Lord has "commended" him by building the church at Corinth through him (13-14). Paul has built the church, and he has not thrust himself into another man's field of labor either, as his opponents have done (15). That is the solid and factual vindication of his authority, one that permits him to boast only *of the Lord* (17) and allows him to hope that he will be further vindicated by greater work in a wider field (15-16), as the Corinthians' faith increases and he is free to go on to further labors in the West (*in lands beyond you,* 16). Paul is looking (as his Letter to the Romans makes plain) to Rome and beyond Rome to Spain (see Introduction to Romans).

10:13 *Beyond limit.* This seems to be a hit at the extravagance of the claims with which his opponents had overawed the Corinthians. (Cf. 11:20-21)

11:1-4 PAUL'S REASON FOR BOASTING

11:1-4 To defend the church which he has betrothed to Christ and to protect her from the

gospel from the one you accepted, you submit to it readily enough. ⁵ I think that I am not in the least inferior to these superlative apostles. ⁶ Even if I am unskilled in speaking, I am not in knowledge; in every way we have made this plain to you in all things.

7 Did I commit a sin in abasing myself so that you might be exalted, because I preached God's gospel without cost to you? ⁸ I robbed other churches by accepting support from them in order to serve you. ⁹And when I was with you and was in want, I did not burden any one, for my needs were supplied by the brethren who came from Macedonia. So I refrained and will refrain from burdening you in any way. ¹⁰As the truth of Christ is in me, this boast of mine shall not be silenced in the regions of A·cha′ia. ¹¹And why? Because I do not love you? God knows I do!

12 And what I do I will continue to do, in order to undermine the claim of those who would like to claim that in their boasted mission they work on the same terms as we do. ¹³ For such men are false apostles, deceitful workmen, disguising themselves as apostles of Christ. ¹⁴And no wonder, for even Satan disguises himself as an angel of light. ¹⁵ So it is not strange if his servants also disguise themselves as servants of righteousness. Their end will correspond to their deeds.

16 I repeat, let no one think me foolish; but even if you do, accept me as a fool, so that I too may boast a little. ¹⁷ (What I am saying I say not with the Lord's authority but as a fool, in this boastful confidence; ¹⁸ since many boast of worldly things, I too will boast.) ¹⁹ For you gladly bear with fools, being wise yourselves! ²⁰ For you bear it if a man makes slaves of you, or preys upon you, or takes advantage of you, or puts on airs, or strikes you in the face. ²¹ To my shame, I must say, we were too weak for that!

But whatever any one dares to boast of—I am speaking as a fool—I also dare to boast of that. ²²Are they Hebrews? So am I. Are they Israelites? So am I. Are they descendants of Abraham? So am I. ²³Are they servants of Christ? I am a better one—I am talking like a madman—with far greater labors, far more imprisonments, with

satanic influence of those who proclaim *another Jesus* (4), Paul will play the fool and boast; a holy *jealousy* (2) for the church impels him.

11:2 *betrothed you to Christ.* For the people of God (the church) as the betrothed, or bride, of God or Christ cf. Hos 2:19-20; Eph 5:26-27.

11:3 *Serpent deceived Eve.* Cf. Gn 3:4.

11:4 *Another Jesus.* See Introduction to 1 Co, par. 15.

11:5-6 THE BOAST OF KNOWLEDGE

11:5-6 Though he makes no pretense of rivaling these *superlative apostles* (5) in skilled speech, he will boast of his *knowledge.* (6)

11:6 *Unskilled in speech.* Cf. 1 Co 1:17; 2:4.

Knowledge. For Paul's conception of knowledge, in contrast to that of his opponents, cf. 1 Co 8:1-2.

11:7-15 THE BOAST OF SERVING WITHOUT PAY

11:7-15 He will boast, ironically, of that which has been made a reproach to him, of the fact he *preached God's gospel without cost* to his converts (7). He will not let the insinuation of the false apostles (who evidently interpreted his refusal to accept remuneration as an admission that he lacked full apostolic stature) drive him from this policy, which is dictated by his love for the Corinthians.

11:8-9 *Robbed other churches,* by accepting support from them in their poverty. Cf. Paul's words to the Macedonian church at Philippi, Ph 4:15, 18.

11:10 *This boast of mine.* Cf. 1 Co 9:3-6, 12, 15-18.

11:14 *Satan.* For Satan as the enemy or perverter of true Gospel proclamation cf. Ro 16:20 with 16:17-18.

11:15 *Their end will correspond to their deeds.* They will in the end, when God crushes Satan under foot (Ro 16:20) and renders to all men according to their works (Ro 2:6), be punished as they deserve.

11:16-33 THE BOAST OF THE SERVANT OF CHRIST

11:16-33 Though he is too "weak" to assume the arrogant self-seeking demeanor of his opponents, he will boast of all that they dare boast of—and more. He can claim all that they claim in the way of Judaic descent and Judaic prerogative (22). And he is a better *servant of Christ* (23) than they, better because he is marked (as the Servant Christ was) by toil, suffering, and persecution, worn by the daily pressure of his anxious care for all the churches. He *will boast of the things that show* his *weakness* (30), to the glory of his Lord.

11:18 *Worldly things,* such as power and prestige (20) and descent. (22)

11:22 *Hebrews . . . Israelites . . . descendants of Abraham.* Cf. Introduction to 1 Co, par. 14, and Ph 3:4-5. *Hebrews* here probably designates those Jews who were Palestinian born and retained their mother tongue, in contrast to the Jews of the Dispersion, who adopted Greek, the common lan-

countless beatings, and often near death. 24 Five times I have received at the hands of the Jews the forty lashes less one. 25 Three times I have been beaten with rods; once I was stoned. Three times I have been shipwrecked; a night and a day I have been adrift at sea; 26 on frequent journeys, in danger from rivers, danger from robbers, danger from my own people, danger from Gentiles, danger in the city, danger in the wilderness, danger at sea, danger from false brethren; 27 in toil and hardship, through many a sleepless night, in hunger and thirst, often without food, in cold and exposure. 28And, apart from other things, there is the daily pressure upon me of my anxiety for all the churches. 29 Who is weak, and I am not weak? Who is made to fall, and I am not indignant?

30 If I must boast, I will boast of the things that show my weakness. 31 The God and Father of the Lord Jesus, he who is blessed for ever, knows that I do not lie. 32At Damascus, the governor under King Ar'e·tas guarded the city of Damascus in order to seize me, 33 but I was let down in a basket through a window in the wall, and escaped his hands.

12 I must boast; there is nothing to be gained by it, but I will go on to visions and revelations of the Lord. 2 I know a man in Christ who fourteen years ago was caught up to the third heaven—whether in the body or out of the body I do not know, God knows. 3And I know that this man was caught up into Paradise—whether in the body or out of the body I do not know, God knows—4 and he heard things that cannot be told, which man may not utter. 5 On behalf of this man I will boast, but on my own behalf I will not boast, except of my weaknesses. 6 Though if I wish to boast, I shall not be a fool, for I shall be speaking the truth. But I refrain from it, so that no one may think more of me than he sees in me or hears from me. 7And to keep me from being too elated by the abundance of revelations, a thorn was given me in the flesh, a messenger of Satan, to harass me, to keep me from being too elated. 8 Three times I besought the Lord about this, that it should leave me; 9 but he said to me, "My grace is sufficient for you, for my power is made perfect in weakness." I will all the more gladly boast of my weaknesses, that the power of Christ may rest upon me. 10 For the sake of Christ, then, I am content with weaknesses, insults, hardships, persecutions, and calamities; for when I am weak, then I am strong.

11 I have been a fool! You forced me to it, for I ought to have been commended by

guage of their world. (Cf. Acts 6:5 note)

11:24-25 Five times . . . three times . . . once, etc. Paul adopts the style of the inscriptions in which Hellenistic kings and Roman emperors recorded their exploits. Thus his careful enumeration is formally a "boasting" in the "worldly" style, but since the boasting is wholly concerned with his sufferings, it becomes in substance a tribute to the Lord who has deigned to make him His servant (cf. Acts 9:15-16), the Lord for whom it is an honor to suffer.

11:29 Who is weak, etc.? On Paul's sympathetic concern for the weak, cf. 1 Co 8 and 9:22; Ro 14:1 to 15:13 note.

11:32 Aretas, name of a number of kings of the Nabataean Arabs. Aretas IV (9 B. C.—A. D. 40) held Damascus in A. D. 39—40.

11:33 Let down in a basket . . . escaped. Cf. Acts 9:24-25.

12:1-10 THE BOAST OF VISIONS, REVELATIONS AND A "THORN IN THE FLESH"

12:1-10 He will boast of visions and revelations of the Lord which have been given him; but he again ends by boasting of his weakness, of the affliction (thorn . . . given me in the flesh, 7) which his Lord would not take from him even though he prayed for relief repeatedly, in order that his

Lord's power might be made perfect in the apostle's weakness. He boasts of his weakness, for in his weakness the power of Christ rests on him, and only thus he is strong.

12:2 A man in Christ. Paul after his conversion. Paul is reticent before the mystery of his visionary experiences.

Third heaven. In Judaic tradition, heaven was thought of as consisting of a number of levels, of which the third was the highest.

12:3 Paradise, most likely identical with the third heaven of 12:2. This heavenly Paradise was conceived of as the abode of the souls of the righteous awaiting the resurrection. (Cf. Lk 23:43)

12:7 Thorn . . . in the flesh. It is certain that some form of affliction is meant; just what form it took we have no way of knowing.

A messenger of Satan. For Satan as the imposer of afflictions (under the overruling control of God) cf. Job 2:6-7; as the one who impedes the apostolic mission cf. 1 Th 2:18.

12:8 I besought the Lord. Paul PRAYS to Jesus Christ as naturally as he does to God, strong indication of the deity of our Lord.

12:11-18 THE BOAST OF SIGNS, WONDERS MIGHTY WORKS, SELFLESS SERVICE

12:11-18 Though in his person he is nothing but

you. For I was not at all inferior to these superlative apostles, even though I am nothing. [12] The signs of a true apostle were performed among you in all patience, with signs and wonders and mighty works. [13] For in what were you less favored than the rest of the churches, except that I myself did not burden you? Forgive me this wrong!

14 Here for the third time I am ready to come to you. And I will not be a burden, for I seek not what is yours but you; for children ought not to lay up for their parents, but parents for their children. [15] I will most gladly spend and be spent for your souls. If I love you the more, am I to be loved the less? [16] But granting that I myself did not burden you, I was crafty, you say, and got the better of you by guile. [17] Did I take advantage of you through any of those whom I sent to you? [18] I urged Titus to go, and sent the brother with him. Did Titus take advantage of you? Did we not act in the same spirit? Did we not take the same steps?

19 Have you been thinking all along that we have been defending ourselves before you? It is in the sight of God that we have been speaking in Christ, and all for your upbuilding, beloved. [20] For I fear that perhaps I may come and find you not what I wish, and that you may find me not what you wish; that perhaps there may be quarreling, jealousy, anger, selfishness, slander, gossip, conceit, and disorder. [21] I fear that when I come again my God may humble me before you, and I may have to mourn over many of those who sinned before and have not repented of the impurity, immorality, and licentiousness which they have practiced.

PAUL'S IMPENDING VISIT AND CONCLUSION (13:1-14)

13 This is the third time I am coming to you. Any charge must be sustained by the evidence of two or three witnesses. [2] I warned those who sinned before and all the others, and I warn them now while absent, as I did when present on my second visit, that if I come again I will not spare them—[3] since you desire proof that Christ is speaking in me. He is not weak in dealing with you, but is powerful in you. [4] For he was crucified in weakness, but lives by the power of God. For we are weak in him, but in dealing with you we shall live with him by the power of God.

a fragile vehicle of the power of Christ, Paul is not at all inferior to *these superlative apostles* (11); he can boast of the *signs of a true apostle* (12), *mighty works,* performed in complete selflessness (*in all patience,* 12) as Jesus performed His mighty works, not for Himself but as a gift and blessing for others. In the light of this, the Corinthians cannot give ear to those who interpret his refusal to accept pay as a sign that they were less favored than churches founded by other apostles; neither can they lend credence to the charge that he refused to take pay directly in order to gain it directly, through his helpers and associates; selfless men like *Titus* (18) are the sufficient refutation of that charge. This practice was dictated by fatherly love (14) for them, and he will not depart from it now, even though there are those who misinterpret it as a *wrong* (13) done to the Corinthians.

12:14 *The third time.* Cf. 13:1 and Introduction, par. 2.

12:18 *Urged Titus . . . sent the brother.* Cf. 2:13, 8:18.

12:19-21 REASON FOR PAUL'S BOASTING: THE UPBUILDING OF THE CHURCH

12:19-21 Paul's boasting has not been a decline from the high apostolic independence which he had professed earlier (cf. 5:11 – 6:10 note); he has not been pleading in his own defense before a human court; he has been speaking in *the sight of God . . . in Christ* (19), for his church's edification,

in order that they might repent (21) before Paul's visit and spare him and themselves the grief and humiliation of another "painful" visit. (Cf. Introduction, par. 2)

12:21 *Impurity, immorality,* etc. Cf. 6:14 – 7:1.

13:1-10 PAUL'S IMPENDING VISIT

13:1-10 Paul will come and deal unsparingly with those who refuse to repent; they shall have full proof of the POWER of his apostolic authority (1-4). But, characteristically, the apostle who is strong when he is weak implores the Corinthians not to put his authority to the test. His desire is, not to triumph over them but to upbuild them. He therefore prays that they *may not do wrong* (7), in order that he *may seem to have failed* (7), since he is helpless over against the *truth* of the Gospel and its workings in repentant men (8). Nowhere, perhaps, does the selflessness of Paul's apostolic will and the purity of his apostolic love appear in clearer light than here, where he wills not to demonstrate by severity (10) the power given him by the exalted Christ who speaks in him.

13:1 *Two or three witnesses,* as the Law requires, Dt 19:15; cf. Mt 18:16; 1 Ti 5:19; Heb 10:28.

13:4 *Weakness . . . power.* As in his missionary proclamation (1 Co 2:1-2), so in his pastoral care of the church Paul is determined to know nothing except "Jesus Christ and him crucified." He will be only the servant of the Servant Christ, with His weakness and HIS strength.

5 Examine yourselves, to see whether you are holding to your faith. Test yourselves. Do you not realize that Jesus Christ is in you?—unless indeed you fail to meet the test! 6 I hope you will find out that we have not failed. 7 But we pray God that you may not do wrong—not that we may appear to have met the test, but that you may do what is right, though we may seem to have failed. 8 For we cannot do anything against the truth, but only for the truth. 9 For we are glad when we are weak and you are strong. What we pray for is your improvement. 10 I write this while I am away from you, in order that when I come I may not have to be severe in my use of the authority which the Lord has given me for building up and not for tearing down.

11 Finally, brethren, farewell. Mend your ways, heed my appeal, agree with one another, live in peace, and the God of love and peace will be with you. 12 Greet one another with a holy kiss. 13All the saints greet you.

14 The grace of the Lord Jesus Christ and the love of God and the fellowship of[n] the Holy Spirit be with you all.

[n] Or *and participation in*

13:11-14 CONCLUSION: ADMONITION (11), GREETINGS (12-13), BENEDICTION (14)

13:11 This concluding admonition is summary expression of the will to reconciliation (by way of repentance) which informs the whole letter; the will of God which made Paul an apostle of Christ Jesus (1:1) is a will of *love and peace*.

13:12 *Holy kiss.* Cf. Ro 16:16 note.

13:14 The Trinitarian benediction is a revelation of all that makes obedience to the admonition of v. 11 ("mend your ways," etc.) possible and inescapable. The whole *love of God* which broke in glory upon mankind when the *grace of the Lord Jesus Christ* was manifested in poverty for the enrichment of the world (cf. 8:9), that *love* and *grace,* conveyed by the *Spirit* who unites men with God and with one another (fellowship)—that is the church's resource, alive and working in the apostolic Word; and with it all things are possible.

GALATIANS

INTRODUCTION

The Word of the Lord grows; where it grows, the Lord Jesus Christ is present and at work; and He is always "a sign that is spoken against" (Lk 2:34). Where the Word of the Lord grows, the kingdom of God is present; Jesus once described the presence and working of the Kingdom by comparing it with the working of leaven in dough; where the Kingdom is, there is ferment, disturbance, change, and upheaval. And so it is not surprising and in no way a contradiction of the fact that it is a divine Word if the growth of the Word brings with it tension and rouses conflict, not only between the church and the world but also within the church itself. The first church experienced such tension and conflict when the Word of the Lord began to grow on Gentile soil and the question of the relationship between the converted Gentile and the Christian Jew became an acute question, involving as it did the question of the relationship between the new, universal Gospel and the ancient Law given by God to Israel.

The apostles and the apostolic church knew from the beginning that the Christ is Lord of all and that the Word of the Lord must grow on every soil under heaven. Jesus had made His apostles His witnesses, not only in Jerusalem and all Judea but also in Samaria and to the end of the earth (Acts 1:8). The miracle of Pentecost spelled out in roaring wind, in apportioned flame, and in the gift of a speech that men of every nation could understand as their own the fact that the Spirit was to be poured out on "all flesh," that the Gospel was to go to all men in every tongue, that the promise for the last days, now being fulfilled in the outpouring of the Spirit, was not only to the Jews but also "to all that are far off, every one whom the Lord our God calls to him." (Acts 2:39)

This knowledge did not remain mere theory; nor was it the active possession of only a few. When Samaria received the Word of God preached there by Philip, the Jerusalem apostles acknowledged and welcomed the fellowship of the Samaritans and ce-mented the fellowship between the church of Samaria and the church of Jerusalem by sending Peter and John there to confer on them the gifts of the Spirit in full measure; and the apostles further extended that fellowship by "preaching the gospel to many villages of the Samaritans" (Acts 8:4-25). Philip was prompted by the angel of the Lord to tell the good news of Jesus to the Ethiopian eunuch and to baptize him, thus bringing into the new people of God one who had been doubly excluded from the ancient people of God both by the fact that he was a Gentile and by the fact that he was a eunuch (Dt 23:1). Thus the promise made for just such men through the prophet was fulfilled (Is 56:3-8). Such incidents were surely not isolated—Luke records typical incidents in his compressed account of how the Word of the Lord grew—nor were they unknown or forgotten in Jerusalem.

Another such incident, the conversion of the Gentile Cornelius and his family and friends (Acts 10:1-48), is characteristic of the attitude of the Palestinian church. The account of Luke marks this incident as a turning point, an epochal event. He tells it very fully, with emphasis on the divine guidance given by visions granted to both Peter and Cornelius; he records the sermon delivered by Peter in the house of Cornelius; and he points to the striking manifestations of the Spirit in these Gentile converts, manifestations at which the Jewish Christians were "amazed." Luke also records the fact that Peter's Jewish reluctance to enter a Gentile house had to be overcome (Acts 10:9-16, 27) and that there were those in Jerusalem who were dubious and critical about the step Peter had taken (Acts 11:1-18). For Peter this incident was of decisive and lasting importance, as his reference to it at the Apostolic Council shows (Acts 15:7-9). That the doubts of the men of Jerusalem were not wholly overcome by Peter's answer to their objections (Acts 11:4-18) is evident from the subsequent course of events. Thus there were present in Judaic Christianity two

conflicting impulses, both the will for the inclusion of the Gentiles and a Judaic reluctance to accept the uncircumcised Gentiles as brethren without reservation or limitation.

The beginnings and the seeds of conflict were there. The tension was made acute and brought into the open chiefly by three events: the conversion of Saul, the founding of a predominantly Gentile church at Antioch on the Orontes, and the missionary journey of Paul and Barnabas to Cyprus and the cities of Southern Galatia in Asia Minor. The conversion of the Pharisee and persecutor Saul is marked both in the three accounts of it in Acts (Acts 9:1-19; 22:3-21; 26:9-18) and in Paul's own reference to it in his epistles (Gl 1:15-16; 1 Co 15:8-10; Eph 3: 3, 8; 1 Ti 1:12-16) as a creative act of the sovereign grace of God, an act which made Saul God's "chosen instrument" (Acts 9:15). The history of Saul, or Paul, his Roman name by which he was known in his work among the Gentiles and is remembered in the church, shows us how the Lord of history had prepared His chosen instrument. Paul was a Roman citizen (Acts 16:37; 22: 25); a citizen of Tarsus in Cilicia, no mean Greek city (Acts 21:39); and a Hebrew of the Hebrews (Ph 3:5). Here was a man whose history had fitted him for the task to which the grace of God had called him. He was enabled by it to become all things to all men; he could, in a world dominated politically by Rome, bring the Gospel to men decisively influenced by Greek culture and speaking the Greek language. And he would be the last man to break ruthlessly with Judaic Christianity, even when the question of the relationship between Gentile and Jew in the church made fellowship between Jew and Gentile agonizingly difficult, for he remained in the highest sense a Hebrew of the Hebrews to the last (cf. Ro 9:1-5). In Paul God gave the church the man whose word and work would inevitably heighten the tensions latent there, and also the man who would work wholeheartedly for a salutary resolution of those tensions.

Paul did not found the Gentile church at Antioch; some unnamed Jews, men of Cyprus and Cyrene, did that, or rather the "hand of the Lord" did it through them (Acts 11:20-21). Paul is not quite the lone genius in pioneering Gentile missions and in establishing Gentile churches free from the Law that some romanticizing accounts make him out to be. Neither was he the first to work for contact and communion between the new Gentile community and the older Judaic churches. The Jerusalem church itself did that by sending Barnabas, that "good man, full of the Holy Spirit and of faith" (Acts 11:24), to Antioch. And it was Barnabas who brought Paul to Antioch (Acts 11:25-26). But the influence of Paul's preaching at Antioch must have been deep and decisive. How great Paul's influence was we can measure by the fact that it was Paul whom the brethren chose to go with Barnabas to bring relief to the brethren in Judea during the famine (Acts 11:27-30), and by the fact that the Spirit chose him for the first organized mission to the Gentiles (Acts 13:1-3). It was no doubt largely due to Paul's influence that the church of Antioch remained a church free of the Law, a church that both cultivated a full and active fellowship with the Judaic church and became the base for mission work to the Gentiles.

On the missionary journey that took Paul and Barnabas to Cyprus and Asia Minor (Acts 13—14) Paul emerges as the leader; Luke now calls him by his Roman name Paul (13:9), and now usually speaks of the two men in the order "Paul and Barnabas," whereas previously he has put the name of Barnabas first. From the time of their meeting with the Roman proconsul Sergius Paulus on Cyprus (Acts 13:6-12), Paul is the central figure in Gentile missions and dominates the rest of Luke's account of how the Word of the Lord grew. The conduct of the mission which Paul undertook jointly with Barnabas is characteristic of the ecumenical outlook of Paul. He sought contact with the synagog everywhere and found a ready acceptance of his good news especially among the "devout converts to Judaism" (Acts 13:43) and those Gentiles whom Luke designates as "men who fear God," Gentiles who without actually being full converts to Judaism still were on the fringes of the synagog, attracted by its pure preachment of the sole God and the high character of its moral teaching. Paul sought contact with the synagog and became a Jew to the Jew in his preaching by emphasizing how all God's previous dealings with Israel, from the time of the patriarchs to John the Baptist, have been leading up to and preparing for the message of Jesus as the Messiah, whom Paul now proclaimed to them (Acts 13:26-41). But at the same time he made it startlingly plain that his Gospel was, as the fulfillment of the promises of God, no mere supplement to the

Law, but the end of the Law and the antithesis to it, that the Word of God was now going beyond the confines of Israel into all the world, that through the Savior whom God had brought of David's line *"every one that believes* is freed [literally "justified"] from everything from which you could not be freed by the law of Moses" (Acts 13:39). He threw the doors of the new temple of God wide open to all, to Jew, to proselyte, to Gentile, and gave all men direct access to God, in Christ and simply by faith. He was saying out loud and in so many words what had long been implicit in the miracle of Pentecost, in the evangelization of the Samaritans, and in the conversion of the Ethiopian eunuch, Cornelius, and the Gentiles of Antioch.

As a result there came into the church large numbers of Gentiles, without circumcision, without submitting to the customs of Moses, not by way of Judaism, not as Jewish proselytes, but directly. And these people were, to some extent at least, conscious of the fact that they did not need to come into the church by way of Judaism, that they were full members of the new people of God, just as they were and as God had called them. This was bound to raise questions in the minds of Jewish Christians who had not yet or would not ever grasp the total newness of the New Testament, who could not or would not face all that was implicit in the words of John the Baptist when he said, "God is able *from these stones* to raise up children to Abraham" (Mt 3:9), or all that Jesus had meant when He said, in view of one Gentile's faith, *"Many* will come from east and west and sit at table with Abraham, Isaac, and Jacob in the kingdom of heaven" (Mt 8:11). Not that anyone denied the Gentile the right to membership in the church; the question was rather: *How* was the Gentile to attain such membership? Were all God's ancient ordinances, all the marks and tokens of His covenant with Israel, simply to be discarded by the new and culminating revelation of God in Christ? Was the ancient people of God, the people who claimed Abraham the believer as their father, simply to disappear, lost in the inbreaking wash of Gentile converts? Thus was created the tension in the church which led to the convocation of the Apostolic Council and the writing of Paul's Letter to the Galatians.

The Apostolic Council

The immediate occasion of the Apostolic Council was the arrival at Antioch of Jewish Christian men who insisted that Gentile converts must come into the church by way of Judaism; such men are commonly labeled "Judaizers." These Judaizers came to Antioch with the demand that the Gentile Christians be circumcised "according to the custom of Moses" (Acts 15:1; cf. 15:5), and they demanded circumcision as necessary to salvation: "Unless you are circumcised . . . you cannot be saved" (Acts 15:11). This party, or group, had its forerunners in men of the type who had called Peter to account for entering the house of the Gentile Cornelius (Acts 11:1-18). If Gl 2:1-5 refers, as seems most probable, to Paul's visit to Jerusalem A. D. 46 at the time of the famine (his second visit, Acts 11:30; 12:25), men of this sort had already collided with Paul when they demanded that his Greek companion Titus be circumcised. And Paul had stoutly resisted their demands. At least some of them were converted Pharisees (Acts 15:5). They were, then, a group or party within the church and did not, so far as we can see, expressly deny any part of the Gospel as preached by Paul and the rest. In fact they seem to have claimed the support of the Jerusalem church and the Jerusalem apostles for their demands (Acts 15:24); Luke is perhaps tacitly disallowing their claim when he says that they came "down from *Judea*" (Acts 15:1) and not from Jerusalem.

They were so insistent in their demands, argued so stubbornly and so skillfully with Paul and Barnabas, and so unsettled the minds of the Gentile Christians at Antioch (Acts 15:24) as well as elsewhere in Syria and Cilicia (Acts 15:23) that it was decided to carry the matter to the apostles and elders in Jerusalem (Acts 15:2). At the meeting in Jerusalem, which apparently included not only the apostles and elders but also representatives of the "whole church" (Acts 15:22), the voices of Peter and James, the brother of the Lord, were raised decisively in favor of Gentile freedom from the Law (Acts 15:7-11, 13-21). This was quite in keeping with the position they had previously taken over against Paul's Gospel and his apostolate to the Gentiles A. D. 46 (Gl 2:1-10), and the Judaic church followed their leadership in refusing to impose on the Gentiles "a yoke . . . which neither our fathers nor we have been able to bear" (Acts 15:10). But it must be remembered that for Judaic Christianity the question of the freedom of the Gentiles had two facets. The one half of the question,

Must a Gentile become a proselyte to Judaism in order to be saved? was answered at once and decisively by the council. But the other half of the question needed to be answered also, and that was, What is the relationship between the circumcised, ritually clean Jewish Christian and the uncircumcised, ritually unclean Gentile Christian to be? How are they to live together, and how are they to carry out that act which loomed so large as an expression of Christian fellowship—namely, table fellowship—how are they to eat together? (It should be remembered that the common meal and the celebration of the Lord's Supper were closely connected in the early church.) For the radical Judaizers the answer was of course simple: Let the Gentiles be circumcised and become good Jews. For Jewish men of good will who sought to fulfill the mission to Israel which God had given them (Gl 2:8-9), a mission which made it impossible for them to assume the freedom they had granted to the Gentiles, the answer was anything but simple. And in the light of this fact the words in the letter sent to the churches must be understood, the words, namely, "It has seemed good . . . to us to lay upon you no greater burden than these necessary things: that you abstain from what has been sacrificed to idols and from blood and from what is strangled and from unchastity" (Acts 15:28-29). The "necessary things" requested of the Gentiles are not marked as necessary to salvation and are therefore not a reimposing of the Law upon them; this is a *request* addressed to the Gentiles, a request which asked them to abstain from foods and practices abominable to Jewish feelings, foods and practices which their pagan past and their pagan surroundings made natural and easy for them. It is understandable that abstention from "unchastity" should be included also in the request, when we remember how closely connected unchastity was with pagan worship, pagan festivals, and pagan life generally. The so-called Apostolic Decree is therefore anything but a triumph of Judaic legalism. If a burden of love was laid on the Gentile brethren by it, the Judaic brethren also assumed no light burden in not expecting and asking more. The reception of the letter at Antioch (Acts 15:31) and later on in the province of Galatia (Acts 16:4, 5) shows that the Gentile churches did not view it as a defeat for Gentile freedom: "They rejoiced at the exhortation" (Acts 15:31) and "were strengthened in the faith, and they increased in numbers daily." (Acts 16:5)

The men of the church learned, as the Word of the Lord grew among them, not to use their freedom as an opportunity for the flesh, but through love to "be servants of one another" (Gl 5:13). Thus Christianity was safeguarded against a reimposition of the Law; the very real danger that Christianity might degenerate into a Judaic sect (and so perish with Judaism) was averted. And the unity of the church was preserved; the new Gentile church was kept in contact with the Judaic church, to which it owed the Gospel (cf. Ro 15:27) and was thus kept firmly rooted in the Old Testament Scriptures—a great blessing, for the history of the church has shown how readily alien and corrosive influences beset the Gospel once contact with the Old Testament is lost. To surrender the Old Testament is the first step toward misunderstanding, perverting, and so losing the Gospel of the New Testament.

The Letter of Paul to the Galatians

The struggle was in principle decided by the council at Jerusalem. But that did not mean that the Judaizers were forever silenced or that their influence was completely neutralized. Their claims were decisively rejected by the church at Jerusalem; but they had, apparently, meanwhile gone on to spread their mischief beyond Jerusalem and Antioch in the churches which Paul and Barnabas had established in Southern Galatia on their first missionary journey at Pisidian Antioch, Iconium, Lystra, and Derbe (Acts 13:14). They did so with considerable success, for what they proclaimed was a very plausible sort of substitute for the Gospel which Paul's converts had heard from him. To judge from Paul's polemics against them, they did not in so many words deny any positive teaching that Paul had brought to the Galatians; they acknowledged and proclaimed Jesus as the Messiah, the Son of God, the risen and exalted Lord, the Giver of the Spirit, in whose name is salvation; they did not deny that He would soon return in glory to consummate God's work in grace and judgment. The evidence does not even indicate that they completely ignored or obliterated the cross in its redemptive significance; Paul's repeated and passionate emphasis on the central and all-embracing significance of the cross in his letter does indicate that for them the Messiah of the

cross was overshadowed by the Messiah in glory, that the cross of Christ tended to become an episode which His exaltation counterbalanced and reduced to relative insignificance.

They did not, on their own profession, come to destroy Paul's work, but to complete it (Gl 3:3). The coming of the Messiah, in their proclamation, crowned Israel's history and consummated Israel; it did not therefore by any means signify the end of the Law and such sacred ordinances as circumcision and the Sabbath, which God Himself had ordained as the mark and condition of the covenant between Himself and His people forever. The coming of the Christ did not free men from the Law; the Christ confirmed the teaching of the Law and deepened the obedience which it demanded. Salvation by the mediation of the Christ therefore most assuredly included the performance of the works of the Law. A Christian estate based on faith alone, without circumcision and without the Law, was a very rudimentary and unfinished estate; perfection lay in circumcision and in keeping the Law to which it committed a man. Thus a man became a true son of Abraham and the heir of the blessing promised to Abraham, a member of God's true and ancient people. To dispense with the Law would mean moral chaos, or at best a very dubious and dangerous sort of liberty.

Paul, these men insinuated, had not told them all that was necessary for their full salvation. He was, after all, not an apostle of the first rank, not on a par with the original Jerusalem apostles, through whom he had received his apostolate. His failure to insist on the keeping of the Law was a piece of regrettable weakness on his part, due no doubt to his missionary zeal, but regrettable nevertheless; he had sought to gain converts by softening the rigor of the genuine Gospel of God – he had, in other words, sought to "please men." They, the Judaizers, were now come to complete what Paul had left unfinished, to lead them to that Christian perfection which Paul's Gospel could never give them.

Their attack was thus a three-pronged one. It was (a) an attack on the apostolate of Paul, (b) an attack on the Gospel of Paul as omitting essential demands of God, and (c) an attack which pointed up the moral dangers that would result from a proclamation of salvation by mere faith in an absolutely free and forgiving grace of God.

The attack was subtle; it was also, apparently, an organized attack under a single leadership; Paul refers to one personality as particularly responsible for the harm that had been done in the Galatian churches (Gl 5:10). And the attack was ominously successful, understandably enough. For the converted Jew this new form of the Gospel promised a more relaxed relationship with his unconverted fellow Jews; the Gentile converts would be impressed by the authority of the Jerusalem apostles which the new preachers invoked for their cause. And the zeal of these uncompromising extremists no doubt impressed both Gentile and Jew.

Paul probably heard of the activity of these men and of their incipient success while he was still at Antioch on the Orontes. Since he was about to go up to Jerusalem to thresh out the question raised by the Judaizers with the apostles and elders there, he could not go to Galatia in person, as he might have wished (Gl 4:20), to meet the attack and to combat the danger. He met it by writing the Letter to the Galatians, which is therefore to be dated A. D. 48 or 49.

The letter achieved its purpose; the Galatians joined loyally in the gathering of gifts for the poor in Jerusalem (1 Co 16:1), an undertaking close to Paul's heart as an expression of the unity between Gentile and Judaic Christianity. A certain Gaius of Derbe (in Galatia) was among the representatives of the Gentile churches who accompanied Paul when he took the Gentile offerings to Jerusalem. (Acts 20:4)

The Letter to the Galatians is one of the most personal and autobiographical of the letters of Paul, invaluable for the historical appreciation of his Gospel and his work; it is therefore valuable for the understanding of the growth of the Word of the Lord. We see here that the growth of that Word is genuine human history; the chosen instruments of the Lord are anything but robots – they do their work and the will of the Lord with the passionate intensity of personal involvement. The men who witness to the Christ are laid hold of by the Christ, and their mission becomes flesh of their flesh and bone of their bone.

Scarcely another epistle so emphasizes the "alone" of "by grace alone, through faith alone" as does this fighting exposition of the Gospel according to Paul with its embattled stress on the fact that Law and Gospel confront man with an inescapable, not-to-be-compromised either-or. Paul's Letter to the

Romans expounds the same theme more calmly and more fully and has a value of its own; but there is no presentation of the Gospel that can equal this letter in the force with which it presents the inexorable claim of the pure grace of God. Luther, who had to fight Paul's battle over again, said of Galatians: "The Epistle to the Galatians is my own little epistle. I have betrothed myself to it; it is my Catherine of Bora."

It should be remembered that the letter addresses itself to a very earnest, very pious, and very Christian sort of heresy and crushes it with an unqualified anathema. Our easy age, which discusses heresy with ecumenical calm over teacups, can learn from this letter the terrible seriousness with which the all-inclusive Gospel of grace excludes all movements and all men who seek to qualify its grace.

THE LETTER OF PAUL TO THE

GALATIANS

INTRODUCTORY: SALUTATION, REPROACH, AND CURSE (1:1-10)

1 Paul an apostle—not from men nor through man, but through Jesus Christ and God the Father, who raised him from the dead— 2 and all the brethren who are with me,

To the churches of Galatia:

3 Grace to you and peace from God the Father and our Lord Jesus Christ, 4 who gave himself for our sins to deliver us from the present evil age, according to the will of our God and Father; 5 to whom be the glory for ever and ever. Amen.

6 I am astonished that you are so quickly deserting him who called you in the grace of Christ and turning to a different gospel—7 not that there is another gospel, but there are some who trouble you and want to pervert the gospel of Christ. 8 But even if we, or an angel from heaven, should preach to you a gospel contrary to that which we preached to you, let him be accursed. 9 As we have said before, so now I say again, If any one is preaching to you a gospel contrary to that which you received, let him be accursed.

10 Am I now seeking the favor of men, or of God? Or am I trying to please men? If I were still pleasing men, I should not be a servant[a] of Christ.

Paul's Defense of His Apostolate

1:11 — 2:21

PAUL'S APOSTOLATE: ITS ORIGIN IN GOD (1:11-24)

11 For I would have you know, brethren, that the gospel which was preached by me is not man's[b] gospel. 12 For I did not receive it from man, nor was I taught it, but

---

[a] Or *slave*   [b] Greek *according to man*

1:1-10 The peculiarly impetuous and passionate character of the letter is apparent from the start. After the salutation Paul, without pausing for the thanksgiving and prayer which usually follow (cf., e. g., Ro 1:8-13), breaks into a severe reproach of the Galatians for deserting the Gospel and an unqualified condemnation of the men who have misled them with what purports to be *another gospel* but is in reality a perversion of the one true Gospel. With that he has already begun the theme that is to occupy him through the first two chapters: the defense of his apostolate. Paul is not, as his opponents claim, a man-pleaser who has diluted the Gospel to achieve a quick and cheap success: he is wholly *a servant of Christ*—neither he nor anyone else has authority to change the Gospel of Jesus Christ.

1:1-5 The salutation touches on all three of the themes of the letter: the divine origin and independence of Paul's apostolate *(not from men nor through man)*, chs. 1–2; the centrality of the cross *(who gave himself for our sins)*, chs. 3–4; and the new life which removes men from "the present

evil age," where the compulsion and condemnation of the Law have their necessary place. (Chs. 5–6)

1:2 *All the brethren who are with me.* Paul often associates individuals with himself in the salutation (cf., e. g., 1 Co 1:1; 2 Co 1:1; Ph 1:1; Cl 1:1); only here does he include a group (his co-workers [?], representatives of a congregation or congregations [?]). He is indicating perhaps that what he has to say is not one man's opinion, one apostolic voice. The whole apostolic church is warning them and pleading with them in what follows.

1:11–2:21 In three stages Paul defends his apostolate against the charge that his authority is secondary and derivative ("from men . . . through man," 1:1): his apostolate is divine grace conferred directly on him (1:11-24), recognized as such by the Jerusalem apostles (2:1-10), independent even over against so powerful a figure as Cephas. (2:11-21)

1:11-24 *The gospel . . . preached by me is not man's gospel* (11); Paul's first word concerning his apostolate is a word concerning the Gospel for

---

it came through a revelation of Jesus Christ. [13] For you have heard of my former life in Judaism, how I persecuted the church of God violently and tried to destroy it; [14] and I advanced in Judaism beyond many of my own age among my people, so extremely zealous was I for the traditions of my fathers. [15] But when he who had set me apart before I was born, and had called me through his grace, [16] was pleased to reveal his Son to[c] me, in order that I might preach him among the Gentiles, I did not confer with flesh and blood, [17] nor did I go up to Jerusalem to those who were apostles before me, but I went away into Arabia; and again I returned to Damascus.

18 Then after three years I went up to Jerusalem to visit Cephas, and remained with him fifteen days. [19] But I saw none of the other apostles except James the Lord's brother. [20] (In what I am writing to you, before God, I do not lie!) [21] Then I went into the regions of Syria and Cilicia. [22]And I was still not known by sight to the churches of Christ in Judea; [23] they only heard it said, "He who once persecuted us is now preaching the faith he once tried to destroy." [24]And they glorified God because of me.

PAUL'S APOSTOLATE RECOGNIZED BY THE PILLARS OF THE CHURCH (2:1-10)

2 Then after fourteen years I went up again to Jerusalem with Bar′na·bas, taking Titus along with me. [2] I went up by revelation; and I laid before them (but

[c] Greek in

which he is "set apart" (Ro 1:1), with which his apostolate is so closely identified that he can on occasion refer to it as "my gospel" (Ro 2:16; 2 Ti 2:8; cf. 2 Co 4:3; 1 Th 1:5). This Gospel, the beating heart of his apostolate, he has not received from man; he did not learn it as he learned the Law and the *traditions of* his *fathers* at the feet of Gamaliel (Acts 22:3). Christ came to him by *revelation*, by that act of God in which God alone is active to make Himself known and to make Himself count in man's life (12, cf. 16). No man contributed to that, least of all Paul himself; his willing and running were in violent opposition to God's revelation all the way (13-14, cf. 23). Neither did the first *apostles* contribute anything (17): Paul did not meet *Cephas* (Peter) until 3 years later and then only briefly (18). The *churches . . . in Judea* knew him only by hearsay for 14 years — and they gave all the credit for his conversion to God (*glorified God because of me*, 24). Like them, Paul can attribute his conversion and call to the apostolate only to God's eternal counsels, His sovereignly gracious good pleasure, His *grace* that forgave him his rebellious past and empowered him for his future ministry to the Gentiles (15-16). Paul's autobiography is an echo of Jesus' words to Peter: "Flesh and blood has not revealed this to you, but my Father who is in heaven." (Mt 16:17)

1:11 *For*. Paul is saying, "I am a slave of Christ [10], for God has by His revelation made me His slave."

1:13 *Persecuted the church*. Cf. Acts 8:1-2; 9:1-4; 22:4-16; 26:9-18.

1:14 *Traditions of my fathers* are that body of interpretations of (and additions to) the Law which had grown up around the Law and enjoyed a prestige and authority in Judaism practically equal to that of the Law itself. (Cf. Mt 15:2)

1:15 *Set me apart before I was born*. Paul describes God's control of his existence in terms used by the Lord when He called Jeremiah into His service as His prophet. (Cf. Jer 1:5)

Through his grace. Paul always looks on his apostolate as sheer grace. (Cf. Ro 1:5; 1 Co 15:10; Eph 3:2, 7, 8; 1 Ti 1:14)

1:17 *Arabia*. The kingdom of the Nabataean Arabs extended northward to within a short distance south of Damascus.

1:18 *Cephas*, Aramaic form of "Peter." (Cf. Jn 1:42)

1:19 *Apostles except James the Lord's brother*. According to this translation, James is called *apostle*. He would then belong to that larger group (beyond the Twelve) of apostles who were commissioned by the risen Lord (cf. 1 Co 15:7). But the Greek words may also be translated to read: "I saw none of the other apostles, but I did see James, the Lord's brother."

2:1-10 Paul's second visit to Jerusalem raised the very question which the agitators in the Galatian churches were raising: Had Paul, or anyone, the authority to bring Gentiles into the church without circumcision? The question was bound to be raised, for Paul took with him *Titus*, an uncircumcised Gentile convert (1). And the question was raised — not by the Jerusalem apostles but by *false brethren secretly brought in* (4), men of the same stripe as those now subversively active in Galatia. These Paul resisted for the Gentiles' sake, the Gospel's sake, for the truth's sake, for the sake of the *freedom* with which Christ made men free (5). The pillar of the Jerusalem church made common cause with Paul, recognized the *grace* of God *given* to him in his apostolate to the Gentiles, laid no restrictions on his preaching of the Gospel of freedom (*added nothing to me*, 6), gave him and Barnabas *the right hand of fellowship*, and agreed on a division of labor (9). The only request they made of Paul and Barnabas was that they cement the bond of fellowship between Jewish and Gentile Christians by an active charity (*remember the poor*, 10), a request that Paul met more than halfway.

2:1 *After fourteen years* — 14 years after Paul's

privately before those who were of repute) the gospel which I preach among the Gentiles, lest somehow I should be running or had run in vain. [3] But even Titus, who was with me, was not compelled to be circumcised, though he was a Greek. [4] But because of false brethren secretly brought in, who slipped in to spy out our freedom which we have in Christ Jesus, that they might bring us into bondage— [5] to them we did not yield submission even for a moment, that the truth of the gospel might be preserved for you. [6]And from those who were reputed to be something (what they were makes no difference to me; God shows no partiality)—those, I say, who were of repute added nothing to me; [7] but on the contrary, when they saw that I had been entrusted with the gospel to the uncircumcised, just as Peter had been entrusted with the gospel to the circumcised [8] (for he who worked through Peter for the mission to the circumcised worked through me also for the Gentiles), [9] and when they perceived the grace that was given to me, James and Cephas and John, who were reputed to be pillars, gave to me and Bar′na·bas the right hand of fellowship, that we should go to the Gentiles and they to the circumcised; [10] only they would have us remember the poor, which very thing I was eager to do.

PAUL'S APOSTOLATE: ENCOUNTER WITH PETER (2:11-21)

11 But when Cephas came to Antioch I opposed him to his face, because he stood condemned. [12] For before certain men came from James, he ate with the Gentiles; but when they came he drew back and separated himself, fearing the circumcision party. [13]And with him the rest of the Jews acted insincerely, so that even Bar′na·bas

conversion or after the first visit described in 1:18-19? The whole question of the chronology of Paul's visits to Jerusalem and their relationship to the visits recorded in Acts is a complicated and much-discussed problem whose solution does not contribute much to the understanding of the letter. On the whole it seems best to identify this visit with that of Acts 11:27-30 (rather than with that of Acts 15, as many interpreters do). The revelation referred to in 2:2 would there probably be that given by the prophet Agabus (Acts 11:28): *Barnabas* was with Paul on that visit (Acts 11:30) as well as on that described in Acts 15; and since the visit of Acts 11 was a relief mission (Acts 11:29), the words of the "pillars" to Paul and Barnabas in Gl 2:10 could be rendered, with fidelity to the Greek, as: "They asked us to continue to remember the poor, which very thing I had been eager to do." A private (2:2) discussion concerning the Gospel preached among the Gentiles could well have been held on the occasion of that visit.

2:2 *Run in vain.* Paul knew that if the Jerusalem authorities were not sympathetic to his Gentile mission, his work could be seriously impaired. They had shown a ready and active sympathy with the work done among the Greeks at Antioch (Acts 11:20-26); he hoped for the same sympathy in regard to work further afield. And he was not disappointed in that hope.

2:6 *What they were makes no difference to me.* This seems to conflict with what he has said in 2:2. There Paul obviously set great store by the sympathy and approval of the men of Jerusalem. The point he is making here is that the Gospel, not being a "man's gospel" (1:11), cannot be validated by any man's approval, just as no man, not Paul himself, can alter it and make "another gospel" of it. (1:9)

2:7-9 This administrative measure either did not work out in practice—we find Paul going regularly into the Jewish synagog on his missionary travels (e.g., Acts 13:5, 14) and Peter writing to Gentile churches (1 Ptr)—or, as seems more likely, was never intended as a rigid rule. Paul's road ran westward to the Greek-speaking world; if he encountered Jews on that road, he would inevitably speak the Good News "to the Jew first" (Ro 1:16), and he never forgot his kinsmen even in his mission to the Gentiles. (Ro 11:13-14)

2:9 *Grace.* Cf. 1:15 and the note there.

Pillars. The church is thought of as the structure raised by the Lord Christ (cf. Mt 16:18); in that structure these men are prominent and important.

2:10 *Remember the poor.* For Paul's interest in the collection for the poor in Jerusalem see Ro 15:24-28; 1 Co 16:1-4; 2 Co 8−9; and cf. Acts 24:17.

2:11-21 Paul illustrates the independence of his apostolate by means of an incident in the history of the church at Antioch. When *Cephas* (Peter) by his behavior there first attested the equality and freedom of the Gentile Christians by eating with them and then denied it by withdrawing from table fellowship with them (12), Paul *opposed him to his face* (11). He spelled out for Peter the meaning of his inconsistent behavior, his *insincerity* (13), his evasion of the *truth of the gospel* (14) which *condemned* him (11). Paul bluntly pointed out to Peter, the "first" of the Twelve, what his actions (whether he was conscious of it or not) were saying. They were saying to the Gentile Christians: Unless you *live like Jews* (14), submitting to the Law, you remain unclean *Gentile sinners* (15) unfit for table fellowship with the Jew. These actions were saying to his fellow Jewish Christians: We have sinned by eating with

was carried away by their insincerity. [14] But when I saw that they were not straightforward about the truth of the gospel, I said to Cephas before them all, "If you, though a Jew, live like a Gentile and not like a Jew, how can you compel the Gentiles to live like Jews?" [15] We ourselves, who are Jews by birth and not Gentile sinners, [16] yet who know that a man is not justified[d] by works of the law but through faith in Jesus Christ, even we have believed in Christ Jesus, in order to be justified by faith in Christ, and not by works of the law, because by works of the law shall no one be justified. [17] But if, in our endeavor to be justified in Christ, we ourselves were found to be sinners, is Christ then an agent of sin? Certainly not! [18] But if I build up again those things which I tore down, then I prove myself a transgressor. [19] For I through the law died to the law, that I might live to God. [20] I have been crucified with Christ; it is no longer I who live, but Christ who lives in me; and the life I now live in the flesh I live by faith in the Son of God, who loved me and gave himself for me. [21] I do not nullify the grace of God; for if justification[e] were through the law, then Christ died to no purpose.

Paul's Defense of the Gospel of Free Grace

3:1–4:31

THREE WITNESSES TO THE TRUE NATURE OF LAW AND GOSPEL (3:1-14)

3 O foolish Galatians! Who has bewitched you, before whose eyes Jesus Christ was publicly portrayed as crucified? [2] Let me ask you only this: Did you receive the Spirit by works of the law, or by hearing with faith? [3] Are you so foolish? Having

[d] Or *reckoned righteous;* and so elsewhere   [e] Or *righteousness*

unclean Gentiles; being *justified by faith in Christ* (16) is not enough to make and keep us clean. With that Peter by his actions was saying: Christ is *an agent of sin* (17), for faith in Him has led us into this sin. This amounts to saying: The *grace of God* (21) and the love of the Son (20) manifested in the death of Christ are ineffectual: Christ *died to no purpose* (21). Our baptism is meaningless: We have not *died to the law* by being *crucified with Christ* (19, 20; cf. Ro 6:3-6) *Christ* does not *live in* us (20). Peter did indeed stand condemned: he was *building up again* the Law, to which he had died with Christ; in thus denying the grace of God he was proving himself *a transgressor* (18) of the Law, which bade him love the Lord his God with all his heart.

Paul's words to Peter constitute the transition to the theme of the second major part of his letter, the either-or of Law or Promise, Law or Gospel. (3:1–4:31)

2:11 *He stood condemned,* by his actions. He had divided the church which God had made one in Christ Jesus. (3:26-28)

2:12 *Came from James,* that is, from Jerusalem, where James soon became the acknowledged leader of the church (see Introduction to the Letter of James). It is not said that James sent them to put an end to the table fellowship between Jewish and Gentile Christians; it is not even said that they remonstrated with Peter, Barnabas, and the rest. The mere presence of representatives of the Jerusalem church was enough to remind Peter of the criticism that his action would provoke in the Jewish-Christian stronghold of Jerusalem (cf. Acts 11:1-3) and to make him waver in his freedom.

He ate with the Gentiles. The common meal was a token and expression of fellowship, deeply felt as such; moreover, the Lord's Supper was celebrated in connection with it. (Cf. 1 Co 11:17-34)

2:15 *Gentile sinners.* The phrase represents the attitude of the pious Law-observing Jew toward nations without the Law.

2:19 *Through the law died to the law.* The Christian, "crucified with Christ" (20) in Baptism (Ro 6:3-11), has died *through the law* since it was Christ's obedience to the Law (a whole love for God and for man) that took Him to the cross; he *died to the law* because in Christ's death the condemnation and curse of the Law (cf. 3:13) was executed on man once for all, and the man in Christ is freed from the Law legally, on the Law's own terms, by dying. (Cf. Ro 7:1-6)

3:1-14 First witness: Paul appeals first to the witness of the *experience* (4) of the Galatians. They owe their conversion to the proclamation of the Crucified; and the cross is God's verdict on mankind, His rejection of all the works of man. It is by *hearing with faith* (not by works which the Law commands and rewards) that they have received the Spirit and witness the miracles done among them. They must be *bewitched* to believe that a progression from the Spirit to *flesh* (circumcision), from Gospel to Law, is an advance and not a retrogression. (1-5)

Second witness: He then meets the Judaizers on their own ground by appealing to the witness of the Old Testament concerning Abraham; Abraham is the father of the people of God as a justified believer, and those who are *men of faith* are his true sons, heirs of the blessing promised to all nations. (6-9; cf. Ro 4)

begun with the Spirit, are you now ending with the flesh? 4 Did you experience so many things in vain?—if it really is in vain. 5 Does he who supplies the Spirit to you and works miracles among you do so by works of the law, or by hearing with faith?

6 Thus Abraham "believed God, and it was reckoned to him as righteousness." 7 So you see that it is men of faith who are the sons of Abraham. 8And the scripture, foreseeing that God would justify the Gentiles by faith, preached the gospel beforehand to Abraham, saying, "In you shall all the nations be blessed." 9 So then, those who are men of faith are blessed with Abraham who had faith.

10 For all who rely on works of the law are under a curse; for it is written, "Cursed be every one who does not abide by all things written in the book of the law, and do them." 11 Now it is evident that no man is justified before God by the law; for "He who through faith is righteous shall live";f 12 but the law does not rest on faith, for "He who does them shall live by them." 13 Christ redeemed us from the curse of the law, having become a curse for us—for it is written, "Cursed be every one who hangs on a tree"—14 that in Christ Jesus the blessing of Abraham might come upon the Gentiles, that we might receive the promise of the Spirit through faith.

THE RELATIONSHIP BETWEEN PROMISE AND LAW (3:15-29)

15 To give a human example, brethren: no one annuls even a man's will,g or adds to it, once it has been ratified. 16 Now the promises were made to Abraham and to his offspring. It does not say, "And to offsprings," referring to many; but, referring to one, "And to your offspring," which is Christ. 17 This is what I mean: the law, which came four hundred and thirty years afterward, does not annul a covenant previously ratified by God, so as to make the promise void. 18 For if the inheritance is by the law, it is no longer by promise; but God gave it to Abraham by a promise.

f Or the righteous shall live by faith   g Or covenant (as in verse 17)

Third witness: Paul further appeals to the witness of the Law itself. The Law demands deeds and pronounces a *curse* on all who do not obey it fully. *No man,* though, *is justified before God by the law;* all men are under its curse and can be justified only by the faith which looks to Him who took upon Himself the curse of the Law in our stead. In Him all men, Gentiles as well as Jews, receive the *blessing of Abraham* and the gift of the *Spirit promised* for the last days of fulfillment *through faith.* (10-14)

3:1 *As crucified.* Cf. 2:21. The cross, as God's crushing verdict on man and as His acquittal of man for Christ's sake, has forever excluded man's performance, the way of the Law, as the way of salvation.

3:3 *Are you now ending,* or "being made complete," alluding to the claim of the Judaizers that Paul had preached an "incomplete" gospel in Galatia, one that needed to be supplemented by their teaching. *Flesh* probably refers to circumcision.

3:6 For a fuller treatment of *Abraham* as father of the whole people of God, of all believers both Gentile and Jew, cf. Ro 4 and the notes there. *Thus.* The connecting link in the thought is the answer which the question of 5 expects: "You have received the Spirit because you heard and *believed,* just as Abraham (with whom the history of the people of God begins) also believed and was justified." Therefore you are walking in the footsteps of Abraham, stand before God as he stood,

are justified as he was, and are in the truest sense his sons.

Believed God, etc. Cf. Gn 15:6; Ro 4:3.

3:8 Cf. Gn 12:3

3:10 *Cursed be.* Cf. Dt 27:26. Paul cites freely; the *all things written* is implied but not stated in Dt 27:26. But compare Dt 28:15 ("do all his commandments and his statutes"). For the full horror of the *curse* cf. Dt 28:15-68.

3:11 Cf. Hab 2:4; Ro 1:17; and the notes on those passages.

3:12 *Faith . . . does them.* Salvation by grace through faith and salvation by works are mutually exclusive. (Cf. Ro 4:2-5; 9:32; 11:6)

3:13 *A curse for us.* For a similarly drastic statement of the vicarious atonement cf. 2 Co 5:21.

Cursed be every one. Dt 21:22-23 pronounced this curse on the executed criminal. For Paul, the unconverted Pharisee, this had probably been the greatest stumbling block; he had probably joined in the cry, "Jesus be cursed!" (1 Co 12:3), for how could the Crucified, He whom the Law pronounced accursed, be the Christ, the Lord!

1) 3:15-18 THE PROMISE OF GOD AS A WILL OR TESTAMENT

3:15-18 The blessing of Abraham and the gift of the Spirit do not come by way of the Law (cf. 3:1-14). But the Law is God's law; it is "holy, and the commandment is holy and just and good" (Ro 7:12), for God's will of love is expressed in the Law (5:14, 23). The Law cannot therefore be

19 Why then the law? It was added because of transgressions, till the offspring should come to whom the promise had been made; and it was ordained by angels through an intermediary. 20 Now an intermediary implies more than one; but God is one.

21 Is the law then against the promises of God? Certainly not; for if a law had been given which could make alive, then righteousness would indeed be by the law. 22 But the scripture consigned all things to sin, that what was promised to faith in Jesus Christ might be given to those who believe.

23 Now before faith came, we were confined under the law, kept under restraint until faith should be revealed. 24 So that the law was our custodian until Christ came, that we might be justified by faith. 25 But now that faith has come, we are no longer under a custodian; 26 for in Christ Jesus you are all sons of God, through faith. 27 For as many of you as were baptized into Christ have put on Christ. 28 There is neither Jew nor Greek, there is neither slave nor free, there is neither male nor female; for you are all one in Christ Jesus. 29And if you are Christ's, then you are Abraham's offspring, heirs according to promise.

merely dismissed; it must be seen in its place and time as it functions in God's overall plan for the salvation of man as God has revealed it. God Himself, not Paul, has assigned to the Law its secondary place. God's first word in the history of His people was the *promise* made to Abraham, not the *law* given through Moses. The promise, this basic and primary word to mankind, is a giving word: "I will bless you, and make your name great, so that you will be a blessing . . . in you all the families of the earth shall be blessed" (Gn 12:2-3). The promise says, "I will give" (Gn 12:7). Now, no one can annul a will *once it has been ratified* (by the testator's death); so also the Law, coming centuries after the promise, cannot be thought of as in any way annulling or even modifying His promise (15-18) – "the gifts and the call of God are irrevocable." (Ro 11:29)

3:15 *A man's will.* As RSV note *g* indicates, the same Greek word is used for both *will* and *covenant;* this suggests the comparison. For the promise as covenant, a gracious, freely giving declaration of God which establishes and regulates a relationship between God and man, cf. Gn 17:2-14.

3:16 *Offspring . . . Christ.* From the vantage point of the fulfillment of the promise, Paul sees that there is but *one* offspring of Abraham in whom the promised blessing is finally realized, *Christ,* "the son of Abraham." (Mt 1:1)

3:17 *Four hundred and thirty years afterward.* Cf. Ex 12:40.

Previously ratified. Because the covenant is God's, it is ratified and in force as soon as it is uttered – unlike a human testator's will which is in force only after the testator's death.

3:18 *By the law . . . no longer by promise. Law* ("You shall") and *promise* ("I, God, will") exclude one another (cf. Ro 4:14). God's demanding word and His giving word are reconciled only in the cross. (13)

2) 3:19-29 THE SUBORDINATE, TEMPORARY
　　　　FUNCTION OF THE LAW

3:19-29 The function of the Law was not to annul the promise of God; rather, the Law had a negative

and temporary function in relation to the promise (19, 22), one limited to the nation Israel (20, see the note below). The Law has subserved the gracious purpose of God's promise; it has performed a *custodian's,* or overseer's, service over God's people until the time of the fulfillment of the promise. Now that the new age of *faith* has come (faith in the *promise*), the Law ceases to perform that function.

3:19 *Added.* Cf. Ro 5:20: "Law came in." The Law came after the promise and is of limited duration, controlling the life of God's people *till the offspring* (Christ) *should come.*

Because of transgressions. The Law brought man's sin out into the open as a violation of God's will (Ro 3:20) and so actually served to "increase the trespass." (Ro 5:20; cf. Ro 7:13)

Ordained by angels. Cf. Dt 33:2-4; Acts 7:53. Jew and Judaizer saw in this a mark of the glory of the Law; Paul sees in it a mark of the inferiority of the Law. When God gave His promise for all nations, He spoke directly to Abraham, the father of the people; He gave His law through *angels* and a human *intermediary,* Moses.

3:20 This obscure verse seems designed to make clear the significance of the *intermediary* in the giving of the Law. An *intermediary implies more than one,* namely, the nation Israel, for whom the Law was designed. The Law is limited both in time (19) and in scope, confined to Israel. It is therefore not the first nor the last nor the prime word of the one God of both Jew and Gentile who will justify both by faith. (Ro 3:29-30)

3:21 *If . . . law . . . could make alive.* The Law could not and did not overthrow the reign of death (cf. Ro 5:12, 17), did not make alive men "dead through . . . trespasses and sins" (Eph 2:1; Cl 2:13). The promise, fulfilled in Christ, did.

3:22 *Consigned all things to sin.* God's will and verdict as expressed in *the scripture* imprisoned *all things* under the power of sin; the condemnation covered both man (Ro 3:9-19; 11:32) and man's world. (Gn 3:17-19; Ro 8:20, 22)

3:23-24 Three times in two verses Paul expresses the negative, provisional, subordinate character of the working of the Law, already expressed once

THREE ASPECTS OF SONSHIP CONFIRMING THE GOSPEL OF GRACE (4:1-31)

4 I mean that the heir, as long as he is a child, is no better than a slave, though he is the owner of all the estate; 2 but he is under guardians and trustees until the date set by the father. 3 So with us; when we were children, we were slaves to the elemental spirits of the universe. 4 But when the time had fully come, God sent forth his Son, born of woman, born under the law, 5 to redeem those who were under the law, so that we might receive adoption as sons. 6And because you are sons, God has sent the Spirit of his Son into our hearts, crying, "Abba! Father!" 7 So through God you are no longer a slave but a son, and if a son then an heir.

8 Formerly, when you did not know God, you were in bondage to beings that by nature are no gods; 9 but now that you have come to know God, or rather to be known by God, how can you turn back again to the weak and beggarly elemental spirits, whose slaves you want to be once more? 10 You observe days, and months, and seasons, and years! 11 I am afraid I have labored over you in vain.

12 Brethren, I beseech you, become as I am, for I also have become as you are. You did me no wrong; 13 you know it was because of a bodily ailment that I preached the gospel to you at first; 14 and though my condition was a trial to you, you did not

in 22 ("consigned . . . to sin"): *confined, restraint, custodian.*

3:25 *Faith* is shorthand for the new age in which by faith men are blessed with Abraham (9), are righteous and live by faith (3:11) in the Christ, are released from the curse by Him, receive the Spirit through faith (3:13-14), and are all sons of God and united in Christ Jesus through faith. (3:27-28)

3:26-29 With the fulfillment of the promise in Christ (cf. 16), the distinctions set up by the custodian Law *(Jew, Greek)*, all the distinctions of the "present evil age" (1:4) are done away with *(slave, free, male, female, 28).* The new people of God, all who are *baptized,* stand before God clothed in Christ, as *Abraham's offspring,* heirs *according to the promise* made to Abraham. (Cf. 16)

3:27 *Put on Christ.* We think of clothing as something external, which may or may not express what the clothed person is. Biblical thought generally conceives of clothing as being expressive of the person; one clothed in righteousness, majesty, strength, etc., is righteous, majestic, and strong (cf., e.g., Ps 132:9; 93:1; Is 52:1; 59:17). To put on Christ therefore means that a man is fully and wholly in Him; Christ is His real, true existence. (Cf. 2:20)

3:29 *Christ's . . . offspring . . . heirs.* Cf. 3:16.

4:1-31 This section has a rather miscellaneous character, but the three units of thought are held together by the idea of sonship. (Cf. 4:7, 19, 31)

1) 4:1-11 SONS AND HEIRS

4:1-11 The position of Israel under the Law was that of son and heir, but a minor heir, a child without liberty, no better than a slave. For the Jew to turn from the Gospel of free grace to the Law and its bondage would mean turning from manhood to childhood, from a freedom which the Father Himself has bestowed to a self-chosen slavery. For the Gentile, a turning from the Gospel to the Law would be practically a return to idolatry — he would be worshiping the outworn and

discarded garments of God, not the living God as now revealed in His Son.

4:3 *Elemental spirits of the universe.* Cf. 9, "weak and beggarly elemental spirits." The exact meaning of the word translated as *elemental spirits* (here and in Cl 2:8, 20) is uncertain. The idea of "spirit" is not necessarily included under the term, which basically means simple "element," something rudimentary, as in Heb 5:12 ("first principles"). Whatever the precise meaning of the term may be, Paul's general argument is clear. Paul is pointing up what Israel under the Law and paganism have in common; the Jew under the Law and the Gentile immersed in paganism are both unfree, in contrast to their present freedom in Christ. The Jew under the Law is bound to such elements of the world as "days, and months, and seasons, and years" (cf. 10), subject to physical circumcision, obliged to distinguish between clean and unclean foods, and to offer physical, animal, and cereal offerings. The Gentile in his paganism is enslaved to "weak and beggarly" elemental things — and worse, he is in bondage to gods that "are no gods" (8, Paul does not say this of the Jew under the law of God). But a return to the past is unthinkable for either Jew or Gentile now that they are both free sons of God by God's act in Christ.

4:6 *Abba* is in Jesus' mother tongue the child's familiar and affectionate address to his father; it illustrates the perfect freedom of the Christian's sonship (cf. Ro 8:16-17) and echoes Jesus' own mode of addressing His Father. (Mk 14:36)

4:9 *To know God* and *to be known by God* are two sides of one reality, describing the communion established by God's grace and enjoyed through faith. (Cf. 1 Co 8:2-3)

2) 4:12-20 MY LITTLE CHILDREN!

4:12-20 The Galatians have known what joy it is to be *children* of God in Christ. Paul gave them a new birth with the Gospel of free grace (19). Will they now turn from him whom they once

scorn or despise me, but received me as an angel of God, as Christ Jesus. [15] What has become of the satisfaction you felt? For I bear you witness that, if possible, you would have plucked out your eyes and given them to me. [16] Have I then become your enemy by telling you the truth?[h] [17] They make much of you, but for no good purpose; they want to shut you out, that you may make much of them. [18] For a good purpose it is always good to be made much of, and not only when I am present with you. [19] My little children, with whom I am again in travail until Christ be formed in you! [20] I could wish to be present with you now and to change my tone, for I am perplexed about you.

21 Tell me, you who desire to be under law, do you not hear the law? [22] For it is written that Abraham had two sons, one by a slave and one by a free woman. [23] But the son of the slave was born according to the flesh, the son of the free woman through promise. [24] Now this is an allegory: these women are two covenants. One is from Mount Sinai, bearing children for slavery; she is Hagar. [25] Now Hagar is Mount Sinai in Arabia;[i] she corresponds to the present Jerusalem, for she is in slavery with her children. [26] But the Jerusalem above is free, and she is our mother. [27] For it is written,

> "Rejoice, O barren one who does not bear;
> break forth and shout, you who are not in travail;
> for the children of the desolate one are many more
> than the children of her that is married."

[h] Or *by dealing truly with you*　[i] Other ancient authorities read *For Sinai is a mountain in Arabia*

---

loved so fervently, count him their enemy, and listen to the flattering persuasion of men who woo them now by *making much* of them in order to lord it over them later?

4:12 *Become as I am, for I also have become as you are,* that is, free of the Law. Paul had come to them simply as an apostle of Jesus Christ; he had become "to those outside the law . . . as one outside the law" (1 Co 9:21) and had given them the freedom with which Christ had made him free.

You did me no wrong, when I first came to you in physical weakness.

4:17 *They make much of you.* The Judaizers are wooing them now to win them over; but they want to *shut* them *out* from full membership in the church in order that the Galatians may make much of them, that is, become dependent on them as on the men who can give them all that they need to become true sons of Abraham and members of the people of God—circumcision, the Law.

4:19 *My little children.* Cf. 1 Co 4:15. Paul is like a mother *in travail,* but he does not labor to bring forth children in his own likeness—Paul has no use for Paulinists (ef. 1 Co 1:12-13). His words, his Gospel, are to bring forth Christians, men in whom *Christ* is *formed,* in whom Christ lives. (Cf. 2:20)

4:20 *Change my tone.* Paul has already used a great variety of "tones," ranging from the sharpest denunciation (1:6-9) to warmest appeal (19). If he were *present* with them to hear their questions and to know firsthand their problems, he might find yet another form of speech with which to win them back to the truth.

3) 4:21-31 SONS OF ABRAHAM:
　　　　ISHMAEL OR ISAAC?

4:21-31 Those who seek to win over the Galatians promise them that they will make the Galatians "sons of Abraham" by incorporating

them in Israel (through circumcision, etc.). Paul's reply is: "Abraham had two sons; which son of Abraham will you be, Ishmael or Isaac? If you set store by physical descent from Abraham and want to join his physical descendants, your sonship is that of Ishmael, the son *born according to the flesh,* son of a slave woman who is typical of the covenant of *Mount Sinai* (a covenant which imposed the Law and could no more be God's final redemptive word than the birth of Ishmael could be the fulfillment of the promise to Abraham). That covenant produces slaves; and the slave woman has her counterpart in *Jerusalem,* the enslaved and doomed city of the Jews. True sonship is that of Isaac, born *through promise,* produced by the gracious and creative Word of God, son of the free woman, who is typical of the covenant of freedom and corresponds to the *Jerusalem above* (the redeemed and free people of God). The child of the free woman was persecuted by the child of the slave woman; so also the church is persecuted by Israel. But that does not change the destiny of either one. Those who would be Abraham's sons must go the way of the Gospel and freedom, not the way of enslavement under the Law."

4:21 *The law,* that is, the Book of Genesis, one of the five books of the Law. For the story of Hagar and Ishmael cf. Gn 16 and 21:8-21.

4:23 *Born according to the flesh,* that is, by the devising of man. (Cf. Gn 16:1-4)

4:25 *Hagar is Mount Sinai in Arabia.* The text here is very uncertain. The reading given in RSV note *i* is perhaps to be preferred. In Greek the word for "for" is very similar to the word for Hagar, and this may have led to confusion in copying the text. If we adopt the reading of the note *(For Sinai is a mountain in Arabia),* the sense seems to be: It is right to identify the slavery covenant of Sinai with Hagar, for Mount Sinai

28 Now we,^{j} brethren, like Isaac, are children of promise. 29 But as at that time he who was born according to the flesh persecuted him who was born according to the Spirit, so it is now. 30 But what does the scripture say? "Cast out the slave and her son; for the son of the slave shall not inherit with the son of the free woman." 31 So, brethren, we are not children of the slave but of the free woman.

Paul's Defense of the Gospel: Life in Freedom

5:1 – 6:10

LIFE IN FREEDOM: GENERAL DESCRIPTION (5:1-24)

5 For freedom Christ has set us free; stand fast therefore, and do not submit again to a yoke of slavery.
2 Now I, Paul, say to you that if you receive circumcision, Christ will be of no advantage to you. 3 I testify again to every man who receives circumcision that he is bound to keep the whole law. 4 You are severed from Christ, you who would be justified by the law; you have fallen away from grace. 5 For through the Spirit, by faith, we wait for the hope of righteousness. 6 For in Christ Jesus neither circumcision nor uncircumcision is of any avail, but faith working^x through love. 7 You were running well; who hindered you from obeying the truth? 8 This persuasion is not from him who calls you. 9 A little leaven leavens the whole lump. 10 I have confidence in the Lord that you will take no other view than mine; and he who is troubling you will bear his judgment, whoever he is. 11 But if I, brethren, still preach circumcision, why am I still persecuted? In that case the stumbling block of the cross has been removed. 12 I wish those who unsettle you would mutilate themselves!

^{j} Other ancient authorities read *you* ^{x} Or *made effective*

is in Arabia, the home of Hagar's slave-children, Ishmael and his descendants.

4:26 *The Jerusalem above,* that is, the second covenant (cf. 24), the new covenant of free sonship. (4:7)

4:27 *It is written.* Cf. Is 54:1. The prophetic Word was addressed to Jerusalem, the destroyed, captive, desolate capital of the deported people of God. The city is compared to a *barren* and deserted wife who is promised the miracle of abundant offspring. This promise finds its fulfillment in the church, the new Israel of God (cf. 6:16) that shall triumph over persecution (cf. 29) and increase marvelously.

4:29 *Persecuted.* Cf. Gn 16:12, where it is said of Ishmael: "He shall be a wild ass of a man, his hand against every man and every man's hand against him; and he shall dwell over against all his kinsmen," and Gn 21:9, which was interpreted by Judaic tradition as indicating Ishmael's hostility toward Isaac.

4:30 *Cast out the slave.* Cf. Gn 21:10-12.

To meet the charge that his Gospel of free grace means a breakdown of morality, Paul depicts the life of freedom, first in general terms (5:1-24) and then by concrete examples. (5:25 – 6:10)

1) 5:1-12 FREEDOM AND THE LAW

5:1-12 Freedom and Law are incompatible. Freedom is not a way which man has chosen, but the way which Christ has established. No man may therefore compromise with it; to return to the way of the Law in however slight a measure

(such as submitting to circumcision) is to cancel the Gospel of freedom, is to lose the Christ who has set us free. (1)

5:3 *Bound to keep the whole law.* Once a man goes the way of the Law, he must go the whole way. (Cf. 3:10; Ja 2:10)

5:6 *Faith working through love.* The parallels to this expression in 1 Co 7:19; Gl 6:15 are instructive. The "new creation" (Gl 6:15) means a life of "faith working through love" (Gl 5:6) and so "keeping the commandments of God." (1 Co 7:19)

5:8 *This persuasion,* that is, to accept circumcision and go the way of the Law does not come from Him who called you, for He called you "in the grace of Christ" (1:6) and not with the demands of the Law.

5:11 *Preach circumcision . . . persecuted.* Paul's opponents evidently accused him of compromising on circumcision on occasion; the incident of Timothy's circumcision (Acts 16:3) shows how far Paul was willing to go in becoming a Jew to the Jews "in order to win Jews" (1 Co 9:20). But Paul's stand over against the demand that Titus be circumcised (2:2-5) shows that he never wavered on the matter where "the truth of the gospel" was involved. Here his answer is simply to point to the fact that he is still being persecuted (by Jews and Judaizers); he could easily have avoided persecution by a little compromise – but did not, since circumcision and the cross are mutually exclusive.

5:12 *Mutilate themselves!* Since in Christ circumcision has become meaningless (6), the act is

13 For you were called to freedom, brethren; only do not use your freedom as an opportunity for the flesh, but through love be servants of one another. 14 For the whole law is fulfilled in one word, "You shall love your neighbor as yourself." 15 But if you bite and devour one another take heed that you are not consumed by one another.

16 But I say, walk by the Spirit, and do not gratify the desires of the flesh. 17 For the desires of the flesh are against the Spirit, and the desires of the Spirit are against the flesh; for these are opposed to each other, to prevent you from doing what you would. 18 But if you are led by the Spirit you are not under the law. 19 Now the works of the flesh are plain: fornication, impurity, licentiousness, 20 idolatry, sorcery, enmity, strife, jealousy, anger, selfishness, dissension, party spirit, 21 envy,[k] drunkenness, carousing, and the like. I warn you, as I warned you before, that those who do such things shall not inherit the kingdom of God. 22 But the fruit of the Spirit is love, joy, peace, patience, kindness, goodness, faithfulness, 23 gentleness, self-control; against such there is no law. 24And those who belong to Christ Jesus have crucified the flesh with its passions and desires.

LIFE IN FREEDOM: CONCRETE EXAMPLES (5:25 — 6:10)

25 If we live by the Spirit, let us also walk by the Spirit. 26 Let us have no self-conceit, no provoking of one another, no envy of one another.

6 Brethren, if a man is overtaken in any trespass, you who are spiritual should restore him in a spirit of gentleness. Look to yourself, lest you too be tempted. 2 Bear one another's burdens, and so fulfil the law of Christ. 3 For if any one thinks he is something, when he is nothing, he deceives himself. 4 But let each one test his own work, and then his reason to boast will be in himself alone and not in his neighbor. 5 For each man will have to bear his own load.

6 Let him who is taught the word share all good things with him who teaches.

7 Do not be deceived; God is not mocked, for whatever a man sows, that he will

[k] Other ancient authorities add murder

---

a mere mutilation of the flesh (cf. Ph 3:2). With bitter irony Paul wishes that the devotees of circumcision (mutilation) would go the whole senseless way and emasculate themselves, as the pagan devotees of the goddess Cybele, for instance, did. The cult of Cybele originated in Pessinus in the Roman province of Galatia and would be familiar to the Galatians.

2) 5:13-24 FREEDOM AND THE SPIRIT

5:13-24 Freedom must not be misinterpreted to mean license; freedom means being set free from self to serve one's fellowman (which is the essence of God's will as expressed in the Law).

Freedom means walking, conducting oneself, by the power and leading of the Spirit. It means entering that struggle against the flesh and its desires which a man can wage and win only in the power of the Spirit. It means living a life *led by the Spirit,* a life which moves on a level that the Law's threats and condemnation cannot touch. It means that Christ's death to sin (*crucified,* 24) becomes a reality in those *who belong to Christ.*

5:15 *Bite and devour one another.* The bitter factionalism which the proponents of the Law have brought into the churches threatens to destroy them.

5:17 Cf. Ro 7:15-23.

5:25 — 6:10 Life in freedom means the end of all self-centered pride, the end of provocative self-assertion and envy (5:25-26). It means a life of meek and gentle ministry to the erring, a ministry

performed in the consciousness of one's own frailty (6:1-5). It means loving generosity toward those who teach in the church. (6:6)

As the life in the freedom of faith is a life of love (cf. 5:6), so it also is a life of soberly responsible hope. Freedom in Christ does not absolve a man of responsibility for his action; rather it heightens responsibility. Man will reap what he has sown. God will hold him accountable for what he has in his freedom done with the gift of the Spirit.

5:25 *Walk.* The word implies an orderly, disciplined walking, a being guided by the Spirit.

6:2, 5 *Bear one another's burdens. . . . Each man will have to bear his own load.* Christians serve one another, and yet each man remains individually responsible for his own life's work. "Each of us shall give account of himself to God." (Ro 14:12)

6:4 *Reason to boast . . . in his neighbor,* that is, boasting of one's supposed superiority to one's neighbor.

6:6 It may be that Paul's opponents had used Paul's refusal to accept support for himself as a pretext to cover a callous neglect toward the teachers of the church. Paul always insisted on obedience to the Lord's command "that those who proclaim the gospel should get their living by the gospel" (1 Co 9:14; cf. Mt 10:10; Lk 10:7-8), even though he himself made no use of this right. (1 Co 9:14)

6:7 *God is not mocked* with impunity; His justice will deal with those who flout His will.

also reap. ⁸ For he who sows to his own flesh will from the flesh reap corruption; but he who sows to the Spirit will from the Spirit reap eternal life. ⁹And let us not grow weary in well-doing, for in due season we shall reap, if we do not lose heart. ¹⁰ So then, as we have opportunity, let us do good to all men, and especially to those who are of the household of faith.

CONCLUSION (6:11-18)

11 See with what large letters I am writing to you with my own hand. ¹² It is those who want to make a good showing in the flesh that would compel you to be circumcised, and only in order that they may not be persecuted for the cross of Christ. ¹³ For even those who receive circumcision do not themselves keep the law, but they desire to have you circumcised that they may glory in your flesh. ¹⁴ But far be it from me to glory except in the cross of our Lord Jesus Christ, by which¹ the world has been crucified to me, and I to the world. ¹⁵ For neither circumcision counts for anything, nor uncircumcision, but a new creation. ¹⁶ Peace and mercy be upon all who walk by this rule, upon the Israel of God.

17 Henceforth let no man trouble me; for I bear on my body the marks of Jesus.

18 The grace of our Lord Jesus Christ be with your spirit, brethren. Amen.

¹ Or *through whom*

6:8 *Sows to his own flesh,* that is, expends his energies and life in the kind of activities enumerated in 5:19-21. Similarly, *sows to the Spirit* is illuminated by 5:22.

Corruption, the opposite of *eternal life,* eternal destruction in the judgment of God. The same Greek word is translated "destruction" in 2 Ptr 2:12.

6:10 *Household of faith.* Cf. Mt 10:25, where Jesus calls His disciples "those of his household."

6:11-18 The conclusion, written by Paul's own hand (the rest of the letter was dictated), sums up once more the chief thought of the letter, with special emphasis on the selfish motives of the Judaizers and the selfless, Christ-centered motivation of Paul. The letter closes with a plea that he whom suffering has marked as Christ's own may be spared further agony at the hands of the Galatians and with a benediction on all who *walk by this rule* of the Gospel of freedom and are therefore the true *Israel of God,* true sons of Abraham. (Cf. 3:7, 29)

6:11 The *large letters* may be for emphasis. Some think that the "bodily ailment" to which Paul refers in 4:13 may have been a disease of the eyes (cf. 4:14) which left his eyesight permanently impaired; then the large letters would be necessitated by his imperfect vision.

With my own hand. For Paul's habit of dictating his letters and adding a postscript or a greeting in his own handwriting cf. 1 Co 16:21; Cl 4:18; 2 Th 3:17. In Ro 16:22 the secretary, Tertius, adds a greeting of his own.

6:12 *May not be persecuted for the cross of Christ.* By practising circumcision they continue to identify themselves with Judaism and hope to be tolerated as a sect within Judaism. The *cross* rules out *circumcision,* every concession to legalism, for in the cross Christ has redeemed men from the curse and power of the Law. (Cf. 3:13)

6:14 *The world,* in which man's "good showing," his personal glory, counts and is pursued, ceased to exist for those who believe in the Crucified. They still live in it, as they live in the flesh (2:20), but it does not set standards for them or control their conduct.

6:15 Cf. 5:6; 1 Co 7:19.

6:17 *The marks of Jesus.* In the Greek world devotees or slaves of a deity were marked or tattooed with the sign of their master and so became sacrosanct; Paul calls the scars of his sufferings marks of Jesus which consecrate him to the Lord and should evoke awe and loving consideration for the apostle.

The Captivity Letters

The letters of Paul to the Ephesians, Philippians, Colossians, and Philemon are known as the Captivity Letters because they were all written while Paul was a prisoner, most likely at Rome, in A. D. 59–61. Some scholars date some of the Captivity Letters from Paul's 2-year imprisonment in Caesarea in A. D. 56–58 (cf. Acts 23:11-24, 27). Others date them all from a supposed imprisonment in Ephesus during his ministry there in A. D. 52–55, an imprisonment not mentioned by Luke in Acts but made probable by the troubled character of Paul's Ephesian years. But on the whole the ancient tradition which assigns the Captivity Letters to Rome still seems the most probable.

The Book of Acts tells the moving story of how Paul went up to Jerusalem for the last time bearing gifts from the Gentile churches to the church of Jerusalem, how this Christlike action of ministry to his people in the face of danger and death lead to his arrest in Jerusalem, to his 2-year imprisonment in Caesarea, to his appeal to Caesar, and to the perilous voyage which finally brought him to Rome as he had long been hoping (Ro 1:10-11; 15:23, 32; Acts 19:21) and as his Lord had promised (Acts 23:11), but in a way he had not foreseen, as a prisoner (Acts 28:20). He remained a prisoner in Rome for two years, but the terms of his imprisonment were such that he was not reduced to idleness. He had his own rented quarters and his friends, the emissaries of the churches, and his co-workers had free access to him (Acts 28:31); they could cheer him by their presence and inform him personally of the fortunes and misfortunes of his churches. And the matured wisdom and ageless love of the aging apostle were available to them. We see him, at the end of the Book of Acts, "preaching the kingdom of God and teaching about the Lord Jesus Christ quite openly and unhindered." (Acts 28:31)

Paul's imprisonment was therefore not an interruption of his ministry but an exercise of his ministry. Paul himself viewed it as such: he sees in his sufferings an extension, as it were, of "Christ's afflictions" (Cl 1:24) for the sake of His church; he is a "prisoner for Christ Jesus" on behalf of the Gentiles (Eph 3:1), "a prisoner for the Lord" (Eph 4:1); his imprisonment is an imprisonment for the Gospel (Phmn 13); he is an "ambassador in chains" for the Gospel (Eph 6:19-20); and his trial at Rome is for the "defense and confirmation of the gospel" (Ph 1:7). He sees in his sufferings a part of the grace bestowed on him in the gift of his ministry, and so he rejoices in them. (Cl 1:24; Ph 2:17)

Not least among the fruits which grew on that tree of adversity are the Captivity Letters. In them we have Paul's profoundest proclamation of the all-embracing significance of the Christ (Letter to the Colossians) and of the nature and glory of His church (Letter to the Ephesians), a small but impressive record of how the Gospel can transfigure even mean and sordid aspects of human life (Letter to Philemon), and a letter whose dominant note of hopeful joy in the midst of suffering has through the ages helped keep the church a hoping Advent church even under persecution (Letter to the Philippians).

EPHESIANS

INTRODUCTION

The Letter to the Ephesians is linked by the evidence in the letter itself to the Letter to the Colossians and the Letter to Philemon. Tychicus is the bearer of the letter (Eph 6:21) and will give the readers fuller information concerning the imprisoned apostle (Eph 6:22). Since Tychicus is also the bearer of the Letter to the Colossians, and since Onesimus is returning to Colossae with Tychicus (Cl 4:7-9), the three letters (Ephesians, Colossians, Philemon) have a common historical background; they proceed from Paul's Roman captivity and are to be dated somewhere within the two years of that captivity (A. D. 59—61), perhaps in the earlier part of it.

But was the letter really addressed to the church in Ephesus? The earliest manuscripts do not have the words "in Ephesus" in the salutation (1:1), and their witness is confirmed by that of the early church fathers; the RSV translators had good reason for omitting the words from their revision of the text. Moreover, the letter itself nowhere indicates that Paul and the readers whom he is addressing are personally acquainted with one another; there are passages which indicate the very opposite (Eph 1:15; 3:2). When we consider how long Paul ministered in Ephesus and what close ties that ministry established (Acts 20:36-38), the absence of any personal touches in the letter is very striking. Similarly the letter gives no hint that Paul is personally acquainted with the life of the church—there are no concrete details, no reminiscences of former personal contacts. Paul's letters to the Corinthians, written to a church in which he had worked and with which he was intimately acquainted, present a striking contrast to the Letter to the Ephesians in this respect. One can hardly avoid the conclusion that the letter known as the Letter to the Ephesians was not originally addressed to Ephesus, at least not to Ephesus alone.

The best explanation of the historical background of the letter would seem to be the one suggested as early as the 16th century by Beza, Grotius, and Ussher: When Paul sent Tychicus to Colossae, he at the same time sent a general letter designed especially for a group of churches in Asia Minor which had been evangelized under his supervision during his Ephesian ministry, but had for the most part never been personally visited by him, places like Colossae, Hierapolis, and Laodicea. Tychicus would leave a copy with each church in the towns through which he passed on his way to Colossae, and possibly he transmitted copies to towns which did not lie on his route. In the latter case Paul's promise that Tychicus would inform the churches of his estate (Eph 6:21) would be fulfilled when Tychicus visited these churches after having completed his mission to Colossae. Each copy would bear the name of the church addressed. When Paul's letters were later collected and published, probably at Ephesus, the letter naturally came to bear the title "To the Ephesians," since Ephesus was no doubt included in the number of the churches addressed and was the most prominent among them. Some later copyist then probably inserted the words "in Ephesus" in the salutation to bring the text of the letter into harmony with its title. Some scholars are inclined to see in the letter "from Laodicea" referred to in Cl 4:16 the letter we know as Ephesians. It may be; copying was an onerous task in antiquity, and it would be natural and sensible to make one copy do for the two churches, since Colossae and Laodicea lay only 13 miles apart.

The sending of Tychicus to Colossae thus provided the external occasion for the writing of the circular letter now called the Letter to the Ephesians. What Paul's motives in sending such a letter were, we can infer from the apostolic church's missionary practice and from a statement made by Paul toward the end of the letter itself. The apostolic church always sought contact with newly founded churches. John and Peter were sent to Samaria after the evangelist

Philip had founded a church there (Acts 8:14). Barnabas was sent to the young church at Antioch (Acts 11:22). Paul took representatives of the Jerusalem church with him on his first two missionary journeys (Barnabas, Mark, Silas); he maintained contact with Jerusalem and Judaic Christianity and sought to express and maintain the unity of the Spirit in the bond of peace by means of the Gentile collection for the Jerusalem saints; and he regularly revisited the churches which he had founded. As Paul surveyed his work in the East from the vantage point of his position in Rome, and saw from the reports of his co-workers the temptations and the dangers to which the young churches were exposed, he might well be moved to do by letter what he could not do in person, to go through his territory once more, "strengthening the churches" (Acts 15:41). That would be one motive for writing to the churches in the East.

The other motive was provided by Paul's peculiar situation. Paul in Rome knew himself to be an ambassador for the Gospel, albeit an ambassador in chains (Eph 6:20). Again the strength of the Lord was being made perfect in weakness. The Gentile churches saw the human weakness of the imprisoned apostle to the Gentiles more clearly than they saw the divine strength which worked through him; they had grown dispirited at the news of his imprisonment (Eph 3:13). Moreover, Paul was facing a crisis in his ambassadorship, one that would ask of him all the boldness he could muster (Eph 6:18-20). Paul therefore did two things in his letter. He asked for the intercessions of the churches, thus removing them from the role of lamenting spectators and making them active participants in his great ambassadorial task. And he held up before them the greatness of that task, the greatness of the church which the mighty divine Word proclaimed by him had created and was sustaining. He had just written to the Colossians how God's act in the cross of Christ has made a peace which embraces the universe in all its parts and in all its powers (Cl 1:20); he had just written to Philemon and had seen, in applying the power of the Gospel to heal the breach between master and run-away slave, how that peace heals all man's life and removes its ugly rancors. He now spoke of "Christ our peace" (Eph 2:14) to all the scattered and troubled churches and held before them the greatness of the new people of God which God has created by uniting Jew and Gentile, once enemies, in one church; he held up before them the glory of that one, holy church, thus keeping the churches conscious of their high privilege of unity in Christ and of the obligation which the high privilege of membership in the one church involves. If the Letter to the Colossians is the letter of Christ, the Head of the church, the Letter to the Ephesians is the letter of the church, the body of Christ. Its purpose and outreach are as universal as its destination is general.

Content of the Letter

The Letter to the Ephesians consists of two portions, the first being an exposition of what the church is, the second an exhortation concerning all that membership in the church involves. We can sum up the message of the letter in the words of ch. 2, v. 10: "We are his workmanship, created in Christ Jesus for good works . . . that we should walk in them."

Value of the Letter

Paul is here singing hymns in prison, as he once did at Philippi. It is a hymn rich in content, a hymn which sings of the "manifold wisdom of God" and "the unsearchable riches of Christ." One perceptive modern interpreter has compared the letter with the Letter to the Romans; in both letters, he points out, Paul elaborates the theme stated in 1 Co 1:24, "Christ the power of God and the wisdom of God." Whereas Romans stresses the element of power (Ro 1:16), Ephesians emphasizes the wisdom of God. The church that is always prone to forget that it is God's creation and likes to think of itself as a structure of strength which man in *his* wisdom has reared and can in his wisdom control will do well to immerse itself again and again in this hymn from prison and learn from the ambassador in chains an awed humility in the presence of that awful, divine wisdom.

THE LETTER OF PAUL TO THE

EPHESIANS

The Church: Created in Christ Jesus

1:1 – 3:21

1 Paul, an apostle of Christ Jesus by the will of God,
To the saints who are also faithful[a] in Christ Jesus:
2 Grace to you and peace from God our Father and the Lord Jesus Christ.

DOXOLOGY TO THE FATHER OF OUR LORD JESUS (1:3-14)

3 Blessed be the God and Father of our Lord Jesus Christ, who has blessed us in Christ with every spiritual blessing in the heavenly places, 4 even as he chose us in him before the foundation of the world, that we should be holy and blameless before him. 5 He destined us in love[b] to be his sons through Jesus Christ, according to the purpose of his will, 6 to the praise of his glorious grace which he freely bestowed on us in the Beloved. 7 In him we have redemption through his blood, the forgiveness of our trespasses, according to the riches of his grace 8 which he lavished upon us. 9 For he has made known to us in all wisdom and insight the mystery of his will, according to his purpose which he set forth in Christ 10 as a plan for the fulness of time, to unite all things in him, things in heaven and things on earth.

11 In him, according to the purpose of him who accomplishes all things according to the counsel of his will, 12 we who first hoped in Christ have been destined and appointed to live for the praise of his glory. 13 In him you also, who have heard the word of truth, the gospel of your salvation, and have believed in him, were sealed with the promised Holy Spirit, 14 which is the guarantee of our inheritance until we acquire possession of it, to the praise of his glory.

THANKSGIVING AND PRAYER (1:15-23)

15 For this reason, because I have heard of your faith in the Lord Jesus and your

[a] Other ancient authorities read *who are at Ephesus and faithful*   [b] Or *before him in love, having destined us*

1:1-2 SALUTATION

1:1 On the absence of a place name in the salutation see the Introduction.

1:3-14 The opening doxology (cf. 2 Co 1:3 ff.; 1 Ptr 1:3 ff.) surveys the whole range of God's redemptive blessings: the eternal purpose of God which *chose* and *destined* men to be His own through Christ, to the *praise of His glorious grace* (3-6a); the bestowal of His grace in the redemption wrought by Christ's death and in the proclamation of the *mystery of his will* which shall unite all things in Him *for the praise of his glory* (6-12); the ultimate fulfillment of His redemption, the inheritance which the gift of the Holy Spirit guarantees to the church *to the praise of his glory. (13-14)*

The church comes into being by God's will in Christ. Note the constant recurrence of words denoting God's plan and purpose *(purpose, will, mystery of his will, plan, counsel, chose, destined, appointed)* and the red thread of "in Christ" which runs through the whole doxology.

1:3 *In Christ.* Cf. 4, 6, 7, 9, 10, 11, 13. Paul uses this phrase in a wide variety of applications to indicate the unique significance of Christ in God's

redeeming purpose, action, and the results of His action in the redeemed community now and in the universe at the end of days (1:10). Christ as the comprehensive Representative of mankind is the place where (or Person through whom) God acts for us men and our salvation; He is therefore the place where (the Person in whom) we receive and enjoy all that God's action has bestowed on man.

1:6 *The Beloved*, Christ, the Son beloved of the Father. (Cf. Mt 3:17; 17:5; Cl 1:13)

1:9 *Mystery* indicates that God's great plan for the salvation of man and the restoration of all things can be known only by God's revelation. (Cf. 3:3-5; Dn 2:27-28 and 2:22)

1:10 *Fulness of time.* The time, determined by God, when His redeeming purpose reaches its full measure in the sending of His Son. (Cf. Mk 1:15; Gl 4:4)

1:13 *Sealed,* marked as God's property and assured of His protection. (Cf. 4:30; 2 Co 1:22)

1:14 *Guarantee,* literally "down payment," "first instalment," which in ancient times was a substantial portion of the whole.

1:15-23 Paul *gives thanks* for the faith and love of his readers (15-16) and prays that they may be

358

love[c] toward all the saints, 16 I do not cease to give thanks for you, remembering you in my prayers, 17 that the God of our Lord Jesus Christ, the Father of glory, may give you a spirit of wisdom and of revelation in the knowledge of him, 18 having the eyes of your hearts enlightened, that you may know what is the hope to which he has called you, what are the riches of his glorious inheritance in the saints, 19 and what is the immeasurable greatness of his power in us who believe, according to the working of his great might 20 which he accomplished in Christ when he raised him from the dead and made him sit at his right hand in the heavenly places, 21 far above all rule and authority and power and dominion, and above every name that is named, not only in this age but also in that which is to come; 22 and he has put all things under his feet and has made him the head over all things for the church, 23 which is his body, the fulness of him who fills all in all.

THE GENTILES HAVE PART IN THE REDEMPTION (2:1-10)

2 And you he made alive, when you were dead through the trespasses and sins 2 in which you once walked, following the course of this world, following the prince of the power of the air, the spirit that is now at work in the sons of disobedience. 3Among these we all once lived in the passions of our flesh, following the desires of body and mind, and so we were by nature children of wrath, like the rest of mankind. 4 But God, who is rich in mercy, out of the great love with which he loved us, 5 even when we were dead through our trespasses, made us alive together with Christ (by grace you have been saved), 6 and raised us up with him, and made us sit with him in the heavenly places in Christ Jesus, 7 that in the coming ages he might show the im-

c Other ancient authorities omit *your love*

enabled by the Spirit to comprehend all that God has wrought for them (17): the *hope* which God's call has given them (18), the certainty of the *inheritance* which God's call has promised them (18), and the assurance that God's *power* (19) will carry believers safely through the dark present into future glory (14) — the power which He supremely manifested when He *raised* Jesus Christ *from the dead* and made Him Lord of all and Head *over all things for the church,* the *body* of Christ. (20-22)

1:17 *A spirit of wisdom.* Better "the Spirit of . . ."; the Holy Spirit is meant and is characterized by the gifts, *wisdom* and *revelation,* which He bestows. Cf. Ro 8:15 ("Spirit of adoption"), where v. 16 makes plain that the Holy Spirit is meant, and 2 Co 4:13; 2 Ti 1:7; Heb 10:29. For the connection between *Spirit* and *wisdom* cf. 1 Co 12:8; Cl 1:9; Acts 6:3, 10; between *Spirit* and *revelation* cf. 1 Co 2:10, 12; Eph 3:5.

1:18 *Hearts.* The heart in Biblical usage is the seat and organ not only of feeling, as with us, but of the whole inner life of men, including will and mind; "to say in one's heart" means "to think." (Ro 10:6; Ps 14:1)

Inheritance in the saints. The *inheritance* belongs to the future (cf. 1:14; 1 Ptr 1:4, "kept in heaven for you"), but *in the saints* (in the church) the future blessing is by the gift of the Spirit (1:14) already known and enjoyed. (Cf. Heb 6:4-5)

1:21 *Rule, authority, power, dominion.* Names for angelic powers, whether benign or hostile, taken over from Judaism; they are mentioned in order to assert the incomparable superiority of the Lordship of Christ (cf. Ro 8:38-39; 1 Co 15:24; Cl 1:16; 2:10, 15). For the whole thought cf. Heb 1:4-14.

Name. Title of dignity and honor. (Cf. Ph 2:9)

1:22-23 *Head over all things for the church . . . his body. Head* signifies dominion, lordship (not the intellect as with us). Christ's relationship to His church is more than mere power-dominion over it; He is vitally and organically united with His church and functions personally through it. This unique Lordship is expressed by the head-body image. (Cf. 5:23; Cl 1:18, 24)

Fulness, as being completely "filled" by Christ. *Fills all in all.* For "fill" in the sense of "dominate," "rule," cf. 4:10 and Jer 23:24, where the ideas of rule and omnipresence are combined.

2:1-10 God's universal redemption includes the Gentiles. He has delivered them from death and the dominion of Satan and has raised them to life and glory with the risen and exalted Christ (1-7). All this is unmerited grace, the gift of God received by faith. The church is solely and wholly God's creation, created for good works. (8-10)

2:2 *Walked.* For "walk" as designating "total behavior," "a way of life," cf. v. 10; Ro 6:4; 8:4; 14:5, etc. In Ro 13:13 the word for walk is rightly rendered "conduct ourselves."

Sons of disobedience, disobedient men (cf. 5:6; Cl 3:6). "Son of" is used to designate a man's character or calling ("son of the soil" is a farmer), sometimes his destiny, as in "son of perdition," 2 Th 2:3.

2:3 *We all,* Jews as well as Gentiles. (Cf. Ro 3:9)

2:4 *But God.* Cf. Ro 3:21, "But now . . . ." Salvation is God's "nevertheless" to man's desperate situation under His wrath. This is the first of a series of expressions which underscore the sheer gratuity of salvation (mercy, love, loved, grace, gift, not because of works, created).

measurable riches of his grace in kindness toward us in Christ Jesus. [8] For by grace you have been saved through faith; and this is not your own doing, it is the gift of God—[9] not because of works, lest any man should boast. [10] For we are his workmanship, created in Christ Jesus for good works, which God prepared beforehand, that we should walk in them.

THE GENTILES HAVE PART IN THE REDEEMED COMMUNITY (2:11-22)

11 Therefore remember that at one time you Gentiles in the flesh, called the uncircumcision by what is called the circumcision, which is made in the flesh by hands— [12] remember that you were at that time separated from Christ, alienated from the commonwealth of Israel, and strangers to the covenants of promise, having no hope and without God in the world. [13] But now in Christ Jesus you who once were far off have been brought near in the blood of Christ. [14] For he is our peace, who has made us both one, and has broken down the dividing wall of hostility, [15] by abolishing in his flesh the law of commandments and ordinances, that he might create in himself one new man in place of the two, so making peace, [16] and might reconcile us both to God in one body through the cross, thereby bringing the hostility to an end. [17] And he came and preached peace to you who were far off and peace to those who were near; [18] for through him we both have access in one Spirit to the Father. [19] So then you are no longer strangers and sojourners, but you are fellow citizens with the saints and members of the household of God, [20] built upon the foundation of the apostles and prophets, Christ Jesus himself being the cornerstone, [21] in whom the whole structure is joined together and grows into a holy temple in the Lord; [22] in whom you also are built into it for a dwelling place of God in the Spirit.

THE APOSTLE'S PRAYER FOR THE GENTILES (3:1-21)

3 For this reason I, Paul, a prisoner for Christ Jesus on behalf of you Gentiles— [2] assuming that you have heard of the stewardship of God's grace that was given to me for you, [3] how the mystery was made known to me by revelation, as I have

---

2:10 *Workmanship*, what He has made, created; the same word is translated in Ro 1:20 as "the things that have been made."

For good works, etc. Faith (v. 8) is purely receiving, but it IS a receiving, and therefore faith is inevitably an active faith which *walks* in the good works which God has *prepared* beforehand. Passages like this show how close to each other Paul and James are. (Ja 2:14-26)

2:11-22 Christ by the cross has abolished the Law which divided mankind into Jew and Gentile and excluded the Gentile from the *covenants* and *hope* of Israel. Thus He has created and proclaimed *peace*, the end of the ancient *hostility* between Israel and the Gentiles and the union of Jew and Gentile into one reconciled people of God. The Gentiles are incorporated into the people of God, into the family of God, into the living *temple* of God.

2:12 *Covenants of promise.* The covenant expresses God's gracious will to have fellowship with man, to create a bond (where no "natural" bond exists) between Himself and man, to give fallen man a future and a hope. The basic content of the covenant is, "I will be your God," and this gives all forms of the covenant the character of a promise, whether it be the covenant with Abraham (Gn 17:7-8), with Israel (Ex 24:3-11; cf. 19:3-6), with David (2 Sm 23:5), or the covenant as embodied in the person and ministry of the Servant

(Is 42:6-7), or the promised new covenant (Is 54:10; 55:3; 61:8; Jer 31:31-34; Eze 16:60; 34:25; 37:26). To this the Gentiles were *strangers*, until Christ established the new covenant in His blood. (Mt 26:28; 1 Co 11:25)

2:16 *In one body.* The *one body* of Christ which hung on the cross under the judgment of God for the sins of all (Gl 3:13; 2 Co 5:21) is the atoning basis for the *one body* which is His church (4:4). Because the love of God comprehended all men in that suffering and dying body, there can now be a church composed of Jew and Gentile, a body of the risen Christ, sharing His exaltation and glory. (2:6)

2:17 *He came and preached*, through His apostles, in whose Word His atoning work lives on effectually.

2:18 *Access in one Spirit to the Father.* Cf. Ro 5:1-2; 8:15-16.

2:20 *Prophets.* The word order and 3:5 ("NOW . . . revealed to his . . . prophets") indicate that New Testament prophets are meant. (Cf. 4:11; Ro 12:6; 1 Co 12:28; 14:1-33)

Cornerstone, which determines the form and function of the various parts and of the whole.

3:1-21 As in 1:15 ff., Paul moves from the recital of the blessings bestowed on the Gentiles to a prayer for his Gentile readers (1). He prays that they may comprehend the full measure of the blessings bestowed on them, that they may know

written briefly. 4 When you read this you can perceive my insight into the mystery of Christ, 5 which was not made known to the sons of men in other generations as it has now been revealed to his holy apostles and prophets by the Spirit; 6 that is, how the Gentiles are fellow heirs, members of the same body, and partakers of the promise in Christ Jesus through the gospel.

7 Of this gospel I was made a minister according to the gift of God's grace which was given me by the working of his power. 8 To me, though I am the very least of all the saints, this grace was given, to preach to the Gentiles the unsearchable riches of Christ, 9 and to make all men see what is the plan of the mystery hidden for ages in*d* God who created all things; 10 that through the church the manifold wisdom of God might now be made known to the principalities and powers in the heavenly places. 11 This was according to the eternal purpose which he has realized in Christ Jesus our Lord, 12 in whom we have boldness and confidence of access through our faith in him. 13 So I ask you not to*e* lose heart over what I am suffering for you, which is your glory.

14 For this reason I bow my knees before the Father, 15 from whom every family in heaven and on earth is named, 16 that according to the riches of his glory he may grant you to be strengthened with might through his Spirit in the inner man, 17 and that Christ may dwell in your hearts through faith; that you, being rooted and grounded in love, 18 may have power to comprehend with all the saints what is the breadth and length and height and depth, 19 and to know the love of Christ which surpasses knowledge, that you may be filled with all the fulness of God.

20 Now to him who by the power at work within us is able to do far more abundantly than all that we ask or think, 21 to him be glory in the church and in Christ Jesus to all generations, for ever and ever. Amen.

d Or *by*   *e* Or *I ask that I may not*

fully the incomprehensible love of the Christ who has redeemed them and may thus be filled with all the fullness of the God who has blessed them (14-19). In a long parenthesis (2-13) he dwells on the grace bestowed on him as apostle to the Gentiles, the high privilege of proclaiming to them their inclusion in the new people of God according to the eternal purpose of God now realized in Christ Jesus. This grace gloriously transfigures the suffering which his apostolic task entails. The prayer concludes with a doxology to the God who is greater than our thoughts of Him and our prayers to Him: *To him be glory in the church and in Christ Jesus.* (20-21)

3:1 *A prisoner for Christ Jesus.* Cf. 4:1. The man who is an apostle "by the will of God" (1:1) is captured by that gracious will; he serves as the accredited messenger of Christ, not in spite of his sufferings but in and through them; the *prisoner* Paul is "an ambassador in chains." (6:20, cf. 2 Co 4:7-12; 12:9; Cl 1:24-25; 2 Ti 2:9-10)

3:3, 4, 9 *Mystery.* See 1:9 note.

3:5 *Holy apostles.* The apostles are holy because God has "set them apart" for the Gospel. (Ro 1:1)

3:6 *Partakers of the promise.* Cf. 2:12.

3:7 *Minister,* a servant who provides for the needs of others, such as those who wait on tables.

3:9 *God who created.* For the unity of God the Creator and Redeemer see 2 Co 4:6 and Paul's use of "new creation," 2:10, 15; 4:24; Cl 3:10; 2 Co 5:17; Gl 6:15; cf. Ja 1:18.

3:10 *Principalities and powers.* Cf. 1:21 note.

3:13 *Which is your glory.* Through the apostle's suffering Christ is glorified (cf. Ph 1:20; 2 Co 12:9),

and therein His body, the church, is glorified.

3:14 *Bow my knees.* The usual posture of prayer was standing (Mt 6:5; Lk 18:11, 13); kneeling indicates unusual fervency and urgency of prayer. (Lk 22:41; Acts 21:5)

Every family . . . is named. The word for *family* denotes both "family" and also larger communal groupings derived from a common ancestor, such as a clan or tribe. Every communal grouping in which concord and peace prevail is in some way a witness to Him who is in the truest sense Father, the God of peace and not of disorder (1 Co 14:33), the God whose plan and purpose it is to unite all things in heaven and on earth into one "family" again. (1:10)

3:18 *With all the saints.* Being "rooted and grounded in love" (17), they are united with the whole company of saints, fellow Christians (cf. 1:1), whose varied gifts and graces work together to give all a full comprehension (*breadth and length,* etc.) of the wondrous workings of the love of Christ. (19)

3:20 "Thou art coming to a King,
    Large petitions with thee bring."

3:21 *In the church.* It is an indication of the churchliness of this letter that this is the only doxology in the NT which contains this phrase.

4:1-16 God's call (1) is a call to unity, to the denial of self (2) in the zealous pursuit of unity (3), to the utilization of the varied gifts bestowed by the exalted Christ for the full realization of this unity, that the church may be the mature and perfectly functioning body of Christ, who is its Head. (4-16)

The Church Is Created for Good Works

4:1 — 6:24

DIVERSITY OF GIFTS IN THE SERVICE OF UNITY (4:1-16)

4 I therefore, a prisoner for the Lord, beg you to lead a life worthy of the calling to which you have been called, 2 with all lowliness and meekness, with patience, forbearing one another in love, 3 eager to maintain the unity of the Spirit in the bond of peace. 4 There is one body and one Spirit, just as you were called to the one hope that belongs to your call, 5 one Lord, one faith, one baptism, 6 one God and Father of us all, who is above all and through all and in all. 7 But grace was given to each of us according to the measure of Christ's gift. 8 Therefore it is said,

"When he ascended on high he led a host of captives,
    and he gave gifts to men."

9 (In saying, "He ascended," what does it mean but that he had also descended into the lower parts of the earth? 10 He who descended is he who also ascended far above all the heavens, that he might fill all things.) 11 And his gifts were that some should be apostles, some prophets, some evangelists, some pastors and teachers, 12 to equip the saints for the work of ministry, for building up the body of Christ, 13 until we all attain to the unity of the faith and of the knowledge of the Son of God, to mature manhood, to the measure of the stature of the fulness of Christ; 14 so that we may no longer be children, tossed to and fro and carried about with every wind of doctrine, by the cunning of men, by their craftiness in deceitful wiles. 15 Rather, speaking the truth in love, we are to grow up in every way into him who is the head, into Christ, 16 from whom the whole body, joined and knit together by every joint with which it is supplied, when each part is working properly, makes bodily growth and upbuilds itself in love.

4:3 *Unity of the Spirit.* The unity created and fostered by the Spirit (cf. 4 and 2:18). Vv. 4-6 describe this given unity.

4:4-6 There are seven ones in this description of the unity of the church, seven being the number of completeness and perfection. The first three look to the present: the church is *one body,* alive with the creative vitality of the *one Spirit,* animated by the *one hope* which the Spirit inspires and guarantees (cf. 1:13-14). The next three look to the historical origin of the church; Jew and Gentile came to be united in one church, when they came to *one faith* in *one Lord* (cf. Ro 10:12-13) and were baptized in His name. The last one looks to the ultimate origin of the church, the *one God and Father* who has from everlasting blessed us in Christ (1:3). He is *above all* in "the immeasurable greatness of his power" (1:19), works *through all* for the attainment of His gracious purposes (cf. 1:1, "apostle . . . by the will of God"; 3:2, 7), and dwells *in all* whom the Spirit has made a "dwelling place of God." (2:22)

4:8 Cf. Ps 68:18. Paul makes three interpretive changes as he quotes. First, he transfers the Old Testament utterance concerning God to Christ, as is often done in the New Testament in witness to the faith in His deity. Second, he changes from a second-person address to a third-person statement ("Thou didst ascend"; *he ascended*). Third, and this is most striking, he changes the "receiving gifts among men" of the psalm to *he gave gifts to men.* So bold a recasting of the psalm verse is intended to recall (rather than merely quote) the psalm, which does in fact celebrate God the Victor as the Giver of gifts to His people. (Ps 68:5, 6, 9, 10, 20, 35)

4:9-10 There is no domain or power in all the universe which the suffering and exalted Christ has not subdued. When He gives gifts, He gives out of "unsearchable riches" (3:8) and with absolute authority. For the sense of *fill* cf. 1:23.

4:11 *Apostles . . . prophets . . . evangelists . . . pastors and teachers.* A comparison with 1 Co 12: 27-28 shows that the list is not intended to be exhaustive. The *apostles,* eye- and ear-witnesses and authorized messengers of Christ, are essential to the establishment of church (cf. 2:20, "foundation of the apostles"); through them Christ speaks and gathers His own (Ro 15:18-19; 2 Co 13:3). *Evangelists* spread the apostolic Word abroad (Acts 8:5-40; cf. 21:8); *prophets* guide and enlighten the church in such matters as missions (Acts 13:1-3) and charity (Acts 11:27-30). *Pastors and teachers* attend to the day-by-day nurture and edification of the churches established by the labors of apostle and evangelist.

4:12 *Saints,* all members of the church. "There is on earth a little holy flock or community of pure saints under one head, Christ. . . . I was brought to it by the Holy Spirit and incorporated into it through the fact that I have heard and still hear God's Word." (Luther)

4:15 *Speaking the truth,* or "living of the truth (or the true faith) in love."

4:15-16 *Grow up . . . into . . . the head . . . Christ, from whom.* The reality (what Christ signifies for the church) breaks the limit of the image (*head, body*).

THE RADICAL BREAK WITH THE PAGAN PAST (4:17-24)

17 Now this I affirm and testify in the Lord, that you must no longer live as the Gentiles do, in the futility of their minds; [18] they are darkened in their understanding, alienated from the life of God because of the ignorance that is in them, due to their hardness of heart; [19] they have become callous and have given themselves up to licentiousness, greedy to practice every kind of uncleanness. [20] You did not so learn Christ!—[21] assuming that you have heard about him and were taught in him, as the truth is in Jesus. [22] Put off your old nature which belongs to your former manner of life and is corrupt through deceitful lusts, [23] and be renewed in the spirit of your minds, [24] and put on the new nature, created after the likeness of God in true righteousness and holiness.

WALK IN LOVE, IN THE LIGHT, IN WISDOM (4:25 – 5:20)

25 Therefore, putting away falsehood, let every one speak the truth with his neighbor, for we are members one of another. [26] Be angry but do not sin; do not let the sun go down on your anger, [27] and give no opportunity to the devil. [28] Let the thief no longer steal, but rather let him labor, doing honest work with his hands, so that he may be able to give to those in need. [29] Let no evil talk come out of your mouths, but only such as is good for edifying, as fits the occasion, that it may impart grace to those who hear. [30] And do not grieve the Holy Spirit of God, in whom you were sealed for the day of redemption. [31] Let all bitterness and wrath and anger and clamor and slander be put away from you, with all malice, [32] and be kind to one another, tenderhearted, forgiving one another, as God in Christ forgave you.

5 Therefore be imitators of God, as beloved children. [2] And walk in love, as Christ loved us and gave himself up for us, a fragrant offering and sacrifice to God.

4:17-24 The new life of truth in love (18) calls for a radical break with the Gentiles' pagan past and their pagan surroundings. It means putting on the *new nature, created after the likeness of God in true righteousness and holiness* and putting off the *old nature which . . . is corrupt through deceitful lusts.*

4:17 *Futility of their minds.* Cf. Ro 1:21; 1 Ptr 1:18. *Mind* is here used in the broad sense of "attitude, way of thinking." The *futility* of the mind, its frustrate purposelessness, is defined in v. 18 in terms of a lack of clear judgment ("darkened in . . . understanding"), a distorted vitality exercised in "ignorance," and moral obtuseness or insensibility ("hardness of heart").

4:21-22 *Taught in him.* This unusual phrase probably refers to the instruction which the readers had received after their baptism, when they had "put on Christ" (Gl 3:27) and were *in him* but had yet to learn what their baptismal confession to Jesus as Lord (Ro 10:9) meant, concretely and in detail, for the conduct of their lives. *The truth* which could displace the futile lies that had filled their former life they found in the words and works of *Jesus,* the historical Man who had lived a life not "alienated from the life of God" (18), a truly human life in communion with the life of God.

4:22 *Deceitful lusts.* They promise man heaven and give him hell.

4:24 *Created.* Cf. 2:9-10. *After the likeness of God.* Cf. Gn 1:26-27.

4:25 – 5:20 Christians are "created in Christ Jesus for good works, which God prepared before-hand, that we should *walk* in them" (2:10). This "walking" is here considered from three points of view, as a walking *in love* (4:25 – 5:2); a walking as *children of light* (5:3-14); and a walking *not as unwise men but as wise.* (5:15-20)

1) 4:25 – 5:2 WALK IN LOVE

4:25 – 5:2 Men whose lives are bounded by the Holy Trinity live and move in the domain of love. As men *sealed in the Holy Spirit* (4:30), *as beloved children of God* who imitate their Father (5:1), as men brought near to God by the atoning sacrifice of the *Christ* who *gave Himself up* for them (5:2), they must *walk in love* (5:2). The *neighbor* can no longer be the victim of their self-assertion, to be exploited by their *falsehood* (4:25), assaulted by their *anger* (4:26), diminished by their thieving (4:28), degraded by their *evil talk* (4:29; cf. 31). The neighbor has become precious in their eyes, as the human life in which their love has scope to *give* (4:28), to *impart grace* (4:29), to be *kind* and *tenderhearted,* to *forgive* (4:32).

4:26 *Be angry but do not sin.* There is such a thing as righteous anger, but there is the ever-present danger that it may turn into all-too-human spite.

4:27 *Opportunity to the devil,* for whom the wrath of man affords welcome scope.

5:1-2 For a similar combination of ideas (God's love manifested in Christ's self-giving into death) cf. Ro 5:5-10.

5:2 *Fragrant offering and sacrifice.* For the language of sacrifice in a literal sense cf. Ex 29:18; in a figurative sense, Eze 20:41.

3 But fornication and all impurity or covetousness must not even be named among you, as is fitting among saints. 4 Let there be no filthiness, nor silly talk, nor levity, which are not fitting; but instead let there be thanksgiving. 5 Be sure of this, that no fornicator or impure man, or one who is covetous (that is, an idolater), has any inheritance in the kingdom of Christ and of God. 6 Let no one deceive you with empty words, for it is because of these things that the wrath of God comes upon the sons of disobedience. 7 Therefore do not associate with them, 8 for once you were darkness, but now you are light in the Lord; walk as children of light 9 (for the fruit of light is found in all that is good and right and true), 10 and try to learn what is pleasing to the Lord. 11 Take no part in the unfruitful works of darkness, but instead expose them. 12 For it is a shame even to speak of the things that they do in secret; 13 but when anything is exposed by the light it becomes visible, for anything that becomes visible is light. 14 Therefore it is said,

"Awake, O sleeper, and arise from the dead,
and Christ shall give you light."

15 Look carefully then how you walk, not as unwise men but as wise, 16 making the most of the time, because the days are evil. 17 Therefore do not be foolish, but understand what the will of the Lord is. 18 And do not get drunk with wine, for that is debauchery; but be filled with the Spirit, 19 addressing one another in psalms and hymns and spiritual songs, singing and making melody to the Lord with all your heart, 20 always and for everything giving thanks in the name of our Lord Jesus Christ to God the Father.

BE SUBJECT TO ONE ANOTHER (5:21 — 6:9)

21 Be subject to one another out of reverence for Christ. 22 Wives, be subject to your husbands, as to the Lord. 23 For the husband is the head of the wife as Christ is

2) 5:3-14 WALK AS CHILDREN OF LIGHT

5:3-14 *Children of light,* who have become *light in the Lord* (8), are no longer at home in the murky world of dark, unbridled desire, whether it be sexual desire or the desire for things (3); knowing the love of God (cf. 1-2), they no longer wage the undeclared war against God which is the heart of our evil desires. Neither are they at home in the world of moral *filthiness* (4); they have a clear vision of what is *fitting* in the light and know that God has given them tongues for *thanksgiving* (4). They have a clear vision of God's judgment too; no sophistry can hide the Judge from their eyes (5-6). They can no longer participate in *works of darkness;* they cannot even find a comfortable compromise with them. They must *expose them* (7-11), and so bring men out of the sleep of sin and death into the wakeful day, where *Christ shall give* them *light.* (12-14)

5:5 *Covetous . . . idolater.* Cf. Mt 6:24.

Kingdom of Christ and of God. One kingdom, one royal reign, is meant; *of Christ* probably accents the present manifestations of the reign, *of God* the future kingdom when Christ "delivers the kingdom to God the Father." (1 Co 15:24)

5:10 *Try to learn.* This describes the intelligent operation of the enlightened Christian conscience which determines what is *pleasing to the Lord* in any given situation.

5:11 The word here translated *expose* is regularly used in the New Testament of confronting a man with his sin in order to lead him to repentance. Cf. Mt 18:15 ("tell him his fault"); Jn 3:20 ("exposed"); 8:46 ("convicts"); 16:8 ("convince"); 1 Co 14:24 ("convicted"); 1 Ti 5:20 ("rebuke").

5:12 The shamefulness of the deeds of darkness becomes apparent when they are called by their proper name, not kept secret and not concealed by silly talk and levity. (Cf. 4)

5:13 Light not only exposes; it also overcomes darkness. The words of the children of light proclaim not only judgment but also repentance, faith, and forgiveness, and so what is *exposed by the light* becomes *light.*

5:14 These words are probably quoted from a baptismal hymn.

3) 5:15-20 WALK AS WISE MEN

5:15-20 Christians walk wisely in this evil world; their wisdom is to *understand what the will of the Lord is* (15, 17). And the will of the Lord is that the body of Christ do His work while there is still time (16). The only intoxication in their lives is the intoxication of the *Spirit* manifested in the exuberance of song and thanksgiving. (18-20)

5:18 *Do not get drunk.* The common meal, symbol and expression of Christian fellowship, would naturally include *wine.* 1 Co 11:20-22 shows that this admonition was a needed one.

5:19 *Psalms and hymns and spiritual songs.* It is hardly possible to make clear distinctions between the three types of sacred song here enumerated. The adjective *spiritual* probably applies to all and means "inspired by the Holy Spirit."

5:21 — 6:9 The Christians' reverence for Christ will mold their conduct in the relationship of

the head of the church, his body, and is himself its Savior. ²⁴As the church is subject to Christ, so let wives also be subject in everything to their husbands. ²⁵ Husbands, love your wives, as Christ loved the church and gave himself up for her, ²⁶ that he might sanctify her, having cleansed her by the washing of water with the word, ²⁷ that he might present the church to himself in splendor, without spot or wrinkle or any such thing, that she might be holy and without blemish. ²⁸ Even so husbands should love their wives as their own bodies. He who loves his wife loves himself. ²⁹ For no man ever hates his own flesh, but nourishes and cherishes it, as Christ does the church, ³⁰ because we are members of his body. ³¹ "For this reason a man shall leave his father and mother and be joined to his wife, and the two shall become one flesh." ³²This mystery is a profound one, and I am saying that it refers to Christ and the church; ³³ however, let each one of you love his wife as himself, and let the wife see that she respects her husband.

6 Children, obey your parents in the Lord, for this is right. ² "Honor your father and mother" (this is the first commandment with a promise), ³ "that it may be well with you and that you may live long on the earth." ⁴ Fathers, do not provoke your children to anger, but bring them up in the discipline and instruction of the Lord.

5 Slaves, be obedient to those who are your earthly masters, with fear and trembling, in singleness of heart, as to Christ; ⁶ not in the way of eyeservice, as menpleasers, but as servants*f* of Christ, doing the will of God from the heart, ⁷ rendering service with a good will as to the Lord and not to men, ⁸ knowing that whatever good any one does, he will receive the same again from the Lord, whether he is a slave or free. ⁹ Masters, do the same to them, and forbear threatening, knowing that he who is both their Master and yours is in heaven, and that there is no partiality with him.

THE ARMOR OF GOD AND THE POWER OF PRAYER (6:10-24)

10 Finally, be strong in the Lord and in the strength of his might. ¹¹ Put on the whole armor of God, that you may be able to stand against the wiles of the devil. ¹² For we are not contending against flesh and blood, but against the principalities, against the powers, against the world rulers of this present darkness, against the

f Or *slaves*

this age and will make all these relationships channels for the love of Christ. The family and household relationship of spouses, of children and parents, and of slaves and masters will all have on them the mark of the Christ who is Lord of all. In all three cases Paul first addresses the party of whom subjection and self-abnegation is most obviously required (*wife, children, slaves*) and then proceeds to lay the equally demanding yoke of considerate love on the shoulders of the other party to the relationship.

5:26 *Washing of water with the word,* that is, Baptism, which derives its force and significance from the Word of Christ, who commands it and assigns to it its efficacy and significance. (Mt 28:19)

5:31 Cf. Gn 2:24.

5:32 *This mystery . . . a profound one,* known only by God's revelation, appears to be this: Only the man to whom "the mystery of the gospel" (6:19) has been revealed, only he who has come to know the love of Christ for His church, can know and understand how total a communion of love between man and woman the Creator established in marriage. Some translations render *profound mystery* with "great truth."

6:2 Cf. Ex 20:12.

6:5 *Slaves* were considered a part of the family, or household, and so would naturally be included in a table of duties such as this.

6:6 *Eyeservice.* Service rendered only because and so long as the master's eye is on them.

6:10-24 The church is God's outpost and bridgehead in an alien and still hostile world. The Christians' life is therefore of necessity a life of battle with the powers of Satan. For this battle God prepares them; He gives them knowledge of the unseen and ever-present enemy, gives them strength, and equips them with divine defensive and offensive weapons—His *truth* their cincture, His *righteousness* for their *breastplate,* His *gospel of peace* for their sandals of agility, *faith* for their shield, the hope of *salvation* for their *helmet,* His *word* for their spiritual *sword* (10-17). These weapons they employ with *prayer,* strengthening their ranks by *supplication* for one another (*all the saints,* 18), extending God's conquest by supplication for their apostle that he may proclaim the Word boldly. (19-20)

6:12 *In the heavenly places.* This phrase is used elsewhere of God (1:3), of Christ (1:20), of Christians exalted with Christ (2:6), of angelic principalities and powers (3:10). Its use here of satanic powers indicates that they are transcendent powers (the extreme opposite of localized and recognizable powers of *flesh and blood*) pressing in on man, terrifyingly omnipresent and conquerable only by divine power and weaponry. Cf. "prince of the power of the air, the spirit." (2:2)

spiritual hosts of wickedness in the heavenly places. [13] Therefore take the whole armor of God, that you may be able to withstand in the evil day, and having done all, to stand. [14] Stand therefore, having girded your loins with truth, and having put on the breastplate of righteousness, [15] and having shod your feet with the equipment of the gospel of peace; [16] besides all these, taking the shield of faith, with which you can quench all the flaming darts of the evil one. [17] And take the helmet of salvation, and the sword of the Spirit, which is the word of God. [18] Pray at all times in the Spirit, with all prayer and supplication. To that end keep alert with all perseverance, making supplication for all the saints, [19] and also for me, that utterance may be given me in opening my mouth boldly to proclaim the mystery of the gospel, [20] for which I am an ambassador in chains; that I may declare it boldly, as I ought to speak.

[21] Now that you also may know how I am and what I am doing, Tych′i·cus the beloved brother and faithful minister in the Lord will tell you everything. [22] I have sent him to you for this very purpose, that you may know how we are, and that he may encourage your hearts.

[23] Peace be to the brethren, and love with faith, from God the Father and the Lord Jesus Christ. [24] Grace be with all who love our Lord Jesus Christ with love undying.

6:13-17 The description of the Christian's weapons is strongly colored by phrases from the Old Testament, which recall the weaponry of the Lord (Is 59:17), the Messiah (Is 11:4-5), and the great Servant of the Lord (Is 49:2). Thus the divine character of the Christian's equipment is stressed.

6:19 *Also for me.* Paul constantly sought the intercessions of the churches, one of the ways by which he made it clear that the apostle does not lord it over the church's faith (2 Co 1:24). Cf. Ro 15: 30; 2 Co 1:11; Cl 4:3-4; 2 Th 3:1-2.

6:21-22 See the Introduction.

THE LETTER OF PAUL TO THE
PHILIPPIANS

INTRODUCTION

The Captivity Letters tell of visitors who came from Paul's churches in the East to see Paul in Rome (cf. Colossians and Philemon). One of these was Epaphroditus, and he came from Philippi in Macedonia, the first church founded by Paul in Europe (Acts 16:11-40). Paul, Silas, Timothy, and Luke had arrived in Philippi early in the second missionary journey (A. D. 49—51). Philippi was a Roman "colony," that is, a settlement of Roman soldiers enjoying Roman citizenship, settled at a strategic point in the system of Roman roads for the security of the empire. Apparently not many Jews were there; neither a regular synagog, only a "place of prayer" (Acts 16:13), probably in the open air, at a riverside. It was there that Paul had begun his work. The Lord opened the ear of a proselyte named Lydia to his words, and we may suppose that the house of this wealthy and generous woman became the meeting place of the church (Acts 16:14 - 15). Paul knew "conflict" (Ph 1:30) and suffering in Philippi; he had been beaten and imprisoned without the due process of law to which his Roman citizenship entitled him. He had known not only conflict but also that joy in the midst of conflict and suffering which is the characteristic token of the apostolic and Christian existence (Acts 16:25). And he had experienced triumph in conflict and suffering, the triumph of the Lord whose strength is made perfect in weakness and defeat; he was released from prison and vindicated, and he gained the jailer and his household for the Lord. (Acts 16:25-40)

The church which grew, as the Word of the Lord grew, in Philippi was predominantly Gentile. And it was a church which remained especially near and dear to Paul. It was Paul's firstborn in Europe; the faithful and consecrated Luke remained there when Paul continued on his journey and provided spiritual leadership of a high order; the impetuous generosity of Lydia in the first days evidently set the tone of the church's life for the years that followed.

We recall how she viewed her baptism as an initiation into a life of giving; she told Paul and his companions, "If you have judged me to be faithful . . . come to my house and stay," and "prevailed" on them to comply with her wish (Acts 16:15). The generosity of the Philippians was so genuinely rooted in Christ and His Gospel that Paul felt free to accept gifts from them; he can call them his "partners" in the proclamation of the Gospel (Ph 1:5; 4:15). They supplied his wants in Thessalonica (Ph 4:16) and again in Corinth (2 Co 11:9), and that too at some sacrifice to themselves; Paul told the Corinthians, "I robbed other churches by accepting support from them in order to serve you" (2 Co 11:8). This same actively generous partnership in the Gospel had moved the Philippians (and the other churches of Macedonia) to contribute to the collection for the Jerusalem saints "beyond their means," even in the midst of a "severe test of affliction" and in the depths of poverty. (2 Co 8:1-5)

The coming of Epaphroditus was another link in the golden chain of Philippi's gracious generosity. Still suffering persecution (Ph 1:29), still poor (Ph 4:19), the men and women of Philippi had nevertheless gathered a gift for Paul, probably under the direction of their "bishops and deacons," whom Paul singles out in the salutation of his letter (and only in this letter, Ph 1:1). They had sent the gift to Paul by the hand of one of their number, Epaphroditus, and had instructed him to remain in Rome with Paul as a minister to his need (Ph 2:25). Epaphroditus had delivered the gift and had performed his task of ministry with such self-forgetting devotion that "he nearly died for the work of Christ, risking his life" to complete the service of the Philippian Christians to their apostle. (Ph 2:30)

Date of Writing

These events help fix the date of Paul's Letter to the Philippians more exactly within the limits of his 2-year imprisonment

at Rome (A. D. 59 – 61). There has been time for a series of communications between Rome and Philippi; news of Paul's imprisonment has reached distant Philippi; the Philippians' gift has been gathered, sent, and received; news of Epaphroditus' illness has reached Philippi and has caused great concern there; and news of this concern has again come to Paul and Epaphroditus at Rome. It has been calculated that this series of communications would require a total of at least five or six months; they probably took considerably longer. Moreover, the letter itself indicates that Paul's long-deferred trial is at last in progress (Ph 1:7), that it has proceeded so far that Paul can with some confidence hope for an early release from imprisonment (Ph 1:25; 2:24), though there is still real danger of an adverse verdict and death. All this points to a date toward the close of the 2-year imprisonment, probably to the early months of A. D. 61.

Paul is about to return Epaphroditus to Philippi (Ph 2:25-30); he sends with him a letter in which he gives his partners in the Gospel news of himself, his trial, and his prospects of release; thanks them for their gift; and excuses and commends their messenger Epaphroditus, who through no fault of his own has been unable to carry out fully the ministry entrusted to him. He notices too with pastoral concern and with kindly evangelical tact their internal troubles, a tendency to self-assertion on the part of some, with its consequent tendency to disunity. He encourages them in the persecution which pressed on them from without; and he warns them with passionate sternness of the dangers which threaten them, alerting them to the threat posed by Judaistic and libertine perverters of the Gospel.

Value of the Letter

Among the Captivity Letters, Colossians and Ephesians show us Paul the fighter for the truth, the thinker and theologian, the great strategist of church unity; the Letter to Philemon shows us Paul the man whose whole life is irradiated by the grace and glory of the Gospel. The Letter to the Philippians with its many and various facets is harder to classify; one modern scholar has brilliantly used this letter as an introduction to the whole thought-world of Paul; he sees in it the characteristic union of Paul the believer, Paul the missionary, and Paul the theologian. Perhaps one might best use the bold joy of faith as the common denominator of its multiplicity, faith as Luther once described it: "Faith is a living, resolute, total confidence in God's grace, a trust so certain that it is willing to die a thousand deaths for its belief. And such a trust in God's grace and such knowledge of God's grace make a man joyous, resolute, and robustly cheerful over against God and all God's creatures." An imprisoned apostle writes to a persecuted church, and the keynote of his letter is: "I rejoice. Do you rejoice?" Where under the sun is anything like this possible except where faith is, where the Holy Spirit breathes His wholesome and creative breath? The whole letter is a good illustration of a word Paul used in Ph 4:5, a word which we are obliged to translate with some such term as "forbearance." But "forbearance" expresses only a part of Paul's meaning; the Greek word which he uses points to a princely quality in man, to that largeness of heart, that spacious generosity, that freedom from the cruelly competitive scrabble of this world which only he possesses whose "commonwealth is in heaven," who is heir to all that is Christ's.

THE LETTER OF PAUL TO THE
PHILIPPIANS

1 Paul and Timothy, servants[a] of Christ Jesus,
To all the saints in Christ Jesus who are at Phi·lip′pi, with the bishops[b] and deacons:
2 Grace to you and peace from God our Father and the Lord Jesus Christ.

Thanksgiving and Prayer
1:3-11

3 I thank my God in all my remembrance of you, 4 always in every prayer of mine for you all making my prayer with joy, 5 thankful for your partnership in the gospel from the first day until now. 6And I am sure that he who began a good work in you will bring it to completion at the day of Jesus Christ. 7 It is right for me to feel thus about you all, because I hold you in my heart, for you are all partakers with me of grace, both in my imprisonment and in the defense and confirmation of the gospel. 8 For God is my witness, how I yearn for you all with the affection of Christ Jesus. 9And it is my prayer that your love may abound more and more, with knowledge and all discernment, 10 so that you may approve what is excellent, and may be pure and blameless for the day of Christ, 11 filled with the fruits of righteousness which come through Jesus Christ, to the glory and praise of God.

a Or *slaves*   *b* Or *overseers*

1:1 *Saints* is one of Paul's regular terms for Christians; it marks them as called and claimed by God, to be instruments of His purpose.

For the special mention of *bishops* (overseers) and *deacons* (their assistants, especially in charitable work) see the Introduction.

1:3-11 Paul gives thanks for the Philippians' *partnership in the gospel from the first day until now* and emphasizes the personal character of the bond which this partnership has established between himself and them (3-8). He prays that their *love* may grow and increase and that their *knowledge* and *discernment* may keep pace with their love. (9-11)

1:4 *Joy.* The dominant note of the letter. (Cf. 1:18-19, 25; 2:2, 17-18, 28, 29; 3:1; 4:1, 4, 10)

1:5 *Your partnership in the gospel.* They heard and believed it (1:29); suffered for it (1:28-30); lived and witnessed it (2:15; 4:3); and supported its proclamation (Acts 16:14-15; Ph 2:25, 30; 4:10 ff.; 4:15-16). The Gospel entered their life and controlled it.

1:7 *Partakers with me of grace.* Paul always speaks of his apostolate as grace (Ro 1:5; 1 Co 15:9-10; Eph 3:7-8; 1 Ti 1:14). The apostolic church, which is caught up into his apostolic mission and impetus, shares in that grace.

Imprisonment . . . defense and confirmation of the gospel. Apparently Paul's trial is in progress and has afforded him a welcome opportunity to proclaim the Gospel, clear it of misunderstandings and misinterpretations, and thus plant it firmly on Roman soil. (Cf. 1:12, 16)

1:9-11 Paul implores for his partners in the Gospel the kind of life in Christ which he describes in 3:12-16 as his own: a life of continual forward tension, of ever-deepening apprehension of the Christ who made him His own. Such a life will be one of increasing love and growing knowledge and discernment, a life in which "mind and heart according well . . . make one music," in which love, being motivated by knowledge of Jesus Christ, works intelligently toward clearly conceived goals, capable of distinguishing not only between good and bad but also between better and best. Paul's Letter to the Philippians is the classic expression of such an informed and intelligent love.

1:11 *Fruits of righteousness.* Righteousness is "through faith in Christ, the righteousness from God that depends on faith" (3:9; cf. Ro 1:17; 3:21-31; 2 Co 3:9; 5:21). *The fruits of righteousness . . . come through Jesus Christ* just as the righteousness itself does; the new life of the man declared righteous is His creation, the fruit borne by branches that receive their life from the vine. (Jn 15:5-8)

To the glory and praise of God. The life of all servants of God is, like the life of the Servant Christ, a living doxology. (Cf. 2:11; Jn 15:8)

News from Prison

1:12-26

12 I want you to know, brethren, that what has happened to me has really served to advance the gospel, 13 so that it has become known throughout the whole praetorian guard^c and to all the rest that my imprisonment is for Christ; 14 and most of the brethren have been made confident in the Lord because of my imprisonment, and are much more bold to speak the word of God without fear.

15 Some indeed preach Christ from envy and rivalry, but others from good will. 16 The latter do it out of love, knowing that I am put here for the defense of the gospel; 17 the former proclaim Christ out of partisanship, not sincerely but thinking to afflict me in my imprisonment. 18 What then? Only that in every way, whether in pretense or in truth, Christ is proclaimed; and in that I rejoice.

19 Yes, and I shall rejoice. For I know that through your prayers and the help of the Spirit of Jesus Christ this will turn out for my deliverance, 20 as it is my eager expectation and hope that I shall not be at all ashamed, but that with full courage now as always Christ will be honored in my body, whether by life or by death. 21 For to me to live is Christ, and to die is gain. 22 If it is to be life in the flesh, that means fruitful labor for me. Yet which I shall choose I cannot tell. 23 I am hard pressed between the two. My desire is to depart and be with Christ, for that is far better. 24 But to remain in the flesh is more necessary on your account. 25 Convinced of this, I know that I shall remain and continue with you all, for your progress and joy in the faith, 26 so that in me you may have ample cause to glory in Christ Jesus, because of my coming to you again.

Admonition: A Life Worthy of the Gospel

1:27 — 2:18

UNITY OF SPIRIT (1:27-30)

27 Only let your manner of life be worthy of the gospel of Christ, so that whether I come and see you or am absent, I may hear of you that you stand firm in one spirit,

^c Greek *in the whole praetorium*

1:12-26 The news is good. Paul's trial has made it clear that he is not what his accusers have charged, a seditious disturber of the Roman peace, but what he himself has always claimed, "a prisoner for Christ." Thus the cause of the Gospel has been advanced through his imprisonment and trial (12, 13). The turn which Paul's case has taken has emboldened his brethren to speak the Word of God without fear; and in this Paul rejoices, even though some of these preachers are motivated by selfish and partisan zeal in their preaching (14-18). Paul is convinced that whatever may befall him, life or death, Christ will be glorified through him. His heart's desire is to depart and be with Christ forever; but the duty which he gladly takes upon himself is that he remain in the service of his Lord on earth. And so he looks forward to being released and rejoining his church at Philippi.

1:13 *Praetorian guard,* the soldiery that guarded Paul. They would be struck by the contrast between the charges laid against their prisoner and his deportment and bearing, so completely gracious and noncriminal; and their curiosity would give Paul an opportunity to testify to his cause both before them and, directly or indirectly, also to *all the rest* who might hear of him. The

reading of RSV note c (*in the whole praetorium*) would refer to the residence of the Roman governor in a province; a goodly number of scholars are inclined to think that all or some of the Captivity Letters were written by Paul from Ephesus during an otherwise unknown imprisonment there. In that case the reading of the note would be the more likely, since the word is used in this sense in the NT. (Mk 15:16; Jn 18:28, 33; 19:9; etc.)

1:26 *Glory in Christ Jesus, because of my coming.* Paul's coming to the Philippians will further their faith (cf. 25), and it is of the essence of faith to "pour contempt" on all human pride and to glory and boast in Christ alone. (Cf. 1 Co 1:26-31 and 4:7; Gl 6:14)

1:27 — 2:18 If they are partners in the Gospel, their life must correspond to the Gospel; this will show itself in their unity of spirit (1:27 — 2:2), in humility and self-effacement (2:3-11), and in their attitude as obedient servants of God. (2:12-18)

1:27-30 Unity of spirit is especially important in the face of the persecution which it is their privilege to endure for Christ. No enemy from without can destroy them; God will destroy their enemies. But they can destroy themselves by disunity.

with one mind striving side by side for the faith of the gospel, [28] and not frightened in anything by your opponents. This is a clear omen to them of their destruction, but of your salvation, and that from God. [29] For it has been granted to you that for the sake of Christ you should not only believe in him but also suffer for his sake, [30] engaged in the same conflict which you saw and now hear to be mine.

HUMILITY AND SELF-EFFACEMENT (2:1-11)

2 So if there is any encouragement in Christ, any incentive of love, any participation in the Spirit, any affection and sympathy, [2] complete my joy by being of the same mind, having the same love, being in full accord and of one mind. [3] Do nothing from selfishness or conceit, but in humility count others better than yourselves. [4] Let each of you look not only to his own interests, but also to the interests of others. [5] Have this mind among yourselves, which is yours in Christ Jesus, [6] who, though he was in the form of God, did not count equality with God a thing to be grasped, [7] but emptied himself, taking the form of a servant,[d] being born in the likeness of men. [8]And being found in human form he humbled himself and became obedient unto death, even death on a cross. [9] Therefore God has highly exalted him and bestowed on him the name which is above every name, [10] that at the name of Jesus every knee should bow, in heaven and on earth and under the earth, [11] and every tongue confess that Jesus Christ is Lord, to the glory of God the Father.

[d] Or *slave*

1:27 *Worthy of*, corresponding to; the kind of life the Gospel of Christ calls for and makes possible. Cf. Eph 4:1; Cl 1:10; 1 Th 2:12; 2 Th 1:5, where the standard and dynamic of the new life is expressed in various terms, all of them in the last analysis corresponding to the *gospel* in the present passage: "calling" (Eph), "the Lord" (Cl), "God, who calls you" (1 Th), "the kingdom of God." (2 Th)

For the faith of the gospel. In their firm and unanimous endurance of opposition their own faith is being tested and purified (cf. 1 Ptr 1:6-7); they are mutually strengthening one another in the faith; and the witness of their suffering for Christ's sake (cf. 29) will propagate the faith in others, as Paul's own suffering has done (30) and continues to do. (1:7, 12, 18)

1:28 *A clear omen.* Cf. 2 Th 1:5-10.

1:29 *Granted to you.* For suffering as grace and privilege cf. Mt 5:10-12; Acts 5:41; 1 Ptr 2:20; 4:12-14.

1:30 *The same conflict*, suffering and imprisonment (cf. Acts 16:19-40; 21:27 – 28:31). Paul can speak credibly on suffering, for he speaks from experience.

2:1-11 The admonition to humility is closely related to the preceding. The strong and ancient enemies of unity and pride *(conceit)* and *selfishness*; only where they are displaced by *humility* and self-sacrifice is true unity possible. This self-effacing and self-giving humility is theirs in Christ Jesus, who went a way that was the divine way, the very opposite of the way willed by Satan (to be "like God," Gn 3:5), the Servant-Messiah's way of self-giving (Is 52:13 – 53:12) that took Him to the cross and thus to universal Lordship to the glory of God the Father.

2:1 In the light of 2 Co 13:14, which this verse so strongly resembles, one could paraphrase as follows: "As surely as Christ encourages you in your suffering for His sake, as surely as the love of God impels you, as surely as you participate in the creative and life-giving power of the Spirit – in short, as surely as God's love and compassion are a reality in your lives . . . . " Cf. Ro 12:1, where Paul bases his appeal on "the mercies of God."

2:2 *Complete my joy.* Paul's joy is his confident and resolute yea to the Gospel which proclaims his Lord and extends His Lordship over men; it is his glad amen to the Gospel in its effectual working (1:18-19; 2:17-18) and its effects (1:3; 2:2; 4:1, 10, and here). He rejoices, as he bids the Philippians rejoice, "in the Lord." (3:1; 4:4)

2:2, 5 *Mind* here denotes the whole set and bent of man's will. Cf. Cl 3:1-2, where "seek" and "set your minds" are used as synonyms.

2:5 *Which is yours in Christ Jesus,* that is, by virtue of the fact that Christ Jesus has made you His own (3:12), the fact that you have been incorporated in Him by Baptism and He lives in you; the will of Him who loved you and gave Himself for you has laid claim to your will. (Gl 2:20)

2:5-11 These words are poetry, both in form and content. This and the fact that a number of the expressions used do not occur elsewhere in Paul make it likely that he is quoting an early Christian hymn which both the Philippians and he knew and sang at worship. The successive stanzas adore Christ in His preexistence with God and as God (6), in His humiliation unto death (7-8), in His exaltation and final glory when at His coming the whole universe shall do obeisance before Him. (9-11)

2:6 *In the form of God.* Whatever the precise meaning of these much-discussed words, the general sense is clear from the phrase in which the thought is picked up once more, *equality with God.*

A thing to be grasped, to be used to the full, exploited for His own advantage.

2:7 *Emptied himself.* The phrase probably echoes

OBEDIENT SERVANTS (2:12-18)

12 Therefore, my beloved, as you have always obeyed, so now, not only as in my presence but much more in my absence, work out your own salvation with fear and trembling; [13] for God is at work in you, both to will and to work for his good pleasure.

14 Do all things without grumbling or questioning, [15] that you may be blameless and innocent, children of God without blemish in the midst of a crooked and perverse generation, among whom you shine as lights in the world, [16] holding fast the word of life, so that in the day of Christ I may be proud that I did not run in vain or labor in vain. [17] Even if I am to be poured as a libation upon the sacrificial offering of your faith, I am glad and rejoice with you all. [18] Likewise you also should be glad and rejoice with me.

Paul's Actions on the Philippians' Behalf

2:19—3:1

19 I hope in the Lord Jesus to send Timothy to you soon, so that I may be cheered by news of you. [20] I have no one like him, who will be genuinely anxious for your welfare. [21] They all look after their own interests, not those of Jesus Christ. [22] But Timothy's worth you know, how as a son with a father he has served with me in the gospel. [23] I hope therefore to send him just as soon as I see how it will go with me; [24] and I trust in the Lord that shortly I myself shall come also.

Is 53:12, "He poured out his soul to death," and describes the Servant's complete self-giving; it is a sort of heading over the whole of 7-8.

2:8 *Death on a cross,* the criminal's death in the sinners' stead.

2:9 *Name* tells not only who He is, to distinguish Him from others, but what He is, His significance for others. The name is Lord (11) in the fullest and completest sense of that word. For the New Testament, no other title so sums up the significance of Jesus as Lord. (Cf. Ro 10:9)

2:12-18 The admonitions to unity (1:27-30) and to humility and self-effacement (2:1-11) lead up to and prepare for (*therefore*, 2:12) the admonition to obedient service. As the culminating statement concerning the Servant Jesus Christ in His humiliation was a statement concerning His utter obedience (2:8), so the crowning admonition calls for obedience. First, Paul stresses the quality of that obedience: the *fear* and *trembling* (12) of the servant totally devoted to his Lord and apprehensive of betraying the trust reposed in him and of frustrating the purpose of the God who works in him (13); the complete and unquestioning submission of the servant who is, like Jesus, minded to live by every word that proceeds from the mouth of God (*without grumbling or questioning,* 14; *holding fast the word of life,* 16; cf. Mt 4:4); the servant's active and energetic working in dependence on God (*work . . . for God is at work,* 12-13; *Do . . . that you may be . . . children of God,* 14-15). Second, Paul gives an inspiring picture of the effects of obedient ministry: the obedient, active servants become an extension of the Servant who is the Light of the world (15; cf. Mt 5:14; Lk 2:32; Jn 8:12; 12:35, 46; Is 42:4; 49:4), a light which the opposition and persecution of *a crooked and perverse generation* (15) cannot quench; they shall appear *in the day of Christ* as the crowning glory

of the apostle through whom Christ speaks and works (16); the life of the obedient servants, their working faith, becomes a living sacrifice, a spiritual worship offered to God (17; cf. Ro 12:1); and so they come to know the whole joy of faith (cf. 1:20), Jesus' own joy in ministry fulfilled. (Jn 15:11)

2:12-13 *Work out your own salvation . . . for God is at work.* This is the classic expression of the logic of faith and grace; faith is "faith which works through love" (Gl 5:6), not in order to win the favor of God but because it is rich in the possession of His favor and strong by virtue of His grace continually bestowed. (Cf. 3:12; Mt 4:17; 1 Co 15:10; 1 Th 4:7; Cl 1:29; Heb 13:20-21)

2:17 *Libation upon the sacrificial offering.* For the *libation* of wine which accompanied the daily burnt offering cf. Ex 29:38-46; Nm 28:1-10; Jl 1:9. For the imagery of sacrifice applied to the apostolic ministry cf. Ro 15:16.

2:19—3:1 Paul is sending Timothy, the most selfless and dependable of his co-workers, to the Philippians. He will cheer Paul by a fresh and firsthand report of them and will be genuinely concerned for their welfare. And Paul himself hopes to come to them shortly (2:19-24). He is sending the Philippians' emissary, Epaphroditus, back to Philippi, with thanks to God for sparing his life (which he has risked in serving Paul), with warm commendation of the work which he has done, and with the request that his church receive him and honor him in the Lord (2:25-30). Paul concludes his admonitions with a final call to joy in the Lord. (3:1)

2:19 *In the Lord Jesus.* Paul's will and work are wholly dominated by the Lord whom he serves; he can therefore hope and plan only in communion with Him. (Cf. 24; 1 Co 16:7)

Timothy. See the Introduction to First Timothy,

25 I have thought it necessary to send to you E·paph′ro·di·tus my brother and fellow worker and fellow soldier, and your messenger and minister to my need, 26 for he has been longing for you all, and has been distressed because you heard that he was ill. 27 Indeed he was ill, near to death. But God had mercy on him, and not only on him but on me also, lest I should have sorrow upon sorrow. 28 I am the more eager to send him, therefore, that you may rejoice at seeing him again, and that I may be less anxious. 29 So receive him in the Lord with all joy; and honor such men, 30 for he nearly died for the work of Christ, risking his life to complete your service to me.

3 Finally, my brethren, rejoice in the Lord. To write the same things to you is not irksome to me, and is safe for you.

Christian "Perfection": Warning and Instruction

3:2—4:1

WARNING AGAINST JUDAIZERS (3:2-11)

2 Look out for the dogs, look out for the evil-workers, look out for those who mutilate the flesh. 3 For we are the true circumcision, who worship God in spirit,ᵉ and glory in Christ Jesus, and put no confidence in the flesh. 4 Though I myself have reason for confidence in the flesh also. If any other man thinks he has reason for confidence in the flesh, I have more: 5 circumcised on the eighth day, of the people of Israel, of the tribe of Benjamin, a Hebrew born of Hebrews; as to the law a Pharisee,

ᵉ Other ancient authorities read *worship by the Spirit of God*

and for Timothy's mission cf. 1 Co 4:17; 1 Th 3:1-2.

2:23 *How it will go with me,* that is, in the trial. (Cf. 1:19-26)

2:25 *Epaphroditus.* Otherwise unknown. Paul calls him *fellow soldier* because he has shared hardship and danger with him.

3:1 *To write the same thing,* etc. It is difficult to determine whether these words refer to the repeated command to rejoice which precedes them or to the warning which follows. The words *is safe for you* seem to go more naturally with the warning.

3:2—4:1 Paul warns against two perversions of the Gospel, two false ideas of Christian "perfection" (3:12), that of legalistic Judaizers (3:2-11) and that of libertine *enemies of the cross of Christ* (3:17-21), who "pervert the grace of our God into licentiousness" (Jude 4). Between the two warnings he portrays himself, the man in Christ, as the true example of Christian perfection or maturity. (3:15)

3:2-11 With a vehemence which is in startling contrast to the cheerful serenity of the rest of the letter, Paul warns against his old and persistent enemies, the Judaizers, who had once created such havoc in the churches of Galatia (see the Introduction to Galatians) and elsewhere and were, apparently, still at work. He turns against them every boast and every claim with which they bolstered their position. They who called the uncircumcised Gentiles unclean *dogs* are themselves unclean scavenger "dogs"; they who insist on works as the way to salvation are themselves *evil-workers,* disturbing the faith and peace of the church. The circumcision of which they boast as the token of the covenant Paul bitterly terms a meaningless mutilation of the flesh;

what circumcision once signified, namely, membership in the people of God, is no longer to be found in circumcision but in Christ (3:3). Paul uses himself, the Israelite and former Pharisee, as an example of how all the old Israelite prerogatives and privileges have become meaningless in the presence of Christ and the righteousness which man can find only in Him. Paul here (3:9) gives his sharpest and most eloquent definition of the *righteousness from God,* a dominant motif in his Letter to the Romans.

3:2 *Mutilate the flesh.* This gains added point if it is remembered that such mutilation actually excluded a man from "the assembly of the Lord." (Dt 23:1)

3:3, 4 *Flesh* here signifies what a man "naturally" is by virtue of his descent, birth, and upbringing—as opposed to what God's mighty grace makes possible, gaining and knowing Christ, being found in Christ, having righteousness through Him, sharing His resurrection life (8-11). If Paul were to boast of being a descendant of Benjamin, he would be boasting in the flesh; but he glories in Christ.

3:3 *The true circumcision.* For the church as the true covenant people of God cf. Ro 2:29; 4:16, 23; Gl 3:7; 4:28; 6:16.

Worship God in spirit. Perhaps better with RSV note *e, worship by the Spirit of God.* (Cf. Jn 4:24)

3:5 *A Hebrew born of Hebrews.* Paul's family, though resident in the Greek city Tarsus (Acts 21:39) and distinguished by Roman citizenship (Acts 22:28), remained strictly faithful to the ancient ways of their ancestral religion and retained the Hebrew (Aramaic) language which many Jews living in the Dispersion soon forgot.

6 as to zeal a persecutor of the church, as to righteousness under the law blameless. 7 But whatever gain I had, I counted as loss for the sake of Christ. 8 Indeed I count everything as loss because of the surpassing worth of knowing Christ Jesus my Lord. For his sake I have suffered the loss of all things, and count them as refuse, in order that I may gain Christ 9 and be found in him, not having a righteousness of my own, based on law, but that which is through faith in Christ, the righteousness from God that depends on faith; 10 that I may know him and the power of his resurrection, and may share his sufferings, becoming like him in his death, 11 that if possible I may attain the resurrection from the dead.

TRUE CHRISTIAN PERFECTION (3:12-16)

12 Not that I have already obtained this or am already perfect; but I press on to make it my own, because Christ Jesus has made me his own. 13 Brethren, I do not consider that I have made it my own; but one thing I do, forgetting what lies behind and straining forward to what lies ahead, 14 I press on toward the goal for the prize of the upward call of God in Christ Jesus. 15 Let those of us who are mature be thus minded; and if in anything you are otherwise minded, God will reveal that also to you. 16 Only let us hold true to what we have attained.

WARNING AGAINST THE ENEMIES OF THE CROSS (3:17 — 4:1)

17 Brethren, join in imitating me, and mark those who so live as you have an example in us. 18 For many, of whom I have often told you and now tell you even with

3:6 *Blameless.* By the standards that he then applied, which were those of his fellow Jews (cf. Gl 1:14). For Paul's integrity as Jew and Pharisee cf. 2 Ti 1:3.

3:7 *Counted as loss,* because they had led him to oppose Christ in His body, the church.

3:8 *Knowing Christ.* As the sequel shows, this knowing is personal encounter and fellowship with Christ, having Him as Lord of one's life, gaining Him, being found in Him (9), believing in Him, etc. Knowing Christ, or God, and being known by Him come to the same thing. (Cf. 1 Co 8:2-3; 13:12; Gl 4:9)

3:9 *Righteousness of my own . . . righteousness from God.* For the contrast cf. Ro 10:3. For righteousness as God's gift, the whole of the salvation bestowed by Him, cf. Mt 5:6; 6:33; Ro 1:17; 3:21-31; 1 Co 1:30; 2 Co 3:9; 5:21.

3:10-11 For suffering and dying with Christ as the way and transition to life with Him cf. Ro 8:17; 2 Co 4:10-17; 2 Co 13:4; 2 Ti 2:11-12; and Jesus' word to His disciples, Mt 16:25.

3:12-16 In a passage which provides the link between his warning against the Judaizers and his warning against the "enemies of the cross of Christ" (3:17-21), both of them people who had arrived and talked of their "perfection," Paul gives a remarkable description of the Christian life as a constant and never-finished straining forward toward that which God's grace holds out to the believer in Christ: *I press on to make it my own, because Christ Jesus has made me his own* (3:12). Paul sees Christian perfection and Christian maturity in just this ever imperfect and ever renewed appropriation of the gift of God in Christ.

3:14 The picture is that of a runner competing for a prize, all tensed and concentrated energy.

God's call ushers man "into the fellowship of His Son, Jesus Christ" (1 Co 1:9), a fellowship which grows deeper as it is appropriated and lived and is perfected in the glory of the world to come (cf. 3:21); toward this the whole Christian life moves, toward the full realization of the "hope that belongs to your call." (Eph 4:4)

3:15-16 Revelation is given in increasing measure as it is gratefully received and used, according to Jesus' word, "To him who has will more be given, and he will have abundance." (Mt 13:12)

3:17 — 4:1 Since Paul describes this group only enough to condemn them, we cannot be absolutely sure of their identity. He had spoken of them to the Philippians often (3:18), and they could readily identify them. Paul is probably pointing to men of the kind whom he had had to deal with at Corinth (see Introduction to Letters to the Corinthians) — the proud, secular, superspiritual men of knowledge who said, "We belong to Christ," and yet emptied the cross of its content, who on the basis of their higher "knowledge" came to terms with sin and made the church at home in the world by conforming it to the world. Paul had put an end to their influence at Corinth, but they apparently continued their activities elsewhere, and not without success. Paul reminds the Philippians (who as Roman "colonists" had their citizenship in the distant and splendid city of Rome) where their true home lies and where their heart should be: *Our commonwealth is in heaven, and from it we await a Savior, the Lord Jesus Christ* (3:20). They cannot boast in the flesh, the things of this world, like the Judaizers, or make this world their real home, like the enemies of the cross. In the pure hope of the Gospel they *stand firm . . . in the Lord* (4:1), who is Lord of the future and better world.

tears, live as enemies of the cross of Christ. [19] Their end is destruction, their god is the belly, and they glory in their shame, with minds set on earthly things. [20] But our commonwealth is in heaven, and from it we await a Savior, the Lord Jesus Christ, [21] who will change our lowly body to be like his glorious body, by the power which enables him even to subject all things to himself.

4 Therefore, my brethren, whom I love and long for, my joy and crown, stand firm thus in the Lord, my beloved.

The Whole and Healthy Life of Peace

4:2-9

2 I entreat Eu·o'di·a and I entreat Syn'ty·che to agree in the Lord. [3]And I ask you also, true yokefellow, help these women, for they have labored side by side with me in the gospel together with Clement and the rest of my fellow workers, whose names are in the book of life.

4 Rejoice in the Lord always; again I will say, Rejoice. [5] Let all men know your

3:17 *Imitating me.* For the apostle as object of imitation (which involves a recognition of his authority as emissary and spokesman of Christ) cf. 1 Co 4:16; 11:1; Gl 4:12; 1 Th 1:6; 2 Th 3:7, 9. In Eph 5:1 God Himself is the object of imitation.

3:18 *Enemies of the cross.* A man becomes an enemy of the cross when he ignores God's fearful and costly judgment on human sin in the death of His Son. The cross makes impossible any compromise with sin.

3:19 *Their god is the belly.* They live for the satisfaction of their physical appetites and passions. (Cf. Ro 16:18)

They glory in their shame. They glory in their "freedom," which is actual degrading licentiousness, as in the mark of their superior spirituality. (Cf. 1 Co 6:12-13; 1 Co 5:2, 6 and Jude 4, 8, 10, 13 16, 18, 19)

3:21 *Change our lowly body.* Cf. Ro 8:23; 1 Co 15:43, 49, 53. Man is redeemed, all of him as he came from the Creator's hand.

4:1 *My . . . crown.* When they appear "pure and blameless" before Christ at His coming (1:10), that will be the apostle's crowning glory. (2:16; cf. 1 Th 2:19)

4:2-9 The hope for the return of the Lord and the glory of the world to come (3:20-21) does not make the Christian indifferent toward this life and its problems and duties. Rather, the return of the Lord gives life now, with its problems and decisions, its full significance; the light of His coming falls upon the present and fills it, for all its dangers and difficulties, with joy and peace. *Euodia* and *Syntyche,* who have fallen out, are to settle their differences *in the Lord,* whom they have proclaimed together, whose coming will judge all violators of His peace; one whom Paul addresses as *yokefellow* is to help them find their way back to one another—their quarrel is not their individual concern only but concerns the whole church, all *whose names are* inscribed in God's *book of life* (2-3). The whole and undivided

church is to *rejoice in the Lord,* whose coming is *at hand;* their high hope is to give them a blithe and princely generosity (*forbearance,* 5) toward all men. Their grateful prayer to God is to be the cure for all anxiety and care. Thus the *peace of God* will guard (*keep,* 7) their *hearts* and *minds* more surely and securely than the Roman garrisons keep the Roman peace at Philippi (4-7). They cannot treat this poor present world with indifference or contempt; whatever in it is *just, pure, lovely, gracious,* etc., is deserving of their sympathetic thought. These things cannot be their ultimate norm and standard; they cannot set their minds on earthly things (3:19) in this sense. But the apostolic Gospel which Paul has proclaimed and lived among them, their true and only norm for action (*do,* 9), will equip them for a positive and discerning appreciation of these things, e. g., the Roman sense for the beneficence of law and the veteran's loyalty to his state. And God who is God of peace and not of confusion (1 Co 14:33) will *be with* them as they pursue this course. (8-9)

4:2, 3 *Euodia, Syntyche,* and *Clement* are otherwise unknown. The *true yokefellow* is evidently an especially trusted co-worker of Paul's at Philippi.

4:3 *The book of life* as a symbol of God's elective love (those who names are in it are His elect, objects of His love, enrolled among the citizens of the city of God) is found frequently in both Testaments. (Cf. Ex 32:32-33; Ps 69:28; 138:16; Is 4:3; Dn 12:1; Ml 3:16; Lk 10:20; Heb 12:23; Rv 3:5; 13:8; 17:8; 20:12, 15)

4:5 *Forbearance.* The Greek work is difficult to reproduce in English; it signifies the gracious condescension of a superior, one so sure of his strength and greatness that he is above the competitive scramble that makes men selfish and cruel; such the Christians are as heirs of the world to come, and as such they are to act to all sorts and conditions of men.

forbearance. The Lord is at hand. 6 Have no anxiety about anything, but in everything by prayer and supplication with thanksgiving let your requests be made known to God. 7And the peace of God, which passes all understanding, will keep your hearts and your minds in Christ Jesus.

8 Finally, brethren, whatever is true, whatever is honorable, whatever is just, whatever is pure, whatever is lovely, whatever is gracious, if there is any excellence, if there is anything worthy of praise, think about these things. 9 What you have learned and received and heard and seen in me, do; and the God of peace will be with you.

Thanks for the Philippians' Gift
4:10-20

10 I rejoice in the Lord greatly that now at length you have revived your concern for me; you were indeed concerned for me, but you had no opportunity. 11 Not that I complain of want; for I have learned, in whatever state I am, to be content. 12 I know how to be abased, and I know how to abound; in any and all circumstances I have learned the secret of facing plenty and hunger, abundance and want. 13 I can do all things in him who strengthens me.

14 Yet it was kind of you to share my trouble. 15And you Phi·lip′pi·ans yourselves know that in the beginning of the gospel, when I left Macedonia, no church entered into partnership with me in giving and receiving except you only; 16 for even in Thes·sa·lon′i·ca you sent me help*f* once and again. 17 Not that I seek the gift; but I seek the fruit which increases to your credit. 18 I have received full payment, and more; I am filled, having received from E·paph′ro·di·tus the gifts you sent, a fragrant offering, a sacrifice acceptable and pleasing to God. 19And my God will supply every need of yours according to his riches in glory in Christ Jesus. 20 To our God and Father be glory for ever and ever. Amen.

f Other ancient authorities read *money for my needs*

4:7 *Passes all understanding.* Surpasses all attempts of human thought and devising to obtain security. *Peace* in Biblical language is often more than cessation of hostilities; it expresses that wholeness which the grace of God creates when it sets all right, the divinely normal order of things. Cf. Paul's usual greeting of "grace and peace" and especially Ro 5:1 ff. in which Paul expands on the idea of "peace with God." *Peace* is seen as similarly active and powerful in Cl 3:15.

4:10-20 Paul expresses his joy at this fresh token of their concern for him; it has supplied, not so much his physical need (Christ has given him strength to rise above that) as his need of their love—they have *shared* his *trouble* (10-14). He appreciates their gift as one more example of their partnership in the Gospel (cf. 1:5, 7) and as a *fragrant offering, a sacrifice acceptable and pleasing to God*, whom they serve in serving him who is apostle by the will of God (cf. Cl 1:1) and servant of His Son (Ph 1:1). He promises them that His God, the rich and generous Rewarder of all who seek Him with no thought of reward, will *supply* their *every need*; their giving will not make them poor but rich. To Him belongs all glory. (15-20)

4:11 *Content,* that is, self-sufficient; only, Paul's sufficiency is from his Lord (13), not from himself.

4:15 *The beginning of the gospel,* when it was first preached among you and proceeded southward from your home, *Macedonia.* (Cf. Acts 16:11 – 17:15)

Partnership with me in giving and receiving. Paul contributed the Word; they contributed to his support. Paul usually refused to take support from churches which he founded (2 Co 11:7; 12:13; 1 Th 2:5-9), although he knew himself to be entitled to it (1 Co 9:7). His motive was the desire to avoid all appearance of self-seeking (1 Th 2:5; 2 Co 12:17-18), to put no "obstacle in the way of the gospel of Christ" (1 Co 9:12). In the case of the Philippians he made an exception, and they supported Paul so regularly (cf. v. 16; 2 Co 11:8-9) that Paul can call their relationship a business partnership, using the language of commerce to describe it. The phrase cited above was technical for "in settlement of a mutual account"; in v. 17 *to your credit* could be rendered "credited to your account," and in v. 18 *I have received full payment* is the ancient formula for having "received in full."

4:18 *A fragrant offering.* Cf. Ex 29:18; Lv 1:9; 2:2; 3:5, etc.

CONCLUSION (4:21-23)

21 Greet every saint in Christ Jesus. The brethren who are with me greet you. ²²All the saints greet you, especially those of Caesar's household.

23 The grace of the Lord Jesus Christ be with your spirit.

4:21-23 Paul sends greetings, as at the beginning (1:1), to *every saint*, all members of the church at Philippi, from *the brethren who are with him* (probably his own associates), and from *all the saints* (probably members of the church at Rome) and concludes with the benediction or *grace*.

4:22 *Those of Caesar's household*, slaves or freedmen of the imperial house, servants at the emperor's court rather than members of his family. Many of them occupied positions of some importance both in Rome and in the provinces of the empire.

COLOSSIANS

INTRODUCTION

Among those who came to Paul and were welcomed by him during his Roman imprisonment was Epaphras. He came from Colossae, a city in Asia Minor some 125 miles east of Ephesus. He brought Paul news of the Gentile church that had been founded there, probably by Epaphras himself (Cl 1:5-8), working under the direction of Paul or at least with Paul's full approval (Cl 1:7). He had good news to bring. He could speak warmly of the Colossians' faith and of their love; the Gospel had grown and borne fruit in Colossae as everywhere (Cl 1:6). But what had brought Epaphras to Rome was his anxiety for the church at Colossae, not his pride in it. The Christians of Colossae and of neighboring Laodicea were still holding to the Gospel which they had received; but that pure loyalty was being threatened and undermined. The church was threatened by a new teaching that was in many ways strikingly similar to the Gospel Epaphras had preached there. Both the new teaching and the Gospel originally preached in Colossae proclaimed a non-national universal religion. Both recognized the great gulf that exists between God and natural man. And both proffered a redemption which would bridge that gulf. But the new teaching was in the last analysis an utter distortion of the Gospel Epaphras had proclaimed. He sensed the difference but could not, perhaps, analyze and define it well enough to be able to oppose it effectively. He therefore appealed to Paul, wise in the ways of Greek and Jew alike, keen in insight, and ready to do battle for the truth. Would Paul help him?

It is difficult to get a clear and consistent picture of the heresy which threatened Colossae, for Paul in his Letter to the Colossians does not so much oppose it argumentatively as overwhelm it by confronting it with the whole riches of the true Gospel of Christ. It seems to have been a religion of self-redemption of the "gnostic" type. Built on a Jewish or Jewish-Christian basis, it was a fusion of Greek and Oriental ideas and combined at least three elements. One of these elements was theosophic, that is, the new teaching claimed to have and to impart an occult, profound knowledge derived from God; Paul speaks contemptuously of a "tradition" and a "philosophy" (Cl 2:8). Another element was ritualistic; stress was laid on circumcision (Cl 2:11); questions of food and drink, festivals, new moons, and sabbaths were deemed important (Cl 2:16). A third element was ascetic; Paul speaks of prescriptions of abstinence ("Do not handle, Do not taste, Do not touch," Cl 2:21) and of a "rigor of devotion," of "self-abasement," and of "severity to the body" (Cl 2:23). We are left to conjecture how these elements were combined into a system.

Paul's references to the "worship of angels" (Cl 2:18) and to "elemental spirits of the universe" (2:8, 20) indicate what was the heart of the danger in this teaching. Other powers besides the Christ were being proclaimed and invoked as mediators between God and man; the ritual and ascetic aspects of this religion probably represent means of placating or of obtaining contact and communion with these powers. What Epaphras, with a sound Christian instinct, surely sensed and what Paul clearly saw was this: *the new teaching called into question and obscured the unique greatness of the Christ and the complete sufficiency of His atonement.* What made this heresy all the more dangerous was the fact that it claimed not to supplant but to supplement the Gospel which the Colossians had received. The new teaching would, so the new teachers claimed, carry the Colossian Christians beyond their rudimentary Christianity to fullness and perfection; hence Paul's repeated emphasis on the fact that the Colossians are complete and full in the Gospel which they have received, that in the Christ whom they know they can find all the treasures of divine wisdom. (2:2, 3, 9, 10; cf. 1:28)

Value of the Letter

"As for you," Joseph told his brothers, "you meant evil against me; but God meant

it for good" (Gn 50:20). The new movement at Colossae meant evil, for it was an attack, all the more vicious because it was not a frontal attack, on the fact that dominates the whole New Testament, the sole Lordship of the Lord Jesus Christ. But God meant it for good; He gave us in Paul's Letter to the Colossians a proclamation of the Lord Jesus Christ in unparalleled fullness and depth. The church that in its creed intones, "God of God, Light of Light, very God of very God, begotten not made, being of one substance with the Father," is indebted not least to this letter.

The Letter to the Colossians is also a striking fulfillment of the promise of Jesus to His disciples, "Every scribe who has been trained for the kingdom of heaven is like a householder who brings out of his treasure what is new and what is old" (Mt 13:52). The apostles of Jesus are not merely disciples of a rabbi, whose sacred duty it is to pass on their master's words unchanged. They are witnesses to Him who has all authority in heaven and on earth, and they have the Spirit as His gift, the Spirit who leads them into all truth and thus glorifies the Christ. At the time of the church's need the Spirit opened up to Paul dimensions of the glory of the Christ which the new people of God had not apprehended so fully before; this strengthened their loyalty to the Gospel.

THE LETTER OF PAUL TO THE

COLOSSIANS

INTRODUCTION: SALUTATION, THANKSGIVING, AND PRAYER (1:1-14)

1 Paul, an apostle of Christ Jesus by the will of God, and Timothy our brother, 2 To the saints and faithful brethren in Christ at Co·los'sae:
Grace to you and peace from God our Father.

3 We always thank God, the Father of our Lord Jesus Christ, when we pray for you, 4 because we have heard of your faith in Christ Jesus and of the love which you have for all the saints, 5 because of the hope laid up for you in heaven. Of this you have heard before in the word of the truth, the gospel 6 which has come to you, as indeed in the whole world it is bearing fruit and growing—so among yourselves, from the day you heard and understood the grace of God in truth, 7 as you learned it from Ep'a·phras our beloved fellow servant. He is a faithful minister of Christ on our[a] behalf 8 and has made known to us your love in the Spirit.

9 And so, from the day we heard of it, we have not ceased to pray for you, asking that you may be filled with the knowledge of his will in all spiritual wisdom and understanding, 10 to lead a life worthy of the Lord, fully pleasing to him, bearing fruit in every good work and increasing in the knowledge of God. 11 May you be strengthened with all power, according to his glorious might, for all endurance and patience with joy, 12 giving thanks to the Father, who has qualified us[b] to share in the inheritance of the saints in light. 13 He has delivered us from the dominion of darkness and transferred us to the kingdom of his beloved Son, 14 in whom we have redemption, the forgiveness of sins.

The Sufficiency of Christ and the Gospel

1:15 — 2:23

THE FULL GLORY OF CHRIST, THE SON OF GOD (1:15-23)

15 He is the image of the invisible God, the first-born of all creation; 16 for in him all things were created, in heaven and on earth, visible and invisible, whether thrones

[a] Other ancient authorities read *your* [b] Other ancient authorities read *you*

1:1-14 Paul gives *thanks* for the Colossians' *faith* and *love,* a love inspired and sustained by the *hope laid up for you in heaven.* He assures them that the *gospel* which has produced this in them, which they have heard from *Epaphras,* is the true, universal, powerful, and productive Gospel preached *in the whole world,* proclaiming and conveying the *grace of God in truth* (the Gospel which needs no supplementation by "philosophy" and "human tradition," cf. 2:6-8).

Paul *prays* that they may grow in the *knowledge* of this Gospel, a knowledge of God's gracious *will* (not of empty speculations) which produces a life rich *in every good work, increasing* as it is employed in the service of the *Lord,* the *beloved Son* of God, King of a *kingdom* whose subjects *have redemption, the forgiveness of sins,* now and the hope of an *inheritance* in the bright future world of God (*in light,* 12). Paul prays that God the Father, who has given them their present blessing and their glorious future, may strengthen them to endure with *patience* the pressure of the present

and that the lives of the Colossians, lived in the *power* bestowed by Him, may be an unbroken song of thanksgiving to Him.

1:1 For *Timothy* as cosender (hardly coauthor) of letters to churches cf. the salutations of 2 Co, Ph, 1 and 2 Th, Phmn.

1:2 *Saints,* Christians, those whom God has by His call (cf. Ro 1:7; 1 Co 1:2) consecrated for Himself and His purposes.

1:7 *Epaphras.* See the Introduction.

1:9 *Spiritual,* produced by the Holy Spirit.

1:13 Cf. Paul's words to King Agrippa, Acts 26:18.

1:15-23 The mention of God's beloved Son, who is God's redemption and forgiveness in person (1:13-14), leads over to a mighty hymn in praise of Christ in His full glory as Creator and Redeemer. Paul holds before the eyes of the church all that they have in Him whom Epaphras (1:7) proclaimed to them: He is God's *image,* the perfect manifestation of the *invisible God; the first-born of all creation,* the Mediator of creation, antecedent to and

or dominions or principalities or authorities—all things were created through him and for him. [17] He is before all things, and in him all things hold together. [18] He is the head of the body, the church; he is the beginning, the first-born from the dead, that in everything he might be pre-eminent. [19] For in him all the fulness of God was pleased to dwell, [20] and through him to reconcile to himself all things, whether on earth or in heaven, making peace by the blood of his cross.

21 And you, who once were estranged and hostile in mind, doing evil deeds, [22] he has now reconciled in his body of flesh by his death, in order to present you holy and blameless and irreproachable before him, [23] provided that you continue in the faith, stable and steadfast, not shifting from the hope of the gospel which you heard, which has been preached to every creature under heaven, and of which I, Paul, became a minister.

THE FULL GLORY OF THE GOSPEL (1:24 — 2:5)

24 Now I rejoice in my sufferings for your sake, and in my flesh I complete what is lacking in Christ's afflictions for the sake of his body, that is, the church, [25] of which

Lord over all created beings, including all angelic powers *(thrones, dominions, principalities, authorities)*. As He is Lord of creation, He is also *head* of *the church;* as He is *the first-born of all creation,* He is also *the first-born from the dead,* the Lord in whom all mankind may find life everlasting. *In him all the fulness* of the God who willed man's redemption graciously dwelt; in obedience to that will He went into the depths of a criminal's violent death *(blood of his cross)* to restore man and all man's fallen world to God. He is *in everything . . . pre-eminent;* in His kingdom (1:13) they are secure—no powers of darkness have power to harm them there.

1:15 *Image of the invisible God.* Cf. 2 Co 4:4; Heb 1:3. In Him the invisible God has made Himself known, not only in the Word but in a Person (cf. Heb 1:1-2); He has condescended to men in audible, visible, palpable form (1 Jn 1:1), in the flesh common to all men (Jn 1:14). In the Son men may behold Him who sent Him, the Father. (Jn 12:45; 14:9)

Firstborn of all creation. As v. 16 indicates, this does not put Christ among God's creatures, but asserts His superiority and primacy over them.

1:16 *Created.* For Jesus Christ as Mediator of creation cf. 1 Co 8:6; Jn 1:3; Heb 1:2; Rv 3:14.

Thrones, dominions, etc. Names common to Judaism and the New Testament of angelic or demonic powers that are thought of as in some sense controlling the universe. The false teachers apparently assigned to them power independent of Christ (2:8) and held them to be objects of worship (2:18). Paul, in proclaiming Christ as their Creator, roundly asserts His Lordship over them and so already indicates the irrelevance and wrongness of any angel worship. For the names cf. Ro 8:38; 1 Co 15:24; Eph 1:21; 3:10; Cl 2:10, 15.

Created . . . for him, to serve His gracious purpose of establishing God's reign, challenged by man's sin. Our Lord's miracles document His sovereign control over all creation during His sojourn on earth. As exalted Lord He reigns over all creation (Mt 28:18; Ro 8:39; Rv 5:13), will bring all creation home to God (Ro 8:19-22), and shall receive the homage of universal creation. (Ph 2:10-11)

1:17 *All things hold together.* Cf. Eph 1:22; Heb 1:3.

1:18 *Head of the body, the church.* Cf. Eph 1: 22-23 and Cl 2:19. The idea of intimate and vital connection between Christ and His people, the church, is obvious; not so obvious perhaps is the thought that the head is not the seat of intelligence, as with us, but is a symbol of power and lordship (cf. 1 Co 11:3; Eph 5:23); the head is even thought of as the source of life and growth. (Eph 4:16; Cl 2:19)

First-born from the dead. Christ's resurrection is THE resurrection, the basis and the beginning of the resurrection of all who are His. Cf. especially 1 Co 15:20-23. Christians have a "living hope" of eternal life "through the resurrection of Jesus Christ from the dead." (1 Ptr 1:3; cf. 1 Co 6:14; 1 Th 4:14)

1:19 *The fulness of God.* The whole grace *(was pleased)* and power of God was at work in Him; the triumph over death (18) is total, the reconciliation (20) complete. There is no need to supplement it in any way: "In him the whole fulness of deity dwells bodily, and you have come to fulness of life in him." (2:9)

1:21-23 This Christ in all His glory is the Colossians' Christ; He is their Reconciler; He will *present* them *holy and blameless* in the judgment, justified. They need not seek Him in any new and mystical ways, for He has come into the *flesh* in real humanity and found them. They need only *continue in the faith* and remain steadfast in the *hope of the gospel,* the old known Gospel, the universal Gospel for all the world proclaimed by Paul who is "apostle of Jesus Christ by the will of God." (1:1)

1:21 *Estranged and hostile.* Cf. Eph 2:12; 4:18; Ro 5:6-10.

1:23 *Gospel . . . preached to every creature,* to the whole world. Cf. 1:6 and Mk 16:15. Paul probably uses *creature* here to indicate that the Gospel preached to man is good news both for man and for man's world. (Cf. v. 20; Ro 8:19-21)

1:24 — 2:5 The Colossians have this Christ as their Reconciler and Justifier in the Gospel and in it alone (cf. 1:23). The Gospel is therefore infinitely precious; Paul *rejoices* to *suffer* in its behalf as he

I became a minister according to the divine office which was given to me for you, to make the word of God fully known, 26 the mystery hidden for ages and generations *c* but now made manifest to his saints. 27 To them God chose to make known how great among the Gentiles are the riches of the glory of this mystery, which is Christ in you, the hope of glory. 28 Him we proclaim, warning every man and teaching every man in all wisdom, that we may present every man mature in Christ. 29 For this I toil, striving with all the energy which he mightily inspires within me.

2 For I want you to know how greatly I strive for you, and for those at La·od·i·ce'a, and for all who have not seen my face, 2 that their hearts may be encouraged as they are knit together in love, to have all the riches of assured understanding and the knowledge of God's mystery, of Christ, 3 in whom are hid all the treasures of wisdom and knowledge. 4 I say this in order that no one may delude you with beguiling speech. 5 For though I am absent in body, yet I am with you in spirit, rejoicing to see your good order and the firmness of your faith in Christ.

c Or *from angels and men*

toils with Christ-inspired *energy* to proclaim it. The Gospel is universal in its scope and power, proclaiming the revealed secret of God (*mystery,* 27) far beyond the limits of His ancient people, bestowing the riches of the glory of His grace on the *Gentiles;* it is present and powerful for *every man,* to make *every man mature in Christ.* God did not intend it for a coterie, and no coterie can claim it as its own. The Gospel is complete and sufficient, the sure ground of *hope* (1:27; cf. 1:23), *faith,* and *love* and the source of all *understanding* and *knowledge.* Any pretense of a higher knowledge, beyond the Christ proclaimed in the Gospel, is delusion and deceit, for in Christ *all the treasures of wisdom and knowledge* are to be found. In the power of this Gospel the church can be (what the Colossians now are) an ordered and disciplined army of God.

1:24 *I rejoice in my sufferings,* etc. The difficulty of this passage lies particularly in the phrase *complete what is lacking in Christ's afflictions.* That Christ's redemptive suffering and death need no supplementing is clear from 1:20-21 and 2:9-15 and the whole tenor of the letter, which opposes the idea that the work of Christ needs any supplementation by any human effort ("philosophy," ritual performance, or ascetic rigors). It is clear, moreover, that Paul looks upon his sufferings as suffering in union with Christ, as is all Christian suffering (Ro 8:17), a participation in the afflictions of Him who is persecuted when His church is persecuted (Acts 9:4), that this suffering of his is essential to his "divine office" as proclaimer of Christ (Acts 9:16), is gladly accepted as such (cf. Ph 2:17), and redounds to the benefit of the church (cf. 2 Co 1:5-7; 4:10-12; Eph 3:13). One had, perhaps, best leave open the question whether *what is lacking* refers to the destined afflictions of Christ in His church generally (Mt 24:6; Rv 6:11), a "quota" of suffering to be filled by those who "through many tribulations . . . must enter the kingdom of God" (Acts 14:22), or whether Paul rejoices, more specifically, in the thought that he by his suffering reduces the church's share in the destined tribulations. The essential thought, on either interpretation, remains that suffering for

the Gospel's sake is a positive, creative contribution to the life of the church.

1:25 *Divine office.* To speak the *word of God,* to reveal God's mystery—this is God's own work (Dn 2:27-28); man can do so only if God appoints and empowers him (1:1; 1:29). For the apostolic Word as Word of God or of Christ cf. 1 Th 2:13; Ro 15:18; 2 Co 13:3.

1:26-27 *The mystery.* Cf. 2:2; 4:3. From its first occurrence in the Bible onward (Dn 2:28), the word *mystery* has two connotations. First, the *mystery* is a mystery, or secret, because only God can reveal it; but He does reveal it—it is His "open secret" which He wills ultimately to share with all mankind. In the New Testament it is constantly associated, as here in Colossians (1:27; 4:3-4), with verbs like "make known" or "reveal" (cf., e. g., Mt 13:11; Mk 4:11; Ro 16:25-26; Eph 3:3-5). Second, the content of the *mystery* is God's hidden governing of all history toward the establishment of His reign (Dn 2:31-45). This culminates in the sending of His Son, the offense of His cross, and the triumph of His resurrection (Mt 13:11, 16-17; Ro 16:25-26; 1 Co 2:1-2 [RSV note *c*], 7; Eph 1: 7-9; 3:3-4, 9; 6:19; 1 Ti 3:16); it will be "fulfilled"; carried to its triumphant conclusion, when God's seventh and last trumpet sounds (Rv 10:7) and "the kingdom of the world has become the kingdom of our Lord and of his Christ." (Rv 11:15)

1:26 *Hidden from ages and generations,* in Israel, the nation entrusted with the oracles of God (Ro 3:2), into whose life, history, and worship the coming Christ cast shadows before Him to prefigure and announce His coming. (2:17)

1:28 *Every man . . . every man . . . every man.* The mystery, the Gospel, the Christ are there for all men, Gentile or Jew. Perhaps Paul is also aiming at the tendency of the errorists to create an exclusive clique within the church.

2:2 *Understanding . . . knowledge.* Cf. 1:9.

2:3 *Are hid.* The *treasures of wisdom* are hidden in the Crucified, overlaid by the offense and foolishness of the cross (1 Co 1:23), but revealed to faith by the Spirit. (1 Co 2:6-13)

2:5 *Good order . . . firmness.* The words have military associations.

THE REFUTATION OF THE COLOSSIAN HERESY (2:6-23)

6 As therefore you received Christ Jesus the Lord, so live in him, [7] rooted and built up in him and established in the faith, just as you were taught, abounding in thanksgiving.

8 See to it that no one makes a prey of you by philosophy and empty deceit, according to human tradition, according to the elemental spirits of the universe, and not according to Christ. [9] For in him the whole fulness of deity dwells bodily, [10] and you have come to fulness of life in him, who is the head of all rule and authority. [11] In him also you were circumcised with a circumcision made without hands, by putting off the body of flesh in the circumcision of Christ; [12] and you were buried with him in baptism, in which you were also raised with him through faith in the working of God, who raised him from the dead. [13]And you, who were dead in trespasses and the uncircumcision of your flesh, God made alive together with him, having forgiven us all our trespasses, [14] having canceled the bond which stood against us with its legal demands; this he set aside, nailing it to the cross. [15] He disarmed the principalities and powers and made a public example of them, triumphing over them in him.[d]

[d] Or *in it* (that is, the cross)

2:6-7 Paul has one weapon of offense: Christ. In the opening admonition (6-7) he bids the Colossians base their whole existence on Him. He is the soil in which they have struck root, from which they continue to draw nourishment and strength. He is the foundation on which the growing structure of their life rests and rises. In Him they have the firmness of faith which Paul rejoiced to behold (*established*, 7; cf. 5), in Him, the Christ whom they know, for whom they continually give thanks to the Father. (1:12)

2:6 *Received Christ Jesus*. The proper object of *received* is the Gospel or "the word of God" (cf. 1 Co 15:1, 3; Gl 1:9, 12; 1 Th 2:13; cf. 4:1 and 2 Th 3:6); but the Gospel is a power (Ro 1:16) which bestows what it proclaims and so to receive the Gospel is to receive Christ Jesus.

Live in him. The word here translated "live" (literally "walk") is used by Paul, in common with the Old Testament and Judaism, with a great variety of modifiers to designate the whole bent and tenor of man's life. Only here does he use the phrase *in him* with it, another indication of the Christ-centeredness of this letter.

2:8-15 Christ is the norm of all teaching (*according to Christ*, 8; cf. 7, "as you were taught"), for in Him God has given them all that is His to give: the *whole fulness of deity* incarnate for us men and for our salvation, *fulness of life* under Him who is Lord over all powers, a life which no *elemental spirits of the universe*, no *rule* or *authority* dare challenge or attack, life as members of the new people of God (*circumcision of Christ*, 11). It is the life of the risen Christ that they share by virtue of their baptism, just as they shared thereby His death. With Christ God has *made* them *alive*, as forgiven men, beyond the reach of their dead past, beyond the accusation of the unfulfilled Law that stood against them as their damning certificate of indebtedness, for in the *cross* God *canceled* that *bond* and published its cancellation. Now that their guilt is gone, the *principalities and*

powers have no hold on them; they participate in Christ's *triumph* over them. The Gospel is Christ all the way (*in Him,* four times; *with Him,* twice; circumcision *of Christ*). Any pretentiously speculative theology (*philosophy*) which departs from Him as the all-controlling norm by substituting *human tradition* for divine revelation is *empty deceit,* a pseudo-gospel without content. It cannot lead them to life and freedom; it can only entrap and exploit them (*makes a prey of you*).

2:8 *Philosophy* is used more broadly than in current usage to include what we should call theosophy or (loosely) theology, any comprehensive view of God, man, and the world.

Elemental spirits of the universe, supernatural powers (sometimes identified in ancient thought with the stars) thought of as controlling the universe. But the idea of *spirits* is not necessarily associated with the word in question, and the phrase could be translated "principles of this world"; it would then indicate the earthbound, human character of this theology controlled by crude this-worldly ideas.

2:9-10 *Whole fulness of deity dwells bodily,* in a form in which man can comprehend, know, and love, a form communicable to man so that he receives *fulness of life.*

2:11-12 *Circumcision* was once the prerequisite and mark of membership in the ancient people of God (Gn 17:9-14), the token and seal of God's covenant with Abraham (Ro 4:11). It admitted a man to the blessings of the covenant and committed him to the claims of the covenant (Dt 10: 16; Jer 4:4; cf. Dt 30:6; Ro 2:25). Circumcision has been surpassed and superseded by the *circumcision of Christ*, by *baptism*, God's own act of *putting off* man's *body of the flesh*, that is, his old sinful nature (cf. Ro 6:6), by *burying and raising* him with Christ, the inclusive Representative of mankind. A return to circumcision now is both meaningless and impious, for it ignores this final and triumphant act of God.

16 Therefore let no one pass judgment on you in questions of food and drink or with regard to a festival or a new moon or a sabbath. 17 These are only a shadow of what is to come; but the substance belongs to Christ. 18 Let no one disqualify you, insisting on self-abasement and worship of angels, taking his stand on visions, puffed up without reason by his sensuous mind, 19 and not holding fast to the Head, from whom the whole body, nourished and knit together through its joints and ligaments, grows with a growth that is from God.

20 If with Christ you died to the elemental spirits of the universe, why do you live as if you still belonged to the world? Why do you submit to regulations, 21 "Do not handle, Do not taste, Do not touch" 22 (referring to things which all perish as they are used), according to human precepts and doctrines? 23 These have indeed an appearance of wisdom in promoting rigor of devotion and self-abasement and severity to the body, but they are of no value in checking the indulgence of the flesh.*e*

Life in the All-Sufficient Christ

3:1 — 4:6

SEEK THE THINGS THAT ARE ABOVE, WHERE CHRIST IS (3:1-17)

3 If then you have been raised with Christ, seek the things that are above, where Christ is, seated at the right hand of God. 2 Set your minds on things that are above,

e Or *are of no value, serving only to indulge the flesh*

2:16-19 Christ is the only and all-controlling norm of all worship. The foods and festivals of Israel foreshadowed Him and have significance only in that foreshadowing; they cannot now constitute the *substance* of worship — only Christ can do that, for He is the fulfillment of all the promises of God: the clean food for the new Israel, Bread and Water of life (Jn 6:35-51; 7:37), their sabbath rest (Heb 4:9), their Passover (1 Co 5:7-8). He is the Head from whom His body derives its functioning unity and godly growth. The only *self-abasement* that has any validity is self-abasement before Him; any *worship of angels* that obscures Him is human pride in religious disguise. Whoever does not hold fast to Him as *Head* has lost the standard of *judgment* and the right to judge any pious manifestation of true faith; he cannot set himself up as umpire and *disqualify* those who run the course which Christ has laid out for them. (Cf. 1 Co 9:24-27; Ph 3:12-16)

2:18 *Angels,* perhaps to be identified with the "elemental spirits" of 2:8 and 20.

Sensuous mind. Literally "mind of the flesh."

2:20-23 Christ is the only norm for the Christian's relationship to the *world* of creaturely things, things that men *handle, taste,* and *touch.* *With Christ* the Christian has died to that world and has been raised into the world of God (cf. 3:1); that world can never again be a threat to him or a norm for his conduct, the object of fearfully detailed *regulations* which govern his relationship to them as to powers (*elemental spirits,* 20) that have a decisive influence on him. Such ascetic regulations, *human precepts and doctrines,* are, for all their appearance of wise and strenuous piety (23), a manifestation of the *flesh,* that is, of self-seeking, self-assertive man seeking to do for himself what God in Christ has done for him.

2:22 *Things which all perish as they are used.* This and the phrase *human precepts* indicate that Paul is thinking of the words of Jesus, Mt 15:9, 17.

2:23 The reading of RSV note *e* (*serving only to indulge the flesh*) seems preferable, since Paul is throughout this section (8-23) stressing the "fleshly" (humanly proud and self-assertive) character of the superior piety of the Colossian errorists ("empty deceit . . . human tradition," 8; "puffed up . . . by his sensuous mind," 18; "human precepts and doctrines," 22).

3:1 — 4:6 As Christ is the whole Gospel and the whole refutation of all distortions of the Gospel (1:15 — 2:23), so He is the whole basis and power of the new life of those who believe in Him. His name (*Christ, Lord, Lord Jesus, Lord Christ*) occurs 15 times in the 31 verses of this section.

3:1-17 The reality of the Christian life is to be seen in Christ; nothing is more real than the fact that Christians have died with Him, have been raised with Him, and share the glory of His life in God. But that glory is as yet a hidden glory; until the Christ *who is* their *life appears,* its glory is a reality to be realized and manifested in a life whose bent and intent (*seek,* 1; *set your minds,* 2) is a militant no to *what is earthly,* to the old world to which the Christian has died; a no to the old world of erotic self-assertion (5) and economic self-assertion (*covetousness,* 5), to the old world of heroic self-assertion (8), the old world of devious self-assertion, the lie (9), the old world in which ethnic, religious, cultural, and social divisions fragment mankind (11). The Christian has *died* to all that (3) in Christ; and this death is realized in his putting *to death* of all that. His resurrection to glory is realized in his enacted yea to God's re-creating act (10); his continual putting on (12) of the garment in which God's elective love (12) has

not on things that are on earth. 3 For you have died, and your life is hid with Christ in God. 4 When Christ who is our life appears, then you also will appear with him in glory.

5 Put to death therefore what is earthly in you: fornication, impurity, passion, evil desire, and covetousness, which is idolatry. 6 On account of these the wrath of God is coming.ᶠ 7 In these you once walked, when you lived in them. 8 But now put them all away: anger, wrath, malice, slander, and foul talk from your mouth. 9 Do not lie to one another, seeing that you have put off the old nature with its practices 10 and have put on the new nature, which is being renewed in knowledge after the image of its creator. 11 Here there cannot be Greek and Jew, circumcised and uncircumcised, barbarian, Scythian, slave, free man, but Christ is all, and in all.

12 Put on then, as God's chosen ones, holy and beloved, compassion, kindness, lowliness, meekness, and patience, 13 forbearing one another and, if one has a complaint against another, forgiving each other; as the Lord has forgiven you, so you also must forgive. 14And above all these put on love, which binds everything together in perfect harmony. 15And let the peace of Christ rule in your hearts, to which indeed you were called in the one body. And be thankful. 16 Let the word of Christ dwell in you richly, teach and admonish one another in all wisdom, and sing psalms and hymns and spiritual songs with thankfulness in your hearts to God. 17And whatever you do, in word or deed, do everything in the name of the Lord Jesus, giving thanks to God the Father through him.

CHRIST THE LORD OF THE HOUSEHOLD (3:18 — 4:1)

18 Wives, be subject to your husbands, as is fitting in the Lord. 19 Husbands, love your wives, and do not be harsh with them. 20 Children, obey your parents in everything, for this pleases the Lord. 21 Fathers, do not provoke your children, lest they become discouraged. 22 Slaves, obey in everything those who are your earthly masters, not with eyeservice, as men-pleasers, but in singleness of heart, fearing the Lord. 23 Whatever your task, work heartily, as serving the Lord and not men, 24 knowing that from the Lord you will receive the inheritance as your reward; you are serving the Lord Christ. 25 For the wrongdoer will be paid back for the wrong he has done, and there is no partiality.

ᶠ Other ancient authorities add *upon the sons of disobedience*

clothed him. He speaks his yea to God's love in a life of compassionate, meek, forgiving love (12-14), a life in which the *peace of Christ* (the soundness and health which His reconciliation has produced) controls all relationships (15), where His potent *word* is the indwelling power that produces salutary and grateful song (16), where *everything* is done *in the name of the Lord Jesus* — what the incarnate Lord is, has done, and signifies for man is the source and power of it all. (17)

3:1 *Raised with Christ.* Cf. 2:13. For the thought and particularly the significant combination of the indicative (what God has done) and the imperative (what the believer now should and can do by the grace of God) cf. Ro 6:1-14 and the notes there. Both here and in Eph 2:6 Paul goes one step beyond what he has said in Ro 6 by speaking of the Christian's resurrection as already accomplished (cf. the future tense in Ro 6:8). But Paul can speak in Ro 8:30 of the future glorification of the believer as an accomplished fact ("glorified"), which comes to the same thing.

Seated at the right hand of God, in power and majesty coequal. (Cf. Ps 110:1)

3:4 *Appear with him in glory.* Cf. Ph 3:20-21; 2 Th 1:10.

3:5 *Put to death.* Cf. Ro 6:11.

3:10 *New nature . . . renewed in knowledge after the image,* etc. For the new creation cf. 2 Co 5:17; Gl 6:15; Eph 2:10, 15; 4:24. *In knowledge* — it was the lure of "knowledge" that led man down the path of rebellion against the God who had created him in His image (Gn 3:5-6). That path led him to alienation from God, enmity toward God (1:21), darkened understanding, and a futile mind (Eph 4:17-18). In Christ, the obedient Man, the fearful rebellion of man is ended and its results are healed; man can again know God and be known by Him (1 Co 8:2-3; Gl 4:9); man can find in Christ "all the treasures of wisdom and knowledge." (2:3)

3:11 *Scythians,* natives of the region which is now southern Russia, were reputed in antiquity to be the most *barbarian* of the barbarians.

3:13 *As the Lord has forgiven.* Cf. Jesus' answer to Peter's question on forgiveness, Mt 18:21-35.

3:16 *Word of Christ . . . teach . . . admonish . . . wisdom.* This corresponds exactly to what Paul has described as his own task in 1:28. The apostolic church is to be an "imitator" of the apostle. (Cf. 1 Co 4:16; 11:1; Gl 4:12; Ph 3:17; 1 Th 1:6; 2 Th 3:7, 9)

3:18 — 4:1 The hidden glory of the new life manifests itself in the ordinary household relationships of wife and husband, children and

4 Masters, treat your slaves justly and fairly, knowing that you also have a Master in heaven.

VIGILANCE IN PRAYER, WISDOM TOWARD THE WORLD (4:2-6)

2 Continue steadfastly in prayer, being watchful in it with thanksgiving; 3 and pray for us also, that God may open to us a door for the word, to declare the mystery of Christ, on account of which I am in prison, 4 that I may make it clear, as I ought to speak.

5 Conduct yourselves wisely toward outsiders, making the most of the time. 6 Let your speech always be gracious, seasoned with salt, so that you may know how you ought to answer every one.

CONCLUSION: PERSONAL MATTERS (4:7-18)

7 Tych'i·cus will tell you all about my affairs; he is a beloved brother and faithful minister and fellow servant in the Lord. 8 I have sent him to you for this very purpose, that you may know how we are and that he may encourage your hearts, 9 and with him O·nes'i·mus, the faithful and beloved brother, who is one of yourselves. They will tell you of everything that has taken place here.

10 Ar·is·tar'chus my fellow prisoner greets you, and Mark the cousin of Bar'na·bas (concerning whom you have received instructions—if he comes to you, receive him), 11 and Jesus who is called Justus. These are the only men of the circumcision among my fellow workers for the kingdom of God, and they have been a comfort to me. 12 Ep'a·phras, who is one of yourselves, a servant*g* of Christ Jesus, greets you, always remembering you earnestly in his prayers, that you may stand mature and fully assured in all the will of God. 13 For I bear him witness that he has worked hard for

g Or *slave*

---

parents, slaves and masters. The glory is hidden; things remain as they were, the old order of subordination and obedience lives on. And yet all is new, for Christ has become Lord over both the obedient and the obeyed.

3:22 *Slaves* were considered a part of the household. Cf. the notes on Paul's Letter to Philemon for the New Testament attitude toward slavery.

4:1 *Masters.* The Greek word is elsewhere translated "lord."

4:2-6 The new life is a vigilant life of continual *prayer,* particularly prayer for the progress of the apostolic *word,* the proclamation of the *mystery of Christ* (3-4). The new life is itself a proclamation of the mystery to the world (*outsiders,* 5), a witness which calls for the gift of wisdom (5, cf.1: 9-10) and for speech marked by Christian taste and tact (*seasoned with salt,* 6).

4:3 *Door for the word,* that is, a missionary "opening." The Word is thought of as living and actively moving. (Cf. 1:26; 2 Th 3:1)

4:7-18 The last paragraphs deal with the sending of Tychicus, bearer of the letter, and the return of the Colossian slave Onesimus; convey greetings; direct an exchange of letters between Colossae and the neighboring town of Laodicea; and charge Archippus to fulfill his ministry. Paul concludes with a greeting written with his own hand, a renewal request for their intercessions, and a brief benediction. These are personal matters, to be sure; but with Paul there is no cleavage between personal and official aspects of his life.

4:7 *Tychicus* of Asia accompanied Paul on his last journey to Jerusalem (Acts 20:4) and was the bearer of the Letter to the Ephesians also (Eph 6:21; see the Introduction to that letter). We catch a glimpse of his later activity as Paul's co-worker in Tts 3:12 and 2 Ti 4:12.

4:9 *Onesimus.* See the Introduction to Philemon. In calling this embezzling runaway slave *the faithful and beloved brother, who is one of yourselves,* Paul is bidding the Colossians put into practice the injunction of 3:13: "As the Lord has forgiven you, so you also must forgive," totally, with no rancorous remembrance of past failings.

4:10 *Aristarchus* of Thessalonica is called *fellow prisoner* (literally "prisoner of war") as one who shares difficulties and dangers with Paul, the soldier (1 Co 9:7; 2 Co 10:3) and prisoner (Eph 3:1; 4:1; Phmn 1, 9) for Christ. He had been seized by the mob at Ephesus (Acts 19:29) and accompanied Paul on the dangerous last voyage to Jerusalem (Acts 20:4) and to Paul's Roman imprisonment (Acts 27:2). He is listed among Paul's fellow workers in Phmn 24 also.

Mark. See the Introduction to Mark's Gospel. Cf. Acts (where he is called John Mark, John, or Mark) 12:12, 25; 13:13; 15:37-39; Phmn 24; 2 Ti 4:11.

4:11 *Jesus . . . Justus.* Known only from this passage. *Of the circumcision,* i. e., Jewish. This implies that Epaphras (12), Luke, and Demas (14) were of Gentile birth.

4:12 *Epaphras.* Cf. 1:7; Phmn 23 and the Introduction.

4:13 *Laodicea and Hierapolis* with Colossae constituted a triangle of neighboring towns in the Lycus valley.

you and for those in La·od·i·ce′a and in Hi·er·ap′o·lis. ¹⁴ Luke the beloved physician and Demas greet you. ¹⁵ Give my greetings to the brethren at La·od·i·ce′a, and to Nympha and the church in her house. ¹⁶And when this letter has been read among you, have it read also in the church of the La·od·i·ce′ans; and see that you read also the letter from La·od·i·ce′a. ¹⁷And say to Ar·chip′pus, "See that you fulfil the ministry which you have received in the Lord."

18 I, Paul, write this greeting with my own hand. Remember my fetters. Grace be with you.

4:14 *Luke.* Mentioned only here and in 2 Ti 4:11 and Phmn 24 in NT. Cf. Introduction to Luke.

Demas. Known only from this passage, 2 Ti 4:10, and Phmn 24.

4:15 *Nympha.* Known only from this passage.

The church in her house. For the house-church (the usual form in the first days of the church) cf. Acts 2:46; Ro 16:5 (the grouping of names in Ro 16:15-16 suggests house-churches also); and Phmn 2.

4:16 For the theory that *the letter from Laodicea* is the work which we know as the Letter to the Ephesians see the Introduction to Ephesians.

4:17 *Archippus,* called "fellow soldier" by Paul in Phmn 2. He may have been Philemon's son. We can only guess as to the exact nature of the ministry which he had *received from the Lord.*

4:18 *With my own hand.* Cf. 1 Co 16:21; Gl 6:11; 2 Th 3:17. Paul dictated the body of his letters, Ro 16:22.

THE FIRST LETTER OF PAUL TO THE

THESSALONIANS

INTRODUCTION

The Letters to the Thessalonians are part of that history of the growth of the Word of the Lord we commonly designate as Paul's second missionary journey. It took Paul, with his new companions Silas and Timothy, to Europe. The heart of this was the apostle's 18-month ministry in the great commercial center of Corinth. That ministry was preceded by a revisitation of the churches of Syria and Cilicia and of the Galatian churches founded on the first missionary journey; by missionary work in the European cities of Philippi, Thessalonica, and Berea, work again and again cut short by the malice of superstitious avarice or by the plottings of jealous Jews; and by missionary activity at Athens, the great cultural center of Greece. It was followed by a brief exploratory visit to Ephesus which prepared for Paul's long ministry there on his third missionary journey.

The Word of the Lord sped on and triumphed (2 Th 3:1) in Europe, but in its peculiarly divine way. It sped on surely but not without opposition; it triumphed with the inevitable triumph of a work of God, but its history is not the history of an easy and effortless triumph — it is a history marked, rather, by the persecution, suffering, and internal difficulties of the human bearers and the human recipients of the Word. The history of the second missionary journey has left its mark on the Letters to the Thessalonians. Paul's companions on the journey, Silas (Paul calls him by his Roman name Silvanus) and Timothy, join in the sending of both letters. Paul's opening words in the first letter are a commentary on the history that brought him to Thessalonica: "We know, brethren beloved by God, *that he has chosen you*; for our gospel came to you not only in word, but also in power and in the Holy Spirit and with full conviction" (1 Th 1:4-5). Paul knew from his own experience that the existence of the church at Thessalonica was due not to human planning and devising, but to the elective love of God which had become his-

tory in Paul's mission to Europe. Paul would recall, as he wrote these words, how he and his companions had been led, uncomprehending but obedient, by God's own hand and by the Spirit of Jesus (Acts 16:7) past the province of Asia, which would have seemed the logical next step on their missionary way, past Mysia, away from Bithynia, to Troas, to receive there the vision which summoned them to Europe (Acts 16:9); he would recall, too, how persecution had pushed him on with illogical haste from Philippi to Thessalonica. When Paul spoke of the elective love of God to the Thessalonians, he was not uttering a theoretical tenet of his faith; he was uttering what God had woven into the living texture of his faith by a history in which he, Paul, had himself acted and suffered.

Paul bore the badge of suffering, which was the mark of his apostolate, when he came to Thessalonica from Philippi. The Paul and Silvanus who took to "praying and singing hymns to God" in the jail at Philippi after being beaten by the magistrates (Acts 16:24) had learned to see in their sufferings not the defeat but the triumph of the Word of the Lord; and they spoke the Word in Thessalonica with the robust and confident courage of men who know that they are bearers of the Word of God (1 Th 2:13) — and they did not conceal from their Thessalonian hearers that their word would put the imprint of suffering on the church of God in Thessalonica, too (1 Th 1:6; 2:14; 3:3-4; 2 Th 1:4-7). No small part of that suffering was due to the rancor of unbelieving Jews; and this, too, finds expression in the letter. (1 Th 2:14-16)

Paul experienced anew on this journey the power and activity of Satan, who plants weeds where the Lord plants good seed. Forced to leave Thessalonica before his work there was really finished, he tried again and again to return to the young church — "but Satan hindered us," he writes (1 Th 2:18; cf. 3:5). He experienced also the power for order and discipline which God had

set into the world in the form of the Roman government (cf. Ro 13:1-7); his Roman citizenship had procured him an honorable release from prison at Philippi (Acts 16: 37-39), and the power of Rome was to stand between him and Judaic malice again at Corinth (Acts 18:12-17), when the proconsul Gallio refused to entertain the ambiguous and invidious Jewish charges against him. When Paul spoke to the Thessalonians of the power that restrains the antichristian attack on God and God's people (2 Th 2:6-7), he was writing revelation which God had given him, to be sure; but God had written that revelation into the history and the experience of Paul the apostle, too.

The Founding of the Church at Thessalonica

Thessalonica was the kind of place that Paul usually chose for an intensive and prolonged ministry. It was the capital of the Roman province of Macedonia and the residence of the Roman proconsul, commercially important as a harbor town, and an important communications center lying on the *Via Egnatia,* the road which connected Rome (by way of Dyrrachium) with Byzantium and the East. It was thus naturally fitted to become a missionary center, a point from which the Word of the Lord, once established in men's hearts, might readily "sound forth." (1 Th 1:8)

Paul arrived with his companions Silas and Timothy (one representing the old Jerusalem church; the other, half Jew and half Greek, representing the young church in Galatia) at Thessalonica in A. D. 50 and began his work, as usual, in the synagog. According to Luke (Acts 17:2), Paul's work in the synagog lasted "three sabbaths," and Luke records no further activity in Thessalonica. But Paul's own account of his work as missionary and as pastor of the new church in Thessalonica (1 Th 2:1-12) suggests a more prolonged ministry among the Gentiles after the break with the synagog had taken place (Acts 17:5). This is confirmed by a notice in Paul's Letter to the Philippians, where he recalls that the Philippians *twice* sent money for his needs when he was at Thessalonica (Ph 4:16). Luke's account in Acts is therefore a highly compressed one; he gives an impression of Paul's ministry at Thessalonica by indicating only the initial and the final stages of his work there.

The break with the synagog came early; the ministry among the Gentiles was per- haps prolonged for several months. The congregation at Thessalonica was therefore, as the Letters to the Thessalonians also indicate, predominantly Gentile (1 Th 1:9; 2:14; cf. Acts 17:4). The life of that congregation was from the first a vigorous one marked by the characteristically Christian joy which even severe trials cannot quench, an active faith which documented itself in a far-reaching missionary witness (1 Th 1:3, 7 f.), a brotherly love which Paul can speak of as taught them by God Himself (1 Th 4:9-10), and an intense hope which longed for the return of "Jesus who delivers us from the wrath to come" (1 Th 1:10; cf. 4:13 ff.). Paul says of them (and Paul's generous recognition of what God has wrought in men never degenerates into empty flattery) that they "became an example to all the believers in Macedonia and in Achaia," all Greece (1 Th 1:7). Only, they were still little children in Christ, good and gifted children, but not mature and stable men, when Paul was forced to leave them. (Acts 17:5-10; 1 Th 2:17)

Occasion of the First Letter

Paul proceeded southwest from Thessalonica to Berea; and from there, when Jews from Thessalonica stirred up opposition to him in Berea also (Acts 17:10-13), to Athens. After a brief ministry there, which brought him into contact with the philosophy of the Greeks, he went on to Corinth, where a vision of the Lord bade him remain and work in depth. And remain he did—for almost two years. Meanwhile the church at Thessalonica remained in his thoughts and his prayers, and he was filled with a deep and restless anxiety for the brethren of whom he was "bereft . . . in person not in heart" (1 Th 2:17). Would they stand fast under the persecution which had come upon them? Would they misunderstand his departure and his continued absence from them? In this connection it is well to remember that Paul and his companions were not the only propagandists and pleaders for a cause that traveled the Roman roads in those days; they were part of a numerous and motley troup of philosophers, rhetoricians, propagandists for various foreign and domestic cults, missionaries, charlatans, and quacks who went from town to town, all intent on getting a hearing, all eager for money or fame or both. These usually came and went, never to be heard from again. Paul would in the popular mind

be classified with them. And Paul in Thessalonica, A. D. 51, was not yet the apostle Paul as the church has learned to see him since; he was simply a hitherto unknown little Jew who had come and gone, like hundreds of brilliant and persuasive men before him. The church of Thessalonica would of itself not be minded to classify Paul thus; but his enemies would, and they would thus undermine his apostolic authority and with it the faith in the Gospel with which he was identified as apostle.

Paul's anxieties and fears were well founded. And he could not return to Thessalonica, although he attempted to do so more than once, to relieve his anxieties and to do the work that would obviate the dangers which gave rise to them. Satan hindered him (1 Th 2:18); we can only guess as to what form this hindering took. Finally, when he could no longer endure the suspense, he sacrificed the aid and companionship of Timothy (a real sacrifice, for Paul's was a nature that needed the presence of friends and brethren) and sent him to Thessalonica, both to strengthen the faith of the church and to learn firsthand how they fared. (1 Th 3:1-5)

Neither the account in Acts nor Paul's account in his first letter makes it clear whether Timothy first joined Paul at Athens and was sent back to Thessalonica from there or whether Paul, alone at Athens, directed Timothy by letter to revisit Thessalonica before rejoining him at Corinth. At any rate, when Timothy returned from Thessalonica to Paul at Corinth with the good news of the Thessalonians' faith and love and fidelity to Paul (1 Th 3:6), it meant for Paul the release from a long and agonizing tension. He threw himself with new vigor into his work at Corinth (Acts 18:5), and he wrote the letter which we call First Thessalonians. This letter is Paul's response to Timothy's report, a long thanksgiving for the good news which Timothy had brought, a thanksgiving which looks back over the whole history of the Thessalonian church since its founding and is at the same time a vindication of the purity and sanctity of his motives as their apostle and pastor (chs. 1–3). The thanksgiving is followed by a series of admonitions suggested by Timothy's report. Paul is doing by letter what he could not do face to face; he is supplying what is lacking in their faith. (Cf. 1 Th 3:10)

Timothy would have reported that these Christians in a Gentile environment, and in a Greek harbor town at that, where the idea of sexual purity was a complete novelty, were having difficulty in maintaining the chastity a life of faith demands; that their past made it difficult for them to shed at once and altogether the unscrupulous craftiness which they had hitherto regarded as normal and prudent; that their fervent hope easily degenerated into an excited and irresponsible enthusiasm which led them to neglect the tasks and duties of daily life; that their imperfect grasp of the hope which the promised return of the Christ gave them made them despondent regarding their kin and brethren who had died before that return; that their hope was not content to be pure hope and leave the times and seasons of fulfillment in God's hands but sought to calculate and predict; that their life as a community bound together by faith and love and hope was not without its frictions and difficulties. To these difficulties Paul's warm and pastoral heart responded with a wisdom and a love that only the Spirit of God can bestow.

The first three chapters give us a particularly vivid picture of Paul the missionary and pastor at work in a young Gentile church—how the Word of the Lord grows on pagan soil.

The value of the hortatory section may be measured by the fact that these two brief chapters have furnished no less than three Epistles in the ancient church's pericopal system, the Epistle for the Second Sunday in Lent (1 Th 4:1-7) and the Twenty-fifth and Twenty-seventh Sundays After Trinity. (1 Th 4:13-18; 5:1-11)

Few letters offer more sustenance for the hope of God's people than this one; besides the two great sections on the lot of the dead in Christ (4:13-18) and on the times and seasons of the Lord's return (5:1-11), note the fact that practically every major section in the letter ends on the note of the return of the Lord. (1 Th 1:10; 2:12, 16, 19; 3:13; 5:23)

THESSALONIANS

SALUTATION (1:1)

1 Paul, Silvanus, and Timothy,
To the church of the Thessalonians in God the Father and the Lord Jesus Christ:
Grace to you and peace.

Thanksgiving for the Word of God in Thessalonica

1:2 — 3:13

THE FOUNDING OF THE CHURCH AT THESSALONICA (1:2 — 2:12)

2 We give thanks to God always for you all, constantly mentioning you in our prayers, [3] remembering before our God and Father your work of faith and labor of love and steadfastness of hope in our Lord Jesus Christ. [4] For we know, brethren beloved by God, that he has chosen you; [5] for our gospel came to you not only in word, but also in power and in the Holy Spirit and with full conviction. You know what kind of men we proved to be among you for your sake. [6]And you became imitators of us and of the Lord, for you received the word in much affliction, with joy inspired by the Holy Spirit; [7] so that you became an example to all the believers in Macedonia and in A·cha′ia. [8] For not only has the word of the Lord sounded forth from you in Macedonia and A·cha′ia, but your faith in God has gone forth everywhere, so that we need not say anything. [9] For they themselves report concerning us what a welcome we had among you, and how you turned to God from idols, to serve a living and true God, [10] and to wait for his Son from heaven, whom he raised from the dead, Jesus who delivers us from the wrath to come.

2 For you yourselves know, brethren, that our visit to you was not in vain; [2] but though we had already suffered and been shamefully treated at Phi·lip′pi, as you

1:1 *Silvanus* and *Timothy*, Paul's co-workers on the second missionary journey and cofounders of the church at Thessalonica. See the Introduction.

1:2 — 3:13 The first three chapters are an unusual expansion of the thanksgiving with which Paul usually opens his letters. In grateful reminiscence Paul looks back to the time of the founding of the church (1:2 — 2:12), to the time of persecution (2:13-16), to the time of his separation from the Thessalonians (2:17 — 3:5), gives thanks for the good news which Timothy's report concerning them has brought (3:6-10), and includes a prayer. (3:11-13)

1:2 — 2:12 Paul recalls the coming of the Gospel to Thessalonica, the Thessalonians' exemplary reception of the Word, and the missionary impact of their example (1:2-10). He dwells on his own behavior as apostle (courageous, pure in motive, unselfish, and gentle, 2:1-8) and as their pastor — his selfless devotion in supporting himself by the toil of his hands while he tended them with a father's care. (2:9-12)

1:3 *Faith . . . love . . . hope.* For this triad as summary of man's life as a Christian cf. 5:8; 1 Co 13:13; Cl 1:4-5; Heb 10:22-24.

Work of faith. Faith, in Paul as in James, must inevitably manifest itself in deeds, as "faith working through love." (Gl 5:6; cf. Ja 2:14-26)

1:4 *He has chosen you.* Cf. 2 Th 1:13. Paul's experience on the second missionary journey had powerfully brought home to him that God's elective love in its mysterious working brings men to faith. See the Introduction.

1:6 *Imitators of us and of the Lord.* The apostle (with his co-workers) can be the object of imitation only because Christ works through him (Ro 15:18) and speaks in him (2 Co 13:3). For Christ as recipient of the Word cf. Jn 17:8; Rv 1:1. For the apostle as object of imitation cf. 1 Co 4:16; 11:1; Gl 4:12; Ph 3:17; 2 Th 3:7, 9.

1:8 *Word of the Lord sounded forth.* Cf. 2 Th 3:1.

Macedonia and Achaia. The northern and southern halves of Greece, the two provinces into which the Romans had divided Greece.

1:9-10 An instructive summary of Paul's missionary preaching to Gentiles, with its penetrating appeal to the conscience of man (*the wrath to come;* cf. 2 Co 4:2). The triad of faith (*turned to God*), love (*serve*), and hope (*wait for his Son*) is heard again.

2:2 *Suffered . . . at Philippi.* Cf. Acts 16:19-39.

know, we had courage in our God to declare to you the gospel of God in the face of great opposition. 3 For our appeal does not spring from error or uncleanness, nor is it made with guile; 4 but just as we have been approved by God to be entrusted with the gospel, so we speak, not to please men, but to please God who tests our hearts. 5 For we never used either words of flattery, as you know, or a cloak for greed, as God is witness; 6 nor did we seek glory from men, whether from you or from others, though we might have made demands as apostles of Christ. 7 But we were gentle*a* among you, like a nurse taking care of her children. 8 So, being affectionately desirous of you, we were ready to share with you not only the gospel of God but also our own selves, because you had become very dear to us.

9 For you remember our labor and toil, brethren; we worked night and day, that we might not burden any of you, while we preached to you the gospel of God. 10 You are witnesses, and God also, how holy and righteous and blameless was our behavior to you believers; 11 for you know how, like a father with his children, we exhorted each one of you and encouraged you and charged you 12 to lead a life worthy of God, who calls you into his own kingdom and glory.

THE TIME OF PERSECUTION (2:13-16)

13 And we also thank God constantly for this, that when you received the word of God which you heard from us, you accepted it not as the word of men but as what it really is, the word of God, which is at work in you believers. 14 For you, brethren, became imitators of the churches of God in Christ Jesus which are in Judea; for you suffered the same things from your own countrymen as they did from the Jews, 15 who killed both the Lord Jesus and the prophets, and drove us out, and displease God and oppose all men 16 by hindering us from speaking to the Gentiles that they may be saved—so as always to fill up the measure of their sins. But God's wrath has come upon them at last!*b*

a Other ancient authorities read *babes*   *b* Or *completely*, or *for ever*

In the face of . . . opposition. Cf. Acts 17:1-8.

2:3 *Error,* illusion, self-deception.

Uncleanness, impure motives.

2:4 *God who tests our hearts.* Paul implicitly compares himself to the prophet Jeremiah, who committed his cause to God when persecuted (Jer 11:20, cf. 18-19). In Gl 1:15 Paul speaks of his call to the apostolate in language taken from Jeremiah's description of his call. (Jer 1:5)

2:5 *Cloak for greed,* that is, noble language that conceals the speaker's intention of getting money out of his hearers. (Cf. Acts 20:33)

2:8 *Share . . . our own selves.* Cf. 2 Co 12:15; Ph 2:17.

2:9 *Worked night and day.* Cf. Acts 18:3; 20: 34-35; 1 Co 4:12; 9:6, 12, 14-18.

2:11 *Father.* At the very beginning, in their infancy, he was their gentle nurse (2:7); as they advanced, he became their father, who trained and reared them.

2:12 *Calls.* The present tense is significant. The once-for-all initial call (e. g., Ro 8:30; 1 Co 1:9; Gl 1:6; 1 Th 4:7) which brings man under the reign of God *(kingdom)* and sets him on the road to *glory* is continually renewed in the Word, which becomes his daily nurture. Cf. 5:24; the once-accepted converting Word of God continues to work in the believers. (2:13)

2:13-16 Paul gratefully recalls how the Thessalonians received the apostolic Word as the very *word of God* which it is, how that divine Word evinced its power in them by enabling them to endure persecutions comparable to those endured by the churches of Judea.

2:14 *From your own countrymen,* Gentiles, since the church at Thessalonica was predominantly Gentile (see the Introduction). Persecution at Thessalonica originated with the Jews, but they succeeded in inflaming the Gentile townsmen and officials against the new Christian community. (Acts 17:5-9)

2:15-16 It would be easy to dismiss these words as an anti-Semitic outburst prompted by the rancor of a Jewish renegade. But it is to be noted (a) that the statement simply takes up Jesus' indictment of His countrymen *(killed . . . the prophets,* cf. Mt 23:37); (b) that it is a straightforward record of what happened in the history of Jesus, the Judaic church, and Paul's missionary work; and (c) that Paul incurred and endured Judaic enmity just because his love for the Jew and his faith in the promises of God compelled him to proclaim the Gospel "to the Jew first" (Ro 1:16; Acts 12 to 28), a practice which he continued in the face of persistent rejection and persecution. For Paul's unquenchable love for his people cf. Ro 9:1-3; 10:1.

2:16 *Fill up the measure of their sins.* Cf. Gn 15:16. The whole tragedy of Israel is contained in the fact that Paul is forced to describe them in the language the Lord had used of the pagan nation He drove out of Canaan to provide a home for His people.

God's wrath has come upon them. The hardening

THE TIME OF SEPARATION (2:17 – 3:5)

17 But since we were bereft of you, brethren, for a short time, in person not in heart, we endeavored the more eagerly and with great desire to see you face to face; [18] because we wanted to come to you—I, Paul, again and again—but Satan hindered us. [19] For what is our hope or joy or crown of boasting before our Lord Jesus at his coming? Is it not you? [20] For you are our glory and joy.

3 Therefore when we could bear it no longer, we were willing to be left behind at Athens alone, [2] and we sent Timothy, our brother and God's servant in the gospel of Christ, to establish you in your faith and to exhort you, [3] that no one be moved by these afflictions. You yourselves know that this is to be our lot. [4] For when we were with you, we told you beforehand that we were to suffer affliction; just as it has come to pass, and as you know. [5] For this reason, when I could bear it no longer, I sent that I might know your faith, for fear that somehow the tempter had tempted you and that our labor would be in vain.

TIMOTHY'S GOOD NEWS (3:6-10)

6 But now that Timothy has come to us from you, and has brought us the good news of your faith and love and reported that you always remember us kindly and long to see us, as we long to see you—[7] for this reason, brethren, in all our distress and affliction we have been comforted about you through your faith; [8] for now we live, if you stand fast in the Lord. [9] For what thanksgiving can we render to God for you, for all the joy which we feel for your sake before our God, [10] praying earnestly night and day that we may see you face to face and supply what is lacking in your faith?

PRAYER (3:11-13)

11 Now may our God and Father himself, and our Lord Jesus, direct our way to you; [12] and may the Lord make you increase and abound in love to one another and to all men, as we do to you, [13] so that he may establish your hearts unblamable in holiness before our God and Father, at the coming of our Lord Jesus with all his saints.

which has befallen Israel (Ro 11:7-10, 25) is God's judgment on Israel's unbelief and is as such a token and foretaste not only of the fall of Jerusalem but of the final judgment, "the wrath to come." (1:10)

2:17 – 3:5 Paul recalls his longing to see the church of Thessalonica again, his repeated attempts to return to them (frustrated by Satan), and finally the sending of Timothy to establish them in their faith and to bring him word concerning their faith.

2:18 The vehemence of Paul's assurance is probably due to the fact that his enemies sought to discredit him by saying that he had left his converts to face persecution alone while he had taken to his heels.

Satan hindered us. What form the satanic opposition took can only be conjectured. One likely suggestion is that Paul could not return to Thessalonica without endangering his former host, Jason, from whom the city authorities had taken security to keep the peace. Any disturbance resulting from Paul's return would put Jason in jeopardy. (Acts 17:9)

2:19 *Crown of boasting,* a mark of honor and distinction of which I can boast or in which I can exult. (Cf. 2 Co 1:14)

3:3-4 Cf. Mt 5:10-12; Acts 14:22. Neither Jesus nor his apostle ever fostered the illusion that the church is an island of tranquillity.

3:5 *The tempter* (Satan, cf. Mt 4:3) *had tempted you* successfully.

3:6-10 Paul rejoices at and gives thanks to God for their steadfastness in faith and love and their loyalty to himself.

3:6 *Brought us the good news.* Paul uses the word commonly used for proclaiming the Gospel; their continued faith and love are God's working, and news of His gracious activity is "gospel.".

3:10 *Supply what is lacking in your faith.* This is what Paul does or at least begins to do in chs. 4 and 5. Here, as in 1:3 ("your work of faith"), Paul is thinking of faith as operative and productive.

3:11-13 As is usual in Paul's letters, the long thanksgiving is followed by an intercessory prayer. Paul prays that God and the Lord Jesus may direct his way back to Thessalonica and that the Lord may establish the hearts of the Thessalonian believers in love and hope.

3:11 *Lord Jesus* is the object of prayer, strong evidence for His deity.

3:13 *With all his saints,* literally "holy ones"; probably angels are meant. (Cf. Zch 14:5; Mt 25:31)

Exhortations and Conclusion

4:1 — 5:28

MORAL EXHORTATIONS FOR INDIVIDUALS (4:1-12)

4 Finally, brethren, we beseech and exhort you in the Lord Jesus, that as you learned from us how you ought to live and to please God, just as you are doing, you do so more and more. [2] For you know what instructions we gave you through the Lord Jesus. [3] For this is the will of God, your sanctification: that you abstain from unchastity; [4] that each one of you know how to take a wife for himself*x* in holiness and honor, [5] not in the passion of lust like heathen who do not know God; [6] that no man transgress, and wrong his brother in this matter,*c* because the Lord is an avenger in all these things, as we solemnly forewarned you. [7] For God has not called us for uncleanness, but in holiness. [8] Therefore whoever disregards this, disregards not man but God, who gives his Holy Spirit to you.

9 But concerning love of the brethren you have no need to have any one write to you, for you yourselves have been taught by God to love one another; [10] and indeed you do love all the brethren throughout Macedonia. But we exhort you, brethren, to do so more and more, [11] to aspire to live quietly, to mind your own affairs, and to work with your hands, as we charged you; [12] so that you may command the respect of outsiders, and be dependent on nobody.

CONCERNING THOSE WHO ARE ASLEEP (4:13-18)

13 But we would not have you ignorant, brethren, concerning those who are asleep, that you may not grieve as others do who have no hope. [14] For since we believe that Jesus died and rose again, even so, through Jesus, God will bring with him those who have fallen asleep. [15] For this we declare to you by the word of the Lord, that we who are alive, who are left until the coming of the Lord, shall not precede those who have fallen asleep. [16] For the Lord himself will descend from heaven with a cry of command, with the archangel's call, and with the sound of the trumpet of God. And the dead in Christ will rise first; [17] then we who are alive, who are left, shall be caught up together with them in the clouds to meet the Lord in the air; and so we shall always be with the Lord. [18] Therefore comfort one another with these words.

c Or *defraud his brother in business*　*x* Or *how to control his own body*

4:1-12 The admonitions ᴛᴏ sexual purity (1-8), to brotherly love (9-10), and to quiet industry (11-12) were probably prompted by Timothy's report.

4:1 *To please God* involves the idea of willing service to Him. (Cf. 1:9; Cl 1:10)

4:2 *Through the Lord Jesus,* on His authority.

4:3 *Unchastity.* Sexual immorality is meant.

4:5 *Heathen who do not know God.* The OT uses this phrase of the heathen, in contrast to Israel (Ps 79:6; Jer 10:25); the "heathen" Thessalonians have become the new Israel of God who know God.

4:8 *Who gives his Spirit to you,* or "into you," that is, "into your hearts" (cf. Eze 36:27). The promise given to ancient Israel has become a reality in the new Israel. With the gift of the Spirit, God gives the power to do what He commands.

4:9 *Taught by God.* Mt 18:32-33, with the preceding parable (23-31), is the best commentary on this phrase.

4:11 *Live quietly.* Cf. 2 Th 3:11-12.

4:12 *Respect of outsiders.* The vitality of the Christian hope excited the curiosity and interest of men (cf. 1 Ptr 3:15), but if the hope made idlers and busybodies of those who held it, it would soon become an object of derision.

4:13 For the occasion and need for this admonition see the Introduction.

4:14 *Jesus ... rose again ... through Jesus.* Here, as everywhere in the NT, the resurrection of Jesus is the sole and whole basis for the hope of eternal life. His resurrection is the resurrection of the dead (cf. 1 Co 15:12-22; 2 Co 4:14). He is "the resurrection and the life." (Jn 11:25)

4:15 *By the word of the Lord.* No known word of Jesus corresponds exactly to what Paul is saying here. Paul may be quoting a saying of Jesus not recorded in our gospels, as he does in Acts 20:35.

4:17 *Meet the Lord ... be with the Lord.* For all the dramatic splendor which marks Paul's portrayal of the Lord's return (16), the Christian hope here remains, as always in the NT, personal, a hope for full communion with our Lord.

4:18 *Comfort one another.* Cf. 5:11. Thus, by being spoken from man to man, the Word of God proclaimed by the apostle continues to work in the believers. (2:13)

THE TIMES AND SEASONS OF THE LORD'S RETURN (5:1-11)

5 But as to the times and the seasons, brethren, you have no need to have anything written to you. 2 For you yourselves know well that the day of the Lord will come like a thief in the night. 3 When people say, "There is peace and security," then sudden destruction will come upon them as travail comes upon a woman with child, and there will be no escape. 4 But you are not in darkness, brethren, for that day to surprise you like a thief. 5 For you are all sons of light and sons of the day; we are not of the night or of darkness. 6 So then let us not sleep, as others do, but let us keep awake and be sober. 7 For those who sleep sleep at night, and those who get drunk are drunk at night. 8 But, since we belong to the day, let us be sober, and put on the breastplate of faith and love, and for a helmet the hope of salvation. 9 For God has not destined us for wrath, but to obtain salvation through our Lord Jesus Christ, 10 who died for us so that whether we wake or sleep we might live with him. 11 Therefore encourage one another and build one another up, just as you are doing.

EXHORTATIONS FOR CONGREGATIONAL LIFE (5:12-22)

12 But we beseech you, brethren, to respect those who labor among you and are over you in the Lord and admonish you, 13 and to esteem them very highly in love because of their work. Be at peace among yourselves. 14 And we exhort you, brethren, admonish the idlers, encourage the faint-hearted, help the weak, be patient with them all. 15 See that none of you repays evil for evil, but always seek to do good to one another and to all. 16 Rejoice always, 17 pray constantly, 18 give thanks in all circumstances; for this is the will of God in Christ Jesus for you. 19 Do not quench the Spirit, 20 do not despise prophesying, 21 but test everything; hold fast what is good, 22 abstain from every form of evil.

CONCLUSION (5:23-28)

23 May the God of peace himself sanctify you wholly; and may your spirit and soul and body be kept sound and blameless at the coming of our Lord Jesus Christ. 24 He who calls you is faithful, and he will do it.

5:1-11 The coming of the Day of the Lord is as incalculable (thief) as it is certain (travail). Its coming does not call for a calculating curiosity but vigilance and sobriety; for nothing less than salvation, life with Christ, is at stake.

5:1-2 Times and the seasons. Like Jesus (Mt 24:3-4, 36-44; Acts 1:7), Paul will not enter into the question of times and seasons at all; there is a gentle irony in you . . . know well (literally "exactly")—the Christian's "exact" knowledge of the Day of the Lord is that its time is unknowable. For thief in the night cf. Mt 24:43; Lk 12: 39-40; 2 Ptr 3:10; Rv 3:3; 16:15.

5:3 Travail. The point of comparison is inevitability.

5:5 Sons of. To be "son of" something means that you have your nature and destiny determined by it (cf. Eph 2:2; 5:6; Cl 3:6; 2 Th 2:3), as a child derives its character and place in life from its parents.

5:6-7 Cf. Ro 13:11-14.

5:8 For the whole armor of God cf. Eph 6:13-17.

5:10 Whether we wake or sleep, whether we are among the living or the dead at the coming of the day of the Lord. Paul is touching once more on the thought of 4:13-18. For Christ as Lord of the living and the dead by virtue of His atoning death and resurrection cf. Ro 14:8-9.

5:11 See 4:18 and the note there.

5:12-22 Paul exhorts the congregation to a loving recognition of its leaders because of their work (12-13); to a life of loving and patient ministry to one another (14-15); to a worship of continual joy, prayer, and thanksgiving (16-18); to a full but discerning use of the gifts of the Spirit. (19-22)

5:19-20 Not quench the Spirit . . . prophesying. Apparently Paul is inculcating a proper appreciation of both the "enthusiastic" manifestations of the Spirit, such as speaking with tongues, and the more sober and sobering gifts, such as the plain instructive and edifying speech of prophecy. For a fuller treatment see 1 Co 12 and 14.

5:21 Test everything. Cf. 1 Co 14:29, where the church is told to "weigh what is said" by the prophets, and 1 Jn 4:1.

5:22 Every form of evil, even when it appears in "spiritual" guise.

5:23-28 The second half of the letter is rounded out by an intercessory prayer very similar to that of the conclusion of the first half (23-24; cf. 3: 11-13). This is followed by a request for the church's intercession, greetings, instruction for the public reading of the letter, and a closing benediction. (25-28)

5:23 Spirit and soul and body, the total human being as a unity of his renewed capacity for communion with God (spirit), his natural vitality (soul), and his physical existence (body).

5:24 Calls. See note on 2:12.

25 Brethren, pray for us.
26 Greet all the brethren with a holy kiss.
27 I adjure you by the Lord that this letter be read to all the brethren.
28 The grace of our Lord Jesus Christ be with you.

5:27 We see here the beginnings of the liturgical use of the apostolic letters. Cf. Cl 4:16, where Paul prescribes an exchange of letters between churches. Why Paul should be so emphatic in entreating that all should hear the letter is not apparent; perhaps there was a tendency to break up into cliques. (Cf. 5:13)

5:28 Paul's closing benediction in his epistles always contains the same thought, but the form varies from epistle to epistle.

THE SECOND LETTER OF PAUL TO THE

THESSALONIANS

INTRODUCTION

For the history of the Thessalonian church see the Introduction to First Thessalonians. The Second Letter to the Thessalonians was evidently written not long after the first, perhaps a few months later, A. D. 50, at Corinth. According to reports which reached Paul at Corinth (we do not know how; perhaps the church wrote to Paul), the Christians of Thessalonica were still standing firm under persecution (2 Th 1:4), but false notions concerning the "coming of our Lord Jesus Christ and our assembling to meet him" (2 Th 2:1) had gained currency in the church. Those who advocated these notions apparently appealed to some alleged prophetic utterance ("spirit") or teaching or writing of Paul's to support them (2 Th 2:2). The resultant excited, almost hysterical expectation (2 Th 2:2) had led some to abandon their regular occupation and to lead an idle and disorderly life in dependence on the charity of the church (2 Th 3:6-12). Others, it would seem, struck by the high demands of the first letter (the demand that they be found "blameless" at the coming of the Lord, 1 Th 3:13; 5:23), had grown fearful and despondent concerning the coming of the Christ; for them, they felt, it would mean not deliverance but judgment and destruction.

Paul's second letter is his answer to this situation in the church at Thessalonica. It therefore sounds two notes. For those who indulge in overheated fantasies concerning the last times there are sobering words that point to the events which must necessarily precede the coming of the Christ in glory (2 Th 2:1-12). For the despondent and the fearful there is an eloquent and reassuring recognition of the new life which God has worked in them and a comforting emphasis on the certainty of their election by God (2 Th 1:3-12; 2:13-15). Paul turns the church from both excitement and despondency to that sober and responsible activity which is

the hallmark of the genuinely Christian hope: The hoping church turns from preoccupation with itself to God; the church must pray, pray "that the word of the Lord may speed on and triumph" (2 Th 3:1); and the hoping church must work — work for its living in sober industriousness and for its own health as the church of God by disciplining and correcting all whose life is a departure from the apostolic Word and example and therefore a denial of the real character of the church. (3:6-15)

Second Thessalonians is an outstanding example of the spiritual tact of the apostle, which enables him to quell the fevered excitement of a hope grown hysterical without quenching the fervor and the life-shaping force of that hope and to instill sobriety without robbing the Christian hope of its intensity, leaving both fear and faith to do their salutary work in man. His emphasis on working industry in this connection (an emphasis which he spelled out in his life too by supporting himself) is a part of the apostolic recognition of the order established by God the Creator and remains one of the great safeguards of Christian sanity over against all falsely spiritual contempt for the gifts and claims of God's created world.

The eschatological teaching is an amplification and an enrichment of what Paul has given the church in the first letter, particularly in ch. 2. The passage renews and explicates the warning of Jesus, who taught His disciples that wheat and weeds must ripen together till the harvest; it reminds the church that the satanic counterthrust is inevitable and constant wherever God's Word grows and God's reign is established, that any shallow ecclesiastical optimism which bows the knee to the idol of Progress and any churchly piety which becomes comfortably at home in this world is a denial of the revelation on which the life of the church is built.

THE SECOND LETTER OF PAUL TO THE

THESSALONIANS

1 Paul, Silvanus, and Timothy,
To the church of the Thessalonians in God our Father and the Lord Jesus Christ:
2 Grace to you and peace from God the Father and the Lord Jesus Christ.

Thanksgiving, Assurance, and Prayer

1:3-12

3 We are bound to give thanks to God always for you, brethren, as is fitting, because your faith is growing abundantly, and the love of every one of you for one another is increasing. 4 Therefore we ourselves boast of you in the churches of God for your steadfastness and faith in all your persecutions and in the afflictions which you are enduring.

5 This is evidence of the righteous judgment of God, that you may be made worthy of the kingdom of God, for which you are suffering—6 since indeed God deems it just to repay with affliction those who afflict you, 7 and to grant rest with us to you who are afflicted, when the Lord Jesus is revealed from heaven with his mighty angels in flaming fire, 8 inflicting vengeance upon those who do not know God and upon those who do not obey the gospel of our Lord Jesus. 9 They shall suffer the punishment of eternal destruction and exclusion from the presence of the Lord and from the glory of his might, 10 when he comes on that day to be glorified in his saints, and to be marveled at in all who have believed, because our testimony to you was believed. 11 To this end we always pray for you, that our God may make you worthy of his call, and may fulfil every good resolve and work of faith by his power, 12 so that the name of our Lord Jesus may be glorified in you, and you in him, according to the grace of our God and the Lord Jesus Christ.

Two Admonitions Concerning the Day of the Lord

2:1-17

BE NOT QUICKLY SHAKEN IN MIND (2:1-12)

2 Now concerning the coming of our Lord Jesus Christ and our assembling to meet him, we beg you, brethren, 2 not to be quickly shaken in mind or excited, either

1:3-12 Paul gives thanks for the ever-increasing faith and love of the Thessalonians and for their steadfastness under persecution (3-4). The fidelity and righteousness of God, he assures them, make their present suffering His pledge that they shall participate in the final deliverance, when those who do not obey the Gospel and oppress the church shall perish in the judgment of the Lord Jesus (5-10). Paul prays that God, who has called them, may in His grace and power foster and make fruitful the faith which His call has created, to the glory of their Lord, who shares His glory with them. (11-12)

1:5 *Evidence* or "a clean omen" (cf. Ph 1:28), *of the* (future) *righteous judgment.*

Made worthy of the kingdom. For suffering as

God's gracious discipline to prepare His own for the glory of the Kingdom cf. Ro 5:2-5; 8:17-18, 28; 2 Co 4:17.

1:7 *Grant rest with us.* Paul too is suffering (cf. 3:2) and can therefore speak credibly concerning their suffering.

2:1-12 Paul speaks from a pastoral concern. Some utterance of his concerning the imminent character of the coming of the Day of the Lord (cf. 1 Th 5:1-3) had been misinterpreted to mean the Day of the Lord had already come, with the result that the responsible sobriety of Christian hope (1 Th 5:8) had given way to hysterical excitement and irresponsible idleness (cf. 3:11). His words are intended to restore the hope of the church to health and vigor (1-2). What he has to

by spirit or by word, or by letter purporting to be from us, to the effect that the day of the Lord has come. ³ Let no one deceive you in any way; for that day will not come, unless the rebellion comes first, and the man of lawlessness*a* is revealed, the son of perdition, ⁴ who opposes and exalts himself against every so-called god or object of

a Other ancient authorities read *sin*

say concerning the great apostasy (rebellion) and the revelation of the man of lawlessness as signs of the coming of the Day of the Lord is no novelty but a repetition of what he had taught during his ministry in Thessalonica (5), a part of the basic instruction which bade his converts "wait for" the coming of God's "Son from heaven" (1 Th 1:10). That instruction, as Paul himself asserted (1 Co 15:11), was the common stock of all apostolic preaching, the proclamation of Christ in His significance "in accordance with the scriptures" (1 Co 15:3-4). The OT speaks of a great counterthrust to the kingdom of God in the last days, a demonic counterkingdom concentrated and incarnated in a historical figure (cf. Eze 38–39); Daniel sees in Antiochus Epiphanes IV, the Seleucid king who sought to stamp out Israel's worship of the God of her fathers and sparked the Maccabean revolt, one such incarnation (Dn 7: 23-27; 8:23-25; 11:36-37; cf. 9:27; 12:11). The warning issued by Daniel lived on in Jewry, and the expectation of the counter-Messiah, or Antichrist, was very much alive in Israel in the time between the Testaments. Jesus' parable of the weeds and the wheat takes up this OT expectation of a diabolical counterkingdom which appears in religious guise, hard to distinguish (in its beginnings) from the kingdom of God (Mt 13:24-30, 36-43). And Jesus speaks more explicitly in His discourse on last things of false Christs who will come in His name with marvelous manifestations of power to deceive His elect (Mt 24:5, 23-24). He employs the language of Daniel (Dn 9:27; 11:31; 12:11) to warn His disciples of "the desolating sacrilege" whose shadow shall fall across "the holy place" and empty it of worshipers (Mt 24:15). It was of this aspect of the "word of the Lord" that Paul had spoken and now speaks, as of something familiar to his readers, as John does in 1 Jn 2:18, 4:3. His speech is therefore succinct and allusive, for us somewhat "hard to understand." (2 Ptr 3:16)

Paul first speaks (3-8) of the sequence of the terrible events which must precede the coming of the Day of the Lord. There will be a great *rebellion* headed by and concentrated in a figure who is called *the man of lawlessness*, one who rebels so radically against God that he deifies himself and therefore dooms himself (*son of perdition*, 3). The great counterthrust works in hiddenness and secrecy at first, as *the mystery of lawlessness*; and God's merciful governance of history will raise up a power and a person to restrain it (*what is restraining*, 6; *who now restrains*, 7). But the hour will come when *the lawless one will be revealed* (8), to work openly and freely — and to be judged and destroyed. (8)

Paul then dwells on the satanic character of the lawless one (9-12). First, his great weapon is the satanic lie (cf. Jn 8:44); the Antichrist is

pseudo-Christ, a satanic perversion of the Christ of God: he has a *coming* (9), to imitate and oppose the *coming* of Christ (8); *signs and wonders* (9), to imitate and oppose the Christ "attested . . . by God with mighty works and wonders and signs" (Acts 2:22); a *mystery of lawlessness* (7) to imitate the "mystery of Christ" (Eph 3:4; Cl 4:3); a potent and persuasive lie (*pretended signs*, 9; *wicked deception*, 10; *strong delusions . . . what is false*, 11), to imitate and oppose the *truth* (10, 12) of the Gospel of Christ. Second, like all the workings and incarnations of Satan, *the man of lawlessness* cannot escape the sovereign control of God. There is no uneasy balance of power between the satanic and the divine; the man of lawlessness must, unwittingly and unwillingly, serve God's purposes. Through him God executes His judgment, that fearful judgment which delivers up men who will not love the truth to the lie which they desire. Only those become victims of the potent lie who "suppress the truth" (Ro 1:18) and so invoke the wrath of God.

Just wherein Paul saw the first workings of the mystery of lawlessness we cannot say; perhaps it was the deification of the Roman emperor as it had manifested itself in Caligula (A. D. 37–41). Nor do we know just what or whom he had in mind when he spoke of a restraint and a restrainer: perhaps it was the benign power of Roman law and order which made seas and roads safe for the bearers of the Gospel and permitted the Word of the Lord to "speed on and triumph" (3:1). Nor do we know how far he was permitted to look into the future toward the final historical manifestation of the mystery of lawlessness and its judgment. Paul wrote, prophetically, to sober men's hope and to alert men to the realities of the history in which they live. The men of the Lutheran Reformation responded responsibly to that alert when they looked upon the papacy and saw there the marks of the man of lawlessness. A responsible church is called on to do in this our day what they did, with faith and fear, in theirs.

2:2 By spirit, an utterance inspired by the Holy Spirit. Perhaps someone with the gift of prophecy interpreted Paul's preaching in a sense not intended by him; if so, Paul is calling on the church to "test" the prophetic utterance. Cf. 1 Th 5:21 and the note there.

Letter purporting to be from us. Cf. 3:17. Perhaps a forged letter is meant. But Paul may be simply warding off a misinterpretation of his first letter.

2:3 Son of perdition, doomed to perish. For the idiom "son of," as indicating a man's nature and destiny, cf. 1 Th 5:5; Eph 2:2; and the notes on those passages.

2:4 Temple of God, the church (cf. 1 Co 3:16-17; Eph 2:21), where God is known and worshiped. The man of lawlessness is usurper.

worship, so that he takes his seat in the temple of God, proclaiming himself to be God. [5] Do you not remember that when I was still with you I told you this? [6]And you know what is restraining him now so that he may be revealed in his time. [7] For the mystery of lawlessness is already at work; only he who now restrains it will do so until he is out of the way. [8]And then the lawless one will be revealed, and the Lord Jesus will slay him with the breath of his mouth and destroy him by his appearing and his coming. [9] The coming of the lawless one by the activity of Satan will be with all power and with pretended signs and wonders, [10] and with all wicked deception for those who are to perish, because they refused to love the truth and so be saved. [11] Therefore God sends upon them a strong delusion, to make them believe what is false, [12] so that all may be condemned who did not believe the truth but had pleasure in unrighteousness.

STAND FIRM (2:13-17)

13 But we are bound to give thanks to God always for you, brethren beloved by the Lord, because God chose you from the beginning[b] to be saved, through sanctification by the Spirit[c] and belief in the truth. [14] To this he called you through our gospel, so that you may obtain the glory of our Lord Jesus Christ. [15] So then, brethren, stand firm and hold to the traditions which you were taught by us, either by word of mouth or by letter.

16 Now may our Lord Jesus Christ himself, and God our Father, who loved us and gave us eternal comfort and good hope through grace, [17] comfort your hearts and establish them in every good work and word.

Exhortations to Intercession and Discipline

3:1-15

3 Finally, brethren, pray for us, that the word of the Lord may speed on and triumph, as it did among you, [2] and that we may be delivered from wicked and evil men; for not all have faith. [3] But the Lord is faithful; he will strengthen you and guard you from evil.[d] [4]And we have confidence in the Lord about you, that you are doing and will do the things which we command. [5] May the Lord direct your hearts to the love of God and to the steadfastness of Christ.

6 Now we command you, brethren, in the name of our Lord Jesus Christ, that you keep away from any brother who is living in idleness and not in accord with the tradition that you received from us. [7] For you yourselves know how you ought to imitate us; we were not idle when we were with you, [8] we did not eat any one's bread without paying, but with toil and labor we worked night and day, that we might not burden any of you. [9] It was not because we have not that right, but to give you in our conduct

[b] Other ancient authorities read *as the first converts*   [c] Or *of spirit*   [d] Or *the evil one*

2:8 *Slay him with the breath of his mouth.* Cf. Is 11:4.

2:10, 12, 13 *Truth,* the Gospel. (Cf. Gl 2:5, 14; Eph. 1:13; Cl 1:5)

2:12 *Truth . . . unrighteousness.* Cf. Ro 2:8.

2:13-17 The Antichrist and the counterkingdom cannot shake or make questionable the sovereign reign of the triune God; to Him Paul gives thanks for His gracious work in the Thessalonian believers, past (*chose,* 13; *called,* 14), present (*sanctification . . . belief in the truth,* 13), and future (*to be saved,* 13; *obtain the glory,* 14). In the presence of His gracious majesty Paul can bid his readers *stand firm* in the truth which he has transmitted to them (15). With Him Paul intercedes, with the Giver of *eternal comfort and good hope,* the God of *love* and *grace,* to keep His church in Thessalonica strong in heart and steadfast *in every good work and word.* (16-17)

2:15 *Traditions.* For the Gospel (and instruction for conduct derived from it) as *tradition,* received from the Lord and delivered or transmitted to others, cf. 1 Co 11:2, 23; 15:3; 2 Th 3:6; cf. Heb 2:3.

2:16-17 Unlike the prayer in 1 Th 3:11-13, this one contains no request that Paul may be enabled to return to Thessalonica. Paul had meanwhile received the vision which bade him remain in Corinth. (Acts 18:9-11)

3:1-15 Paul turns the mind of the church from overexcited, idle hope to the work of the apostolic church; he asks for the church's intercessions on his behalf, now that his work is opposed and threatened by *wicked and evil men;* assures the church once more of the aid and protection of their *faithful Lord* and of his, Paul's, confidence in their obedience; and implores for them the gift of love and steadfast hope. (1-5)

A last *command* deals with the disciplining of

an example to imitate. [10] For even when we were with you, we gave you this command: If any one will not work, let him not eat. [11] For we hear that some of you are living in idleness, mere busybodies, not doing any work. [12] Now such persons we command and exhort in the Lord Jesus Christ to do their work in quietness and to earn their own living. [13] Brethren, do not be weary in well-doing.

14 If any one refuses to obey what we say in this letter, note that man, and have nothing to do with him, that he may be ashamed. [15] Do not look on him as an enemy, but warn him as a brother.

CONCLUSION: BENEDICTION AND AUTOGRAPH GREETING (3:16-18)

16 Now may the Lord of peace himself give you peace at all times in all ways. The Lord be with you all.

17 I, Paul, write this greeting with my own hand. This is the mark in every letter of mine; it is the way I write. [18] The grace of our Lord Jesus Christ be with you all.

brethren who disobey the apostolic *tradition* and ignore the apostle's own *example* by living lives of *idleness* at the expense of others. The church's treatment of them is to remind them, forcefully yet fraternally, that they are by their disobedience excluding themselves from the fellowship which the apostolic Word has created. (6-15)

3:16-18 Paul dictated his letters (cf. Ro 16:22) and added a final greeting in his own handwriting (1 Co 16:21; Gl 6:11). This autograph conclusion is to serve as a mark of identification should there by any doubt about the genuineness of a letter. (Cf. 2:2)

The Pastoral Letters

INTRODUCTION

The Name "Pastoral"

The name "Pastoral" has been applied since the 18th century to the letters addressed to Timothy and Titus; the title had been applied to First Timothy alone as early as the 13th century by Thomas Aquinas. This designation marks the letters as directed to "pastors" or shepherds of the church and as dealing with the office of the pastor. It is more properly applied to First Timothy and to the Letter to Titus than to Second Timothy. Second Timothy has pastoral elements in it, but is basically a personal letter and in a class by itself. First Timothy and Titus are official letters, addressed not only to the recipient in each case but also to the churches to which these men were being sent, and they cover the whole range of church life: offices in the church, the worship life of the church, the care of souls, and especially the combating of error which threatens the health of the church. The official character of the letters is seen in their form also; the usual Pauline thanksgiving at the beginning is replaced by words which indicate that the content of the letter is a repetition in writing of oral instructions already given—a common feature in official letters (1 Ti 1:3; Tts 1:5). The personal communications usually found at the close of Pauline letters are either absent entirely, as in the Letters to Timothy, or kept extremely brief, as in the Letter to Titus. The style of the letters likewise reflects this "official" character: We have here terse and pointed directions delivered with apostolic authority; the doctrinal background and basis of the directions are given in pointed and pregnant formulations designed to be readily grasped and remembered; some of them are "sure sayings," probably already familiar to the churches. (1 Ti 1:15; 3:1; 4:9; Tts 3:8)

Historical Background of the Pastoral Letters

Since we do not have the help of the Book of Acts for the period in which the writing of the Pastoral Letters falls and must reconstruct the history of this period entirely from hints given in the letters themselves, the order of events must remain somewhat doubtful; even an approximate dating of them is difficult. The following is a probable reconstruction of the course of events:

1. That Paul was released at the end of the 2-year imprisonment recorded in Acts 28:30 (A. D. 61) seems certain; there is really no evidence at all that his first Roman imprisonment ended in martyrdom. Paul apparently did not remain long in Rome after his release; the jealousies and frictions to which he alludes in Philippians (Ph 1:15-17) would make it advisable for him to leave soon.

2. Whether Paul ever carried out his intention of going to Spain (Ro 15:28) must remain doubtful. The Captivity Letters say nothing of an anticipated Spanish voyage, and the Pastoral Letters likewise say nothing of that undertaking. Neither did the Spanish church preserve any tradition which attributed its origin to the missionary work of Paul. On the other hand, Paul's journey to Spain is attested by early and reliable Roman sources like the Letter of Clement of Rome to the Corinthians (I, vv. 5-7), written within a generation after the events (A. D. 96), and the Muratorian Canon (about A. D. 175). The apocryphal Acts of Peter (written about A. D. 200) also refers to the Spanish voyage of Paul; and no one in antiquity seems to have questioned it. If Paul did make the voyage, it was probably soon after his release from imprisonment A. D. 61.

3. Paul intended to revisit his former mission fields in Asia and Macedonia (Phmn 22; Ph 2:24); the Pastoral Letters indicate that he carried out this intention. He returned to the East by way of Crete, where he remained for a time as missionary. He left Titus in charge of the task of consolidating the church there when he himself proceeded eastward. (Tts 1:5)

4. Paul may have touched at Ephesus; if he did, he could not have remained there long. The instructions which he gave Timothy, whom he left in charge at Ephesus, indicate that much work still remained to be done there. (1 Ti 1:3)

5. Paul himself proceeded from Ephesus to Macedonia, and from there he wrote First Timothy. (1 Ti 1:3)

6. Paul wrote the Letter to Titus either from Macedonia just before his departure for Nicopolis or during the journey to Nicopolis, where he planned to spend the winter. There were several prominent cities called Nicopolis; the one referred to in the Letter to Titus is probably Nicopolis in Epirus. Titus was to join Paul in Nicopolis when relieved in Crete by Artemas or Tychicus. (Tts 3:12)

7. During the interval between the writing of the Letter to Titus and Second Timothy Paul visited Troas, Corinth, and Miletus. (2 Ti 4:13, 20)

8. Paul was again arrested (whether in the East or at Rome can hardly be made out) and imprisoned at Rome. This time his imprisonment was much more severe than A. D. 59—61, and he saw no hope of an acquittal. In Second Timothy he summons his "beloved child" to him once more before the end.

9. This second imprisonment in Rome ended in the martyrdom of Paul. It took place under Nero, certainly, but hardly during the great Neronian persecution A. D. 64. Paul would hardly have summoned Timothy, the man to whom he looked for the faithful continuation of his work, to a certain death in Rome; neither would it be like Paul to lament that none of the Roman Christians had stood by him at his first hearing if those Christians were at that time dying for their faith. The writing of Second Timothy and Paul's death must be dated either before the great persecution under Nero, perhaps A. D. 63, or later, perhaps even so late as A. D. 67, the last year of Nero's reign.

THE FIRST LETTER OF PAUL TO

TIMOTHY

INTRODUCTION

Paul, on his way to Macedonia, has left Timothy at Ephesus with instructions to "charge certain persons not to teach any different doctrine" (1 Ti 1:3). Paul does not describe this "different doctrine" systematically; but from his attacks on it in 1:3-7; 4:1-3, 7; 6:3-5, 20-21 and from the tenor of his instructions for the regulation of the life of the church, it is clear that Timothy must do battle with a form of "Gnosticism," an early stage of that heresy which was to become in its fully developed form the most serious threat to the church in succeeding generations. Gnosticism is not so much a system as a trend or current of thought which produced a great variety of systems, often by combining with some already existing religion. It was therefore present and active as a corrupting force long before the great Christian-Gnostic systems of the second century appeared; we have already seen one example of it in the heresy which threatened the church at Colossae.

Basic to all forms of Gnosticism is a dualistic conception of reality, that is, the view that what is spiritual, nonmaterial, is of itself good and what is material or physical is of itself bad. This view affects man's whole attitude toward the world of created things. The dreary details of Gnostic speculation on the *origin* of the material universe need not concern us here. It may suffice to note:

a. that the world is no longer viewed as God's good creation, as the Scriptures view it (that is, a world which God created, fallen with fallen man but redeemed with man and destined to be transfigured with him, Ro 8:19-22); rather, the created world is viewed as in itself alien and hostile to God because it is matter and not spirit;

b. that man's desperate predicament, his alienation from God, is no longer seen as being due to his sinful rebellion against God, but to the fact that he is entangled in the world of matter;

c. that redemption consists in being freed from the material world in which man dwells and is entangled. This liberation can come about only by knowledge (Greek, *gnosis,* hence the name of the heresy); this knowledge must be imparted to man by revelation from a higher world;

d. the mission of the Savior-God is to impart this knowledge not to all men, but to a select few who will pass it on to those who are "worthy";

e. that those who have knowledge, the "gnostics," must free themselves from the influence of matter by abstaining from certain foods and from marriage. (Sometimes the negative attitude toward things physical and material had the opposite effect and led to a supreme indifference to things physical and material, so that, for instance, the sexual life of man was considered to be morally indifferent.)

Such a trend of thought would lead inevitably to an utter distortion of all that "the glorious gospel of the blessed God" (1 Ti 1:11) proclaimed. God the Creator disappears – all the good gifts of food and drink which He gives are suspected and feared; all the salutary orders which He has established in this world (marriage, family, government) are despised and ignored. The Old Testament, which rings with glad adoration of the God who made the heavens and the earth and blesses man within the orders of this world, must either be ignored or have its obvious sense interpreted away by allegorizing "myths and endless genealogies." The Law becomes the arena of speculation and vain discussions, not the voice of God which calls the sinner to account and condemns him. In terms of this kind of thought, there can be no real incarnation of the Son of God; for how can the divine, which is spiritual, enter into union with matter, which is of itself evil? And when sin is not recognized as man's guilt, there can be no real redemption either. Where knowledge is made central in the religious life of man and self-redemption by way of ascetic exercise is made the way of salvation, there is no possibility of that pure Christian love that "issues

from a pure heart and a good conscience and sincere faith" (1 Ti 1:5). A narrow and sectarian pride takes its place (1 Ti 6:4, 20; cf. 1:3-7). Where the teaching office becomes a wordy, speculative, disputatious purveying of "knowledge" to a select coterie of initiates, it is bound to become corrupted; it appeals to the pride, selfishness, and mercenary instincts of men, and the teacher becomes that ghastly, demon-ridden caricature of the true teacher which Paul has described in 1 Ti 4:1-2.

Timothy's task will be to let the fresh and wholesome winds of "sound doctrine" into the house of God, whose air has been infected by the morbid and infectious mists of this *gnosis*. To the demonic denial of God the Creator and the rejection of His good gifts he must oppose the glorious Gospel of the blessed God "who gives life to all things" (1 Ti 6:13), the God whose every creation still has on it the mark of His primeval "Very Good!" (Gn 1:31) and is even in its fallen state "consecrated by the word of God and prayer" (1 Ti 4:5). To "godless and silly myths" he is to oppose the grateful adoration of the Creator. To the Gnostic misuse of the Law he must oppose the right and lawful use and let the sinner hear the fearful verdict of God in order that he may give ear to God's acquittal in His Gospel. (1:8-11)

To the rarefied and unreal Christ of Gnostic speculation he must oppose "the *man* Christ Jesus" (1 Ti 2:5), the Christ Jesus who really entered into history under Pontius Pilate (1 Ti 6:13) and died a real death on the cross for the sins of all men (1 Ti 2:6). He must present this Christ as the whole content of the truth which the church upholds and guards, the mystery of God "manifested *in the flesh*" (1 Ti 3:16). To Gnostic self-redemption by means of knowledge and ascetic self-manipulation he must oppose redemption as the sole act of the Christ who came into the world, not to impart higher knowledge but "to save sinners" (1 Ti 1:15), the Christ "who gave Himself as a ransom for all" (1 Ti 2:6). To Gnostic exclusiveness he must oppose the all-embracing grace of God, and to their narrow sectarian pride he must oppose the Gospel of universal grace (1 Ti 2:4) and thus make of the church a church which can pray wholeheartedly for *all* men (1 Ti 2:1), a church which lives in the "love that issues from a pure heart and a good conscience and sincere faith." (1 Ti 1:5)

To the imposing picture of the Gnostic teachers, these brilliant, speculative, disputatious, and mercenary men, he must oppose the picture of the true teacher. He must, first of all, himself *be* that picture; he dare not let himself be drawn down to the level of his opponents and fight demonic fire with fire; he must do battle, "holding faith and a good conscience" (1 Ti 1:19); he must, as a good minister of Jesus Christ, not allow himself to be infected by what he opposes but must continue to be "nourished on the words of faith" (not knowledge) "and of the good doctrine" which he has followed hitherto. He must train himself, athlete-like, in godliness (1 Ti 4:6-7). Thus he will be able to fight the good fight of faith as a "man of God," standing in the succession of Moses and the prophets, singly devoted to God's cause (1 Ti 6:11-12; cf. 6:3-10), laying hold even now of that eternal life which shall be his in fullness at the appearing of the Lord Jesus Christ (1 Ti 6:11-15). He must himself be all that the Gnostic teachers are not; and he is to see to it that the men who oversee the church's life and administer the church's charity, the bishops and deacons, are men of like character. They need not be brilliant men; they must be good men. It is enough if a bishop be "an apt teacher" (1 Ti 3:2); he need not be a brilliant speaker or a captivating personality. The qualifications which Paul sets up for bishops and deacons are singularly sober and down to earth; but the moral standards which he sets up for them are awesomely high (1 Ti 3:1-13). Paul wants men whom the grace of God has "trained," as he puts it in his Letter to Titus (2:11-12), seasoned, selfless, wise, and gracious men whose faith has borne fruit in their homes, in their marital fidelity, and in the training of their children. (1 Ti 3:2, 4, 12)

Timothy had a great piece of work assigned to him. And he was a good man for the task. He was both Jew and Greek (Acts 16:1). He had lived with the Old Testament from childhood (2 Ti 3:15). Prophetic voices had assigned him to this "good warfare" (1 Ti 1:18). God had given him the requisite gifts for it (1 Ti 4:14), and his whole history had been one that fostered those gifts. He had been Paul's almost constant companion for a dozen years (Acts 16:1 ff.). The apostolic "pattern of sound words" (2 Ti 1:13) had become a part of his makeup, and the apostolic example had been constantly before him (2 Ti 3:10, 11, 14). Paul had employed him as his emissary before this, though never for

so extended and difficult a mission as this one. When Paul was prevented from returning to Thessalonica, he sent Timothy to the young and troubled church to establish the believers in their faith and to exhort them (1 Th 3:1-2). He had sent Timothy to Corinth during that troubled period when the Corinthians were becoming drunk on the heady wine of the new teaching, to remind them of the apostle's "ways in Christ" (1 Co 4:17; 16:10). He had sent him to Philippi from Rome during the time of his imprisonment and had commended him to the Philippians with the finest tribute that can be paid to a servant of God in the Gospel: "I have no one like him, who will be genuinely anxious for your welfare. They all look after their own interests, not those of Jesus Christ. But Timothy's worth you know, how as a son with a father he has served with me in the gospel." (Ph 2:20-22)

If Paul was a fond father to Timothy, he was not a blind one. He knew his beloved child's weaknesses: Timothy was still young and apparently conscious of it as a handicap (1 Ti 4:12). He was inclined to be timid (cf. 1 Co 16:10-11; 2 Ti 1:7). Besides, his health was not of the best; his stomach troubled him, an ailment not uncommon among sensitive and conscientious young men of God. (1 Ti 5:23)

Therefore Paul writes Timothy a letter which sums up once more the oral instructions already given him (1 Ti 1:3). This letter will give his work the sanction and authority of Paul, "an apostle of Christ Jesus by command of God our Savior and of Christ Jesus our hope" (1 Ti 1:1). Paul is in effect telling the church of Ephesus what he had once told the Corinthians: "He is doing the work of the Lord, as I am. So let no one despise him." (1 Co 16:10-11)

TIMOTHY

SALUTATION (1:1-2)

1 Paul, an apostle of Christ Jesus by command of God our Savior and of Christ Jesus our hope,

2 To Timothy, my true child in the faith:

Grace, mercy, and peace from God the Father and Christ Jesus our Lord.

The Gnostic Heresy Corrupts the Doctrine of the Church

1:3 – 3:16

THE INDICTMENT (1:3-7)

3 As I urged you when I was going to Macedonia, remain at Eph'e·sus that you may charge certain persons not to teach any different doctrine, 4 nor to occupy themselves with myths and endless genealogies which promote speculations rather than the divine training[a] that is in faith; 5 whereas the aim of our charge is love that issues from a pure heart and a good conscience and sincere faith. 6 Certain persons by swerving from these have wandered away into vain discussion, 7 desiring to be teachers of the law, without understanding either what they are saying or the things about which they make assertions.

THE TRUE PROCLAMATION OF LAW AND GOSPEL (1:8-20)

8 Now we know that the law is good, if any one uses it lawfully, 9 understanding this, that the law is not laid down for the just but for the lawless and disobedient, for

a Or *stewardship*, or *order*

1:1-2 *An apostle.* Paul need not present his apostolic credentials to Timothy, his *true child in the faith,* of course; but the letter is an official one intended also for the church at Ephesus and is to undergird the authority of Timothy. See the Introduction and the note on 6:21.

1:3 ff. The letter falls into three major sections (I. 1:3 – 3:16; II. 4:1 – 6:2; III. 6:3-21). Each section is introduced by an indictment of the Gnostic heresy (1:3-7; 4:1-5; 6:3-10), which is followed by positive instruction on how the evil described in the indictment is to be combated and overcome.

1:3 – 3:16 Paul does not give a detailed description of the *different doctrine;* but he indicates clearly what its tendency is (which makes his indictment all the more valuable for the church of later days in the necessary task of theological self-examination and self-criticism). The doctrine which Timothy is to combat is, first, speculative, a human search for knowledge, not God's revelation which enters into and shapes men's lives (*training*) and is received and progressively appropriated *in faith,* in a grateful and obedient receiving (1:4). It is, second, loquacious and disputations, a matter of *vain discussion* (6) which leads nowhere and effects nothing worthwhile, whereas the *charge* (5) received by Paul and by all proclaimers of the Gospel aims at solid, practical

goals: *faith* in a God who saves and forgives, the *good conscience* of the forgiven man, the *pure heart* of unalloyed devotion which divine forgiveness can create in man, the *love* which grows on the soil of sincere faith and the good conscience and pure heart which faith gives a man (5). The *different doctrine* is, third, a "different gospel" (cf. Gl 1:6; 2 Co 11:4) and therefore no gospel at all (Gl 1:7); its proponents desire to be *teachers of the law* (7) and want to effect by prohibitions and prescriptions (cf. 4:3; Tts 1:14) what only *the glorious gospel of the blessed God* (11) can create. Paul's indictment (1:3-7) makes clear that there can be no compromise with this different doctrine, which corrupts both Law and Gospel; Timothy must *wage the good warfare* (1:18) of God against it. He will do so by proclaiming the Law as law (1:8-11) and by proclaiming the Gospel with which the apostle has been entrusted, the Gospel of the sheer overflowing grace of our Lord which Paul knows from profoundest personal experience (1:11-17), the Gospel which he commits to Timothy as to one whom the Spirit of God has marked out for this ministry (1:18-20). But since the Gospel is not a theory but a power which produces a life to be lived, Timothy's good warfare will also be concerned with the worship of the church (2:1-15) and with its organization (3:1-13). The Gospel,

the ungodly and sinners, for the unholy and profane, for murderers of fathers and murderers of mothers, for manslayers, [10] immoral persons, sodomites, kidnapers, liars, perjurers, and whatever else is contrary to sound doctrine, [11] in accordance with the glorious gospel of the blessed God with which I have been entrusted.

12 I thank him who has given me strength for this, Christ Jesus our Lord, because he judged me faithful by appointing me to his service, [13] though I formerly blasphemed and persecuted and insulted him; but I received mercy because I had acted ignorantly in unbelief, [14] and the grace of our Lord overflowed for me with the faith and love that are in Christ Jesus. [15] The saying is sure and worthy of full acceptance, that Christ Jesus came into the world to save sinners. And I am the foremost of sinners; [16] but I received mercy for this reason, that in me, as the foremost, Jesus Christ might display his perfect patience for an example to those who were to believe in him for eternal life. [17] To the King of ages, immortal, invisible, the only God, be honor and glory for ever and ever.[b] Amen.

18 This charge I commit to you, Timothy, my son, in accordance with the prophetic utterances which pointed to you, that inspired by them you may wage the good warfare, [19] holding faith and a good conscience. By rejecting conscience, certain persons have made shipwreck of their faith, [20] among them Hy·me·nae′us and Alexander, whom I have delivered to Satan that they may learn not to blaspheme.

THE DIVINE TRAINING THAT IS IN FAITH: WORSHIP (2:1-15)

2 First of all, then, I urge that supplications, prayers, intercessions, and thanksgivings be made for all men, [2] for kings and all who are in high positions, that we

[b] Greek *to the ages of ages*

as the *divine training that is in faith* (1:4), is to produce and form a church which is in its whole life and all its manifestations the *pillar and bulwark of the truth* (3:15), the place where and the means through which there is exhibited for all men to see the creative grace of her incarnate and exalted Lord. (3:16)

1:3-7 See the note on 1:3—3:16 above.

1:4 *Myths and endless genealogies.* Just what these were is impossible to say. Some think of fanciful Judaic elaborations on the Old Testament, others of Gnostic speculations. The adjective *endless* is an indication of the apostle's low opinion of this kind of theological activity, an opinion that comes out plainly in the words "speculations" (4) and "vain discussion." (6)

1:5 *Our charge,* the obligation to proclaim the Gospel, laid on Paul (11) and on Timothy (18), and to be enjoined upon those teaching a different doctrine. (3)

1:7 *Teachers of the law.* Cf. 4:1-3; Tts 1:14.

1:8-20 Timothy is to combat and overcome the threatening corruption of doctrine by recognizing and proclaiming the true function of the Law, by using the Law *lawfully,* in accordance with its own intent (of opposing and exposing sin and condemning the sinner) and in the light of the *glorious gospel of the blessed God* (8-11), by which God makes men *just,* clear of the compulsion and condemnation of the Law (8). Timothy is to proclaim the Gospel with which Paul has been *entrusted* (11) as the antidote to the corrupted gospel of the false teachers, for Paul's own apostolate is the clearest Gospel of divine grace written into the life of undeserving man (12-17). Timothy can take up *the good warfare* (18) confidently, for God has taken the initiative in his ministry as in

Paul's; His Spirit moved men to the *prophetic utterances* which *pointed* to him for this mission (18). He has cause for fear only if he ceases to believe the Gospel which he proclaims or violates his *conscience* by falsifying the Gospel and so *making shipwreck of* his *faith,* as *Hymenaeus and Alexander* have done. (18-20)

1:8 *We know,* etc. Cf. Ro 7:12, 16.

1:9-10 The list of transgressors follows the order of the Decalog, with six instances for the first table of the Law and eight for the second table. Paul gives extreme cases of transgression (e. g., *murderers of fathers* for the Fourth Commandment) to emphasize the negative character of the Law.

1:12-17 Cf. 1 Co 15:9; Gl 1:15; Eph 3:7-8.

1:13 *I had acted ignorantly.* This did not make him guiltless, but he had not placed himself outside the sphere of Jesus' prayer from the cross (Lk 23:34) by deliberate rejection of known and acknowledged truth, as the false teachers are doing, 4:1-2; 6:5. (Cf. Heb 6:4-8; 10:26-31)

1:18 *Prophetic utterances which pointed.* Cf. Acts 13:1-3 for a similar operation of the Spirit in prophecy.

Warfare. Cf. 1 Co 9:7; 2 Ti 2:3-4.

1:20 *Hymenaeus.* Cf. 2 Ti 2:17-18. *Alexander* may be identical with the Alexander mentioned in 2 Ti 4:14-15.

Delivered to Satan, for punishment (cf. Job 2:6). Exclusion from the church, excommunication, is meant, 1 Co 5:3-5, 13. Perhaps the imposing of bodily suffering is also implied. (1 Co 5:5, "destruction of the flesh"; Acts 13:11)

2:1-15 Timothy is to oppose and overcome the corrupting influence of the false teaching by so ordering the worship of the church that its prayers

may lead a quiet and peaceable life, godly and respectful in every way. ³ This is good, and it is acceptable in the sight of God our Savior, ⁴ who desires all men to be saved and to come to the knowledge of the truth. ⁵ For there is one God, and there is one mediator between God and men, the man Christ Jesus, ⁶ who gave himself as a ransom for all, the testimony to which was borne at the proper time. ⁷ For this I was appointed a preacher and apostle (I am telling the truth, I am not lying), a teacher of the Gentiles in faith and truth.

8 I desire then that in every place the men should pray, lifting holy hands without anger or quarreling; ⁹ also that women should adorn themselves modestly and sensibly in seemly apparel, not with braided hair or gold or pearls or costly attire ¹⁰ but by good deeds, as befits women who profess religion. ¹¹ Let a woman learn in silence with all submissiveness. ¹² I permit no woman to teach or to have authority over men; she is to keep silent. ¹³ For Adam was formed first, then Eve; ¹⁴ and Adam was not deceived, but the woman was deceived and became a transgressor. ¹⁵ Yet woman will be saved through bearing children,ᶜ if she continuesᵈ in faith and love and holiness, with modesty.

ᶜ Or *by the birth of the child*   ᵈ Greek *they continue*

---

may be an expression of the all-embracing grace of God proclaimed in the Gospel and a recognition of government as a salutary functioning of the law of God (1-7). Prayers are to be said in the peaceable and forgiving spirit which the one Mediator between God and man has enjoined in the Fifth Petition (8). The conduct and demeanor of the worshipers is to be a recognition of the sanctity of the position which the Creator has assigned to woman. (9-15)

2:1 *First of all.* Worship is of supreme importance as the bridge between doctrine and action, the means whereby all life is hallowed so as to become worship. (Cf. Ro 12:1)

All occurs six times in six verses as an emphasis on the universality of the Gospel and as a protest against the sectarian exclusiveness of the Gnostic heresy, which produced an intellectual in-group. The church faces and loves the world.

2:2 *For kings.* Cf. Jer 29:7; 1 Ptr 2:13-17.

2:5 *One mediator.* One only, Christ Jesus, not Moses, not any of the intermediate beings which Gnostic speculation interposed between God and man. Jesus alone has mediated the whole grace of God's new and perfect covenant for all. (Cf. Heb 8:6; 9:15; 12:24)

The man. Cf. Ro 5:12-19; 1 Co 15:21-22, 45-49.

2:6 A clear echo of Jesus' word on His life and death as a vicarious redemption for "many." Paul changes the Hebraic "many" of Mt 20:28 and Mk 10:45 into "all" for Greek ears, since in Hebrew usage "many" can be used for "all." (Cf. Ro 5:18 with 19, where "all" and "many" are used interchangeably.)

The testimony . . . borne. The redeeming act in Christ and the proclamation of it to men are but two phases, or aspects, of one saving act of God (cf. 2 Co 5:18-19; Eph 1:7-9; 2:13-16 with 17). In 2 Ti 1:10 and Tts 1:2-3 the second phase serves as a shorthand designation for the whole.

2:7 *I am not lying.* Evidently Paul's apostolic authority was being questioned in Ephesus, as it had been earlier, for example, in Galatia. (Cf. Gl 1—2)

2:8 *Lifting holy hands.* The uplifted hand (palm upward) was the common gesture of prayer in antiquity.

Without anger or quarreling. Cf. Mt 6:12; Mk 11:25.

2:9-15 Paul had special occasion to speak of woman's place in the worship of the church; the false teachers were introducing ascetic rigors regarding food and marriage (4:3). Nothing less than the goodness of God's good creation, including marriage, was at stake. Paul is fighting to preserve the divine order which honors and fosters both man and woman in their individuality, as man, as woman. He points first to creation (13) and the Creator's intention to create woman as "a helper fit" for man (Gn 2:18). Then he points to the Fall, where the very qualities that make woman glorious as "a helper fit" for man (her pliability and openness to suggestion) proved her downfall (Gn 3:1-6). These two facts support the statement which denies the office of public teaching with its exercise of *authority over men* to woman (12). Paul finally (15) points to the sphere where woman's powers and gifts have full and free scope, the rearing of children (one which modern psychology with its discovery of the crucial importance of the first five years of a man's life has exalted); there she may walk in faith, love, and modest holiness toward the salvation which she shares equally with man (cf. Gl 3:28). Whoever sees in this an indication of "male superiority" or "female inferiority" has not yet learned to bow in adoration before the Creator who has made all things well and is certainly not thinking in terms of "the glorious gospel of the blessed God." (1:11)

2:15 *Will be saved through bearing children.* The Greek preposition here translated *through* is a flexible one; it can indicate not only mediation or agency but also attendant circumstances; Paul uses the same preposition in 2 Co 2:4 to say that he wrote a letter with tears, weeping as he wrote. This seems the more natural sense here too; woman will find salvation by *faith* in the sphere of activity assigned to her by her Creator. The

THE DIVINE TRAINING THAT IS IN FAITH: ORGANIZATION (3:1-16)

3   The saying is sure: If any one aspires to the office of bishop, he desires a noble task. [2] Now a bishop must be above reproach, the husband of one wife, temperate, sensible, dignified, hospitable, an apt teacher, [3] no drunkard, not violent but gentle, not quarrelsome, and no lover of money. [4] He must manage his own household well, keeping his children submissive and respectful in every way; [5] for if a man does not know how to manage his own household, how can he care for God's church? [6] He must not be a recent convert, or he may be puffed up with conceit and fall into the condemnation of the devil;[f] [7] moreover he must be well thought of by outsiders, or he may fall into reproach and the snare of the devil.[f]

[8] Deacons likewise must be serious, not double-tongued, not addicted to much wine, not greedy for gain; [9] they must hold the mystery of the faith with a clear conscience. [10] And let them also be tested first; then if they prove themselves blameless let them serve as deacons. [11] The women likewise must be serious, no slanderers, but temperate, faithful in all things. [12] Let deacons be the husband of one wife, and let them manage their children and their households well; [13] for those who serve well as deacons gain a good standing for themselves and also great confidence in the faith which is in Christ Jesus.

[14] I hope to come to you soon, but I am writing these instructions to you so that, [15] if I am delayed, you may know how one ought to behave in the household of God,

[f] Or *slanderer*

---

interpretation given in RSV note *c* (*by the birth of the child,* that is, Christ) is a possible rendering of the Greek but hardly fits the context.

3:1-16 Timothy is to oppose and overcome the corrupting influence of the false teachers by providing for *bishops* and *deacons* whose conduct, example, and influence shall be a living embodiment of the fact that the church is *the pillar and bulwark of the truth,* the truth, namely, of the Gospel which proclaims Christ as the Savior of men by a real incarnation that ties Him to the *flesh,* to the *nations,* and to the *world* — not the Christ of Gnostic speculation who has no real contact with man. The true Gospel proclaims both His complete manhood and His total Godhead, His humiliation and His exaltation; He is the embodiment of the grace of God which saves man and transforms his life to one of uprightness and godliness. (Cf. Tts 2:11-14)

3:1 *Bishop* means "overseer" of a congregation; the modern "pastor" is closer to it than the sense that bishop has acquired in church language. The kind and quality of the "overseeing" implied may be gathered from the fact that Peter applies the term along with "Shepherd" to Christ Himself (1 Ptr 2:25, well translated as "Guardian" there). The overseer-shepherds derive their authority and character from the chief Shepherd. (1 Ptr 5:1-4)

3:2 *Husband of one wife.* This is aimed not at remarriage after the death of one's spouse but at concubinage and the virtual polygamy of illicit divorce.

Hospitable. The bishop would be called on to receive delegates of other churches and traveling missionaries. (3 Jn 5 ff.)

3:6 *Recent convert . . . conceit . . . condemnation of the devil.* A man still immature in faith would be particularly liable to the besetting sin of the clergy, pride; and the Accuser (Rv 12:10; Zch 3:1; cf. Lk 22:31) would be quick to bring his charge and demand punishment.

3:7 *Reproach and the snare of the devil.* A known tainted past may rise up to discredit the bishop and the community which he represents. He may be driven either to despair or to some rash and wrong action; in either case he proves easy prey to the devil.

3:8 *Deacons* (the word means "servant, one who waits on another," and is a title of honor, cf. Mt 20:26) provided for the poor and the ill in the congregation.

3:9 *The mystery of the faith,* the revealed Gospel, (cf. v. 16). Since Christian charity is care for the whole man, the deacon is not merely a "practical" functionary; he must be a man of Christian spirituality, able to apply the Gospel to man's need in the various areas of life.

3:10 *Also be tested.* Implies that bishops too underwent careful scrutiny before appointment, as 2, 4, 6, 7 imply.

3:11 *The women.* Either the wives of the deacons or, more probably, deaconesses. (Cf. Ro 16:1)

3:13 *Gain a good standing,* literally "a step," which may mean either that in doing God's work of mercy they draw closer to God and so learn to speak the Gospel ever more confidently, or that they grow in stature and influence by the faithful exercise of their office and so, matured and emboldened, advance to the office of bishop. The two interpretations are not mutually exclusive.

3:15 *One ought to behave.* The *one* is very broad, including Timothy himself (cf. 4:12), teachers (1:3-4), men and women, bishops, deacons, deaconesses in their relationship to one another and to the Father of the house in the household of God.

which is the church of the living God, the pillar and bulwark of the truth. [16] Great indeed, we confess, is the mystery of our religion:

> He[h] was manifested in the flesh,
> vindicated[i] in the Spirit,
>   seen by angels,
> preached among the nations,
> believed on in the world,
>   taken up in glory.

The Gnostic Heresy Corrupts the Life of the Church

4:1 — 6:2

THE INDICTMENT (4:1-5)

4 Now the Spirit expressly says that in later times some will depart from the faith by giving heed to deceitful spirits and doctrines of demons, [2] through the pretensions of liars whose consciences are seared, [3] who forbid marriage and enjoin abstinence from foods which God created to be received with thanksgiving by those who believe and know the truth. [4] For everything created by God is good, and nothing is to be rejected if it is received with thanksgiving; [5] for then it is consecrated by the word of God and prayer.

[h] Greek *Who;* other ancient authorities read *God;* others, *Which*   [i] Or *justified*

3:15 *Pillar and bulwark of the truth.* The properly functioning church exhibits and supports the truth by which its members live and move and have their being, the truth being nothing less than the incarnate and exalted Christ Himself. To use another Pauline image, in beholding the body of Christ, the church, men can come to know Christ.

3:16 *The mystery of our religion.* A mystery because only God can reveal it and has in these last days revealed it; for Christ ·as the mystery in person cf. Cl 1:27; 2:2. The content of the revelation is unfolded in the following six lines, probably an early Christian hymn, pithy and pointed as a message inscribed in stone, a remarkable contrast to the "endless genealogies" (1:4) and "vain discussion" (1:6) of the Gnostics. Six passive verbs describing six mighty acts of God sum up the Gospel which we know from the four gospels and Acts. The Son of God *was manifested in the flesh;* He became the Servant of God and in a human life lived God's will of atoning love for man; that Servant-life brought Him under the judgment of God and veiled His Godhead so completely that men standing by His cross could tauntingly demand that He *vindicate* Himself by descending from it. He cried out and died on the cross and left His vindication in His Father's hands. And God did vindicate Him. In the power of the invincible life of the *Spirit,* manifested at His conception (Mt 1:18, 20), His baptism (Mt 3:16), His temptation (Mt 4:1-10), in His proclamation (Lk 4:14, 18), and in His triumph over satanic powers (Mt 12:28) — in that power He rose from the dead (Ro 1:4). *Angels* beheld what no human eye could see; the angels who had hailed His birth (Lk 2:13) set a table in the wilderness for the obedient Son

(Mt 4:11), hovered over Him in legions as He walked on earth (Jn 1:51; Mt 26:53). They proclaimed God's vindication of His Son and Servant to the disciples and prepared them for their meeting with the risen Lord (Mt 28:5; Lk 24:4-7). He, the vindicated Son of God in power, sent them out to the *nations* under His command and empowered by the Spirit (Mt 28:19; Lk 24:47). There in the alienated and hostile *world* the crowning miracle took place — the nations who had been far off were brought near; they *believed* on the Christ and came into the household of God (Eph 2:19). The Christ lives and reigns; when He was *taken up* from earth, He was enthroned at the right hand of the Father, *in glory.* That is the mystery of our religion. That is why there can and must be a "household of God," a "church of the living God," on earth. That is why worship and ministry can and must be so pure and powerful. That is why Timothy and all who believe on the incarnate Lord must and can wage the good warfare for the truth.

4:1 — 6:2 The appearance of these false teachers is a first fulfillment of the Spirit's warning for the latter days. Their teaching, for all its pretensions to rigorous piety, is a demonic denial of the goodness of God's creation (4:1-5). Timothy is to oppose and overcome this corrupting influence — *take heed to yourself and to your teaching;* let his food be the sound and wholesome food of the Gospel, his exercise to *train . . . in godliness.* Thus nurtured and trained, let him perform his duties soberly, scrupulously, and strenuously, fixing his hope in the living God, using to the full the gift which God has given him, and setting an *example in speech and conduct, in love, in faith, in purity* (4:6-16). His treatment of various age groups and classes in the church is to safeguard the

TAKE HEED TO YOURSELF AND TO YOUR TEACHING (4:6-16)

6 If you put these instructions before the brethren, you will be a good minister of Christ Jesus, nourished on the words of the faith and of the good doctrine which you have followed. 7 Have nothing to do with godless and silly myths. Train yourself in godliness; 8 for while bodily training is of some value, godliness is of value in every way, as it holds promise for the present life and also for the life to come. 9 The saying is sure and worthy of full acceptance. 10 For to this end we toil and strive,*j* because we have our hope set on the living God, who is the Savior of all men, especially of those who believe.

11 Command and teach these things. 12 Let no one despise your youth, but set the believers an example in speech and conduct, in love, in faith, in purity. 13 Till I come, attend to the public reading of scripture, to preaching, to teaching. 14 Do not neglect the gift you have, which was given you by prophetic utterance when the council of elders laid their hands upon you. 15 Practice these duties, devote yourself to them, so that all may see your progress. 16 Take heed to yourself and to your teaching; hold to that, for by so doing you will save both yourself and your hearers.

HOW ONE OUGHT TO BEHAVE IN THE HOUSEHOLD OF GOD (5:1 – 6:2)

5 Do not rebuke an older man but exhort him as you would a father; treat younger men like brothers, 2 older women like mothers, younger women like sisters, in all purity.

j Other ancient authorities read *suffer reproach*

soundness of the life of the church. He is to deal with young and old as with his kinfolk in the household of God (5:1-2). His treatment of widows who receive support from the church is to be both wisely realistic and lovingly respectful (5:3-16). He is to honor the elders who do their work faithfully; he is to deal soberly and conscientiously with those who fail in their duties (5:17-25). He is to remind slaves that their relationship to their masters, particularly Christian masters, is not abrogated by their freedom in Christ, but is hallowed by it; they are to serve all the better for serving freely. (6:1-2)

4:1-5 For a general description of the heresy see the Introduction.

4:1 *The Spirit . . . says.* For prophecies concerning the rise of false prophets and perversions of Christianity cf. Mt 24:11; Mk 13:22; Acts 20:29-30; 2 Th 2:9-10; and for a later date, Rv 13.

Deceitful spirits . . . demons. For the demonic-satanic character of all false religion cf. 1 Co 10:20-21; of perversions of the Gospel particularly, 2 Co 11:3-4, 13-15; 2 Th 2:9-10; 2 Ti 2:26.

4:2 *Consciences . . . seared,* scarred and calloused by compromise with sin (cf. Eph 4:19). The word *seared* can also mean *branded,* that is, marked as slaves of the devil. (Cf. 2 Ti 2:26)

4:3 *Forbid marriage.* For the positive appreciation of marriage which Paul opposes to this cf. 2:15; 3:2, 4-5, 12; and the whole conception of the church as the family of God, 3:15; 5:1-2.

4:4 *Everything . . . good.* Cf. Gn 1:4, 10, 12, 18, 26, 25, 31. To reverse God's own verdict of "very good" is to speak a demonic no to the Creator, now revealed as Savior (1:1; 2:3) to "those who believe." (3)

Received with thanksgiving, from the hand of the Creator, the Father of the household to whom

all look for food (Ps 145:15-16), as the man Jesus did. (Mt 15:36; Lk 24:30, etc.)

4:5 *Consecrated by the word of God,* both the word spoken by God at creation (Gn 1:31) and the word of Scripture incorporated in the table prayer.

4:6 *Brethren.* The picture of the family of God still dominates. (Cf. 3:15; 5:1-2)

4:10 *Strive,* like athletes in a contest, continuing the metaphor of training (8). (Cf. 1 Co 9:24-27; 2 Ti 2:5; 4:7-8)

Especially of those who believe, since in them His will to save reaches its goal.

4:12 *Your youth.* Timothy was probably in his thirties; "youth" covered the period when a man was liable to military service, extending to the 40th year.

4:14 Cf. 1:18. The reference is to Timothy's ordination and commissioning. Cf. 2 Ti 1:6, where Paul speaks of himself as having ordained Timothy. Whether the reference is to two different occasions or whether Paul joined the elders in the laying on of hands can hardly be made out.

4:16 Cf. 1 Co 9:22-23.

5:1 – 6:2 See the analysis of 4:1 – 6:2 given at 4:1 – 6:2. The household of God embraces young and old (5:1-2), widows (5:3-16), elders with their special authority and responsibility (5:17-25), and slaves (6:1-2). The idea of the family of God runs through the whole unit, and in the section on the treatment of widows Paul is at pains to safeguard the ties and duties of the natural family (5:4, 8, 16). There is no conflict of interest between membership in the family of God and in the natural family.

5:3-16 Care for the widow was from of old well established in the life of the church. God is celebrated in the OT as "Father of the fatherless and protector of widows" (Ps 68:5, cf. Dt 10:18) and

3 Honor widows who are real widows. ⁴ If a widow has children or grandchildren, let them first learn their religious duty to their own family and make some return to their parents; for this is acceptable in the sight of God. ⁵ She who is a real widow, and is left all alone, has set her hope on God and continues in supplications and prayers night and day; ⁶ whereas she who is self-indulgent is dead even while she lives. ⁷ Command this, so that they may be without reproach. ⁸ If any one does not provide for his relatives, and especially for his own family, he has disowned the faith and is worse than an unbeliever.

9 Let a widow be enrolled if she is not less than sixty years of age, having been the wife of one husband; ¹⁰ and she must be well attested for her good deeds, as one who has brought up children, shown hospitality, washed the feet of the saints, relieved the afflicted, and devoted herself to doing good in every way. ¹¹ But refuse to enrol younger widows; for when they grow wanton against Christ they desire to marry, ¹² and so they incur condemnation for having violated their first pledge. ¹³ Besides that, they learn to be idlers, gadding about from house to house, and not only idlers but gossips and busybodies, saying what they should not. ¹⁴ So I would have younger widows marry, bear children, rule their households, and give the enemy no occasion to revile us. ¹⁵ For some have already strayed after Satan. ¹⁶ If any believing woman[l] has relatives who are widows, let her assist them; let the church not be burdened, so that it may assist those who are real widows.

17 Let the elders who rule well be considered worthy of double honor, especially those who labor in preaching and teaching; ¹⁸ for the scripture says, "You shall not muzzle an ox when it is treading out the grain," and, "The laborer deserves his wages." ¹⁹ Never admit any charge against an elder except on the evidence of two or three witnesses. ²⁰As for those who persist in sin, rebuke them in the presence of all, so that the rest may stand in fear. ²¹ In the presence of God and of Christ Jesus and of the elect angels I charge you to keep these rules without favor, doing nothing from

[l] Other ancient authorities read *man or woman;* others, simply *man*

the OT enjoins care and concern for the widow (Dt 24:17; Is 1:17). The first organized charity of the church arose out of concern for the widow (Acts 6:1-6). Paul is here not so much enjoining care for the widow as regulating it; apparently the generosity of the church in this respect had been widely abused, and there was danger of a churchly pauperism. Hence the note of sobriety and caution here: a list (9) is to be kept of widows qualified by age, need, and character to receive support from and (perhaps) render service in the church (9-10); in the light of past experience the enrollment of younger widows is discouraged (11-15); and the duty of family members to provide for their own and not shift their obligations over to the church is stressed. (4, 8, 16)

5:5 Cf. Lk 2:37.

5:10 *Brought up children,* both her own and orphaned children.

Washed the feet of the saints. This would be part of the *hospitality* mentioned (cf. Lk 7:44), but adds the note of humble, self-denying service, after the example of Christ (Jn 13:14-17). The *saints* are traveling Christians in need of hospitable ministry.

5:12 *Their first pledge,* not to remarry, made when enrolled in the list of widows.

5:17-25 Since Paul is in this unit not dealing with church offices (as in ch. 3), it would be better to translate the word rendered *elders* with the nontechnical term "older men" (as in 5:1) both in

17 and 19. (In fact, the nontechnical sense would fit Tts 1:5 also, so that the "office" of elder is not necessarily present in the Pastoral Letters at all, although found elsewhere in the NT, Acts 14:23; 1 Ptr 5:1 ff.). Paul is instructing Timothy on how to deal with a group of men whose place in the household of God gave rise to special problems. They enjoyed especial prestige, and leaders and teachers were normally drawn from their ranks (17). They would therefore be open to invidious attack; and in case of wrongdoing on the part of these grave and respected men, disciplinary action would be unusually difficult. Paul therefore insists on the honor due them (17-18) and protection from irresponsible attack (19). He goes on to remind Timothy that the salutary discipline of the erring prescribed by Jesus applies to them too and should be exercised without partiality but with due deliberation and especial care. (20-25)

5:17 *Double honor,* perhaps both esteem and financial support.

5:18 Dt 25:4; Lk 10:7; cf. 1 Co 9:9, 14.

5:19 Cf. Mt 18:15-17; Dt 19:15; 2 Co 13:1.

5:20 *Presence of all.* Cf. Mt 18:17: "Tell it to the church."

5:21 For a similar solemn adjuration cf. 2 Ti 4:1, where the reference to the Last Judgment is more explicit than here. But the reference to the Last Judgment is unmistakable here too: God will "judge the secrets of men by Christ Jesus" (Ro 2:16), who will come to judge "in his glory, and all

partiality. 22 Do not be hasty in the laying on of hands, nor participate in another man's sins; keep yourself pure.

23 No longer drink only water, but use a little wine for the sake of your stomach and your frequent ailments.

24 The sins of some men are conspicuous, pointing to judgment, but the sins of others appear later. 25 So also good deeds are conspicuous; and even when they are not, they cannot remain hidden.

6 Let all who are under the yoke of slavery regard their masters as worthy of all honor, so that the name of God and the teaching may not be defamed. 2 Those who have believing masters must not be disrespectful on the ground that they are brethren; rather they must serve all the better since those who benefit by their service are believers and beloved.

The Gnostic Heresy Corrupts Its Teachers

6:3-21

Teach and urge these duties. 3 If any one teaches otherwise and does not agree with the sound words of our Lord Jesus Christ and the teaching which accords with godliness, 4 he is puffed up with conceit, he knows nothing; he has a morbid craving for controversy and for disputes about words, which produce envy, dissension, slander, base suspicions, 5 and wrangling among men who are depraved in mind and bereft of the truth, imagining that godliness is a means of gain. 6 There is great gain in godliness with contentment; 7 for we brought nothing into the world, and *m* we cannot take anything out of the world; 8 but if we have food and clothing, with these we shall be content. 9 But those who desire to be rich fall into temptation, into a snare, into many senseless and hurtful desires that plunge men into ruin and destruction. 10 For

m Other ancient authorities insert *it is certain that*

the angels with him" (Mt 25:31). Timothy is to exercise judgment in the sobering consciousness that he, too, will be judged.

Elect angels, as opposed to fallen angels. (2 Ptr 2:4; Jude 6)

5:22 *Hasty in the laying on of hands,* either in ordination (remembering what may ensue if an unworthy candidate is ordained, cf. 3:10) or as a gesture of forgiveness toward the disciplined sinner (be sure that his repentance is serious and likely to prove lasting).

5:23 A parenthetical remark suggested by the word "pure" (22). Timothy's present practice of total abstinence from wine is not only bad for his health; it may also give the impression that he is seeking purity, as the Gnostics sought it, by abstinence. (Cf. 4:3)

5:24-25 What a man is, good or bad, will out sooner or later; therefore deliberate thoroughness is in order both in testing a man before ordination and in the process of disciplining the errant.

6:1 *May not be defamed.* Cf. Tts 2:10, where the same thought is put positively.

6:3-21 Men who have broken with the *sound words of our Lord Jesus Christ* and *wandered away from the faith* become conceited, ignorantly and morbidly contentious, *depraved in mind and bereft of the truth* which they have spurned. Their self-centered and self-seeking bent manifests itself most obviously in their avarice, which proves their ruin; they have lost the faith and the peace of a good conscience (3-10). Timothy is to oppose

and overcome this corrupting influence by being a true *man of God,* combining a militant zeal for God's cause with love and gentleness, finding his whole riches in the *eternal life* to which he has been *called* (11-12); by unalloyed obedience to the *commandment* which his baptism and ordination have imposed on him, in a career of selfless ministry until the return of the Lord Jesus Christ, who will reward and judge His servants (13-16); by faithfully *guarding* the truth which has been *entrusted* to him, remembering that the key to it is not a vaunted *knowledge* but *faith* (20-21). Verses 16-19 are a parenthetic general warning suggested by the example of the corrupt teachers. Not only teachers are exposed to the temptation of avarice; the *rich* are to be admonished to find their true riches in God, in generous deeds, and in the life to come, which is life indeed.

6:3-10 Paul has applied Jesus' simple test for false prophets ("You will know them by their fruits," their output, Mt 7:16) to the teaching promulgated by the false teachers (1:3-7) and to the life produced in their followers (4:1-5). He now applies the test to the character of the teachers, the person identified with the teaching. There has been some anticipation of this, inevitably, in the preceding indictments. (1:6; 4:2)

6:5 *Bereft of the truth.* They have opposed the truth (2 Ti 3:8), turned away from listening to the truth (2 Ti 4:4), rejected the truth (Tts 1:14). Their guilt becomes their doom; God deprives them of the truth. (Cf. Mt 13:12; Ro 1:28 and 1:18)

The following Bible verses after 6:19 were omitted by mistake:

20 O Timothy, guard what has been entrusted to you. Avoid the godless chatter and contradictions of what is falsely called knowledge, 21 for by professing it some have missed the mark as regards the faith.

Grace be with you.

the love of money is the root of all evils; it is through this craving that some have wandered away from the faith and pierced their hearts with many pangs.

11 But as for you, man of God, shun all this; aim at righteousness, godliness, faith, love, steadfastness, gentleness. 12 Fight the good fight of the faith; take hold of the eternal life to which you were called when you made the good confession in the presence of many witnesses. 13 In the presence of God who gives life to all things, and of Christ Jesus who in his testimony before Pontius Pilate made the good confession, 14 I charge you to keep the commandment unstained and free from reproach until the appearing of our Lord Jesus Christ; 15 and this will be made manifest at the proper time by the blessed and only Sovereign, the King of kings and Lord of lords, 16 who alone has immortality and dwells in unapproachable light, whom no man has ever seen or can see. To him be honor and eternal dominion. Amen.

17 As for the rich in this world, charge them not to be haughty, nor to set their hopes on uncertain riches but on God who richly furnishes us with everything to enjoy. 18 They are to do good, to be rich in good deeds, liberal and generous, 19 thus laying up for themselves a good foundation for the future, so that they may take hold of the life which is life indeed.

6:11 *Man of God.* Cf. 2 Ti 3:17. The phrase is used in the OT to denote bearers of God's Word: Moses, Ps 90 (superscription), Dt 33:1; prophets, 1 Sm 2:27; 1 K 13:1; 2 K 1:9-10; 4:16, etc. Jesus aligned His disciples with the prophets, Mt 5:12.

6:12 *You made the good confession,* at your baptism or your ordination or perhaps both.

6:13 *God who gives life.* Over against the false teaching (4:3) Paul again asserts the majesty of the Creator, as he recalls His goodness in v. 17.

Christ . . . Pontius Pilate . . . good confession. Over against Gnostic myths of a Christ too heavenly to be a real man, Paul asserts the Christ who appeared in history, before a Roman governor. Over against those who flout "the sound words of our Lord Jesus Christ" (6:3) he reminds Timothy that they are the words of One who sealed His testimony with His blood. (Jn 18:37, cf. 36)

6:19 *For the future,* that is, for the world to come. (Cf. Mt 6:19-20; Lk 12:33; 16:9)

6:20 *Contradictions of what is falsely called knowledge,* Gnostic antitheses to the sound teaching of the apostles and their Lord.

6:21 *With you.* The *you* is plural, an indication that the letter is intended for the church as well as for Timothy. See the Introduction.

TIMOTHY

INTRODUCTION

Paul writes from prison in Rome. He has been a prisoner for some time: Onesiphorus, a Christian of Ephesus, had already sought him out and visited him in Rome (2 Ti 1: 16-17). There has already been one hearing, at which Paul was deserted by all men and yet, with the Lord's help, so successfully defended himself that he "was rescued from the lion's mouth" (2 Ti 4:16-17). But Paul has no hope of ultimate acquittal; he is at the end of his course. And he is virtually alone; only Luke is with him. He longs to see "his beloved child" Timothy once more and bids him come to Rome before the winter makes travel by sea impossible (2 Ti 1:4; 4:9, 21). But he must reckon with the possibility that Timothy may not reach Rome in time; and so he must put in writing all that he hopes to tell Timothy in person if and when he arrives. The letter is thus, as Bengel has put it, Paul's "last will and testament" in which he bids Timothy preserve the apostolic Gospel pure and unchanged, guard it against the increasingly vicious attacks of false teachers, train men to transmit it faithfully, and be ready to take his own share of suffering in the propagation and defense of it. The most personal of the Pastoral Letters is therefore in a sense "official" too; for Paul cannot separate his person from his office. The man who has been "set apart for the gospel of God" (Ro 1:1) remains one with that Gospel in life and in death.

Date of writing: A. D. 65 – 67.

THE SECOND LETTER OF PAUL TO

TIMOTHY

SALUTATION (1:1-2)

1 Paul, an apostle of Christ Jesus by the will of God according to the promise of the life which is in Christ Jesus,
2 To Timothy, my beloved child:
Grace, mercy, and peace from God the Father and Christ Jesus our Lord.

Paul's Appeal: Rekindle the Gift Within You

1:3-18

3 I thank God whom I serve with a clear conscience, as did my fathers, when I remember you constantly in my prayers. 4As I remember your tears, I long night and day to see you, that I may be filled with joy. 5 I am reminded of your sincere faith, a faith that dwelt first in your grandmother Lois and your mother Eunice and now, I am sure, dwells in you. 6 Hence I remind you to rekindle the gift of God that is within you through the laying on of my hands; 7 for God did not give us a spirit of timidity but a spirit of power and love and self-control.

8 Do not be ashamed then of testifying to our Lord, nor of me his prisoner, but share in suffering for the gospel in the power of God, 9who saved us and called us with a holy calling, not in virtue of our works but in virtue of his own purpose and the grace which he gave us in Christ Jesus ages ago, 10 and now has manifested through the appearing of our Savior Christ Jesus, who abolished death and brought life and immortality to light through the gospel. 11 For this gospel I was appointed a preacher and apostle and teacher, 12 and therefore I suffer as I do. But I am not ashamed, for I know whom I have believed, and I am sure that he is able to guard until that Day what has been entrusted to me.*a* 13 Follow the pattern of the sound words which you have heard from me, in the faith and love which are in Christ Jesus;

a Or what I have entrusted to him

1:3-18 Paul introduces his appeal with thanksgiving for the bond of affection which has united him and Timothy, with an expression of his strong desire to see him again, and with a grateful recollection of the sincere faith that dwells in him (3-5). His appeal to Timothy is threefold: to *rekindle the gift of God* within him and so make full proof of the Spirit of *power and love and self-control* dwelling in him (6-7); to continue his task of witnessing to the Lord whom they both serve, to remain unashamedly loyal to the imprisoned apostle and ready to *share in suffering for the gospel* in the assurance that the gracious power of God which has overcome death and has sustained Paul in the faithful discharge of his appointed task will empower him too (8-12); to hold fast and guard the truth which Paul has committed to him, by the power of the Spirit who dwells in him as He dwells in Paul (13-14). Paul concludes his appeal by pointing to the warning example of *all . . . in Asia* who have failed him and to the heartening example of the kind and courageous Onesiphorus. (15-18)
1:3 *Serve with a clear conscience,* perhaps in contrast to the false teachers who have rejected

conscience (1 Ti 1:19) and have seared and corrupted consciences. (1 Ti 4:2; Tts 1:15)
As did my fathers. For Paul's insistence on the integrity of his piety as a Pharisee cf. Ph 3:6.
1:5 Cf. Acts 16:1-3. For Timothy's rearing in the faith cf. 3:15.
1:6 *Rekindle.* The gift of God is a spiritual gift (cf. v. 14; 1 Co 12:1). For the Spirit pictured as fire cf. Acts 2:3; 1 Th 5:19; Rv 4:5.
The laying on of my hands. Cf. 1 Ti 4:14.
1:8 *Ashamed.* Cf. Ro 1:16.
1:9 *Gave us in Christ Jesus.* Cf. Eph 1:3-4.
1:11 The *preacher* (or "herald") proclaims the Gospel; the *apostle* (commissioned messenger) disseminates it; the *teacher* applies it to daily living as "the divine training that is in faith." (1 Ti 1:4; cf. 1 Ti 2:7)
1:12 *What has been entrusted to me,* the Gospel in its purity and the whole future of the apostolic church. God will have a care for His Word and His people (cf. 2:19). But there is much to be said for the rendering given in RSV note a: *what I have entrusted to him,* i. e., Paul's life, the reference to Paul's suffering, his expectation of death (4:6-8) on the one hand, and the divine triumph over death

14 guard the truth that has been entrusted to you by the Holy Spirit who dwells within us.

15 You are aware that all who are in Asia turned away from me, and among them Phy·gel'us and Her·mog'e·nes. 16 May the Lord grant mercy to the household of On·e·siph'o·rus, for he often refreshed me; he was not ashamed of my chains, 17 but when he arrived in Rome he searched for me eagerly and found me—18 may the Lord grant him to find mercy from the Lord on that Day—and you well know all the service he rendered at Eph'e·sus.

Paul's Charge: Entrust the Word to Faithful Men

2:1 – 4:8

ENTRUST THE TRUTH TO FAITHFUL MEN (2:1-13)

2 You then, my son, be strong in the grace that is in Christ Jesus, 2 and what you have heard from me before many witnesses entrust to faithful men who will be able to teach others also. 3 Share in suffering as a good soldier of Christ Jesus. 4 No soldier on service gets entangled in civilian pursuits, since his aim is to satisfy the one who enlisted him. 5 An athlete is not crowned unless he competes according to the rules. 6 It is the hard-working farmer who ought to have the first share of the crops. 7 Think over what I say, for the Lord will grant you understanding in everything.

8 Remember Jesus Christ, risen from the dead, descended from David, as preached in my gospel, 9 the gospel for which I am suffering and wearing fetters like a criminal.

(1:10) on the other, and the usage of the Greek word translated as *what has been entrusted* combine to favor this translation.

1:15 *Phygelus and Hermogenes* are otherwise unknown; they were probably former co-workers of Paul, from whom he might expect aid and support in time of need.

1:16-18 *Onesiphorus* is otherwise unknown; Paul's tribute to his energetic and fearless love remains his only but enduring monument. He was apparently dead at the time when Paul wrote. (Cf. 18)

1:18 He who found the prisoner will *find* mercy in the judgment (cf. Mt 25:36 and 34). Paul's prayer is for the given gift of Christ, mercy for those whom God's mercy has made merciful. (Mt 5:7)

2:1 – 4:8 The theme of this unit is stated in 2:2: *What you have heard from me . . . entrust to faithful men who will be able to teach others also,* the "apostolic succession" of sound apostolic teaching, the only apostolic succession that the NT knows. These faithful men are not as prominent in what follows as one might expect, although it is clear that they are not forgotten. Cf 2:14 *(remind them);* 2:21 *(if any one purifies himself);* 2:24 *(the Lord's servant);* 3:12 *(all . . . will be persecuted);* 4:8 *(all who have loved his appearing).* The reason for this is not far to seek; in all his letters Paul manifests a strong consciousness of how "personal" the apostolate is; how the grace of the Lord lays claim to and employs the whole person with all his powers, experiences, and actions; how a man must be what he proclaims lest he "put an obstacle in the way of the gospel of Christ" (1 Co 9:12). He therefore speaks freely of himself; and he can say quite without vanity, "Be imitators of me, as I am of

Christ" (1 Co 11:1). What holds for the apostle holds for all men entrusted with the apostolic Word of witness. Paul is therefore speaking of the training of *faithful* apostolic *men,* not only when specifically issuing instructions concerning them but also when he speaks of himself (2:8-10; 3:10-11, 14; 4:6-8) and of the man that Timothy ought to be (2:3-13, 15-16, 22-23; 3:14-17; 4:1-2, 5). In all this he is saying to the faithful men entrusted with the Gospel: "Join in imitating me, and mark those who so live as you have an example in us." (Ph 3:17)

2:1-13 Timothy can train and inspire faithful men only if he is himself faithful, ready to endure hardships and toil with a soldier's single loyalty, an athlete's rigorous self-discipline, and a farmer's strenuous industry (1-7). This he can do in the strength which is to be found in the risen Christ, who has given Paul the courage to suffer imprisonment and disgrace for the sake of God's elect. Timothy is to work and suffer in the faith that union with Christ in suffering and death is the assurance of union with Him in life and glory. (8-13)

2:2 *Heard . . . before many witnesses,* at his ordination or commissioning when he was pledged to the apostolic truth and "made the good confession in the presence of many witnesses." (1 Ti 6:12)

2:7 *Think over.* Paul does not spell out the application of the three pictures for Timothy. The Lord whom he serves will give him the insight he needs. (Cf. Ph 3:15-16)

2:8 Cf. Ro 1:3-4. Both passages are probably a quotation or an echo of an early creed.

2:9 *The word of God is not fettered.* See the notes on 4:10-12 and 4:17.

But the word of God is not fettered. [10] Therefore I endure everything for the sake of the elect, that they also may obtain salvation in Christ Jesus with its eternal glory. [11]The saying is sure:

If we have died with him, we shall also live with him;

[12]　　if we endure, we shall also reign with him;

　　　if we deny him, he also will deny us;

[13]　　if we are faithless, he remains faithful—

for he cannot deny himself.

TRAIN FAITHFUL MEN TO DEFEND THE TRUTH (2:14-26)

14 Remind them of this, and charge them before the Lord[b] to avoid disputing about words, which does no good, but only ruins the hearers. [15] Do your best to present yourself to God as one approved, a workman who has no need to be ashamed, rightly handling the word of truth. [16]Avoid such godless chatter, for it will lead people into more and more ungodliness, [17] and their talk will eat its way like gangrene. Among them are Hy·me·nae′us and Phi·le′tus, [18] who have swerved from the truth by holding that the resurrection is past already. They are upsetting the faith of some. [19] But God's firm foundation stands, bearing this seal: "The Lord knows those who are his," and, "Let every one who names the name of the Lord depart from iniquity."

[b] Other ancient authorities read God

2:11 *The saying is sure.* Cf. 1 Ti 1:15; 3:1; 4:9; Tts 3:8. What follows is probably a quotation from an early Christian hymn; note the rhythmic language and the parallelism.

Died . . . live. Cf. Ro 6:8.

2:12 *Endure . . . reign.* Cf. Ro 8:17; 1 Ptr 4:17.

Deny. Cf. Mt 10:32-33; Rv 3:5.

2:13 *He remains faithful.* His "overflowing" (1 Ti 1:14) grace breaks the symmetry of the song; He who taught His disciples to pray daily for forgiveness (Mt 6:12) will not *deny himself;* they shall find forgiveness through Him. (Cf. Ro 8:34)

2:14-26 Timothy is to warn these faithful men against sinking to the level of their opponents in their defense of the truth; they love disputes about words, but the teacher of the church is not to be a debater (14). Timothy can do this effectively only if he himself is an honest workman of the Lord, not like Hymenaeus and Philetus with their godless, cancerous, and disturbing teaching (15 to 18). He must, moreover, do his work in the believing confidence that God's truth cannot be overcome, that God will protect and vindicate His own (19). If he obeys the imperative of God's elective grace, he will become a pure and precious vessel fit for God's noblest uses. As such he will be able to rise above stupid controversies and create faithful men in his own image (20-23), servants of the Lord who can overcome error with apt teaching, with kindly, forbearing, gentle correction, in the faith and hope that God can grant their opponents repentance and deliver them from the devilish lie which intoxicates and ensnares them. (24 to 26)

2:14 *Them,* the "faithful men" of v. 2.

Does no good, i. e., does not convert the opponent, while the church *(hearers)* is shaken in the faith.

2:17 *Hymenaeus* is mentioned as a blasphemous teacher, excommunicated by Paul, in 1 Ti 1:20; *Philetus* is otherwise unknown.

2:18 *Holding that the resurrection is past already.* The resurrection of the dead is meant. Their teaching was a distortion of the idea that the Christian participates in Christ's death and resurrection through his baptism (Ro 6:3-11). By making the resurrection a purely inner, spiritual experience they evaded the thought of the resurrection of the body, which was offensive to Greek thinking (Acts 17:32. The Greek depreciated the body and thought of it as the prison of the soul, from which the immortal soul was released by death). Their teaching was therefore a demonic denial of the goodness of God's creation (1 Ti 4:1-5), a blasphemous attack on the Creator. (1 Ti 1:20)

2:19 *Foundation.* The truth on which the church is built (Eph 2:20), thought of as living and working in its witnesses *(those who are his).*

Seal, mark of God's ownership and therefore of His protection. (Cf. Eph 1:13)

"The Lord knows those who are his." Quoted from Nm 16:5, where the RSV translates rightly, "The Lord WILL SHOW who is his," for the Hebrew word "know" bears that dynamic sense. The words were spoken by Moses when one Korah and his companions challenged the leadership of Moses and Aaron. In the ordeal that ensued (Nm 16:5-35), Korah and his company were destroyed when "the earth opened its mouth and swallowed them" (Nm 16:32) because they had "despised the Lord" (Nm 16:30). As in the days of Moses, so now (cf. 3:8) those who despise the Lord and rebel against His apostles will be dealt with by the judgment of God.

"Let every one, etc." This is not a direct quotation of any one OT passage but a sort of summarization of a number of them (cf. Is 52:11; 26:13). The thought that acknowledging the God of the covenant as Lord *(names the name of the Lord)* commits a man to a life of righteousness under the blessings of His covenant is basic to the whole OT.

20 In a great house there are not only vessels of gold and silver but also of wood and earthenware, and some for noble use, some for ignoble. 21 If any one purifies himself from what is ignoble, then he will be a vessel for noble use, consecrated and useful to the master of the house, ready for any good work. 22 So shun youthful passions and aim at righteousness, faith, love, and peace, along with those who call upon the Lord from a pure heart. 23 Have nothing to do with stupid, senseless controversies; you know that they breed quarrels. 24And the Lord's servant must not be quarrelsome but kindly to every one, an apt teacher, forbearing, 25 correcting his opponents with gentleness. God may perhaps grant that they will repent and come to know the truth, 26 and they may escape from the snare of the devil, after being captured by him to do his will. *c*

THERE WILL COME TIMES OF STRESS (3:1-9)

3 But understand this, that in the last days there will come times of stress. 2 For men will be lovers of self, lovers of money, proud, arrogant, abusive, disobedient to their parents, ungrateful, unholy, 3 inhuman, implacable, slanderers, profligates, fierce, haters of good, 4 treacherous, reckless, swollen with conceit, lovers of pleasure rather than lovers of God, 5 holding the form of religion but denying the power of it. Avoid such people. 6 For among them are those who make their way into households and capture weak women, burdened with sins and swayed by various impulses, 7 who will listen to anybody and can never arrive at a knowledge of the truth. 8As Jannes and Jambres opposed Moses, so these men also oppose the truth, men of corrupt mind and counterfeit faith; 9 but they will not get very far, for their folly will be plain to all, as was that of those two men.

CONTINUE IN WHAT YOU HAVE LEARNED (3:10-17)

10 Now you have observed my teaching, my conduct, my aim in life, my faith, my patience, my love, my steadfastness, 11 my persecutions, my sufferings, what befell me at Antioch, at I·co′ni·um, and at Lystra, what persecutions I endured; yet from them all the Lord rescued me. 12 Indeed all who desire to live a godly life in Christ Jesus will be persecuted, 13 while evil men and impostors will go on·from bad to worse, deceivers and deceived. 14 But as for you, continue in what you have learned and have firmly believed, knowing from whom you learned it 15 and how from childhood

c Or *by him, to do his* (that is, God's) *will*

2:21 *If any one purifies himself,* i. e., obeys the imperative of God's elective grace: "Depart from iniquity." (19)

2:22 *Youthful passions,* in this context not erotic desires but youth's tendency to passionate partisanship, impatient pride, intellectual delight in controversy, etc.

2:24 *The Lord's servant.* Cf. Isaiah's prophecy of the Servant (Is 42:2), fulfilled in Jesus, Mt 12:17-21, esp. v. 19.

2:26 *Escape from,* literally "return to sobriety and so escape from."

Snare of the devil. For the demonic-satanic character of false religion generally cf. 1 Co 10:20-21; of perversions of the Gospel particularly cf. 2 Co 11:3-4, 13-15; 2 Th 2:9-10; 1 Ti 4:1.

3:1-9 Timothy is to do his work in the sobering conviction that times and men will grow worse and that opposition to the truth will increase. The only alleviating feature of this dark future is that the folly of those who oppose the truth will expose itself.

3:1 *In the last days.* Cf. 4:3; 4:1.

3:5 *Form of religion.* This may include both a correct creed and proper religious observances that have no influence on men's daily life.

3:6-7 This is probably an allusion to current activities of heretical teachers, the exact nature of which escapes us. Perhaps they cultivated the acquaintance of fashionable and flighty women whose "interest in religion" made them perpetually curious about the latest religious fad. (Cf. 4:3)

3:8 Jewish tradition assigned the names *Jannes* and *Jambres* to the Egyptian sorcerers who opposed Moses when he appeared before Pharaoh (Ex 7:11, 22; 8:7). Their opposition to the truth took the form of a counterfeit of the truth.

3:10-17 Timothy is to do his work in the solid assurance that he has the equipment needed for his difficult and dangerous task in the example of Paul, in the apostolic teaching he has received, and in the inspired Scriptures which are able to *instruct* man *for salvation through faith in Christ Jesus.*

3:11 *What befell me at Antioch,* etc. Cf. Acts 13:14-52; 14:1-20; 16:1-5. Timothy's home was in *Lystra,* and the memory of his first experience with the suffering of an apostle would be particularly vivid.

3:15-17 There is hardly another passage which sums up so succinctly and powerfully the convic-

you have been acquainted with the sacred writings which are able to instruct you for salvation through faith in Christ Jesus. [16]All scripture is inspired by God and[d] profitable for teaching, for reproof, for correction, and for training in righteousness, [17] that the man of God may be complete, equipped for every good work.

DO THE WORK OF AN EVANGELIST (4:1-8)

4 I charge you in the presence of God and of Christ Jesus who is to judge the living and the dead, and by his appearing and his kingdom: [2] preach the word, be urgent in season and out of season, convince, rebuke, and exhort, be unfailing in patience and in teaching. [3] For the time is coming when people will not endure sound teaching, but having itching ears they will accumulate for themselves teachers to suit their own likings, [4] and will turn away from listening to the truth and wander into myths. [5]As for you, always be steady, endure suffering, do the work of an evangelist, fulfil your ministry.

[6] For I am already on the point of being sacrificed; the time of my departure has come. [7] I have fought the good fight, I have finished the race, I have kept the faith. [8] Henceforth there is laid up for me the crown of righteousness, which the Lord, the righteous judge, will award to me on that Day, and not only to me but also to all who have loved his appearing.

Paul's Request: Come to Me Soon

4:9-22

[9] Do your best to come to me soon. [10] For Demas, in love with this present world, has deserted me and gone to Thes·sa·lon'i·ca; Crescens has gone to Galatia,[e] Titus to Dal·ma'tia. [11] Luke alone is with me. Get Mark and bring him with you; for he is very useful in serving me. [12] Tych'i·cus I have sent to Eph'e·sus. [13] When you come, bring

[d] Or *Every scripture inspired by God is also*　[e] Other ancient authorities read *Gaul*

tions of our Lord and His apostles concerning the OT. These are: (1) The OT achieves its true utterance (says what it means) only in living connection with the NT Gospel, as witness to the righteousness of God manifested in Christ Jesus (Ro 3:21). Only the ear of faith *(faith in Christ Jesus)* hears its true utterance; only the believer in Christ Jesus experiences its power to effect God's radical deliverance of man from his desperate situation *(salvation)*. (2) The Scriptures have this power because they are the product and the instrument of the Spirit of God *(inspired by God;* cf. 2 Ptr 1:19-21). (3) As such they are *profitable,* useful, performing a function. Being the work of the Spirit, whose creative possibilities begin where man's possibilities end, they can give man what man cannot give himself: *teaching,* knowledge of the will and ways of the God of illimitable power, wisdom, and goodness; *reproof,* the exposure and conviction of sin which make a man cry out, "Woe is me! For I am lost," in the presence of his holy God (Is 6:5); *correction,* the raising up of man to life and ministry where man has failed and totally collapsed (Is 6:6-8); *training in righteousness*—the inspired Word takes man in hand, lays the gentle yoke of his Savior God upon him, puts his reckless life in order, and makes of him a *man of God . . . complete, equipped for every good work.* (17)

4:1-8 Timothy is to fulfill his ministry strenuously, insistently, courageously in the face of men's indifference to sound teaching and in spite

of their itching desire for false teaching; he is responsible, not to men but to the Christ who will return to judge all men. It is Timothy who must now do the work of an evangelist. Paul's course is run, his fight finished; he looks to the reward that awaits him and all faithful men who look in love for their Lord's appearing, His return to reign.

4:5 *Always be steady,* literally "be sober in all things."

4:6 *Sacrificed.* Cf. Ph 2:17.

4:8 *Crown of righteousness. Righteousness,* the final verdict of the God who "justifies him who has faith in Jesus" (Ro 3:26), is the *crown.* Cf. "crown of life," Ja 1:12.

4:9-22 *Come to me soon* (9). Paul's longing for his beloved child (cf. 1:4), a longing intensified by loneliness *(Luke alone* of all his co-workers is with him, 11), and his desire to impress on Timothy once more face to face the greatness and the glory of the task which is now his to carry on break forth in the urgent request that Timothy come to him in Rome. So intense is his feeling that he repeats the request in the midst of the greetings at the end: *Do your best to come before winter.* (21)

4:10 *Demas, in love with this present world,* rather than with the future "appearing" (8) of his Lord. Demas is otherwise unknown.

4:10-12 These verses, along with v. 20, provide an instructive commentary on 2:9: "The word of God is not fettered." Paul continues to deploy his workers *(Crescens, Titus, Tychicus)* with his accustomed energy and draws in new forces

the cloak that I left with Carpus at Troas, also the books, and above all the parchments. [14]Alexander the coppersmith did me great harm; the Lord will requite him for his deeds. [15] Beware of him yourself, for he strongly opposed our message. [16]At my first defense no one took my part; all deserted me. May it not be charged against them! [17] But the Lord stood by me and gave me strength to proclaim the message fully, that all the Gentiles might hear it. So I was rescued from the lion's mouth. [18] The Lord will rescue me from every evil and save me for his heavenly kingdom. To him be the glory for ever and ever. Amen.

19 Greet Prisca and Aq·ui·la, and the household of On·e·siph'o·rus. [20] E·ras'tus remained at Corinth; Troph'i·mus I left ill at Mi·le'tus. [21] Do your best to come before winter. Eu·bu'lus sends greetings to you, as do Pudens and Linus and Claudia and all the brethren.

22 The Lord be with your spirit. Grace be with you.

(Mark). Crescens is otherwise unknown; for Titus see the Introduction to the Letter to Titus. For Tychicus see the Introduction to the Captivity Letters and cf. Acts 20:4; Eph 6:21; Cl 4:7; Tts 3:12; perhaps he is to relieve Timothy at *Ephesus.* For Mark see the Introduction to his gospel.

4:13 *Cloak.* Paul's prison was no doubt a cold place.

Books . . . parchments. The first may be documents that would be useful to Paul in his trial; the latter probably were parts of the OT.

4:14 *Alexander.* Both the person and the event referred to are otherwise unknown. Alexander may be identical with the Alexander of 1 Ti 1:20; but the name was a common one, and it is difficult to see why the excommunicated false teacher of 1 Ti 1:20 should be identified as the *coppersmith* here.

4:16 *My first defense.* See the Introduction. Possibly the words refer to the earlier trial of Paul in A. D. 61, in which Paul was acquitted and released for further work in his mission to the Gentiles. (Cf. v. 17)

May it not be charged. Paul prays as Jesus prayed (Lk 23:34) and as Stephen prayed. (Acts 7:60)

4:17 *That all the Gentiles might hear it.* Whether the reference is to Paul's earlier trial or to a first hearing in his present trial, Paul appeared before the tribunal of Caesar as "an ambassador in chains" (Eph 6:20) and presented the cause and

claim of Christ to the Gentiles. (Cf. Ph 1:12-18)

Lion's mouth, symbol of deadly peril. (Ps 22:21)

4:18 A reminiscence of the Lord's prayer. (Mt 6:13)

4:19 *Prisca and Aquila.* Cf. Acts 18:2-3, 18, 24-26 (Luke uses the diminutive form of Prisca's name, Priscilla); Ro 16:3-4; 1 Co 16:19.

Onesiphorus. Cf. 1:16-18.

4:20 *Erastus.* Cf. Acts 19:22; the Erastus of Ro 16:23, called "the city treasurer," is hardly the same person.

Trophimus. Cf. Acts 20:4; 21:29.

4:21 *Before winter,* when travel by sea was suspended (cf. Acts 27:12; 28:11). If Timothy waits until shipping is resumed in the spring, he will not find Paul alive.

Eubulus . . . Pudens . . . Linus . . . Claudia and all the brethren. Probably members of the church at Rome. Linus appears as second bishop of Rome (after Peter) in ancient lists. The others are unknown. If they were among those who failed Paul at his first defense (16), Paul's mention of them here (as brethren!) is evidence that Paul could forgive completely, as his Lord did when He called the disciples who had failed Him "my brethren." (Mt 28:10)

4:22 *Grace be with you.* The *you* is plural; Paul is greeting the church at Ephesus, perhaps more particularly the "faithful men" (2:2) to whom Timothy is to entrust the apostolic teaching. *Grace* is the apostle's last word.

THE LETTER OF PAUL TO

TITUS

INTRODUCTION

The Letter to Titus is quite similar to First Timothy in its occasion, purpose, and content and can therefore be treated rather briefly here. Paul had worked for a while as missionary on the island of Crete together with Titus, the prudent, able, and tactful Gentile companion who had rendered him such valuable services at the time when the relationship between the Corinthian church and Paul had been strained to the breaking point (2 Co 2:13; 7:6 ff.; 8:6; 12:18). At his departure from Crete Paul left Titus in charge of the task of consolidating and organizing the newly created Christian communities. His task resembled that of Timothy at Ephesus in that the faith and life of the church were being endangered by the rise of false teachers of a Gnostic type, more pronouncedly Judaic in their teaching than those at Ephesus (Tts 1:14; 3:9). The situation was further complicated in Crete, however, by the fact that in these newly founded Christian communities solid organization was lacking and the pagan environment was particularly vicious (1:5, 12, 13). Whereas Timothy was to restore order in established churches, Titus had to *establish* order in young churches. It was a task which called for all his courage, wisdom, and tact. Paul wrote to Titus to encourage him in this difficult assignment, to aid him in combating the threatening heresy, to advise him in his task of organizing and edifying the churches and, not least, to give Titus' presence and work in Crete the sanction and support of his own apostolic authority. This last intention of the letter is evident in the salutation of the letter, which dwells on Paul's apostolate (1:1-3), and in the closing greeting, "Grace be with you *all*" (3:15), which shows that the letter addressed to Titus is intended for the ear of the churches also.

Time and place of writing: about A. D. 63 in Macedonia or en route to Nicopolis.

TITUS

1 Paul, a servant[a] of God and an apostle of Jesus Christ, to further the faith of God's elect and their knowledge of the truth which accords with godliness, 2 in hope of eternal life which God, who never lies, promised ages ago 3 and at the proper time manifested in his word through the preaching with which I have been entrusted by command of God our Savior;

4 To Titus, my true child in a common faith:
Grace and peace from God the Father and Christ Jesus our Savior.

Amend What Is Defective
1:5-16

5 This is why I left you in Crete, that you might amend what was defective, and appoint elders in every town as I directed you, 6 if any man is blameless, the husband of one wife, and his children are believers and not open to the charge of being profligate or insubordinate. 7 For a bishop, as God's steward, must be blameless; he must not be arrogant or quick-tempered or a drunkard or violent or greedy for gain, 8 but hospitable, a lover of goodness, master of himself, upright, holy, and self-controlled; 9 he must hold firm to the sure word as taught, so that he may be able to give instruction in sound doctrine and also to confute those who contradict it. 10 For there are many insubordinate men, empty talkers and deceivers, especially the circumcision party; 11 they must be silenced, since they are upsetting whole families by teaching for base gain what they have no right to teach. 12 One of themselves, a prophet of their own, said, "Cretans are always liars, evil beasts, lazy gluttons." 13 This testimony is true. Therefore rebuke them sharply, that they may be sound in the

[a] Or *slave*

1:1-4 The salutation is unusually detailed; like that of Paul's Letter to the Romans, written to a church which did not know the apostle personally, it dwells on the nature and function of the *apostle*, his place in the eternal counsels of God the Savior (the age-old promise now fulfilled, manifested, and proclaimed) *to further* the *faith, knowledge,* and *hope* of *God's elect.* For the purpose of this full exposition of the apostolate see the Introduction.

1:2-3 *Promised . . . manifested.* Cf. 2 Ti 1:9-10; Eph 3:5.

1:5-16 Titus is to supply the immature churches with sober and responsible leadership by appointing *elders* (5) to oversee (*bishop,* 7) the life of the church; they are to be men of unimpeachable character (*blameless,* 6), exemplary in their family life (6), and fitted by their disciplined and gracious maturity to function as *God's steward* (7), firmly grounded in *sound doctrine,* able to instruct the faithful and confute the contradictor (9). This last quality is especially important in Crete, where the church is exposed to the pernicious teachings of men who *profess to know God (gnosis),* but *deny him by their deeds* (16), insubordinate, loquacious, deceitful, mercenary men of Jewish-Christian

background (*circumcision party,* 10) who purvey speculative theology (*myths,* 14) and impose human commands of abstinence in the name of higher knowledge and higher purity. These men *must be silenced* (11), for their teaching reveals their ignorance of God and the impurity of their minds. (15-16)

1:5 *Elders* designates the leaders according to the age group from which they are drawn; *bishop* (7) describes them according to their function, that of being overseers. (Cf. Acts 20:28)

1:6-9 Cf. 1 Ti 3:1-7 and the notes there.

1:10-16 The description of the false teachers is very similar to those of 1 Ti 1:3-11; 4:1-11; 6:3-10; 2 Ti 2:14-18, which help toward the understanding of what is very briefly indicated here; the peculiarity of the situation in Crete sets this passage off from the others (12). For a general description of the Gnostic heresy see the Introduction to First Timothy.

1:12 *A prophet of their own.* The quotation was commonly attributed to the sixth-century poet and religious reformer Epimenides, himself a Cretan and so a valid witness to their national character, which had a bad reputation in antiquity generally.

1:13 *Rebuke . . . that they may be sound in the*

faith, [14] instead of giving heed to Jewish myths or to commands of men who reject the truth. [15] To the pure all things are pure, but to the corrupt and unbelieving nothing is pure; their very minds and consciences are corrupted. [16] They profess to know God, but they deny him by their deeds; they are detestable, disobedient, unfit for any good deed.

Sound Doctrine and Sound Living

2:1 — 3:8

THE TRAINING GRACE OF GOD IN DAILY LIFE (2:1-15)

2 But as for you, teach what befits sound doctrine. [2] Bid the older men be temperate, serious, sensible, sound in faith, in love, and in steadfastness. [3] Bid the older women likewise to be reverent in behavior, not to be slanderers or slaves to drink; they are to teach what is good, [4] and so train the young women to love their husbands and children, [5] to be sensible, chaste, domestic, kind, and submissive to their husbands, that the word of God may not be discredited. [6] Likewise urge the younger men to control themselves. [7] Show yourself in all respects a model of good deeds, and in your teaching show integrity, gravity, [8] and sound speech that cannot be censured, so that an opponent may be put to shame, having nothing evil to say of us. [9] Bid slaves to be submissive to their masters and to give satisfaction in every respect; they are not to be refractory, [10] nor to pilfer, but to show entire and true fidelity, so that in everything they may adorn the doctrine of God our Savior.

[11] For the grace of God has appeared for the salvation of all men, [12] training us to renounce irreligion and worldly passions, and to live sober, upright, and godly lives in this world, [13] awaiting our blessed hope, the appearing of the glory of our great God and Savior[c] Jesus Christ, [14] who gave himself for us to redeem us from all iniquity and to purify for himself a people of his own who are zealous for good deeds.

[15] Declare these things; exhort and reprove with all authority. Let no one disregard you.

[c] Or *of the great God and our Savior*

faith. The aim of rebuke is to free men of error and to restore their faith to health. Cf. Mt 18:15: "You have gained your brother."

1:14 *Jewish myths,* probably allegorical interpretations of the Old Testament in support of Gnostic speculation.

1:14-15 *Reject the truth . . . all things are pure.* The truth which these men reject is that enunciated by Jesus when He rejected Judaic tradition (Mk 7:6-8) and "declared all foods clean." (Mk 7:19)

1:15 *To the pure,* etc. This echoes Jesus' teaching concerning what defiles a man (Mk 7:18-23). The pure man is the new man in Christ who receives with thanksgiving everything created by God and enjoys it with a clear conscience (cf. 1 Ti 4:5; Ro 14:14, 20). The *corrupt and unbelieving* men cannot feel at home in God's good creation because they know neither their Savior nor their Creator. (Cf. v. 16)

2:1-15 Titus is to let *sound doctrine* (1) make sound the whole life of man. He is to instruct men of all ages and classes by word and example (7-8) in that wholesome conduct of life which God's universal grace in Christ has made possible; the life of the redeemed people of God is to be a living preachment of that enabling grace; even the life of the slave may adorn the doctrine of God our Savior. (10)

2:10 *Adorn the doctrine,* as a fruitful tree adorns the soil on which it grows.

2:11-14 This is the pithiest and most comprehensive statement on the grace of God to be found in the Pauline letters. It looks back to God's spontaneous act (*appeared,* 11) of love in Jesus Christ, His act of universal radical deliverance (*salvation*) for the redemption of mankind (14). It looks to the future, to the fulfillment of the *blessed hope* given by that redemption (13). But the chief emphasis is on the present. God's saving grace is a *training* grace (12) which makes man's life sound in every respect. Under the benign sway of this grace (cf. Ro 6:14) man's relationship to himself is one of self-control (*sober,* 12); to his fellowman, one of justice (*upright,* 12); and to his God, one of piety (*godly,* 12). God's grace fulfills His ancient intention and promise of a people redeemed and purified for a life of service to Him. (14; cf. Ps 130:8; Eze 37:23)

2:15 *Reprove,* that is, call to repentance. The new life of the new people of God does not "come naturally," but is a life of constant repentance, as Luther declared in the first of his Ninety-five Theses.

REBORN FOR OBEDIENCE, COURTESY, GOOD DEEDS (3:1-8A)

3 Remind them to be submissive to rulers and authorities, to be obedient, to be ready for any honest work, 2 to speak evil of no one, to avoid quarreling, to be gentle, and to show perfect courtesy toward all men. 3 For we ourselves were once foolish, disobedient, led astray, slaves to various passions and pleasures, passing our days in malice and envy, hated by men and hating one another; 4 but when the goodness and loving kindness of God our Savior appeared, 5 he saved us, not because of deeds done by us in righteousness, but in virtue of his own mercy, by the washing of regeneration and renewal in the Holy Spirit, 6 which he poured out upon us richly through Jesus Christ our Savior, 7 so that we might be justified by his grace and become heirs in hope of eternal life. 8 The saying is sure.

The Exclusion of Unsound Teaching

3:8b-11

I desire you to insist on these things, so that those who have believed in God may be careful to apply themselves to good deeds;*d* these are excellent and profitable to men. 9 But avoid stupid controversies, genealogies, dissensions, and quarrels over the law, for they are unprofitable and futile. 10 As for a man who is factious, after admonishing him once or twice, have nothing more to do with him, 11 knowing that such a person is perverted and sinful; he is self-condemned.

d Or *enter honorable occupations*

3:1-8a Sound doctrine produces sound civic life. Members of God's new people are to be obedient to governmental authority, active and energetic in the pursuit of the civic good, showing all men that gentle and winning Christian courtesy which has been engendered in them by the *goodness and loving kindness of God* our *Savior* (4). His saving, justifying, renewing work (5-7) equips believers for their profession: *good deeds.* (8)

3:2 *Gentle.* The word translated *gentle* suggests the graciousness of a superior, one who is above the pressure of cruel competitiveness; it is a gentleness born of strength.

Courtesy is a good rendering here for a word elsewhere rendered as "meekness" (Ja 1:21; 3:13). It is the considerate and kindly attitude of one who knows that it is God who makes the decisions and confidently leaves the ultimate decisions to Him.

3:3-7 This second passage on the redeeming love of God (cf. 2:11-14) with its emphasis on the complete absence of merit or deserving on the part of the redeemed serves to counteract cold Christian smugness toward non-Christians. We dare not despise non-Christians or write them off as being of no consequence; to do so would be to deny the mercy of Him who did not write us off.

3:5-7 God's saving act is detailed in the order in which the Christian has experienced it. In Baptism he has been buried with Christ and has risen to new life with Him; the blessings of the cross and resurrection are his by this *washing of regeneration* (Ro 6:3-14). In Baptism he has received the Holy Spirit, who leads him into all truth and glorifies for him the Christ into whose name he has been baptized (Jn 16:13-14). Under the Spirit's tutelage he realizes ever more fully what it means to be justified by grace, to have a present unburdened by past guilt, and to live in the resilient

hope of eternal life. For a similar sequence cf. 1 Co 6:11.

3:8b-11 Men who live and work in the wholesome light of *excellent and profitable* (8) sound teaching have neither taste nor time for endless, useless, and morbid theological debate. They do their duty toward the man who makes propaganda for his error and gathers followers for it (*factious,* 10). They confront him with the truth and call him to repentance (*admonishing,* 10). If he refuses repeated admonition, they must exclude him from the church, for he has condemned himself by persisting in his sinful perversion of the truth and has excluded himself from their fellowship. (11)

3:8 *Who have believed,* that is, have come to faith and are believers.

3:9 *Genealogies.* Cf. 1 Ti 1:4. These probably refer to speculative and fanciful interpretations of Old Testament history. They are *unprofitable and futile* because they do not employ the inspired Scriptures for the purpose for which they were given, to "instruct" men "for salvation through faith in Christ Jesus." (2 Ti 3:15-17)

3:10 *Factious,* creator and leader of a faction, one of those "who create dissensions and difficulties, in opposition to the doctrine which you have been taught" (Ro 16:17). The Greek word has given us the term "heretic," and these verses are the classical definition of the heretic.

3:10 *Once or twice.* The procedure is to be that prescribed by Jesus, Mt 18:15-17.

3:11 *Perverted and sinful . . . self-condemned.* Since he has both turned aside from the true course and has refused the admonition that would restore him, he stands condemned by his own actions and must be left to the judgment of God. (Cf. 1 Co 5:5, 12-13)

CONCLUSION: INSTRUCTIONS, GREETINGS, BENEDICTION (3:12-15)

12 When I send Ar'te·mas or Tych'i·cus to you, do your best to come to me at Nic·op'o·lis, for I have decided to spend the winter there. 13 Do your best to speed Zenas the lawyer and A·pol'los on their way; see that they lack nothing. 14And let our people learn to apply themselves to good deeds,*d* so as to help cases of urgent need, and not to be unfruitful.

15 All who are with me send greetings to you. Greet those who love us in the faith. Grace be with you all.

3:12-15 Titus is to rejoin Paul in Nicopolis when Artemas or Tychicus comes to relieve him (12). He is to help Zenas and Apollos, the bearers of this letter, on their way (13). The Cretan Christians, too, are to do their part in supporting these missionaries (14). Paul and his co-workers send greetings to Titus and all believers in Crete.

3:12 *Artemas.* Unknown.

Tychicus. Cf. Acts 20:4; Eph 6:21; Cl 4:7-9; 2 Ti 4:12.

Nicopolis, probably in Epirus. See the Introduction to the Pastoral Letters.

3:13 *Zenas the lawyer.* Probably a converted Jewish scribe.

Apollos. Cf. Acts 18:24-28; 1 Co 1:12; 3:4-6, 22; 16:12.

3:15 *With you all.* At least the substance of this letter is intended for all the Christians in Crete.

THE LETTER OF PAUL TO

PHILEMON

INTRODUCTION

During his 2-year imprisonment in Rome Paul "welcomed all who came to him" (Acts 28:30). Among the many who sought out Paul was one disreputable character, and Paul "welcomed" him too, the slave Onesimus. Onesimus had run away from his master Philemon of Colossae, lining his pockets for the journey with his master's goods, as was the usual practice with runaway slaves (Phmn 18). Somehow he reached Rome, and somehow he came into contact with Paul. Paul's welcome for poor Onesimus must have been a warm one, for he converted the young runaway and became very fond of him. Paul would gladly have kept Onesimus with him, for he was now living up to his name (Onesimus means "useful") in his devoted service to Paul. Since the slave's master Philemon was also a convert of Paul's, bound to him by a sacred and enduring tie, he might have made bold to do so. But Paul honored all human ties, including the tie which bound slave to master, as hallowed in Christ (Cl 3:22 ff.; Eph 6:5 ff.). He therefore sent Onesimus back to Colossae with Tychicus, the bearer of his Letter to the Colossians (Cl 4:7-9), and wrote a letter to his master in which he bespoke for the runaway a kindly and forgiving reception. We can measure the strength of the bond between the apostle and his converts by the confidence with which Paul makes his request of Philemon, a request all the more remarkable in the light of the fact that captured runaways were usually very harshly dealt with. Paul goes even farther: he hints that he would like to have Onesimus back for his own service. (13, 14, 20, 21)

Brief and personal though it is, the Letter to Philemon affords two valuable Christian insights. First, there is no line of cleavage between the official Paul, the apostle, and the person Paul; for both, life has one content and one meaning: "For me to live is Christ." Luther portrays Paul as being a "Christ" to Onesimus, "pleading the cause of the runaway as Christ has pleaded ours. For we are all His Onesimi, if we believe it." A man who believes and knows that he has come back to God as God's runaway slave and has been welcomed as a son, such a man can write the Gospel into life's minutiae as naturally and gracefully as Paul does in this letter.

Second, the Letter to Philemon illustrates the apostolic and Christian attitude toward social problems. Paul does not plead for Onesimus' liberation. There is nothing like a movement to free slaves, even Christian slaves of Christian masters, either here or elsewhere in the New Testament. But a Gospel which can say to the master of a runaway slave that he is to receive him back "for ever, no longer as a slave, but more than a slave, as a beloved brother" (Phmn 15-16), has overcome the evil of slavery from within and has therefore already rung the knell of slavery.

428

THE LETTER OF PAUL TO
PHILEMON

GREETINGS (1-3)

1 Paul, a prisoner for Christ Jesus, and Timothy our brother,
To Phi·le′mon our beloved fellow worker 2 and Ap′phi·a our sister and Ar·chip′pus our fellow soldier, and the church in your house:
3 Grace to you and peace from God our Father and the Lord Jesus Christ.

THANKSGIVING AND PRAYER (4-7)

4 I thank my God always when I remember you in my prayers, 5 because I hear of your love and of the faith which you have toward the Lord Jesus and all the saints, 6 and I pray that the sharing of your faith may promote the knowledge of all the good that is ours in Christ. 7 For I have derived much joy and comfort from your love, my brother, because the hearts of the saints have been refreshed through you.

PAUL'S PLEA FOR HIS CHILD ONESIMUS (8-20)

8 Accordingly, though I am bold enough in Christ to command you to do what is required, 9 yet for love's sake I prefer to appeal to you—I, Paul, am ambassador[a] and now a prisoner also for Christ Jesus—10 I appeal to you for my child, O·nes′i·mus, whose father I have become in my imprisonment. 11 (Formerly he was useless to you, but now he is indeed useful[b] to you and to me.) 12 I am sending him back to you, sending my very heart. 13 I would have been glad to keep him with me, in order that he might serve me on your behalf during my imprisonment for the gospel; 14 but I preferred to do nothing without your consent in order that your goodness might not be by compulsion but of your own free will.

15 Perhaps this is why he was parted from you for a while, that you might have him back for ever, 16 no longer as a slave but more than a slave, as a beloved brother, especially to me but how much more to you, both in the flesh and in the Lord. 17 So if you consider me your partner, receive him as you would receive me. 18 If he has

_____
[a] Or an old man   [b] The name Onesimus means useful or (compare verse 20) beneficial

1-3 *Timothy* had been with Paul during his 3-year ministry in Ephesus and no doubt was acquainted with many Christians of the province of Asia, such as *Philemon,* his wife *Apphia,* and his son *Archippus,* who had a special ministry at Colossae (Cl 14:17) and so is singled out as *fellow soldier* of the apostle.

4-7 Paul gives thanks for Philemon's faith and love and prays that they may continue their effectual witness. Philemon seems to have recently distinguished himself by a work of love which *refreshed the hearts of the saints.* Paul is about to request another such refreshment of heart for himself. (20)

6 The *knowledge* which Philemon's love born of faith is to promote may be the knowledge which his witness produces or increases in others. The thought might, however, also be that Philemon's own knowledge is deepened as his faith is demonstrated and exercised in love.

8-20 Paul appeals to Philemon to receive Onesimus again, now more than a slave to him, a beloved brother forever. Paul lets Philemon know

how greatly he cherishes this child of his imprisonment and hints pretty broadly that he would like to have him back in his own service; after all, Paul argues, Philemon owes him more than the gift of a slave could repay—as Paul's convert he owes his very life and self to Paul. (19)

10 Cf. 1 Co 4:15: "I became your father in Christ Jesus through the gospel."

14 *Your goodness* here means the generous action of making Paul a gift of the "useful" Onesimus.

16 Onesimus has become *a beloved brother* to his master *both in the flesh,* that is, in his legal-human position as a slave, and *in the Lord,* as fellow member in the church, the body of Christ. These words are a concrete application of what Paul has taught the churches in Cl 3:11; 3:22—4: 1; and Eph 6:5-9; cf. 1 Ti 6:1-2; Tts 2:9-14.

17 Philemon is Paul's "beloved fellow worker" (v. 1), "his brother" (v. 7), and his *partner* (v. 17; cf. Ph 1:5). In v. 19 Paul speaks of him as owing his very existence to Paul. So strong is the bond created by the Gospel.

wronged you at all, or owes you anything, charge that to my account. [19] I, Paul, write this with my own hand, I will repay it—to say nothing of your owing me even your own self. [20] Yes, brother, I want some benefit from you in the Lord. Refresh my heart in Christ.

21 Confident of your obedience, I write to you, knowing that you will do even more than I say. [22]At the same time, prepare a guest room for me, for I am hoping through your prayers to be granted to you.

CONCLUDING GREETINGS (21-25)

23 Ep'a·phras, my fellow prisoner in Christ Jesus, sends greetings to you, [24] and so do Mark, Ar·is·tar'chus, Demas, and Luke, my fellow workers.

25 The grace of the Lord Jesus Christ be with your spirit.

19 The language here is that of a formal IOU. This is probably a touch of humor. Paul hardly had the means to compensate Philemon for the loss which he had sustained through Onesimus. But the second half of the verse is serious truth clothed in the language of familiar friendship; since Philemon was once "dead in trespasses" (Cl 2:13) and came "to fulness of life" in Christ (Cl 2:10) through Paul's proclamation of the Gospel, he owes himself, the true self that will live forever, to Paul.

21-25 Paul bespeaks Philemon's hospitality for the time of his release and return to Colossae, transmits the greetings of his visitors and fellow workers at Rome, and closes with a benediction.

22 *To be granted to you,* that is, by being released from imprisonment and so becoming free to revisit the churches of Asia.

23-24 The names mentioned here all occur in Cl 4:10-14. The term *fellow prisoner* means literally "fellow prisoner-of-war." It is used figuratively to indicate that Epaphras is voluntarily sharing his hardships as a soldier of Christ.

THE LETTER TO THE
HEBREWS

INTRODUCTION

1 The Letter to the Hebrews is surely a part of the story of how the Word of the Lord grew and prevailed. Here if anywhere in the New Testament we are made conscious of the fact that God's speaking is a mighty onward movement, an impetus of revelation designed to carry man with it from glory to glory. And here it is impressed on us that if a man resists that impetus, he does so at his own deadly peril; we are warned that stagnation and retrogression invite the destroying judgment of God. But the letter is itself also the proof that God does not abandon the weak and sickly stragglers of His flock; He sends forth His Word and heals them.

Destination of the Letter

2 The title "To the Hebrews" is not part of the original letter, but was probably added in the second century when the New Testament letters were gathered into a collection. Moreover, there is no salutation which would identify the readers. The destination of the letter must therefore be inferred from the letter itself. It is not so personal as a letter of Paul's. It is more on the order of a sermon (cf. 13:22, "my word of exhortation"), and it is more literary, with its high stylistic finish and strictly unified theme. Still, it is not merely an essay in letter form, but a genuine letter. It grows out of a personal relationship between the author and his readers. The author has lived among the people whom he is now addressing; and though he is at the time of writing separated from them, he hopes to be restored to them soon (13:18-19, 23). The content of the letter indicates that the readers were Jewish Christians, so that the title given by the men of the second century is not unfitting.

3 Many modern scholars are inclined to see in the readers not Jewish Christians in danger of relapsing into Judaism, but Gentile Christians (or Christians in general) in danger of lapsing into irreligion. And they have often argued their case with considerable ingenuity. But it is difficult to see why the letter should in that case be from beginning to end one great and emphatic exposition of the superiority of the New Testament revelation over that of the Old Testament. Why should an appeal to *Gentile* Christians in danger of apostasy take just this form? Jewish Christians seem to be more likely recipients of the letter.

4 Where these Jewish Christians lived cannot be definitely made out. Italy is the most likely place, and within Italy, Rome. The letter contains greetings to the church from "those who come from Italy" (13:24), evidently from members of the Jewish Christian church who are now with the author and are sending greetings to their home church. This is confirmed by the fact that Hebrews is first quoted and alluded to by Roman writers, namely, Clement of Rome and Hermas. The readers have their own assembly (10:25), but are also connected with a larger group, as the words "greet *all* your leaders and *all* the saints" (13:24) indicate. It has therefore been very plausibly suggested that the recipients were one of the house churches to which Paul refers in Romans. (16:5, 14-15)

Occasion and Purpose of the Letter

5 These Christians had in the past given evidence of their faith and love (6:10). They had stoutly endured persecution themselves and had courageously aided others under persecution (10:32-34). Their believing courage had not failed them in times of crisis; but it was failing them in the longdrawn, unending struggle with sin (12:4). They were growing dispirited and slack (12:12); the continuous pressure of public contempt, particularly the contempt of their fellow Jews (13:13), had revived in them the old temptation to be offended at the weakness of the Christ they believed in, at His shameful death, and at the fact that the Christ did not fulfill their Judaic expectation and "remain for ever" on earth (cf. Jn 12:34) but

was removed from sight in the heavens. They had ceased to progress in their faith (5:11-14) and were neglecting the public assembly of the church which could strengthen them in their faith (10:25). Some had perhaps already apostatized (6:4-8); all were in danger of falling away (3:12) and reverting to Judaism (13:9-14). Judaism with its fixed and venerable institutions, its visible and splendid center in the Jerusalem temple and its cultus, its security and exemption from persecution as a lawful religion under Roman law must have had for them an almost overwhelming fascination.

6 The letter is therefore basically just what its author calls it, a "word of exhortation" (13:22), an appeal to "hold fast the confession . . . without wavering" (10:23; cf. 10:38; 3:14). The author points his readers to Jesus and urges them to look to Jesus, "the pioneer and perfecter of our faith, who for the joy that was set before him endured the cross, despising the shame, and is seated at the right hand of the throne of God" (12:2). They are to consider Him with the eyes of faith and find in Him the strength to overcome their weariness and faintheartedness (12:3). The whole long and detailed exposition of the high priesthood of Christ is anything but a merely informative theological treatise. It is wholly pastoral and practical in its aim and intent. The author is a leader like the leaders whom he describes in his letter (13:17); he is keeping watch not over the theology of his people but over their souls as one who will have to give an account of his leadership.

The Author of the Letter

7 The letter does not name its author, and there is no consistent tradition in the early church concerning its authorship. In the East the letter was regarded either as directly written by Paul or as in some sense owing its origin to Paul. Origen of Alexandria reflects this tradition; he says of the letter: "Its thoughts are the thoughts of the apostle, but the language and composition that of one who recalled from memory and, as it were, made notes of what was said by the master . . . . Men of old times handed it down as Paul's. But who wrote the epistle God only knows certainly." The Western church did not attribute the letter to Paul; Tertullian of Carthage assigned it to Barnabas, while in Rome and elsewhere the letter was anonymous.

8 The fact that the author counts himself and his readers among those who received the Word of salvation at second hand from those who had heard the Lord is conclusive evidence that the author is not Paul (2:3), for Paul appeals repeatedly to the fact that he has seen the Lord and has received the Gospel directly from Him (1 Co 9:1; 1 Co 15:8; Gl 1:11-12). The general character of the theology of the letter and the author's acquaintance with Paul's companion Timothy (13:23) point to someone who moved in the circle of Paul's friends and co-workers. The characteristics of the letter itself further limit the possibilities: they indicate that the author was in all probability a Greek-speaking Jewish Christian, thoroughly at home in the Old Testament in its Greek translation, and intimately acquainted with the whole worship and cultus of the Jews, a man capable, moreover, of the most finished and literary Greek in the New Testament. Barnabas, the Levite from Cyprus (Acts 4:36) and companion of Paul, would be a not unlikely candidate for authorship. Whether Tertullian attributed the letter to him on the basis of a genuine tradition or was making a plausible conjecture, cannot be determined. Apollos, whom Luther suggested as the possible author, is even more likely. He was associated with Paul, though not in any sense a "disciple" of Paul, and Luke in the Book of Acts describes him as a Jew, a native of that great center of learning and rhetoric, Alexandria, an eloquent man, well versed in the Scriptures, and fervent in spirit (Acts 18:24-25), all characteristics that we find reflected in Hebrews.

9 Luther's conjecture remains the most reasonable of all the ancient and modern conjectures, which have attributed the letter to a great variety of authors—Luke, Clement of Rome, Silvanus, Aquila and Priscilla, Priscilla alone, etc. But Origen's word still holds: "Who wrote the epistle God only knows certainly." More important than the man's name is the kind of man he was; he was an earnest teacher of the church, deeply conscious of his responsibility for the church, whom the Holy Spirit moved to employ all his resources of language and learning in order to restore to health and strength the weak and faltering church.

Date of the Letter

10 Since Hebrews is quoted by Clement of Rome in his letter to the Corinthians

of A. D. 96, the letter must be earlier than that date. There is no evidence which enables us to determine exactly how much earlier it was written. Timothy is still alive at the time of writing (13:23), but since he was a young man when Paul first took him as his companion in A. D. 49 (Acts 16:1-3), he may have lived to the end of the first century or beyond. The readers have been converted by personal disciples of the Lord (2:3), and considerable time has elapsed since their conversion: they have had time for development and growth (5:12). Some of their first leaders are now dead (13:7). They have endured one persecution (probably the Neronian persecution A. D. 64) and are apparently facing another (10:36). All this points to the latter half of the first century. Since the author dwells on the fact that the old system of priesthood and sacrifice was destined to be superseded by a greater and more perfect priesthood and sacrifice, it would seem strange that he does not mention the fall of Jerusalem (which put an end forever to the old cultus) if that event had taken place. The argument from silence is strong in this case, and a dating before A. D. 70, probably shortly before, seems very probable. But it should be said that many scholars today are not inclined to attach much weight to this argument; they argue that the author is thinking not of the Jerusalem temple and its cultus, but of the cultus as he knows it from the Old Testament, and date the letter somewhere in the eighties.

Characteristics of the Letter

11 The purpose of the letter is practical, like that of every book of the New Testament; its aim is to strengthen faith and hope, to inculcate stout patience and a joyous holding fast to the Christian confession. The message which provides the basis for the exhortation and the impetus and power for its fulfillment has three primary characteristics. It is founded on the Old Testament; it is centered in Christ; and it is marked by an intense consciousness of the fact that all days since the coming of the Christ are last days.

12 The message is, first, founded on the Old Testament. It is to a large extent an interpretation and exposition of Old Testament Scriptures. It has been likened to a Christian sermon or a series of sermons on selected psalms (2, 8, 95, 110). The letter therefore contains high testimony to the inspiration and authority of the Old Testament Scriptures. In the first verse the whole Old Testament is designated as the very voice of God speaking to men, and throughout the letter words which men of God spoke of old are presented as spoken by God Himself (e. g., 1:5, 6, 13; 5:5) or by Christ (e. g., 2:11-13; 10:5) or by the Holy Spirit. (3:7; 10:15)

13 The author's characteristic use of the Old Testament is that which has been termed the typological use, that is, he sees in the history and the institutions of the Old Covenant events, persons, and actions which are typical, foreshadowings and prefigurings of that which was to become full reality in the New Covenant. In one sense the whole epistle is a set of variations on a theme from Paul: "These [the Old Testament sacral institutions] are only a shadow of what is to come; but the substance belongs to Christ" (Cl 2:17). Thus Melchizedek, both priest and king, is divinely designed to point beyond himself to the great High Priest Jesus Christ (7:1—10:18). The fate of God's people in the wilderness, their failure to attain to the promised Sabbath rest, points beyond itself to the eternal Sabbath rest which awaits the New Testament people of God (3:7—4:13). This view and use of the Old Testament never degenerates into mere allegory; that is, the Old Testament figures are never merely symbols of eternal truths, as in the allegorizing interpretation of the Jewish philosopher Philo; rather, the Old Testament history is always taken seriously as history. As such, as history, it points beyond itself to the last days. This use of Scripture is therefore an eloquent expression of the faith that God is Lord of all history, shaping it for His purposes and leading it toward His great redemptive goal. The Old Testament is therefore of abiding value and enduring significance for the people of God in the last days, for it enables them to see the whole sweep and direction of the mighty redeeming arm of God.

14 The message is, second, centered in Christ. Christ, the Son of God, dominates the whole, and Christ colors every part of the whole. He stands at the beginning of history as the Son through whom God created the world; He stands at the end of all history as the divinely appointed "heir of all things" (1:2). He dominates all history and rules the whole world, "upholding the universe by his word of power" (1:3). He is God's ultimate and definitive Word to man (1:2), and His high-priestly ministry is God's

ultimate deed for man—a whole, assured, eternal deliverance from sin. That high-priestly, atoning ministry spans the whole of Jesus' existence: His entry into mankind, His sacrificial suffering and death, His entering into the heavenly Holy of Holies, His presentation of His sacrifice at the throne of God, and His return in glory to the waiting people of God are all high-priestly acts. (E. g., 2:17-18; 9:11-14; 4:14; 9:28)

15 His high-priestly ministry marks Him as full partaker in the Godhead and as completely one with man. Indeed, no letter of the New Testament is so full of the humanity of Jesus as Hebrews. Since He is both Son of God and a Priest fully one with man, His priesthood and His sacrifice have a real and eternal significance and top and supersede every other priestly ministration. The impress of the incarnate Christ is upon His people; His history of suffering and triumph is their history; His obedience and fidelity to the Father make possible their faithful obedience to God. His entering into the Holy Place gives them access to the throne of God.

16 The message is, third, marked by the consciousness that the days since God spoke in His Son are "these last days" (1:2). Christ has appeared "at the end of the age to put away sin by the sacrifice of himself" (9:26). It is the beginning of the end; the new world of God has become a reality in the midst of the old, and men "have tasted . . . the powers of the age to come" (6:5) even now. What former ages had possessed in an imperfect form, a form which itself pointed to a fuller realization, is now a present blessing—a better covenant (7:22), better sacrifices (9:23), a better possession (10:34), and a better hope (7:19). Men still hope, and the full realization of all that Christ has wrought is still to come. But the Day is drawing near (10:25) when all that is now a sure hope shall be fully realized. This "last days" character of Jesus' work, its eschatological character, gives it a final, once-for-all character and makes the decision of faith one of terrible urgency; eternal issues are being decided now, in faith or unbelief. Man is confronted by an eternal and inescapable either-or. Seen in this eschatological light, the sternness of the warnings in 6:4-8 and 10:26-31, warnings which at first glance seem to preclude the possibility of a second repentance, is not strange. (These warnings seemed to Luther to be "hard knots" and made him dubious about the letter.) God has spoken His last word, and the time is short; men must not be left under the delusion that they can coolly and deliberately sin and then repent in order to sin again. Such sinning is the last step on the way toward apostasy; it is the expression of an "evil, unbelieving heart" (3:12) which cannot find the way to repentance because it has deliberately cut itself off from God, the Giver of repentance.

OUTLINE

I. 1:1—4:13 God's Ultimate Word, Spoken by a Son

    A. 1:1-14 Instruction: The Son Superior to Angels

    B. 2:1-4 Admonition: Do Not Neglect Such a Great Salvation

    C. 2:5-18 Instruction: The Son Made Lower than the Angels

    D. 3:1-6 Instruction: Jesus Worthy of More Glory than Moses

    E. 3:7—4:13 Warning: Harden Not Your Hearts

II. 4:14—10:18 Jesus, the Ultimate High Priest

    A. 4:14—5:10 Instruction: Jesus a True High Priest

    B. 5:11—6:20 Warning and Encouragement

    C. 7:1—10:18 Instruction: Jesus the High Priest

III. 10:19—12:29 Exhortation and Warning

    A. 10:19-25 Exhortation: Draw Near with a True Heart

    B. 10:26-31 Warning: Judgment on Apostasy

    C. 10:32-39 Exhortation: Do Not Throw Away Confidence

    D. 11:1—12:2 Exhortation: Run the Race

    E. 12:3-29 Exhortation to Faith and Fear

IV. 13:1-25 Concluding Admonitions and Close

THE LETTER TO THE

HEBREWS

God's Ultimate Word, Spoken by a Son

1:1 — 4:13

INSTRUCTION: THE SON SUPERIOR TO ANGELS (1:1-14)

1 In many and various ways God spoke of old to our fathers by the prophets; ² but in these last days he has spoken to us by a Son, whom he appointed the heir of all things, through whom also he created the world. ³ He reflects the glory of God and bears the very stamp of his nature, upholding the universe by his word of power. When he had made purification for sins, he sat down at the right hand of the Majesty on high, ⁴ having become as much superior to angels as the name he has obtained is more excellent than theirs.

5 For to what angel did God ever say,
>"Thou art my Son,
>today I have begotten thee"?

Or again,
>"I will be to him a father,
>and he shall be to me a son"?

The pastoral intent of the writer (cf. Introduction, par. 6) dictates the structure of his letter; instruction alternates with words of admonition, warning, and appeal. The statements which expound the surpassing significance of Jesus the Son as God's last Word to man are followed by imperatives which summon men to heed that Word.

1:1—4:13 God has spoken His ultimate Word in His Son, who surpasses all previous mediators of divine revelation (prophets, angels, Moses); therefore give heed to that Word of salvation.

1:1-14 God has climaxed His ancient Word of promise (*prophets*, 1) by His final Word *spoken* in *these last days by a Son* (2). The unique importance of this Word is revealed in the unique greatness of its Bearer, God's Son. SEVEN WEIGHTY STATEMENTS expound the Son's greatness (2-4). He is seen at the end of God's ways as *heir*, Owner, and Ruler of the universe (2). He is seen at the beginning of God's ways, in creation, as partaking in the Creator's action (2). To behold His glory is to see the *glory of God* going forth into the world. To know Him is to know God's *nature* (3). The Son's *word of power* is God's own Word, *upholding the universe* (3). The Son's work, *purification for sins*, is God's proper work (3; cf. Eze 36:25-33). The Son is enthroned in honor on God's own throne (*right hand of the Majesty on high*, 3). His *name*, expressing all that He is and signifies for man, marks Him as *superior to angels*, who declared God's law. (4; cf. 2:2)

SEVEN OT QUOTATIONS (5-13) cite the witness of God's ancient Word concerning the surpassing greatness of the Son. In two passages God speaks of David's son and Lord as His Son (5; cf. Ps 2:7;

2 Sm 7:14). Two passages point up the angels' inferiority to the Son (6-7; cf. Dt 32:43; Ps 97:7). Two passages again hail the Son as the incarnation of God's kingdom, eternally enthroned in the Creator's unchanging Majesty (8-12; cf. Ps 45:6-7; Ps 102:25-27). The seven quotations, like the seven statements, reach their climax in the words of Ps 110:1, which set the King at God's right hand and promise Him victory (13; cf. 3). Angels cannot compete with Him; they can only *serve* His gracious purpose of *salvation.* (14)

1:2 *A Son.* The prophets were true messengers of God, but servants, each entrusted with a portion of the message which was to be fully and finally expressed in the sending of One who was Son in the full sense. (Cf. Mt 21:37; Mk 12:6)

Heir of all things . . . created the world. Paul has the two thoughts in inverse order: "All things were created through him and for him" (Cl 1:16). Cf. also Jn 1:3 and Mt 28:18. Sonship and heirship go together. (Cf. Ps 2:7-8)

1:3 *Bears the very stamp of his nature,* as a coin reproduces the pattern of the die which stamped it.

1:5-13 The author's use of the OT will appear audacious, or even arbitrary, to anyone who does not share his convictions that: (a) the whole OT is the voice of God; (b) Jesus Christ is very God; (c) the whole OT testifies to Him. (Cf. Introduction, pars. 12 and 13; Jn 5:39; Acts 10:43; 2 Co 1:19-20; 2 Ti 3:15)

1:5a Ps 2:7, where God addresses the king on David's throne in words whose full meaning becomes real and apparent in the Son of David, the Son of God.

1:5b 2 Sm 7:14. God's promise to David (through the prophet Nathan) concerning David's succes-

[6]And again, when he brings the first-born into the world, he says,
> "Let all God's angels worship him."

[7] Of the angels he says,
> "Who makes his angels winds,
> and his servants flames of fire."

[8] But of the Son he says,
> "Thy throne, O God,[a] is for ever and ever,
> the righteous scepter is the scepter of thy[b] kingdom.

[9]
> Thou hast loved righteousness and hated lawlessness;
> therefore God, thy God, has anointed thee
> with the oil of gladness beyond thy comrades."

[10]And,
> "Thou, Lord, didst found the earth in the beginning,
> and the heavens are the work of thy hands;

[11]
> they will perish, but thou remainest;
> they will all grow old like a garment,

[12]
> like a mantle thou wilt roll them up,
> and they will be changed.[c]
> But thou art the same,
> and thy years will never end."

[13] But to what angel has he ever said,
> "Sit at my right hand,
> till I make thy enemies
> a stool for thy feet"?

[14]Are they not all ministering spirits sent forth to serve, for the sake of those who are to obtain salvation?

ADMONITION: DO NOT NEGLECT SUCH A GREAT SALVATION (2:1-4)

2 Therefore we must pay the closer attention to what we have heard, lest we drift away from it. [2] For if the message declared by angels was valid and every trans-

---

[a] Or *God is thy throne*   [b] Other ancient authorities read *his*   [c] Other ancient authorities add *like a garment*

---

sors, a promise fully fulfilled in Jesus Christ.

1:6 Words which in their original setting (Dt 32:43) called upon the *angels* to worship the Lord God of Israel as the Avenger and Savior of His people are here applied to the incarnate Son of God, "that all may honor the Son, even as they honor the Father" (Jn 5:23). The OT is quoted according to the Septuagint (an ancient Greek translation of the OT), which differs from the one reproduced in English versions. Recent discoveries indicate that this reading may well be the original one.

1:7 Ps 104:4. God's *angels* ("messengers") appear in various forms, fulfill their service, and vanish. God's Son endures unchanged. (1:8-10)

1:8-9 In Ps 45:6-7 the anointed king of God's people is, as God's vice-regent and executor of His righteousness on earth, called *God* (or his reign is marked as divine, cf. RSV note *a*); being under the favor of God, his reign is destined to endure. This ancient promise found its final Yes in Jesus Christ. (Cf. 2 Co 1:20)

1:10 Ps 102:25-27. Ps 102 is entitled "A prayer of one afflicted, when he is faint and pours out his complaints before the LORD." The psalmist, his existence shattered, can find grounds for hope only in the God who endures when all else passes away. He will arise and have pity on His people,

so that all "nations will fear the name of the LORD, and all the kings of the earth" will bow before His glory (Ps 102:12-15). In Jesus Christ God did arise and help and lead all peoples to worship Him; and the words of Ps 102 are fitly applied to the Son.

1:13 Ps 110:1. God addresses His anointed king. It was with the words of this psalm that Jesus Himself had stated His Messianic claim most powerfully. (Cf. Mt 22:41-46 note)

Stool for thy feet, symbol of conquest. (Cf. Jos 10:24)

1:14 *Ministering spirits.* The angels who worship (6) the Son are sent forth to *serve* man, with whom the Son has identified Himself and to whom He has given *salvation.*

2:1-4 Even the Law, *declared by angels,* imposed fearful penalties on *every transgression or disobedience;* how much the more does God's final Word of *salvation* confront its hearers with a dreadful alternative for those who *neglect* it; for they are rejecting the Word of Christ, the attestation of His apostles, the witness of the *God* who does *wonders,* the working of His *Spirit.*

2:1 *Drift away.* Cf. Introduction, pars. 5 and 6.

2:2 *Declared by angels.* Cf. Acts 7:53; Gl 3:19.

Just retribution. Cf. 10:29, which echoes the language of Nm 15:30-31; 35:30; Dt 17:2-7.

gression or disobedience received a just retribution, [3] how shall we escape if we neglect such a great salvation? It was declared at first by the Lord, and it was attested to us by those who heard him, [4] while God also bore witness by signs and wonders and various miracles and by gifts of the Holy Spirit distributed according to his own will.

INSTRUCTION: THE SON MADE LOWER THAN THE ANGELS (2:5-18)

[5] For it was not to angels that God subjected the world to come, of which we are speaking. [6] It has been testified somewhere,

"What is man that thou art mindful of him,
or the son of man, that thou carest for him?

[7]   Thou didst make him for a little while lower than the angels,
thou hast crowned him with glory and honor,[d]

[8]   putting everything in subjection under his feet."

Now in putting everything in subjection to him, he left nothing outside his control. As it is, we do not yet see everything in subjection to him. [9] But we see Jesus, who for a little while was made lower than the angels, crowned with glory and honor because of the suffering of death, so that by the grace of God he might taste death for every one.

[10] For it was fitting that he, for whom and by whom all things exist, in bringing many sons to glory, should make the pioneer of their salvation perfect through suffering. [11] For he who sanctifies and those who are sanctified have all one origin. That is why he is not ashamed to call them brethren, [12] saying,

"I will proclaim thy name to my brethren,
in the midst of the congregation I will praise thee."

[13]And again,

"I will put my trust in him."

And again,

"Here am I, and the children God has given me."

[d] Other ancient authorities insert *and didst set him over the works of thy hands*

2:5-18 The fact that the Son *was made lower than the angels* (9) takes nothing from His glory and does not call in question His superiority to the angels; rather, it is the essential part of His glory. If in His humiliation He is subjected to the *suffering of death*, He *tastes death for every one* (9) in order that all men may share in the *glory and honor* which *the grace of God* has designed for man (6, 9). He partakes of man's *nature, in flesh and blood,* and dies man's *death* (14) in order to deliver men from the tyranny of the lord of death, *the devil* (14-15). He *suffered* and was *tempted* as One who was destined thereby to become *a merciful and faithful high priest to God . . . to make expiation for the sins of the people* (17). Vicariously and victoriously He has "made purification for sins" (1:3) and therefore is enthroned as Son of God in glory (1:3) and brings the *many sons* of God *to glory*. (2:10)

2:5 *For* points back to 1:14. God's Word (Ps 8, quoted in vv. 6-8) has destined man, not angels, to have dominion in *the world to come;* therefore the Son identifies Himself with man, and the angels are sent forth to serve man.

2:6 *Testified somewhere.* Only here in Hebrews is an OT word introduced as spoken by a man; the vagueness of the reference seems designed to play down the human aspect of its authorship.

2:6-8 The words of Ps 8:4-6 recall Gn 1:26, where the Creator gives man dominion over His creation;

they point forward to the "world to come" in which that dominion will be fully restored to man. In this world *(as it is)* that perfect dominion is not a visible reality but an object of faith and hope.

2:9 *We see Jesus.* In Jesus (marked as man by the use of His human name alone) the believed destiny of man is a reality; He who died *for every one* has risen and has entered into the honor, glory, and dominion designed for man.

2:10 *He* is God, Lord of history and creation *(for whom and by whom all things exist). It was fitting,* in harmony with His revealed nature as holy and righteous God, that He should *bring men to glory* and *salvation,* not by overlooking their sin but by dealing with it. He dealt with man's sin by giving His Son as the *pioneer* of man's salvation, who opens the way and leads the way to salvation. The Son becomes the *perfect pioneer* by *suffering* for man's sin (and dying for man's sin, cf. 14).

2:11 The Son's act of suffering and dying to make "purification for sins" (1:3) is a sacrificial, priestly act (cf. 17); therefore the principle of priesthood applies to Him: priest *(he who sanctifies)* and people *(those who are sanctified)* are both of *one origin,* both are human. (Cf. 5:1, 8-10)

2:11b-13 The three OT passages all emphasize the Son's solidarity with the men for whom He performs His priestly service. Ps 22:22 pictures the righteous Sufferer (the prototype and pre-

14 Since therefore the children share in flesh and blood, he himself likewise partook of the same nature, that through death he might destroy him who has the power of death, that is, the devil, 15 and deliver all those who through fear of death were subject to lifelong bondage. 16 For surely it is not with angels that he is concerned but with the descendants of Abraham. 17 Therefore he had to be made like his brethren in every respect, so that he might become a merciful and faithful high priest in the service of God, to make expiation for the sins of the people. 18 For because he himself has suffered and been tempted, he is able to help those who are tempted.

INSTRUCTION: JESUS WORTHY OF MORE GLORY THAN MOSES (3:1-6)

3 Therefore, holy brethren, who share in a heavenly call, consider Jesus, the apostle and high priest of our confession. 2 He was faithful to him who appointed him, just as Moses also was faithful in*e* God's house. 3 Yet Jesus has been counted worthy of as much more glory than Moses as the builder of a house has more honor than the house. 4 (For every house is built by some one, but the builder of all things is God.) 5 Now Moses was faithful in all God's house as a servant, to testify to the things that were to be spoken later, 6 but Christ was faithful over God's*f* house as a son. And we are his house if we hold fast our confidence and pride in our hope.*g*

WARNING: HARDEN NOT YOUR HEARTS (3:7 – 4:13)

7 Therefore, as the Holy Spirit says,
　　"Today, when you hear his voice,
8　　do not harden your hearts as in the rebellion,
　　on the day of testing in the wilderness,
9　　where your fathers put me to the test
　　and saw my works for forty years.

e Other ancient authorities insert *all*　*f* Greek *his*　*g* Other ancient authorities insert *firm to the end*

diction of the suffering Christ, cf. Mt 27:35, 39, 43, 46; Jn 19:28) as calling men His *brethren* (11). The other two are words of the prophet Isaiah (Is 8:17-18). The prophet had proclaimed the will and Word of the Lord to his people and their king in vain. The prophet binds up his testimony and seals his teaching among his disciples, trusting in God to vindicate His servant the prophet as the bearer of His Word. He and the disciples *(children)* given Him by God will meanwhile stand as living witnesses while "the LORD . . . is hiding his face" from His people (Is 8:17). Even so Jesus met the unbelief and the rejection with which His people responded to Him. He *put* His *trust* in God, as a man can do it, thanked God for the men God had given Him, for His disciples and the church created by their witness (cf. 2:3). Thus He entered fully into His brotherhood with man.

2:14 *The devil has the power of death* because He can accuse sinful man (cf. Rv 12:9-10). When the Son enters mankind and confronts Satan with a human righteousness which the devil cannot accuse, the accuser is "destroyed" and man is set free.

2:17 *High priest.* Cf. 11 note. Here the author states the theme that is to dominate the whole central section of his epistle, 4:14 – 10:18.

The "admonition" portion of this section is touched on lightly in the verse (3:1) which introduces the next instruction, probably because the admonition based on the high priesthood of the Son is to be developed so fully in 10:19 ff.

3:1-6 Jesus is *apostle,* the authorized Messenger or Envoy of God who speaks and acts in His name; He is *high priest* who with intercession and sacrifice represents man before God. As such He can be compared with *Moses,* who delivered God's people from bondage in Egypt (cf. 2:15) as God's spokesman and agent (Ex 3:10-12; 4:10-17) and more than once stood before God as a priestly intercessor for his people (Ex 32:11-14, 30-32; Nm 14:13-19). Both, too, were *faithful* in their service *in God's house* (God's people, His household). Yet Jesus is *worthy of . . . much more glory than Moses.* Whereas Moses served as *servant,* Jesus was faithful *as a Son,* Lord *over God's house as He is Creator of the house (builder).* Whereas Moses' service pointed beyond itself to a greater future *(to testify to the things that were to be spoken later),* Jesus' Word and work ushers in God's final great Today (cf. 3:7, 13, 15; 4:7). The house over which He is Lord in the last days is made up of men of all nations whose *confidence, pride, and hope* is fixed on Him, not on Moses.

3:1 *Apostle* is used as a title of Jesus only here in the NT. But cf. Jn 20:21, where the verb ("sent") used to describe Jesus' own mission is the one from which the noun "apostle" is derived.

3:4 *Builder . . . is God.* As "Builder" of the people of God Jesus is entitled to divine honor, just as He is as Creator of the world. (1:2)

3:5 *Moses was faithful.* Cf. Nm 12:7: "My servant Moses . . . entrusted with all my house."

3:7 – 4:13 Where God builds and blesses His house, when He gives His people an apostle and

10　　　Therefore I was provoked with that generation,
　　　　　and said, 'They always go astray in their hearts;
　　　　　they have not known my ways.'
11　　　As I swore in my wrath,
　　　　　'They shall never enter my rest.' "

12 Take care, brethren, lest there be in any of you an evil, unbelieving heart, leading you to fall away from the living God. 13 But exhort one another every day, as long as it is called "today," that none of you may be hardened by the deceitfulness of sin. 14 For we share in Christ, if only we hold our first confidence firm to the end, 15 while it is said,

　　　　　"Today, when you hear his voice,
　　　　　do not harden your hearts
　　　　　　　as in the rebellion."

16 Who were they that heard and yet were rebellious? Was it not all those who left Egypt under the leadership of Moses? 17And with whom was he provoked forty years? Was it not with those who sinned, whose bodies fell in the wilderness? 18And to whom did he swear that they should never enter his rest, but to those who were disobedient? 19 So we see that they were unable to enter because of unbelief.

4　Therefore, while the promise of entering his rest remains, let us fear lest any of you be judged to have failed to reach it. 2 For good news came to us just as to them; but the message which they heard did not benefit them, because it did not meet with faith in the hearers.ʰ 3 For we who have believed enter that rest, as he has said,

　　　　　"As I swore in my wrath,
　　　　　'They shall never enter my rest.' "

although his works were finished from the foundation of the world. 4 For he has

ʰ Other manuscripts read *they were not united in faith with the hearers*

high priest, the members of His household are tempted to desecrate the gift and so lose it. So it was of old when Israel *left Egypt under the leadership of Moses* (3:16); men hardened their hearts and put God to the test in the wilderness (3:8-9). In their disobedience and *unbelief* (3:19) they provoked God to wrath, forfeited the *rest* He had promised and provided in the Promised Land, and *fell in the wilderness* (3:17-18). So it may be now in the days of "Jesus, the apostle and high priest" of the Christian faith ("our confession," 3:2). Therefore the *Holy Spirit's* warning as recorded in Ps 95 (3:7-11) must be heeded now: *Take care* and *exhort one another*, for the *unbelieving heart and the deceitfulness of sin* threaten still to drive men into apostasy *from the living God.* (3:12-14)

The *promise of entering* God's rest remains (4:1). The unbelief of the men under Moses' leadership destroyed them but did not nullify the promise. The rest which God created by His resting on the seventh day of creation endures; it *remains a sabbath rest for the people of God* (4:9). The promise was not exhausted when *Joshua*, Moses' successor, brought the people into the rest of the Promised Land. God repeated the promise to the people *through* David, in the Psalter, *long afterward* (4:7) and opened up the prospect of a rest greater than Canaan could give. The history of God's promise is cause for salutary *fear* (4:1) and spurs His people on to *strive to enter that rest* (4:11) which Jesus, the Son greater than the servants Moses and Joshua, gives to those *who have believed* (4:3). The promise is forfeited, now as then,

when it meets the *same sort of disobedience* and destroys the disobedient (4:11), for the promise is the live and effective *word of God,* trenchant, penetrating, *discerning*, exposing him who hears it to the inescapable scrutiny of his Judge (*with whom we have to do,* 4:12-13).

3:7-11 Ps 95:7-11. The first half of the psalm is a call to worship the Savior, King, Creator, and Shepherd of Israel (Ps 95:1-6), expressing Israel's "confidence and pride" in her hope (Heb 3:6). The second half, quoted here, is a stern warning that worship without obedience is in vain.

3:8-9 *Rebellion . . . put me to the test.* For the history alluded to here and recalled more explicitly below (16-19) cf. Ex 17:1-7; Nm 14:1-23.

3:12 *Fall away.* The ultimate outrage of conscience which we call apostasy (6:6) is meant. (Cf. Introduction, par. 16)

4:2 *Good news . . . message . . . faith.* The terms in which the story of Israel's hardness of heart and rebellion is told emphasize the parallel between Israel and the NT people of God. The word for *good news* is the verb for "gospeling," evangelizing.

4:3 *We who have believed enter.* "We who have come to faith are in process of entering." For Christians, entry into God's rest is not ONLY future; they taste "the powers of the age to come" (6:5) even now.

4:3-6 *His works were finished . . . God rested . . . it remains for some to enter it* (God's rest). God's movement in creation (from works to rest) is the pattern for His movement in redemption. As He gave men "dominion over the WORKS" of His hands

somewhere spoken of the seventh day in this way, "And God rested on the seventh day from all his works." ⁵And again in this place he said,

"They shall never enter my rest."

⁶ Since therefore it remains for some to enter it, and those who formerly received the good news failed to enter because of disobedience, ⁷ again he sets a certain day, "Today," saying through David so long afterward, in the words already quoted,

"Today, when you hear his voice,
do not harden your hearts."

⁸ For if Joshua had given them rest, God*i* would not speak later of another day. ⁹ So then, there remains a sabbath rest for the people of God; ¹⁰ for whoever enters God's rest also ceases from his labors as God did from his.

11 Let us therefore strive to enter that rest, that no one fall by the same sort of disobedience. ¹² For the word of God is living and active, sharper than any two-edged sword, piercing to the division of soul and spirit, of joints and marrow, and discerning the thoughts and intentions of the heart. ¹³And before him no creature is hidden, but all are open and laid bare to the eyes of him with whom we have to do.

Jesus, the Ultimate High Priest

4:14 — 10:18

INSTRUCTION: JESUS A TRUE HIGH PRIEST (4:14 — 5:10)

14 Since then we have a great high priest who has passed through the heavens, Jesus, the Son of God, let us hold fast our confession. ¹⁵ For we have not a high priest who is unable to sympathize with our weaknesses, but one who in every respect has been tempted as we are, yet without sin. ¹⁶ Let us then with confidence draw near to the throne of grace, that we may receive mercy and find grace to help in time of need.

5 For every high priest chosen from among men is appointed to act on behalf of men in relation to God, to offer gifts and sacrifices for sins. ² He can deal gently with the ignorant and wayward, since he himself is beset with weakness. ³ Because of this he is bound to offer sacrifice for his own sins as well as for those of the people. ⁴And one does not take the honor upon himself, but he is called by God, just as Aaron was.

5 So also Christ did not exalt himself to be made a high priest, but was appointed by him who said to him,

"Thou art my Son,
today I have begotten thee";

⁶ as he says also in another place,

"Thou art a priest for ever,
after the order of Mel·chiz′e·dek."

i Greek *he*

(Ps 8:6), He will give them part in His everlasting Sabbath rest. (Cf. 10)

4:14 — 5:10 There is cause for holy fear in the presence of God's enduring promise (cf. 4:1); but there is even stronger cause for *confidence* (4:16). In *Jesus, the Son of God,* we have a *great high priest,* sympathetic with us in *our weaknesses* (14-15). Through His priestly intercession the awesome throne of God has become the *throne of grace* for us, source of divine *mercy* and *grace to help in time of need.* (16)

Jesus is a true high priest, being a man acting *on behalf of men,* clothed in our humanity, learning a human *obedience* by suffering (5:1-3, 7-9). He has also that other qualification for true priesthood, divine appointment. He is *called, appointed*

by God (5:4-6), *designated by God a high priest after the order of Melchizedek.* (5:10)

5:3 *Sacrifice for his own sins.* Cf. Lv 9:7; 16:6-9. This trait of the OT priesthood is noted not because Jesus' priesthood has anything corresponding to it, but merely to illustrate the humanity of priesthood.

5:4 *As Aaron was.* Ex 28:1.

5:5 *Christ . . . appointed.* The word spoken in Ps 2:7 to the anointed king found its ultimate fulfillment when uttered by the voice from heaven at Jesus' baptism, where the Son of God became one with mankind under the wrath of God in order "to fulfil all righteousness." (Mt 3:13-17)

5:6 *In another place.* Ps 110:4. The same divine word which designated the King as representative

7 In the days of his flesh, Jesus[j] offered up prayers and supplications, with loud cries and tears, to him who was able to save him from death, and he was heard for his godly fear. 8Although he was a Son, he learned obedience through what he suffered; 9 and being made perfect he became the source of eternal salvation to all who obey him, 10 being designated by God a high priest after the order of Mel·chiz'e·dek.

WARNING AND ENCOURAGEMENT (5:11 — 6:20)

11 About this we have much to say which is hard to explain, since you have become dull of hearing. 12 For though by this time you ought to be teachers, you need some one to teach you again the first principles of God's word. You need milk, not solid food; 13 for every one who lives on milk is unskilled in the word of righteousness, for he is a child. 14 But solid food is for the mature, for those who have their faculties trained by practice to distinguish good from evil.

6 Therefore let us leave the elementary doctrine of Christ and go on to maturity, not laying again a foundation of repentance from dead works and of faith toward God, 2 with instruction[k] about ablutions, the laying on of hands, the resurrection of the

[j] Greek he   [k] Other ancient manuscripts read of instruction

of God's victorious power on earth (Ps 110:1; cf. Heb 1:13 note) marked Him out as the Priest who represents man before God. (Cf. 10)

5:7 *Loud cries and tears.* The reference is to Jesus' praying in Gethsemane (Mt 26:36-46) and the human cries wrung from Him by the burden of priestly office, such as those recorded in Mt 17:17 and Jn 12:27.

His godly fear, the humbly submissive reverence which led him to conclude His *prayers and supplications* with, "Nevertheless, not as I will, but as thou wilt." (Mt 26:39)

5:8 *Learned obedience.* One "learns" obedience (makes it one's own) by concrete acts of obedience. This the Son did, by obeying even where obedience meant taking the cup of suffering which man's sin had mixed.

5:9 *Made perfect.* Cf. 2:10. That is, perfectly qualified to be the *source of salvation* to all who obediently confess Him (cf. 4:14) as their High Priest.

5:10 *Melchizedek.* The author indicates the theme he will develop fully in 7:1 — 10:18.

5:11 — 6:20 The author has reached the point where he would develop fully the major theme of his letter: Jesus the High Priest after the order of Melchizedek (5:10). His next words (5:11 — 6:20) show that he feels what many a leader of a less-than-perfect flock has felt. He looks at the PRESENT state of his charges and feels a disappointed dissatisfaction at their stagnant immaturity. They have not advanced as they should and cling to a bottle-fed infancy when they should be advancing to the solid food of maturity. (5:11-14)

His resolve to lead them on to maturity is therefore beset by a crippling fear for their FUTURE. He sees them drifting with the current which sweeps toward *apostasy* (6:6), to that dread extremity of impenitence from which there is no hope of return. (6:1-8)

But then he recalls their PAST and the past (and present) fruitfulness of their love and thus gains the assurance that the God who has begun His

good work in them will carry it through to completion (cf. Ph 1:6). The sure promise of God, made doubly sure by His assuring oath, still holds for them and can realize the full assurance of hope. This Godward look gives him the strength to continue his task of keeping watch over these wavering souls, not "sadly" but "joyfully." (9-20: cf. 13:17)

5:12 *You need milk.* This, like the preceding *you need some one to teach you,* etc., is not merely an objective analysis of the readers' state but an indictment and a reproach. The author does not propose to take them back to the ABC's of Christianity but wills to carry them "on to maturity." (6:1)

5:13 *Word of righteousness* may mean the Gospel. But this meaning hardly fits in with the clause that follows, *for he is a child;* the Gospel is accessible to babes (Mt 11:25). And in 6:1-2 the author concedes that his readers do know the elementary doctrines of Christ. Another possible rendering, "normal, right, mature speech," is therefore preferable. By persisting in childish ways when childhood is past, a man loses his capacity for grasping and expressing the Gospel for the mature, such as is expressed in the doctrine of the priesthood of Jesus.

5:14 *Faculties trained by practice to distinguish.* Cf. Ro 12:2, where Paul describes the growth to Christian maturity as a constant "proving" (a testing and discerning) of what is the will of God.

6:1-2 The readers are to *leave the elementary doctrine,* not in the sense of abandoning it but (as the use of *foundation* shows) of building upon it, using it as the basis for progress. The elementary doctrine is described by six terms arranged in pairs. The first pair speaks of the beginning of the Christian life, the response to missionary preaching (cf. Acts 20:21), which bids men turn *(repentance)* from the evil works of their past, when they "were dead in trespasses" (Cl 2:13), to the God who forgives and renews *(faith).* The next pair speaks of their initiation

dead, and eternal judgment. ³And this we will do if God permits.ˡ ⁴ For it is impossible to restore again to repentance those who have once been enlightened, who have tasted the heavenly gift, and have become partakers of the Holy Spirit, ⁵ and have tasted the goodness of the word of God and the powers of the age to come, ⁶ if they then commit apostasy, since they crucify the Son of God on their own account and hold him up to contempt. ⁷ For land which has drunk the rain that often falls upon it, and brings forth vegetation useful to those for whose sake it is cultivated, receives a blessing from God. ⁸ But if it bears thorns and thistles, it is worthless and near to being cursed; its end is to be burned.

9 Though we speak thus, yet in your case, beloved, we feel sure of better things that belong to salvation. ¹⁰ For God is not so unjust as to overlook your work and the love which you showed for his sake in serving the saints, as you still do. ¹¹And we desire each one of you to show the same earnestness in realizing the full assurance of hope until the end, ¹² so that you may not be sluggish, but imitators of those who through faith and patience inherit the promises.

13 For when God made a promise to Abraham, since he had no one greater by whom to swear, he swore by himself, ¹⁴ saying, "Surely I will bless you and multiply you." ¹⁵And thus Abraham,ᵐ having patiently endured, obtained the promise. ¹⁶ Men indeed swear by a greater than themselves, and in all their disputes an oath is final for confirmation. ¹⁷ So when God desired to show more convincingly to the heirs of the promise the unchangeable character of his purpose, he interposed with an oath, ¹⁸ so that through two unchangeable things, in which it is impossible that God should prove false, we who have fled for refuge might have strong encouragement to seize the hope set before us. ¹⁹ We have this as a sure and steadfast anchor of the soul, a hope that enters into the inner shrine behind the curtain, ²⁰ where Jesus has gone as a forerunner on our behalf, having become a high priest for ever after the order of Mel·chiz′e·dek.

INSTRUCTION: JESUS THE HIGH PRIEST (7:1—10:18)

7 For this Mel·chiz′e·dek, king of Salem, priest of the Most High God, met Abraham returning from the slaughter of the kings and blessed him; ² and to him

ˡ Other ancient manuscripts read *let us do this if God permits*   ᵐ Greek *he*

into the Christian life by the Sacrament of Baptism *(ablutions),* and by the reception of the Spirit, which was often accompanied by *the laying on of hands* (cf. Acts 8:14-18; 19:1-6). The third pair points to the goal of the new life *(resurrection of the dead, and eternal judgment);* it reads like a paraphrase of the early creed which Paul cites in Ro 10:9: "If you confess with your lips that Jesus is Lord and believe in your heart that God raised him from the dead, you will be saved" (from death and the judgment).

6:2 *Ablutions.* The word is similar to but not identical with the word regularly used for Christian Baptism; that, and the fact that it is used in the plural, indicates that the *instruction* pointed up the distinctiveness of Christian Baptism as over against the baptism of John (cf. Acts 19:1-4) or the various ablutions known in Judaism. (Cf. 9:10; Mk 7:4)

6:3 *If God permits.* God's grace CAN do the "impossible" (4); but to "PRESUME upon the riches of his kindness and forbearance and patience" is perilous in the extreme and invites His judgment. (Ro 2:4-5)

6:4-6 For the nature and peril of *apostasy* (6) cf. 10:26-31 and Introduction, par. 16.

6:6 *Crucify . . . on their own account.* Men who have fully known and THEN rejected the blessings won for them by the Crucified have made common cause with those who rejected the Son of God, crucified Him, and uttered mockeries under His cross *(contempt).*

6:10 *God is not so unjust.* God's merciful justice gives to him who has (uses and values) God's previous gifts (Mt 13:12). God is the faithful vinedresser who prunes "every branch that does bear fruit . . . that it may bear more fruit." (Jn 15:2)

Work . . . love . . . in serving the saints. Cf. 10:32-34.

6:12-13 God's *promise to Abraham,* supported by oath, serves as the classic example of encouragement to those who like man endure in *faith and patience* to *inherit the promises.* In the record of Gn 22:16-17 the "unchangeable character of his purpose" (6:17) is clearly seen.

6:18-20 *The hope set before us* (the hoped-for blessing) serves as *anchor of the soul,* holding it firm and steady, lest it "drift away" (2:1) into lethargy and apostasy. The *hope* is Jesus Himself (cf. Cl 1:27), our *high priest* who has entered into the Holy of Holies (God's presence) as our *forerunner* to bring us there too. With the mention of the eternal *high priest . . . after the order of Melchizedek* the author returns to his main theme.

6:19 *Behind the curtain* which separated the *inner shrine* (Holy of Holies) from the rest of the sanctuary. There only the high priest went, and he only once a year. (Lv 16:2, 12; Heb 9:3, 6-7, 25)

7:1—10:18 Jesus is the true High Priest (4:1 to

Abraham apportioned a tenth part of everything. He is first, by translation of his name, king of righteousness, and then he is also king of Salem, that is, king of peace. 3 He is without father or mother or genealogy, and has neither beginning of days nor end of life, but resembling the Son of God he continues a priest for ever.

4 See how great he is! Abraham the patriarch gave him a tithe of the spoils. 5And those descendants of Levi who receive the priestly office have a commandment in the law to take tithes from the people, that is, from their brethren, though these also are descended from Abraham. 6 But this man who has not their genealogy received tithes from Abraham and blessed him who had the promises. 7 It is beyond dispute that the inferior is blessed by the superior. 8 Here tithes are received by mortal men; there, by one of whom it is testified that he lives. 9 One might even say that Levi himself, who receives tithes, paid tithes through Abraham, 10 for he was still in the loins of his ancestor when Mel·chiz′e·dek met him.

11 Now if perfection had been attainable through the Levitical priesthood (for under it the people received the law), what further need would there have been for another priest to arise after the order of Mel·chiz′e·dek, rather than one named after the order of Aaron? 12 For when there is a change in the priesthood, there is necessarily a change in the law as well. 13 For the one of whom these things are spoken belonged to another tribe, from which no one has ever served at the altar. 14 For it is

5:10); more than that, He is Priest of a higher order. His *priestly office* (ch. 7), the better *sanctuary* in which He ministers (ch. 8), and the final and perfect *sacrifice* which He offers (9:1 – 10:18) – all mark Him out as the ultimate High Priest, the Mediator who has established God's new and final covenant, His new and ultimate order of things in which the Law is superseded and God's grace holds free and final sway (7:22; 8:6, 7, 8, 10, 13; 9:15; 10:16, 28; cf. 12:24; 13:20). The whole section, so richly elaborated, is designed to overcome the Judaic tendency to take offense at Jesus at the two points where offense was likeliest and strongest: (1) His "shameful" death on the cross and His present hiddenness (cf. Introduction, pars. 5 and 6); (2) the fact that His life and priestly ministry signified the "end of the law" (cf. Ro 10:4), that law which the Jews revered as the unviolable and eternal Word of God.

7:1-28 INSTRUCTION: MELCHIZEDEK AND AARON PRIESTHOOD OF PROMISE AND LAW

7:1-28 Jesus is High Priest of a higher order, not that of Aaron and Levi established and regulated by the Law, but that of Melchizedek established by the promise of God to endure forever. His priesthood supersedes and antiquates the legal Levitical priesthood.

7:1-10 The eternal priesthood of the Messiah is foretold and promised in Ps 110:4 (cf. Heb 5: 6, 10; 6:20). It is foreshadowed in Gn 14:17-20, in the figure of the priest-king Melchizedek and in the story of his meeting with Abraham. Both what is said and what is left unsaid of Melchizedek in the sacred record mark him as *resembling the Son of God . . . a priest for ever* (3) and as being thus distinct from and superior to those priests who are *descendants of Levi* and derive their authority from the Law. (5)

7:1-3 According to the record, Melchizedek, type (cf. Introduction, par. 13) of Jesus the Messianic Priest, bears SIGNIFICANT NAMES: His titles, *king*

of righteousness and *king of peace* suggest the Messiah to whom eternal priesthood is promised in Ps 110:4. Cf. the Messianic designations, "the LORD our righteousness," Jer 23:6, and "Prince of Peace," Is 9:6. The OT record generally and its prescriptions for priesthood particularly emphasize *genealogy*. There is a SIGNIFICANT SILENCE, however, concerning Melchizedek's descent. He confronts us in Genesis as one who, singularly, has no recorded *beginning of days nor end of life*. Unlike the priests under the Law, he stands in no succession and has no successors but continues in unique and eternal majesty *a priest for ever*.

7:4-10 And he performs SIGNIFICANT ACTIONS: Melchizedek receives tithes from Abraham and *blesses* Abraham. Both are priestly actions; they show that Melchizedek functions as priest even to Abraham, the recipient of the *promises*. Even Abraham, "called the friend of God" (Ja 2:23; cf. Is 41:8; 2 Ch 20:7), needs the mediation and blessing of this eternal priesthood, the priesthood of the "Son of God, a priest for ever" (3), of Him in whom "all the promises of God find their Yes" (2 Co 1:20). Even Abraham, destined by the promise to "inherit the world" (Ro 4:13), acknowledges the surpassing greatness of this priesthood by paying tithes to Melchizedek. Just as Melchizedek's act of blessing marks him as *superior* (7) to Abraham, so Abraham's act of giving him a *tithe of the spoils* (4) is an acknowledgment of Melchizedek's superiority. *See how great he is!* His is the greatness of *our Lord* (14), the Christ. A greatness not derived from *a commandment in the law* and not dependent on the *genealogy* which Law prescribes but inherent in his person by "the power of an indestructible life" (16). He is not, like the *descendants of Levi . . . a mortal* man (8) clothed for a time only in the dignity and power of priesthood; *he lives,* and his life and his priesthood are one; both are everlasting.

7:11-28 The eternal priesthood of Christ as foreshadowed in Melchizedek is acknowledged as

evident that our Lord was descended from Judah, and in connection with that tribe Moses said nothing about priests.

15 This becomes even more evident when another priest arises in the likeness of Mel·chiz'e·dek, 16 who has become a priest, not according to a legal requirement concerning bodily descent but by the power of an indestructible life. 17 For it is witnessed of him,

"Thou art a priest for ever,
after the order of Mel·chiz'e·dek."

18 On the one hand, a former commandment is set aside because of its weakness and uselessness 19 (for the law made nothing perfect); on the other hand, a better hope is introduced, through which we draw near to God.

20 And it was not without an oath. 21 Those who formerly became priests took their office without an oath, but this one was addressed with an oath,

"The Lord has sworn
and will not change his mind,
'Thou art a priest for ever.' "

22 This makes Jesus the surety of a better covenant.

23 The former priests were many in number, because they were prevented by death from continuing in office; 24 but he holds his priesthood permanently, because he continues for ever. 25 Consequently he is able for all time to save those who draw near to God through him, since he always lives to make intercession for them.

26 For it was fitting that we should have such a high priest, holy, blameless, unstained, separated from sinners, exalted above the heavens. 27 He has no need, like those high priests, to offer sacrifices daily, first for his own sins and then for those of the people; he did this once for all when he offered up himself. 28 Indeed, the law appoints men in their weakness as high priests, but the word of the oath, which came later than the law, appoints a Son who has been made perfect for ever.

8 Now the point in what we are saying is this: we have such a high priest, one who is seated at the right hand of the throne of the Majesty in heaven, 2 a minister in

superior by Abraham, the "patriarch" (4) and the ancestor of Levi, the tribe of the priesthood; Levi himself, present in his ancestor Abraham, thus acknowledges the superiority of Christ's priesthood (9-10). All this marks the priesthood of the Law as merely preliminary to Christ's ultimate priesthood. The promise pointed, not to Levi, the tribe designated by the *Law of Moses* as the priestly tribe, but to the tribe of *Judah* (14) from which our Lord was to spring. *Another priest* arises by virtue of God's potent promise, and with His coming the old order passes; the *former commandment,* which established the Levitical priesthood, is *set aside* (18); the introduction of *a better hope* (19) which really effects what priesthood is designed to effect, that is, enable men to *draw near to God,* makes clear the *weakness* and *uselessness* of the old legal order in comparison with the new, how much *better* is the new *covenant* ensured by the ultimate High Priest Jesus Christ. (22)

This new hope and new priesthood is God's promise at work, promise in its purest form, the *oath* of God (20; cf. 6:13-14). In His oath God commits His life to the blessing of man (cf. Gn 22: 15-18). His oath (Ps 110:4) gives man the everlasting Priest, always alive *to make intercession* (23-25), the sinless Son who *offered up himself* in sacrifice *once for all* (27) and thus was *made perfect* as priest, capable of interceding for sinful man *for ever.* (26-28)

8:1-13 INSTRUCTION: JESUS' PRIESTLY MINISTRY IN THE TRUE SANCTUARY, THE HEAVENS, MEDIATING THE NEW AND BETTER COVENANT

The Son's priesthood is of another order than that of the Levitical priesthood and superior to it, as both the promise (Ps 110:4) and prefiguration (Gn 14:17-20) and their fulfillment (7:15-16) show. This superiority is manifest also in the place of His priestly ministration, *heaven* (1), the *true tent* (or *tabernacle*), the *heavenly sanctuary* of which the earthly sanctuary where the descendants of Levi serve is but a *copy and shadow* (5). In that earthly sanctuary the sons of Levi serve and die (cf. 7:23); *in heaven* the Son is a *minister* (2) who lives and reigns (*seated at the right hand,* 1; cf. 1:13), made perfect in His priesthood forever (7:28). As the appearance of the Son as ultimate Priest ushers in a whole new divine order of things (7:12, 18-19), so His ministry in the new heavenly sanctuary involves a new order of things, the promised new and better covenant (7-13). No longer is man thrust into the presence of God by a commandment of the Law; he is drawn near to God under this new priesthood in the new sanctuary by the inner impulse of a renewed mind and heart in which God is known (acknowledged and adored) and His law is inscribed; the reluctance and resistance of sinful man is overcome by

the sanctuary and the true tent[n] which is set up not by man but by the Lord. 3 For every high priest is appointed to offer gifts and sacrifices; hence it is necessary for this priest also to have something to offer. 4 Now if he were on earth, he would not be a priest at all, since there are priests who offer gifts according to the law. 5 They serve a copy and shadow of the heavenly sanctuary; for when Moses was about to erect the tent,[n] he was instructed by God, saying, "See that you make everything according to the pattern which was shown you on the mountain." 6 But as it is, Christ[o] has obtained a ministry which is as much more excellent than the old as the covenant he mediates is better, since it is enacted on better promises. 7 For if that first covenant had been faultless, there would have been no occasion for a second.

8 For he finds fault with them when he says:
> "The days will come, says the Lord,
> when I will establish a new covenant with the house of Israel
> and with the house of Judah;
>
> 9   not like the covenant that I made with their fathers
> on the day when I took them by the hand
> to lead them out of the land of Egypt;
> for they did not continue in my covenant,
> and so I paid no heed to them, says the Lord.
>
> 10   This is the covenant that I will make with the house of Israel
> after those days, says the Lord:
> I will put my laws into their minds,
> and write them on their hearts,
> and I will be their God,
> and they shall be my people.
>
> 11   And they shall not teach every one his fellow
> or every one his brother, saying, 'Know the Lord,'
> for all shall know me,
> from the least of them to the greatest.
>
> 12   For I will be merciful toward their iniquities,
> and I will remember their sins no more."

13 In speaking of a new covenant he treats the first as obsolete. And what is becoming obsolete and growing old is ready to vanish away.

9 Now even the first covenant had regulations for worship and an earthly sanctuary. 2 For a tent[p] was prepared, the outer one, in which were the lampstand and the table and the bread of the Presence;[q] it is called the Holy Place. 3 Behind the second

---

[n] Or *tabernacle*   [o] Greek *he*   [p] Or *tabernacle*   [q] Greek *the presentation of the loaves*

God's creatively renewing forgiveness of sin. (12)

8:2 *Sanctuary and the true tent.* The question of the PLACE of Christ's priestly ministry was an important one for Jewish Christians. The old order to which they were accustomed was visible and impressive; the Holy City with its temple, to which the priests repaired in a continued rhythm of prescribed duties, that lodestone which drew Jews from all over the world for the celebration of the great festivals – ancient, venerable, and celebrated in the songs of Israel – what was there in the new order to replace and surpass it? The answer of Hebrews is: If the Christ, the new High Priest, is invisible, that is because He is in the true sanctuary, in heaven; if He does not appear in the earthly sanctuary, that is because He is too great for that priesthood and its sanctuary. (4)

8:4 *If he were on earth,* etc. The sanctuary in which Christ ministers MUST be in heaven; there is, as it were, no room for Him and His ministry within the old shadow-order of the Levitical priesthood on earth.

9:1 – 10:18 INSTRUCTION: ULTIMATE ATONING
SACRIFICE OF CHRIST

9:1 – 10:18 *But when Christ appeared* (9:11) – with this mighty adversative clause comparable to Paul's "BUT NOW" in Ro 3:21 or his "BUT GOD" in Eph 2:4, Hebrews introduces the climax of its argument concerning the last days, the supreme Word of God spoken by a Son (cf. 1:2), the ultimate High Priest. It has already been declared that the High Priest of the promise holds a higher and more enduring office than was ever given by the Law to the sons of Levi (ch. 7); that He ministers in a greater SANCTUARY than the Law could prescribe or men could erect (ch. 8). Now, the latter proclaims that He offers a better and everlasting SACRIFICE (9:1 – 10:18), *his own blood,* Himself, and thus secures for man what the old order never secured, *an eternal redemption* (9:12). Again and again the author asserts the supremacy of Christ's ultimate atoning sacrifice: The old order itself points beyond its own limitations to the unlimited

curtain stood a tent[p] called the Holy of Holies, 4 having the golden altar of incense and the ark of the covenant covered on all sides with gold, which contained a golden urn holding the manna, and Aaron's rod that budded, and the tables of the covenant; 5 above it were the cherubim of glory overshadowing the mercy seat. Of these things we cannot now speak in detail.

6 These preparations having thus been made, the priests go continually into the outer tent,[p] performing their ritual duties; 7 but into the second only the high priest goes, and he but once a year, and not without taking blood which he offers for himself and for the errors of the people. 8 By this the Holy Spirit indicates that the way into the sanctuary is not yet opened as long as the outer tent[p] is still standing 9 (which is symbolic for the present age). According to this arrangement, gifts and sacrifices are offered which cannot perfect the conscience of the worshiper, 10 but deal only with food and drink and various ablutions, regulations for the body imposed until the time of reformation.

11 But when Christ appeared as a high priest of the good things that have come,[r] then through the greater and more perfect tent[p] (not made with hands, that is, not of

[p] Or *tabernacle*   [r] Other manuscripts read *good things to come*

possibilities of God in the future. Even at the high point in the ancient sacrificial system, the ritual of the Day of Atonement (Lv 16), the fact that only *the high priest . . . and he but once a year* entered the Holy of Holies amounts to a confession that the way into the sanctuary was not yet so wholly and freely accessible as it was to become *when Christ appeared as a high priest of the good things that have come* (9:11), with the sacrifice which alone could *perfect* the *conscience* of sinful man and set him unafraid before his God. That sacrifice is Christ's self-offering (*his own blood,* not that of *goats and bulls,* 9:13); by the death of Christ the testament (covenant) of God takes effect validly and forever, just as a human testator's will, or testament, takes effect at the testator's death (9:15-17). What the shedding of blood in the ancient rites of purification and the sprinkling of blood at the establishment of the covenant at Sinai (18-22) – what that signified and symbolized is full and glorious reality now; with this *shedding of blood* there is forgiveness of sins (9:22). Christ's offering of Himself is unique and unrepeatable – there can be no return to the old and no expectation of anything more. When Christ shall come again, He shall return as Savior, as One whose sacrificial dealing with sin is complete, over and done with (9:28). *The shadow of good things to come* which the Law had (10:1) gives way to the *realities* (10:1) present in Christ, the *high priest of good things that have come* (9:11). Those ancient sacrifices *continually offered year after year* testified, by the very fact that they were repeated, to their own insufficiency; they could not put away sin effectively and forever, as Christ's *sacrifice of himself* (9:26) has done (cf. 10:4). Christ's personal, voluntary offering of His whole self to God (10:5-10) is the unique (10:11-14) final sacrifice (10:15-18). In that sacrifice the ancient promise of the new covenant has been utterly fulfilled. The forgiveness of sin, the goal of all sacrifice, has been attained. There need no longer be and there can *no longer* be *any offering for sin.* (10:18)

9:1-10 For the arrangement and furniture of the *earthly sanctuary* (1) under the *first covenant* cf. Ex 25:8-40. The permanent temple structures which succeeded the wilderness *tent* (2), or tabernacle, retained the basic plan of the first structure.

9:4 *Altar of incense.* According to Ex 30:6, the altar of incense seems to have been located outside the Holy of Holies, in the Holy Place. Perhaps the author is already thinking of the once-a-year ritual of the Day of Atonement (7; cf. Lv 16), when an offering of incense was made in the Holy of Holies (Lv 16:12), in contrast to the daily offering of incense in the Holy Place, and so is led to locate the incense altar within the Holy of Holies.

9:4 *Manna.* Cf. Ex 16:33.
Aaron's rod. Cf. Nm 17:1-11.

9:5 *We cannot now speak in detail.* The author, writing "briefly" (13:22), will not linger over the symbolic significance of the sanctuary furnishings but presses on to what is most significant for his theme, the once-a-year ritual of the Day of Atonement. (6-7; cf. Lv 16)

9:8 *The Holy Spirit indicates,* in the OT Word, which He inspired.

9:9 *Symbolic for the present age.* The full significance of the OT arrangements, which reveal the limitations of the old order, can be grasped only now when Christ has "opened the new and living way" into the very presence of God. (10:19)

9:10 *The time of reformation,* the time of Christ's high priesthood, when the Law's "shadow of good things to come" is replaced by "the true form of these realities" (10:1; cf. Cl 2:17), "the good things that have come" (9:11), when the merely ritual cleansing provided by *regulations for the body* is replaced by the internal "purification for sins" (1:3) which can "perfect the conscience" (9:9) and give man true access to God.

9:11 *Not made with hands . . . not of this creation.* Not of human manufacture and therefore not limited by the external character of created materials. For the idea of a true sanctuary *not made with hands* see the words of Jesus, Mk 14:58; Jn 2: 19-21; and of Stephen, Acts 7:48; cf. Is 66:1-2.

this creation) [12] he entered once for all into the Holy Place, taking[s] not the blood of goats and calves but his own blood, thus securing an eternal redemption. [13] For if the sprinkling of defiled persons with the blood of goats and bulls and with the ashes of a heifer sanctifies for the purification of the flesh, [14] how much more shall the blood of Christ, who through the eternal Spirit offered himself without blemish to God, purify your[t] conscience from dead works to serve the living God.

[15] Therefore he is the mediator of a new covenant, so that those who are called may receive the promised eternal inheritance, since a death has occurred which redeems them from the transgressions under the first covenant.[u] [16] For where a will[u] is involved, the death of the one who made it must be established. [17] For a will[u] takes effect only at death, since it is not in force as long as the one who made it is alive. [18] Hence even the first covenant was not ratified without blood. [19] For when every commandment of the law had been declared by Moses to all the people, he took the blood of calves and goats, with water and scarlet wool and hyssop, and sprinkled both the book itself and all the people, [20] saying, "This is the blood of the covenant which God commanded you." [21]And in the same way he sprinkled with the blood both the tent[p] and all the vessels used in worship. [22] Indeed, under the law almost everything is purified with blood, and without the shedding of blood there is no forgiveness of sins.

[23] Thus it was necessary for the copies of the heavenly things to be purified with these rites, but the heavenly things themselves with better sacrifices than these. [24] For Christ has entered, not into a sanctuary made with hands, a copy of the true one, but into heaven itself, now to appear in the presence of God on our behalf. [25] Nor was it to offer himself repeatedly, as the high priest enters the Holy Place yearly with blood not his own; [26] for then he would have had to suffer repeatedly since the foundation of the world. But as it is, he has appeared once for all at the end of the age to put away sin by the sacrifice of himself. [27]And just as it is appointed for men to die once, and after that comes judgment, [28] so Christ, having been offered once to bear the sins of many, will appear a second time, not to deal with sin but to save those who are eagerly waiting for him.

10 For since the law has but a shadow of the good things to come instead of the true form of these realities, it can never, by the same sacrifices which are continually offered year after year, make perfect those who draw near. [2] Otherwise, would they not have ceased to be offered? If the worshipers had once been cleansed, they would no longer have any consciousness of sin. [3] But in these sacrifices there is a reminder of sin year after year. [4] For it is impossible that the blood of bulls and goats should take away sins.

[5] Consequently, when Christ[v] came into the world, he said,
> "Sacrifices and offerings thou hast not desired,
> but a body hast thou prepared for me;
[6]　　in burnt offerings and sin offerings thou hast taken no pleasure.
[7]　　Then I said, 'Lo, I have come to do thy will, O God,'
> as it is written of me in the roll of the book."

[s] Greek *through*　[t] Other manuscripts read *our*　[u] The Greek word here used means both *covenant* and *will*
[p] Or *tabernacle*　[v] Greek *he*

9:13 Cf. Lv 16:6-7, 15-16; Nm 19:1-22.

9:14 *Through the eternal Spirit,* as the sinless Son of God (cf. Ro 1:4) and the Servant of God who does His atoning work in the power of the Spirit of God (Is 42:1; Is 53). The Spirit at work in Christ's sacrifice there reveals "the depths of God." (1 Co 2:10)

9:15-16 *Covenant . . . will . . . death.* The same Greek word is used for both *covenant* and *will,* and the author makes use of this to show how the *death* (blood) of Christ is essential to the establishment of the *new covenant* of the forgiveness of sins. (Cf. 22)

9:19-20 Cf. Ex 24:6-8.

9:22 *Almost everything.* For exceptions per-mitted by the Law cf. Lv 5:11 and Nm 16:46; 31: 22 f.; 31:50.

Shedding of blood . . . forgiveness. Cf. Lv 17:11.

9:24 *Heaven itself.* Cf. 8:1.

9:26 *Sacrifice of himself.* Cf. 7:27. This statement sums up the superiority of Christ's sacrifice as a total self-offering, the oblation of His life ("own blood," 9:12; "body," 10:10) and the devotion of His will. (10:4-9)

9:27 Christ's sacrifice has the once-for-all finality of a man's *death* and *judgment,* with the amazing difference that His death leads to deliverance from judgment ("save," 28).

10:5-7 Ps 40:6-8 according to the Septuagint (ancient Greek translation), which differs from

8 When he said above, "Thou hast neither desired nor taken pleasure in sacrifices and offerings and burnt offerings and sin offerings" (these are offered according to the law), 9 then he added, "Lo, I have come to do thy will." He abolishes the first in order to establish the second. 10And by that will we have been sanctified through the offering of the body of Jesus Christ once for all.

11 And every priest stands daily at his service, offering repeatedly the same sacrifices, which can never take away sins. 12 But when Christ[w] had offered for all time a single sacrifice for sins, he sat down at the right hand of God, 13 then to wait until his enemies should be made a stool for his feet. 14 For by a single offering he has perfected for all time those who are sanctified. 15And the Holy Spirit also bears witness to us; for after saying,

16   "This is the covenant that I will make with them
       after those days, says the Lord:
       I will put my laws on their hearts,
       and write them on their minds,"

17 then he adds,

       "I will remember their sins and their misdeeds no more."

18 Where there is forgiveness of these, there is no longer any offering for sin.

Exhortation and Warning

10:19—12:29

EXHORTATION: DRAW NEAR WITH A TRUE HEART (10:19-25)

19 Therefore, brethren, since we have confidence to enter the sanctuary by the blood of Jesus, 20 by the new and living way which he opened for us through the

[w] Greek *this one*

Hebrew but conveys the essential point that total self-devotion is the ultimate, essential sacrifice.

10:16-17 Cf. Jer 31:33-34. The significance of the promise of the new covenant has been dwelt on in 8:6-13.

10:19—12:29 The instruction of 4:14—10:18 has been eloquently rich and full; the exhortation is correspondingly vigorous, urgent—and filled with a deadly serious concern. The author evinces himself as one who has heard attentively the witness to Jesus which brought God's "great salvation" to him and as inspired by the Spirit who lived and worked in that witness (2:3-4); by that Spirit Jesus lives and works in his words. Jesus planted both confident faith and holy fear in His disciples when He told them, "To him who has will more be given, and he will have in abundance; but from him who has not, even what he has will be taken away" (Mt 13:12). That same combination of faith and fear lives in the author's heart, and he implants it in the hearts of his readers too. He invites them to draw near to God wholeheartedly and actively by the "new and living way" which their High Priest has consecrated for them (10:19-25) and at the same time warns them against "not having," not possessing and using, God's ultimate gift, repeating his earlier (6:1-8) warning against apostasy (10:26-31; cf. Introduction, par. 16). He bids them recall the believing steadfastness of their former days when the light of God's salvation first broke upon them, for their encouragement he calls the roll of ancient men

of faith and bids his readers look to Jesus, the Pioneer and Perfecter of their faith, and so to run with perseverance the race they must run, cheered on by the great cloud of witnesses who ran the race before them (10:32—12:3). He teaches them to see even in their present sufferings the hand of the God who gives, the Father who disciplines every child whom He receives as His own (12:4-11). He urges them to repent of their past slackness and to grow strong again before (again the note of holy fear is sounded) the time for repentance be forever past. The final splendor of God's gracious speaking is more awesome than were the terrors of Mount Sinai when the Law was given (12:18-24). To refuse Him who is speaking NOW is to ignore the final warning spoken from heaven itself and invites the judgment of Him who, though He gives to all who will receive and have the gift, a kingdom that cannot be shaken, will prove a consuming fire to all who will not offer Him the acceptable worship which is His due. (12:25-29)

10:19-25 The *true heart* (22) is the heart of one whose eye is fixed on Jesus the *great priest* (19-21) and can therefore *draw near* to God in confident *faith* (22) and unwavering *hope* (23), living a life of responsible *love* (24) in the fellowship of the worshiping church.

10:20 *Curtain . . . his flesh.* The curtain is the curtain which divides the Holy Place from the Holy of Holies (9:3). Jesus has opened up the way into the innermost sanctuary, into the very presence of God, through the curtain of His human

curtain, that is, through his flesh, 21 and since we have a great priest over the house of God, 22 let us draw near with a true heart in full assurance of faith, with our hearts sprinkled clean from an evil conscience and our bodies washed with pure water. 23 Let us hold fast the confession of our hope without wavering, for he who promised is faithful; 24 and let us consider how to stir up one another to love and good works, 25 not neglecting to meet together, as is the habit of some, but encouraging one another, and all the more as you see the Day drawing near.

WARNING: JUDGMENT ON APOSTASY (10:26-31)

26 For if we sin deliberately after receiving the knowledge of the truth, there no longer remains a sacrifice for sins, 27 but a fearful prospect of judgment, and a fury of fire which will consume the adversaries. 28A man who has violated the law of Moses dies without mercy at the testimony of two or three witnesses. 29 How much worse punishment do you think will be deserved by the man who has spurned the Son of God, and profaned the blood of the covenant by which he was sanctified, and outraged the Spirit of grace? 30 For we know him who said, "Vengeance is mine, I will repay." And again, "The Lord will judge his people." 31 It is a fearful thing to fall into the hands of the living God.

EXHORTATION: DO NOT THROW AWAY CONFIDENCE (10:32-39)

32 But recall the former days when, after you were enlightened, you endured a hard struggle with sufferings, 33 sometimes being publicly exposed to abuse and affliction, and sometimes being partners with those so treated. 34 For you had compassion on the prisoners, and you joyfully accepted the plundering of your property, since you knew that you yourselves had a better possession and an abiding one. 35 Therefore do not throw away your confidence, which has a great reward. 36 For you have need of endurance, so that you may do the will of God and receive what is promised.

37   "For yet a little while,
     and the coming one shall come and shall not tarry;
38   but my righteous one shall live by faith,
     and if he shrinks back,
     my soul has no pleasure in him."

39 But we are not of those who shrink back and are destroyed, but of those who have faith and keep their souls.

---

life and body (flesh) destroyed in sacrifice for the sinner's sake.

10:21 *Over the house of God.* Cf. 3:6.

10:22 *Draw near,* for worship and service.

Hearts sprinkled . . . bodies washed. The OT ceremonial washings (cf. 9:13-14; Ex 30:20; Lv 16:4) furnish the picture for the effectual sanctification of the whole man in Baptism.

10:25 *The Day,* of the return of Christ and judgment. (Cf. 1 Co 3:13)

10:26-31 Cf. Introduction, par. 16, and 6:4-8. The harsh warnings on apostasy are the negative counterpart to the warm and winning invitation of 19-25, prepared for, however, by the mention of the "Day" in 25.

10:26 *There no longer remains a sacrifice for sins.* The apostate has *deliberately* and against better *knowledge* rejected the one, final sacrifice provided by God (29). (Cf. 2 Ptr 2:20-21)

10:28-29 For the aggravated offense of sinning against God's ultimate "great salvation" cf. 2:1-3.

10:28 Cf. Dt 17:2-6; also Nm 15:30.

10:29 *Spurned . . . profaned . . . outraged.* All three verbs emphasize the deliberate (26) character of apostasy against knowledge of the truth.

Outraged the Spirit. Cf. Mt 12:31-32 note; Mk 3:28-30.

10:30 *Vengeance is mine.* Dt 32:35-36.

10:32-39 Again, as in 6:9-10, the author looks to his readers' past and finds there a joyous stamina of faith (32-34) which is encouraging to him and can be an incentive to them. *Therefore do not throw away your confidence* (35). The light that shone on them at their conversion (32) has illumined dark days for them; in that light they can still endure, *do the will of God and receive what is promised* (36). In the *little while* before their Lord's return (37), they need not be among the number of the apostates who *shrink back and are destroyed;* they can stand in the ranks *of those who have faith* and live (38-39) by God's promise.

10:37-38 Hab 2:3-4 is quoted according to the Septuagint (ancient Greek version most commonly used in the Greek-speaking church). This differs considerably from the Hebrew as translated in English versions, but the cardinal point (the unbreakable connection between faith, righteousness, and life, 38) is not affected thereby.

EXHORTATION: RUN THE RACE (11:1 – 12:2)

11 Now faith is the assurance of things hoped for, the conviction of things not seen. [2] For by it the men of old received divine approval. [3] By faith we understand that the world was created by the word of God, so that what is seen was made out of things which do not appear.

4 By faith Abel offered to God a more acceptable sacrifice than Cain, through which he received approval as righteous, God bearing witness by accepting his gifts; he died, but through his faith he is still speaking. [5] By faith Enoch was taken up so that he should not see death; and he was not found, because God had taken him. Now before he was taken he was attested as having pleased God. [6]And without faith it is impossible to please him. For whoever would draw near to God must believe that he exists and that he rewards those who seek him. [7] By faith Noah, being warned by God concerning events as yet unseen, took heed and constructed an ark for the saving of his household; by this he condemned the world and became an heir of the righteousness which comes by faith.

8 By faith Abraham obeyed when he was called to go out to a place which he was to receive as an inheritance; and he went out, not knowing where he was to go. [9] By faith he sojourned in the land of promise, as in a foreign land, living in tents with Isaac and Jacob, heirs with him of the same promise. [10] For he looked forward to the city which has foundations, whose builder and maker is God. [11] By faith Sarah herself received power to conceive, even when she was past the age, since she considered him

11:1 – 12:2 When Moses led Israel into the Promised Land, he set before them "life and death, blessing and curse" and bade them choose life (Dt 30:19-20). The same choice confronts the wandering people of God in the last days; and the choice-of-life is faith (10:39). The whole record of God's dealing with man in the OT, from creation onward, is one long demonstration of the crucial necessity of "having faith." Only by faith can man live by the invisible realities of God and enter upon God's future (11:1). The record of the men of old shows that man can live only by faith in the sunlight of God's favor (11:2). Only by faith, indeed, can man live in God's world as God's creature at all, for only faith can know that the world is God's creation and the theater of His royal rule over His creation (11:3); only the invisible sway of God's Word makes it possible to "draw near" to God; to live in His world without heeding His Word is a "shrinking back" from Him that leads to destruction (cf. 10:39). Three men are singled out from the generation before the Flood: *Abel* (4), *Enoch* (5), and *Noah* (7). *By faith* each of them *received divine approval.* (4, 5, 7; cf. 2)

The OT record of the patriarchs is a record of their faith. *By faith Abraham obeyed* (8) when God called him and entered into God's invisible future (cf. 13-16) on the pilgrimage whose goal is the eternal *city* of God (9-10). *By faith* Abraham dared to sacrifice the son of the promise when God *tested* him (17); and his faith was not put to shame (19). *Isaac* and *Jacob* invoked the future which they saw and knew only *by faith* (20, 21) upon their sons and sons' sons when they blessed them.

The record of the Exodus, the heart of the faith by which Israel was to live for centuries, is a record of faith (22-29). *Joseph* would not seek immortality for his body in the skill of Egyptian embalmers; he committed himself to the unseen, hoped-for future deliverance of his people (21) by giving *directions* that his body be joined to his believing people's pilgrimage. Five times (23, 24, 27, 28, 29) the career of *Moses* is characterized as a career of faith. *By faith* God's *people crossed the Red Sea as if on dry land* (29) when the visible superiority of *the Egyptians* perished. The story of Israel's entry into the Land of Promise is the story of faith, whether it be the faith of a great leader like Joshua capturing *Jericho* (30) or of a pagan harlot like *Rahab* (31). There is not time to call the entire roll, to tell the whole story of the power of faith as shown in mighty heroic acts (32-35) or in the enduring of hardships and death (35-38). And God has kept all these ranks of faithful men poised and waiting for the final fulfillment of His promises till now! He has done us the honor of joining us to them that all might be *made perfect* together. (39-40)

11:1 *Assurance of things hoped for,* inner certainty concerning them.

11:3 *Things which do not appear,* the will, Word, and working of God, which cannot be rationally or empirically demonstrated.

11:4 *He is still speaking.* He lives on and speaks in the pages of the OT, and his witness is an incentive to all subsequent believers. He is one in that "great cloud of witnessess" of which 12:1 speaks.

11:5 *Enoch.* Cf. Gn 5:21-24, esp. 24.

11:6 *Rewards those who seek him.* Cf. Am 5:4, 6.

11:7 *Noah . . . took heed.* Gn 6:13-22.

He condemned the world. His faithful obedience to God's Word (Gn 6:22) was a living indictment of the heedlessness of the doomed world round about him (cf. Gn 6:5-7). For this use of "condemn" cf. Mt 12:41,42.

11:8 *Obeyed when . . . called.* Cf. Gn 12:1-8.

11:11 *Sarah . . . power to conceive.* Cf. Gn 17:19; 18:11-14; 21:2.

faithful who had promised. 12 Therefore from one man, and him as good as dead, were born descendants as many as the stars of heaven and as the innumerable grains of sand by the seashore.

13 These all died in faith, not having received what was promised, but having seen it and greeted it from afar, and having acknowledged that they were strangers and exiles on the earth. 14 For people who speak thus make it clear that they are seeking a homeland. 15 If they had been thinking of that land from which they had gone out, they would have had opportunity to return. 16 But as it is, they desire a better country, that is, a heavenly one. Therefore God is not ashamed to be called their God, for he has prepared for them a city.

17 By faith Abraham, when he was tested, offered up Isaac, and he who had received the promises was ready to offer up his only son, 18 of whom it was said, "Through Isaac shall your descendants be named." 19 He considered that God was able to raise men even from the dead; hence, figuratively speaking, he did receive him back. 20 By faith Isaac invoked future blessings on Jacob and Esau. 21 By faith Jacob, when dying, blessed each of the sons of Joseph, bowing in worship over the head of his staff. 22 By faith Joseph, at the end of his life, made mention of the exodus of the Israelites and gave directions concerning his burial.*

23 By faith Moses, when he was born, was hid for three months by his parents, because they saw that the child was beautiful; and they were not afraid of the king's edict. 24 By faith Moses, when he was grown up, refused to be called the son of Pharaoh's daughter, 25 choosing rather to share ill-treatment with the people of God than to enjoy the fleeting pleasures of sin. 26 He considered abuse suffered for the Christ greater wealth than the treasures of Egypt, for he looked to the reward. 27 By faith he left Egypt, not being afraid of the anger of the king; for he endured as seeing him who is invisible. 28 By faith he kept the Passover and sprinkled the blood, so that the Destroyer of the first-born might not touch them.

29 By faith the people crossed the Red Sea as if on dry land; but the Egyptians, when they attempted to do the same, were drowned. 30 By faith the walls of Jericho fell down after they had been encircled for seven days. 31 By faith Rahab the harlot did not perish with those who were disobedient, because she had given friendly welcome to the spies.

32 And what more shall I say? For time would fail me to tell of Gideon, Barak,

* Greek *bones*

11:12 *Stars of heaven . . . grains of sand.* Cf. Gn 15:5-6; 22:17; 32:12.

11:13 *What was promised,* that is, the final last-days fulfillment of the promise. (Cf. 33)

Strangers and exiles. Cf. Gn 23:4, where Abraham so describes himself when negotiating for the purchase of a burial plot for Sarah—his possession of the Promised Land was still one of "the things hoped for" when he had no room in it even to bury his dead!

11:16 *Their God,* "the God of Abraham . . . Isaac . . . Jacob." (Ex 3:6,15; 4:5)

11:17 *Abraham . . . was tested.* Cf. Gn 22:1-10.

11:18 *Descendants be named.* Cf. Gn 21:12.

11:19 Cf. Ro 4:17.

From the dead . . . he did receive him back. Since the Word of God determines what a man is, Isaac, as designated for sacrifice by God's command, was already among the dead.

11:20 *Isaac invoked future blessings.* Cf. Gn 27: 27-29, 39-40.

11:21 *Jacob . . . blessed . . . sons of Joseph.* Cf. Gn 48:8-22.

Bowing . . . over the head of his staff. The phrase is taken from Gn 47:31, following the Greek translation (Septuagint).

11:22 *Joseph.* Cf. Gn 50:24-25; Ex 13:19.

11:23 *Was hid . . . by his parents.* Cf. Ex 2:2 and 1:22. Their faith could not abandon a child born under the promises of God.

11:25 *Fleeting pleasures of sin.* The sin would have been the one that so much exercises the author's concern, namely, the apostasy; cf. 6: 1-8 notes and 10:26-31.

11:26 *Suffered for the Christ.* Suffering for the sake of the future promised to God's people is suffering for the Christ; the Christ is the future of His people.

11:27 *Not . . . afraid of the anger of the king.* These words make it clear that Moses' second departure from Egypt (rather than his first fearful departure in Ex 2:15) with his people is meant, when he told the panicking Israelites, "Fear not, stand firm, and see the salvation of the LORD." (Ex 14:13)

11:28 *Kept the Passover.* Cf. Ex 12:21-28, 29-30.

11:29 *Crossed the Red Sea.* Cf. Ex 14:21-31.

11:30-31 *Walls of Jericho fell down . . . Rahab.* Cf. Jos 2:1-21; 6:22-25.

11:32 *Gideon.* Cf. Ju 6—8.

Barak. Cf. Ju 4—5.

Samson. Cf. Ju 13—16.

Samson, Jephthah, of David and Samuel and the prophets—³³ who through faith conquered kingdoms, enforced justice, received promises, stopped the mouths of lions, ³⁴ quenched raging fire, escaped the edge of the sword, won strength out of weakness, became mighty in war, put foreign armies to flight. ³⁵ Women received their dead by resurrection. Some were tortured, refusing to accept release, that they might rise again to a better life. ³⁶ Others suffered mocking and scourging, and even chains and imprisonment. ³⁷ They were stoned, they were sawn in two,ʸ they were killed with the sword; they went about in skins of sheep and goats, destitute, afflicted, ill-treated— ³⁸ of whom the world was not worthy—wandering over deserts and mountains, and in dens and caves of the earth.

39 And all these, though well attested by their faith, did not receive what was promised, ⁴⁰ since God had foreseen something better for us, that apart from us they should not be made perfect.

12 Therefore, since we are surrounded by so great a cloud of witnesses, let us also lay aside every weight, and sin which clings so closely, and let us run with perseverance the race that is set before us, ² looking to Jesus the pioneer and perfecter of our faith, who for the joy that was set before him endured the cross, despising the shame, and is seated at the right hand of the throne of God.

EXHORTATION TO FAITH AND FEAR (12:3-29)

3 Consider him who endured from sinners such hostility against himself, so that you may not grow weary or fainthearted. ⁴ In your struggle against sin you have not yet

ʸ Other manuscripts add *they were tempted*

Jephthah. Cf. Ju 11 — 12.

David. Cf. 1 Sm 16 — 30; 2 Sm 1 — 24; 1 K 1 — 2:11.

Samuel. Cf. 1 Sm 1 — 12; 16:1-13.

11:33 *Conquered kingdoms.* E. g., Gideon overcame the Midianites against overwhelming odds; Jephthah defeated the Ammonites; David conquered the Philistines.

Enforced justice. Cf. what is said of David's reign in 2 Sm 8:15.

Received promises. Cf., e. g., God's promise to Gideon, Ju 6:16: "I will be with you, and you shall smite the Midianites as one man."

Stopped the mouths of lions. Cf. Dn 6.

11:34 *Quenched raging fire.* Cf. the three men in the fiery furnace, Dn 3:25.

Escaped the edge of the sword. Cf. Ps 144:10; 1 Sm 18:11.

Won strength out of weakness. Cf. Ju 16:28.

Became mighty in war. Cf. 1 Sm 17.

Put foreign armies to flight. This may refer either to exploits of great leaders, such as those referred to in 11:32, or to the victories over foreign power recorded in the apocryphal books 1 and 2 Mac.

11:35 *Women received their dead by resurrection.* Cf. 1 K 17:17-24; 2 K 4:25-37.

11:35-38 offer examples of great endurance sustained by faith. Some of the examples were probably suggested by cases of heroic suffering by the faithful during the Maccabean revolt recorded in 1 and 2 Mac.

11:37 *Sawn in two.* According to Judaic tradition, Isaiah suffered this fate under the wicked king Manasseh, who "shed very much innocent blood." (2 K 21:16)

11:38 *The world was not worthy.* They were too good for the wicked "world" (men without God

and opposed to His will) which persecuted them and made wandering outlaws (cf. 11:37) of them.

11:39 *Well attested by their faith.* Cf. 11:1 — 12:2 note.

11:40 *Something better,* namely, the new and better covenant with all the blessings that full forgiveness entails. (Cf. 8:6, 8-12)

12:1 *Lay aside every weight,* anything that would weigh down, encumber, and slow down the runner in his course. Faith involves renunciation.

Sin which clings so closely, like an encumbering garment which slows the runner's stride.

12:2 *The joy . . . set before him.* For the *joy* of Jesus, His delight in fulfilling His Father's will and delivering man, cf. Jn 15:11; 17:13; see also Jn 4:35-38.

Is seated, in triumphant majesty. Cf. 1:3; 10:12; Ps 110:1.

12:3-29. The double note of confident faith and holy fear runs through the close and climax of the last long exhortation which began at 10:19. There are many grounds for the triumphant certainty of faith. There is Jesus, who has run our race and fought our fight before us and for us, one with us in His manhood (note the use of the human name alone, Jesus, 2), who faced the *hostility* of the *sinners,* to whom He ministered, and was obedient *to the point of shedding blood* (4), unshaken to the end in His "assurance of things hoped for" and His "conviction of things not seen" (11:1; cf. 12:2). There is the God whom, through Jesus, we know as Father, who *addresses* us *as sons* (5) and bids us accept discipline and chastisement from His fatherly hand (5-6; Pr 3:11-12) as the sure token of our sonship (7-8). His discipline and chastisement are a better thing than what our less wise and sometimes arbitrary (*at their pleasure,* 10)

resisted to the point of shedding your blood. 5And have you forgotten the exhortation which addresses you as sons?—

"My son, do not regard lightly the discipline of the Lord,
nor lose courage when you are punished by him.

6　　　For the Lord disciplines him whom he loves,
and chastises every son whom he receives."

7 It is for discipline that you have to endure. God is treating you as sons; for what son is there whom his father does not discipline? 8 If you are left without discipline, in which all have participated, then you are illegitimate children and not sons. 9 Besides this, we have had earthly fathers to discipline us and we respected them. Shall we not much more be subject to the Father of spirits and live? 10 For they disciplined us for a short time at their pleasure, but he disciplines us for our good, that we may share his holiness. 11 For the moment all discipline seems painful rather than pleasant; later it yields the peaceful fruit of righteousness to those who have been trained by it.

12 Therefore lift your drooping hands and strengthen your weak knees, 13 and make straight paths for your feet, so that what is lame may not be put out of joint but rather be healed. 14 Strive for peace with all men, and for the holiness without which no one will see the Lord. 15 See to it that no one fail to obtain the grace of God; that no "root of bitterness" spring up and cause trouble, and by it the many become defiled; 16 that no one be immoral or irreligious like Esau, who sold his birthright for a single meal. 17 For you know that afterward, when he desired to inherit the blessing, he was rejected, for he found no chance to repent, though he sought it with tears.

fathers could give us, and they bear better fruit: life (9) and the *peaceful fruit of righteousness to those who have been trained by* them (11). From Him we can seek and find new strength for *drooping hands* and *weak knees* (12); when we grow weary, strength to help one another along straightened paths, strength to heal the lagging *lame* and help them on their way in *peace* and *holiness* (14). The prospect that greets the marchers is a splendid and heartening one: no longer the terrors that accompanied the giving of the Law on Sinai (18-21) but the festal triumph of the gathered people of God in *the city of the living God,* assembled with *angels* and archangels and all the company of heaven around *Jesus, the mediator of the new covenant* by virtue of His *sprinkled blood* (24), inheritors at last of *a kingdom that cannot be shaken.* (28)

But we are not yet what we then shall be, *just men made perfect* (23), and we still have need of the salutary discipline of holy fear. We need the Word that warns us of the danger of growing *weary or fainthearted* (3), that will not let us forget God's Word to His sons regarding their chastisement (5-11). We need the Word that wakens us to our responsibility toward our fellows, lest they and we both *fail to obtain the grace of God* (15). We need the warning against growing bitter and resentful under the benign pressure of God's hand, lest the "root of bitterness" grow up into a spreading noxious weed which troubles and defiles (15). We need to be reminded of the tragic instance of *Esau,* lest we like him take the cash and let the credit go, forfeiting the blessing that we shall one day seek in vain *with tears* (16-17). We need to be reminded that in *the city of the living God* which is the goal of our journeying there is *a judge who is God of all* (23), whose scrutiny no one and nothing can escape. We dare not forget

that He *who is speaking* to us now and is warning us from heaven (25) is the omnipotent Lord of the future whom we dare not refuse, least of all now when He is poised for that last act of His which *will shake not only the earth but also the heaven.* Our gratitude *for receiving a kingdom that cannot be shaken* (28) is real gratitude only if we look to the great Giver *with reverence and awe* (28). *Thus,* as men impelled by faith and hallowed by fear, we can *offer acceptable worship.* (28)

But the somber note of fear does not drown out the glad note of faith. Even when we are confronted with the ultimate terror of God as a *consuming fire,* we are permitted to remember that He remains *our God* (29) and are reminded that He becomes consuming fire only when we in our self-will will not let Him be our God.

12:5-6 Pr 3:11-12.

12:9 *Father of spirits.* God is so called in contrast to human, physical fathers, to indicate the surpassing character of His Fatherhood.

12:12 *Drooping hands . . . weak knees,* both signs of the exhausted runner. (Cf. 12:1)

12:13 *Make straight paths.* The picture is changed from that of a runner in a race to that of the pilgrim people of God marching over difficult terrain, where the *lame* would sustain injury unless their fellow marchers cared for them.

12:14 *Strive for peace with all men.* Peace within the fellowship of the church is meant. Where there is discord, there cannot be that care for one another which is enjoined in the following.

12:15 *"Root of bitterness."* The phrase is taken from the Greek version of Dt 29:18. The Hebrew text has "a root bearing poisonous and bitter fruit" (RSV). Dt 29:18 warns against apostasy.

12:16 *Esau . . . sold his birthright.* Cf. Gn 25:29-34.

12:17 *He was rejected.* Gn 27:30-40.

18 For you have not come to what may be touched, a blazing fire, and darkness, and gloom, and a tempest, [19] and the sound of a trumpet, and a voice whose words made the hearers entreat that no further messages be spoken to them. [20] For they could not endure the order that was given, "If even a beast touches the mountain, it shall be stoned." [21] Indeed, so terrifying was the sight that Moses said, "I tremble with fear." [22] But you have come to Mount Zion and to the city of the living God, the heavenly Jerusalem, and to innumerable angels in festal gathering, [23] and to the assembly[z] of the first-born who are enrolled in heaven, and to a judge who is God of all, and to the spirits of just men made perfect, [24] and to Jesus, the mediator of a new covenant, and to the sprinkled blood that speaks more graciously than the blood of Abel.

25 See that you do not refuse him who is speaking. For if they did not escape when they refused him who warned them on earth, much less shall we escape if we reject him who warns from heaven. [26] His voice then shook the earth; but now he has promised, "Yet once more I will shake not only the earth but also the heaven." [27] This phrase, "Yet once more," indicates the removal of what is shaken, as of what has been made, in order that what cannot be shaken may remain. [28] Therefore let us be grateful for receiving a kingdom that cannot be shaken, and thus let us offer to God acceptable worship, with reverence and awe; [29] for our God is a consuming fire.

Concluding Admonitions and Close

13:1-25

13 Let brotherly love continue. [2] Do not neglect to show hospitality to strangers, for thereby some have entertained angels unawares. [3] Remember those who are in prison, as though in prison with them; and those who are ill-treated, since you also are in the body. [4] Let marriage be held in honor among all, and let the marriage bed be undefiled; for God will judge the immoral and adulterous. [5] Keep your life free

[z] Or *angels, and to the festal gathering and assembly*

He found no chance to repent. Another rendering of the Greek is possible and indeed probable. The "no chance to repent" could refer to the fact that Isaac could not withdraw the blessing once he had bestowed it on Jacob (Gn 27:37, cf. 35) and the whole might be rendered: "He found no chance to change his father's decision."

Tears Gn 27:34, 38.

12:18 *What may be touched,* i. e., a physical place like Sinai. For the terrors of Sinai cf. Ex 19:12-22; 20:18-21; Dt 4:11-12; 5:22-27.

12:20 Cf. Ex 19:12-13.

12:21 *"I tremble with fear."* Cf. Dt 9:19, where, however, Moses' fear is occasioned by his discovery of the golden calf and the people's apostasy. Cf. Acts 7:32 for a similar phrase describing Moses in his encounter with God.

12:23 *Assembly of the first-born* probably refers to angels, created before man and occupying a place of honor in the "city of the living God, the heavenly Jerusalem." (22)

12:24 *Mediator of a new covenant.* Cf. 8:6; 9:15.

Sprinkled blood that speaks more graciously. The well-known hymn verse is an apt commentary:

Abel's blood for vengeance (Gn 4:10)
Pleaded to the skies;
But the blood of Jesus
For our pardon cries.

12:25 *They did not escape,* that is, the people Israel, Ex 19:21, 24. For the thought cf. 2:1-4.

12:26 Cf. Hg 2:6, where the words refer to God's last coming to glorify His abode.

12:29 *Fire* is a common Biblical symbol of divine judgment in both the OT and the NT. Cf., e. g., Am 1:4, 7, 10, 12, 14; 2:2, 5; 7:4; Mt 3:10, 11.

13:1-6 TRUE LOVE AND FALSE

13:1-6 The first set of admonitions encourages the readers to *continue* in true *love:* love for brothers in the family of God, both the known and near and those from afar *(hospitality);* actively sympathetic love for the prisoner and the persecuted *(ill-treated);* pure conjugal love *(marriage).* The threat of God's judgment upon those who violate the sanctity of wedded love (4) provides the transition to the warning against false love, *love of money,* which is mistrust and unbelief toward Him who has promised His help.

13:2 *Hospitality,* not merely cordial sociability but a ministry of love to traveling, persecuted, and missionary fellow Christians. (Cf. 3 Jn 8; Ro 12:13)

Entertained angels, as Abraham and Lot did. (Gn 18:1-8; 19:1-3)

13:3 *In prison . . . ill-treated.* Cf. 6:10; 10:32-34.

Since you also are in the body, and therefore yourselves liable to suffering.

13:5 *"I will never . . . forsake you."* The promise of God which sustained Joshua when he led the wandering people of God into Canaan (Jos 1:5; Dt 31:6-8) will sustain God's people on their last journey to their eternal city. (Cf. 13:14)

from love of money, and be content with what you have; for he has said, "I will never fail you nor forsake you." 6 Hence we can confidently say,

> "The Lord is my helper,
> I will not be afraid;
> what can man do to me?"

7 Remember your leaders, those who spoke to you the word of God; consider the outcome of their life, and imitate their faith. 8 Jesus Christ is the same yesterday and today and for ever. 9 Do not be led away by diverse and strange teachings; for it is well that the heart be strengthened by grace, not by foods, which have not benefited their adherents. 10 We have an altar from which those who serve the tent[a] have no right to eat. 11 For the bodies of those animals whose blood is brought into the sanctuary by the high priest as a sacrifice for sin are burned outside the camp. 12 So Jesus also suffered outside the gate in order to sanctify the people through his own blood. 13 Therefore let us go forth to him outside the camp, and bear the abuse he endured. 14 For here we have no lasting city, but we seek the city which is to come. 15 Through him then let us continually offer up a sacrifice of praise to God, that is, the fruit of lips that acknowledge his name. 16 Do not neglect to do good and to share what you have, for such sacrifices are pleasing to God.

17 Obey your leaders and submit to them; for they are keeping watch over your souls, as men who will have to give account. Let them do this joyfully, and not sadly, for that would be of no advantage to you.

18 Pray for us, for we are sure that we have a clear conscience, desiring to act

[a] Or *tabernacle*

13:6 Cf. Ps 118:6, expressing the confident boast of the man who though "pushed hard" by his enemies (13) and "sorely chastened" by the Lord (18), found in Him his strength and song and salvation." (14)

13:7-19 CONCERNING LEADERS IN THE CHURCH

13:7-19 Three admonitions concern *leaders* in the church. The first and longest (7-16) deals with the leaders, now dead (7), who *spoke . . . the word of God* to them. The second (17) concerns their present leaders in their pastoral function as men *keeping watch over* their *souls*. The third takes the form of a request by the author of the letter for the intercession of the church. (18-19)

13:7-16 The readers are to honor the memory of the *leaders* who first taught them *the word of God* (cf. 2:3) by following in the footsteps (*imitate*, 7) of their *faith;* for their faith, like their teaching, was centered and fixed in Christ. Christ abides unchanged. His first witnesses may die, and *diverse and strange teachings* may attempt to distort Him or becloud His glory; yet He remains the *same for ever* (8). In Him they will continue to find the *grace* which will keep the *heart* strong and firm in faith (9); in Him they will find the strength they need, not in *foods* (as the authors of the diverse and strange teachings apparently claim). These foods were apparently connected with the old order of the Law and its cultus which "made nothing perfect" (7:19; 9:9-10) and therefore never *benefited their adherents* (9) as the grace of God in Christ can benefit His adherents now. That old order had sacrifices in which people and priests had the *right to eat* (10) of the sacrificial animal. But that was never the procedure in the case of the *sacrifice for sin* (11) on the Day of Atone-

ment, where the *bodies of those animals* were *burned outside the camp* (11; cf. Lv 16:27). And the once-for-all sacrifice of *Jesus* was such a sacrifice for sin, for He suffered on the Day of Atonement *in order to sanctify the people through his own blood* and was consumed by the fire of suffering *outside the gate* of Jerusalem (12). The *altar* on which Christ's blood was offered offers His adherents *grace*, not food; those who cling to the old order and will not in faith recognize the new (*those who serve the tent*, or *tabernacle*, 10) *have no right to eat* (10) there; for they seek food, not grace. No new teaching can force Jesus back into the old and doomed Jerusalem, back into the old order of unprofitable foods. Men must continue to seek Him where He is to be found, in the new *city which is to come* (14), the new Jerusalem (cf. 12:22-24). For the Christian Jew that meant a painful break with the past and with the majority of his people, who will *abuse* him as a renegade to the faith and the God of his fathers (13). But he need not fear that his worship life has become poorer because he has broken with the splendid cultus of old Israel. There is left him a true *sacrifice . . . pleasing to God* (15-16), sacrifice that his OT itself approved (Ps 50:14, 23; Hos 14:2; cf. Ps 51:15-17): the sacrifice of praise to God and beneficence to man. (15-16; cf. Ja 1:27; 1 Ptr 2:5)

13:7 *Life,* that is, their mode of life, their fidelity to their Lord which made the *outcome* of their life a triumphant one, perhaps a martyr's death.

13:17 *To give account.* Cf. 1 Ptr 5:2-4.

Of no advantage to you. A leader hampered by the disobedience of his people, doing his pastoral duty *sadly,* cannot give his people the full benefit of his leadership.

13:18 *A clear conscience.* Only a leader with

honorably in all things. [19] I urge you the more earnestly to do this in order that I may be restored to you the sooner.

20 Now may the God of peace who brought again from the dead our Lord Jesus, the great shepherd of the sheep, by the blood of the eternal covenant, [21] equip you with everything good that you may do his will, working in you[b] that which is pleasing in his sight, through Jesus Christ; to whom be glory for ever and ever. Amen.

22 I appeal to you, brethren, bear with my word of exhortation, for I have written to you briefly. [23] You should understand that our brother Timothy has been released, with whom I shall see you if he comes soon. [24] Greet all your leaders and all the saints. Those who come from Italy send your greetings. [25] Grace be with all of you. Amen.

[b] Other ancient authorities read *us*

a clear conscience can lay a justified claim to the intercessions of his people. (Cf. 2 Co 1:11-12)

13:20-25 CLOSE

13:20-25 The author's own intercession for his readers (20-21), an appeal to *bear with* his *word of exhortation* (22), news concerning his own and Timothy's coming to them (23), greetings (24), and a brief benediction (25) conclude the letter.

13:20-21 The intercession invokes the *God* who has created and bestowed *peace* (that perfect health and soundness in the relationship between God and man which He desires) by the death and resurrection of His Son. *Through Jesus Christ* and His covenant sacrifice He has created His people; through Him, the *great shepherd,* He will preserve His people, equipping them for all that is *pleasing in his sight.*

13:20 *Shepherd . . . covenant.* Cf. Eze 37:24-27.

13:22 *Word of exhortation* would be for Jewish-Christian ears the equivalent of "sermon." Cf. Acts 13:15, where the term is so used in the synagog.

Briefly. The letter is brief in comparison with the extended discourse and discussion which his presence (19, 23) with them would make possible.

13:23 The mention of *Timothy,* long an associate of Paul, suggests that the author, too, was associated with Paul. The fact that Timothy is mentioned alone, with no reference to the man with whom he was identified lifelong so closely, indicates that Paul was no longer among the living.

13:24 *Those . . . from Italy.* Cf. Introduction, par. 4.

THE LETTER OF

JAMES

INTRODUCTION

The Letter of James is addressed to Jewish Christians. The words of the salutation, "To the twelve tribes in the Dispersion" (1:1), in themselves do not necessarily mark the readers as Jewish, since the New Testament constantly appropriates the titles and attributes of Israel for the New Testament people of God (cf. Gl 6:16; Ph 3:3; 1 Ptr 1:1, 17; 2:9-10; Rv 7:4 ff.; 14:1); but these words are part of the generally Judaic coloring of the letter. The situation presupposed among the Christians addressed in the letter—that of a poor, tired, oppressed, and persecuted church—corresponds to what we know of the Jerusalem church of Acts 1—12; and what held for Jerusalem very probably held for other Jewish churches in Palestine and in the Dispersion also. The sins which the letter particularly deals with are the sins of Judaism in their Christianized form; the problem of sexual license, for instance, which looms so large in Gentile Christianity and is constantly dealt with in letters addressed to Gentile churches, is not touched on here, while the prime sin of Israel under the leadership of scribe and Pharisee, that of cleavage between profession and practice (Mt 23:3), which evoked Jesus' most stringent polemics, is scored heavily by James. The place of worship is called by the same name as the Jewish synagog (2:2), a practice which was long observed in Judaic Christianity but was never frequent elsewhere in Christendom. The author takes all his examples from the Old Testament (Abraham, Rahab, Job, the prophets, Elijah), and this tells us something about the readers as well as the author.

Date of the Letter

The letter is apparently addressed to Judaic Christians of the early days, during the period covered by Acts 1—12. The church is still firmly enmeshed in Judaism, a part of historic Israel, so much so that one modern scholar has argued that the letter is addressed to *all* Israel, stressing all that Christians and Jews have in common, and is in-tended to be a missionary appeal, by way of admonition and a call to repentance, to all Jews. Although this theory amounts to an overstatement of the case and can hardly be accepted in the form in which it is advanced, it does call attention to the essentially Judaic character of the persons addressed, and it recognizes the fact that there are portions in the letter which address the readers particularly as members of historic Israel (4:1 ff.) and passages which are apostrophes directed to the Judaic world around the church rather than admonitions spoken directly to the church (4:13-17; 5:1-6). Judaism has not yet definitely expelled the new community. Furthermore, there is no indication in the letter of the tensions and difficulties which arose when Gentiles came into the church in large numbers, those tensions which gave rise to the Apostolic Council (Acts 15) and occasioned Paul's Letter to the Galatians. A date prior to Paul's first missionary journey is therefore most probable, about A. D. 45; and the phrase "twelve tribes of the Dispersion" is intended to designate the new people of God at a time when it consisted primarily of converted Jews.

Author of the Letter

The only indications of authorship in the letter are the name James in the salutation and the general tone and character of its content. If we ask which of the various men named James in the New Testament could expect to be recognized and identified when he calls himself simply "James, a servant of God and of the Lord Jesus Christ" (1:1) and could speak with such massive authority to Judaic Christianity as he does in this writing, the most probable answer is: James, the brother of the Lord. (The much-debated question whether the brethren of the Lord were His cousins, half brothers, or full brothers need not detain us here; the last alternative, that they were the children of Joseph and Mary, would seem to be the most probable; that they were his half brothers is

possible; the theory that makes them his cousins is beset by almost insuperable difficulties.)

This James had, like his brothers, refused to accept his brother as the Christ during His lifetime (Jn 7:5). It was not apparently until the risen Lord appeared to him that his doubts were overcome and he became the servant of Him whom he henceforth called "the Lord Jesus Christ" (cf. 1 Co 15:7; Acts 1:14). Active in the life of the church from the beginning, he seems to have confined his work to Jerusalem. Possibly he undertook missionary journeys within Palestine, like his brothers (1 Co 9:5). At any rate, it was in Jerusalem that he became and remained prominent. As early as A. D. 44 he was the acknowledged leader of the Jerusalem church, as Peter's words in Acts 12:17 show. About to leave Jerusalem after his deliverance from jail, Peter bids the people assembled in Mary's house tell of his release and departure "to James and to the brethren." At the Apostolic Council the voice of James is the final and decisive voice in the discussion (Acts 15:13-29). When Paul at the end of his third missionary journey reports to the Jerusalem church and brings the gifts of the Gentile church to the saints at Jerusalem, he reports to James (Acts 21:18). The picture we have of James in Acts is confirmed by what we find in the letters of Paul; Paul can refer to him simply as "James" and reckon on being understood (1 Co 15:7); he practically ranks him with the apostles in Gl 1:19, and even mentions him before Peter and John as one of the "pillars" of the church (Gl 2:9). James is, for Paul, so integral a part of the life of the Jerusalem church that he can describe Jerusalem Christians who came to Antioch by saying, "Certain men came *from James*" (Gl 2:12). Jude can in his letter identify himself to his readers by calling himself "brother of James." (Jude 1)

A later Jewish-Christian tradition preserved for us by Eusebius (*HE* II, 23, 4) pictures James as a paragon of Judaic piety in the sense that he was deeply interested in and devoted to the ritual side of that piety; but none of the New Testament notices of him confirms this. He is, according to the New Testament, a Christian Jew devoted to his mission to Israel and therefore faithful to the temple and to the Law so long as the temple stands and there is an Israel that will hear him. Reliable tradition has it that he was faithful to his people to the end and

died a martyr's death A. D. 66. So strongly had his piety and his love for his people impressed men that even pious Jews called him the Just and saw in the Jewish wars and the fall of Jerusalem God's righteous visitation on Israel for putting this righteous man to death.

Occasion of the Letter

The Epistle of James shows that the author is acquainted with the situation of his readers, but none of the references is so specific that it enables us to point to any particular event or set of circumstances as the immediate occasion for writing. Still, it is probably not accidental that the epistle opens with a summons to find cause for joy in "various trials" (1:2) and closes with an admonition to restore the brother who "wanders from the truth" (5:19). The "twelve tribes" are under the twin pressures of poverty and persecution; they are tempted to grow depressed, bitter, and impatient—depressed at the fate of the doomed people of which they remained a part, a fate which loomed ever more clearly and more terribly against the stormy skies of Palestine; bitter at the fact that they were offering the grace of God in vain to this doomed people; and impatient for the "times of refreshing" and the establishing of all things (Acts 3:19-21) which the resurrection of Jesus Christ from the dead had promised and assured.

They were tempted, in this apathetic slackening of their energies, this declension in their Christian stamina, to relapse and accommodate their life to the life of the world which pressed on them from every side and sought to put its mark and impress on them. For them accommodation to the "world" meant, of course, accommodation to the Judaism from which they had escaped, Judaism with its distorted piety, its encrusted and inactive faith, its superficial and fruitless hearing of the Word, its arrogant and quarrelsome "wisdom," its ready response to the seduction of wealth, its mad thirst for liberty. The danger of apostasy was for members of this church anything but remote and theoretical; it was immediate and real. (5:19-20)

In such a situation, in a church beset from without and within, faced with the necessity of constant correction and discipline, it is small wonder that the love of many grew cold, that the church was troubled by inner dissensions, that men were ready to speak against and to judge one another, that the

spontaneous mutual ministrations of the first glad days were in danger of lapsing and being forgotten.

Content of the Letter

To these Judaic churches in this characteristically Judaic situation the leader of Judaic Christianity addressed a thoroughly Judaic letter, or rather a homily in letter form; for the letter is a letter chiefly in form —and even the letter form is not complete; the personal conclusion, characteristic of Paul's letters, is absent here. A phrase like *"Listen,* my beloved brethren" (2:5) shows that we have to do with a writing that is simply the extension of the spoken "implanted word"; and the whole style of the letter bears this out. The leader and teacher whose word is the vehicle of the will of God to the Jerusalem church is speaking to the Judaic churches in Judea, Samaria, Galilee, Syria, Cilicia—perhaps the letter went even farther afield than that.

The "miscellaneous" character of James' admonitions has often been exaggerated, sometimes in the interest of theories concerning the origin of the book. This miscellaneous character is more apparent than real, being due to the Semitic habit of thought which sets down related thoughts side by side without explicitly coordinating them or subordinating one to the other as we are accustomed to do. James' call to repentance breaks down on closer investigation into six rather massive units, each of which again usually has two aspects.

THE LETTER OF

JAMES

1 James, a servant of God and of the Lord Jesus Christ,
To the twelve tribes in the Dispersion:
Greeting.

Turn to God, the Giver of Perfect Gifts

1:2-27

TURN TO THE GOD WHO PERFECTS YOU BY TRIAL (1:2-18)

2 Count it all joy, my brethren, when you meet various trials, 3 for you know that the testing of your faith produces steadfastness. 4And let steadfastness have its full effect, that you may be perfect and complete, lacking in nothing.

5 If any of you lacks wisdom, let him ask God, who gives to all men generously and without reproaching, and it will be given him. 6 But let him ask in faith, with no doubting, for he who doubts is like a wave of the sea that is driven and tossed by the wind. 7, 8 For that person must not suppose that a double-minded man, unstable in all his ways, will receive anything from the Lord.

9 Let the lowly brother boast in his exaltation, 10 and the rich in his humiliation, because like the flower of the grass he will pass away. 11 For the sun rises with its scorching heat and withers the grass; its flower falls, and its beauty perishes. So will the rich man fade away in the midst of his pursuits.

12 Blessed is the man who endures trial, for when he has stood the test he will receive the crown of life which God has promised to those who love him. 13 Let no one say when he is tempted, "I am tempted by God"; for God cannot be tempted with

1:1 James begins with an obeisance to *God and . . . the Lord Jesus Christ;* he stands in the same relation to both; he is *servant,* totally devoted to both in the obedience of faith. And he speaks to the new Israel, the *twelve tribes* of the new age who have not yet reached their eternal home but live as scattered exiles in this world (*in the Dispersion;* cf. 1 Ptr 1:1; Ph 3:20). He speaks as the servant of the Lord, the prophets (Am 3:7), spoke of old to God's people, and their message is also his, the call to repentance: "Turn" (cf., e. g., Jer 25:5). This turning is both a turning from evil and a turning to the Lord who makes repentance possible (Lm 5:21) and bestows His forgiveness and blessing on the penitent. (Jl 2:12-14)

Twelve tribes. For the NT church as the new Israel cf. Gl 6:16; Ph 3:3; 1 Ptr 1:1, 17; 2:9-10; Rv 7:4 ff.; 14:1.

1:2-18 Turn from your folly (5), from your wavering double-mindedness (6-8), your doubt of God's goodness, your Judaic fatalism which attributes man's sin to God. (13-15)

Turn to your God and find in Him the power to speak a glad assent to the trials which He sends you (2); find in Him the tried and tested faith which gives steadfastness (3) and perfection (4); find in Him, by the prayer of faith, the wisdom which will enable you to bear your trials (5), a wisdom which enables the poor man to see in his

poverty his exaltation (9) and gives to the rich man the power to see his greatness elsewhere than in himself and his riches (10-11). Turn to God and find in Him the unchanging Giver of all good gifts, the Giver of the supreme gift of new birth by His Word, a rebirth which is the beginning and pledge of creation's rebirth (18). Thus empowered, endure your trials manfully and joyfully and receive from Him the crown of life. (12)

1:2 *Joy.* Cf. 5:10-12.

1:3 *Faith.* When Christians are put to the test, faith is being tested. Faith is of central importance for James. (Cf. ch. 2)

1:5 *Wisdom* in the Scriptures is a gift of God (charismatic), centered in God and practical, having to do with management of life. One might describe it as the ability to see God steadily and see Him whole, in all aspects of one's life, even in trial and suffering, as here.

Ask . . . given. Cf. Mt 7:7.

1:10-11 Cf. Is 40:6-8, where the contrast to man in his frailty and transience is the "word of our God" which "will stand for ever." The Word of God plays a significant part in this chapter, 1:18, 21, 22, 23, 25 ("perfect law").

1:12 *Crown of life.* Life, eternal life in a glory bestowed by God, is the crown.

1:13 Trial and temptation lie close together; God's testing of faith can be the occasion of the

evil and he himself tempts no one; [14] but each person is tempted when he is lured and enticed by his own desire. [15] Then desire when it has conceived gives birth to sin; and sin when it is full-grown brings forth death.

16 Do not be deceived, my beloved brethren. [17] Every good endowment and every perfect gift is from above, coming down from the Father of lights with whom there is no variation or shadow due to change.[a] [18] Of his own will he brought us forth by the word of truth that we should be a kind of first fruits of his creatures.

TURN TO THE GOD WHO IMPLANTED HIS WORD AMONG YOU (1:19-27)

19 Know this, my beloved brethren. Let every man be quick to hear, slow to speak, slow to anger, [20] for the anger of man does not work the righteousness of God. [21] Therefore put away all filthiness and rank growth of wickedness and receive with meekness the implanted word, which is able to save your souls.

22 But be doers of the word, and not hearers only, deceiving yourselves. [23] For if any one is a hearer of the word and not a doer, he is like a man who observes his natural face in a mirror; [24] for he observes himself and goes away and at once forgets what he was like. [25] But he who looks into the perfect law, the law of liberty, and perseveres, being no hearer that forgets but a doer that acts, he shall be blessed in his doing.

26 If any one thinks he is religious, and does not bridle his tongue but deceives his heart, this man's religion is vain. [27] Religion that is pure and undefiled before God and

[a] Other ancient authorities read *variation due to a shadow of turning*

temptation to refuse God's loving discipline and to depart from Him. *"I am tempted by God."* The rabbis attributed to God the creation of the evil impulse in man (for which the Law was given as the cure), and the Qumran sect held a similar view. James' warning would be particularly relevant to Jewish Christians. (Cf. 16, "Do not be deceived.")

1:14-15 *Own desire.* Man is responsible for the uncanny sequence that leads with the inevitability of conception, gestation, and birth to *death.*

1:17 *Father of lights,* Creator (cf. Jb 38:28). God ordained the lights to "be for signs and for seasons" (Gn 1:14, 18); they are the most certain thing in creation, yet even they undergo *variation* and *change;* God's giving, His will of grace, is more certain than the most certain of His creations.

1:18 James is referring to the supreme gift of God to His new 12 tribes, namely, new birth, new life. 1 Ptr 1:3 connects this gift explicitly with "the resurrection of Jesus Christ from the dead"; and the resurrection of the "Lord of glory" (2:1) constitutes the unspoken presupposition of James word.

Word of truth, the Gospel. (Cf. 1 Ptr 1:22-25; Eph 1:13; Cl 1:5)

1:19-27 Turn from the pride which breaks out in self-assertive speech before it has heard the good Giver out, turn from the anger which resents His judgment on man's sins (19), from the filthiness and wickedness which insulates a man against the wholesome fires of God's judgment and against the life-giving warmth of His grace (21). Turn from speaking to hearing, from self-assertive anger to the meekness which hears God out on His terms (19-21), turn to God and receive from His Word the righteousness which God alone can work (20), receive it in a repentance which strips off the filth and wickedness of self and in

its naked helplessness receives from God salvation of the soul. (21)

When you have so heard the Word in repentance and faith, turn from the self-deception which thinks that God's Word is a word to be contemplated, that a man may hear God's Word without being moved by it (22, 26); turn from such mere and forgetful hearing of His Word (22, 24, 25) to a persevering and vital hearing of it, turn to a doing of the Word which God's great gift has made for you a perfect law of liberty, a law which sets you free for God and for your fellowmen (25), that law which leads man to a pure and undefiled worship of God, which hallows his speaking, makes his deeds deeds of mercy, and sets him apart from the defilement and the doom of this dark world. (26-27)

1:19 *Know this,* that God is the generous (1:5), unchangingly sure Giver of every good gift (1:17) and that His supreme gift of new life comes to man by His Word (1:18). Therefore the hearing (and doing) of this Word is of such critical importance.

1:20 *Righteousness of God.* Since a meek hearing does "work" this righteousness, and since the Word is one which does God's own work of saving men's souls (21), the righteousness of God can hardly be anything but His redeeming righteousness of which both the OT (e. g., 1 Sm 12:7, where the word for righteousness is translated "saving deeds") and St. Paul (Ro 3:21) speak. Cf. also Jesus' beatitude on those who hunger and thirst for righteousness. (Mt 5:6)

1:25 *Perfect law ... of liberty.* This description of God's Word is in a series with the life-giving "word of truth" (18) and the "implanted word which is able to save" (21). It is therefore best taken as signifying the Gospel in its transforming and formative impact on man's life.

1:26-27 *Religious ... religion ....* The word used

the Father is this: to visit orphans and widows in their affliction, and to keep oneself unstained from the world.

Turn to the True and Active Faith

2:1-26

TURN: BREAK WITH PARTIALITY TOWARD THE RICH (2:1-13)

2 My brethren, show no partiality as you hold the faith of our Lord Jesus Christ, the Lord of glory. 2 For if a man with gold rings and in fine clothing comes into your assembly, and a poor man in shabby clothing also comes in, 3 and you pay attention to the one who wears the fine clothing and say, "Have a seat here, please," while you say to the poor man, "Stand there," or, "Sit at my feet," 4 have you not made distinctions among yourselves, and become judges with evil thoughts? 5 Listen, my beloved brethren. Has not God chosen those who are poor in the world to be rich in faith and heirs of the kingdom which he has promised to those who love him? 6 But you have dishonored the poor man. Is it not the rich who oppress you, is it not they who drag you into court? 7 Is it not they who blaspheme the honorable name which was invoked over you?

8 If you really fulfil the royal law, according to the scripture, "You shall love your neighbor as yourself," you do well. 9 But if you show partiality, you commit sin, and are convicted by the law as transgressors. 10 For whoever keeps the whole law but fails in one point has become guilty of all of it. 11 For he who said, "Do not commit adul-

stresses the manifestations or exercise of religion, religion in action, and might be rendered "a worshiper . . . worship."

1:27 *Pure and undefiled.* James uses the language of OT cultic worship to describe the new worship in Spirit and truth, as Paul does, Ro 12:1; cf. 1 Ptr 2:5.

Visit orphans and widows. Visit is not mere sociability but active sympathy and assistance. *Orphans and widows,* those who are most in need of help and least capable of repaying, are especial objects of God's love.

2:1-13 Turn from a partiality which fawns on the rich and dishonors the poor (1-3), for that is for you a cleavage of yourself and a transgression of your Lord's command of "Judge not" (4); it involves an impious judgment on the poor and a false and unrealistic judgment on the rich. (5-7)

Turn from the pious self-justification which pleads the law of love to excuse partiality toward the rich (8); free yourselves of the last traces of the Judaic theory of compensation, which seeks to offset the transgression of one commandment with the fulfillment of another (9-11); turn from the mercilessness which you can conceal from yourselves but will not be able to conceal from God in the Judgment. (12-13)

Turn to the Lord Jesus Christ, who will bestow the glory of the kingdom of God on the poor and has made the poor rich even now as heirs of the Kingdom (1, 5), who lifts those who believe in Him above the petty difference between rich and poor. Rise in faith to the vision which sees men, both poor and rich, with the eyes of God, the poor as heirs of God, the rich as the oppressors of the people of God and the blasphemers of the holy name pronounced on the believer at his baptism (5-7). Return to a real and repentant confronta-

tion with the will of God — see in the law of love the royal law which gives meaning to all the commandments and includes them all; and remember that you will be judged under the law of liberty, that law which sets you free for God and for your fellowman; remember that only a faith whose work is mercy can hope for mercy in the merciful judgment of God. (8-13)

2:1 *Faith of,* perhaps better, "faith in." As Jesus Christ is on a par with God, He is like God the object of faith. As God in the OT is called "King of glory" and "God of glory" (Ps 24:7; 29:3), so *Lord of glory* is a title of deity applied to Jesus.

2:4 *Made distinctions among yourselves.* Better, "are at odds with yourself, waver in your own mind." The Christian assembly as a whole is contradicting its own deepest convictions of faith when it fails to look on the poor with the eyes of God.

2:5 *Poor . . . kingdom.* Cf. Mt 5:3; 1 Co 1:26-29.

2:6 *The rich. Rich* is not a purely economic designation (cf 1:10; 5:1-6). The rich man whom James condemns is the man who seeks to secure his existence by means of secular guarantees with no thought for God or man, like the rich fool of Jesus' parable (Lk 12:15-21), "who lays up treasure for himself, and is not rich toward God."

2:7 *Name . . . invoked over you.* An allusion probably to baptism in the name of Jesus Christ, and the phrase could also be rendered: "That honorable name which was pronounced over you." The persecutors of the church met the confession "Jesus is Lord" with the anathema "Jesus be cursed!" (Cf. 1 Co 12:3)

2:8 *Royal law,* the law as interpreted by Jesus, who is the kingdom of God in person. (Cf. Mt 22: 34-40)

tery," said also, "Do not kill." If you do not commit adultery but do kill, you have become a transgressor of the law. [12] So speak and so act as those who are to be judged under the law of liberty. [13] For judgment is without mercy to one who has shown no mercy; yet mercy triumphs over judgment.

TURN FROM MERE PROFESSION TO AN ACTIVE FAITH (2:14-26)

14 What does it profit, my brethren, if a man says he has faith but has not works? Can his faith save him? [15] If a brother or sister is ill-clad and in lack of daily food, [16] and one of you says to them, "Go in peace, be warmed and filled," without giving them the things needed for the body, what does it profit? [17] So faith by itself, if it has no works, is dead.

18 But some one will say, "You have faith and I have works." Show me your faith apart from your works, and I by my works will show you my faith. [19] You believe that God is one; you do well. Even the demons believe—and shudder. [20] Do you want to be shown, you **shallow man**, that faith apart from works is barren? [21] Was not Abraham our father justified by works, when he offered his son Isaac upon the altar? [22] You see that faith was active along with his works, and faith was completed by works, [23] and the scripture was fulfilled which says, "Abraham believed God, and it was reckoned to him as righteousness"; and he was called the friend of God. [24] You see that a man is justified by works and not by faith alone. [25] And in the same way was not also Rahab the harlot justified by works when she received the messengers and sent them out another way? [26] For as the body apart from the spirit is dead, so faith apart from works is dead.

2:12 *Law of liberty.* Cf. 1:25 and the note there.

2:13 *Mercy triumphs over judgment.* Cf. Mt 5:7, where Jesus promises mercy in the Judgment to the merciful, and Mt 25:31-46, which is Jesus' commentary to the beatitude on the merciful.

2:14-26 Turn from a merely verbal faith, for a faith that exhausts itself in words is as useless as a charity that exhausts itself in gracious phrases (14-16); turn from a faith that is in reality no faith at all, but dead (17) and unable to save. (14)

Turn: Cease trying to excuse yourselves with a pious sophistry which makes an impossible cleavage between faith and works by distributing them as several gifts, faith to one man, works to another (18); this reduces faith to a merely intellectual grasp of truths about God—demons have that kind of faith, and they know that it cannot save them; they shudder at the judgment that is to come upon them. (19)

Turn from this delusion about your barren faith, a faith as impotent and inactive as a corpse (20, 26). Turn to that faith which is a living faith and must needs evince itself in works (18), a faith which justifies because it is a faith that commits a man wholly to his God and is therefore a working faith, such a faith as Abraham's was: he was ready to give to God the best gift God had given him, his son. Abraham's faith was active in his works and found its fullest expression in works (21-22). In the fact that believing Abraham showed in deed that he held God dearer than God's dearest gift there was seen the full meaning of the words, *Abraham believed God, and it was reckoned to him as righteousness* (23). Abraham, the believing friend of God, was friend in word and deed, and so one can even say that man is justified by works and not by faith alone, for faith is never alone, as even the example of Rahab shows: Hers was a

simple and unfinished faith, and yet this believing woman, with her stained and ruined past, acted out her faith in works, and she too was thus justified by works as one whose faith made her the doer of the will of God. (25)

Turn to the faith which is the creation of the God who is God of the living and not of the dead, a faith that is a body animated by a living soul, not a corpse. (26)

2:18 *You . . . I.* One person . . . another person.

Show you my faith. Note that James does not say "Show you my works"; he is interested in faith.

2:19 *You do well.* Ironic.

The demons believe—and shudder. Cf. Mt 8:28-29.

2:21 *Offered his son.* Gn 22:1-19.

2:22 This and v. 26 are James' carefully measured statements on faith as working faith. Statements like 19 and 24 are more in the nature of argumentative "shockers" designed to shatter the complacency of those who argue for a workless faith.

Completed, in the sense that an apple tree is completed when it produces what God intended and created it to produce, apples. One modern translator renders, "Found its highest expression in" instead of *was completed.*

2:23 Gn 15:6; Is 41:8; 2 Ch 20:7.

Fulfilled. Not in the sense that a prediction proved true, for Gn 15:6 is not a prediction; rather, the Word of God which imputed righteousness to Abraham's faith documented itself in deeds and so found its full expression when he feared God and obeyed His voice. (Gn 22:12, 18)

2:25 *Rahab the harlot.* Rahab's sinful past is not glossed over, as it was in Judaic legends concerning her. For the story of Rahab cf. Jos 2:1-24;

Turn, Teachers in the Church, to God-given Wisdom

3:1-18

TURN FROM YOUR SINFUL SELVES TO GOD (3:1-12)

3 Let not many of you become teachers, my brethren, for you know that we who teach shall be judged with greater strictness. 2 For we all make many mistakes, and

6:1-25. For her faith cf. particularly Jos 2:8-11.

At the time of the Reformation the place of James in the church's canon (the collection of sacred books which are authoritative for the faith of the church) was again questioned, not only by Luther but also by Roman Catholic scholars such as Erasmus and Cajetan. Luther's objection to James is based chiefly on the section Ja 2:14-26, which to Luther seemed to be in irreconcilable conflict with Paul and the Gospel of salvation by grace through faith without the works of the Law. But James' words on faith and works are not aimed at Paul; neither do they really contradict Paul's teaching. The idea that faith is merely the certainty that God is one (2:19) has nothing to do with Paul; neither was Paul the first to see in Abraham the exemplar of saving faith — the rabbis had done that before him, as had Jesus Himself (Mt 8:11; Jn 8:56). The polemics of James *may* be directed at a watered-down and distorted version of Paul's Gospel, such as might have been reported in Jerusalem from Antioch when Paul was preaching there (Acts 11:25-26). But it is more likely that James is combating not a doctrine but a practical threat to faith that came to his readers from their Judaic past and surroundings. Jesus had said of the teachers of Judaism that they professed without practicing (Mt 23:3) — what would be more natural than a recurrence of this Judaic fault in a Christianized form in Judaic Christianity? It should be noted, moreover, that the bold but monumentally simple argument of James would be pitifully weak, if not malicious, as a refutation of Paul's teaching. And the James whom we know from his letter is neither weak intellectually nor malicious morally. James is not attacking Paul.

Neither does James, at bottom, contradict Paul. Both Paul and James are moved to speak by love. Paul emphasizes the fact that our salvation is wholly God's grace and entirely His doing and that faith is therefore first and foremost pure receiving. Paul will leave no desperate sinner outside God's call of grace. James emphasizes the fact that faith is union and communion with God and commits us wholly, with all our thoughts and all our doing, to God; James will allow no brother to destroy his faith and himself by making of faith an intellectual acceptance of doctrinal propositions and emptying it of love and works. Paul speaks to the sinner's desperation; James speaks to Christian complacency. When James is speaking to the repentant sinner, he makes no mention of works but bids such a one in his desperation draw near to God, in the assurance that God will draw near to him like the father of the returning prodigal son

(Ja 4:8). James describes man's redemption as a new birth from God, solely by the will and Word of God (Ja 1:18); and he describes God's love for man as God's sole and sovereign choice, as God's election (Ja 2:5). Paul, on the other hand, can combine his own characteristic emphasis with that of James in a single sentence: "By grace you have been saved through faith; and this is not your own doing, it is the gift of God — not because of works, lest any man should boast. For we are his workmanship, *created in Christ Jesus for good works,* which God prepared beforehand, that we should walk in them." (Eph 2:8-10)

The same Luther who objected so strenuously to James' conception of justification by faith has given us a description of faith which would delight the heart of James: "Faith is a divine work in us, which transforms us and gives us a new birth from God (Jn 1:13) and kills the old Adam. . . . Oh, it is a living, busy, active, and mighty thing, this faith; it cannot but be ever doing good. Faith does not ask if there are good works to be done, but has done them before one can ask and is ever a-doing. But whoever does not do such works is a man without faith; he goes groping about in search of faith and good works and knows neither what faith nor what good works are." And the first of Luther's theses, which makes repentance the beating heart of the Christian existence, might serve as a title to the Letter of James. The presence of this letter in the canon is a perpetual reminder to the church not to misconstrue Paul by making him the advocate of a lazy and workless faith, a reminder to hear and be guided by the real Paul, the Paul who entreats us "not to accept the grace of God in vain." (2 Co 6:1)

Turn from the blithe self-assurance which presses boldly into the teaching office, unmindful of the fearful responsibility imposed on human frailty by that office (1-2); consider what a struggle is involved in the control of the tongue (2), what fearful power for evil this small member wields, how fierce and untamable this ruthless evil, this very embodiment of the godless world, is (3-6). Turn from the delusion that any man can tame this evil — man is lord of creation but is not master of his tongue (7-8). Turn from that unnatural cleavage of the soul which makes the tongue the means by which men both bless God and curse man, the creature made in the image of God (9-12). Since *no man* can tame the tongue, turn to Him who alone can overcome the evil in man. (This is implicit in *no human being can tame the tongue;* the positive side of the call to repentance is really expressed in 3:13-18.)

3:1 *With greater strictness.* Cf. Lk 12:48.

if any one makes no mistakes in what he says he is a perfect man, able to bridle the whole body also. ³ If we put bits into the mouths of horses that they may obey us, we guide their whole bodies. ⁴ Look at the ships also; though they are so great and are driven by strong winds, they are guided by a very small rudder wherever the will of the pilot directs. ⁵ So the tongue is a little member and boasts of great things. How great a forest is set ablaze by a small fire!

6 And the tongue is a fire. The tongue is an unrighteous world among our members, staining the whole body, setting on fire the cycle of nature,*b* and set on fire by hell.*c* ⁷ For every kind of beast and bird, of reptile and sea creature, can be tamed and has been tamed by humankind, ⁸ but no human being can tame the tongue—a restless evil, full of deadly poison. ⁹ With it we bless the Lord and Father, and with it we curse men, who are made in the likeness of God. ¹⁰ From the same mouth come blessing and cursing. My brethren, this ought not to be so. ¹¹ Does a spring pour forth from the same opening fresh water and brackish? ¹² Can a fig tree, my brethren, yield olives, or a grapevine figs? No more can salt water yield fresh.

TURN FROM EARTHLY WISDOM TO GOD (3:13-18)

13 Who is wise and understanding among you? By his good life let him show his works in the meekness of wisdom. ¹⁴ But if you have bitter jealousy and selfish ambition in your hearts, do not boast and be false to the truth. ¹⁵ This wisdom is not such as comes down from above, but is earthly, unspiritual, devilish. ¹⁶ For where jealousy

b Or *wheel of birth*   *c* Greek *Gehenna*

3:2-5 The three images used to illustrate the power of the tongue (*bit, rudder, small fire*) all stress slight cause and great effect; the third (fire) adds the huge destructiveness of the effect. The tongue is thought of as the expressive instrument of the will.

3:6 *Unrighteous world.* The world, with its contempt for the poor whom God has chosen (2:5) and its ruthless and insatiable passions which drive it into opposition to God (4:1-4), defiles the Christian from without (1:27); the tongue, the instrument of communication with the world, defiles (*staining*) from within. (Cf. Mt 15:11, 18-20)

Set on fire by hell. Since *hell* (*Gehenna*) in Biblical usage is the place of punishment (not the abode of Satan), the thought here seems to be that the tongue is so evil that the fires of the future judgment already envelop it. (Cf. Lk 16:24)

3:9 *The likeness of God* (Gn 1:27) is referred to in Gn 9:6 to justify capital punishment for murder. James' use of the idea here reflects Jesus' teaching that the commandment "You shall not kill" is violated when the tongue is used to injure one's fellowmen. (Mt 5:21-22)

3:12 Cf. Mt 7:16 for the same image.

3:13-18 Turn from a wisdom which in its selfish bitterness creates divisions and produces every vile practice and thus gives the lie to the truth which God has given you in His Word of truth (13-16). Turn from a wisdom that is earthly, unspiritual, and devilish (15). Turn to God, who gives true wisdom and understanding, who alone can save man from his fruitless and arrogant wisdom and give him true wisdom characterized by meekness and productive of good (13), a wisdom whose purity attests its divine origin, an active

and graciously productive wisdom that goes its way in the certitude and candor of faith (17). Turn in the strength of this wisdom to a life devoted to the making of peace, as teachers who by their words and deeds plant seeds which grow and ripen into righteousness. (18)

3:13 Wisdom, like faith, must have *works* if it be genuine.

The *meekness of wisdom.* Meekness is essential to the conception of wisdom. Meekness is closely related to "the fear of the Lord," which the OT declares to be the beginning of wisdom (Ps 111:10; cf. Pr 1:7; Jb 28:28). Jesus' beatitude on the meek is practically a quotation from Ps 37 (Mt 5:5; Ps 37:11), and Ps 37 is a portrait of meekness. Meekness is centered in God; the meek man trusts in the Lord and does good (Ps 37:3), delights in the Lord (4), commits his way to the Lord and trusts His way (5), is still before the Lord and waits patiently for Him (7), knowing that the steps of a man are from the Lord (23), and takes refuge in Him (40). Jesus called Himself meek (Mt 11:29) and entered Jerusalem as the meek King promised by Zechariah (Mt 21:5; Zch 9:9). In meekness man receives the Word that has power to save his soul (Ja 1:21), and in meekness he receives wisdom from above, as God's gift (Ja 1:5). Meekness is therefore the extreme opposite of the harsh egoism that is characteristic of human wisdom. (Ja 3:14, 16)

3:14 *False to the truth.* A jealously selfish and ambitious wisdom contradicts the Word of truth, the Gospel, to which the Christian owes his new life (1:18), and is a wandering from the truth, which brings death to the soul. (5:20)

3:15 *From above,* coming to men as God's good gift. (Cf. 1:17)

and selfish ambition exist, there will be disorder and every vile practice. [17] But the wisdom from above is first pure, then peaceable, gentle, open to reason, full of mercy and good fruits, without uncertainty or insincerity. [18]And the harvest of righteousness is sown in peace by those who make peace.

Turn to God, the Giver of the Spirit and All Grace

4:1-12

TURN FROM ASSIMILATION TO THE WORLD TO GOD (4:1-10)

4 What causes wars, and what causes fightings among you? Is it not your passions that are at war in your members? [2] You desire and do not have; so you kill. And you covet[d] and cannot obtain; so you fight and wage war. You do not have, because you do not ask. [3] You ask and do not receive, because you ask wrongly, to spend it on your passions. [4] Unfaithful creatures! Do you not know that friendship with the world is enmity with God? Therefore whoever wishes to be a friend of the world makes himself an enemy of God. [5] Or do you suppose it is in vain that the scripture says, "He yearns jealously over the spirit which he has made to dwell in us"? [6] But he gives more grace; therefore it says, "God opposes the proud, but gives grace to the humble." [7] Submit yourselves therefore to God. Resist the devil and he will flee from you. [8] Draw near to God and he will draw near to you. Cleanse your hands, you sinners, and purify your hearts, you men of double mind. [9] Be wretched and mourn and weep. Let your laughter be turned to mourning and your joy to dejection. [10] Humble yourselves before the Lord and he will exalt you.

TURN FROM THE WORLD'S EVIL-SPEAKING (4:11-12)

11 Do not speak evil against one another, brethren. He that speaks evil against a brother or judges his brother, speaks evil against the law and judges the law. But if you judge the law, you are not a doer of the law but a judge. [12] There is one lawgiver and judge, he who is able to save and to destroy. But who are you that you judge your neighbor?

[d] Or *you kill and you covet*

3:17 The word translated *gentle* is used to describe the free, generous graciousness of a superior, such as a prince or king or God. *Open to reason* might perhaps better be rendered as "compliant," having a ready ear for the pleas of men. The seven adjectives sound like a description of the Christ of the gospels, who is "the wisdom of God." (1 Co 1:24)

3:18 Cf. Dn 12:3; Is 32:16-17.

4:1-10 Turn from the world's passionate wars and fierce fightings (1-2). Turn from the world's worldly, self-centered, and therefore fruitless prayers (3). Turn from your friendship with the world which is infidelity to God and enmity against Him, and turn from the devil, the author of all enmity against God (4, 7). Turn from your impurity and double-mindedness, from your secular laughter and your worldly joys. (8-9)

Turn to the God who has made His Spirit to dwell in you and yearns jealously for that Spirit—you dare not receive the grace of God in vain (5). Turn to God, who opposes the proud but gives grace to the humble, who will welcome all who penitently draw near to Him (6, 8). Turn to the God who exalts those who speak a resolute no to the devil and thus submit to God and humble themselves before Him. (7, 10)

4:4 *Unfaithful creatures,* literally "adulteresses." (Cf. Hos 1–3; Mt 12:39; 16:4; Mk 8:38)

4:5 *Yearns jealously.* God, who gave the Spirit, desires the fruits of the Spirit, "love, joy, peace, patience, kindness, goodness, faithfulness, gentleness, self-control." (Gl 5:22)

Scripture. The quotation cannot be identified.

4:6 *More grace.* God's promise is greater than His threat.

Gives grace to the humble. Pr 3:34.

4:7 The best commentary on this verse is the account of the temptation of our Lord, Mt 4:1-11.

4:8 *Double mind,* divided between God and the world.

4:10 *Humble yourselves.* Cf. Mt 18:4; 23:12; Lk 14:11; 18:14; Ph 2:8-9.

4:11-12 Turn from that refined form of murder (cf. 2), the malicious word against your brother (11). Turn from your quarrel with God, which is what your words against your brother come to; for when you condemn your brother, you condemn God's law, which demands of you a whole and unbroken love for your brother (11). Turn in fear to Him who has power to destroy, the one Lawgiver and Judge whose office you dare not usurp (12). Turn in faith and hope to Him who is able to *save* as well as to destroy. (12)

Turn from the World in Its Haughty Self-assurance

4:13—5:6

TURN FROM THE WORLD'S SELF-ASSURANCE IN PLANNING (4:13-17)

13 Come now, you who say, "Today or tomorrow we will go into such and such a town and spend a year there and trade and get gain"; 14 whereas you do not know about tomorrow. What is your life? For you are a mist that appears for a little time and then vanishes. 15 Instead you ought to say, "If the Lord wills, we shall live and we shall do this or that." 16As it is, you boast in your arrogance. All such boasting is evil. 17 Whoever knows what is right to do and fails to do it, for him it is sin.

TURN FROM THE WORLD'S ACCUMULATION OF WEALTH (5:1-6)

5 Come now, you rich, weep and howl for the miseries that are coming upon you. 2 Your riches have rotted and your garments are moth-eaten. 3 Your gold and silver have rusted, and their rust will be evidence against you and will eat your flesh like fire. You have laid up treasure*e* for the last days. 4 Behold, the wages of the laborers who mowed your fields, which you kept back by fraud, cry out; and the cries of the harvesters have reached the ears of the Lord of hosts. 5 You have lived on the earth in luxury and in pleasure; you have fattened your hearts in a day of slaughter. 6 You have condemned, you have killed the righteous man; he does not resist you.

e Or *will eat your flesh, since you have stored up fire*

4:12 *Who are you . . . ?* Mt 7:1-5; Ro 2:1; 14:4.

4:13—5:6 This section does not address the church directly but rather addresses itself indirectly to the world in the midst of which the church lives, just as the OT prophets do with the "nations" round about Israel. Note that (a) the address "brethren," found in every other section of the epistle, does not occur here; (b) the brusque and peremptory expression *come now* (4:13 and 5:1) occurs only in this section. The warning to the world is, of course, significant to the church in the world; the church lives in the midst of the world, is threatened by the world, and can be infected by the world. Also, the church is thus kept aware of the fact that God's call to repentance is a universal call, as universal as the grace of God, with whom nothing is impossible, not even the conversion of the ungodly rich. But because it is the world that is primarily addressed here, the positive aspects of the command to "turn" are here only implicit.

4:13-17 Turn from the secular self-assurance of the trader, who lays his plans under the delusion that man is lord of his tomorrows, forgetting the frailty and transience of all human life and forgetting Him who is Lord of the morrow (13-17). Turn to the Lord who rules all life and all its tomorrows and learn to say *"If the Lord wills"* in all your planning (15), for to know the Lord and not to live constantly under His Lordship is sin. (17)

4:15 This is another example of the meekness of which James speaks in 3:13. See note there.

4:17 The reader can no longer plead ignorance; he has been warned.

5:1-6 Turn from the world's callous and brutal pursuit of riches, its heaping up of possessions beyond any conceivable need, its fat and wanton luxury; for the rich live luxuriously under the very shadow of judgment, unmindful of the fact that the last days are already upon them, that the slaughter-day of judgment (Jer 12:3) is imminent, that day on which their treacherously gotten and unused wealth will rise up to witness against them. They employ the Law to kill the righteous man, as they used it to condemn and kill the Righteous One, and they find in the patient submission of the righteous the assurance that all is well.

5:1 *Rich.* Cf. 2:6, where the antithesis to the rich are those "rich in faith" (2:5), and the note there.

5:3 *Evidence against you,* in the Final Judgment. (Cf. 8-9)

For the last days, literally "in the last days." All days since the coming of the Christ, the Lord of glory, are "last days." (Heb 1:2)

5:4 *Lord of hosts.* This title, expressive of the high majesty and the illimitable power of the God who has rank on rank of powers at His disposal, is frequently used by the prophets in threats of judgment (cf. e. g., Am 4:13; 6:14; 9:5; Nah 2:13; 3:5); for the *Lord of hosts,* as Judge of those "who oppress the hireling in his wages" cf. Ml 3:5.

5:6 *The righteous man.* There may be a reference to Jesus as the Righteous One here. (a) "Righteous One" occurs as a Messianic designation of Jesus in Acts 3:14; 7:52; 22:14 (all in an early Palestinian setting) and in Is 53:10 as a designation of the Suffering Servant who by His vicarious death makes "many to be accounted righteous." (b) The death of the righteous is accomplished by legal means *(condemned)*; it is judicial murder. (c) The second half of the verse would then be read as a question: "Does He not resist you?" (i. e., as your Judge). This would give point to the "therefore" of v. 7. "Therefore," James would be saying, "since the Righteous One has suffered before you and for

Turn to the Returning Lord

5:7-20

7 Be patient, therefore, brethren, until the coming of the Lord. Behold, the farmer waits for the precious fruit of the earth, being patient over it until it receives the early and the late rain. 8 You also be patient. Establish your hearts, for the coming of the Lord is at hand. 9 Do not grumble, brethren, against one another, that you may not be judged; behold, the Judge is standing at the doors. 10 As an example of suffering and patience, brethren, take the prophets who spoke in the name of the Lord. 11 Behold, we call those happy who were steadfast. You have heard of the steadfastness of Job, and you have seen the purpose of the Lord, how the Lord is compassionate and merciful.

12 But above all, my brethren, do not swear, either by heaven or by earth or with any other oath, but let your yes be yes and your no be no, that you may not fall under condemnation.

LET YOUR WHOLE LIFE BE ATTUNED TO HIS COMING (5:13-20)

13 Is any one among you suffering? Let him pray. Is any cheerful? Let him sing praise. 14 Is any among you sick? Let him call for the elders of the church, and let them pray over him, anointing him with oil in the name of the Lord; 15 and the prayer of faith will save the sick man, and the Lord will raise him up; and if he has committed

you and God has highly exalted Him, therefore endure patiently until He returns as Deliverer (8) and Judge. (9)

5:7-12 Turn from the impatience of the wavering heart (7-8). Renounce all grumbling against the brother; all our attempts to have the last word now show that we have forgotten Him who will come to have the last word soon (9). Renounce all swearing; when we invoke the presence of the Lord on some of our words, we show that we have forgotten the coming Lord who is the remembering witness of our every word. (12)

Turn to the patience of the farmer who waits but knows why he must wait and what he waits for—the precious harvest which crowns his year with festal joy (7-9). Turn to the comforting knowledge of the Lord's ways given you in the Scriptures, to the example of the prophets who spoke the Word of the Lord as you are speaking it now, who suffered for that speaking as you are suffering now, who suffered with a patient endurance which you must emulate; for you know from the example of Job what the purpose of the Lord in all man's suffering is; you know Him as the compassionate and merciful Lord (10-11), and you know that steadfastness under His Lordship brings a great reward (11). Turn to that speaking which always has the end in view, so that your every word to your brother is a word of love and your simple yes and no is an oath spoken in the presence of Him who comes to judge and to reward. (9, 12)

5:7 *The Lord.* Jesus Christ, so also in 8. In both cases the word for coming is that regularly used in the NT of our Lord's second coming.

The early and the late rain. The early rain in autumn and the late rain in spring were both essential to the success of agriculture. The early rain prepares the ground for plowing and seeding; the late rain helps mature the grain. The OT

praises God as the Giver of both. (Dt 11:14; Jer 5:24; Jl 2:23).

5:10 Cf. Mt 5:11-12.

5:11 *Job.* Cf. Jb 1:21-22; 42:10-17.

5:12 Cf. Mt 5:34-37.

5:13-20 Turn: Let every aspect of your life, your suffering and your joy, be hallowed by the Word of God and by prayer. (13)

Turn: Let the life of the church be one of ministering love to the sick, a love which deals with suffering man in the believing confidence that forgiveness and healing are THERE by God's giving, there for the reaching hand of the prayer of faith; faith can pray as Elijah prayed. (14-18)

Turn: Let the love of the seeking Shepherd live in you, that love which pursues the brother who has wandered from the truth and brings him back, back from death to life, from sin to the forgiveness of sins. (19-20)

5:14 *Elders of the church,* probably the officials called by that name, men whose experience with affliction and prayer gave them the Christian stamina necessary for intercession on behalf of men oppressed by both illness and the consciousness of their sins. For the office of elder cf. Acts 11:30; 14:23; 15:2, 4, 6, 22-23; 16:4; 20:17, 28; 21:18; 1 Ti 5:17-18; Tts 1:5-9; 1 Ptr 5:1-4.

5:14 *Anointing him with oil in the name of the Lord.* For the use of oil in the treatment of illness cf. Is 1:6; Eze 16:9; Mk 6:13. Probably medical treatment is all that is meant; such treatment is undertaken in the name of the Lord, at His command and invoking His aid. Another possibility is suggested by Lk 7:46, where it is implied that anointing the head with oil is a way of welcoming a guest. Then the anointing would be an assurance to the sick man that he is not separated from the church whose assembly (2:2) he cannot attend for common prayer and praise and participation in

sins, he will be forgiven. [16] Therefore confess your sins to one another, and pray for one another, that you may be healed. The prayer of a righteous man has great power in its effects. [17] E·li′jah was a man of like nature with ourselves and he prayed fervently that it might not rain, and for three years and six months it did not rain on the earth. [18] Then he prayed again and the heaven gave rain, and the earth brought forth its fruit.

19 My brethren, if any one among you wanders from the truth and some one brings him back, [20] let him know that whoever brings back a sinner from the error of his way will save his soul from death and will cover a multitude of sins.

the Supper of the Lord: he is one with them and all members suffer with him (cf. 1 Co 12:26). In any case it is the prayer of faith, not the oil in itself, that restores the sick man, because it effectively invokes the aid of the Lord. (15)

5:16 *Prayer of a righteous man.* Cf. 15, "prayer of faith." Righteousness and faith are closely linked for James, as they are for Paul.

5:17 *Elijah.* Cf. 1 K 17:1; 18:1; 18:42-45; Lk 4:25.

5:20 *Cover a multitude of sins,* that is, bring about forgiveness for the erring brother's sins. For this sense of cover cf. Ro 4:7 (Ps 32:1-2). For the authority to pronounce God's forgiveness to the penitent sinner cf. Mt 18:15, 18; Lk 17:3. We have reason to feel that one of the two coordinated thoughts *(save, cover)* should be subordinated: "Will save his soul from death by covering a multitude of sins"; cf. 5:10, where SUFFERING and patience amounts to what we should call PATIENCE amid suffering. The interpretation frequently suggested that the one who brings back an erring brother thereby secures the forgiveness of his OWN sin can hardly stand, for it is without parallel in the NT.

THE FIRST LETTER OF

PETER

INTRODUCTION

It is because the Word of the Lord comes from God to man as a pure gift and as creative grace that it lives and grows from man to man. On the night in which He was betrayed Jesus foretold the failure of His disciples. Satan, He said, would sift them like wheat in the hope and to the intent that they might prove chaff to be burned in the unquenchable fire. On that occasion Jesus gave Peter, who was to fail most signally, a special proof of His love: "Simon, Simon," He said, "I have prayed for you that your faith may not fail" (Lk 22:31-32). That forgiving love of Jesus laid the divine claim of grace on Peter even then, on the principle that he who is forgiven much shall love much (Lk 7:47). Jesus went on to say, "And when you have turned again, strengthen your brethren" (Lk 22:32). Because he had failed and had been forgiven, because he knew both the fragility of man's resolves and the strength of divine grace, Peter was fitted for the task of strengthening his brethren. We find him doing this in his letters as the strengthener of persecuted brethren (1 Ptr) and as the strengthener and warner of brethren whose hold on the Christian hope is growing weak. (2 Ptr)

Occasion of the First Letter of Peter

This letter is addressed to the Christians of five provinces of Asia Minor. Peter calls them "exiles of the Dispersion" (1:1), a term which suggests "the dispersion of the Jews" and might naturally be thought to imply Jewish Christian readers, especially since Peter was primarily the apostle to the circumcised (Gl 2:7-9). But the letter itself shows that the readers have a Gentile background (e. g., 1:14; 2:9-10; 4:3-4); they are therefore "exiles of the Dispersion" in a figurative sense, strangers and sojourners on this earth (1:17; 2:11), dispersed in an unbelieving world. There is nothing to indicate that Peter and his readers knew each other personally.

The Christians addressed are undergoing some form of persecution (3:16-17) and are perhaps being threatened by an even severer form of persecution (4:12-19). They are being slandered, ridiculed, and suspected of disloyalty to the state (4:14, 16; 4:4; cf. 2:13-17); but there is nothing to indicate a full-scale official persecution. We hear nothing of a demand for emperor worship, for instance; nor is there any hint of confiscation of property, imprisonment, or martyr's death. Yet it is a time of severe trial; they are going through a "fiery ordeal" (4:12), perhaps the first great ordeal they have been called on to endure, since they are finding it "strange" (4:12). And Peter writes to them out of the riches of the grace which he has himself experienced, out of the fullness of the glorious hope which Christ has implanted in him, to encourage them in steadfast endurance in the strength of that grace and for the sake of that hope. He writes to admonish them to a life which befits the great salvation that is in store for them. He writes in order to make these afflicted men see once more the full, eternal dimensions of the true grace of God in order that they may stand fast in it. (5:12)

Place and Time of Writing: Silvanus' Part in the Letter

Peter sends greetings to his readers from her "who is at Babylon, who is likewise chosen" (5:13). This no doubt refers to a church (the Greek word for church is feminine), and the church referred to is in all probability the church at Rome. Christianity seems to have taken over this name for Rome from late Judaism. Babylon had been branded by Old Testament prophecy as the embodiment of world power at enmity with God and His people. Peter is, in using this name for Rome, reminding his readers that the hostile world which now has power to impose the fiery ordeal on the scattered and homeless people of God is doomed to destruction under the judgment of God. The letter was thus written at Rome.

The place of writing helps fix the time of writing. There is no reason to doubt that

Peter did reach Rome and did die a martyr's death there. But Peter did not reach Rome until the latter years of his life, after Israel had been called to repentance and had been called in vain. Since the persecution to which the letter refers does not seem to be an official one like that under Nero and since Peter can still call for solid loyalty to the state (2:13-17), a date before the Neronian persecution of A. D. 64 is probable.

As for the circumstances which prompted Peter to write to Gentile churches, some of which had their origin in Paul's missionary labors, one can only guess. A recent commentator on First Peter has made a suggestion which is probable and attractive, to the effect that Peter may have written at Paul's suggestion. Paul, about to leave for Spain in A. D. 61 or 62, having heard of the situation of the churches of northern Asia Minor, laid it on Peter's heart to write to them a circular letter, just as Paul himself had written somewhat earlier to a group of churches in Asia Minor (Letter to the Ephesians). This receives some confirmation from the fact that Silvanus, Paul's longtime companion, had a part in the writing of the letter. Peter's words, "By [or "through"] Silvanus, a faithful brother as I regard him, I have written briefly to you" (5:12), probably indicate that he was more than merely a secretary to Peter. Perhaps he acted as translator; Peter as a Galilean would know Greek but was doubtless more at home in Aramaic. Or perhaps Silvanus worked more freely, carrying out Peter's general instructions as to content and submitting his work to Peter's supervision, a practice not uncommon in ancient letter writing. Silas as the trusted companion of Paul and a man endowed with the gift of prophecy (Acts 15:32) may have been called into the consultation between Peter and Paul when the letter was planned and was thus acquainted with its purpose and content from the outset.

Special Value of the Letter

First Peter is often and rightly called the Letter of Hope. Hope in the full Christian sense of a serene and confident dependence on God, hope based on the unshakable certainty of the resurrection of the dead which is begun and guaranteed in the resurrection of Jesus Christ, hope as a mighty energizing power for the whole life of men in the church is certainly a dominant note of the letter. But such convenient catchword summaries are necessarily oversimplifications and can serve to conceal from the student the variety and riches of the letter. These qualities of variety and richness have been noted by many students. Erasmus called it "an epistle sparse in words, crammed with content." The comprehensiveness of the letter is taken into account by those scholars who have suggested that the section 1:3—4:11 represents a baptismal homily, or address, which laid before the newly converted all that their new life in the church conferred on them as God's gift and all that it asked of them as the response of faith and hope to that gift. Others have taken the whole letter as a record of an early Christian service of worship, beginning with an address to the newly baptized converts (1:3—4:11) and concluding with an address to the whole church (4:12—5:11). A modern New Testament scholar makes the penetrating comment that the compressed fullness of the letter marks it as the production of a *worker* who knows how to utilize his time; he sees in the "luminous" power of Peter's sentences the hallmark of that composed and settled intellectual strength which results from a life of constant prayer. Luther included First Peter in his list of the prime and capital books of the New Testament. Anyone looking for a key book which will unlock for him the meaning of the whole New Testament would do well to give his days and nights to this letter.

THE FIRST LETTER OF

PETER

SALUTATION (1:1-2)

1 Peter, an apostle of Jesus Christ,
To the exiles of the Dispersion in Pontus, Galatia, Cap·pa·do'ci·a, Asia, and Bi·thyn'i·a, 2 chosen and destined by God the Father and sanctified by the Spirit for obedience to Jesus Christ and for sprinkling with his blood:
May grace and peace be multiplied to you.

The Exultation of Hope

1:3-12

3 Blessed be the God and Father of our Lord Jesus Christ! By his great mercy we have been born anew to a living hope through the resurrection of Jesus Christ from the dead, 4 and to an inheritance which is imperishable, undefiled, and unfading, kept in heaven for you, 5 who by God's power are guarded through faith for a salvation

1:1-2 The salutation follows the ancient letter form (sender, recipients, greetings) but is crammed with specifically Christian content. The sender presents himself as *apostle* — eyewitness (5:1) and called and authorized representative — *of Jesus Christ,* in whom Christ Himself speaks (Mt 10:40; 2 Co 13:3). The recipients are marked as under the abundant blessing of the triune God *(Father, Spirit, Jesus Christ).* And the greeting, familiar to us from the letters of Paul, invokes on the readers an ever-increasing measure of the free, undeserved favor of God *(grace)* and of that sound and healthy well-being which God's grace creates *(peace,* cf. 5:14).

1:1 *Exiles of the Dispersion.* The term *Dispersion* was applied from the Babylonian Captivity onward to the Jews living scattered abroad in the world, far from their homeland (cf. Jn 7:35). In the NT the term (cf. Ja 1:1) and the idea are applied to Christians living in this world, far from their true and eternal home. (Cf. 1:17; 2:11; 2 Co 5:6; Ph 3:20; Cl 3:1-4 and 2:20)

Pontus, Galatia, etc. The letter is designed to circulate in a series of Roman provinces, beginning at Pontus, south of the Black Sea, moving southward to Galatia and *Cappadocia,* then westward to *Asia* and northward to *Bithynia.*

1:2 *Chosen and destined.* Literally "FORE-chosen and PRE-destined." The uncaused, free elective love of God, antecedent to man's history and independent of man's deserts or efforts, is the strongest possible assurance and comfort amid trials. (Cf. Ro 8:28-39)

Sanctified by the Spirit. Sanctified belongs to the same word-family as "holy" (cf. 1:16). The Holy Spirit consecrates, sets apart, men for God and empowers them to lead lives of *obedience* to His will as revealed in His Son. (Cf. Ro 8:2-4)

Sprinkling with his blood. The once-for-all atoning sacrifice of Christ (1:18-19) avails constantly to restore the Christian to communion and fellowship with God whenever he fails in his obedience (cf. 1 Jn 1:8-9; 2:1-2). *Sprinkling with . . . blood* recalls Ex 24:7-8, the establishment of God's covenant with His people and their response: "We will be obedient." The new covenant is established by the blood of Christ (Mt 26:28) and evokes the obedience of faith.

1:3-12 The opening doxology rings with the high confidence of triumph over death which fills the whole NT. By God's great mercy Christians have been born anew to a living hope through the resurrection of Jesus Christ from the dead, to a sure and eternal inheritance in Christ (3-5), who has accomplished the salvation which the prophets promised and desired (10-12). No suffering can dim this joyous hope or quench their love for Christ or shake their faith in Him. (6-9)

1:3 *Born anew.* For the new life in Christ as a new birth cf. 1:23; Jn 3:3, 7, 8; Ja 1:18; 1 Jn 2:29; 3:9; 4:7; 5:1, 4, 18.

1:4 *Inheritance.* Israel's inheritance was the promised land of Canaan (Dt 4:21; 19:14; Jos 1:6; Jer 3:19), a good land but, because of the sins of Israel, defiled by idolatry, withered by drought, and overrun by invaders. The new land of promise, the new heavens and earth, will be forever exempt from all that.

1:5 *Guarded.* The living, valid hope of the Christian is doubly safeguarded; the inheritance is kept safe for them in heaven (4) and those who hope are guarded by God as with a strong body of soldiery. For the military term cf. 2 Co 11:32; for the thought, Ph 4:7.

Salvation. The final, ultimate deliverance. (Cf. 1:9; 2:2; Ro 13:11; 1 Th 5:8, 9; Heb 9:28)

ready to be revealed in the last time. 6 In this you rejoice,[a] though now for a little while you may have to suffer various trials, 7 so that the genuineness of your faith, more precious than gold which though perishable is tested by fire, may redound to praise and glory and honor at the revelation of Jesus Christ. 8 Without having seen[b] him you[c] love him; though you do not now see him you[c] believe in him and rejoice with unutterable and exalted joy. 9As the outcome of your faith you obtain the salvation of your souls.

10 The prophets who prophesied of the grace that was to be yours searched and inquired about this salvation; 11 they inquired what person or time was indicated by the Spirit of Christ within them when predicting the sufferings of Christ and the subsequent glory. 12 It was revealed to them that they were serving not themselves but you, in the things which have now been announced to you by those who preached the good news to you through the Holy Spirit sent from heaven, things into which angels long to look.

The Ministry of Hope

1:13 — 4:6

LIVING HOPE: MINISTRY OF OBEDIENT CHILDREN (1:13 — 2:3)

13 Therefore gird up your minds, be sober, set your hope fully upon the grace that is coming to you at the revelation of Jesus Christ. 14As obedient children, do not be

[a] Or *Rejoice in this*   [b] Other ancient authorities read *known*   [c] Or omit *you*

1:6 *Suffer . . . trials.* For the difficulties and dangers besetting the Christians addressed cf. the Introduction.

1:7 *Redound to praise and glory and honor,* primarily of God. Cf. 4:11; Eph 1:6, 12, 14; Ph 2:11, but with the suggestion (since the recipient of the praise and glory and honor is not specified) that the believers too participate in them. (Cf. 4:13-14; 5:1, 4, 10)

Revelation of Jesus Christ, at His second coming. (Cf. 1:13; 4:13; 1 Co 1:7; 2 Th 1:7)

1:10 *The prophets.* For the OT prophets as belonging to the "not-yet" of the time before the coming of Christ cf. Mt 13:17. This passage attests strongly the unity of the OT and the NT; one revelation, one Spirit, one Christ bind them together.

1:11 *What . . . time.* Cf. Dn 12:6 ff.

The Spirit of Christ. As the Christ, before His incarnation, was Mediator of creation (Jn 1:3; Cl 1:16; Heb 1:2), so He was active also in the inspiration of the prophets who foretold His coming. For the activity of the preexistent Christ cf. also 1 Co 10:4, 11; Eph 1:3-5.

Sufferings of Christ and . . . glory. Cf. especially Is 52:13 — 53:12. The idea of *sufferings* and *subsequent glory* is also suggested by the fact that in many Messianic promises the figure of the future Deliverer appears against a dark background of judgment and misery: Is 9:1-7; Is 11:1 ("stump" of Jesse; cf. the threats of the preceding ch.); Mi 5: 1-4. Cf. Lk 24:25-26.

1:12 *Angels long to look.* For the angels' interest and activity in God's redeeming activity cf. Heb 1:14 and the manifold ministrations of the angels in Revelation.

Through the Holy Spirit. The inspiration of those who proclaim the fulfillment corresponds to the inspiration of the prophets who predicted the grace (10) to come in Christ.

1:13 — 4:6 God's gift of a living hope claims the Christians wholly; every aspect of their existence is colored and shaped by it. The living hope becomes a lived hope. It claims them as children (1:13 — 2:3), as the new people of God (2:4-10), as men who have become aliens and exiles in this world. (2:11 — 4:6)

1:13 — 2:3 God's gift of a new birth to a living hope makes them children of God who obey and serve Him in the sober and alert vigilance of that hope (1:13-14). Their conduct reflects the holiness of the Father who gave them life by His call (1:15-16). They honor their Father in lives of holy fear, for they know the fearful cost of the redemption which a righteous God has provided; it cost the life of the Lamb of God (1:17-21). Since they owe their new life to the living Word of God, their lives express God's will of love which the Word reveals: in obedience to it they love their brethren (1:22-25). They make the Word the constant nurture of their lives and grow in stature as sons of God destined for salvation. (2:1-3)

1:13 *Gird up,* as men gird up their robes in preparation for vigorous action. (Cf. Lk 12:35)

Grace. The substance of the prophetic promise (10) is also the object of their hope.

Revelation of Jesus Christ. Cf. v. 7.

1:14 *Children.* The conception of Christians as children of God colors this whole section. Cf. 1:17 ("Father"); 1:23 ("born anew"); 2:2 ("newborn babes"); the contrast with their old life is expressed in like terms (1:18, "ways inherited from your fathers").

Ignorance, their pagan past. (Cf. Acts 17:30; Eph 4:18)

conformed to the passions of your former ignorance, [15] but as he who called you is holy, be holy yourselves in all your conduct; [16] since it is written, "You shall be holy, for I am holy." [17]And if you invoke as Father him who judges each one impartially according to his deeds, conduct yourselves with fear throughout the time of your exile. [18] You know that you were ransomed from the futile ways inherited from your fathers, not with perishable things such as silver or gold, [19] but with the precious blood of Christ, like that of a lamb without blemish or spot. [20] He was destined before the foundation of the world but was made manifest at the end of the times for your sake. [21] Through him you have confidence in God, who raised him from the dead and gave him glory, so that your faith and hope are in God.[d]

22 Having purified your souls by your obedience to the truth for a sincere love of the brethren, love one another earnestly from the heart. [23] You have been born anew, not of perishable seed but of imperishable, through the living and abiding word of God; [24] for

> "All flesh is like grass
> and all its glory like the flower of grass.
> The grass withers, and the flower falls,
25   but the word of the Lord abides for ever."

That word is the good news which was preached to you.

[d] Or *so that your faith is hope in God*

1:15-16 Holiness is God's gift; His effective call sets men apart for Himself; makes them His "called saints," literally His "called holy ones" (cf. Ro 1:7; 1 Co 1:2); this given holiness claims from men and makes possible for men a holy life, a life lived to God; they are "sanctified" (made holy) "for obedience" (1:2). Thus the just requirement of the Law (1:16; Lv 11:44-45) is fulfilled in those who walk according to the Spirit. (Ro 8:4)

1:17-19 *Father . . . fear.* The great mercy (3) of the Father is His infinite and costly condescension, the condescension of Him who remains the impartial Judge who spared not His own Son but delivered Him up for us all (Ro 8:32), made Him the Ransom for many (18; cf. Mt 20:28), and provided the atoning sacrifice (19). He is therefore to be served with *fear* (17); just because His grace is so lavish and costly a grace, man dare not desecrate it by misprizing or squandering it (cf. Ph 2:12). "There is forgiveness with thee, that thou mayest be feared." (Ps 130:4)

Invoke as Father. Probably referring to the Lord's Prayer. (Mt 6:9; cf. Ro 8:15; Gl 4:6)

Fear implies reverential awe and, above all, obedience. Cf. Gn 22:12, 18; 2 Co 5:11; 7:1, 15.

Lamb without blemish or spot. Suggests the Passover lamb (Ex 12:5) by whose blood Israel was delivered from the judgment of God when the first-born of Egypt perished. (Ex 12:12-13; cf. 1 Co 5:7)

1:21 *Your faith and hope are in God,* based on divine reality and therefore certain. God has chosen and destined them (2), has given them new birth (3), is guarding them with His power (5), has provided the liberating ransom (18) and the atoning sacrifice (18) which He predestined from everlasting and manifested at the end of time (20), has *raised* Christ from the dead and glorified Him (21). In obeying Christ (2), in loving Him and be-

lieving in Him (8), in heeding the prophetic Word inspired by the Spirit of Christ (12), in hoping for the grace that comes at the revelation of Jesus Christ (13), they are fixing their *faith and hope . . . in God.* They come to the Father through Him. (Cf. Jn 14:6)

1:22 – 2:3 The readers love Christ and believe in Him without having seen or seeing Him (8); their faith has come from what they heard, the *good news* (25) which effectually bestows what it announces. That living *truth* (22), heard and heeded, has purified them, made them fit for converse and communion with God. Since this is personal communion, it involves responsibility. The living Word produces living men who love one another as *brethren* having one merciful Father (22) and grow in stature as sons of God by the nurture of *pure spiritual milk* (2:2); the Word of God that gave them life sustains their life. It is noteworthy that the first concrete applications of the demand "You shall be holy" (15) are love (cf. 1 Co 13:13) and growth – "The Christian life is not a having-become but a becoming" (Luther; cf. Ph 3:12-15). The emphasis on brotherly love and growing maturity prepares for the idea of the corporate priesthood of the whole people in 2:4-10.

1:24 Cf. Is 40:6-9. The Word that sustained Israel when, buried in the Babylonian Captivity, her future hung solely on the creative Word of God with no human and earthly probabilities to guarantee it – that Word is fitly applied to the church of exiles (1:1, 17; 2:11) which lives on a future made certain only by the Word of God.

Flesh. Man (including man in his most impressive and powerful manifestations, cf. Is 31:1-3) in his frailty and transience.

1:25 *The Lord.* The OT passage has "our God"; Peter is applying the passage to Christ and His good news.

2 So put away all malice and all guile and insincerity and envy and all slander. ² Like newborn babes, long for the pure spiritual milk, that by it you may grow up to salvation; ³ for you have tasted the kindness of the Lord.

LIVING HOPE: MINISTRY OF THE NEW PEOPLE OF GOD (2:4-10)

4 Come to him, to that living stone, rejected by men but in God's sight chosen and precious; ⁵ and like living stones be yourselves built into a spiritual house, to be a holy priesthood, to offer spiritual sacrifices acceptable to God through Jesus Christ. ⁶ For it stands in scripture:

"Behold, I am laying in Zion a stone, a cornerstone chosen and precious,
and he who believes in him will not be put to shame."

⁷ To you therefore who believe, he is precious, but for those who do not believe,

"The very stone which the builders rejected
has become the head of the corner,"

⁸ and

"A stone that will make men stumble,
a rock that will make them fall";

for they stumble because they disobey the word, as they were destined to do.

9 But you are a chosen race, a royal priesthood, a holy nation, God's own people,ᵉ that you may declare the wonderful deeds of him who called you out of darkness into

ᵉ Greek *a people for his possession*

2:2 *Salvation.* As in 1:5 and 9, ultimate salvation. Growth continues until the day when they shall be acknowledged and proclaimed by God as His sons. (Mt 5:9)

2:3 Cf. Ps 34:8, which is again quoted at 3:10-12. *Lord,* the OT designation for the covenant God of Israel is here, as often, applied to Jesus (cf. v. 4)—strong witness to His deity.

2:4-10 By being joined to Christ, the living Stone to whom Scripture points as the Rock of salvation for all who believe and the Stone over which unbelief stumbles and falls—by being joined to Him they become living stones in a new and better temple, priests who offer acceptable sacrifices of praise to the God who has called them out of darkness into His marvelous light, to be His own people, a holy nation of kingly priests to serve and glorify Him.

2:4-5 These verses state the theme of the passage; the thought of v. 4 is further developed in vv. 6-8, that of v. 5 in vv. 9-10.

2:5 *Spiritual house . . . spiritual sacrifices.* The Holy Spirit produces the new habitation of God (cf. Eph 2:22) and makes possible the new and acceptable sacrifices, for He lives and works in the OT Word (1:11) and in the NT Gospel (1:12) and so sanctifies (1:2) men for obedience to Jesus Christ.

2:6 The quotation (Is 28:16) reinforces the idea of v. 4, "in God's sight chosen and precious." In Isaiah God opposes His way of deliverance to that of the unscrupulous and worldly rulers of Jerusalem, who have made lies their refuge and have taken shelter in falsehood and hope to escape destruction by shrewd political alliances (Is 28: 14-15). His way is the way of divine justice and righteousness (Is 28:17) and calls for faith (Is 28:16; cf. 7:9; 30:15). That way is ultimately

Christ, God's final No to the wisdom and power of men. (1 Co 1:18-25)

2:7 The line of demarcation between God's people and the world is no longer national or racial but is drawn between faith and unbelief. Ps 118:22 elaborates the idea of "rejected by men" in v. 4. Ps 118 celebrates the steadfast love of the Lord who has given victory and deliverance against all human probabilities (10-14) to His king and people. The triumph is His and His alone (23-24; cf. 5-9). Jesus had used these words to express to the leaders of Israel His confidence that God would vindicate Him and lead Him to victory despite their rejection of Him (Mt 21:42). Peter now saw fulfilled in the Gentile churches of Asia Minor the prediction Jesus had made on that occasion: "The kingdom of God will be taken away from you and given to a nation producing the fruits of it." (Mt 21:43)

2:8 Cf. Is 8:14-15. In Isaiah it is the God of Israel Himself who becomes "a stone of offense and a rock of stumbling to both houses of Israel" when they refuse to go the way of faith (cf. Is 7:9) and of obedience in holy fear to which He has summoned them. In Christ Israel and all men are once more, and finally, confronted by the covenant God who asks of them only faith but can accept nothing less than faith. (Cf. Ro 9:32-33)

Disobey the word. Christ is accepted or rejected in the inspired Word that brings Him into men's lives (1:12, 25). *As they were destined to do:* Even in his revolt against God man does not escape the all-encompassing governance of God.

2:9 Cf. Ex 19:5-6; Dt 7:6; Is 43:21; 45:4-6; 61:6. All the glory that was Israel's, all that God by His covenant intended Israel to be, has now passed to the Israel of God (Gl 6:16) composed of men of all nations: the new people is elect and special,

his marvelous light. 10 Once you were no people but now you are God's people; once you had not received mercy but now you have received mercy.

LIVING HOPE: MINISTRY OF ALIENS IN THIS WORLD (2:11−4:6)

11 Beloved, I beseech you as aliens and exiles to abstain from the passions of the flesh that wage war against your soul. 12 Maintain good conduct among the Gentiles, so that in case they speak against you as wrongdoers, they may see your good deeds and glorify God on the day of visitation.

13 Be subject for the Lord's sake to every human institution,ᶠ whether it be to the emperor as supreme, 14 or to governors as sent by him to punish those who do wrong and to praise those who do right. 15 For it is God's will that by doing right you should put to silence the ignorance of foolish men. 16 Live as free men, yet without using your freedom as a pretext for evil; but live as servants of God. 17 Honor all men. Love the brotherhood. Fear God. Honor the emperor.

18 Servants, be submissive to your masters with all respect, not only to the kind and gentle but also to the overbearing. 19 For one is approved if, mindful of God, he endures pain while suffering unjustly. 20 For what credit is it, if when you do wrong and are beaten for it you take it patiently? But if when you do right and suffer for it you take it patiently, you have God's approval. 21 For to this you have been called, because Christ also suffered for you, leaving you an example, that you should follow in his steps. 22 He committed no sin; no guile was found on his lips. 23 When he was reviled, he did not revile in return; when he suffered, he did not threaten; but he trusted to him who judges justly. 24 He himself bore our sins in his body on the tree,ᵍ that we might die to sin and live to righteousness. By his wounds you have been healed. 25 For you were straying like sheep, but have now returned to the Shepherd and Guardian of your souls.

3 Likewise you wives, be submissive to your husbands, so that some, though they do not obey the word, may be won without a word by the behavior of their wives, 2 when they see your reverent and chaste behavior. 3 Let not yours be the outward adorning with braiding of hair, decoration of gold, and wearing of fine clothing, 4 but let it be the hidden person of the heart with the imperishable jewel of a gentle and

ᶠ Or *every institution ordained for men*   ᵍ Or *carried up . . . to the tree*

its function mediatorial (priests) and doxological.

2:10 The words which Hosea had used (Hos 2:23; cf. 1:10) in an amazing promise of mercy to a people who had forfeited every right to be called God's people, Israel (Hos 1:2-9), is used by Peter as it is by Paul (Ro 9:25) to proclaim God's mercy to the Gentiles.

2:11−4:6 Their new position as God's priestly and special people sets them apart as aliens and exiles in this world. They are therefore called on to live amid an alien and hostile mankind in such a way that their life is a witness which silences slander and can lead men to glorify God (2:11-12). This applies to their every social relationship, as subjects to civil authorities (2:13-17); as servants, especially where servitude involves undeserved suffering meekly borne after the example of Christ (2:18-25); as spouses (3:1-7); as members of the Christian community united in love and humility (3:8). As heirs of God's blessing their function in the world is to bless, not to return evil for evil (3:9-12). Though the witness and ministry of blessing involves them in undeserved suffering, no harm can come to them if they take Christ for their Lord, their example, and their Savior and with Him pass through suffering to glory (3:13-22), for by suffering they can learn to speak Christ's

triumphant No to the flesh and His whole Yes to the will of God. (4:1-6)

2:11 *Exiles.* Cf. 1:1, 17. *Aliens and exiles* are under close scrutiny in the land of their exile.

Wage War. For sin as a militant power cf. Ro 7:23.

2:12 *Day of visitation,* the day when God turns their hearts to Himself. On that day they will thank God for the *good deeds* which played a part in bringing about their conversion (cf. Mt 5:16). For *visitation* in the sense of God's gracious approach to man cf. Lk 19:44. For the verb "visit" in the same sense cf. Lk 1:68; 7:16.

2:13-14 Cf. Ro 13:1-7; Tts 3:1.

2:18-25 *Servants.* House slaves are meant. The equality and honor accorded the slave in the Christian community was in striking contrast to the position of the slave in the Gentile community, where he was generally esteemed a thing rather than a person. The slave's witness was therefore especially important, and the demand laid on him is a staggeringly high one. The motivation is correspondingly profound and rich: they are to find the model and the power for their conduct in Christ, the Suffering Servant (22, 24; cf. Is 53), who died to make them whole men, and in the Good Shepherd and Guardian of their souls (25),

quiet spirit, which in God's sight is very precious. ⁵ So once the holy women who hoped in God used to adorn themselves and were submissive to their husbands, ⁶ as Sarah obeyed Abraham, calling him lord. And you are now her children if you do right and let nothing terrify you.

7 Likewise you husbands, live considerately with your wives, bestowing honor on the woman as the weaker sex, since you are joint heirs of the grace of life, in order that your prayers may not be hindered.

8 Finally, all of you, have unity of spirit, sympathy, love of the brethren, a tender heart and a humble mind. ⁹ Do not return evil for evil or reviling for reviling; but on the contrary bless, for to this you have been called, that you may obtain a blessing. ¹⁰ For

> "He that would love life
> and see good days,
> let him keep his tongue from evil
> and his lips from speaking guile;
> 11   let him turn away from evil and do right;
> let him seek peace and pursue it.
> 12   For the eyes of the Lord are upon the righteous,
> and his ears are open to their prayer.
> But the face of the Lord is against those that do evil."

13 Now who is there to harm you if you are zealous for what is right? ¹⁴ But even if you do suffer for righteousness' sake, you will be blessed. Have no fear of them, nor be troubled, ¹⁵ but in your hearts reverence Christ as Lord. Always be prepared to make a defense to any one who calls you to account for the hope that is in you, yet do it with gentleness and reverence; ¹⁶ and keep your conscience clear, so that, when you are abused, those who revile your good behavior in Christ may be put to shame. ¹⁷ For it is better to suffer for doing right, if that should be God's will, than for doing wrong. ¹⁸ For Christ also died[h] for sins once for all, the righteous for the unrighteous, that

[h] Other ancient authorities read *suffered*

who has set their futile (cf. 1:18) lives in order.

3:6 Cf. Gn 18:12, where the word for *lord* is translated as "husband" in the RSV.

3:7 *The weaker sex.* In common parlance this phrase has come to have a derogatory sense. But it is human male pride that made it depreciatory, not Peter. He uses it to commend woman to man's love and care; the second half of the verse makes clear how high a place he assigns to woman, as does the NT generally. (Cf. Gl 3:28; Cl 3:11, 19)

3:9 *Evil for evil,* etc. Cf. 2:23; Lk 6:27-28; Ro 12: 14, 17.

Obtain a blessing. Gl 3:9, 29; Gn 12:2.

3:10-12 Cf. Ps 34:12-16. Peter quotes from the third section of Ps 34, an admonition to "depart from evil, and do good; seek peace, and pursue it." The admonition is based on the experience of the goodness of the Lord (v. 8; cf. 1 Ptr 2:3) which the psalm celebrates with the joyfulness that characterizes the letter of Peter. (Ps 34:1-10)

3:15 *The hope that is in you.* The buoyancy of the Christian hope must have made a deep impression on the men of late antiquity, which was marked by a deep hopelessness. The golden age lay in the past, not the future. The Roman poet Horace, even when called on to celebrate the glories of the new age ushered in by Augustus, never quite managed to grow warm about the future: "Our parents' age, worse than that of our grandfathers, has produced us, inferior to them and destined to bring forth an even more vicious progeny,"

he wrote, damning four generations in three short lines.

3:18-22 The main drift of this much-debated passage is clear. As in 2:21-25, Peter appeals to the example of Christ (18 ff.) to enforce and establish what he has said in 13-17. The suffering, triumphant, and exalted Christ is the basis for his triumphant question in v. 13, for the beatitude on those who "suffer for righteousness' sake" which echoes Jesus' own words (14a, cf. Mt 5:10), for the commands to endure sufferings untroubled and unafraid (14b), with Christ enthroned in the temple of their hearts, persisting amid suffering in their witness to the hope that inspires them, maintaining a clear conscience in behavior that can silence the slanders of those who revile them (14b-16). When Peter in summary says, *It is better to suffer for doing right, if that should be God's will, than for doing wrong* (17), he is not stating an abstract and general principle; he is proclaiming Christ the Lord (cf. 15). Concerning Him, the supreme Zealot "for what is right" (13), the great Sufferer "for righteousness' sake" (14, 17), Peter makes three major statements. The first statement is clear (18): Christ's suffering and death was vicarious (*the righteous for the unrighteous*) and atoning (*bring us to God*). The third statement (22) is also clear: The risen Christ *has gone into heaven;* He is enthroned at the *right hand of God* with all powers in subjection to Himself. But what does the second statement signify

he might bring us to God, being put to death in the flesh but made alive in the spirit; [19] in which he went and preached to the spirits in prison, [20] who formerly did not obey, when God's patience waited in the days of Noah, during the building of the ark, in which a few, that is, eight persons, were saved through water. [21] Baptism, which corresponds to this, now saves you, not as a removal of dirt from the body but as an appeal to God for a clear conscience, through the resurrection of Jesus Christ, [22] who has gone into heaven and is at the right hand of God, with angels, authorities, and powers subject to him.

4 Since therefore Christ suffered in the flesh,[i] arm yourselves with the same thought, for whoever has suffered in the flesh has ceased from sin, [2] so as to live for the rest of the time in the flesh no longer by human passions but by the will of God. [3] Let the time that is past suffice for doing what the Gentiles like to do, living in licentiousness, passions, drunkenness, revels, carousing, and lawless idolatry. [4] They are surprised that you do not now join them in the same wild profligacy, and they abuse you; [5] but they will give account to him who is ready to judge the living and the dead. [6] For this is why the gospel was preached even to the dead, that though judged in the flesh like men, they might live in the spirit like God.

[i] Other ancient authorities add *for us;* some *for you*

(19-21)? *He went and preached to the spirits in prison* (19) — what sort of "preaching" is meant, and who are the *spirits in prison?*

Many, perhaps most, interpreters see in the *spirits in prison* a reference to men who have died, specifically those who perished in the Flood (20), supreme examples of disobedience to God's call, and interpret the preaching as a saving proclamation of the Gospel. The second statement as a whole would then assert the universal efficacy of Christ's atoning death and resurrection. But grave difficulties beset this view of the passage: It is difficult to find parallels to the spirits (without modifiers) in the sense of the spirits of the departed dead. If the preaching was a saving proclamation, one would expect to hear that the spirits, or some of them, were saved by it; but of this the text says nothing. The context speaks only of the saving of *a few,* Noah and his family (20). It seems preferable therefore to take *spirits* in the well-documented sense of supernatural evil powers. (Cf. Mt 8:16; 12:45; Mk 9:20; Lk 9:39; 10:20; 11:26; Acts 16:18.) The word translated *preached* in itself means simply "proclaimed"; it is most commonly used in the NT of Gospel proclamation, but occurs also of the proclamation of the Law (Acts 15:21; Ro 2:21; Gl 5:11), or in a general sense (Rv 5:2). The second statement then would assert the triumph of Christ over the demonic powers to whom He proclaimed their defeat and deposition (cf. Cl 2:15). This gives a natural and climactic sequence: atonement, triumph, enthronement.

3:18 *Once for all.* This emphasizes both the everlasting efficacy of His sacrificial death (cf. Heb 9:26, 28; 10:10, 14) and the fact that "death no longer has dominion over him." (Ro 6:9-10)

Flesh . . . spirit, cf. Ro 1:4. In the *flesh,* in full and suffering humanity, He went to His death and endured the infliction of it upon Himself in all its bitterness. The *spirit,* which He committed to His Father's hands, was kept safely there. (Lk 23:46; cf. 2 Ti 1:12)

3:19 The phrase translated *in which* could as

well be rendered "in the course of which," referring not to *spirit* alone but to the whole of His Passion, death, and quickening. The proclamation to the spirits then took place between His death and resurrection, as it is stated in the Apostles' Creed.

3:20 *Who . . . did not obey.* This may refer to the fallen angels of Gn 6:1-4. In the structure of Genesis they constitute the third and final example of that ever-increasing "wickedness of man" (Gn 6:5) which led to the judgment of the Flood, the first being Cain (Gn 4:1-16) and the second, Lamech (Gn 4:23-24; cf. 2 Ptr 2:4-5; Jude 6). Jewish tradition made much of the incident as indicating the origin of demonic powers.

3:20-21 These verses are formally a digression from the main theme; but the digression serves the general purpose of the admonition to endure suffering (a) by pointing up the seriousness of the hour, comparable to the *days of Noah* in which *few* were saved when the disobedient perished (cf. our Lord's last-days admonition, Mt 24:37-39; Lk 17:26-27) and (b) by offering the comfort of *baptism, which . . . now saves* (as the ark once saved), giving men part in the *resurrection of Jesus Christ.* (Cf. Ro 6:3-5)

3:21 *Appeal to God for a clear conscience.* The candidate for baptism undergoes baptism in the hope and assurance that God will thereby forgive him all his trespasses. (Cl 2:12-13)

3:22 *Authorities . . . powers,* names for supernatural powers whether good or evil, angelic or demonic. Here evil powers seem to be meant. (Cf. v.19)

4:1-6 This section is parallel to the preceding (3:13-22), but the thought shifts from the Christ on the cross to the Christ of Gethsemane, who spoke a whole Yes to *the will of God* (2) which presented to Him the cup of suffering and death, although His whole manhood (*flesh,* 1) cried out for preservation and life (Mt 26:42). Peter bids his readers *arm* themselves with that *same thought* (1), to let the mind of the Christ who died for them be their mind, to think His thought, to

The Sobriety of Hope
4:7—5:11

7 The end of all things is at hand; therefore keep sane and sober for your prayers. 8Above all hold unfailing your love for one another, since love covers a multitude of sins. 9 Practice hospitality ungrudgingly to one another. 10As each has received a gift, employ it for one another, as good stewards of God's varied grace: 11 whoever speaks, as one who utters oracles of God; whoever renders service, as one who renders it by the strength which God supplies; in order that in everything God may be glorified through Jesus Christ. To him belong glory and dominion for ever and ever. Amen.

12 Beloved, do not be surprised at the fiery ordeal which comes upon you to prove you, as though something strange were happening to you. 13 But rejoice in so far as

will His will. They are to arm themselves, for this is a fighting matter, a struggle against the grain. The way they are to go is against their Gentile past, and the past is hard to shake (3), it is a minority way, with the suasion of the masses against it and exposed to the *abuse* of the majority (4). And it is, apparently, a discredited way; those among them who heard the good news of the living hope have died like all other men. The final futility of death came to them as it came to the discredited Messiah in whom they hoped; like Him, they were *judged in the flesh like men* (6). But the resurrection of Jesus Christ triumphantly gives the lie to all that. He lives enthroned at the right hand of God (3:22), *ready to judge the living and the dead* (4:5). Those who have abused the Christ in abusing the Christian hope *will give account to him* (5); those who have hoped in Him and have armed themselves with His thought shall *live,* as He lives (cf. 3:18), *in the spirit like God.* (6).

4:1 *Whoever has suffered,* etc. The only way to have done with sin is the way of suffering, which Christ has gone *for us* (the reading given in RSV note *i* should probably be adopted). Cf. Ro 6:2, 7. Communion with Him takes the Christian, too, down the road of suffering.

4:6 This verse seems designed to answer the question with which Paul deals in 1 Th 4:13-18, the question which oppressed some early Christians: "What of those who have died before our Lord's return — will they have part in the promised glory?" As 1 Co 15 shows, there were those who presumed to say no to that question.

4:7—5:11 The living hope is exuberant, attended by an "unutterable and exalted joy" (1:8). But it is not a witless intoxication; the command, "Be sober," is heard as early as 1:13. And this aspect of hope is particularly prominent in the closing admonitions of the letter (cf. 4:7; 5:8). The approaching end of all things calls for a sober vigilance in prayer, a life of love and mutual ministry, to the glory of God through Jesus Christ (4:7-11). It alerts Christians to see in their sufferings both a sharing in the suffering of Christ (and therefore a guarantee of their future participation in His glory) and also the sign and dawn of the approaching Last Judgment (4:12-19). It calls for

a sober and responsible congregational life: the elders are to exercise their shepherd's office with a pure zeal, conscious of their responsibility to the Chief Shepherd who is about to be manifested. The church is to submit obediently to the elders. All are to be clothed in humility (5:1-5). It calls on all to submit to the governance of God and to trust in His care, to be vigilant and firm in resisting the devil in the assurance that suffering is the normal lot of God's people and that the God of all grace will sustain them and in due time exalt them. (5:6-11)

4:7-8 *End . . . prayers . . . love.* The prayer, "Thy kingdom come," or "Maranatha" ("Our Lord, come!" 1 Co 16:22; Rv 22:20), and the prayer, "Thy will be done" (love), belong together. For the connection between expectation of the end and love cf. Ro 13:8-11; Heb 10:23-25; and 1 Co 13:8-13.

4:8 *Love covers a multitude of sins.* Love proves *unfailing* in the face of the brother's sins; it can forgive 70 times 7 times (Mt 18:22). He who prays the second petition of the Lord's Prayer cannot but pray the fifth petition too, both halves of it. (Cf. Ja 5:20)

4:9 *Hospitality,* a much-needed service rendered to traveling Christians and missionaries. (Cf. 3 Jn 5-8; Ro 12:13; 1 Ti 3:2; 5:10; Heb 13:2)

4:10 *Good stewards.* This removes all pride and therefore all harshness from Christian ministrations. Cf. 1 Co 4:7, and for the whole question of the gifts of the Spirit and the responsible employment of them for the benefit of the church, Ro 12:3-8 and 1 Co 12—14.

4:11 *Renders service.* The word is used particularly of supplying the physical needs of the poor in the church. Cf. Acts 6:1 ff., where the RSV renders it as "daily distribution."

Glorified . . . glory. In the active love of the church the future glory of God (when every knee shall bow in adoration before Him) is anticipated; He is, in the church, to be even now what He shall one day be manifestly and universally, "all in all." (Cf. Eph 4:6)

4:12 *Surprised . . . strange.* For suffering as the normal and inevitable lot of the church in this age cf. Lk 6:22-23, 26; Acts 14:22; 1 Th 3:4.

Ordeal . . . comes. What was before a possibility (3:13 ff.) is now an actuality. (Various conjectures

you share Christ's sufferings, that you may also rejoice and be glad when his glory is revealed. 14 If you are reproached for the name of Christ, you are blessed, because the spirit of glory*j* and of God rests upon you. 15 But let none of you suffer as a murderer, or a thief, or a wrongdoer, or a mischief-maker; 16 yet if one suffers as a Christian, let him not be ashamed, but under that name let him glorify God. 17 For the time has come for judgment to begin with the household of God; and if it begins with us, what will be the end of those who do not obey the gospel of God? 18And

"If the righteous man is scarcely saved,
where will the impious and sinner appear?"

19 Therefore let those who suffer according to God's will do right and entrust their souls to a faithful Creator.

5 So I exhort the elders among you, as a fellow elder and a witness of the sufferings of Christ as well as a partaker in the glory that is to be revealed. 2 Tend the flock of God that is your charge,*k* not by constraint but willingly,*l* not for shameful gain but eagerly, 3 not as domineering over those in your charge but being examples to the flock. 4And when the chief Shepherd is manifested you will obtain the unfading crown

j Other ancient authorities insert *and of power*
k Other ancient authorities add *exercising the oversight*
l Other ancient authorities add *as God would have you*

---

have been made to explain this shift from possibility to actuality. The most probable is that Peter, having closed his letter with a doxology and an "Amen" at 4:11, was moved to add a postscript when he received news from Asia Minor that the situation there had worsened and the to-be-expected *fiery ordeal* had begun.)

4:13 *Rejoice.* Cf. Mt 5:11-12; Acts 5:41; Ja 1:2 ff.

Share Christ's sufferings. Cf. Ro 8:17; 2 Co 1:5; Ph 3:8-11; Cl 1:24; 2 Ti 2:12.

His glory is revealed. Cf. 1:7, 13; 5:1.

4:14 *Spirit of glory. Spirit* should be capitalized; the Holy Spirit is characterized by the gift which He bestows (*glory;* cf. "Spirit of sonship," Ro 8:15). The Spirit is the beginning and guarantee of the blessings of the world to come (cf. 2 Co 1:22; 5:5; Eph 1:14); those who "have become partakers of the Holy Spirit and have tasted . . . the powers of the age to come" (Heb 6:4-5) – they have a foretaste of the future glory amid the sufferings of this age.

4:16 *As a Christian.* It is curious that the term which has become the commonest designation for followers of Christ occurs only three times in the NT. The name was first applied to disciples of Jesus in Antioch (Acts 11:26), is found in the mouth of the skeptical king Herod Agrippa II (Acts 26:28), and here in 1 Ptr, and seems to be the name applied to the church by hostile outsiders. Originally it may have been a term of mockery.

4:17 If the church undergoes a fiery ordeal (12), that is an indication that the end of all things is at hand (7); for the judgment which overtakes the *household of God,* the church (cf. 1 Ti 3:15), is the last preliminary to the Last Judgment (cf. Jer 25:29; Eze 9:6). This thought has a double value for the church: (a) It assures the church that her suffering is not blind chance but has a meaningful place in God's activity (cf. note on v. 12); (b) it warns the members of the church that to seek to escape suffering by renouncing the faith is fatally senseless; they will escape present suffering only to find certain doom.

4:18 *Where will . . . appear?* What will become of him? The verse is a quotation from Pr 11:31 in the form given by the ancient Greek translation of the OT (Septuagint), which differs from the present Hebrew text as translated in the RSV. For the thought cf. Lk 23:31.

4:19 *Entrust their souls to a faithful Creator.* As Jesus did on the cross (Lk 23:46; cf. 1 Ptr 2:23). A *faithful* God will not betray His trust, and He who willed and created the life of man has the will and the power to preserve it.

5:1 *Elders.* As the context shows ("tend the flock," 2) a general designation for officials exercising pastoral care. (Cf. Acts 20:17, 28)

Fellow elder . . . witness . . . partaker in the glory. Although Peter in quiet humility joins the ranks of the elders and does not stand on his dignity as apostle, he cannot be silent concerning the grace given him as *witness of the sufferings of Christ.* Some see in the phrase *partaker in the glory . . . to be revealed* an allusion to Peter's presence at the Transfiguration (Mt 17:1-8), where he was eyewitness to "honor and glory from God the Father" (2 Ptr 1:17) that was to be Christ's beyond the cross and was a *partaker* in it in the sense that he had a firsthand experience of it. This has considerable probability.

5:2 *Tend.* For a picture of all that a shepherd's care involved cf. Is 40:11 and Eze 34:1-6, 11-16; the latter is also the background and prototype of our Lord's words in Jn 10:1-16.

Flock of God. Cf. Eze 34:31.

5:3 *Examples.* For the idea of leadership by example and the related idea of imitation cf. 1 Co 4:16; 11:1; Ph 3:17; 1 Th 1:6; 2 Th 3:7-9; 1 Ti 4:12; Tts 2:7.

5:4 *Chief Shepherd,* Christ the Good Shepherd. (Jn 10:11, 14; cf. Heb 13:20)

Unfading crown, unlike the festal crown or the Greek athlete's crown of victory, which was of leaves or flowers that soon withered away.

of glory. ⁵ Likewise you that are younger be subject to the elders. Clothe yourselves, all of you, with humility toward one another, for "God opposes the proud, but gives grace to the humble."

6 Humble yourselves therefore under the mighty hand of God, that in due time he may exalt you. ⁷ Cast all your anxieties on him, for he cares about you. ⁸ Be sober, be watchful. Your adversary the devil prowls around like a roaring lion, seeking some one to devour. ⁹ Resist him, firm in your faith, knowing that the same experience of suffering is required of your brotherhood throughout the world. ¹⁰And after you have suffered a little while, the God of all grace, who has called you to his eternal glory in Christ, will himself restore, establish, and strengthen *m* you. ¹¹ To him be the dominion for ever and ever. Amen.

CONCLUSION (5:12-14)

12 By Silvanus, a faithful brother as I regard him, I have written briefly to you, exhorting and declaring that this is the true grace of God; stand fast in it. ¹³ She who is at Babylon, who is likewise chosen, sends you greetings; and so does my son Mark. ¹⁴ Greet one another with the kiss of love.

Peace to all of you that are in Christ.

m Other ancient authorities read *restore, establish, strengthen and settle*

5:5 *Clothe yourselves ... with humility,* as Jesus did (Jn 13:4) to Peter's dismay. (Jn 13:6-8; cf. 12-20)

God opposes .... Cf. Pr 3:34; Ja 4:6.

5:6 *Humble ... exalt.* The quotation from Proverbs in 5:5 connects the two ideas of humility toward one another (5) and humility before God.

Mighty hand. The mighty hand of God which once delivered His people out of the house of bondage in Egypt (Dt 9:26, 29; 26:8) is still mighty to save, and He will lead His people home in the last great Exodus, in spite of all diabolic opposition. (8)

5:7-9 Humility toward God is not an abject groveling before Him but profound and grateful trust in Him (7); it does not reduce man to fatalistic apathy but gives him power and courage for vigilant and heroic action. (8-9)

5:7 *Cast ... on him.* Cf. Ps 55:22; Mt 6:25-32; Lk 12:22-31.

5:8 *Prowls around like a roaring lion.* The threat posed by the devil is not underestimated: he is everywhere, powerful, bent on destruction.

5:10 *Little while ... eternal glory.* Cf. Ro 8:18; 2 Co 4:16.

5:12-14 The conclusion takes gracious notice of Silvanus' help in the composition of the letter, sums up its purport in one pithy statement, conveys the greetings of the church at Rome (Babylon) and of Mark, enjoins the kiss of love, and bestows the benediction of peace.

5:12 *Silvanus* is the Latinized form of Silas, prominent member of the early Jerusalem church, prophetically endowed (Acts 15:38), entrusted with an important mission (Acts 15:22-23), thereupon companion and co-worker of Paul. (Acts 15:40—18:5; 2 Co 1:19; 1 Th 1:1; 2 Th 1:1)

5:13 *She who is at Babylon ... likewise chosen.* The church at Rome. See the Introduction.

5:13 *My son Mark.* Mark the evangelist, called *son* because converted by Peter. (Cf. 1 Co 4:15; Phmn 10)

5:14 *The kiss of love,* elsewhere called the "holy kiss" (Ro 16:16; 1 Co 16:20; 2 Co 13:12; 1 Th 5:26), later became a regular part of the Communion liturgy. The origin of the practice is not known; it probably derives from the exchange of kisses between members of a family frequently mentioned in the OT and expresses the family solidarity of the "household of God."

PETER

INTRODUCTION

The historical contours of the First Letter of Peter are tolerably distinct; we can answer with considerable assurance most of the questions that historical inquiry raises concerning it. The second letter, however, is wrapped in mystery, and the reconstruction of its historical background is beset at almost every point with perplexing uncertainties. While the first letter's place in the canon has always been an assured one, that of the second letter has been disputed, with the weakest historical attestation of any book in the New Testament. There are some faint indications that the letter was known and used in the second century, but there is no unmistakable evidence that it was known and used in the church before the time of Origen (A. D. 185 to 254), who uses the letter and considers it apostolic, but is aware of the fact that its place in the canon is in dispute. The authenticity of the first letter, though questioned by modern critical scholarship, is actually quite solidly established by the external and internal evidence, whereas the authenticity of the second letter was questioned even in the early church and is denied by the great majority of scholars today. The circle of readers for whom the first letter was intended is clearly defined by the letter itself; the address of the second letter is very general: "To those who have obtained a faith of equal standing with ours" (1:1), and leaves the location of the readers uncertain. The words, "This is now the *second letter* that I have written to you, beloved" (3:1), make it likely but not certain that its destination is the same as that of the first letter. Concerning the time and place of writing of the second letter we can only say that it must be dated toward the close of Peter's life and that it was therefore probably written from Rome. We can see what sort of tendencies and difficulties occasioned the second letter, but we cannot fix them as to place and time with any precision.

Content of the Second Letter of Peter

If all else is uncertain, there is no uncertainty about the intent and the message of the letter. Like the First Letter of Peter, it is written in the service of Christian hope. The letter has, to be sure, often been called the Epistle of Knowledge, and "knowledge" is a prominent motif in the letter; but knowledge is not being emphasized and imparted for its own sake, but for the purpose of strengthening the Christian hope and defending it against the attack of error and to preserve it from the corrosion of doubt (cf. 1:3 with 1:8 and 11; 3:17-18). If the first letter is designed to keep hope alive and strong in men under the stress of persecution, the second letter is designed to maintain hope pure and strong in men whose hope is threatened by false teaching and is in danger of being weakened by doubt.

THE SECOND LETTER OF

PETER

SALUTATION (1:1-2)

1 Simeon[x] Peter, a servant and apostle of Jesus Christ,
To those who have obtained a faith of equal standing with ours in the righteousness of our God and Savior Jesus Christ:[a]

2 May grace and peace be multiplied to you in the knowledge of God and of Jesus our Lord.

The Greatness of the Christian Hope

1:3-11

3 His divine power has granted to us all things that pertain to life and godliness, through the knowledge of him who called us to[b] his own glory and excellence, 4 by which he has granted to us his precious and very great promises, that through these you may escape from the corruption that is in the world because of passion, and become partakers of the divine nature. 5 For this very reason make every effort to supplement your faith with virtue, and virtue with knowledge, 6 and knowledge with self-control, and self-control with steadfastness, and steadfastness with godliness, 7 and godliness

---

[x] Other authorities read *Simon*   [a] Or *of our God and the Savior Jesus Christ*   [b] Or *by*

1:1 *Faith of equal standing with ours.* If the letter is addressed to Gentiles, *ours* may refer to Jewish Christians. Cf. Acts 15:9, where Peter says that God "made no distinction between us [Jews] and them [the Gentiles], but cleansed their hearts by FAITH." Otherwise *ours* would refer to the apostles; the faith of those who believed the apostolic Word is as valid as the faith of the eye- and ear-witness. (Vv. 16-18)

Righteousness of our God. His saving righteousness, revealed in the Gospel to every one who has faith, Jew and Greek. (Ro 1:16)

1:2 *Grace and peace.* Cf. 1 Ptr 1:2.

Knowledge, not merely intellectual apprehension but a knowing that involves the whole man and is a communion between the knower and the known. (Cf. 1:3, 8, 9; 2:20; Cl 1:9-10)

1:3-11 The Christian hope bestows a great gift; the great and precious promises of our God and Savior Jesus Christ call men into communion with Him and into the glory and excellence of His eternal kingdom (3-4); cf. v. 11. The Christian hope makes a great claim on men; the possession of this hope calls for a life of strenuous sanctification. (5-11)

1:4 For the *promises* of God as the motivation and means of a new life see 2 Co 7:1 (cf. 6:16-18). In the divine promise the Word of promise and the blessing promised are one, for the Word effectually imparts what it says.

Corruption . . . in the world because of passion. Cf. 1 Jn 2:16.

1:5 *Make every effort.* Cf. 1:3, "His divine power has granted us all things." (In the Greek *every* and

all are expressed by the same word.) This is the logic of the Gospel: God's free and all-sufficient giving motivates and makes possible the wholehearted *effort* of man's response to it. Paul's words in Ph 2:12-13 are perhaps the classic expression of it: "Therefore [since Christ has gone the way of the servant for us to the cross] . . . WORK OUT your own salvation . . . for God is at WORK in you, both to will and to work for his good pleasure."

1:5-7 *Supplement your faith.* Supplement, as the fruit of a tree "supplements" the tree. But the translation is somewhat misleading. The word means "furnish" or "provide," and there is a preposition ("in") with *faith;* it would be preferable to render: "In your faith provide virtue" (i. e., let your faith provide, or produce, virtue) and continue the whole series (5-7) in the same way. The whole series describes, in chain-reaction form, the flowering and fruitage of faith; the qualities selected for emphasis are all in antithesis to the characteristics of the false teachers who pervert the way of truth (ch. 2) and deny the heart of the Christian hope (3:3-4): *virtue* is set over against their wrongdoing (2:13); true living *knowledge* which gives *grace and peace* and all that *pertains to life and godliness* (1:2-3) is set over against their brutish ignorance (2:12); *self-control* is set over against their greed and licentiousness (2:2, 3, 10, 12, 13, 14, etc.); *godliness* over against their brash and blasphemous impiety (2:1, 10, 12); *brotherly affection* and *love,* over against their self-seeking propagation of destructive heresies (2:1), their ruthless exploitation of the church. (2:3, 14, 18)

483

with brotherly affection, and brotherly affection with love. [8] For if these things are yours and abound, they keep you from being ineffective or unfruitful in the knowledge of our Lord Jesus Christ. [9] For whoever lacks these things is blind and shortsighted and has forgotten that he was cleansed from his old sins. [10] Therefore, brethren, be the more zealous to confirm your call and election, for if you do this you will never fall; [11] so there will be richly provided for you an entrance into the eternal kingdom of our Lord and Savior Jesus Christ.

The Certainty of the Christian Hope

1:12 — 2:22

THE CHRISTIAN HOPE AND THE PROPHETIC WORD (1:12-21)

[12] Therefore I intend always to remind you of these things, though you know them and are established in the truth that you have. [13] I think it right, as long as I am in this body,[c] to arouse you by way of reminder, [14] since I know that the putting off of my body[c] will be soon, as our Lord Jesus Christ showed me. [15]And I will see to it that after my departure you may be able at any time to recall these things.

[16] For we did not follow cleverly devised myths when we made known to you the power and coming of our Lord Jesus Christ, but we were eyewitnesses of his majesty.

[c] Greek *tent*

1:8-9 *The knowledge of our Lord Jesus Christ* is living, personal knowledge of Him; one possesses it by using it, acting on it, living it; otherwise it is lost. "To him who has will more be given, and he will have in abundance; but from him who has not, even what he has will be taken away." (Mt 13:12; cf. Cl 1:9-10)

Was cleansed, through Baptism.

1:10 God's *call*, which brings the eternal love of His *election* into man's life, is *confirmed* when it does not remain an idea or something learned from the catechism but is allowed to do its proper work and produces a life "worthy of the calling." (Eph 4:1)

1:12-21 The Christian hope is guided and sustained by the inspired OT prophetic Word, now made sure by the apostolic witness to the majesty of Christ, the fulfillment of prophecy.

1:12 *Therefore*, since their life can be effective and fruitful now (8) and can lead to the eternal kingdom (11) only if *the truth that* they *have* remains their constant and ever-increasing possession.

Remind. Cf. Ro 15:15; 1 Jn 2:21; Jude 5.

1:14 *Our Lord . . . showed me.* Jn 21:18-19.

1:15 *These things:* All that the apostolic witness has given to the church: the knowledge of God and of Jesus our Lord (2), the precious and very great promises (4) that enable men to become partakers of the divine nature (4) and to enter into the eternal kingdom of our Lord and Savior Jesus Christ. (11)

1:16-21 "These things" (15) are invaluable and indispensable and must be preserved, not because the apostles were great religious geniuses who clothed their dreams and aspirations in *cleverly devised myths* but because it was given them to be

eyewitnesses of great acts of God (16). In the Transfiguration (17-18) they beheld the *majesty of our Lord Jesus Christ* (16), the anticipation of that power, *honor and glory* (17) which would be His as the Father's gift at His second *coming* (16); there they heard the *voice* of the *Majestic Glory* and learned the full intent of God's word to His anointed King (*my beloved Son,* 17; cf. Ps 2:7) and the full significance of His word concerning His Spirit-filled Servant (*with whom I am well pleased,* 17; cf. Is 42:1); there in the Lord Jesus Christ, in God's Son and Servant, they saw God's Word accomplishing that which He purposed and prospering in the thing for which He sent it (Is 55:11). Now the apostles have the *prophetic word,* on which their hope of the final and universal triumph of the Son and Servant depends, *made more sure,* buttressed by fact and fulfillment (19). This Word is their gift to the church; this Word is a *lamp* unto men's feet and a light for their path by which they can confidently walk in dark places until the great *day dawns* whose light makes lamps superfluous, the time when the light within them (*morning star . . . in your hearts*) will answer to the light that falls upon them from without and prophecies, their service done, will pass away. (1 Co 13:8)

God is His own interpreter and makes plain what His Word intends; when men twist the Scriptures (cf. 3:16) and impose their *own interpretation* (20), they do so to their own destruction (3:16), for they darken God's lamp and lay unholy hands on the handiwork of the *Holy Spirit,* who *moved* men to utter what their own *impulse* never prompted; under His inspiration the prophets spoke *from God* (21); they could say: "Thus says the Lord."

17 For when he received honor and glory from God the Father and the voice was borne to him by the Majestic Glory, "This is my beloved Son,[d] with whom I am well pleased," 18 we heard this voice borne from heaven, for we were with him on the holy mountain. 19And we have the prophetic word made more sure. You will do well to pay attention to this as to a lamp shining in a dark place, until the day dawns and the morning star rises in your hearts. 20 First of all you must understand this, that no prophecy of scripture is a matter of one's own interpretation, 21 because no prophecy ever came by the impulse of man, but men moved by the Holy Spirit spoke from God.[e]

THE CHRISTIAN HOPE AND FALSE TEACHERS (2:1-22)

2 But false prophets also arose among the people, just as there will be false teachers among you, who will secretly bring in destructive heresies, even denying the Master who bought them, bringing upon themselves swift destruction. 2And many will follow their licentiousness, and because of them the way of truth will be reviled. 3And in their greed they will exploit you with false words; from of old their condemnation has not been idle, and their destruction has not been asleep.

4 For if God did not spare the angels when they sinned, but cast them into hell[f] and committed them to pits of nether gloom to be kept until the judgment; 5 if he did not spare the ancient world, but preserved Noah, a herald of righteousness, with seven

[d] Or my Son, my (or the) Beloved
[e] Other authorities read moved by the Holy Spirit holy men of God spoke   [f] Greek Tartarus

1:17-18 Transfiguration. Mt 17:1-8; Mk 9:2-8; Lk 9:28-36; the mountain is called holy because it was the scene of revelation. (Cf. Gn 28:16-17)

1:19 For the OT as the book of the NT church's hope cf. Ro 15:4.

2:1-22 The Christian hope need not be shaken by the godless false teachers who shall come, for the church is forewarned of their coming, knows that their condemnation is sure, and is assured that the Lord knows how to rescue the godly from trial. (9)

To understand the violence of the language, the sternness of the strictures, and the severity of the threats of this section, one must bear in mind how plausible an imitation of Christianity the proclamation of these false teachers must have seemed to many, especially to the unsteady souls (14) of men recently converted from paganism (18). They operated in false words (3), with great and legitimate catchwords of Christianity like freedom (19), a conception close to the heart of the Gospel (cf. Jn 8:32, 36; Ro 8:2, 21; 2 Co 3:17; Gl 4:26, 31; 5:1). How readily this idea of freedom lent itself to distortion and falsification can be seen from warnings like Gl 5:13 and 1 Ptr 2:16. The gift of liberation from sin (Ro 6:18, 22) easily became the license to sin (Ro 6:1; cf. 3:8). And for recently converted pagans the prospect of slipping back, with a good conscience, into the easy vices of their past must have been enticing (14, 18) indeed. The danger was acute; the church needed to be told in no uncertain terms that these teachings were wholly vicious and that any compromise with these teachers was impossible.

2:1 False prophets . . . among the people, Israel, Dt 13:1-5. (Cf. Mt 7:15; 24:4-5, 11, 24; Acts 20:28-31)

False teachers among you. Cf. Mt 7:15; 24:4-5, 11, 24; Acts 20:28-31; 2 Ti 3:1-9.

Denying the Master who bought them. Cf. Jude 4. They may call Him "Lord, Lord," but their lives are a contradiction of His will and Word. (Cf. Lk 6:46)

Bought them. Cf. especially 1 Co 6:19-20 for the idea that Christ's redeeming act obligates to a pure life. Cf. also 1 Co 7:23; Gl 3:13; Rv 5:9; 14:3-4. The purchase idea is akin to that of ransom and redemption. (Mt 20:28; 1 Ptr 1:18-19)

2:2 Way of truth . . . reviled. Outsiders, who cannot distinguish between true Christianity and false, judge the way of truth by the lives of these men and their followers and condemn it.

2:3 Condemnation . . . destruction. The Word of God which condemns them and threatens their destruction is thought of as an active, vigilant power waiting to pounce on them.

2:4-10a Three OT examples (angels who sinned, 4; a flood, 5; Sodom and Gomorrah, 6) support the thesis that the Lord knows how . . . to keep the unrighteous under punishment until the day of judgment (9), while the examples of Noah (5) and Lot (7) offer proof for the comforting assurance that the Lord knows how to rescue the godly from trial (9). Cf. Jude 6-8.

2:4 Hell (RSV note f: Tartarus). The term Tartarus is borrowed from the Greeks, who used it to designate a subterranean place where divine punishment was visited on the wicked dead.

Angels. Cf. Gn 6:1-4; Jude 6; 1 Ptr 3:19-20.

2:5 Noah, a herald of righteousness. Noah proclaimed righteousness by "walking with God" (Gn 6:9), obedient to His will and Word (Gn 6:22), in the midst of a generation whose every thought "was only evil continually" (Gn 6:5). Jewish tradition elaborated on Noah as proclaimer of righteousness.

Flood. Gn 6:5 − 8:12.

other persons, when he brought a flood upon the world of the ungodly; 6 if by turning the cities of Sodom and Go·mor′rah to ashes he condemned them to extinction and made them an example to those who were to be ungodly; 7 and if he rescued righteous Lot, greatly distressed by the licentiousness of the wicked 8 (for by what that righteous man saw and heard as he lived among them, he was vexed in his righteous soul day after day with their lawless deeds), 9 then the Lord knows how to rescue the godly from trial, and to keep the unrighteous under punishment until the day of judgment, 10 and especially those who indulge in the lust of defiling passion and despise authority.

Bold and wilful, they are not afraid to revile the glorious ones, 11 whereas angels, though greater in might and power, do not pronounce a reviling judgment upon them before the Lord. 12 But these, like irrational animals, creatures of instinct, born to be caught and killed, reviling in matters of which they are ignorant, will be destroyed in the same destruction with them, 13 suffering wrong for their wrong-doing. They count it pleasure to revel in the daytime. They are blots and blemishes, reveling in their dissipation,*g* carousing with you. 14 They have eyes full of adultery, insatiable for sin. They entice unsteady souls. They have hearts trained in greed. Accursed children! 15 Forsaking the right way they have gone astray; they have followed the way of Ba′laam, the son of Beor, who loved gain from wrong-doing, 16 but was rebuked for his own transgression; a dumb ass spoke with human voice and restrained the prophet's madness.

17 These are waterless springs and mists driven by a storm; for them the nether gloom of darkness has been reserved. 18 For, uttering loud boasts of folly, they entice with licentious passions of the flesh men who have barely escaped from those who live in error. 19 They promise them freedom, but they themselves are slaves of corruption; for whatever overcomes a man, to that he is enslaved. 20 For if, after they have escaped the defilements of the world through the knowledge of our Lord and Savior Jesus Christ, they are again entangled in them and overpowered, the last state has become worse for them than the first. 21 For it would have been better for them never to have known the way of righteousness than after knowing it to turn back from the holy commandment delivered to them. 22 It has happened to them according to the true proverb, The dog turns back to his own vomit, and the sow is washed only to wallow in the mire.

g Other ancient authorities read *love feasts*

2:6 *Sodom and Gomorrah.* Gn 19.

2:9 *Keep . . . under punishment until the day of judgment.* Cf. 4. For the thought that the wicked dead suffer punishment prior to the Last Judgment cf. Lk 16:23-28.

2:10a *Authority,* that of the Lord and Master, Jesus Christ.

2:10b-11 Jude 8-9 goes into more detail on this. These emancipated, licentious, greedy, lying, and proud men rush in where angels fear to tread; men hardened in sin lose their awe for God's judgment and are insensitive to Jesus' warning, "Judge not." (Mt 7:1)

2:12 This emphasis on the brutish, *animal* character of the false teachers has a special point in the light of the fact that many of the libertine errorists who arose in the church laid claim to a special "spirituality."

2:13 *Revel in the daytime.* Even pagan public opinion frowned on this.

Blots and blemishes on the Christian community, in whose common meals they still share (*carousing with you;* cf. 1 Co 11:20-22, 33-34).

2:14 *Accursed children!* Literally "children of the curse," "accursed ones"; cf. Mt 25:41. Cf. "children of the promise," Ro 9:8; Gl 4:28; "chil-

dren of wrath," Eph 2:3; "children of light," Eph 5:8.

2:15-16 *Balaam.* Jude 11; Nm 22—24.

Ass. Nm 22:21-32.

2:17 *Waterless springs,* unproductive of good.

Mists driven, unstable and unreliable.

Nether gloom . . . reserved. Cf. vv. 4 and 9.

2:19 *Slaves . . . enslaved.* For the enslavement to sin see Jn 8:34; Ro 6:16, 20; cf. Gn 4:7.

2:20-21 *Last state . . . worse . . . than the first.* The sin against the light, apostasy in the face of known and acknowledged truth, has unforeseeable consequences. One of Jesus' sternest parables is a warning against this sin. (Mt 12:42-45; cf. also Heb 10:26, 31)

2:21 *Holy commandment.* For *commandment* as expressing the whole of the Christian proclamation, with the emphasis on the fact that it claims man for Christ, cf. 3:2; 1 Ti 6:14; Mt 28:20 ("all that I have commanded you"); and Paul's use of "law" in Ro 8:2 ("law of the Spirit of life in Christ Jesus") and "charge" in 1 Ti 1:5. James's "law of liberty" (1:25) is similar.

2:22 *The dog.* Pr 26:11.

The scoffers who say, "Where is the promise of his coming?" simply ignore the fact that the God

The Delayed Fulfillment of the Christian Hope

3:1-18

"WHERE IS THE PROMISE OF HIS COMING?" (3:1-7)

3 This is now the second letter that I have written to you, beloved, and in both of them I have aroused your sincere mind by way of reminder; 2 that you should remember the predictions of the holy prophets and the commandment of the Lord and Savior through your apostles. 3 First of all you must understand this, that scoffers will come in the last days with scoffing, following their own passions 4 and saying, "Where is the promise of his coming? For ever since the fathers fell asleep, all things have continued as they were from the beginning of creation." 5 They deliberately ignore this fact, that by the word of God heavens existed long ago, and an earth formed out of water and by means of water, 6 through which the world that then existed was deluged with water and perished. 7 But by the same word the heavens and earth that now exist have been stored up for fire, being kept until the day of judgment and destruction of ungodly men.

"THE LORD IS NOT SLOW ABOUT HIS PROMISE" (3:8-10)

8 But do not ignore this one fact, beloved, that with the Lord one day is as a thousand years, and a thousand years as one day. 9 The Lord is not slow about his promise as some count slowness, but is forbearing toward you,[h] not wishing that any should perish, but that all should reach repentance. 10 But the day of the Lord will come like a thief, and then the heavens will pass away with a loud noise, and the elements will be dissolved with fire, and the earth and the works that are upon it will be burned up.

[h] Other ancient authorities read *on your account*

---

who once judged the world by water can and will judge the world by fire.

3:1 *Sincere,* pure, a mind inaccessible to the alien influences and sinful desires which slacken or frustrate obedience to the commandment of the Lord and Savior. (2)

Reminder. Cf. 1:12-15.

3:2 *Commandment,* in the same comprehensive sense as in 2:21.

3:3 *In the last days.* For the thought that opposition to the truth is itself a sign of the last days cf. 1 Ti 4:1-2; 1 Jn 2:18.

Scoffers . . . following their own passions. This emphasis on passions indicates that the scoffers are identical with, or at least related to, the false teachers of ch. 2. Paul had to combat the same combination of libertinistic "freedom" and the denial of the Christian hope (1 Co 6 and 15): Hope and purity live together. (1 Jn 3:3)

3:4 *Where is . . . ?* What has become of it? It has not been fulfilled.

Coming. Cf. 1:16.

Fathers, the first Christian generation.

All things have continued. The argument from the regularity and continuity of the created order is met with the reference to God's Word, which created and controls that order. (5-6)

3:5 *Out of water and by means of water.* The thought of this difficult phrase seems to be an echo of the creation account in Genesis. The earth emerged from the waters (Gn 1:2) when God separated the upper and nether waters by means of the firmament (Gn 1:6-8) and gathered the

nether waters together into one place. (Gn 1:9-10; cf. Ps 24:2)

3:7 *Fire . . . judgment.* Cf. 10-12. *Fire* is frequently used in the OT Scriptures as a symbol of God's punitive and destructive wrath, sometimes in connection with His final judgment, e. g., Zph 1:18; 3:8; Ml 4:1. The *fire of judgment* is here pictured as destroying not the world but *ungodly men.* This should be kept in mind for the interpretation of 10-12.

3:8-10 The church is to see in the Lord's delay a missionary command: the delay is the forbearance of the God who wills the salvation of man and would have all men come to repentance.

3:8 *With the Lord.* To speak of "delay" in connection with the Lord's coming is to impose human standards on the Lord, to try to fit Him into categories which are not His (Ps 90:4). A genuinely Christian hope will not seek to master God thus; it will not be curious about the Lord's timetable but will be concerned about His purpose. (9)

3:9 The Lord's purpose is clear; He would have *all* men *reach repentance* and live; and that gives the waiting and hoping church its direction and goal — and its solemn responsibility, in the face of which the question of the time of His coming fades into insignificance. (Cf. 11, 12, 15)

3:10 *Like a thief.* With this image, emphasizing the "unexpectedness" and suddenness (Mk 13:36; Lk 21:34) of His coming, Jesus cut off all attempts at calculating the time of His return (Mt 24:43; cf. 36). It is echoed by Paul (1 Th 5:2) and John. (Rv 3:3; 16:15)

"WHAT SORT OF PERSONS OUGHT YOU TO BE" (3:11-18)

11 Since all these things are thus to be dissolved, what sort of persons ought you to be in lives of holiness and godliness, 12 waiting for and hastening[i] the coming of the day of God, because of which the heavens will be kindled and dissolved, and the elements will melt with fire! 13 But according to his promise we wait for new heavens and a new earth in which righteousness dwells.

14 Therefore, beloved, since you wait for these, be zealous to be found by him without spot or blemish, and at peace. 15And count the forbearance of our Lord as salvation. So also our beloved brother Paul wrote to you according to the wisdom given him, 16 speaking of this as he does in all his letters. There are some things in them hard to understand, which the ignorant and unstable twist to their own destruction, as they do the other scriptures. 17 You therefore, beloved, knowing this beforehand, beware lest you be carried away with the error of lawless men and lose your own stability. 18 But grow in the grace and knowledge of our Lord and Savior Jesus Christ. To him be the glory both now and to the day of eternity. Amen.

[i] Or *earnestly desiring*

3:10 *Will be burned up*. If this is the correct text, the total annihilation of the present world is meant, while the rest of the NT speaks rather of a restoration of creation (e. g., Ro 8:19-22). But the best attested text is the very difficult "will be found," which may mean that *the earth and the works* of man that both adorn and disfigure the earth will be exposed to the fire of God's judgment, be refined and purified, and emerge as God's "new heavens and a new earth" (13). The universe will pass through fearful convulsions (*dissolved*, 10, "melt," 12) as Jesus foretold (Mt 24:29). But God's goal for His creation, over which He once spoke His "very good" (Gn 1:3; 1 Ti 4:4), is not extinction but restoration and transfiguration.

3:11-18 The church is to see in the Lord's delay a summons to a life of sanctified, tense, and vigilant expectancy, a life characterized by growth in grace and knowledge of our Lord and Savior Jesus Christ.

3:11 *What sort of persons*. This is the center of gravity in all the NT teaching of last things from John the Baptist and Jesus onward.

3:12 *Hastening the coming of the day,* by living a life and proclaiming the truth which will enable men to reach repentance. (9)

Elements, the various parts of which the world is composed.

3:13 *Heavens* and *earth* indicate the continuity of the world to come with God's first creation (Gn 1:1), our world. The otherness of the coming world is expressed by *new,* a word characteristic of the new quality of all that pertains to the world to come. Cf. Mt 26:29; 2 Co 5:17; Eph 4:24; Heb 10:10; Rv 2:17; 3:12; 5:9; 14:3; 21:1-2; 21:5; for the whole expression cf. Is 65:17; 66:22; Rv 21:1.

Righteousness dwells. In the world to come God's will shall be done on earth as it is in heaven. All the ruin and frustration with which man's sin has disfigured God's good world will have passed away. (Cf. Ro 8:19-22)

3:15 *Forbearance . . . salvation*. Cf. 9; Ro 2:4.

So also . . . Paul wrote. Characteristic words of Paul on the urgency of the last days are Ro 13: 12-14; 1 Co 7:29-31; 1 Th 5:1-11.

Wisdom. Cf. 1 Co 3:10; also 1 Co 2:6; 3:18.

3:16-17 *Some things . . . hard to understand*. Paul's critics at Corinth conceded that his letters were "weighty and strong" (2 Co 10:10) but apparently asserted that the Gospel was "veiled" by the rich profundity of his thought and language (2 Co 4:3). Paul himself complains that men have maliciously misinterpreted his bold language on the free grace of God (Ro 3:8; cf. 6:1), and it is probable that the false teachers of ch. 2 did the same thing and are here alluded to as *the ignorant and unstable* (cf. 2:12, 17); certainly the designation *lawless men* fits them.

3:18 *Day of eternity,* the day of the Lord (10) which ushers in eternity. The church asserts and proclaims the still-hidden divine glory of its Lord even now.

RELATIONSHIP BETWEEN 2 PETER AND JUDE

The relationship between 2 Peter and the Letter of Jude is usually considered one of the strong arguments against the authenticity of 2 Peter. The Letter of Jude and the second chapter of 2 Peter are so similar in language and thought that there is obviously a historical connection between the two; they can hardly have originated altogether independently of each other. Most scholars today argue that 2 Peter is the later of the two documents and has incorporated the Letter of Jude. The arguments used to prove the dependence of 2 Peter on Jude cannot be discussed in detail here. But it should be noted that this theory of borrowing on the part of a second-century writer leaves a good many unanswered questions. For example, if Jude is the earlier document and 2 Peter the later, why is it that Jude's account of the false teachers is the darker and more sinister of the two? In Jude the false teachers are compared not only to Balaam, but also to Cain and Korah—why should a second-century writer, engaged in so desperate a struggle against such a dangerous heresy that he must invoke the name of Peter in order to combat it, tone down the indictment of Jude? Note also that Jude twice (4 and 17) refers to an older apostolic writing which predicts the errorists who at Jude's time are present in the church. 2 Peter answers to that document; it predicts future errorists (2:1, 3) whose coming and working Jude notes as present in his time. It would seem to follow that Jude knew and prized as apostolic a document which must have been very similar to the second chapter of our 2 Peter. If 2 Peter is not apostolic but later than Jude, the original apostolic document referred to by Jude (4 and 17) must have been lost early without leaving a trace.

THE FIRST LETTER OF

JOHN

INTRODUCTION

The Gospel of John was to some degree polemical. It was probably not directly occasioned by false teaching, but some characteristic accents and features of the gospel are most readily understood as John's answer to a false teaching which perverted the true Gospel. The First Letter of John is wholly and vigorously polemical. It is aimed at false teachers, and although the letter never enters into a detailed refutation of their error, much less a full presentation of their teaching, the general character of the heresy can be ascertained with tolerable accuracy from hints given in the letter.

The false teachers had arisen in the church: "They went out from us," John writes, "but they were not of us; for if they had been of us, they would have continued with us; but they went out, that it might be plain that they all are not of us" (1 Jn 2:19). At the time when John wrote, they had separated themselves from the church — or had been expelled by the church: "You are of God, and have overcome them," John tells the church (1 Jn 4:4). They had apparently constituted themselves as a separate community, and they continued to make vigorous propaganda for their cause (cf. 2 Jn 7, 10) and still constituted a threat to the church. (1 Jn 2:27; 3:7)

They were a real threat, for they were very "religious" men. They were "spiritual" men and claimed the prophetic authority of the Holy Spirit for their teaching (1 Jn 4:1). They propagated a high and solemn sort of piety which claimed immediate communion with God and operated with slogans like "I know Him," "I abide in Him," "I am in the light" (1 Jn 2:4, 6, 9), and "I love God" (1 Jn 4:20). They probably felt themselves and professed themselves to be a new elite in Christendom, the "advanced" type of Christian. John is probably referring to them in his second letter when he speaks of those who "go ahead" and do not abide in the doctrine of Christ (2 Jn 9). It was no wonder that they deceived many and that many who remained in the church were perhaps not fully convinced that the church had been in the right when it separated itself from them. Or there might well have been some who were still secretly attracted to this brilliant new theology.

They deceived many, these new teachers. But they could not deceive the heart of John, for his heart was in fellowship with the Father and with His Son Jesus (1 Jn 1:3). The eyes that had seen the Word of life in the flesh (1 Jn 1:1) saw these men for what they were. They are, in John's clear vision of them, not prophets of God but false prophets (1 Jn 4:1); their words are inspired not by the Spirit of truth but by the spirit of error (1 Jn 4:6); they are not the Christ's, but the very embodiment of the Antichrist of the last days (1 Jn 2:18), impelled and informed by the spirit of the Antichrist (1 Jn 2:22; 4:3), who inspires the lie.

What was this lie? They denied not the deity but the full humanity of the Christ. They denied that Jesus, the man in history, was the Christ, the Son of God (1 Jn 2:22; cf. 4:3; 4:15; 5:5); they denied that Jesus was the Christ who had come "in the flesh" (1 Jn 4:2; cf. 2 Jn 7). We get a hint of how far this denial went in the words of John which state positively the significance of the Christ who came in the flesh: "This is he who came by water and blood, Jesus Christ, not with the water only but with the water and the blood" (1 Jn 5:6). These words are in themselves somewhat obscure; but they become clearer against the background of the heresy which they combat. That heresy was most probably the heresy of Cerinthus and his followers, of which Irenaeus has left us a description (*Adv. Haer.* I 26, 1). Cerinthus, according to Irenaeus, taught that Jesus was a man among men, a superior man but still merely man, the son of Joseph and Mary; at His baptism the "heavenly Christ" descended on Him in the form of a dove and enabled Him to reveal the hitherto unknown God and to perform miracles; at His Passion, however, the "heavenly Christ" again left

Jesus, and only Jesus the man suffered and died. In other words, the Christ came "by water" (the baptism of Jesus). The cross of Jesus, the shed blood of the Son of God, which the apostolic witness celebrated as the crown and culmination of the ministry of Christ, was thus ignored or relegated to the background. The blood of Jesus, the Son of God, was no longer the blood which "cleanses us from all sin." (1 Jn 1:7)

Where the cross is not taken seriously, sin is no longer taken seriously either. Men whose proud piety centers in their assumed *knowledge* of God and ignores the cross in which God has revealed Himself as both the Judge of sinful man and the Forgiver of sinners can think of sin as something that need not concern them; they can deceive themselves and say that they have no sin; they can say, "We have not sinned," and thus make a liar of God, who has in the cross declared that all men have sinned (1 Jn 1:8, 10) and has in the cross given His Son as the "expiation . . . for the sins of the whole world" (1 Jn 2:2). Such a piety can be comfortable in this world; the offense of the cross is gone, and the lives of Christians are no longer a walking indictment of the sins of the world. The world, which does not recognize the children of God, but rather hates them (1 Jn 3:1, 13), can come to terms with these men and with the Christ whom they proclaim: "They are of the world, therefore what they say is of the world, and the world listens to them." (1 Jn 4:5)

Over against these men John asserts with all the concentrated power that this inspired Son of Thunder can command the full reality of the incarnation, the fact that life and communion with God are to be found in Jesus, the Christ who came and died for man's sin in the flesh, or they will not be found at all; that any claim to know and love God which does not produce a life of righteousness and love is a blank lie; that the child of God cannot ever, without denying himself and his God, be at home in the world which is in the power of the Evil One. The letter is controversial and polemical, but it is not merely or one-sidedly polemical. John meets the danger which threatens the church by a powerfully positive restatement of what the Christian life really is, a passionate appeal to recognize in action the full measure of the gift and the full extent of the claim of that grace of God which has given man fellowship with the Father and the Son.

First John is a letter written to Christians, to men whose faith is being endangered by heresy and is being tried by temptation. Although the usual letter forms (salutation, close, etc.) are missing, it is nevertheless a genuine letter written for a specific situation by a father in Christ to his "children," and it is pervaded by an intense personal and pastoral concern for these "children." In its white-hot passion for the truth, for a Christian Gospel and a Christian life that is genuine, whole, and uncompromised, it remains a tonic and bracing word for the church always. It summons a church grown easy and comfortable to bethink itself penitently of the basic facts and the basic laws of its existence. Nowhere is black so black and white so white as in this letter; the antithesis of truth-lie, Christ-Antichrist, God-devil leaves the church no possibility of doubt as to where she must stand. And the letter likewise leaves no doubt that the church *can* stand where she must stand; the greatness of God's enabling gift is lettered out in pithy statements which are as profound as they are brief and pointed. Perhaps no New Testament book of like compass has furnished so many brief sayings, sayings that Christian men can lay up in their hearts, to live by and to die on, as this First Letter of John. (E. g., 1:5, 8; 2:2, 9-11, 15-17, 23; 3:1-2; 4:1-3, 7-12, 19; 5:3-5, 11-12)

THE FIRST LETTER OF

JOHN

THE REVELATION (1:1-4)

1 That which was from the beginning, which we have heard, which we have seen with our eyes, which we have looked upon and touched with our hands, concerning the word of life— 2 the life was made manifest, and we saw it, and testify to it, and proclaim to you the eternal life which was with the Father and was made manifest to us— 3 that which we have seen and heard we proclaim also to you, so that you may have fellowship with us; and our fellowship is with the Father and with his Son Jesus Christ. 4And we are writing this that our*a* joy may be complete.

The Tests of the Christian Life

1:5—5:12

THE FIRST STANDARD (1:5—2:27)

5 This is the message we have heard from him and proclaim to you, that God is light and in him is no darkness at all. 6 If we say we have fellowship with him while

a Other ancient authorities read *your*

The utterances of the letter do not move forward step for step in a straight line but circle, spiral fashion, around three great themes, with a continued enrichment of the thought at each turn. Consequently, there is considerable overlapping, both in the major divisions and in the subdivisions; no formal outline is a wholly satisfactory guide to the content of the letter. It is, in the last analysis, best appropriated by giving oneself to its movement with energetic sympathy and without too much concern for grasping it structurally. But as a first introduction to the letter the outline given in these notes may prove useful. It is adapted from the work of an English and a German scholar who, working independently of each other, arrived at the same analysis of the content. According to it, the letter begins with a statement of the revelation which God has given in this Son (1:1-4) and then proceeds to apply three tests to the Christian life as it is lived in the light of this revelation. This revelation furnishes three STANDARDS according to which Christian life is tested: (1) "God is light" (1:5); (2) "We are God's children now" (3:2); and (3) "God is love" (4:8). According to these standards three TESTS are applied to the Christian life: The test of righteousness, the test of love, and the test of true belief. All three of them occur in each of the three major divisions of the letter.

1:1-4 God has spoken His ultimate Word, the *word* of *eternal life,* in the audible, visible, palpable historical reality of His incarnate Son. With that Word He has admitted man to fellowship with Himself and has placed men into *fellowship* with one another. This revelation lives and works on in the spoken and written word of the first witnesses to the incarnation.

For the whole paragraph cf. Jn 1:1-18.

1:4 *Our joy may be complète.* Cf. Jn 15:11. The joy of the apostolic witnesses, like that of the Son Himself, is made full when God's will is done, the will that none be lost from the fellowship which He has created. (Cf. Jn 17:12-13)

1:5—2:27 *God is light and in him is no darkness at all* (1:5). Fellowship with God means walking in the light (1:7); test yourselves to know whether you are walking in the light.

1:5—2:6 THE TEST OF RIGHTEOUSNESS

1:5—2:6 Walking in the light means facing the fact of your *sins* (which are exposed by the light), confessing your sins, and receiving forgiveness by the atoning death *(blood)* of Christ. Only thus is fellowship with God a genuine fellowship.

1:5 *Light . . . darkness.* Men who live in an electrically lighted world and know little of the uncertainties and terrors of darkness cannot appreciate this image as the ancients did. For John, Jesus Christ *is* the Light, cf. 2:8, and Jn 1:4, 5, 7, 8, 9; 3:19-21; 8:12; 9:5; 12:35, 36, 46; when he says that God is *light,* he is pointing to God as manifested in His only Son, the Giver of grace, truth, life, and sonship. The light both blesses freely and obligates; men are called upon to believe in the light, walk in the light, and become "sons of light" (Jn 12:36); that is, their whole nature and all their action is to be determined by the light. *Darkness* is similarly not merely a state but a power, waging a battle against the light (Jn 1:5), doomed (1 Jn 2:8) but not yet annihilated, blinding

492

we walk in darkness, we lie and do not live according to the truth; 7 but if we walk in the light, as he is in the light, we have fellowship with one another, and the blood of Jesus his Son cleanses us from all sin. 8 If we say we have no sin, we deceive ourselves, and the truth is not in us. 9 If we confess our sins, he is faithful and just, and will forgive our sins and cleanse us from all unrighteousness. 10 If we say we have not sinned, we make him a liar, and his word is not in us.

2 My little children, I am writing this to you so that you may not sin; but if any one does sin, we have an advocate with the Father, Jesus Christ the righteous; 2 and he is the expiation for our sins, and not for ours only but also for the sins of the whole world. 3And by this we may be sure that we know him, if we keep his commandments. 4 He who says "I know him" but disobeys his commandments is a liar, and the truth is not in him; 5 but whoever keeps his word, in him truly love for God is perfected. By this we may be sure that we are in him: 6 he who says he abides in him ought to walk in the same way in which he walked.

7 Beloved, I am writing you no new commandment, but an old commandment which you had from the beginning; the old commandment is the word which you have heard. 8 Yet I am writing you a new commandment, which is true in him and in you, because*b* the darkness is passing away and the true light is already shining. 9 He who says he is in the light and hates his brother is in the darkness still. 10 He who loves his brother abides in the light, and in it*c* there is no cause for stumbling. 11 But he who hates his brother is in the darkness and walks in the darkness, and does not know where he is going, because the darkness has blinded his eyes.

12 I am writing to you, little children, because your sins are forgiven for his sake.

b Or *that* *c* Or *him*

men (Jn 2:11) and claiming their love and loyalty. (Jn 3:19)

1:7-8 The *light* which overcomes man's sins necessarily exposes sin. (Cf. Jn 3:20)

1:7 *Blood*, of the Lamb of God, the final sacrifice for sin. (Jn 1:29; 1 Jn 5:6)

1:9 *Faithful and just.* God is *faithful* in that He holds to His promises, to which He has spoken His Yea in Jesus Christ (2 Co 1:19-20). He is *just* in that He does not overlook sin but has dealt with it righteously and effectually in the atoning death of Jesus, His Son. (Cf. Ro 3:24-26)

1:10 *Make him a liar.* When God gave His Son for the world's life, the Sacrifice for the WORLD's sin (Jn 3:16; 1:29), He declared all men guilty. (Cf. 2:2)

2:1 *Advocate.* Cf. Ro 8:34 for Christ as Intercessor at the right hand of God.

2:2 *Expiation.* The rendering of the KJV, "propitiation," is preferable in that it keeps alive the essential thought that sin is personal rebellion against God and invokes His wrath, which is averted by the sacrifice that God Himself in His great love provides. (4:10)

2:3-6 "Walking in the light" means keeping God's commandments, keeping His *word* in *love* and walking as Christ walked.

2:4 *"I know him,"* like "I abide in him" (cf. 6), is apparently one of the slogans of the false teachers. John points out that knowledge of God without obedience is a self-contradiction, a lie.

2:5 *Love for God is perfected.* His love for God finds full and adequate expression, reaches its goal.

2:6 *Way in which he walked,* namely, Jesus Christ, who could say "I do know him [the Father] . . . and I keep his word." (Jn 8:55)

2:7-17 THE TEST OF LOVE

2:7-17 The exposition of the test of love follows the scheme of Jesus' twin commandment of love (cf. Mt 22:34-40), love for neighbor (*brother,* 7-11) and love for God (15-17). The latter commandment is preceded by a brief reminder of all that motivates and enables the readers to love God with all their hearts: the forgiveness of sins, knowledge of the eternal Christ and of the Father who sent Him, victory over the Evil One in the power of the Word of God. (12-14)

2:7-8 *Old commandment . . . new commandment.* The *commandment* of love is *old;* it goes back to Christ (Jn 13:34), and the readers have known it as long as they have known Christ. And yet it is *new,* for Christ not only restored the Law's old commandment of love; by His self-giving love He has created a new situation, with new possibilities of obedience and fulfillment: as the commandment is fully realized and done *(true) in him,* so it can become a live reality in those who know Him. With the coming of Christ, the *light,* the new world of God has become a reality in the midst of the old *(already shining),* and the abiding reality of this new world is love. (Cf. 1 Co 13:8, 13)

2:10 *No cause for stumbling.* Cf. 11, the effect of darkness. If the rendering of RSV note *c (in him there is no cause for stumbling)* is adopted, the meaning would be: He who loves his brother will be a living witness to his faith, not an obstacle or offense to the faith of others.

2:12-17 Walking in the light means loving the *Father,* not the dying and doomed *world* separated from Him by its *lust* and *pride.*

2:12-15 With an effective monotony of repetition John brings home to his readers the unshakable

13 I am writing to you, fathers, because you know him who is from the beginning. I am writing to you, young men, because you have overcome the evil one. I write to you, children, because you know the Father. 14 I write to you, fathers, because you know him who is from the beginning. I write to you, young men, because you are strong, and the word of God abides in you, and you have overcome the evil one.

15 Do not love the world or the things in the world. If any one loves the world, love for the Father is not in him. 16 For all that is in the world, the lust of the flesh and the lust of the eyes and the pride of life, is not of the Father but is of the world. 17And the world passes away, and the lust of it; but he who does the will of God abides for ever.

18 Children, it is the last hour; and as you have heard that antichrist is coming, so now many antichrists have come; therefore we know that it is the last hour. 19 They went out from us, but they were not of us; for if they had been of us, they would have continued with us; but they went out, that it might be plain that they all are not of us. 20 But you have been anointed by the Holy One, and you all know.*d* 21 I write to you, not because you do not know the truth, but because you know it, and know that no lie is of the truth. 22 Who is the liar but he who denies that Jesus is the Christ? This is the antichrist, he who denies the Father and the Son. 23 No one who denies the Son has the Father. He who confesses the Son has the Father also. 24 Let what you heard from the beginning abide in you. If what you heard from the beginning abides in you, then you will abide in the Son and in the Father. 25And this is what he has promised us,*e* eternal life.

26 I write this to you about those who would deceive you; 27 but the anointing which you received from him abides in you, and you have no need that any one should teach you; as his anointing teaches you about everything, and is true, and is no lie, just as it has taught you, abide in him.

d Other ancient authorities read *you know everything*   *e* Other ancient authorities read *you*

Gospel certainties which are the motive and basis of their love for God. The *children* are the church as a whole. (John repeatedly addresses his readers as "little children" or "children," 2:1, 28; 3:18; 4:4; 5:21). They can and should love God with all their heart because their *sins are forgiven* for Christ's sake (12); the evil they have done, being forgiven, no longer blocks their way to the light (cf. Jn 3:20), and they know God as their way to the light and their forgiving *Father* (13). The *fathers*, backbone of the church, mature Christians with settled convictions, know *him who is from the beginning,* the "word of life" (1:1), who brought them into their enduring fellowship of love with God (1:3). The *young men,* the hope and future of the church, have won a victory over the *evil one* in the years when victory is most difficult; they know that they have found the strength for that victory in the *word of the God,* who first loved them in order that they might love Him. (4:10, 19)

2:15 *Do not love the world.* As 16 makes plain, the "way of the world" (its lust, greed, and pride) is meant. For the absolute opposition between "world" and God cf. Ja 4:4.

2:16 *Pride of life,* or "pride in one's possessions." (The word here translated "life" can also mean "means of livelihood" and is rendered as "goods" in 3:17). The rich farmer of Jesus' parable (Lk 12:16-21), the "rich" of Ja 5:1-6, and all the devotees of conspicuous consumption suggest themselves as illustrations.

2:18-27 THE TEST OF TRUE BELIEF

2:18-27 Walking in the light means holding to the Christ revealed from the beginning as the incarnate Christ, *Jesus* (22); it means rejecting the lie of the Antichrist who in denying the incarnate Son denies the Father too.

2:18 *The last hour.* For the appearance of pseudochristian and antichristian powers as a mark of the beginning of the end cf. Mt 24:5, 11, 24; 1 Ti 4:1; 2 Ti 3:1; 2 Ptr 3:3; Jude 18.

Antichrist . . . many antichrists. Cf. 22, "the antichrist"; 4:3, "the spirit of antichrist . . . ." John does not say whether he identifies the many antichristian teachers with THE Antichrist of whom the church has been warned (cf. 2 Th 2) or sees in them precursors of the Antichrist. The important thing is that the church recognize and reject their antichristian teaching.

2:19 For a summary of the origins and character of the false teachers see the Introduction.

2:20 *Anointed* (cf. 27), endowed with the Holy Spirit, who leads into all truth (Jn 16:13). For anointing in this sense cf. 2 Co 1:21.

The Holy One, Christ. Cf. Mk 1:24; Lk 4:34; Jn 6:69; Rv 3:7.

You all know. The *all* is emphatic, rejecting the claim to special knowledge put forward by the false teachers. (4)

2:22 *Jesus,* asserting the full manhood of Christ. (Cf. 4:2; 2 Jn 7; Jn 1:14)

2:25 Cf. Jn 17:1-3.

2:27 Cf. 20 and note there.

28 And now, little children, abide in him, so that when he appears we may have confidence and not shrink from him in shame at his coming. ²⁹ If you know that he is righteous, you may be sure that every one who does right is born of him.

3 See what love the Father has given us, that we should be called children of God; and so we are. The reason why the world does not know us is that it did not know him. ² Beloved, we are God's children now; it does not yet appear what we shall be, but we know that when he appears we shall be like him, for we shall see him as he is. ³And every one who thus hopes in him purifies himself as he is pure.

4 Every one who commits sin is guilty of lawlessness; sin is lawlessness. ⁵ You know that he appeared to take away sins, and in him there is no sin. ⁶ No one who abides in him sins; no one who sins has either seen him or known him. ⁷ Little children, let no one deceive you. He who does right is righteous, as he is righteous. ⁸ He who commits sin is of the devil; for the devil has sinned from the beginning. The reason the Son of God appeared was to destroy the works of the devil. ⁹ No one born of God commits sin; for God's*f* nature abides in him, and he cannot sin because he is*g* born of God. ¹⁰ By this it may be seen who are the children of God, and who are the children of the devil: whoever does not do right is not of God, nor he who does not love his brother.

f Greek *his*　　*g* Or *for the offspring of God abide in him, and they cannot sin because they are*

2:28—4:6 *We are God's children now* (3:2). Fellowship with God means being God's children; test yourselves to know whether you are born of God.

2:28—3:10 THE TEST OF RIGHTOUSNESS

2:28—3:10 The Son of God, through whom you have become children of God, *appeared to take away sins* (3:5), *to destroy the works of the devil* (3:8); being *born of God* therefore means a radical antagonism to the evil (*who has sinned from the beginning,* 3:8), and a total aversion from sin (3:9). Those who sin are *children of the devil,* not *children of God.* (3:10)

2:28-29 These verses form the transition from *abide in Him* (28; cf. 2:24, 27) to the idea of the following section that being born of God means doing *right.*

2:28 *When he appears.* The thought of the imminent return of Christ adds urgency to the repeated appeal to *abide in Him.*

3:1 *Know,* in the full sense of "recognize, acknowledge, be in harmony with"; cf. 3:13, where the world's attitude is called "hate," and Jn 16:2-3.

3:2 *Shall be like him,* like Christ, sons in freedom and glory. (Cf. Jn 12:26; 8:18, 21, 29; Ph 3:21; Cl 3:4)

3:3 *Hopes . . . purifies himself.* This unbreakable connection between hope and purity of life, between the confidence in the returning Christ that looks to Him for everything and the resolute self-committal that devotes everything to Him, is the hallmark of all NT teaching on hope, from John the Baptist to John the prophet on Patmos.

3:4-10 Nowhere is the test of righteousness more rigorously applied than here. In the light of misleading and plausible false teaching (*let no one deceive you,* 7) which dodges and minimizes the seriousness of sin, John makes two major assertions and draws the inescapable inferences

from them. First, *sin is lawlessness,* violation of the holy will of God (4). God took sin so seriously that He sent His sinless Son into death *to take away sins;* to cancel the guilt and take away the power of sin (5). Faith in Him (*abides in him . . . seen . . . known him,* 6) cannot coexist with sinning. Second, *sin is of the devil* (8), is diabolical revolt and enmity against God. God sent His Son into death to liberate men from their diabolical imprisonment in revolt (8) and to make them His obedient sons (9). To sin is to deny God as your Father and to recommit yourself to the paternity and tyranny of the devil. Sin is sin, and righteousness is righteousness in fact and act (7, 10), and nothing and no one can make sin innocent or righteousness a matter of indifference. (Cf. Ro 3:31; 8:4)

3:4 Cf. 5:17.

3:8 Cf Jn 8:44.

3:9 *God's nature,* literally "seed"; the indwelling Spirit is probably meant as the presence and power of God.

3:9 *He cannot sin.* Cf. Ro 6:2. This statement seems to be a flat contradiction of 1:7-10. Both statements deal with sin, not abstractly and in general but in relationship to the atoning work of Christ (1:7, "blood"; 3:5, 8). Both are fighting words directed against the attempt to minimize sin, either by denying the presence of it or by trying to make it smell sweeter by another name. The relationship between the two statements might be stated thus: Unless sin is faced for what it is, as the hideous abnormality described in 3:4-10, there can be no genuine confession of sins as demanded in 1:7-10. Where sin is accepted as "normal," there is no confession and absolution, no fellowship with God and man, no church. (1:6-7)

3:10 *Nor he who does not love his brother.* Transition to the next unit, 3:11-24, the test of love.

11 For this is the message which you have heard from the beginning, that we should love one another, 12 and not be like Cain who was of the evil one and murdered his brother. And why did he murder him? Because his own deeds were evil and his brother's righteous. 13 Do not wonder, brethren, that the world hates you. 14 We know that we have passed out of death into life, because we love the brethren. He who does not love abides in death. 15Any one who hates his brother is a murderer, and you know that no murderer has eternal life abiding in him. 16 By this we know love, that he laid down his life for us; and we ought to lay down our lives for the brethren. 17 But if any one has the world's goods and sees his brother in need, yet closes his heart against him, how does God's love abide in him? 18 Little children, let us not love in word or speech but in deed and in truth.

19 By this we shall know that we are of the truth, and reassure our hearts before him 20 whenever our hearts condemn us; for God is greater than our hearts, and he knows everything. 21 Beloved, if our hearts do not condemn us, we have confidence before God; 22 and we receive from him whatever we ask, because we keep his commandments and do what pleases him. 23And this is his commandment, that we should believe in the name of his Son Jesus Christ and love one another, just as he has commanded us. 24All who keep his commandments abide in him, and he in them. And by this we know that he abides in us, by the Spirit which he has given us.

4 Beloved, do not believe every spirit, but test the spirits to see whether they are of God; for many false prophets have gone out into the world. 2 By this you know the Spirit of God: every spirit which confesses that Jesus Christ has come in the flesh is of God, 3 and every spirit which does not confess Jesus is not of God. This is the

3:11-24 THE TEST OF LOVE

3:11-24 The Son of God *laid down his life for us* (16); thereby He laid upon all sons of God His commandment that they *should love one another* (11). To believe in the name of God's Son and to love one another as sons of God, these two cannot be separated from each other. To hate, as Cain hated, is to be a murderer and a child of the devil and to abide in death. To love, as Christ loved, in deed and in truth, is to be a child of God, with a child's confidence before God, the assurance of being heard by Him.

3:11 *Message.* The commandment is so organically connected with the Gospel message that it can be called by the same name. Cf. 23, where "commandment" is used to cover both faith and love.

3:12 *Cain.* Gn 4:7-8 *Why? . . . his own deeds were evil.* It is characteristic of the evildoer that he hates the light and all who walk in the light. (Cf. 13 and Jn 3:20)

3:14 Cf. Jn 5:24. *Because* introduces the reason why *we know,* not why *we have passed out of death.*

3:15 Hates . . . murderer. Cf. Mt 5:21-22.

3:19-20 *By this,* by loving in deed and truth (18) and so having God's love abiding in us (17), *we shall* know that *the truth* which sets men free from sin and self (cf. Jn 8:32) has sway over us and determines our actions. Then the accusation of our consciences (*hearts,* 19, 20) will fall silent before the testimony of our deeds and, much more, before the mightier testimony of our God, whose love lives in our hearts. In that love He is mightier (*greater*) than our faltering human hearts; that love is the awesome love of the God who forgives (Ps 130:4), the love of Him who says, "I will not

execute my fierce anger . . . FOR I am God and not man, the Holy One in your midst" (Hos 11:9), the love whose measure our hearts cannot take. (Ro 5:6-8)

3:20 *He knows everything.* Cf. Mt 25:31-45, where the Son of Man, as divine Judge, knows and values deeds of love which those who did them would not dare to plead in their own behalf.

3:24 *The Spirit.* The mention of the Spirit serves a twofold function. It makes clear that our assured consciousness of God's love in our lives is not our own subjective mood-making but God's own work; and it provides a transition to 4:1-6, with its antithesis between "the Spirit of God and . . . the spirit of antichrist." (2, 3)

4:1-6 THE TEST OF TRUE BELIEF

4:1-6 God's final revelation has been the Word made flesh (4:2; cf. 1:1-4; Jn 1:14). This revelation has drawn the line of division between children of God and the world. Christ and Antichrist, true prophecy and false prophecy, the Spirit of truth and the spirit of error, the Spirit of God and the spirit of Antichrist, these confront one another in absolute antithesis. The test of true belief is therefore clear and simple; whether or not a man believes the final Word of God as God has spoken it, as the Word spoken *in the flesh* (4:2), determines whether a man is a child of God. (Cf. 2:18-27)

4:1 *Test the spirits.* Since both true and *false prophets* claim the inspiration of the Spirit for their utterances, the church must weigh and test their utterances, especially where errorists lay claim to a higher "spirituality" as they did and do. (Cf. 1 Th 5:19-21; 1 Co 12:10; 14:29; 1 Ti 4:1)

4:3 *Jesus,* the human historical figure, "flesh."

spirit of antichrist, of which you heard that it was coming, and now it is in the world already. 4 Little children, you are of God, and have overcome them; for he who is in you is greater than he who is in the world. 5 They are of the world, therefore what they say is of the world, and the world listens to them. 6 We are of God. Whoever knows God listens to us, and he who is not of God does not listen to us. By this we know the spirit of truth and the spirit of error.

THE THIRD STANDARD (4:7–5:12)

7 Beloved, let us love one another; for love is of God, and he who loves is born of God and knows God. 8 He who does not love does not know God; for God is love. 9 In this the love of God was made manifest among us, that God sent his only Son into the world, so that we might live through him. 10 In this is love, not that we loved God but that he loved us and sent his Son to be the expiation for our sins. 11 Beloved, if God so loved us, we also ought to love one another. 12 No man has ever seen God; if we love one another, God abides in us and his love is perfected in us.

13 By this we know that we abide in him and he in us, because he has given us of his own Spirit. 14And we have seen and testify that the Father has sent his Son as the Savior of the world. 15 Whoever confesses that Jesus is the Son of God, God abides in him, and he in God. 16 So we know and believe the love God has for us. God is love, and he who abides in love abides in God, and God abides in him. 17 In this is love perfected with us, that we may have confidence for the day of judgment, because as he is so are we in this world. 18 There is no fear in love, but perfect love casts out fear. For fear has to do with punishment, and he who fears is not perfected in love. 19 We love, because he first loved us. 20 If any one says, "I love God," and hates his brother, he is a liar; for he who does not love his brother whom he has seen, cannot[h] love God whom he has not seen. 21And this commandment we have from him, that he who loves God should love his brother also.

[h] Other ancient authorities read *how can he*

4:4 *Have overcome them*, since the Son of God has "overcome the world" (Jn 16:33) and the prince of this world. (3:8; cf. Jn 12:31; 14:30; 16:11)

4:5 *Of the world*. They partake of the nature of the world in its estrangement from and opposition to God, think its thoughts, and speak its language; they are in tune with the times. (Cf. Jn 15:19)

4:7–5:12 *God is love* (4:8). The three tests (of righteousness, love, and true belief) recur in this section but not in the same order as in the first and second. Rather, the idea that all three are related and inseparable is stressed; therefore the three tests in this section interlock and overlap. The test of love is clearly seen in 4:7-12, 16-21; the test of righteousness in 5:1-5; the test of true belief in 4:13-15; 5:6-12.

4:7-12 THE TEST OF LOVE (Cf. 2:7-17; 3:11-24)

4:7 *Love one another*. The emphasis here, as throughout the letter, is on the mutual love of brothers within the church. This emphasis is dictated by the situation of the church; a church which has passed through a life-or-death struggle for the truth and has been hurt and shaken by the departure from its ranks of men once cherished as brothers in the faith (2:19) is in grave danger of settling into cold distrust, abandoning the love which it had at first (Rv 2:4; cf. Mt 24:12). It is clear that this fraternal love is not thought of as

excluding universal love; if it did, the love of God for the world (9) could not serve as the exemplar and source of this love. Cf. also Jn 13:35, where the love of the disciples for one another is portrayed as their witness to all men.

4:12 *No man has ever seen God*. This thought comes in somewhat abruptly here; its place in the argument is made clear in 20.

4:13-15 THE TEST OF TRUE BELIEF (Cf. 2:18-27; 4:1-6)

4:13 *Spirit*. For the connection between the Spirit and true belief cf. 4:1-2 and Jn 14:26; 15:26-27; 16:7-15; note the designation "Spirit of truth," Jn 14:17; 15:26; 16:13; 1 Jn 4:6; 5:6.

4:16-21 THE TEST OF LOVE

4:16 *So we know and believe*. The unbreakable connection between true belief and love is indicated here.

4:17 *As he is*. He who believes in Jesus is like Him in that God abides in him and he in God (15); therefore he need not fear the Judgment.

4:18 *Fear* is here not the wholesome fear of mingled awe and obedience (e. g., Ph 2:12), but abject terror at the impending judgment. For *punishment* in connection with the Last Judgment cf. Mt 25:46.

4:21 *Commandment . . . love*. The organic connection between love and righteousness (5:1-5) is indicated.

5 Every one who believes that Jesus is the Christ is a child of God, and every one who loves the parent loves the child. 2 By this we know that we love the children of God, when we love God and obey his commandments. 3 For this is the love of God, that we keep his commandments. And his commandments are not burdensome. 4 For whatever is born of God overcomes the world; and this is the victory that overcomes the world, our faith. 5 Who is it that overcomes the world but he who believes that Jesus is the Son of God?

6 This is he who came by water and blood, Jesus Christ, not with the water only but with the water and the blood. 7And the Spirit is the witness, because the Spirit is the truth. 8 There are three witnesses, the Spirit, the water, and the blood; and these three agree. 9 If we receive the testimony of men, the testimony of God is greater; for this is the testimony of God that he has borne witness to his Son. 10 He who believes in the Son of God has the testimony in himself. He who does not believe God has made him a liar, because he has not believed in the testimony that God has borne to his Son. 11And this is the testimony, that God gave us eternal life, and this life is in his Son. 12 He who has the Son has life; he who has not the Son of God has not life.

CONCLUSION (5:13-21)

13 I write this to you who believe in the name of the Son of God, that you may know that you have eternal life. 14And this is the confidence which we have in him, that if we ask anything according to his will he hears us. 15And if we know that he hears us in whatever we ask, we know that we have obtained the requests made of him. 16 If any one sees his brother committing what is not a mortal sin, he will ask, and God*i* will give him life for those whose sin is not mortal. There is sin which is mortal;

i Greek *he*

5:1-5 THE TEST OF RIGHTEOUSNESS
(Cf. 2:18-27; 4:1-6)

5:1-2 *Believes . . . loves . . . obey his commandments.* Here the interconnection of true belief, love, and righteousness is made clear.

5:3 *Commandments are not burdensome.* Cf. Mt 11:30. Not because they are easy to fulfill, but because the child of God has been given the power to fulfill them. (4)

5:4-5 *Whatever is born of God.* Referring both to Jesus Christ and to all who become children of God by *faith* in Him (cf. 5). By faith in Him they enter into His victory over the *world* (Jn 16:33), over the spell cast by the world's lust and pride (2:16), and over the Evil One who rules in the world. (5:19)

5:5 Again the close connection between righteousness and true belief *(believes)* is indicated.

5:6-12 THE TEST OF TRUE BELIEF

5:6 *By water and blood.* For the connection between this statement and the heresy of Cerinthus see the Introduction. The Son of God has overcome the world by identifying Himself with man in the whole compass of His mission, from His baptism *(water)*, the beginning of His public ministry, to His death on the cross *(blood)*; therefore His resurrection is the resurrection of man, eternal life for man.

5:7 *Spirit is the truth.* Just as Jesus can speak of Himself as the truth (Jn 14:6), so the Spirit who glorifies Him (Jn 16:14) by His witness can be called the truth.

5:8 *Three witnesses, the Spirit, the water, and the blood.* The historical facts as interpreted by the Spirit; this describes the four gospels and for that matter the whole of the NT witness to Jesus, the Son of God. *And these three agree.* The Spirit works with the facts and holds men to the facts; there is no Christian "spirituality" which can ignore them. (Cf. 4:2-3)

5:9 *Testimony of men,* according to the law that demands "two or three witnesses." (Dt 19:15)

5:10 *Has the testimony in himself,* by the operation of the Spirit, concerning whom Jesus gave the promise, "He will be in you." (Jn 14:17)

5:13-21 Like the gospel (Jn 20:31), 1 John closes with a statement of purpose (13), which is followed by a postscript. (14-21; cf. Jn 21)

5:14-17 These verses reiterate the assurance of 3:21-22 that prayer is heard. The assurance here is even stronger (15) and is directed specifically to intercession for an erring brother. But the assurance and promise is restricted to intercessions *for those whose sin is not mortal* (16). *Mortal sin* is not defined, but the context of the letter suggests that the sin of the false teachers and their followers is meant. The question would naturally arise in the church: May we still intercede for those who have gone out from us, for men who have broken our sacred fellowship, who have resisted the witness of the Spirit (5:7), despised the blood that atones for us (5:6; cf. Heb 10:29), given themselves to the spirit of Antichrist and error (4:3-4)? Is prayer for them still a prayer according to God's will (5:14)? Is not their sin the unforgivable blasphemy against the Spirit of which Jesus warned (Mt

I do not say that one is to pray for that. [17]All wrongdoing is sin, but there is sin which is not mortal.

18 We know that any one born of God does not sin, but He who was born of God keeps him, and the evil one does not touch him.

19 We know that we are of God, and the whole world is in the power of the evil one.

20 And we know that the Son of God has come and has given us understanding, to know him who is true; and we are in him who is true, in his Son Jesus Christ. This is the true God and eternal life. [21] Little children, keep yourselves from idols.

12:31), and have they not removed themselves from the sphere and power of Christian intercession for the sinner, which always presupposes that repentance is still possible, as it is necessary? John's answer is marked by great reserve; he will not command such intercession. But he does not forbid it and gives no simple rule to be mechanically applied (and misused); each renewed Christian mind must in each case "provide what is the will of God, what is good and acceptable and perfect." (Ro 12:2)

5:18-21 Amid the doubt which successful heresy can raise and amid the hurt which the departure of men who once were brothers in the faith inflicts on men whose faith lives in love, even amid these the church can remain unshaken and unafraid. For the church is certain that those born of God will be preserved from *sin* and the *evil one* (18), certain that there can be no compromise between the church and the world (19), certain that in the Son of God she has the true revelation of God and eternal life, for Jesus Christ *is the true God and eternal life* — any worship which excludes Him is idolatry. (20-21)

THE SECOND LETTER OF

JOHN

INTRODUCTION

The Second Letter of John is addressed
by one who calls himself simply "the elder"
to "the elect lady and her children" (v. 1).
This is probably a figurative way of addressing a church (the word for church is feminine
in Greek), rather than a literal address to
some Christian woman and her children. The
very broad statement of the salutation,
"whom I love in the truth, and not only I
but also all who know the truth" (v. 1) is
more suitable to a church than to an individual. The expression in v. 4, "I rejoiced
greatly to find some of your children following the truth," is most naturally understood
of a church, some of whose members had resisted the inroads of the heresy which was
then ravaging the church of Asia Minor. The
greeting of v. 13, "The children of your elect
sister greet you," also seems to be more
naturally taken as a greeting from a sister
church in whose midst the elder is writing.
And finally, the content of the letter (the
renewal of the commandment of love and a
stern warning against false teachers) seems
eminently suitable as a message to a church.
Besides, if the "elect lady" is an individual.
why is she not named, as Gaius is named in
Third John?

The letter was occasioned by the activity of
false teachers, most probably the same group
that John dealt with in his first letter. There
is the same emphasis on the commandment
of love (5-6), the same emphasis on the reality of the incarnation of the Son of God (His
"coming . . . in the flesh," 7), the same designation of the false teaching as deceit
and the work of the "antichrist" (7), the same
insistence on the fact that no one can know
the Father except through the incarnate
Son (9). The letter contains one of the
sternest warnings in the New Testament
against participating in or furthering the
activities of those who pervert the Gospel
(10-11). It is this furthering of the work of
the false teachers that is referred to, of
course, in the words, "Do not receive him
into the house or give him any greeting"
(10); evangelists were dependent on the
hospitality of Christians as they moved from
place to place, as Third John shows; they had
no missionary fund to draw on.

The second letter is probably to be dated
about the same time as the first. The designation "elder" would seem to indicate
that John had outlived his generation and
had become the grand old man of the church
in Asia Minor.

THE SECOND LETTER OF

JOHN

1 The elder to the elect lady and her children, whom I love in the truth, and not only I but also all who know the truth, 2 because of the truth which abides in us and will be with us for ever:

3 Grace, mercy, and peace will be with us, from God the Father and from Jesus Christ the Father's Son, in truth and love.

4 I rejoiced greatly to find some of your children following the truth, just as we have been commanded by the Father. 5And now I beg you, lady, not as though I were writing you a new commandment, but the one we have had from the beginning, that we love one another. 6And this is love, that we follow his commandments; this is the commandment, as you have heard from the beginning, that you follow love. 7 For many deceivers have gone out into the world, men who will not acknowledge the coming of Jesus Christ in the flesh; such a one is the deceiver and the antichrist. 8 Look to yourselves, that you may not lose what you*a* have worked for, but may win a full reward. 9Any one who goes ahead and does not abide in the doctrine of Christ does not have God; he who abides in the doctrine has both the Father and the Son. 10 If any one comes to you and does not bring this doctrine, do not receive him into the house or give him any greeting; 11 for he who greets him shares his wicked work.

12 Though I have much to write to you, I would rather not use paper and ink, but I hope to come to see you and talk with you face to face, so that our joy may be complete.

13 The children of your elect sister greet you.

a Other ancient authorities read *we*

1 *The elder.* See Introduction. Some scholars identify the author of 1 and 2 Jn, who calls himself *the elder* (as well as the unnamed author of 1 Jn) with a rather shadowy figure, the elder John, referred to by Papias, a second-century church father of Hierapolis in Asia Minor. But the identification is highly uncertain, and the very existence of this second (elder) John is questionable.

Truth is used in the comprehensive and dynamic sense familiar to us from the fourth gospel (e.g., Jn 1:17; 8:32; 14:6) and 1 Jn (e.g., 1:6, 8; 3:19) both here and in 2 and 4. Truth is, practically, all that Jesus Christ is, does, and signifies for man; truth is therefore not only known but followed (4) and done. (Jn 3:21; 1 Jn 1:6)

4-11 The letter to Ephesus (Rv 2:1-7, the church which in its honest zeal for purity of teaching "abandoned the love it had at first," illustrated the necessity of combining the commandment of love with the warning against false teaching.

7 Cf 1 Jn 2:22

8 *What you have worked for.* The elder is concerned lest all the God-given energies with which they have "worked out their salvation with fear and trembling" (Ph 2:12) should have been expended in vain, that all the "toil and patient endurance" (Rv 2:2) with which they have combated error and clung to the truth should fail of the *full reward* which is promised to the faithful. (Cf. Rv 2:7, 10-11, 26-28; 3:5, 12, 21)

9 *Who goes ahead.* Progress *in the doctrine of Christ* is essential (cf. 1 Ptr 2:2); a supposed "progress" beyond Him who is God's final and definitive Word (Heb 1:1) is fatal pride and deadly error.

12 *Joy.* Cf. 1 Jn 1:4; Jn 15:11.

501

JOHN

INTRODUCTION

The Third Letter of John gives us another glimpse into the apostolic activity of John in his latter years. If the first and second letters dealt with heresy, the third letter deals with a missionary problem. The recipient of the letter, "the beloved Gaius," had distinguished himself by his loyal support of some traveling evangelists (5-8). These evangelists had meanwhile reported to their home church, probably at Ephesus, and had there testified to the love which Gaius had shown them (6). He had done so in the face of grave difficulties; a certain Diotrephes had sought, and was at the time of writing still seeking, to put himself in control of the church to which Gaius belonged and had refused to welcome the missionary brethren. He went even farther than that and sought to stop those who wished to receive the missionaries and "put them out of the church" (9-10). In so doing he was consciously opposing the elder himself. (9)

Content of Third John

John in his letter warmly commends Gaius, who has by his support of the missionaries shown himself as a "fellow worker in the truth" (8); at the same time he commends to Gaius the bearer of the letter, Demetrius, who is probably the leader of a group of evangelists (12). Since a letter to the church dominated by Diotrephes has not had the desired effect, John promises to come himself and to deal with Diotrephes and to put an end to his malicious "prating." (9-10)

When the Lord called Paul to be His apostle, He said, "I will show him how much he must suffer for the sake of my name" (Acts 9:16). What the Lord said of Paul held for all the apostles; they remained servants and sufferers to the end. John never became his serene highness, the lord of the church of Asia; he remained the apostle of the Crucified, with no power but that of the Word with which he was entrusted, the contradictable Word of the Gospel. He lived and worked "in honor and dishonor, in ill repute and good repute" (2 Co 6:8). The New Testament has preserved the record of the apostle's dishonor too; these things are written for the apostolic church and for our learning.

The third letter probably dates from the same period as the first and second letters. Some scholars think that the letter to the church referred to in v. 9 may be our Second John. This cannot be either proved or disproved.

THE THIRD LETTER OF

JOHN

1 The elder to the beloved Gaius, whom I love in the truth.

2 Beloved, I pray that all may go well with you and that you may be in health; I know that it is well with your soul. 3 For I greatly rejoiced when some of the brethren arrived and testified to the truth of your life, as indeed you do follow the truth. 4 No greater joy can I have than this, to hear that my children follow the truth.

5 Beloved, it is a loyal thing you do when you render any service to the brethren, especially to strangers, 6 who have testified to your love before the church. You will do well to send them on their journey as befits God's service. 7 For they have set out for his sake and have accepted nothing from the heathen. 8 So we ought to support such men, that we may be fellow workers in the truth.

9 I have written something to the church; but Di·ot're·phes, who likes to put himself first, does not acknowledge my authority. 10 So if I come, I will bring up what he is doing, prating against me with evil words. And not content with that, he refuses himself to welcome the brethren, and also stops those who want to welcome them and puts them out of the church.

11 Beloved, do not imitate evil but imitate good. He who does good is of God; he who does evil has not seen God. 12 De·me'tri·us has testimony from every one, and from the truth itself; I testify to him too, and you know my testimony is true.

13 I had much to write to you, but I would rather not write with pen and ink; 14 I hope to see you soon, and we will talk together face to face.

15 Peace be to you. The friends greet you. Greet the friends, every one of them.

1 *Gaius* was a very common Roman name. This Gaius cannot be identified with others of the same name mentioned in the NT. (Acts 19:29; 20:4; Ro 16:23; 1 Co 1:14)

3 *The truth of your life,* literally "your truth." He *follows the truth* so wholeheartedly that his life has become a document in which the truth is inscribed for all men to read.

6 *Send . . . on their journey.* This term seems to have become almost technical as a designation for the furtherance and support of missionaries.

(Acts 15:3; Ro 15:24; 1 Co 16:6; Tts 3:13)

12 *Demetrius.* See the Introduction.

From the truth itself. This probably means that some Christian prophet, impelled by the Spirit of *truth,* marked Demetrius out for his missionary task. Cf. Acts 13:2, where the Holy Spirit so designates Barnabas and Saul.

15 *Friends.* Found only here as an expression of Christian solidarity ("brothers" being the common term): perhaps a reminiscence of Jesus' use of "friends." (Jn 15:13-15; cf. Lk 12:4)

THE LETTER OF
JUDE

INTRODUCTION

The author, "Jude. a servant of Jesus Christ and brother of James" (1), is probably the brother of our Lord, mentioned together with James in Mk 6:3 and Mt 13:55. James, the brother of our Lord and head of the Jerusalem church, was probably the only James (after the early death of the apostle James, the Son of Zebedee) prominent enough to serve as identification; and the brothers of Jesus, James and Jude, are the only *pair* of brothers bearing those names that we know from New Testament times. Jude can hardly be the apostle of that name; aside from the fact that he does not designate himself as apostle, the manner in which he speaks of the apostles in v. 17 makes it clear that he does not claim to be one of them. One may wonder why he does not call himself "brother of Jesus"; but the brothers of Jesus remembered their Brother's word: "Whoever does the will of my Father in heaven is my brother" (Mt 12:50); they knew that faith alone establishes the tie which binds a man to Jesus and makes him an obedient son of God.

The Letter of Jude was occasioned by the appearance and activity of men who answered Paul's question, "Are we to continue in sin that grace may abound?" (Ro 6:1) in a way that was the very opposite of Paul's. They saw in the freedom which Christ had won for men not a liberation from sin but the liberty to sin. They perverted the free grace of God into licentiousness, thus denying their Master and Lord (4), who bade men follow Him in purity of heart. Moreover, they proclaimed this ungodly liberty quite openly, even arrogantly (8, 13, 16, 19). Far from breaking with the church, they carried on their propaganda within it; having "gained admission secretly" (4), they joined in the fellowship of the common meal (12) and created divisions *within* the church with their teachings (19). For teachers they evidently were, or claimed to be; Jude calls them clouds, from which men expect water (12); the church evidently was led to expect refreshment and life from their

words. Jude does not deign to enter into a discussion of whatever system of teaching these men may have used to support their distorted conception of Christian liberty; he speaks of their "dreamings" (8), which would seem to indicate that they were speculative in their theology, or perhaps appealed to a special revelation by visions to support their claims. Jude centers his attack on the impiety of these "ungodly persons" (4); he is following the guidance of Jesus, who told His disciples, "You will know them by their fruits" (Mt 7:16). He points to the evil fruits of this bad tree; the vehemence with which he does so is an indication that these were persuasive and impressive men, all the more dangerous to the church because they would not break with the church whose Lord they denied (4). Jude therefore insists that the church break with them. He rouses holy fear in his readers as he calls on them to do battle for "the faith," for all that their Lord and His apostle had given them (3). They are to avoid all contact and compromise with the false teachers lest they fall under the fearful judgment of God which they know so well from their Old Testament; for that judgment will surely destroy these destroyers of the church of God (5-7; cf. 13-15). Even the attempt to save those brethren who are wavering between the new error and the old truth is to be made in this holy fear: "Have mercy with fear." (23)

But fear is not Jude's only resource; he also instills the high confidence of faith. His readers know from the ancient word of Enoch and from the apostolic Word of these last days (14-15; 17-18) that these arrogant, contentious, and mercenary blasphemers are doomed; they will perish in their pride (4, 11, 14-15). And, above all, the church is secure in the love of God which will preserve her for "Jesus Christ" (1) when He returns. And so the letter closes with a doxology filled with the exuberant confidence of hope. (24-25)

Jesus gave His disciples only one simple

test by which to distinguish false prophets from true prophets: "You will know them by their fruits" (Mt 7:16). The test seems almost absurdly simple when one considers the history of error in the church, error in its ever-new and plausible disguises. But this little, powerful Letter of Jude is living proof that Jesus' confidence in His followers was not misplaced. Endowed with the Spirit of Jesus, Jude rightly saw and soundly declared that what these ungodly men were producing as the newest theology in A. D. 70—80 was not a fruit of the Spirit. The church was greatly aided by Jude's word in her second-century struggle with the Gnostic heresy. Our own century is evidence that the impulse to pervert the grace of God into licentiousness is a perennial plant which must be eradicated ever and again. The church will find in Jude an honest gardener to help her in this painful but necessary task.

JUDE

1 Jude, a servant of Jesus Christ and brother of James,
To those who are called, beloved in God the Father and kept for Jesus Christ:
2 May mercy, peace, and love be multiplied to you.

3 Beloved, being very eager to write to you of our common salvation, I found it necessary to write appealing to you to contend for the faith which was once for all delivered to the saints. 4 For admission has been secretly gained by some who long ago were designated for this condemnation, ungodly persons who pervert the grace of our God into licentiousness and deny our only Master and Lord, Jesus Christ.*a*

5 Now I desire to remind you, though you were once for all fully informed, that he*b* who saved a people out of the land of Egypt, afterward destroyed those who did not believe. 6And the angels that did not keep their own position but left their proper dwelling have been kept by him in eternal chains in the nether gloom until the judgment of the great day; 7 just as Sodom and Go·mor′rah and the surrounding cities,

a Or *the only Master and our Lord Jesus Christ*
b Ancient authorities read *Jesus* or *the Lord* or *God*

1-2 THE SALUTATION: ASSURANCE
IN THE FACE OF THREATENING EVIL

1-2 There is a strong note of assurance in both the description of the persons addressed (1) and the greeting (2). The struggle to which Jude calls them (3) need not terrify them. The eternal love of God has effectually reached them in His call (cf. Ro 8:28-30); it is now their safe abode, and by it they will be *kept for Jesus Christ,* that is, for the day when He returns to judge mankind and to gather in His own. Compare Paul's prayer in 1 Th 3:11-13 and 5:23-24.

1 The description of the persons addressed is so general that we can do little more than guess who the readers were or where they were situated. According to Paul (1 Co 9:5) the brothers of Jesus were active in missionary work, and we may imagine that the persons addressed are a congregation or a group of congregations founded by Jude himself; he knows their situation and feels a pastoral responsibility for them.

2 "To him who has will more be given" (Mt 13:12). The *mercy, peace, and love* of God which is theirs as men called by Him will be theirs in increasing measure. "But from him who has not, even what he has will be taken away" (Mt 13:12); they can lose these blessings if they will not face and fight the evil that has crept into their midst. It is this evil that Jude unmasks and describes in the body of his letter.

3-4 THE EVIL UNMASKED

3-4 The evil is a radical one, a threat to the very roots of the Christian existence: *our common salvation, the faith which was once for all delivered to the saints, the grace of our God, our only Master and Lord, Jesus Christ.* The danger is all the greater for being as yet an unperceived danger; it

has crept into the church *secretly* in a Christian guise.

3 No Christian teacher has a natural taste for controversy; he is forced into it by his concern and responsibility for *our common salvation.*

The *faith . . . delivered to the saints* is the creed which contains and conveys the interpreted facts that are the substance of belief. We may think of such early catechetical summaries of apostolic teaching as the one cited by Paul in 1 Co 15:3-11 and the materials which we now have in the four gospels. That the OT too constituted an integral and authoritative part of this *faith* is shown by the Letter of Jude itself and by the whole NT. Since God's act in Christ is His final Word (Heb 1:1-2), the *faith* is delivered *once for all;* there is no going beyond it. (Cf. 2 Jn 9)

4 *Long ago . . . designated,* by ancient prophecy (14-15) and the predictions of the apostles. (17)

5-16 THE EVIL DESCRIBED AND JUDGED

5-7 Jude draws on the faith once for all delivered to the saints, on the OT, to remind his readers of God's unsparing judgment on unbelief and disobedience such as confronts the church in the teaching of these ungodly persons (4). The judgment strikes and dooms all evil, whether it be the unbelief of Israel in the wilderness (5), the disobedience of angels (6), or the flagrant and perverse immorality of Sodom and Gomorrah. (7)

5 Cf. Nm 14, especially v. 11, for the unbelief of the people. For a similar use of Israel's infidelity as a warning to the church cf. 1 Co 10: 1-13; Heb 3:7 — 4:11.

6 For the mysterious story of the angels who *left their proper dwelling* see Gn 6:1-4.

7 See Gn 19. Gn 19:5 is the background of our ugly word "sodomy."

which likewise acted immorally and indulged in unnatural lust, serve as an example by undergoing a punishment of eternal fire.

8. Yet in like manner these men in their dreamings defile the flesh, reject authority, and revile the glorious ones.[c] 9 But when the archangel Michael, contending with the devil, disputed about the body of Moses, he did not presume to pronounce a reviling judgment upon him, but said, "The Lord rebuke you." 10 But these men revile whatever they do not understand, and by those things that they know by instinct as irrational animals do, they are destroyed. 11 Woe to them! For they walk in the way of Cain, and abandon themselves for the sake of gain to Ba'laam's error, and perish in Korah's rebellion. 12 These are blemishes[d] on your love feasts, as they boldly carouse together, looking after themselves; waterless clouds, carried along by winds; fruitless trees in late autumn, twice dead, uprooted; 13 wild waves of the sea, casting up the foam of their own shame; wandering stars for whom the nether gloom of darkness has been reserved for ever.

[c] Greek glories   [d] Or reefs

8-13 Undeterred by these warnings from the past (yet, v. 8), these godless persons go their arrogant way, defying all authority (8), unwilling to leave judgment to God, as even the archangel Michael did (9), but arrogating it to themselves (10). There is to the eye of faith something bestial in the way they rush into their own destruction (10), pursuing the way of the killer Cain, the mercenary prophet Balaam, and the rebel Korah (11). Such they are to the forewarned eye of faith. On the surface they do not look so horrible as all that; they take part in the fellowship of the church's love feasts, the common meal sometimes associated with the celebration of the Lord's Supper (12), as all good churchmen do. But this deceptive appearance need deceive no one: their participation in the common meal, designed to be an expression of selfless mutual love, is just another coarse expression of their self-centered arrogance, of a piece with their demeanor as teachers who promise much but give nothing, like waterless clouds (12) that give no rain, trees that yield not fruit (12) or stars (13) that give the sailor no guidance. Inconstant as waves of the sea, shameless in their shame, they invite the judgment of God. (13)

8 The false teachers defile the flesh by their sexual license. For a similar example of "spiritual" emancipation (based on the false idea that Spirit and flesh have nothing to do with each other) and for Paul's judgment upon it cf. 1 Co 6:12-20. They reject authority when they deny Jesus Christ as their only Master and Lord (cf. 4). They are willing to accept Christ as Liberator and Giver of the Spirit but will not accept Him as the Lord who said, "TEACH them to observe all that I have commanded you" (Mt 28:20). In so doing they withdraw from the authority of His apostles (cf. 17) and of the OT too. They revile the glorious ones, the angels, messengers and ministers of God, guardians and preservers of God's order in the world. Perhaps Jude is recalling the word of Jesus in Mt 18:10, where He speaks of the angels of the "little ones" (those who need the help and guidance of the church) as having constant access to God;

this word is part of Jesus' warning to those who despise these little ones and cause them to sin (cf. Mt 18:5-9). When the false teachers try to mislead unwary, simple Christians, they are flouting the authority of the angels whom God has given for their protection.

9 The false teachers have less awe for the judgment of God than the angels themselves. Even the archangel Michael, in his contention with the devil, remembered the word of God which said, "Vengeance is mine, I will repay, says the Lord" (Ro 12:19: Dt 32:35). The phrase The Lord rebuke you occurs in Zch 3:2 as a rebuke to Satan when he brings his accusation against Joshua the high priest. The story of Michael's contention with Satan for the body of Moses is, according to the witness of early church fathers, taken from a work called Assumption of Moses written about A. D. 30, now imperfectly preserved. According to it, Michael was charged with the burial of Moses; Satan claimed the body on the ground that Moses was a murderer, having slain an Egyptian (Ex 2:12). Michael left the judgment to God, who intervened on Moses' behalf.

11 The way of Cain, the murderer of his brother, appears in 1 Jn 3:12 as the very antithesis of the way enjoined by Jesus ("that we should love one another," 1 Jn 3:11). It is therefore a fitting description of the conduct of men who deny our only Master and Lord, Jesus Christ (4), and are blemishes on the love feasts of the followers of Jesus.

Balaam, the prophet hired by Balak to curse Israel (Nm 22 – 24), who for the sake of gain attempted to go against his own inspired convictions, is the prototype of men who claim special revelation ("dreamings," 8) and act from mercenary motives (16). It was also the counsel of Balaam which misled Israel into licentious idolatry. (Nm 31:16; 25:1-2; Rv 2:14)

Korah is a striking OT example of those who reject authority (8). He headed a rebellion against the authority of Moses and Aaron and was destroyed by the judgment of God. (Nm 16:1-35)

12 Twice dead, because, once rescued from death by the Gospel (cf. Eph 2:1-10), they have returned

14 It was of these also that Enoch in the seventh generation from Adam prophesied, saying, "Behold, the Lord came with his holy myriads, [15] to execute judgment on all, and to convict all the ungodly of all their deeds of ungodliness which they have committed in such an ungodly way, and of all the harsh things which ungodly sinners have spoken against him." [16] These are grumblers, malcontents, following their own passions, loud-mouthed boasters, flattering people to gain advantage.

17 But you must remember, beloved, the predictions of the apostles of our Lord Jesus Christ; [18] they said to you, "In the last time there will be scoffers, following their own ungodly passions." [19] It is these who set up divisions, worldly people, devoid of the Spirit. [20] But you, beloved, build yourselves up on your most holy faith; pray in the Holy Spirit; [21] keep yourselves in the love of God; wait for the mercy of our Lord Jesus Christ unto eternal life. [22]And convince some, who doubt; [23] save some, by snatching them out of the fire; on some have mercy with fear, hating even the garment spotted by the flesh.[e]

24 Now to him who is able to keep you from falling and to present you without blemish before the presence of his glory with rejoicing, [25] to the only God, our Savior through Jesus Christ our Lord, be glory, majesty, dominion, and authority, before all time and now and for ever. Amen.

[e] The Greek text in this sentence is uncertain at several points

to the old way of sin and death (cf. 2 Ptr 2:21). For *uprooted* as a picture of God's judgment cf. Mt 15:13.

14-16 They have the prophetic word of Enoch against them, these sensual, self-seeking, loud-mouthed men who can never get all they want and all that they think they deserve, for all their brash pushing and contriving. The Lord will convict and condemn them when He appears for judgment.

14-15 The words of Enoch are quoted from the apocryphal Book of Enoch (1:9); its language is echoed also in v. 6. Jude's use of apocryphal books, like Enoch and Assumption of Moses, has troubled some men in both the ancient and the modern church. Unnecessarily, it would seem. The fact that an inspired author uses a story from the Assumption to illustrate a point and cites from Enoch a statement on the divine judgment which echoes many OT passages does not necessarily mean that he regards the whole books, with all their strange and bizarre features, as authoritative and inspired. Paul quotes even pagan writers with approval (e. g., Menander in 1 Co 15:33 and Epimenides in Tts 1:12) to make a point.

17-23 THE DEFENSE AGAINST THE EVIL

17-23 The men called by God and kept for Jesus Christ (1) are not without defense. They have the apostolic Word and face the evil forewarned and open-eyed (17-18); they have the *faith* once and for all delivered to them as the firm foundation on which their house of life may be built (20); they have the Spirit to inform their prayers (20); they have the love of God to sustain them in the bright hope of the return of their Lord, the hope of eternal life (21). Thus furnished for defense, they need not fall prey to the sectarian divisions produced by worldly, unspiritual men (19); they can even take the offensive and undo, in pure mercy and holy fear, at least some of the

evil these ungodly persons have produced. (22-23)

17-18 The *predictions of the apostles* quoted in the following verse are not found in exactly that form in any of the apostolic writings. The quotation reflects such passages as Acts 20:29-30; 1 Ti 4:1 ff.; 2 Ti 3:1 ff.; 2 Ptr 3:3; cf. 1 Jn 2:18-23; 4:1-3.

19-21 The *most holy faith* is inviolable: no one dare lay profane hands on it, for the whole majesty of the Trinity is contained in it *(Spirit, God, Lord Jesus Christ)*.

20 *Pray in the Holy Spirit.* Cf. Ro 8:15-16, 26-27; Eph 6:18.

21 For *mercy* in the Last Judgment cf. 2 Ti 1:18, Ja 2:13. Jesus promised mercy in the Judgment to the merciful (Mt 5:7; cf. 25:31-45). The latter part of the verse therefore leads directly to the admonition of vv. 22-23, to deal mercifully with those entangled in the lies of the libertine teachers.

23 The *fire* from which the faithful Christians are to snatch their erring brothers is the fire of God's judgment that is threatening to destroy them (cf. Am 4:11; Zch 3:2). *The garment spotted by the flesh* is a strong expression to indicate that even the slightest contact, even an apparently external contact, is to be avoided.

24-25 DOXOLOGY: CONFIDENCE OF VICTORY OVER EVIL

24-25 The closing doxology repeats and intensifies the note of assurance with which the letter began. The church has good reason to fear (cf. 23); she has no reason to despair. There is One who has the power to bring her safely and triumphantly through all the temptations that beset her into His glorious presence at the Judgment, the Savior God whose eternal glory, majesty, dominion, and authority are all in the service of His mercy, which shall pronounce her blameless on that day. She shall hear Jesus Christ her Lord say, "Come unto Me!"

THE

REVELATION TO JOHN

(The Apocalypse)

INTRODUCTION

Occasion and Purpose

Revelation is, in form, a letter addressed to seven churches in the Roman province of Asia (Rv 1:4), complete with salutation and closing benediction (Rv 1:4; 22:21). The situation which called forth the writing is made clear by the writing itself: the churches are being troubled by false teachers (Rv 2:6, 14-15), slandered and harassed by Jews, the "synagogue of Satan" (Rv 2:9; 3:9), and are undergoing a persecution (Rv 1:9) which has already cost the lives of some faithful witnesses (Rv 2:13; 6:9-10) but has not yet reached its height (Rv 6:11). To these churches John, himself in banishment on the island of Patmos "on account of the word of God and the testimony of Jesus" (Rv 1:9), writes the account of the visions given to him there, the record of "the revelation of Jesus Christ, which God gave him to show to his servants" (Rv 1:1). He writes in order to strengthen them in their trials, both internal and external, to hold before them the greatness and the certitude of their hope in Christ, and to assure them of their victory, with Christ, over all the powers of evil now let loose on the world and, to all appearances, destined to triumph on earth. The book is thoroughly practical, like all the books of the New Testament, designed to be read in the worship services of the churches, as the first of the seven beatitudes which the book pronounces shows: "Blessed is he who reads aloud the words of the prophecy, and blessed are those who hear, and who keep what is written therein; for the time is near." (Rv 1:3)

Time and Place of Writing

Irenaeus' statement (*Adv. Haer.* V, 30, 3) that Revelation was written toward the close of the reign of the emperor Domitian (A. D. 81−96) gives us the most probable date for the book, A. D. 95 or 96. Domitian was the first Roman emperor to make an issue of emperor worship; and since the emperor cult was propagated with great zeal in the province of Asia, the collision between the emperor who laid claim to men's worship as "Lord and God" and those who would call no one Lord but Jesus and would worship Him alone proved to be inevitable in Asia. That John should have been banished from Ephesus to Patmos, off the coast of Asia, "on account of the word of God and the testimony of Jesus" (Rv 1:9), that Antipas should have died a martyr's death at Pergamum in Asia (Rv 2:13), that the souls of men who had been slain for the witness they had borne should cry aloud for vindication (Rv 6:9-10)−all this fits in naturally with the historical situation in Asia in the latter years of Domitian's reign. The payment of divine honors to the emperor was made the test of loyalty; the Christian had to refuse, and that refusal made him liable to the penalty of death. The visions given to John made it unmistakably plain to the churches why the Christian had to refuse and die; and these visions wrote out in letters of gold and fire the promise that such dying was not defeat but triumph, a triumph which man shared with the Lamb that was slain, with Him who is King of kings and Lord of lords, whose people go His way through death to victory and royal reign.

The Literary Form of the Book

Revelation, with its visions of riders, trumpets, and bowls, of dragon and beasts, its use of number symbolism, and its mysterious and suggestive style generally, strikes the modern reader as strange and bizarre, and he is inclined to agree with Luther when he says, "My spirit cannot adapt itself to this book." Much in the book that puzzles us today was familiar to John's first readers; much that we can gain access to only by laborious study and by a gradual process of sympathetic immersion into this alien world spoke directly to them. They had been familiarized with the imagery of John's vision by a form of Judaic religious literature known as "apocalyptic." Apoc-

alyptic elaborated certain elements or aspects of Old Testament prophecy found in such passages and books as Isaiah 24–27, Zechariah 9–14, Ezekiel, Joel, and Daniel. It sought to interpret all history on the basis of purported visionary experiences of the author. It was especially interested in eschatology, that is, in the end of history and the ushering in of the world to come. It utilized pictures, allegories, and symbols (which soon became traditional); numbers, colors, and stars were in these images endowed with a profound significance. Books of this type were the Book of Enoch, the Book of Jubilees, Fourth Esdras, and Assumption of Moses.

Formally, Revelation belongs to this class; apocalyptic, as it were, furnished the familiar vocabulary of its speech. But Revelation is set apart from the general run of apocalyptic literature by profound differences. Apocalyptic itself drew heavily on the Old Testament; John draws even more heavily. No other New Testament book can compare with it in the number of allusions to the Old Testament; Revelation is saturated with the Old Testament. In fact, it is the Old Testament itself and not apocalyptic that constitutes the immediate background and the richest source for Revelation. Revelation is at bottom much more deeply akin to the Old Testament than it is to the apocalyptic which it resembles so strongly on the formal side. Other differences are equally striking. Apocalyptic works are generally pseudonymous; that is, they claim some great figure from Israel's past, such as Enoch, as author; and the past course of history as known to the actual author is made a prediction in the mouth of the purported author. John, however, writes in his own name. Apocalyptic has speculative interests and seeks to calculate the times and seasons of the world's last days and the world's end. John has no such speculative interest; he does not aim to satisfy men's curiosity but to give them hope and courage, and he does not attempt to calculate the approach of the end. "I come quickly" is the burden of the revelation of Christ as given to John. The visions of apocalyptic betray their origin; they are the fantasies of men. The visions of John have on them the stamp of genuine visionary experience; they are not products of the study. If apocalyptic may be termed literary meditation on prophetic themes, Revelation is genuine prophecy, a prophecy which uses

apocalyptic motifs and forms insofar and only insofar as they are legitimate explications of Old Testament prophetic themes and are germane to its own thoroughly Christ-centered proclamation. The Lord in speaking through John speaks in the tongues of men; but He does not think the thoughts of men.

The peculiar advantage or virtue of utterance in this form lies not in the precision and clarity with which the utterance can be made, but in the power with which the thing said can be brought to bear on the whole man—on his mind, his imagination, his feelings, his will. His whole inner life is caught up in the moving terror and splendor of these visions; and the course and bent of his life are determined by them as they could hardly be determined by any other kind of communication. But just this characteristic of the book has given rise to widely divergent interpretations of the book; men have attempted, usually in a one-sided fashion, to be more precise in their interpretation of the book than the book itself by its very nature can be. One group of interpreters has fixed on the fact that the visions have their occasion and basis in real historical events and interprets the book wholly in terms of what had already happened at the time of writing; they see no real prediction anywhere in it, but merely an interpretation of past events in the guise of prediction. This, of course, ignores the prophetic claim of the book itself. Others refer everything but the content of the first three chapters to the very end of time, to the period immediately preceding the advent of Christ, and think of it as still awaiting fulfillment. This ignores the fact that for the author himself all time since the ascension of Christ is the time immediately preceding the advent of Christ and makes the book largely irrelevant for the very people for whom it was first written. Others again see in the visions a more or less detailed predictive portrayal of the successive events of universal history or of the history of the church to the end of time; here again one must ask how such a series of predictions was to be of any aid and comfort to the troubled churches of Asia A. D. 95. Still others renounce all attempts to relate the message of the book *directly* to history and see in the visions rather the enunciation of general principles which will hold good throughout history. But the book itself, with its life-and-death involvement in the crisis of A. D.

95, is anything but the enunciation of abstract principles.

Each of these attempts to interpret the book is, in its one-sidedness, a falsification. A true interpretation will, with the first group, look for the roots of the work in the history contemporary with it, for the book was obviously written for the church's encouragement and strengthening at a certain time and place. It will, with the second group, recognize the fact that the prophecy embraces all time between the now of the church and the return of the Lord of the church. It will, with the third group, take seriously the relevance of the book to all history; but it will, with the last group, be inclined to see in it not a blueprint of history but a divine light that strikes history and illumines where it strikes, a pointing finger of God to guide men through history and judgment to the end. If the book is so viewed and so taken to heart, its value for the church and the individual will not depend on the completeness of one's comprehension of every detail of its imagery.

Value of the Book

To men sitting in the quiet of their studies and to the church at peace in the world the Revelation to John presents difficulties and often brings perplexities. Others in the church have used the book to feed their fevered dreams. But the book did not originate as a book to be coolly pondered or as food to feed the dreams of idle men. It is the cry of victory raised for the cause of Christ when His cause seemed doomed — what was this pitifully weak assembly of nobodies to oppose the might of Rome? This book took the word of Jesus, His beatitude upon the persecuted, with absolute seriousness and wrote it into the history of the church when it was clearly becoming a bloody history: "Rejoice and be glad, for your reward is great in heaven!" And so it has happened again and again in the history of the church that when all secular securities were swept away and all human guarantees of triumph were lost, men turned to this book. They turned to this book, which looks with the same unperturbed clarity of vision on the face of Satan and on the face of God and His Anointed and sees written in both the triumph of God and His Christ. Men have turned to this book and have found the strength not only to endure but to sing. The doxologies of the Book of Revelation have echoed in the church most mightily just when men as men could find no cause for songs of praise.

Content of the Revelation to John

Revelation is a carefully constructed and elaborately articulated whole in which the number seven is the dominant unit. An outline such as the following, which views the whole work as a series of seven visions, therefore commends itself as probable. It also seems to be clear that there is a major break between the third and fourth set of visions. This break is constituted not so much by a change of theme as by a change in the vantage point from which the theme is viewed and treated. Important for the understanding of the whole is the observation that each of the units (with the possible exception of the first) spans the whole period between the present and the return of the Lord Jesus, so that we have a set of parallel presentations of the same basic fact and truth, cumulative in effect as each presentation brings in a new aspect of the same basic theme. There is progression in the sense that the end of all things is portrayed with increasing fullness as the visions progress (return of the Lord, last judgment, the new world of God). We have here the same "spiral" thought pattern that is characteristic of the Gospel and the First Letter of John.

OUTLINE

I. 1:1-8 Introduction

II. 1:9 — 11:19 The First Three Visions: The Church of Christ and the Powers of This World

    A. 1:9 — 3:22 First Vision: the Exalted Christ in the Midst of His Church: the Seven Letters

    B. 4:1 — 7:17 Second Vision: the Seven Seals

    C. 8:1 — 11:19 Third Vision: the Seven Trumpets

III. 12:1–22:5 The Last Four Visions: Christ the Lord of the Church and the Powers of Darkness

    A. 12:1–14:20 Fourth Vision: The Attack of the Satanic Anti-Trinity and the Advancing Triumph of Christ

    B. 15:1–16:21 Fifth Vision: the Seven Bowls

    C. 17:1–19:10 Sixth Vision: the Fate of Babylon, the Anti-Church

    D. 19:11–22:5 Seventh Vision: Judgment and Renewal

IV. 22:6-21 Conclusion

THE

REVELATION TO JOHN

(The Apocalypse)

INTRODUCTION (1:1-8)

1 The revelation of Jesus Christ, which God gave him to show to his servants what must soon take place; and he made it known by sending his angel to his servant John, 2 who bore witness to the word of God and to the testimony of Jesus Christ, even to all that he saw. 3 Blessed is he who reads aloud the words of the prophecy, and blessed are those who hear, and who keep what is written therein; for the time is near.

4 John to the seven churches that are in Asia:
Grace to you and peace from him who is and who was and who is to come, and from the seven spirits who are before his throne, 5 and from Jesus Christ the faithful witness, the first-born of the dead, and the ruler of kings on earth.

To him who loves us and has freed us from our sins by his blood 6 and made us a kingdom, priests to his God and Father, to him be glory and dominion for ever and ever. Amen. 7 Behold, he is coming with the clouds, and every eye will see him, every one who pierced him; and all tribes of the earth will wail on account of him. Even so. Amen.

8 "I am the Alpha and the Omega," says the Lord God, who is and who was and who is to come, the Almighty.

1:1-8 The introduction to the visions consists of three parts: a title to the whole book (1-3), an epistolary salutation (4-5a), and a threefold statement of praise, promise, and assurance concerning *Jesus Christ* and His *God and Father.* (5b-8)

1:1-3 The title indicates the source of the *revelation (Jesus Christ, God,* 1), how the revelation is mediated *(angel, servant John, all that he saw,* 1, 2), and how it is to be received *(keep what is written,* 3). There is a strong stress on the last-days urgency of the message of the book *(must soon take place,* 1; *time is near,* 3).

1:1 *Of Jesus Christ, which God gave him.* For Jesus as both Recipient and Giver of revelation cf. Mt 11:25-27; Jn 3:35; 5:20-24, 26-27; 7:16; 8:28; 12:48-49; 16:15; 17:1-8.

Servants, a common OT title of the prophets; cf. 1:3 ("prophecy"); 10:7; 11:18.

1:2 *Word of God* unites this prophet's witness with that of the OT prophets (so richly reflected in his words); testimony of Jesus Christ marks his word as part of the Word of God spoken "in these last days by a Son" (Heb 1:2); and all that he saw refers to the peculiar visionary form in which the word was given to him.

1:3 *Blessed,* the first of seven beatitudes in Rv. (Cf. 14:13; 16:15; 19:9; 20:6; 22:7; 22:14)

Reads aloud, in the worship service, where the letter is to be heard by the assembled faithful. (Cf. Cl 4:16)

Keep. Prophecy is not designed to satisfy curiosity; it opens up the future in order that men may know and obey the will of God which shapes that

future. Only those who hear in faith and hope will read this book profitably. Cf. 1, "to show to his SERVANTS."

1:4-5a The salutation has the form familiar to us from the letters of Paul (cf. Ro 1:1-7; Gl 1:1-3). The whole book is a letter, a personal, purposeful, practical word to the church.

1:4 *Asia,* the Roman province in western Asia Minor is meant.

Seven spirits, the one Holy Spirit as given to and active in the seven churches. (Cf. 2:7, 11, etc.)

1:5 The *faithful witness* refers to the Christ who became incarnate and died (Jn 18:37); the *first-born of the dead,* to the Risen One; and the *ruler of kings,* to the exalted Christ at the right hand of God.

1:5b-8 The salutation opens out into a doxology to the Christ who died and rose and rules (cf. 5a), whose *love* has *freed* men *from* their *sins* and so has created the new Israel, the royal priestly people of God (5b-6; cf. Ex 19:6; Is 61:6). The promise speaks of the return of Christ as the Son of Man to judge and reign (Dn 7:13, *coming with the clouds;* cf. Zch 12:10). The word of assurance (8) is spoken by the *Lord God* Himself: however dreadful "what soon must take place" (1) may prove to be, nothing escapes His control who is the Beginning and the End of all things *(Alpha . . . Omega);* the kings and priests of God may stand firm in the assurance that they are in the hands of *the Almighty.*

1:8 *Alpha . . . Omega,* the first and last letters of the Greek alphabet.

First Three Visions: The Church and the Powers of This World
1:9 — 11:19

FIRST VISION: THE SEVEN LETTERS (1:9 — 3:22)

9 I John, your brother, who share with you in Jesus the tribulation and the kingdom and the patient endurance, was on the island called Patmos on account of the word of God and the testimony of Jesus. 10 I was in the Spirit on the Lord's day, and I heard behind me a loud voice like a trumpet 11 saying, "Write what you see in a book and send it to the seven churches, to Eph'e·sus and to Smyrna and to Per'ga·mum and to Thy·a·ti'ra and to Sardis and to Philadelphia and to La·od·i·ce'a."

12 Then I turned to see the voice that was speaking to me, and on turning I saw seven golden lampstands, 13 and in the midst of the lampstands one like a son of man, clothed with a long robe and with a golden girdle round his breast; 14 his head and his hair were white as white wool, white as snow; his eyes were like a flame of fire, 15 his feet were like burnished bronze, refined as in a furnace, and his voice was like the sound of many waters; 16 in his right hand he held seven stars, from his mouth issued a sharp two-edged sword, and his face was like the sun shining in full strength.

17 When I saw him, I fell at his feet as though dead. But he laid his right hand upon me, saying, "Fear not, I am the first and the last, 18 and the living one; I died, and behold I am alive for evermore, and I have the keys of Death and Hades. 19 Now write

---

1:9 — 11:19 Rv is a word of prophecy (1:3), a revelatory word. In this word God makes Himself known and makes Himself count in the life and history of His people. He gives men eyes to see (in the present and in the future) what the eye of man cannot see and hearts that can conquer where victory seems impossible. He gives men eyes and hearts to see and believe the reign of God and His Anointed where that reign is anything but a transparent and palpable reality. Thus He enables men to believe "in hope against hope." (Ro 4:18)

1:9 — 3:22 Christ, Victor over death and Lord of the church, appears to His prophet in blazing divine majesty, overwhelms him, restores him, and commissions him to write to the seven churches in His name (1:9-20). In the seven letters the church, under the blessing, power, and judgment of the exalted Christ, is asked to do the impossible in an intolerable situation (perversion of the Gospel from within, persecution to the death from without). Christ places on His church the inexorable claim of His grace: No compromise! No compromise with falsehood or with loveless-ness, no compromise over against the satanic (*synagogue of Satan,* 2:9; *Satan's throne,* 2:13; 3:9; *deep things of Satan,* 2:24), no compromise with compromisers (*Nicolaitans,* 2:6, 15), no compromise with sloth, indifference, or lukewarmness. He *who conquers* (2:11), and he alone, has the great promises of the Lord of the church. (Chs. 2 — 3)

1:9-20 THE PROPHET'S INAUGURAL VISION

1:9 *Patmos,* a small island off the SW. coast of Asia Minor, 30 miles south of Samos, used as a place of banishment by the Roman emperors.

1:10 *In the Spirit,* for this term for inspiration cf. Mt 22:43, where it is used of the inspired psalmist.

1:11 *Seven churches.* The seven cities mentioned

all lay on a Roman road which ran northward from *Ephesus* to *Pergamum* and then turned inland and southward to *Thyatira, Sardis, Philadelphia, Laodicea;* all were assize towns and centers in which the cult of the emperor was fostered. What the Spirit said to these *seven churches* could be readily transmitted to other churches in the area. The *seven* are to be thought of as representative of the whole church; note the recurrent phrase, "What the Spirit says to the churches," 2:7, 11, etc.

1:12 *Lampstands.* Cf. 20 note.

1:13-16 The appearance of the exalted Christ is described in terms taken from OT descriptions of the *son of man* (Dn 7:13), of a mysterious heavenly figure in Dn 10 who reveals the future to Daniel (Dn 10:5-6), and of God Himself (cf. Dn 7:9; Eze 1:24, 26-27). Thus there is a strong stress on the deity of Christ, in close connection with the emphasis on the humanity which took Him into man's death. (18)

1:16 *Seven stars,* symbol of universal sovereignty, found on Imperial Roman coins.

1:17 *Fell ... as though dead.* The APPEARANCE of Christ expresses His majesty and purity, His searching eye and inescapable tread, His overwhelming and piercing word of judgment; before it the prophet collapses, as Isaiah did in the presence of the Lord of hosts. (Is 6:5; cf. Eze 1:28; Dn 10:7-9; Ju 6:22-23)

1:17-18 *Fear not.* In the WORDS of Christ His divine, eternal power *(the first and the last, living one)* is seen to be in the service of His love. He who in love *died* for men (cf. 1:5, "blood") lives *for evermore* to release men from the power of *Death.*

1:18 *Keys of,* authority over. (Cf. Mt 16:19)

Hades, the realm of the dead. (Cf. Mt 16:18)

1:19 *What is* refers to the contents of chs. 2 — 3; *what is to take place hereafter,* to the succeeding visions.

what you see, what is and what is to take place hereafter. [20]As for the mystery of the seven stars which you saw in my right hand, and the seven golden lampstands, the seven stars are the angels of the seven churches and the seven lampstands are the seven churches.

2 "To the angel of the church in Eph′e·sus write: 'The words of him who holds the seven stars in his right hand, who walks among the seven golden lampstands.

2 "' I know your works, your toil and your patient endurance, and how you cannot bear evil men but have tested those who call themselves apostles but are not, and found them to be false; [3] I know you are enduring patiently and bearing up for my name's sake, and you have not grown weary. [4] But I have this against you, that you have abandoned the love you had at first. [5] Remember then from what you have fallen, repent and do the works you did at first. If not, I will come to you and remove your lampstand from its place, unless you repent. [6] Yet this you have, you hate the works of the Nic·o·la′i·tans, which I also hate. [7] He who has an ear, let him hear what the Spirit says to the churches. To him who conquers I will grant to eat of the tree of life, which is in the paradise of God.'

8 "And to the angel of the church in Smyrna write: 'The words of the first and the last, who died and came to life.

1:20 *Mystery,* what can be known only by divine revelation. (Cf. 17:6-7)

Stars . . . lampstands . . . angels . . . churches. Both the stars and the lampstands signify the church. The seven stars, symbol of universal dominion, point to the angels, the church as a divine reality, as it is in God's eyes and therefore really is and eternally shall be. The lampstands point to the churches as a historical reality, functioning on earth at a certain time and place as the light of the world (Mt 5:14; Ph 2:15-16). These two aspects of the church cannot be separated; when Christ addresses the church in Ephesus, for instance, He speaks to the "angel of the church" (2:1). His words of recognition, rebuke, correction, threat, and promise addressed to the angel of the church are telling the church to be in its human actions what the church by divine action is, somewhat as we rebuke and encourage with the words, "Be yourself." The close connection between angel and lampstand is seen very clearly in 2:5: If the angel will not repent, the lampstand will be removed.

2:1-7 THE LETTER TO EPHESUS

2:1-7 The seven letters all have the same structure. (a) After the command to write, Christ designates and describes Himself as the Author of the letter; the self-designation usually picks up some feature from the inaugural vision of 1:9-20. (b) The Lord of the church addresses the church in words of diagnosis (praise and rebuke) and exhortation. (c) The summons to vigilant hearing (*He who has an ear,* 7) either precedes or follows. (d) The word of promise given *to him who conquers,* to the repentant and obedient church.

2:1 *Ephesus,* capital of the province of Asia and its greatest city, of outstanding political, commercial, religious, and cultural importance. Paul's extended and successful ministry there is sketched in bold strokes in Acts 19:1 – 20:1; cf. also Paul's farewell words to the elders of Ephesus in Acts 20:17-35.

Stars . . . lampstands. Cf. 1:12, 13-16, 20 notes.

2:2-6 The church is unreservedly praised for its unwearied zeal in contending "for the faith which was once for all delivered to the saints" (Jude 3) but is called on to *repent* of its decline in *love,* a failing that threatens the very existence of the church (5). The bitterness of necessary controversy has embittered its heart; the church has forgotten that "love . . . is not irritable or resentful . . . bears all things, believes all things, endures all things." (1 Co 13:5-7)

2:2 *Apostles,* true witnesses to the Lord Christ. (Cf. 2 Co 11:13-15)

2:6 *Works of the Nicolaitans.* There can and must be a hatred of evil *works,* without hatred of the men who do them. The *Nicolaitans* (cf. 2:14-15) advocated and defended a compromise with the paganism that surrounded the church in the public festivals of the city and in many social and civic associations. For the Gentile reaction of hurt surprise at the fact that Christians abstained from such associations cf. 1 Ptr 4:3-4; the temptation to compromise for the sake of peace and public approval must have been strong.

2:7 To *conquer* is to obey the Lord of the church who speaks to the church by His Spirit and to return in the power of the Spirit to a love like that of Jesus Christ, in whom a faithful witness to the truth and a self-expending love were perfectly united (cf. 1:5-6). The Christian's victory is a partaking in His victory *(I will grant).*

Eat of the tree of life, find that true eternal life which man's sin had forfeited (Gn 2:9; 3:22-24) and return to a life of unbroken fellowship with God in *paradise.* (Cf. 22:2, 14, 19)

2:8-11 THE LETTER TO SMYRNA

2:8-11 For the structure of the letter cf. 2:1-7 note.

2:8 *Smyrna,* an ancient and famous city 40 miles north of Ephesus, a great commercial center proud of its emperor cult, with a considerable Jewish population.

First and . . . last, etc. Cf. 1:17-18. The eternal

9 " 'I know your tribulation and your poverty (but you are rich) and the slander of those who say that they are Jews and are not, but are a synagogue of Satan. 10 Do not fear what you are about to suffer. Behold, the devil is about to throw some of you into prison, that you may be tested, and for ten days you will have tribulation. Be faithful unto death, and I will give you the crown of life. 11 He who has an ear, let him hear what the Spirit says to the churches. He who conquers shall not be hurt by the second death.'

12 "And to the angel of the church in Per'ga·mum write: 'The words of him who has the sharp two-edged sword.

13 " 'I know where you dwell, where Satan's throne is; you hold fast my name and you did not deny my faith even in the days of An'ti·pas my witness, my faithful one, who was killed among you, where Satan dwells. 14 But I have a few things against you: you have some there who hold the teaching of Ba'laam, who taught Balak to put a stumbling block before the sons of Israel, that they might eat food sacrificed to idols and practice immorality. 15 So you also have some who hold the teaching of the Nic·o·la'i·tans. 16 Repent then. If not, I will come to you soon and war against them with the sword of my mouth. 17 He who has an ear, let him hear what the Spirit says to the churches. To him who conquers I will give some of the hidden manna, and I will give him a white stone, with a new name written on the stone which no one knows except him who receives it.'

18 "And to the angel of the church in Thy·a·ti'ra write: 'The words of the Son of God, who has eyes like a flame of fire, and whose feet are like burnished bronze.

Lord of life and Victor over death speaks with authority to the persecuted church facing death, urging faithfulness unto death and promising the crown of life. (10)

2:9 *Poverty . . . rich.* Cf. Ja 2:5.

Jews . . . synagogue of Satan. By committing themselves to the satanic lie *(slander)* and to the murderous satanic will they have forfeited their right to be called the people of God (cf. Jn 8:44). Jewish opposition to the church persisted in Smyrna; Jews took a leading part in the martyrdom of Polycarp, bishop of Smyrna, in A. D. 155.

2:10 *Ten days,* a relatively short period of time (Gn 24:55; Dn 1:12, 14); the main emphasis is on the fact that the time of *tribulation* is measured and controlled by God.

2:11 *Second death,* the final eternal separation from God and His life, described in 20:14 and 21:8 as eternal torment in "the lake of fire." (Cf. Mt 10:28)

2:12-17 THE LETTER TO PERGAMUM

2:12-17 For the structure of the letter cf. 2:1-7 note.

2:12-13 *Pergamum,* to the north of Smyrna, a city renowned for the rich variety of its pagan cults, a strong center of the Imperial cult (worship of the Roman emperor). Here, where the satanic power that lurks behind every idol (1 Co 10:19-20) was so powerfully entrenched *(Satan's throne . . . where Satan dwells),* the decision of the church for the Lord Jesus and against all other "lords" (1 Co 8:5-6) was particularly difficult and dangerous. The church had already experienced the shock of martyrdom *(Antipas . . . my faithful one . . . was killed)* and was in especial need of the powerful *words of him who has the sharp two-edged sword,* His recognition (13), His warning (14-16), and His promise (17). *My faith,* faith in Me as Lord *(name).*

2:14-15 *Balaam* once brought about the fall of God's people by enticing them into the lascivious worship of Baal of Peor (Nm 31:15-16; cf. Nm 25:1-3); the *Nicolaitans* with their *teaching* (cf. 2:6 note) posed a similar threat to God's people now. For the history of Israel as warning and instruction for the new people of God cf. 1 Co 10:1-22.

2:17 *Hidden manna . . . new name.* Those who have in fidelity to Christ refused to compromise with satanic pagan idolatry by eating food sacrificed to idols (14) will be fed with food from heaven by Christ Himself in the world to come; those who have held fast to His name (13) will receive from Him a *new name,* that is, a new eternal status and being in the world to come. For the sense of *new name* cf. Is 62:1-4.

Hidden, invisible to unbelief, known to faith but not yet seen. "Hope that is seen is not hope. For who hopes for what he sees? But if we hope for what we do not see, we wait for it with patience." (Ro 8:24-25)

White stone. The image is probably that of an amulet engraved with a divine name which assures the wearer of safety and well-being. (Cf. 3:12)

Which no one knows except him who receives it. Only by the grace of God, through His Spirit, does man come "to know the love of Christ which surpasses knowledge." (Eph 3:14-19)

2:18-29 THE LETTER TO THYATIRA

2:18-29 For the structure of the letter cf. 2:1-7 note.

2:18 *Thyatira,* the smallest of the seven cities addressed, lay to the SE. of Pergamum. The church receives high praise for its living and flourishing faith (19) but is sternly rebuked and warned for its tolerance of a false "prophetess" whose seductive teaching leads men to compromise with

19 " 'I know your works, your love and faith and service and patient endurance, and that your latter works exceed the first. 20 But I have this against you, that you tolerate the woman Jez'e·bel, who calls herself a prophetess and is teaching and beguiling my servants to practice immorality and to eat food sacrificed to idols. 21 I gave her time to repent, but she refuses to repent of her immorality. 22 Behold, I will throw her on a sickbed, and those who commit adultery with her I will throw into great tribulation, unless they repent of her doings; 23 and I will strike her children dead. And all the churches shall know that I am he who searches mind and heart, and I will give to each of you as your works deserve. 24 But to the rest of you in Thy·a·ti'ra, who do not hold this teaching, who have not learned what some call the deep things of Satan, to you I say, I do not lay upon you any other burden; 25 only hold fast what you have, until I come. 26 He who conquers and who keeps my works until the end, I will give him power over the nations, 27 and he shall rule them with a rod of iron, as when earthen pots are broken in pieces, even as I myself have received power from my Father; 28 and I will give him the morning star. 29 He who has an ear, let him hear what the Spirit says to the churches.'

3 "And to the angel of the church in Sardis write: 'The words of him who has the seven spirits of God and the seven stars.

" 'I know your works; you have the name of being alive, and you are dead. 2Awake, and strengthen what remains and is on the point of death, for I have not found your works perfect in the sight of my God. 3 Remember then what you received and heard; keep that, and repent. If you will not awake, I will come like a thief, and you will not know at what hour I will come upon you. 4 Yet you have still a few names in Sardis, people who have not soiled their garments; and they shall walk with me in white, for

---

licentious paganism surrounding them. (20-23)

Son of God . . . eyes . . . feet. The church is confronted with the high majesty of the Judge (cf. Jn 5:25-29). The scrutiny of His fiery eye "searches mind and heart" (23); and He advances toward judgment on *feet . . . like burnished bronze,* feet that no power can resist or stay.

2:20 *Jezebel.* The name of King Ahab's Tyrian queen, who corrupted the religion of Israel with "the harlotries and the sorceries" of her native gods Baal and Astarte (2 K 9:22; 1 K 16:31-32; 18:19), is fittingly applied to the *prophetess* who, like the Nicolaitans (2:6, 15), was corrupting the life of the new people of God.

2:22-23 *Sickbed,* condign punishment for the bed of *adultery.*

Those who commit adultery with her are those who have come under the spell of her beguiling doctrine but are not yet completely carried away by it; for them repentance is still possible. *Her children* are those who have absorbed her teaching so completely that they are wholly like her, immoral and impenitent (cf. 21); them the Judge will *strike . . . dead* in their guilt.

2:24 *Deep things of Satan.* The adherents of the prophetess spoke of their peculiar "enlightened" tenets (which distinguished them from simple and decent God-fearing folk) as the *deep things* of God; the prophet John fearlessly calls them by their right name.

2:26 *My works,* the good works which Christ both commands and enables them to do.

2:26-27 In language taken from Ps 2:8-9 Christ promises the faithful a part in His own eternal Messianic reign. (Cf. 3:21)

2:28 *The morning star,* the star Venus, which symbolized worldwide dominion.

3:1-6 THE LETTER TO SARDIS

3:1-6 For the structure of the letter cf. 2:1-7 note.

3:1 *Sardis,* an ancient Lydian city south of Thyatira with a long and brilliant past, important in Roman times as an industrial center, seat of a Roman provincial court, and site of a temple for emperor worship. The church seems to have been untroubled by persecution and not tested by internal struggle. Its besetting sin was religious and moral apathy.

3:1-2 *Seven spirits . . . seven stars.* Christ not only has dominion over the churches (*stars* 1:16, 20), He has the fullness of the creative power of the Spirit (cf. 1:4) as His gift to the churches. He can therefore bid the *dead* church of Sardis *awake and strengthen what . . . is on the point of death,* for He gives what He commands by His gift of the Spirit.

Dead . . . works. Cf. Ja 2:26.

Not . . . perfect. Literally "not fulfilled." God has created the church "for good works" which He Himself "prepared beforehand, that we should walk in them" (Eph 2:10). Good works not done are like prophecy unfulfilled; God's purpose for man is being thwarted, His grace is being received in vain. (2 Co 6:1)

3:3 *Remember,* recall and relive.

I will come like a thief. Cf. Jesus' word concerning His final coming, Mt 24:43, echoed once more in Rv 16:15.

3:4 *Soiled their garments,* by infidelity to their Lord.

they are worthy. [5] He who conquers shall be clad thus in white garments, and I will not blot his name out of the book of life; I will confess his name before my Father and before his angels. [6] He who has an ear, let him hear what the Spirit says to the churches.'

7 "And to the angel of the church in Philadelphia write: 'The words of the holy one, the true one, who has the key of David, who opens and no one shall shut, who shuts and no one opens.

8 " 'I know your works. Behold, I have set before you an open door, which no one is able to shut; I know that you have but little power, and yet you have kept my word and have not denied my name. [9] Behold, I will make those of the synagogue of Satan who say that they are Jews and are not, but lie—behold, I will make them come and bow down before your feet, and learn that I have loved you. [10] Because you have kept my word of patient endurance, I will keep you from the hour of trial which is coming on the whole world, to try those who dwell upon the earth. [11] I am coming soon; hold fast what you have, so that no one may seize your crown. [12] He who conquers, I will make him a pillar in the temple of my God; never shall he go out of it, and I will write on him the name of my God, and the name of the city of my God, the new Jerusalem which comes down from my God out of heaven, and my own new name. [13] He who has an ear, let him hear what the Spirit says to the churches.'

14 "And to the angel of the church in La·od·i·ce′a write: 'The words of the Amen, the faithful and true witness, the beginning of God's creation.

15 " 'I know your works: you are neither cold nor hot. Would that you were cold or hot! [16] So, because you are lukewarm, and neither cold nor hot, I will spew you out of my mouth. [17] For you say, I am rich, I have prospered, and I need nothing; not knowing that you are wretched, pitiable, poor, blind, and naked. [18] Therefore I

3:5 *White garments* symbolize vindication and victory. (Cf. 6:11)

Book of life, in which the names of the citizens of the city of God are enrolled. (Cf. Ex 32:32-33; Ps 69:28; Dn 12:1; Lk 10:20; Ph 4:3; Heb 12:23)

I will confess his name. An echo of Jesus' words, Mt 10:32.

3:7-13 THE LETTER TO PHILADELPHIA

3:7-13 For the structure of the letter cf. 2:1-7 note.

3:7-13 To *Philadelphia,* the church which despite its *little power* in means and prestige has been faithful (8) and enduring in obedience to the Word of the Lord (10), the *holy* and faithful *(true)* Lord promises missionary opportunity and triumph (8-9) and preservation in the coming universal *hour of trial* (10). *He who conquers* (12) shall have his enduring place of honor in the living *temple of . . . God;* God will acknowledge him as His own *(name of my God),* enroll Him among the citizens of the *new Jerusalem,* the *city of . . . God;* he shall share in the glory of Christ the Conqueror *(my . . . new name)*—all this as the free gift of the Christ who with Messianic authority *(key of David,* 7) *opens* the kingdom of heaven to all believers.

3:7 *Philadelphia,* SE. of Sardis, strategically located and situated in a fruitful land, was a rich and commercially important city. The church there was neither rich nor "important"—but faithful.

Key, symbol of authority (cf. Mt 16:19 note; Is 22:22), here of the authority to admit or exclude men from the Kingdom.

3:8 *Open door,* of missionary opportunity (cf.

1 Co 16:9; 2 Co 2:12). Others take it of the door to the Kingdom (cf. 7 and 12); but the promise of the conversion of the hostile Jews (9) seems rather to suggest missionary success.

3:9 *Synagogue of Satan.* Cf. 2:9 note.

3:10 *Hour of trial . . . coming on the whole world.* The following visions depict this hour of trial (seals, 4:1—8:1; trumpets, 8:2—11:21; bowls, 15:1—16:21) as growing ever more intense. Visions such as 7:1-17 depict the preservation of the faithful.

3:12 *Pillar in the temple.* Perhaps an allusion to a custom of Philadelphia, where citizens who had deserved well of the state had pillars set up in their honor in a local temple.

3:14-22 THE LETTER TO LAODICEA

3:14-22 For the structure of the letter cf. 2:1-7 note.

3:14 *Laodicea,* SE. of Philadelphia, was a rich city renowned as a center of commerce, banking, and cloth manufacture, seat of a medical school. The church there seems to have taken color from its environment and to have become self-satisfied, secure in itself, "lukewarm." Laodicea had forgotten what Philadelphia remembered, that the Kingdom is promised to the poor in spirit. (Mt 5:3)

3:18 *Buy,* in the sense of Is 55:1-2, "without money and without price." Cf. the gracious assurance of v. 20 and the lavish promise of 21. The threat of 16 ("spew you out") is to make them receptive for the promise of 19-21.

3:18 *Gold . . . garments . . . salve,* alluding to the banking, manufacture, and medicine which had

counsel you to buy from me gold refined by fire, that you may be rich, and white garments to clothe you and to keep the shame of your nakedness from being seen, and salve to anoint your eyes, that you may see. ¹⁹ Those whom I love, I reprove and chasten; so be zealous and repent. ²⁰ Behold, I stand at the door and knock; if any one hears my voice and opens the door, I will come in to him and eat with him, and he with me. ²¹ He who conquers, I will grant him to sit with me on my throne, as I myself conquered and sat down with my Father on his throne. ²² He who has an ear, let him hear what the Spirit says to the churches.' ''

SECOND VISION: THE SEVEN SEALS (4:1 — 7:17)

4 After this I looked, and lo, in heaven an open door! And the first voice, which I had heard speaking to me like a trumpet, said, "Come up hither, and I will show you what must take place after this." ²At once I was in the Spirit, and lo, a throne stood in heaven, with one seated on the throne! ³And he who sat there appeared like jasper and carnelian, and round the throne was a rainbow that looked like an emerald. ⁴ Round the throne were twenty-four thrones, and seated on the thrones were twenty-four elders, clad in white garments, with golden crowns upon their heads. ⁵ From the throne issue flashes of lightning, and voices and peals of thunder, and before the throne burn seven torches of fire, which are the seven spirits of God; ⁶ and before the throne there is as it were a sea of glass, like crystal.

And round the throne, on each side of the throne, are four living creatures, full of eyes in front and behind: ⁷ the first living creature like a lion, the second living creature like an ox, the third living creature with the face of a man, and the fourth living creature like a flying eagle. ⁸And the four living creatures, each of them with six wings, are full of eyes all round and within, and day and night they never cease to sing,

made Laodicea rich — and "lukewarm." The Laodiceans had spent their money "for that which is not bread" and their "labor for that which does not satisfy." (Is 55:2)

3:19 *Zealous,* the opposite of "lukewarm." (16)

3:20 *Hears my voice and opens the door.* This is a pictorial explanation of "repent" (19); *hears* includes the idea of "obeys."

3:20-21 *Eat with him . . . sit with me on my throne.* Both the picture of the common meal and that of the shared reign emphasize the completeness of personal communion with Christ, what it means to be "forever with the Lord."

4:1 — 7:17 The vision of the seven seals tells the church that compromise is neither necessary nor possible. The evils that sweep around the church (including the satanic thrust into the church) are no wild chance, no irrational vagaries of fate, no secular uncertainties with which men may come to terms. No, in all this God, the *one seated on the throne* (4:2), is reigning (ch. 4); in all this Christ, the slain Lamb, is opening the seals of God's book, executing His counsels (ch. 5). Though the riders of ruin go forth, though the martyrs cry, though the structure of the universe topples till men grow desperate in the face of God's judgment (ch. 6) — nevertheless the preservation of the church and the eternal vindication of God's saints are sure, for they are part of God's royal will (ch. 7). "Your God reigns," the prophet proclaims to the church; "unite your will with His."

4:1-11 ONE SEATED ON THE THRONE

4:1-11 God, the omnipotent Creator, is manifested in splendor, receiving the adoration of the whole creation, over which He rules.

4:1 *After this.* The visions turn from the interpretation of the present (chs. 2 — 3) to the future of the world and the church.

4:2 *Throne.* For the throne as symbol of God's reign cf. Ps 11:4-6; 29:10; 47:8; 80:1; 99:1; 103: 19-22; Is 6:1; Eze 1:26; Dn 7:9.

4:3 *Rainbow* recalls God's covenant of compassionate forbearance with every living creature after the Flood (Gn 9:13-16). The God who sits enthroned on high, the dread Judge of Sinai (cf. Ex 19:16), separated from men by the "sea of glass" (6), is nevertheless a God of grace. (Cf. Eze 1:28)

4:4 *Twenty-four elders* probably represent the people of God as they are in God's intent, in Christ, made alive, raised up, and seated in heavenly places (Eph 2:6), glorified (Ro 8:30) in God's presence *(white garments, golden crowns).* Others think of them as a superior class of angels especially close to God, familiar with His counsels (cf. 5:5; 7:13). But multiples of twelve usually refer to the people of God. (Cf. 7:4-8; 21:12, 14)

4:5 *Fire . . . seven spirits.* Cf. 1:4. The fostering warmth, the light, and the constant motion of fire make it an apt symbol of the genial Spirit through whom God communicates to man.

4:6 *Sea of glass.* Cf. v. 3 note; 15:2; Ps 104:3; Eze 1:22.

4:6-8 *Four living creatures* combines features of the seraphim of Is 6:2 and the cherubim of Eze 1:5, 18. They represent nature in the service of the Almighty; the lordly power of the *lion,* the solid strength of the *ox,* the skill and intelligence of *man,* the tireless speed of the *eagle* are at His

"Holy, holy, holy, is the Lord God Almighty,
who was and is and is to come!"

⁹And whenever the living creatures give glory and honor and thanks to him who is seated on the throne, who lives for ever and ever, ¹⁰ the twenty-four elders fall down before him who is seated on the throne and worship him who lives for ever and ever; they cast their crowns before the throne, singing,

¹¹   "Worthy art thou, our Lord and God,
to receive glory and honor and power,
for thou didst create all things,
and by thy will they existed and were created."

5 And I saw in the right hand of him who was seated on the throne a scroll written within and on the back, sealed with seven seals; ² and I saw a strong angel proclaiming with a loud voice, "Who is worthy to open the scroll and break its seals?" ³And no one in heaven or on earth or under the earth was able to open the scroll or to look into it, ⁴ and I wept much that no one was found worthy to open the scroll or to look into it. ⁵ Then one of the elders said to me, "Weep not; lo, the Lion of the tribe of Judah, the Root of David, has conquered, so that he can open the scroll and its seven seals."

6 And between the throne and the four living creatures and among the elders, I saw a Lamb standing, as though it had been slain, with seven horns and with seven eyes, which are the seven spirits of God sent out into all the earth; ⁷ and he went and took the scroll from the right hand of him who was seated on the throne. ⁸And when he had taken the scroll, the four living creatures and the twenty-four elders fell down before the Lamb, each holding a harp, and with golden bowls full of incense, which are the prayers of the saints; ⁹ and they sang a new song, saying,

"Worthy art thou to take the scroll and to open its seals,
for thou wast slain and by thy blood didst ransom men for God
from every tribe and tongue and people and nation,

¹⁰   and hast made them a kingdom and priests to our God,
and they shall reign on earth."

¹¹ Then I looked, and I heard around the throne and the living creatures and the elders the voice of many angels, numbering myriads of myriads and thousands of thousands, ¹² saying with a loud voice, "Worthy is the Lamb who was slain, to receive

---

disposal. Man thus appears twice in this vision, among the creatures and as a member of the people of God, created AND redeemed.

4:10-11 *Cast their crowns,* to indicate that their *glory and honor and power* is theirs purely as a gift from God, their Creator and Lord.

4:11 *To receive glory.* God receives His glory when man acknowledges Him as God and adores Him, "gives glory to God."

5:1-14 THE SLAIN LAMB AND THE SEALED
          SCROLL

5:1-14 The counsels of God are a sealed book, an unknown and dreadful secret for sinful man and his fallen world. The prophet weeps when the strong angel's challenge goes unanswered and the world is left without a future and a hope. There is hope in One only, in the slain and triumphant Messiah; He can take the book and reveal and execute the counsels of God. His appearance evoked a triple chorus of adoration from the living creatures and elders, from myriads of angels, and from every creature in God's world. The last song, that of the creatures, unites praise for the Lamb with praise for God the Enthroned, thus marking the Lamb as in majesty coequal with God and linking ch. 5 closely with ch. 4.

5:1 For the *scroll* as a symbol of God's counsels cf. Eze 2:9 – 3:3; Rv 10:2-11.

5:5 *Lion . . . Root of David.* Both are OT designations for the Messiah who was to come. *Lion* stresses His conquering power (Gn 49:8-10); *Root of David* speaks of the lowly and unpromising beginnings of One who shall triumph solely in the power of the Spirit of the Lord. (Is 11:1-2; cf. 3-10)

5:6 *Lamb . . . slain.* Cf. Is 53:7; Jn 1:29, 35 notes. The atoning sacrifice of Christ's death is the key to all the counsels of God.

Seven horns, symbol of all-encompassing power.

Seven eyes . . . seven spirits, symbols of the penetrating insight of Him who "shall not," like human rulers, judge merely "by what his eyes see" and of that "wisdom and understanding . . . counsel and might . . . knowledge and fear of the Lord" with which He shall establish God's rule of righteousness and restore the peace of Paradise on earth. (Is 11:2-9)

5:8 *Incense . . . prayers.* Cf. Ps 141:2. The suffering church is assured that the *prayers of the saints,* Christians, are heard before the throne of God and the Lamb.

5:9 *Ransom,* set free by payment, redeemed. (Cf. Mt 20:28 note)

5:12 *To receive power,* etc. (Cf. 4:11 note)

power and wealth and wisdom and might and honor and glory and blessing!" [13]And I heard every creature in heaven and on earth and under the earth and in the sea, and all therein, saying, "To him who sits upon the throne and to the Lamb be blessing and honor and glory and might for ever and ever!" [14]And the four living creatures said, "Amen!" and the elders fell down and worshiped.

6 Now I saw when the Lamb opened one of the seven seals, and I heard one of the four living creatures say, as with a voice of thunder, "Come!" [2]And I saw, and behold, a white horse, and its rider had a bow; and a crown was given to him, and he went out conquering and to conquer.

3 When he opened the second seal, I heard the second living creature say, "Come!" [4]And out came another horse, bright red; its rider was permitted to take peace from the earth, so that men should slay one another; and he was given a great sword.

5 When he opened the third seal, I heard the third living creature say, "Come!" And I saw, and behold, a black horse, and its rider had a balance in his hand; [6] and I heard what seemed to be a voice in the midst of the four living creatures saying, "A quart of wheat for a denarius,*a* and three quarts of barley for a denarius;*a* but do not harm oil and wine!"

7 When he opened the fourth seal, I heard the voice of the fourth living creature say, "Come!" [8]And I saw, and behold, a pale horse, and its rider's name was Death,

a The denarius was a day's wage for a laborer

5:13 *Every creature.* All creation, which shall share in the glory of redeemed man, anticipates that hour of "glorious liberty" in this song. (Cf. Ro 8:19-21)

6:1-17 SIX SEALS OPENED

6:1-17 The opening of the seals is not merely the revelation of God's purposes but also the execution of them. What follows now, after the Lamb's decisive act and the universal exultation which it evoked, is disturbing: not an immediate triumph of God and the Lamb but the usual sequence of disasters that make human history. At the opening of the first seal the Antichrist, opponent and imitator of Christ, rides forth, *conquering and to conquer* (2). At the breaking of the second seal the red horse of war rides forth *to take peace from the earth* and to bring death (3-4). The opening of the third seal ushers in a season of scarcity (5-6). And the fourth seal signifies the triumph of the rider on the pale horse, *Death* (7-8). All this is marked as being under God's control, to be sure; God's *living creatures* utter the command that lets these fearful riders range (1, 3, 5, 7), and the power they have *was given* them by the Lord God Almighty (2, 4, 8). But this is not God's final victory. It is therefore no wonder that at the opening of the fifth seal the martyrs are heard crying out to God for vindication, asking that the God for whom they have died hallow His name by rendering judgment in their favor. They are given an anticipatory vindication in the white robe of glory but are given to know that the End is not yet (9-11). The End is in view at the opening of the sixth seal, when a convulsed universe heralds a judgment of God so terrible that men, even the greatest and mightiest, call on the mountains to fall on them and cover them; extinction is preferable to facing the wrath of God and the Lamb. (12-17)

6:2 *White horse.* The crowned victorious *rider* on the white horse RESEMBLES the victorious Christ as portrayed in 19:11-21, superficially at least. But his weapon is the *bow,* which in Eze 39:3 is the weapon of Gog, the great enemy of the people of God in the last days (Eze 38 – 39). Moreover, he appears in a series of sinister figures. The figure is best understood, therefore, as the Antichrist, both opponent and imitator of Christ. On this understanding we find in the first four seals the same sequence as in the words of Jesus concerning the last days in Mt 24:5-10 – (1) misleading by false Christs; (2) wars; (3) famines; (4) death (by persecution in Mt 24:9, which is taken up in the fifth seal here). Others take the first rider to be Christ Himself, or the victorious Gospel (cf. Mk 13:10); still others think of a triumphant militarism such as that of the Parthians, an Eastern people who had inflicted a memorable defeat on Roman forces in A. D. 62. But the interpretation given above seems to fit the text and context best. For the figure of Antichrist cf. ch. 12. For the deceptive and misleading appearance of the antichristian power cf. "the synagogue of Satan" (2:9; 3:9), "throne of Satan" (2:13), and "the deep things of Satan." (3:24)

6:6 A *denarius* represents a day's wage for a laborer (cf. Mt 20:2); a *quart of wheat* is a day's ration for a man. A day's work would just keep a man alive on wheat; if he bought the cheaper *barley,* he would have something for his family also, but hardly enough. The inflationary price of food has been estimated as being 8 to 16 times normal prices.

Do not harm oil and wine. The luxuries of life are available – for those who can afford them; the small man is hardest hit, as is usual in times of dearth.

6:8 *Death* is the power to which all men must succumb in this age; *Hades* is the realm or kingdom of death, to which unbelieving men are committed while those who die in the Lord (14:13) are delivered from it. (Cf. Mt 16:18 note)

and Hades followed him; and they were given power over a fourth of the earth, to kill with sword and with famine and with pestilence and by wild beasts of the earth.

9 When he opened the fifth seal, I saw under the altar the souls of those who had been slain for the word of God and for the witness they had borne; 10 they cried out with a loud voice, "O Sovereign Lord, holy and true, how long before thou wilt judge and avenge our blood on those who dwell upon the earth?" 11 Then they were each given a white robe and told to rest a little longer, until the number of their fellow servants and their brethren should be complete, who were to be killed as they themselves had been.

12 When he opened the sixth seal, I looked, and behold, there was a great earthquake; and the sun became black as sackcloth, the full moon became like blood, 13 and the stars of the sky fell to the earth as the fig tree sheds its winter fruit when shaken by a gale; 14 the sky vanished like a scroll that is rolled up, and every mountain and island was removed from its place. 15 Then the kings of the earth and the great men and the generals and the rich and the strong, and every one, slave and free, hid in the caves and among the rocks of the mountains, 16 calling to the mountains and rocks, "Fall on us and hide us from the face of him who is seated on the throne, and from the wrath of the Lamb; 17 for the great day of their wrath has come, and who can stand before it?"

7 After this I saw four angels standing at the four corners of the earth, holding back the four winds of the earth, that no wind might blow on earth or sea or against any tree. 2 Then I saw another angel ascend from the rising of the sun, with the seal of the living God, and he called with a loud voice to the four angels who had been given power to harm earth and sea, 3 saying, "Do not harm the earth or the sea or the trees, till we have sealed the servants of our God upon their foreheads." 4And I heard the number of the sealed, a hundred and forty-four thousand sealed, out of every tribe of the sons of Israel, 5 twelve thousand sealed out of the tribe of Judah, twelve thousand of the tribe of Reuben, twelve thousand of the tribe of Gad, 6 twelve thousand of the tribe of Asher, twelve thousand of the tribe of Naph´ta·li, twelve thousand of the tribe

A *fourth of the earth*. The judgments of God depicted in the vision of the seven seals are still partial and preliminary, designed to call men to repentance. (Cf. 8:7, 9, 11, 12, "a third"; 3:20)

6:9 *Under the altar*. The slaying of God's witnesses has not been mere senseless butchery; their dying had a meaning and purpose, as a sacrifice offered to their God. (Cf. Ph 2:17; 2 Ti 4:6)

6:10 The honor of their *Sovereign Lord* is at stake in their death, and so they commit their cause to Him "who judges justly," as Christ did. (1 Ptr 2:23)

6:16 *Wrath of the Lamb*. He who in His great love was slain and by His blood did ransom men for God (5:9) will at the End appear as Judge of all who have despised and rejected His love.

7:1-17 INTERLUDE: THE NUMBERED SAINTS
        AND THE REDEEMED MULTITUDE

7:1-17 "The great day of their wrath has come, and who can stand before it?" (6:17) is the frantic question to which desperate men can find no answer. The prophet is given a twofold answer. First, the vision of the 144,000 members of the completed people of God, numbered by God and marked as His everlasting own by His seal, assures him and the church that nothing and no one can pluck God's elect from His hand—THEY shall be able to stand (1-8). Second, the vision of the innumerable multitude from among all nations assures him and the church that the grace of God which has

cleansed them by the blood of the Lamb will bring them safely out of the last great tribulation which still awaits them (cf. 6:11) and enable them to stand before their Judge unafraid; more than that, His grace will bring them into a new life of enraptured adoration, a life of perpetual worship (*serve*, 15) before the throne in the temple of God, a life of consummated salvation in which the agonies of their present creaturely life are no more: no hunger, no thirst, no blasting heat, no tears any more, but fulfilled life in the shelter of God's presence and under the everlasting kindly care of their Good Shepherd (9-17). Now the seventh seal can be opened (8:1) and God's winds of judgment can be let loose upon the earth (7:1-3). God's people can endure to the end.

7:1 For the *four winds* as instruments of God's judgment cf. Jer 49:36.

7:2 *Rising of the sun*, a quarter of good omen. Paradise lay in the east (Gn 2:8), and in Judaic tradition the Messiah was expected to come from the east.

The *seal* marks them as God's property and under His protection; the *living God* is the acting God, no inert idol but mighty to save. For God's sealing as His act of protecting His own faithful ones amid judgment cf. Eze 9:4.

7:4 The number 12 is the number of the people of God, once the 12 tribes of Israel, now made up of men from every nation. The number 10 is the number of the rounded whole (10 Egyptian

of Ma·nas′seh, 7 twelve thousand of the tribe of Simeon, twelve thousand of the tribe of Levi, twelve thousand of the tribe of Is′sa·char, 8 twelve thousand of the tribe of Zeb′u·lun, twelve thousand of the tribe of Joseph, twelve thousand sealed out of the tribe of Benjamin.

9 After this I looked, and behold, a great multitude which no man could number, from every nation, from all tribes and peoples and tongues, standing before the throne and before the Lamb, clothed in white robes, with palm branches in their hands, 10 and crying out with a loud voice, "Salvation belongs to our God who sits upon the throne, and to the Lamb!" 11And all the angels stood round the throne and round the elders and the four living creatures, and they fell on their faces before the throne and worshiped God, 12 saying, "Amen! Blessing and glory and wisdom and thanksgiving and honor and power and might be to our God for ever and ever! Amen."

13 Then one of the elders addressed me, saying, "Who are these, clothed in white robes, and whence have they come?" 14 I said to him, "Sir, you know." And he said to me, "These are they who have come out of the great tribulation; they have washed their robes and made them white in the blood of the Lamb.

15   Therefore are they before the throne of God,
        and serve him day and night within his temple;
        and he who sits upon the throne will shelter them with his presence.

16   They shall hunger no more, neither thirst any more;
        the sun shall not strike them, nor any scorching heat.

17   For the Lamb in the midst of the throne will be their shepherd,
        and he will guide them to springs of living water;
        and God will wipe away every tear from their eyes."

THIRD VISION: THE SEVEN TRUMPETS (8:1 — 11:19)

8 When the Lamb opened the seventh seal, there was silence in heaven for about half an hour. 2 Then I saw the seven angels who stand before God, and seven

---

plagues, 10 commandments, etc.). 144,000 expresses the full number of the people of God under His watchful providence.

7:9 The innumerable *great multitude* is the same as the numbered tribes of Israel, seen from another point of view. While the 144,000 stresses the certainty of God's elective purpose, the innumerable *multitude* expresses the overwhelming greatness of His ultimate triumph.

Palm branches were carried by the festal crowds at the Feast of Booths (or Tabernacles), the feast of ingathering and thanksgiving for the harvest, the feast that commemorated the time when Israel dwelt in booths when God brought them up out of Egypt (Lv 23:33-43). Zch 14:16 contains a special promise that the Gentiles should one day partake in it.

7:10 *Salvation,* the accomplished deliverance of the Exodus of the last days (cf. 9 and Ex 15:1-2), is solely the act of God in Christ. (Cf. Eph 2:8-10)

7:14 *The great tribulation,* well known from the OT (Dn 12:1) and the words of Jesus. (Mt 24:21)

7:16-17 The language and thought of the OT, always a major influence in Rv, are especially prominent here. (Cf. Is 49:9-10; Ps 121:6; Eze 34:23; Ps 23; Is 25:8)

8:1 — 11:19 The opening of the seventh seal introduces, not the expected End but a new series of visions which surveys once more the time from the Now of the church to the End (11:15-19). The church must be prepared to remain uncompro-

misingly steadfast amid even sterner visitations than the vision of the seals had foretold. What the church trembles at now is but the beginning of the travail which precedes the world's rebirth (cf. Mt 24:8). The seals are followed by the trumpet blasts of God, judgmental visitations which warn mankind and call on men to repent (cf. 9:20-21). These visitations first strike man's world—the earth, the sea, the living waters, sun and moon and stars; they are still partial (*a third,* 8:7, 9, etc.), but under their impact the solid comfort of man's creaturely existence grows fragile and uncertain (ch. 8). These are followed by visitations in which the demonic, uncanny character of the powers employed by God becomes apparent, visitations which make increasingly plain the helplessness of man (locusts from the bottomless pit and innumerable troops of infernal cavalry, 9:1-19). The church is not permitted to hope for "better times," for man is pictured as remaining impenitent and obdurate over against God's trumpet calls (9:20-21). Before the seventh trumpet (as before the seventh seal, ch. 7) there is an interlude (chs. 10—11) which assures the church that amid all this God's purposes are ripening fast; there shall be no more delay and the salutary, steadying voice of prophecy shall still be heard (ch. 10). The pseudo-church may be abandoned to its fate, but God's protecting hand will be over the true church (11:1-2), and the church's witness will continue in martyr-triumph (11:3 ff.).

trumpets were given to them. ³And another angel came and stood at the altar with a golden censer; and he was given much incense to mingle with the prayers of all the saints upon the golden altar before the throne; ⁴ and the smoke of the incense rose with the prayers of the saints from the hand of the angel before God. ⁵ Then the angel took the censer and filled it with fire from the altar and threw it on the earth; and there were peals of thunder, voices, flashes of lightning, and an earthquake.

6 Now the seven angels who had the seven trumpets made ready to blow them.

7 The first angel blew his trumpet, and there followed hail and fire, mixed with blood, which fell on the earth; and a third of the earth was burnt up, and a third of the trees were burnt up, and all green grass was burnt up.

8 The second angel blew his trumpet, and something like a great mountain, burning with fire, was thrown into the sea; ⁹ and a third of the sea became blood, a third of the living creatures in the sea died, and a third of the ships were destroyed.

10 The third angel blew his trumpet, and a great star fell from heaven, blazing like a torch, and it fell on a third of the rivers and on the fountains of water. ¹¹ The name of the star is Wormwood. A third of the waters became wormwood, and many men died of the water, because it was made bitter.

12 The fourth angel blew his trumpet, and a third of the sun was struck, and a third of the moon, and a third of the stars, so that a third of their light was darkened; a third of the day was kept from shining, and likewise a third of the night.

13 Then I looked, and I heard an eagle crying with a loud voice, as it flew in mid-heaven, "Woe, woe, woe to those who dwell on the earth, at the blasts of the other trumpets which the three angels are about to blow!"

9 And the fifth angel blew his trumpet, and I saw a star fallen from heaven to earth, and he was given the key of the shaft of the bottomless pit; ² he opened the shaft of the bottomless pit, and from the shaft rose smoke like the smoke of a great furnace, and the sun and the air were darkened with the smoke from the shaft. ³ Then from the smoke came locusts on the earth, and they were given power like the power of scorpions of the earth; ⁴ they were told not to harm the grass of the earth or any green

---

The beast from the abyss (11:7, announcing the theme of chs. 12 — 14) shall gain no lasting victory (11:11-12). At the sound of the seventh trumpet a song is heard in heaven which already celebrates the triumph of the Lord and His Christ (11:14-18). This song announces the themes of the second half of Rv (chs. 12 — 22): God and His Christ have become kings over the world with a reign that no satanic powers can long contest (chs. 12 — 14). The time has come to judge the dead (ch. 20), to reward the saints (chs. 21 — 22), and to destroy the enemies of God who destroy the earth (chs. 17 — 19). God's ultimate grace of the covenant and His ultimate judgment are in view. (11: 19)

8:1-12 THE FIRST FOUR TRUMPETS

8:2 *Stand before,* an OT expression for "are in the service of."

Trumpets were in the Biblical world more means of signaling than a musical instrument, used in the temple worship, in warfare, sounded at the accession of kings. The prophets spoke of the trumpet blast which would herald the coming of the Day of the Lord (Jl 2:1; Zph 1:16), and the NT speaks of the trumpet which shall herald the return of Christ and the resurrection of the dead (Mt 24:31; 1 Co 15:52; 1 Th 4:16). Here the trumpets speak of God's becoming King and the coming of the End.

8:3-5 *Prayers of all the saints* are welcomed and

sped on to God by God's angels. When the saints pray, "Thy kingdom come," they pray for judgment on all that opposes the coming of God's kingdom; hence the *peals of thunder,* etc.

8:7 *Hail . . . on the earth* recalls seventh plague on Egypt, Ex 9:23 ff.

8:9 *Sea became blood.* Cf. the first Egyptian plague, Ex 7:20 ff.

8:11 *Wormwood,* bitter and poisonous. (Cf. Jer 9:15)

8:12 Cf. the ninth Egyptian plague, Ex 10:21-23.

8:13 — 9:21 THE FIFTH AND SIXTH TRUMPETS

8:13 *Eagle.* For the eagle (or vulture) as a bird of ill omen cf. Hos 8:1.

9:1-3 The prophet sees a bright object *(star)* descended from heaven; on closer view this bright object is seen to be one of God's bright ministers *(he);* similarly the *smoke* from the *bottomless pit* is seen to be a dark swarm of *locusts.*

9:1 *Bottomless pit,* cf. 11; 20:1, 3. The wrath of God removes the barrier which His long-suffering patience has placed between the dark infernal world and man; man is exposed to powers he can no longer explain away as "the usual course of history" or "natural catastrophes." Man is made to feel his helplessness before the wrath of God.

9:3 *Locusts.* Cf. the eighth Egyptian plague, Ex 10:1-20, and Jl 1 — 2, which show how fearful a thing even a plague of natural locusts could be.

9:4 *Seal of God.* Cf. 7:3-4.

growth or any tree, but only those of mankind who have not the seal of God upon their foreheads; [5] they were allowed to torture them for five months, but not to kill them, and their torture was like the torture of a scorpion, when it stings a man. [6]And in those days men will seek death and will not find it; they will long to die, and death will fly from them.

7 In appearance the locusts were like horses arrayed for battle; on their heads were what looked like crowns of gold; their faces were like human faces, [8] their hair like women's hair, and their teeth like lions' teeth; [9] they had scales like iron breastplates, and the noise of their wings was like the noise of many chariots with horses rushing into battle. [10] They have tails like scorpions, and stings, and their power of hurting men for five months lies in their tails. [11] They have as king over them the angel of the bottomless pit; his name in Hebrew is A·bad′don, and in Greek he is called A·pol′lyon. [b]

12 The first woe has passed; behold, two woes are still to come.

13 Then the sixth angel blew his trumpet, and I heard a voice from the four horns of the golden altar before God, [14] saying to the sixth angel who had the trumpet, "Release the four angels who are bound at the great river Euphrates." [15] So the four angels were released, who had been held ready for the hour, the day, the month, and the year, to kill a third of mankind. [16] The number of the troops of cavalry was twice ten thousand times ten thousand; I heard their number. [17]And this was how I saw the horses in my vision: the riders wore breastplates the color of fire and of sapphire[c] and of sulphur, and the heads of the horses were like lions' heads, and fire and smoke and sulphur issued from their mouths. [18] By these three plagues a third of mankind was killed, by the fire and smoke and sulphur issuing from their mouths. [19] For the power of the horses is in their mouths and in their tails; their tails are like serpents, with heads, and by means of them they wound.

20 The rest of mankind, who were not killed by these plagues, did not repent of the works of their hands nor give up worshiping demons and idols of gold and silver and bronze and stone and wood, which cannot either see or hear or walk; [21] nor did they repent of their murders or their sorceries or their immorality or their thefts.

10 Then I saw another mighty angel coming down from heaven, wrapped in a cloud, with a rainbow over his head, and his face was like the sun, and his legs

[b] Or *Destroyer* | [c] Greek *hyacinth*

9:4-11 Three things distinguish these infernal locusts from the familiar locusts: (a) they attack, not vegetation but men, inflicting a pain like that of the bite of a *scorpion,* so intense that those smitten long for death; (b) their grotesquely horrible appearance; (c) their leader, the *angel of the bottomless pit, Abaddon,* the Destroyer.

9:5 *Five months,* the life-span of the locust.

The poisonous bite of the *scorpion* was proverbial (cf. 1 K 12:11; Eze 2:6). The scorpion is associated with "the power of the enemy" (Satan) in the word of Jesus, Lk 10:19.

9:11 *Abaddon* was in the OT a name for the PLACE of destruction, often associated with Sheol, the realm of the dead (cf. Jb 26:6; 28:22; Pr 15:11; Ps 88:11). Here it is a personal power of destruction.

9:12-19 The *troops of cavalry,* 200 million strong, are even more pronouncedly supernatural-demonic than the locusts, and their power of destruction greater (*killed,* 18). The only link with history is the mention of the *Euphrates* (14). Israel had experienced destructive judgments of God from beyond the great river (cf. Is 8:5-8), and in the Roman world men trembled for the security of the empire when they looked to the east.

9:20-21 God in His wrath has powers at His disposal which are so uncannily overwhelming that man can only throw himself on His mercy in repentance. This man refuses to do; he clings to his ungodliness (idolatry, 20) and his unrighteousness (21) in spite of all. (Cf. Ro 1:18)

9:20 *Works of their hands,* idols which their hands have made. (Cf. Hos 14:3)

10:1 — 11:19 INTERLUDE: ASSURANCE FOR THE CHURCH

10:1 — 11:13 Whatever the difficulties in interpreting the details of this vision, the main points of God's assurance to the church are plain: the oath sworn by the mighty angel assures the church that "the Lord is not slow about his promise as some count slowness" (2 Ptr 3:9), that He will fulfill all that He has promised (10:1-3). The bitter scroll eaten by the prophet is the renewal of his prophetic commission and assures the church that she shall not lack the guidance of the prophetic Word in the time of the third great woe (10:8-11). The vision of the measured temple assures the true church of God's protection and warns the church against compromise: the false church will perish (11:1-2). The church's task and destiny in the last days is pictured in the career of the two witnesses who call mankind to repentance

like pillars of fire. ² He had a little scroll open in his hand. And he set his right foot on the sea, and his left foot on the land, ³ and called out with a loud voice, like a lion roaring; when he called out, the seven thunders sounded. ⁴And when the seven thunders had sounded, I was about to write, but I heard a voice from heaven saying, "Seal up what the seven thunders have said, and do not write it down." ⁵And the angel whom I saw standing on sea and land lifted up his right hand to heaven ⁶ and swore by him who lives for ever and ever, who created heaven and what is in it, the earth and what is in it, and the sea and what is in it, that there should be no more delay, ⁷ but that in the days of the trumpet call to be sounded by the seventh angel, the mystery of God, as he announced to his servants the prophets, should be fulfilled.

8 Then the voice which I had heard from heaven spoke to me again, saying, "Go, take the scroll which is open in the hand of the angel who is standing on the sea and on the land." ⁹ So I went to the angel and told him to give me the little scroll; and he said to me, "Take it and eat; it will be bitter to your stomach, but sweet as honey in your mouth." ¹⁰And I took the little scroll from the hand of the angel and ate it; it was sweet as honey in my mouth, but when I had eaten it my stomach was made bitter. ¹¹And I was told, "You must again prophesy about many peoples and nations and tongues and kings."

11 Then I was given a measuring rod like a staff, and I was told: "Rise and measure the temple of God and the altar and those who worship there, ² but do not measure the court outside the temple; leave that out, for it is given over to the nations, and they will trample over the holy city for forty-two months. ³And I will grant my two witnesses power to prophesy for one thousand two hundred and sixty days, clothed in sackcloth."

4 These are the two olive trees and the two lampstands which stand before the

---

(*sackcloth*, 11:3) with all the power of an Elijah and a Moses, in their defeat by the beast from the bottomless pit, in their triumphant ascent into heaven. (11:3-13)

10:1 The *rainbow* indicates that the *mighty angel*, for all his blinding majesty and terrifying voice, is a messenger of the covenant God of mercy. (Cf. 4:3 note)

10:4 *Seal up what the seven thunders have said.* For the seven thunders as a manifestation of "the God of glory" cf. Ps 29. God remains sovereignly free in His revelation; the prophet is permitted to record, not everything but what the church needs to know, and what the church needs to know is contained in the angel's oath, 5-7.

10:7 *The mystery of God* is God's whole purpose for the world, to be known only by His revelation as it interprets His royal reign in history, moving toward His gracious goal. (Cf. Dn 2)

Announced, literally "told as good news." The *trumpet* of the *seventh angel* ushers in the third woe (8-11; cf. 11:14) for the impenitent but brings the good news of God's fulfilled purpose to the faithful.

10:8-11 For the taking and eating of the scroll as descriptive of the prophet's inspiration cf. Eze 2:8 — 3:3; Jer 15:16. The prophet can only receive the word from God; but once he has received it, it becomes a part of him. The receiving of the word is *sweet*, for the prophet is thus admitted into personal communion with God; it is *bitter* because the prophet is compelled to pronounce judgment on a rebellious world and the unfaithful church.

10:8 The *scroll* is *open* because the Lamb has opened the seals of God's book (ch. 5), and His secret has become an "open secret" since the coming of Christ.

10:9 The *scroll* is *little* as contrasted to the scroll in the hand of God in ch. 5, which contained the whole counsel of God; its content is confined to God's FINAL action in dealing with "peoples and nations and tongues and kings" (11), either the material of 11:1-13, or all of ch. 11, or more probably the remainder of Rv.

11:1-2 The *temple* is not the Jerusalem temple, destroyed 26 years before the writing of Rv, but signifies the church (cf. 1 Co 3:16; 2 Co 6:16). The *measuring* of the temple marks it off as God's property, sacrosanct and protected. The *court outside the temple* is the false or apostate church abandoned by God, as the ancient temple was when Israel went after false gods. (Cf. Is 63:10-19)

Forty-two months (cf. 1,260 days, 3), the 3½ years of the terrible reign of Antiochus IV (168 to 165 B. C.), when the temple was desecrated, became the measure for the duration of a period of oppression and affliction in Judaic tradition. (Cf. Dn 7:25; 12:7)

11:3 *Sackcloth*, sign of penitential mourning (cf. Jon 3:5-10; Mt 11:21). They preach repentance.

11:4 *Two olive trees . . . two lampstands.* The imagery is freely adapted from Zch 4:3, 11-14 (where the reference is to the political and the priestly leader of God's people) and marks the two witnesses as authorized representatives of God, active in His service, *stand before*. (Cf. 8:2 note)

Lord of the earth. 5And if any one would harm them, fire pours from their mouth and consumes their foes; if any one would harm them, thus he is doomed to be killed. 6 They have power to shut the sky, that no rain may fall during the days of their prophesying, and they have power over the waters to turn them into blood, and to smite the earth with every plague, as often as they desire. 7And when they have finished their testimony, the beast that ascends from the bottomless pit will make war upon them and conquer them and kill them, 8 and their dead bodies will lie in the street of the great city which is allegorically[d] called Sodom and Egypt, where their Lord was crucified. 9 For three days and a half men from the peoples and tribes and tongues and nations gaze at their dead bodies and refuse to let them be placed in a tomb, 10 and those who dwell on the earth will rejoice over them and make merry and exchange presents, because these two prophets had been a torment to those who dwell on the earth. 11 But after the three and a half days a breath of life from God entered them, and they stood up on their feet, and great fear fell on those who saw them. 12 Then they heard a loud voice from heaven saying to them, "Come up hither!" And in the sight of their foes they went up to heaven in a cloud. 13And at that hour there was a great earthquake, and a tenth of the city fell; seven thousand people were killed in the earthquake, and the rest were terrified and gave glory to the God of heaven.

14 The second woe has passed; behold, the third woe is soon to come.

15 Then the seventh angel blew his trumpet, and there were loud voices in heaven, saying, "The kingdom of the world has become the kingdom of our Lord and of his Christ, and he shall reign for ever and ever." 16And the twenty-four elders who sit on their thrones before God fell on their faces and worshiped God, 17 saying,

"We give thanks to thee, Lord God Almighty, who art and who wast,
    that thou hast taken thy great power and begun to reign.

18   The nations raged, but thy wrath came,
    and the time for the dead to be judged,
    for rewarding thy servants, the prophets and saints,
    and those who fear thy name, both small and great,
    and for destroying the destroyers of the earth."

19 Then God's temple in heaven was opened, and the ark of his covenant was seen within his temple; and there were flashes of lightning, voices, peals of thunder, an earthquake, and heavy hail.

[d] Greek *spiritually*

11:5-6 The power of the two witnesses (the witnessing church) is portrayed in terms that recall the mighty deeds of Elijah (2 K 1:10, 12; 1 K 17:1) and Moses. (Ex 7:17, 19)

11:7 The *beast,* Antichrist, or the antichristian power. (Cf. ch. 13)

11:8 *Great city,* apparently the same as the "holy city" of v. 2, the apostate people of God which has (like the Jerusalem that *crucified* the Lord Jesus) become the enemy of God and must therefore be called by names like *Sodom* and *Egypt,* typical opponents of the divine will.

Allegorically, or "spiritually"; that is, those enlightened by the Spirit know its true name and nature.

11:9 The refusal of burial adds degradation to defeat. (Cf. Jer 8:2; 22:18-19)

11:13 *Gave glory to . . . God,* by confessing their sin (cf. Jos 7:10; Jn 9:24). Here, in the word of assurance to the church, it becomes clear that there will be exceptions to the general rule of man's impenitence (cf. 9:20-21); through His witnessing church God will "by all means save some." (1 Co 9:22)

11:14-18 The *third woe* is not pictured at all; the *voices in heaven* and the *twenty-four elders* in their songs anticipate the outcome of that final woe: the manifest, uncontested, and eternal reign of the *Lord and of his Christ,* when divine judgment and grace have done their work.

11:17 *Who art and who wast.* There is any longer no need to say "who art to come." The promise of His coming has been fulfilled, the prayer of the church has been answered.

11:19 *Temple . . . opened . . . ark of his covenant . . . seen.* God is no longer hidden from men's eyes in the Holy of Holies enthroned unseen upon the *ark. His covenant* promise ("I will be your God") is forever fulfilled, and those that love Him see Him face to face.

12:1 — 22:7 To see and grasp fully the futility of any attempt at compromise, the church must be given eyes to see the satanic background of history, to look into the depths beneath the apparently solid surface, solid only to the unwarned, unrepentant, unexpectant eye. The deeper reality of history is the irreconcilable conflict between God and Satan, between God's kingdom and the satanic

Last Four Visions: Christ and the Powers of Darkness

12:1 — 22:5

FOURTH VISION: ANTI-TRINITY AND CHRIST (12:1 — 14:20)

12 And a great portent appeared in heaven, a woman clothed with the sun, with the moon under her feet, and on her head a crown of twelve stars; [2] she was with child and she cried out in her pangs of birth, in anguish for delivery. [3] And another portent appeared in heaven; behold, a great red dragon, with seven heads and ten horns, and seven diadems upon his heads. [4] His tail swept down a third of the stars of heaven, and cast them to the earth. And the dragon stood before the woman who was about to bear a child, that he might devour her child when she brought it forth; [5] she brought forth a male child, one who is to rule all the nations with a rod of iron, but her child was caught up to God and to his throne, [6] and the woman fled into the wilderness, where she has a place prepared by God, in which to be nourished for one thousand two hundred and sixty days.

[7] Now war arose in heaven, Michael and his angels fighting against the dragon; and the dragon and his angels fought, [8] but they were defeated and there was no longer any place for them in heaven. [9] And the great dragon was thrown down, that ancient serpent, who is called the Devil and Satan, the deceiver of the whole world—he was

counter-kingdom. This history, hinted at in the first half of Rv (2:9; 3:9; 2:13, 24; 9:1, 11; 11:7), is the subject of the second half.

12:1 — 14:20 The birth of the Messianic Child and the history of His persecuted church are nothing less than the final working out of the primal struggle that began with the fall of man in Gn 3. This history is the history of the assault of the enemy, furious but futile, on the Messiah and the Messianic people of God. (Ch. 12)

Satan is the imitator of God (cf. 2 Co 11:3-4, 13-15); he constitutes himself an anti-trinity (dragon, first beast, second beast) in opposition to the Father, Son, and Spirit. The satanic will becomes incarnate in historical powers which threaten to make the world too small for the people of God; Jesus' promise that the meek shall inherit the earth seems an uncertain word over against the might of these overwhelming and seductive powers. (Ch. 13)

But the ultimate triumph of Christ and His church is not called into question. The 144,000 faithful who have His Father's name inscribed on their brows sing their new song of victory on Mount Zion. Somber angelic voices call all men to repentance as they proclaim an eternal Gospel, announce the fall of Babylon (the anti-church, cf. ch. 17), and pronounce a curse on all who submit to the beast (the Antichrist). The golden-crowned Son of Man is seen reaping His ripened harvest and executing the bloody judgment of His vintage on the earth. (Ch. 14)

12:1, 3 The word *portent,* occurring here for the first time in Rv, marks the beginning of a new series of visions.

Woman symbolizes the people of God from whom the Messiah sprang; her splendor *(sun, moon, stars)* is from the heavenly world, God's gift to her. (By contrast, the anti-church Babylon, pictured as a harlot, has her ornaments from the lower world, the earth and the sea, 17:4). The

twelve stars recall the 12 tribes. (Cf. 7:4-8)

12:2 *Pangs of birth.* Cf. Mi 5:3.

12:3-4 *Dragon,* "that ancient serpent . . . Devil and Satan" (9), killer of men and father of the lie (Jn 8:44), is the inveterate opponent by nature of the Messianic Child whose coming means God's grace and truth for men (Jn 1:17); he is poised to destroy Him. The *ten horns* indicate his great power, the *seven diadems* his claim to royalty as "ruler of this world." (Jn 14:30)

12:4 *Swept down a third of the stars.* His terrible power has made inroads even on the heavenly world (cf. Dn 8:10). These fallen stars are the dragon's angels. (7)

12:5 The verse is practically a quotation of Ps 2:7-9 and definitely identifies the Child as the Messiah. The whole victorious career of the Messiah is summed up in the words *was caught up to God and to his throne;* Jesus similarly sums up His whole life's work in its triumphant conclusion: "I go to the Father." (Jn 16:10)

12:6 The Christ is at the right hand of God; the church is still in *the wilderness,* on earth far from her true and lasting home, like Israel far from Canaan. There God provides for her, as He did for Israel, until the time of affliction (1,260 days, cf. 11:1-2 note) is past. (The story of the woman is continued in 12:13-17.)

12:7-12 The church lives, imperilled and apparently helpless, in the wilderness; but God's saints can look forward confidently to ultimate victory and security and can face the prospect of martyrdom (11) and the last wrathful attack of the devil with serenity, for they know they face a defeated enemy. The decisive battle has been fought. Satan has lost his place as *accuser* of men before God (10), for the *blood* of the Lamb has atoned for man's guilt. The great and decisive reality now is, not the devil's short season of wrath but *the salvation and the power and kingdom of our God and the authority of his Christ.*

thrown down to the earth, and his angels were thrown down with him. [10]And I heard a loud voice in heaven, saying, "Now the salvation and the power and the kingdom of our God and the authority of his Christ have come, for the accuser of our brethren has been thrown down, who accuses them day and night before our God. [11]And they have conquered him by the blood of the Lamb and by the word of their testimony, for they loved not their lives even unto death. [12] Rejoice then, O heaven and you that dwell therein! But woe to you, O earth and sea, for the devil has come down to you in great wrath, because he knows that his time is short!"

13 And when the dragon saw that he had been thrown down to the earth, he pursued the woman who had borne the male child. [14] But the woman was given the two wings of the great eagle that she might fly from the serpent into the wilderness, to the place where she is to be nourished for a time, and times, and half a time. [15] The serpent poured water like a river out of his mouth after the woman, to sweep her away with the flood. [16] But the earth came to the help of the woman, and the earth opened its mouth and swallowed the river which the dragon had poured from his mouth. [17] Then the dragon was angry with the woman, and went off to make war on the rest of her offspring, on those who keep the commandments of God and bear testimony to Jesus. And he stood[e] on the sand of the sea.

13 And I saw a beast rising out of the sea, with ten horns and seven heads, with ten diadems upon its horns and a blasphemous name upon its heads. [2]And the beast that I saw was like a leopard, its feet were like a bear's, and its mouth was like a lion's mouth. And to it the dragon gave his power and his throne and great authority. [3] One of its heads seemed to have a mortal wound, but its mortal wound was healed, and the whole earth followed the beast with wonder. [4] Men worshiped the dragon, for he had given his authority to the beast, and they worshiped the beast, saying, "Who is like the beast, and who can fight against it?"

[5] And the beast was given a mouth uttering haughty and blasphemous words, and it was allowed to exercise authority for forty-two months; [6] it opened its mouth to

---

[e] Other ancient authorities read *And I stood*, connecting the sentence with 13.1

12:10 *Accuser.* He has no power over man because man has found in the man Jesus (who comprehends all men in Himself by His love) a love for God and an obedience to Him which the seducer could not destroy even in death. Jesus could say concerning him as He went to the cross: "He has no power over me." (Jn 14:30)

Our brethren. For the bond that unites angels and men, created by one God to serve Him as sons, cf. 22:8-9.

12:13-17 The church's position in the world wears a double aspect. She knows in faith that victory is hers; she HAS conquered by the blood of the Lamb (cf. 11). On the other hand, she knows of Satan's great wrath and has good cause for fear. The prophet's word of assurance to her is that the dragon cannot harm her; the God who led His ancient people safely through the sea and nourished them with manna in the wilderness will deliver her from the flood and will feed her.

12:14 *Time, and times, and half a time.* Still another way of expressing the 3½ years or 1,260 days. (Cf. Dn 7:25; Rv 11:1-2 note)

12:17 *The rest of her offspring.* The church appears as both inviolable and under attack. Therefore she is represented both by the *woman* and by *the rest of her offspring,* those whom Jesus claims as His brothers. (Heb 2:11; cf. Ro 8:29)

13:1-18 As Satan is anti-God, so he has his anti-Christ, a world power in which his opposition

to God becomes incarnate (the first *beast,* 1-10). As the Holy Spirit witnesses to Christ and glorifies Him (cf. Jn 15:26; 16:14), so there is a satanic anti-Spirit to witness to the Antichrist and to glorify him. (*Another beast,* 11-18)

13:1 *Beast rising out of the sea.* As the prophet looked out over the sea from Patmos (cf. 1:9), he looked toward Rome. Rome, the great world power with its deified emperor making a totalitarian claim on the loyalties of men, was the hostile world power confronting men in A. D. 96 and is the model for the beast as portrayed by the prophet. Its characteristic features reappear in subsequent history.

Ten horns, etc., point up the impressive, organized power of the Roman state.

Blasphemous name, e. g., the title favored by the emperor Domitian, "Lord and God."

13:2 Features that characterize successive world powers in Dn 7:1-6 are combined to characterize this world power.

13:3 *Mortal wound . . . healed.* The Antichrist is an imitation of the real Christ; he has apparently triumphed over death, like the slain Lamb. (Cf. 1:18; 5:6)

13:5 *Was given . . . was allowed.* Cf. 7, 14, 15. The use of the passive voice indicates that God remains in control of this wild satanic rebellion and sets limits to it (*forty-two months,* cf. 11:1-2 note). The reign of Antichrist is limited; He "who

utter blasphemies against God, blaspheming his name and his dwelling, that is, those who dwell in heaven. [7]Also it was allowed to make war on the saints and to conquer them.[f] And authority was given it over every tribe and people and tongue and nation, [8] and all who dwell on earth will worship it, every one whose name has not been written before the foundation of the world in the book of life of the Lamb that was slain. [9] If any one has an ear, let him hear:

[10]   If any one is to be taken captive,
              to captivity he goes;
          if any one slays with the sword,
              with the sword must he be slain.

Here is a call for the endurance and faith of the saints.

11 Then I saw another beast which rose out of the earth; it had two horns like a lamb and it spoke like a dragon. [12] It exercises all the authority of the first beast in its presence, and makes the earth and its inhabitants worship the first beast, whose mortal wound was healed. [13] It works great signs, even making fire come down from heaven to earth in the sight of men; [14] and by the signs which it is allowed to work in the presence of the beast, it deceives those who dwell on earth, bidding them make an image for the beast which was wounded by the sword and yet lived; [15] and it was allowed to give breath to the image of the beast so that the image of the beast should even speak, and to cause those who would not worship the image of the beast to be slain. [16]Also it causes all, both small and great, both rich and poor, both free and slave, to be marked on the right hand or the forehead, [17] so that no one can buy or sell unless he has the mark, that is, the name of the beast or the number of its name. [18] This calls for wisdom: let him who has understanding reckon the number of the beast, for it is a human number, its number is six hundred and sixty-six.[g]

14 Then I looked, and lo, on Mount Zion stood the Lamb, and with him a hundred and forty-four thousand who had his name and his Father's name written

---

[f] Other ancient authorities omit this sentence   [g] Other ancient authorities read *six hundred and sixteen*

---

sits upon the throne and the Lamb" shall have "honor and glory and might for ever and ever." (5:13)

13:7 *War on the saints.* Cf. "on the rest of her offspring," 12:17 note.

13:8 *Book of life.* Cf. 3:5 note. Those *written . . . in the book of life* are God's elect, whom nothing and no one can separate from the love of God in Christ Jesus. (Cf. Ro 8:28-39)

13:10 Cf. Jer 15:1-2. The church's mission is to suffer and die (cf. 6:11), not to offer violent resistance *(slays with the sword).* But the allusion to Jer 15:1-2 indicates that another reading suggested by some ancient authorities may be preferable. That reading is: "If any one is TO BE SLAIN with the sword, with the sword he must be slain," repeating the idea of the first half of the verse.

13:11 *Beast . . . out of the earth.* When the prophet on Patmos looked landward, he looked toward Asia Minor, where the cult of the deified Roman emperor had its most avid practitioners and propagandists. There the anti-Spirit is doing his work of glorifying the Antichrist.

Lamb . . . dragon. Cf. Jesus' description of the false prophet, Mt 7:15. However "religious" he may sound, this spirit is unmistakably the spirit of the *dragon,* Satan.

13:14-15 *Allowed.* The anti-Spirit too remains under God's overruling control. (Cf. 13:5 note)

13:16-17 With his *mark* the beast claims men as completely as God makes men His own by His

seal (7:3); by means of economic sanctions *(buy or sell),* he seeks to make men dependent on himself for their existence.

13:18 *Number of the beast* (666 or 616). Much ingenuity has been expended on the deciphering of this cryptic number, but no one solution has won general acceptance. It was probably used as a precautionary measure to prevent an utterance which could be construed as treasonable from falling into hostile Roman hands. The threefold six may indicate a threefold falling short of seven, the number of perfection; the anti-trinity is branded as a sorry imitation of the Trinity.

14:1-20 In God's mysterious governance of history the enemy has been "allowed to make war on the saints and to conquer them" (13:7); but the enemy's victory is as hollow as his claim to deity is false. Once more, just when the anti-trinity appears invincible, the suffering and dying church is assured of triumph: God's elect appear singing the new song that only they can know, the pure in heart, the redeemed who have not compromised with the satanic lie (1-5). Once more the church hears angelic voices announcing the impending judgment on all who have exchanged the truth of God for the lie of Babylon and the beast (6-11). Once more the church is permitted to behold the fearful alternative to the final harvest-home: the final vintage and the treading of the winepress of the wrath of God. (17-20)

14:1 *Mount Zion.* All that God has promised

on their foreheads. ²And I heard a voice from heaven like the sound of many waters and like the sound of loud thunder; the voice I heard was like the sound of harpers playing on their harps, ³ and they sing a new song before the throne and before the four living creatures and before the elders. No one could learn that song except the hundred and forty-four thousand who had been redeemed from the earth. ⁴ It is these who have not defiled themselves with women, for they are chaste;ʰ it is these who follow the Lamb wherever he goes; these have been redeemed from mankind as first fruits for God and the Lamb, ⁵ and in their mouth no lie was found, for they are spotless.

6 Then I saw another angel flying in midheaven, with an eternal gospel to proclaim to those who dwell on earth, to every nation and tribe and tongue and people; ⁷ and he said with a loud voice, "Fear God and give him glory, for the hour of his judgment has come; and worship him who made heaven and earth, the sea and the fountains of water."

8 Another angel, a second, followed, saying, "Fallen, fallen is Babylon the great, she who made all nations drink the wine of her impure passion."

9 And another angel, a third, followed them, saying with a loud voice, "If any one worships the beast and its image, and receives a mark on his forehead or on his hand, ¹⁰ he also shall drink the wine of God's wrath, poured unmixed into the cup of his anger, and he shall be tormented with fire and sulphur in the presence of the holy angels and in the presence of the Lamb. ¹¹And the smoke of their torment goes up for ever and ever; and they have no rest, day or night, these worshipers of the beast and its image, and whoever receives the mark of its name."

12 Here is a call for the endurance of the saints, those who keep the commandments of God and the faith of Jesus.

13 And I heard a voice from heaven saying, "Write this: Blessed are the dead who die in the Lord henceforth." "Blessed indeed," says the Spirit, "that they may rest from their labors, for their deeds follow them!"

14 Then I looked, and lo, a white cloud, and seated on the cloud one like a son of man, with a golden crown on his head, and a sharp sickle in his hand. ¹⁵And another angel came out of the temple, calling with a loud voice to him who sat upon the cloud, "Put in your sickle, and reap, for the hour to reap has come, for the harvest of the earth is fully ripe." ¹⁶ So he who sat upon the cloud swung his sickle on the earth, and the earth was reaped.

17 And another angel came out of the temple in heaven, and he too had a sharp sickle. ¹⁸ Then another angel came out from the altar, the angel who has power over fire, and he called with a loud voice to him who had the sharp sickle, "Put in your sickle, and gather the clusters of the vine of the earth, for its grapes are ripe." ¹⁹ So the angel swung his sickle on the earth and gathered the vintage of the earth, and threw it into the great wine press of the wrath of God; ²⁰ and the wine press was trodden outside the city, and blood flowed from the wine press, as high as a horse's bridle, for one thousand six hundred stadia.ⁱ

ʰ Greek *virgins*   ⁱ About two hundred miles

concerning His Anointed will come true; He WILL set His Anointed on His holy hill, in triumph over His enemies. (Ps 2:1-6)

His . . . and his Father's name written on their foreheads, not the mark of the beast. (Cf. 13:16; 14:9)

14:4 *Chaste* (virgins). For the virgin as a symbol of unsullied fidelity cf. 2 Co 11:2-3 and the contrast to the "impure passion" inspired by Babylon, 14:8, called "harlot" in 17:1, 5.

14:6-7 The fact that God still calls to men, His creatures, warning them not to repeat the sin of Adam by overleaping the boundary between creature and Creator (Gn 3), that is *gospel.*

14:8 *Babylon.* Cf. chs. 18 — 19.

14:10 *In the presence of . . . angels and . . . the Lamb.* This underscores the justice of their punishment; neither the angels through whom God warned and wooed them (6 ff.) nor the Lamb once slain for them will intercede for them.

14:13 *Henceforth,* from now and when they are being more and more sorely tried.

Their deeds follow them. They will be remembered in the judgment, when the books of men's lives lie opened before the Judge. (22:12; cf. Mt 25:31-46)

14:14 *One like a son of man,* Christ. (Cf. 1:13)

14:15 *Harvest.* For the harvest as the ingathering of God's people cf. Mt 9:37; Jn 4:35.

14:20 *Blood flowed.* The monstrous river of

FIFTH VISION: THE SEVEN BOWLS (15:1 — 16:21)

15 Then I saw another portent in heaven, great and wonderful, seven angels with seven plagues, which are the last, for with them the wrath of God is ended.

2 And I saw what appeared to be a sea of glass mingled with fire, and those who had conquered the beast and its image and the number of its name, standing beside the sea of glass with harps of God in their hands. ³And they sing the song of Moses, the servant of God, and the song of the Lamb, saying,

"Great and wonderful are thy deeds,
O Lord God the Almighty!
Just and true are thy ways,
O King of the ages!*ʲ*

4 Who shall not fear and glorify thy name, O Lord?
For thou alone art holy.
All nations shall come and worship thee,
for thy judgments have been revealed."

5 After this I looked, and the temple of the tent of witness in heaven was opened, ⁶ and out of the temple came the seven angels with the seven plagues, robed in pure bright linen, and their breasts girded with golden girdles. ⁷And one of the four living creatures gave the seven angels seven golden bowls full of the wrath of God who lives for ever and ever; ⁸ and the temple was filled with smoke from the glory of God and from his power, and no one could enter the temple until the seven plagues of the seven angels were ended.

16 Then I heard a loud voice from the temple telling the seven angels, "Go and pour out on the earth the seven bowls of the wrath of God."

2 So the first angel went and poured his bowl on the earth, and foul and evil sores came upon the men who bore the mark of the beast and worshiped its image.

3 The second angel poured his bowl into the sea, and it became like the blood of a dead man, and every living thing died that was in the sea.

4 The third angel poured his bowl into the rivers and the fountains of water, and they became blood. ⁵And I heard the angel of water say,

"Just art thou in these thy judgments,
thou who art and wast, O Holy One.

6 For men have shed the blood of saints and prophets,
and thou hast given them blood to drink.
It is their due!"

ʲ Other ancient authorities read *the nations*

---

blood points to the monstrosity of the sin which provoked God's judgment on it.

15:1 — 16:21 The mounting impiety of the world under satanic domination and the uttermost straits of the church call for the last judgmental blows of God within history before the Last Judgment, which concludes all history. These blows are represented by the outpouring of the seven bowls of wrath. For all their parallelism with the seven seals (chs. 4 — 7) and the seven trumpets (chs. 8 — 11), the bowls have a character of their own. They are related to the content of chs. 12 — 14 (15:2; 16:2, 10, 13, dragon, beast, false prophet = second beast) and 16:13, 19 points forward to the next unit (judgment on Babylon and the two beasts, chs. 17 — 19). Above all, these blows of God are characterized as climactic. There is a climactic stress on the fact that God's judgments are in the service of His redemptive will (15:3-8) and a climactic stress on the justice of God's judgmental action (15:3-4; 16:5-7). And the reaction of men is climactic; no longer are they merely

desperate (6:15-17) or impenitent (9:20-21); they now *cursed the God of heaven* (16:9, 11, 21). A heavenly voice speaks a climactic word: *"It is done!"* (16:17)

15:1 *Another portent.* Cf. 12:1, 3. The birth of the Messiah, the dragon's attack on the Messianic Child, and the bowls of wrath are portents of the world's last days.

15:2-4 God had delivered His people from Egypt by acts of judgment on their oppressors. God's final deliverance is pictured in colors taken from that event, the Exodus. As of old, His people stand by the sea, victorious and free, and the *song of Moses* (Ex 15) is taken up into the *song of the Lamb,* which praises God the Deliverer, now revealed as the Deliverer not only of Israel but of *all nations.*

15:5 *Temple . . . opened.* The ministers of God's judgment proceed from the place where God wills to be graciously present among His people (Ex 40:34-38); His judgments subserve His mercy.

15:8 *Smoke . . . glory of God.* Cf. Is 6:4.

[7]And I heard the altar cry,
    "Yea, Lord God the Almighty,
    true and just are thy judgments!"

8 The fourth angel poured his bowl on the sun, and it was allowed to scorch men with fire; [9] men were scorched by the fierce heat, and they cursed the name of God who had power over these plagues, and they did not repent and give him glory.

10 The fifth angel poured his bowl on the throne of the beast, and its kingdom was in darkness; men gnawed their tongues in anguish [11] and cursed the God of heaven for their pain and sores, and did not repent of their deeds.

12 The sixth angel poured his bowl on the great river Euphrates, and its water was dried up, to prepare the way for the kings from the east. [13]And I saw, issuing from the mouth of the dragon and from the mouth of the beast and from the mouth of the false prophet, three foul spirits like frogs; [14] for they are demonic spirits, performing signs, who go abroad to the kings of the whole world, to assemble them for battle on the great day of God the Almighty. [15] ("Lo, I am coming like a thief! Blessed is he who is awake, keeping his garments that he may not go naked and be seen exposed!") [16]And they assembled them at the place which is called in Hebrew Ar·ma·ged'don.

17 The seventh angel poured his bowl into the air, and a loud voice came out of the temple, from the throne, saying, "It is done!" [18]And there were flashes of lightning, voices, peals of thunder, and a great earthquake such as had never been since men were on the earth, so great was that earthquake. 19 The great city was split into three parts, and the cities of the nations fell, and God remembered great Babylon, to make her drain the cup of the fury of his wrath. [20]And every island fled away, and no mountains were to be found; [21] and great hailstones, heavy as a hundredweight, dropped on men from heaven, till men cursed God for the plague of the hail, so fearful was that plague.

SIXTH VISION: THE FATE OF BABYLON, THE ANTI-CHURCH (17:1 — 19:10)

17   Then one of the seven angels who had the seven bowls came and said to me, "Come, I will show you the judgment of the great harlot who is seated upon many waters, [2] with whom the kings of the earth have committed fornication, and with

---

16:9 *Give him glory.* Cf. 11:13 note.

16:12-16 Only the assembling of the armies of the *kings of the whole world . . .* for *battle* is told here; the battle is pictured in 19:19-21.

16:12 *Euphrates.* Cf. 9:12-19 note.

16:13 *Like frogs.* The sense is obscure.

16:14 *The great day.* Cf. 6:17: "great day . . . of wrath."

16:15 *I am coming like a thief.* The voice of Christ (cf. Mt 24:43; Lk 12:39; Rv 3:3) is heard unexpectedly in warning. Even when His return is near, it will not seem near; the huge armies arrayed against God would rather seem to indicate that victory and the End are still far off. Hence His call to vigilance.

16:16 *Armageddon.* This *Hebrew* name can be rendered "hill of assembly" (cf. Is 14:13-14) or "His (God's) fruitful mountain," referring to Mount Zion, from which help comes for God's people (Jl 2:32; 3:16-17, 21). Some translate "Mountain of Megiddo," referring to Mount Carmel — the city Megiddo, lying six miles from the base of the mountain, had been the scene of the victory won against fearful odds over the Canaanites by Deborah and Barak (Ju 5:19). The idea would then be that God's final victory would be similarly unexpected and astonishing. But since Mount Carmel is nowhere else identified by

reference to Megiddo, this interpretation, too, remains uncertain.

17:1 — 19:10 The announced theme of this vision is "the judgment of the great harlot" (17:1). In 17:1-18 the nature of this antichristian power, especially the connection between the harlot and the beast, is described and God's intention to destroy the harlot is announced. The next section (18:1-24) predicts and describes the judgment: Heavenly voices are heard proclaiming the doom of Babylon and bidding God's people to escape from her doom (1-8); kings, merchants, and shipmasters are heard lamenting the fall of the mighty and luxurious city (9-20); and a mighty angel is seen hurling a huge stone into the sea, an action symbolizing the overthrow of the city "drunk with the blood of the saints and . . . martyrs of Jesus" (21-24). The final section (19:1-10) brings the response of God's saints, *a great multitude in heaven,* to the overthrow of the persecuting power: a triple hallelujah of praise to the God who has by His judgment delivered them and invited them to the pure marriage supper of the Lamb.

17:1-18 THE HARLOT AND THE BEAST

17:1-18 The church has been (12:1 ff.) and will again be (19:7-8; 21:2, 9) pictured as a woman;

the wine of whose fornication the dwellers on earth have become drunk." ³And he carried me away in the Spirit into a wilderness, and I saw a woman sitting on a scarlet beast which was full of blasphemous names, and it had seven heads and ten horns. ⁴ The woman was arrayed in purple and scarlet, and bedecked with gold and jewels and pearls, holding in her hand a golden cup full of abominations and the impurities of her fornication; ⁵ and on her forehead was written a name of mystery: "Babylon the great, mother of harlots and of earth's abominations." ⁶And I saw the woman, drunk with the blood of the saints and the blood of the martyrs of Jesus.

When I saw her I marveled greatly. ⁷ But the angel said to me, "Why marvel? I will tell you the mystery of the woman, and of the beast with seven heads and ten horns that carries her. ⁸ The beast that you saw was, and is not, and is to ascend from the bottomless pit and go to perdition; and the dwellers on earth whose names have not been written in the book of life from the foundation of the world, will marvel to behold the beast, because it was and is not and is to come. ⁹ This calls for a mind with wisdom: the seven heads are seven mountains on which the woman is seated; ¹⁰ they are also seven kings, five of whom have fallen, one is, the other has not yet come, and when he comes he must remain only a little while. ¹¹As for the beast that was and is not, it is an eighth but it belongs to the seven, and it goes to perdition. ¹²And the ten horns that you saw are ten kings who have not yet received royal power, but they are to receive authority as kings for one hour, together with the beast. ¹³ These are of one mind and give over their power and authority to the beast; ¹⁴ they will make war on the Lamb, and the Lamb will conquer them, for he is Lord of lords and King of kings, and those with him are called and chosen and faithful."

15 And he said to me, "The waters that you saw, where the harlot is seated, are peoples and multitudes and nations and tongues. ¹⁶And the ten horns that you saw, they and the beast will hate the harlot; they will make her desolate and naked, and

the anti-church, too, appears under the figure of a woman, but a woman who is the extreme opposite of both personifications of the church. The woman of ch. 12 is adorned with ornaments of heaven (sun, moon, stars); the harlot is bedizened with ornaments taken from the earth and sea *(purple, scarlet, gold, jewels, pearls)*. The woman becomes the mother of the Messiah for the world's salvation (12:5). The harlot is like Babylon, the ancient enemy of God's people who dominated the world and corrupted what it dominated; she is *mother of harlots and of earth's abominations* (17:5). The bride is bound to Christ, in fellowship with God; the woman seated on the beast is a harlot, without ties or loyalties, alienated from God and persecutor of God's people. The woman has only God for her Protector in the wilderness (12:6) and the bride belongs to the unseen Christ who has been taken up to the throne of God (12:5); the harlot has wealth, luxury, and the visible and palpable power of the beast and the kings of the earth for her support.

That power is an uncanny imitation of God and Christ, with a mysteriously persistent vitality *(was, and is not, and is to ascend,* 8; cf. 1:4, 17-18) which casts a spell on men (8, 13). But it is a power massed in opposition to the Lamb (14) and so is doomed to *go to perdition* (8, 11). The beast and its subservient powers will in the end carry out God's purpose and fulfill His *words* (17); they *will hate the harlot* (as irrationally as they once were infatuated by her) and destroy her.

17:1 *Many waters.* This feature, taken from the situation of ancient Babylon, is interpreted al-

legorically in 15 as peoples, multitudes, tongues.

17:2 The *kings of the earth* have purchased her favors by submitting to her rule (cf. 13) and have been corrupted by her.

17:3 *Blasphemous names.* Cf. 13:1 note.

Heads . . . horns. Cf. 9, 10, 12.

17:4 *Cup . . . of abominations.* Perhaps a contrast to the "cup of blessing" (1 Co 10:16) of the Lord's Supper is implied.

17:5 *Name of mystery.* Cf. 7. Only the eye enlightened by God's revelation can see this opulent, voluptuous, and powerful figure for what she is: enemy of the people of God *(Babylon)* and corrupter of mankind *(mother of harlots,* etc.).

17:6 *Drunk with the blood.* She revels in bloodshed; Christians would remember how the emperor Nero had made his massacre of Christians in A. D. 64 a "circus entertainment," as a Roman historian calls it.

I marveled greatly. He had expected to see judgment (1), not this voluptuous and mighty figure, sure of herself. (Cf. 18:7)

17:7-18 The *mystery of the woman, and of the beast* remains something of a mystery. Rome *(seven mountains,* 9; *great city,* 18) a succession of Roman emperors *(seven kings,* 10) and kings who had become subjects of the Roman Empire *(ten kings,* 12-13) constitute the background and furnish the colors for the prophecy. So much is clear. Not so clear is the utterance of 11; the *eighth* seems to point to the return of a Roman emperor who has already appeared in history but will reappear. Perhaps the figure of Nero is the historical point of contact here. Nero had

devour her flesh and burn her up with fire, [17] for God has put it into their hearts to carry out his purpose by being of one mind and giving over their royal power to the beast, until the words of God shall be fulfilled. [18]And the woman that you saw is the great city which has dominion over the kings of the earth."

18 After this I saw another angel coming down from heaven, having great authority; and the earth was made bright with his splendor. [2]And he called out with a mighty voice,

"Fallen, fallen is Babylon the great!
It has become a dwelling place of demons,
a haunt of every foul spirit,
a haunt of every foul and hateful bird;

3   for all nations have drunk[k] the wine of her impure passion,
and the kings of the earth have committed fornication with her,
and the merchants of the earth have grown rich with the wealth of her wantonness."

[4] Then I heard another voice from heaven saying,
"Come out of her, my people,
lest you take part in her sins,
lest you share in her plagues;

5   for her sins are heaped high as heaven,
and God has remembered her iniquities.

6   Render to her as she herself has rendered,
and repay her double for her deeds;
mix a double draught for her in the cup she mixed.

7   As she glorified herself and played the wanton,
so give her a like measure of torment and mourning.
Since in her heart she says, 'A queen I sit,
I am no widow, mourning I shall never see,'

8   so shall her plagues come in a single day,
pestilence and mourning and famine,
and she shall be burned with fire;
for mighty is the Lord God who judges her."

9 And the kings of the earth, who committed fornication and were wanton with her, will weep and wail over her when they see the smoke of her burning; [10] they will stand far off, in fear of her torment, and say,

"Alas! alas! thou great city,
thou mighty city, Babylon!
In one hour has thy judgment come."

11 And the merchants of the earth weep and mourn for her, since no one buys their cargo any more, [12] cargo of gold, silver, jewels and pearls, fine linen, purple, silk and scarlet, all kinds of scented wood, all articles of ivory, all articles of costly wood, bronze, iron and marble, [13] cinnamon, spice, incense, myrrh, frankincense, wine, oil, fine

---

[k] Other ancient authorities read *fallen by*

---

embodied the persecuting power of Rome to a terrible degree. He had died in mysterious circumstances, and popular belief held that he was hidden somewhere in the East and would one day return. The persecuting power which Nero represented will appear again, in more terrible form, for the eighth is "abnormal," breaking the limits of "normal history," which can be structured in a scheme of sevens. This is the final concentration of the antichristian power doomed to go to perdition (11). The harlot Babylon is both dependent on this power (3) and destroyed by it (16). The anti-church has its seeds of destruction within itself. The point of 12 remains obscure.

17:17 The *words of God* are the real, enduring,

and decisive power in history. (Cf. Is 40:6-8)

18:1-24 "FALLEN, FALLEN IS BABYLON THE GREAT!"

18:1-24 Cf. the paraphrase at 17:1—19:10. The judgment on Babylon is the most broadly depicted; men needed full assurance that the great city, despite all its appearance of solid permanence, could not endure.

18:2 *Dwelling place of demons.* Demons were thought to haunt desolate places. Cf. the demoniacs "who lived among the tombs." (Mk 5:3)

18:4 *Another voice,* that of Christ, since He refers to *my people* and is distinguished from God. (5, 8)

flour and wheat, cattle and sheep, horses and chariots, and slaves, that is, human souls.
14   "The fruit for which thy soul longed has gone from thee,
     and all thy dainties and thy splendor are lost to thee, never to be found again!"
15 The merchants of these wares, who gained wealth from her, will stand far off, in fear of her torment, weeping and mourning aloud,
16   "Alas, alas, for the great city
     that was clothed in fine linen, in purple and scarlet,
     bedecked with gold, with jewels, and with pearls!
17   In one hour all this wealth has been laid waste."

And all shipmasters and seafaring men, sailors and all whose trade is on the sea, stood far off 18 and cried out as they saw the smoke of her burning,
     "What city was like the great city?"
19And they threw dust on their heads, as they wept and mourned, crying out,
     "Alas, alas, for the great city
     where all who had ships at sea grew rich by her wealth!
     In one hour she has been laid waste.
20   Rejoice over her, O heaven,
     O saints and apostles and prophets,
     for God has given judgment for you against her!"

21 Then a mighty angel took up a stone like a great millstone and threw it into the sea, saying,
     "So shall Babylon the great city be thrown down with violence,
     and shall be found no more;
22   and the sound of harpers and minstrels, of flute players and trumpeters,
     shall be heard in thee no more;
     and a craftsman of any craft
     shall be found in thee no more;
     and the sound of the millstone
     shall be heard in thee no more;
23   and the light of a lamp
     shall shine in thee no more;
     and the voice of bridegroom and bride
     shall be heard in thee no more;
     for thy merchants were the great men of the earth,
     and all nations were deceived by thy sorcery.
24   And in her was found the blood of prophets and of saints,
     and of all who have been slain on earth."

19 After this I heard what seemed to be the loud voice of a great multitude in heaven, crying,
     "Hallelujah! Salvation and glory and power belong to our God,
2   for his judgments are true and just;
     he has judged the great harlot who corrupted the earth with her fornication,
     and he has avenged on her the blood of his servants."
3 Once more they cried,
     "Hallelujah! The smoke from her goes up for ever and ever."
4And the twenty-four elders and the four living creatures fell down and worshiped God who is seated on the throne, saying, "Amen. Hallelujah!" 5And from the throne came a voice crying,
     "Praise our God, all you his servants,
     you who fear him, small and great."
6 Then I heard what seemed to be the voice of a great multitude, like the sound of many waters and like the sound of mighty thunderpeals, crying,
     "Hallelujah! For the Lord our God the Almighty reigns.
7   Let us rejoice and exult and give him the glory,

19:1-10 "HALLELUJAH!
     FOR THE . . . ALMIGHTY REIGNS"

19:1-10 Cf. the paraphrase at 17:1—19:10.

19:7 *Bride.* Cf. 21:2, 9. The church is here described under a new figure, since the church's union and communion with the Lamb (cf. 9) is to be stressed.

for the marriage of the Lamb has come,
and his Bride has made herself ready;

8   it was granted her to be clothed with fine linen, bright and pure"—
for the fine linen is the righteous deeds of the saints.

9 And the angel said[l] to me, "Write this: Blessed are those who are invited to the marriage supper of the Lamb." And he said to me, "These are true words of God." [10] Then I fell down at his feet to worship him, but he said to me, "You must not do that! I am a fellow servant with you and your brethren who hold the testimony of Jesus. Worship God." For the testimony of Jesus is the spirit of prophecy.

SEVENTH VISION: JUDGMENT AND RENEWAL (19:11 — 22:5)

11 Then I saw heaven opened, and behold, a white horse! He who sat upon it is called Faithful and True, and in righteousness he judges and makes war. [12] His eyes are like a flame of fire, and on his head are many diadems; and he has a name inscribed which no one knows but himself. [13] He is clad in a robe dipped in[m] blood, and the name by which he is called is The Word of God. [14]And the armies of heaven, arrayed in fine linen, white and pure, followed him on white horses. [15] From his mouth issues a sharp sword with which to smite the nations, and he will rule them with a rod of iron; he will tread the wine press of the fury of the wrath of God the Almighty. [16] On his robe and on his thigh he has a name inscribed, King of kings and Lord of lords.

17 Then I saw an angel standing in the sun, and with a loud voice he called to all the birds that fly in midheaven, "Come, gather for the great supper of God, [18] to eat the flesh of kings, the flesh of captains, the flesh of mighty men, the flesh of horses and their riders, and the flesh of all men, both free and slave, both small and great." [19]And I saw the beast and the kings of the earth with their armies gathered to make war against him who sits upon the horse and against his army. [20]And the beast was

[l] Greek he said   [m] Other ancient authorities read sprinkled with

19:8 It was granted her to be clothed with fine linen . . . the righteous deeds of the saints. All that the church has, including righteous deeds, is the gift and work of God (Cf. Ph 2:12-13 note). Therefore the dead are in the last judgment "judged . . . by what they had done." (20:12)

19:10 Worship. Overwhelmed by the greatness of the revelation which the angel (9) has mediated (cf. 17:1), the prophet offers to give him divine honor. The angel's refusal shows how the line between the Author of revelation and the agents of revelation is carefully safeguarded.

For the testimony of Jesus is the spirit of prophecy. The angel is fellow servant of other (human) witnesses. Jesus speaks by them through the Spirit of truth. (Cf. Jn 14:26; 16:14)

19:11 — 22:5 The satanic opponents of Christ appeared in the order: dragon, first and second beast, the harlot Babylon. They are judged and destroyed in the opposite order: Babylon (chs. 17 — 18), first and second beast (19:11-21), the dragon (20:1-10). When the dead have been judged and the "last enemy" (1 Co 15:26), death, has been destroyed (20:11-15), then the new world of God appears, the new heaven and new earth, the new Jerusalem, full of splendor, light, and life, wherein God's communion with His own is fully and forever consummated. (21:1 — 22:5)

1) 19:11-21 CHRIST TRIUMPHANT OVER THE TWO BEASTS

19:11-21 The true Rider on the white horse

(whose gruesome parody appeared at the opening of the first seal, 6:2) now appears. Four names express the fullness of His saving significance. He is Faithful and True (11), the Fulfiller of all the promises of God. He has a name . . . which no one knows but himself, expressing the mystery of His oneness with God, which makes His presence the very presence of God among men (12). He is called The Word of God (13), God's uttered light, life, grace, and truth for men (cf. Jn 1:4, 14). His name is King of kings and Lord of lords (16), before whom no Antichrist or antichristian emperors can stand. (17:21)

19:12 Eyes are like a flame. Cf. 1:13-16 note. Many diadems. He is Lord of all.

19:13 Robe dipped in blood. He is marked as Victor from the outset. Cf. Is 63:1-6, which is again echoed in 15 ("tread the wine press").

19:14 The armies of heaven appear, not as armed for battle but in the robes of victory; so sure is the outcome of the battle.

19:15 Mouth . . . sharp sword . . . rod of iron. Echoes of Messianic prophecies. (Is 11:4; Ps 2:8) Tread the wine press. Cf. Is 63:1-6. "The Father . . . has given all judgment to the Son." (Jn 5:22)

19:17-18 The angel's invitation to this great supper of God is the grim counterpart to the beatitude on those "invited to the marriage supper of the Lamb." (9)

19:19 Armies gathered. The attack planned in 16:12-16 is now to be executed.

19:20 The beast was captured. That is the whole

captured, and with it the false prophet who in its presence had worked the signs by which he deceived those who had received the mark of the beast and those who worshiped its image. These two were thrown alive into the lake of fire that burns with sulphur. [21]And the rest were slain by the sword of him who sits upon the horse, the sword that issues from his mouth; and all the birds were gorged with their flesh.

20 Then I saw an angel coming down from heaven, holding in his hand the key of the bottomless pit and a great chain. [2]And he seized the dragon, that ancient serpent, who is the Devil and Satan, and bound him for a thousand years, [3] and threw him into the pit, and shut it and sealed it over him, that he should deceive the nations no more, till the thousand years were ended. After that he must be loosed for a little while.

4 Then I saw thrones, and seated on them were those to whom judgment was committed. Also I saw the souls of those who had been beheaded for their testimony to Jesus and for the word of God, and who had not worshiped the beast or its image and had not received its mark on their foreheads or their hands. They came to life, and reigned with Christ a thousand years. [5] The rest of the dead did not come to life until the thousand years were ended. This is the first resurrection. [6] Blessed and holy is he who shares in the first resurrection! Over such the second death has no power, but they shall be priests of God and of Christ, and they shall reign with him a thousand years.

7 And when the thousand years are ended, Satan will be loosed from his prison [8] and will come out to deceive the nations which are at the four corners of the earth,

---

description of the battle; the attack was doomed to failure.

False prophet describes the second beast according to his activity as spokesman for the first beast. (Cf. 13:11 ff.)

Lake of fire, the place of eternal punishment. Cf. Mt 25:41 and the description of Gehenna, Mk 9:43, 47-48.

2) 20:1-10 THE OVERTHROW OF THE DRAGON

20:1-10 The overthrow of the dragon is accomplished in two stages. The first stage, the binding of Satan for 1,000 years (1-3), corresponds to the defeat of Satan at the birth of the Messiah (12:7-9). The 1,000 years are the era of the hidden but real reign of Christ, the time of His hidden triumph (hidden under the cross) and the time of the hidden triumph of His church, hidden under martyrdom but in reality a life and reign with Christ (4-6). The hidden triumph becomes a manifest triumph at the end of the 1,000 years, when Satan is permitted to make his last desperate assault and is consigned to everlasting torment in the lake of fire.

20:1 *Bottomless pit.* Cf. 9:1, 11; 11:7; 17:8.

20:2 *Bound him.* Cf. Jesus' word concerning the binding of the "strong man" (Satan) by His (Jesus') coming and the manifestation of that victory in His power over the demons, Mt 12:28-29. Jesus speaks also of Satan as fallen (Lk 10:17-19), cast out (Jn 12:31-32), and judged (Jn 16:11) by His, Jesus', faithful and mighty ministry.

20:3 *Deceive the nations no more.* Since the truth of God has appeared in Jesus (Jn 1:17) to unmask and overcome the satanic lie (Jn 8:44), no one NEED be deceived by him any more; only those who have "refused to love the truth" are condemned to be subject to the "strong delusions"

of Satan, to "believe what is false" (2 Th 2:9-11). Cf. also 19:20, where it is said that those who "had received the mark of the beast," i. e., submitted to him, were deceived by the "signs" worked by the "false prophet."

20:4 *Thrones . . . judgment.* The language echoes Dn 7:9, 22, 26-27 and recalls the substance of Daniel's vision: "the Ancient of Days came, and judgment was given for the saints of the Most High, and the time came when the saints received the kingdom." (Dn 7:22)

The souls (cf. 6:9 "souls of those . . . slain," etc.) are those who have lost their life for Christ's sake and now find it in a life and reign with Christ, according to His promise. (Mt 16:25; Jn 12:25-26)

20:5 *The rest of the dead,* those resurrected for judgment. (Cf. 12)

The first resurrection. Their life and reign with Christ NOW is an anticipation of the resurrection and the life of the world to come. Cf. Jn 5:24-25; 12:26, 32; and Jn 11:23-26, where Jesus directs Martha's thoughts away from "the resurrection at the last day" and turns them to Himself as the present resurrection and life.

20:6 *The second death,* defined in 14 as the eternal torment of "the lake of fire."

They shall reign. It is probably significant that the words "on earth" contained in the promise to the priestly people in 5:10 are not repeated here. This reign during the 1,000 years is not yet the ultimate reign on earth, the new earth of the world to come.

20:8 *Gog* appears in Eze 38—39 as the last great enemy of the people of God, destroyed by God in battle. *Magog* is, in Eze, his land; whether the term is here used in the same way ("Gog and his land, his people") or whether Magog is also a personal name, can hardly be made out.

that is, Gog and Magog, to gather them for battle; their number is like the sand of the sea. [9]And they marched up over the broad earth and surrounded the camp of the saints and the beloved city; but fire came down from heaven[n] and consumed them, [10]and the devil who had deceived them was thrown into the lake of fire and sulphur where the beast and the false prophet were, and they will be tormented day and night for ever and ever.

11 Then I saw a great white throne and him who sat upon it; from his presence earth and sky fled away, and no place was found for them. [12]And I saw the dead, great and small, standing before the throne, and books were opened. Also another book was opened, which is the book of life. And the dead were judged by what was written in the books, by what they had done. [13]And the sea gave up the dead in it, Death and Hades gave up the dead in them, and all were judged by what they had done. [14] Then Death and Hades were thrown into the lake of fire. This is the second death, the lake of fire; [15] and if any one's name was not found written in the book of life, he was thrown into the lake of fire.

21 Then I saw a new heaven and a new earth; for the first heaven and the first earth had passed away, and the sea was no more. [2]And I saw the holy city, new Jerusalem, coming down out of heaven from God, prepared as a bride adorned for her husband; [3] and I heard a loud voice from the throne saying, "Behold, the dwelling of God is with men. He will dwell with them, and they shall be his people,[o] and God himself will be with them;[p] [4] he will wipe away every tear from their eyes, and death shall be no more, neither shall there be mourning nor crying nor pain any more, for the former things have passed away."

[n] Other ancient authorities read *from God, out of heaven*, or *out of heaven from God*
[o] Other ancient authorities read *peoples*   [p] Other ancient authorities add *and be their God*

20:9 *Camp of the saints* and *beloved city* (cf. 21:2, 9) both designate God's people, the church.

Fire came . . . consumed. Again (cf. 19:20) there is really no battle. The already defeated foe (20: 1-3) is destroyed.

3) 20:11-15 THE LAST JUDGMENT

20:11 *Throne,* symbol of judgment. (Cf. 4 and Mt 19:28)

Earth and sky fled away. The present heaven and earth, marred by man's sin (Ro 8:20-22), cannot stand before the Judge as they are. They must disappear in their present form ("The FORM of this world is passing away," 1 Co 7:31) to make way for the new, transfigured heaven and earth. (21:1)

20:12 *Books . . . book of life.* Both the book of life and the books which record men's deeds *(what they had done)* are significant in the Judgment. Man is saved and acquitted solely by the grace of God, which has chosen him freely and inscribed his name in the book of life; but the book of each man's life will show whether a man has really received that grace and has not received it in vain, whether God's gracious Word has by its power brought forth fruit for God. This same double emphasis on God's free grace and man's responsibility under that grace appears in Jesus' portrayal of the Last Judgment, Mt 25:31-46 ("Come, O blessed of my Father, inherit the kingdom PREPARED FOR YOU," and "You DID it to me"; cf. Ph 2:12-13).

20:14 *Lake of fire.* Cf. Mt 25:41: "the eternal fire PREPARED FOR THE DEVIL and his angels." When man opposes God, he makes the devil's doom his own.

4) 21:1 — 22:5 THE NEW WORLD OF GOD

21:1 — 22:5 The new world of God is restored creation (*new heaven and a new earth,* 1). And it is consummated communion between God and man; therefore it is a *holy city,* a new city of God, *Jerusalem,* united with the *Lamb* as His *Bride* (2, 9). There God dwells with men and shall be their everlasting Comforter (4). The promise made to the Messiah, "I will be his father, and he shall be my son" (2 Sm 7:14), will be fulfilled for all who dwell in the holy city (7). The appointments and dimensions of the new Jerusalem are twelve and multiples of twelve; the city is the perfect embodiment of the community-creating will of God who chose *the twelve tribes* of Israel and of the Lamb who appointed the *twelve apostles* (12, 14). There is *no temple in the city* (symbol and embodiment of God's communion with His people), for the city has more than the temple — the immediate presence of the *Lord God the Almighty and the Lamb* (22). The new community of God embraces all *nations* (24, 26); men of all nations shall *worship* Him together, *see his face,* and bear His *name* upon their brows (22:3-4). And all *shall reign* with Him *for ever and ever* (22:5). All that is sad and ugly and false is banished from this city (21:4, 8, 27; 22:3); the new world in which righteousness dwells is full of brilliant beauty (gems!), full of *light* (21:23, 24, 25), God's own light (22:5), full of life (*water of life,* 21:6; 22:1; *tree of life,* 22:2), and perfect health. (22:2)

21:1 *The sea was no more.* The ancient world dreaded the sea for its violence and treachery (cf. Ps 107:23-28; Is 57:20; Eze 28:8). That God should be Lord even over this untamable element

5 And he who sat upon the throne said, "Behold, I make all things new." Also he said, "Write this, for these words are trustworthy and true." 6And he said to me, "It is done! I am the Alpha and the Omega, the beginning and the end. To the thirsty I will give from the fountain of the water of life without payment. 7 He who conquers shall have this heritage, and I will be his God and he shall be my son. 8 But as for the cowardly, the faithless, the polluted, as for murderers, fornicators, sorcerers, idolaters, and all liars, their lot shall be in the lake that burns with fire and sulphur, which is the second death."

9 Then came one of the seven angels who had the seven bowls full of the seven last plagues, and spoke to me, saying, "Come, I will show you the Bride, the wife of the Lamb." 10And in the Spirit he carried me away to a great, high mountain, and showed me the holy city Jerusalem coming down out of heaven from God, 11 having the glory of God, its radiance like a most rare jewel, like a jasper, clear as crystal. 12 It had a great, high wall, with twelve gates, and at the gates twelve angels, and on the gates the names of the twelve tribes of the sons of Israel were inscribed; 13 on the east three gates, on the north three gates, on the south three gates, and on the west three gates. 14And the wall of the city had twelve foundations, and on them the twelve names of the twelve apostles of the Lamb.

15 And he who talked to me had a measuring rod of gold to measure the city and its gates and walls. 16 The city lies foursquare, its length the same as its breadth; and he measured the city with his rod, twelve thousand stadia;q its length and breadth and height are equal. 17 He also measured its wall, a hundred and forty-four cubits by a man's measure, that is, an angel's. 18 The wall was built of jasper, while the city was pure gold, clear as glass. 19 The foundations of the wall of the city were adorned with every jewel; the first was jasper, the second sapphire, the third agate, the fourth emerald, 20 the fifth onyx, the sixth carnelian, the seventh chrysolite, the eighth beryl, the ninth topaz, the tenth chrysoprase, the eleventh jacinth, the twelfth amethyst. 21And the twelve gates were twelve pearls, each of the gates made of a single pearl, and the street of the city was pure gold, transparent as glass.

22 And I saw no temple in the city, for its temple is the Lord God the Almighty and the Lamb. 23And the city has no need of sun or moon to shine upon it, for the glory of God is its light, and its lamp is the Lamb. 24 By its light shall the nations walk; and the kings of the earth shall bring their glory into it, 25 and its gates shall never be shut by day—and there shall be no night there; 26 they shall bring into it the glory and the honor of the nations. 27 But nothing unclean shall enter it, nor any one who practices abomination or falsehood, but only those who are written in the Lamb's book of life.

22 Then he showed me the river of the water of life, bright as crystal, flowing from the throne of God and of the Lamb 2 through the middle of the street of the city; also, on either side of the river, the tree of lifer with its twelve kinds of fruit, yielding its fruit each month; and the leaves of the tree were for the healing of the nations. 3 There shall no more be anything accursed, but the throne of God and of the Lamb shall be in it, and his servants shall worship him; 4 they shall see his face, and his name shall be on their foreheads. 5And night shall be no more; they need no light of lamp or sun, for the Lord God will be their light, and they shall reign for ever and ever.

CONCLUSION (22:6-21)

6 And he said to me, "These words are trustworthy and true. And the Lord, the

q About fifteen hundred miles
r Or the Lamb. In the midst of the street of the city, and on either side of the river, was the tree of life, etc.

---

was cause for special awe and wonder (Ps 46:1-3). The dread of a world turned against man will disappear in God's new world.

21:16 *Length and breadth and height are equal,* like that of the Holy of Holies in the temple (1 K 6:20). The whole city has become the innermost sanctuary of God's dwelling.

21:17 *Man's measure, that is, an angel's.* Since

the angel is a "fellow servant" of men (19:10; 22:9), he measures with the same standard. Why this should be expressly mentioned here remains obscure.

21:24, 26 All that is bright and best of creation returns home to the Creator, to His glory.

22:6-21 The book closes, as it began (1:4-5), as a letter, a personal urgent word of Christ to His

God of the spirits of the prophets, has sent his angel to show his servants what must soon take place. [7]And behold, I am coming soon."

Blessed is he who keeps the words of the prophecy of this book.

8 I John am he who heard and saw these things. And when I heard and saw them, I fell down to worship at the feet of the angel who showed them to me; [9] but he said to me, "You must not do that! I am a fellow servant with you and your brethren the prophets, and with those who keep the words of this book. Worship God."

10 And he said to me, "Do not seal up the words of the prophecy of this book, for the time is near. [11] Let the evildoer still do evil, and the filthy still be filthy, and the righteous still do right, and the holy still be holy."

12 "Behold, I am coming soon, bringing my recompense, to repay every one for what he has done. [13] I am the Alpha and the Omega, the first and the last, the beginning and the end."

14 Blessed are those who wash their robes,[s] that they may have the right to the tree of life and that they may enter the city by the gates. [15] Outside are the dogs and sorcerers and fornicators and murderers and idolaters, and every one who loves and practices falsehood.

16 "I Jesus have sent my angel to you with this testimony for the churches. I am the root and the offspring of David, the bright morning star."

17 The Spirit and the Bride say, "Come." And let him who hears say, "Come." And let him who is thirsty come, let him who desires take the water of life without price.

18 I warn every one who hears the words of the prophecy of this book: if any one adds to them, God will add to him the plagues described in this book, [19] and if any one takes away from the words of the book of this prophecy, God will take away his share in the tree of life and in the holy city, which are described in this book.

20 He who testifies to these things says, "Surely I am coming soon." Amen. Come, Lord Jesus!

21 The grace of the Lord Jesus be with all the saints.[t] Amen.

[s] Other ancient authorities read *do his commandments*   [t] Other ancient authorities omit *all;* others omit *the saints*

church; the concluding benediction is one commonly used by Paul in his letters (e. g., 1 Co 16:23; 2 Co 13:13; 2 Th 3:18). Three times Jesus' urgent word is heard: *I am coming soon* (7, 12, 20). He comes, the Revealer, whose Word must be heard and heeded (7). He comes, the Recompense, the First and Last who has spoken the first word of grace and will speak the last word of judgment (12-13). He comes, Jesus the incarnate Christ *(root and offspring of David),* the Dawn of salvation *(morning star)* in whom His people have already tasted the powers of the world to come (16). Three times the word of longing response is heard, *Come.* The Spirit-filled church *(Spirit and the Bride,* 17) cries, *Come;* the prophet John prays, *Amen. Come, Lord Jesus* (20); and every one who hears the prophetic word is bidden to join in that prayer (17). When the church, endowed with "eternal comfort and good hope" (2 Th 2:16) through the grace of the Lord Jesus, has become the longing church, the purpose of Rv has been accomplished. The longing church can in the vitality of her hope live in obedience to the Word of God, without adding thereto or taking therefrom (7, 18-19); can in holy fear recognize the fearful alternatives to her appointed way and shun them (11, 15); can live a life of continual repentance by washing her robes (14) and drinking of the freely given waters of life (17) and so come at last to the tree of life and enter the holy city by the gates. (14)

22:7 Cf. 1:3.

22:8-9 Cf. 19:10 note.

22:11 *Let the evildoer,* etc. The issues are clear, by the light of the revelation given; a man may and must choose his way. No one can plead ignorance. The beatitude of 14 and the invitation of 17b make it clear that repentance is still possible; the *filthy* can become clean and the water of life is available without price for the *evil* man who turns from his ways.

22:15 *Dogs* were considered unclean animals; the OT uses the term *dog* of a sodomite. (Dt 23:18)

22:16 *Root and . . . offspring of David.* Cf. Is 11:1. *Star.* Cf. Nm 24:17.

22:18-19 Cf. Dt 4:2; 13:1; 29:20.

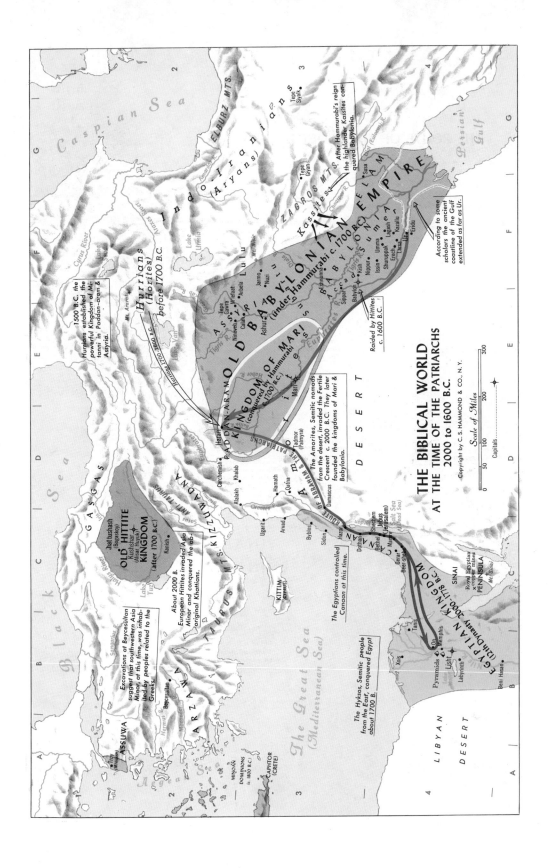

THE BIBLICAL WORLD
AT THE TIME OF THE PATRIARCHS
2000 to 1600 B.C.

Copyright by C. S. HAMMOND & CO., N. Y.

Scale of Miles
0   50   100   200   300

Capitals.................

Hurrians 1500 B.C. the
established the powerful Kingdom of Mi-
tanni in Paddan-aram &
Assyria.

After Hammurabi's reign,
the highlander Kassites conquered Babylonia.

According to some
scholars the ancient
coastline of the Gulf
extended as far as Ur.

Raided by Hittites
c. 1600 B.C.

The Amorites, Semitic nomads
from the desert, invaded the Fertile
Crescent c. 2000 B.C. They later
founded the kingdoms of Mari &
Babylonia.

Excavations at Beycesultan
suggest that southwestern Asia
Minor, at this time, was inhab-
ited by peoples related to the
Greeks.

About 2000 B.
European Hittites invaded Asia
Minor and conquered the ab-
original Khattians.

The Egyptians controlled
Canaan at this time.

The Hyksos, Semitic people
from the East, conquered Egypt
about 1700 B.

O L D   B A B Y L O N I A N

E M P I R E

(under Hammurabi c. 1700 B.C.)

KINGDOM OF MARI
(conquered by Hammurabi
c. 1700 B.C.)

PADDAN-ARAM

OLD HITTITE
KINGDOM
(after 1700 B.C.)

EGYPTIAN KINGDOM
(12th Dynasty 2000-1776 B.C.)

Caspian Sea

Black Sea

The Great Sea
(Mediterranean Sea)

Aegean Sea

Persian Gulf

DESERT

LIBYAN   DESERT

SINAI
PENINSULA

Hurrians (Horites)
before 1700 B.C.

Indo-Iranians
(Aryans)

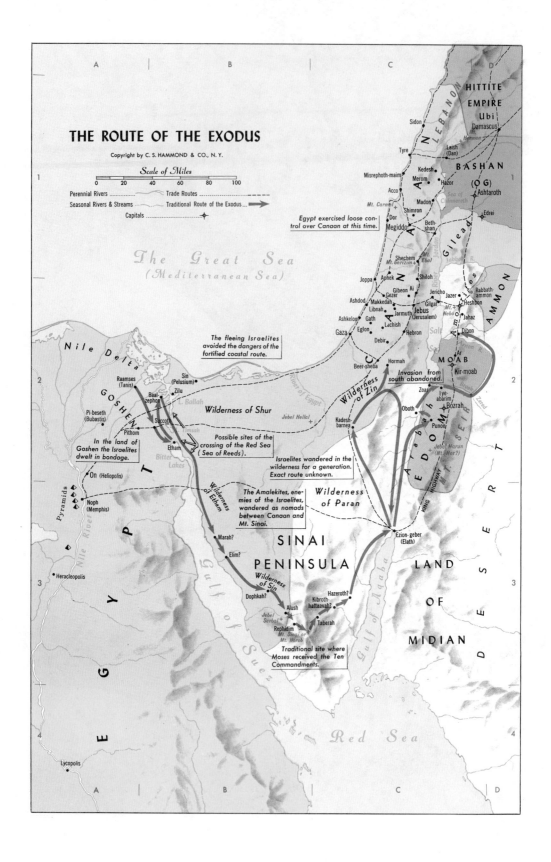

THE ROUTE OF THE EXODUS

Copyright by C. S. HAMMOND & CO., N. Y.

Scale of Miles

0   20   40   60   80   100

Perennial Rivers ....
Seasonal Rivers & Streams ......
Capitals ....✦

Trade Routes ....
Traditional Route of the Exodus ...➤

Egypt exercised loose control over Canaan at this time.

The fleeing Israelites
avoided the dangers of the
fortified coastal route.

The Great Sea
(Mediterranean Sea)

Nile Delta

Invasion from
south abandoned.

Possible sites of the
crossing of the Red Sea
(Sea of Reeds).

In the land of
Goshen the Israelites
dwelt in bondage.

Israelites wandered in the
wilderness for a generation.
Exact route unknown.

The Amalekites, ene-
mies of the Israelites,
wandered as nomads
between Canaan and
Mt. Sinai.

Wilderness
of Paran

SINAI
PENINSULA

LAND

OF

MIDIAN

Wilderness
of Sin

Traditional site where
Moses received the Ten
Commandments.

Red Sea

HITTITE
EMPIRE
Ubi
Damascus

BASHAN
(OG)

Place names

Sidon
Tyre
Leish (Dan)
Kedesh
Misrephoth-maim
Merom
Hazor
Acco
Ashtaroth
Edrei
Mt. Carmel
Shimron
Madon
Dor
Megiddo
Beth-shan
Gilead
Shechem
Mt. Gerizim
Mt. Ebal
Shiloh
Joppa
Aphek
Rabbath-ammon
AMMON
Gibeon
Gezer
Jericho
Jazer
Heshbon
Ashdod
Makkedah
Gilgal
Mt. Nebo
Libnah
Jebus (Jerusalem)
Jahaz
Ashkelon
Gath
Jarmuth
Lachish
Dibon
Gaza
Eglon
Hebron
Debir
Beer-sheba
Hormah
MOAB
Kir-moab
Wilderness
of Zin
Zoar
Iye-abarim
Oboth
Bôzrah
Punon
Kadesh-barnea
EDOM
Jebel Harun
(Mt. Hor?)
Ezion-geber
(Elath)
KING'S HIGHWAY
MT. SEIR
DESERT

Raamses (Tanis)
Sin (Pelusium)
Zilu
Baal-zephon
L. Ballah
GOSHEN
Pi-beseth (Bubastis)
Pithom
Succoth
River of Egypt
Jebel Hallal
Wilderness of Shur
Etham
L. Timsah
Bitter Lakes
On (Heliopolis)
Pyramids
Noph (Memphis)
Wilderness of Etham
Heracleopolis
Marah?
Elim?
Gulf of Suez
Dophkah?
Alush
Jebel Serbal
Rephidim
Mt. Sinai or Mt. Horeb
Hazeroth?
Kibroth-hattaavah?
Taberah
Gulf of Aqaba

EGYPT

Lycopolis

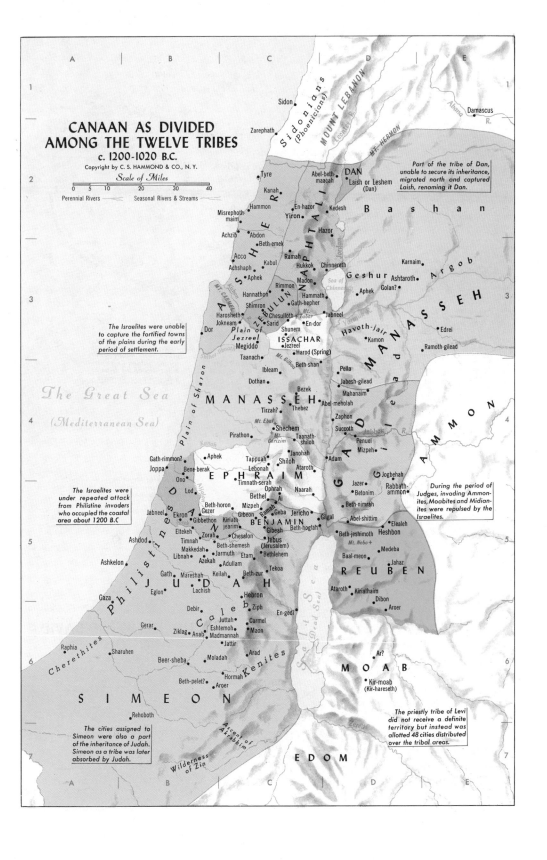

CANAAN AS DIVIDED
AMONG THE TWELVE TRIBES
c. 1200-1020 B.C.

Copyright by C. S. HAMMOND & CO., N. Y.

Scale of Miles

0 5 10   20   30   40

Perennial Rivers   Seasonal Rivers & Streams

Part of the tribe of Dan, unable to secure its inheritance, migrated north and captured Laish, renaming it Dan.

The Israelites were unable to capture the fortified towns of the plains during the early period of settlement.

The Israelites were under repeated attack from Philistine invaders who occupied the coastal area about 1200 B.C.

During the period of Judges, invading Ammonites, Moabites and Midianites were repulsed by the Israelites.

The cities assigned to Simeon were also a part of the inheritance of Judah. Simeon as a tribe was later absorbed by Judah.

The priestly tribe of Levi did not receive a definite territory but instead was allotted 48 cities distributed over the tribal areas.

The Great Sea
(Mediterranean Sea)

Sidon
Zarephath
Sidonians (Phoenicians)
MOUNT LEBANON
Leontes R.
MT. HERMON
Abana R.
Damascus

Tyre
Kanah
Hammon
Misrephoth-maim
Achzib
Abdon
Beth-emek
Acco
Achshaph
Aphek
Haroseth
Jokneam
Dor

Abel-beth-maacah
DAN
Laish or Leshem (Dan)
En-hazor
Kedesh
Yiron
Hazor

Bashan

MT. CARMEL
Kishon R.
ASHER
NAPHTALI
Ramah
Hukkok
Chinnereth
Kabul
Madon
Rimmon
Hannathon
Shimron
Gath-hepher
Hammath
ZEBULUN
Chesulloth
Sarid
Jabneel
Mt. Tabor
Shunem
En-dor

Geshur
Ashtaroth
Golan?
Aphek
Karnaim
Argob
MANASSEH
Edrei

Sea of Chinnereth
Jordan

Plain of Jezreel
ISSACHAR
Megiddo
Taanach
Ibleam
Dothan
Jezreel
Harod (Spring)
Beth-shan
Mt. Gilboa

Havoth-jair
Kamon
Ramoth-gilead

Plain of Sharon
Shihor-libnath R.

MANASSEH
Tirzah?
Thebez
Bezek
Mahanaim
Abel-meholah
Pella
Jabesh-gilead

Mt. Ebal
Shechem
Mt. Gerizim
Pirathon
Taanath-shiloh
Janohah
Zaphon
Succoth
Penuel
Mizpeh
Jabbok R.
GAD
Gilead

AMMON

Kanah R.
Gath-rimmon?
Aphek
Tappuah
Shiloh
Lebonah
Ataroth
Adam
Joppa
Bene-berak
Ono
EPHRAIM
Timnath-serah
Ophrah
Naarah
Jazer
Betonim
Jogbehah
Rabbath-ammon
Lod
Bethel
Mizpeh
Beth-nimrah
Beth-horon
Gezer
Gibeon
Ramah
Geba
Jericho
Abel-shittim
Elealeh
Jabneel
Ekron
DAN
Gibbethon
Kiriath-jearim
BENJAMIN
Gibeah
Gilgal
Heshbon
Eltekeh
Zorah
Chesalon
Jebus (Jerusalem)
Beth-hoglah
Beth-jeshimoth
Mt. Nebo
Ashdod
Timnah
Makkedah
Beth-shemesh
Bethlehem
Baal-meon
Medeba
Libnah
Jarmuth
Etam
Jahaz
Azekah
Adullam
Tekoa
REUBEN

Ashkelon
Gath
Mareshah
Keilah
Beth-zur
PHILISTINES
Eglon
Lachish
Hebron
Ataroth
Kiriathaim
Dibon
Gaza
JUDAH
Debir
Ziph
En-gedi
Aroer
Gerar
Juttah
Carmel
Caleb
Ziklag
Anab
Eshtemoh
Maon
Madmannah
Jattir
Arad
Raphia
Sharuhen
Cherethites
Beer-sheba
Moladah
Ar?

Salt (Dead) Sea

MOAB
Kir-moab (Kir-hareseth)

Beth-pelet?
Aroer
Hormah
Kenites

SIMEON
Rehoboth

Wilderness of Zin
Ascent of Akrabbim

EDOM
Zered R.

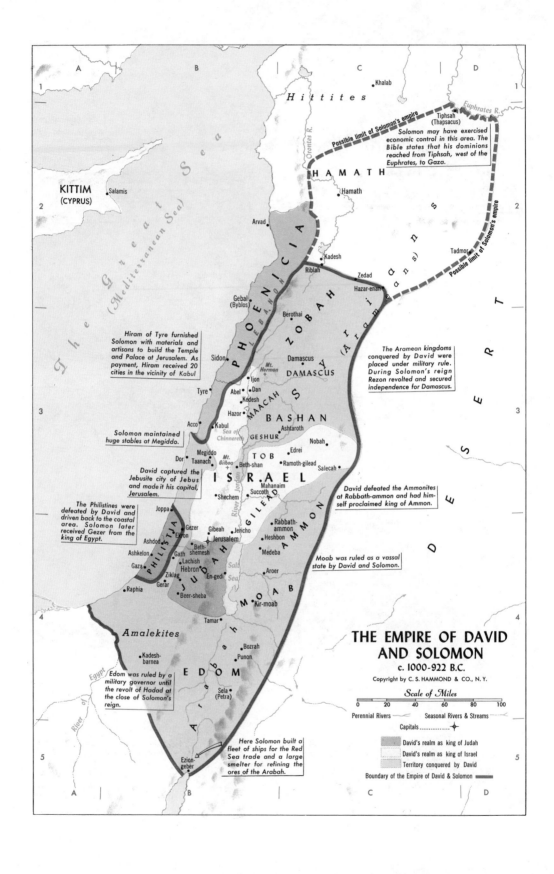

THE EMPIRE OF DAVID
AND SOLOMON
c. 1000–922 B.C.

Copyright by C. S. HAMMOND & CO., N. Y.

Scale of Miles

0   20   40   60   80   100

Perennial Rivers   Seasonal Rivers & Streams

Capitals .... ✦

David's realm as king of Judah
David's realm as king of Israel
Territory conquered by David
Boundary of the Empire of David & Solomon ▬▬▬

Map labels:

Hittites
Khalab
Euphrates R.
Tiphsah (Thapsacus)

Possible limit of Solomon's empire

Solomon may have exercised economic control in this area. The Bible states that his dominions reached from Tiphsah, west of the Euphrates, to Gaza.

HAMATH
Hamath
Arvad
KITTIM (CYPRUS)
Salamis

The Great Sea (Mediterranean Sea)

Kadesh
Riblah
Zedad
Hazar-enan
Tadmor

Possible limit of Solomon's empire

Gebal (Byblos)
Berothai
ZOBAH

PHOENICIA
LEBANON

The Aramean kingdoms conquered by David were placed under military rule. During Solomon's reign Rezon revolted and secured independence for Damascus.

Hiram of Tyre furnished Solomon with materials and artisans to build the Temple and Palace at Jerusalem. As payment, Hiram received 20 cities in the vicinity of Kabul.

Sidon
Mt. Hermon
Ijon
Damascus
DAMASCUS
Tyre
Abel Dan
Kedesh
Hazor
MAACAH
BASHAN
Acco
Kabul
Ashtaroth
GESHUR
Nobah
Sea of Chinnereth

Solomon maintained huge stables at Megiddo.

TOB
Edrei
Megiddo
Mt. Gilboa
Beth-shan
Ramoth-gilead
Salecah
Dor
Taanach

ISRAEL

David captured the Jebusite city of Jebus and made it his capital, Jerusalem.

Mahanaim
Succoth
GILEAD
Shechem

David defeated the Ammonites at Rabbath-ammon and had himself proclaimed king of Ammon.

Joppa

The Philistines were defeated by David and driven back to the coastal area. Solomon later received Gezer from the king of Egypt.

Gezer
Gibeah
Jericho
Rabbath-ammon
Heshbon
AMMON
Ekron
Ashdod
Beth-shemesh
Jerusalem
PHILISTIA
Gath
Lachish
Ashkelon
Medeba
Gaza
Hebron
Ziklag
En-gedi
Gerar
Beer-sheba
JUDAH
Salt Sea

Moab was ruled as a vassal state by David and Solomon.

Aroer
Raphia
Tamar
MOAB
Kir-moab

Amalekites

Bozrah
Kadesh-barnea
Punon

River of Egypt

EDOM

Edom was ruled by a military governor until the revolt of Hadad at the close of Solomon's reign.

Sela (Petra)

Arabah

Here Solomon built a fleet of ships for the Red Sea trade and a large smelter for refining the ores of the Arabah.

Ezion-geber

DESERT

Orontes R.

(Arameans)

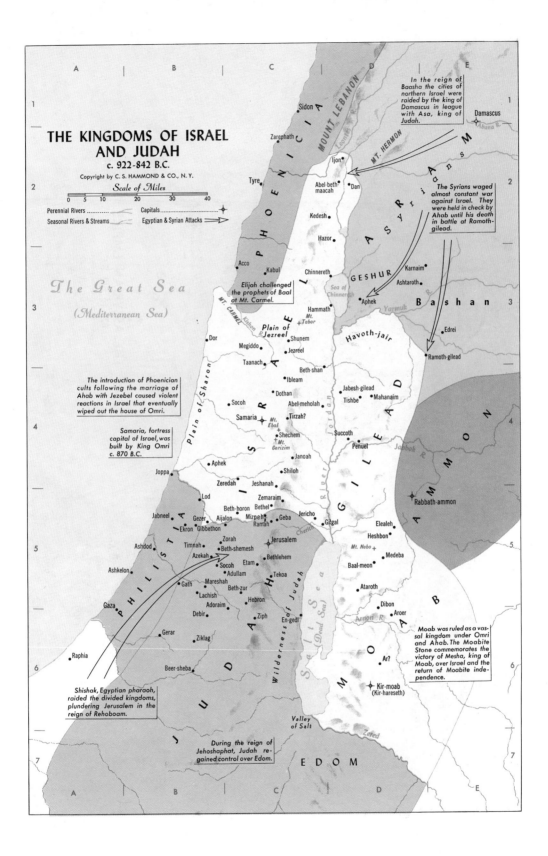

THE KINGDOMS OF ISRAEL AND JUDAH
c. 922-842 B.C.

Copyright by C. S. HAMMOND & CO., N. Y.

Scale of Miles

0   5   10   20   30   40

Perennial Rivers ....
Seasonal Rivers & Streams ~~~~~
Capitals .... ✦
Egyptian & Syrian Attacks ⟶

The Great Sea
(Mediterranean Sea)

In the reign of Baasha the cities of northern Israel were raided by the king of Damascus in league with Asa, king of Judah.

The Syrians waged almost constant war against Israel. They were held in check by Ahab until his death in battle at Ramoth-gilead.

Elijah challenged the prophets of Baal at Mt. Carmel.

The introduction of Phoenician cults following the marriage of Ahab with Jezebel caused violent reactions in Israel that eventually wiped out the house of Omri.

Samaria, fortress capital of Israel, was built by King Omri c. 870 B.C.

Moab was ruled as a vassal kingdom under Omri and Ahab. The Moabite Stone commemorates the victory of Mesha, king of Moab, over Israel and the return of Moabite independence.

Shishak, Egyptian pharaoh, raided the divided kingdoms, plundering Jerusalem in the reign of Rehoboam.

During the reign of Jehoshaphat, Judah regained control over Edom.

PHOENICIA

MOUNT LEBANON

MT. HERMON

Damascus

Sidon

Zarephath

Tyre

Ijon

Abel-beth-maacah · Dan

Kedesh

Hazor

Acco

Kabul

Chinnereth

Sea of Chinnereth

GESHUR

Karnaim

Ashtaroth

Aphek

Bashan

Edrei

Ramoth-gilead

MT. CARMEL

Kishon

Dor

Plain of Jezreel

Hammath

Mt. Tabor

Shunem

Megiddo

Jezreel

Havoth-jair

Taanach

Beth-shan

Ibleam

Dothan

Jabesh-gilead

Socoh

Abel-meholah

Tishbe

Mahanaim

Samaria

Mt. Ebal

Tirzah?

GILEAD

Shechem

Mt. Gerizim

Succoth

Aphek

Janoah

Penuel

Jabbok R.

Shiloh

Joppa

Zeredah

Jeshanah

Lod

Zemaraim

Beth-horon

Bethel

Jabneel

Gezer

Aijalon

Mizpeh

Geba

Jericho

AMMON

Rabbath-ammon

Ekron

Gibbethon

Ramah

Gilgal

Elealeh

Ashdod

Zorah

Jerusalem

Heshbon

Mt. Nebo

Timnah

Beth-shemesh

Medeba

Azekah

Bethlehem

Socoh

Etam

Baal-meon

Ashkelon

Adullam

Tekoa

PHILISTIA

Gath

Mareshah

Beth-zur

Ataroth

Lachish

Hebron

Dibon

Aroer

Gaza

Adoraim

Arnon R.

Debir

Ziph

En-gedi

Gerar

Ziklag

JUDAH

Wilderness of Judah

Salt Sea (Dead Sea)

B

Raphia

Beer-sheba

MOAB

Ar?

Kir-moab (Kir-haresheth)

Valley of Salt

Zered

EDOM

ISRAEL

River Jordan

Cherith

Plain of Sharon

Wilderness of Judah

ASSYRIANS / Syrians

Abana R.

Yarmuk

Zippori

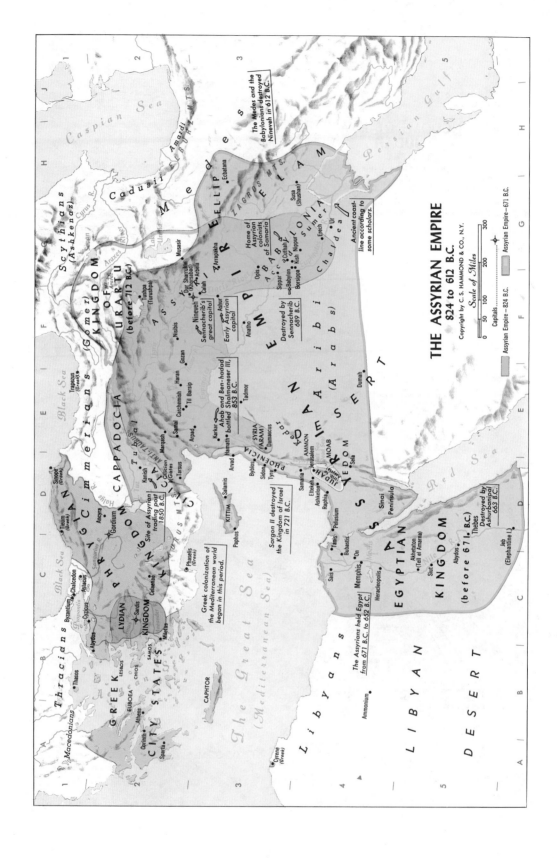

THE ASSYRIAN EMPIRE
824 to 612 B.C.
Copyright by C. S. HAMMOND & CO., N.Y.

Scale of Miles
0 50 100   200   300

Capitals
Assyrian Empire – 824 B.C.
Assyrian Empire – 671 B.C.

The Medes and the
Babylonians destroyed
Nineveh in 612 B.C.

Ancient coast-
line according to
some scholars.

Home of
Assyrian
colonists
of Samaria

Destroyed by
Sennacherib
689 B.C.

Early Assyrian
capital

Nineveh
Sennacherib's
great capital

Site of Assyrian
trading post
1850 B.C.

Greek colonization of
the Mediterranean world
began in this period.

Sargon II destroyed
the Kingdom of Israel
in 721 B.C.

Ahab and Ben-hadad
battled Shalmaneser III,
853 B.C.

The Assyrians held Egypt
from 671 B.C. to 652 B.C.

Destroyed by
Ashurbanipal
663 B.C.

EGYPTIAN
KINGDOM
(before 671 B.C.)

LIBYAN

LIBYAN

DESERT

Caspian Sea

Black Sea

Black Sea

The Great Sea
(Mediterranean Sea)

Red Sea

Persian Gulf

Scythians
(Ashkenaz)

Cadusii

Medes

ELLIPI

ELAM

Thracians

Macedonians

Cimmerians
(Gomer)

KINGDOM
OF
URARTU
(before 712 B.C.)

PHRYGIAN
KINGDOM

CAPPADOCIA

CILICIAN
KINGDOM

LYDIAN
KINGDOM

GREEK
CITY STATES

KITTIM

CAPHTOR

A   S   S   Y   R   I   A   N   E   M   P   I   R   E

BABYLONIA

Sumer

Chaldea

Akkad

SYRIA
(ARAM)

PHOENICIA

JUDAH

ISRAEL

EDOM

N   E   F   U   D   (A r a b s)

Keder

A   r   i   b   i
(A r a b s)

S   Y   R   I   A   N   D   E   S   E   R   T

Sinai
Peninsula

DESERT

Sinope
(Greek)

Trapezus
(Greek)

Amisus

Ancyra

Gordium

Celaenae

Sardis

Abydos

Phaselis
(Greek)

Miletus

SAMOS

CHIOS

LESBOS

EUBOEA

Athens

Corinth

Sparta

Byzantium

Chalcedon

Astacus

Cyzicus

Lampsacus

Thasos

Cyrene
(Greek)

Ammonium

Tushpa
(Turushpa)

Musasir

Dur Sharrukin
(Khorsabad)

Calah

Arbela

Arrapkha

Ashur

Nisibis

Gozan

Haran

Carchemish

Samal

Marqasi

Arpad

Karkar

Hamath

Arvad

Byblos

Sidon

Tyre

Samaria

Eltekeh
Ashkelon

Jerusalem

Raphia

Sela

Til Barsip

Tadmor

Damascus

AMMON

MOAB

Dumah

Anatho

Opis

Sippar
Cuthah

Babylon
Borsippa

Kish

Nippur

Erech

Ur

Susa
(Shushan)

Ecbatana

Heracleopolis

Memphis

On

Bubastis

Sais

Tanis

Pelusium

Akhetaton
(Tell el Amarna)

Siut

Abydos

Thebes

Jeb
(Elephantine I.)

Ammori

Paphos

Salamis

Kanish

Gaza

Tarsus

Cilician
Gates

Kedesh

Zagros Mts.

Anti-Taurus

Taurus Mts.

Halys R.

Sangarius R.

Araxes R.

Cyrus R.

Tigris R.

Euphrates R.

Lake Van

Lake Urmia

JUDAH AFTER THE FALL OF ISRAEL
c. 700 B.C.

Copyright by C. S. HAMMOND & CO., N.Y.

Scale of Miles
0   5   10   20   30

Perennial Rivers ....
Seasonal Rivers & Streams ....
Capitals ....

The Great Sea

(Mediterranean Sea)

Sennacherib conquered Phoenicia, with the exception of Tyre, in 701 B.C.

After Samaria fell, the Ten Tribes were taken away to Assyria, where they disappeared from the pages of history. Syrians and other peoples were brought into Samaria and became the Samaritans of the Bible.

With the conquest of Samaria in 721 B.C. by Sargon II, the Kingdom of Israel came to an end.

In 701 B.C. Sennacherib captured 46 cities of Judah as he pushed down toward the Egyptians, defeating them at Eltekeh.

In 701 B.C. Jerusalem was besieged, though not taken, by Sennacherib.

Ammon, Moab and Edom fell to the Assyrian Esarhaddon in 680 B.C., but they were never held long enough to be organized as regular provinces of the empire.

Raphia   Here Sargon II defeated the Egyptian army in 720 B.C.

Judah was never a province of Assyria. Throughout Assyrian domination, it preserved a nominal independence under its own king, though paying tribute regularly and homage when it was required.

PHOENICIA

MOUNT LEBANON

MT. HERMON

DAMASCUS

QARNINI

Bashan

HAURAN

GALILEE

MT. CARMEL

Plain of Jezreel
MEGIDDO

Plain of Sharon

Du-ru

SAMARIA

GILEAD

AMMON

PHILISTIA

J U D A H

Salt Sea (Dead Sea)

MOAB

EGYPTIAN KINGDOM

EDOM

Place names
Sidon
Zarephath
Tyre
Achzib
Acco
Ramah
Jotbah
Gath-hepher
Jokneam
Dor
Megiddo
Taanach
Jezreel
Dothan
Samaria
Shechem
Mt. Ebal
Mt. Gerizim
Shiloh
Aphek
Joppa
Lod
Jabneh (Jabneel)
Ekron
Gezer
Beth-horon
Bethel
Ai
Michmash
Jericho
Gilgal
Gederoth
Gibbethon
Eltekeh
Aijalon
Gibeon
Ramah
Geba
Anathoth
Gibeah
Nob
Ashdod
Beth-shemesh
Timnah
Jerusalem
Libnah
Adullam
Tekoa
Gath
Moresheth-gath
Mareshah
Lachish
Hebron
Adoraim
Debir
En-gedi
Gaza
Gerar
Beer-sheba
Ijon
Abel-beth-maacah
Dan
Kedesh
Hazor
Chinnereth
Sea of Galilee
Aphek
Ashtaroth
Karnaim
Hammath
Mt. Tabor
Shunem
Beth-shan
Pella
Mahanaim
Edrei
Ramoth-gilead
Rabbath-ammon
Heshbon
Mt. Nebo
Elealeh
Medeba
Jahaz
Dibon
Aroer
Ar?
Kir-moab (Kir-hareseth)
Zoar
Raphia

Leontes R.
Abana R.
Pharpar R.
Jordan R.
Yarmuk R.
Jabbok R.
Jordan River
Arnon R.
Kishon R.

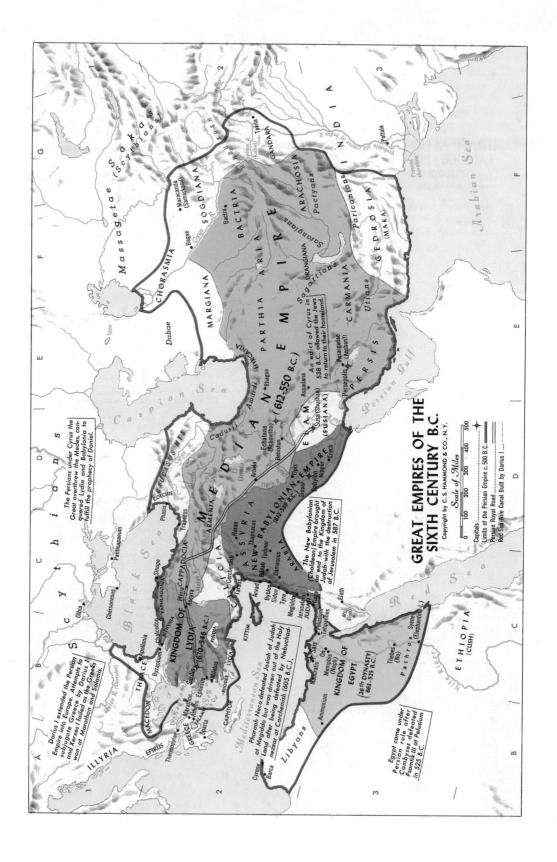

GREAT EMPIRES OF THE SIXTH CENTURY B.C.

Copyright by C. S. HAMMOND & CO., N.Y.

Scale of Miles

0   100   200   300   400   500

Capitals ....
Limits of the Persian Empire c. 500 B.C.
Persian Royal Road ....
Red Sea-Nile Canal Built by Darius I ....

The Persians under Cyrus the Great overthrew the Medes, conquered Lydia and Babylonia to fulfill the prophecy of Daniel.

An edict of Cyrus in 538 B.C. allowed the Jews to return to their homeland.

The New Babylonian (Chaldean) Empire brought an end to the Kingdom of Judah with the destruction of Jerusalem in 587 B.C.

Darius I extended the Persian Empire into Europe. Attempts to subjugate Greece by Darius I and Xerxes I foiled as the Greeks won at Marathon and Salamis.

Pharaoh Neco defeated Josiah of Judah at Megiddo but was driven out of the Holy Land after being defeated by Nebuchadnezzar at Carchemish (605 B.C.).

Egypt came under Persian rule after Cambyses defeated Psamtik III at Pelusium in 525 B.C.

MEDIAN EMPIRE (612-550 B.C.)

PERSIAN EMPIRE

NEW BABYLONIAN EMPIRE (612-539 B.C.)

KINGDOM OF LYDIA (670-546 B.C.)

KINGDOM OF EGYPT (26th DYNASTY 663-525 B.C.)

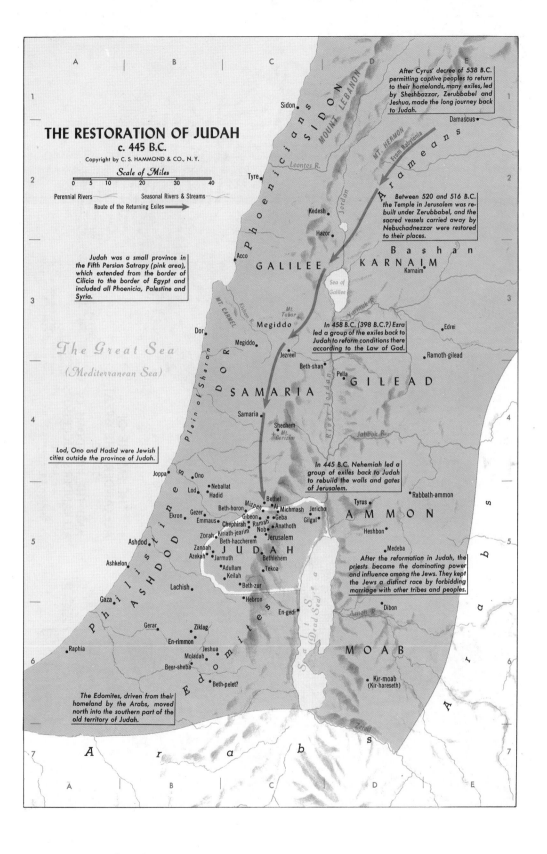

THE RESTORATION OF JUDAH
c. 445 B.C.

Copyright by C. S. HAMMOND & CO., N. Y.

Scale of Miles

0 5 10   20   30   40

Perennial Rivers ―――――

Seasonal Rivers & Streams ――――

Route of the Returning Exiles ――――▶

After Cyrus' decree of 538 B.C. permitting captive peoples to return to their homelands, many exiles, led by Sheshbazzar, Zerubbabel and Jeshua, made the long journey back to Judah.

Between 520 and 516 B.C. the Temple in Jerusalem was rebuilt under Zerubbabel, and the sacred vessels carried away by Nebuchadnezzar were restored to their places.

Judah was a small province in the Fifth Persian Satrapy (pink area), which extended from the border of Cilicia to the border of Egypt and included all Phoenicia, Palestine and Syria.

In 458 B.C. (398 B.C.?) Ezra led a group of the exiles back to Judah to reform conditions there according to the Law of God.

Lod, Ono and Hadid were Jewish cities outside the province of Judah.

In 445 B.C. Nehemiah led a group of exiles back to Judah to rebuild the walls and gates of Jerusalem.

After the reformation in Judah, the priests became the dominating power and influence among the Jews. They kept the Jews a distinct race by forbidding marriage with other tribes and peoples.

The Edomites, driven from their homeland by the Arabs, moved north into the southern part of the old territory of Judah.

The Great Sea
(Mediterranean Sea)

SIDON

MOUNT LEBANON

Phoenicians

Aramaeans

MT. HERMON

From Babylonia

Sidon

Damascus

Tyre

Leontes R.

Kedesh

Hazor

Bashan

KARNAIM

Karnaim

Acco

GALILEE

MT. CARMEL

Sea of Galilee

Jordan

Kishon R.

Mt. Tabor

Megiddo

Dor

Megiddo

Jezreel

Beth-shan

Pella

Edrei

Ramoth-gilead

DOR

Plain of Sharon

SAMARIA

GILEAD

Samaria

Shechem

Mt. Gerizim

River Jordan

Jarmuk R.

Jabbok R.

Joppa

Ono

Lod

Neballat

Hadid

Bethel

Mizpeh

Ai

Michmash

Jericho

Tyrus

Rabbath-ammon

AMMON

Beth-horon

Gibeon

Geba

Gilgal

Ekron

Gezer

Emmaus

Chephirah

Ramah

Anathoth

Heshbon

Zorah

Kiriath-jearim

Nob

Ashdod

Beth-haccherem

Jerusalem

Medeba

Zanoah

Azekah

Jarmuth

Bethlehem

Ashkelon

Adullam

Tekoa

Keilah

Dibon

Lachish

Beth-zur

Gaza

Hebron

En-gedi

Amon R.

Gerar

Ziklag

En-rimmon

Jeshua

MOAB

Raphia

Moladah

Beer-sheba

Kir-moab
(Kir-hareseth)

Beth-pelet?

Philistines

ASHDOD

Edomites

Salt Sea (Dead Sea)

Zered

Arabs

A   r   a   b   s

Arabia

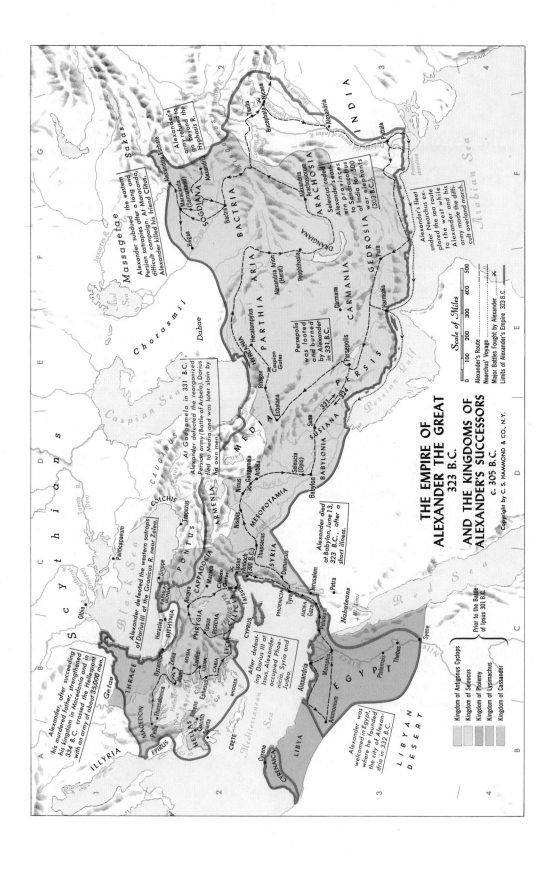

THE EMPIRE OF
ALEXANDER THE GREAT
323 B.C.
AND THE KINGDOMS OF
ALEXANDER'S SUCCESSORS
c. 305 B.C.

Copyright by C. S. HAMMOND & CO., N.Y.

Scale of Miles
0 100 200 300 400 500

Alexander's Route ....
Nearchus' Voyage ....
Major Battles Fought by Alexander ✕
Limits of Alexander's Empire 323 B.C. ━━━

Kingdom of Antigonus Cyclops
Kingdom of Seleucus
Kingdom of Ptolemy   Prior to the Battle
Kingdom of Lysimachus   of Ipsus 301 B.C.
Kingdom of Cassander

Alexander, after succeeding
his murdered father, strengthened
his kingdom in Macedonia and in
334 B.C. crossed the Hellespont
with an army of about 35,000 men.

Alexander defeated the western satraps
of Darius III at the Granicus R. near Zelea.

After defeat-
ing Darius III at
Issus, Alexander
occupied Phoe-
nicia, Syria and
Judea.

Alexander was
welcomed in Egypt,
where he founded
the city of Alexan-
dria in 332 B.C.

At Gaugamela in 331 B.C.
Alexander defeated the reorganized
Persian army (Battle of Arbela). Darius
fled to Media and was later slain by
his own men.

Alexander died
at Babylon, June 13,
323 B.C., after a
short illness.

Persepolis
was looted
and burned
by Alexander
in 331 B.C.

Alexander subdued the eastern
Persian satrapies after a long and
difficult campaign. At Maracanda,
Alexander killed his friend Clitus.

Alexander's
army refused to
go beyond the
Hyphasis R.

Seleucus ceded
Alexander's east-
ern provinces
to Sandracottus
to India for 500
war elephants
(303 B.C.)

Alexander's fleet
under Nearchus ex-
plored the sea route
to the west while
Alexander and his
army made the diffi-
cult overland march.

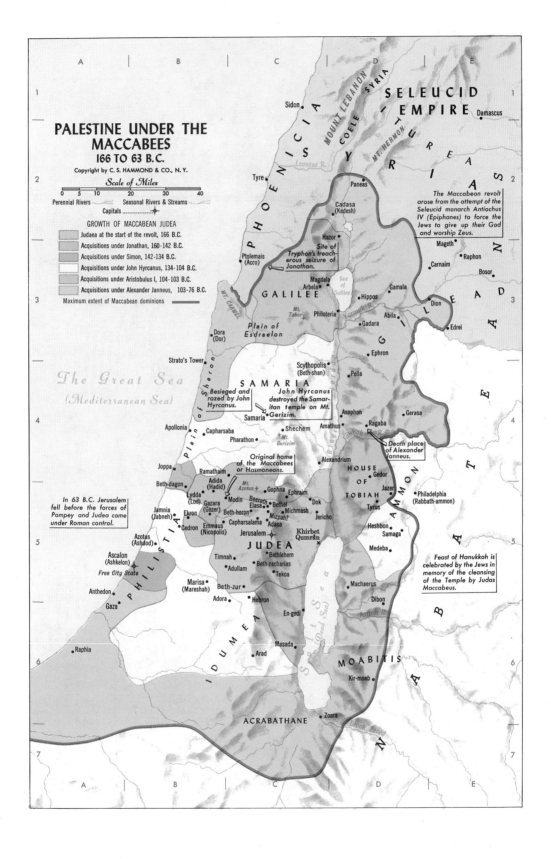

PALESTINE UNDER THE MACCABEES
166 TO 63 B.C.

Copyright by C. S. HAMMOND & CO., N.Y.

Scale of Miles

0 5 10   20   30   40

Perennial Rivers _____   Seasonal Rivers & Streams _____

Capitals .... ✦

GROWTH OF MACCABEAN JUDEA

Judaea at the start of the revolt, 166 B.C.

Acquisitions under Jonathan, 160-142 B.C.

Acquisitions under Simon, 142-134 B.C.

Acquisitions under John Hyrcanus, 134-104 B.C.

Acquisitions under Aristobulus I, 104-103 B.C.

Acquisitions under Alexander Janneus, 103-76 B.C.

—— Maximum extent of Maccabean dominions

The Maccabean revolt arose from the attempt of the Seleucid monarch Antiochus IV (Epiphanes) to force the Jews to give up their God and worship Zeus.

Besieged and razed by John Hyrcanus.

John Hyrcanus destroyed the Samaritan temple on Mt. Gerizim.

Original home of the Maccabees or Hasmoneans.

Death place of Alexander Janneus.

In 63 B.C. Jerusalem fell before the forces of Pompey and Judea came under Roman control.

Feast of Hanukkah is celebrated by the Jews in memory of the cleansing of the Temple by Judas Maccabeus.

SELEUCID EMPIRE

Damascus

Sidon

MOUNT LEBANON

COELE SYRIA

MT. HERMON

Leontes R.

Tyre

PHOENICIA

Paneas

Cadasa (Kedesh)

Hazor

Site of Tryphon's treacherous seizure of Jonathan.

ITUREA

Mageth

Raphon

Carnaim

Bosor

Ptolemais (Acco)

Magdala

Arbela

Sea of Galilee

Gamala

GALILEE

MT. CARMEL

Mt. Tabor

Philoteria

Hippos

Dion

GILEAD

Abila

Edrei

Dora (Dor)

Plain of Esdraelon

Gadara

Ephron

Strato's Tower

Scythopolis (Beth-shan)

Pella

SAMARIA

Plain of Sharon

Samaria

Mt. Gerizim

Shechem

Amathus

Asophon

Ragaba

Gerasa

Apollonia

Capharsaba

Pharathon

Joppa

Ramathaim

Beth-dagon

Adida (Hadid)

Lydda (Lod)

Gazara (Gezer)

Modin

Mt. Azotus

Beeroth

Ephraim

Gophna

Bethel

Dok

Michmash

Alexandrium

HOUSE OF TOBIAH

Gedor

Jazer

Philadelphia (Rabbath-ammon)

AMMON

Ekron

Beth-horon

Jamnia (Jabneh)

Mizpah?

Jericho

Tyrus

Cedron

Emmaus (Nicopolis)

Capharsalama

Adasa

Jerusalem

Khirbet Qumrân

Heshbon

Samaga

Azotus (Ashdod)

JUDEA

Medeba

Ascalon (Ashkelon)

Free City State

Timnah

Bethlehem

Beth-zacharias

Tekoa

Machaerus

Dibon

Anthedon

Marisa (Mareshah)

Adullam

Beth-zur

MOABITIS

Gaza

Adora

Hebron

En-gedi

Raphia

IDUMEA

Arad

Masada

Kir-moab

Salt Sea (Dead Sea)

Arnon R.

ACRABATHANE

Zoara

Brook Arabah

The Great Sea (Mediterranean Sea)

PHILISTIA

Jordan River

Yarmuk R.

GALAAD

BATANEA

SYRIA

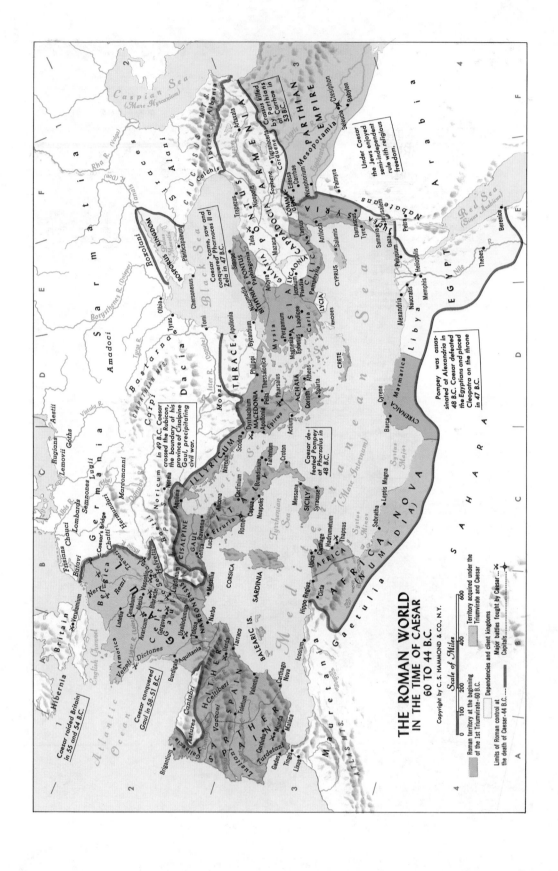

THE ROMAN WORLD
IN THE TIME OF CAESAR
60 TO 44 B.C.

Copyright by C. S. HAMMOND & CO., N.Y.

Scale of Miles

0   100   200   400   600

Roman territory at the beginning
of the 1st Triumvirate–60 B.C.

Territory acquired under the
Triumvirate and Caesar

Dependencies and client kingdoms

Limits of Roman control at
the death of Caesar–44 B.C.

Major battles fought by Caesar

Capitals

Caesar raided Britain
in 55 and 54 B.C.

Caesar conquered
Gaul in 58–51 B.C.

In 49 B.C. Caesar
crossed the Rubicon,
the boundary of his
province of Cisalpine
Gaul, precipitating
civil war.

Caesar de-
feated Pompey
at Pharsalus in
48 B.C.

Caesar came, saw and
conquered Pharnaces II at
Zela in 47 B.C.

Crassus killed
by Parthia at
Carrhae in
53 B.C.

Under Caesar
the Jews enjoyed
semi-independent
rule with religious
freedom.

Pompey was assas-
sinated at Alexandria in
48 B.C. Caesar defeated
the Egyptians and placed
Cleopatra on the throne
in 47 B.C.

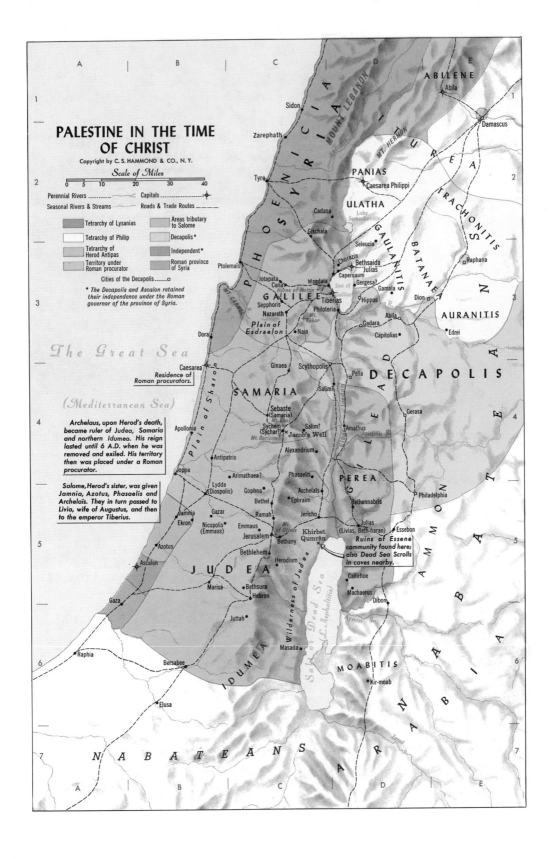

PALESTINE IN THE TIME OF CHRIST

Copyright by C. S. HAMMOND & CO., N. Y.

Scale of Miles
0 5 10 20 30 40

Perennial Rivers .... Capitals ....
Seasonal Rivers & Streams .... Roads & Trade Routes ......

Tetrarchy of Lysanias
Tetrarchy of Philip
Tetrarchy of Herod Antipas
Territory under Roman procurator
Areas tributary to Salome
Decapolis *
Independent *
Roman province of Syria

Cities of the Decapolis ....

* The Decapolis and Ascalon retained
their independence under the Roman
governor of the province of Syria.

Archelaus, upon Herod's death,
became ruler of Judea, Samaria
and northern Idumea. His reign
lasted until 6 A.D. when he was
removed and exiled. His territory
then was placed under a Roman
procurator.

Salome, Herod's sister, was given
Jamnia, Azotus, Phasaelis and
Archelaïs. They in turn passed to
Livia, wife of Augustus, and then
to the emperor Tiberius.

The Great Sea

(Mediterranean Sea)

ABILENE
Abila
Damascus
Sidon
Zarephath
Tyre
PANIAS
Caesarea Philippi
ITUREA
MT. HERMON
ULATHA
Lake Semechonitis
Cadasa
Gischala
TRACHONITIS
GAULANITIS
BATANAEA
Seleucia
Raphana
Chorazin
Bethsaida Julias
Capernaum
Jotapata
Cana
Horns of Hattin
Magdala
Gergesa?
Gamala
AURANITIS
Ptolemais
Sea of Galilee
Sepphoris
Tiberias
Hippos
Dion
Edrei
GALILEE
Nazareth
Philoteria
Abila
MT. CARMEL
Mt. Tabor
Gadara
Capitolias
Plain of Esdraelon
Nain
Dora
Ginaea
Scythopolis
Pella
DECAPOLIS
Caesarea
Residence of Roman procurators.
SAMARIA
Salim?
Gerasa
Sebaste (Samaria)
Mt. Ebal
Sychem (Sychar?)
Mt. Gerizim
Salim?
Amathus
Jabbok R.
GILEAD
Jacob's Well
Plain of Sharon
Apollonia
Alexandrium
Antipatris
Arimathaea?
Phasaelis
PEREA
Joppa
Lydda (Diospolis)
Gophna
Archelaïs
Philadelphia
Jamnia
Gazar
Bethel
Ephraim
Bethennabris
AMMONITES
Ekron
Nicopolis (Emmaus)
Ramah
Jericho
Julias (Livias, Beth-haran)
Essebon
Emmaus
Mt. of Olives
Khirbet Qumran
Azotus
Jerusalem
Bethany
Ruins of Essene community found here; also Dead Sea Scrolls in caves nearby.
Ascalon
Bethlehem
Herodium
Callirhoe
JUDEA
Marisa
Bethsura
Hebron
Machaerus
Dibon
Gaza
Wilderness of Judea
Dead Sea (L. Asphaltitis)
Juttah
MOABITIS
Masada
Kir-moab
Raphia
Bersabee
IDUMEA
Sea of
Arnon R.
ARABIA
Elusa
N A B A T E A N S
Zered

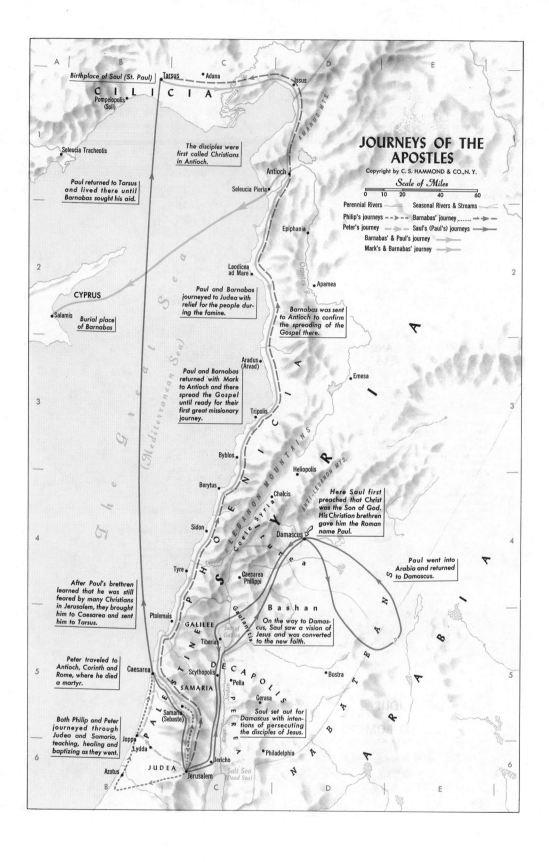

JOURNEYS OF THE APOSTLES

Copyright by C. S. HAMMOND & CO., N. Y.

Scale of Miles

0   10   20   40   60

Perennial Rivers   Seasonal Rivers & Streams

Philip's journeys - - - →   Barnabas' journey ......→

Peter's journey   Saul's (Paul's) journeys →

Barnabas' & Paul's journey →

Mark's & Barnabas' journey →

CILICIA

Birthplace of Saul (St. Paul) — Tarsus   • Adana

Pompeiopolis (Soli) •

• Issus

The disciples were first called Christians in Antioch.

Seleucia Tracheotis •

Paul returned to Tarsus and lived there until Barnabas sought his aid.

Antioch

Seleucia Pieria •

Epiphania •

CYPRUS

Laodicea ad Mare •

• Apamea

Paul and Barnabas journeyed to Judea with relief for the people during the famine.

Barnabas was sent to Antioch to confirm the spreading of the Gospel there.

• Salamis

Burial place of Barnabas

Aradus (Arvad) •

• Emesa

Paul and Barnabas returned with Mark to Antioch and there spread the Gospel until ready for their first great missionary journey.

Tripolis •

PHOENICIA

Byblos •

Heliopolis •

Berytus •

Chalcis •

Here Saul first preached that Christ was the Son of God. His Christian brethren gave him the Roman name Paul.

Sidon •

Damascus •

Tyre •

Caesarea Philippi •

Paul went into Arabia and returned to Damascus.

After Paul's brethren learned that he was still feared by many Christians in Jerusalem, they brought him to Caesarea and sent him to Tarsus.

Ptolemais •

Bashan

GALILEE

Sea of Galilee

Tiberias •

On the way to Damascus, Saul saw a vision of Jesus and was converted to the new faith.

Peter traveled to Antioch, Corinth and Rome, where he died a martyr.

Caesarea •

Scythopolis •

DECAPOLIS

• Bostra

Pella •

SAMARIA

Gerasa •

Both Philip and Peter journeyed through Judea and Samaria, teaching, healing and baptizing as they went.

Samaria (Sebaste) •

Saul set out for Damascus with intentions of persecuting the disciples of Jesus.

Joppa •

Lydda •

Jericho •

• Philadelphia

Azotus •

JUDEA

Jerusalem

Salt Sea (Dead Sea)

The Great Sea (Mediterranean Sea)

SYRIA

Coele-Syria

LEBANON MOUNTAINS

ANTI-LEBANON MTS.

AMANUS MTS.

Orontes R.

ARABIA

NABATRA

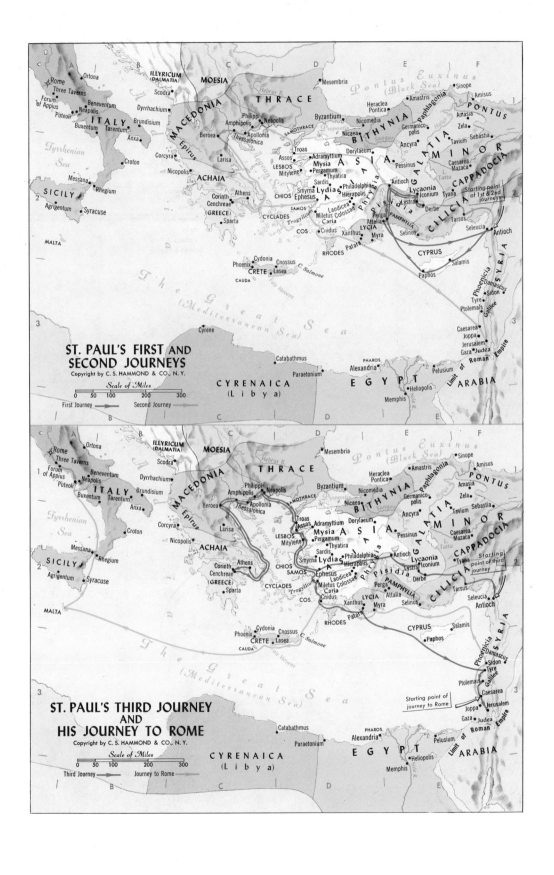

ST. PAUL'S FIRST AND
SECOND JOURNEYS
Copyright by C. S. HAMMOND & CO., N.Y.
Scale of Miles
0 50 100   200   300
First Journey ⟶   Second Journey ⟶

ST. PAUL'S THIRD JOURNEY
AND
HIS JOURNEY TO ROME
Copyright by C. S. HAMMOND & CO., N.Y.
Scale of Miles
0 50 100   200   300
Third Journey ⟶   Journey to Rome ⟶

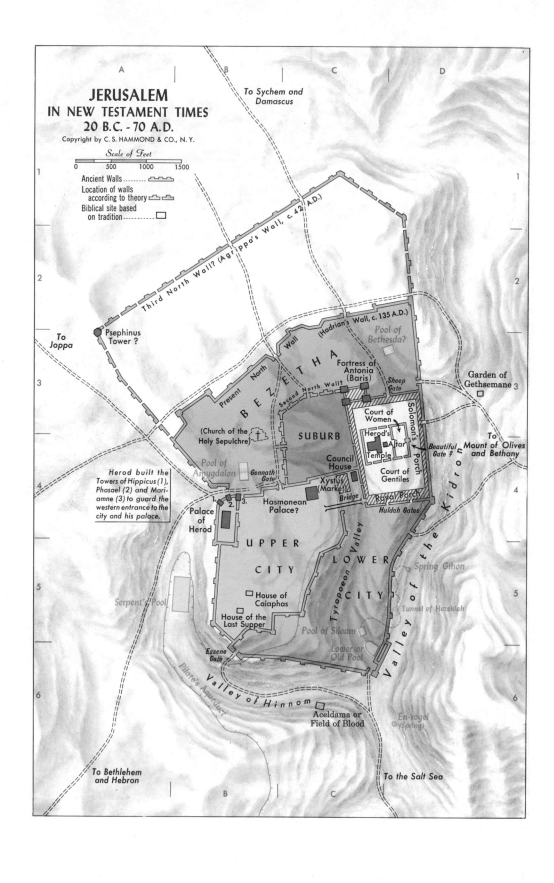

JERUSALEM
IN NEW TESTAMENT TIMES
20 B.C. - 70 A.D.
Copyright by C. S. HAMMOND & CO., N. Y.

Scale of Feet

0   500   1000   1500

Ancient Walls ....
Location of walls
according to theory ....
Biblical site based
on tradition ....

To Sychem and
Damascus

Third North Wall? (Agrippa's Wall, c. 42 A.D.)

To
Joppa

Psephinus
Tower ?

(Hadrian's Wall, c. 135 A.D.)

Pool of
Bethesda?

BEZETHA

Present

North

Second North Wall?

Wall

Fortress of
Antonia
(Baris)

Sheep
Gate

Garden of
Gethsemane

(Church of the
Holy Sepulchre)

SUBURB

Court of
Women

Solomon's Porch

Herod's
Altar

To
Mount of Olives
and Bethany

Pool of
Amygdalon

Gennath
Gate

Council
House

Temple

Court of
Gentiles

Beautiful
Gate ?

Herod built the
Towers of Hippicus (1),
Phasael (2) and Mari-
amne (3) to guard the
western entrance to the
city and his palace.

Xystus
(Market)

Bridge

Royal Porch

Huldah Gates

Palace
of
Herod

Hasmonean
Palace?

UPPER

CITY

LOWER

Lo Valley

Spring Gihon

Tyropoeon Valley

CITY

Valley of the Kidron

Serpent's Pool

House of
Caiaphas

Tunnel of Hezekiah

House of the
Last Supper

Pool of Siloam

Essene
Gate

Lower or
Old Pool

Pilate's Aqueduct

Valley of Hinnom

Aceldama or
Field of Blood

En-rogel
(Spring)

To Bethlehem
and Hebron

To the Salt Sea